WILLIAM LYON PHELPS

WILLIAM LYON PHELPS

AUTOBIOGRAPHY
WITH LETTERS

OXFORD UNIVERSITY PRESS

NEW YORK LONDON TORONTO

1939

Printed in the United States of America

TO MY WIFE
ANNABEL

ACKNOWLEDGEMENT

I EXPRESS my thanks to the Macmillan Company for permitting me to quote from some of my books published by them, especially *Teaching in School and College*, *The Twentieth Century Theatre*, *Essays on Modern Dramatists*, and *Essays on Things*: to E.P.Dutton and Company for permission to quote from my book *Appreciation*: to the Liveright Publishing Corporation for permission to quote from my book *The Excitement of Teaching*: and to the editors of the *Yale Review*, *Delineator* and *Cosmopolitan* for permission to reprint some of my articles with revisions: especially am I grateful to Charles Scribner's Sons, who have most generously allowed me to quote copiously from my monthly articles 'As I Like It' which I contributed to *Scribner's Magazine* during fourteen happy years.

PREFACE

On *Friday* 20 *April* 1781 '*Somebody said the life of a mere literary man could not be very entertaining.* JOHNSON. "*But it certainly may. This is a remark which has been made, and repeated, without justice; why should the life of a literary man be less entertaining than the life of any other man? Are there not as interesting varieties in such a life? As* a literary life *it may be very entertaining.*"' *Johnson had previously meditated on the same question, for in* The Idler *he had written,* '*It is commonly supposed that the uniformity of a studious life affords no matter for narration; but the truth is, that of the most studious life a great part passes without study.* . . . *he is born and married like another man; he has hopes and fears, expectations and disappointments, griefs and joys, and friends and enemies.*' (*Powell-Hill edition of Boswell's* Life of Johnson, IV:98.)

Even if a literary life should not be entertaining to others, this particular one has been prodigiously entertaining to him who has lived it.

The lack of order, coherence, symmetry in this book is owing neither to accident nor to laziness; it is the way I chose to write it. Novels of particular communities or of particular lives often seem untrue because the novelist endeavours to form the events into a plot, with development and climax; whereas life itself has nothing but a time-line; and even that is reduced to a semblance of order only by the artificial divisions of clock and calendar. And the individual time-line is continually broken by memory and by anticipation. The pleasure of good conversation would be destroyed if conversations were 'organized' —forced to proceed in a definite direction, instead of being brittle, broken by interruptions. Dean Briggs used to say that Donne, as a poet, was like an unruly bird dog; 'he chases every wild thought that flies out of the thicket.' His poems are more interesting than an orderly epic on transcendentalism in twelve books, specifically condemned by another great poet.

Furthermore it is possible that readers who admire consistency may think I am either superficial or insincere in my admiration for writers of antagonistic and irreconcilable views. But intellectual curiosity annihilates consistency. How is it possible to be consistent in such a tragi-comedy as this world where God Himself seems so inconsistent? I love authors who give me stimulation and delight. Strong convictions should be accompanied by tolerance for other views and keen interest in them. Intellectual excitements like other excitements gain by variety. Some of my favourite modern authors are Browning and Schopenhauer, Barrie and Strindberg, Hardy and Chesterton, Housman and Francis Thompson, Dickens and Emily Brontë, Henry James and Dumas, Stevenson and George Moore, Swift and Emerson, Ibsen and Rostand, Goethe and Dr. Johnson, Mill and Carlyle, and in reading works of genius I am perhaps a little like Emerson's yellow-breeched philosopher, leaving the chaff and taking the wheat.

In reading the autobiography of a famous contemporary, I was mildly astonished to observe that he gave the names and addresses of all persons who had entertained him at week-ends and had shown him kindness in other ways. It troubles me that I cannot do this. If I should include the names of all my friends who have shown me hospitality and added to my happiness by their generosity and unselfishness, this book would be three times its present size and would in many places read more like a catalogue than a biography. Surely such specifications are unnecessary. My friends know that no matter how great or many may be my limitations, I am not lacking in appreciation.

To those who wonder ('Sir, you may wonder') why I print

so many letters, thus losing continuity and proportion, let me say this book would never have been written if it were not for the large number of letters from persons more important than the author. In this instance the Scripture text is reversed; the letter giveth life. Among the variety of things that have contributed to my happiness one of the most salient is my good fortune in having met so many distinguished writers. I am a hero-worshipper. Thus I am grateful for permission to print these epistles.

When I have finished reading the proofs, I hope that some persons may read the book. As for me,

> *I am afraid to think what I have done:*
> *Look on't again I dare not.*

W.L.P.

Branford College,
* Yale University,*
*   All Souls Day 1938.*

CONTENTS

CONTENTS xiii

CONTENTS

CONTENTS

CONTENTS

INTRODUCTION

In looking back, I should have to change somewhat the famous words of Landor:

> I strove with none, for none was worth my strife.
> Nature I loved, and next to Nature Art:
> I warmed both hands before the fire of life:
> It sinks, and I am ready to depart.

Very fine, no doubt; although, written by Landor, the first four words have an oddity all their own. To fit my own case, I should have to say

> I strove with none. I always hated strife.
> Nature I loved, and God and Man and Art:
> I warmed both hands before the fire of life:
> It sinks, yet I'm not ready to depart.

The vast majority of persons are compelled to live without prodigious adventures and without the gratification of most of their transient desires; yet ordinary circumscribed existence can be exciting.

For although I have lived what is called a sheltered life, it has been anything but dull. Daily existence has often been thrilling. Apparently I have been and am much happier than most men and women. My happiness certainly has never come from resignation. It has been said that the happiest men and women in the world are those who have good health, a sufficient income, *and no ambition*. This would probably be true if we meant by happiness a quiet enjoyment of existence with the absence of worry or unsatisfied desire. I do not know whether I envy such people or not; I sometimes envy their calmness and self-control.

But I am not that kind of man at all; I have always been eaten up with ambition, I have had the longings described by Faust as he sat at his desk in the moonlight, and I worry about innumerable little things. I have never had a placid temperament. I have had two prolonged attacks of nervous prostration, one at the age of twenty-six and one at the age of fifty-nine, and my religious faith remains in possession of the field only after prolonged civil war with my naturally sceptical mind. Yet I have certainly lived a happy life.

Since I have lived without great adventures and yet with many mental alarms and excursions, why have I been so happy?

It is fortunate there are people of adventurous, pioneering, exploring blood, who love to go into deserts, trackless forests, appalling jungles, and mingle with savage or primitive races. They write, and we share their adventures without danger or inconvenience. I suppose there is no one who has less of the frontiersman in him than I. If I had all my expenses paid and a salary in addition, nothing would induce me to visit equatorial Africa or Mary Byrd Land. I have no desire to climb hitherto unclimbed mountains. Instead of being the first man up a mountain, I had rather be the last one; the mountain does not interest me particularly until it has had human associations. I agree with G.K.Chesterton who said, 'I will lift up mine eyes unto the hills but I will not lift up my carcass thither.' Fleet Street gives me a keener thrill than any lonely heights. Hot jungles and trackless snows may be beautiful, but to me they are not so beautiful as the Grand Central Station illuminated, or the North River by night, or Fifth Avenue by day or Fleet Street before sunset. I am a man of the city, and I like theatres, music, newspapers, and cultivated men and women. It may be that savages have admirable traits, but

I am sure they are not so agreeable or so trustworthy or so interesting as any number of men and women I know in New Haven, Connecticut, and Huron County, Michigan.

Perhaps the chief source of my happiness lies in my gift of appreciation. I must have been born with it. When I was a child, everything unusual excited me; now that I am old, everything usual has about the same effect.

When I was six, and Christmas gifts were distributed in school, the present for me was placed on my desk. It is curious that I have forgotten what it was but have not forgotten my emotion. I was so overcome with awe and wonder and joy at receiving it that I looked at it in absolute silence, being unable to articulate. The foolish teacher said, 'Why, Willie, don't you like your present?'

After I had entered the Hartford High School at the age of thirteen, I was playing football with the huge crowd at recess, was knocked down, trampled on, and covered from head to foot with dirt and dust. No one paid any attention to me, except Clarence Wickham, the champion athlete of the school. He it was and no other, who picked me up, dusted me off, set me on my feet. I was not only 'lifted,' I was 'exalted.'

Montaigne said, 'Whatever are the benefits of fortune, they yet require a palate fit to relish and taste them.' Happiness is more dependent on the mental attitude than on external resources. This would be an absurdly obvious platitude, were it not for the fact that ninety-nine out of a hundred persons do not believe it.

I have always had a keen relish for agreeable sensations. Even as a little child, I responded gratefully—and usually with surprise—to any acts of kindness or to any courtesies from older people. And I well remember, when I was in the High School, calling upon Mr. Stiles T.Stanton of Stonington, a member of the legislature, to ask him to serve as a judge in the Prize Declamations. If he had looked at me contemptuously, and said 'I'm busy,' I should not have been surprised; he treated me, however, neither with contempt nor with condescension, but as if I were an equal. This may seem a small thing, but I have never forgotten it. He was a gentleman.

All kinds of outdoor games, winter and summer, were an inexpressible delight. And even as a little boy, I was intensely *conscious* of all this. In the midst of sliding downhill in the moonlight, or playing ball in summer, I would say to myself, 'Isn't this wonderful?' and in my adolescence, I remember saying to a girl, 'Isn't it great to be young?'

I mention these details, because the majority of persons do not so *consciously* enjoy their youth or any other thing while they have it. In a world filled with misfortunes, losses, drawbacks, and suffering, most persons seem to take good health, sanity, food and drink, wives and husbands, for granted; and appreciate them only too late. Not so with me. I seemed to have in the midst of enjoyment an inner knowledge of my enjoyment, an awareness of happiness; as often, in the midst of a public lecture, I make a remark that I never had thought of before; and while the audience is digesting it, I say to myself, 'How in the world did you ever think of that?'

When, at the age of six, I went to Barnum's circus, and 'the greatest show on earth' lasted from two o'clock till five, the three hours were undiluted bliss. I remember not only the gorgeous spectacle, but the joy with which I regarded it.

In his admirable *Life of Webster*, Dr. Fuess says there are two classes of men; those who get up in the morning rather heavy, sluggish, and perhaps depressed, gradually during the day become more alive, and finally in the evening are sparkling and vivacious—and the other kind, who are happiest and most lively at breakfast. Now I have always, from earliest childhood even until now, belonged to this latter class.

Like most boys and girls, I hated to go to bed in the evening, yet was forced to go at an early hour. Bedtime meant fun was over; no more excitement till the next day. Waking in the morning was full of promise. 'No dream's worth waking,' Browning said. I remember a picture in our house of a mother carrying a baby in her arms. The room was illumined only by a crepuscular light, and it was impossible to tell whether this twilight was of the dawn or of the coming night. I remember looking at that hundreds of times, and always hoping that it was the dawn. Then the child would have the day before it full of wonderful things, instead of nothing to look forward to. And indeed I have almost always felt a touch of sadness at nightfall; and almost always eagerness in the early morning. The best thing ever said about heaven in the Bible is that there is no night there. I have always wished—and now that I am old, I wish it with tenfold intensity—that sleep were not necessary. I have always begrudged the time we have to spend in sleeping or— too common an experience with me—vainly trying to sleep. If it were physically possible and my strength and above all, my eyes would permit, I should like to spend all the daylight in work and play, and read all night.

Bertrand Russell says it is a mistake to suppose that those who sleep well are spiritually inferior; perhaps this is true. There is perhaps no reason why we should consider our sufferings as a sign of superiority. Yet there is truth in what Goethe said:

> Who never ate his bread in sorrow,
> Who never spent the darksome hours
> Weeping and watching for the morrow,
> He knows ye not, ye Heavenly Powers!

That blessings brighten as they take their flight may be true with many persons; possibly they do not realize the happiness of health until they lose it, or the happiness of travel, sport, conversation, love, adventure, or what you will, until old age. But that has never been so with me. Waking in the morning, I always looked forward with joy to teaching my first class at college; waiting on the tennis court for my partners to appear, I was filled with active pleasure; and in the midst of innumerable experiences I have not only consciously, but self-consciously enjoyed them.

I am afraid if I continue in this vein, I shall become intolerable; but as this is an autobiography, it seems necessary to emphasize these emotions, as they are truly characteristic.

I have no doubt my ardent religious faith is largely responsible for the happiness that I have found in mere living; but it is not wholly responsible. G. K. Chesterton was profoundly religious and Arnold Bennett was certainly not. Yet it would be difficult to say which of these two men lived with more gusto. Arnold Bennett's attitude toward life was a chronic wonder, amazement, delight; the innumerable gadgets of modern existence pleased him prodigiously. And Mr. Chesterton used to say that he hoped he would never be too old to stare at everything; and that the most important emotion to preserve in maturity was *the enjoyment of enjoyment*.

The difference between my happiness as a child and my happiness as a man, is that in childhood I always wanted some excitement to take me out of the routine. The resumption of routine was often accompanied by a devastating if temporary sinking of the heart. With what ecstasy my brothers and I got through school on Friday afternoon and then went away to spend the week-end with my Aunt Libbie at Stratford! But how my heart sank as I had to go back to school on Monday morning!

Then Saturday was the golden day of the week. Now in a

certain sense every day is Saturday. Then I was always hoping for something different to happen. Now my hope is that nothing different will happen. I hope only I may be able to keep in sufficient health or vigour to go on with the routine. And I enjoy the hot bath in the tub as I used to enjoy the old swimming hole.

So, as I look back on childhood and youth, happy though I was, I have no regret that they are irrecoverable; I have no sentimental yearning for the past. I ran and skipped and leaped through those bright halls

Es glänzt der Saal, es schimmert das Gemach

and advanced into other rooms quite different but more interesting; because there was not only more to appreciate, but my powers of appreciation had developed.

My enjoyment of the best in music, art, and books does not detract from my enjoyment of more simple things; though I enjoy the best more than the second best. I am transported by the symphonies of Beethoven and by the operas of Wagner. Yet that does not lessen my enjoyment of Gilbert and Sullivan, of a drum and fife corps, of a brass band. As I grow older I find Shakespeare more thrilling, more enchanting; yet I relish a good detective story. I shall never forget my excitement in seeing Richard Mansfield as Richard III; yet I still love the circus and everything in it.

AUTOBIOGRAPHY
WITH LETTERS

AUTOBIOGRAPHY
With Letters

I

EARLY CHILDHOOD

I WAS born at the south-east corner of Elm and Church Streets, in New Haven, Connecticut, on Monday the second of January 1865.

Both my parents were of Connecticut stock; my father came in a direct line from William Phelps, who settled in Windsor, Connecticut, in 1636; my mother's mother was named Sophia Lyon; she was born in Stratford, Connecticut. On her side of the family I am remotely descended from Sir John Lyon, of Scotland, who was married in 1376; he was an ancestor of the Earl of Strathmore, and my Aunt Libbie used to exhibit the Lyon family coat-of-arms bearing the thistle. I am a lineal descendant of Theophilus Eaton, the First Governor of the Colony of Connecticut in 1638. I mention these things, not because I am proud of my Scottish and Connecticut descent, for why should I be proud of something with which I had nothing whatever to do?

The marriage of my father, the Rev. Sylvanus Dryden Phelps (born in Suffield, Conn., 1816) and my mother, Sophia Emilia Lyon Linsley (born in Stratford, Conn., 1823) took place in 1847. My father was a large, powerful man, who developed strength and self-reliance as a boy. His father, a farmer, died when the boy was only twelve. The family were very poor and my father had to do a man's work on the farm. He supported himself through school and college, walking over a hundred miles from Suffield to Providence, to enter Brown University. He had immense vigour and never seemed to suffer from anything resembling 'nerves.' When he was seventy-eight, he used to dive and swim in water that was too cold for many younger men.

My mother was highly-strung, and sometimes suffered from acute nervous despondency. But most of the time she was in high spirits and full of gaiety. She was insatiably fond of playing games and was so amiable, so kind, so sympathetic, so warm-hearted, that she was intensely beloved by innumerable individuals. She was an ideal pastor's wife, visiting the sick and the poor, always conducting the adult class in Sunday School, and for more than thirty years she wrote two columns weekly for a religious journal. She was one of the most lovable persons I ever knew and her death in 1903 was the greatest sorrow of my life.

My parents had five children. The eldest, Sophia, was born in 1848 and died at the age of twenty-two. A son James I never saw. My oldest brother, the Rev. Dryden William Phelps was born in 1854 and died in 1931. He was never married. My brother Arthur, the Rev. Dr. Arthur Stevens Phelps, two years older than I, was born in 1863 and is living in California. Arthur and I were as close together as two boys could possibly be; growing up together, sharing everything. He was married to Miss Blanche Stroud, and both their children are married; the Rev. Dr. Dryden Linsley Phelps is a professor in West China and his sister Céleste is married to William Fogg Osgood, Professor of Mathematics at Harvard.

It took my parents six months after my birth to find for me a name satisfactory to them and the family; for some time I was called Frank Mansfield. Finally, as I learn from my mother's letters to her sister, I was named William Lyon, after my great-grandfather, a Colonel of the Governor's Footguards during the American Revolution, and one of the founders in 1792 of the New Haven Bank. His portrait hangs today in the Directors Room. His son, my mother's uncle, was also named William Lyon.

My mother's father, the Reverend James H. Linsley, who died in 1843, was a very interesting person. He was a strictly orthodox evangelical clergyman and also an authority in natural history, especially in conchology. His immense collection of shells, arranged with their Latin names in his minute handwriting, attracted many scientific visitors to his home in Stratford; he also collected and mounted many birds. He had a passion for natural history, and for many branches of scientific research, as such matters were then understood. The other side of his mind was religious and theological, what we should now call Fundamentalist; and he was fanatical on the subject of temperance. He founded or helped to found the first Total Abstinence Society in Stratford; and I have seen the childish signatures of his two children, my mother and my aunt, affixed before they were six years old to a document in which they promised to abstain from intoxicating liquor. My aunt had a good singing voice and took lessons. One day Mr. Linsley found lying on the piano a song she had just learned; it was Jonson's 'Drink to me only with thine eyes.' He told her such a song was not fitting for a young lady to sing. He then erased the word *Drink* and wrote in the word *Eat*; henceforth she sang it 'Eat to me only with thine eyes.'

I have been informed that some psychiatrists today urge parents not to teach their children the familiar prayer 'Now I lay me down to sleep,' because it will suggest to the infant mind the thought of death and thus inspire fear at bedtime. The hard-boiled Puritan babies of New England got out of that prayer agreeable relaxation; they handed the responsibility over to God and went to sleep peacefully. I wonder what the psychiatrists would say to the verses my maternal grandmother, Mrs. Linsley, had for her mental furniture, for on the wall of a room in my house hangs a sampler, wrought by her little hands in 1790, when she was about five years old. It contains this cheerful poem:

> There is an hour when I must die,
> Nor do I know how soon 'twill come:
> A thousand children young as I,
> Are called by death to meet their doom.

The Puritans were determined not to let even children forget the certainty of death and the uncertainty of its hour. If they heard the laughter of children, they felt something ought to be done about it. And yet as carriers of gloom-germs, they were perhaps not so effective as our modern atheistical novelists. The Puritans felt that life was serious, but they had faith in the ultimate rightness of things; they believed this was God's world and that its darkness would be followed by eternal sunshine. Serious views of life seemed to them rational. But the modern pessimist, with no philosophy of life, and with no hope for humanity either here or hereafter, is as fully determined not to let us have any fun. The moment we try to enjoy ourselves we are called sternly to order. Now I cannot see that tears have any higher intellectual value than laughter; there may be as much cerebration in a comedy as in a tragedy. The Puritans believed that out of a dark soil bright flowers would spring; the modern pessimist offers us no flowers, but more dirt.

I am sorry my mother was brought up to regard drinking, smoking, card-playing, dancing, theatre-going, as wicked. I mean I am sorry for her. She would have loved cards and the theatre. She played many other indoor games and she went with delight to concerts and other entertainments. But neither my mother nor my father ever saw a play in the theatre or ever touched a playing-card.

One might naturally think that, brought up as I was in so intensely religious a household, where my father was the

Benavente in the Browning Chair, New Haven, 18 March 1923

Fortieth Wedding Day
Augusta, Georgia

*My Father's House at 44 High Street, New Haven, 1868.
Mother and brother Arthur in lower window; sister (died 1871)
in upper window; brother Dryden over the door; and Father at
fence with me*

Leaving Honolulu, July 1916
J.R.Galt (Yale 1889) *our host*

At the Henry Ford birthplace, 1931. Reading from left to right: Mrs. Phelps, Henry Ford, Mr. Phelps, Mrs. Ford, my brother-in-law, Frank Hubbard, and Mrs. Frank Hubbard

*William Lyon Phelps, aged 8
Taken in New Haven*

My Caddie at Augusta, Georgia

William Lyon Phelps at his desk in New Haven

pastor of the church and my mother the teacher of the adult Bible class, where we invariably attended two services and usually three on Sunday and the weekly prayer-meeting, and where no games and for a long time no secular reading were allowed on Sunday, my childhood would have been unhappy. On the contrary, my childhood and that of my brothers was very happy indeed. The intensity of my parents' religious convictions gave significance to their enjoyment of daily life. They abounded in good humour, and it seems to me now that the house was full of laughter. We frequently entertained guests; in those days a clergyman on his travels never went to an hotel, but always to some other clergyman's house. One of my earliest recollections is lying in bed and hearing from below the resounding laughter of my mother, as she talked with some visitor or caller.

It is always difficult to state with accuracy how far back in one's life one can remember; it is probable that many of our earliest reminiscences are in fact reminiscences of what we have been told. I feel sure of only one or two facts. I had a long illness that lasted for months, during which my fourth birthday occurred. My parents told me in later years that I was a sickly child, that they feared I would not live, and that finally in this long illness I was at the point of death more than once. Apparently this illness was a climax; for after I recovered, I grew into healthy boyhood and I suppose that during my life I have been more active than the average person.

I have a distinct recollection of my father coming into the room while I was in bed during this long illness, and bringing me a little tack-hammer as a present.

We had moved into a new house when I was three, and I remember a photograph's being taken of the house and of the entire family. I had on a white dress and was laughing as my father held me on top of the iron fence. My mother, sister, and brothers were in the windows. This house stands today, 44 High Street, New Haven; it is a square, brick house, with what was then called a French roof.

My sister Sophie died of typhoid fever when she was twenty-two; I was only six. I have missed her all my life. She was not beautiful, but she possessed extraordinary charm and the undergraduates at Yale were frequent visitors. As a 'kid brother' I must have been a nuisance; I came into the room interrupting agreeable conversation, and was sometimes bribed by the particular young man of the moment to go away and stay away. I have seen some of the letters Sophie wrote to her college friends and others; they reveal wit, intelligence, and charm. Although she was not formally engaged, I think she would have married the young man who called most frequently.

Men who love only once are among the rarest specimens of the human race; but there was another young man, who despite positive and repeated refusals from my sister, persisted in asking her to marry him. He had fought in the Civil War, had been wounded, and was a hero to my brother Arthur and me. A bullet had passed through his body, just above the hip. We were never tired of examining this scar, and putting our fingers into the hole in his side. We asked him endless questions about his battles. 'How did you feel when the bullet went through you?' He said he laughed.

When my sister was in the coffin on the morning of the funeral, and my mother and I were in the room, this young Lieutenant entered quietly and without noticing us, went to the dead girl and kissed her on the forehead. I asked my mother, 'Why did he kiss her? She's dead.' 'He kissed her because he loved her.' 'Well, was she going to marry him?' 'No.' 'How do you know that?' 'Because she told him she never would marry him.'

This man became a physician and lived to be over ninety.

He was never married and apparently never thought of any other woman. I used to see him at intervals of ten years or so; and he never talked about anything except my sister, and told me he was certain of being united with her in the next world. He said she was his Beatrice.

My sister, being so much older than my brother Arthur and I, had the unpleasant task of frequently taking care of us during the absence of our parents. We were a noisy, mischievous pair of small boys, and must have given her no end of trouble. Yet I never remember her saying a single disagreeable or angry word, though on one occasion she felt it her duty to whip us both. We were brought up on corporal punishment, a good thing for us. When I was either four or five years old, I strayed away and got lost somewhere down on Chapel Street, half a mile or so from home. Finally a policeman spoke to me, and eventually obtained the street and number of my home. I had disappeared about eleven o'clock in the morning and it was between three and four when the policeman brought me to the front door. I fully expected a whipping; my sister was the only person in the house. Perhaps the others were looking for me. Instead of whipping and scolding me, she greeted me with affection. Then she said, 'You must be very hungry,' and brought me some cold pudding. I recall my surprise at this unexpectedly agreeable reception and the ambrosial taste of that pudding.

My sister died on a winter morning just before dawn. I was wakened by a commotion in the house, and said to myself, 'Sophie must be dead.' Then my mother came into the room, almost insane with grief, crying out 'My God! My God!' I whispered to my father, 'What makes Mama swear so?' and my father told me, 'She is not swearing; she is praying.'

Two days later, when I was told that I was to be taken to the funeral, I leaped up and down and shouted and laughed in glee. I was not rebuked for this. My parents knew I had no real notion of the tragedy of my sister's death, and that the excitement of going somewhere in a carriage overcame every other sensation. It was the first time I had ever been in a hack, as we called it. I have no clear recollection of the interment; but I remember on the way back from the funeral, my brother Arthur, aged eight, burst into tears, and was comforted by my mother.

I miss my sister much more now than I did sixty years ago.

Here is a letter from my mother to 'Libbie,' written when I was nearly three years old.

NEW HAVEN, DEC. 10TH, 1867

MY DEAR DARLING SISTER,

Last night Willie was naughty and slapped me. I took him in my lap and tried to convince him how bad it was to strike his own Mamma. I said, 'Who takes all the care of little Willie?, makes and mends all his little clothes,' etc. He said 'There aint none body does.'

Arthur and Willie are now clearing the snow off the sidewalk. You ought to see them with their shovels at work

At the age of four or possibly five, I came very near losing my life. Incredible as it may seem, a dose of arsenic had been laid on the library floor in a corner, to exterminate mice. My brother and I were crawling around on the carpet, while my father at his stand-up desk was preparing his sermon. We found the arsenic, thought it was sugar or something edible, and we stuffed a handful into our mouths. It tasted so unpleasant we began spitting it out and our father turned around to see what was the matter. He had us at the kitchen sink in a moment, and we expelled what was left and washed and gargled. Apparently we had swallowed nothing, for we never felt any internal unpleasantness. But I can taste it still—it was such a surprise.

I was reminded of this experience when I saw the play

Madame Bovary in New York in December 1937. When Constance Cummings stuffed her mouth full of arsenic, it looked exactly both in colour and in quantity like the arsenic I took so many years ago. I am glad the resemblance went no further.

When I was about six years old, playing with other boys on top of a lattice in the garden ten feet high, one of my playmates humorously pushed me off. Had I landed on my neck, I should have been killed. But I fell on my shoulder. I went into the library where my father was writing a sermon, and he found I could not lift the arm. He took me to our neighbour, the famous surgeon Dr. Francis Bacon, who examined the arm, said nothing was broken, but that I must wear a sling for a week. It is impossible to describe the rapture this gave me. To wear a sling! To go to school every day, with my arm in a sling, the envy of every boy. A hero decorated by a Commander-in-Chief for gallantry in action could not have felt more pride.

EARLY EDUCATION

I was sent to a private school on York Street, Monday, 4 October 1868; I was three years old; I am not sure whether it was then called a kindergarten; I have no recollection of hearing that word until many years later. The teacher, a Miss Morse, was kind. My father used to come for me at the end of the morning session. Once, as we walked home through a tremendous snowstorm, I was curiously interested in the spectacle of two men on the sidewalk, who were so drunk that they kept falling down. It seemed to me they were doing it for our entertainment, and I thought it was rather nice of them.

From the age of three to the age of five I attended Miss Morse's private school. When I was five I entered the regular public district Grammar School, called after the famous lexicographer, Webster School. I was the youngest and smallest boy in the establishment, and was in daily fear of the Irish lads, whom we called Micks. The boys and girls in this school represented every layer of society in New Haven; for on Crown Street dwelt many families of considerable affluence, while Oak Street and Morocco Street belonged to the slums.

The small boy is naturally a dirty little animal; I can say truthfully that although I have frequently been disgusted, I have never been shocked since I was nine years old. Dostoevski says the average schoolboy uses language that would make a drunken sailor blush, which describes accurately the daily talk I heard during recess and after hours in this school. The most blasphemous and obscene expressions came trippingly on the tongue and were used apparently with no sense of bravado, but as the common staple of conversation. Many of our modern novelists instead of being 'frank' or 'realistic' seem to me rather juvenile. They remind me of the small talk of small boys at the Webster School.

When I was five years old, I was invited to a children's party which became tempestuous. I was chasing a girl running from room to room, dodging in and out among the other children. She made a dash into the hall running straight toward the closed door that led into the street. Just as it seemed as if she must crash into it, she leaped to one side and I went headlong into this portal. I had raised my right arm to seize her, and this arm plunged through the large glass pane in the door. So far as I can remember, I felt no hurt, but an astonishing stream of blood spirted from my wrist. I had cut two arteries. The ladies screamed and dragged me hysterically to a wash basin, and turned the faucet on my arm; but the blood covered them and the basin and it seemed as if it would cover the room. I never saw so much flowing blood, bright arterial red, and as I remember, it seemed to come in tremendous jets (I had been running violently), that spouted several feet. Unquestionably I should have died in not many minutes; but my mother, who was in another part of the house, hastened into the room, drew me into a chair and closed her hand on my wrist above the cut and hung on with desperation. She called out 'You must get a doctor immediately!' In those days there was no telephone, no speedy means of transportation. Some-one had to find a carriage and drive a long distance; it was nearly an hour before Dr. Pierpont came. I cannot remember saying anything. My mother had checked the flow of blood—why no bandage or tourniquet was used I shall never understand. The Doctor sewed up my wrist with wire, then bandaged it heavily, and said that if anything happened in the night, he must be sent for. The huge scar on my wrist is there now; and I always smile when any physician attempts to feel my pulse; for he tries the right arm first and cannot understand why no pulse is discernible.

One night about this time—it may have been shortly after this accident—I dreamed that Jesus Christ was sitting on a white cloud whilst I and others were standing below gazing at him. Suddenly he called in a loud voice, 'Willie Phelps, come here!' When I told my parents at breakfast of this dream, which I thought rather charming, they looked very grave.

I have no recollection of learning to read; when I entered this school at the age of five, I could read aloud with ease, and it was only a five-syllabled word like 'particularly' that gave me any difficulty. I had a naturally good ocular memory for words and three times in the 'spelling down' matches I was the last survivor. Pride goeth before a fall; for on the fourth contest, I was one of the first to go down. The teacher pronounced the word *gem*, which I had never heard and had no recollection of having seen. I spelled it *jem*.

In later years my heart ached for those women teachers. The filth and dirt the boys brought into the schoolroom, the insolent manner in which they answered the teacher's questions, the ribald laughter that resounded on occasions skilfully prepared to produce it! No boy ever rose to recite without finding crooked pins, or tacks (and I remember one file) put in his chair to greet his down-sitting—then came the exaggerated howl of pain and rage, the backhanded blow, the teacher's vain remonstrance. Spitballs flew around the room, falling on the just and on the unjust.

One of the bigger and tougher boys ceased to be a problem at school, for he was arrested for rape, and sent to jail. His crime and his fate were for many months a subject of conversation.

I have often wondered whether I was really a physical coward at school or whether, because of my tender years and tiny size, my awareness of incapacity made me timid. However that may be, one of the innumerable advantages of growing up is getting rid of chronic fear. Because I was easily terrified, my heroes were naturally the tough boys and they never suspected my worship. At Christmas we all exchanged gifts anonymously, and then at a certain moment, every boy and girl opened the package on his desk. I had made my gift to the roughest and most dare-devil lad in the room. His desk was not far from mine; and when we both opened our parcels, he sneered at me and mine, insisting that he had got a much better present than the one that fell to me. I did not dare tell him I was his benefactor.

He was secretly my hero, because when most of the boys were whipped by the teacher, they cried, and he always laughed out loud. The harder she struck him, the more he laughed. I have never got over my admiration and wonder at this spectacle. When we were whipped, we had to hold out a hand, and the teacher hit it with a rattan stick. He would hold out his hand, and when she was through, he would offer the other one, laughing with delight. There were nine or ten whippings every day.

An excellent illustration of the mystery of personality was in daily evidence. There were twelve rooms. Every room had a female teacher and these twelve disciples in turn were ruled by a male principal. Every teacher and every boy and girl in the building were in mortal terror of this man; he was legendary. He dwelt apart in some throne room aloft; and it was quite possible to spend a year at the school and never set eyes on him. But his invisible presence was a terrific actuality. The teachers seldom appealed to the Supreme Court. Thus, I shall never forget my amazement one day while my tough hero was getting an unusually prolonged whipping from the teacher and treating it with more than usual risibility, she suddenly lost patience and said, 'I will send you up to Mr. Lewis.' My hero collapsed; his mirth changed to pleading terror. 'Oh, don't send me to Mr. Lewis! I'll do anything you say, only don't please send me to Mr. Lewis!'

What Mr. Lewis did to these lads no one ever knew, but strange tales came from these mysterious interviews. Perhaps he never laid hands on them; just looked at them until they were petrified with fear. He was the one salvation of the women teachers, and for over forty years he presided over that whirlwind of childish savagery, disorder, corruption, and sin, and somehow made citizens out of that unpromising material. One day, coming out after school was over, he spoke to me kindly, with a smile. I was in such terror I could say nothing; but as soon as I got around the corner I ran for my life.

Once in a while he would walk through our schoolroom, without looking at anybody or speaking a word. The most absolute silence marked his advent. He seemed to me of colossal size. Years afterwards, when I returned to New Haven, I marvelled at his tiny frame and puny appearance. Was this grey-haired little man the ogre of my childhood? For the strange thing is, that even in the vile language used at recess, no boy even then took his name in vain. John Lewis was a genius of discipline.

My father had been pastor of the First Baptist Church in New Haven for nearly thirty years; and in 1874, when I was nine, he accepted a call to the Jefferson Street Baptist Church in Providence, Rhode Island. Here we lived first at 34 Carroll Street and later at 5 Francis Street. At first I attended a district or grade school, very similar to the Webster School at New Haven; and here, at the

age of ten, I fell in love with a schoolmate, Ella Henries
—I wonder where she is now? She knew I loved her,
though in her presence I was tongue-tied, 'such was my
faint heart's sweet distress.' I call it love, because I had
the symptoms described in the mediaeval romance writers,
and they were good diagnosticians. I kissed her once only
and that was in the game post-office, and it was a miserable
effort. I shakingly aimed at her mouth and side-swiped
her on the cheekbone.

During the year and a half we lived in Providence, I was
'converted.' There were revival meetings at our church,
and one evening, when the Reverend Doctor Bixby had
been preaching, I stood up when they called for the unconverted. It was not an explosive experience, but I did
feel very happy. My brother and I were baptized by immersion by my father in March 1876; thus I have been a
member of the Baptist denomination in 'good and regular
standing' for over sixty years. One of the reasons I have
never deserted the fold is that the Baptists have no creed,
no ritual, no church organization; there is indeed no Baptist Church, only a collection of Baptist churches. No
organization has any control over any Baptist unit, any
more than the New York University Club has over the
Chicago University Club. Now while I admire the beauty
of a ritual and often attend Mass in a Catholic Church, I
am such an individualist that I feel more at home among
Baptists, Congregationalists, and Quakers.

Here for a few months in Providence I had my first intellectual awakening. I made progress with a rapidity that
in retrospect is inexplicable. There was an excellent private
school at the top of the hill opposite Brown University,
called the University Grammar School, kept by the brothers Merrick and Emory Lyon. It was an expensive school,
but in some way my father managed to enter my brother
Arthur and me (my oldest brother Dryden, after a year

at Yale, had accompanied the family to Providence and was an undergraduate at Brown) at a reduced rate. We entered this school in the Autumn of 1875, when I was ten, and left it in the Spring of 1876, when the family moved to Hartford.

I have often wondered what my mental development would have been had we remained in Providence. I should have been prepared for college at the age of fifteen, possibly fourteen, and would undoubtedly have entered Brown.

I was once more the youngest and the smallest boy in school. The oldest boys were some of them full-grown, wore side-whiskers and moustachios, and came from wealthy or aristocratic families. Doctor Lyon, a remarkable teacher, took a personal interest in me, and suddenly I developed a fierce and unquenchable thirst for learning. We were in school about six hours daily except Saturday and I often studied six hours a day at home. I was making fast progress in Latin, French, History, English composition, public speaking; and if I had stayed at that school two years I should either have learned more than I learned in the next six years or I should have had some kind of breakdown.

Friday mornings we had 'Declamation exercises,' when every boy, except those excused for some reason, spoke a piece he had learned by heart. I had no difficulty in learning the eighty-eight stanzas of 'Horatius at the Bridge,' and I remember it took me twenty minutes to speak them. It must have bored the school almost beyond endurance. Here too I had the opportunity to speak Browning's poem 'Hervé Riel' before he published it. Browning, abandoning his usual custom, printed it in the *Cornhill Magazine* in 1871, and gave the hundred pounds he received to the suffering inhabitants of Paris. Later, in the year 1876, he published it in the volume *Pachiarotto*. Well, I was turning over the pages of Monroe's *Sixth Reader* to find a good

poem for declamation; and I found that. I had never heard
of the author but the poem pleased me; and I recited it in
1875. As in my later professional career I spent more time
teaching Browning than any other author, it interests me
to recall this early episode.

It may be that my extraordinary progress in the acquisition of knowledge came from the blessed fact that in the
University Grammar School, I was, for some unknown
reason, free of mathematics, the curse of my subsequent
life at school and at college. Apart from an hour called
'Mental Arithmetic' which seemed more like an amusing
game than anything else, I had no mathematics. All my
studies I found absorbing, exciting; they made an equally
strong appeal to my interest and to my ambition.

In this school I was also getting a much-needed social
education, though it did not last long enough to reform
my bad manners. Possibly because the other boys were
so much older or because they had all been so well brought
up, I cannot remember hearing any bad language during
the winter of my stay. They seemed to me young gentlemen
of finished elegance, and I felt uncouth; like a savage who
had wandered into a civilized home. Perhaps I was more
like a savage who had been converted by some missionary;
I was very religious, but devoid of tact or even the rudi-
ments of good social behaviour.

For my own sake, I am sorry that my earliest sermons
are lost. It would amuse me to read them. I wished to
imitate my father; I wanted to be like him in every way.
I wanted to excel at athletic games, I wanted a gun to go
shooting, I wanted a desk of my own and solitude for
writing, I wanted to be a preacher and public orator. When
I was eight years old, I began to preach sermons to the
family on Sunday afternoons and I kept this up for two or
three years. I wrote these sermons out on 'sermon paper'
and every Sunday afternoon I conducted a regular service,

the audience consisting of my father, mother, and two brothers. I remember how desperately hard it was for me to think up enough material to fill four pages of manuscript. The family assembled, with a perfectly straight face, for I was tremendously in earnest; I read the hymns before they were sung, and preached a sermon, which whatever it lacked in literary merit, was uncompromisingly orthodox. The family managed to listen seriously, until, one afternoon while reading a hymn I came to the line

Deep horror then my vitals froze

and I had the misfortune to pronounce the word as 'vittles.' The family burst into roars of uncontrollable laughter. I was hurt and I believe that ended my first efforts as a preacher. I could see nothing funny in it, and their attempts to explain the connotation of cold storage were lost on me, as I had never seen the word *victuals*.

My other early attempts at public recitals were more fortunate; I became every summer a public entertainer. In those days two classes of people went to Saratoga Springs—race-track gamblers and ministers of the Gospel. In common with other ministers, my father stayed in boarding-houses; the race-track people, whom we never met, stayed at one of the three enormous hotels that were famous all over the world, The Grand Union Hotel, The United States Hotel, and Congress Hall. It was solemnly whispered to me that at these hotels some of the millionaires paid five dollars a day!

The larger boarding-houses had some kind of entertainment every evening—music, elocution, and what not. I had learned a comic song, part sung, part recited (wasn't it by Gus Williams?) called 'Mygel Schneider's Party,' and the Manager of the boarding-house, hearing me singing it for fun one day, got me to sing it in public every night for the entertainment of the guests. I was devoid of self-consciousness, and sang this absurd piece nightly without the slightest embarrassment or fear. If I had to enter a room containing people engaged in animated conversation, I was overwhelmed with embarrassment; but I could get up before a big audience and speak or recite or sing without even a shadow of fear. I have never had stage-fright, possibly because I began to speak so early.

Henry Ward Beecher said he never walked on a platform or a pulpit without stage-fright, though it disappeared the moment he began to speak. I often say to myself just before walking on the stage in a crowded auditorium, 'Why am I not frightened?' but even that question does not disturb me. I reflect, 'You ought to be scared; you would have more respect for yourself if you were scared;' but try as hard as I may, it is all in vain. I am straining at the leash.

Beginning with 1895, I have given every year many public lectures outside of my work in the classroom; and my annual *courses of lectures* in New Haven, New York, Brooklyn, Philadelphia, and Connecticut cities I have particularly enjoyed. I think everyone who lectures frequently to large audiences enjoys it; but I think very few feel such thrilling delight as I invariably do. Whether I give it or not, I always receive inspiration. Furthermore, I love these audiences; I have for them an intimate, almost a family affection. I call them my children; in the Brooklyn Institute my Sunday children; in the Town Hall, Manhattan, my Saturday children; in New Haven, my Tuesday children; in the Forum, my Philadelphia children. Often while I am travelling in Europe or in remote parts of the United States, some person will speak to me saying, 'I am one of your Sunday children,' and it is like meeting a relation or a college classmate. There is an intimacy between my audiences and myself that adds much to the pleasure of addressing them. I am grateful to them and to all the people everywhere who have honoured me by their presence and attention. It has also been an especial pleasure to speak to academic audiences in various universities; and to conventions of school-teachers and librarians, all of us engaged in a common cause and proud of our profession.

BOYHOOD EXPERIENCES

AT Providence, 12 November 1875, when I was ten years old, I was examined by Dr. Emory Lyon at the University Grammar School, in *Eaton's Common School Arithmetic*; and a day or two later by Harmon S.Babcock in Latin and Geography. I was examined also in French by Dr. Lyon.

I wrote the following note at Providence, 14 March 1876. 'I was examined by Deacon Hall, Mr. Benson, and Papa, to be baptized. This happened Thursday, Feb. 24, 1876. I told my experience to the church, Feb. 25, 1876. I was baptized with Miss Whaley, Mrs. Allen, Lincoln Rose, my brother Arthur, on Feb. 27, 1876, Sunday eve. Papa preached the night I was baptized on Sodom and Gomorrah. It was a very solemn sermon. The text was "And Lot pitched his tent toward Sodom." He repeated some poetry of Arthur Coxe's. I remember that the sermon was so interesting, that I utterly forgot all about the baptism.'

After the sermon when my father called for the first person to come forward to be baptized, no one moved. Finally he said 'Let the first one come!' No one moved, so I stepped forward. I should have been baptized last, because the water in the baptistery would not have been nearly so deep; the clothes and the robes of each person take up a great deal of water. I remember distinctly that when I put my foot in, I gasped aloud, and the lady playing the organ looked at me in amazement. My father led me and the water came up to my chin.

Two years later, when I was graduated from the

West Middle District School at Hartford, the Principal, Mr. D.P.Corbin, addressed the graduating class as follows:

'Don't be so *foolish* as to study Saturday, so *wicked* as to study Sunday, and so *crazy* as to study early Monday morning.'

Thursday, Friday, Saturday, 26, 27, 28 October 1876, my parents took the whole family to the Centennial in Philadelphia. I kept a diary while there. The things that I remember most distinctly are the huge Corliss engine, which Mr. Corliss would not allow to run on Sunday, and the delicious taste of butter at a French restaurant. We were wandering about the grounds and entered a French restaurant for lunch; I could not imagine why the butter tasted so much better than any I had ever known. It was the first time I had ever tasted saltless butter; but during the last sixty years I have got saltless butter whenever possible.

On top of the Ohio State Building appeared one day in the open air before an enormous crowd, Rutherford B.Hayes, candidate for President of the United States. He was introduced by General Hawley, Senator from Connecticut. Near me, on the ground, and in the midst of this throng, sat a woman suckling her child. It was the first time I had consciously seen a woman's breast; and it was a strange spectacle. The mother was as indifferent to Hayes's eloquence and to the enthusiasm of the crowd as was her child.

One of the sights of the Centennial was in Agricultural Hall, where on a perch stood a bald headed eagle called Old Abe. He had gone through the four years of the Civil War, as a pet of the Union Soldiers, and had escaped unscathed. 'Some of the rebels had shot at him,' I wrote. Again: 'Then to Machinery Hall, then to Main Building, where I saw a model of Chaos (*sic*) the greatest pyramid of Egypt.'

The glass-blowers were surrounded by throngs, and thousands of model glass slippers were sold. We brought home two. One I have now; the other, some thirty years after its purchase, I threw against the wall and smashed, in a rage at losing a game of billiards.

I did not see another World's Fair until 1893, when my wife and I went to Chicago. I do not believe there has ever been an Exposition anywhere in the world that compares with that one in beauty and dignity. No witness will forget the Court of Honour at night.

Incidentally, our first view of the new University of Chicago was from the top of the Ferris Wheel; and the one Gothic quadrangle looked academically impressive. The only person we met in front of it a half-hour later was the President, William R.Harper. He was, as usual, full of enthusiasm for the future of the university, for the future of Chicago, for the future of the human race.

The following letter is worth reading, because it reveals the character and personality of my father, and because it shows some of the difficulties that have always beset young ministers in small churches. The man to whom my father wrote this letter was so discouraged by the smallness of his salary and the conditions accompanying it, that he was considering leaving the ministry altogether and accepting an agency as a travelling salesman.

NEW HAVEN, MARCH 13, 1851

DEAR BR. GORHAM:

I have been to the Board Meeting at Norwich, & would suggest that they have unanimously appointed you as the Minister for Humphreys-ville, & very anxious for you to remain there. I also procured for you an order on the Treasurer for the amount of your salary up to the present time *Eighty-four Dollars*, & what money was on hand then, *Fifty-five dollars*, was paid for you & I have it here awaiting your order. The rest you can get any time on application to the Treasurer. Now this $84 is a snug little sum for your labors for less than two months & a half. At least it is better than nothing. And with your present salary, *due to be paid promptly*, you may not complain very much, till Providence gives you a better portion.

Your letter received Tuesday morning I liked very much, with some slight exceptions. You say you know or I know that I would not consent to do as you are doing, that is preach for the salary & the people you are preaching for. I will tell you what I did do, after I got ready for the Ministry. I was invited to settle with a little church worshiping in a poor hall, a small congregation, & on a salary of less than four hundred, & I considered it a fair chance to begin with. But for reasons, disconnected with the salary, place etc., I engaged to supply another church for nearly six months at the rate of about $300 a year, & I did so; & there preached a year for the church of which I am now Pastor at $400. And if I were not a Pastor, I would again, yes preach at Humphreysville, as you are doing, unless called elsewhere by Providence. I had as much debt to pay as you, & paid it faster on a small salary & few expenses, than it would be possible for me to do now.

I fully believe you will rue it, if you accept any agency, even if a larger salary is proposed. Think of increased expenses; what if you should be sick among strangers! If well, you would have no certain dwelling place. You would often get the cold shoulder, or your cause would, & if you didn't have the *blues* worse than anything you have yet experienced, then you would be more fortunate than some I know of. Suppose you should take an agency, at $600 a year. Depend upon it you would not be as well off at the end of the year as you would to remain where you are. I do not think your temperament suited to an agent. It is not absolutely necessary to stay in Humphreysville. Pastoral relations change in the Spring often, & if duty calls elsewhere I presume some favorable opening will be presented for you. Besides, things are not to be in your village as they are now long. A good House of Worship is very soon to be built & paid for, & then there will be a good congregation, & soon a flourishing Church by God's blessing. Your present improved style of preaching, & your determination to excel, will attract no doubt a delighted audience for you, & result in the conversion of many. You know it wants a strong man, & faithful Minister just at your point in the Naugatuck Valley, where there is so much ungodliness, practical infidelity. No place in this world is a Paradise, & the most favored of God's ministers meet with things that almost crush their hearts. Suppose I should tell *all* my experience even as it is at this time. My present salary does not cover all the expenses of my family, & I am compelled to deny myself in many things that I feel as though I ought to have. But if God blesses my labors, I *hope* for improvement.

I would not put the slightest obstacle in the way of any blessing for I have the kindest & deepest interest & affection for you. But I was surprised & pained, on hearing from you, just after you had commenced a new era in the manner of preaching, etc. that you were writing to your friends in different parts, proposing to abandon the ministry for the sake of *expecting* a little more salary. I felt that you were doing what would be an injury to you & disastrous to some extent to the cause of religion. Your motives may be good; but others would not look with your eyes. May God speed you in the right course, with his richest blessing.

Yours affectionately,

S. D. PHELPS

INTERLUDE ON CATS

I HAVE always been an idolater of cats. Idolater is the accurate word; and perhaps only those will understand my devotion in whom, as in me, the love of cats is inborn. I once heard a famous scientist in a public lecture say that most children are afraid of anything that has fur on it; and their fear, he explained, is owing to the fact that some forty thousand years ago furred animals were dangerous to the hairless human children; and a feeling therefore rose which had become instinctive, persisting long after the original reason for it had ceased to exist. This statement, like many other remarks of scientific men, I heard with profound scepticism.

My father, my mother, and my aunt took no interest in cats, and would have been undisturbed had they known they would never see one again. Yet I cannot remember the time when any cat, no matter how humble in origin and in social station, failed to arouse in me breathless adoration. Even the dirtiest alleycat was an object of worship.

Many persons love cats; but have they had these intimations of felinity in earliest childhood? How shall I describe this cat-worship? As a baby I loved every piece of fur. My oldest brother had a fur hat; night after night I slept with it. I called it the cat-hat. My aunt Libbie had a tippet of ermine. I used to hug this article, and kiss it frantically. My aunt at first was touched when she came into the room and found me kissing her ermine, because she thought it was evidence of my love for her. She discovered it was nothing of the kind; and she was even more puzzled than disappointed. I loved my aunt and she was good to me; but when she asked me if I kissed the ermine because it was hers, I shouted with the disconcerting candour characteristic of childhood, 'No! No!' and kissing the fur with renewed vigour, I called it 'Kitty! Pussy!' Even today I long to stroke every piece of fur I see. No doubt many visitors thought I was insane. Perhaps they were right. Only if I was, I have never recovered. In addressing women I admired I added the termination *cat* to their names; thus Elizabeth became Lizcat, Olivia Livcat, Madelene Madcat, Alice Alleycat, and Helen Hellcat.

I have always envied professionals I have seen enter the cages of lions and tigers and stroke cats eight feet long!

Of all domestic animals the cat is the most beautiful and the most graceful. His anatomy is precisely adapted to his needs; and although he takes only a hundredth as much athletic exercise as a dog, he is always in perfect condition. Whoever saw a housemaid exercising a cat? There is no other beast who from a position of absolute relaxation can spring with accuracy and with no preliminary motion. The cat does not have to wind up like a baseball pitcher, or get 'set;' he transmutes potential energy into kinetic energy with no visible effort.

When a cat aims at the top of a fence or the surface of a table, he usually succeeds at the first effort, unlike the dog, who will try and continue to try long after the impossibility of attainment has been demonstrated to a spectator. The cat's economy of effort is as remarkable as his judgement of distance; you cannot persuade him to try for any mark beyond his reach. The cat catches birds on the ground by outguessing them and by a final spring faster than flight; but if the bird has risen in the air, the cat makes no attempt at pursuit, which he knows to be futile and undignified. But the dog will run after flying birds to the limit of exhaustion.

The amazing activity of the cat is delicately balanced by his capacity for relaxation. Every household should contain a cat, not only for decorative and domestic values, but because the cat in quiescence is medicinal to irritable, tense, tortured men and women. In spite of all the physicians and hospitals and books that are endeavouring to induce men and women to 'relax'—continued energy seems to be required in order to keep quiet—few human beings understand the art of repose. They cannot let go.

Now when the cat decides to rest, he not only lies down; he pours his body out on the floor like water. It is reposeful merely to watch him. The average man looks up from the morning newspaper and roars at the folly and stupidity of our law-makers; then he happens to see the family cat, who seems to put to the householder every day the Emersonian question—'So hot, my little Sir?'

The beauty and grace and agility of the cat's body are equalled by his intellectual and spiritual nature. It is often said by those who have no affection for cats that cats have no affection; this is a slander. A youth tried to convince an old man that cats were without affection, saying the cat loves you only because he wishes to get something out of you. It isn't really love. 'Ah,' replied the sage, 'when you are as old as I am, you will call that love.'

The dog is a good fellow and jolly companion, but he does not compare in intellectual power with the cat. The cat has an acute mind, an inflexible will, and a patience almost divine. If the cat wishes to leave the room, he makes no fuss about it and does not annoy you with vocal importunities; he selects a position near the door. Now you may change his position but you cannot change his purpose; his purpose is to leave the room; and he knows that opportunities come to those who are ready. He pretends he has dismissed the matter from his mind; but when someone happens to open the door, the cat departs.

The patience of the cat in hunting is one reason why he seldom returns empty-clawed. A hole in the ground will arouse terrific enthusiasm in a dog; he will bark frantically and dig vigorously; but unless something happens within five minutes, his ardour cools; he goes away and forgets. If a cat decides there is game in a certain spot he does not advertise his presence; he waits for the prey to make the first move and he can outwait any other living thing.

One reason men have always liked dogs is that the dog flatters us with fawning servility; it is agreeable to be received with such demonstrations of affection. But the devotion of the dog has been overpraised. What a dog wants is entertainment. He is easily bored, cannot amuse himself, and demands excitement. His ideal is a life of active uselessness. That the dog is devoted only to his master is a myth. He is devoted to anyone in whose company he finds entertainment. I had to be disillusioned before I accepted this truth. My first dog was a noble Irish setter who apparently could not bear to have me out of his sight; he cared nothing for guests or strangers; if I left the room he instantly followed me. I felt proud of this, and often thought what a noble, faithful fellow he was. But one day I fell into a sickness and had to stay in bed two weeks. For an hour or so on the first day he remained in my room. But there were other men in the house. One of them took the dog for a walk and alienated his affections. The dog never came near me, but pretended to be pleased when I recovered.

Even the famous 'one-man' dogs are fed by the one man. Yet I feel like a traitor in calling attention to these moral defects. How can I help loving a creature so affectionate, so demonstrative, so responsive? I can't. It is only my love of truth that compels me to say that in dignity and neatness the dog does not compare with the cat. The dog is a jolly good fellow; he leaps joyously upon you, places his muddy paws on your shirt-front, and after swimming, postpones the shaking of his frame until he is within close range. Indoors he wags his tail violently, knocking down vases and ornaments and leaving a trail of wreckage. The cat, on the other hand, after delicately showing affection by rubbing gently against one's ankles, springs without apparent effort to a narrow shelf covered with fragile objects and never displaces anything. His extraordinary mental and physical poise is shown by the astounding fact that he can sleep with assurance on the top of a fence only two inches broad, or indeed far aloft on the trim branch of a tree.

The superiority of the cat is shown most convincingly in his intellectual resources. You may love a dog but the cat commands your respect. His infinite capacity to keep still makes him good company for many quiet hours. The dog, as someone has said, is always on the wrong side of the door.

The ability of the cat to entertain himself was shown in a striking essay which appeared about forty years ago in the *Yale Literary Magazine*; it was written by an undergraduate, Ray Morris, who later demonstrated his ability to write equally well on other themes. He emphasized the cat's intellectual resources.

I have observed this fact so often that it may be in my comments I shall unwittingly borrow from my memory of Mr. Morris's essay. If you leave the dog outside the front door only for a moment, while you are looking inside for something, he is in a flutter of nerves; he barks, whines, and scratches in an agony of desolation. But if you kick the cat out of the house with a kind of final gesture, he remains thoughtful a moment as if to say, 'Now I *had* planned to spend the afternoon indoors; but it is possible that it is more hygienic in the garden. I will sleep until there are further developments.'

The cat, although he has not the super smelling power of

the dog, has an astonishing faculty of finding his way to the place he has chosen to reach. A man who owned a magnificent cat was told by his neighbours that if he did not kill the animal before Saturday night, they would do it for him; for the cat had shown a fondness for their chickens. He was at a loss what to do. A friend advised him to take the cat to the most complicated corner in the city of Boston, somewhere near Scollay Square. There the streets are so crooked and twisted that no stranger has ever found his way without enquiry; he should leave the cat there, would never see him again, and would have no cause for worry, since the place abounded in grocery shops where someone would gladly take in the animal. The owner was asked a month later if he had done this and with what result. He replied, ' What a place that was! if I had not followed the cat, I should never have got home.'

To a man individual liberty is the greatest blessing; to a dog it is the last word in despair. He is happy only in slavery. Hence he sticks to a master even though he is treated badly. The more one beats him, the greater is his servility. If you wish to keep a cat you must treat him with respect. The cat is essentially free. He has never been entirely tamed. He will not stand physical ill-treatment and you must not laugh at him when he comes down from a tree, the only thing he does ungracefully. The Egyptians, with their endless patience, were the only people who succeeded in turning him into a domestic animal, and heaven only knows how many centuries they spent on the task.

Men resemble dogs; women are more like cats. A large part of men's activity is physical; they spend much time in running around, and they demand excitement. Women manage somehow to entertain themselves in a way incomprehensible to the male mind.

It is a pity that dogs take no interest in washing themselves; it would help in passing the time. It is a constant resource for a cat. If there is nothing else going on or if the cat is wakeful, he can always wash himself. To a cat self-washing is a means of cleanliness, an athletic exercise, a pastime, a fine art, a religious ritual. I have seen a cat go into a frenzy of ablution.

How strange it is that to a cat's tongue, corrugated like the blade of a golf-niblick, heat should be unendurable. The cat always waits for hot food to cool.

You can guess what a dog is thinking about and what he will do next, both of which divinations fail with the cat. The eyes of a cat do not betray his mind. He has such a patrician reserve that when he does show affection it is enormously flattering. When you want a dog to come to you instantly, you shout at him. Try that on the cat.

It is often said that the dog is more intelligent, because he learns tricks so easily. But is this good evidence? You command a dog to 'sit up' and the poor fellow thinks he has to do it. The average cat throws off, pretends unconquerable limpness of body and stupidity of mind, and an inability to understand what is wanted. Of course he understands only too well. Why sit up? There is nothing in it.

But cats, alas, are as mortal as dogs. It may be that they have nine lives, but as my friend George Stanleigh Arnold says, it is always the ninth that they lose.

No man in the world understood cats better than the famous playwright, William Gillette. After I had printed an article on cats, I received from Mr. Gillette the following letter:

> Surely it must be evident to you that those who attack a person for appreciating the wonderful traits and beauties of cats are grossly and absolutely ignorant, and also pitiably prejudiced regarding them, and in addition are the resident members of a class which prefers abject unreasoning worship and cloying servility to unconquerable independence and rare judgment of character.
>
> And surely you know what good company you are in—and I am

not referring to myself alone in reminding you of this—in the appreciation of cats. Even old Voltaire took the trouble to say 'Beware of the woman who does not like cats'—and although I have sometimes failed to beware of her, I nevertheless enjoy having that testimony to Mr. V.'s attitude on the question.

What I really wanted to say was not the foregoing (which is really foregone, as there can be no argument about it)—but the following:

There are three things which I really think you would do well to touch upon when you next take up this subject:

1. The absolute necessity of cats for the preservation of birds. There is unlimited testimony from scientific sources that, for the few birds that are caught and devoured by cats, there are millions whose lives are saved by the destruction of their enemies.

2. The unquestionable possession of some sort of extra 'sense' which enables cats to be aware of the attitude—or even more than the attitude, of a human mind, where it concerns themselves. I have experimented a great deal in this direction, and cannot avoid the conclusion that cats are either mind readers (when they want to be) or that they have such a wonderful appreciation of exterior symptoms that they arrive at the mental processes via that route.

3. I have forgotten this one for the moment; but I want to tell you this; it was very important and it would be a good thing for you to consult me before you do anything further on this subject—and also possibly (for all I know) on any other.

P.S. Although I have taken considerable time in trying to remember what the third point was, it has not yet occurred to me. For a substitute, however, let us say that it was the exquisite sense of comedy possessed by the family under discussion—comedy of the very highest known altitude. Though I have not considered the matter, it seems to me that no other animal is possessed of such an exquisite and fastidious sense of humour—not even man himself.

Finally, although there are many persons who are afraid of dogs, they are not really afraid of dogs—they are afraid of being bitten. But the uncanny and unearthly nature of the cat is shown by the fact that many brave men and women are in terror if there is a cat in the room. It is not fear of what the cat might do—it is fear of the Cat. Lord Roberts, the great soldier, had an unconquerable fear of cats. Cosmo Hamilton wrote (*Unwritten History*),

He dined once at the country house of a mutual friend, rose in the middle of dinner, ran out into the garden, and stood trembling on the lawn because a yellow-eyed Angora kitten had poked an inquisitive head around the door. His fear was well-founded; for the next moment the kitten would have leaped on his knee. Cats have a sure instinct for those who fear or dislike them, and they will invariably leap upon them or rub against them, in the endeavour to dispel prejudice.

The late Doctor James Hosmer Penniman of Philadelphia wrote an exquisite little book on cats called *The Alley Rabbit*. He received a letter from William Gillette, written in his castle, 'Seventh Sister.'

I have bestowed upon you the highest honor in the repertoire of the Seventh Sister Establishment. I have named a cat after you and it wasn't a gelding either but a fine sturdy Thomas cat. This superb animal has been baptized, not with the name of James alone but with your middle and last names as well. Also we call him Doc for short, and the old boy seems perfectly delighted, throwing his tail about in the air with joyful jerks—which is a darn sight more than you could do. Ever since we have been addressing this cat as Dr. James Hosmer Penniman, he has been leaving carefully selected rats on the Seventh Sister Penniman Memorial Library.

On 21 January 1928 I received the following letter from Mr. W.A.Way, from Grey Institute, Port Elizabeth, Cape Colony.

I wonder whether you noticed in Mr. Fletcher's Memoir of A.D.Godley which appears in Godley's *Reliquiae* (Oxford University Press) the concluding words 'he shared with many wise persons a most intelligent and comprehensive affection for the whole race of cats.' Godley, who was editing the Oxford Magazine when I was up, is I suppose the happiest and cleverest and most scholarly of all writers and parodists. (He died at 70 in 1925) so that you are again in excellent company!

I received the picture of a cross-eyed cat, the pet of Mrs. Muriel Frey, of San Francisco. Had anyone knowledge of any other cat thus peculiar? My own white cat,

Miss Frosty Evans of Philadelphia, had one blue and one green eye, attracting the attention of biologists. Men and women with one blue and one brown eye are not uncommon, but the blue-and-green combination is rare.

Only a few years ago I was delighted to learn from a philosopher and scholar, author of many books, and my intimate friend, the late Dr. Henshaw Ward, that a cat had been named after me. He wrote from North Carolina in the winter of 1933:

My dear Billy:

This afternoon, when I called on Professor C.A.Lloyd of the Biltmore Junior College, I was astonished to hear Mrs. Lloyd say, 'Oh, here is William Lyon Phelps.' Then a gray cat trotted from behind me, and I was amused.

But after I had heard the story of the name I realized that it is not amusing. It is an idyll—as I will show you. When this cat was a kitten and before he was christened, the boy who owned him happened to read some passage of yours in which you express your admiration for cats. The boy exclaimed, 'Any one who can write so understandingly about cats ought to have one named after him.' The boy was entirely serious. The animal is always called 'Dr. Phelps' by the whole family.

RUFUS H. PHELPS

I HAVE never owned any dog except Irish setters; three of whom have been named Rufus. The one whom I describe here was the second to bear his name, and he belongs in this autobiography because he was the most literary dog in the world. Rufus was Irish, he was red-headed, he was a good fighter after he had exhausted diplomatic formalities; therefore it was natural that he should have been born during the World War, and on the anniversary of the Battle of the Boyne, still celebrated as a bellicose occasion.

He was born 12 July 1917 and died 28 June 1931, having nearly attained the venerable dog's age of fourteen.

Bernard Shaw celebrated 12 July 1928 by writing his own name for us in one of his books and under it 'Rufus's Birthday.' But the two never met.

When we had the honour of entertaining Joseph Conrad in our house in New Haven, Rufus displayed adoration. He fawned upon him, shook hands, and gazed into the face of the seaman with intense earnestness. Mr. Conrad responded with strokes and caresses. That was an unforgettable scene when the old seadog conversed so intimately with the dog of the fields.

On the first occasion when John Galsworthy entered our library, and sat at my desk, Rufus came in. He ran to Mr. Galsworthy, and although he had never seen him before, greeted him as if both were intimate friends. Mr. Galsworthy, who had an Irish setter of his own three thousand miles away, immediately knelt on the floor, clasped the dog around his neck, and kissed him fervently on the brow.

Hugh Walpole, on various visits to America, established a close friendship with Rufus, and told him many interesting facts about dogs he himself had written in England, to which Rufus listened with attention.

When Mr. and Mrs. G. K. Chesterton stayed at our house, Rufus immediately showed recognition of the genius of the famous Englishman, putting his paw up as if to say, 'We understand each other perfectly.'

Joseph Conrad was not the only amphibious writer who appreciated Rufus. When the dog was hardly more than a puppy—though he had already given unmistakable signs of coming intellectual distinction—John Masefield happened to be in my library. The two had not conversed more than a few moments when it seemed as if they had grown up together; and W. B. Yeats greeted Rufus as a fellow-countryman.

Rufus admired men of letters; and his taste was by no means narrow. It was all one to him whether his friend was a poet, a dramatist, a novelist, or essayist; all Rufus asked was that he write *something*, and that something of international fame. In this one respect, it is possible that he incurred the obloquy of being regarded as a snob. Socially speaking, all dogs are snobs; but I prefer to regard the particular homage that Rufus paid to distinguished writers, not as a mark of snobbery, but as penetrating literary criticism. He discriminated between the near-great and the great; reserving his highest favours to those who stood highest.

After his death, Rufus became a legendary figure. The story of his filling the post of librarian is well known. We have many new books lying on our library table; our neighbours and friends enter at the front door, select what books they wish to read, and depart. It was reported that those who showed literary discrimination in their selections were affectionately greeted by Rufus; those who took inferior books received snarls and snorts. This is, I regret to say, apocryphal.

6

THREE BLESSINGS

EARLY in the year 1876 my father received an invitation from Hartford, Conn., to become editor and proprietor of the *Christian Secretary*, a weekly periodical representing the Baptist denomination. Among denominational periodicals this stood high, having been founded in 1822. My father had always been a contributor, having caught at an early age (by seeing his contributions in type) what Oliver Wendell Holmes called 'lead poisoning.' His first work as an editor was in his schooldays at the Connecticut Literary Institution at Suffield, when he and another boy edited the school paper. My father loved everything that had to do with a newspaper office; he knew how to set type, and in our house in New Haven, he had a printing press and several cases of type.

He was sixty years old, and though he was in constant demand as a preacher, he knew the average congregation preferred younger pastors; there was every reason why he should go to Hartford. Accordingly, in the Spring of 1876 the family moved to the capital city of Connecticut, where he rented a house at 137 Sigourney Street.

Although the break in my formal education, in my being forced to leave the University Grammar School at Providence, set me back at least two years, in every other way the move to Hartford was for me fortunate; and in three definite ways.

My father had always had a large private library, but apart from some standard sets of classics, the library was almost entirely theological. Now, however, as he was in charge of a weekly journal with a good circulation, the publishers sent him for review new books on every subject. So our house was filled with the latest novels, essays, poems, histories, biographies, and books of travel. What this meant to me it is not necessary to emphasize. I had always read everything I could lay my hands on; and now, for the next fifteen years, from the age of eleven to the age of twenty-six, I had God's plenty. But my efforts were not confined to reading. When I was fourteen, I read among the new books, Higginson's *Young Folks' Book of American Explorers*, and my father asked me to review it for the paper! He put in a prefatory note giving the name and age of the new literary critic. This was the first book I ever reviewed in print; the first of many thousands, for I never stopped from that day to this.

When I was sixteen, seventeen, and eighteen, some books which had an influence on me were the successive volumes of the American Statesmen Series, edited by John T. Morse, Jr., who was still active at the age of ninety-six. I was led by these to read other works in American political history, and when, at the age of seventeen, I read Daniel Webster's speech of the Seventh of March 1850, I was completely converted to Webster's point of view; although I had been taught by my parents and by everyone else who mentioned the subject, to believe the opposite. It pleases me today that the best authorities on American history believe that the speech of the Seventh of March, which ruined Webster in New England, was the wisest, most far-seeing, most patriotic, most unselfish action of his career.

I shall never forget the evening in 1882 when I sat down under the gas-light to read Froude's *Life of Carlyle*. This book became a lifelong inspiration; Carlyle's writings and books about Carlyle have had a continuous influence on me. I read *Sartor Resartus* before going to college; in a later chapter I shall speak of the effect of Carlyle's *Heroes*; in 1884 when I was a sophomore appeared *Obiter Dicta*, the book that made Augustine Birrell famous; the first essay in it was on Carlyle, and I read it with excitement. About forty years later, when I was slowly recovering from a nervous breakdown I began to read David Alec Wilson's monumental *Life of Carlyle*; it had a good deal to do with my convalescence, because I became so absorbed in it I forgot my despondency; I read every word of the six volumes as they appeared in successive years. Although Mr. Wilson hated Froude I cared nothing about that controversy. I have always been grateful to Froude for arousing my interest in Carlyle when I was seventeen, and grateful to Mr. Wilson for bringing out his work just when I needed it most.

Not only do I owe my initial reading of Carlyle to Froude, but it was through this biography that I began to read a far greater writer, Goethe. Carlyle talked so much of Goethe that I read his translation of *Wilhelm Meister* before I was eighteen. It interested me enormously; the first composition I wrote for the Yale undergraduate *Literary Magazine* was on Philina. I have always been very fond of Philina, and think Wilhelm failed to appreciate her. She was not morally impeccable, but she illuminates every scene in which she appears and when she leaves the story it is like the death of Mercutio.

In my Junior year at college I went to hear the Emma Abbott Opera Company in *Mignon*. I had no idea the Mignon was the Mignon of my beloved novel; but when I saw the characters (so intimately familiar to my mind) appear on the stage, Wilhelm, Philina, Laertes, Friedrich, and the rest, I had a succession of thrills, and this opera has always had for me an especial fascination.

While I was still a schoolboy, I read Bayard Taylor's

translation of *Faust*, not only the best of the numerous translations of that work, but one of the greatest translations of any work. Of course I could not understand much of *Faust*; but it is well for boys and girls to read some authors and some books that are beyond their stage of development. I was conscious of greatness, as one obtains through shifting clouds transient views of the Matterhorn.

I *live* with Goethe as I live with Shakespeare and with Browning. Browning made the poet Cleon say that after his death his soul would be in men's hearts. Although Cleon himself got no comfort out of this, Goethe's soul has been in my heart for fifty years. I suppose I think of him every day of my life.

I have the highest intellectual respect for those three towering men of genius of the eighteenth century—Goethe, Voltaire, Benjamin Franklin, all of whom, fortunately for the world, lived to be over eighty. They were lovers of liberty and were more civilized than the majority of educated persons today.

Incidentally, in my boyhood I became fond of the offices and composing room of the *Christian Secretary*. I used to go there many times outside of school hours, set type from a 'stick,' distribute type, and fold papers every Tuesday afternoon as they came from the big press.

Like many boys of those days, I owned a small printing press, run by hand, on which I printed cards and various trivialities. My first appearance as an editor was at the age of twelve. With the assistance of another small boy, Charles A. Kellogg as 'publisher,' I edited *The Midget* and indeed wrote the entire first number, including the advertisements. I contributed an original poem, the first instalment of a novel called *Captain Chas. Plympton* (a naval officer who got into action in the first paragraph) and various items of local news. We returned the money extracted from subscribers, as the first number was also the last.

The second definite benefit that I received from our residence in Hartford was social, and of great value. The difference in the public schools in Hartford from those I had attended in New Haven and Providence was as great as if I had been in another world. I do not believe there has ever been any Grade School or any Public High School anywhere in America, equal to the West Middle District School and the High School of Hartford in the seventies and eighties.

My parents were more concerned with my spiritual and intellectual development than they were with my social behaviour; rather the opposite of most parents today, who think that if their children are healthy and have good manners, nothing more will be required. In my case what I needed was dancing-school, and my aunt in vain implored my parents to send me there, for I was the only boy among my playmates in Hartford—literally the only one—who did not know how to dance. But my parents believed that dancing, along with theatres and cards, was wicked. I could not help learning something about social behaviour from the boys in the Hartford schools; for while some of them were dissipated and smutty in conversation, nearly all of them were well-dressed and had what seems to me now (by comparison with my own) the manners of French diplomats. Perhaps I can give an idea of the social prestige of the Public High School when I affirm that there was not a single boy or girl in Hartford eligible to enter the High School who was anywhere else, except for one reason, deficiency of brains. It was emphatically *the thing* to go to the Public School.

The third definite benefit that I received from outside was the intimate friendship and influence of Frank Gay. When my father took over the *Christian Secretary*, one of the young men who worked in its office was Frank Gay, who was then about eighteen. He became a member of our family; he had a room to himself, and ate his meals with us. He was mainly self-educated; but although I spent two years at Harvard and over forty at Yale and came into intimate contact with the finest specimens of American youth, I can say honestly that I have never known a more perfect gentleman than Frank Gay. He was intelligent, was widely read, had an almost infallible taste in literature and the fine arts, was good-natured and full of fun, and yet had a quiet dignity that made him, wholly unconsciously, a model of good behaviour. Six or seven years older, his influence on me was very great. I never heard him mention religion, but he was a church-member, and he adored my mother; he could not have loved her more if he had been her own flesh and blood.

Having had to work hard for his living when many other boys of his age were in High School preparing for college, he was not an athlete; he never played any games; but I, who have always been a playboy, got plenty of that recreation at school. Frank Gay used to talk with me about books, music, the theatre, and other matters of serious import; and his example was as powerful as his precepts. He was ambitious, and after some months in our house and at the office, he secured a position in a Hartford Library, where he was rapidly promoted, soon to be the head of the Watkinson Library, and became one of the famous Librarians of America.

When I was twelve, I went to the Library one day, to take out the *Outward Bound* Series of Oliver Optic, and Frank Gay asked me why I read so much trash. I replied that I read it because I liked it. He then suggested that I read Shakespeare; I rather resented this, because I thought he was like a physician giving me a prescription. He then proposed that I should read one play by Shakespeare and that if I did not like it, he would never ask me to read another, and furthermore would keep me informed as to every new book by Oliver Optic that came to the Library. This seemed to me a fair proposal. He gave me *Julius Caesar*. I read this with such excitement that I went on to read others, and then, after reading fifteen or twenty plays, partly because I wanted to, partly out of bravado, I read the Complete Works. My taste was not very good; I enjoyed *Titus Andronicus* more than I enjoyed *Hamlet* and for obvious reasons; but the stories in Shakespeare filled me with delight; and became part of the furniture of my boyish mind.

These three influences, the new books that came for review, the social manners of my schoolmates, and the direct guidance of Frank Gay, deserve especial mention.

7

FIRST DIARY

HERE are extracts from a diary I kept in 1879, aged 14. I printed in large inky letters the following on the first page:

DIARY OF WILLIAM LYON PHELPS
CONTAINING WITHIN ITS PAGES A PERSONAL ACCOUNT OF
HIS EVENTFUL AND INTERESTING (to him) LIFE

I certainly had a happy childhood in Hartford. Over and over again I wrote, 'I had a splendid time all day.' 'Lots of fun today.' Occasionally these happy reflexions were interrupted by adverse comments on school and on my teachers, who for the most part, were kind enough. 'Miss K——, (big fool), thought I was doing something, and moved my seat. I think she is a FOOL. . . . Had a tremendous snowfight on Asylum Ave. After supper, sung some. I read *Little Lights Along Shore*. I finished the book. The next book I intend to read is the *Odyssey*.'

I attended a boys' prayer-meeting. 'I led. I read the 53d Chapter of Isaiah. We had 18 there. Sam Coit said, "How splended it would be if we could say, as Paul said, 'I have fought the good faith.'" He got matters mixed up.' *Saturday, Jan.* 11, 1879. 'Played all day. Too tired to write any more.'

Sunday, Jan. 12. 'Went to church this morning, and Mr. Emerson preached, but I did not give good attention.'

Monday, Jan. 13. 'This evening, just before supper, I got caught in Berryman's sled, and accidentally, the word

48

(Damn) escaped my lips. Berryman said something about speaking in meeting. I told him I did not mean to swear, that the word was accidental, but I must see him some more about it.'

Tuesday, Jan. 14. 'Saw Berryman, and fixed it all right.'

Here are other entries for the same month.

'Studied a very little on my Algebra this evening, and could not get a single example. Yours truly.'

'This evening, a mouse ran in the buttery, and I nearly hit him with a boot. We must have a cat. When I think of the dear departed Thomas, I feel as tho' no cat could equal him in catlike beauty, skill and strength.'

I bought a book from my brother about this time, and on the flyleaf I wrote, 'Sold to him by his darling brother.'

The Principal of the Hartford High School was Joseph Hall, and he surprised me one day. 'However cross or strict Mr. Hall may be in school, he is a bully fellow out of it. At the junction, he and Joe came along in a sleigh, and Mr. Hall asked me if I did not want to hook on. He waited for me, and then we went off. I got off a little beyond the Congregational Church.' (Rev. Joseph Twichell's.)

Every day we took our sleds to school and tried to hook on sleighs. We usually succeeded and thus got hauled through the snow all the way to school and back again, both for morning and afternoon sessions; a method of locomotion not to be sneezed at.

The silver lining. 'It rained a good deal last night, spoiling the sleighing, but making it splendid for snow-balling.'

And here is an entry (28 *Jan.* 1879) that, apart from the original spelling, expresses my present sentiments. 'Finished the *Odyssey* this evening. I like it very well, though it is not near as much to my liking as the ILEAD.'

Sunday, Feb. 2, 1879. 'Ed Tuller asked me to lead the young people's meeting, and after some hesitation, I accepted . . . I hope I shall lead well. My voice is changing.'

Feb. 6. 'Been sick all day, and did not go to school. I went out and snowballed a little this p.m. . . . I went to the Institute and got *Love me little, love me long,* and *Hard Cash,* both by Chas. Reade.'

Friday, Feb. 7. 'Headache still continues, and I did not go to school.'

Saturday, Feb. 8. 'Headache does not trouble me today. I went sliding on Dummy's Hill . . . At 9 o'clock p.m., I took a splendid bath, not having bathed since before Thanksgiving.'

Feb. 13. 'Drydie (my brother) brought home from the Institute *White Lies,* by Reade, and *Frank, the Young Naturalist,* by Fosdick. Mama will not let me read any more of Reade's, but I read the other nearly thro'.'

Feb. 19. 'I read the entire book of Psalms today. This morning I finished *Jean Teterol's Idea,* (by Cherbuliez), and in the afternoon and eve. read 2 books of *The Gunboat Series. (Frank on a Gunboat,* etc.) . . . Mama and Papa went to Governor Andrews' party, and Mama looked beautiful dressed in green silk.'

Feb. 21. 'This p.m. I finished my Bible for the 2nd time, and got $1.28 for it.'

Feb. 24. 'I don't know what *is* the matter with me. I have a headache every day from morning till night. To the horrors of headache was added the thick darkness of toothache.'

7 *March.* 'Went to prayer meeting at Tyng's house. Something was the matter with me, for I laughed all through. I felt very bad, but it could not be helped.'

2 *May.* Mr. and Mrs. John M. Ney took us with their children for a long drive to Glastonbury, where we got trailing arbutus and ate wintergreen. 'I think I shall always

remember this afternoon with pleasure, I had such a splendid, nobbie, bully, etc. time.' (And I always have remembered it.)

10 *May*. 'Yesterday Papa got me a bully spring suit, that only cost $5. I don't see how he got it so cheap. Everybody guesses about $10 as its price.'

14 *May* 1879. 'Miss Kipp, to whom we recite Grecian History, is bully. I thought she was going to be duced bad. We recite Caesar to Childs, who is quite good. Algebra to Knibloe. They have got an infernal idea in regard to Latin this year. They make us learn the Latin by heart. No use in it whatever.'

23 *May*. 'Bought and ate a pound of dried apples, which nearly made me puke and be sick.'

8 *June*. 'Ajax (our white cat) had a fight with a rat, killing him. Her eye is so swollen it is almost closed, and she is so weak and sick this morning, that she can hardly walk and won't eat. She is better this p.m., and eats. I hope she will live.'

9 *June*. 'I am about sure Ajax will live. *Beata et felix Felis!*'

10 *June*. At a church supper. 'After supper, some of the ladies played Fan Drill, charging 20 cents admission. Mama treated us to it, and I thought it was worth about 2 cts. They made over $20 on it.'

11 *June*. 'Bullard fell off a fence and hurt his arm, tomorrow or today, I forget which, as this diary was written some days after.'

9 *July*. Our literary club. 'Kellogg's composition was on Forepaugh's Difficulties in getting animals for his show. Bullard's was on The Youth of Washington. Mine was on Capt. Pedge Hash. Kellogg roared several times at his own wit. It was a pretty fair meeting.'

13 *July*. 'Finished *Litlte Men* this p.m. I think it spoilt both *Little Women* and *Little Men* not to have Jo marry Laurie.'

Wednesday, 16 *July* 1879. This was the day of the famous tornado at Wallingford, Conn., the only one in our history until 1938. 'Today it was the hottest day it has been in 25 years. It was intolerable. Bronson and I had our lemonade stand out at 7 o'clock, to get the start of Paton and Berryman. They were terrible mad when they found us there. We hauled in 63 cents. Went swimming at about 10'clock, and stayed in 2 hours and a half. The water was bully. The weather was still and hot, when suddenly the clouds covered the sky, and there was a tremendous wind. It was one of the most fearful winds I ever saw. A great tree was blown down across our swimming place and one near Cushman's factory. Anna Bullard was reading a book on her piazza, when the wind dashed the book out of her hand, for 5 or 4 feet. The Bullards gave me some lemon ice and cream, which was very good. There were several tornadoes out West, and heavy thunder-storms.'

17 *and* 18 *Oct.* 'This morning, George Peters (afterwards astronomer at the U.S. Naval Observatory in Washington) and I walked to Cottage Grove. We lugged a hatchet, two infernal blankets, lunch, and my gun, with ammunition. On the way, we killed a ground sparrow, a warbler. When we got there, we felled trees, and built a hut, in the thick woods. I killed a Downy Woodpecker. We slept comfortably all night. We heard an animal and loaded our gun in the night. The next morning shot a ground sparrow, a warbler, and a bluebird. We got home about one p.m. I shot an English sparrow on the way home. Had perfectly splendid fun.'

19 *Oct.* 'Dr. Stone's father was suddenly killed, and he has left town for the place where his father lived. So Mr. Minor preached today. I think he looks like an owl.'

31 *Oct.* 'Our Greek teacher, Mr. Perrin, is a bully fellow.'

17 *Nov.* 'Arthur and I have had headaches all day. Arthur got his from football. But I'll be darned if I know how I got mine.'

About this time my brother Arthur and I learned Hog Latin, where each word is spelled out and is unintelligible unless one knows the key; for example: SUSHASHYOU-TUTYOUPUP means Shut up. 'As I was standing at the foot of the staircase in Batterson's Block, a group of factory or office girls came out together, and to my surprise they were all cursing and swearing in Hog Latin. GUGOD-UDDADAMUMYOU means G—— D—— you! As they did not imagine anyone could understand what they were saying, they were very much astonished when I called out in the same language, "Shut up!"'

24 *Nov.* 'I began a small manuscript paper this morning, entitled the *Hartford Daily.* I got 4 subscribers.'

26 *Nov.* 'Edited my paper this a.m. Kicked football this p.m.'

27 *Nov.* Thanksgiving. 'Had a bully day. Skated all the morning on Sharp's. It is splendid.' One of the boys who skated with us was Charlie Dillingham, who afterwards became the famous theatre manager. Even as a boy, he had the enthusiasm so characteristic of his later years. I remember his saying that day at Sharp's, 'I'd rather skate than eat.'

3 *Dec.* 'Read *Castle Foam* all day. It is a dreadfully melancholy book. If I owned it, I'd pitch it in the fire.'

11 *Dec.* 'Read *The Woman in White* all day, pretty near.'

28 *Dec.* A rather pessimistic story of this particular Sabbath Day. 'Went to Church, Sunday School, and both meetings in the evening. As old fool —— would not be superintendent any more, old Bullet-headed —— was elected. Other officers the same. Weather warm. A tremenjous thaw. Spoilt sleighing. Spoilt coasting. Spoilt skating.'

2 *Jan.* 1880. 'My birthday today. (15.) Got splendid presents. From Mama, a checker-board and men, a great box of tools, fifty cents, two books, and a candy. Dryden, an elegant pocket-book. From Papa, 1 doz. collars. From Arthur, figuring pack, his watch and key. Papa also gave me a watch chain.'

9 *Jan.* Here came melancholia, which lasted some weeks. 'This noon and afternoon I felt dreadfully. Awful bad, somehow. I was glad when Libbie came.' (My aunt Miss Elizabeth Linsley, who came for a visit from her home in Stratford.)

10 *Jan.* 'Had the same horrible feeling this a.m. Finished Jules Verne's *Tribulations of a Chinaman*. Went hunting with Al Talcott. Shot a nuthatch and a sparrow. I hope Libbie will stay a great while.'

15 *Jan.* 'Could not eat anything, hardly. A very sick feeling. Dr. G.Pierrepont Davis gave me a prescription, and after school, I got the stuff in the shape of one enormous pill. Had to wait for it about three-quarters of an hour, and wound up by losing it. Drydie got it over again in l'evening. Took huge pill. Went down like a bullet.'

16 *Jan.* 'O how much better I feel!'

2 *Feb.* 'February has 5 Sundays this month, which has not happened for 30 years, and will not happen again for forty years.' Forty years seemed an immense distance ahead, at that time. But the year 1920, which produced its five Sundays in February according to my prophecy, now seems a good while ago.

We never paid any attention to climate or to seasons but went out shooting in ice and snow and rain and mud.

28 *Feb.* 'Frank (Hubbard), Pete (George Peters) and I had a good hunt today. I killed two warblers, one bluebird, and a nuthatch. Frank knocked over a magnificent robin. He picked him on the wing. His breast and guts were a bright red. Frank also shot a bluebird and blue jay, the

latter falling into a mudpuddle, and receiving some hurt thereby. When we got home I stuffed Frank's bluebird and my robin which Frank gave me. I could not get the wire through the knee joint, so I did not mount them.'

Much of our shooting was done in what is now a densely populated part of Hartford. Curious that we should have found robins and bluebirds, etc., in February.

8 *March*. 'This morning I cleaned out my meadow-lark, preparatory to stuffing him. This noon I fixed his eyes with shoe-buttons. Fred Keep came over this evening and put the wires up his legs. I then finished him up, and mounted him on a board. He looks splendid, and is in a natural position.'

14 *March*. 'Read *Hal, the Story of a Clodhopper*, by W.M.F.Round, all the p.m.' Round was a popular author in those days.

People who lived in Hartford many years ago will remember that when the horse cars came up the hill from the railway station to the junction of Farmington and Asylum Avenues, an extra horse was put on for that brief climb. The man in charge of him had to walk back and begin over again with the next car. This he did all day, and it was not what one would call 'a rowdy life,' which may explain his ill temper.

18 *March*. 'Clad Wiley accidentally hit (with a snowball) the old Irishman that takes up the extra horse to go up the hill with the horsecar. The old devil immediately turned around, and picking up a couple of rocks, hurled one at my head. I managed to dodge it, but he came running up, and nabbing me by the throat, he drew back his fist, and I thought I was a gone-cat. I told him over and over again that I didn't hit him, but that only made him wilder. *Denique* he went away, leaving a track of mud across my face, where he had hit me. We got it off.'

20 *March.* 'Did not go hunting today. Why not? None of your bizness. Snowballed all day. Had bully fun. Finished *In Silk Attire*, by William Black.'

Beginning with January of this year 1880, my marks at school, which had been low for three years, suddenly jumped up to nearly perfect, and I never had any trouble with school or college marks the rest of my life (except that I was not good in mathematics in college).

25 *March.* 'Rec'd my marks for this month today. 9.9 in Latin, 9.9 in Algebra, 9.8 in Latin (another course), 9 in Reading. Reading does not count. Whole average, Nine-Nine!' Perfect was 10.

Thus one continual worry and terror, which had pursued me like Black Care for three years, was permanently eliminated.

1 *April.* 'Glory of glories! Miss Snowball Jackson Diable, alias Mrs. Tiger Tomcat, hatched precisely one kitten today! It is an image of its father, Mr. Tiger Tomcat. In the Geyser Box! The kitten's name is Epaminondas Alcibiades Pentacosiomedimni. It is awful cunning.'

17 *April.* 'Fished all day in West Hartford with Rich Hubbard. We caught 15 bullheads and three eels. One or two of the bullheads were a foot long.'

Some difficulties with a prayer-meeting at the High School.

25 *May.* 'We had a boys' meeting in the little German recitation room, as of yore. Jim Reynolds led, and Lou Robinson, Hiram Loomis, Wilson, Dan Bidwell, Shipman Major, Ned Fellowes and some others were present. The meeting was ruined by Dan, who made funny speeches, called Jim "Mr. Goodell," and so forth, throughout the meeting. I spoke and prayed.'

5 *June* 1880. 'I saw the ball game between Company K and the nine made up with Sedgwick pitcher, F. Johnson catcher, W. T. Redfield 1st base, Henry Welch, 2d base,

Rob Way 3d base, Dan Glazier shortstop, Deming left field, Arthur Shipman and later Jim Reynolds right field, and Kong, center-field. Company K came out one run ahead.' 'Hen' Redfield was one of the stars for Company K.

9 *June*. 'Went to Christian Home for supper tonight. Had stacks of fun. C. Abell, Goodnow, Derrick, Josh Allen, Frank and Charles Cooley, Hooker etc. were there. Good supper.'

REFLEXIONS ON ANIMALS

PERHAPS the surest test of civilization is man's attitude toward animals. Ill treatment of animals is not necessarily the sign of deliberate cruelty in the torturer; it is more often an indication of a defective imagination, an inability to understand. Francis Parkman in *The Oregon Trail* spoke of the cruelty to birds and other animals by the Indians, especially by the Indian children, who showed no remorse or shame after those abominable practices. Many peasants with primitive minds treat animals badly; the paradox is that we call it brutality. Also, the sense of humour in some children needs cultivating; they laugh at insanity, at the sound of a foreign language, at a dog with a can tied to his tail.

Of course, it is possible for children to become over-sentimentalized. This attitude is well indicated by the familiar anecdote of the small boy looking at the picture of Christian martyrs delivered to the lions: 'Oh, look, Mama, that dear little lion in the corner isn't getting anything!' When I was a child, I woke up one night, and wept when I thought of the warm comfort of my bed and my kitten on the hard kitchen oilcloth. In the same way, those who condemn quail, partridge, and duck-shooting are, I think, over-sentimental. The only consistent attitude would be that of the vegetarian to abstain from fish, flesh, and fowl. And even then it would require only a slight stretch of the imagination to sympathize with potatoes which possibly suffer horribly when torn up by the roots.

If it is wicked to shoot quails for the table, then it is more wicked to eat chickens; for one keeps and feeds chickens only to betray them. One might easily work oneself into a frame of mind where one who eats chickens is a traitor and a murderer. After all, the child and men and women are of more importance and value than any animal; there is no sentimentality in the New Testament on this or on any other point. After reminding his audience that God never forgets a sparrow, Our Lord remarked that we are of more value than many sparrows.

When Robert Browning and others said that they would rather die than have any dog or cat suffer in order that they might be relieved from pain, these men of genius were not squarely meeting the issue. What they should have done was to balance their own children against dogs and cats.

Yet as we grow older, we are less and less willing to take the life of any animal wantonly. Why is this? Is it because we know the value of life, is it because toleration—live and let live—is the result of intellectual development, or what is the reason? Recently as we were playing golf, a large, harmless, black snake crawled across the fairway. The caddies were unanimous for death, and the four players for acquittal.

I used to wonder why it was as a small boy that I delighted in shooting and killing birds, any bird, edible or otherwise, for I was not cruel by nature, and could not bear to see any animal ill-treated or in pain. Yet, when I was too small to own a gun, I would get up at dawn, armed with David's implement, and try to kill robins and bluebirds. On the rare occasions when I succeeded, I felt thrills of joy, unshaded by regret. Later, when I owned a gun, it was much the same. It was only in riper years that I never shot except at something that I wanted to eat, or at something predatory. Apart from the pleasure of hunting, which is instinctive in every boy, I finally found the true explanation; I found it in an early novel by Zona Gale. A girl is out walking with one of 'nature's noblemen,' and when he killed a beautiful bird, she rebuked him sharply, much to his bewilderment, for he was no more conscious of guilt than was Parsifal when he killed the swan. In response to her question, he said that he wanted to see the bird *nearer*. Zona Gale's explanation is the true one. Not only did I feel a thrill when I shot a bird, but another, keener and quite different thrill when I held the dead body in my hand. The bird is an elusive creature, apparently inaccessible; one never has him near enough to examine completely and leisurely; hence the desire to hold him.

Now those were the days before the Kodak; hunting with opera-glass and camera is better for the boy and much better for the birds. Yet that same element of destructiveness characteristic of boys is also characteristic of adults who have matured only bodily. Every deserted building has its windows broken. Small boys and stupid men really do love to smash things. I was impressed when a contractor, who employed thousands of workmen, told me that when his men were engaged in construction work of any kind, work that meant creating and developing something, most of them worked mechanically, slowly and without zeal; but when the order came to demolish a tall building, they worked with enthusiasm—smashing, tearing, destroying.

9

EARLY FRIENDSHIPS, MARK TWAIN, AND BILLIARDS

WHEN my parents in the Spring of 1876 decided to move to Hartford, they unconsciously arranged my marriage, which was to take place nearly seventeen years later. I first met my wife when I was eleven years old.

At the West Middle School in Hartford there was a boy two years older than I whose name was Frank Watson Hubbard. We became friends and there has never been a cloud on our friendship during sixty years.

His father, Langdon Hubbard, was living in Huron County, Michigan, whither he had gone originally from Connecticut as a pioneer, and was engaged in an extensive lumbering business. There were no facilities out there for education; hence he had sent his three children, Frank, Richard, and Annabel to Hartford, where they lived with three maiden aunts, and had entered the West Middle School.

Frank and I became inseparable. We were both fond of outdoor games and especially of shooting. He owned a long, single-barrel, muzzle-loading shotgun, and equipped with this primitive implement, we spent entire Saturdays in the pursuit of robins, meadowlarks, yellowhammers, and other songbirds, which, I hasten to add, we always brought home, cooked, and ate with relish. I remember one winter day, when we were out in the fields and woods, we became very hungry, and made an excellent meal off English sparrows. The wild country over which we hunted extended from Woodland Street to Talcott Mountain.

The next year when I was twelve, my father allowed me to buy a double-barrelled muzzle-loading shot gun, which I bought from Charlie Shepard for six dollars. My conservative breast crossed by straps holding powderhorn and shotpouch, I thought I resembled Hawkeye.

It was owing to this gun that I became a criminal, sought by the police and by detectives, and that for the first and last time in my life, a price was set on my head. It happened in this way. I was shooting with a schoolmate, George Peters. We became separated in the woods along the banks of Hog River. Suddenly I saw, sweeping around a bend in the stream, a flock of white ducks, which I supposed to be wild. I let them have both barrels, killing two and mortally wounding three. Attracted by the report, George came up, and was overcome with horror. I fully expected him to be envious of my wonderful good luck; but instead of that, he cried, ' What have you done? Those are Mark Twain's prize ducks. If you are caught, he will put you in jail. Run for your life!'

My flush of joy turned to the icy sweat of fear. I slipped around through the woods to Frank Hubbard's house, and told him he was the only friend I had in the world. He advised me to reach home by roundabout ways, and not to come near Hog River for some time. I got home safely.

The next morning I read in the Hartford newspaper a prominently displayed notice from Mark Twain, offering a substantial financial reward for the apprehension of the 'miscreant' who had killed his white ducks. Here I was, a criminal, sought by the police, with a price set on my head. For several months I avoided Hog River and was in terror. Years later, when I became acquainted with Mark Twain, I never dared to tell him of this particular episode; for although he was the world's greatest living humorist, there were certain subjects to which his sense of humour did not extend.

Mark Twain's house stood on Farmington Avenue, near Forest Street; his neighbours were Harriet Beecher Stowe, Charles Dudley Warner, and William Gillette. His house had been built according to his own ideas, with the kitchen in front, so that the cook and housemaids would not have to run through the living-rooms and hall to see a procession go by. The billiard room was on the top floor and a tiny balcony projected from one of the windows; nearly all dwellings built in the eighteen-seventies had abscesses of that kind. I often used to see Mark Twain standing in his shirt-sleeves on that balcony, the eternal cigar in his mouth and a billiard cue in his hand. While his opponent was playing, Mark would come out for air. Billiards was his only athletic exercise; he always said, 'Never stand up when you can sit down; never sit down when you can lie down.'

However, I frequently saw Mark Twain on the street; for although he was fond of driving with his wife and children in an open carriage, he must have walked down town every clear day, for I saw him often. He was so conspicuous that the jest of G. K. Chesterton applies perfectly. Some admirer said to the Englishman, 'It must be wonderful just to take a walk and have everybody know who you are.' 'Yes,' replied Chesterton, 'and if they don't know, they ask.' The Englishman had been made noticeable by nature; the American by deliberate choice. His dark brown hair was long, and fell in masses around his neck, having apparently received his personal attention. In cold weather, instead of an overcoat, he wore a jacket of sealskin, with the fur side outside; in walking, he had the rolling gait of a sailor. He was distinguishable a long way off. People stopped when he passed them, and remained as if hypnotized, staring after his diminishing figure. Those who had seen him before found him well worth seeing again; those who had never seen him asked the nearest by-stander (sometimes me) who he was, and their already awakened curiosity received a lift by the answer.

Although the name Mark Twain was familiar to all Americans, he had in those days more notoriety than fame. I do not believe there was anyone in Hartford who knew then what we know now, that he is one of the world's great literary artists. He was a funny man, and people were fond of him because he made them laugh. His most intimate friend was the Reverend Joseph H.Twichell, pastor of the Asylum Avenue Congregational Church; and Mark, though he had lost all religious belief, usually attended church. Mr. Twichell was universally beloved in Hartford for his sincerity and courage.

At church-meetings, held on some weekday night, Mark frequently entertained the audience, which crowded the room every time it was announced that he would speak. I remember on one occasion, as Mr. Twichell preceded him up the stairs leading to the platform, the audience burst into tumultuous applause. Mark, pointing to Twichell's back, called out to the audience, 'He thinks it's for *him*.'

Three of these occasions I remember very well indeed, though none of us knew that we were listening to a man of genius. First, I heard him read in 1876 from the novel just published, *Tom Sawyer*; he chose the episode of Tom's fight with the citified boy. Second, I heard him read from *Huckleberry Finn* from manuscript, some time before the year 1885, when it was published. Third, I heard him recite his own ghost-story *The Golden Arm*, and I remember the shriek of surprised horror that rose from the audience when he reached the climax.

He was the greatest master of the art of public reading then living, though we did not know it. It was an art he studied with infinite pains, and later wrote about with great detail, telling others who wished to cultivate it of the immense importance of the *pause*. The same scrupulous accuracy that made him so careful of dialect and italics in everything he prepared for publication (I have examined many of his pencilled notes on the margins of his proof-sheets) made him pay the utmost attention to the proper emphasis in reading aloud. He told us in *Tom Sawyer* and elsewhere of his disgust with pulpit-reading of the Bible and of hymns, where no attention was paid to the meaning of the passages.

In the seventies and eighties Mark's favourite poet was Browning; he used to say he could make any so-called obscure passage transparently clear merely by reading it aloud. His daughter Clara allowed me to examine his copies of Browning; they are covered with his pencil marks to indicate how they should be read. In Hartford a club was formed which met regularly to hear him read Browning's poetry. How I wish we had gramophone records!

On 23 February 1887, he wrote in pencil, 'Remark dropped after finishing "Easter Day"—& requested to "write it down."

'One's glimpses & confusions, as one reads Browning, remind me of looking through a telescope (the small sort which you must move with your hand, not clock-work): You toil across dark spaces which are (to your lens) empty; but every now & then a splendor of stars & suns bursts upon you & fills the whole field with flame.'

Here is a letter he wrote, first printed a few years ago by Benjamin De Casseres in a thin volume called *When Huck Finn Went Highbrow*—limited to 125 copies.

HARTFORD, DEC. 2/87

MY DEAR MRS. FOOTE:

Well, people & things do swap places in most unexpected ways in this world. Twenty years ago I was a platform-humorist & you a singer of plaintive Scotch ballads that were full of heart-break &

tears. And now we have changed places. You are platform-humorist (among other things), & I am reader to a Browning class! I can't imagine a completer reversal of roles than this. I hope you find your changes as pleasant as I do mine, and that you are as willing as I to let the thing remain as it is; for I wouldn't trade back for any money.

Now when you come to think of it, wasn't it a curious idea—I mean, for a dozen ladies of (apparently) high intelligence to elect me their Browning-reader? Of course you think I declined—at first; but I didn't. I'm not the declining sort. I would take charge of the constellations if I were asked to do it. All you need in this life is ignorance & confidence; then success is sure. I've been Browning-reader forty-two weeks, now, & my class has never lost a member by desertion. What do you think of that, for a man in a business he *wasn't* brought up to?

I wonder if—in one particular—your experience in your new avocation duplicates mine. For instance, I used to explain Mr. Browning—but the class won't stand that. They say that my reading imparts clear comprehension—& that is a good deal of a compliment, you know; but they say the poetry never gets obscure till I begin to explain it—which is only frank, & that is the softest you can say about it. So I've stopped being expounder, & thrown my heft on the reading. Yes, & with vast results—nearly unbelievable results. I don't wish to flatter anybody, yet I will say this much: put me in the right condition & give me room according to my strength, & I can read Browning so Browning himself can understand it. It sounds like stretching, but it's the cold truth. Moral: don't explain your author; read him right & he explains himself.

I wish you every possible success, & shall be as glad as your own heart to hear that you have won it.

Sincerely your friend

S. L. CLEMENS

It seems strange today that his literary reputation was so long delayed. He would undoubtedly have been more famous if he had not been so funny. Calvin Coolidge, who was Class Humorist on his graduation from Amherst, observed that funny men never got anywhere in politics; he made up his mind he would never be funny again.

Mark in the eighties and even in the nineties was so

generally regarded as a professionally funny man that contemporary critics and historians of American literature
ranked him with Josh Billings and Artemus Ward and Pe-
troleum V.Nasby, never where he belonged—with Emerson and Hawthorne.

Yet his humour often had an undertone of either common sense or philosophy or both. I can see him now as I
saw him when I was thirteen years old, addressing the
graduating class at the West Middle School, saying in his
slow drawl, 'Boys and girls, the subject of my remarks today is Methuselah. Methuselah lived to be 969 years old;
but what of that? There was nothing doing. He might as
well have lived to be a thousand. You boys and girls will
see more in the next fifty years than Methuselah saw in his
whole lifetime.'

There was probably more universal interest in the personality of Mark Twain than in any other American writer,
living or dead. The whole world read him and the whole
world loved him. No other writer ever succeeded in making
an assumed name so truly a household word. George Eliot
and Anatole France had nothing like the range of his reputation nor do they seem so sure of immortality. George
Eliot belongs to English literature and Anatole France belongs to French literature; Mark Twain belongs to the
world.

Had he lived and died as a pilot on the Mississippi, his
personality might have made him a legendary figure; had
he succeeded in his mining enterprises in Nevada, he might
now be remembered as one of our Western pioneers. It was
only by an accident that he became a literary man; and it
was only when the colossal force of his mighty genius found
its full expression in *Tom Sawyer* and in *Huckleberry Finn*
that he was able to produce imperishable masterpieces.

He did everything possible to escape his fate and fame.
Had the Civil War not stopped passenger traffic on the

river, he would have continued contentedly as a pilot, for he had reached the summit of his ambition—the pilot was the king of the Mississippi. Had he not failed of becoming a mining millionaire by a few minutes, he would have enjoyed his fortune with his friends on the frontier.

Even as a writer, Mark Twain almost always miscast himself. He thought that *Joan of Arc* was his masterpiece, for he had done his best to make it so. (Barrett Wendell said shrewdly that Shakespeare probably thought his own finest work was *Coriolanus*.) Mark Twain wanted to be a philosopher, but somehow cheerfulness kept breaking in.

The worst case of stage-fright I have ever witnessed happened at Unity Hall one night in the presence of Mark Twain. George W. Cable, from the deep South, a writer quite unlike Erskine Caldwell or William Faulkner, had acquired a national reputation through his novels, *The Grandissimes* and others. He made his first appearance as a lecturer and reader in Hartford, and was brilliantly introduced to the crowded house by Mark Twain. The applause was deafening. Mr. Cable stood up, looked at the audience, and could not even open his mouth. He was petrified by fear. He stood there motionless for what seemed an eternity, and he would have been there yet if Mark Twain had not risen, seized one of Cable's books which was fortunately on the platform, opened it, found a place, thrust it into Cable's hand and told him to read.

The only respect in which I resembled Mark Twain was in my passion for billiards. Unfortunately billiards was inseparably associated with the saloon, where I went seldom and always furtively. But when I was fourteen, Frank Hubbard discovered a man who wished to sell a small billiard table—it had rubber tubes for cushions—but the price was prohibitive, twenty dollars. Our total assets were seventy-five cents. Frank told me that his younger sister, Annabel, had received from her father, on his latest visit, a

present of a twenty-dollar gold piece. He had vainly tried
to induce her to part with it, for, as he said, of what possible use could it be to a girl? He made the tactical error of
the brother-and-sister *motif*, and when that failed, he attempted stronger measures with even less success. Then he
asked me to talk with her, saying 'You are more soft-
hearted than I am.' He thought that while he had exhausted logic and threats, my powers of persuasion might
be greater than his; and he thought accurately, for I subsequently persuaded her to become my wife.

I have never forgotten this diplomatic errand. It was
Saturday night; pitch-dark and bitterly cold. I went to his
front door, while he hid outside, and as she came to the
door herself, I placed my face about two inches from hers,
and began in tender whispers. I told her I knew how much
she thought of that twenty dollars, and how natural it was
for her to keep her money, after her brother had spent his;
but that I myself felt it would be simply marvellous on her
part to make this supreme sacrifice. 'Remember you are
not doing it merely for him; my own happiness depends on
getting this billiard table. We have no resources. I shall remember your kindness as long as I live.'

I made only one error in this entreaty. I told her we
should regard it as a loan. The gentle expression on her face
turned for a moment into one of incredulity; this was too
much for even a girl to believe; we could no more have repaid that twenty dollars than we could have liquidated the
national debt.

Instantly I saw that I was stating something which was
not only incredible, but which also chilled the eternal
woman's desire to sacrifice herself for a man. I went back to
the wind-harp stop, and she whispered, 'Just wait a minute.' She went upstairs and returned with the twenty-
dollar gold piece, actually looking almost as radiant as if
she were receiving it. I gave her in return something of no

value; and I also told her there was no girl like her in the whole world.

Armed with this twenty dollars, we hired an expressman to transfer the table from the place of purchase to my house, we agreeing to pay seventy-five cents. He asked for more after the somewhat difficult move was made, but we had wisely made our contract beforehand. The table was hoisted up three flights of stairs, and placed in a small room. It was nearly midnight, too late to play. The next day being Sunday, I was not allowed to touch it, and on Monday morning I had to go to school, from which I was not free till four o'clock. Then we made straight for that billiard table, and played till eleven o'clock, not stopping for the evening meal.

We played for large sums of fictitious money. Frank was taking the regular course in Hannum's Business College, preparatory to a banking career in Michigan. As he was bookkeeper, he secured funds amounting to about thirty thousand dollars, which looked like real money; we divided this into three parts, one for me, one for Frank, and one for a schoolmate, Francis R. Pratt. We used to play billiards for stakes of anywhere from one hundred to five hundred dollars; and I remember on one afternoon Frank Pratt won all my money; whereupon I suggested that we shake dice. I got all my money back and then all of his; he went home penniless and in tears, I having won something like twelve thousand dollars.

If older people had known what we were doing, they would have predicted an evil fate for us in later years. But we had enough excitement gambling with this imitation money to last us for the rest of our lives. I have never played any game for money.

I have played billiards and pocket billiards (pool) all my life and regard it as the best of indoor games. It seems strange to me that when we have taken so many sports from England we should have taken billiards from France. The English game of billiards is almost unknown in America and I have never seen an English billiard table in the United States. Even cricket is more popular with Americans than British billiards.

Not only do I enjoy playing, but also there is no indoor game that I have more pleasure and excitement in watching. When Frank Hubbard and I were small boys in Hartford we saw a great match at the Allyn House between the famous French champion Vignaux and Jake Schaefer (father of the present expert) at the beautiful game of cushion caroms. The highest run ever made was 77, by Sexton, but that night Schaefer ran 70. The masters of billiards in those days were Schaefer, Slosson, Sexton, Sutton, and a little later Napoleon Ives, who some believe was the greatest of them all. The excitement of the game, the bad air, the chalk dust were not good for him; and he died of tuberculosis. He was, I believe, the first expert to use a heavy cue. In the twentieth century I saw many great games played by Willie Hoppe, Schaefer the younger, Horemans, Hagenlacher, Walker Cochran, and others. Willie Hoppe has probably had a longer career in the first flight than any other player in history and seems today unbeatable at 18.1. When he was in Michigan in 1937, he was kind enough to come over to our house and play on the worst table he had ever seen. On the same day he enjoyed golf much more. Like many men who have reached the top in any form of sport, he is a very interesting person, modest and unassuming, full of good talk.

I wish the cushion carom game might be revived. Long runs are sometimes monotonous; long runs are impossible in cushion caroms, and every shot is interesting.

Watching pocket billiards I find equally exciting. I attend the championship matches every year when they are held in New York. Greenleaf, Caras, Ponzi, Rudolph, and others give me continuous thrills. Four hours of this spectacle seem like four minutes.

The champion billiard player, like the concert pianist (and the poet), is born and not made. Continuous practice is essential; but such co-ordination cannot possibly be acquired. I asked Willie Hoppe about this and he said all the practice in the world and from early childhood to maturity could not by itself make a champion.

The most famous men of letters whose sole recreation was billiards were Herbert Spencer and Mark Twain. I should like to have seen a match between them. Spencer I believe swore only once in his life; but the anecdote about his loss of a game to a young man is a classic. His billiard cue is preserved as a sacred relic in London. He was not devoid of humour; for when asked why he would not marry, he replied he was willing to marry any suitable woman. Accordingly they brought a woman to him saying she had a great mind; and left them together for several hours. Spencer said she wouldn't do at all. 'Instead of having a great mind, she has a small mind in constant activity.'

IO

ASTRONOMY

AMONG my extra-curriculum activities in school at Hartford, was astronomy. I have forgotten how my interest in this subject began, but among the new books sent to my father for review was a copy of Simon Newcomb's *Popular Astronomy*; I read that book over and over again. Thomas Mills Day, son of the former editor of the *Hartford Courant*, was a boy at the West Middle School, and his family had come into the possession of a good telescope. I used to go to his front yard, formed by the intersection of Farmington and Asylum Avenues, and there spent many evenings gazing at the firmament.

I wanted a telescope of my own and had no funds. My schoolmate, Arthur Perkins, who had such a talent for scientific pursuits that his subsequently being forced into the practice of the law was a lifelong tragedy, offered to make me a telescope if I would provide the materials, the total cost of which was less than three dollars. He made a tube out of cardboard, painted it black, made a tripod, and with an object glass of two and one-half inches at one end, and an eye-piece at the other, I could see the moons of Jupiter, the crescent of Venus, occultations of stars, and such phenomena. I could not afford an achromatic eye-piece, so I had all the colours for nothing. For years I was passionately devoted to astronomy, and my interest in the subject lasted until I was compelled to take a course in astronomy in college, which was devoted wholly to mathematical calculations; the stars were neither seen nor mentioned. I was so disgusted that for years afterwards I did not consider the subject.

In 1881 I stayed up all night to observe a total eclipse of the moon; and I saw through my telescope two occultations of stars during the eclipse.

But the greatest day with my telescope came when I was seventeen—the sixth of December 1882, when from about nine in the morning till about four in the afternoon I observed the transit of Venus. Hartford was in the best position for this spectacle; two astronomers had been sent over from Germany, and were to cable WOE if the day were cloudy, WONDERFUL if it were wholly clear, and WONDERFUL-WANTING if they missed a contact and yet saw most of the transit.

My schoolmates, Day, Peters, and I had been talking of nothing else for weeks; I carried my telescope to Peters's yard where there would be a more unobstructed view of the sun. His interest in astronomy became professional and permanent, and in later years he was one of the astronomers at the United States Naval Observatory in Washington; Day has a very fine telescope in his home in New Jersey.

The transit of Venus is a very rare spectacle, coming one might say in pairs, with long intervals. There had been one in 1874 about which I knew nothing; there was this one in 1882. The next one will be in 2004, followed by one in 2012, when again there will be an interval of more than one hundred years.

Accordingly on the day before, 5 December, I asked my Latin teacher at the High School if he would kindly excuse me for the next day, as I wished to observe the transit of Venus. Like most persons, he had never heard of it, and viewed me with suspicion. He refused. Then I begged him to let me off, telling him I *must* see it. 'Oh, wait for the next one,' he said. Whereupon I asked him, 'Do you know

when the next one is coming? It will be in the year 2004.'
Then he got stuffy, and said, ' Well, I won't excuse you.' I
determined to be a martyr for the sake of science, and
stayed away from school all day, expecting to be severely
punished and possibly expelled; but I think my teacher
must have looked up the matter or consulted the Principal,
who knew something about astronomy, for when I returned to school no reference was made to my deliberately
defiant absence.

When the black disc of the planet approaches the outer
limb of the sun, the moment the two curves touch is called
the First Contact; when it touches the inner side at the last
moment before beginning its journey across the flaming expanse, it is the Second Contact; when, about seven hours
later, it has almost completed its transit, and touches the
inner curve on the other side of the sun, it is the Third Contact; and when it has fully completed its journey, and
touches the outer limb of the sun, not to repeat this performance for nearly 122 years, that is the Fourth Contact.
(I am glad that the horrible verb 'to contact' was then
unknown.)

The last two contacts show an apparent link or drop
uniting for a moment the small disc of Venus with the huge
disc of the sun, as if they shook hands on meeting and again
at parting. On this December day in 1882, the First Contact, at about nine in the morning, was partially cloudy;
but then the sky cleared and was cloudless all day, making
observations perfect. The 'link' or 'drop' in the afternoon
was very distinct.

All day long, the black disc of Venus, looking like a
smaller tennis ball, stood out plainly on the face of the sun;
many years later, 14 November 1907, I observed a transit
of Mercury, which looked like a golf ball. Transits of Mercury are fairly frequent, the next one occurring 11 November 1940.

That day in 1882 was one of the great days of my life; the spectacle was amazing in itself, and the thought that no one living would ever see it again lent a peculiar air of solemnity to the scene.

When I became a member of the American Philosophical Society, founded by Benjamin Franklin, I immediately associated myself with the astronomers, telling them I was the most enthusiastic non-mathematical astronomer in the world; that I loved the sea and sailing ships, but could not understand navigation; that I loved the stars, but could not comprehend even elementary mathematics. They received me with affection if not with respect; and I am pleased to be the only person not an astronomer making the annual dinner-pilgrimage at the hospitable home of Mr. and Mrs. Gustavus Wynne Cook, where there is probably the finest amateur observatory on the face of the earth.

In 1937 I made a pilgrimage with these astronomers to see the great telescope being made near Philadelphia for the California observatory; and as we were looking at this giant and meditating on the fact that in these days of mass production, here was one individual mechanism that took years to build, I told Harlow Shapley, Head of the Harvard University Observatory, that I, as an astronomer, had two advantages over him. This telescope costs about seven million dollars, whereas mine of 1882 cost less than three dollars; secondly, although his astronomical knowledge compared to mine was in about the same ratio, I had seen a transit of Venus, which he had never seen and never would see, even if he lived to be a hundred.

Logically, although not chronologically, I might mention here some other experiences with astronomers; for I have known many astronomers intimately. My lawn tennis partner in New Haven, Frederick L. Chase (we won second prize in the open doubles in the New England championship tournament), was an astronomer, and could play whist with us only on stormy evenings.

When I was lecturing at the University of California in the summer of 1908, I had the pleasure of visiting the great Lick Observatory on the top of a neighbouring mountain. The late Dr. W.W.Campbell and Robert Grant Aitken were Heads of this observatory and intimate friends of mine, whilst one of their predecessors, E.S.Holden, was one of the best friends I ever had, with whom I kept up an epistolary conversation until his death. Well, on my visit in 1908, Dr. Aitken told me that when in April 1906 San Francisco was slowly being destroyed by fire, he turned the great telescope directly on the city and felt as if he were looking down into Hell. There was no wind; immense districts of the city were steadily and inexorably being consumed by unconquerable and prodigious flames. He looked on with horror, unable to help.

The great astonomer George Ellery Hale was a very dear friend. He and Mrs. Hale were exceedingly kind to us when I was lecturing at the Los Angeles branch of the University of California in the summer of 1919. They took us to the summit of Mount Wilson (5,900 feet) where we saw and looked through the largest telescope in the world, the 100-inch reflector. That was the first time I saw the moons of Saturn; and the cluster in Hercules was a marvellous spectacle. We had a jolly supper with the staff; and as we descended the mountain late in the night, the lights of Pasadena made almost as gorgeous a display as anything we had seen aloft. Two bonds united Dr. Hale and me, apart from his knowledge and my love of astronomy. He worshipped cats, owned a magnificent feline; and he read a good many detective novels every month.

At one of the regular meetings of the American Philosophical Society, Professor Miller of Swarthmore College told me a remarkable story of Richard Croker, one of the most famous politicians of America, for many years the inscrutable Chief of Tammany Hall and absolute political boss of New York. Prof. Miller was Professor of Astronomy at the University of Indiana during the years when Croker was at the height of his fame in metropolitan politics; one night the telephone rang, and Miller was informed that Richard Croker was speaking. 'You don't mean Richard Croker of New York?' 'The same.' 'What can I do for you?' 'I am passing through Indiana and I thought you might be willing to let me look through the telescope.' He was cordially invited and the two men went into the observatory. Mr. Croker's remarks showed a fair knowledge of amateur astronomy. After the telescope had been turned on various objects, Mr. Croker wished to see the nebula in Orion, and was informed that would not be visible until about two o'clock in the morning. 'I shall be glad to wait for it,' said the Tammany Chief. Accordingly they stayed and after seeing it, and expressing his thanks, Mr. Croker remarked, 'I like the stars; they are dependable.'

To turn from the sublime to the ridiculous aspect of astronomy: the late Judge Elbert Hamlin, one of my pupils in the class of 1896, took as an undergraduate the course in astronomy offered by Professor William Beebe. On the final examination one of the questions was 'How many moons has Saturn?' Hamlin guessed, wrote down too many and was flunked. About fifteen years later, he happened to see in the morning paper that some additional satellites had been discovered, making the total number what he had placed on his exam paper. Immediately he sent a long telegram to Professor Beebe, quoting the newspaper cutting. 'Fifteen years ago you flunked me not knowing that my knowledge of Saturn exceeded yours. And your flunking me was a tragedy for Yale. There was the golden opportunity which would have given Yale University immortality in science by announcing a discovery fifteen years ahead of all other institutions of learning. I can forgive you for the personal insult, but it is difficult to forgive you when we remember what my discovery would have meant in adding prestige to Yale.'

Professor Beebe was delighted with this telegram; and I wish I could remember his reply.

II

MOODY AND SANKEY

WHEN I was fifteen, D.L.Moody and Ira Sankey came to Hartford and for many weeks held evangelistic services in the Rink. Although Americans, their great reputation had been made in England, and they came to the United States in the full flush of fame. Sankey had an uncultivated, almost hoarse baritone, but his singing was indescribably affecting. An audience of thousands in absolute stillness heard him sing 'The Ninety and Nine' or 'What Shall the Harvest Be' or the terrifying 'Almost Persuaded,' and no one ever forgot him. Moody was the greatest professional evangelist I ever heard. He had no mannerisms, very few gestures, and seldom raised his voice to a shout; but his deep and unaffected piety, his apposite figures of speech, his humour, his solid common sense, his thrilling earnestness, made him amazingly effective. He did great good and as he hated hysteria and sensationalism, he never did any harm. He was a man of genius. In later years I got to know him intimately, both at his school at Northfield and during his visits to Yale; it was impossible to talk with him without feeling his sincerity and his knowledge of human nature. The following incident changed the life of Sir Wilfred Grenfell, who as a young medical student had attended a big revival meeting out of curiosity. Moody asked a local clergyman to lead in prayer. The man went on praying until Grenfell started to leave. Suddenly, in the midst of this prayer, Mr. Moody spoke out in a loud voice. 'While the Rev. Dr. —— is praying, let us unite in singing

Hymn Number —.' It was sung with gusto. Then Grenfell
stayed for the sermon. When Moody was old, I asked him
one day if he would preach the following Sunday in our
church. He said, 'I will give you the answer a girl made to
a young man. He asked her, "Will you marry me?" and
she replied, "You have good judgement but bad luck."'

When I was an undergraduate, he preached one Sunday
at Yale. Attendance was compulsory and the attention to
the average sermon was not very keen; and most sermons
were no longer than twenty minutes. Mr. Moody preached
for one hour, and held the breathless attention of the students.

One of the best effects of his prolonged visit to Hartford
in 1878 was on the various pastors of the city; they were
roused to new zeal and the increase of membership was evident in every church.

The meetings conducted by Moody and Sankey were followed in Hartford by those directed by the Rev. George F.
Pentecost and the singer George C. Stebbins, who composed many tunes that became well known and in the
twentieth century are frequently sung over the radio. He is
still living and on 26 February 1938 celebrated his ninety-
second birthday.

83 HIGH STREET
CATSKILL, N.Y.

DEAR PROF. PHELPS.

Your gracious telegram of birthday greetings touches my heart
very deeply, and your recalling the meetings in Hartford conducted
by Dr. Geo. F. Pentecost, just 60 years ago at this time of year, gives
me great pleasure, and I am deeply grateful to you for it.

You do me great honor to speak of the singing in those meetings so
kindly, and also of the contribution I have made to the service of song
in the intervening years, and I thank you for it most sincerely. If you
can recall any of the songs I sang alone in those meetings, it occurs to
me it would be 'The Green Hill,' for that is the one most called for that
whole season, partly because the musical setting was new, it having

been composed for a special service in the Baptist Church of which Dr. Pentecost was then pastor in Boston in late 1877. By way of parenthesis, as you might say, I have very often seen recently that song referred to as being used in broadcasting programs of my songs by various radio stations in honor of my birthday, which has not been the case in former services on my birthday, to such an extent I had thought it had dropped out of the thought of the people.

Coming back to the meeting in Hartford, it was at that time that 'Evening Prayer'—Saviour, breathe an evening blessing—had its first introduction by its being sung by the large Male Choir that had been assisting Moody and Sankey in their great meetings there. The music of which is the first of all my compositions that came into general use. Dr. Pentecost followed Moody and Sankey there, as already intimated, and also in New Haven in the spring following. While there I had the pleasure of meeting your honored father, who gave me the opportunity of visiting with him on several occasions and who gave me copies of several hymns, which I appreciated very sincerely. I have many times recalled him and those occasions when singing his justly famous hymn 'Saviour Thy Dying Love' which, with the splendid musical setting by Dr. Lowry, I have sung uncounted number of times and always with blessing to myself, for it is one of the best hymns for the regular church service and for prayer meetings, and all deeply spiritual services to be found in any church hymnals, certainly of those I have known.

With hearty congratulations to Mrs. Phelps and yourself for having known and walked with each other since your early years, I am sincerely and gratefully yours,

GEO. C. STEBBINS

An immediate effect of these services on my schoolmates and me was that we organized and kept up for years 'The Boys' Prayer-Meetings,' which were held for an hour one evening every week at private houses. My father and mother highly approved of these, but my aunt Libbie was ironically amused, though she was astonished at their continuance for so long a period.

12

CHINESE SCHOOLMATES

THE fact that in Hartford, both in the District School and in the High School some of my most intimate friends were Chinese boys seems strange as I look back. When I entered the West Middle School, I found a considerable number of Chinese boys there; it seemed natural to have them for playmates. This may have been partly owing to the attractive qualities of these Orientals, and their genius for adaptation.

A distinguished Chinese gentleman and scholar, Yung Wing, was living in Hartford, and it was through his influence that this large group of Chinese boys came there to study and to learn American ways. Every one of them was a patrician, of good family in China, and had as a rule much more spending money than most of the Americans. They had excellent manners, were splendid sportsmen, alert in mind, good at their studies, good at athletics. I do not think I have ever known a finer group of boys and young men. After graduating from the High School at Hartford, they entered Yale, when suddenly the command came from China, and they were all forced to return home.

These boys were dressed like us, except that they wore long queues. When they played football, they tucked these queues inside their shirts and sometimes tied them around their heads; for if the queue got loose, it afforded too strong a temptation for opponents. All our games were of course new to them, but they became excellent at baseball, football, hockey on the ice, then known as 'shinny,' and in fancy skating they were supreme. When the bicycle was invented, the first boy at school to have one was Tsang; and I can see him now, riding this strange high machine up Asylum Avenue.

I remember them individually; King, Kong, Se Chung, Kai Kah Wong, Chuck, Cho, Tsang, and all the rest. Mun Yew Chung, a little older than the majority of them, was in the class of 1883 at Yale, where he was universally respected. He became coxswain on the Yale crew, and steered the boat in the races as coolly as if he were out for a practice spin. It is said that he was told he must swear at the oarsmen to make them row their best; for he usually sat in his place in silence. Swearing did not come naturally to him, for he was grave and impassive; but finally, being told he must curse them, he would, at the most unexpected moments, and without any emphasis mechanically utter the monosyllable 'damn!' whereat the crew became so helpless with laughter, they begged him to desist. He was coxswain of the victorious Yale crews of 1880 and 1881; and at some Yale-Harvard meeting many years later, when a Harvard man expressed doubt as to whether Mun Yew Chung had even seen a university boat race, much less taken part in it, the Chinese suavely confessed he had never seen a Harvard crew row; and after a pause, explained that they were always behind him. Mun Yew Chung became a prominent statesman in China, and occasionally visited the United States as a diplomatic representative of his country.

I can well remember, when we used to 'choose up sides' at football, how the first choice invariably went to Se Chung, a short-thick-set boy, built close to the ground, who ran like a hound and dodged like a cat. What Se Chung had in grace and speed, Kong had in bull strength. Built broad and strong, eternally good-natured and smiling, he would cross the goal line, carrying four or five

Americans on his shoulders. In baseball, Tsang was a great pitcher, impossible to hit; King was a tower of strength to any nine, and even little Chuck, much younger than the others, took to a baseball as an infant takes to the bottle. My most intimate friend at the High School was a splendid Chinese boy named Cho—dignified and serious, who even at that time was more a sophisticated man of the world than I shall ever be. To hear that young gentleman translate Caesar in the classroom was a liberal education. Every Saturday Cho and I used to go shooting in West Hartford, after meadowlarks and yellowhammers. He had a huge gun that weighed over twelve pounds, which he would carry uncomplainingly all day long; and bring down birds on the wing at a prodigious distance. When these boys, to our infinite regret, were recalled to China, Cho gave me his great gun as a pledge of eternal friendship. In China he entered the Navy, and where he is now I wish I knew. We kept up a fitful correspondence for some years.

These boys not only excelled us Americans at athletics; you should have seen them cutting the double eight and the grapevine! They cut us out in other ways that caused considerable heart-burnings. When the Chinese youth entered the social arena, none of us had any chance. Their manner to the girls had a deferential elegance far beyond our possibilities. Whether it was the exotic pleasure of dancing with Orientals, or, what is more probable, the real charm of their manners and talk, I do not know; certain it is that at dances and receptions, the fairest and most sought-out belles invariably gave the swains from the Orient the preference. I can remember the pained expressions on the faces of some of my American comrades when the girls deliberately passed them by and accepted the attentions of Chinese rivals with a more than yielding grace. Personally, I rather enjoyed this oft-recurring situation, for my father and mother would not permit me to learn to dance, and this racial struggle appealed to my dramatic instinct. And the Orientals danced beautifully.

Thus the pleasant recollections of my boyhood are full of Chinese memories: and although, by the time I entered Yale, these fine fellows had gone home, I vainly hoped they might return. There was only one Oriental in my college class, Yan Phou Lee, who had an amazing command of English, and whose articles in the '*Lit*,' and speech at the Junior Exhibition, and later on the Commencement stage, attracted attention far outside academic walls.

13

MY AUNT

I HAVE often wondered why a maiden aunt is more worldly-minded than one's mother, but it is usually the case; I was pleased to read in Alice James's *Journal* under date of 1 December 1889, 'Prof. Farlow asking at the club table one night "Why is every man's aunt so entirely different from his mother?"'

The Reverend James H.Linsley, whom I mentioned, had only two children, Elizabeth Lyon Linsley, born 1821, and my mother, born 1823. Elizabeth was never married, refusing many offers, for after her father died in 1843 and my mother was married in 1847, she stayed home and took care of her mother, who lived until 1865. We children never called her anything but Libbie; she would not have allowed us to call her Auntie. Libbie had certain peculiarities and oddities, as nearly all people have who live alone; and after 1865 she lived alone in the great house in Stratford, Conn., where she and my mother were born. She paid us frequent visits and some of the happiest days of my life were spent at her house, when my brothers and I went there for weekends.

Her influence on me (and on my brothers) was wholly beneficial, for she supplied everything I did not get at home; and if she had been permitted would have accomplished much more. Although she lived from 1821 to 1896, she belonged in her mind and tastes to the eighteenth century. At heart she was a rationalist, thoroughly disliked evangelicanism, thought revivals vulgar, and although she invariably attended divine service and was a good judge of sermons, never joined any church. She kept Saturday night as faithfully as any Puritan; and gave supper parties Sunday evening to show her colours. Pope seemed to be her favourite poet. She never surrendered to any form of Victorianism. She kept all the beautiful early eighteenth-century furniture with which her house was filled (it is in my house now); and although all her neighbours and friends (including us) thought she was eccentric and perverse in not liking the massive ugliness of the Victorian period, nothing had any effect on her. She was right and she knew she was right, though she fought a solitary battle. She went to the theatre and to the opera, and tried in vain to induce her sister to let us go; for month after month she implored my parents to send us to dancing-school, for she knew that although our souls were saved, our bodies were gawky and clumsy. It is entirely owing to her that my teeth are regular and good; for when we were small boys, she took more interest in our teeth than in our souls, and took us to the dentist frequently and stayed with us there many weary hours. She was interested in every detail of our lives, and longed to have us happy and natural, and did her best to make us so. She studied the art of conversation as she studied the art of singing, and she seemed to prize good manners and good breeding and good taste above everything. She was proud of her ancestry and of her home; and she had a will of iron. I think she loved us three boys more than she loved anything else on earth.

Among other things I learned from her, I learned some consideration for others. When I was about eight years old, spending a week-end at her house, a middle-aged man called one evening, and after a polite skirmish with my aunt, he devoted his attention to me. At that time I happened to be excited about boats, and the visitor discussed the subject in a way that I found charming. After he left, I

spoke of him with enthusiasm. What a man! and how tremendously interested in boats! My aunt informed me that
he was a New York lawyer; that he cared nothing whatever about boats—took not the slightest interest in the
subject. 'But why then did he talk all the time about
boats?' 'Because he is a gentleman. He saw you were interested in boats, and he talked about the things he knew
would interest and please you. He made himself agreeable.'

Libbie was thoroughly familiar with Shakespeare. When
she came to our house for a prolonged visit, I always—at
her request—slept with her. She was a lonely woman, no
doubt, and liked to have me in the room. I slept with her till
I was fourteen or fifteen, and took it for granted, though
like most elderly people, she woke up early, and woke me
up too. I had recently read the complete works of William
Shakespeare, and from five in the morning until six-thirty,
we discussed the characters and plots with ardour. We did
this on every one of her visits for several years; I learned
a great deal. She used frequently to mention 'his profound
knowledge of the human heart;' this remark meant nothing to me, for I knew and cared nothing about the human
heart; what interested me in Shakespeare were the good
stories and the dashing gentlemen. The only time I ever
shocked her was once when I expressed unlimited enthusiasm for the *Taming of the Shrew*, and for the way in which
Petruchio treated Katherine. This pleased my small boy
nature immensely, to see this smarty girl put in her place.
On this question my aunt reasoned with me in vain.

My aunt used to tell me again and again that I was a
combination of a small boy and of a man of forty; and I
now see that she was right.

One day I had been reading in the Bible the story of
Jephthah's daughter and how she went upon the mountains to bewail her virginity. I did not fully understand
this; but I was impressed by it, and still more impressed by

the sensation I caused in a room full of people on that evening, when I regarded my aunt, who for some reason seemed to be depressed, and suddenly in the general silence I shot at her this question—'Are you bewailing your virginity?'

Long before the days of popular magazines which told an ignorant public what to wear, what to say, and what to think, how did she, living alone in a village, become infallible on the proper appearance of boys? When we received from somebody a few brightly-coloured silk handkerchiefs, and thought them far more 'tony' than white linen ones, she earnestly although vainly tried to persuade us they were vulgar; and where did she learn the following fact—which distinguishes as by a label the gentleman from other males? She solemnly told me, 'When the barber cuts your hair, never, never allow him to shave the back of your neck!' and I never have.

How I wish that by some miracle we might when we ourselves are old, talk with our parents and our aunts and uncles from an equality of age! There is always this gulf of generations. I suppose the attitude of a man or woman who was born when his parents were twenty-one, must be different when he is forty-five and they are sixty-six, from that of one, who, like me, cannot remember either his father or mother except when they were grey. Yet even so, does any boy ever regard his mother as a woman or remember she was a girl? Barrie brought this out in *Alice Sit by the Fire.* She isn't a woman; she is 'mother.' That is why Hamlet was so unspeakably shocked by his own mother's sensuality.

14

EXPERIENCES AT GRAMMAR SCHOOL

ALTHOUGH the transfer from Providence to Hartford was in many ways so beneficial, much loss came through the change of schools; for no matter how much parents may gain by removing from one city to another, there is almost always a loss for the children. The rapid growth in positive learning that I had made in a few months at the University Grammar School in Providence was balanced by a loss of two years in Hartford. And indeed during the next three years, with the exception of some brilliant flashes, I was, for the first and last time in my life, rated among the dull, backward, incompetent schoolboys, receiving very low marks, and finally, having to drop back a year. This was a strange and unpleasant experience; and even now, as I look back upon it, not altogether explicable.

It is possible that puberty had something to do with it. For it was during the years from twelve to fourteen that I was at my worst so far as getting good marks in studies was concerned. Or it may be that poor teaching had something to do with it, for my brother Arthur, two years older than I, who was for a time in the same classes and with the same teachers, had a somewhat similar experience; from this he as suddenly emerged, went on to graduate from High School with honours, writing an original Greek poem, and to take Phi Beta Kappa at Yale.

Mathematics always helped to keep me back; they were the curse of my life at school and college, they had more to do with my unhappiness than any other one thing, and I bitterly regret the hours, days, weeks, months, and years that I was forced to spend on this wholly unprofitable study. I shall return to this later with more venom.

In Hartford the school year began in April; we had just arrived in the Spring of 1876; and my brother Arthur and I were placed in Room Number Ten of the West Middle District School. Outside of school hours I was a great reader; and my head was stuffed full of battle-romances. I used to draw with my pencil on the inside covers of my text books two knights fighting, with one of them impaled by the spear, while the blood flowed copiously from the wound. One day, the teacher walking down the aisle, spied these pictures; and to my amazement she burst into a violent rage; in the presence of the well-filled room, she called me a dirty, vile, filthy boy, and expressed as much abhorrence for me as if I had been a criminal. I could not understand such an explosion of wrath; but she had a bad temper anyhow, and I supposed she was angry because she had caught me wasting some of my time in nonsensical drawings. It was not until years later that the real reason for her rage came to me. This teacher thought my pictures were obscene! She took the spear-head and the flow of blood for something else. She never forgave me; she hated me after that, and I found it impossible to please her, or to get anything like a good mark.

If she had asked me to stay after school, and quietly talked to me about my supposed obscenities, my frank amazement would have convinced her; but no, she had to condemn me publicly. This, and other unjust treatment that I received occasionally, convinced me that it was better in dealing with pupils, to make any mistake rather than punish the innocent.

I think during the two years that I spent at the West Middle School and the first year at the High School, my inability to get good marks puzzled my teachers more than it did me. I read aloud so easily, I wrote such good compositions, I spoke more intelligently than most of my classmates, I remembered the words and music of every song and hymn we were taught, and yet I got low marks. Some of my teachers used to talk with me outside of school hours; I can see now that they were impressed by my general intelligence and by my low standing.

A curious thing happened at the end of the first year. We had a written examination in ten or eleven subjects. We had been told that if we got a total mark above Five we should jump a room and go into the highest room, Number 12. That if we got above Four we should advance one room, and that if we fell below Four we should remain another year where we were. I announced myself as a candidate for leaping to Room Number 12. Well, the first examination was Arithmetic. I worked and wrote steadily during the allotted two hours. My mark on this examination was .04, four-tenths of one; nobody received a lower mark. I remember that the Principal, who was not an unkind man, came to me and said it was ridiculous for me to think of leaping a room; that I should probably remain where I was for the rest of my life. I made no reply, for what was there to say?

The next examination was in history, and I received the highest mark in the room. History was as real to me as my own life, and I described the death of General Wolfe on the battlefield of Quebec as if I had been an eye witness. When the Principal was shown this paper, he was flabbergasted. My total average for all the exams was 5.5, and together with my brother, I landed in the highest room, and became a Senior. During the whole of the next year, my curse was Arithmetic; I remember working four hours one evening on a question in 'Partial Payments' for the next day, and getting it wrong. I believe the standard of graduation from the West Middle School was *relatively* higher than that of any other institution I have seen. We had to take three complete exams *in all the studies*, and unless one's total was above five, one was not allowed to graduate, and one could not receive a diploma. Many failed every year. I squeezed through with an average of 5.2.

The twenty-four hours before 'graduating exercises' were among the unhappiest of my life. The reason for this may seem ridiculous, but my agony was real. All the boys and girls who were to receive diplomas were carefully drilled to march in to the auditorium two by two, first the girls, then the boys. The Principal, in addressing us, said there was an odd number of boys and an odd number of girls. Instantly I had the presentiment that he would select me to walk in with the odd girl. My worst fears were immediately confirmed. 'The girls will walk in two by two, then Willie Phelps and Alice Post will follow arm in arm, then will come the boys.' I could not have felt worse had he announced my execution.

My own sufferings in childhood and boyhood from bashfulness and self-consciousness were so acute, that I have ever since had profound sympathy for any bashful boy or girl. Older people laugh at this, which is brutal; one might as well laugh at a boy writhing in physical torment. I went to the Principal immediately after this meeting, and begged him to give the assignment to some boy who would not mind; but the Principal, probably thinking I was cowardly and needed discipline, refused to let me off. That afternoon, at the dress rehearsal, we went through with this processional. I have ever since been grateful to Alice Post (now Mrs. Haight). I supposed of course she would approach me with loathing. She came with the most gracious smile, as if she regarded walking in with me as an honour and a delight! I did not like to be rude to her, for of course there was nothing personal in my attitude. She took my arm as if I were a duke, and we went through with it. She talked with me like a woman of the world. Yet all that night I saw myself entering the auditorium, the only boy with a girl, and the entire audience grinning at me. I seriously thought of running away. But just before the exercises were to begin, I learned to my overwhelming joy and relief, that one of the girls was taken ill, hence Alice was to walk in with one of her own sex, and I marched in alone, at the head of the boys. I was thirteen years old, and the smallest boy in the class.

I did not dislike girls; they seemed to me remote and mysterious beings; in their presence I was hopelessly confused and tongue-tied. Sometimes while walking on the street, if I saw one a hundred yards away whom I knew and to whom therefore I must take off my hat, I would dive into a side street, or hide in a yard until she had safely passed. I longed to meet girls on equal terms; I longed to talk and laugh with them, and be at ease in their presence; and how I envied the boys who managed this with no embarrassment! With me it was the moth and the star.

On the stage at graduation exercises that day I suffered from another difficulty that often afflicted me, and from which I learned to understand others. I could not stop laughing. There was as much mirth in this laughter as if I had been over a slow fire; I did not want to laugh, but I could not help it. It was sheer nervousness. I understood then and I understand now why there are certain people who laugh in church, laugh at funerals, laugh during serious conversations.

It must not be thought that I was an unhappy, morose, or solitary youth. Quite the opposite. I felt absolutely at ease with other boys of my age, I played all the outdoor games with enormous gusto, I went swimming 'with the gang' every day in warm weather, I loved expeditions in the woods, camping out, and all that sort of thing. I was one hundred per cent Boy—but in the presence of girls or on solemn and formal occasions, I often did the wrong thing. I was often afraid in the church prayer-meetings that I should laugh, not because anything struck me as funny, but just because I did not want to laugh. This is a curse that particularly afflicts bashful, self-conscious, imaginative boys and girls.

So far as scholarship is concerned, my life as a schoolboy was so remarkable in its brilliance and in its stupidity (for at one time I was at the head of the class and at another at the foot) that it may be worth recording. Ten and eleven years old, at the school in Providence, I attracted amazement from both teachers and schoolmates by brilliant achievements; I seemed far ahead of my years in intellectual maturity. At the age of fourteen I was so low in standing, though working desperately hard, that I had to go back a whole year, and join the class below; a bitter humiliation. Then suddenly everything became easy again, and with the exception of mathematics, I had no more difficulties, but stood among the leaders at school and college.

The autobiography of the famous playwright and actor Sacha Guitry called *If Memory Serves* (translated by Lewis Galantière) has such interesting comment on boyhood education that it is worth consideration by parents. It seems that the boy Sacha was frequently transferred from one prep school to another; he went to *eleven*. And so, from the age of six to the age of eighteen, he was without any real education at all, and after that, made no pretence of seeking any. His peregrinations however gave him opportunities for observation of teachers, pupils, lessons, and methods; and his summary is

The time we lose in school is lost during the most precious period of our lives. . . . I am convinced that we are extremely intelligent between the ages of eight and fourteen years, and that most of us are less so between fourteen and twenty, much less. . . . I am quite ready to agree that the professors in our institutions of higher education are superior people, but I insist that it is at the beginning of our education that we should be confided to remarkable men. If, from our earliest years, we were given the taste for work, we should thereafter learn soon enough what our needs are; for I believe that we learn easily and usefully what we need. . . .

All the originality that we possess between the ages of eight and fourteen—our natural aptitudes, our individual gifts—are dead at the time of our eighteenth year. Of course these gifts may return later, but what time lost!

There may be another reason apart from inefficient teaching; for Goethe, in *his* autobiography says children 'generally promise more than they perform: and it seems that Nature, among the other roguish tricks that she plays us, here also especially designs to make sport of us. . . . The child, considered in and for himself, with his equals, and in relations suited to his powers, seems so intelligent and rational, and at the same time so easy, cheerful, and clever, that one can hardly wish it further cultivation. If children grew up according to early indications, we should have nothing but geniuses; but growth is not merely development; the various organic systems which constitute one man spring one from another, follow each other, change into each other, supplant each other, and even consume each other; so that after a time, scarcely a trace is to be found of many aptitudes and manifestations of ability.'

I wonder if this does not partially explain the disappointment many parents and teachers feel in so many cases of unfulfilled 'promise,' and the regret that so many old persons feel as they look back on their own life. When I was a child, I could amuse groups of other boys and even of adults by telling long stories improvised without hesitation; if early promise meant later performance, I ought to have been a novelist or dramatist. But, unlike the late A.C.Benson, I do not feel broken-hearted. Of course I envy distinguished creative writers, but why cry for the moon? I have had too good a time to cry for anything. Goethe's words of wisdom comfort me, and perhaps they may comfort others.

Yet why so many brilliant little boys and girls, and why so many dull old men and women? Who explains it more accurately, Guitry, Wordsworth, or Goethe?

Mr. Guitry also says something that applies I think not only to the education of children, but to that of college undergraduates. It seems to me ridiculous that in most colleges today lectures and recitations are regarded as a penalty for the dull and lazy; all the students are trying to get on the 'Dean's list' which means that if they are sufficiently intelligent or industrious, they will not have to attend classes regularly. The implication, of course, is that they are more brilliant than their teachers; and should not have to be forced to listen to the stupidity of specialists. I had always insisted that college classes should be so conducted that those who are dull or lazy or incompetent should be refused the privilege of attending them. They should be forced to study alone or with a private tutor until they can show sufficient ability to be readmitted. Therefore I was pleased by Sacha Guitry's statement,

> Classwork should be passionately interesting. Of course for this we should have to have passionately interested teachers, people convinced of the beauty of their mission—and not poor crocks whose chief characteristics are their mediocrity and commonplaceness.
>
> I dream of the time when a master will be able to say to a pupil, 'You behaved badly, and I shall punish you. You will not be allowed to attend class.' *Vous n'avez pas été sage, tantôt. Pour votre punition, vous n'assisterez pas à la classe.*

My standing in graduating from the West Middle District School was so low and my scholarship record during the preceding years (1876–7) had been so poor, that the Principal said I was not fitted to enter the High School and that I ought to remain at West Middle and take its Senior year over again. This was a gloomy prospect, for in spite of my miserable marks, I was ambitious. Although the Principal was a man whom we respected, in this particular matter his judgement was not so good as that of a boy only a little older than I, whose own marks were so low he had difficulty in remaining in the High School. This was Morris Penrose, and I shall always be grateful to him. He advised me to enter the High School; saying that even if I were dropped and forced to spend five instead of four years there, it would be far better for my development to spend them in the High School in a more mature environment than to repeat a year with the little boys and girls in the District School. This advice seemed to me sound and seems so still; I determined to follow it if it should be possible. But the immediate problem was, could I enter the High School?

I had supposed, unless one had the permission of the District School Superintendent to enter the High School, one was not allowed to try the entrance examinations; and he would not give permission either to my brother Arthur or to me. Thus, for two weeks after leaving the West Middle, we were despondently looking forward to re-entering the class at our old Grammar School.

I shall never forget the April morning in 1878, when a boy came running to our house in Sigourney Street, and told us that any boy or girl in Hartford was free to try the entrance exams for the Public High School; they were open to anyone, and they would begin in fifteen minutes! If he had not found us at home that morning or if he had come later, we should have lost a year. We ran down Asylum Avenue as fast as our legs would carry us, got there just in time, took the whole series of entrance exams—found them much easier than the ones we had had at the West Middle —and so both passed triumphantly into the High School.

15

THE HARTFORD PUBLIC HIGH SCHOOL

I ENTERED the Hartford Public High School in April 1878, and found it difficult to keep up with my studies. There was a printed monthly report, which gave the exact standing of every pupil in the school. This report was public, was sent to all the parents, so that the precise position in scholarship of every boy and girl in the school was known. If one's average fell below Five for three months, one was dropped into the lower classes; and if one was in the lowest class, one was dropped from the school. In the next Spring my average fell below Five. The Principal, Joseph Hall, sent for me, and told me I should have to go. I suggested we were nearly at the end of the school year, when everyone had to take the final examination; that I be allowed to try this. He immediately granted my request and to his amazement I successfully survived this ordeal and entered the next class.

But in the Autumn of the following year (1879) I fell so low in my studies that my case was hopeless. There seemed to be a cloud over my mind, so that I could not properly learn anything, though I tried hard. I became discouraged; and I had bad luck with one of my teachers who was anything but sympathetic. She thought I was a shirker and a loafer. I withdrew from the school in November, feeling my disgrace keenly. My parents must have been terribly disappointed, but they were unbelievably kind. Not a word of reproach; perhaps they saw how disconsolate I was.

In January I re-entered the High School, and in the

lower class. For some weeks I suffered from a depression so profound that I should have been glad to die. To see my former classmates going to their recitations, while I was doing the first year over again, seemed intolerable. But, by the mercy of God, I was assigned to a room presided over by Miss Mary Mather, a young and very attractive woman. She must have observed my sorrowful countenance, for while she never asked me what was the matter, her attitude was extremely sympathetic. She was kind; she was encouraging. Suddenly a cloud seemed to pass from my mind.

Studies that had seemed impossibly difficult became easily comprehensible; I obtained high marks with less than half the effort it had previously cost me to get low ones. I astounded my parents, teachers, and former classmates by going to the top row; my name frequently came at the head on the monthly reports, and from that time, shortly after my fifteenth birthday (1880) to the age of twenty-six, when I passed my last examination, I was always among the honour students.

Miss Mary Mather was as shy as she was kind. She suffered from acute nervousness, and it must have been torture to her often in the schoolroom. I think I was the only one of her pupils who came near understanding her. Some days she would begin to laugh, would vainly try to stop, would shake with laughter, and once or twice have to dismiss the class. The other boys were naturally amused by this; but I knew what hell she was passing through. Some years after this she was overcome by a nervous affliction, and died.

But I can say of her what the Pope said of Pompilia, that not even in Heaven could she be any more of an angel than she was on earth. It is one of the innumerable mysteries of life that a woman like Mary Mather, who was wholly kind, sympathetic, and lovely, should have had to suffer such nervous depression.

In Junior and Senior year at the High School, we had a teacher who made a profound impression. This was Winfred R. Martin, six feet four, with a large red beard. He was the exact opposite of a routine hearer of recitations; and at first we boys rebelled against his methods, because 'he asked questions that were not in the notes.' He was one of the most learned men I have ever known and he never published a line. He had an overwhelming passion for the acquisition of knowledge; and had no other ambition. To publish would have taken time which he used to learn something more. Every Saturday he took the train to New Haven, to study Sanskrit with the greatest scholar in the world, William Dwight Whitney. And after he got to the point where he could not endure High School teaching any more, he went to Tübingen and stayed there until he had won his doctor's degree. Later he became Professor of Ancient and Modern Languages at Trinity College, Hartford, where he was happy. He taught Sanskrit, Arabic, the Semitic languages, Greek, Latin, French, German, and Italian. He was never married and his highest happiness was in learning.

Occasionally I went to his rooms in Hartford and called on him, something I never did with any other teacher. I bored him horribly, but I came away from those interviews feeling inspired. I can see him in my mind's eye as plainly as I saw him in the classroom nearly sixty years ago. I remember his translation of the famous passage in Virgil's eclogues. He spoke it just once in the classroom, and it printed on my mind in imperishable type. The passage begins

Tale tuum carmen nobis, divine poeta

'O divine poet, your song is to me as deep sleep upon the grass to the weary, as in summer's heat to slake one's thirst from a springing rivulet of clear water.'

When I was an undergraduate at Yale, I became acquainted with Floyd R.Smith of the class above me, a famous half-mile runner. Fifty years later I met him in New Jersey, and discovered that before Martin came to the High School at Hartford, Smith had him as teacher of Latin and Greek in the High School at Jersey City. Replying to my request, he wrote me as follows:

I remember well the day he told us that he was going to leave, to go to the Hartford High School. So you were the looters that pilfered our treasure chest. Boy, but he was a teacher, the best of all we met on our way. He embodied for me all of the romance and service of teaching.

When, on one occasion, we were fed up on the Gallic Wars, he closed his textbook and turned to Froissart with some such comment as this: 'Froissart would have described in detail each of these patriotic murders. Caesar disposed of all of them with one ablative absolute, omnibus occisis (I believe), and devoted the rest of his column to the glorification of Julius Caesar—a great reporter, that Caesar.' He took us with Froissart on his journey through England, Scotland, Italy and finally to Aquitaine in the retinue of the Black Prince.

Our reward for enduring the monotony of Xenophon's parasangs was his personally-conducted tour to Jane Austen's pre-Victorian England. *Sense and Sensibility*, *Pride and Prejudice* for a time at least, displaced *Diamond Dick* and *Murderous Moses*.

One of the most dramatic and enduring by-products of that course in Latin and Greek was our introduction to the old Norse Vikings. Romance in golden trappings. I used to stare at him in a transport of admiration. He seemed to me to be one of them, with his six-foot stature, his commanding brow and his blond beard. We boys spoke of him as Old Man Martin, for he must have been at least thirty when we knew him—past ninety now if living. I wonder who else remembers him.

I met him in my Freshman year, on Chapel Street, and he took me to lunch. He was then taking a post-graduate course in Sanskrit, I believe. Why didn't Yale grab him?

16

WALKING, WORKING, FROGS, LOVE

SEVEN years after I was graduated from the High School I was again to meet Martin—not in New Haven but in Paris—and we had more than one meal together. Of that meeting, more anon.

When I was in the High School, George William Curtis, one of the most fastidious and exquisite gentlemen who ever appeared on a public platform, delivered an address on civil service reform in Hartford. Of this address I heard only three words but I can see him now and hear his voice as plainly as if he were in the room. He appeared on the platform in full evening dress, immaculate and graceful, with the grey side-whiskers of the period. He examined his manuscript, said 'Ladies and Gentlemen'—at that moment I fell asleep and was awakened by the applause one hour later.

It was a winter night and I had been coasting all the afternoon. There was a silver dollar in my pocket and when the big sled turned over, as it did when we were rounding a curve, that silver dollar was embedded in my hip and for a month I wore on my leg the circular impression of the U.S.A.

I did an immense amount of walking in my schooldays; several times walking the 37 miles between Hartford and New Haven in a day; the first time when I was only eleven. When I was sixteen I spent the Easter week vacation with my pal, Frank Hubbard, walking 100 miles in five days, from Hartford to Norwich to New London and Saybrook, taking the boat from Lyme to Hartford at one o'clock in the morning.

In the Easter vacation of my Sophomore year in college, my classmate John Norton Pomeroy, of San Francisco, and I walked from New Haven up along the Housatonic River into the northwest corner of the State.

And a few days after Commencement in 1887, my classmates George Pettee, Horace Hart, Tom Penney, and I walked over 200 miles from New Haven to the White Mountains; we stopped a few days at Northfield, and heard Moody the evangelist, and were also fortunate in hearing Professor Henry Drummond deliver for the first time his address *The Greatest Thing in the World*, which Moody persuaded him to publish. It was translated into all the languages of Europe.

Only one day in my life have I performed severe manual labour from dawn till nightfall, and that was enforced. When we were living in Providence, and I was ten years old, our closest friend and playmate was a boy named Lincoln Rose, whose father was a missionary in India; Lincoln was living with a deacon in the church. This deacon was a curious mixture—as perhaps we all are—of piety, coarseness, kindness, and severity. He was orthodox of the orthodox; his speeches and prayers in public were eloquent; on his farm he was a hard driver, and yet saw that the men he employed were well fed. I remember one winter night, when we were having a 'social' at our church, with abundant food and agreeable entertainment, this deacon went out on the street, and brought in the policeman who had to be out all night, found him a place at the table, and said 'Captain, you sit here and make a good meal.' I remember plainly how that policeman gratefully ate that hot oyster broth.

Yet one day when I saw this deacon directing work on his farm, I was amazed to hear him use obscene language in shouting at a dog. It was many years before golf had caused devout people to curse fluently, and I had forgotten how such apparent inconsistencies had always been true of human nature. 'Out of the same mouth proceedeth blessing and cursing,' wrote the apostle St. James. At a football game in New Haven one day, an undergraduate left his seat and came near a friend of mine, and said 'I don't mind ordinary profanity; but that old man up there with whom I was sitting has kept up such a stream of blasphemies that I can't stand it. I don't know who he is.' On pointing him out, he was told that was the Reverend Doctor —— a sincere and devoted clergyman from another city, who exerted a particularly fine influence on boys. He was well known for his terrific excitement at all athletic games; but this undergraduate could not believe he was really a clergyman. He was, though.

Well, about that day's work. After we had moved to Hartford, Lincoln Rose wrote to my brother and me, inviting us to spend a day with him on the farm managed by the deacon, and where he worked every day for the same wages customarily paid boys. 'Sonny, how much do you get for hoeing those potatoes?' 'Don't get nothing, but get hell if I don't do it.'

We arrived in the evening, stayed the night, rose early, and we supposed that as we were visitors, the deacon would let Lincoln off for one day, and we would all three have a good time playing together. Quite otherwise. The deacon told us to come right along to the hayfield. We did not return to the house for noonday dinner; a lunch was brought to us in the fields. We pitched hay until dark and my hands were covered with blisters; as the twilight finally came on, and we took the last load to the barn, we were sent up to the upper storey of the barn to level off and smooth out the enormous heaps of hay. I can feel now the hot, close, stuffy air of that barn-room in the gathering darkness, and the stifling feeling of the hay and straw in my eyes, ears, and throat.

Of course we received no money for this work and no thanks. Either the deacon thought it was good for us to be made to work, or he thought he had a good opportunity to get two more hands for nothing. And how he did drive us all day! 'Hurry up there, I'm right on your heels!'

The next morning, as we returned to our home in Hartford, we were so stiff and sore we could hardly move; but our physical aches and pains were nothing to our bitter resentment. It seems funny enough, now, our planned holiday with Lincoln; but it was not funny then. I have never done a day's work since, so far as manual labour is concerned.

Some of the happiest hours in my boyhood in Hartford I owe to the late Pliny Jewell. His brother Marshall Jewell, several times Governor of Connecticut, was the handsomest old man I ever saw. To see him on horseback, with his ruddy complexion, snow-white hair and pointed white imperial, with his unassuming patrician elegance, looking like a Duke of the *ancien régime*, was a sight never to be forgotten. His brother Pliny, a charming, kindly old gentleman, lived in a beautiful house on Farmington Avenue, with extensive and well-kept gardens. On this estate was a pond which froze solid every winter. Mr. Jewell had printed a number of cards inscribed SKATING TICKET and he gave one to every boy in the neighbourhood he felt would not abuse the privilege. What fun we had on that pond! I remember when I was twelve years old I finished one evening *David Copperfield*. I went over to the pond in the bright moonlight. I was alone. I skated around and around repeating aloud over and over again, 'O Agnes O my soul!'

I used to go over occasionally to the pond in the summer twilight, to see Mr. Jewell with his frogs. A servant would bring out a large armchair and place it on the border of the little lake. Then the old gentleman came, took his seat deliberately, and began to ring a large dinner-bell. As the mellow tones filled the air, the frogs would emerge from the water and group themselves expectantly yet respectfully around Mr. Jewell, who fed them with bits of bread, which they received courteously. I had never discriminated among frogs; but to this gentleman every one of those frogs was an individual, and he had named them all. The largest was called Laura Matilda, and was his favourite. I have seen Laura draw near his armchair, take a bit of bread delicately from his fingers, eat it and then wipe her mouth daintily, like the Prioresse in Chaucer.

In my Senior year at the Hartford High School, I was elected Class Orator, and on Class Day I delivered my oration, 'Perils of the Republic.' I thought this was filled with original ideas; and I was chagrined when an older man asked me what subject I was going to discuss, and on hearing it, he said, 'Poor old Republic; it always catches it at Graduation Exercises!' I was then a convinced Federalist, believing in a strong centralized national government. My four perils were the Saloon, the polygamy threat in the State of Utah, a too small navy, and illiteracy among our Southern people. This speech was delivered with sincere passion in the Spring of 1883; and the first paragraph shows how much more fortunate our country was then than it is now.

> The country is now in a state of unexampled prosperity. Our revenues greatly exceed our expenses; the national debt is being rapidly decreased; the Treasury is overflowing.

And there was no income tax.

The two public days of graduation came later in the month. On the first, eight boys and girls were selected from the whole school to compete for prizes in declamation. I spoke Macaulay's 'Battle of the Lake Regillus.' For the boys, the first prize was awarded to Clarence A. Barbour, later President of Brown University, and one of the foremost platform speakers in America; the second prize, to my delight, was awarded to me, and now I am Public Orator of Yale University.

On the whole, the last three years of my life in the High School were very happy. It is true that I suffered from love-melancholy; but as Sienkiewicz said there were some physical tortures so horrible that they seemed at moments like monstrous delight, so this love-melancholy was so profound that it had a certain grave charm like the loneliness of mountain scenery at twilight.

My two love-affairs were both hopeless. I fell in love with a girl at school and remained in love with her for more than two years, without ever meeting her or speaking to her. How amazed she would have been had she known! Later in Senior year there was another, whom I knew and talked with awkwardly and tongue-tied, who seemed to me incredibly beyond my low level of existence, although she tossed me frequent notes and once when she did not know I was looking at her, I saw her kiss a sprig of pussy willow I had given her. But I was a faint-heart.

I always think of the Hartford High School with loyal affection; it was a first-rate school. And I can understand how Maurice Baring felt about Eton. As it is quite the fashion in modern novels to look back with disgust at one's days in school and to represent the atmosphere there as barbaric, cruel, and stupid, the loyal strain in Maurice Baring's temperament comes as a refreshing change:

I cannot deal with the experience of others. I can only deal with my own. I haven't the slightest pretence of impartiality, nor the slightest desire to see the question steadily, and, seeing it whole, I am a violent, an unblushing, an unrepentant partisan. About my own experiences and my own feelings with regard to Eton I have no doubt whatsoever. I enjoyed Eton wholeheartedly and unreservedly: I enjoyed it all from the first to the last moment. If I had my life to live over again, I should like all that piece back with nothing left out. . . . I do not want Harrow to win the Eton and Harrow match either this year, next year or ever. I do not believe that any other school is as good as Eton—not nearly as good. I do not believe that Eton is quite different now from what it used to be. I believe that Eton is just the same; but even if she is not, even if she has changed for the worse, I believe her to be better than any other school. (*Lost Lectures*)

His saying he did not want Eton ever to lose the cricket match will be understood by most school and college graduates. Although the great poet Alfred E. Housman failed to get his degree at Oxford and was Professor at Cambridge so many years, he always wanted Oxford to win the boat-race. In microscopic imitation of so mighty a genius, I was never more emotionally devoted to Yale than while I was teaching at Harvard and enjoying its intellectual and social atmosphere; never more wild with partisan fervour than when the Yale athletic teams came to Cambridge. Returning to the Harvard Yard from a Yale victory, one of my Harvard pupils said, 'Mr. Phelps, I never saw anyone look so happy as you do now.'

17

GOING TO THE THEATRE

My mother never allowed me to attend any theatrical performances. As I had read all of Shakespeare at the age of twelve, I was eager to see a Shakespeare play, especially as Edwin Booth was then in his prime, and appeared annually in Hartford. Ordinarily, parents would be pleased if their children wished to see a play by Shakespeare; not so with ours. Finally, when I was eighteen, Thomas W. Keene, a melodramatic actor, came to Hartford to play *Macbeth*. I had a private interview with my father, and told him how passionately I desired to see this play. Finally he gave me fifty cents and said I might go, only I must say nothing about it to mother. 'We men must stand together' Accordingly, that night I sneaked off, and with some other boys sat in the gallery and for the first time in my life saw a play on the stage. I was thrilled. When I came home, I found my mother sitting up for me; she had discovered where I had been; her sorrow was great and sincere; she felt that I had committed some dreadful sin; I saw it was no use even to consider the matter further. It is difficult to write about this without giving a false impression of my mother. She was never grim, never harsh; she was all tenderness and also full of fun; but the theatre was wrong, and Christians did not deliberately do what they knew was wrong.

That autumn, however, I entered Yale; and as I had never promised that I would not go to the theatre, I went fairly often. I saw George C. Miln play *Hamlet*. It has often been said that no one has ever entirely failed who has played the part of Hamlet. After having seen Miln, I know this statement is not true. It was interesting to see an actor deliver Hamlet's advice to the players while breaking every rule so definitely expressed.

Of the thirty-seven plays of Shakespeare, I have seen all but five, and I hope to see them all before I die. I have not seen *The Two Gentlemen of Verona*, *Timon of Athens*, and the three parts of *King Henry VI*.

The Shakespearean performances that made the deepest impression on me: Richard Mansfield as King Richard III, Edwin Booth as Shylock, and Maurice Evans as King Richard II. Evans's unabridged *Hamlet* in 1938 I regard as the greatest production of the greatest play in the world.

With the exception of the Passion Play at Oberammergau, I have never been more thrilled than by Sarah Bernhardt in *La Tosca*; hers was the finest exposition of the art of acting I have ever seen. That was in 1892.

Among other theatrical performances I shall never forget are *Les Caprices de Marianne* at the *Comédie Française*, Maeterlinck's *Schwester Beatrix* and Gorki's *Nachtasyl* in Germany, Ernst von Possart in *Faust* and Henry Irving's production of *Faust*, Féraudy in *Les Affaires sont les Affaires*, Mrs. Pat Campbell as Magda, Hermann Bahr's *Das Konzert* (Munich), Maude Adams as Peter Pan, Nazimova as Hedda Gabler, William Gillette, Louis Calvert, and Helen Hayes in *Dear Brutus*, Katharine Cornell as Elizabeth Barrett and Saint Joan, *Die Fünf Frankfürter*, *The Old Lady Shows Her Medals*, *Mary Rose*, the New York New Theatre Company in Galsworthy's *Strife* and in Maeterlinck's *The Blue Bird*, Louis Calvert's stunning performance in Besier's *Don*, Granville-Barker's production of *The Doctor's Dilemma* and *Androcles*, Granville-Barker's play *The Madras House* at the Neighborhood Theatre in

New York, the Theatre Guild's production of St. John Ervine's *John Ferguson* and *Jane Clegg*, Mr. Hampden's
Cyrano, and I suppose I could mention forty or fifty more.

The theatre has been one of the greatest pleasures of my
life; and I have been a drama critic fifty years. When I
reached the age of twenty-one, there was no more audible
objection to my going to the theatre, and I celebrated my
freedom by publishing a long criticism of Wilson Barrett's
Hamlet in the *Yale Literary Magazine* for March 1887.

I have had the good fortune to see and hear most of the
great actors of the world. On the whole, I think the combination of play and acting that made the deepest impression was the Passion Play at Oberammergau, which I saw
for the first time in 1890. Everything combined to make
this occasion memorable. It was my first journey in Europe; I was twenty-five; there was no railroad to Oberammergau; no shriek of the locomotive stabbed the sacred silence; and the peasants had not lost their pristine simplicity.

Furthermore I sat down in front, directly before the
stage, with nothing over my head but the sky. When it
rained, as it did three or four times during the day-long
performance, we let it rain. We did not know or care
whether we were wet or not. When one sits twenty or
thirty rows back in the more expensive seats, as I did on a
subsequent occasion, one has hundreds of tourists with
their opera-glasses between one and the stage. But sitting
directly in front, I forgot it was a play. I was in Palestine.

And of all the events in the tragedy, from eight in the
morning till five in the afternoon, the supreme moment for
me was not the Crucifixion, for I had steeled myself in advance. It was a moment during the procession to the cross.
There were seven hundred actors on the stage, from the
smallest children to the oldest men and women. On not
one face did I see indifference, inattention, or any assumed

expression. They themselves were *living* the scene, which is why I was living it with them. The small boys, as they picked up stones to throw at the Son of God, screamed, 'To the cross with the Galilean!' I have beheld many mob scenes, but none like this. The turbulent, frenzied throng moved incoherently and noisily along with their victim. Directly behind him was a group of women, shaken with grief, and sobbing. Suddenly the weary and blood-stained Sufferer stopped and turned around; and at that moment the raging, excited mob became still. In this awful silence Jesus spoke to the women:

> Daughters of Jerusalem, weep not for me, but weep for yourselves, and for your children. For, behold, the days are coming in which they shall say, Blessed are the barren, and the wombs that never bare, and the paps that never gave suck. Then shall they begin to say to the mountains, Fall on us; and to the hills, Cover us.

Omitting the Passion Play, which is produced with a sincerity founded on faith, a sincerity beyond the reach of the most consummate art, I think one of the supreme moments on the professional stage was that when Edwin Booth as Shylock advanced on the helpless Antonio. This I saw in Detroit in the year 1887; and I knew then why Booth was called the greatest American actor.

It was the trial scene; the judge had apparently given the relentless Shylock full power over his victim. Shylock had been whetting the shining knife on the sole of his shoe; looking up from time to time at the face of Antonio with hellish hatred—impatient of the legal delays, and of the appeal for mercy. When the judge apparently granted the final permission, saying:

> And you must cut this flesh from off his breast;
> The law allows it, and the court awards it—

Shylock, baring his wolfish fangs in a frenzy, cried out: 'Most learned judge! a sentence!' and then, with an expression of ferocity that I can never forget, he sprang at Antonio, screaming:

'Come, *prepare!*'

So long as I live, I shall see that face and hear that word, '*prepare!*'

One of the greatest of modern actors and certainly the most intellectual, was Richard Mansfield. When he was a young man, I saw him as King Richard III. It was a stunning performance all through; but the high moment came in the dawn ushering in the last day of the usurper's life. King Richard had been tormented all night by terrible dreams, in which appeared the apparitions of the men and women he had murdered. Finally, in the doubtful twilight preceding sunrise, Catesby called him.

The king came to the front of the tent, so obsessed by the awful ghosts of his dreams that he was not sure whether this figure in shining silver armour was real or merely another horror. The king said nothing; he advanced slowly, slowly toward his retainer, and finally reached out his groping hands; the moment he touched the solid armour and knew the figure was real, he embraced him and in a voice of indescribable relief he whispered, 'Oh, *Catesby!*'

The greatest woman actor I ever saw was Sarah Bernhardt, who made a deeper impression on me than Duse. I saw the divine Sarah many times, in classic and in modern plays. She was surely at her best in melodrama; for while she had all the resources of a magnificent artist, and her voice of gold could give significance and beauty to any poetry or prose, she was primarily a tragedian of action; the more passionate the scene, the more effective she became. I shall never forget *La Tosca*. She was inspired; she seemed to rejoice in the plenitude of her powers. Even in her tenderest love scenes she purred like a tiger, and her fingers clasped and unclasped in her lover's hair with the lazy movements of a great cat.

She was at her best in the dinner scene with Scarpia. She had reluctantly promised to grant Scarpia's demands if he would write out the paper which would save her lover. As he turned his back to her while writing out the note, she looked wildly over the wreck of the dinner table. Suddenly she saw a knife. Her eyes glared. She seized the knife and in order to steady her nerves, poured herself a glass of wine, which flowed over the top of the glass and all over the tablecloth. Then with the knife behind her back, she awaited the approach of Scarpia. He came toward her, smiling in the security of triumph. As he extended the paper toward her, she sprang at him like a wildcat and drove the knife into his breast.

Henry Irving never impressed me as a Shakespearean actor; like Sarah Bernhardt, he was at his best in melodrama. Those who, like me, had the good fortune to see him in *The Bells*, *The Lyons Mail*, *Louis XI*, saw Irving at the height of his power. I think his finest scene came in *The Bells* when he sat gibbering on the floor with the accursed sleighbells ringing in his ears.

Ellen Terry during many years was the favourite actress among English-speaking people; but although I saw her many times, she never gave me a thrill. She always seemed to be her charming self. I saw her as Margaret in *Faust*, yet I cannot remember her appearance or her voice.

Magda, by the late Hermann Sudermann, is a grand opportunity for the display of acting. The title role was played by Duse, Bernhardt, Modjeska, Mrs. Pat Campbell, by all the feminine stars. A supreme moment for me occurred at the beginning of the second act, one fearfully hot summer night in the uncomfortable little Royalty Theatre in Soho. Mrs. Campbell's acting was so magnificent that we forgot the heat. She was the prima donna who had left Main Street a long time before, and fresh from her triumphs, revisits her humble home. It is a stuffy little parlour, where it is clear nothing interesting has ever happened or can happen. Magda's mousey sister, a commonplace 'home-body,' dressed in unbecoming and cheap attire, is waiting alone in this depressing environment. Suddenly the opulent, voluptuous Magda foams into the room. She stops. She looks at the dreadful changeless furniture. Then she looks at her sister. Then she kisses her. Not a word was spoken, but I found that I was crying.

Louis Calvert was an actor of genius. I saw him many times—in the New Theatre as old Anthony in Galsworthy's *Strife*, in the Theatre Guild, as the butler in Barrie's *Dear Brutus*, as Andrew Undershaft in Shaw's *Major Barbara*. Under Winthrop Ames's direction in the New Theatre, he appeared in Rudolph Besier's play, *Don*. He was describing his conversion to Christianity, although at the moment he held a pistol in his hand:

> When I found salvation after many years of sin—oh, the blessedness of it! I was walking near the Marble Arch on a winter's afternoon, and I stopped to listen to a poor man who told of the Lord's infinite goodness and mercy. And all of a sudden, like a sunrise at sea, God lit up my soul. . . .

At that moment I actually saw the sunrise on Calvert's face, and I can see it now.

The most beautiful woman I ever saw on the stage was Mary Anderson as Rosalind. By a bit of bad luck, I missed seeing Coquelin as Cyrano, although I had the pleasure of meeting Coquelin at dinner in New York at the house of Mr. George A. Glaenzer. He was most gracious. John Bigelow, over ninety, was smoking a fat cigar and chattering vivaciously with Coquelin in French at one o'clock in the morning.

One day in New York in the Autumn of 1887, I saw Irving's fine production of *Faust* in the afternoon, and Possart's production in German in the evening. The scenic effects in Irving's performance I have never seen equalled, despite the advance in mechanical devices during the last fifty years. Mr. Alexander was good as Faust, Ellen Terry unimpressive as Margaret, Irving at his best in the tragically ironical part of Mephistopheles, as he conceived it. That evening I went down in the Bowery to the old Thalia Theatre, and there saw a totally different conception of Mephisto; for Possart made his chief characteristic *Roguishness*. The audience roared with laughter and relished the interpretation. Here God was seen on the stage as plainly as in the old Mysteries or in *Green Pastures*. The curtain rose showing cloudy effects; there was God, a man with a white beard and a sonorous bass voice, with the three archangels—buxom German girls. Later, when I saw Possart in the same role in Munich, the government did not allow God to appear in person—his voice was heard. Herr Possart told me the Catholic Church would not permit it.

That night when I heard the play in New York, the German audience was in a state of continual excitement; they gave demonstrations in mirth, and in vociferous applause. The audience seemed to be religiously divided, the Catholics downstairs, the Protestants in the gallery; and once I thought there was going to be a fight. When Mephisto spoke of the Church's having a capacious stomach for the receipt of money and treasure, the people in the gallery greeted this with loud laughter and tremendous applause; the people on the floor with hissing and imprecations which were kept up for some time. The passage that aroused this rumpus was

> Die Kirche hat einen guten Magen,
> Hat ganze Länder aufgefressen,
> Und doch noch nie sich übergessen;
> Die Kirch' allein, meine liebe Frauen,
> Kann ungerechtes Gut verdauen.

Years later, in Munich, I became well acquainted with Possart, who was the Intendant of the Royal Theatres. I told him of the day in New York when I had seen Irving's Mephisto in the afternoon and his in the evening. He laughed and said that Irving, wishing to show him a courtesy, sent one of his representatives to the Thalia Theatre, had him placed in a box with a huge wreath which he was publicly to present to Possart. Now in Irving's version as in the opera, the first scene is Faust alone in his study. So when the curtain rose, and the first scene was the Prologue on the theatre and that was followed by the Prologue in Heaven, the bewildered emissary left and reported to Irving that they were not playing *Faust* that night but some other piece the name of which he did not know.

On one of Irving's appearances in New Haven, I had the pleasure of meeting Mr. Bram Stoker, then known as Irving's manager, now far better known as the author of *Dracula* (1897). Mr. Stoker was genial; he apologized for not taking me upstairs in the hotel to see Irving; the actor had left word that no one under any circumstances was to be permitted to see him. Mr. Stoker died in 1912, and twenty years later I had the pleasure of meeting Mrs. Stoker on a Hellenic pilgrimage in the Aegean Sea. She kindly invited me to come to tea when we should both be in London. I spent a delightful afternoon at her house, meeting among other interesting people, Mr. Cunninghame-Graham, for whose literary art I have absolute reverence. He was then over eighty, tall and slender, with an Elizabethan pointed beard, and looking like a great Elizabethan gentleman. It was difficult to realize, talking with this quiet, unassuming patrician, that for many years he had played so great a part in the wildest and most dangerous frontier life. I remember when the conversation turned on Bernard Shaw, his saying, 'No one can form any accurate estimate of Mr. Shaw without emphasizing first of all his most characteristic trait, his personal *kindness.*'

Here is a letter Cunninghame-Graham wrote me from Ceylon:

THE HOTEL SUISSE
KANDY, CEYLON
JAN. 30, 1934

DEAR WM. LYON PHELPS

Your too kind letter & the press cutting have just reached me. I hasten to reply & to apologize for delay. In answer to your far too flattering reference to our brief too brief meeting, I can only say, that the pleasure was mutual, & that I felt extremely honoured in making your acquaintance.

Again thanking you & hoping we may meet again

Yrs sincerely,

R. B. CUNNINGHAME-GRAHAM

P.S. A jolt on a bronco, in early years, has made my writing very bad.
R. B. C. G.

During the last seven or eight years, exclusive of opera and motion pictures, I have seen about fifty plays annually; my appetite grows by what it feeds on. Though I suppose I am the only white man who has never written a play, some of the happiest afternoons and evenings of my life have been passed in witnessing plays—pure, flawless delight that remains as a permanent addition to memory. The theatre is one of the greatest blessings of humanity, and I feel an unpayable debt of gratitude to dramatists, managers, and the innumerable actors and actresses who have given me so much pleasure. I shall never become sufficiently sophisticated to lose the keen anticipation of a night at the play. I am not ashamed to confess that I love the preliminary moments, the crowded house of men and women, who have left their troubles; the lights, the proleptic music; the sudden darkness; the ascent of the curtain;—these will thrill me so long as I am conscious.

Of all the pages of Addison, I like most the famous description of Sir Roger at the play. 'As soon as the house was full, and the candles lighted, my old friend stood up and looked about him with that pleasure which a mind seasoned with humanity naturally feels in itself at the sight of a multitude of people who seem pleased with one another, and partake of the same common entertainment.'

And perhaps no one has ever better expressed the purpose and goal of entertainment in the theatre than Doctor Johnson when he said of his friend Goldsmith's new play *She Stoops to Conquer*, 'I know of no comedy for many years that has so much exhilarated an audience, that has answered so much the great end of comedy—making an audience merry.'

18

CLYDE FITCH

ONE person who unites in my memories schooldays and
the theatre was Clyde Fitch, a classmate in the High
School, who appeared on the monthly reports as William C. Fitch. He was even at the age of fourteen a complete individualist; he was unlike any other boy I had ever
seen. He hated outdoor games and would have nothing to
do with them; instead of speaking our dialect, he spoke
English accurately and even with elegance; he was imma-
culately, even exquisitely clothed; he made no friendships
among the boys and it was evident that he regarded us as
barbarians, which we were; we showed it in many ways and
particularly in our treatment of him. He seemed to be an
impossible person. We treated him exactly as the undergraduates at Oxford ten years earlier had treated Oscar
Wilde; they threw him in the Cherwell and wrecked the
beautiful decorations of his rooms in Magdalen.

Every morning at 'long recess' we ran out into the school
yard and played football furiously for twenty minutes;
Fitch remained in the schoolroom, writing notes on per-
fumed paper and tossing them to the girls; he seemed to be
deep in correspondence during most of the school hours.
I remember sitting next to him in the class in Caesar,
and despite the ever imminent danger of being suddenly
called upon to recite—which he did easily and well—I
observed he was engaged in the rapid composition of a
letter on light blue paper; when he had finished it to his
satisfaction he tossed it with surprising accuracy to a

maiden who was waiting to receive it. He was fourteen years old.

To us he seemed quite impossible; but how offensive we must have seemed to him! When we came in from football, streaming with sweat, stewing in our own juice, and sat down beside this immaculate person, whose very hair looked clean, what inner repugnance he felt we never knew; he never betrayed his soul to boys.

Once, while I was talking with him in his house in New York, he went back of his own accord to our schooldays. 'I knew, of course, that everybody regarded me as a sissy; but I would rather be misunderstood than lose my independence. The only concession I ever made was this: on stormy days, my mother forced me to wear overshoes to school, which I hated, and I knew it would not do to appear rubber-shod before the other boys. So I always hid these offensive things before reaching school, and put them on again on my way home. I hated football, baseball; was bored to death by all sports; and I did not see why I should do things I hated to do merely to conform to public opinion.'

Judged by the standards most people use in estimating success, he was right and all the rest of us were wrong; for in later years we are credibly informed that his annual income was $250,000 a year. So he finally won the respect of the Philistines. The wife of Andrea del Sarto thought her husband was an ass, because he spent his time painting pictures, instead of acting like a man; but other people, she must have reflected, were even greater asses, because they paid real money for these things.

If my memory serves me, Miss Elsie de Wolfe once expressed her amazement that Clyde Fitch should know more about women than they knew about themselves. She said that at a rehearsal her cue was to walk upon the stage in high emotion; she did so; but her inner complacency was jarred by the playwright's voice coming out of the dark

auditorium: 'That isn't the way to walk in order to express
your feelings in this scene; I'll show you.' He did; he walked
on, and she saw immediately that he was right and she was
wrong. She could not understand his insight; but I could,
for I went to school with him. During the long recesses
when we were playing football he was spending those minutes with the girls, for he instinctively knew that they had
more to teach him than we. That is where he laid the foundation of his success as a dramatist, even as Richardson
learned how to write novels by composing letters for the
village maids.

After High School we did not meet again until about
1900. He had gone to New York, earned a living as a private tutor, wrote some short stories, and finally succeeded
in getting one or two curtain-raisers on the stage. In 1890
he became famous with his play *Beau Brummel*, superbly
acted by Richard Mansfield.

In 1900 or 1901 he invited me to his house in New York
and we were intimate friends for the rest of his life. I succeeded in inducing him to lecture at Yale, and the enthusiasm of the undergraduates pleased him.

Fitch was one of the best talkers in private or in public I
have ever heard. One night in New Haven, I invited a
group of ten undergraduates (The Pundits) to meet him
at dinner in my house. After dinner, the students sat literally at his feet in my library, while he kept up a stream of
brilliant talk until one o'clock, when it was time to take his
train to Boston.

He told me an interesting story of Oscar Wilde. Before
the public scandal Wilde's perversion was known by many
men of letters. One day when Fitch was driving in his
victoria along Piccadilly, he was hailed from the pavement
by Wilde; he drew up to the kerb, and Wilde entered the
carriage saying, ' Why is it, Clyde, that you don't come to
see me any more?' and Fitch replied, 'Oh, Oscar, you know

the reason perfectly well.' They conversed for half an hour in friendly fashion, and Fitch did not see him again until after his release from prison. Then some friend told him that Wilde was living in a small cottage at Dieppe and that he would appreciate it if Fitch called on him. Accordingly Fitch crossed the channel and found Wilde all alone in a small building near the sea. In the evening Wilde said, 'I'll read you a poem I have just written.' A tremendous storm of wind and rain was raging and to the accompaniment of rain and hail beating on the windowpanes, Wilde read from manuscript the whole of *The Ballad of Reading Gaol*.

In June 1909 Fitch spoke to my Yale undergraduate class in contemporary drama. He had just completed a new play, *The City*. He described the plot and characters, saying that on his return from Europe he would begin rehearsals. On 4 September he died in France; and when *The City*, the most successful of all his successes, had its first performance in December, the following lines had for me a tragic significance unintended by the author:

Why, it was only a minute ago he was there, talking with me! It doesn't seem possible——that now——he's dead——.

19

LOOKING FORWARD TO COLLEGE

THE only subject on which my father and I ever violently disagreed was on the place where I should 'go to college.' Indeed, for a short time during my second year in High School, discouraged by mathematics, I told him I would not go to college at all; he was so horrified that I never brought up the matter again. But as to the particular college, we had a daily combat for three years before he gave in, and that for the Biblical reason—it was because of my importunity. My father was not only a graduate of Brown University, he was also a Trustee; he regarded his election as Trustee as the highest honour of his life. My oldest brother Dryden had been graduated at Brown in 1877; and in the midst of my struggle with my father, my brother Arthur was sent to Brown, only one year before I was due. But this fact, instead of putting a quietus on my hopes, stimulated me to further efforts; so that I gave my father no rest, day or night.

I wanted to go to Yale. As a little boy in New Haven I had seen the undergraduates walking the streets like gods. Any allusion to Yale in the newspapers made my heart beat faster (it does still), and I followed every athletic event from afar, once in a while going to New Haven to see a game. But there was much more in my longing than athletic sentiment. I *knew* I needed the intellectual and social stimulus of a great university. I had never been away from home; I was brought up strictly in the Baptist denomination; I was backward in everything that is included in *savoir vivre*, and my intellectual life was more intense than broad. Brown is a great university today, and even in the eighties its long and noble history—it was founded in 1764—and its Faculty gave it high standing; but as compared with Harvard or Yale, it was then parochial; and I knew Yale was a better place for me. When I began my fight to enter Yale, my father never dreamed I should be successful; he told me at the beginning to dismiss the subject from my mind. He quite reasonably said that as a Trustee of Brown, one of his duties was to persuade as many parents as possible to send their boys there; and what if his own son went to Yale? My mother thought I ought to go to Brown, because its religious influence would be better for me than the more liberal atmosphere of Yale. The only ally I had was my aunt Libbie; and she could give no practical support.

I cannot remember the exact moment when my father capitulated; but I think he weakened in July 1882, the year before I was to graduate from the High School. My brother, with some other boys, was to camp out at Lake George, where we had both been the preceding summer. I volunteered to remain in the office, give up camping and my vacation, and work on the paper with my father, if he would finally consent to let me go to Yale; the consent could not have been final, because it was not really settled till some months later. But I remember with what a sinking of the heart I saw my brother and my friends leave for the camp. Alas, for my good resolutions! after about ten days in the office, I became very ill with an attack of malaria, and as soon as I got better, the doctor ordered me off to Lake George.

The hardest of all for my father to endure was this; when in the Spring of 1883 it was finally decided that I could go to Yale, my brother Arthur, who was then finishing his Freshman year at Brown, felt he must be treated as well as I. So my father had to explain to the authorities at Brown that as I was going to Yale, he would have to take Arthur out and remove him also to Yale. This really was a terrible blow; and I must say the President at Brown seemed fully to understand and made it easy rather than more difficult for the transfer to be made. Arthur's standing was so high that he entered the Sophomore year at Yale without any difficulty, his year at Brown receiving full credit, and he was graduated from Yale in 1886, a member of Phi Beta Kappa.

20

THE ROBBER

FRANK HUBBARD, my playmate at the West Middle School in Hartford, had gone to Michigan, to begin his life-work with his father; he wrote, asking me to come out and spend the summer of 1883 before I was to enter Yale. I had never been west of the Adirondacks, and was glad of this opportunity. I took a train to Niagara Falls, sat up all night in the day-coach, and spent the morning at the Falls, where the greatest of all swimmers, the famous Captain Webb, had lost his life in the whirlpool a few days before; many of the residents still believed he would turn up safe and sound. At noon I took a train across Canada to Sarnia, and as that was long before the railway tunnel had been made, I reached Port Huron on the ferry, stayed at the old Huron House overnight, and at six the next morning took the steamer *Milton D. Ward* for Huron City, my destination. The boat stopped at Lexington, Port Hope, etc., and reached Huron City at six in the evening, a voyage of exactly twelve hours. There the dock was half a mile long, and after my long trip from Hartford, I was glad to see Frank at the landing place.

The most exciting thing that happened during this summer in Michigan was a 'hold-up' and robbery. There was a country store, owned by Frank's father, and managed by the bookkeeper, Austin Case. Every evening Frank and I spent in this store, talking with Mr. Case, with customers, and casual visitors. One Saturday night, between nine and ten, when every one else had left, and we three were in the back office engaged in conversation, we heard the outer door of the store open, and footsteps approaching. We thought nothing of this, for the store contained the United States Post Office, and we supposed some farmer had come for his mail. Imagine our amazement when there came into the small enclosure where we were huddled in the corner, a masked man! He was tall, and just below his eyes hung a copious black false beard, which masked his features. Pointing a revolver at us he uttered quietly three words, and I can hear them now—'Open that safe.' During the day fifteen hundred dollars had been deposited in the safe; he must have known this, and he must also have looked in the window, and seen that we were together in one corner, so that he could command our position as easily as if he were controlling one man. For a moment I thought some yokel was playing a practical joke, because the beard was so grotesque; but I was quickly undeceived. The robber was directly in front of me; behind me was Mr. Case, and a few feet to one side stood Frank.

Was I afraid? I was in mortal terror. The blood in my body seemed to change into ice water, and my fear was horribly accentuated by the screams of the bookkeeper, who implored the robber not to shoot. The revolver was not more than three feet from my face; looking at it, I could see the bullets in the chambers; I saw also that the hammer was raised and the man's forefinger on the trigger. I did not dare to make the slightest motion, for fear the robber might instinctively or even accidentally press the trigger, in which case I should have died at the age of eighteen. Mr. Case was ten years older, he was well-dressed and we were in old muddy clothes, having spent the day out shooting; it never occurred to the robber that anyone but Mr. Case would have the key to the safe, whereas it lay in Frank's pocket. The robber could not bear to go away without the money he had come for; and repeatedly declared he would kill the bookkeeper if the safe were not opened. But the bookkeeper, in complete hysteria, finally convinced him that he did not have the key; and Frank was so calm that fortunately the robber did not guess its location. Finally, after what seemed an eternity, the robber asked for my watch. He did not allow me to give it to him. I placed it on the counter and he shovelled it into his pocket, while keeping the muzzle of that accursed weapon on my face; he took Frank's watch, and then backed into the store, telling Mr. Case to follow him. The till was opened and he took the eighteen dollars it contained. Then he backed out of the front door, and immediately we heard the galloping hoofs of his horse. I never saw him again, though we looked far and wide in the days and nights that followed. Some months later, however, as I was sitting in my college room in New Haven, the postman brought me my watch. The robber had been caught and sentenced to prison for twenty years.

I have read many detective novels where men remain calm while facing a loaded pistol; and I had often imagined myself getting the best of a burglar, if he should ever attack me. But on this one occasion I was so afraid, that I was careful to do or say nothing that might make the situation any worse.

My first sensation after he had left us was one of rage; had it been possible to kill him, I should have shot him without any compunction. In looking back on it, however, I am not sure whether that black rage was because of our being robbed or because I was ashamed of having been so afraid. I lost my watch but I also lost my self-respect; yet I do not really see what I could have done. The wild thought passed through my mind while I was facing the pistol—'suppose I leap right upon him, the three of us will overpower him, only I shall be dead.' Today I am glad of two things; I am glad I did not spring at him, and glad also I had no opportunity to kill him.

COLLEGE DAYS AT YALE

Ihr bringt mit euch die Bilder froher Tage,
Und manche liebe Schatten steigen auf.

IT would be difficult to exaggerate the eagerness with which I looked forward to college. If I had been away at boarding school, the transition would not have been so violent. But I had always come home every day from attendance at public school; and it seemed to me that going away from home to college, and living there with the other undergraduates, would be paradise. I was happy at home, I loved my parents who were very kind to me, and yet I longed to get away. Boys and girls long to leave home; boys love to go away to college and girls love to have a separate apartment with the key in their sole possession.

There are two reasons, which only partially explain it. The first is that although the average child loves his parents, he does not love them half so much as they love him. This is true, as he will find out when he has children of his own. The tragedy is that the presence of children is necessary to the parents' happiness, while the son or daughter, though loving the parents, gets on very well in their absence. The greatest novel ever written on the eternal theme of the Younger Generation is Turgenev's *Fathers and Children*; and although individual parents and individual sons may be quite unlike the parents and their son Bazarov, the feeling on both sides is about the same. The love of many parents for their children is mingled with terror; terror that the youth may outgrow the parents' point of view, fear that he may be bored at home, fear that the solicitude shown to prevent this may only increase it.

The second reason is that young people hate the round of expected events, hate a routine; they love the absence of restraint; and they find this freedom more with their mates than with their family.

However this may be, no prisoner ever desired freedom more than I desired to go to college. On the few occasions when I went to New Haven at the age of fifteen or sixteen to see a football game, my excitement during the contest, great as it was, was not nearly so great as it was while I was walking down Chapel Street after the game was over. I was in this huge crowd of undergraduates; then when we reached the college buildings, I had to keep on to the railway station to take the train for Hartford, while these marvellous beings entered the college gates. If I should ever see the blessed angels entering Paradise with myself shut out, I could hardly envy them more. To think that these young men lived together in dormitories, ate their meals together, shared their studies and their sports!

And here again, at least during the first year, realization was not inferior to my hopes. Later there came something of a disillusion which Browning expressed so perfectly in his poem *Pauline*, written when he was twenty; the first part of the passage does not overstate my glow of anticipation as I gazed afar at college towers, but the second part— the disillusion—was in my case only partly true.

As some world-wanderer sees in a far meadow
Strange towers and high-walled gardens thick with trees,
Where song takes shelter and delicious mirth
From laughing fairy creatures peeping over,
And on the morrow when he comes to lie
For ever 'neath those garden-trees fruit-flushed
Sung round by fairies, all his search is vain.

First went my hopes of perfecting mankind,
Next—faith in them, and then in freedom's self
And virtue's self, then my own motives, ends
And aims and loves, and human love went last.
I felt this no decay, because new powers
Rose as old feelings left—wit, mockery,
Light-heartedness; for I had oft been sad,
Mistrusting my resolves, but now I cast
Hope joyously away.

My brother Arthur and I roomed on the top floor of North Middle College, in the Old Brick Row; his company was of course congenial to me, but it was a bad arrangement for him. He should have roomed with some member of his own class; it was hard enough for him to enter at the beginning of his Sophomore year, but it made conditions much harder to be surrounded with Freshmen.

I found college life wildly exciting; and the differences between this and my previous school experiences did not lose their novelty. The four classes were forced to attend morning chapel at ten minutes past eight—a splendid thing; there we Freshmen sat in our assigned places, saw the mighty Gods of the football field come down the aisle, and realized that we too, belonged; we were a part of all this. To me it was exciting to have college classes on Saturday morning and on other afternoons at five o'clock, in rooms illuminated by gas jets. Never in my life had I attended school on Saturday; and to go to a class at five in the afternoon was almost as remarkable as if we had gone at five in the morning.

Class sentiment at Yale was then at its height; in our class rush against the Sophomores, in our crew race against the other classes, in our class baseball game against Harvard, I would at any moment gladly have died for my class flag. (This sentiment is obsolete today.) When our class crew beat the Sophomores, we carried every member of our eight up Chapel Street, and had a huge bonfire on the campus. In the Rush against the Sophomores, held on a field more than a mile from college, I had all my clothes torn off, except my shoes and socks. A Junior lent me a linen 'duster,' and clad only in that, I walked a mile through the streets to college, thrilled with pride and delight; on the campus, one of my Professors looked at me as if I had been a decayed fish. But I had fought for '87!

It was an interesting spectacle in New Haven, in the days when attendance on daily morning chapel was compulsory, to see, between five minutes and ten minutes past eight, the throngs of students sprinting toward the university house of worship. With many of them the art of dressing, eating breakfast, and running to chapel illustrated the irreducible minimum of time.

As the philosopher Thales in the seventh century before Christ said that the most difficult thing in the world was to know oneself, I think it pertinent to state that there was one undergraduate, who, although consistently unable to know his lessons, knew himself better than most philosophers. Having been informed that no further absences from chapel would be excused, he placed a placard on his bedroom door to attract the attention of the janitor. In large letters was printed the command, 'Wake me up at a quarter before eight; it is important; never mind what I say or if I make no response; be sure and wake me up at quarter before eight.' Then under this injunction, 'Try again at half-past nine.'

It was well for me that I went to Yale. I had never met anyone from our Southern States until I entered college; I had never heard the Southern accent on the lips of a white man. I remember how strange and yet how pleasant that accent sounded when spoken by my classmates from Louisiana, South Carolina, and Georgia. There were also five men in my class from San Francisco; every locality in the country was represented.

Among the most agreeable and most profitable hours in my four years were those I spent in long walks with classmates; we thought nothing of twenty miles. These long journeys on foot, with good conversations and amusing adventures, are as obsolete nowadays as Roman chariots.

Persons who live in magnificent scenery do not always appreciate it. I remember one late afternoon on our New Hampshire excursion, as we entered a vale between mountains, a young farmer asked us where we came from. I answered, 'Connecticut.' He uttered *Connecticut*! as if it were Mesopotamia! and added, 'I wish I could see Connecticut.' 'But,' said I, 'we have no mountains like these in Connecticut.' 'Oh, damn these mountains!' And it appeared that he had never been outside of that valley.

I had entered college intending eventually to become a lawyer; I read some law in leisure moments, and occasionally visited city courtrooms. I had visions of myself winning great cases in crowded courtrooms, and then entering politics, and becoming a United States Senator; for a boy of eighteen, I was deeply read in American political history. There was no moment in my college course when with a theatrical gesture I 'renounced the law,' but becoming more and more interested in literature, I was, in spite of my ambitions, slowly, at first imperceptibly, but finally, drawn entirely away from legal studies or ambitions.

Most of our classrooms were dull and the teaching purely mechanical; a curse hung over the Faculty, a blight on the art of teaching. Many professors were merely hearers of prepared recitations; they never showed any living interest, either in the studies or in the students. I remember we had Homer three hours a week during the entire year. The instructor never changed the monotonous routine, never made a remark, but simply called on individuals to recite or to scan, said 'That will do,' put down a mark; so that in the last recitation in June, after a whole college year of this intolerable classroom drudgery, I was surprised to hear him say, and again without any emphasis, 'The poems of Homer are the greatest that have ever proceeded from the the mind of man, class is dismissed,' and we went out into the sunshine. Two Freshmen instructors shone by contrast; a young teacher of Latin named Ambrose Tighe, who left Yale in a few years, and had a fine career as a lawyer and member of the legislature in Minnesota. He tried to teach us Roman history as well as Latin grammar; he talked about Horace as though Horace were a man about town, and he himself looked and acted like a man of the world. I remember his saying that he would like to teach us Lucretius, but that he did not know enough; 'for,' said he, 'in comparison with Lucretius, the entire works of Horace and Virgil sink into insignificance.' The older members of the Faculty looked upon Mr. Tighe with suspicion. He made Latin interesting; and they got rid of him.

One of our instructors in Greek, the opposite in all respects of the Greek teacher I have mentioned, was Horatio Reynolds; he had a defective leg, and was by us affectionately called 'step-and-a-half,' shortened to 'Steppy'— while later college generations always spoke of him as 'Limpy.' He was universally beloved. He told us we ought to read some Greek history outside of the classroom. Therefore for several months, I stayed up one hour later, and every night from ten to eleven, I read Grote's *History of Greece*—one of the best things I ever did.

We had only Latin, Greek, and Mathematics until the last few weeks of Freshman year; then Professor Cyrus Northrop taught us Hill's *Rhetoric*. It was Northrop's last year at Yale, as he had just been elected President of the University of Minnesota, where he made a great reputation. He was universally respected and beloved, and died at nearly ninety years of age. I called upon him in Minneapolis when he was eighty-seven; remembering the opening of Plato's *Republic*, I asked him how it felt to be so old; was he as happy as he was in youth or middle age? He said, 'I am just as happy now as I ever was, only there is such a short time left.' That night he made a speech at the Yale Alumni Dinner; it was a masterpiece—brief, witty, incisive.

Well, in the Spring of 1884, when he was teaching us Freshman Rhetoric, he announced that every one must select some essay—any essay— write a synopsis of it, and bring it to the classroom. I had never read Carlyle's *On Heroes and Hero Worship*; and I chose for my 'effort' the chapter called 'The Hero as Man of Letters.' I chose this because I thought it would be good for me. It was.

There are spiritual experiences we would not have missed for anything. They are worth more than years of routine existence. In an hour the soul rises to a higher plane, and, despite temporary lapses, one can never live again permanently on the lower level. The mind leaps to an elevation. That afternoon in my room on the top floor of old North Middle, as I absorbed 'The Hero as Man of Letters,' I was caught up into an ecstasy. There is no other word which truly describes my state of mind. The pages of the book seemed to me aflame, and the fire consumed me utterly. When I came to read my paper in the classroom, the spell was still upon me. I trembled with excitement, and could hardly read the words I had written. Professor Northrop, who had probably expected a perfunctory report, looked at me with astonishment. His talent for ironical comment had made him a terror both to slackers and to gushers; if he had chilled my holy enthusiasm with his famous icy disdain, I should never have forgiven him. But apparently he discerned that my uncontrollable enthusiasm was sincere; that I was really under the domination of the genius of Carlyle. I have not forgotten his brief but emphatic word of commendation.

At the end of my first year in college, my parents decided to move from Hartford to New Haven, so that my brother and I were to live at home while continuing our studies. This was the worst thing that ever happened to me during the four years at Yale. I heard their decision with dismay, a sinking of the heart. It was impossible to explain this feeling to them, without hurting their feelings intolerably. Yet I went as far as I dared. I begged them not to give up their pleasant social life in Hartford. Besides, my father would have to take the train every morning to Hartford and the train back in the evening, in order to continue his editorial work. But in those days every editor had a pass on the railway, so transportation cost him nothing. There were two reasons which induced them to make this change of residence. One was the expense; it was cheaper for them to have us live at home than to pay for our board; but the strongest reason was the unhappiness of our mother in our absence. She could not bear to have us away.

Those seemed good and sufficient reasons to my parents; and how could I explain that they were destroying my college life? For surely the curriculum to which I was faithful was only a part of a great experience; I wished to be independent, to live in a college dormitory, and be master of my time. Furthermore, a student in New Haven was at a serious disadvantage among his mates; the others, who came from afar, belonged to the college; he merely attended recitations and went home like a boy in High School. How I envied the students who came from San Francisco!

Nearly all undergraduates enjoy Freshman year the least and Senior year the most; with me my happiest year was the Freshman, for it was the only time when I had an actual share in the full life of the place. It was a very humble share, for I was a Freshman, and I was obscure; but after all, I belonged.

In our Freshman year two distinguished visitors from England were introduced by the President at morning chapel. One day Lord Chief Justice Coleridge spoke to us a few moments on the study of the classics; and I remember his saying that *every day since he had been graduated from Oxford*, he had read something in Greek or Latin; and he was one of the busiest men in the world. He was then sixty-three.

One morning the President introduced Matthew Arnold; all I can remember is a large man with conspicuous dark whiskers, a strong English accent (I had never previously heard any one so pronounce the word *years*) who made a complimentary remark saying that young men like us would be carrying the burden of civilization in future years.

Oscar Wilde had given a lecture in New Haven the year before I entered college; he was entertained by the daughters of Professor Whitney, who took him to a masquerade ball, where three persons came dressed as Oscar Wilde. He did not seem to mind. They asked him if he would like to dance. He replied, 'No; I used to dance; now I dine.'

In Sophomore year I had three memorable experiences, which are comparable to the excitement I had as a Freshman with Carlyle. In our Greek course we studied Sophocles's *Oedipus Rex* with Professor Frank B. Tarbell. He was then in his thirties, and the type of man more common at Oxford or Cambridge than in an American university. He was an elegant and fastidious scholar, precise and dignified in his manner and speech. He never had a frivolous moment. He was not popular with the undergraduates and for two reasons; he had only contempt for laziness and stupidity; and the depressing Faculty atmosphere of official formality, which I shall speak of later, prevented him from sharing with the students the riches of his mind. Yet he had already been discovered by some of the more ambitious undergraduates; they had sought him out, and got him to meet a few of them informally. These were in the class above ours, so that we were prohibited from attending these meetings; but rumours began to circulate about college that Professor Tarbell was a quickening intellectual force. In my Senior year he gave three courses open to only a few students; two of these, *Ancient Philosophy* and Mill's *System of Logic*, I count among the most powerful inspirations of my mental life. The third was an oddity which Tarbell gave only once, and no one has ever repeated. It was called *The Logic of Chance*. I loved the study of logic and hated the study of mathematics. Alas, I soon found this course was largely mathematics. Among the few students was Irving Fisher, today a famous mathematical economist. Even as an undergraduate he knew much more about mathematics than Mr. Tarbell, and constantly corrected the instructor in the classroom; to Tarbell's credit, so far from resenting this, he gave every sign of appreciation.

I have always regretted the lack of one course which perhaps I might have had. In our Junior year Mr. Tarbell announced a course in Greek history, open to the one hundred and fifty members of our class. As I was the only one who elected it, it was withdrawn. But if I had only gone to him, and insisted that he give it for one pupil! It would have been a tremendous experience.

He was too independent for the Faculty standards of those days; his superiors told him he was teaching the students philosophy when he should be teaching Greek grammar; and they refused to reappoint him, just at the time when he was becoming an intellectual stimulus to many. I think his departure was the most severe loss Yale sustained for many years. To him it was a tragedy. He was a lonely, awkward bachelor, diffident and shy; we were afraid he would obtain no position anywhere. And he loved Yale with all his heart.

He secured a subordinate post in the Classical Faculty at Harvard; and a few years later, when I went to Harvard as a graduate student, I renewed my acquaintance with him. He told me the number of students at Harvard electing Greek was so rapidly diminishing that he had received notice his appointment could not be renewed; he had been offered the five-year directorship of the American School at Athens, but he could not bear to leave America for so long a time.

President Harper was about to open the University of Chicago; I wrote him about Tarbell; he immediately telegraphed Tarbell, offering him a professorship. Tarbell accepted, and spent the rest of his days until the age of retirement at the University of Chicago, where he was honoured and beloved and happy. I do not think Tarbell ever knew the source of that telegram, but I look back upon it with unalloyed satisfaction.

It may be that Tarbell's unorthodox views on religion had something to do with the unwillingness of the Yale authorities to retain his services. There was an annual Day of Prayer for Colleges; many of the recitations were omitted, and a speaker from the Faculty, chosen by the students, addressed each class separately. The Freshmen had first choice, and invariably chose Professor Northrop, who was very impressive; in our Sophomore year we had Professor Frank Abbott, who later had a distinguished career at Chicago and Princeton; in Junior year we had Tarbell, and I shall never forget the sudden shock in one of the sentences of his address. After giving us valuable advice, he said, ' And then you must remember that in all dangers, depressions, and difficulties you have always one Friend; one Friend always faithful, to whom you can go with confidence at any time, in the assurance that you will find solace and inspiration; a Friend that will never desert you, a Friend always accessible; I refer of course to—*Books.*'

In the Autumn of my Sophomore year, we were studying the *Oedipus Rex*; Tarbell gave out a number of subjects for essays, which we were required to write and submit to him. He assigned to me the subject 'Does Sophocles represent Oedipus as suffering for sin?' In preparation for this, I sat down and read through at a sitting the entire play in the original; a memorable experience. Then I read many of the commentaries of various British scholars and liked none of them until I found the Irishman Mahaffy's, which seemed to my young mind full of common sense. I wrote an essay in which I maintained the negative position; there was no sin here, it was a tragedy of fate. I was requested to read it in the classroom. Professor Tarbell asked me to come to his dormitory room and talk it over, and he began by saying, 'Well, the highest compliment you can pay any essay is to say it is worth criticizing.' And he proceeded to criticize it, greatly to my edification. He hated exaggeration in any form. He hated inaccuracy. I have never known anyone else who combined to so high a degree the love of truth with the ability to speak it. Once I heard a rumour that a friend of both of us had been drinking too much; I asked Tarbell for the facts. At first he said the circumstances were so unusual that it might not be possible to contribute anything of value to the discussion. But I insisted, whereupon he replied, 'I think it must be admitted that excessive indulgence in potations has temporarily impaired his health.' The man eventually made a complete recovery.

After Tarbell died and his brother John died, his watch and his Phi Beta Kappa key came to me; they are among my most treasured possessions.

The other powerful influence in the Autumn of my Sophomore year was in English literature, and probably had much to do with my turning from law. There was no instruction in the English language and literature in the first two years at Yale, except a few months in Rhetoric with

Professor Northrop in Freshman year and three months in a manual of English literature in the winter term of Sophomore year.

But one November day in Sophomore year the entire class was rounded up in one room and addressed by Mr. McLaughlin, tutor in English. He placed on the board twelve subjects and announced that every member of the class must hand in before Christmas an original essay on one of these topics; furthermore, there would be first, second, and third groups of prizes. None of these subjects appealed to me; and as we were leaving the room, I asked my classmate John Pomeroy, which subject he had selected. He replied, 'The twelfth, of course.' Now the twelfth and last was 'Tennyson's analytical power as shown in *Maud*.' I said, 'But I have never read *Maud*.' 'Neither have I,' he replied, 'but it is the only subject worth the attention of an intelligent man.' That was the way we used to talk about the Faculty!

I decided, with some eccentricity, that before writing my essay, I would read the poem. I shall never forget the afternoon in my father's house when I read *Maud* for the first time. I entered the room one kind of man and left it another kind of man. When one passes through a profound spiritual experience, although one is apparently unaware of one's surroundings at the time, they are indelibly impressed on the memory. I thought nothing of it then, but I remember now the weather of that cold November afternoon, the location of the desk in the room and the angle at which I sat in my chair at that desk. I had always been fond of narrative verse, I had read all of Shakespeare, but I do not think I had any real appreciation or understanding of pure poetry until the day I first read *Maud*.

It did not come on the first reading. I read the poem through rapidly from beginning to end, and was not impressed. But I was ambitious; I wanted to win a prize. I knew I must feel intensely about this poem if I were to write well about it; accordingly I began to read it through the second time, and with more attention.

I cannot tell why one particular line converted me. But in the beginning of the second part, the duel scene, after the neurotic hero has shot Maud's big brother, the line

Was it he lay there with a fading eye?

suddenly transformed me from a Philistine to a lover of poetry. I saw the scene at dawn; I heard the singing birds; I breathed the odour of the woods and flowers in the garden; I saw the white figure of Maud in her party dress fleeing in horror through the shrubbery; I saw the handsome big brother dying, and the lover standing stupidly with the smoking pistol in his hand. I knew in that moment the significance of poetry; that the poet is the interpreter for us of the beauty of nature and of the passions of man. There was another garden in front of me, besides the one described in the poem. It was the garden of Poetry; the gates opened wide, I entered, and I never came out.

I shall always be grateful to this poem, for it was the means of my conversion; I escaped from the gall of bitterness and the bond of Philistine iniquity, into the kingdom of light. And after all, it is a great poem. In his novel, *The Old Man's Youth*, William De Morgan, speaking of passionate love, called *Maud* 'the poem which goes further to describe this frame of mind than anything else in English, or out of it.'

I felt an exaltation when in morning chapel President Porter read aloud the names of the four men in the Sophomore Class who had won first prizes—Kent, Lee, Phelps, Pomeroy. William Kent was the best natural writer in college; in later years he became a member of Congress and a philanthropist; Lee was a Chinese student of remarkable ability; John Pomeroy became a professor of Law.

Because I was a first prize winner, I was asked by one of the Editors of the *Yale Literary Magazine* to write an essay for that journal; there was nothing I wanted to do more than that; accordingly I wrote an essay on Philina, the coquette in Goethe's *Wilhelm Meister*. But the editors from the Senior Class rejected it, saying none of them had ever heard of the novel.

With the ten dollars prize money, I bought Mommsen's *History of Rome*. And I read it.

In the second term of our Sophomore year we took up the study of *The Clouds* by Aristophanes. On the first day we were met by our instructor, Doctor Walter Bridgman, whom we never saw after that first meeting; he took typhoid fever. A graduate student, only two years out of college, filled the vacancy and taught us for six months. His name was Joseph Lewis, a brilliant man. He had a brother among the undergraduates named Charlton M. Lewis, who later became my beloved colleague as a professor of English literature. Young Joseph Lewis was then in perfect health and Walter Bridgman had typhoid fever; but in two or three years Lewis was dead of tuberculosis and Bridgman is alive today at the age of nearly eighty.

I did not admire the way Aristophanes treated Socrates in *The Clouds*; I had read Plato's *Apology*, *Crito*, and some other works, and Socrates was my hero. I was delighted when I discovered that Aristophanes's play was voted a failure by what corresponded to the Pulitzer Prize Judges of that year, 423 B.C. Accordingly, when it was suggested by Mr. Lewis that we write essays on any subject connected with *The Clouds*, I called my essay 'The Didactic Methods of Aristophanes as Shown in *The Clouds*.' I have not often been thrilled by my own compositions, either while writing them or afterwards. But I finished my essay with this paragraph, and a thrill came over me while I was writing the last sentence. I was twenty years old.

There is therefore no reason why we should reverse the decision of the Athenian judges, who pronounced the play a failure. Its wit and even its earnestness do not save it. The man who is befouled is to us almost the incarnation of virtue. The figure of the poet, piteously begging the Athenians for the prize, contrasts harshly with the solitary grandeur of Socrates standing before his accusers, perfectly calm in the contemplation of the grave.

I left the essay at Mr. Lewis's rooms, and the next day I received an urgent invitation to visit him; he was quite overcome by that last sentence, and asked me how in the world I had ever happened to think of it. I could not tell him; while I was writing, I *saw* those two men addressing the Athenians, one pleading for a prize, the other refusing to plead for his life.

In my Sophomore year I was not very happy. These three essays were the three most important events for me. Mathematics were the curse of my existence. For six months, three hours a week, we had a course in Mechanics. Toward the close of every hour, the professor gave out a problem, and said that as soon as we had finished, we were to hand it to him, and leave the room. I tried every time, three times a week for six months; I never shirked it and never took a 'cut.' Not once in the whole six months did I obtain a correct solution.

It has always seemed strange to me that in the revolt against the required studies of Latin and Greek—a revolt that began in America in the eighties, and became successful in the early years of the twentieth century—no one ventured to attack the requirement of the study of Mathematics. It was thought Latin and Greek were useless and mathematics valuable and practical. The truth is that for every occupation except one for which higher mathematics are a prerequisite, like civil engineering, Greek and Latin are more *useful*. For the preacher, the lawyer, the physician, the journalist, and for nearly all business men, the classics are definitely more important than mathematics. Training in the ancient languages, with the accompanying culture and history, with the aid given to the mastery of expression in English—where in comparison stands the binomial theorem?

I believe in the equal dignity of all studies. But it is absurd for a university to require neither Latin nor Greek for a degree and yet insist on the higher mathematics. I have no doubt that for those who have a natural aptitude, mathematics are valuable as intellectual discipline and training, whether one will make practical use of them or not. But for those who have no gift and no inclination, mathematics are worse than useless—they are injurious. They cast a blight on my childhood, youth, and adolescence. I was as incompetent to deal with them as is a child to lift a safe. I studied mathematics, because I was forced to do so, faithfully and conscientiously from the age of three to the age of twenty-one, through my Junior year in college. After 'long division,' nearly every hour spent on this subject was worse than wasted. The time would have been more profitably spent in manual labour, in athletics, or in sleep. These studies were a brake on my intellectual advance; a continuous discouragement and obstacle; the harder I worked, the less result I obtained. I bitterly regret those hours and days and weeks and months and years which might have been profitably employed on studies that would have stimulated my mind instead of stupefying it!

I remember after a year spent on Chauvenet's *Geometry* in college, I looked up the name of the author to discover whether or not he was still living; and when I found that he was no more, I wrote on the title-page of his accursed book, 'Thank God, he's dead!'

I was always an ambitious student, and wished to excel; therefore it was necessary for me to put more time and effort on mathematics than on any other study. Even so, my grade in mathematics was never distinguished in college, and I could not possibly have been graduated with honours had I not in other studies stood very high.

But while I was unhappy, my fate was not nearly so tragic as that of hundreds of other boys. There have been hundreds who were deprived of the advantage and the privilege of a college education because of their inability to obtain a passing mark in mathematics. They were sacrificed year after year to this Moloch.

I am aware that Henry Adams lamented the fact that in his education there had not been more and higher mathematics; but surely his view of life was sufficiently pessimistic without that added bleakness.

I am glad that of all the essays and compositions I wrote during the four years in college, and I wrote a great many, I never submitted one before handing it in to any other person for correction, suggestion, or advice. No doubt my essays would have been improved had I done so; but I am glad I depended only on myself.

In the summer vacation of 1885, at the end of my Sophomore year, I went to Michigan on a visit to my friend Frank Hubbard; his sister Annabel had come there to live in the Autumn of 1884. And here I am, fifty-three years later, in the summer of 1938, writing at my desk in this same Michigan house, with my wife Annabel in the next room.

My greatest single ambition in college was to become a member of the editorial board of the *Yale Literary Magazine*. This is not only the oldest college journal; it is the oldest monthly magazine in America. It had been founded in 1836 by a group of students, chief among whom was William M. Evarts of the class of 1837; later he became one of the greatest American lawyers, and Secretary of State in the cabinet of President Hayes.

There had always been five editors, chosen from the

Junior class, who edited the *Lit.* in their Senior year. Election was by ballot, the entire Junior class assembling for the purpose; and competition was always keen. I had seen copies of the magazine before entering college, and modestly hoped that some day I might be chosen. Talking with a group of my classmates in Freshman year, I expressed my hope, but also my belief that I could never win; they were so certain of my success that I rashly promised them all a good dinner if I should be elected two years later; they remembered this promise at the proper time. Yet at the beginning of my Junior year, with the election only five months away, I had abandoned hope. I had submitted compositions in Freshman and in Sophomore year, and none had been accepted. But at the opening of the Autumn term of Junior year, one of the editors, Arthur Shipman, urged me to try. To my delight, I succeeded in getting two compositions into the October issue, and an original story into the November one; but as all three of my compositions, a story, an essay, and a poem, were rejected for the December number, my hopes sank again.

It was not considered proper for any candidate to attend the meeting of the class when the election took place; I waited in my room for news of the balloting. In an hour two or three of my friends came shouting under my window that I was elected; and although, of the five successful candidates, I received the least number of votes, I was elevated to the seventh heaven of bliss. John Norton Pomeroy and William Kent of California, Andrew F. Gates of Connecticut, and Charles H. Ludington of New York, were the other four; of the first two I have already spoken. Ludington became a high official in the Curtis Publishing Company of Philadelphia, and Gates a successful lawyer and member of the State Legislature; Gates and I are the only ones yet alive.

As a rule, editors wrote less after the election than before. It was the other way with me; and once safely on the board, I wrote continuously for a whole year, essays, stories, poems. It was good practice. In studying the play *King Henry IV*, the character of the Welsh chieftain, Owen Glendower, whom Hotspur ridiculed so cruelly, took hold of my imagination, and to one of the numbers of the *Lit.* I contributed the following Sonnet:

GLENDOWER

'I can call spirits from the vasty deep:'
The starry fires are under my control;
To me the future is an open scroll
Unfurled by angels in my golden sleep.
Kings tremble at my name; and women weep
In piteous terror as my chariots roll
To bloody battles; the funereal toll
Foretells the harvest I am come to reap.
I have a part in God's almighty power!
My voice will calm the surly ocean's swell,
And hush the boisterous winter's icy breath.
My joy is in the combat's dreadful hour:
I fear no foe in earth or heaven or hell;
And laugh in mockery at grinning death.

In the Spring of Junior year I competed with other members of the class for the Junior Exhibition prizes; eight men were chosen, who delivered their successful compositions in public, the winner to receive the Junior Exhibition (later called the Ten Eyck) prize. No subjects were announced; one could write on anything one chose. I wrote on 'Goethe as a Religious Teacher;' for although I was then forced to read Goethe in translations, I had, since I was seventeen, been reading *Wilhelm Meister*, *Faust*, the shorter poems, *Truth and Poetry*, *Iphigenia*, *Götz von Berlichingen*, *Werther*, and many other works. This competition aroused great excitement in those days, because the winner was usually elected to a Senior Secret Society. I was chosen among the eight and spoke my piece; I did not win, but the work in preparation for this essay was of great value.

I was told by some of the judges afterward that I should have won had I spoken better; and indeed, I spoke very badly, in a monotonous manner, and as if I did not believe what I was saying, though it came from my heart. I learned by my failure the importance of earnestness and emphasis in public speaking. The reason for my dullness on the platform was that a member of the Faculty (who for some cause I never discovered disliked me intensely), ridiculed me before the other men, while we were getting instructions from him about the preparation of our pieces for the great day. The unexpectedness of this attack and the virulence with which it was uttered, destroyed my confidence.

In my Sophomore year, after I had definitely given up the idea of becoming a lawyer, I wasted a good deal of time wondering what I should do; and one day I asked an older man for his advice. 'You have nearly three years before you graduate; you should not give the matter a thought; you cannot make any decision until the emergency comes; haven't you got a lesson for tomorrow? Sit down and study it.' This was the first I had heard of the advice, 'Live one day at a time.' It seemed to me sound, and I followed it.

So in the last term of my Senior year, with Commencement only a few weeks away, I could not make up my mind what profession to follow. But I had narrowed it to three things—the ministry, journalism, teaching. In those days there was no unemployment for any man of average health and intelligence, who had no bad habits; so one really could choose. I talked with the editor of a daily newspaper, who offered me a job as reporter then and there —take it or leave it—at twelve dollars a week; but as he would not wait one month for me to graduate, I left it.

As it turned out, however, my life has been spent in the practice of all three professions; and indeed at this moment, I am a teacher, a preacher, and a journalist.

22

THE YOUNGER GENERATION

I HAVE known six younger generations. I have looked forward, I have looked around, I have looked back. I may add that I have looked back only professionally, in the endeavour to understand the young men whom I teach. Personally, I have looked back very little. When I was a child, I wanted to be a man. When I was a young man, I wanted to be a mature man. And after I had descended into the vale of years, I did not, as apparently many do, look back with longing to the days of my youth. It is always the new experience I am seeking; I am wasting no time in the vain endeavour to recapture the irrecoverable past.

It does not disturb me that the body grows old. But when does one himself grow old? I think I can state accurately the exact moment when a person passes into old age. It is the moment when in solitude one's thoughts regularly turn more to the past than to the present or future. In the matchless Shakespearean phrase, the *stealing steps of age* overtake our slowing bodies; but they can never catch up with an alert mind.

When I was a little boy in the grammar school, the seniors looked to me like demi-gods; no truly great man today can seem to me quite so wonderful as those giants. They were fourteen years old. As a child, playing in the streets, I looked with envy on the college undergraduates. They were dressed in those days like a modern stage caricature of a professor. They wore frock coats, tall hats, and whiskers, yet they were in the heyday of their youth.

Good, bad, and indifferent they were. One degenerate offered me an unpardonable insult; another seemed angelic. I lost the ball I was playing with; and seeing my dismay, he bent down to me, gave me a quarter, and told me to go to the nearest store and buy a new ball. In an instant I rose from despair to rapture. I wonder if my benefactor is still alive. I wish I knew his name.

Fifty years ago I knew the younger generation by personal and intimate contact; I was among my contemporaries. Today, although I am with them every day, what do I really know about them? When someone asks me if the young men of today drink more than formerly, I am the very last man to possess the necessary knowledge. That some of them get drunk is certain; but they never came into my classroom drunk, they never called upon me while drunk.

Those who believe the present younger generation have bad habits should consider former times. In the eighteenth century, excessive drinking was the rule. Faculty and students got drunk together. Before the Civil War in America there was an immense amount of drinking. The growth of athletic games has had much to do with the improvement in personal habits. When I was an undergraduate, there was certainly a good deal of drunkenness, though not comparable to the excesses of earlier days.

The younger generation in my time had a narrow and provincial outlook. They were interested mainly in the affairs of their own little world. They were mainly Philistines: they had little respect for scholarship, were innocent of culture, knew nothing of good music or art, and cared not at all for international affairs.

A large number of modern undergraduates have travelled in Europe; they are acquainted with good literature, good music, good plays; they know not only books, but the editions of books; many of them indulge in intelligent conversation. In all these things there has been an advance. A lady from out of town told me she came to New Haven to attend an important concert. She hurried into a restaurant to get a hasty meal. She had happened to enter one filled with students; and she supposed the conversation at the tables around her would be devoted to athletics, motion pictures, and automobiles. She was amazed to find that most of the talk was excellent, interesting conversation on interesting themes.

There is a straightforward frank honesty about young people today that commands admiration. Outwardly they are not so religious; it would be impossible to maintain prayer-meetings and religious exercises, which, even though they were slimly attended in the old days, were still a recognized part of college life. But I suppose the younger generation today *think* more about religion than they used to. They are eager to find out the truth about everything, and cannot be put off with any subterfuge. If people today are worried about the large amount of religious scepticism in college, they should remember that youth has always been more or less sceptical. It has outgrown some of the things it has been taught in childhood, and it has not yet reached a maturer view. The *Yale Literary Magazine* for the year 1879 contained an article called 'Religious Skepticism in College,' written by an undergraduate, which, if printed word for word today, would be considered up to date. There is an attitude toward religion worse than either scepticism or hostility; indifference. There is certainly today a good deal of outspoken scepticism and a certain amount of downright antagonism. But there is not so much indifference.

Dr. Cyril Norwood, Headmaster of Harrow School, in his book, *The British Tradition in Education*, mentioned five pillars as its foundation: religion, discipline, culture, athletics, public service.

Whatever we may think of the first four, there is no doubt that the last is an essential article in the creed of modern youth. They do not want to lead a selfish life. They really long to be useful to their community, to their country, to the world. They may not always listen eagerly to the gospel of orthodox religion; but to the gospel of selfishness they will not listen at all. If you should tell them merely to make the most of themselves, that the wisest life is a life of personal aggrandizement, they would look upon you with scorn. My hope is that life in the world will not dull the beauty and freshness of their ideals; that they will not become callous; that they will not compromise with their conscience. When they have reached middle age, will they still hold fast to these ideals? If so, the world will be safe in their hands.

We must remember that in every age the average member of the older generation has looked with distrust on the new. Why is this? Is it because as we grow older, we grow out of sympathy with youth, forget our own youth, and delude ourselves with the idea that boys and girls should be as sober and self-restrained as their teachers? Remember the splendid warning of Browning, which he put into the mouth of the great Pope of Rome:

> Irregular noble scapegrace—son the same!
> Faulty—and peradventure ours the fault
> Who still misteach, mislead, throw hook and line,
> Thinking to land Leviathan forsooth,
> Tame the scaled neck, play with him as a bird,
> And bind him for our maidens! Better bear
> The King of Pride go wantoning awhile,
> Unplagued by cord in nose and thorn in jaw,
> Through deep to deep, followed by all that shine,
> Churning the blackness hoary.

Is it because we are jealous? We must soon leave active participation in the great game of life, and we cannot bear to have the game go on, played by our successors? The younger generation, said Ibsen, are knocking at the door. Shall we wait for them to break it down, or shall we admit them gladly?

I think the chief reason older people shake their heads dubiously over the younger generation is that there has been a steady increase of informality. Easy intimacy of manners seems to many serious elders akin to promiscuity in morals. 'I don't know what our girls are coming to!' If any one is depressed today over what one thinks may be a shocking loss of modesty, if any one thinks that our boys are irresponsible and our girls without reticence, let me insist that this is the way the younger generation has always seemed to venerable eyes. Now if the typical representatives of the older generation had always been right, the world would have gone to the dogs long ago; for in every period of history, prophets have announced that the world is bound dogward.

Homer remarked constantly on the degeneracy of the young men of his time, as compared with their noble and splendid ancestors. Someone dug up a rock in Egypt that had been buried about three thousand years. On it was an inscription, which a scholar interpreted. It announced that contemporary young men were effete, not at all like the hardy fellows of the good old times.

Before the Great War, I heard constantly from older men the statement that college boys were no good; that they were lazy, irresponsible, not serious, unfitted for an emergency. Then came the war, and these same boys endured hardships that no Spartan or no Roman could have sustained. Furthermore, if they were used to luxuries, think what they gave up; whereas, in the days of our ancestors, going to war was in many respects like going on a picnic. The difference between ancient wars and the Great War may be summed up in a phrase: *From campfires to poison gas.* Yet there was only one thing modern boys were afraid of; they were afraid they would not get there in time.

There is a passage in the gospel of St. Luke older people should consider. It is a prophecy of the coming young man, John the Baptist: 'And he shall go before him in the spirit and power of Elias, to turn the hearts of the fathers to the children.'

Some fathers are trying to make their sons resemble them. Is it not possible that one reason for the misunderstanding between the older and the younger generation arises from the fact that we do not turn our hearts to them?

If a son or a daughter shock the parents by announcing he has lost his religious faith, it will not do to sneer or to laugh. Profound sympathy and intellectual respect are what will help.

And there is something that will help far more. If a son says he no longer believes in the Christian religion, what is the only convincing reply? *It is, to live like a Christian.* This is more difficult than any verbal rejoinder. But the life is the only proof. From love and dependence on parents, children quickly pass to criticism. If fathers and mothers will illustrate the standards they profess, they will not have to worry.

To those numerous members of the older generation who fear that the young people are going to the devil, I recommend the following paragraph in a letter I found in the *Memoir of Lady Rose Weigall,* written 24 July 1862. The italics are hers.

> I sat at dinner by the Duke of Hamilton, who inquired much after you. He is still wonderfully handsome, and I was much struck by his *gracefulness* in dancing, which he did with several other middle-aged after dinner. It was a contrast to the *slouching walk* which the young men call dancing.

One day when I was expounding to undergraduates Tennyson's 'Locksley Hall Sixty Years After,' in which he lamented the loss of female reticence, reverence, and modesty, for the 'maiden fancies' were 'wallowing' in 'Zolaism,' I threw out the general query, 'Why is it that the older generation have always thought the younger generation were going to the devil?' and one of the students, Dana Von Schrader of St. Louis replied, 'Perhaps the younger generations would have gone to the devil, if the older generations had not always thought they were going there.'

And at about the same time, another undergraduate sought my advice alone after class. He was a good fellow, neither affected nor priggish. He spoke quite seriously. 'I am going home for the Christmas vacation, and I wish you would tell me what to do. I have no desire to drink; I simply don't like it and don't want to drink. But what shall I do? I don't want to hurt father's feelings.'

No satisfactory novel has ever been written of college life, and only one first-rate story of school life, *Tom Brown's Schooldays*, which combines local realism with the spirit of eternal boyhood.

As there is no good novel of college life, so is there only one good play, *Alt Heidelberg*. And never did a successful drama start less promisingly. When the curtain rose on the opening night, managers, actors, and author feared the worst. The playwright remarked, 'If this piece has as many performances as it has had rehearsals, I shall be content.' But to the amazement of all back of the curtain, the play scored a smashing success, and is apparently an immortal classic. It is not only frequently produced at the repertory theatres of Germany, it has also been translated into many languages. Richard Mansfield and later the New Theatre Company played it in America, and in 1924 it had a long run at the Porte-Saint-Martin in Paris. Like *Tom Brown* it has the perfect combination of realistic local conditions with the undying spirit of youth. Any man or woman who can see *Old Heidelberg* without a lump in the throat has ceased to be human.

The social life of America has changed so much since the eighties that those times seem almost as remote as the Middle Ages. And as the colleges are close to the national life, they have been borne along on the current. What were once regarded as luxuries are now considered necessities— how many who are sixty years old had the custom in the eighties of ordering in a hotel a 'room with bath'? Compare the number of city-dwellers who formerly owned a horse and carriage with those who now own an automobile.

Toward the end of the eighties, the colleges lost their monastic character, and became huge 'business propositions,' the change being noticeable in the daily activities of the College President. President Hadley's immediate predecessors at Yale were Noah Porter and Timothy Dwight. He said when he called upon President Porter, he usually found him reading Kant; when he called on President Dwight, he found him reading a balance-sheet. It is unfortunate that the modern undergraduate so seldom has an opportunity to see or speak with the President. Over a hundred years ago, Timothy Dwight the First used to meet the members of the Senior Class once a week—they asked him questions on any subject in the universe, and he answered them. Some of these were published, and it is interesting to see that they were largely the topics that are discussed today—freedom of the press, religious scepticism, war, international relations, censorship of the theatre, etc. Despite the size of modern classes, I think the College President might meet once a week all Seniors who cared to come, and conduct a question box. The President is usually a scholar and a man of the world; a weekly meeting of this kind might be of value, and ought to be a relief to the President from the importunate cares of finance.

Although the undergraduate today has a wider range of

activities than in the eighties, in one respect the earlier age was happier. College life ought to be different from the life of the world, and in those days it was. The men depended on one another for their chief happiness; they took long walks, and had interminable discussions. Football was an *athletic* event. For days before it, they discussed it, and after the game, if their college won, they celebrated together; if they lost, they analysed the tragedy. Today in practically every college in America, a football game is not primarily an athletic event, it is a social event. The game is a two-hour interval in forty-eight hours of dancing.

Changes in social life have affected the professors more than the students. Nearly all of my college teachers wore frock coats made of broadcloth, and their manner to the students was icily formal; today the professor appears in the classroom in sport clothes, talks and dines familiarly with students, plays golf and tennis with them, and comes into close and friendly relations. There was one way in which the old-time professor got into 'closer contact' with the undergraduate than now. Every member of the Faculty was then a policeman; it was his duty to stop disorder, and there was plenty of it to stop. The Reverend Ezekiel Robinson, President of Brown in the eighties, was over six feet in height, with long legs and arms; one winter night he heard a disturbance in front of his house, which stood at the top of a steep hill. He rushed out; the students scattered; he ran after one luckless individual, and just as the fugitive rounded the corner, the President caught him in the seat of the pants with a kick of such force and accuracy that the student was projected down the slope with terrific speed. In that sense the Faculty then came into close contact with the 'student body.'

23

INTERLUDE: *HIC ET UBIQUE*

When I was seven or eight years old, as I was walking up Chapel Street, New Haven, amid the crowd of shoppers, I saw an old man, with a white beard, old and ragged and looking feeble and cold and hungry, asking individuals in a piteous tone, 'Won't you give an old man a penny?' Feeling very sorry for this wretched beggar, I stood and watched him. All of a sudden he came over to me and bending down low to my little face, he whispered, 'Don't you worry about me. I'm all right and I've got plenty of money.' Then he raised the lower part of his beard, revealing the face of a healthy young man. He followed this gesture by drawing from his pocket a canvas bag containing a pint of cash, filled to the brim with silver coins. I looked at this in amazement. At that moment another passer came along; and my beggar went right up to him and said in heart-rending tones, 'Won't you give an old man a penny?'

This was my first revelation of human duplicity. I did not give him away. But why did he take this chance? Was it because he could not endure the expression on my face? Was it merely because I was a child?

Many years later, as I was standing in line to buy a ticket at a railway station, I marvelled at the sublime patience, the sweet courtesy, the undeviating politeness with which the ticket-seller answered foolish questions. Three or four women preceded me and each one of them asked this man repeatedly superfluous, almost idiotic questions. To each

one he gave a sweet smile and answered with perfect courtesy. When I finally reached him, I said, 'I can't help admiring the courtesy and patience you show in answering so
many unnecessary questions.' A transformation came over
him. He said, 'Jesus Christ! Jesus Christ! some day I'll
break their Goddamned necks!'

My remark seemed to touch a nerve in this apparently
calm man.

Why do oral corrections of our manners so enrage us?
Mr. William Walker of Albany sent me a cutting from an
English newspaper. A municipal orchestra concert was
being given at Folkestone. Mr. C.E.Mumford, an alderman, a borough magistrate, and member of the Kent
County Council, entered the room, took a seat at a table,
ordered coffee, and began to read a book. In order to get a
better light, he turned his back to the players, and was
quietly enjoying himself, reading and listening to the
music. Two men immediately approached him; one called
him a damned cad, and the other said he was insulting the
audience and the orchestra by sitting with his back to the
stage, and insisted that he be forcibly ejected. Alderman
Mumford, like many men in a similar predicament, became more and more angry the longer he reflected on this
lesson in etiquette. He said to a reporter:

> I am a peaceful old man of 71, but at the time I felt like hitting
> both men. I went into the building to enjoy the music, and to read my
> book, and I did not think that I was doing any harm by reading or
> sitting as I did. I am taking legal advice in the matter.

Self-constituted censors of other people's behaviour are
irritating. It is curious into what a frenzy of rage they can
drive their victims, and how lasting is the sense of injury. I
met a man who told me that in a New York restaurant occupied only by men he removed his coat, whereupon a

waiter told him to put it on. He swore horribly while telling this. When Sir Sidney Lee was in this country, he lit his pipe while sitting in a man's club. He was told that pipes were not allowed. He never recovered from the shock. Many years ago I had finished my meal in a hotel 'coffee-room' in Norwich, England, and while waiting for the waiter to bring my bill, I lit a cigar. An Englishman at an adjoining table came to me and said: 'You should remember there are ladies present.' I was too astonished to make any reply. But as soon as I got outside, I found I was boiling with rage. Even now I cannot think of the incident with calm. I suppose there is so much vanity in all of us we resent fiercely unsolicited lessons in etiquette.

But why should any one regard it as an insult to be mistaken for one who does honest work? Coming down to breakfast at seven in a Philadelphia hotel, I saw a man bending over the unlighted newspaper stand. I asked: 'Are these today's New York papers?' He turned around resentfully and said: 'I don't know any more about it than you do.' He thought I thought he was the paper man. The more the idea penetrated his mind, the angrier he became, and he added stuffily: 'How would I know any more about it than you?' Of course he ought to have said, 'How *should* I know?' But the time for giving him a lesson in English grammar seemed inopportune; so I merely said: 'Sir, your face seemed so intelligent that I thought you could answer any question I should be able to ask.' He snorted. But why should he be angry? Once, when I entered a theatre and stood at the top of the aisle, a man and his girl approached; he shoved his tickets into my hands and demanded that I show him his seats. I answered: 'I'd do it in a minute, if I had the least idea where they were.' Then he profusely apologized, and his companion becomingly blushed. But why apologize? I was not angry—why should I be? At a

social function in New Haven, a freshman handed the
plate containing the remnants of his food to a New York
multimillionaire, thinking him to be the butler. The great
capitalist, leader of Newport society, instead of throwing
the plate in the boy's face, took it without comment and
carried it away.

Many 'good' Americans seem to be troubled by the vast
number of English authors who come here to lecture, are
eagerly and copiously entertained, return to their native
land with much money, for which in some cases they have
given nothing except their digestion. The thing certainly
has its amusing side, especially when the 'lecturer' knows
nothing of the art of public speaking, looks at the audience
quizzically, begins his remarks by saying he has nothing to
say and takes an hour to prove it. But why be offended?
Attendance is voluntary. Some say acidly, that if we sent
our authors over there, they would not receive either
money or hospitality. Perhaps not; yet Mark Twain found
it easy to obtain both. At this moment we have no Mark
Twain; and while reading Franklin, I hit upon the possible
reason why Americans entertain overseas visitors so energetically. In a note appended to his *Remarks concerning the
Savages of North America*, Franklin said, 'It is remarkable
that in all Ages and Countries Hospitality has been allow'd
as the Virtue of those whom the civiliz'd were pleased to
call Barbarians. The Greeks celebrated the Scythians for it.
The Saracens possess'd it eminently, and it is to this day
the reigning Virtue of the wild Arabs. St. Paul, too in the
Relation of his Voyage and Shipwreck, on the island of
Melita says the Barbarous People shewed us no little kindness; for they kindled a fire, and received us every one.'

Europeans generally believe that American wives are too
dominant; but Doctor F.T.Wright of Arizona told me he

saw the following framed motto in the window of a house in Berlin:

Ich bin der Herr im Hause und was meine Frau sagt, wird gemacht!

ARNOLD BENNETT AND THE EDUCATION OF GIRLS

My friend and former Yale pupil, Thomas E. Murray, Jr., of Brooklyn, gave me a photostat of this letter; a reply to one his brother Joe had written Mr. Bennett, describing the accomplishments of his five daughters.

75, CADOGAN SQUARE, S.W.1
21st December 1929

DEAR MR. MURRAY,

Thank you for your letter. Your story of your father is very interesting. Your story of the young ladies is more than interesting. It is, to me, distressing. Young ladies ought in my opinion to be brought up to do something more than play the piano and dance and ride and talk French. My view is that everyone, however rich, and beautiful, ought to be brought up to earn his or her own living. Also that all women who have any notion of getting married ought to learn to be professional housekeepers in every department of this vast and difficult task.

All good wishes,

Yours sincerely,

ARNOLD BENNETT

Quite often one hears the expression 'I don't know anything about music, but I like, etc.' An unexpected variation on this well-worn theme saluted my ears from a clever woman in a town in northern Connecticut. She had returned from the service at church, and remarked casually: 'I don't know anything about music, but I hate our choir.'

I do not pretend to have any ability as an architect, plumber, or carpenter. But if I were making the furniture and furnishings of a house, I should lower all the desks and elevate all the wash-basins. This applies also to the kitchen sink, where many good women have strained their backs. A great number of people get writer's cramp and neuritis by writing either in too low a chair or on too high a desk. The effort of writing is increased by every additional half-inch added to the height of the desk. That ought to be self-evident, yet every desk I see is too high.

On the other hand, one bends over double to wash one's hands; wash-basins should be elevated. Furthermore, nearly all faucets just barely project over the rim of the basin, so that it is impossible to get one's hands under them to catch the falling water. They should stick out at least three inches.

I advise those who dislike puns not to read this. Our tennis-courts in New Haven are near Bradley Street, where among many other members of the college faculty lived my friends Professor and Mrs. Frank Porter. One day, while I was playing tennis with my colleague Jack Crawford, a strong south wind brought an appetizing odour of grilling beefsteak from the direction of Bradley Street. I wondered from which house so delightful a thing came, and Jack said it must be coming from the Porter house.

The most embarrassing question I ever received in public was from the late Don Marquis, whom I greatly admired. I asked him to give a lecture at Yale on the Francis Bergen Memorial Foundation, and a huge audience appeared. After introducing him, I left the platform, and took a seat in the auditorium. In the middle of his lecture, he remarked that some writers had declared that they found first-rate composition not only delightful but easy; that all the common talk of the terrible and distasteful labour was absurd; that the satisfaction of having written well made the work pleasant. 'I do not agree with them,' said Marquis; 'to write well is extremely hard work. *Don't you find it so, Mr. Phelps?*' This is like the question in court, 'Have you stopped beating your wife?' You cannot answer either Yes or No. Nor did I.

The relativity of immorality in books is shown by the following.

While visiting at the house of a friend, I happened to open idly a volume of the *International Cyclopœdia* and came upon this article on Alexandre Dumas, who gave the world the incomparable story of *The Three Musketeers*.

> Altogether it may be said that the appearance in literature of a writer like Dumas is a portentous phenomenon; and the avidity with which his immoral fictions are devoured, is the most severe condemnation of modern, and especially French, society that could well be pronounced.
>
> *Dumas Fils.* Who has unhappily followed in the footsteps of his father. . . . His principal work is *La Dame aux Camélias*—a novel on which is founded the notorious opera *La Traviata*. It is one of the most audaciously immoral works in existence.

This volume is dated 1892.

There is a whole philosophy of life in a missed short putt, and it makes for pessimism. One does not need to know what a putt is to understand what I mean. For what I mean is this. It is strange that men and women should be so constituted that they can do things easily when the doing of them is of no importance; whilst the moment it becomes essential the doing of them becomes a thousandfold harder. To knock a golf-ball into a hole two feet away is so easy that the ordinary man or woman, while practising alone, could probably do it two hundred times successively; but when a championship depends upon sinking a two-foot putt, there is no one who is not in danger of missing it.

There seems to be a curse on humanity, which lessens ability when it is most needed. Why should the intense desire to do a thing reduce a man's ability to do it? In a perfect world, it would be just the other way around; the more important the crisis, the greater would be the performer's skill. But among the children of men, a consuming eagerness to accomplish something—no matter what it may be —usually makes its accomplishment far more difficult. This is why 'Casey at the Bat' is at once one of the most pessimistic poems in the language and one of the truest to human nature. Why is it easy to walk on a plank at an elevation of two feet and difficult at higher elevations? Why do the most skilful surgeons turn from operating on members of their own family? Why do the greatest orators only seldom rise to an occasion? Why is it that in the complete works of Wordsworth, only a fourth part is good? Why is it that Shakespeare, who had a command of language so marvellous that he seemed to be able to find the right word without effort—why is it that only about seven of his plays are generally read and about thirty neglected? Why is it that the greatest humorists cannot be funny when they most strenuously wish to be? Why did Richter say that every great poet goes to his grave with his best poems unwritten? Why are so few happy retorts made in conversation? Why does the after-dinner speaker make his most brilliant speech on the way home?

I am entirely of the opinion expressed by Heywood Broun in his *Pieces of Hate* concerning after-dinner oratory. I regret that this institution survived the war. It will, I am afraid, survive everything except the treatment recommended by Mr. Broun. Most speakers hate it, most audiences hate it; it has no real friends, and yet it goes on its devastating course. Having to speak at a public dinner in Chicago, I found my place at that pillory of torment, the speakers' table; and there, seeing a magnificent man in evening dress, I gave him my name and grasped his hand with what cordiality I could command. He replied: 'I'm the head waiter, sir.' 'Shake hands again, old man,' I cried; 'you don't know how I envy you!'

Instead of having a long stupefying dinner, followed by long, stupefying speeches, how much better it would be, if we really wished to hear the senator, or the ambassador, or the captain of industry, if we could meet and hear him and, at the conclusion of the oratory, sit down together and enjoy a good dinner! And we should all have a subject for conversation. Furthermore, the speaker would not dare to talk indefinitely. I remember being obliged on one occasion to preside at a 'business men's banquet;' there were five speakers; the third spoke two hours and thirty minutes. I was sorry for the fourth and fifth, but still more sorry for myself, for my post of honour made escape impossible.

Sitting next to one of the other speakers at a public banquet, I observed he ate nothing, and in reply to my enquiry, he said he spoke better from abstinence. 'Ah, but what an error,' I replied; 'for then, if your speech is a failure, you have lost everything.'

At the famous dinner in honour of the seventieth birthday of Mark Twain, he stated that he bought his cigars by the barrel; that some of them had belly-bands, and some not. The little paper band around the cigar is a nuisance, and in endeavouring to pick it off with the fingernail, one frequently inflicts on the cigar a mortal wound. Years ago I made an attack in public on the cigar-band. Among the many letters I received was one from Tampa: 'This nefarious practice was begun years ago by manufacturers of the famous 5-cent variety. Gradually it was imposed on the better grades as an act of protection. Now, however, there is a tendency away from it. I live in Tampa, where we make over 1,500,000 cigars every day. You will find many styles of the better sort coming out now without bands.'

Dr. W.C.Hovey of Nokomis, Illinois, wrote that the bands came from Cuba, where Spanish ladies smoked cigars, so that 'Their pretty fingers might not be stained by coming into contact with the tobacco.'

What has become of the spelling SEGAR, so common in America fifty years ago? To my astonishment, it appeared in *Action at Aquila* (1938), by Hervey Allen.

A poignant sorrow is that I cannot blow rings. I have given the matter serious attention and prolonged practice; and by making horrible grimaces, I can once out of fifty times emit a circle. Yet some of my friends, without looking any worse than usual, can send ring after ring into the air. Professor Barrett Wendell of Harvard, after shooting a succession of rings, would, with astonishing muzzle velocity, shoot a final one through the whole row,

> As right through ring and ring runs the djereed
> And binds the loose, one bar without a break.

In my youth only Catholic and Episcopal clergy could smoke with impunity; others would lose their posts. I remember my own contrition and my respect for a Congregational clergyman, the Reverend Edward Reed of Holyoke, Mass., father of Professor Edward B.Reed of Yale, who, after dinner lit a cigar and I stupidly said, 'I suppose you find a smoke soothing after a day's hard work,' and he replied with a laugh, 'No, that has nothing to do with it; *I love the nicotine.*' This reply would have pleased Mr. Chesterton.

Why is it that a tailor is usually eager to please his men clients, whilst a dressmaker tyrannizes over her woman customers and treats them with royal disdain? A pretty question that might lead to much speculation.

One of the worst foes to human happiness is the fresh-air crank. I love fresh air as much as anybody, but I love it where it belongs—outdoors. I do not like too much of it in the house, and I particularly hate the combination of in-and-outdoor air, because the ingredients are never kindly mixed. I hate a wind blowing across a library-table, and I hate a draught down the back of my neck. One of my grievances against the fresh-air crank is that he has a positive genius for the inopportune. Just when I am absolutely comfortable in a warm interior on a winter day, and can laugh from my security at the cold, some crank is sure to say: 'Don't you think it is very close here?' He walks across the room and opens a window on the back of my neck, letting in the poisonous chill. For in a public meeting or anywhere else the fresh-air crank always opens the window on somebody else's back. He then returns to his safe chair, and says: 'That's better.' Once a friend of mine remarked on closing an open window, 'I've got only one drop of blood in my whole body, and I want that to circulate.'

A reprehensible habit is that of a host who gives a dinner-party and arranges that the guests immediately after the feast is over shall repair to a room that would answer admirably for cold storage. After eating, one is naturally cold, and should go into a warm room. This is proved by the fact that if an open fire is burning on the hearth of the room to which the dinner-guests adjourn, every one instinctively makes for that fire. Usually a large man reaches it first, stands with his back to it, and addresses the company.

Dining-rooms and their successors should never be cold. (There is only one thing worse than a cold dining-room, and that is a cold bathroom.) I felt a strong affection for a convivial and cheerful guest, who, at a dinner-party, in the midst of winter, when the host enquired, 'Shall I open a window?' replied: 'No! Shut all the windows and open all the bottles.'

We are told it is unhealthy to be in a warm room. But how much better it is to be unhealthy and comfortable, than to be healthy and miserable. My advice to the fresh-air crank is to stay outdoors, where he belongs, for he has never been civilized. If he must enter the house or the hall, and must have fresh air, let him open the window on his own back; and let us hope that he catches a terrific cold.

I have often admired the placidity and repose of the American cow. She has a philosophical calm never attained by man. In a forty-acre lot I saw one cow sitting in quiet dignity, and in an unruffled manner contemplating not only the sole item on her eternal bill-of-fare, but *all the meals* she would eat during the next four months. Suppose you or I between breakfast and luncheon were compelled to gaze at the entire accumulation of food we were to eat during the next hundred days! and not only gaze at it, but be surrounded by it! Yet the cow did not seem to mind. She looked off and beyond her food, apparently absorbed in agreeable meditations. Victor Cherbuliez, in his charming novel, *L'Idée de Jean Têtérol*, said: 'All cows are alike; there is in their eyes something fixed and eternal, a silent dream of fresh grass.' Men and women can dream of food only in its absence; but the fortunate cow has both her dreams and their realization.

Yet here is a curious thing. If I had the same food for lunch and dinner every day the monotony would become intolerable; yet I have the same bill-of-fare for breakfast every day and enjoy it so much that I should not like it changed in any particular. And breakfast is my favourite meal. I am hungrier for that than for any other repast. I know in advance what I am going to have not only on a particular morning but on every morning for the rest of my life. If I knew now that I was to have the same breakfast every morning for the next six hundred years, I should re-joice.

Browning's Pied Piper refuses to remain in the misty mid-region of legend. Recently in Budapest a piper appeared who, according to the press despatches, saved a section of the city from a plague of rats by bewitching the animals with music. Then the city authorities refused to pay the piper. The *New York Herald Tribune* informed me that a young veteran of the A.E.F., John Rogoff, is the Pied Piper of the East Side. Mr. Rogoff goes into a cellar, whistles in a peculiarly compelling fashion, and out come the rats. They stream towards him and eat from his hands. He gave a demonstration of his power to a sceptical ob-server, who, after counting seven rats in thirty seconds, incontinently fled. He was afraid, not of the beasts, but of the whistling. 'It had a strange influence on him. He was afraid he'd get up and snatch a piece of bread himself.'

Why do old people eat so much? Many families have some aged and worn-out member, who has to be supported, and who seems to the supporters a prodigious consumer of food. Old Isaac was swindled by that unscrupulous mother-and-son combination, Rebekah and Jacob—swindled through his lust for meat. The reason the aged and the idle eat so much is that meals are the chief events in the day. To an active man or woman good food is agreeable, but the eater is not primarily interested in it; he has been busy up to meal-time, and is thinking of what he has to do the moment the repast is over. Sometimes indeed, no matter how ex-cellent the luncheon, it is an interruption in an absorbing occupation, which is why most Americans could not endure afternoon tea. Do you think I would stop my work or my golf for that? But to venerable and idle persons, who have nothing to do except look forward to the next meal, this is a sacred rite, not to be taken carelessly or hastily. Observe how particular everyone (except the seasick) is about food on an ocean liner, or while travelling anywhere. Some unsympathetic critics say that those who complain about their meals on shipboard probably have not very good ones at home. Of course; that is precisely why they complain when meals are all-important. It is not so surprising that tourists often remember a certain place in Europe because there they had a marvellous dinner. And there is point to what Oscar Wilde said: 'I hate people who are not serious about their meals.'

Nothing is more astonishing to people of the twentieth century than to read of the enormous meals consumed by people in the eighteenth. Those who have read *The Diary of a Country Parson* edited by John Beresford, were astounded by the huge dinners and yet they were part of the daily programme. In his case it was almost pathetic to see how as he grew old he increased his daily doses of rhubarb and began vaguely to wonder if it were not just possible that a quart of port wine might not be good for the gout.

But as late as July 1859 in the extreme heat of midsummer the following dinner card shows what a Yale class consumed at the Old Tontine Hotel in New Haven.

SOUP
Mock Turtle

FISH
Salmon, boiled; Lobster Sauce

ROASTS
Rib of Beef, Chicken, Giblet Sauce; Spring Ducks, Apple Sauce
Ham, Champagne Sauce
Broiled
Leg Mutton, Caper Sauce. Smoked Tongue. Capon, Oyster Sauce

COLD ORNAMENTAL DISHES

Boned Turkey, au Truffes, garnished with Jelly
Mayonnaise de Volaille, à la Parisienne
Langue de Boeuf, decorated
Lobsters, au Naturel
Pig's Head Cheese

CONDIMENTS

Spanish Olives, Worcestershire Sauce, Chow Chow, Brandied Cherries
Pickles   French Mustard

ENTRÉES

Côtelettes d'Agneau, grillé, au Champignons
Fillet de Boeuf, piqué, au Purée de Pomme de Terre
Spring Chicken, broiled, à la Hollandaise
Lambs' Frie, breaded, à la Printanière
Tame Pigeons, stewed in Port Wine
Vol au Vent, garnished with Oysters

VEGETABLES

Stewed Tomatoes   Green Corn   Squash   New Beets
New Potatoes   Mashed Potatoes

PASTRY AND CONFECTIONERY

Montauk Lighthouse
Champagne Jelly, Charlotte Russe, Currant Jelly Slices, Fancy Jelly
Peach Tartelettes, Cup Custards, Vanilla Candy, Swiss Meringues
Fruit Pudding, Wine Sauce; Apple Pie; Peach Pie; Blackberry Pie

DESSERT

Pyramids of Vanilla Ice Cream, Forms of Pine Apple ice
Almonds, English Walnuts, Filberts, Brazil Nuts, Figs, Prunes
Raisins, Peaches, Blackberries
Tea and Coffee

Those who believe that contempt is an indication of intellectual superiority should remember a saying by Alfred De Vigny: '*Il n'y a pas un homme qui ait le droit de mépriser les hommes.*'

It is curious how differently people regard human beings. Some, upon entering a trolley-car, hate every one else in the vehicle; some look upon the crowd at a street corner with disgust; it must be wonderful to have such a sense of superiority. It is amusing to enter a fashionable hotel, and as you advance to the office desk, followed by your travelling bags, to glance for a moment at those individuals who, having already been there some days, now gaze at you from their settled and comfortable chairs. They look at you as though you were garbage. In the same way, many people, travelling in foreign lands, hate all fellow-countrymen whom they meet. This scorn used to distress me, just as I used to be disturbed by the contempt of a waiter in a hotel or a butler in a fashionable mansion; now I am only amused.

When one thinks of the vast folly displayed in human history, it is easy to despise human nature; but when one thinks of the many individuals who, with little money, little education, little ability, nevertheless put up a brave front and meet the day's work with uncomplaining serenity, human nature seems sublime.

Still, there is an intellectual pleasure in reading a brilliant review of the human scene which Bunyan called Vanity Fair. Rose Macaulay's novel, showing that the younger generation is always just that, is well worth an attentive perusal. Satire is valuable provided we apply it first of all to ourselves; then we shall not only enjoy it, but make it profitable. I found Miss Macaulay's *Potterism* delectable; I perceived that there was not only a streak of potterism in every human being, but a large percentage of it in my own mind.

The most agreeable place to read books is on the train. One is comparatively safe from interruption, one cannot be annoyed by the telephone, one almost always has a good light both by day and by night. Two suggestions: in general in the U.S.A. sit on the right side of the train; then you will usually have no track outside your window. On the left side, freight-trains, running in the same direction, keep intervening between you and the light, and it usually seems as if every freight-train were at least four miles long. When your railway car has finally passed it, and you hear the maddened snort of the freight locomotive, maddened because you have escaped, your own train then stops at a station just long enough to permit the entire freight-train to pass, when once more you begin the tedious process of overhauling it. Therefore, sit on the right side of the train. Secondly, ride backward, if you can. It is easier on the eyes. In this attitude, the trees, poles, and landscape fade gently and gracefully away, whereas sitting forward, they rush furiously and directly into your defenceless face.

Of course, there are exceptions to this. A stranger, walking through the grounds of an American university, encountered a tall, magnificent specimen of young manhood, and enquired, 'Do you row on the University crew?' 'No,' replied the student, 'it makes me sick to ride backward.'

Apart from typographical errors, modern books contain many misspellings. The word most often misspelled by the best authors and publishers is *ecstasy*; and the *name* that suffers most often is Shakespeare's *Jaques*. There is no authority for writing *ecstacy*; and to write *Jacques* is not only to give the wrong name, but to ruin Shakespeare's rhythm. Yet in a work by that arch-corrector of other men, the late J. Churton Collins, I found *Jacques*; and in his book on *Hamlet*, published in 1922 by Professor Clutton-Brock of Oxford, I note the same ghastly blunder. There are two quite different men in *As You Like It* named *Jaques*, but there is no *Jacques*.

I am appalled by the soggy weight of nearly all books published during the last ten years. There has been a steady change for the worse. Before the war, I could tell whether a book were published in America or in England, merely by 'hefting' it; British books were light, American heavy. But then came a great improvement on the part of our American publishers; books on this side of the water were as light as those in England.

About ten years ago, both English and American books became equally detestable in their stupendous weight. To read them is not an intellectual, but a gymnastic exercise; one needs the wrists of an orang-outang to hold them. And as everyone reads in bed, there is a chance for a serious accident. Should the book fall out of one's hands while one is sleepy, it might easily kill or permanently injure the half-conscious victim.

Furthermore, such excess baggage prevents one from carrying many books when travelling, thus lessening the sales; and until recently prevented one from buying them as presents and sending them to distant friends, for the postage often cost more than the book.

Aesthetically, these heavy volumes are vulgar, and the publishers should be ashamed of them. There is a charm in a light-weight volume; it invites perusal; it seems attractive, congenial, well-bred, a valued guest in the house. But these heavy-weight elephantine tomes are as depressing as soggy porridge.

Even as we have many humorous books consisting only of the 'boners' made on exam papers, I think an anthology of typographical errors would be side-splitting. One of the most diverting was given by Charles Towne in his entertaining autobiography. Ella Wheeler Wilcox had sent to the magazine which he edited a poem in which the climax was contained in the following line:

My soul is a lighthouse keeper

but it was printed in the magazine

My soul is a light housekeeper

Mrs. Wilcox told him exactly what she thought of him and of his magazine.

Perhaps the most fascinating typographical error I ever heard of was described, curiously enough, by Herbert Spencer. A devout Christian woman wrote a book upholding self-sacrifice and toward its close came this sentence. '*Pour bien comprendre l'amour, il faut sortir de soi.*' In the irrevocable book it appeared thus: '*Pour bien comprendre l'amour, il faut sortir le soir.*'

Which reminds me of an incident that happened to the American novelist William Henry Bishop at a restaurant in Belgium. He told me that the waiter brought him a lobster so small that Bishop was disgusted. He lifted it up and said, '*C'est pour rire.*' The waiter then also lifted it up, to his amazement smelt of it and said gravely, '*Vous avez raison, Monsieur; c'est pourri.*'

An excellent typographical error (sent me by Clayton Crawford) was in Hearst's *Seattle Post-Intelligencer*: 'The Missionary Sisters of the Sacred Hearst.'

I suppose the only publications in the world containing no typographical errors are the Authorized Version of the Bible and railway time-tables.

The late Walter Raleigh, Professor of English literature at Oxford, was seventy-eight inches tall and every inch a man. He chafed terribly under academic forms and restrictions, and seemed always to wish to speak his mind. When, after his death, his letters were published, we found he hated Gladstone, Morley, God, clergymen, Thackeray, Augustine Birrell, George Borrow, Carlyle, Ibsen, Macaulay, Shaw; his black-list is a roll of honour. But he was sincere; and his judgements often shrewd. I heard him lecture in Oxford and later at Yale, and he was so conventional and mild, I was quite unprepared for the downrightness and humour of the unofficial man.

Occasionally, however, in these epistles, he wrote comments of extraordinary ineptitude. Of a book by Barrett Wendell: 'a work that might have been begotten by a German Doctoral Thesis on a Young Men's Christian Association.' In the entire universe the two things most alien to Wendell's mind and tastes, the two things he hated most, were German Doctoral Theses and the Y.M.C.A.

After Raleigh lectured at Yale he departed for Princeton, and we sent word that whoever should meet him at the train could not miss him on account of his great height. Well, there was another big fellow on that train who had an American sense of humour and ready speech. The train drew in at dusk; a huge man stepped off, and the Princeton Professor asked, 'Are you Sir Walter Raleigh?' Instantly the man replied, 'No, I am Christopher Columbus.'

A distinguished physician who has spent his entire life in the South and has always had negro servants devoted to him, told me that all the white man knows of the negroes is what the negroes are willing to impart. He said that negroes, when among themselves, talk in a manner entirely different from the way in which they speak to white men.

Shortly after this conversation, I read in one of Somerset Maugham's books that white men really know nothing about the thoughts of Orientals, and in response to a question of mine as to whether the dark-skinned men know us any better than we know them, I received the following interesting letter.

MAY 21 (1936)

Victoria Palace Hotel
Paris

DEAR PROFESSOR PHELPS

Thank you for sending me your brief article. The answer to your final question—do the dark-skinned men see right through us?—is no. I am convinced of that. Do you think I, who was born in France and have lived here for years, know a Frenchman as a Frenchman knows him? Not for a minute.

Yours sincerely,

W. S. MAUGHAM

Perhaps the best retort I have ever heard of occurred when Thackeray was a candidate for Parliament, and was opposed by Edward Cardwell. The two competitors happened to meet in the course of the campaign, and after a friendly discussion, Thackeray said it would be a good fight, 'and may the best man win.' 'Oh, I hope not!' said his rival.

As a rule Barnum knew the American public loved to be gulled. It was a shame *not* to take the money. His genius consisted in knowing exactly how to swindle them. He swindled them in a way that called forth their admiration, affection, and delight. When I was a small boy in New Haven, one of the sideshows in his circus advertised 'a cherry-coloured cat,' which you had to pay extra to see. No one had ever heard of such a phenomenon, and accordingly crowds streamed into the tent. What they saw was an ordinary black cat, a common enough sight on any street. 'What does this mean?' they enquired of the attendant; receiving the dry answer, 'Some cherries are black.' Now Barnum had accurately known in advance exactly what would happen. Instead of becoming enraged and demanding their money back, they all grinned foolishly, ejaculated the then equivalent of 'Stung again!' immediately went out and implored every one they met on no account to miss seeing the cherry-coloured cat. The result was an enormous intake. In this case I happened to know the cat. It lived in a house at the corner of York and Chapel Streets, belonging to Mrs. Sanford. The day before the circus reached town, the cat disappeared. The day after, the cat was returned to the house, with a ribbon around its neck, bearing a card, 'With Mr. Barnum's compliments.' So that his 'overhead' was nil. Every cent he took in was as 'velvet' as the cat's fur.

On another occasion he put up inside a part of the tent a large sign TO THE EGRESS which pointed to an alley in canvas. Crowds streamed there expecting to see some wild woman; they reached the outer air and found they had to pay their entrance fee over again. The result was as the great man had foreseen. 'Isn't that just like him?'

If, on leaving a shop in Paris, you say 'Bon Jour,' the person addressed says 'Au Revoir' and if you say 'Au Revoir' the rejoinder is 'Bon Jour.' Parisians dislike parrot talk.

This reminds me of the laconic inscription on a tomb in Vevey, Switzerland:

LOUIS BONJOUR
1841–1896
AU REVOIR

I heard of an American who had a fanatical hatred of superfluities of speech and who requested the shortest possible inscription (in verse) on his tomb. It is a pity he could not have lived long enough to see it.

THORPE'S
CORPSE

The Gentleman ought not to become obsolete. John Galsworthy, in his fine drama *The Skin Game*, emphasized the real danger of fighting. The danger is that in a skin-for-skin contest, gentility will prove to be worth nothing; for it will be sacrificed in the desire for victory. Or, in other words, if the enemy cheats, we must cheat too. During the World War the worst possible argument for reprisals always seemed to me to be one constantly urged; namely, that we must treat the enemy as he treats us. In other words, we must allow our foes to determine our own moral standards, and imitate them in the very things that gave us the reason for fighting them. There is where we can take a lesson in manners from Julius Caesar. In that interesting little volume *The Marginal Notes of Lord Macaulay*, containing extracts from the comments Macaulay jotted down on the margins of the books he read, Sir George Otto Trevelyan quoted the following: Cicero had written Caesar a letter expressing his grateful appreciation for the clemency shown by the latter to his captured foes, and Caesar replied to this epistle in words which contained, so Macaulay used to say, the finest sentence ever written: 'I triumph and rejoice that my action should have obtained your approval. Nor am I disturbed when I hear it said that those whom I have sent off alive and free will again bear arms against me; for there is nothing which I so much covet as that I should be like myself and they like themselves.' And on the margin of the book by that sentence, Macaulay wrote: 'Noble fellow!'

Yet for over fifty years it has been the fashion to sneer at Macaulay. When I was a Freshman at Yale in 1884, I remember that Professor Cyrus Northrop, who was the embodiment of dignity, yet who was always called affectionately by the students 'Guts' or 'Gutsy,' saying impressively in the classroom, 'Gentlemen, I am somewhat behind the age in my admiration for Macaulay.' I quoted this remark in print a dozen years ago, and Dr. Lawrence Abbott, Editor of the *Outlook*, wrote me that he was ignoble enough to find great pleasure and satisfaction in his writings. He had recently read all through again Macaulay's *History of England*. At that moment I received a letter from the fastidious scholar T.S.Perry of Boston, who mentioned his suddenly renewed enthusiasm for Macaulay. He added that he had just called on a friend, who said, although the matter had not been brought up in the conversation, 'I have had a sudden reversion to the worship of Macaulay!' Mr. Perry added

> It is certainly a curious bundle of coincidences. Now does T.B.M. perhaps just released from Purgatory, try to boom his reputation in this world, working in some mysterious way through our exceptionally open minds? Or do our thoughts just flow into our minds (and out again) from some great sea of thought, entirely without our control? I have often wondered whence come the thoughts that flow into my mind entirely without my doing anything about it. They flow in like a tide. Just now a certain T.B.M. matter seems straying in the universe and gets into our thoughts.

I am grateful to Macaulay for many things; and I admire him for saying that he would rather have written two lines in Goethe's great lyric than anything else in the history of literature.

> Und Marmorbilder stehen und sehen mich an:
> Was hat man dir, du armes Kind, getan?

Most professional pessimists are happy men (except Swift); most professional humorists are not. Josh Billings usually cried copiously while composing, God knows why. A man who called on him in a newspaper office while he was hurriedly writing manuscript for the importunate printer, was told he must wait; Billings was writing and crying. His friend was sympathetic and wished to know the cause of his grief. 'Oh, nothing; he always cries while writing.' At that moment the boy came out of the room with the fresh copy; the manuscript was doubly wet with ink and tears; his friend glanced at it and read, 'Nothing can cure a man of laziness; but a second wife will sometimes help.'

I am sorry for those whose work has in it nothing of the spirit of adventure; but I remonstrate with those who, although their work is individual and creative, still regard it as drudgery. I was talking ten years ago with one of the leading singers of the Metropolitan Opera House. She said: ' The public have a completely mistaken idea of the life of a prima donna; they think it must be wonderfully happy, filled with pleasure, meeting the gayest people, having constant excitement, being taken out to dinner every night. As a matter of fact, it is a life of the hardest and most unremitting toil, scarcely any fun at all.' Did she not make the cardinal error of forgetting that the chief fun of her life lay in the work itself? It ought to be a delight to interpret before enthusiastic audiences masterpieces of music.

Most persons are afraid to confess either that they are happy or that they enjoy their work. Some are superstitious, and fear that if they say they are happy, some jealous and mysterious force will take their happiness away; others are so afflicted by the insidious disease of self-pity that they have acquired the habit of regarding themselves as protagonists in tragedy. Two weeks of influenza would make their ordinary daily activities seem more alluring.

Like millions of others, I have often wondered what was the expression on Pilate's face and the tone of his voice as he uttered the famous question *What is truth?* Bacon wrote 'What is truth? said jesting Pilate.' Surely he was not jesting. He may have been indifferent or impatient, but not jocose. I feel certain that Bacon had in mind there the

Pilate of the Mystery Plays, which he, like Shakespeare, had seen in his youth, for in them Pilate was sometimes represented as a jester. Even as Shakespeare took his Herod from the Mysteries, Bacon probably took his Pilate. Pilate was a Roman, a practical politician, and was confused and dismayed that in this terrible emergency, instead of thinking of some way to save himself from a horrible death, the prisoner began to talk about truth. 'What's truth at a time like this? Don't you see you are in terrible danger? You don't want truth. You want a practical scheme to get you out of this fix.'

In August 1924 my elder colleague, Professor Henry A. Beers, wrote me the following letter about this:

It happened that I was occupying the same cottage at Chatham that I had occupied in 1917. The lady who owns the shebang has a library consisting of four volumes; two copies of the Bible, a book about Cape Cod, and the biography of a whilom missionary and sea captain. In 1917 I read the book of Job. This summer I was reading Isaiah when your commentary arrived. I have been intrigued like you, about those words of Pilate, 'What is truth?' I do not believe, in spite of Bacon, that they were spoken in jest. It may be that the translation ought to run 'What is the truth?' i.e., 'What is the truth in this particular case? the truth which you say you have come into the world to teach?' But if the translation, as we have it, is idiomatically correct, may not Pilate have meant something like this: 'You say you have come to preach the truth, but what *is* truth? Truth, my young friend, is a hard thing to discover. Here are the Jews who believe in Jehovah, and who want me to crucify you: and there are my countrymen who believe in Jove; and the philosophers and poets of Greece and their Roman followers who don't believe any popular mythology or theology. There is Plato e.g. and there is Lucretius who thinks the universe a concourse of fortuitous atoms, etc. I tell you, my young friend, truth is hard to come at.'

When Madame Nazimova first came to this country in the Russian company headed by Orlenev, and played Ibsen in Russian, the company were in financial straits. Not one of them could speak a word of English; but their performance of *The Master Builder* was so impressive that the opaque language was really no obstacle. Nathan Haskell Dole, of Boston, who translated the works of Tolstoy, gave an afternoon reception for the company in Boston; and with the hope that they might be patronized by society and thus receive some financial support, he invited to meet them the Cabots and the Lowells and the rest of the fashionable Back Bay. This meeting began under difficulties; none of the Americans could speak Russian and no member of the company could speak English, but after some smiling and amicable gestures, a fashionably dressed lady appeared who spoke fluently both Russian and English. She was called Mrs. Brown, or something like that, and saved the situation by her charm and grace of manner and by her continual flow of good talk. Finally she departed with the Russian company and, after she had gone one of the Cabots or Lowells asked, 'Who was that charming woman who spoke so beautifully and showed such ease of manner?' and Mr. Dole replied, 'Why, don't you know who that was? That was Emma Goldman.'

If there is at times a certain condescension in foreigners, the Europeans are even more fanatical worshippers of American movie stars than we. In 1924 little Jackie Coogan arrived in London and went to the Savoy Hotel. I took a short walk in the Strand, and on my return I thought the hotel was on fire. There was an enormous crowd in front of it, which blocked the pavements. Later in the day he was taken to the place where occurs daily the picturesque changing of the guard. His motor-car was rushed by women; they climbed onto the running-boards, and insisted on grabbing his small frame. Four policemen finally succeeded in pushing them off; and it was necessary to take the actor into the building, whence he escaped by a secret passage. Such is the appeal of Soloism; such is the power of advertising.

When years ago Charlie Chaplin arrived at Southampton, women broke the windows of his taxi so that they might take hold of him.

My beloved senior colleague at Yale, Professor Henry A. Beers, could have been one of the best short story writers in America if he had had any ambition. He published one volume of short stories called *A Suburban Pastoral.* The title to the book was the title of the initial story. This story, when I first read it, made an indelible impression because it was so true to life and so contrary to the typical magazine story. He described how a young man took his girl in New Haven for a walk out on the salt marshes near the city. The hero was not an athlete; he was unfortunately obliged to wear spectacles. He had not yet asked the girl to marry him but it was evident they were in love with each other and sooner or later a formal engagement seemed certain.

They were botanizing on the meadows and stayed out a little too long so that as they walked into the city dusk was already falling. They had to pass through the slums before getting into the civilized part of Chapel Street. In front of a saloon stood a group of toughs and as the man and girl approached, an ominous, premonitory silence fell, the calm before the storm. The man felt this danger keenly and attempted to hurry their footsteps but the girl, apparently unaware of any tension, seemed positively to saunter. Just as they got opposite the group the crowd of toughs began to hurl insults. The man made no reply but finally one of the men took a quid of tobacco out of his mouth and threw it. It caught the girl on the cheek. She wiped it off with loathing. Her escort turned around and faced the crowd in impotent rage. The crowd dared him to come on, calling him 'four-eyes' and 'sissy' and then the girl made the one unforgivable remark which closed their romance for ever. She said, 'Oh, how I wish a man were here!'

The difficulty was that her escort had imagination. He knew he was no match for that crowd. Through his mind passed the impulse to attack them, in which case he knew that he would be knocked down and trampled on and the girl would be at their mercy. He saw so plainly the results of action that there was no action. Nothing further happened. They walked home together without the exchange of a word.

Now there is the essence of tragedy; pure realism. In the magazine story her escort would have been a magnificent athlete. He would have acted instantly; he would have knocked down two or three of the toughs and escorted the lady home in triumph. But this happens as a rule only in magazine stories. In real life the toughs will not play up to the hero and allow him to have his will. What does a woman expect of a man at such a time?

Of course there are certain persons without physical fear who would have commanded the situation. Had the girl been accompanied by a genius like Lord Clive, he would have emerged from this ordeal in triumph, but her escort was just an ordinary gentleman who thought more of the girl's ultimate welfare than of his own reputation. Hence he lost her for ever.

I thought of this situation one Sunday evening when I was an undergraduate taking a walk about dusk outside of New Haven with a classmate of mine, Ernest Caldwell, who I think was entirely without physical fear, but lacked imagination. Furthermore he was strong. We happened to walk by a group of tough boys who were younger than we, but there were a good many of them. One of them hurled an insult. I thought it best to take no notice of this but Caldwell turned instantly, walked into the middle of the group and hit the biggest boy a blow on the face. For one moment I had the horrible impulse to run, to which fortunately I did not yield. The curious thing is that not a single word was spoken. Caldwell said nothing, he simply struck, rejoined me, and we walked on together. I expected every moment a stone in the back but nothing happened. The crowd was so overawed that they not only did nothing, they said nothing. Now if Caldwell had hesitated even half a second, we should have been torn to pieces but it was his instant resolution that gave him command of the situation.

When I was ten years old, at Sunday School in Providence, there was indelibly impressed upon my mind the folly and futility of *farewells*; and since that day I have never indulged in the luxury of emotional language as an accompaniment to a supposedly final separation. Sunday Schools opened and closed with 'General Exercises;' and on one Sunday, after the lessons were over, the Superintendent (Mr. Horton) rang the bell and called the whole assembly to attention. A young man who had for some years taught a class was about to leave us and he wished to say a few words of farewell. He had secured a position in New York and this would be his last day with the School and with his class. He was sincerely affected; although we should never meet again in this world, he hoped we should all see one another in Heaven. I did not feel the bourne from which no traveller returns was adequately represented by New York; it did not seem to me beyond the range of possibility that somebody in this large Sunday School might at some time once more see Mr. Blank. He, however, thought otherwise, and took an affecting farewell, as he looked into our faces for the last time. Well, during the week he lost this job in New York and the very next Sunday was back in his accustomed place teaching his class; I myself felt

like a fool to see him there, and could only dimly imagine
how *he* must feel.

Saying Goodbye is one of the fine arts; Maupassant has
demonstrated what might happen to one who after a prolonged farewell, returns for his forgotten umbrella; but
even where the hosts are really sorry to have the guest depart, it is best not to stretch the scene. How often one says
goodbye with thanks, and then the hosts say, 'But we are
coming to the station with you!' 'Now don't do that,' I
beg; 'I shall find the train all right.' But with a mistaken
sense of hospitality, they insist, and accompany me to the
railway station; the train is an hour late; it is one of the
longest hours in life, mine and theirs; one finally descends
to idiotic remarks, 'See the steam coming out of that engine!' and when one's train 'at long last' arrives, the relief
is equally welcome on both sides.

'*Ten Men Love What I Hate*'

I am amused when I see myself described as one who likes
everything. Here is a partial list of things I hate: Musical
comedies, over-long novels in the shape of trilogies, free
verse when it is not poetry, all forms of simplified spelling,
especially *thru*, female legs in the daily news, personal
items from Hollywood, hypocritical enthusiasm from radio
announcers, books written by 'tough guys,' biographies
where the author feels more important than his subject,
night clubs, postum, buttermilk, cauliflower, parsnips,
vegetable marrow, panatella cigars, good meat plastered
with thick gravy, paint on young faces, pageants, the
pronunciation of JOAN with two syllables, the spelling
Vergil, the substitution of hand-me-down words for thinking, such as *complexes*, *mother-fixation*, *defence-mechanism*,
escapist, *wish-belief*, accenting of *positively* and *evidently*
on the third syllable, and the following words: *Angle* (used
inaccurately), *message*, *gubernatorial*, *pools* for *eyes*, *wailed*

for *replied*, *contact* as a verb, *wistful* (for Charlie Chaplin). I particularly hate the word *gotten*. I was pleased when a man telegraphed his wife 'Have gotten tickets for the theatre' and the telegram was received 'Have got ten tickets for the theatre' and she showed up in the lobby with eight eager friends.

And I hate the whole group of novelists whom I call the Medlar Novelists—the medlar is a fruit that becomes rotten before it is ripe.

24

WILLIAM GRAHAM SUMNER

THE two most brilliant teachers on the Yale Faculty were both in the department of Political Economy, William Graham Sumner and Arthur Twining Hadley, later President of the University. Sumner was then in his prime, in the middle forties; he was a tremendous personality. His classroom was a battlefield; he encouraged intellectual resistance from the students, and loved to fight out every disputed point. As his greatest pupil and literary executor, Professor A.G. Keller, used to say, 'It was an eager and nipping air that blew on those heights. If you brought any bit of research to Sumner, he would ask three questions: Is it true? How do you know it? What of it?'

Sumner frequently gave us statements from the newspapers and printed books, asking us to point out their fallacies. He hated sentimentality, vague idealism, and would tolerate no loose or untidy thinking. If the main purpose of the teacher is not to impart instruction, but to arouse and increase the power of thinking—and I believe it is—he was the best teacher we had. I elected every course he offered in my Senior year and in the two graduate years that followed. Later, when I became a member of the Faculty, I got to know him very well. We went together one night to see the Russian actress Madame Nazimova, in Ibsen's *Master Builder*, which some humorist has called 'the piece that passeth understanding.' As we came out, he said, 'All I can make out of this play is, that a young woman induced a man to climb a tower; he was fool enough to do it, and broke his neck.'

Because he was an absolute free-trader, and taught free trade and constantly ridiculed the doctrine of protection, many of the older alumni feared he would corrupt our minds, and letters came frequently to the authorities, urging that he be expelled from the University.

Sumner was as severe with himself as he was with others. He told me that when he was in his thirties he used to smoke ten cigars a day; on a certain occasion, he was looking over the household bills for expenses, and found that for the preceding three months his own bill for cigars was exactly equal to the amount he had spent on groceries for the family; 'and I was a professor of political economy. I paid that bill and never smoked again.'

His course on the Political and Financial History of the United States I took for two years as a graduate student; the political part interested me greatly; the financial part was beyond my comprehension. I have never been able to understand any treasurer's report. The two columns always come out exactly even at the bottom. One day he put on the board a bank statement; suddenly he singled me out and said, 'What do you think of that, Phelps?' I ventured the remark, 'Professor, the bank seems to me in an excellent condition.' Professor Sumner replied, 'We are all grateful for your valuable opinion; that bank closed its doors that afternoon.' In financial matters I seem to be exactly the opposite of Daniel Webster. He was the greatest authority on public finance but was unable to pay his bills. I cannot understand public finance but have never been in debt.

Sumner had the same attitude toward the study of philosophy and metaphysics as that previously held by Benjamin Franklin, who said, 'I quitted that study for others more satisfactory.' Only, while Franklin parted from it genially, on good terms, Sumner never forgave himself for the years he spent on it in his youth nor could he ever forgive professional philosophers. He was always ridiculing them.

Years later, when I was a member of the Faculty, I was sitting directly behind Sumner, when the calling of a new professor of philosophy was the subject under discussion. In his customary downright manner, Sumner addressed the meeting. 'Philosophy is in every way as bad as astrology. It is a complete fake. Yale has a great opportunity now to announce that she will take the lead and banish the study of philosophy from the curriculum on the ground that it is unworthy of serious consideration. It is an anachronism. We might just as well have professors of alchemy or fortune-telling or palmistry.'

The Faculty would not agree to this, so the discussion was resumed. The professor who was making the report on the candidate said he was not sure of the new man's position on Pragmatism. While he was talking, I observed that the back of Sumner's neck was becoming a fiery red, sure indication of a coming explosion. He turned around, looked at the speaker and barked 'What's that you say?' 'Pragmatism,' was the reply. Sumner gave a derisive snort—'Pragmatism!' Then a professor of Greek thought it time for a rebuke, and said reproachfully, 'I think it very unworthy for any of us to ridicule the terminology employed in any other study. All our specialities have their terminology, and I must say—' Sumner grunted, 'Huh, I feel as if I were in Sunday School.'

One day I was at a railway restaurant and took a seat directly behind Professor Sumner. He was quite unaware of my presence. He was eating a large wedge of mince pie, growling over it like a fierce dog. Suddenly he stopped eating, and soliloquized aloud, 'The less I eat of that pie the better I shall feel!' I laughed; he whirled around and said, 'What, you there?' To change the subject, I remarked that I had seen in the papers his name mentioned as a candidate for the Presidency of Yale. 'Nothing in it; nothing at all.' 'Aren't you in the hands of your friends?' 'I should say not! Nothing on earth would induce me to give up the freedom of a professorship for such a job as college president.'

On the very first day we met him in an undergraduate class, he alluded to Henry George's *Progress and Poverty* and stated that a certain paragraph in it contained a fallacy. Toward the close of the hour, he said that we must bring in the next time a written comment on his lecture. I looked up the passage in Henry George, thought (at that time) that Henry George was right and Sumner wrong, and said so on my paper. He read my contribution aloud (without embarrassing me by saying who wrote it) and remarked, 'Although this man is mistaken, I am giving him the highest mark in the room; because he looked up the reference in order to verify it.'

On other occasions, however, he treated me with devastating irony, which I deserved.

25

HENRY DRUMMOND AND SCHOPENHAUER

In the Baptist denomination one could receive a preaching licence from one's church; so a few months after graduation, I went to Hartford, preached a trial sermon in the Asylum Avenue Baptist Church, and was given a licence to preach.

About this time, a woman asked me how I should like to spend my life if I could fashion it according to my desire. I replied that I should like to work hard at some form of intellectual activity from breakfast until luncheon; to spend the afternoon in violent athletic exercise, playing some game; and in the evening to enjoy myself socially, going out to dinner, attending the theatre, conversing, or quietly reading; and that is in general the way I have spent my whole life.

Not knowing exactly what line to take after graduation, and suddenly being offered the position of Secretary of the Yale University Young Men's Christian Association, with an attractive room—which later George Santayana said was the best room he had seen on his visit to Yale—the opportunity to spend half my time as a graduate student, and a salary of seven hundred and fifty dollars, I accepted this, and have never regretted it.

In a few weeks after the opening of the Autumn term, I became intimately acquainted with Professor Henry Drummond of Scotland, the most effective university speaker on religion I have ever heard. His book *Natural Law in the Spiritual World* (1883) had made a sensation;

so in 1887, when he came to America on a speaking tour among the colleges, there was widespread curiosity to hear him. He happened to be at Hartford; I went by train there, had an interview, and he agreed to come to Yale and give a series of addresses. He particularly wanted to speak at Sunday morning chapel, where all the students were required to attend. But the President of the University would not allow him to conduct this service, because he was not an ordained clergyman. He was so disappointed at this refusal, that he came near staying away altogether; but I persuaded him to come, and there was a tremendous crowd at the Sunday afternoon voluntary service. He spoke again that evening, and every night the next two weeks.

I have never seen so deep an impression made on students by any speaker on any subject as that made by Henry Drummond at Yale in the Autumn of 1887. He was a gentleman and a scholar; his method was new, fresh, original. He spoke in quiet, conversational tones, never raised his voice, made no gestures, but was intensely in earnest. He changed the emphasis from death to life. 'We come not to save your souls, but to save your lives. We want you to be Christians, not because you might die tonight, but because you are going to live tomorrow.'

After fifty years, I can still see his face and hear his voice. Mommsen said the eloquence of Cicero was the eloquence of rounded periods, whereas the eloquence of Caesar was that of deeply felt thought. Could any comparison more fitly describe the difference between conventional pulpit oratory and that of Henry Drummond? Every word he spoke was born of years of thought and study and knowledge and meditation. We hung on his words as though they were the Bread of Life.

He told us too much introspection was bad; to keep our eyes not on ourselves, but on the Master. By contemplation of Him, we might gradually be transformed into His likeness. He told us of a little group of young missionaries who went into a far country and never mentioned religion either in speeches or in conversation. They engaged in business and tried to live like the Master. After a year of this, the natives kept coming to their house to find out the guiding principle of their lives, what they believed that made their daily conduct different from others and kept them so cheerful.

Drummond said the reason a consistent Christian seems eccentric to the man in the street is because he *is* eccentric; his life revolves around a different centre from the common centre of self-interest. *Take my yoke upon you.* The yoke is not a badge of servitude, but a convenience, a method of carrying the burden in an easier manner, so that the burden seems light. Jesus had been a carpenter. He made yokes. He knew what He was talking about. He did not mean we should take an additional burden but that we should adopt His method of carrying the burden. The yoke is not an infliction on the ox; it helps the ox to draw the burden without being galled and with less effort. And what is our burden? Some calamity or sorrow? No; the burden is the burden of everyday life, with its cares, perplexities, problems, and worries. If we take the easy yoke and adopt Christ's way of life, the burden will be lighter.

For Drummond's whole emphasis was on Christianity as a way of life. At Northfield in the summer of 1888, Mr. Moody invited him to take a daily, active part in the meetings. Nothing could have better illustrated 'church unity' than that partnership; nothing could have been better evidence of the common sense and spirituality of both men. Moody was an uneducated Fundamentalist who believed every word of the Bible was true; Drummond was a professor of geology, who had been educated in the universities of Scotland and Germany. No two men could have been wider apart in their attitude toward theology. But both were sincere and devout followers of the same Master; and each had deep respect and affection for the other.

The influence of Drummond's visits to Yale—for he came several times in the next few years—lasted from 1887 to the World War. Those successive generations of students had usually as their undergraduate leaders men who took a prominent part in the religious life of the University. I have never seen anything like it; a foreign student told me it would have been inconceivable if he had not witnessed it.

Drummond sought out the leaders of undergraduate life, the principal athletes, the most popular men socially; many of them became earnest, devoted Christians; I can see now a big fellow, member of the University crew, standing up, giving his testimony, with the tears running down his face. Drummond was persuasive; he said we do not need advocates for the Christian religion, but *witnesses*. He kept conference-hours every day, and individual students talked with him. There was no hysteria, no undue excitement, but hundreds of men were really converted, and a good many members of the Faculty.

Drummond persuaded the students to organize little groups of what he called deputations; these went out to other colleges and preparatory schools and talked; the work spread all through the Universities of the East. In the Spring of 1888 three undergraduates came from Princeton to address the students at Yale. They had been carefully chosen by Drummond. One was Winthrop M. Daniels, the valedictorian of his class and now Professor at Yale; one was Robert M. Speer, member of the football team, who was to have a splendid career in the ministry; the third was the most famous football player in the country, Hector Cowan, who could not make a speech, but who was a national hero in athletics. These three men were true to form. Daniels made a brilliant intellectual speech, full of closely reasoned thought; Speer made a charming, persuasive talk, with the very grace of oratory; Cowan, an enormous fellow, stood up, with the sweat running down his face. There was much curiosity to hear what he would say. He stood looking at us a long while, overcome with stage-fright. Then he said, 'I feel more at home on the football field than making a speech; and I guess that'll be about all,' and sat down. But the sacrifice he had made in coming, and his evident sincerity, made a deep impression.

The greatest spiritual influence in my life during my first year as a graduate student was the contact with Henry Drummond; the greatest intellectual stimulus the philosophy of Schopenhauer.

Professor George T. Ladd gave a course on Schopenhauer's work *The World as Will and Idea*. There were about twenty-five students and nearly all of us became college professors. I had always been fond of reading philosophy; and at this time I thought seriously of devoting my life to it. What stopped me eventually was my lack of knowledge of the scientific side in physiological psychology. My interest in philosophy was and is largely literary. I would rather read the writings of Santayana than those of Wundt.

With the single exception of Plato, Schopenhauer is the most interesting writer on philosophy I have ever read. *The World as Will and Idea* is a masterpiece of thought, beauty, wit, humour, and literary style. It is a treatise on human nature and the fine arts; it opened my eyes, and the world has never seemed the same since. While studying that work I could almost feel myself passing from boyhood to manhood. I grew up. I have always been grateful to Lord Haldane and to his collaborator Mr. Kemp for translating Schopenhauer; we should not have studied the original. I hate to think what my life would have been without Schopenhauer; this great pessimist added so much to my happiness. He illuminated every subject he touched and he touched them all. The sincere pessimists—Swift, Schopenhauer, Hardy, Housman—give me extraordinary pleasure. Mentally, I have lived with Schopenhauer fifty years, and find him a charming companion, brilliant and stimulating.

In my serious philosophical studies, I loved Schopenhauer, I had deep respect for Kant, I thought Eduard von Hartmann crude, and Fichte incomprehensible. —

In that short-lived London weekly periodical of the nineteenth century, *Literature*, I read a diverting dialogue in the Elysian Fields between Edward King and Arthur Henry Hallam. One of them said to the other (I haven't seen the article for forty years) something like this. 'What lucky fellows we are! we died too soon to accomplish anything, and we should have been forgotten, if we had not had the good fortune each of us to be the friend of an immortal poet; thus we are both immortal figures on earth; and incidentally, I like my mausoleum much better than yours.' 'I can't possibly agree with you on that,' replied the other with some heat; and a long controversy followed which took the form of a comparison of the literary merits of *In Memoriam* and *Lycidas*.

I myself would suggest that *In Memoriam* is a horizontal poem and *Lycidas* a vertical; the former covers far more ranges of human nature and there is in it something that appeals to everyone. *Lycidas* is an austere solitary peak, reaching a height not only quite beyond Tennyson, but beyond any other English poet except Shakespeare. As a rule, I love the poetry of human nature much more than poetry rising into sublimity from meditative rapture or through an ethereal imagination. Thus, of the four greatest poets of all time, I read Homer and Shakespeare and Goethe far more than I read Dante. Yet to *Lycidas* I make an unconditional surrender; in the presence of its perfection other great poems seem for the moment second-rate.

Yet for eternity I do not think I should choose for a travelling companion either Tennyson or Milton. Tennyson was a great poet, but I do not think he had an interesting mind; and as for Milton, well, I would rather talk with Benjamin Franklin than with George Washington.

If it is possible to do so in the next world I should like to give a succession of small dinner parties where Browning and Schopenhauer could discuss the philosophy of music, for they held and advanced the same views on this subject; the question of optimism and pessimism would in the new environment have a humour all its own; where Barrie and Strindberg, both masters of the theatre, could discuss the eternal feminine in the new light thrown upon that interesting subject; where Hardy and Chesterton could discuss literature and G.K.C. could say, 'I told you so;' where Goethe and Dr. Johnson, who respectively hated and loved controversy, could discuss the respective merits of Eckermann and Boswell—what did Johnson really think of Boswell?—and agree on one theme anyhow, that conversation and not oratory is a true revelation of intelligence; where Rostand could tell Ibsen that he was the only great dramatist in a half-century on earth who owed him nothing; where Dickens could tell Emily Brontë that if he had lived long enough to finish *Edwin Drood* and she had lived long enough to read it, she would have liked it; where Housman and Francis Thompson would at first look at each other and say nothing; but after awhile they would begin to discuss the name and nature of poetry; where Henry James would analyse the motives of angels and Dumas exaggerate their resulting actions; where Stevenson would tell Moore a romantic tale and Moore forget (until too late) where he was; where Mill would wonder how the other half lived and Carlyle would say it served them right; where Swift, looking back on earth, would say that they were a pernicious race of little odious vermin, and Emerson would smile serenely and say, 'But you see everything worked out perfectly according to the divine plan.'

26

BROWNING

INASMUCH as I have read books since I was four years old, it is natural enough that various authors have profoundly affected my mind and character. I have already expressed something of the debt I owe to Shakespeare, to John Stuart Mill, to Carlyle, to Tennyson's *Maud*, to Goethe, to Schopenhauer; to the Authorized Version of the Bible it is impossible to express similar indebtedness. The individual authors just mentioned came at a time in my boyhood and adolescence when they supplied what was needed; but the Bible was from the start an integral part of myself; and it would be as absurd to attempt an estimate of what I owe to it as it would be to appraise what I owe to my lungs or to my heart.

I shall always be grateful to Mill and Carlyle and Schopenhauer, although I was never the disciple of any one of them. It was the influence of Browning's poetry that became paramount. His view of life irresistibly appealed to me. So far as a humble individual can share the philosophy of a mighty genius, Browning's philosophy is my own; his ways are my ways and his thoughts are my thoughts. He was and is for me what Bentham was for Mill. I am a Browningite.

I have mentioned that when I was ten years old I declaimed at school his poem 'Hervé Riel'; but the author's name meant nothing to me then or for the next ten years. In my Senior year at college, in a general course in English literature, we had three or four lessons in Browning, which aroused in me definite aversion. This aversion was increased by the widespread adoration of the poet, by the notoriety of the Browning societies in London and in Boston, and by other eccentric propaganda. The disciples of Browning whom I met were acutely uninteresting.

I was still sufficiently a Philistine to believe not only that Browning was far from being a great poet; I thought also that his influence on the art of poetry was evil. Yes, I was like thousands of my elders who should have known better; the same critics who maintained that whatever Browning was he was certainly not a poet were those who insisted that Wagner could not write music and that Ibsen could not write plays. This attitude toward these three men of original genius seems idiotic today, but in the eighties (among English-speaking people), it was not uncommon. Professor F.J.Child of Harvard, then the foremost English scholar in America, told me seriously in 1890 that Wagner was a charlatan who would soon be forgotten and that those who admired him were full of ridiculous affectations.

In 1886 the famous American tragedian, Lawrence Barrett, was announced to appear in New Haven in *Julius Caesar* (his most successful Shakespearean role was Cassius). I bought a ticket, and was looking forward to the performance, when members of the Yale Faculty and some other citizens got up a petition and asked Mr. Barrett to substitute Browning's *A Blot in the 'Scutcheon*. I was furious at seeing the work of this impostor preferred to a Shakespearean masterpiece. I went to the box-office, got my money back and boycotted the show. I regretted that piece of folly for fifty years.

My father, as Editor of the *Christian Secretary*, received for review the new Riverside six-volume edition of Browning's works; and I decided to read them. They, and they alone, were the means of my conversion. The way to appreciate beauty is to keep looking at it, to appreciate music is to keep listening to it, to appreciate poetry is to keep reading it. I read and read, and gradually changed from aversion to an admiration not much this side of idolatry.

For a few weeks in 1890 I acted as private tutor of the two sons of the railway king, George M. Pullman. They were about ten years old; and I lived with them in a house on the seacoast of New Jersey. After they went to bed, I read every night in *The Ring and the Book*. The *Athenæum* was right when it saluted the poem on its first appearance (1869) with these words: 'It is the most precious and profound spiritual treasure that England has received since the death of Shakespeare.'

We have the greatest affection for those authors who have contributed most to our spiritual development; who have added to our faith, courage, and happiness. A great deal of my *happiness* I owe to Browning.

It was natural, therefore, as soon as I became free to teach at Yale what I wanted to teach, that I should have devoted more time to the teaching of Browning than to any other author. I began in the session of 1897–8 with a course in Chaucer and Browning, remembering what Landor had said to his young contemporary:

> Since Chaucer was alive and hale
> No man hath walked along our roads with step
> So active, so inquiring eye or speech
> So varied in discourse.

Landor had made the exception of Shakespeare, who belonged not to England, but to the world.

Thirty-four students elected this course. The next year I changed it to *Tennyson and Browning*, known to successive generations of Yale undergraduates as 'T and B.' In the last year I gave it, 1932–3, it was elected by 550.

From 1898 to 1933, I had the pleasure of introducing the poetry of Browning into the lives of hundreds of young men; and while naturally not all of them shared my enthusiasm, a large number of them kept up their reading of Browning in after years. It has been good for them, as it was for me.

27

BEGINNING TEACHING

ONE day in the Spring of 1888 Doctor John Meigs, Head Master of the great Hill School at Pottstown, Pa., entered my room and offered me a position as teacher. I told him I had no experience. 'You will get it with us.' At that time the Hill School had no superior in America and I was flattered by the offer, especially as a good salary came with it. We talked it over, and I was about to accept, when I thought I had better ask what subject he expected me to teach. 'Mathematics.' Then I knew the Hill School was not for me. I told him I was incapable. 'But these are elementary mathematics.' I said there were no elementary mathematics; I had had a wide experience, and had never seen any. 'Can't you teach arithmetic?' 'No, Sir; it would be taking money on false pretences.' He laboured with me for a long while, and finally went away sorrowful. I was not very happy myself; but in two or three weeks Mr. William Lee Cushing entered the same room, and said he was about to found a new school for boys at Dobbs Ferry, N.Y., to be called Westminster School, and wanted me to teach there. 'What subject?' 'Anything you like.' I liked all the history and all the English, and we came to an agreement in a few minutes.

The salary was even better than that from the other school. As there were practically no expenses, I saved enough to help me through another year of graduate study, to give me three months bicycling in Europe, and to leave five hundred dollars for my wedding journey.

I now had the opportunity to try teaching as a career; to find out whether or not I could do it, and whether I should enjoy it.

One afternoon in September 1888, I stepped off the train at Dobbs Ferry on the Hudson River and entered Westminster School. This was the first time I had ever been inside a boarding school, and now I came as a teacher. The next day the boys began to arrive, and although with only one exception they were under seventeen, they were for the most part more sophisticated than I. They were certainly more at home away from home; for I had never been away from home except during my Freshman year in college.

The Headmaster was a big, powerful athletic man in the late thirties. I have never known a more honest, upright, sincere, straight-forward individual; all the boys respected him, and I cannot conceive of a more satisfactory Head. There was at the beginning only one other teacher besides me; this was Edward Farrington, who had just been graduated from Yale. After Christmas, another teacher joined the staff—Mr. Buffum of the Amherst class of 1884, a great baseball player. The first night at school Mr. Cushing called Farrington and me into his study, and divided the entire work into three equal parts; thus taking, in addition to all the executive work and cares and responsibilities, exactly as much teaching, discipline and supervision as was assigned to Farrington and to me.

My first night at Westminster School I lay broad awake until it was time to get up in the morning; it seemed to me there were trains every few minutes and the freight-siding near the school gave me the opportunity to hear each freight car start separately after the pull of the engine. But these continuous noises never bothered me again.

During the school year I was busy nearly every waking moment. The only time I had free was Tuesday and Sunday afternoons. We rose at seven, and at every meal I presided over a table of boys. Teaching was from eight till one; in the afternoon, games and athletic exercises. In the evenings, presiding over study hour, where absolute quiet had to be maintained; then the supervision of the small boys with their nightly baths. Thus from seven in the morning until ten at night I had not a free moment, except on Tuesdays and Sundays. Sometimes I became weary of the companionship of so many little boys, though I was fond of them; and merely to relieve my mind, I would take a train on Tuesday afternoon to New York, walk the streets and mingle with crowds of men and women.

Sunday mornings I took a group of boys to the Episcopal Church, where I was supposed to maintain order. They never gave me any trouble; and I enjoyed the Episcopal service, which never previously had I heard on two consecutive Sundays. Immediately after church, I taught a class of girls about fifteen or sixteen years old, in the Presbyterian Sunday School; they were quick-witted and clever and I enjoyed it. The cleverest of them, Isabel Niven, subsequently became the mother of Thornton Wilder, the novelist and dramatist, and is now a fellow-citizen of mine in New Haven.

In going to Westminster School as a teacher, I had two main objects—to earn some money and to find out whether or not I could teach. I did not expect to enjoy the year. I thought it would be drudgery and that I might be a failure. But I enjoyed the year enormously. I had not the slightest trouble maintaining discipline, I had a warm affection for the boys, I kept in magnificent condition through constant physical exercise, and I had the subsequent life-long friendship of Mr. and Mrs. Cushing and their children, one of whom today is Tom Cushing, the playwright. He was a little boy during my year at the school; and he used to beg me to read aloud the blood-curdling stories of Edgar Allan Poe, to which he listened with delight.

It was fortunate that I was even more fond of outdoor games than the boys themselves, for half the day was spent playing. I was never quite good enough to become a member of the Varsity during my undergraduate days, but I had tried for various teams; and I could play baseball, football, lawn tennis, and hockey better than any boy in the school. In those days teachers were allowed to play on prep school teams; thus I was not only the coach of all the athletic organizations in Westminster School, I was also pitcher on the nine, half-back on the football team, etc. We practised every afternoon and no boy enjoyed it more than I. We won all our football games with other schools and lost only one baseball game.

Mrs. Cushing was exceedingly kind to me, and I owe much of my musical education to her. She played Beethoven for me on the piano, and occasionally took me to a concert in New York. There for the first time I heard the Ninth Symphony, conducted by Walter Damrosch. On another occasion, she took me to hear the great Hans von Bülow, who played Chopin's nocturne in G Major. Altogether, this was a rich year in my life; although I was so busy I did not read three books through.

She also did a good deal for my social education, for I was still crude, very crude indeed. She begged me to stand up straight, and added, 'But I know you won't; only idiots stand straight.'

The year was also memorable for me, because I had one accident and one narrow escape from instant death. In the early Spring, workmen were cutting down trees to clear the ground for an addition to the school buildings. I begged them to let me cut down one tree; I succeeded in doing this, and when the tree was felled, thought I was through. But one of the workmen told me I must trim all the branches.

My heart was beating at a great rate, and I was covered
with sweat. My axe went through one of the twigs, through
the lacing of my shoe, and down deep into my foot. The
blood gushed out in floods. I got to the piazza, and for the
first time in my life, fainted clean away. I went through the
experience of dying; it was interesting. Mr. Cushing and
Mr. Farrington were bending over me, binding up the
wound. Suddenly the distant trees and the landscape began to fade; and the curious thing is, that although for
some time I could hear every word spoken by those near
me, I could see absolutely nothing. Then I said to myself,
'I am dying,' and passed away completely. I have since
learned that it is a common experience for very sick persons not to be able to see anything, but to have their hearing if anything sharper than normal. A man will lie on the
bed apparently totally unconscious, and yet hear every
word spoken by anyone in the room. Wills have sometimes
been altered as a result of this.

Browning, who noticed everything, has two parenthe-
tical stanzas in 'Childe Roland to the Dark Tower Came'
which ironically illustrate this interesting fact.

> As when a sick man very near to death
> Seems dead indeed, and feels begin and end
> The tears and takes the farewell of each friend,
> And hears one bid the other go, draw breath
> Freelier outside, (' Since all is o'er,' he saith,
> ' And the blow fallen no grieving can amend;')
>
> While some discuss if near the other graves
> Be room enough for this, and when a day
> Suits best for carrying the corpse away,
> With care about the banners, scarves and staves:
> And still the man hears all, and only craves
> He may not shame such tender love and stay.

My other experience at Westminster School, the escape
from instant death, though it left me uninjured, was

terrible. One morning after Mrs. Cushing had gone to the station to take the train to New York, Mr. Cushing gave me a note for her, suggesting that if I ran straight down the bank to the tracks and along to the station, I could reach her before the train started. This short cut we had occasionally taken.

It was a crisp, cold, windy morning. I ran at full speed down the steep hill to the tracks. On the opposite track an express train was coming along very fast, making a tremendous clatter; I had my foot out to spring on the empty track between me and this train, when a drop of water came into my eye. I made an impatient ejaculation and waited a tenth of a second, to wipe my eye before running ahead; and in that speck of time, another express train, running at full speed in the opposite direction, and which I had not heard on account of the racket made by the train on the other track, came within two inches of my body. I was blown over backwards by the wind of its advance. Had it not been for that drop of water in my eye, I should have stepped directly in front of the locomotive. Even as it was, my foot was within a few inches of the track. That was fifty years ago. I should have missed a great deal.

28

GRADUATE STUDIES AND SPORT

IT is commonly said that during the first few years after birth we learn more than in any later period of equal duration; but it seems to me that during the ten years from 1883 to 1893 I made more mental progress than in any other decade of my life.

I passed from boyhood to manhood. I entered the University in 1883, was graduated in 1887 with special honours in English and in Philosophy and with Phi Beta Kappa; then followed a year's graduate study with the tremendous experience of Schopenhauer; and during that year my religious faith was permanently directed and inspired by Henry Drummond. The next year I taught in a boys' school, a valuable experience which also determined my life work; another year of graduate study with a summer in Europe, and on a bicycle; then came residence at Harvard, the first year as a graduate student. I took the degrees of M.A. at Harvard and Ph.D. at Yale; in my second year at Harvard began my professional work as a college teacher. In 1892 I began teaching at Yale; in 1893 published my first book, *The Beginnings of the English Romantic Movement*; and in the Christmas vacation of 1892–3 I was married.

As I look back on those ten years, a great deal seems to have happened. I began them as a boy, uncertain of the future; I ended them as a married man, living in my house, a member of the Yale Faculty, and the author of a book.

I enjoyed my year of teaching so much at the West-minster School that it settled for me the question of my life-work. I had no further doubts; only I felt sure I should be more happy and more successful teaching in a univer-sity than in a secondary school. Accordingly, I declined the urgent invitation to remain at Dobbs Ferry, and hav-ing obtained a scholarship in the Graduate School at Yale, I went there for the academic year of 1889–90.

On the whole, this was the unhappiest year of my life; and mainly because of one misfortune. My living with those little boys had made me hungry for learning. I was in splendid physical condition. I was twenty-four years old, and I was free to devote myself exclusively to my studies, looking forward to them with unspeakable eagerness. On the very first night of the term, and without any prelimi-nary warning, my eyes suddenly gave out. I had never worn glasses in my life, and had hardly ever been con-scious that I had eyes. I had never taken the slightest care of them, studying all through college under a flaring jet of gas. Now I suddenly found that after reading three or four minutes, my eyes felt as if they were full of needles; and even when I was not reading they were abnormally sensi-tive to light, so that I could not face any artificial light or even a window. I had no idea what was the matter; but of course it was a case of acute conjunctivitis; and if the treatment for that had been understood at the time, I think I could have found complete relief. I went to the leading oculist in New Haven, who said I had astigmatism, put bella donna in my eyes which kept them out of action for two weeks, and prescribed glasses, saying that when the accommodation of the eyes became normal and I used the glasses, I should be all right. He did nothing to relieve the inflammation. Well, I found at the end of those two weeks that my eyes were just as bad with the glasses as they had been without them.

For five or six months I was miserable. In perfect health otherwise, I could read only ten minutes at a time. I could not go to the theatre, to evening entertainments, to anything; lights tormented my eyes. Thus, after four o'clock in the afternoon, I simply sat in a chair in the darkest corner of the room, waiting for bedtime.

After nearly six months of this, I went to the greatest oculist in America, Doctor Knapp in New York. After an hour's minute examination, he said 'Throw away your glasses; there is nothing whatever the matter with your eyes.' When I told him that the New Haven physician said I had astigmatism, he replied 'That's nothing; everybody has astigmatism.'

I went back to New Haven without the glasses and that night at a dinner-party, for the first time in many months, the lights did not hurt my eyes. I hoped they were cured; but after a few weeks, the trouble returned; and I went back to the glasses, after trying others that were even worse. The following summer I spent in Europe, and when I went to Harvard in the Autumn, I paid a visit to the famous oculist in Boston, Doctor Myles Standish. I told him that my whole career and lifelong happiness depended on my getting relief; and indeed I had thought that I should probably have to give up my plans for the life of the mind, and get a job as lumberjack or something like that in the Far West. Doctor Standish said the astigmatism was so slight that many persons with much more of it never wore glasses; but inasmuch as I suffered so intensely, he would have frankly to guess at prescribing glasses which might or might not be of assistance. I left his office with a heavy heart; but as a matter of fact, his glasses helped me more than anything else I had tried, and I found I could do a reasonable amount of work. The magnifying power of these glasses was so slight that I was constantly forgetting them as I saw exactly as well without them; but if I left them off for reading, the eyestrain began again. I have never understood why my eyes should have been so intolerably weak that year, or why I could not get relief. But I would rather go through life without legs than with such eyes.

And here is a strange thing, which may help to explain some of the almost miraculous effects wrought by Christian Science, by the teachings of the late M. Coué, by hypnotic suggestion, and by other forms of mental influence.

One evening in that unhappy winter, when my eyes were at their worst, I was invited to address two or three hundred undergraduates. At the appointed hour I took my seat on the platform. The hall was illuminated by a huge ring of gas-jets suspended from the ceiling. The lights hurt my eyes so that while sitting on the platform I was compelled to look at the floor. Yet during my speech, which lasted from thirty to forty minutes, my eyes felt absolutely strong and without a semblance of pain, and I could look directly at these lights without any blinking whatever. Then when the assembly was over, my eyes were again weak.

I thought then, that if some way could be found by which my mind could be kept strongly concentrated on something, not for forty minutes but for a week, I might be cured. For clearly it was a case of the mind triumphing over a bodily illness.

For I have had similar experiences. Crossing the ocean in June 1935, I had an attack of lumbago so severe that I could walk only with great difficulty and could not stand up straight. I was asked to give a lecture on shipboard. I spoke for one hour. As soon as I began to speak, every trace of pain and stiffness left my body; I stood up straight, moved about with perfect flexibility while talking, and when the lecture was over, walked away to my stateroom with ease. For a moment I thought I was cured. But the trouble then resumed its sway.

In one respect the misfortune with my eyes may have been a good thing for me; on that account, my work as a graduate student the second year at Yale was not brilliant, and the College Faculty, who had the power of appointment, did not reappoint me to a scholarship. I needed one more year of graduate work to get my degree of Doctor of Philosophy, and told the Faculty that if I did not get a scholarship at Yale, I should go to Harvard. I think they believed I was bluffing; for my father and mother lived in New Haven, I could stay with them, and I had no friends at Harvard. I shall not forget the night toward the end of June and the close of the academic year, when I called on President Dwight—to discover the results of the Faculty meeting on scholarships. He was very kind and considerate, but said there were only a few scholarships and they must be distributed around. I told him I should write to Harvard that night. 'Oh, I wouldn't do that,' he said; 'you can get along here and you have only one more year.' I wrote to Harvard at once and got Professor Henry A. Beers to write a letter of recommendation. By return of post, I received a letter from the Harvard authorities, saying that I should be given a Shattuck scholarship, which would pay my tuition, and that if I had only applied earlier, I should have received something better. This was the first of many favours received from Harvard; and with these favours there was always a hearty encouragement.

Thus, it is possible that if the miserable condition of my eyes had not prevented me from doing first-rate work, I should have received another scholarship at Yale; and thus never would have studied at Harvard. While I am certain that my going to Yale as an undergraduate was the best thing I could possibly have done, I am equally certain that after six years of Yale, my going to Harvard was for me the best thing imaginable. Out of my disappointment came a tremendous benefit; for my life at Harvard was greatly advantageous. I cannot find words to express what this change in academic residence meant in my development.

In the summers of 1888 and 1889 I went to Chautauqua at the invitation of George E. Vincent, then the executive manager, who later has had such a distinguished educational and professional career. Professor (afterwards President) W. R. Harper, who was giving regular courses of instruction at Chautauqua, also urged me very strongly to go. But although I took courses there in French and German, and listened to lectures and concerts, my real reason for going was the splendid opportunity the place offered to play baseball. The most famous college athlete in America was my intimate friend and Yale undergraduate associate, Amos Alonzo Stagg, the greatest baseball pitcher in Yale's history and an All-American end in football. He was the Captain and Coach of the Chautauqua nine, and in 1888 offered two prizes, one in fielding and one in batting for the whole season. Herbert Moore won the fielding prize and I won in batting. My prize was a copy of the Complete Poems of Byron and I still look with pride on the inscription on the flyleaf.

> W. L. Phelps
> From his Friend
> A. A. Stagg
> Chautauqua 1888. Batting average, 389.

In the summers of 1937 and 1938 I visited Chautauqua for the first time in nearly fifty years and met Bert Moore, who won the fielding prize on that nine in 1888; and Emmet Flanders, the catcher. He showed courage and skill in catching Stagg's pitching.

Among speakers who visited Chautauqua in those two

summers, were Professor H.H.Boyesen of Columbia and Professor J.P.Mahaffy of Trinity College, Dublin. The former gave a lecture on George Eliot, in which he said that he once had a conversation with the Russian Turgenev and George Eliot's husband, George Henry Lewes. The discussion turned on the novels. Boyesen thought *Middlemarch* was the best, Turgenev said *The Mill on the Floss*, and Mr. Lewes, like a loyal husband, said *Daniel Deronda*. Boyesen said that George Eliot was totally without physical charm. 'She had a face like a horse, and if you will imagine a very sad horse, you will get her expression correctly.'

The Irishman Mahaffy, then about fifty years old, gave a course of lectures in Chautauqua, and I had many good talks with him. We attended a public banquet together and he scandalized the crowd by calling for wine, and saying in a loud voice that it was ridiculous to have a dinner without wine. At that time nearly everybody at Chautauqua was 'temperance' and not a drop of liquor was ever sold on the premises or permitted. I walked back from the dinner with Mahaffy in the moonlight, at two o'clock in the morning. I told him that in my Sophomore year at Yale I wrote an essay on Sophocles, and that I had read many criticisms written by professors at Oxford and Cambridge, and found them all more learned than sensible; at the last I had got hold of his essay which seemed to me full of wisdom. 'What is the matter with those scholars?' I asked. 'Why,' said Mahaffy, 'they live secluded lives; they are pedants; they know Greek perfectly, but they don't know anything whatever about human nature.'

I then told him how much I had enjoyed reading Schliemann's *Troja* and how greatly I admired A.H.Sayce's Introduction. 'Yes, Sayce is a fine scholar and a good man; but the poor fellow is dying of consumption. He will hardly live out the present year (1889).' Sayce lived till 1933, dying at the age of 88! He survived Mahaffy fourteen years, Mahaffy dying in 1919 at the age of eighty.

Sayce's *Reminiscences* (1923) is an interesting autobiography. In the first sentence he says he was born coughing and had coughed ever since. Probably the constant exposure in the open air in his archaeological expeditions kept him alive. After he retired from his professorship at Oxford, he spent the last years in the impossible climate of Scotland. *Venienti occurrite morbo!* Sayce's *Reminiscences* is full of good stories. Herbert Spencer, as everyone knows, told the whole world about his ill health, and particularly about his insomnia, which he dwelt on frequently and with unction, representing himself as a martyr. Sayce says that one night he and Spencer had to share the same room in an inn, and that the moment Spencer got into bed he must instantly have fallen asleep, for he began to snore and kept it up with such volume all night, that Sayce could not sleep a wink. In the morning, Spencer got out of bed wearily, and said he hadn't been able to sleep at all; he had lain awake the entire night.

I wrote to Sayce expressing my admiration for his autobiography.

8 CHALMERS CRESCENT,
EDINBURGH
June 9 '26

DEAR SIR,

Somewhat belatedly let me thank you much for your kind & encouraging letter of April 2. I am but just returned to my Scotch residence from the East & your letter has now been put into my hands. It makes me feel that my work has not been altogether in vain.

Yours sincerely

A. H. SAYCE

BICYCLING IN EUROPE

TRAVELLING was cheaper then than now; and the dollar of course bought more. I set apart five hundred dollars for my first trip to Europe. First class fare round trip, $105; purchase of a bicycle in Brussels, $80; clothes bought in London $50; all travelling expenses in Europe, $250; and I had fifteen dollars in my pocket when I arrived in New York.

We sailed on an old, small, and cheap steamer of the Red Star Line, the *Waesland*, Captain Grant. We left New York harbour Wednesday, 25 June 1890, at eleven in the morning.

There were five in our party; my Yale classmates, George D. Pettee and Horace Hart, and two graduate students at Yale, John Strong and H. Austin Aikins. All are now living except Hart.

Pettee became Head Master of the University School in Cleveland, Aikins professor of philosophy at Western Reserve University, and Strong a clergyman. I shall always be glad that my first voyage to Europe was on a very small steamer with only one deck and that we sailed directly from New York to Antwerp *without any stops*.

On the modern luxury liners, it is quite possible to spend every day on one of the decks and never see the ocean. But with our small ship lying low in the water we lived very close to the sea, and the deck was frequently awash. On the fourth day out we had the biggest storm I have ever seen; one day four or five of us on deck were hit by a terrific wave, knocked down, and all went sprawling and submerged, coming to a sudden stop somewhere in the scuppers. In the midst of this storm a little boy died, and was buried at sea; only a very few of us could attend the funeral on account of the violent motion of the ship. I stood by the Captain while he read the funeral service; and I could hear only an occasional word through the screaming wind and the roaring waves.

It was a voyage of eleven days; I shall never forget the landing at Antwerp. On Sunday afternoon, we sailed up the Scheldt with the beautiful green grass on both sides and the picturesque windmills turning. We docked at Antwerp at five o'clock; landed (it seemed) almost in front of the cathedral.

In addition to the pleasure of having on board five Harvard students, equalling in number our five Yale men, with whom we played exciting matches of shuffle-board and sang songs, there were several members of college faculties whose conversation I listened to with keen enjoyment.

One of these was an extraordinarily shy but exceedingly learned research scholar in linguistics, Philippe Marcou of Harvard, to whom I became attached, and whom I saw frequently during the following year at Cambridge, Mass. One day the conversation turned on favourite passages in poetry and music, and I remarked that I could not explain my preference, but that there was one passage in the Ninth Symphony coming immediately after the divine *Adagio Molto e Cantabile* which Beethoven gave to the second violins, that affected me more deeply than any other phrase in music. Doctor Marcou said, 'That has always been my favourite.' Nothing perhaps unites people more than such preferences; and from that moment I loved the man. There were two professional musicians on board, Professor Amsberg and Professor Himmelsbach of

Philadelphia. One day there was a grand debate between them on an ideal subject for discussion, because the propositions cannot be proved. Herr Amsberg said Mozart was as great a composer as Beethoven; that *Don Giovanni* was the greatest opera ever written; and that anyhow vocal music was greater than instrumental. All three of these propositions were vigorously denied by Professor Himmelsbach, who insisted that everything in human nature could be found in the first eight symphonies of Beethoven, and that instrumental music could express emotions far beyond the range of the voice. They argued with abundant illustrations for two hours, at the end of which each had convinced himself; an interesting discussion, coming from professionals.

For the first time in my life I met men who spoke various languages fluently; and how I envied them! Marcou spoke English, French, German, and Spanish with ease. A Belgian merchant who seemed to have travelled everywhere spoke six languages fluently and went from one to another without apparent difficulty. It was interesting to me to meet these cosmopolitans, because most Americans, when they do speak a foreign language, speak it as if it *hurt*, as the average tenor sings.

Although I have always been sensitive to new impressions and increasingly so with advancing years, I must confess I have never been able to recapture the rapture of that first voyage to Europe. To me the arrival in the Old World was such a succession of thrills that I cannot find words to express my emotions; the landing, the walking about Antwerp that first Sunday night, the journey to Brussels and Cologne, the beginning of the bicycle excursion,—I was in a continuous excitement. The first night of our bicycle excursion we spent at Bonn; and I remember looking out of my hotel window before going to bed, and wondering if it were not all a dream from which I should awaken. 'Is it possible that I am really here in a German city?'

In Brussels for the first and last time in the whole three months we engaged a guide to show us the town. This man took us immediately to the house of ill fame. It was apparently in a respectable part of the city, certainly not in the slums; there was nothing to distinguish this house from any other; it was simply one in a rather long block of good-looking residences. A well-dressed woman came to the door and we were shown into an empty room where there was a piano. In a few moments seven girls appeared, one of whom was a negro; they were suggestively dressed, but to me and I believe to my companions they were not in the least tempting though they tried to be. Whenever I read of the beauty and grace and charm of harlots—for I suppose there is no class of women described more sentimentally—I think of these Brussels prostitutes. They were dull and stupid; they had no conversational gifts; they were devoid of charm; a man would have to be quite drunk to desire them; and we were very glad indeed, after paying a few francs for a bottle of wine, which seemed to be expected as tribute, to leave the girls and the room and house and breathe the open air again. Our guide was sadly disappointed by our virtue; I suppose he had a commission from the house.

In Brussels we bought our bicycles, and took the train for Cologne. Here we entered the cathedral about eight in the morning and did not emerge for five hours. We listened to a religious service which lasted about an hour; then we explored every nook and cranny of the vast structure and climbed to the top of one of the towers, over five hundred feet.

It is not matter for astonishment that the modern drama had its origin in the Catholic Church of the Middle Ages; the difference between worship and drama is a difference mainly of *intention*. I had an opportunity that morning at Mass to witness the distinction. It so happened that I sat between a devout German Catholic and some foreign tourist. The German worshipped reverently; the tourist had a pair of binoculars which he turned curiously on the priests and the choir from beginning to end.

From Cologne we bicycled along the bank of the Rhine and near Bingen *an early dream came true*. When we were Sophomores in college, Pettee and I had attended an illustrated lecture by John L.Stoddard, probably the most successful lecturer who ever lived. When it was announced in any American city that his course of six illustrated lectures would be given, the line used to form in front of the auditorium forty-eight hours before the box-office was opened.

Pettee and I were in the top gallery and the lowness of our purse may be known by the altitude of the seats. When the stereopticon picture showed the river Rhine, I turned to Pettee in the gallery and whispered, 'I'll shake hands with you to stand on that very spot within seven years.' We shook hands solemnly. Neither of us had any money; my father was a Baptist minister and his father kept a general store in a New England village. But that night we knew that if we were both alive, we should see the Rhine. Five years later we leaned our bicycles up against the roadside, looked out on the river, and the dream came true. 'Remember that night in the dark theatre? Well, here we are!'

At the University of Heidelberg we heard a lecture by the famous Kuno Fischer. It was a hot summer day and there seemed to be no air at all in the lecture room, very much as Browning described the German university in 'Christmas Eve.' All the windows shut tight; I think they had not been opened for thirty years. I had supposed that German professors lectured to their students in a dry, impersonal manner. I was in for a surprise. At precisely quarter past four Fischer walked briskly into the room to the accompaniment of foot-applause from the students; he hung his hat on a peg, began speaking almost before he reached his place behind the desk, and without a scrap of notes, poured out a lava-like flow of burning eloquence, gesticulating violently, reaching tremendous heights of oratory, descending to the most bitter ironical denunciations; and occasionally being overcome by sentiment, his voice would break and his eyes fill with tears. The subject was Leibniz, and I have never seen anyone before or since get into such a storm of passion over Leibniz.

Kuno Fischer was an old man then, short, fat, with scanty white hairs on the two sides of his bald head. His face was clean shaven, his mouth very wide, his nose hardly bigger than a button. But his bearing had such dignity and sincerity and his broad forehead gave such intellectual power to his expression that his nose was unable to spoil his face.

Toward the close of his lecture he reached a climax of eloquence; his eyes blazed; his voice thundered. Suddenly as the clock in the hall struck five, he stopped almost in the middle of a sentence, and walked swiftly out of the room while the students stamped. In delivering his lecture he spoke with such torrential speed that I understood hardly anything; and yet, after the space of more than forty-five years, that lecture remains vividly in my mind. I can see and hear him as distinctly as if I were now in the room.

We wheeled along through the Rhineland to Strassburg, and from there through the Black Forest; in the little village of Offenburg I was impressed by a huge statue to Sir Francis Drake, erected in honour of his having introduced potatoes into Europe.

One day, the weather being very bad, we took a train for some thirty miles, and there being no one else in the compartment, we all began to sing; the guard came along, and said that if we sang, we must pay fifty pfennigs extra.

On Saturday afternoon, 26 July, we went to Oberammergau; in those days the train went only part way, and we climbed the mountain in a springless wagon, receiving a series of terrific jolts. The next day Sunday dawned clear and bright. We rose at five, and after coffee and rolls in the kitchen of the cottage where we stayed, we went to Mass, and at half-past seven entered the theatre. Our seats were in the second row, directly in front of the stage, with nothing over us but the sky. The play began at eight, with a recess from 11.30 to 1.30, and closed at 5.15. Then we walked and ran all the way down the mountain and caught a train for Munich.

During the last fifty years I have seen the most famous actors in the world, from Salvini to those now living; but I have never seen any play or any acting that affected me so uncontrollably as the Passion Play at Oberammergau. I shall always be glad that our seats were close to the stage, in spite of the fact that during the showers that fell at intervals, we were drenched. During the entire day in 1890, I felt not as if I were seeing a play, but as if I were taking part in the most tremendous series of events in human history.

The Crucifixion was not the most effective part of the play; it was marred by the too realistic breaking of the legs of the thieves, which was grotesque. But the scene in the morning when Jesus bade farewell to his mother, and she asked, 'When shall I see you again, my son?' and we knew it would be on the cross—the spectators close to me were sobbing aloud and the tears rolled down my face.

There was also one moment in the performance not rehearsed. Heavy clouds came up during the conversation between Jesus and Herod; and when Herod with a sarcastic smile asked Jesus a question, the Saviour looked silently at the sky and there was a tremendous crash of thunder. An answer from heaven.

In this year of 1890 there was a tragedy within the tragedy. Every young man in Oberammergau hopes some day to be chosen for the part of Christus; and every young girl hopes to be chosen for the Blessed Virgin. This year the girl selected for the role was engaged to be married; her lover insisted that the marriage take place that Spring, in which case she could not appear in the play. She begged him to wait until the Autumn, explaining that to appear as Mary the Mother would glorify her whole life. The young peasant became very angry at this and told her she must choose between the play and him; she chose the play. His pride was greater than his love; he forsook her and made a hasty marriage. All summer long she played the part of Mary with her own heart pierced with sorrow, and in the Autumn she took the veil.

From Munich we went to Switzerland and in daredevil mood we pushed our bicycles up to the top of the Furka Pass. At the beginning of the climb the temperature was about ninety; at the top, where we stayed over night, it was midwinter, snow all around and the road frozen solid. It was the first day of August. The next morning we started bicycling down the mountain, making the spiral curves with the greatest difficulty. Some native bicyclists hitched a small fallen tree to the rear mudguard, dragging that after them as a break. We strapped the brakes down; the whole thing was a foolhardy proceeding and I know I had two or three very narrow escapes from going over the precipice. Once I fell on the very edge and looked straight down some two thousand feet.

When we first started in Germany, I noticed that the German wheelmen all carried a whip in a socket attached to the handlebar; and I was informed it was for defence against dogs. We soon found out that some form of preparedness was necessary. I do not know why the dogs hated cyclists with such fury. Everywhere we met men with carts drawn by huge and savage dogs; these dogs would frequently break away from their masters and come tearing after us, hauling their carts after them. And free dogs seemed equally hostile. I tried the whip, I tried carrying a pocket-full of stones, but the best expedient I finally discovered to be the simplest. When the wild dog got very close and tried to bite my leg, I leaned over and spit in his eye. With some practice I became accurate. It never failed. Dogs that paid no attention to whips or stones stopped instantly when they got this dose.

During that whole summer I never got over my amazement at the excellence of the roads. Except in cities and in private estates, there was not a single good road in America in 1890. Ruts and dust and mud but never anywhere a hard smooth surface. When I was told that in Europe the roads were good everywhere and that for hundreds of miles the macadam was perfect, I did not believe it, and every day it was a fresh surprise. I had taken so many long tramps in America and had never seen or expected to see a good road that these magnificent highways astounded me. They were much better then than they are now, for the automobile had not been invented and there were no trucks or lorries to spoil the surface. The best of all the roads were the great *Routes Nationales* in France, made by Julius Caesar and improved by Napoleon. We travelled many miles through the deserted French countryside without seeing a house or a man; yet five of us could ride abreast on a road as smooth as a billiard table.

The only dangerous wheeling we had was in Switzerland, and as I look back on that I wonder I escaped with my life; but coming over the Jura mountains from Geneva into France we had some tedious climbs and some thrilling coasts—running down for miles. Auxonne is a town I never heard mentioned, but I shall never forget our entrance into that tiny mediaeval city; it was heavily fortified; we pushed our wheels between two immensely thick walls and over several moats to effect an entrance. Americans on the roads in 1890 were an object of intense interest; all the school-children everywhere stopped to ask us questions, and near Auxonne a poor old woman who had been gathering herbs was so fascinated by our having come from far away America that she talked with us for a long time. She asked if I would accept a glass of wine, whereupon she fetched a bottle from some corner of her clothing. I drank and she refused to take any compensation. The kindhearted old girl said she had a son in the wine business.

When we entered Dijon, we went to the Hotel de la Cloche, and found that Phillips Brooks had just registered. I asked the clerk if it were really the great preacher and he said volubly, 'Yes, Dr. Brooks has just arrived with his two daughters!' What a public scandal if it had been true! And what ammunition it would have furnished to his antagonists the next year when they endeavoured to prevent his election as Bishop.

At Montbard, the birthplace of the famous eighteenth-century scientist Buffon, we stopped for the night. After dinner, I wandered out alone in the twilight, and came to the castle. The great gates to the estate being open, I entered and found a land of enchantment. Never have I seen any allusion to the Castle at Montbard so that its beauty came upon me as a stunning surprise. I thought the place more beautiful than Heidelberg; and the extensive park and gardens were in perfect order. No one was visible. I had the beauty of the place to myself; and in the deepening dusk the gardens about the ancient grey walls seemed to be filled with friendly ghosts.

> A moment after, and hands unseen
> Were hanging the night around me fast.

I expected to see these *revenants* but I saw neither the quick nor the dead. Surely the *Genius Loci* must be there, but he gave no visible or audible sign.

Near the Castle Tower in the dusk, I had a beautiful prospect of the town, with the lights beginning to appear in the houses. I longed to stay in the Enchanted Ground another hour, but fearing that some retainer might close the gates, I returned reluctantly to the inn. But 'I had caught for a moment the powers at play.' It is indeed impossible for me adequately to describe the emotion I felt in that crepuscular solitude.

In Paris a few days later we went to the opera to hear *Faust*. Before the curtain rose a gentleman with a big beard whose seat was directly in front of us, turned around and said he had recognized my voice. It was Doctor Winfred R. Martin, my inspiring teacher of Virgil in the Hartford High School nearly ten years before. He told us we were in luck that night, because a beautiful American girl from Maine named Emma Eames, who had just made her début and was the sensation of Paris, was to sing Marguerite. She was indeed passing fair to see and her glorious voice haunts me still. She had not then sung in America but in the years to come I was to hear her over and over again; and in later years was to have (as I have now) the privilege of her intimate friendship. She has always been my favourite prima donna, even though her contemporaries were the most extraordinary group of sopranos the world has ever known. I shall always remember that night in Paris, when I first saw her in the radiance of her youth and beauty (she was twenty-five) and heard that voice of gold. By great good fortune, the Mephistopheles was young Pol Plançon, one of the greatest bassos of all time, whom also I was to hear so many nights in America. They sang in that sensational trio in the last act with such wealth of tone that the audience insisted on an encore; I was shocked by their acquiescence.

In Rouen, a city I was to visit often in the future, I found that I did not agree with those who had told me the church of Saint Ouen was more beautiful than the Cathedral—beautiful they both are, but I found the Cathedral, outside and in, overwhelming. We crossed the Channel from Dieppe so that we might first enter England in Newhaven, for both my companion and I, Horace Hart, were natives of New Haven in America. In London at Westminster Abbey the grave of Browning was covered with fresh flowers. He had been there only about six months.

In London I had my first subway journey in the world, in the London 'Underground' as it was called. The smoke and smell and din were terrific, but it was exciting. At a Promenade Concert in Covent Garden a woman, fat, fair, and more than forty, appeared on the stage, and I wondered why that ancient ruin was permitted to exist. But when she opened her mouth, a flood of gorgeous tones filled the room. It was magnificent singing; and finally, in response to repeated encores, she sang 'Home, Sweet Home.' It was Belle Cole, of whom I had never heard, and whom I have never forgotten. Sims Reeves, the great tenor, very old, sang in a way that charmed the vast audience, who idolized him.

I rode my bicycle the whole length of Piccadilly without a dismount, a feat I should not attempt in these latter days. But I loved those wood pavements of London. In our boarding house at Portman Place, an English physician sat next me at dinner, and said 'You an American? Why, you don't talk through your nose.'

On a Sunday, I went across the river to Newington Butts, to hear the Rev. Charles Spurgeon, most famous Baptist preacher in the world. His Tabernacle, built to accommodate his audiences, held an audience that morning of about six thousand. There was no organ and no instrument; the congregation sang with gusto. His text was, 'Lord, I am unworthy that thou shouldest come under my roof.' The language of the sermon was simple and sincere; his manner intensely earnest; his voice could be distinctly heard. I remember his saying something like this: 'Did I earnestly follow God many years ago? I don't care tuppence whether I did or not. I am following Him *now*.'

I came across the river on top of a bus over Westminster Bridge, thinking of Wordsworth's Sonnet which he composed 3 September 1802 on the roof of a coach on that same bridge. But the 'mighty heart' of London was never lying still in my time.

On 3 September 1890, however, I found myself as solitary as Wordsworth. Since 25 June, when we set sail from New York, I had had jolly companionship. But here, Horace Hart only being left of the original five, and he wishing to go to Edinburgh and caring nothing about Stratford-on-Avon, we separated, and words cannot describe my melancholy loneliness, from which, however, I completely recovered in two days. I would no more have visited England without seeing Stratford than I would have read Shakespeare and skipped *Hamlet*. That night I went again to Covent Garden and a young girl, Miss Grimson (where is she now?) was the piano soloist in Mendelssohn's Concerto in G Minor, which, curiously enough, I have never heard since. It was her first appearance; she was horribly nervous, and toward the end, she forgot. The orchestra stopped, and her music was handed to her. A few hissed, but this hissing was drowned in tremendous applause; and at the close, she was recalled three times. The audience did their best to cheer her, but how she must have suffered! Years later, while sitting with my friend, the late W. J. Henderson, music critic of the *New York Sun*, the great Madame Samaroff, who was giving the cycle of Beethoven Sonatas, forgot the music in the middle of the Hammerklavier Sonata. She laughed aloud, asked the audience to excuse her, went back stage and returned in excellent humour with her music, and finished the piece triumphantly. Bill Henderson told me he had more than once seen a famous pianist forget; but that they had always tried to fasten the blame on the piano or on somebody else; this was the first time when the artist frankly confessed to a lapse in memory. She was so great she could afford to do it; anyhow, she did, and won the devotion of the audience.

Cardinal Newman had died on 11 August, nearly ninety years old, and the shop windows were full of his portraits, and the hymn 'Lead, Kindly Light' was being sung and quoted every day. It is interesting to remember that Charles Kingsley and John Henry Newman, whose public debate attracted so much attention, and who wrote so many volumes in prose, will both be longest remembered for one lyrical poem by Newman, and three by Kingsley. The greatest hymn in our language is *Lux Benigna*, and 'The Three Fishers,' 'The Sands o' Dee,' and 'O that We Two Were Maying' will live forever. Newman's hymn, like the Lord's Prayer, can be sincerely uttered by anyone who feels religious aspiration, no matter what his theological position may be.

I had just bought a copy of a new edition of Rossetti's Poems and his lyrical translation of songs in Victor Hugo's *Burgraves*, one of the finest translations ever made by one great poet from another, haunted me so that I kept shouting it aloud when alone.

I

Through the long winter the rough wind tears;
  With their white garment the hills look wan.
      Love on: who cares?
      Who cares? Love on.
My mother is dead; God's patience wears;
  It seems my chaplain will not have done.
      Love on: who cares?
      Who cares? Love on.
The Devil, hobbling up the stairs,
  Comes for me with his ugly throng.
      Love on: who cares?
      Who cares? Love on.

II

In the time of the civil broils
    Our swords are stubborn things.
A fig for all the cities!
    A fig for all the kings!

The Burgrave prospereth:
    Men fear him more and more.
Barons, a fig for his Holiness!
    A fig for the Emperor!

Right well we hold our own
    With the brand and the iron rod,
A fig for Satan, Burgraves!
    Burgraves, a fig for God!

I spent several evenings in Hyde Park and found the speeches tremendously interesting. It was a strict case of the survival of the fittest. Every orator had a group around him, but if he for a moment lost his inspiration, a rival speaker only a few yards away, would capture half his audience. One speaker asserted loudly that he did not believe in royalty—'Of course I have nothing personally against the Queen; she does her best, according to her lights,' to which the crowd listened with indifference. Not far away a debate was in progress between a venerable

white-bearded atheist and an evangelical Oxford undergraduate. Here was Radical Old Age against Youthful Conservatism. Each man was accompanied by seconds, who
held books for his principal, while a third man held a lamp,
so that each of the antagonists could refer to and read from
his particular authority. The crowd took a deep interest in
this; but it was a sporting interest, exactly like that in any
athletic struggle. The skill of the contestants was more interesting than the question at issue; controversies are usually uninstructive.

Saturday 6 September was a red-letter day. I started out
alone on my bicycle at ten o'clock, wheeled through Hammersmith, Hounslow, and Colnbrook to Windsor, crossing
the Thames at a lovely place where there was a fine view of
the castle; and I soon saw the landscape from the top of the
Round Tower. After walking about Eton, I bicycled to
Stoke Poges, where I saw the churchyard of Gray's
'Elegy' as one sees visions in a dream—for my spirit
seemed to leave my body, and I was elevated into ecstasy.
The time and the place. The lovely September afternoon
was drawing to a close; there was not a breath of wind and
in this twilight calm I saw the churchyard, the yew tree,
the rugged elms, the graves, and the whole quiet scene not
changed since Gray described it. I fell on my knees, carried
away by my emotions.

On that same afternoon I did homage at the grave of
William Penn. He is buried in the small enclosure of a quiet
country house and lies with his family, a small headstone
containing only the words

WILLIAM PENN: 1718.

Nearby I entered the cottage at Chalfont St. Giles, where
Milton wrote part of *Paradise Lost*, and where the furniture
remains as he left it. I also made a pilgrimage from the tiny
cottage of the uncompromising Milton to the spacious man-

sion of the compromising Waller, and read the inscription;
thirty-eight years later I read it again in company with
G.K.Chesterton, whose house was only a few feet away.

That evening in the Red Lion at High Wycombe I met
an English gentleman who was also an enthusiast on English poetry, and we talked till a late hour. Next morning
(Sunday) I bicycled to Oxford, entering the town as the
bells were knolling men to church. I took a seat in All
Saints, and heard the Public Orator preach a dry sermon.
It was the Rev. Dr. W.W.Merry, whose name at any rate
was quite familiar to me, as he was the editor of the textbook of Homer that I had studied in my Freshman year at
Yale. I remember perfectly after all these years the expression on his face in the pulpit. He looked very unhappy. The
subject of the sermon was *Gratitude*!

Oxford was even more beautiful than I had anticipated.
At the hotel I met Billy Brown, who was graduated from
Yale the year before me (now the Rev. Professor Dr. William Adams Brown, of Union Theological Seminary,
author of many admirable books). Billy and I went out
for an evening walk at Oxford and found ourselves in the
midst of St. Giles's Fair. Two or three damsels pushed
feather dusters in our faces, so we bought similar weapons
and enjoyed the occasion. Universal licence prevailed in
the thick crowds, but with the utmost good nature everywhere. This was my first experience of an English Fair, and
it reminded me every moment of Ben Jonson's *Bartholomew
Fair*, which I had studied at Yale.

Wheeling on to Stratford, I stopped to read on a big
monument the following inscription:

6 MILES

To Shakespere's town whose name
Is known thro' all the earth
To Shipston 4, whose lesser name
Boasts no such poet's birth.

I saw all the sights at Stratford and fell in love with the town. In the twilight I hired a rowboat and rowed for an hour on the Avon.

Next day I walked to Shottery and talked with an old lady in the famous cottage; she was Mrs. Baker and claimed to be a descendant of the Hathaways. On my way I passed many children going to school, with shining morning faces. In my inn at Stratford I had in my bedroom gaslight, the first time I had had anything except kerosene or candles in a bedroom since leaving New York in June.

I wheeled on to Coventry, seeing Warwick Castle and Kenilworth on the way and at dusk came in sight of the 'three tall spires.' Next day I visited the George Eliot country, seeing the little farmhouse where she was born, the church at Astley, which I suppose is the one in *Scenes from Clerical Life*, and entered the spacious grounds at Griff, where she lived for twenty years; her brother was living there then. The old gardener, who remembered her perfectly, was well supplied with anecdotes, and I found his conversation interesting.

On the way to Birmingham I had an alliterative lunch by the road, consisting of Crackers, Cheese, Cakes, Chocolate, and Cider. At the Theatre Royal I heard Wilson Barrett in *Hamlet*, whom I had heard in New Haven three years before. The house was jammed and when he appeared the cheering was tremendous. I sat in the top gallery among crowds of men, many of whom had never read the play and were ignorant of its plot. How I envied them! they were spellbound. When Hamlet drew his sword on the King at prayer, a man next me whispered, 'Now he's going to kill him!' and his disappointment was acute; and Hamlet's reasons seemed to him flimsy.

In Shrewsbury I had cakes and ale with a young Welshman, who was so hospitable that he invited me to come to his house near Snowdon and stay there till I sailed for

America; and I should have been glad to accept, if only I had had the time. I visited the scene of the Battle of Shrewsbury (1403) and thought of Falstaff and Hotspur.

I heard an organ recital in Chester Cathedral that impressed me more than any similar performance in my life. Curiously enough, there are in the cathedral two battle-flags brought from Bunker Hill!

On Sunday morning, 14 September, in company with three young Englishmen, we wheeled to Hawarden to see Gladstone in church. Mr. Gladstone entered at a side door and sat in the chancel. If only he had read the lessons, and I could have heard that marvellous voice! Just before the sermon he took a seat in the front pew in order to hear better. The preacher was pompous, well nourished, red-faced, and said nothing worth remembering; yet I remember his saying that if people gather together and put up a meeting-house, that cannot possibly be called a Church; the only true Church is the Church of England. After service I hurried around in front. Mr. Gladstone soon appeared. As he came out he recognized some acquaintance with a smile on his old face, that reminded me of sunlight on a cliff. As he came close to me, I took off my cap, and he acknowledged the salute. He was then nearly eighty-one and walked with the ease and grace of youth. As I was looking at his receding figure, an Englishman whispered in my ear, 'You are looking at the greatest man England has ever produced.' I knew better than that; but I thought then and I think now that I was looking at the greatest living statesman in the world.

In the afternoon I wheeled away into Wales, passing into a wild and desolate country, with grand mountain views in the distance. Passing through St. Asaph, where Mrs. Hemans is buried, I coasted along down to the seashore, with splendid mountain views on the left and the wide sea on the right. Wheeling through a rocky defile past a castle,

I caught up with a young Englishman and we travelled along side by side, and that night we shared the same room in the Stanley Hotel at Llandudno. Walking out together, we saw sitting at an open window, Carmen Sylva, the famous poet-queen of Rumania. Ellis and I spent the next day climbing around Llandudno in magnificent weather, enjoying the holiday crowds and the stunning views of mountains and sea. I bade farewell to him in the late afternoon and took the boat for Liverpool and the bicycle trip was over.

My journey alone through England was in some respects the most interesting of the summer. I was really almost never alone, for I was constantly running across Englishmen who in five minutes seemed like old friends. English people in their own country are perhaps more friendly than anywhere else. It would be impossible anywhere to find any persons more so; it was my daily experience.

Aikins and Hart, who had started with me in June, appeared, and we all three embarked on the small *City of Chester* on 17 September, and in nine days we reached New York.

30

LIFE AT HARVARD

L'amitié jette des racines bien profondes dans les cœurs honnêtes.
—*Vingt Ans Après.*

ON the first day of October 1890 I arrived in Cambridge
and went to my rooms at 22 Winthrop Street. My roommate was Arthur Gordon (now the Reverend Doctor) who
was a son of the Reverend Doctor A.J.Gordon of Boston,
one of the greatest pulpit orators in America, and an intimate friend of my father. Arthur was six or seven years
younger than I, and was in the Junior Class at Harvard
College; thus he used the rooms only during the day, returning to Boston every evening. He was the best of company, always cheerful; and I wished very much he could
have lived in the rooms as I did, for I missed him in the
evenings, and was lonely. Fortunately he had two lovely
and charming sisters, Elsie and Helen.

In going to Harvard I made up my mind that I would
learn all I could, not only from my studies and teachers,
but also from my new associations. There were many Yale
men studying in the Harvard Law School; it was a strong
temptation to see them, but I resolutely avoided them and
all former friends and everything that in any way reminded
me of past years. This life at Harvard was a new experience, and I determined to get the most out of it. Thus I ate
at a table in Memorial Hall, roomed with a Harvard undergraduate, cultivated Harvard acquaintances, and altogether behaved as if I had never heard of Yale.

The one exception to all this was a fortunate one; my own beloved Yale classmate, William A.Setchell, later for many years Head of the Department of Botany at the University of California, was then beginning his famous career as a teacher of botany at Harvard. He was at my table in Memorial Hall, and his assistance and advice during those first few months was of the greatest value to me. He and I had been devoted friends at Yale, and had taken midnight walks together; it was delightful to find this one old friend in new surroundings.

On my second day at Harvard I called on the professors under whom I was to study; and first of all on Professor Francis J.Child, known to the students as 'Stubby' Child. He hated to be interrupted in his home in Kirkland Street, but he was kind and considerate. At that time it was considered both by the Faculty and students in the Harvard Graduate School, that everyone who took advanced studies in English must spend nearly all his time on philology. Thus I found the students were all studying Anglo-Saxon, the history of the English language, Historical English Grammar, Old Norse, Gothic, and what not; furthermore, the Doctor's theses were on linguistic subjects. I asked some of these men if they really preferred to write on such themes. 'No, of course not; but you can't write a doctor's thesis in literature.' I replied that my thesis would have nothing whatever to do with philology. They regarded me with a mixture of incredulity, wonder, and envy.

Now when I called on Professor Child, he began to make out a programme for me consisting of the unpalatable subjects mentioned above. I told him I had had one year of Anglo-Saxon at Yale, and that would have to last me all my life. But he said I must have these other linguistic studies. I told him I had the highest respect for those studies and for the professors who taught them; but that they did not interest me. I wished to confine myself to English literature. He was so astounded at this and perhaps thought I was not taking graduate work seriously or was lazy or dilettantish or something, that he became rather severe; and my career at Harvard very, very nearly came to an end on the second day. I finally said, 'Professor Child, I have come to Harvard to study literature under you and your colleagues; if you refuse to allow me to take the studies I came here for, I shall take the first train back to New Haven.' Suddenly his whole manner changed. 'You go ahead and take anything you like. It is refreshing to find a graduate student who knows what he wants.'

Accordingly the first year I took Shakespeare with Professor Child; the History and Principles of English Versification, with Dean L.B.R. Briggs (God bless his heart!); Elizabethan Drama, with Mr. George Pierce Baker, who nearly forty years later was to be my colleague at Yale and Head of the Department of Drama; and a course in research in eighteenth century literature, where I reported my results every week or so to Professor Barrett Wendell. In the following year I took Chaucer under Professor Kittredge; Elizabethan literature (outside drama) under Professor Wendell; and English literature of the seventeenth century, under Dean Briggs.

This was the last year of my life that I was exclusively a student; I remember what a strange sensation it was in June 1891, when, on taking my examinations on the year's work at Harvard, I reflected that I had been going to school and taking examinations from the age of three to the age of twenty-six, and now I should never have to take an exam again! One chapter in my life had closed. Preparation was over. The professional work of my life would begin in the Autumn.

Although this was my last year as a registered student, it was the only year when I had been able to concentrate on my favourite studies; thus, until my breakdown in health, it was the happiest year of my life since my Freshman year at Yale. As an undergraduate at Yale, there were hardly any courses in English literature; and even in the Yale Graduate School, there were not sufficient courses in English, so that I took philosophy, history, and economics as well. But now, at Harvard, I had only the studies I wanted. My eyes grew better all the time, and although I lived like a hermit, had hardly any exercise and no recreation, I was happy.

Once more, as has so often happened in my life, realization was better than anticipation. I went to Harvard as an experiment, thinking it would be good for me, but not expecting to enjoy it. It was like a new lease of life. I felt like Andrea del Sarto at the court of François Premier. There was a keen intellectual atmosphere created not only by the members of the English Department, but by a Department of Philosophy which I suppose was the most brilliant that has ever existed—William James, Josiah Royce, George Santayana, George Herbert Palmer, Hugo Münsterberg; I knew these men and heard them give public lectures. On Sunday afternoons I went occasionally to the house of Professor Nathaniel Shaler, who was a brilliant talker on anything and everything; Charles Eliot Norton was in his prime, and his *obiter dicta* in his famous course in Fine Arts were reported all around the place. There was a vitality indescribable. Bliss was it in that dawn to be alive.

At our eating table in Memorial Hall, we had good conversation. My seatmate was John Matthews Manly of South Carolina, now one of the foremost English scholars in the world. Other men were Charles Davenport, now the famous biologist, and Charles M. Bakewell, subsequently my colleague at Yale and a member of Congress. Nearly all the men were from the South, and they were so good to this particular Yankee that they elected me an honorary member of the Southern Club and on the occasion when they gave a public dinner to Thomas Nelson Page and Hopkinson Smith, I was the only Northern man present. I remember how queer old Professor Toy looked with his enormous white beard; because while he might have been the model for a portrait of Hosea, his cigarette in that beard seemed incongruous. The Southern students at my Harvard table were Logan H. Roots, now Bishop in China; Andrew Patterson, later Dean at the University of North Carolina; David Houston, later University President and member of President Wilson's cabinet; Francis Caffey, now United States District Judge for Southern New York; William J. Battle, later Dean at the University of Texas; Augustus Long, later of the English Department at Princeton; and Collier Cobb, later Professor of Geology at the University of North Carolina. These Southern young gentlemen became my most intimate friends, and perhaps being such an unmitigated 'damyankee' I may have been in a way as good for them as they certainly were for me. One day, with that brilliant young Southerner, whose early death was such a loss to his country, William G. Brown, we all walked together from Cambridge to Salem, and visited the historical places.

Other men at the table and good friends of mine were Brace Chittenden, later a professor of Mathematics, and his brother Percy, one of the very few who did not enter academic life; Dickinson Sargent Miller, later Professor of Philosophy; his eccentric friend Hodder, afterwards professor at Bryn Mawr; and William E. Ritter, later Professor of Zoology at the University of California.

The Harvard professor with whom I came most closely in contact was Barrett Wendell; we became intimate friends; he was very kind to me, and I shall always think of him with grateful affection. In many ways he was the most peculiar man on the Harvard Faculty and President

Eliot waited a good many years before promoting him to a full professorship. It speaks well for Harvard—it is indeed meant by me to be the highest possible compliment to Harvard, both to the authorities and to the undergraduates—that in the nineties Harvard was the only university in America that could or would have kept Wendell. There have been some universities (not Yale and not Harvard) where the oddities, indiscretions, and other characteristics of professors as revealed in the classroom have been a source of revenue to students whose love of money has been more acute than their sense of honour. These students, ignoring the fact that things said in the classroom are not for publication, have furnished to the papers sensational statements made or supposed to be made by their teachers; and as college professors are generally 'news,' these indiscretions form what the newspapers call a 'story.' To the everlasting credit of Harvard undergraduates, I never knew of a single one of Wendell's remarks or acts being supplied by them for public consumption. They had much good-natured fun with him in the articles and in the pictures of the *Harvard Lampoon*, but that was all in the family; and if there had been any talk of letting Wendell go, these students would have been the first to rise in his defence.

A stranger meeting Barrett Wendell for the first time would have thought he was impossible. He had the most exaggerated 'English accent' I have ever heard either from an Englishman or any one else. He spoke like the stage caricature of an Englishman. Where he originally acquired this accent I do not know; but it had become a part of himself. I never caught him off his guard; nor did I ever hear him speak in any other fashion in the classroom, on the public platform, in general conversation, or in the bosom of his family. On the street people stopped and stared at him, arrested by these strange sounds.

Apparently he never was aware of the attention he commanded.

In describing the exaggerated 'English accent' of some Englishmen, H.G.Wells called it the 'whinnying voice.' I have sometimes wondered if the great Jonathan Swift had not chosen his Houyhnhnms after first hearing the conversation of cultivated Englishmen. Now Wendell had that whinnying voice; beginning very high with a slight stammer, and then descending in a rapid cascade of sound.

Wendell was like the English too, in his love of a cold room. His famous 'office' in Grays 18, in the Harvard Yard, never had steamheat, only an open fire, and even in winter the windows were open; so that later, when we had meetings of the English Faculty there, the aged Professor A.S.Hill, famous as the author of Hill's *Rhetoric*, always wore his fur overcoat.

Wendell's peculiarities seemed at first like affectations; yet I have never known any teacher of English composition who showed more common sense. For many years he carried the all but intolerable burden of reading and correcting themes, day after day. His room was filled with these compositions; they were all over the table and on the chairs, and when he lay down on the sofa, to get a little rest, he used a bunch of themes for a pillow. However picturesque and bizarre his own manner and way of expression, he never tolerated affectation in the compositions of his students. Ruthlessly he combed out of them every bit of 'fine writing,' every trace of insincerity, and taught them how to express themselves clearly and with economy of words. His book *English Composition* is the best treatise on the art of writing I have ever seen, and certainly the only one I read through from first page to last with undiminished interest.

Furthermore, Wendell, although very sensitive, was extraordinarily modest; so modest that it was almost painful;

one hardly knew what to say. At my first interview with him, when I came as a graduate student, he said 'I don't know anything,' and a few days later he said, 'You have probably already taken my measure.' It took me some time to find out what he meant. He meant he felt out of place in a modern German-trained American college Faculty, surrounded as he was by research scholars and philologists. He had never studied Anglo-Saxon, he knew no German, he had never studied for the degree of Doctor of Philosophy, which had in general become the sole gateway to college teaching. But he knew English literature thoroughly, was an admirable critic, and was thoroughly at home in the Latin, French, and Italian languages.

On that Harvard English Faculty, one could hardly imagine five men more unlike than Professor Francis Child, A.S.Hill, L.B.R.Briggs, George Lyman Kittredge, and Barrett Wendell. But they got along together beautifully, with mutual respect, admiration, and affection.

During my first year at Harvard I saw Wendell frequently; during the second year I saw him every day. Except at meals, or in the lecture-room, I never saw him when he was not smoking or preparing to smoke; at a time when in many colleges it would have been fatal for a member of the Faculty to take a drink, Wendell insisted on having alcohol—as he called it—with his meals; and how he shocked Professor Coy of Andover, at a school dinner there, by taking a bottle from his pocket! Wendell hated hypocrisy; and he said no one should refrain under any circumstances from drinking at a public dinner, if it was his custom to drink at all.

Probably no man ever loved his children more than he; but he loved also not to show this emotion. I came into his room one day and the following dialogue took place.

P. 'How are your children, Mr. Wendell?'
W. 'Oh, just at this moment I believe they have scarlet fever.'

P. 'Why, that's terrible!'

W. 'Yes, and you know scarlet fever is often followed by Bright's disease, idiocy, and such things.'

P. 'How fearful!'

W. 'Well, that's the sort of thing that lends interest to the game, you know.'

They all got well.

At another time he was explaining to me that he very seldom saw his children, as he left the house so early and came home just at dinner-time, when they had had their supper and had gone to bed.

P. 'Do you really love your children, Mr. Wendell?'

W. (After a long period of consideration) 'Ye-es, but not when the first one came. It was so exceedingly rudimentary.'

Once, when I was in his room, Dean Briggs came in.

B. 'How are you getting on with your book, Wendell?'

W. 'I shall finish it next Sunday.'

B. 'Why, do you work on Sunday?'

W. 'Of course; it's the best day to work; the only day free of interruption.'

B. 'Well, merely putting it on the lowest possible ground, Wendell, the lowest possible ground, that of health, I should think you would find it well to have one day of rest.'

W. 'My dear fellow, that's the highest possible ground.'

He came at my invitation to Yale to speak at the banquet celebrating the sixtieth anniversary of the founding of the *Yale Literary Magazine*. Unfortunately there was one Yale student present who was quite drunk. I introduced Wendell saying that he had consented to come to the enemy's country. Wendell rose and whinnied, 'The enemy's country! My God, what is that?' and immediately the drunken man, catching the pitch with precision, gave loudly a perfect imitation. I suffered agony; Wendell paid no attention to the interruption and went on with an admirable speech.

At the celebration in 1901 of the two hundredth anniversary of the founding of Yale, for which elaborate preparations had been made, we had invited as guests at our house William Dean Howells, Thomas Bailey Aldrich, Dean Briggs, and Professor Wendell. Wendell's *A Literary History of America* had recently appeared and only a short time before the celebration, the *North American Review* contained an article by Howells attacking this book with such severity that it would be impossible for the two men to meet. Howells thought the book was the work of a snob, and being very democratic himself, he said what he thought about it and its author. Fortunately neither Howells nor Wendell knew that the other had been invited; so the University authorities arranged for Howells to go elsewhere, and Mr. and Mrs. Wendell came to us.

Wendell loved life intensely; he loved his family, his home in Boston, his colleagues and students, and his friends in the Tavern Club and elsewhere; and I remember his saying to me on the occasion of this 1901 visit, 'Do you realize we've got only about fifteen more years of all this?'

The well-deserved honours that came in later years were most gratifying to him. The famous Clark lectureship at Cambridge University, his residence for a year in France as Exchange Professor, his election to the American Academy of Arts and Letters. He died in 1921.

It seems trivial enough now, but in the year 1896 Harvard and Yale had some dispute over athletics, so that for a brief interval there was a suspension of contests; in that same year Wendell and I collaborated on an edition of the play *As You Like It* to be used in schools; he wrote the introductory matter and I supplied the notes. At his suggestion, we both signed this dedicatory sentence, written by him.

At a time when such differences as declare themselves between the two oldest colleges of New England are unduly emphasized, it is a singular pleasure to bear part in any work which shall help to show how truly Harvard and Yale are at one.

B.W.
W.L.P.

February, 1896.

Professor L.B.R. Briggs was then about thirty-five and had recently been made Dean of Harvard College. At a little distance he looked like an undergraduate, and to the very end of his long life he had a certain boyish charm. It has been my good fortune to know many men of upright and unselfish and indeed of noble character; I never knew a better man that Dean Briggs. He was a Saint; and his saintliness was equalled by his modesty and his common sense and his effervescent humour. His sympathy for the weaknesses of humanity was matched by his sensitive conscience. Hence he was an ideal Dean. He loved the undergraduates and he believed in discipline. He was universally respected by his colleagues and by all classes of students; and some of those whom he expelled from Harvard remained his friends for life. The influence of this man on innumerable individuals cannot be exaggerated.

He was never robust and he had a chronic trouble with his throat. It seems to me he had a sore throat for fifty years. But he allowed nothing to interfere with his duties; and we met him outdoors in the worst of sleety weather, clad in his long overcoat with the flying cape, bent on some errand of duty or unselfishness.

One of the best things in my life was my intimate friendship with Briggs. Just as I always felt ignorant when talking with Professor Kittredge, so I always felt morally unworthy while talking with Dean Briggs; yet both men somehow or other made it easy for me.

After I had been at Harvard as a graduate student two months, I was awarded a Morgan Fellowship, a great honour in itself, and yielding an income of five hundred dollars a year. I did not find out until much later, that Dean Briggs, hearing there was to be a vacancy, had spent an entire afternoon in snow and sleet, walking about Cambridge, calling on various members of the Committee, and obtaining their support for this Fellowship.

Usually, when men are driven by an inflexible sense of duty, they are somewhat grim. The extraordinary thing about Briggs was that although no Puritan was ever more uncompromising, no sinner ever had more personal charm. What Mr. Morse said of John Quincy Adams would apply to Briggs—'the temptation to perform his duty was always strong; and if the duty were a particularly disagreeable one, the temptation became ungovernable.'

When Rollo Brown's *Life of Briggs* was published, I wrote to Briggs about it; and received the reply, 'I told him to wait until after my death and then not to do it.'

When Briggs reached the age limit of retirement and became Professor Emeritus, he carried out a plan that I recommend to all lonesome or unoccupied Emeriti. I would do it myself if I were not so busy. He elected two courses in the classics at Harvard exactly as if he were an undergraduate, attended every class exercise, and faithfully prepared every lesson.

As I was a graduate of Yale and had had comparatively little training in English studies, and at Harvard was competing with graduate students who had had four years of English, I expected to be outstripped by some of my competitors. Imagine my satisfaction, then, at the end of the year in June, when the marks of all the students were printed for distribution, to discover that not only did I have an 'A' in all four of my graduate courses, but that in three of them, I was the only person with this distinction. One of my fellow-students, now a professor of English, said to me, 'Damn you! it's owing entirely to you that I got a B instead of an A. I was told that in any ordinary year my work was good enough to have won an A; but that yours was so much better he had to put you in a class by yourself.'

In the Shakespeare course Professor Child addressed the class just before returning the bluebooks containing our exam papers, which he had himself corrected, annotated, and marked. He said, 'Many of you no doubt think you are going to get a good mark; but in this exam absolute accuracy is essential; I cannot give a high mark except to those papers that show a thorough and precise knowledge.' I thought to myself, 'This means that probably the best I can expect is a C plus.' My book was handed back to me. It was marked A, and under this letter Professor Child had written

Excellent book!

And it was legible, so there could be no mistake. His handwriting was so bad that once a student, on receiving a composition back from him, said, 'Professor Child, I did not think my composition was anything remarkable, but was it so horrible as all this?' 'What do you mean?' asked the professor. 'Why, Sir, look; at the end of my composition you have written *My God*!' Child looked at it and said, 'That isn't *My God*; that's *Very Good*.'

During my first year at Harvard I lived more like a recluse than ever before or since. I worked three hours a day on my doctor's thesis; then I had in addition the regular courses of study to carry through. As soon as I had finished a meal in Memorial Hall, I returned directly to my room or went into the College Library. Feeling that such a life was too selfish, I used to go on Sunday mornings with Logan Roots and Francis Caffey and a few others to the Boston docks where we visited the ships, and attempted some evangelistic and other helpful work with the sailors. Usually we were received kindly by these men, though with some bewilderment mixed with commiseration; and once we were emphatically told by a sea-captain to get out and stay out. Although this was rather humiliating, I secretly sympathized with him. He had not asked us to call.

The other philanthropic work I did was in connexion with the Boston Associated Charities. I was assigned to take charge of a destitute family, to visit them regularly, and find out their needs and how much assistance was necessary. I kept this up for two years and how I did hate it! But the people in charge of the organization were invariably kind to me, and when I told them that I could not see that I was accomplishing anything, they assured me that I was. The poor family at any rate were always affectionate, and the Irish widowed mother paid me a charming compliment, saying, 'I hope you'll live till I'm tired of yer!'

My room at 22 Winthrop Street faced the North; no ray of sunlight ever entered it. It was imperfectly heated by a defective furnace in winter, as the poor woman who kept the house could not afford sufficient fuel. Studying hour after hour in this gloomy room I acquired malaria, which I had not had for five or six years. Every day I suffered from what Burton is always talking about in *The Anatomy of Melancholy*—flushing and chills. I had what the country people used to call 'dumb ager.' I felt my face and head getting hot and chills creeping up my spine. I was taking no exercise and had no recreation. I was absorbed only in study, determined to finish my thesis by the first of May.

A woman on the other side of the double house, whose room was next to mine, was learning both to sing and to play the piano. When her voice became exhausted she rested it by her piano exercises until it was sufficiently refreshed to begin singing again.

In addition to these difficulties, the husband of the woman who was my landlady was dying of tuberculosis. This was in the year 1891, and none of us knew—certainly not his physician—what to do. What they actually did was to keep the windows of his room where he sat all day hermetically sealed so that no draught could injure him. Being entirely ignorant of the danger of infection, I used to go into this close and stuffy room, and sit by this man's side and have long talks with him. I must have inhaled ten thousand germs but nothing happened to me; he was evidently dying, and did die while I was staying in the house.

In the early Spring, obsessed by the work I was doing on my Doctor's thesis and by the fear that I should not finish it in time, I became afflicted with insomnia. This became so severe and so long-continued that finally I went back to my parents' house in New Haven to rest. But what people need who suffer from sleeplessness is not rest but diversion; and there was no diversion. I suffered so much that I really do not care to write about it. But it was a remark made by Professor Beers of Yale that did me more good than any physician or any medicine. I went to him and said that I had hoped to have my thesis completed by the first of May, which was the time for submitting it, but that I feared I should have to give up my degree that year, as I was in such poor health. He merely remarked, 'You have already done enough work on your thesis to deserve your degree, and you will get it anyway. Hand in your incomplete work at the proper time, and you will receive your degree at Commencement. You can polish it and if necessary add to it next year.' I do not think that he ever knew what he did for me; for I might have had a complete and prolonged breakdown.

But his statement took a tremendous load off my mind. I returned to Harvard immediately, and although I felt that I wrote that thesis not in ink but in blood, I finished it some time before the date, and did not have to ask any favours.

During those weeks of depression, before temporarily

giving up and going to New Haven for rest, and while at
New Haven, although in no danger of suicide, I constantly
longed to die. If any robber then had pointed a pistol at me
in the night, I should have regarded him as my best friend.
I am always sympathetic with sufferers from 'nerves' or
from melancholia or depression, for I know the particular
part of hell they are in. And I feel when any young person
commits suicide that if someone could only have been with
him or if he could only have got through that month of
misery, he might have had before him forty or fifty years
of happiness.

DR. EDWARD CONSTANT SEGUIN (1843–98)

One day in the early summer of 1891, while I was slowly
recovering, I wrote to Dr. Seguin in New York, asking for
an appointment. He telegraphed that he was sailing for
Europe on the next day; he could see me if I called early in
the morning. I got to his house before his office was opened,
and was the first in what soon became a long line of patients. I was tremendously impressed in the hour's conversation with him. He apparently took a great interest in
my case, and asked if I had, when in good health, been a
sound sleeper. I told him that never since childhood had I
slept both long and well and that only once in my life had
I slept until nine o'clock in the morning. 'You are a man
who requires comparatively little sleep; it is an error for
you to go to bed early. Do not go to bed before midnight;
but get up early.'

As I was going to Harvard that autumn to begin my
work as a teacher and would have a college room, he told
me to be sure and have a roommate so that I would never
be alone at night. He urged me also to have a lighted
candle always by the bedside (electric lights were very
rare then) because one usually has to get up to extinguish
a gas light and that brings one too fully awake. 'Read

until you are sleepy, the moment you feel sleepiness blow out the candle, and if you wake in the night, read some more.' Then he gave me a prescription of sulphonal, telling me not to use it except for severe and prolonged insomnia. Merely talking with Dr. Seguin did me so much good that I took no drug for several weeks and then used his prescription only once. There was something about him that seemed to give me new courage and strength.

I did not know then of the terrific tragedy he had suffered about nine years before, when his wife killed herself and her three small children, but that tragedy lent additional force to his remarks when I later reflected on them. He said with quiet emphasis, 'I am a great believer in the power of the human will. The will can be cultivated and strengthened so that one can actually control not only one's conduct but one's thoughts. For example, I can decide when I go to bed the exact hour when it is necessary for me to wake and I wake exactly at that hour; whether it is four or five or seven or eight. I never have to be called no matter how necessary or important it may be for me to get up at a certain hour, and I have never used an alarm clock.'

I tried this myself but the difficulty was that if it were necessary for me to rise at five or six to catch a train or for any other reason, and I depended on my will, I always woke up two or three hours too soon.

Dr. Seguin made as great an impression on me as did any specialist I have ever consulted. He was born in Paris, the son of a distinguished psychiatrist. His father brought him to the United States when he was seven. He was a graduate of the College of Physicians and Surgeons in New York and he became profoundly interested in the study of nervous diseases. He went to Paris in 1869 and studied under the greatest specialists in the world, Charcot and others. In 1894, three years after I had consulted him, he had the first symptoms of an illness of the brain. He knew it was fatal although he lived four years. He made a special study of his own disease for the benefit of others.

A curious, disagreeable, and for many years inexplicable effect of taking sulphonal or any of its kindred soporifics I will mention, because although I feel sure it is unusual, there may be others who are similarly affected and do not know the cause.

I took one dose of the sulphonal in a glass of hot milk at four in the afternoon. I noticed absolutely no effect. I went out and about as usual, took a walk with a friend that evening, and went to bed without feeling sleepy at ten. But the next moment (as it seemed) it was seven in the morning; it was the best night's sleep I had had in years, and I experienced no unpleasant effects.

Nearly ten years later when I was in London, I had a prolonged case of sleeplessness, and took sulphonal from a new prescription. In a few days I began to itch terribly; far worse it was than mosquito or flea bites. Then big discoloured blotches broke out on my ankles and wrists. I consulted a London physician, a good general practitioner. He did not use the word but it was clear he thought I had syphilis. He told me my condition was serious; he thought I was going to be an invalid. I was certain it was not syphilis, because never in my life have I run any chance of taking it; I told the physician that in two weeks I was planning a bicycle trip, and he said that would be entirely out of the question. Well, I knew he was mistaken. In a few days the trouble entirely disappeared and I was perfectly well. Three years later I took some sulphonal with exactly the same result; but I did not connect the itching and blotches with the sleep-mixture. It never occurred to me. Some years after that, the same thing happened again; and being at that time in the company of one of the most distinguished physicians in the world, Dr. William Welch of Johns Hopkins, I showed him the blotches on my wrist, and asked him if he knew of any cause for such things. He was entirely at a loss to account for them; I doubt if even in his long practice, he had ever seen anything just like them. It is possible, of course, that *he* thought I had syphilis. He had no solution to offer and no remedy.

But a few years after that, the same result following the same medicine, I discovered the cause for myself. I suddenly remembered that whenever in previous years I had taken sulphonal or trional or anything like that, it was followed by this horrible itching and hideous blotches. I knew then that I must never take these things, for the results of the remedy, although temporary, were worse than the malady.

Yet in conversation since then with many excellent physicians, it is clear to me that they are for the most part unacquainted with the cause of these symptoms, so that I think such results are rare. But if some other persons have had them, heaven only knows what remedies the doctors have prescribed! The medicines—both external and internal—prescribed for me by that London physician did no good at all.

The Yale and Harvard Commencements in the year 1891 came on the same day; and on that day I received the degree of Master of Arts from Harvard and Doctor of Philosophy from Yale. Although I had looked forward to the doctorate for years I decided to take my degree in person at Harvard; for I had already had one degree at Yale and had never seen a Harvard Commencement. So on that June day, in Sanders Theatre at Cambridge I received my diploma from President Eliot and became an alumnus of Harvard as well as of Yale.

I had determined to stay at Harvard another year; and in the Spring of 1891 I had been reappointed to the Morgan Fellowship. But only a few days after receiving this honour, Professor Wendell asked me if I would be his Assistant during the coming year and read all the daily themes in his course which was known as English twelve, at a salary of six hundred dollars. There were two reasons—apart from the pleasure of the work and Wendell's company—which induced me to accept. It was a six hundred dollars clear because tuition was free to teachers; this would turn out therefore to be two hundred and fifty more dollars than I should have from the Fellowship. But the chief reason was that it made me a member of the Harvard English Department, on the teaching staff. I had no position elsewhere, thought it probable that I should get a job in some Western university, and I could get a better position if I went from the Harvard Faculty rather than as a student without experience.

All appointments at Harvard—great and small—were made by President Eliot; and I had an interesting interview with him. Although a good many Yale graduates went to the Harvard Law and Medical Schools, very few went there for anything else; he was interested in the reasons that brought me to the Harvard Graduate School and in my impressions of the life there. He asked me many questions, and told me I was appointed. I asked him 'Is my title to be Assistant or Instructor?' 'It will be Assistant.' 'But, Sir, it will be a great deal better for me if I can have the name *Instructor*; for I suppose this will be my only year at Harvard. I must be on the lookout for a full-time teaching position somewhere, and if I can call myself an Instructor at Harvard, it will be of great value.' He smiled and said 'Your title will be Assistant.' 'But, Sir, the man who has just had this very same job is called on the Catalogue Instructor.' 'No he isn't, he is Assistant.' 'If you will look him up, Sir, you will see that he is Instructor.' He rang and ordered a copy of the Catalogue brought to him. 'To my very great surprise, Mr. Phelps, I find you are right; he is called Instructor. It must have been an error, and I will see that it never happens again.' Then we both laughed.

Thus I began my work in the Autumn at Harvard as Assistant in English; but after about three weeks, I received a letter from Yale, informing me that I had been appointed Instructor in English at Yale, and suggesting that I begin my work immediately. During the two years preceding, I had hoped for this appointment more than for anything else. Now I felt it had come too late. I was settled in my room at Harvard, 54 Thayer Hall in the College Yard, I had begun my work as a member of the Harvard teaching force, and although I felt that if I refused this Yale offer it would kill my chances of ever going there, it seemed to me right to refuse.

I called on President Eliot. He was rather astonished at my receiving such an offer in the midst of term, and this is what he said: 'You are entirely free to go if you wish; whenever Harvard appoints a man for a certain term, the University is bound, but the man is not. The University must keep you and pay you till the expiration of your term, but every man who teaches at Harvard is free to go anywhere else, at any moment, and without notice. I will therefore not urge you to stay; but if you do decide to stay at Harvard, we shall raise your salary to the amount equal to that of the Yale offer, for which of course you will do some more work.'

'*And my title will be Instructor?*'

He laughed and said 'Your title will be Instructor.' I replied, 'I am grateful for your kindness and I shall stay this year at Harvard.' So before the first of November my salary was raised to one thousand dollars (my college room was free) and my title was Instructor in English.

I wrote the Yale authorities, thanking them for the offer, saying I should have accepted had it been offered before the opening of the term, explaining that I felt I should now remain for the present year where I was. And when I had posted that letter, I felt that I should never have the chance to teach at Yale.

Getting my roommate that second year at Harvard was rather interesting. Several men I had met at Harvard asked if I would room with them, but for various reasons I declined. Then a man from Bucknell University said a friend of his was coming to Harvard from that college to spend his Senior year, and take the Bachelor's degree the following June. He spoke in the highest terms of the great ability of this young man, added that owing to his aggressive personality he might be difficult to get along with, but if I waived that, I should find him interesting. I have never seen anyone I could not get along with, so I wrote a letter to him, remembering that Schopenhauer had said that a man's character is more clearly revealed by a letter than by an interview. His name was Ralph Charles Henry Catterall.

The letter I received pleased me; and we immediately agreed to become roommates at Harvard. I never saw him until we were in the room together. The following September (1891) he reached Cambridge a few hours before me, and when I entered the room, there he was; we introduced ourselves, and from that moment until he died in my house in Michigan in 1914 there was no cloud on our friendship. We were absolutely congenial. He was specializing in history, saying he loved literature too much to make the study of it professional. He had an astonishingly good memory. If I quoted any passage from English poetry, he immediately gave chapter and verse. He had an exceedingly interesting mind; I was always happy and contented in his company, and it pleases me to remember that his becoming my roommate changed the course of his life. I introduced him in Boston to the girl who became his wife. At the end of the college year, I wrote to President Harper of Chicago, urging him to grant Catterall a fellowship in the Graduate School. This was given; Catterall went there, took his doctor's degree, became Instructor and Assistant Professor of History at the University of Chicago, and some years later was called to a full professorship at Cornell, where he had enormous success as a teacher and as a member of the community. He made a tremendous impression on the students. His wife was Helen Honor Tunnicliff of Macomb, Illinois; she had studied law at the University, had taken her degree, and was an accomplished musician. I had met her while she was studying music in Boston. They were married in 1896 and often visited us in our country home in Michigan. We spent part of our Sabbatical year with them in Paris in 1903. In 1912, while travelling in Europe, he had a stroke; from this he seemed to have recovered, and with his son, Ralph T. Catterall, now a lawyer in Richmond, Virginia, he came to our house in Michigan in July 1914. On that first evening he seemed to be in excellent health, but during the night a second stroke came and in two days he was dead.

He was one of the most interesting men I have ever known; and one of the most brilliant.

One day, near the close of my first year at Harvard, Charles Davenport, now the famous biologist, asked me if I would accept the Presidency of the Harvard Graduate Club. This was a club of graduate students, who had regular meetings for social and intellectual purposes, and invited members of the Faculty to address them. I felt flattered and accepted with alacrity. I enjoyed my administration; it brought me into close contact with students in a variety of departments and also with some distinguished men who spoke to us. During the year, I secured as speakers President Eliot, Charles Eliot Norton, Thomas Sergeant Perry of Boston, Frank Tarbell, and others. President

Eliot seemed surprised that the Presidency, instead of being given to one of the two hundred Harvard graduates, was given to the only Yale man in the Harvard Graduate School; and this led to frequent and rather intimate conversations with him.

One of the most interesting young men on the Harvard Faculty was Lewis Gates, Instructor in English. He was a recluse; he lived in his room on the Yard, never took any exercise, never went into society, and stayed up nearly all night with his books. His only release from his studies was music; he played the piano well, and had a good knowledge of instrumentation. He was one of the best classroom lecturers at Harvard; and I think would have become one of the distinguished literary scholars of America, if it had not been for the tragic mental disease that eclipsed his splendid intelligence. I told Wendell how much I admired Gates, and asked some questions about him. Wendell replied that while everyone admired Gates, no one knew him; that it was impossible to know him; that he resisted every attempt at acquaintance. It seemed to me that while Gates doubtless valued his independence, his seclusion was the result of shyness. I therefore called upon him, and discovering his love of music, proposed that we go to the opera together. We became intimate friends; several times we went to Grand Opera in Boston and walked back to Cambridge at one o'clock in the morning, a good time for intimate talk. I shall never forget those conversations. I became immensely fond of him, and I really think I brought a little happiness into his solitary existence. I have found very often that men who are said to be averse to society or sour-minded, are really only shy; I have never known one who did not gratefully and affectionately respond to friendly advances.

One night at the close of *Lohengrin*, as Jean de Reszké departed for the magic land whence he had come, Gates whispered to me, 'There goes the Ideal! it can never stay!'

A few years later, being in Cambridge for the day, I called on Gates, and to my amazement found him with a tennis racket in his hand; 'Why, I thought you hated all games.' 'I cannot begin to tell you how I hate them; I loathe tennis; but the doctor tells me I must let up on work, and have some exercise every day.' He looked very despondent; it was the beginning of his decline.

I made the most of the propinquity of Boston. Although my financial resources were slender, I never missed a good opportunity at the theatre, at concerts, and at the opera. During the season of 1890–91, Booth and Barrett made a prolonged stay, and I heard them in *Julius Caesar*, *Othello*, and other plays. With about forty other Harvard students, I acted as supe, being a Roman senator, one of the 'skin' guards, a gentleman-in-waiting on Desdemona, etc. Lawrence Barrett was exceedingly kind to us. While waiting to go on, he talked to us in the wings about Harvard, about our plans for the future, and was most gracious. The regular Boston stage hand who had us in charge was an abominable and foul-mouthed ruffian. We hardly knew what to do with him; but once, just as Mr. Barrett was going on as Cassius, and this brute shoved three or four of us out of his way, he immediately took the man by the shoulder and said, 'It is fortunate that you are dealing with young gentlemen; if they were as brutal and bestial as you are, they might seriously injure you; the only thing that saves you is their good breeding. I advise you not to put it to any further strain.' The bully was cowed and slunk off. It was as dramatic as anything on the stage. We were all in the wings, the play was going on; there was Mr. Barrett in full Roman armour, speaking in an impressive whisper to this tough, while we, clad as ancient Romans, looked on in amazement.

Lawrence Barrett's greatest part was Cassius; he completely dominated the stage in the famous tent scene. As Othello he was also very fine. But as Iago—for one night Booth and Barrett exchanged roles—he was curiously miscast. He almost never took that part; the great combination was Barrett's Othello and Booth's Iago. However, he noticed everything; one of us, as a Roman senator, kept his eyeglasses on, and Mr. Barrett whispered in the midst of the scene while we were all on the stage, 'Take off those eyeglasses!'

A popular slogan at Harvard in those days was 'To Hell with Yale!' Some Harvard Freshmen had it printed on their stationery. One evening, when I went in with about forty Harvard students to supe in *Julius Caesar*, one of the actors, who knew more about acting than about undergraduates, coached us in the wings. 'Remember you are the Roman mob; be rough, unruly, turbulent, jostle each other!' Imagine saying that to a group of students. No sooner had we got on the stage than our 'mob' in the Forum degenerated into a free fight; we slugged and shoved each other unmercifully. The actor who had coached us looked from the wings aghast at his too faithful pupils; he kept shaking his fist at us and stage-whispering 'You damn fools! you damn fools! behave yourselves! what the hell do you think you are?' This roused us to fresh efforts; and the audience at all events showed no lack of appreciation. I thought we were going to steal the show.

This same actor had told us that when Mark Antony mentioned the will of Caesar, we were to shout hoarsely in unison,

We'll hear the will! we'll hear the will!

I cannot say whether these Harvard students had deliberately prepared the following effect, or whether one happened to say it and the others joined in; but whether planned or impromptu, no sooner had Antony mentioned the will, than these rascally academic supes all shouted

To Hell with Yale! to Hell with Yale!

If the essence of humour be incongruity, I do not know of any more incongruous spectacle than this mob, clad in Roman togas, shouting that famous slogan. The audience in the first seven or eight rows, hearing it distinctly, went into convulsions.

I was selected among the supes as one of six, called the 'skin guards,' as we were dressed only in rough, furry, and horribly filthy skins, to carry the dead body of Brutus from the stage. We had of course the utmost reverence for the great Edwin Booth; and I am glad to remember that in this rather difficult undertaking we made no mistake. In full view of the audience we picked him up, and carried him tenderly back into the wings, and deposited him in a large armchair. He put his hand affectionately on my shoulder and said, 'Well done, boys!' which made us very proud. Thus I have not only appeared on the professional stage with Edwin Booth but have literally supported him.

I attended two meetings of the Harvard Religious Union, a group of undergraduate and graduate students who met to discuss matters concerning religion. At the first meeting, Professor Toy, the famous scholar in the Semitic languages, who I believe taught in the Harvard Divinity School as well as in the Graduate School, was the speaker of the evening. He threw overboard everything usually associated with Christian theology. In answering questions from the audience, one student asked 'Do you believe in prayer?' to which, after some consideration, Professor Toy replied 'No; prayer is unscientific; at any rate, if any words are used. Perhaps the nearest approach to a true prayer would be a sigh.'

Yet at another meeting, Professor George Herbert Palmer was the speaker. He defended belief in the miracles recorded in the New Testament, saying he thought there was a real difference between those in the Gospels and those in the books of the Old Testament. A man might rationally reject the latter, and yet believe in the stories of the Gospels.

With reference to Professor Toy's remarks on prayer, there was a story current at Harvard in my time, which may be apocryphal, and yet is pertinent and amusing. The number of students in the Divinity School was so small that about half the rooms in the dormitory were occupied by Sophomores in the College. The Divinity students were often shocked by the alcoholic enthusiasm of Sophomores, returning from Boston late at night; but the shock was nothing to that received by the Sophomores, when they asked the candidates for the Christian ministry about their religious beliefs. At the end of the year, the Sophomores, on being asked if they wanted to continue occupying rooms in the same building with the Divinity men, answered, 'No! we don't want to room with those damned atheists!'

The professors in the Philosophical Department were so distinguished that there was general and frequent discussion of philosophical questions by undergraduates and indeed by all members of the academic community. It was announced that Professor Royce would give a series of lectures on metaphysics; on the opening night the spacious hall was so crowded that many were standing and many could not get in at all; the second lecture was given in a much larger room with the same result; all the subsequent lectures in the series were given in Sanders Theatre.

Although I shall always be grateful to Harvard for giving me an appointment as Instructor, and although my year of teaching was advantageous to me in every way, nothing would have induced me to consider a reappointment. I did not believe in the Harvard system of compulsory English compositions or in the enormous labour required of the instructors. The only subject required of Harvard undergraduates was the writing of compositions; this was required of every Freshman, every Sophomore, and at least for part of the year, of every Junior. The result was that a large number of men on the Faculty spent nearly all their time and energy in reading and correcting these themes; it seemed to me that this work was not University work at all, and that any primary schoolma'am would probably have been more efficient in the correcting job. That a man should graduate from Harvard with honours, spend two years in advanced study in the Graduate School, then a year of research in Europe—only to correct spelling, grammar, paragraphing, etc., seemed to me a hideous waste of time and energy. Furthermore, although many of these Freshmen and Sophomores wrote abominably when forced to sit in a room and compose a theme on an assigned subject, whenever they wrote a letter asking excuse on account of sickness, their style was correct and respectable. I knew of no work anywhere that so well illustrated the law of diminishing returns as this forced English composition.

I believed then and I believe now, that *elective courses* in advanced composition for men who wished to cultivate the art of writing and loved it, were exceedingly valuable; there were such courses at Harvard offered to picked men by Professor Briggs and Professor Wendell which were most profitable. After I had taught at Yale a few years, I sent up to Professor Wendell a collection of themes written by my Yale Sophomores, in connexion with their studies in English literature; these men had never received any college training in English composition; but I felt sure that technically their themes would be as good as those written by Harvard Sophomores, though the latter were thoroughly trained in technical composition. Mr. Wendell read them and wrote me that they were in every way equal to the work of Harvard Sophomores.

The only men on the Harvard English Faculty who were excused from reading themes were Professor Child and Professor Kittredge; and these men, with Wendell, did not believe in the required system. The most bitter expressions came from the venerable Professor Child, usually regarded as the foremost English scholar in America. For many years he had been forced to read hundreds and hundreds of undergraduate compulsory compositions; he said the system was bad for both students and teachers. He regretted the enormous amount of time and energy he had thus wasted. One day I met him in the Yard, and he asked me what I was doing; I replied, 'Reading themes.' He looked at me affectionately and said, 'Don't spoil your youth.'

During the entire academic year at Harvard, I read more than eight hundred themes every week; I read all day and a good part of the night. Once I was sick for two days, and a substitute read for me, because even one day's lapse made it impossible to keep up.

Now I do not regret this one year; far from it. I had the most pleasant associations with my colleagues on the Harvard Faculty, and my principal work brought me into close contact with one hundred and thirty representative Harvard Juniors and Seniors. Professor Wendell gave a course, where the men wrote long themes for him every two weeks and a one-page theme every day. My job was to read the dailies; and as these students wrote a diary I became intimately acquainted with them; furthermore, many came to see me for individual conferences. A splendid group of young men—frank, honest, humorous, they wrote of their daily doings and of their thoughts on all subjects. It was a great experience for me—I became devotedly attached to these Harvard undergraduates.

Professor Briggs said I was the only man in the world intimately acquainted with both Harvard and Yale undergraduates. Some of these men became lifelong friends. Frederick Winsor, Head of the Middlesex School at Concord; Oswald Garrison Villard, editor of the New York *Nation*; David D. Wells, a young novelist who died at the dawn of his fame; H. G. Pearson, Professor at the Massachusetts Institute of Technology; De Lancey Howe, author of *The Star of Umbria* and other books.

Among my Sophomore theme-writers, I gave out at the end of the year only two 'A's;' one of these to Lindsay Todd Damon, now Professor of English at Brown University; the other to Edwin F. Edgett, later the accomplished literary editor of the *Boston Transcript*.

Another great delight of that year of teaching was the weekly meeting of the English instructors in Wendell's room at Grays 18—A. S. Hill, Briggs, Gates, Lathrop, Hurlbut, Arthur Carey. We had good times discussing the work.

PRESIDENT HARPER

During that year of 1891-2, Doctor W. R. Harper was travelling about the country, visiting all the Universities, selecting men for his Faculty for the new University of Chicago, which was to open in the Autumn of 1892. There was a fluttering in academic roosts, whenever it was rumoured he was coming; for he offered to Heads of Departments the then extraordinary salary of seven thousand dollars; and there were many stories of fabulous things that were going to happen. I spent a whole day with him at Harvard and accompanied him on his successful expedition to Newton, where he captured Professor Burton, a Biblical scholar. President Harper offered me an instructorship at

fifteen hundred dollars, which I accepted. Two months
later I received an offer from Denison University at Granville, Ohio, at eighteen hundred, with living expenses fifty
per cent lower. I wrote to President Harper about this, and
I gathered from his reply that I was entirely free to accept
that offer if I wished. I declined it. In the Spring I was
asked by President Dwight of Yale to come to New Haven
for a conference. He immediately offered me fifteen hundred dollars, with the stipulation that I should not be required to do any teaching of English composition, but only
of literature. He said however, 'You must decide now, on
the spot, whether you will or will not take this position; I
do not want you to go to President Harper, and then come
back here, with a larger offer from him.' I replied, 'I will
take the position.' I began work that year, September 1892,
and remained at Yale forty-one years, automatically becoming Emeritus in June 1933.

When I wrote to Doctor Harper, I got a telegram telling
me not to accept the Yale offer until I had talked with
him; but I explained it was settled. He did not like this,
but I wrote him that I had fully understood from our correspondence on the Denison matter, that I was free to accept any offer. Thus the offer from Denison University,
in all probability, changed the course of my life. If I had
not had Dr. Harper's letter as a precedent, I should of
course have felt bound not to accept the offer from Yale
until I had communicated with him; he might have told
me that I was not free to go; thus I should have begun
teaching at the University of Chicago, and might never
have received another offer from Yale. Or if I had, the financial inducements at Chicago would perhaps have been so
great that I should have felt compelled to remain there.

William Rainey Harper, the organizer and first President
of the University of Chicago, was in educational affairs a
man of genius. Although he died in his fiftieth year, he had

lived longer than most men. He took his B.A. degree at the age of fourteen, his degree of Doctor of Philosophy at the age of nineteen, and was married in the same year. He was the hardest worker I have ever known, and I have known many. He went to bed at one, and rose at six. He never took a vacation; he played no games, had no hobbies or avocations, and no recreations of any kind. He was always apparently in high spirits, enjoyed himself enormously, and was boiling over with enthusiasm. I suppose there never was a greater teacher. For some years he was on the Yale Faculty, teaching Hebrew to the Divinity students and the English Bible to the undergraduates. He revolutionized the study of the Bible in America; and gave courses of public lectures on the subject at various universities and large cities. His students were aflame with enthusiasm. He started more young men studying the Hebrew language than any ten teachers have ever done before or since. He made them think the Hebrew language was more important than any other subject, ancient or modern. I asked him once how many times he had taught the first verse of the Hebrew Bible; and I forget how many thousand times he mentioned. I asked, 'Are you always full of enthusiasm for it?' 'Not always; but when I am not enthusiastic, I create the enthusiasm.'

He was tremendously happy in his home life. He told me that he was married at the age of nineteen, with no resources. 'During the first few years of our married life, there were a number of times when neither my wife nor I was able to write a letter, because we could not buy a postage stamp. But we never regretted the marriage.'

To enter any of the classes he taught at the Divinity School was a memorable experience. The students crowded into the room as eagerly as men go to a great athletic contest or to hear a great opera singer.

No other man could have accomplished what he brought

to pass at the University of Chicago. Starting with no buildings, no library, no Faculty, no students, in a very few years the University of Chicago became one of the leading universities of the world.

President Harper died of cancer; when the case was hopeless, he exhibited magnificent courage; but his son told me, 'I have never known any man who wanted to live so much as my father.' For several months he lingered, giving everyone an example of faith and uncomplaining cheerfulness.

I saw him often during his years of administration; he was always the same—full of gusto. Before any plans were known, and while he was engaged in active teaching at Yale and I was a student there, he had astonished me one day, when I was alone with him, by telling me that Mr. Rockefeller had provided funds for the founding of a great American university; then he asked, as if my opinion were important (it was a way he had with everyone) 'Where should this University be founded?' I replied without any hesitation, 'Chicago.' 'Oh, no,' he said, 'by no means; that's not the place at all. Try again.' 'Well, then,' I said, 'if Chicago is impossible, some place in the Mississippi valley.' 'Why, you're still further off. Can't you do better than that?' 'No, I give it up.' Then Doctor Harper said, 'There is only one place in America for this new University, if it is to be the institution I have in mind; it must be in New York City.' I was amazed. 'New York? Why, there are three great universities there now.' 'All the better,' said he, 'all the better.' What caused the change in plans I never knew; but once Chicago was selected, 'there is no place in the world like Chicago!'

In some way, President Harper combined immense courage and unlimited energy with extraordinary modesty. It was a rare combination of assurance of success without even the faintest trace of conceit. He always had what the poet Vaughan called high humility. A very beautiful character.

31

TEACHING AT YALE

I BEGAN regular work as a full-time Instructor in English at Yale in the Autumn of 1892. The College was nearly two hundred years old, but this was the first time that English literature had ever been taught to Freshmen. I was given one-third of the class from September to Christmas, another third from Christmas to Easter, and the last section from Easter to June; so that I was to meet intimately in small divisions, three hours a week, all the members of the incoming class of 1896. I was twenty-seven years old and looked eighteen. When I came to the door of the lecture-room and found it locked, one or two Freshmen waiting there, naturally taking me for a classmate, said 'Oh, the Prof hasn't got here yet.' When I took a key from my pocket and unlocked the door, they looked at me in amazement.

I taught the Freshmen *As You Like It*, *Macbeth*, and *King Henry IV, Part I*. I enjoyed the work unspeakably; and at the end of the Autumn term, when the first alphabetical third of the class found that they were to have no more English until Sophomore year, they sent to me a delegation headed by John Berdan (now Professor of English at Yale) asking me if I would continue to teach a volunteer class in the evening. I agreed to this—though it was an unprecedented thing at Yale. Accordingly for the next three months, I met a large group of Freshmen one evening a week and taught them English poetry of the nineteenth century.

At the end of Freshman year, I was directed to continue the teaching of English to this same class of 1896 in their Sophomore year. It was for Sophomores an elective study, but all except three men took it. I had one-half of the class until February and the second half for the rest of the year. Our friendly and intimate relations were still further strengthened. Then, when they became Juniors, I began to offer elective courses in addition to my work with the lower classes; many took these courses, so that I really taught them for four years. When they graduated in June 1896, they presented me with a large silver cup.

I suppose there has never been a member of the Yale Faculty who knew intimately every member of a large class as I knew these men; and although they are now over sixty, my friendship with them has only been strengthened by time. As it happened, this class, the first I taught at Yale in regular daily work, contributed more men to the Yale Faculty than any other class in Yale's history; so that a considerable number of my first pupils became my colleagues.

The intense affection between these undergraduates and their young teacher was refreshingly exceptional because of the traditional teaching at Yale. To me my methods seemed simply natural and unaffected; to some of my older colleagues on the Faculty they seemed revolutionary, deliberately sensational.

About a year before I began my work at Yale, an older member of the alumni asked me what profession I had chosen, and I said, 'Teaching.' To which he replied, 'Oh, that's too bad. The novelty of the thing will appeal to you during the first year, and you will think it is fine; then you will fall into a rut, teach in a routine fashion like all the rest, and become merely mechanical. Furthermore, you will be cut off from active life among men and women, and will never know anything about the world.'

I have always been glad that I received that challenge before I began work; for I made up my mind then and there that I would never allow myself to become a routine teacher, that I would try to make every recitation an event in the lives of the students, and anyhow, an event in my own life. Despite innumerable errors and shortcomings, I can honestly say that although I have often taught and lectured badly, I have never done it mechanically; and in my last year of teaching, at the age of sixty-eight, I found it as thrilling and delightful as during the earliest days.

During those early days, the students were eighteen and I was twenty-seven; during the last year, the students were twenty and twenty-two and I was sixty-eight. Between us there was that immense gulf of years; in addition to which, the after-war morality and new points of view would seem to make it impossible for the students and me to stand on common ground. Thus, during those last few years, if the undergraduates had regarded me as an amiable anachronism, I should not have liked it, but I should not have resented it. But, as my own enthusiasm for teaching was if anything stronger in old age than in youth, I found—really to my amazement—that my intimate relations with the members of the classes of 1933 and 1934 and 1935 were about what they had been with those of 1896. Perhaps nothing pleased me more than an editorial in the *Yale Daily News* during the Spring of 1933, which said that the students then in college were probably closer to Professor Phelps than had been the men of the early nineties. Whether this were true or not, I loved to hear it!

The reason my teaching in 1892 seemed to my older colleagues revolutionary was that Yale was a place where traditions counted enormously. In the traditional teaching at Yale, formality was the rule. Nearly all the members of the Faculty wore dark clothes, frock coats, high collars; in the classroom their manners had an icy formality;

humour was usually absent, except occasional irony at the expense of a dull student. It was quite possible to attend a class three hours a week for a year, and not have even the remotest conception of the personality of the man behind the desk. The teachers seemed to believe this was the only method by which discipline could be enforced and maintained.

There was a blight, a curse on the teaching, unfortunate both for teachers and pupils. Instructors who were thirty years old had the classroom manner of old men; I remember how astounded I was at discovering that one whom we all believed to be venerable was thirty-eight. These men certainly gave no indication of enjoying teaching; and of course the students found no joy in learning.

I will give two illustrations. There was one of our professors who was like the rest in merely hearing recitations and marking them; he never made comments and never betrayed emotion. One day I happened to meet a lady who was his contemporary, who had known him well when he was an undergraduate. She told me that he was the life of every party, outdoors or in; that whenever there was a picnic or an excursion anywhere, if they could get him, success was assured; that he was the finest and wittiest and most delightful conversationalist she had ever known. I told her she must be thinking of someone else; but no, this was the man. It was incredible. Officially he was one person and on other occasions he was another.

The most extraordinary case however, and yet different from the majority only in degree, was that of a professor whom it was my misfortune to have in Freshman, Sophomore, and Junior year. He never gave the slightest indication of having any human emotion, like sympathy, humour, consideration. He was a remorseless machine in the classroom, holding us down by iron discipline; it was impossible for me or any other student to penetrate the barrier between this man and the class he taught; and there was a steadily disagreeable attitude on his part that made us hate him. If he had died during my undergraduate years, I should have rejoiced greatly. Not only was this man icily contemptuous in the classroom, he made himself obnoxious to the students by interfering with many of their extra-curricular activities; so that for at least thirty years successive generations of undergraduates regarded him with hatred.

It was not until some years after my graduation, and after I had become a member of the Faculty, that I discovered he was generous, kind, considerate. He was also full of fun, delighting in jokes and ridiculous puns. The special papers that he used to write for a club were full of original wit.

Now this man was Jekyll and Hyde. Unofficially he was absolutely lovable; officially he was detestable.

He was a martyr to his theory of discipline. He ought to have been admired and loved by all those generations of youth; and how they would have loved him if he had given them a chance, and how he would have appreciated their affection and their esteem! Instead of that, this tender-hearted man had the tragedy of knowing that year after year he was hated and despised.

I mention these things because they help to explain why my teaching seemed revolutionary and sensational; I simply made up my mind that I should be exactly the same man in the classroom as out of it; there would be no detectable difference. I would assume that the undergraduates and I were equally interested in the subject, and that we were studying it together. Thus I was not sensational; I was natural.

But as in the old days of rhetorical oratory, when any exceptional individual spoke from the platform in a natural, easy, conversational manner, it seemed astounding; when

an actor on the stage, dispensing with conventional mannerisms, spoke and acted with unaffected naturalness, the
result was amazing; so my natural manner in the classroom
produced an effect that must be called startling. The response from the students indicated it.

Informality in college teaching is common enough now;
but in the nineties at Yale, it was almost unheard of.

Informality does not necessarily mean any loss of dignity; it may mean simply that one throws away all pretence. I began to teach with absolute naturalness; later in
my public addresses, in my sermons in church, in my dinner speeches, in my orations at funerals, I have never
changed. Whether I am talking to two persons or to two
thousand, my manner is exactly the same. As a great deal
is said about the technique of public speaking, I will say
that this is all the technique I know. But whenever I address a strange audience, there is always that same opening
shock. I can feel it; it is not unpleasant. I never begin with
conventional platitudes and generalities; no matter how
large the audience may be, I always feel as if I were talking
to each one separately. 'This only is the witchcraft I have
used.'

The year 1892 was memorable personally. I finished my
year of instruction at Harvard in June. I began my career
as a teacher at Yale in September and remained in active
service until retired by age in 1933. After finishing reading
my first exam papers as a teacher in December, I took
the train to Michigan. On Wednesday, 21 December 1892
at high noon, I was married to Miss Annabel Hubbard in
the house at Huron City where I am now writing (1938),
and we have lived happily ever after. The Rev. Jacob
Horton of Port Huron, assisted by my brother, the
Rev. Dryden W. Phelps, performed the ceremony.

Neither my wife nor I had ever been South, so we decided
to take our wedding journey in what was described as the

Sunny South. We went to Asheville, North Carolina; and the day after we arrived, the thermometer fell to zero and stayed there for a week. We therefore went to Boston, where we were comfortable, stopping at Washington on the way.

On our return to New Haven, early in January, I was pleased to find that the Freshmen whom I had taught from September to the Christmas vacation had made us a beautiful wedding present, the *Complete Works* of James Russell Lowell.

After I had been teaching a few weeks, there was a meeting of the Freshman Faculty, most of whom were much older than I. I was informed that my marks were too high. To which I replied that the Faculty were at liberty to make a horizontal reduction if they wished, but that this Freshman class was very remarkable and I believed they had earned those grades. The older men naturally were amused and wished to know how I could pronounce the class to be remarkable, when it was the first class I had taught. I told them I was sure of the fact. They decided to let my grades remain. Two years later this very class entered more members of Phi Beta Kappa than had ever been known at Yale, and in the years following, as I have said, this same class contributed more members to the Yale Faculty than any other class in Yale's history before or since.

I have always been grateful that my first experience in Yale teaching should have been with this really amazing class of 1896; and in later years I had as my colleagues in the English Department Professors John Chester Adams, John Milton Berdan, George Henry Nettleton; in other departments Herbert E. Hawkes in Mathematics, now and for many years past the famous Dean of Columbia University, known and admired by all men; Albert G. Keller, Professor of the Science of Society, the distinguished successor of W.G.Sumner; Hollon A.Farr, Professor of German, and for many years a high official in the Dean's office; Rudolph Schevill, who taught romance languages, and for many years has been Professor at the University of California; Professor Christopher Coleman, Professor of History in Butler College, Indianapolis; Rowland Cox, Instructor in Surgery, Columbia University; Sherwood O. Dickerman, Professor of Greek at Williams College; Edward L.Durfee, who became Instructor in History at Yale; Jay G.Eldridge, who for many years has been Professor of German and Dean of the University of Idaho; Clarence V.Fowler, Instructor at the U.S.Naval Academy; Herbert E.Gregory, Professor of Geology at Yale; William M.Hess, for some years Recorder at Yale; Frederic B. Johnson, Bursar of Yale; Robert S.McClenahan, President Assiut College, in Egypt; William C.Morgan, Professor of Chemistry, Reed College, Oregon; Henry A.Perkins, Professor of Physics, Trinity College, Hartford; Fred O. Robbins, for some years Instructor in French at Yale; L.R.Scarborough, President of Southwestern Baptist Theological Seminary, in Texas; Charles P.Sherman, for many years Assistant Professor of Roman Law at Yale Law School; M.J.Spinello, for some years Instructor in Romance Languages, University of California; Douglas Stewart, Director of the Carnegie Museum, Pittsburgh; Canon Anson Phelps Stokes, for many years the famous Secretary of Yale University; Chauncey W.Wells, Professor of English at the University of California.

Haec sunt mea ornamenta! and I have mentioned only those who became members of College Faculties. Many others became teachers in Secondary Schools. I believe such a scholastic record for a college class after graduation is extraordinary. It was a good class for me to meet in my first essay at teaching at Yale.

During the whole four years my relations with this class

remained intimate. Outside of the classroom I played tennis and hockey and whist with them. The famous 'Bridgeport Tennis Tournament' will be remembered by every man who took part.

When they came to graduate, Elbert Hamlin headed a committee who called at my house and said the Class wished to present me with a Cup. I told them I was deeply gratified, but that there must be no public presentation and no announcements in the papers. I did not tell them, but the reason was that my popularity with this class had aroused jealousy and hatred from some older members of the Faculty, and that a public ceremony of presentation might cost me my position. Hence the magnificent cup was left at my house by a small group one afternoon when I was away.

There is no doubt that in those days (1880–1900) popularity with the students was a serious handicap; if promotion to professorships had been in the power of the President and Corporation, as it was in most other American universities, it would have been otherwise; but the Permanent Professors on the Faculty had the power of election; thus it was in some ways like being admitted to a very select club. It was easier to be elected if one were an 'available' candidate; that is, if one had not attracted undue attention; but extreme popularity made the ruling powers feel that the candidate must have stooped to conquer. Professor Sumner used to say it was often easier for a man from another college to receive an appointment than for a man on the ground; 'the latter's faults we know, and all we know of the distant man is that he has faults, but as we do not know what they are, we forget their certain existence.'

I had already as an undergraduate witnessed what I have always regarded as disasters for Yale. Mr. Ambrose Tighe, who taught us Latin in our Freshman and Sophomore years made his classroom so interesting that he incurred the displeasure of the higher powers, and was released. Frank Tarbell, our Instructor in Greek and Logic, was released just when his influence was becoming really profound. Tarbell later was very happy at Chicago, with his colleagues in the classics and in archaeology, and with his intimate friends Robert Herrick, William Vaughn Moody, Robert Lovett, and John Manly, of the English Department.

Now, after I had taught at Yale for seven or eight months, I was warned by several professors that my stay would be short; some were friendly, and merely told me to look out; others were quite the reverse, and gave me distinctly to understand that I could never look for promotion. Every time I received an offer elsewhere, I was earnestly advised to take it. I do not believe any member of the Faculty ever received so many invitations to leave Yale that came *from the inside*. One of my superiors told me that if I went on, I should be like Ambrose Tighe (my hero) whom he mentioned with contempt, and would share his fate.

After four years as Instructor, however, I was promoted to an Assistant Professorship, but only after a fierce battle in the Faculty, which was not settled until Commencement Day! Three years later an endowment for a Professorship in English Literature was given to Yale, and it had to be filled; a younger colleague of mine, and one who had had much shorter service was appointed. (I am glad that my friendship with him was never injured by this; we were dear and intimate friends till his untimely death.) But when this appointment came up to the President and Corporation, they, feeling it to be unfair to me, ratified it and at the same time unanimously elected me as well, and sent the two names back to the Faculty. The Faculty rejected me, and the letter I got from President Dwight that evening was one of the severest disappointments of my life. He said that his own disappointment was very great; and I knew that he had pleaded with the Faculty during a long session urging that I be appointed along with my colleague. And he added in his letter to me that what distressed him most was that he believed that now I could never become a Professor at Yale. This letter I received at night and my suffering was so intense from the shock of it that I was actually in physical agony. Nor did I get a good night's sleep for many weeks.

There were, however, two Professors, Frank K. Sanders and E. H. Sneath, who wrote me personal letters, telling me they were sure I should eventually win promotion. And two years later (1901) the election took place.

Apart from the jealousies, heart-burnings, and whisperings, which are characteristic of every University community as they are of every military post, I think that the older professors in those days honestly felt that what every young instructor needed was repression, 'taking down,' that encouragement and praise would be bad for him. Certain it is that for years the affection and enthusiasm I received from my students was balanced by the hostility that came from those who had my Yale future in their power. Words of encouragement were few and far apart.

Fortunately for me, the Senior Professor of English Literature at Yale College when I began to teach was Henry A. Beers. He was nearly twenty years older than I, had entered the law after he had been graduated from Yale, and after a brief and uncongenial experience in New York, had been called back to the University. Although he had spent a year of study at Heidelberg, he was totally unlike the conventional German-trained English scholar typical everywhere in America during the twenty years preceding the World War. At Heidelberg he had studied both Goethe's *Faust* and metaphysics with the eloquent Kuno Fischer;

and he had thoroughly enjoyed himself with the students. Professor Beers was a man entirely without ambition, without the slightest itch for publicity, without any talent for self-advertising. He never professed to be a research scholar in the approved Germanic style; but in reality he was one of the most profound and accurate scholars on the Faculty. He was thoroughly at home in Greek, Latin, Italian, French, German, Anglo-Saxon. In addition to courses covering all the range of English literature from Chaucer to contemporaries, he gave courses in Italian on the *Purgatorio*, and in Anglo-Saxon. And for an entire year I attended with immense profit a voluntary course that he gave in *Faust*, where he read the entire poem aloud in German, translated it, and commented.

He was entirely free from the meaner vices, so commonly found among actors, singers, military officers, and college professors. *He had absolutely no jealousy*. It made not the slightest difference to him what anybody thought about anybody else. Although he never made a religious profession of any kind, he loved only the best in men and in art. He was quietly pessimistic about life, never asking or expecting much, and viewing the world with an unobtrusive and infallible sense of humour. I have never seen him emotionally excited about anything; I never heard him raise his voice; I never heard him roar with laughter. His profound knowledge of literature and his fine taste were a good corrective for me when I was a graduate student. I was too easily excited and given to exaggeration of loves and hates.

I have never known a more agreeable companion. He was perfect; only one had to draw him out. He never cared for games of any kind; he loved to be at home with his wife and numerous children; and like some other men who were near-sighted, he was an excellent amateur botanist. He loved dogs and cats and was kind-hearted. It is really impossible to describe him; I have never known any one like him.

But it was a good thing for me that this quiet-tempered, reticent man, so innately noble, should have been my Senior officer.

Had he had any ambition, he would have been one of the best known of contemporary creative writers. His volume of short stories called *A Suburban Pastoral* is written with delicate art; his volumes of original poems are full of beauty and quiet music; his humorous publications, *The Ways of Yale* and others were a delight to the vast number of Yale graduates. His most important work on scholarship, *History of Romanticism*, was a contribution to the subject.

After I had taught Freshmen and Sophomores for two years, 1892–4, Professor Beers gave me permission to offer an elective open to Seniors and Juniors, members of the class of 1895 and 1896. Accordingly I offered a course in Elizabethan Drama, which was taken by one hundred and thirty men. Thus I had the pleasure of becoming acquainted with the Seniors and also of carrying on my work with the class of 1896 in their Junior year.

One day after I had finished a lecture on Marlowe's *Doctor Faustus*, and had spoken incidentally with enthusiasm of the playing of Mephistopheles in Gounod's *Faust* by Edouard de Reszké, who was on that very day appearing in New York, an undergraduate told me of his own rapturous admiration for that great artist, and asked my advice. He said that he was to take his degree in June, and that the one ambition of his life was to be an opera singer. His parents, however, were bitterly opposed to this, thinking it was not a career for a young American. 'What do they want you to do?' 'They want me to be a business man.' 'Very good; as soon as you graduate, go to New York, get a job in some business; then hire a first-rate teacher, and take singing-lessons at night. In a few months he will tell you whether you have only a parlour voice or whether you really can aspire to the operatic stage. If the former be true, you will be glad to remain in business; if the latter, your parents will certainly consent to your professional career, and if they don't, what of it?'

He followed my advice; and before six months he was well started as a singer, in a few years he was invited to become a member of the Metropolitan Opera House company, and after the final departure of Edouard de Reszké, he not only took his role as the King in *Lohengrin*, but also showed me with pride his royal robe—under the collar was written the name Edouard de Reszké. The mantle of the great Polish basso had thus literally descended on Herbert Witherspoon.

Herbert had a brilliant career on the stage, later became the Head of a school of music, and in 1935 was chosen Manager of the Metropolitan Opera; but before he could begin his work, suddenly died.

There was another undergraduate in this first course I gave in Elizabethan Drama, a Junior named Alexander Smith Cochran. He was shy and reticent; and I had no means of knowing whether or not the course had made any impression upon him. Nor did I know anything about him personally; or that he was a millionaire in his own right.

Some ten years after his graduation he wrote me from England, saying that the course in Elizabethan Drama had awakened in him an acute interest in the literature of the period; that he had amused himself with collecting some rare books; and that in a few days he would send me his manuscript catalogue. I really was quite unprepared for what followed; for every month I receive letters from persons who think they own books of great value, which are worth perhaps five dollars.

When I got Cochran's catalogue, I was astounded. He

had books that were worth several hundred thousand dollars, Shakespearean quartos, a copy of the first edition of the *Sonnets*, of Bacon's *Essays*, and so on. The next year he wrote me again, saying he was coming to America, that he had in mind an original plan, and would wait until we could discuss it together. His plan was a good one. He wished to found at Yale an Elizabethan Club, because the one thing he had most missed at Yale was good conversation; that if there were an undergraduate club, with a remarkable library as a nucleus, he thought students who loved literature and the arts would be glad to meet there, and talk informally and naturally about literature, both with their contemporaries and with congenial members of the Faculty. He would donate the club building, the library, and an endowment.

He asked me to find a suitable building. I found one and told him the owner wanted seventy-five thousand dollars. 'I'll buy it,' said Cochran, and he did. A vault was built for the books, one hundred thousand dollars was given for endowment and the Club opened its doors in the Autumn of 1911. It is one of the most successful organizations connected with the University. Later Cochran went over to England on a special journey, and in advance of the auction, bought all four folios of Shakespeare from the Huth Library.

The club has been addressed by many distinguished men of letters from Europe and America. No one who was present will ever forget the address by Sir William Osler on Burton's *Anatomy of Melancholy*.

From the start, the club has been fortunate in having the services and counsel of Andrew Keogh, the distinguished librarian (now Emeritus) of Yale University.

I regard the late Alexander Smith Cochran as one of Yale's greatest benefactors.

Commemorating the one hundredth anniversary of the

death of Keats, the club invited Miss Amy Lowell to address the members. The undergraduates were interested in what she would say and also hoped that she would run true to form and smoke a cigar; for most of them had never seen a woman with a cigar in her mouth. Miss Lowell made an admirable and scholarly address and described her Keats original manuscripts and early editions, after which the meeting became informal. It is difficult to describe what followed without giving an impression of vulgarity; and Miss Lowell was downright but never vulgar. She lit and kept in her mouth during conversation a huge black cigar, which fascinated the group of students who surrounded her. One asked her, 'Miss Lowell, what do you think of Rabindranath Tagore?' Without removing the cigar from her mouth, Miss Lowell said 'He's a charlatan.'

The reading of exam papers was the only part of my academic work that I disliked; it was drudgery. Until I was sixty, however, I read every paper myself, over five hundred twice a year. Once in a while a gleam of humour brightened the task. In discussing the Mediaeval Mystery Plays, I had described the costumes of the players, God, the Devil, Pilate, and so on, and the realistic jaws of Hellmouth, in front of which were the damned souls, persons dressed in black tights with yellow stripes. Several months later, in setting the exam, I put down as one of the questions, 'Describe the costumes worn by the players in the Mysteries,' and one man wrote 'The Damned Souls wore Princeton colours.'

On another occasion, in the course in Tennyson, I innocently set the question, 'What ultimately became of Dora?' and a student wrote 'She died.'

For only one year the Freshmen were required to listen to a series of lectures on Oriental history; they did not suppose there would be any final examination. But being told about two weeks from the end of the course that they

Our House in New Haven

Westminster School Baseball Nine, Dobbs Ferry, N.Y. 1889
Mr. Phelps in centre

Attending Yale-Harvard ball game, Alumni Day, 1933

Huron City, Michigan

William Lyon Phelps and Thornton Wilder
110 *Whitney Avenue, New Haven,* 5 *March* 1929

Professor Henry A. Beers, '69, and
Professor William Lyon Phelps, '87 (1915)

Reading. Seven Gables, 1938

Rufus and I, 1938

must all be ready for a written test, most of them decided
to substitute imagination for memory. I wish I had a complete collection of the written answers. They ran somewhat
like this:

Q. Enumerate the four members of a certain dynasty.
A. I will enumerate them: Number One, Number Two, Number
   Three, Number Four.
Q. Can you give the ancestors of Cleopatra?
A. I can.

The senior class statistics, where every member of the
graduating class had to write a series of answers to a questionnaire, used to be a general release of humour. To the
question, How far back can you trace your ancestry?
Jimmy Jenkins replied, I can trace my ancestry about a
mile, after a light fall of snow.

To the question, 'How many athletic prizes have you
taken?' Stevenson ('Nutty Steve') replied, 'I took three
of my roommates' cups, but I returned them.'

There were these replies to the question 'What is your
favourite character in fiction?' 'Saul of Tarsus.' 'Yale
Democracy.' 'Napoleon, as conceived by Professor——.'
One of the humorists wrote, 'It is ridiculous to say there
is no democracy at Yale. Why, even the most aristocratic
Yale student will speak to a poor working girl, right on the
street.'

After I had been teaching at Yale for about a year, I received a letter from the President of Bryn Mawr College in
Pennsylvania saying that I was being considered as a possible member of the English Department at that institution, with the request that I would meet the President at a
certain day and hour in a hotel in New Haven. The letter
was typewritten and signed in a bold hand, 'M.Carey
Thomas.' I supposed the President was a man, and I replied, beginning my letter 'Dear Sir,' that I should be very

glad to be at the appointed place at the appointed time. I got there first and when the lady walked in, I saw that I had made a blunder, and remarked that after such an unpardonable mistake I supposed there would be no use in negotiations. Miss Thomas brushed this aside, saying that it was a mistake that happened so often in her correspondence that she had ceased to pay any attention to it.

She was a business-like woman and told me exactly what she expected of me in case I was invited to Bryn Mawr and accepted. She had read my book *The Beginnings of the English Romantic Movement* and liked it; from what she had heard of my teaching at Yale she was favourably impressed. She then asked me many questions about my ideas of scholarship and of teaching English literature. We talked for over an hour and got along very well. Then as she rose to end the interview, she said, 'Well, I like your ideas very much, and there is only one more question. What are your views on religion?' I smiled and replied, 'I don't think there will be any difficulty on that point. I should not have been regarded as orthodox by the old-fashioned Calvinists of fifty years ago, but I am a Christian and a member of an evangelical church.' To my amazement, a look of intense disappointment, almost of horror, came over her face. 'I am deeply distressed to hear this. I am most anxious that our girls be left with entirely free and open minds. I do not want them unduly influenced by religious doctrines or biased by any theological or superstitious views. This is a serious drawback, Mr. Phelps. Do you think, if you should be called to our Faculty, that you could keep your religious prejudices out of the classroom?' I replied that I understood that I was to be hired as a teacher of English, and not as an evangelist.

We parted amicably, although the interview had begun inauspiciously with my blunder and ended with her disappointment. However, in a few days I received a very kind letter from President Thomas, offering me a good position. I considered it carefully and declined, mainly because I preferred to teach young men rather than young women.

A short time after this, I told President Dwight of Yale confidentially of this interview. He was very much astonished and laughed heartily as he replied, 'It has always been my experience that those teachers who are religious never mention it in the classroom, whereas those who are antagonistic to religion are always talking about it to the students.'

President Thomas was at that time beginning her career as Executive even as I was beginning as a teacher. She became one of the most distinguished of American college presidents and her intellectual ability combined with her capacity for leadership gave her a permanent place in the history of American education. Apparently, however, she never got over her dislike of religious enthusiasm; for a friend of mine, sitting at the same table with her many years later, in the dining-room of an ocean steamer, observed that while she was enjoying her meal, she had propped up in front of her a novel by A.S.M.Hutchinson, which she was reading apparently with increasing disapproval. All of a sudden Miss Thomas spoke in a determined voice: 'Steward, take this book and throw it out of the window!'

One day in the Spring of 1895 I called on Professor Beers and told him that I should like to give a course on Modern Novels, confining the subject-matter entirely to contemporary works. Rather to my surprise and greatly to my pleasure, he gave his immediate assent to this, saying there was no reason why the literature of 1895 could not be made as suitable a subject for college study as the literature of 1295.

Thus was inaugurated what I believe was the first course in any university in the world confined wholly to contemporary fiction. I called the course *Modern Novels*. It was open to Seniors and Juniors, and was elected by two hundred and fifty men.

It was a good time to begin the serious academic study of contemporary prose fiction, for the preceding year 1894 was remarkable for the appearance of new novels many of which belong to literature: *Trilby, Lord Ormont and His Aminta, Esther Waters, The Ebb Tide, The Jungle Book, Life's Little Ironies, Jude the Obscure* (serially), *Pudd'nhead Wilson, Pembroke, The Prisoner of Zenda, The Dolly Dialogues, Under the Red Robe;* and Conrad's first novel *Almayer's Folly* was in press. Hall Caine's *The Manxman* and Mrs. Humphry Ward's *Marcella* also appeared in this same year. Although they both attracted immense attention from the public and intellectual respect from the critics, both novelists were unimportant and ephemeral, and for exactly opposite reasons.

When I gave the first lecture in the Autumn, I hoped the course would attract no attention outside of academic halls; for in those days, newspaper notoriety was often fatal to a university career. It is hard to say just how this publicity began, for I gave out no interviews, nor did I mention the subject anywhere; but a notice in the New Haven newspapers was quickly followed by a whole column in the *New York Times*, and it seemed as if every newspaper in the country followed suit. The usual headline was

THEY STUDY NOVELS

and a page was devoted to the revolutionary theme. Editorials usually appeared in the same issue. The vast majority of newspaper comment was favourable; but there were some editorial writers who looked with disapproval on the course, the separate novels studied, and the young instructor. The news of this amazing addition to the curriculum travelled across the ocean; the course was gravely condemned in a full column editorial in the London *Daily*

Telegraph, and the following delightful parody appeared in *Punch* (Autumn 1895), called

A NOVEL EDUCATION

The tutor of St. Mary's, Cambridge, was sitting in his rooms after Hall interviewing a succession of undergraduates.

'Sit down, please, Mr. Jones,' he said to the last comer; 'I wish to speak to you very seriously on the subject of your work. The College is not at all satisfied with your progress this term. For instance, Professor Kailyard tells me that your attendance at his lectures has been most irregular.'

'Well, Sir,' said Jones, fumbling with the tassel of his cap, 'I didn't think they were important—'

'Not important? How do you expect to be able to get up difficult authors like Crockett and Maclaren unless you've attended a course of lectures on Scotch dialect? Do you know the meaning of "havers," "gabby," or "yammering"? I thought not. Then your last paper on "Elementary Besantics" was very weak. Have you really been giving your energies to your work, or have you been frittering away your time over other books?'

Jones looked guilty, but said nothing.

'Ah,' resumed the Don, 'I see how it is. You've been wasting your time over light literature—Homer and Virgil, and trash of that sort. But you really must resist temptations of that kind if you wish to do creditably in the Tripos. Good evening.'

Jones departed, to be succeeded by another undergraduate.

'I sent for you, Mr. Smith,' said the Tutor, 'because—though your work on the older writers is pretty good—your acquaintance with modern realism is quite insufficient. You will attend the course of anatomy lectures at the hospital, please. You can't study your "keynotes" intelligently without them.'

A third student made his appearance in the doorway.

'Mr. Robinson, I'm sorry to say that your work is unsatisfactory. On looking at your Mudie list, I find that you've only taken out ten novels in the last month. In order to see whether you can be permitted to take the Tripos this year, I'm going to give you a few questions, the answers to which must be brought me before Saturday. You will find pen and ink on that table. Kindly take down the following questions, as I dictate them.'

The tutor cleared his throat, and began:

'Question one. Explain "P.W.D. accounts," "a G.T.," "G.B.T.

shin-bones." Trace the bearing of the history of Mowgli on the Dar-
winian theory.

'Question two. "The truth shall make us free." Give context, and
comment on this statement. Conjugate, in accordance with the library catalogue, *The Woman who*—, noting which of the tenses are
irregular.

'Question three. "There were two Trilbys" (Trilby, Part VIII).
Explain this statement. What had Mr. Whistler to do with it?

'Question four. Give the formulae for the employment of (a) the
Mad Bull; (b) the Runaway Horse; (c) the Secret Marriage. What
would you suggest as the modern equivalents of these?

'Question five. Rewrite the story of *Jack and Jill*,—(a) in Wessex
dialect; (b) as a "Keynote"; (c) as a "Dolly Dialogue."

'That will do for the present,' concluded the tutor. And, as his
pupil left the room, he seated himself at the writing-table and began
Chapter XXIX of his 'Prolegomena to *Three Men in a Boat.*'

Then letters began to come in from everywhere; I could
not afford a Secretary and I had no time to answer them.
So I had printed an answer, which I had to send out at
least three times every day for a year.

When I gave the semi-annual examination at Christmas
on the material covered during the first term, the best paper I received was from a member of the Senior Class,
Clarence Day, who forty years later was to become universally known as the author of *Life with Father*. Clarence
was regarded with affection by his classmates but the chief
impression he made on them was as an eccentric; he was
voted on graduation the most eccentric member of the
class. He had an extraordinary collection of pipes. I felt
quite sure of his success in literature and told him so.
Not long after graduation, however, he became afflicted
with a lifelong disease, arthritis, which had the double effect of completely crippling him and at the same time
being exquisitely painful. For over thirty years he showed
daily heroism in not allowing this tragedy to conquer his
spirit or destroy his creative energy. Yet during the few
years that elapsed between graduation and the arthritis it

is somewhat surprising that he was not murdered. He journeyed into the States beyond the Mississippi, carrying several hundred cards that he had had beautifully printed. When accosted by strangers in the train, he would after a little conversation silently present one of these cards; they bore inscriptions like this—'I will not take up any more of your valuable time. That remark of yours about the weather is very original,' etc.

Although the undergraduates apparently enjoyed both the course and the writing of a weekly critical theme, which I made obligatory, and although the newspaper comment was on the whole highly favourable, the majority of the older professors gave me distinctly to understand that unless I dropped the course at the end of its first year, I should myself be dropped from the Faculty. President Timothy Dwight, always the best friend I had among my superiors, sent for me, and advised me not to continue the course another year. I told him that I fully believed in the value of the course, but that I had no illusions as to my place in the university. 'You are the President—you are my chief and it is only a pleasure to obey you.' I knew that he had only my welfare in mind. Then the Dean of the college, Henry P. Wright, sent for me and made the following remark: 'If your course had been a failure there would have been no objection to its continuance.'

I had no desire to pose as a martyr and I hoped that the silent omission of the course for the following year would not be observed; but unfortunately it was. Learning that emissaries from the New York papers were on their way to New Haven to interview me, I left town and for a week only my wife knew where I was. On my return, the teapot-tempest had somewhat subsided, and to all the newspaper men I stated that I had voluntarily given up the course for one year. This was at least technically true; for the President had told me that I had a perfect right to continue it if I wished, only he advised me as a friend to conform to the judgement of my superiors.

Two years later I gave a course in American literature, in which I included all the American novels I had discussed in the previous course; and five years later I gave a course, the first of its kind, I believe, in any university, which was confined to contemporary dramatists.

My term as Instructor expired with the Novel course; and the Professors, perhaps relenting, perhaps pleased with my determination to avoid publicity connected with the withdrawal of that course, promoted me to an Assistant Professorship for five years. I learned this fact on Commencement Day. So that I began my work as Instructor at Yale with the Freshmen of the Class of 1896, and on the day this class was graduated, I ceased to be an 'Instructor' and became an Assistant Professor. At the expiration of my term in 1901, I was promoted to a full professorship, and a few months later, was made Lampson Professor of English literature, which position I held until my retirement, when I became Professor Emeritus.

William Lampson was a Yale graduate of the class of 1860, who lived at Leroy, N.Y. He left in his will money for three professorships, one in Greek, one in Latin, one in English, the balance of his estate to pay for the erection of a Yale building for lectures and recitations. This was an admirable bequest, as it provided for the foundation of three professorships and released money for current expenses. Thus for thirty-five years my salary came from the estate of a man whom I had never seen. I did what I could to make his name known, and kept a large portrait of him in my college office. I have always felt grateful to him and wished that I could have known him personally. His estate provided for an annual salary for every one of the three professorships of four thousand dollars a year. This was in 1901 the maximum salary for a full professor at Yale.

I was told on a cold morning of February that the professors were to meet that afternoon and recommend me for a professorship. I had to lecture at Madison, New Jersey, that evening. I came back over the ferry at New York near midnight; the river was filled with huge blocks of ice. I reached New Haven at half-past two in the morning. My wife greeted me with the glorious news of my promotion and had a supper ready of oysters and champagne. I wrote in my diary, 'I am very happy. My future is settled.' A number of professors called on me the next day, and said that whatever opposition there had been to me in the past was entirely dead, and that the Faculty were wholly appreciative. This gave me unspeakable delight.

Although their discussions were secret, several of them told me of one amusing incident that was too good to keep. A dignified and elderly Professor of Latin said in the meeting, 'Well, I am going to vote for Mr. Phelps, but there is just one thing about him I don't like. I wish he had a little more dignity. Everyone calls him Billy.' There was a moment's pause which was suddenly broken by the decisive and harsh voice of Professor William Graham Sumner, 'They call me Billy, too!' Everyone roared with laughter, and that remark made my calling and election sure. Professor Sumner was regarded as the most distinguished man on the Faculty; the students and his colleagues were somewhat in awe of him; yet by the undergraduates and alumni he was always spoken of as 'Billy' Sumner.

President Eliot of Harvard used to say that as he grew older he became in the eyes of the undergraduates steadily younger. When at the age of thirty-five he was elected President of Harvard, he said everyone called him 'Old Eliot'; but when he was eighty years old, walking across the Harvard Yard one night, two undergraduates passed, and he heard one of them say, 'I wonder what Charlie is doing out so late?'

A typographical error gave me an unexpected honour. A Boston newspaper alluded to me as *Lampoon* Professor at Yale. The Harvard *Lampoon* quoted this item, and said, 'With pardonable pride Lampy points out that his favourite son has been doing rather well, even at Yale.' Well, I am proud to represent a Harvard institution *in partibus infidelium*.

On Saturday 2 November 1895 I gave a lecture on 'The Modern Novel' before the Saturday Morning Club of New Haven, which was the beginning of my work as a public lecturer. On the same day I received twelve guineas from London for my editorial work on the plays of Chapman (Mermaid Series).

Early in my career, I was introduced to a large audience by a chairman who said, 'Several times we have secured distinguished men and their lectures have been a total failure; tonight we decided to get a man who is not distinguished but who we know can speak well;' and while the first half of the last clause was certainly true, it aroused general merriment. I certainly enjoyed it.

Introductions are an art. 'We had hoped to have Mr. Phelps here last year, but fortunately he could not come.' 'He is a speaker of word-wild fame.' One rather pompous chairman asked me what he should say. 'Please don't make a speech; just say that the speaker of the evening is Mr. Phelps of Yale.' But unfortunately he had prepared a series of superlatives, at the close of which he said, 'I now have the honour of presenting to you Mr. Yelps of Fale.'

Many poets confine their public appearances to reading from their works, often very badly; the best public reader of his own poems I have ever heard is Alfred Noyes. Yet once in a while, when I have persuaded an author to give a lecture, he has enjoyed the occasion enormously; he had not known what a thrilling experience it can be.

I am inclined to think that while writing helps lecturing,

lecturing is bad for writing. The same applies to teaching. A man's teaching is improved if he writes books, but his style in writing is apt to suffer by teaching often or before large classes. Of the mighty army of school and college teachers, how few are successful novelists, poets, or playwrights! The art of teaching and the art of writing are alike only in that they use the same alphabet. There the resemblance stops. One profound difference is that in composition a man is solitary, he is alone in the room; whereas in teaching and lecturing the more crowded the room, the greater the stimulus.

Many writers, whose compositions are boldly aggressive, are very shy, reticent, bashful, almost timid in conversation; which is natural enough, though at a first meeting one cannot repress a feeling of surprise.

I remember, after reading many things by Rebecca West, I had the pleasure of meeting her, and it seemed incredible that this shy, timid, tiny creature with the whispering voice, could be the author of such defiances. By the way, Mr. Van Druten's play made from her story *The Return of the Soldier*, which I saw in London, affected me more uncontrollably than almost anything else I ever saw on the stage. I not only wept copiously during the scenes, I sobbed aloud between the acts!

Although the art of writing is probably deservedly regarded as superior to the art of public speaking (and the writer may be remembered by the preservation of his words in print, whereas the lecturer, like the actor, will be forgotten) it is certain that a really good lecturer is rarer than a really good writer. There are ten expert writers to one expert public speaker. First-rate public speaking is uncommon.

In my work as a college teacher, apart from my continuous interest in the subjects I have taught, ranging from Chaucer to contemporary writers, perhaps the most gratifying thing is the number of intimate friendships with those who have been my undergraduate pupils. I taught at Yale forty-one years, averaging four hundred students a year. If we multiply our hundred by forty-one, we shall come near the number of personal friends that I have possessed. Some deductions from this large number must of course be made. There are some students on whom I have made no impression; either because they did not care for the subjects I taught, or because they did not care for the way in which I taught them. There have been some—not many, I think—who have hated me. As I look back over these years, I see clearly why I must unavoidably have produced on some students an unfavourable impression. My ebullient enthusiasm, however sincere and unaffected, rasps the nerves of temperaments wholly unlike mine. If a man be cold, sceptical, or cynical, anyone with high-hearted emotional fervour cannot help arousing irritation. Some of these adverse critics have had good minds and some have had dull and sluggish minds; but I know that I have succeeded in arousing from them only hostility. I cannot take credit for this, as a teacher might if he were hated for his austerity. I am sorry for it, yet I could not, in order to please a few, change either my nature or the methods of teaching that seemed to me both natural and in general, effective. If I had pleased only the loafers and did not have the intellectual respect of many good students, then I should know that I was unworthy, not fit to hold a professorship in a great university.

But it is certain that the vast majority of the men that have been in my classroom (including the able students) have enjoyed being there, and have had for the rest of their lives a strong affection for me. I am just as certain of this as I am of the dislike of the (comparatively) very few.

This means that in every town of any size (and in many tiny villages) in the United States I have at least one intimate friend. This is surely an immense reward for the years of teaching.

A temperament like mine, that is easily excited, accompanied by an equally easy loquacity, has the defects of its qualities. But, however much or little I may have contributed to the happiness of others, my almost infinite capacity for appreciation has enormously contributed to my own happiness.

I do not know that I could make entirely clear to an outsider the pleasure I have in teaching. I had rather earn my living by teaching than in any other way. In my mind, teaching is not merely a life-work, a profession, an occupation, a struggle: it is a passion. I love to teach. I love to teach as a painter loves to paint, as a musician loves to play, as a singer loves to sing, as a strong man rejoices to run a race. Teaching is an art—an art so great and so difficult to master that a man or a woman can spend a long life at it, without realizing much more than his limitations and mistakes, and his distance from the ideal.

In a novel published in 1930, *Green Isle,* by Alice Duer Miller, I found the story and the characters interesting, but the following paragraph more interesting than either:

> Strangely enough there is nowhere the average person can go to learn how to live his daily life. Children are taught Latin and astronomy, but no school or college tells them how to clear their mind for a decision, how to tell certain psychological, or even psychopathic types, and how to deal with them; how, for any individual, to draw the line between idleness and serenity, between overwork and fullness of life, between sweet charity and being every man's dupe. Everybody needs such instruction, something halfway between religious precepts and practical talks to salesmen. Women need it particularly, for they do not get, as early as men do, the experience of the business world.

It is quite true, that even among the prodigious number of things professionally taught in some universities today, like cream-separating, nursing, scene-painting, advertising, fertilizing, short-story writing, and among the increasing number of 'business colleges,' 'schools of journalism,' 'schools of the drama,' there are no graduate schools devoted to the art of living, and no professional teachers employed to specialize in Life.

Yet the paradox is that the less practical, the less 'efficient' the particular subject and the particular method of teaching may be, the more the average person will learn how to live his daily life. In a course on electrical engineering, taught by a first-class teacher to a picked class of superior pupils, there will probably be little knowledge gleaned on how to prepare one's mind for a decision, and how to distinguish between sweet charity and being every man's dupe. But in a course in Greek literature, the students may learn little if their proficiency is determined by the ease with which they can read Greek at sight; but they cannot help learning something—and some of them will learn much—about the art of living.

It is curious that many people believe in the importance of what they call vocational and practical courses, and regard the study of great literature as merely ornamental, a pretty accomplishment in seminaries for young ladies. As a matter of fact, nothing is more essential in the proper furnishing of a man's mind than a knowledge of the world's best literature. Literature is the immortal part of history. Literature is the interpretation of human life.

It is unfortunate that the majority of pupils in high schools and colleges do not study literature with the concentrated attention they give later to vocational and professional studies. They do not see the connexion between 'liberal' studies and success in life, but they ought to.

I asked a successful engineer in Boston, a man who is at the head of enterprises with scores of young engineers working under him, this question: 'What studies in college would you advise for one who intends to become a civil engineer?' He replied without any hesitation, 'Anything so long as it has no connexion with engineering.' He told me that those who came to him from technical schools with no liberal education began at first to surpass those who had studied literature and other general subjects. But in a few years the truly 'educated' young men went ahead, because they had imagination, interesting minds, and a knowledge of human nature.

I should not urge boys and girls to read good books because it will make them successful lawyers, physicians, engineers, business men; it is better to be a good father, a good husband, a good son, a good brother, a good friend, than to achieve material success; it is better to be an interesting personality than to be an efficient machine. But just as a physician who has an admirable ' bedside manner ' is more successful than one who carries an atmosphere of chill, so it is certain that a knowledge of human nature, with the sympathy, tolerance, and understanding that should accompany such knowledge, is an asset for success in any calling where one comes into contact with people.

I had a conversation some twenty years ago with a cultivated Englishman, Mr. E. Nelson Fell. He attended one of the most famous schools in the world, Eton, which prepares one for the university. But Mr. Fell did not proceed to the university. He found that Eton prepared him for life. He became a business man, and was sent into a remote part of Russia, where as Superintendent of a vast enterprise, he had under his direction several hundred Russian peasants, *muzhiks*. His educational preparation for this undertaking consisted of the Greek, Latin, Mathematics he had at school.

He not only was obliged to have a thorough knowledge of the immense construction work on which he was engaged; but also he had to manage these peasants, who had adult bodies and infantile minds. Every day he had to make sudden and important decisions; every day he had to draw the line between charity and imposition; every day he had to diagnose correctly psychological and even psychopathic types. His efforts were crowned with success; the enterprise was profitable from the financial point of view, and the peasants, despite occasional outbreaks, were devoted to him heart and soul. He told me that he regarded his years at Eton as the most valuable training he could possibly have had for this particular task. He thought it more valuable than any special training in business management, the psychology of labour, or 'personality.' Apparently he learned at Eton something that was not part of the curriculum—he learned the very things that Mrs. Miller says no school or college imparts.

No matter how many false prophets have gone out into the world, no matter if some of them are in University faculties, no matter if every fundamental principle not only in religion, but in morals and, what seems to some more important, in economics, is publicly challenged, there is no doubt in my mind that schools and colleges are now, even more than ever, the homes of idealism. And this idealism shows itself particularly where there is freedom of thought and liberty of expression. The ideal of service does not mean an enforced and standardized patriotism. I believe the best patriots are those who have the courage and the brains to think for themselves and to declare their opinions, even though those opinions may run counter to received community sentiment. No university is worthy of the name, that does not, with all its discipline and culture, encourage its students to think for themselves. Let them in later years sacrifice their money for the public good; but they should not sacrifice their convictions for anything.

This matter was expressed with his customary felicity by Sir James Barrie, in his address called *The Entrancing Life*, delivered on his installation as Chancellor of Edin-

burgh University in 1930, and now available in print. He
discussed the aim of Scottish universities: the 'needs of
the genius of the Scottish people.'

> Those needs are that every child born into this country shall as far
> as possible have an equal chance. The words 'as far as possible' tar-
> nish the splendid hope, and they were not in the original dream. Some
> day we may be able to cast them out. It is by Education, though not
> merely in the smaller commoner meaning of the word, that the chance
> is to be got. Since the war various nations have wakened to its being
> the one way out; they know its value so well that perhaps the only
> safe boast left to us is that we knew it first. They seem, however, to
> be setting about the work with ultimate objects that are not ours.
> Their student from his earliest age is being brought up to absorb the
> ideas of his political rulers. That is the all of his education, not merely
> in his academic studies but in all his social life, all his mind, all his
> relaxations; they are in control from his birth, and he is to emerge
> into citizenship with rigid convictions which it is trusted will last
> his lifetime. The systems vary in different lands, but that seems to be
> their trend, and I tell you they are being carried out with thorough-
> ness. Nothing can depart more from the Scottish idea, which I take
> to be to educate our men and women primarily not for their country's
> good but for their own, not so much to teach them what to think as
> how to think, not preparing them to give as little trouble as possible
> in the future but sending them into it in the hope that they will give
> trouble.

So far from being a dull routine, teaching is to me the
most adventurous, the most exciting, the most thrilling of
professions. It has its perils, its discouragements, its successes, its delights. Browning says, 'It's an awkward thing
to play with souls;' and whenever I enter a classroom
filled with young men, I think of them not as a class or as a
group, but as a collection of individual personalities more
complex, more delicate, more intricate than any machinery. Not only is every student an organism more sensitive
than any mechanical product; every student is infinitely
precious to some parent or to some relative who may be
three thousand miles away. That is why the teacher should

never use irony or sarcasm or the language that humiliates; that is why he should never take the attitude of suspicion or depreciation. The officials at the United States Mint, the Head of a diamond mine, the President of a metropolitan bank are not dealing with material so valuable as that in the hands of the teacher. Their mistakes are not so disastrous as his; their success is not so important. The excitement of teaching comes from the fact that one is teaching a subject one loves to individuals who are worth more than all the money in the world.

In the year 1896 the daily round of lectures and recitations was enlivened by a manuscript poem received from one of the foremost living poets. Two undergraduate literary clubs had been formed and were holding regular meetings—the Stevenson Club and the Kipling Club. The members were confined to Sophomores of the Class of 1898. I was asked to be a member of the Stevenson Club and I accordingly met regularly with them. We contributed together fifty pounds toward the Stevenson memorial in Edinburgh. The Kipling Club did much better. Its President was Gouverneur Morris, now and for many years a popular American novelist. This Sophomore wrote to Mr. Kipling in Vermont, inviting him to attend the 'annual' banquet of the Kipling Club. One day young Morris came racing up to me on the Yale campus waving a manuscript. Perhaps no man of genius ever made a more gracious and generous response to an invitation from a college undergraduate than Rudyard Kipling had made with this poem.

Morris had the poem printed in the issue of the *Yale Literary Magazine* for May 1896; and that issue immediately became enormously valuable as a genuine first edition of Kipling. This whole matter has been admirably

discussed in a pamphlet written by the distinguished journalist, Julian S.Mason, of the Class of 1898 and a member
of that Kipling Club. This pamphlet was printed in 1937
by the Yale Library Associates of the Yale University
Press, together with a photostat copy of Kipling's handwriting, for the entire poem was written in pen and ink and
signed by the author. Here is the poem.

> Attind ye lasses av Swate Parnasses
> An' wipe my burnin' tears away
> For I'm declinin' a chanst av dinin'
> Wid the bhoys at Yale on the foorteenth May.
>
> The leadin' fayture will be liter-ature,
> (Av a moral nature as is just an' right)
> For their light an' leadin' are engaged in readin'
> Me immortial Worruks from dawn till night.
>
> They've made a club there an' staked out grub there
> Wid plates an' napkins in a joyous row,
> An' they'd think ut splindid if I attinded
> An' so would I—but I cannot go.
>
> The honust fact is that daily practise
> Av rowlin' inkpots, the same as me
> Conshumes me hours in the Muses' bowers
> An' laves me divil a day to spree.
>
> Whin you grow oulder an' skin your shoulder
> At the World's great wheel in your chosen line,
> Ye'll find your chances, as Time advances,
> For takin' a lark are as slim as mine.
>
> But I'm digressin'. Accept my blessin',
> An' remember what ould King Solomon said,
> That youth is ructious an' whiskey's fluxious,
> An' there's nothin' certain but the mornin' 'head.'

On 25 March 1898 I accompanied the Yale undergraduate expeditionary force of debaters in an invasion of

Princeton. Yale won the debate; but the 'most notable feature' as the newspapers correctly stated, was the banquet that followed; at the head table sat two Presidents of the United States, though we thought there was only one. President Patton of Princeton presided; at his right sat Grover Cleveland, at his left James H. Eckels of Chicago, who had been Controller of the Currency; the Honourable William L. Wilson, who was in Cleveland's cabinet, and at this time President of Washington and Lee University; Woodrow Wilson, professor at Princeton; the great historical scholar, J. F. Jameson, then of Brown; the Hon. Everett Wheeler of New York; and the Hon. James Alexander, President of the Equitable Assurance Society of New York; last and least, myself. All made speeches, and when I was called on, it was three o'clock in the morning. I was brief.

I obtained the signatures of the distinguished speakers on my dinner-card. The only writing implement I had was a tiny gold pencil, no bigger than a match. I shall never forget Cleveland's quizzical look as he took that tiny pencil in his enormous hand; he looked at the pencil and then at me, before he looked at the space where he was to write.

MR. CLEVELAND'S SPEECH (*NEW YORK MAIL AND EXPRESS*, 26 MARCH 1898)

My association with Princeton is so new that, with that devotion which generally characterizes a new investiture, I am much cast down. I supposed when I was honored by Princeton in their request to come to the debate tonight that it merely foretold pleasant things. I did not suppose I would be called upon to mourn for a Princeton defeat. But I am in that position. In law when we are defeated there are two courses open. We may either appeal or go to the hotel and swear at the Court. We cannot appeal in this case, however, and as for swearing at the Court, the proprieties of the occasion demand that it should be done in such a private way as to make it hardly worth while to undertake it at all. I take considerable comfort out of the debate tonight—that is, I take all the comfort I can. I am, however, just like the old woman who, at her husband's funeral, said that inwardly she was as mad as anybody.

I was glad they did not introduce us to the grill room of this inn tonight instead of the dining room. Indeed, there remains a bare chance that I may save a little of moral character and a slight vestige of good Presbyterianism. Yale had to work for all she got tonight. But we take joy in the fact that there are other days, and we can feel like the old confederate going home, who said his people had killed as many of the enemy as they had of them.

I am proud of our boys. I am very proud of them; and we shall not forget them. I am proud of the character of this contest, which was a contest of wit and brains and practice and mental work. We can say to our friends of Yale that they cannot carry home an exclusive pride in their men. We feel a pride in them, too. They belong to the brotherhood of collegians, and they have demonstrated, along with our boys, that they are not behind-hand in developing talent that is sure to tell in the future for the good of our fellow beings and the welfare of mankind. I know the character of collegians too well not to know that after an occasion of this kind there is no sharpness in defeat nor any undue glorification in victory. Such contests as tonight fit men for good citizenship, and I hope hereafter that this sort of contest will have its proper number of innings, as it certainly should have, and we promise our friends of Yale that we will give them additional innings, and under new circumstances in the future.

32

MY FIRST BOOK

THE title of my Doctor's thesis and of my first book was *The Beginnings of the English Romantic Movement. A Study in Eighteenth Century Literature.* It was really the fulfilment of a boyish dream; for the first literary problem to arouse my interest made appeal in my schooldays at Hartford. I was reading a good deal of literature of the Age of Anne, comparing it in my mind with the romances of Walter Scott. What caused that extraordinary change in the tone and fashion of poetry and prose? As a boy, I made up my mind that some day I would find out.

In the Spring of 1890 Professor Beers at Yale suggested that I take for the subject of my thesis the history of English Romanticism. No subject could possibly have interested me more. That summer I was enjoying my first visit in England; and I went to the British Museum to read for a few days. Although I was twenty-five years old, I looked like a boy, and was dressed in bicycle clothes. The man in the Librarian's office at first refused to give me a ticket, telling me that English schoolboys were not allowed in the Reading Room, and that I must not come there to read for my exams. I told him I was an American and a college graduate and was twenty-five years old. He did not believe this; and finally asked, 'Will you swear that you are over twenty-one?' Accordingly I swore, and signed on some dotted line, and was very reluctantly given access to the Reading Room for two days.

At the time I was amused but amused very much more

three years later; for in 1893 appeared the book for which I had begun reading on that September day in London, and to my delight, Doctor Richard Garnett wrote me a long personal letter of congratulation, saying he had read the new book, had ordered a copy for the British Museum, and wished to congratulate the author.

I did all the research work on this book in the Harvard College Library, but Professor Beers was kind enough to send me the manuscript of his lectures on English Romanticism, which were of especial help to me in order and method. When my thesis was finished and before it was taken to Yale, Professor Barrett Wendell read it, and insisted that I must publish it as a book. I had had no intention of publishing it, being content to have finished it; for as another graduate student remarked, 'I have finished my thesis; and if God will forgive me, I will never write another.'

The next year I asked Professor Beers if he had any objection to my publishing it, for although my thesis confined itself to beginnings and closed with the year 1765, and his lectures extended all through the nineteenth century, I felt I might be stealing some of his thunder. He immediately urged me to print, saying he might never publish and that if he did, it would be some years hence.

Professor Wendell gave me a letter to Scribner's, and the manuscript was given to the famous critic, W. C. Brownell, to read. I had a pleasant talk with him and with Mr. Charles Scribner, not knowing how closely intimate would be my friendship with both men in later years. Mr. Brownell declined the book as he thought it a work of special research and not suited to the general reader. It is the only book of mine ever declined by a publisher. His judgement seemed good and yet the future proved him mistaken, as the book after forty years continues to sell some copies annually. It had to be reprinted many times.

When Professor Kittredge heard it had been rejected, he wished to read it, and he urged Ginn and Company of Boston to publish it, which they did in the autumn of 1893. I well remember my excitement when the first proofs arrived. Kittredge's kindness did not stop there; for he reviewed the book in *The Nation*.

It received a very good press in the United States, Great Britain, France, and Germany. The only qualifying clause in the chorus of praise was that the book was too mechanical. Professor Edward Everett Hale in his review said that no scholar henceforth could get along without it, but that Doctor Phelps treated books as if he were cataloguing shells. And a very favourable French review (by Joseph Texte) said the style of the book was *un peu sec*, something no-one has ever said since of anything I published.

I conclusively proved in this book that the English Romantic movement began, not in the last quarter of the eighteenth century, but before 1750; that its beginnings were unconscious and instinctive, in contrast to the French romantic movement in the nineteenth century. For the French movement was a fight, led by some men of genius, against the national literary instinct, whereas the English movement was the assertion of the national romantic temperament in literature, held in bondage for a short time by men of genius in the Age of Anne. Even at the zenith of their glory, the signs of revolt were plainly visible.

I shall never know whether, after this gratifying initial success, I ought to have continued in research work in literary history or not. I had the satisfaction of having made an addition to orderly knowledge, which even the most fanatical believer in 'special research' was compelled to treat with respect.

As I look back, the thing that I most regret was the amount of time during the best years of early middle age that I gave to the *editing* of authors; this was sound scholarly work, but it took an immense amount of time, and it would have been better if I had devoted those years to writing original works.

But I was asked to edit the Selections from the Works of Thomas Gray, and although I succeeded in making my text closer to the originals than any edition that had appeared since Gray's death, and although the value of my book was greatly increased by a fine chapter contributed by Professor Kittredge on 'Gray's Knowledge of Norse,' in which he pointed out some appalling errors by Gosse, I doubt if the whole year I spent on this book was worth while. One of the best things about it was that it brought me a close epistolary friendship with the late Reverend D.C.Tovey of Worplesden Rectory, Guildford, England. In his edition of Gray's poems, he expressed his gratitude to the edition by Professors Phelps and Kittredge of Yale College (*sic*), and in his later edition of Gray's *Letters* he began his preface as follows:

> If I had their permission, I should like to dedicate this volume to four kindly correspondents whom it has never been my privilege to meet, but to whose encouragement in this, or comments on my previous work on Gray, I am much indebted. These are Professors Hales and Dowden on this side of the Atlantic, and Professors Phelps and Kittredge on the other. I am able to face once more some adverse and captious criticism, in the belief that my labours on Gray seem to them neither superfluous, nor, in spite of errors and oversights which, of all students of the poet they are best able to detect, unscholarly.

This led to a correspondence that lasted until his death. The most interesting statement in the following letter is the allusion to his son Donald, who more than justified his father's faith in him. He is now Sir Donald Francis Tovey, Reid Professor of Music in the University of Edinburgh, music editor for the *Encyclopedia Britannica*, composer of many pieces of music and author of important books.

WORPLESDEN RECTORY
GUILDFORD
May 4, 1901

MY DEAR SIR,

Ever since the receipt of your kind letter I have been alternately reproaching myself for not acknowledging it (or *did* I acknowledge it after all) and invoking a murrain on the yokels who misinformed you about Worplesden. I am on the way from Guildford to London. You must have passed my station in going up to town. It would have been a real delight to me to welcome you and Mrs. Phelps to my parson's fare, if you would have stayed to accept it.

I am sending you a few *errata*. I have sent the like to Professor Kittredge. Are you coming here again?

Yours ever

D. C. TOVEY

Are you a musician? My son Donald is making a name for himself both in England and Germany, as a pianist and composer. I daresay you will see him in America in a year or so.

The allusion in this letter to the misdirection was owing to the fact that my wife and I, bicycling from Devonshire to London in 1900, in passing through Guildford had in vain tried to find Worplesden Rectory and were sadly misdirected.

The Reverend Mr. Tovey, Professor Kittredge and I were in complete agreement about the standing of Sir Edmund Gosse as a scholar. As a literary critic, Gosse had a deservedly high reputation, but his immense British reputation as a scholar seems mysterious and inexplicable. Mr. Tovey, himself a scrupulous scholar, was never given to over-statement. In one of his letters he wrote me: 'I have gleaned more misinformation from the works of Edmund Gosse than from any other writer, ancient or modern.'

My edition of Gray led me into a series of editorial tasks which used up a vast amount of time and energy. Thackeray's *English Humourists of the Eighteenth Century* of which the British Museum did not contain a first edition, the Complete Novels of Samuel Richardson, the Works of Jane Austen, Stevenson's Essays, the Best Plays of Chapman for the Mermaid Series (I was pleased to be in that company) were some of the tasks that occupied my spare time in term and in vacation for fifteen precious years between 1894 and 1909!

My revolutionary course in Modern Novels at Yale had a permanent effect on my life and career; and it is impossible for me to say whether I chose rightly or wrongly. What I am certain about, however, is that the way I chose contributed to my happiness and to a less extent, naturally, to that of others.

In 1907, Mr. George P. Brett, head of the great publishing firm of the Macmillan Company in New York, asked me to call. He suggested that I write a book on Modern Novelists, for which he would give me a favourable contract on the spot, without waiting to see a page of manuscript. This subject appealed to me, for while it could scarcely be called research, it was more interesting to me than reading the works of authors who were not worth reading at all, whose sole value lay in their possible indication of literary movements. For in the summer of 1900, I had done an immense amount of work in the British Museum and in the Bodleian at Oxford, on the history of the English Drama in the eighteenth century. I do not regret this, because the conditions of work were delightful, and the field, from the point of view of research, was sufficiently rich. But from every other point of view, the material was dust and ashes.

So, two years later, after due reflexion, I accepted Mr. Brett's generous offer—I shall always be grateful to him—and wrote a book called *Essays on Modern Novelists*. There were separate essays, most of which I first printed in the *North American Review*, the *Forum*, the *Independent*, and other periodicals, on Thomas Hardy, William De Morgan, Mark Twain, Kipling, Alfred Ollivant, Howells, Stevenson, Björnson, Sienkiewicz, Sudermann, and Mrs. Humphry Ward. All of these authors were living, except Stevenson.

I admired these novelists, except Mrs. Ward. My essay on her novels was the ungracious attempt to destroy her reputation as a great novelist. It seems strange enough today that she ever was so regarded; but when I wrote my essay, she was almost universally considered, both in England and in America, as a writer of genius, and as one of the permanent figures in the history of the English novel. I had the highest respect for her mental ability, for her literary conscience, for the nobility of her character; but I thought her novels showed more industry than inspiration, and were without a spark of genius.

I have always enjoyed appreciative rather than destructive criticism; Goethe said the prime qualification of a critic was enthusiasm. But the contemporary appraisals of the novels of Mrs. Ward seemed to me ludicrously wrong. I will quote here the first and the last paragraphs of my essay.

It is high time that somebody spoke out his mind about Mrs. Humphry Ward. Her prodigious vogue is one of the most extraordinary literary phenomena of our day. A roar of approval greets the publication of every new novel from her active pen, and it is almost pathetic to contemplate the reverent awe of her army of worshippers, when they behold the solemn announcement that she is 'collecting materials' for another masterpiece. Even professional reviewers lose all sense of proportion when they discuss her books, and their so-called criticisms sound like publishers' advertisements. Sceptics are warned to remain silent, lest they become unpleasantly conspicuous. When *Lady Rose's Daughter* appeared, the critic of a great metropolitan daily remarked that whoever did not immediately recognize the work as a masterpiece thereby proclaimed himself as a person incapable of judgement, taste, and appreciation. . . .

Mrs. Ward is an exceedingly talented, scholarly, and thoughtful woman, of lofty aims and actuated by noble motives; she is hungry for intellectual food, reading both old texts and the daily papers with avidity. She has a highly trained, sensitive, critical mind,—but she is destitute of the divine spark of genius. Her books are the books of today, not of tomorrow; for while the political and religious questions of today are of temporary interest, the themes of the world's great novels are what Richardson called 'love and nonsense, men and women'—and these are eternal.

My book appeared in January 1910. It went through a number of editions, had a large sale for some years, and has not yet joined the overwhelming majority of the extinct. After twenty-eight years, the publisher's statement shows that during the last year many copies were sold!

Among the reviews that greeted its first appearance, I liked best the one written by Francis Hackett in Chicago—even if he did say that I occasionally hit the walls of my own mind.

Most of the reviewers were amazed that a book of essays on contemporary writers should come from a university professor; and indeed there were still many, probably the majority, of the academic men who did not know and did not care anything about living writers.

Of the senior professors of English literature at Yale, Professor Beers and Professor Thomas R. Lounsbury held exactly opposite views concerning the work I was doing. Mr. Beers gave me encouragement, and Mr. Lounsbury thought I was wasting my time on trivial matters. He wanted me to edit the complete works of Ben Jonson, or write a biography of old Ben, or if I must be modern, to write a biography of Browning.

Mr. Lounsbury enjoyed a great reputation as a scholar. He was an ornament to Yale, and we were proud of him. Furthermore, he was full of humour and common sense, a delightful companion, and favourite among the New York literati; but he cared nothing for European contemporaries. I do not believe he ever read a line of Ibsen, or of Tolstoy. His anthology of American poetry (1912) called the *Yale Book of American Verse*, will still delight the judicious reader by the wit and irony of its preface; he ridiculed Longfellow's 'Psalm of Life,' saying, 'The last place a rational man would choose for leaving a permanent footprint would be on the sandy beach bordering an ocean. . . . this particular young man seems to have been very young. He is advised by his heart to be a hero not only in the battle but in the bivouac. If the psalmist had thought it worth while to reply, he would doubtless have informed the young man that the bivouac, in the modern sense of the word, affords little opportunity for one to show himself a hero, and that the best thing he could do would be to act like one of the dumb driven cattle which his heart warns him not to imitate, and lie down and go peacefully to sleep. Yet with these views about the poem itself, I insert it in this collection in deference to a sentiment in which I do not share.'

For the same reason he included Bryant's 'Waterfowl' which he rightly regarded as second-rate.

The 'bivouac' particularly got on Mr. Lounsbury's nerves, for he fought as a private soldier at the battle of Gettysburg. He told me that in the roar of the battle, when his brigade were told to lie down for a few minutes, nearly every man fell asleep!

Yet, despite the wit and humour and common sense of this preface, the fact remains that the anthology included seven poems of Aldrich, seven of Gilder, seventeen of Holmes, nine of Stedman, and one of Whitman, and that one 'O Captain!' When someone praised that poem to Old Walt, he exclaimed, 'O *damn* My Captain!'

I mention all this because Mr. Lounsbury was the furthest possible from the dry-as-dust pedant, which makes his attitude toward contemporary writers and contemporary criticism all the more evidential of the then academic mind.

I well remember also his saying to me over and over again, and always with emphasis, that it was ridiculous to judge of the value of a college professor by what his students thought of him. They were not qualified to judge. It was only what other professors thought of him that should count; for they were his peers. Certainly, from the point of view of research, that is true. But, alas, their opinions were often affected by vanity and by jealousy.

It seemed to me that there were a sufficient number of professors dealing with the remote past, and doing 'original research.' While it would be a calamity for any university if all the professors of English literature were like me, I felt there was room in this vast body of scholars for one man who should devote at least part of his time to contemporary literature; even as the professors in every branch of *science* knew the latest discoveries. I therefore decided to go ahead.

In 1911 I published *Essays on Russian Novelists*, the first American critical work dealing with this subject. Not knowing Russian, I had to read many of these novels in French and German. Constance Garnett's incomparable translations of Dostoevski and Tolstoy and Chekhov had not appeared; Artsybashev's sensational *Sanin* I read in German. However, I knew that all the books I dealt with would soon appear in English; and my aim was to induce American and British readers to become familiar with some of the greatest works in the history of prose fiction.

The volume included separate essays on Gogol, Turgenev, Tolstoy, Dostoevski, Gorki, Chekhov, Andreev, Artsybashev, Kuprin, with some remarks on Garshin.

The value of these two books was increased by the

bibliography supplied for each by my friend, Mr. Andrew Keogh, Librarian of Yale University.

In 1915 I produced a critical work on Browning, and in 1932 I republished it with enough additional matter almost to double its size. It is meant to be both a commentary on many of the short poems and an introduction to the study of the poet; intended for the general reader. A review that gave me particular pleasure was by the Irishman Robert Lynd, who said, 'This book will introduce readers to a new world of excitement,' for that is exactly what I hoped to accomplish.

Other books I have published are *The Advance of the English Novel*, *The Advance of English Poetry in the Twentieth Century*, *Human Nature in the Bible*, and *Essays on Books*. The last-named appeared in 1914, just after war broke out in Europe. It drew a favourable review in *The Nation*, written I suspect by Paul Elmer More. He headed his review with the caption

REST AMONG THE PEDANTS

and went on to say that during the shambles in Europe pedants showed us how and where to take refuge. To be called a pedant in that particular journal gave me keen pleasure.

In addition to more than twenty-five original books, only one of which was intentionally humorous, I have written articles in a great variety of periodicals.

Most of my writing has been done in the Long Vacation in my summer home in Michigan, where we enjoy isolation and the absence of a telephone. We rise at six every morning, which gives me five good hours at my desk before lunch. If there were only no letters to write! The absence of letter-writing, said Mark Twain, was one of the things he was most eagerly looking forward to in hell.

Inasmuch as I have owed so much in my development

to the series of volumes called *American Statesmen* which
I read when I was seventeen, edited by John T. Morse, Jr.,
I had an intense desire to meet this famous biographer.

16 FAIRFIELD STREET
BOSTON
April 3 1929

My dear Professor Phelps:

I have often wished that I might have the pleasure of meeting a
gentleman of whom I have heard so much, and so pleasantly, as I
have of you. Your scheme for giving me that opportunity is most
welcome, and I shall await you next Saturday forenoon.

Very sincerely yours

JOHN T. MORSE, JR.

This letter was written in longhand, legible as large type.
Mr. Morse was then 89. When I knocked, he was playing
the typewriter vigorously; he seemed to spring across the
room. I had an hour's good talk. His sight and hearing
were perfect, his movements around the room were as active as if he had been thirty, and his mind equally alert.

33

PROFESSORS

IT is rather exciting to live in a small town like New Haven or Cambridge and to be aware of the fact that there is no field of human knowledge, no frontier of speculative thought, no department of the fine arts, where some member of the university faculty is not an authority. If you stand at one street-corner long enough, you will meet a fellow-citizen who can converse intelligently with Einstein, another who knows the latest discoveries in astronomy, another who can tell you about the electron, another familiar with the so-called prehistoric animals, another who can give an intelligent opinion on ancient or modern literature, another who can conduct a symphony orchestra without the score, etc., etc. The 550 members of the Yale faculty, for example, include experts on every department of knowledge. Any time I want to know anything about anything, I use the telephone, and I do not have to tackle the toll line. The amount of actual knowledge possessed by a group of men living in New Haven is almost as vast as the universe itself.

Sometimes, while my students in English literature were entering the classroom, I could not help thinking what an immense variety of instruction was to be imparted in various rooms during the next hour—in physics, chemistry, anthropology, economics, painting, architecture, law, musical composition, biology, zoology, botany, theology, metaphysics, ancient and modern languages, physiology, anatomy, calculus, drama, theatre, government, international politics, constitutional and financial history, and so on. And the life-philosophies of the professors are almost as different as their fields of instruction. One is a strong nationalist, and believes in big armies and navies; one is an ardent pacifist; one is a free-trader, one is a protectionist; one believes in the capitalistic form of government, one is a communist; one is an orthodox Christian, one is antagonistic to all forms of religious belief; there are also Roman Catholics, every shade of Protestant, and Jews. The university world is a microcosm of the world of thought.

And in practical affairs there is almost as much diversity. There are professors who can sail a ship across the ocean, there are those who can drive the Twentieth Century locomotive from New York to Chicago, there are those who can run a bank, stock-exchange, or machine shop, build a suspension bridge, preside over a court of law, paint a portrait, construct a cathedral, compose a sonata. It is exciting to live in such a group.

Today the pews and the pulpit, the students and the teachers, the voter and the office-holder, are nearer together.

The curious thing is, that in those olden times, when the members of the faculty displayed a front of dignified authority, there were frequent outbreaks of disorder, in the classroom and out of it. Teachers were often chosen for their ability as policemen. Now the question of order and good behaviour is never even considered, because there is no occasion for it. Students are as well-behaved in the classroom as in church. In those days, it was so customary to throw coal through a tutor's windows, that he used to say, 'My salary is a thousand dollars, and coal thrown in!'

When I was an undergraduate, it was part of every instructor's duty, if he had a room on the campus, to maintain order. It was not an uncommon sight, in the midst of an uproar at night, to 'spot' a professor in his nightgown, hiding behind a tree, and taking down names of those unfortunate students whose faces were revealed by the bonfire. Then someone yelled, 'Faculty!' and there was a scattering.

Imagine President Seymour or President Conant making such a connexion!

The old-fashioned 'stage' professor has gone forever. The familiar caricature expressed what was the common conception among the populace; a professor was a learned fool. He was a dungeon of remote and unimportant knowledge, without common sense, at home only in the classroom or in his researches. He might be treated with outward respect by the unregenerate, but with a secret contempt—at best, tolerance.

Now that the professor is a man of the world, conforming in appearance and manners to the conventions of society, there is perhaps some danger that he will go too far toward the other extreme. Religion and morality used to be generally associated with teaching. Many modern teachers are so eager to avoid the odour either of learning or of earnestness, that they sometimes adopt an air of flippant sophisticated ironical scepticism. Whatever place irony may have in certain forms of literary composition, it should never characterize the teacher. Teaching should be productive; irony is sterile. A teacher should believe in the subject and in the object; he should believe that his subject is all important, and that the pupil is worthy of his best efforts.

J. M. Barrie told me that he thought jealousy, rather than the love of money, was the root of all evil; he had seen so much misery caused by it. And I suppose jealousy is the love of oneself. High-minded scholars ought to be above such weaknesses; but there are many teachers who cannot endure to hear a colleague praised. Often, when some member writes a fine book or attains success in the classroom, he receives praise from every one except from his fellow-teachers.

In Germany I once saw an amusing play, *Privatdozent*, where, to the infinite entertainment of the audience, college faculty meetings were a part of the show, and what was still more amusing, meetings of professors' wives who took a hand in college politics. Here the really estimable and successful teacher was turned down, and an unworthy man promoted.

But of course there are weaknesses, sin, and vices, wherever there are men and women. And for my part, I rejoice that my life has been spent in an academic circle. We often hear of college friendships, the word being invariably applied to relations between undergraduates. But there are friendships equally strong among members of the faculty, and more enduring as well, for they live together longer. Living with college teachers is to live with men who are intelligent, cultivated, sympathetic, attractive, and on the whole, better and happier than the general run of men in other occupations. Especially *happier*. I brought a New York business man to take lunch in the Graduates Club in New Haven, and he said, 'How happy everybody seems in this place!'

President Hutchins of the University of Chicago recently made an address, which deservedly received wide comment, in which he praised the wisdom and foresight of college professors. They are indeed a fine body of men, because they are searching for the truth and eager to impart it. I am happy and proud to be in their company.

34

GEORGE SANTAYANA

IN the Department of Philosophy at Harvard in 1891 were William James, Josiah Royce, George Herbert Palmer, George Santayana, and Hugo Münsterberg, a quintet of striking personalities, each differing from the other four in many convictions and opinions, while dwelling together in fraternal harmony. Apart from their distinction as scholars, every one was a literary artist. They all knew how to write, not merely with force and with what clearness is possible on such themes, but with that beauty of expression that belongs only to consummate mastery of style. And the best *writer* among them, although he was overshadowed by the reputation of his older colleagues, was George Santayana.

I was invited one evening to attend the regular 'experience meeting' held periodically in the nineties by the Department of Philosophy. At these small assemblies—which were analogous to confessional prayer-meetings—various teachers and students in philosophy gave in the frankest manner a history of their bringing up, and a statement of their present attitude toward life, thought, and religion. The evening it was my good fortune to be present was a red-letter occasion, for the three speakers were young Santayana, still in his twenties, a fiery evangelical preacher, and a Japanese Buddhist. It was like a world's congress of religions on a small scale. Mr. Santayana, who seemed to me the last word in culture, refinement, and suavity, gave in quiet tones, half-smiling all the while, a beautifully expressed statement of a philosophical attitude which would have cost him his job at any other American college. 'If I had to define my position, I should call myself an atheist and a pessimist.' During this flow of exquisite language, it was clear to me that a storm was brewing in the evangelical mind, whose owner, by the way, was a German. As soon as the testimony was completed, this preacher was asked for his 'experience,' and he exploded. 'Before beginning my remarks, I wish to say emphatically that I regard Mr. Santayana's attitude with thorough contempt.' This made a small sensation; but the face of the gentleman attacked betrayed nothing except polite interest. The speaker was passionately sincere, but as Dryden wrote of Jeremy Collier, 'I will not say "The zeal of God's house has eaten him up"; but I am sure it has devoured some part of his good manners and civility.' He was, however, permitted to proceed without protest. 'I have been *converted*'—he glared around the room—'oh, I know how ridiculous that word sounds at Harvard, but'—at this point Professor Royce interrupted, and asked, 'Won't you tell us exactly your experience of Christian conversion, so that we can understand it psychologically?' which, indeed, he did. When he had concluded, the Buddhist, whose Oriental face had, to an Occidental observer, remained inscrutably impassive during the entire evening, gave a statement of his religious philosophy. In one evening, then, I heard a Spaniard, a German, and a Japanese express with commendable frankness points of view as far apart as the cluster of Hercules from the Charles River. Such was the quickening and exciting intellectual atmosphere in the Harvard Philosophical Department, in which Mr. Santayana was developed and to which he contributed. He remained an instructor nine years, an assistant professor another nine years and then, shortly after he had been promoted to a professorship, voluntarily withdrew, and went to live in Europe, where I had much good talk with him. He left Harvard to the sharp regret both of the students and of his colleagues.

Perhaps Mr. Santayana's breadth of view and intellectual charity are shown most of all in the fact that he has always honoured me with his friendship, which, as it has survived so many things, I hope will survive this book. I really believe in the Incarnation—that the Son of God is not only the Saviour of the world, but that He will eventually save it—and I can conceive of no mental or religious outlook that could be to my friend more crude or naïve. Possibly he enjoys points of view so different from his own, being quietly conscious of rational superiority. I remember his visit to me after I returned to Yale. He had never 'stopped off' at New Haven, and perhaps he had much the same idea of Yale as was not uncommon at Harvard. Berlin looked down on Oxford, Oxford looked down on Harvard, Harvard looked down on Yale, Yale looked down on— anyhow he came. We had splendid Autumn weather, the regular thing at New Haven (*advt.*), and I took him through the buildings, to college chapel, to a football game. I took him to the top of East Rock and showed him all the kingdom of Yale, and the glory of it. When he returned to Cambridge he published a charming article in the *Harvard Literary Monthly*, which called forth an immediate protest from the *Harvard Crimson*. 'Why, if a stranger should read Mr. Santayana's essay he might think Yale was superior to Harvard, which of course it isn't.'

Mr. Santayana was born in Madrid and brought up as a Roman Catholic. His parents were Spanish; he came to America when he was nine years old and was graduated from Harvard in 1886. While his father was living, he used to spend every summer in Spain, and he is as bilingual as it is possible for anyone to be. He began a translation of *Don Quixote*, which I am glad he abandoned; it would have been beautifully done, but what is the use of translating books when you can write masterpieces?

Logan Pearsall Smith, one of the best of anthologists, made judicious extracts from the writings of Santayana. He found in Mr. Santayana's books

> much writing like that of the older essayists on large human subjects, which seemed to me more interesting and in many ways more important than anything I found in the works of other contemporary writers. I soon fell into the way of copying out the passages that I liked, and thus I gradually formed a collection of little essays on subjects of general interest—art and literature and religion.

My only regret is that Mr. Smith did not include some of the author's poems. Not only is Mr. Santayana, even in his prose and in his philosophy, essentially a poet, but he has written and published many of the finest sonnets to be found in contemporary literature.

All honestly written philosophy is difficult reading for the average mind; it therefore gains by being presented in short pieces, the intervals allowing the reader to rise to the surface to breathe.

There is, indeed, a certain resemblance between Schopenhauer and Santayana; both have a passion for the life of reason, for art, literature, and music, and both have such a control of literary style that they make expression of thought a thing of beauty. Both belong more to literature than to philosophy; there is no doubt that the prodigious influence of Schopenhauer is owing more to the charm of his writing than to its truth. His style—admirably rendered into English by Lord Haldane—is a pliant slave to the author's will, now sparkling with wit and humour, now imperiously impressive with solemn earnestness.

Mr. Santayana's Essays are the fruit of long contemplation and of original thinking. They could not have been written by a pure Anglo-Saxon; they come from a mind essentially Latin in race, Catholic in training, and saturated with mediaeval scholastic philosophy.

He loves serenity and dignity of mind; it is not surprising, therefore, to find him unsympathetic to the turbulent and passionate Browning. But why should the hostility to Browning's philosophy make him incapable of appreciating Browning's poetry? I do not care much for Mr. Santayana's philosophy, but that does not prevent me from enjoying and admiring the literary art with which it is dressed. It is a corpse arrayed in shining garments. The faint suggestion of intellectual snobbism is seen in the following remark on the works of the great British poet. 'They not only portray passion, which is interesting, but they betray it, which is odious.' How plainly I can hear him say that! No man can understand everything, and I fear that Mr. Santayana does not understand Browning, though he thinks him particularly easy to understand. Browning had a gust for life, enormous vitality—qualities that in all civilized society have irritated the patrician; and Mr. Santayana cannot endure Browning's love of life; Browning must seem like a vulgarly cheerful fellow who slaps you on the back. To our philosopher a wise man will never covet immortality in the Christian sense; he might not accept the offer of any life anywhere. This is true pessimism; with all the author's delight in reason—an amazing gift to man—it is quite possible that he would prefer non-existence:

> Nothing can be meaner than the anxiety to live on, to live on anyhow and in any shape; a spirit with any honour is not willing to live except in its own way, and a spirit with any wisdom is not overeager to live at all.

If Mr. Santayana really understood the art of Browning, he could not have said 'the love he describes has no wings.'

> O Lyric Love, half angel and half bird,
> And all a wonder and a wild desire—

It would seem to me that if love is half angel and half bird it can hardly be said to lack wings.

Of religion he always speaks tolerantly, believing that the religious instinct represents man's ideal; there should never be such a thing as religious controversy, any more than we should argue with a lover about his taste. Hence Mr. Santayana has little sympathy with the 'liberal' element either in the Catholic or Protestant Church. The liberals are talking as though there were some basis of truth in religious belief, whereas, of course, it is a matter of poetry and emotion, like love of country. Why bring Raphael up to date? He himself loves the Catholic Church and its beautiful ritual, and in his own interpretation believes that every man should be religious, but not for a moment will he admit that the Catholic Church or any other has a fact foundation. As it is impossible to represent fairly the position of a philosopher on any subject, I had better quote,

> It could never have been a duty to adopt a religion not one's own—any more than a language, a coinage, or a costume not current in one's own country. The idea that religion contains a literal, not a symbolic, representation of truth and life is simply an impossible idea. Whoever entertains it has not come within the region of profitable philosophising on that subject.

It is much the same with his view of immortality. He is an unbeliever in any life beyond the grave, or in the continuance of personality; but he believes that the best part of us is immortal—that is, our influences and our share in the scheme of the universe; and he seems to take comfort in this thought. But, according to this system, the worst part of us must be equally immortal with the better; in order to believe that such immortality was agreeable, one would have to believe that the majority of human actions and thought make for goodness, which I am quite sure he does not believe at all. This is sentimentalism; if the better part survives in our friends, family, or influence—it is really they that survive, and they only for a short time. We do not survive. To Shakespeare himself, in this philosophy, it can make no possible difference five seconds after his death whether he wrote *Hamlet* or whether he spent his days as a drunken sot. Mr. Santayana says that we all ought to be willing to die for our children, or for art, or for our country; but Renan said, 'I am quite willing to die; only I should like to know whether death will be of any use to me.' And surely he was an honourable man.

I am not sure whether Mr. Santayana now calls himself atheist or not; but his philosophy is anti-Christian. To him man is a very small part of the universe, and it seems to him vulgar and conceited to think otherwise; but the whole stress of Christianity is on the importance (to God) of every individual man, woman, or child. In practice, Mr. Santayana believes that everyone should cultivate his mind to the utmost, in order to reach a position of philosophical quietude whence he can survey (like God) all human history and the vain passions and delusions of men, himself serenely (and consciously) superior to the common herd; but Christianity teaches that all men are brothers, and that the highest happiness consists in helping others rather than ourselves. He is better than his creed, as I am worse than mine.

But just as he finds religion beautiful, so do I find his books beautiful like lovely architecture, painting, or music. And it is the honest and noble effort of a man who is determined to make the best of the worst; who wishes to live the life of pure reason, but who is at heart a poet, loving everything beautiful and radiant.

His position in our day seems to me not unlike that of the poet Cleon created by that 'barbarian,' Robert Browning. Cleon summed up in his own person and achievements Greek life and thought; the intellect and art and beauty of the ancient world. He despised St. Paul, as Mr. Santayana despises evangelists. Only, so far from finding his philosophy a means for removing the sting from death, he said (quite correctly) that death was much more terrible to the cultivated philosopher than to the savage.

> Say rather that my fate is deadlier still,
> In this, that every day my sense of joy
> Grows more acute, my soul (intensified
> By power and insight) more enlarged, more keen;
> While every day my hairs fall more and more,
> My hand shakes, and the heavy years increase—
> The horror quickening still from year to year,
> The consummation coming past escape
> When I shall know most, and yet least enjoy—
> When all my works wherein I prove my worth,
> Being present still to mock me in men's mouths,
> Alive still, in the praise of such as thou,
> I, I the feeling, thinking, acting man,
> The man who loved his life so overmuch,
> Sleep in my urn.

So, if I were to look over the world today to find one man who summed up in his mind the best of human culture, both ancient and modern, who knew how to express his ideas in language that gives delight to the eye and to the ear, who represents the highest point attainable by study, thought, and contemplation—I should take the author of those books, which represent so much that is dignified and splendid, the last word of modern civilization, powerless to save the world. For, in the power of changing human lives, this beautiful book is like the Northern Lights, making darkness visible; whereas the simple words of the Gospel are like the genial sun at noonday, giving illumination and warmth to the meanest creatures on the globe.

Doctor William Fogg Osgood, for many years Professor of Mathematics at Harvard, now Emeritus, remembers Santayana very well as a boy, for they were in the same class at the Boston Latin School for four years. As seems natural enough, Santayana cared nothing for athletic games, and showed little ambition at that time to excel in scholarship. He was of course interested in the English language and in the history of Rome. 'Latin came easily to him, and French was like a dialect of Spanish.' I can understand that he cared nothing for mathematics or physics and did only enough to pass; but I am rather astonished that in those boyhood days he showed neither brilliance nor ambition in Greek, especially as 'we had the world's best teacher, Arthur Irving Fiske, Harvard '69.'

In Paris I had good walks and talks with Santayana. He is a philosopher, and lives what I suppose is the true life of a philosopher, though I should find it intolerably lonely. Still, he has what very few people have today, leisure for meditation. All his books are born of long hours of solitary, uninterrupted thought. Though I think he enjoys his own society better than that of other people, he is an admirable conversationalist and a perfect table companion. In a rather dingy restaurant on the Boulevard S.Michel we talked of literature, morals, and religion.

The English are the leanest race in the world; one seldom sees a fat Englishman, yet many of them eat four square meals every day. And when you do see a fat Englishman you will find that he carries his weight remarkably well. Mr. Santayana told me a new story of the famous Oscar Browning, of King's College, Cambridge. He ate seven meals a day. There are people who wake up in the middle of the night and cannot fall asleep again until they have eaten something. But O.B. set his alarm clock at three in the morning in order that he might wake and eat a herring! Then at seven o'clock tea and various eatables were brought to his bedside. At eleven he had a snack two hours before lunch. At four-thirty, high tea with plenty of food. He then ate nothing till dinner, an elaborate affair in many courses, and with a variety of wines. His seventh and last meal was a hearty supper, which he took just before going to bed. He lived to be eighty-three.

In August 1920, the *New York Times Book Review* published a long article by me on Mr. Santayana's *Little Essays*. In this I said his position among English and American philosophers was somewhat similar to that of Schopenhauer in German philosophy, since both of them owed their great reputation largely to the beauty and charm of their literary style, Schopenhauer being one of the few really great masters of German prose and Santayana having no living superior in his mastery of English style.

I then, perhaps mistakenly, compared Mr. Santayana's statements about immortality and religion with those of Lord Morley, as it seemed to me that Morley was absolutely frank in his complete disbelief of any future life, while Mr. Santayana's phrases about it seemed to me not absolutely frank. I also thought it strange that, when he had such a love for Dickens, he should have such a strong dislike for Browning. In all these matters he very courteously and very clearly shows that I somewhat misrepresented his position.

PARIS, SEPT. 8, 1920

DEAR PHELPS

I am much pleased to have your letter and your review of the *Little Essays*. All the first part of it makes me feel as if I were reading an obituary notice by anticipation, and I can almost imagine some Phi Beta Kappa orator, in the not very distant future, spreading this sort of roseate sunset glow over my uneventful history and limping personality. I don't object to the headlines; Harvard in the 1890's being me, and America Today being you: and I think the view of the Yard has much the same quality of cautious idealization. Yours is not a cubist portrait of your humble servant, nor yet a Dutch inventory of his features and circumstances. I think it is very good and fair, if one allows for the friendly partiality you do not disguise, and also for a certain glamour or pathos of distance that already bathed our memories of youth. The only fact that is wrong is your saying that my mother was an American: she was Spanish—we never spoke English together—but had been first married (in Manila) to one of the Boston Sturgis's, so that my half-sisters and half-brother belonged to that once prosperous and always agreeable tribe: and it was in consequence of this connection, and money matters concerned in it, that we went to live in America. A point of interpretation where I feel you are also somewhat misled, or at least reticent, is in regard to my reasons for leaving Harvard. Weariness had something to do with it, but weariness with lectures and with the "problems" of technical philosophy rather than with college committees, on which I seldom appeared. They knew I was no good at business! But my chief motive was a lifelong desire to live in Europe and—which is only possible here—to be left alone. In respect to higher things, most of what you say pleases and satisfies me greatly, especially your mention of Schopenhauer: that is to hit the nail on the head. There are only two points in which perhaps you don't understand me: it seems to me unfair to suggest that, unlike the wizzened Morley, I am not frank about immortality; a scholar like you ought to know that the platonizing or Spinozistic things I say about it, taken in an ideal sense, are the *original motif* of this doctrine in the European tradition: the notion of ghosts or of resurrection has been merely confused with it, and it is no compromise or hedging on my part to separate the two views once more. The other point is about liking life, and the poets who relish it. My disgust at Browning is not because he loves life or has it abundantly, but because he doesn't love it (as Dickens does, for instance) for what is *good* in it, but for what is bad, tawdry, and pretentious. I protest against being called a snob; what I love is what is simple, humble, easy, what ought to be common, and it is only the bombast of false ambitions and false superiority, that I abhor.

Before the war I was on the point of going to give some lectures at the University of Wisconsin and at Columbia, but I doubt now whether I shall ever cross the Atlantic again. I have my head-quarters here, and go away at intervals. Last winter I was in Italy, now I go to Spain, and I was in England throughout the war. All places, where there is an arm-chair within and something human to see without, are much the same, and I lead the same life everywhere. You will find me somewhere on the beaten track whenever you next come to these parts.

Yours sincerely

G. SANTAYANA

In 1928 Mr. Santayana told me he had begun writing a novel but that it would not be published until after his death. At Harvard in the old days he had been conspicuous in social life in Boston, and much sought after; but in Europe he was leading the life of a true philosopher, very simply and never going out in the evening. He was however most genial and affectionate. On 17 August we lunched in a restaurant and talked about ethics, Goethe, Schiller, and Emerson. He said that an ethical life could be lived much better without religion than with it.

In the autumn I preached a sermon at Yale, in which I quoted his Sonnet beginning

> O world, thou choosest not the better part!
> It is not wisdom to be only wise,
> And on the inward vision close the eyes,
> But it is wisdom to believe the heart.
> Columbus found a world and had no chart,
> Save one that faith deciphered in the skies:
> To trust the soul's invincible surmise
> Was all his science and his only art.

I wrote him that I had quoted this poem in the pulpit and he replied

ROME, NOV. 2, 1928

DEAR BILLY—

You always bring with you, even if you come only by the post, a sort of Gulf Stream of warmth and kindness. I have said that old Sonnet (written in 1884) over to myself—I find that I still remember it—and although the words are too much spaced, thinly scattered over an empty waste, like the scrub oaks over a ploughed field, which in Spain are called a wood, yet the whole is perfectly limpid, and I can imagine that emitted in a rotund voice in a hushed religious atmosphere (do people still cough in the Yale Chapel?) it might have a good effect. In any case, I appreciate your appreciation, and I hope our combined exhortation will encourage your young people to have Faith—in themselves!

I have been in Spain—no harm resulting—and afterwards at

Strong's in Fiesole: now I am trying to bend all my remaining energies to finishing vol. II of Realms of Being.—Affectionate greetings
to you both from your old friend

G.S.

In February 1932 my wife and I sailed to Greece, but
before starting I wrote, hoping to meet him in Rome. We
met there in April and he invited us for lunch at a restaurant, the windows of which commanded a magnificent
view. Every afternoon I took long walks with him and his
conversation was, if possible, more stimulating than ever.
As a rule he was visible only between four and six; he wrote
steadily in his room from early in the morning until four,
and after six he retired. But he was kind enough to break
his rule for that one luncheon, and he seemed to enjoy
being with us. Tea and long walks in the afternoon he particularly enjoyed, for I am sure he knew that he had done
a good day's work. I asked him again about the novel; he
was proceeding rapidly with it, but he still felt sure it would
not be published until after his death.

HOTEL BRISTOL, ROME,
Jan. 4, 1932

DEAR BILLY—

Much better than a hurried cruise in a moving, rolling, smoking
and crowded boat would be a quiet luncheon on one of the Eternal
Hills (we may forget that the Vincinal has been removed) of Rome,
namely, the Aventine, to which I invite you both in advance, without
prejudice to other meetings. All that is necessary is that you should
come here on your way to Naples, as I presume you would in any
case.

Your journeys are so many and so energetic that you must often
have been in Rome before; but you will find the old sights probably
mellowed in an eye that has kept watch over New Haven, Conn.
(you see I can quote poetry too, and better than Browning's) and
also many new improvements. I confess I envy you going to Athens
and the Greek islands; but not in the Queen Mary. If I were younger

I should go, alone and solitary for several months; but as it is, I try to make up in memory and fancy what is wanting in leg-power.

I will not give you any news of myself, or ask for any of you, in the hope of soon seeing you.

Yours sincerely

G. SANTAYANA

I knew that he had delivered a lecture at the invitation of some learned academy at The Hague, but I thought it was about Erasmus. I am glad I made the error, for it drew from him the following letter.

HOTEL MIRAMONTI,
CORTINA D'AMPERESSO
July 10, 1933

DEAR BILLY—

Not Erasmus, Spinoza! But even that is not accurate. I went last September to the Hague, where they had a meeting in honour of the tercentenary of Spinoza's birth, and I read a paper which is only attached to Spinoza by way of the zenith: for, mind you, though physically every zenith is at a hopelessly different point from every other, spiritually the nearer anyone gets to his own zenith, the nearer he is to everybody else's. This paper is to appear in a polyglot volume entitled *Septimana Spinozana* which was to have been issued last November, but is still delayed. Perhaps it will appear by November next.

As I approach 70 (December next the venerable number will be complete) I feel that I may abandon the future more and more to Providence. I go on working, but without being at all confident that it will be possible, or would be best, for me to accomplish anything special. At present, I am crawlingly proceeding with my 'novel': this is something nobody else could do, since it gives the *emotions* of my experiences, and not my thoughts or experiences themselves: whereas *The Realm of Truth* or *The Realm of Spirit* might perfectly well be described by some future writer better than I should do it. However, I am very well, and not worried by the crisis or the collapse of the dollar: it makes me much poorer on paper, but I had a broad margin to my budget and as yet have no need of changing my way of living; and it is not impossible, if I should live ten years more, that I might finish my whole programme.

This place—where I have spent three previous summers—is really delightful: warm enough in the sun to make the system exude its waste substances, and cool enough at night to kill all mosquitoes and even flies. Besides the Dolomites are highly picturesque, the peasants also, and the people at this hotel very tolerable—since I don't have to speak to them. The trouble is that on September 1st winter sets in, and I shall have to move to Venice or elsewhere until it is time to return to my Roman diggings.

Well: You at Great Yale are probably being carried sky-high on the crest of twenty enthusiasms at least. Don't break your neck, and God bless you!

Kindest regards.—Come again to Rome: it is improving yearly more than if it were in America. You will be astonished.

Yours ever

G.S.

He changed his mind about publishing the novel, fortunately for the public; and in the winter of 1935–6 it appeared first in England and then in America. Curiously enough, although he has a very high reputation in England, the novel did not make a sensation there; but in America it had an enormous sale, and received favourable reviews from the leading critics. I was enchanted with the literary style and with innumerable observations, because they revealed the great artist and the great mind; but I thought his characters lacked vitality. I wrote a long review for *Scribners* and the following correspondence took place.

HOTEL BRISTOL, ROME
Feb. 16, 1936

DEAR BILLY—

Your letter about *The Last Puritan* was one of the first that reached me, but I have put off thanking you for it until others began to come, so that I could have a certain background on which to place your judgement, other than my own necessarily internal or *a priori* view; because the hardest thing for an author, especially when he has lived as long as I have with his characters—45 years—is to conceive how they will seem to other people, when conveyed to them only by *words*. I have pictures, quite as distinct as memories; and my characters *speak to me*, I don't have to prompt them. This doesn't contradict the fact which you mention, and I point to in the *Epilogue*, that these characters speak my language, and are in some sense masks for my own spirit. On the contrary, that makes, or ought to make, them more living, since they are fetched from an actual actor on the stage, for their social parts. And I think you are partly wrong, like so many other critics, when you suggest that my characters are ghostly and not 'living.' Even the admitted literary character of their talk is not incompatible in the drama, with individuality in tone and temper. Of course, I don't always succeed; yet I think, if you drop all preconceptions or clichés, you will find that there is a good deal of individuality in the way my characters talk, within the frame of what you might call my *metre*. It is my writing, but it is their sentiment. Only the book is very long, it can't leave distinct images if not allowed to settle. The great point is, as with poetry, to get the mind docile and free for suggestion, and then the dramatic spell will work. At least, that is what I can't help feeling, and what is confirmed by various witnesses. One notices Mrs. Darnley's special speech; another tells me he can *hear* Rose talk; . . . surely Irma and Mrs. Alden are not echoes of myself.

However, that isn't the point that matters most in the book or in your letter. You say I don't love life, and that faith is necessary. Very true: I don't love life unconditionally; but I enjoy the 'mere living,' (as Browning has it) when I am in good health, which is most of the time: and I enjoy the episodes, unless I am rudely prevented from doing so. If you have my *Dialogues in Limbo*, and will look at pp.156–161, you will find Socrates and me defining the matter exactly. It was Oliver, not I, who didn't love life, because he hadn't the animal epicurean faculty of enjoying it in its arbitrariness and transiency. He was a Spiritual man, incapacitated to be anything else, like Christ, who wouldn't be a soldier or athlete or lover of women or father of a family (or, even, though I don't say so in the book, a good believing Christian). Now that is a magic vocation, like the vocation of the poet: it demands sacrifice and devotion to a divine allegiance: but poor Oliver, ready for every sacrifice, had nothing to pin his allegiance to. He was what the rich young man in the Gospel would have been if he had been ready to sell his goods and give to the poor, but then had found no cross to take up and no Jesus to follow. Faith, as you say, is needed; but faith is an assurance inwardly prompted, spring-

ing from the irrepressible impulse to do, to fight, to triumph. Here
is where the third sloppy wash in the family tea-pot is insufficient.
And without robustness an imposed intellectual faith wouldn't do:
it would only make a conventional person. You say you can't understand how I seem to hold my own in the world without faith, and
almost without the world. It is quite simple. I have the Epicurean
contentment, which was not far removed from asceticism; and besides I have a spiritual allegiance of my own that hardly requires
faith, that is, only a humorous animal faith in nature and history,
and no religious faith: and this common sense world suffices for *intellectual satisfaction*, partly in observing and understanding it, partly
in dismissing it as, from the point of view of spirit, a transitory and
local accident. Oliver hadn't this intellectual satisfaction, and he
hadn't that Epicurean contentment. Hence the vacancy he faced
when he had 'overcome the world.' *Basta*. Thank you a thousand
times for your friendship.

G.SANTAYANA

On receiving this admirable letter, I asked his permission
to print it in *Scribners*, as it made the best commentary on
the book that I had seen.

By his lack of 'faith' I meant not only faith in God, but
faith in life, such as, for example Sacha Guitry has, who
dedicated his autobiography to *La Vie*. I also said that not
one of the characters in his novel was what I should call
'good.'

HOTEL BRISTOL, ROME
March 16, 1936

DEAR BILLY—

Yes, of course you may print my letter; not that I remember what
I wrote, because my memory disdains to record recent events, but I
can trust you to leave out any indiscreet passages. . . .

There is something which I probably didn't say in my letter that
I wish you would discuss some day in your 'As I Like It' articles.
An important element in the *tragedy* of Oliver (not in his personality,
for he was no poet) is drawn from the fate of a whole string of Harvard
poets in the 1880's and 1890's—Sanborn, Philip Savage, Hugh
McCulloch, Trumbull Stickney, and Cabot Lodge: also Moody, al-

though he lived a little longer and made some impression, I believe, as a playwright. Now, all those friends of mine, Stickney especially, of whom I was very fond, were visibly killed by the lack of air to breathe. People individually were kind and appreciative to them, as they were to me, but the system was deadly, and they hadn't any alternative tradition (as I had) to fall back upon; and of course, as I believe I said of Oliver in my letter, they hadn't the strength of a great intellectual hero who can stand alone.

I have been trying to think whether I have ever known any 'good' people such as are not to be found in my novel. You will say 'There's me and Annabel: why didn't you put *us* into your book to brighten it up a little?' Ah, you are not novelesque enough: and I can't remember anybody so terribly good in Dickens except the Cheeryble Brothers, and really, if I had put anyone like that in they would have said I was 'vicious,' as they say I am in depicting Mrs. Alden. But Irma was what I think good: she wasn't sillier than we all are, except that we keep our silliness quiet. And Oliver was very good: I don't think you like *good* people really, only *sweet* people—like Annabel and you!

G.S.

My acquaintance and subsequent friendship with Mr. Santayana I count among my blessings. Despite our divergence in *Weltanschauung*, I honour him and I love him. His essay on Dickens (in *Soliloquies in England*) is the finest interpretation I have ever read; I have never recovered from my astonishment at his admiration for that particular author. It was natural that Chesterton should love Dickens; but Santayana? I thought Santayana would be repelled by what he would consider Dickens's vulgarity. But no critic has ever written of Dickens with more sympathy and enthusiasm. I asked him how these things might be; and he told me that during the war he was in England. In spare moments he tried to do some reading and soon found that Dickens was the only writer he could read. His essay tells us why.

35

THOMAS SERGEANT PERRY

WHILE I was a boy in high school, I read Mr. Perry's admirable book *English Literature in the Eighteenth Century*. His treatment of the subject produced a permanent impression, and about eight years later when I was a graduate student at Harvard, he was kind enough to invite me to lunch at his house in Boston. Mr. Perry was a great linguist and after he was seventy years old learned Russian and finally read it with ease. He said he thought he had accomplished more than Cato, who learned Greek at eighty. Mr. and Mrs. Perry brought up their children to speak European languages; I remember my amazement at this lunch at their house when the baby girl had a tantrum and was removed from the room, crying and protesting *in French*. I had not supposed any American children took French so seriously or so naturally. That baby is now the wife of Mr. Joseph C. Grew, the accomplished American ambassador to Japan; formerly ambassador to Turkey and to France.

Mr. Perry was a scholar who loved learning for its own sake; he had little ambition and disliked publicity. His intellectual curiosity was insatiable and his letters to me were always interesting. In the seventies he had known Turgenev well in Paris and at that time he produced an English translation (from the French version) of one of his novels. He had an unqualified admiration for the writings and for the personality of Chekhov; and as he grew older he felt that America was intellectually immature and steadily growing more vulgar.

Mrs. Perry, a niece of James Russell Lowell, was a painter, whose professional career extended over many years. In the early days Howells was an intimate friend and in the twentieth century Edwin Arlington Robinson. She painted their portraits.

The Perrys lived abroad for years, and in 1906 we spent a day with them at Giverny. We had tennis doubles and Perry, who was sixty-eight years old, said he preferred singles. I asked if he were not afraid such a contest might kill him. 'But what a glorious death to die!' He (like me) read with avidity all the accounts of the great tennis matches. He read every word in *American Lawn Tennis*, which he called the best magazine in America.

When letter-writing had become almost a lost art, Mr. Perry was a master; his letters, of which I received at least one every week for fifteen years (how I miss them!) were full of charm. One day he had been reading Chekhov's letters to his wife (the famous actress Madame Knipper), and while Mr. Perry felt that they were too intimate to print, he could not help enjoying them.

> Since the letters are printed I most gladly read them. I find them touchingly delightful. You know my sworn devotion to Chekhov, and now it is renewed. They sent me the book from the Public Library, and along with it one that treats of certain states of mind among our fellow-citizens. Its title is 'The Raven on the Skyscraper,' by Veronica and Paul King. . . . It is a ghastly record of our sins, and a confirmed optimist like you will feel its injustice, but a professional pessimist like me will revel in it. Of course it is one-sided, but even then there is a lot of one-sided vulgarity and indecency and brag in this half-ripe, half-rotten country and we are all miserable sinners. Look however at the Chekhov book. It is delightful.

In response to my request, he wrote to me about Emerson: 'I wonder if any one knew him well, as men commonly know one another. I certainly did not, though I saw him several times, first as a boy of 10 when I saw him lecture and he looked like his early portrait, long, lean, lank but with the face of a communicative angel; then in 1862, a Freshman taken to the shrine by his son, a classmate. When I was a tutor, he came to my room on some vaguely understood overseer business. A friend of mine, a senior, was in my room who, I told him, fell on his belly with awe and wriggled from the room like a serpent, for there was, with all his simplicity, his habit of rocking, of eating pie, of coddling each elbow with the other hand, an aura of greatness that was most imposing. Every one felt it. He and Monet— very unlike—gave me the impression of greatness—it's a splendid feeling. Then soon after our marriage L. and I paid a visit to R.W.E. and I could give you details of his talk (about Swinburne e.g.) if writing were easier. Then I heard his lectures (though earlier) at Harvard College.'

Mr. Perry told me of one conversation with Emerson that made a tremendous impression. Emerson came into the room where he was, and began speaking with animation of a friend who had suddenly fainted away. His eyes glowing with excitement, Emerson said 'He fell in a swound,' pronouncing the word to rhyme with *ground*. Swound is a word one *sees* often, but for the first and last time in his life, Perry heard it spoken. The greatness of the speaker, his 'sad sincerity,' his utter unconsciousness of using an unusual expression, combined to make the remark unforgettably striking.

HANCOCK
NEW HAMPSHIRE
June 25, 1927

DEAR P,

If you want to read a real book (as you have probably done already) take *Trader Horn* (Simon & Schuster); it will delight you. It is full of the real stuff & makes almost all other bks. seem like theatre programmes. I am tired or I wd. go on for half an hour.

I reproached Robinson for giving you & not me the *Torrent*, the rare first egg he laid. I bo't the other bk. Dec. 12, '97, I believe, having taken it up in the bk. shop & found it worthy. I can't remember what exact lines fascinated me, for soon after I was off to Japan.

T.S.P.

I had written him that I possessed autographed copies of the first two books by Edwin Arlington Robinson.

36

PLAYING GAMES

I HAVE always been a playboy and have wasted (if you like) a large proportion of my life playing games, but I have had such an enormous amount of fun in competitive sport that I find it difficult to regret the time I have given to it. I began playing baseball when I was five and kept at it until I was forty-five; then, although broken tendons in the leg quickly healed, I decided to quit. I have never played any game, outdoors or in, for money; for my excitement in games, my joy in winning, my sorrow in defeat, have always been so intense that no additional stimulus has been necessary.

I do not really regret the lost time. I regret in learning games that I did not take them more seriously. If I were to live my life over again, I should get early enough good instruction in golf and lawn tennis, especially in the latter. I have never risen above mediocrity in any sport except long distance running, though I have won a fair share of prizes. In 1887, when I was twenty-two, I won the cross-country championship of Yale, running nine miles in fifty-four minutes. There were twenty-three starters. I ran in fourth or fifth place for half an hour, then I increased the pace, and passed every man but one, who was so far ahead of me I could not see him. And indeed, if he had not been an inexperienced Freshman, four years younger than I, he would have won. I did not get a sight of him until about three-quarters of a mile from the finish, when I not only saw him but also saw he was running well. I knew then the only way I could beat him would be to pass him just

once, a hundred yards or so from the finish, and to pass
him with a burst of speed so that he would think I had
much in reserve. With great difficulty I gained on him;
then as I got nearer to him, although I was completely exhausted, I summoned my will power, and on sheer nerve, I
dashed past him. He gave a grunt and acquiesced, evidently thinking I had saved everything for the home
stretch. In reality, although 'all in,' I went 'all out,' and
fell across the finish line, not unconscious, but unable to
move. In a few moments he came in relatively fresh.

I did no training for this race; I was always in good condition and in those days never smoked or drank. An hour
before the race, I ate a hearty meal, finishing with a large
wedge of apple pie.

In college I was not good enough to win a place on the
University nine, but I made the 'second' nine, called the
Yale Consolidated.

The summers in Huron County, Michigan, where I am
now writing these words, were largely spent in playing
ball until I was over forty; and our nine, the Huron City
nine, made up chiefly of members of the U.S. Coast Guard,
won the championship of the County in 1897.

The most exciting moment in all the years I played baseball, happened one summer day in 1893 at Harbor Beach
(then called Sand Beach) when I played third base for Bad
Axe against the Sand Beach nine. Many times have I
struck out with men on bases; and here was the stage set
for great drama, which happens so often in story-books
and so seldom in life. It was the last half of the ninth
inning. Our opponents were exactly three runs ahead. We
had three men on bases, but two were out when I went to
bat. I got two strikes. Apparently no chance of our winning! I can hear the voice of the enemy catcher now (Al
Knapp remembers it as well as I do; he was the catcher
and I see him every summer). 'Put one right over; the big

stiff can't hit it!' I saw the pitcher wind up and the ball approaching. I had no confidence left; I fully expected to strike out. But with the strength of despair, I swung my bat with all my might. To my amazement I saw the ball going on a line over the centre fielder's head. It brought in four runs and won the game, and as I crossed the plate, I had the greatest single thrill of my life. This famous hit made history; it is still talked of and written about in that part of the world.

The love of most men for sport and their absorbing interest in it cannot perhaps be defended rationally; it is an instinct going deeper than reason. Men like W.H.Hudson, Bernard Shaw, and others to whom sport was abhorrent, were without 'sporting blood.' Yet the fact that the majority of men turn first of all to the sporting page in the newspaper can be accounted for on the ground that the first page is usually a record of failures—failures in business, failures in the art of living together, failures in citizenship, in character, and many other things; whereas the sporting page is a record of victories. It contains some good news, a commodity so rarely found on the first page. During the World War, I was travelling somewhere on the train and in the early morning the Chicago newspapers were brought to us; we all grasped them eagerly. Sitting next to me was an Episcopal clergyman in clerical dress. He paid no attention whatever to the war news, but turned feverishly to the sports pages.

In 1892 I was reading aloud the news to my father. My father was an orthodox Baptist minister; he was a good man and is now with God. I had never heard him mention a prize fight and did not suppose he knew anything on that subject, or cared anything about it. So when I came to the headline CORBETT DEFEATS SULLIVAN I read that aloud and turned over the page. My father leaned forward and said earnestly 'Read it by rounds!'

I began to play lawn tennis in 1882, played a good deal, but not regularly, in college, and after I became a member of the Yale Faculty and joined the New Haven Lawn Club in 1892, I played daily. On 30 May 1896 Dr. Fred Chase (the astronomer) and I reached the finals in the New England Tennis Championship, and won second prizes; we were beaten by Malcolm Chace and Arthur Foote, both of them famous players. In 1904 I entered the Bavarian tournament at Munich, and with my partner Bernhard Fünfstück won first prize in men's doubles (*Herren Doppelspiel mit Vorgabe*). We received handsome silver cups. In this same tournament I won first prize in Veteran singles, open only to those who were more than thirty years old! I was thirty-nine. In the finals I played against an Austrian Count, who had me five–love in the first set. He never won another game, however, as I defeated him 7–5, 6–0. I got another silver cup, first prize singles, *Veteranenspiel*.

In 1912 at Mentone, in Southern France, with my French partner M.Arnal, I won first prize in the men's handicap doubles. Although I was forty-seven years old, this was the best playing in doubles I had ever performed; we had a long, hard road to the finals, every match being close.

The New Haven Lawn Club was the only club in America, so far as I know, where tennis was played in the open air with deep snow on the ground, and a temperature at zero or below. We had a court made of wooden planks, laid down every Autumn at the end of the season. The snow was shovelled off, and I have never enjoyed tennis more than in the crisp winter air. I do not know why other clubs did not follow our example. Later, we built two concrete courts, and continued to play tennis all through the winter.

Although in all games I have always played to win, have been elevated by victory and depressed by defeat, the playing has always been mingled with abundant hilarity. My delight in games has made it impossible for me to keep my mouth shut. I am afraid that persons playing tennis on adjoining courts have often been annoyed by the stream of talk and nonsense. My innumerable tennis partners and opponents will remember (not unkindly, I think) the laughter and talk and bad puns that have accompanied our games of tennis and golf. The almost oppressive silence in which most persons play games is foreign to my nature. This silence is characteristic not only of great experts, but of ordinary players and duffers.

I have had the pleasure of seeing many of the greatest players of the world, not only in tournaments but in practice; the only ones who talk and laugh a good deal are Tilden and Perry and Borotra. I remember watching Crawford and Quist playing practice sets with others for several hours. Crawford never smiled and when he spoke, at rare intervals, it was almost a whisper. Quist had the expression of a chief mourner at a funeral. No doubt they enjoy playing and prefer silence; but with me, physical exercise in outdoor games has always stimulated an irrepressible effervescence.

Many of the happiest afternoons of my life were spent playing tennis with my colleagues on the Yale faculty and other friends at the New Haven Lawn Club. For thirty years I gave a series of twenty Tuesday afternoon public lectures in New Haven which began at quarter past four; so every Tuesday afternoon I used to play tennis beginning at two and watch the clock carefully to see just how much time would be left to bathe and change and reach the lecture hall. During the month of September, while we were living in Michigan, I looked forward to these tennis matches with such eagerness that I used to write to Professor Jack Crawford, my regular partner, to Mr. Stanley Williams, to Mr. Lewis Bronson and others, so that on the first Tuesday of the term three men would be sure to be there at the Lawn Club at two o'clock for our first game.

We had a special terminology for various strokes. Because a famous Yale football player, Otis Guernsey, had won a game with Princeton in the last moment by a long kick that trembled on the cross-bar and finally fell on the other side, every net-cord shot was called a 'Guernsey,' and was greeted by shouting that word—unintelligible to spectators. Innumerable other expressions known only to the initiated were employed to punctuate exciting moments in our games, so that these doubles, in which I took part until I was seventy, mingled violent physical exercise with a continuous torrent of vocal hilarity. Even now when I look at that clock on the Lawn Club grounds which I used to watch with such intensity, I feel a pang that I shall never again take part in these exciting and joyful contests. Of all the things I regret most at being forced to abandon because of old age, lawn tennis would come first and I shall always be grateful to the following men, colleagues of mine on the Yale faculty, whose companionship in this magnificent sport gave me such intense pleasure for more than twenty years: Jack Crawford, A. K. Merritt, George Nettleton, A. G. Keller, Fred Luquiens, Stanley Williams, Arthur Corbin, Stewart Mims, Charles Warren, Jack Adams, Karl Young, W. C. Abbott, Howard Church, and others.

On 1 Sept. 1905 my brother-in-law, Frank W. Hubbard, and I went to Brainerd, Minnesota, to visit Alfred K. Merritt, the Yale Registrar, and there for three days we had the finest prairie-chicken shooting I have ever enjoyed. Although these birds are as big as hens and rise from short stubble, it is impossible to see them until they do rise. Of course no sportsman would ever shoot them except on the wing; but why are they never seen ten yards away in stubble two inches high?

I have never been a bridge player because learning the modern game takes more time than I am able to give, but I am devoted to the old-fashioned game of duplicate whist, which almost no one plays today. For thirty years three of my colleagues on the Yale faculty, A. K. Merritt, the Registrar, A. G. Keller, Professor of the Science of Society, and John M. Berdan, Professor of English, have played duplicate whist, Merritt and I playing against Keller and Berdan. We have never played for any stake because we are so eager to win and so anxious not to lose that the excitement needs no further stimulation. Furthermore we never play in the evening because if I should play this game in the evening, I should not sleep all night. None of us can afford to waste a morning at it, and if the weather is good we should rather be outdoors than playing any game inside. But when the weather is bad and we all four have an afternoon free we play; to play the twenty-four boards back and forth takes about three hours. We have had an enormous amount of delight out of these stormy afternoons and candour forces me to admit that Keller and Berdan have, during a period of thirty years, won more games than Merritt and I, though not enough to prevent a continuous white-hot excitement every time we begin.

We have a formula for telephonic invitations to these whist battles. When the weather is horrible, I call up these three colleagues, announcing *This is the day the Lord hath made!* which is immediately understood as an invitation. Professor Keller cut that text in Hebrew out of some Semitic journal, whereupon my friend and colleague, Professor Charles C. Torrey, was kind enough to letter it out for me in the original Hebrew, on a long card, and this placard stands over us as we play.

In later years we added to this Faculty Whist Club Mr. Edwin Oviatt, Professor J. C. Adams, Professor F. B. Luquiens, Professor C. B. Tinker; it is an interesting fact that a majority are members of the class of 1896, whom I first met in 1892 and with whom I kept up intimacy all my life.

Speaking of cards, the former pastor of our church in New Haven one morning when I was present unconsciously demonstrated his own innocence and the guilt of the congregation. In the middle of his sermon, he remarked, 'Members of this church should never play bridge for money. It is not the amount that matters, it is the principle of the thing. It is wrong. Even if you play for a very small stake, it is still wrong. Even if you play for a trivial stake, for a merely nominal stake, even if you play for *only five cents a point*, it is still wrong.' The gasp of horror that went over the audience gave them away. I have often wondered what would have happened to this excellent man if he had ever followed the example of Dean Inge. The Dean said he did not believe in playing cards for money, but that just a few times, to help out a party, he had played for very small stakes. I am sure the Dean knew exactly what he was doing, but the American. . . .

All men can be divided into two classes; those who are excited over playing games and those who are not. It is, of course, from the rational point of view absurd to feel bad because one is beaten; and absurd to rejoice over a victory. No one knows better than I that what one should chiefly enjoy is the pleasant exercise, the good companionship; and after the match is over one should not then care either for victory or defeat. But how impossible such a philosophical attitude!

One illustration will suffice for all. When I was an undergraduate perhaps the greatest scholar on the Yale faculty was William Dwight Whitney, who was regarded both in Europe and America as the leading authority on Sanscrit. His home was constantly visited by students because of its hospitable, social, and stimulating atmosphere; no better conversation could be had anywhere in New Haven. I remember when a Freshman I first entered their sitting room and found not only the three charming young girls, his daughters, and their sweet-tempered and affectionate mother, but the great scholar himself. He looked the part, with snow-white hair and beard and unaffected dignity. He rose from his chair and greeted me, a humble Freshman, as if I were somebody.

Now this gentleman was, as I remarked, one of the most famous scholars in the world and his speciality was in the remote field of Oriental languages. In manner he was calm, self-collected and courteous. But I discovered that his physician had forbidden him to play any game whatever—croquet, halma, checkers, or cards—because he was so excited and so depressed by defeat that it was bad for his health.

I don't know how others would feel on receiving such information; but my respect and affection for the man, when I heard this, were increased an hundred fold.

I know how to enjoy demonstratively and how to enjoy in silence. In playing games I am noisy, except when another is addressing or hitting a golf ball; but my intense, ecstatic enjoyment of symphony orchestras and the operas of Wagner finds me immobile and silent. Never have I committed the mortal sin of nudging my neighbour at music; for there is only one sin worse than that, which is humming a melody when it is sung or played on the stage. Apparently there have always been persons who either consciously (to show off) or unconsciously, commit this unpardonable sin. Chard Smith, in his entertaining and valuable work, *Annals of the Poets* (1935) reminds us of what Dr. Johnson said of the poet Matthew Prior: 'One day he sat at the Paris opera by a man who was so transported that he accompanied the principal performer with his own voice. Prior began to vituperate the actor so loudly and eloquently that his French neighbour, ceasing from his own song, began to protest, saying that the performer was among the greatest singers of the age. "I know all that," replied Prior, "*mais il chante si haut, que je ne sçaurois vous entendre.*"

The first game of golf I ever played was at Providence, my companions being Professors John M. Manly and Edmund Delabarre, of Brown University, on 17 May 1896. Our scores for the nine holes were Delabarre, 68, Manly, 95, and mine 87. I did not play again until the summer of 1897, on a course of four or five holes at Port Austin, Michigan. In the Spring of the next year, 1898, I joined the Golf Club in New Haven and on 21 October 1899 I won the championship of the New Haven Country Club, defeating T. S. Woolsey, Jr., in the final round of 36 holes.

I became a fanatical golf player and forsook lawn tennis altogether. For those first years of the century, 1900–03, we paid no attention to the season or to the weather. We played golf in rain, hail, snow, sleet and in every week of the year. If the snow was very deep, we wore hip rubber boots and used a red ball. We were insane and had a good time.

In 1903 my wife and I went to Europe for a year. There was no golf either in France or Germany, so I took up tennis again, and grew to enjoy it so much that when we returned to Yale in the Autumn of 1904 I played only tennis for some years. Then I took up golf again, and gave about an equal amount of time to both games until I was seventy years old. I should have played either one of these games better had I given up the other; but I should not have had so good a time.

A few years ago I wrote an article on golf, which some day I hope to expand into a small book, with the title *Thirty Years of Looking Up*. One of my former students,

Leonard Kennedy of the class of 1909, gave me the perfect quotation from Browning's *Childe Roland*.

> For, looking up, aware I somehow grew
> 'Spite of the dusk, the plain had given place
> All round to mountains—with such name to grace
> Mere ugly heights and heaps now stolen in view.
> How thus they had surprised me,—solve it, you!
> How to get from them was no clearer case.

In the year 1925 we spent nearly four months at Augusta, Georgia, while I was convalescing from a breakdown. I played golf in foursomes about three times a week with the great Walter J. Travis. He was the first American-trained golfer ever to win the amateur championship of Great Britain; that was in 1904, and it was many years before an American succeeded again. The English, in those days, were not accustomed to see invaders win championships, and his victory was regarded as a national disaster. After his death, the following fine tribute appeared in the London *Times*.

> He never came back again, and among the thousands who watch golf today there are few who saw him play; but that ominous, almost sinister little figure with the black cigar and the Schenectady putter is still familiar to the imagination of all British golfers.
>
> Mr. Travis had a formidable rather than an engaging personality. He kept himself to himself; he played silently and dourly: . . . we were inclined to say that he ought to have been beaten. Yet one solid, uncompromising fact sticks in my head—namely that when Mr. Travis had reached the final, we were afraid, mortally afraid, that Mr. Travis was going to win. . . .
>
> It is his putting that has become legendary, and it was wonderful. . . . I never have seen, however, such utter consternation as was produced by Mr. Travis's putting in that final at Sandwich, nor any putting that had about it such a suggestion of black magic. This was enhanced, no doubt, by the man himself. As he stood there after the stroke, still as a statue, watching the ball with those in-

scrutable eyes of his pursuing its inexorable course, he seemed a
wizard to be burned at the stake. . . . As a game-player he had
essential greatness.

As he stood there after the stroke—many players walk right
after their putt up to the hole; Mr. Travis knew better
than that. Indeed, most golfers would have profited by
playing with Mr. Travis, for he believed in adhering rigidly
to the rules of the game, not conceding putts, and not allowing other players and caddies to stroll ahead of the man
who was to make the next shot.

But, after all, the best thing about Mr. Travis was not
his golfing—the best thing was himself, his mind, his character. He had an interesting mind, a great range of information on many subjects, and was one of the best conversationalists I ever knew. I loved the man, and do honour his
memory.

It is possible that playboys like myself are intellectually inferior to those whose main delight is a solitary
walk; botanical strollers at all events are self-reliant; they
have resources of their own. They need no companions and
no apparatus; they commune with nature, and instead of
trying to escape from themselves, they do just the opposite;
they loaf and invite themselves; and yet—heaven forgive
me!—I glory in my shame. For while the pleasure of sport
consists largely in human companionship, still I love the
sport for its own sake. I have reached an age where in
playing golf I put the weather first, the company second,
and the game third. I had rather play a rotten game in good
weather than a good game in rotten weather. Yet even so I
had rather play golf alone than take a walk alone.

I respect all men who love to potter around in a garden,
but for me such diversion would be a bore. When I talk
with a respectable citizen and ask him the familiar question what he does for exercise or recreation, and he says

he spends an hour in the garden before breakfast and another hour when he returns home from the day's work, I look upon him humbly as a superior intelligence, but I would not imitate him. If I were obliged to mess around in a garden, even though I were so successful as to behold the desired fruit of my labours, I should feel unutterably depressed.

Alex Herd, perhaps better known as Sandy Herd, the famous professional and golf teacher, author of that admirable book, *My Golfing Life*, wrote me a letter so full of enthusiasm for the game that it must be quoted:

> I can assure you when I was a boy at school in my dear old home in St. Andrews, I used to follow all the old champions around the links, watching every shot they played, and admired their skill, and also as men I admired them. It used to give me pleasure once when I was old enough to carry their clubs; what an honour I thought it was! Then they used to gather outside old Tom Morris's shop at night and talk of the great matches that they had played and how they had lost and won championships. I used to stand with my ears and mouth wide open, drinking every word in.
>
> I used to dream of golf. I would get up at four o'clock every morning and play a round of golf before work, and after my hard day's work was over, I would play another round at night. And every putt I played, I would say to myself, 'Got this to win the championship,' little thinking that one day I would achieve that honour.
>
> Golf is a game one must have at heart. One must love it and think it all out as to how to become a champion. One must practise for everlasting, and we can never quite master its wonderful illusive ways.
>
> I love America I like the kind way I was received. I was treated with kindness itself and given all hospitality beyond my dreams.

I love fresh woods and pastures new, but I love them more with a golf club in my hand. If, instead of going out with three good fellows to play golf, I went out alone to find the trailing arbutus or something like that, I should not be happy.

And there is another thing about solitary walking in which I am sure my experience is not unique. I can play eighteen holes of golf, which means three hours of walking, I can play three sets of tennis doubles, which means an hour and a half of violent exercise, without fatigue; over and over again I have felt less tired at the end than when I began. But if I go for a slow saunter with or without companionship, I become exhausted. My back aches horribly, and my legs feel as if they were going to sever their connexion with my frame. And when at last I do sit down, instead of a pleasant fatigue, I feel as if I should never smile again. There is only one fatigue worse than that; it is where some obliging person shows you the 'sights' of a town, or the interior of a museum.

The majority of creative writers are not playboys; they care nothing for outdoor or indoor games. So far as I can find out, Browning never took part in any athletic contest; his chief physical exercise was playing the piano, horseback riding, walking (he never took a cab if he could help it), and, up to the time of his marriage, dancing. Elizabeth expressed her surprise that the author of *Paracelsus* should dance the polka all night. Tennyson played no games; his chief exercise consisted in booming out his own poems in his sea-captain's voice, or taking the dogs for a walk on the edge of the cliffs. In answering the stock question, ' What is your chief recreation?' Bernard Shaw wrote, ' Anything except sport,' and George Moore wrote, ' Religion.'

My oldest brother, Dryden William, eleven years older than I, was entirely different from my brother Arthur and me, for he hated all games, never learned how to swim or even to whistle, never fired a gun or a pistol; but had an accomplishment in which he excelled anyone I have ever seen or heard of. He could definitely remember something that had happened *every day of his life* after the age of five. For example: in the year let us say 1890, if you asked him 'What did you do February 17, 1868?' he could tell you within three minutes.

Once in a dime museum I saw a man, regarded as a freak, who received a good salary for his ability in calculation. If you told him the day of the month and the year when you were born, he would in a few minutes give you the day of the week. By this accomplishment alone, he earned his living. I told him I was born on the second of January 1865. He turned to a big blackboard, made calculations with a piece of chalk, and said 'You were born on Monday,' which was correct.

I mention this because what he succeeded in doing with the help of a blackboard, my brother Dryden did much faster in his head. 'What did you do on February 17, 1868?' By some mysterious process inexplicable to me, but which lasted only about twenty seconds, he would say 'That was a Wednesday' (if it was) and he would then describe the weather and something he had done. I never knew him to fail. Nor was he ever mistaken. One of his favourite tricks was to visit the New Haven cemeteries and correct by his memory dates that were cut on the tombstones. He was invariably right.

Dryden was a tremendous walker; and occasionally my brother Arthur and I went out with him. When I was a small boy, we walked from New Haven to Hartford in one day, nearly forty miles by road. I did that repeatedly before and during college. One day in Freshman year, my classmate, George D. Pettee, and I rose at three in the morning to see how far we could walk in one day. If it had not been for unfavourable weather conditions, we should have done seventy-five miles. As it happened, fifty was the best we could manage. It turned out to be the hottest day in the year; and along about three in the afternoon, we were caught in the severest thunder-storm I ever saw. Before we could reach any shelter, we were drenched. The lightning seemed to play all about us, and a ball of fire struck the ground not fifty yards away. We crawled into a shed, and when the storm ceased, we felt like Rip Van Winkle waking from his twenty years of slumber; we were so wet, so soggy, so cramped, and so stiff, we could hardly move.

When I was sixteen, in company with one of my Chinese schoolmates, I used to run two or three miles every evening. I had read with interest Blaikie's then famous book, *How to Get Strong and How to Stay So*, and one of his recommendations was to run three miles daily. Accordingly, this Chinese boy and I would meet after dark and run out to West Hartford and back. I am glad I did this; it has had a beneficial effect all my life.

In 1882 I saw my first University football game, Yale against Columbia. Yale won easily, but the feature of the game was the number of drop-kick goals made by E. L. Richards, Jr., of Yale. His father was Professor of Mathematics at Yale, and Chairman of all athletic committees. In fact, he was far more interested in athletics than in mathematics. He maintained that activity in athletics could always be accompanied by success in scholarship if the students would plan their time properly. He was proud when his son, Eugene, of the class of 1885, gave such a magnificent illustration of his father's precepts! For Eugene was Chairman of the *Yale Literary Magazine*, Captain of the University football team, and Phi Beta Kappa with philosophical oration (highest honour group).

He and his mate at half-back, Wyllys Terry, were sadly missed after they were graduated in 1885; and that autumn, Frank Peters of the class of 1886 had to develop a green team. Henry Ward Beecher, grandson of the famous divine, was quarter-back; freshmen like Woodruff, 'Pa' Corbin, Charley Gill, Billy Bull, before they were graduated became among the most famous athletes in America;

but it was a green team, and when Princeton came to play the final game with Yale in November, very few believed Yale had any chance at all. Yet Yale should have won. The green team outplayed the Princeton veterans. Watkinson dropped a goal from the field, which then counted five points, and the score remained Yale 5, Princeton 0, until a few minutes before the end. Yale had possession of the ball and was gaining slowly but just enough to keep it, that is, just enough to be assured of victory, when deep in Princeton territory, Yale punted, no one knows why.

The ball bounded wide to one side, and Lamar, the Princeton half-back, caught it on the run, sprinted past the entire Yale team, ran nearly the length of the field without a single Yale player near him, and made a touchdown. No spectator will ever forget 'Lamar's run.' The Princeton crowd rushed deliriously on the field; one man kissed Lamar on both cheeks, and there was pandemonium. Peters threw himself on the ground and tore his hair. I have often read in books of people in grief tearing their hair, but this is the only time I ever saw it.

The score was then Yale 5, Princeton 4, but we felt sure that the Princeton quarter-back would make his place-kick successfully. He did; Dick Hodge stepped up to the ball with as much confidence as if nothing depended on it, and kicked the ball straight between the posts; Yale 5, Princeton 6, the final score. Dick played quarter-back, his brother Hugh end. Both boys had been members of my class at the Hartford High School; their older brother Aspinwall, and their younger brother Sam, also were members of the Princeton University football teams.

At that time we of Yale were heartbroken. But in subsequent years I have always been glad Lamar made that victorious run and won undying fame. For a few years after graduation, he heroically and unselfishly lost his life in the endeavour to save someone from drowning.

Lamar of Georgia—one of the immortals in football.

Although Harvard is perhaps Yale's greatest athletic rival, no game with Harvard has been so thrilling as two twentieth century games with Princeton. I shall remember these as long as I live, and they are as bright in my memory as if they had happened yesterday.

The first of these two games that I have in mind was played 16 November 1907. Ted Coy was then full-back for Yale, Tad Jones was half-back, Howard Jones end, Ray Biglow tackle and captain. Before the game the Princeton team was thought to be superior, and during the entire first half Princeton outplayed Yale with such ridiculous ease that if they had tried a little harder they might have scored another touchdown. They went through the Yale line as easily as if they had been playing against small boys and made a touchdown and goal, counting seven points, and then, when they got near the Yale goal a second time and might easily have made another touchdown, Harlan drop-kicked a goal from the field in an almost contemptuous fashion, not even looking to see whether the ball had gone over the bar or not. This gave a score of Princeton 10, Yale 0, and it seemed as if they would defeat Yale by about 40 points.

When the teams came out for the second half, I said to my neighbour, 'Well, we hardly got hold of the ball in the first half, but, although we are going to be beaten, we shall have the ball for a few moments because Princeton has the kick-off.' But to my amazement and disgust Princeton recovered the kick-off so that Yale didn't even have that small solace.

From that moment the game was all Yale! It seemed as if the teams had changed uniforms. I have never seen such a revolution between the two halves of a football game. This was the golden day in the spectacular career of Ted Coy, one of the greatest football players of all time. He stood far back of the line, receiving a long pass from centre and then started around the end, apparently without interference. Every Princeton man who got in his way was knocked down, not by the interference but by Coy himself. He was inspired; he was a demon; he was a Juggernaut. It was not long before Yale was down in Princeton territory. Then Tad Jones held the ball close to the ground, apparently for Coy to kick, but Coy picked it up and ran over the line for a touchdown. The score was then 10–6. After kicking, Coy started again on his rampant run, and this time the entire Yale team went over the goal line, overwhelming Princeton like an avalanche. Cheers turned to groans, however, when it was learned that the touchdown was not allowed. But in a few moments Yale had the ball again and carried it over for another touchdown, making the score Princeton 10, Yale 12. Even now, looking back after all these years, it seems unbelievable and indeed it was almost miraculous. There is no explanation for it, for although Ted Coy played splendidly during the next two years of his college course, he never reached the heights of the second half of the Princeton game of 1907. Thirty years later Biglow told me that it was sheer inspiration felt by all the team as they came out for the second half.

In an address I made to the students between this game and the game with Harvard on the following Saturday, which Yale won 12–0 but which had not a single spectacular feature, I told them (all witnesses of that Princeton game) that for the rest of their lives, any time that they were despondent or discouraged, they would feel a tide of joy arising in their hearts when they thought of that score 12–10.

The other Princeton game was played at Princeton 14 November 1936. Two years previously Yale had beaten a Princeton team, which was at least twice as good as Yale, by a score of 7–0. In 1935 Princeton had beaten Yale with ridiculous ease at New Haven by the largest score ever made by Princeton against Yale. And when the teams lined up in 1936, the betting was in favour of Princeton.

I had a ticket for this game but was uncertain whether to attend or not. I lectured at Town Hall in New York at 11 o'clock that morning; the weather was perfect, and as soon as I finished the lecture I caught a train for Princeton after the excursion trains had gone, and by running from the train got a taxicab and reached the stadium two minutes after the game had begun. Here until nearly the end of the first half it was all Princeton. The score was Princeton 16, Yale 0. Then Charlie Ewart, one of the smallest men on either side, caught a punt and ran 30 yards through the Princeton team. This run had a stimulating effect. A few minutes later Clint Frank threw a pass of about 55 yards that was caught by Kelley as he was running full speed down the centre of the field. Kelley had hands that were like gigantic claws; he pulled that ball down out of the air and over his shoulder, for he was running, of course, in the same direction as the flying ball. He got rid of two Princeton opponents and went unmolested over the line. All through the second half Yale continued scoring. Yale was ahead of Princeton until early in the third quarter when Princeton got another goal. A few minutes before the end of the game Yale made a final touchdown, making the score Yale 26, Princeton 23. Then Jack White of Princeton got the ball, went through the entire Yale eleven, bound for a certain touchdown, when Al Wilson, Yale half-back, came from the extreme left side of the field, coming apparently out of nowhere, running with terrific speed, and pushed Jack White out of bounds not very far from the goal. This saved the game for Yale because there was not time to make another score for Princeton.

On the whole, it was the most spectacular game I have

ever seen, because I was certain that if the game had lasted ten minutes longer, more scoring would have been done.

All of Yale's athletic relations with Princeton, despite the intense rivalry, have been marked by unclouded friendship.

I have seen but one six-day bicycle race and then only for half an hour, which was quite enough for me, though not for twenty thousand others. It was one o'clock in the morning but I was the only man in the throng who seemed to be aware of it.

I wish that the six-day go-as-you-please on foot could be revived, as in these days of physical development and scientific training it would be interesting to see what the human body could endure. In the eighties, although there was no radio to attract the attention of millions, these six-day races in New York were first page news every day in every newspaper in America.

I remember when the English champion Charles Rowell came over announcing he would endeavour to run 600 miles in six days, something that had never been done. He trained by running forty miles daily, just a warming up. In March 1881 he started with the other competitors in Madison Square Garden at midnight Sunday night and on the first day he ran 150 miles. I have often wished that he had later tried for a twenty-four hour record, for although he meant this to be only the first of six days, no other man has ever run so far in one day. His leading competitor I believe covered 130. In the first three days, that is by Wednesday midnight, he had covered more than 350 miles and the bookmakers refused to take any more bets on him, as he seemed to have the race won. But on the very next day (Thursday) he withdrew. He was unable to continue and said it was owing to his having done too much the first day. An Englishman named Hazael won and covered 600 miles by ten o'clock Saturday night. He was an international hero. Two years later Rowell again competed in New York and this time did not go nearly so far in the first day. He completed 602 miles in the six days but alas, an Irishman named Fitzgerald did 610. Among the great six-day runners of those days were also Cameron, who called himself Noremac, Hughes and a negro named Hart. The trick of course was to find the minimum of sleep during the week. Too little was fatal; too much meant defeat.

When the Olympic Games were revived in 1896, they were appropriately held at Athens and I have always been glad that the Marathon (26 miles 385 yards) was won by a Greek and was actually run from Marathon to Athens, over the course presumably taken by Pheidippides in 490 B.C. This race immediately became popular, particularly in America, where it is run in various localities every year. A Boston shoe-maker for some years gave with every pair of running shoes a printed copy of Browning's poem *Pheidippides*. One of the most famous Marathon runners in America is Clarence De Mar, who has won the Marathon repeatedly with long intervals between victories. In 1928, knowing he was a Sunday School teacher, I invited him to come to New Haven and address a meeting of Yale undergraduates on a Sunday evening. He made an admirable speech.

On the preceding day, although I believe he was forty years old, he had once more won the Marathon race. He showed no stiffness, lameness, or exhaustion when he arrived in New Haven. He made a fine address, and when I took him to the station where he was to take the four-hour train journey to Boston, arriving late at night, he refused to allow me to buy a Pullman seat, saying he preferred the day coach!

37

JOURNEY TO EUROPE

THE last year of the nineteenth century began in Connecticut with a tremendous snowstorm in a temperature of 15 degrees. The next day I celebrated my thirty-fifth birthday by playing billiards in the morning and hockey on the ice in the afternoon and duplicate whist in the evening.

The next night I took the steamer *Richard Peck* for Providence and from there the morning train to Boston. The South Station at Boston on Summer Street, near where Emerson was born in 1803, had recently been completed and was called the 'largest in the world.' I went out to Cambridge and saw my old friends and former colleagues on the Harvard Faculty, lunching with Kittredge, dining with Briggs, talking with Santayana and Robinson and Gates and Barrett Wendell. I had a long talk with President Eliot about conditions at Yale and at Harvard; I explained the method of election at Yale, how I had been elected Professor by the Corporation but the Faculty had refused to agree, so the election was void. He wished to know what objection the Faculty had. 'Well, I had often made imprudent remarks,' to which he said, 'Prudence is not a desirable quality in a college professor.' He seemed astounded that at Yale the Faculty had more power than the Corporation, and gave me definitely to understand that at Harvard one man made all the appointments. I was never more impressed by his energy and determination and air of authority, though I had also never seen him in a more gracious and kindly and cheerful mood; so that I was astonished when, on my saying as I rose to go, 'I hope, President Eliot, I may always come and talk with you when I am in Cambridge,' to hear him reply, 'The next time you come I may not be here.' 'Why, are you going to resign?' 'Resign? Resign? Certainly *not*. But, Mr. Phelps, I am sixty-six years old.' To see him there, the embodiment of health and vigour, and yet feeling death near, made me laugh aloud. He lived twenty-six years after that, sound in body and mind, and died at the age of ninety-two.

A few weeks after I saw him, I received a letter from him, saying it was probable that I should be invited to become a member of the Harvard Faculty. He knew I preferred to remain at Yale if I were allowed to, but this letter gave me immense encouragement, for it removed worry about the future.

On the eleventh of January I heard Paderewski, then in the plenitude of his powers, play the *Sonata Appassionata* as I had never heard it before; at the conclusion of the programme, as an encore, he played Liszt's Rhapsody No. 2, my favourite. Many regard this as 'hackneyed,' but I am so constituted that works of genius never grow stale. I had heard Paderewski in Boston on his first visit to America and I heard him many times after 1900. But for some reason, I was more thrilled by this particular performance than by any other. The very next time I heard him play the Second Rhapsody was 38 years later in his famous motion picture.

On the fifth of April I was one of the Judges for the Ten Eyck Prize Speaking by men of the Junior Class. On the first ballot I voted for Arthur Gleason, and after a hot session lasting over an hour, he received the prize. After his graduation in 1901, he became a distinguished journalist, and his early death was a severe loss.

On the sixth and seventh of April Harry Vardon, being on his first visit to America, played exhibition matches at the Yale Golf Course. This was the first time Americans had had an opportunity to see high-grade golf; it was a revelation and seemed miraculous. On the second day, playing the best ball of two undergraduates, he made a 71, which no one before or since ever equalled on that course. One of his student opponents was Eb Byers of Pittsburgh, who afterwards became National Amateur Champion of America. Vardon was silent even for a golf-player; but when Tim Cheney, who played against him on the first day, put on gloves, Vardon enquired, 'What's the matter? Are the lad's hands cold?' Vardon, a big fellow, used clubs that were light and even dainty in appearance. Many bought them after his visit, but were unable to use them effectively. He had little amenity. On a certain course in Connecticut, as he and his local opponents were leaving the home green and had reached the piazza of the club-house crowded with spectators, one of the 'home players' asked him 'And what do you think of our course, Mr. Vardon?' His answer was awaited in an intense silence. After mature deliberation came the reply, 'With one exception, it is the worst in the world.'

After my bicycle trip through Europe in the summer of 1890, I did not cross the ocean again until 1900, when my wife and I spent three months in England with two weeks on the Continent. Crossing over on the slow and steady cattle-ship *Menominee*, we had some interesting fellow-passengers, Professor Jeremiah Jenks and family and Santayana.

On 11 July of that summer we saw Queen Victoria, as she drove along Constitution Hill. The Queen had come to London that morning from Windsor. In the afternoon we went to The Green Park, and stood at the kerb. A few mounted men in uniform preceded her, and then came the Queen in a little, low, open pony phaeton, coming so close to where I stood that I could have touched her as she passed. She was eighty-one years old, with snow-white hair, and wore large dark spectacles. She was herself not impressive to look at, being short, dumpy, and fat. But to me she was tremendously impressive as Queen and Empress of India, and because of her long reign—the longest of any monarch in English history, and one of the longest in ancient or modern times. As I stood uncovered, I felt both reverence and wonder; she had known all the intellectual giants of the Victorian age, in politics, in literature, in science.

That same morning we had attended a wedding in St. Martin's-in-the-Fields. The American Ambassador, Joseph H. Choate, was there, and took a seat directly in front of us. He turned around and whispered to me, 'Is the bride pretty?' 'Not very' I said. My old college roommate at Harvard, Professor Ralph Catterall, was best man. Immediately after the entrance of the bride, we all sat down, and the Ambassador fell into a deep sleep and did not awaken until the loud music of Mendelssohn at the close.

The most impressive performance at the London theatres we saw that summer was that of Mrs. Patrick Campbell as Magda. She was magnificent, and I shall remember her appearance and her voice as long as I live. Thirty-two years later I persuaded her to give a lecture at Yale; she still had her glorious voice, and she imitated various types of women merely by the quality of tone. She recited Browning's short poem *Wanting—is what?* in a manner that was better than a hundred annotations. She stayed at our house, accompanied by her dog, smoked big cigars, and said she wished to hear me give a literary lecture.

At its close she said, 'Why, you *love* people. It is unmistakable, in the way you look at the audience, in the way you talk.' When I said Goodbye to her the next day, she said 'You are going to kiss me, aren't you?'

THE BARCLAY

Dec. 10/32   111 EAST 48TH STREET

My Dear Dr. Phelps,

This word is to send you and your wife my love, and beg you not to forget me.

You don't know how happy and proud I was that I pleased you. And I never told you how much I enjoyed your lecture and marvelled at your most blessed, kindly and intelligent way of meeting your fellow creatures.

I wish I had that gift. I feel always a stranger—talking to strangers —when I get on to the platform. Horrid for me isn't it?

Thank your dear wife and you for your friendliness. What a wonderful people you are for putting people at their ease, making them feel comfortable.

Yours affectionately,

(If I may)   Beatrice Stella Campbell

Cyril Maude, who also in later years became a good friend and was in our house in New Haven, we saw that summer in *The School for Scandal*. A very fine performance it was, with Winifred Emery.

I worked every day in the British Museum, and among the famous scholars was the great historian Gardiner. He was very kind to Catterall, lending him his notes. One Sunday in Marylebone Church we heard the Rev. H.R.Haweis, whose books on music I had read in my boyhood. He was a curious figure of a man, apparently not more than five feet high, and very untidy. The poor fellow was also lame. But he preached with tremendous vigour on China, expressing the fervent wish that Great Britain would take a 'strong line,' etc.

On 25 July, a terrifically hot day, 96 degrees, we went to the House of Commons, where the Hon. James Bryce was kind enough to give us tickets to the gallery. He said it would be a dull day, and we looked for merely routine business. But, the Boer War was in progress, and anything might happen. In the midst of a dull afternoon, and a sparsely inhabited House, somebody got up and moved that the Secretary of State for Foreign Affairs, Joseph Chamberlain, have his salary reduced. A thrill of excitement went through the assembly; men came crowding in from the lobby, and in a few moments the House was packed. The men on the Irish benches were unruly, filled with ungodly mirth, giving every Conservative speaker except the leaders ironical applause; they were enjoying themselves tremendously.

A youngish man, in the late thirties, rose and was listened to by all with respect. He spoke with intense earnestness. The Englishman next to me in the gallery whispered 'There is the coming man, he will be famous some day. His name is Lloyd George.' Courtney rose and spoke against the war. He was interrupted by someone who called him unpatriotic. Courtney enquired 'And what is your definition of patriotism?' The answer was given and Courtney remarked 'I think patriotism will survive the gentleman's definition of it.'

Joseph Chamberlain spoke with fervour and force for an hour, defending himself, his party, and the country. He was of course listened to with attention, though with manifest disapproval from the opposition and Irish benches. Sir Henry Campbell-Bannerman from the front opposition bench, made a short speech, in which he said that on this particular question he would not vote at all, but expressed his abhorrence of the war. Labouchère, Sir Edward Grey, and Sir Robert Reid spoke. John Morley sat on the front bench of the opposition (the corner seat) and how eagerly I longed to hear him speak! He said not a word, however, but listened to the defenders of the war with an ironical smile. James Bryce spoke for the opposition, and finally Mr. Balfour rose, and in his suave, easy, cultivated, smiling fashion, ridiculed Sir Henry Campbell-Bannerman.

Who would have believed then that in a few years C.B. would be Prime Minister?

Thirty-eight years after that field day in the House of Commons, I was engaged in general conversation with my friend, Charles MacInnes, K.C., of Toronto. I do not know why I mentioned hearing that debate in 1900, but I had no sooner mentioned it, than MacInnes exclaimed 'Why I was there on that day myself!' We compared notes and found that we had both been equally impressed and had remembered accurately everything.

When C.B. was Prime Minister, some important person wrote him a letter about a political crisis. C.B. replied that at the moment his wife was very ill, and that her health meant more to him than the whole British empire.

My wife and I spent a month working in the Bodleian. Mr. Fortescue, the Keeper of the Printed Books in the British Museum, had said 'I will give you a letter to the Librarian of the Bodleian at Oxford; he is an ass, but you must not mind that.' He was certainly eccentric, and looked at me as if I were a decayed fish, but I had no trouble with him. At Oxford I had a delightful afternoon with Morfill, the professor of Russian. His literary enthusiasms pleased me, especially because we agreed. Turgenev was his favourite novelist and Donne almost his favourite English poet. He read aloud to us many of his translations from the Russian, and also an original poem he had written to his cat.

At Cambridge we had 'lodgings' for the first and last time in my life; it was a new experience to have meals brought in and served in our sitting-room. I wished to visit the Pepys library at Magdalene, and had sent a letter to Professor Alfred Newton, the zoologist. When I called upon him, each was surprised by the other's appearance. All he knew of me was that I was a university professor. As I was thirty-five years old and looked like an undergraduate, he could hardly believe I was the man he was awaiting. He himself looked antediluvian, and could walk only with the aid of two canes. After he had recovered from the shock of my youthful appearance, he was kind and considerate, and it was thrilling to examine the volumes in cipher in Pepys's handwriting. I was permitted to examine other books in that library; one of them had on the flyleaf the autograph of Francis Drake!

One afternoon I called on the famous scholar W. W. Skeat, and had good talk with him about Chaucer and other matters. I asked him why he, a Cambridge professor, had his Chaucer printed at the Oxford Press, calling it the Oxford Chaucer. He laughed heartily and said it was because he got more money out of it.

We went over to the Continent that summer and on 19 August saw the Passion Play. I called on and talked with many of the players I had seen ten years before, Mayer who had been Christus three times and was now Choregus, Zwink who was Judas again, though he had told me in 1890 he would not live another ten years, and the St. John who was 28 years old, taking the part for the second and last time. I was not so deeply impressed by the 1900 performance as I had been in 1890—perhaps because it was the second time.

Coming back through Germany, we were admitted to the cathedral at Speyer when they were opening the graves of the Emperors—an extraordinary spectacle. We saw the great sapphire ring of Henry IV.

On 30 August we had a perfect day on the Rhine, taking the steamer from Mainz to Cologne. As we passed Bonn, I noticed a large building on the shore, with the sign *Frauen-Klinik*. A German and his wife with whom I had been engaged in conversation, gazed on this edifice with especial attention. Then the German said to me, 'My first wife died in that building.' It was rather difficult to know how to reply to that statement. I could not say 'How sad!' for his second wife was with him. And the remark did not call for hilarity or congratulations. Suddenly I thought of one of the most useful words in the German language. I said '*So?*'

When we had entered the train at Nuremberg for Munich on our way to the Passion Play, we found in the compartment a fine looking American father and son, the boy about eighteen. The sign on the railway carriage said *Nach München*. As we were waiting for the train to start, the boy asked his father, 'Does *nach* mean *not*?' 'Yes.' 'Well, then, we must get off,' and they began to haul down their baggage. I asked them where they wished to go, and they said Munich. 'Stay where you are, then!' 'But this train says it is not going to Munich.' I explained the meaning of the word *nach*, and then, wishing to make it easier for them, I said to the boy, 'I suppose you have not studied any German.' 'Oh, yes,' said he, 'I have just passed my entrance exam in German for the Sheffield Scientific School at Yale.'

We started our bicycle trip through southern England on Sunday 2 September, wheeling down Holborn through Cheapside and crossing London Bridge without once having to dismount. The Bow Bells were striking noon. That night we stopped at Rochester, heard Dean Hole preach in the cathedral, and the next morning we called on him. While we were waiting in a room filled with books, I glanced over the shelves, expecting to see works on theology, philosophy, and literature; of the hundreds of books in that room every one was apparently on some form of athletic sport. The Dean entered, a magnificent figure. Over eighty years of age and over six feet in height, with a great mane of snow-white hair, he was gracious and hospitable. He invited us to lunch, but we could not stay. He seemed pleased to know that I came from Yale; said he had immensely enjoyed a visit to Yale, and that he thought Yale was closer to Englishmen than any other American university.

Two weeks later on our bicycle trip, we went to Moor Park in Surrey to see the place where Swift and Stella lived at Sir William Temple's. A wealthy American gentleman from Connecticut had leased the place and was living there. He was most cordial, but wondered why we were particularly interested. When I told him it was on account of Swift and Stella, he laughed and said that although he had been living there a year, he had never heard of either of them. 'I like this place because there is good shooting. I can knock down half a dozen rabbits every morning before breakfast.' He invited us to stay and take tea on the terrace and we had a most agreeable time.

Jane Austen died at Winchester, 18 July 1817. She is buried in Winchester Cathedral and the house where she died is very near the vast church.

We had a curious experience in front of this house. It was a cloudless morning. I asked my wife to take a picture of the front of the house; accordingly the camera was pointed at the front door. This door was closed and there was no one in front of it or near it. The camera clicked.

But when the picture was developed there was a woman dressed in black standing close to the door. We have no explanation whatever for this, so we have decided to call the unknown the ghost of Jane Austen. It was such a clear day that every corner of the porch and of the front door appeared in sharp relief; we could almost have seen a fly. There was absolutely nothing; but there stands the woman in the picture.

On 7 September we bicycled across the Isle of Wight; coming to Tennyson's home at Farringford in the late afternoon, we found the place closed and a care-taker said it would be open to visitors only on the regular day. He was deaf to entreaties and other more practical methods of persuasion. But while he was uttering prohibitions, I saw two ladies enter the gate; and I asked them if we might also enter in, explaining that I had the honour of teaching the poet's works to American undergraduates. They were both relations of the poet, and very kindly took us about the spacious grounds, showing us Tennyson's favourite haunts, his cliff walk, and the place where he wrote *Maud*.

Not long after that, I was talking with two nuns about Tennyson, and they told me that one day in the eighties they were looking at Farringford and that a big man with a beard and smoking a pipe, spoke to them, and asked them if they would like to enter. It was the poet. He took them over the grounds, invited them to his study, and then asked, 'Which of my poems shall I read to you?' They were too overcome to choose; so he read aloud the whole of the *Morte d'Arthur*. They never forgot that tremendous experience; but they also told me that while he was conversing with them immediately after the reading, he stood so close to them that he blew copious clouds of tobacco smoke from his pipe directly into their faces, utterly unaware of the effect; and that one of the sisters as a result was violently sick for two hours after the interview.

On Sunday 29 July I called on the famous Boswell scholar, G. Birkbeck Hill (1835–1903), whose edition of the *Life* far surpassed in value all those that had preceded it. He was 65 years old, and looked feeble; but he was working hard every day and night, and like so many other Englishmen, in the evenings did his minute textual work by the light of candles.

He insisted on my staying to supper. He said the regret of his life was that he had begun scholarly work so late and now 'there was not much time left.' He envied all young scholars. I told him of my admiration for the work of his son-in-law (Mr. Crump) for his admirable editorial work on Landor; Mr. Hill spoke of him with admiration and affection.

I shall never forget Mr. Hill's expressions of tragic grief over the Boer War; he was, like so many other first-rate men of that time, wholly opposed to it. He could not speak of it without crying. The tears ran down his face as he exclaimed 'This wicked, cruel war!'

It was of course a pleasure for me to give him the references he asked for in the following letter.

I, THE WILDERNESS,
HOLLY HILL,
HAMPSTEAD, N.W.
Nov. 18, 1902

MY DEAR PROFESSOR PHELPS,

I should have thanked you earlier for the trouble you have taken about the quotation had I not been in the greatest affliction when I received your letter. My dearest wife died on October 30, after a long illness. We had prayed for her release, so much had she suffered, but when the blow fell it was very grievous. We were but a boy and a girl when we were engaged—forty-eight years ago.

I am supported by the love of my children—never had a man better. In my grandchildren I find also great comfort, so that I do not feel desolate. I am taking up the broken threads of my work as well as I can. During many weeks I could do nothing; but in occupation I shall find great relief. I must try to get my edition of the Lives finished, though it seems to have lost most of its interest.

May I trouble you with another question. Emerson, in Letters and Social Aims 1885, p. 55, says that Ben Jonson said that "Donne for not keeping accent deserved hanging." Can you give me the reference? My edition of Jonson is of 1756. I easily found in it your reference.

You may be interested in the following quotation from Henry Crabb Robinson's Diary, i.340 (Aug. 3, 1811): "I made use of the expression poor Coleridge. 'He is,' said Lamb, 'a fine fellow, in spite of all his faults and weaknesses. Call him Coleridge; I hate *poor*, as applied to such a man. I can't bear to hear such a man pitied.' He then quoted an expression to the same effect by (I think) Ben Jonson or Bacon."

Will you give my kindest remembrances to Professor and Mrs. Lounsbury and their son. I know I shall have their sympathy. It is a pleasure to know that you and Mrs. Phelps are to visit England next year.

Yours very sincerely,

G. BIRKBECK HILL

We returned to America in time for the opening of the Autumn term. On 20 October I went to New York to see a special matinée of Browning's *In a Balcony*. Mrs. LeMoyne was the Queen, Otis Skinner played Norbert, and Constance was played by the beautiful young Eleanor Robson (now Mrs. August Belmont). I had expected to see in Browning's one-act poem only a literary curiosity, but to my surprise the play was thrilling. After the curtain the three players were recalled ten times, and then Mrs. LeMoyne, who was too hoarse to speak, whispered something to Otis Skinner, who came to the footlights and said 'Mrs. LeMoyne wishes to tell the audience never to make fun of Browning again.' Although it was intended to give only this one performance, the success was so overwhelming that the three actors went on tour, playing nightly until the end of June, when one of the final performances was given in New Haven, and I had the pleasure of hearing the play again. In May 1912, on the occasion of the celebration of the centenary of Browning's birth in London, I heard an English company give the same play, and since then I have heard it in New York and elsewhere five or six times; and always it has made a profound impression on the audience.

On the last night of the nineteenth century, 31 December 1900, my wife and I went to Trinity Church on the Green in New Haven, and at midnight while the audience were on their knees, the chimes played *Lead Kindly Light* and so began a new century.

38

THOMAS HARDY

NEARLY fifty years ago I read my first novel by Thomas Hardy. This experience I have often tried in vain to forget. When I was feeling ill, I opened a novel with the agreeable title *A Pair of Blue Eyes*. After I had read about two hundred pages, it appeared that the heroine and the two heroes were in a most unpleasant predicament; I myself saw no way out; but I had read so many novels where unpromising situations were neatly changed that I read on in a fool's paradise, thinking the author would exert his magic in the right way. I have since often advised those who read this novel to stop when they are about two-thirds of the way through, and then ask themselves this question—What is the worst possible way in which this story can reach a conclusion? No reader can imagine an ending more shatteringly tragic than the one provided. When I came to that last page, I threw the volume across the room; I vowed I would never read another novel by Thomas Hardy; I went to bed and stayed there one week. Such was the effect produced on me by a pair of blue eyes. Within a year I had read every one of his books.

He seemed to me the foremost living English novelist and to belong to the great tradition. Hence I was eager to meet him.

As it turned out, I forced myself upon his leisure in a way that I suppose is unpardonable; and yet, although I repent some of my sins, I have never felt any regret for this.

On our bicycle tour in 1900, which had begun in London, we reached Dorchester in the moonlight Saturday evening, 8 September, and put up at the King's Arms. Sunday morning I walked to Hardy's house, Max Gate, and found a large sign on the front door, 'Not at home.' Accordingly, I knocked, and when I asked the maid if Mr. Hardy were at home, she replied with another question. She pointed to the sign and asked if I could read. I asked in turn if she could, and if so, what were her favourite books? She was taken aback and perhaps thought I was insane. I explained that I knew I had no business to be there, but that I was an American who adored her master; and if she would explain to him that I was not a newspaper reporter, that I wished to see him only for a few moments, I should never forget her kindness. I never have. She went to the door of a room that I was to enter myself twenty-eight years later and knocked. Soon she returned and said Mr. Hardy would see me at three o'clock.

At three I was at the front door again and just in front of it was Thomas Hardy. He was sixty years old. Like me, he was clad in knickerbockers, with an aged jacket and a straw hat, the only Englishman I ever saw with that head-gear. He was small and slight in stature and figure, looking rather frail and depressed, with grey face and grey moustache. We sat down on a bench in the open air. Although at this first interview he neither laughed nor smiled, he was, after the first moments, exceedingly gracious, kindly, and sympathetic. He was grave rather than sad. He spoke of the wickedness of shooting game birds, of killing any animals; 'wickedness' was the word he used. I reminded him of Emerson's poem beginning 'Hast thou named all the birds without a gun?' but somewhat injured the effectiveness of the quotation and my own reputation by confessing that I often went shooting in America.

Discussing literature, I told him that I should have

known by the structure of his novels that he had been a practising architect; even if he had not used architects as leading characters in *A Laodicean* and *A Pair of Blue Eyes*; that the structure of his novels was evidence enough, and that the manner in which buildings were described, as in *Two on a Tower*, revealed the architect. He said *A Laodicean* contained more of the facts of his own life than anything else he had ever written. That was published in 1881; during its composition he was dangerously ill, and did not believe he could recover. He thought it was his last illness, and perhaps that was why he put in so much of himself. (It would have interested him during those painful weeks of illness if he had known that he was to live on forty-seven years.)

He said he thought the novelist ought always to *tell a story*; that a novel should be constructed with a definite plot.

He then asked me what I thought of his poetry; he had published his first volume of verse, *Wessex Poems*, only two years past, in 1898, with illustrations made from his own drawings. I wish I had then liked the poems as I do now; I could not believe they stood so much higher than the novels in his own estimation, that they were so close to his heart. He was evidently pained when I told him that of course I found them interesting reading, but that I felt they were not so great as his works in prose. He spoke quite strongly about this. He thought they were far superior to any of his novels and that many of his more discerning friends had told him so. I did not know then what I knew in later years, that he had ceased to care about his novels; he did not wish to discuss them. He wished to be considered and remembered only as a poet. Instead of a great novelist writing verse as an avocation, he wished to be regarded as an English poet, who had written some stories in prose. It may be that posterity will so remember him. He had at all events the dearest wish of his life granted. His career as a novelist lasted twenty-five years; his career as a poet, beginning when he was fifty-eight, lasted thirty years. And although he did not publish poetry until late in life, he had been writing verse since boyhood.

I have always regretted that none of his subsequent volumes of poems was, like the first one, adorned with pictures by his own hand. I admire the illustrations he provided for *Wessex Poems*.

We talked for three-quarters of an hour. I had stood up to go after a few minutes, but he had urged me to stay. Finally, when I was taking leave, he asked, 'Is your wife with you?' and when I told him, he asked 'Why didn't she come?' I replied that she did not have the nerve. He cordially invited us both to tea with Mrs. Hardy and himself the following afternoon at five o'clock.

I told him I would rather do that than anything else on earth, but that we were both on a schedule, that in a few days we had to sail for America, and that we had reserved the following day for bicycling all over the country described in his novels, and I did not see how we could do that and still come to tea. He said, 'Leave it this way; Mrs. Hardy and I will be in the garden anyhow at five o'clock tomorrow. If you and Mrs. Phelps can come, we shall be glad to see you; and if you don't appear, we shall quite understand.'

Walking back to the King's Arms, I had an inspiration. The sky was clear and I remembered the harvest moon was due. I suggested to my wife that we bicycle all night through the Hardy country, reach Salisbury, and take the train back to Dorchester, thus accomplishing both objects—seeing the literary landscape and having tea with the Hardys. All we should lose would be a night's sleep. Without a moment's hesitation she agreed, and about five o'clock we mounted our bicycles and wheeled to Puddle-town (the Weatherbury of *Far From the Madding Crowd*). We entered the old church and studied the inscriptions on the graves in the churchyard. Then we went on to Egdon Heath. We reached the vast and sinister Heath just as day was giving way to darkness and saw it exactly as it is described in the early pages of *The Return of the Native*.

In fact, precisely at this transitional point of its nightly roll into darkness the great and particular glory of the Egdon waste began, and nobody could be said to understand the heath who had not been there at such a time. . . . The sombre stretch of rounds and hollows seemed to rise and meet the evening gloom in pure sympathy, the heath exhaling darkness as rapidly as the heavens precipitated it. And so the obscurity in the air and the obscurity in the land closed together in a black fraternization towards which each advanced half-way.

The place became full of a watchful intentness now; for when other things sank brooding to sleep the heath appeared slowly to awake and listen. Every night its Titanic form seemed to await something; but it had waited thus, unmoved, during so many centuries, through the crises of so many things, that it could only be imagined to await one last crisis—the final overthrow.

And while we were looking at this tremendous scene and thinking of the words describing it, suddenly the full moon rose and flooded the dark waste with silver light. That was one of the unforgettable moments of our lives.

We wheeled on through the silent night. There were no clouds, there was no wind and we never met a human being. It was as if we were alone in a dead world illumined by the moon. The outlines of churches stood out in the strong light as clear as noonday. We caught a little sleep toward dawn at a wayside inn. Then we pushed on to Salisbury, and reached the railway station only a few minutes before the train left. I gave our wheels to a man in uniform, asking him to keep them for us till the next day; and we entered the train for Dorchester.

At five o'clock we walked into the gardens at Max Gate. Mr. and Mrs. Hardy were there. Mr. Hardy said, 'Oh, then, you didn't take your bicycle trip!' 'But we did!' and when we explained, he held up both hands in amazement, and exclaimed 'These Americans!'

Mr. Hardy was almost covered with cats. Three or four cats were on various parts of his person, other cats were near at hand, and I noticed saucers of milk placed at strategic points in the shrubbery. 'Are all these your own cats?' 'Oh, dear, no, some of them are, and some are cats who come regularly to have tea, and some are still other cats, not invited by us, but who seem to find out about this time of day that tea will be going.' I said I was a fanatical cattist and was enchanted to have their company.

Mr. Hardy told me that at any time he could dig almost anywhere in his garden and find Roman remains, that once he had found the skeleton of a Roman soldier with his armour and other implements. I reflected that whenever he sat at his desk to write, he was competing not only with his contemporaries, but with twenty centuries. I think these centuries of human habitation gave to his writing a grave sincerity that perhaps it could not have had in a newly-settled land.

Mrs. Hardy was an artist, and in the house she was kind enough to show us many of her pictures. I told her I thought her husband was the greatest of living English writers. She said she liked his earlier novels better, and did not care much for the latest ones. I suppose she had in mind *Jude the Obscure*. She was a devout, orthodox Christian, and in those days some of his later work rather shocked her, I think. I then told her what he himself had said on the previous day about *A Laodicean*. 'Yes, when he wrote that he thought he was on his deathbed. He was suffering terribly, and dictated the whole novel to me, being too ill to hold a pen'.

Mr. Hardy was even more genial on this afternoon than during our conversation of Sunday. He was kindness itself, and seemed to be in almost radiant humour. We stayed two hours, and we shall never forget such kindness and hospitality.

That evening at the King's Arms we sat at dinner with a young lady who was the daughter of the famous publisher Kegan Paul. She said she would have given anything to have that interview with the Hardys, but she added 'I should never have had the brass to go there.' There was also at table a young Englishman, Mr. Eaton, of Cambridge, who walked with us to the train the next morning, and was exceedingly amiable.

Mrs. Hardy died in 1912; in 1914 he was married again. The second Mrs. Hardy not only made the last fourteen years of his life happy, but her inspiration was so strong that he continued to write and publish original poems up to the very end. He was extremely fortunate in both marriages, and in a short poem he paid a beautiful tribute.

> But soon or later, when you hear
> That he has doffed this wrinkled gear,
> Some evening, at the first star-ray,
> Come to his graveside, pause and say:
>
> ' Whatever his message—glad or grim—
> Two bright-souled women clave to him';
> Stand and say that while day decays;
> It will be word enough of praise.

Well, late one afternoon I stood by his grave at Dorchester in company with Mrs. Florence Hardy; and she told me that on the same day that his ashes were placed in Westminster Abbey, his heart was placed in this grave with his first wife.

After these two September days in 1900 I did not see Dorchester again until September 1928; then I spent a day there with Mrs. Hardy and stroked the beautiful cat that had been given to him toward the end of his life. She said that up to his last very brief illness, Mr. Hardy showed no sign of physical or mental decline. He took long walks, his hearing was perfect, he could read all he wanted to, and he composed poetry almost up to the last day. He died in his eighty-eighth year.

In May 1932 we were there again and stayed overnight at Max Gate. We had the pleasure of calling on Mr. Hardy's sister Katherine, a charming woman. Mrs. Hardy showed us the graves in the garden at Max Gate of their favourite dogs and cats. The tombstones were designed by him and the inscriptions prepared.

She told us of his last illness, and of how he asked her to read to him *Rabbi Ben Ezra*; she paused in the middle of the poem, but he signalled to her to read it to the end. He died on the evening of 11 January 1928, and she said that *an hour after his death* she came again to his bedside, and saw on his face such an expression as she had never seen on any human countenance. 'It was a look of radiant triumph such as imagination could never have conceived.'

Mrs. Hardy told us that although her husband was wholly English and wrote almost exclusively on English themes and of English people, he had the deepest conviction of the brotherhood of mankind, and lived consistently in harmony with this creed. During the war there was a large German prison-camp near Dorchester; the prisoners were assigned to various tasks in the neighbourhood. Mr. Hardy took a personal interest in every German prisoner who worked on his place. He gave food and medicines, treating them not only with solicitude for their welfare, but with respect for them as individuals. Now no one was more eager than Mr. Hardy for England's triumph in the war. But his clear intelligence was never clouded by prejudice, and his heart was too big and tender not to be touched by human suffering. It is pleasant to know that these Germans were grateful, that they wrote to their families in Germany about him, and that a letter came back saying that as a result of his consideration, the English prisoners in that part of Germany were receiving better treatment.

Mrs. Hardy told me that 'T.E.Lawrence' was one of their dearest and most intimate friends; that whenever he was in England he always came to their house and stayed with them; and she said with great earnestness, 'In his personal character and habits of life and speech and thought he is more like Jesus Christ than any person I have ever known.'

Mrs. Hardy's biography of her husband, in two volumes, is an admirable work; it tells readers all that readers have a right to know. It has dignity without dulness.

She was kind enough to take us in her motor to have lunch with Mr. and Mrs. St. John Ervine at their home in Seaton, in Devonshire. On the way we stopped at Lyme Regis, and I made the jump in memory of the famous scene in Jane Austen's *Persuasion*.

Mrs. Hardy disliked anything that savoured of chauvinism; she felt that the Religion of Nationalism was evil. At the dinner given by Sir James Barrie in 1928, I sat between Mrs. Bernard Shaw and Mrs. Hardy. I asked Mrs. Shaw in what part of England she was born; and she replied with considerable emphasis, 'Why, I was not born anywhere in England. I am an Irishwoman!'

Mrs. Hardy whispered to me, 'I don't like to hear her say that; I don't see why anyone should be so proud or so glad of their nationality. I am an Englishwoman and love England; but I have sometimes felt that I should have been glad to be of another country.' And I asked, 'Have you felt that way about any particular country?' 'Yes, I have sometimes wished I were French, and at other times I have wished I were an American.'

I think she was really glad to be an Englishwoman, but she felt that nationalism was a danger and that it led to misunderstandings and to war. She was pro-human and had boundless sympathy for humanity.

At the funeral of Hardy in Westminster Abbey in 1928 the choice of pallbearers emphasized the poet and dramatist, rather than the novelist—Sir James Barrie, Bernard Shaw, Rudyard Kipling, Alfred E. Housman, John Galsworthy, Sir Edmund Gosse. Every one of these men, except Mr. Housman, published novels; but Barrie and Shaw were known almost exclusively as dramatists, Galsworthy was as well known as a playwright as a novelist, Kipling was more distinguished for his poetry than his prose, Gosse was a poet and critic, and Housman a lyrical poet.

From the king to the humblest peasant, there was sincere mourning for the death of Hardy; his eminence in four fields of art—architecture, prose-fiction, drama, and lyrical poetry—would have made him a world figure; but the beauty of his character, his sympathy, kindliness, modesty, gentleness, made an equally deep impression.

In the *New York Herald Tribune* for 22 January there was an article by Ford Madox Ford on Thomas Hardy which contained the astounding statement that Ford heard Hardy say he was a practising member of the Anglican Church. To be sure, Samuel Butler said that his own views were the same as those held by the advanced wing of the Broad Church; but the diabolical Butler was a master of irony, and that remark was a two-edged sword. Hardy had less of hypocrisy than of anything else. If he was reported as saying that he loved the church ritual and often attended the services, well and good; he was brought up in the Church, was an ecclesiastical architect, and must have loved the old traditions. Probably no man ever had less respect for God and more respect for His house. But a practising member? Then John Morley was a Fundamentalist and Leslie Stephen an Evangelical Methodist.

I asked Mrs. Hardy about this, and she replied that he never was a practising or believing member of any church; Mr. Ford might have heard Hardy say something sympathetic or appreciative about the church service.

I have always regarded *The Return of the Native* as his masterpiece; it is a desolating tragedy as it stands, but he seems at one time in its composition to have wished to make it even more so. I received the following letter from the American publishers, Harper and Brothers.

MAY 9, 1928

Mr. William Lyon Phelps
Yale University
New Haven, Conn.

DEAR MR. PHELPS:

Mr. Thomas Wells, the editor of our Magazine, has suggested that I write to you as one who knows more about the various editions of Hardy's *The Return of the Native* than anyone else in the country. One of our authors has asked us if we know anything of a note written by Hardy to the effect that Book VI of *The Return of the Native* was added to please the public. Our author says that such a note exists, but no edition can be found which contains it.

I am wondering if you can give us any light on this inquiry.

Sincerely yours,

FRANK S. MACGREGOR

In this letter my knowledge was like Mark Twain's death. But in my copy of Professor Samuel Chew's book *Thomas Hardy as Poet and Novelist*, which had just been published that year (1928) I read the following paragraph (p.40).

One may well question the grim note which Hardy, in the definitive edition of the book (*The Return of the Native*), appended to it, to the effect that only the exigencies of periodical publication caused him to arrange an ending with the marriage of the two children of the heath and requesting readers of 'an austere artistic code' to imagine that Thomasin remained a widow and that Venn disappeared from the country-side.

My younger colleague at Yale, Prof. Richard Purdy, who *is* an authority on Hardy, was kind enough to give me the following information.

By 'definitive edition' Professor Chew must refer to the costly limited and signed Mellstock Edition. The note has not been retained in either the American Harpers or the English Macmillan standard editions—at least the current issues of those editions.

8, ADELPHI TERRACE,
STRAND, W.C.2.
26th March 1929

DEAR PROFESSOR LYON-PHELPS:

I hope that you and Mrs. Lyon-Phelps are both well. I often think of our pleasant meetings. Sir James Barrie was not well at Christmas —a sharp attack of bronchitis—but he is well now—indeed I lunched with him today. He has been the kindest friend possible during the sad days. . . .

I am so glad that you like *Winter Words*. Some of the poems I think are poignant beyond anything else that I have ever read, notably 'He resolves to say no more.' They tear my heart, because I think that if he could have recovered from that illness he could have written more. I miss him more than ever; the thought of returning to Max Gate to live alone there is almost more than I can bear.

With every good wish and my affection to Mrs. Lyon-Phelps and yourself, and my most grateful thanks,

Ever yours sincerely,

FLORENCE HARDY

MAX GATE,
DORCHESTER, DORSET
8th August 1929

DEAR WILLIAM LYON PHELPS:

So many thanks for your letter. It was like a kindly hand stretched across the ocean giving me help and encouragement.

J. M. Barrie is not looking very well, I think, but the hot weather in London has tried him very much, and also the journey to Edinburgh and back the week before last, when he received the freedom of the city, and also he has been looking after someone in a nursing-home who had a bad motor accident. There is no one I know who exerts himself more for any friend who may be ill or in trouble than J.M.B. . . .

My love to you both,

FLORENCE HARDY

MAX GATE,
DORCHESTER, DORSET
4th January 1932.

DEAR PROFESSOR LYON PHELPS,

Your letter was the first I opened on New Year's day. It was so kind of you to write. I do send you and Mrs. Lyon Phelps my very best wishes. I hope I shall see you when you are in England. . . .

I have not seen the Bernard Shaws since that book was published, but Colonel T.E.Lawrence, who saw them off when they left England a fortnight ago says they did not mind the book (I expect that Mrs. G.B.S. disliked it) and that G.B.S. allowed it to be published for the sake of Harris's widow.

I hope you were pleased with Sir James Barrie's little story in the Times. The post that brought me your letter brought also one from his only surviving sister Margaret, and she was very excited about it. The last paragraph I thought very fine. He spent Christmas in Dorset, not here, but at Mells, the home of Lavy Horner, and he is now, I think, at Stanway. He has not been well this autumn but is better now I think—and hope. . . .

I long to go to America, but the force that seems to hold me at Max Gate may perhaps prevent me ever leaving England.

I am grateful—eternally grateful for what you say and write about T.H. I wish I could hear you lecture.

With my love and devotion to you both,

Affectionately,

FLORENCE HARDY

MAX GATE,
DORCHESTER, DORSET
TELEPHONE, DORCHESTER 43
6th November '32

DEAR BILLY—

It was kind of you to write and I loved having news of you both. I hope you are both well. I shall look forward immensely to having your new book on Browning. This is my only address at present. I may go to London later for a few weeks, but that is uncertain. Anything will find me here, and I should be backwards and forwards in any case.

I gave your kind message to my sister-in-law—Katherine Hardy— and she was delighted to know that you remembered her.

I have not seen J.M.B. for a little time, but I had a letter from him a few days ago, asking for news of me as I had not written to him or been to see him for some time. I have been too busy to go to London. But Aircraftman Shaw (Colonel T.E.Lawrence) told me last week that Peter Davies (J.M.B.'s adopted son) had told him that 'Barrie was growing old.' Almost impossible to believe. J.M.B. told me that his visit to Scotland did him a lot of good as the air there suits him so well. I *must* go to see him soon, even if I make a special journey to London for that purpose.

With every good wish and my love to you both,

Affectionately,

FLORENCE HARDY

5, ADELPHI TERRACE,
STRAND, W.C.2.
Sunday, April 29th, '34

MY DEAR BILLY:

Yes, indeed I am in the Adelphi—sitting writing at this moment by a window from which if I raise my eyes I see Cleopatra's needle just in front—& beyond a wonderful view of the Thames, with barges sliding by—& just beneath this room is the beautifully decorated room where Mrs. Garrick gave that famous party to Dr. Johnson, Boswell and others two years after Garrick's death. . . .

Enough of my flat. Thank you so much for sending that cutting, & for the kind words. I did not select the poems. T.H. did. He certainly asked my advice but I think he always held by his own judgment. E.Gosse always thought that *I* selected the poems—but he was wrong.

I am sorry you & Annabel are not to be in Europe this summer as I should have loved to see you both. However, I shall hope to see you in 1935—all being well. Barrie has been keeping pretty well this spring—much better than he was last year. . . .

On Wednesday I go back to Max Gate for a few days but I shall be back here before you receive this I hope—& Max Gate is always a safe address—at least for this year. I do not know about next.

I often think of your jump from the Cobb at Lyme Regis.

All good wishes & love to you both.

Ever sincerely,

FLORENCE HARDY

On 15 May 1937 Mrs. Hardy wrote me she was going into a nursing home 'for a little while.' I thought she had no suspicion of the serious nature of her illness; but my colleague, Richard Purdy, believes she was quite aware of it. It was like her not to complain. Professor Purdy, an admirable research scholar, frequently visited Dorchester in preparation for his studies in Hardy's works; and Mrs. Hardy gave him every assistance possible. He saw her during her last illness. She died of cancer in the Autumn.

Apart from her position as the wife of Thomas Hardy, she was extremely interesting because of herself; she was one of the finest women I have known.

MAX GATE
DORCHESTER, DORSET
16th August 1936

DEAR BILLY:

Your letter, with its generous and characteristic writing was a joy to receive. I hope you are well, and your Annabel. It was so sad that I missed you when you were in London last year. I do not know how that happened. I wish you were coming this summer.

Richard Purdy is on his way to England—indeed I think the boat arrives tonight—for he is due to be in London tomorrow, and I believe he is coming to see me on Tuesday or Wednesday.

I had a visit from Sir James Barrie three weeks ago, and he seemed very well indeed. He did not say much about his play, except that it is to be produced in London in October.

Margaret Kennedy (Mrs. David Davis) asked me some while ago to go with her to the first performance in Edinburgh that month, but I think I will wait until it comes to London. I sincerely hope that Elizabeth Bergner's health will not fail her again.

My husband's sister Katherine Hardy is quite well I rejoice to say, though she has had some slight illnesses early in the year. I see her very often. I told her you had asked after her in your letter, and she was very pleased that you had remembered her, and she said 'I was thinking of him only the other day.' I, too, think of you often, and always when I hear or speak of the Cobb at Lyme Regis, where you walked, and from which you jumped. I hope you will walk there again.

With greetings to you both,

Yours ever,

FLORENCE HARDY

39

ROOSEVELT AND RILEY

AT the Bicentennial celebration of Yale University (founded in 1701) in October, Theodore Roosevelt, who had within a few weeks become President of the United States (McKinley died 14 September) received an honorary degree and made a characteristic speech. In the afternoon he was like a caricature of himself; and yet evidently sincere. I was Head Usher and presented individually to him an interminable line of men. He was not allowed to shake hands with anyone, because McKinley had been shot while doing so; he held his hat in both hands and it was evident that he chafed under the enforced restraint. Whenever a famous athlete appeared in the line and I mentioned his name, the President would release one hand and grasp him around the neck and say 'It's a darned shame I can't shake hands with you, old man!'

Among the men of letters who received honorary degrees, Howells, Aldrich, etc., Mark Twain received the loudest and most prolonged applause.

One of the most picturesque figures was Archbishop Ireland; in his ecclesiastical robes, he attracted much attention.

While I was standing near President Hadley at the evening reception, a delegate from Sweden, covered with medals, was presented. He addressed Hadley *in Latin*, making a fairly long speech. The moment he finished, Hadley replied in equally fluent Latin.

I first met Riley at Indianapolis in the late nineties; some ladies took us to lunch at the Country Club, and before we started, they said the shortest and pleasantest way to drive was through the cemetery, asking us if we had any objection. 'I should like it very much,' said Riley; 'because some day I shall drive there and won't have to come back.' Not long after that, I persuaded Riley to give a reading from his poems at New Haven. I went to his room at the hotel about five o'clock, and found him in a state of absolute hysteria. He was walking up and down in his room like a caged wild beast, shouting out his woes, 'Oh, my God, why did I agree to do this, why, oh, why?' I said, 'After you have had a good dinner, you'll feel better.' 'Dinner? Hear him talk! dinner! I haven't eaten a mouthful all day. I could not possibly eat.'

I thought I had better go, and he screamed 'Don't leave me! stay with me! What will happen to me if you go?' It is impossible to exaggerate his agony of mind; and I wondered why he ever consented to appear in public when it produced such suffering. I tried to tell him that he wasn't going to lecture, did not have to think of anything to say; all he had to do was to recite his poems. It was no use. He remained in this excruciating torture until it was time to go to the lecture, and he was exactly in that same frame of mind behind the curtain, so I feared he would break down. But the instant he appeared before the immense audience, he was wholly at ease, gave a marvellous recital of his poems, and seemed to enjoy doing it; and certainly enjoyed the tumultuous applause. After the lecture, I took him to the Graduates' Club, where, not having eaten anything all day, he ate a huge dinner and was in the highest spirits. I could not help asking him if he always suffered agony during the hours preceding his appearance in public. 'Always.' 'But I should think you would remember that you had done it before and always enjoyed it.' 'No, that doesn't do any good at all.'

Riley was the man of his works. He was kindly, lovable, full of fun, generous, a loyal and devoted friend. He was one of the best men I have ever known, and although he kept up a stream of profanity in conversation, his profanity never seemed vulgar; it was lyrical; and spoken in that soft, gentle voice, seemed a natural manner of emphasis. He never could see anything in the poetry of Walt Whitman. Without raising his voice, he would purl along, 'Old Walt found the —— —— stuff he wrote wasn't worth a —— ——; so he mixed up a lot of —— —— nonsense, and fooled the whole —— —— world.' He was laughing all the time he said this.

The National Institute of Arts and Letters gave Riley the Gold Medal for his poetry. At that time he was very ill, and the medal was sent to him with an appropriate message. I was present at the Institute meeting when the matter was being discussed. It was suggested that at the end of the telegram, three words be added—'God bless you. Some members objected to this, thinking it was not dignified; but finally the blessing was added to the telegram. Riley unexpectedly recovered from this illness; and when I was talking with him one day about the vote on the medal, I remarked that some men thought the message 'God bless you!' was lacking in dignity. 'Then,' said Riley, laughing, 'why didn't they simply send the message "You have been awarded the gold medal for original poetry. God damn you!"'

Riley thought both pessimism and the philosophy of defiance were either affectations or mere arrogance. After he was crippled, someone read aloud to him Henley's familiar lines and when he had finished the last words,

> I am the Master of my fate,
> I am the Captain of my soul,

'The *hell* you are,' said Riley with a laugh.

After Riley had had a stroke, he spent a good deal of time in his automobile being slowly driven around town in Indianapolis. On one of these days, I was with him, when a car passed us containing four or five ladies, everyone wearing the broad hats of the period tied down with veils. Riley looked at them wonderingly and then murmured 'Why do they wear those —— —— hats?'

I asked him if he believed in immortality. He looked at me in amazement. 'Why, of course, we aren't going to die. I shall live right on after my body is buried. There isn't any doubt about it.' And there wasn't in his mind. He had never been interested in spiritualism or in 'messages;' he simply had absolute faith in personal survival.

In response to a request from him, I sent him two essays I had printed on Jane Austen and on Stevenson, and received the following letter:

INDIANAPOLIS, NOV. 28, 1906

DEAR FRIEND: . . . thanks for your just and fine Austen tribute—though her genius is subtly ingenuous as that of Irving in his real characters on the stage—(as hers are on the page). The Stevenson book is just here—so I've barely struck hands with it yet and clapped it on the shoulder. What a man of kidney was R.L.S. No intellectual Bright's disease about that lovely cuss! Lor' don't you love him! Sir Walter, even—for all the start he's got—won't outlast him! And now the pawkie twa o' them are aye toegither! Oh, it's hame!—hame!—hame!—It's there I'm goin' to be, Wi' Weelum Lyon Phelps himsel to gang along wi' me!

All best hails to you and your household, and to your friends that are mine down around 'The Academic Works.' As always your fraternalest,

JAMESY

John Sargent's portrait of Riley in the gallery at Indianapolis is a work of genius. It has that *diablerie* characteristic of his expression when swearing volubly; for I never heard him swear when he was not also laughing. 'When you say that, *smile*.' He looks in the portrait exactly as he must have looked when he described his vain attempt to meet me at the railway station in Indianapolis. He was as helpless as a baby in everything to do with trains or topography. He wrote me that he had gone to the station one hour ahead of time in order to be sure of seeing me, and after all, he failed. He added, 'I could have wept, had not the Almighty given me the blessed gift of cussin'.'

The prophet without honour in his own country was never true of Riley. He was more beloved and honoured in his own town than anywhere else, even though he received a tremendous reception in England. The better he was known personally, the more he was admired. The State of Indiana keeps his birthday as a legal holiday.

In 1902 Yale gave Riley the honorary degree of Master of Arts, the first academic recognition from a great university. I had arranged to entertain him at my house in New Haven, when I had a sudden recurrence of the malady that had laid me low the preceding winter. The physician told me to leave immediately for our summer home in Michigan. My mother and my brother Dryden entertained him, and the Dean of the College, Henry P. Wright, told me that Riley received more applause at Commencement than all the rest of the 'honorary degree' men put together.

NEW HAVEN,
June 26, 1902

Dr. William Lyon Phelps

MY DEAR FRIEND:
   This is all pure magic—Dr. Riley here in your own library writing to you whose presence is so longed for! But Heaven bless you for so promptly going in your health's behalf—besides here in your lovely home I have found your gentle welcoming mother and brother, who gave your home over to me, though I offered them fairest opportunity

to leave me quartered at the hotel—for we arrived late at night and there lodged—going to find your people and explain at 10 next morning.

Well—I just *cannot* realize all that has followed. It is *exchantment*, simply! Professor Beers has been a very brother through it all—and your brother likewise. Dr. Hadley was an inspired man throughout all the ceremonies of yesterday—yea, and last night at reception at Art Building, where your brother took me, 'and the world went well with me then, then, oh then!' But you'll hear of the success of everything through the press and your friends—never a hitch in any particular that I'm aware of. Even read a poem (bran' span fresh and new) though in no wise pertinent to the occasion—which I priorly explained to committee, and they said *Give it*—and I done give it and it seemed to 'go' in really very great shape! We may be going on to New York today, where (utter confidence) I've a new book in press. . . .

All your home-folks send love to you and Mrs. Phelps with this most grateful greeting of your affectionate old friend,

JAMES WHITCOMB RILEY

In 1888 I had seen Riley in the distance at Chautauqua, and this interview with him (author unknown) contains material not easily available elsewhere. It is taken from the 'Walks and Talks' column in Chautauqua Assembly *Daily Herald* of August 1888.

James Whitcomb Riley is a new name on the Chautauqua program, but a name firmly entrenched in public favor by two entertainments which must be counted among the hits of the season. He proved himself such a genius in the field of dialect poetry that he might safely be called the Robert Burns of America. One thing is certain—he is sure of a hearty welcome should he ever visit Chautauqua again. I had a chat with him in his room at the hotel after his last entertainment. I asked him, "How did you happen to choose such a peculiar field." He replied to my question, "I wanted to be an actor, from the time I began to take part in school entertainments in my little native town. When I was a child my father, who was a lawyer and an eccentric man, used to dress me up in quaint clothes and take me to the Court-room. Left to myself I studied the faces of country lawyers and witnesses from the farms, and unconsciously acquired their peculiar dialect. Afterwards I joined a strolling company of actors, but my sense of the histrionic exactness prevented me from reciting what another man had written. I began to create my own characters, language and all, and now and then would acknowledge the authorship. Sometimes I would publish a dialect poem, but no one would give me anything for it until I received a letter from the poet Longfellow concerning one of my poems, in which he said: 'I believe it shows true poetic faculty and insight.' After that it was easy enough—I had at last gained recognition." This interview closed with the remark, "I cannot travel with a trunk. I am continually haunted by the fear that it will be lost; and so I go about the country with a grip. I keep a tenacious hold upon it all day long, and never feel quite safe about it at night. In case there is ever a fearful railway accident, and among the debris is discovered a valise with an arm attached to it firmly, they may bury it without further identification as the fragments of the Hoosier Poet."

40

EVENTS IN 1902

On 3 January 1902, looking out of the windows of the railway berth as we crossed to St. Louis, I saw the Mississippi River for the first time. The broad stream was filled with huge masses of ice.

When I was returning East, W.J.Bryan occupied the seat in front of mine, and wrote incessantly—probably an editorial for *The Commoner*. As I left the train I wished him a happy New Year, and he shook hands cordially.

On Saturday 8 February I played hockey on the ice at Lake Whitney all the afternoon. I was never to play that game again. The next morning I was unpleasantly surprised by a sudden appearance of acute kidney disease. I went to my family physician, Dr. J.P.C.Foster, in whom I had well-placed confidence. He told me, after a laboratory analysis the next day, to take no exercise in the way of games or violent exertion, to give up all outside work except teaching in college, and not to worry. He said he could take me to a New York specialist, but it would not be necessary. Although I did not expect to recover, I went ahead with my regular work in the university, giving up outside engagements; and with occasional setbacks, I became entirely well. But I did not play golf until April and no tennis until the next year and never hockey.

One reason I trusted Dr. Foster, a G.P., was because I knew of the experience of an undergraduate friend of mine

a few years previously. He told me he had some trouble
and wished to know of a good physician. I sent him to
Dr. Foster and said, 'Do exactly what he tells you.' The
Doctor found he had acute Bright's Disease, but insisted
he could cure him. The boy felt he was not progressing
rapidly enough, and wished to see a specialist. Dr. Foster
took him to the most famous man in New York, who after
examination, asked him if he wanted to know the truth.
The boy did; and the specialist told him he could not live
six months. Two years later, he won the mile run in the
university track meet; and is alive and well today.

A grimly amusing thing happened while I was being examined that first evening in Doctor Foster's office. I was
pretty sure that my trouble meant death; I thought I
was doomed. While he was examining me, his daughter in
the next room began to play Chopin's Funeral March. I
burst out laughing and said, 'Doctor, I admire your
daughter's skill on the piano; but do you think she selects
the most appropriate pieces for your office hours?'

On 3 April we had an interesting and beautiful river
journey. We took the steamer *Pocahontas* leaving Norfolk,
Virginia, at seven in the morning, and travelled the whole
day on the river James, reaching Richmond in the evening.
We passed the old tower at Jamestown, thinking of Captain Smith, saw charming old colonial residences like
Westover, and enjoyed the cloudless sunshine.

On 19 April I was a Yale delegate to the inauguration
of President Nicholas Murray Butler of Columbia; the
President of the United States, President Eliot of Harvard,
and Harper of Chicago, made addresses.

On 20 December I went to Denver for the first time, to
address the Yale Alumni dinner, presided over by Ex-
senator Wolcott, who was full of good stories. The weather
at Colorado Springs on Christmas Day was unbelievable.
In the same latitude in Kansas (neighbouring state) it was

two below zero; here it was 80 in the shade, people sitting on the grass, as in summer.

Going out on the old Union Pacific, which I took for sentimental reasons, I was impressed by the immense prairies of western Nebraska, as majestic as the illimitable sea. Returning from Denver, I took the Burlington; the train left at sunset, and as I looked back on Denver, the whole western sky was aflame—El Dorado. There were four or five poor fellows in my car who were sufferers from tuberculosis; I remember particularly one agreeable young man with the too red complexion, who said cheerfully, 'They think I'm very ill; there is really nothing the matter, only a little stomach trouble.' That night he died in his berth.

The hospitality of the Yale men and others in Colorado was warm and generous; and I found it the same when I next visited Denver, 34 years later, in 1936. Only this time what an advance in railway speed! In 1902 my train left Chicago at 5.30 p.m., and arrived in Denver the next evening at midnight. In 1936 I left Chicago at the same hour and arrived in Denver at about eight the next morning. This new stream-lined train often went 115 miles an hour.

In this year 1902 Owen Wister's novel *The Virginian* was published and immediately became a best-seller. Unlike most best-sellers, it has had a steady sale ever since, being today one of the best-known and most widely read American novels of the twentieth century. I called his attention to a tiny slip and to one or two other little specks. The following letter came, and it led to an intimate friendship, broken only by his death 21 July 1938.

SAUNDERSTOWN, R.I. OCT. 8, 1902

MY DEAR SIR:

Thank you most heartily. Shorty could *not* read, and the newspaper either was for Trompas's perusal, or for kindling their fires. The next impression shall benefit by your friendliness. I wish this were the only what you call 'speck'; I find the surface full of them—and of various sorts!

Yours faithfully,

OWEN WISTER

In 1902 Maurice Maeterlinck produced his play *Monna Vanna* which had immediate and widespread success. It was translated into many European languages and was a favourite with playgoers in Continental capitals. It was forbidden in England because the theme turned on the moral problem of whether a wife were justified in giving herself for a night to the commander of an army attacking her country, if by so doing she could save her country from invasion, conquest, and destruction. For the hostile commander promised that if she would come to his tent he would withdraw his army altogether. She agreed to this; feeling that if men were praised for giving their lives for their country, she would deserve even higher praise for sacrificing her honour. This decision, however, did not appeal to her husband who regarded her as a degenerate even for considering such an abominable proposal.

I read *Monna Vanna* early in 1903, and was astonished to see that one of the scenes was so similar psychologically to a scene in Browning's almost forgotten play *Luria* (1846), that I felt it could not be a coincidence. It is only an incidental scene and is not concerned with the main plot; but surely only Browning would ever have conceived it. The fact that both plays deal with the war between Florence and Pisa in the 15th century, that the commander of the Florentine forces is an alien (Moor) was not what impressed me; it was the peculiar psychological twist given to an interview between the Florentine diplomat and Prinzivalle, the Moorish general.

I published an article in the New York *Independent*,

not accusing Maeterlinck of plagiarism, but merely calling attention to the amazing similarity of the two scenes.

James Huneker, at that time drama critic of the *New York Sun*, wrote an article dismissing my absurd discovery as typically professorial pedantic stuff and nonsense. The London *Academy* took the same view. I therefore sent my article to M. Maeterlinck and received the following letter by return of post.

67 RUE RAYNOUARD
PARIS
22 Mars 1903

CHER MONSIEUR

Je viens de lire avec intérêt, ds. *The Independent,* la note que vous avez bien voulu consacrer à *Monna Vanna.* Vous avez parfaitement raison : il y a entre une scène épisodique de mon 2 acte (celle ou Prinzivalle démasque Trivulzio) et l'une des grandes scènes de *Luria* une Similitude que je m'étonne de n'avoir pas vu signaler plus tôt. Je m'en étonne d'autant plus que, loin de cacher cette similitude, j'avais tenu à l'affirmer moi-même en prenant exactement les mêmes villes ennemies, la même époque et presque les mêmes personnages; alors qu'il eut été bien facile de transposer le tous et de rendre l'emprunt méconnaissable, si j'avais eu l'intention de le dissimuler.

Je suis un lecteur assidu et un ardent admirateur de Browning qui est selon moi l'un des plus grands poètes que l'Angleterre ait eus. C'est pourquoi je le considère comme appartenant à la littérature classique et universelle que tout le monde est censé connaître. Il est donc licite et naturel de lui emprunter une situation ou plutôt un fragment de situation, comme on en emprunte journellement à Eschyle, à Sophocle, à Shakespeare; les emprunts, quand il s'agit de poète de cet ordre se font, pour ainsi dire, *coram populo,* et constituent une sorte d'hommage public.

Pour le reste, en mettant à part cet épisode, qui occupe une place si accidentelle et si accessoire qu'on pourrait le supprimer sans que mon drame en fut ébranlé, toute ma pièce s'écarte complètement de la tragédie de Browning et n'a plus rien de commun avec elle. Cette scène s'élève donc dans mon oeuvre comme une sorte de stèle isolée que ma mémoire pieuse y a dédiée au souvenir du poète qui avait créé en mon imagination l'atmosphère où se meut *Monna Vanna*, un souvenir d'un maître entre tous admiré.

Je vous remercie donc bien cordialement de votre amicale communication qui m'a permis d'affirmer ceci, et je vous prie de me croire votre très dévoué

M. MAETERLINCK

I asked his permission to publish his letter and received the following reply:

12 MAI 1903

CHER MONSIEUR:

Votre lettre datée de 26 avril, n'est, je ne sais par quelle erreur de la poste, arrivée qu'hier soir.

Je vous suis très reconnaissant de votre attitude cordiale et très correcte dans cette petite controverse littéraire et je vous en remercie infiniment.

Je ne me souviens plus exactement des termes de ma première lettre—mais comme j'y dis simplement une vérité que je tenais à dire, je ne vois nul inconvenient à ce qu'elle soit publiée telle quelle. Je crois seulement me rappeler que j'y disais que la scène entre Prinzivalle et Trivulzio avait été *empruntée* à Browning. Il serait plus exact de dire qu'elle m'a été *inspirée* par la lecture de *Luria*. C'est d'ailleurs ainsi que ma nouvelle pièce *Joyzelle*, m'a été inspirée par La Tempête de Shakespeare.

S'il semble naturel de chercher un point de départ et un motif d'inspiration dans Shakespeare, pourquoi s'étonnerait-on qu'on le cherche dans Browning?

Merci encore, et croyez-moi, cher monsieur, votre très dévoué

M. MAETERLINCK

The following December (1903) I was in Paris and wrote M. Maeterlinck requesting an interview. He gave me an appointment for six o'clock in the evening. He was living at 67 rue Raynouard. A maid showed me through many long dark corridors and passages, which reminded me of the early plays of the author; finally she knocked at a door, a hearty voice cried '*Entrez!*' and there in a brightly-

lighted room, with a pleasant open fire sat the famous
Belgian at his desk, writing. In view of the mystical
dramas by Maeterlinck, I had expected to see a dreamy
bard. But Maeterlinck was just the opposite. He looked
like a man fond of beefsteak and ale; he was robust and
hearty and genial; perhaps the best word to describe him
would be the word *jovial*. He was most cordial. He offered
me a cigarette, which I lighted and in my embarrassment
I stuck the lighted end in my mouth. Maeterlinck roared
with laughter at my discomfiture, which was the best possible thing he could have done, for I immediately felt on
intimate terms with him, and we had free and intimate
conversation for over an hour. Directly behind him so that
he could reach the books without leaving his chair were
the Elizabethan Dramatists in the then famous Mermaid
Series. The only one missing was the Chapman, which I
had edited myself; and I completed his set the next day,
for which he was grateful. The bookcase seemed to be full
of English and American books; I knew that he had written an introduction to a French translation of Emerson.

I amused him very much by telling him of the account
of his French translation of the Elizabethan play by Ford
(*'Tis Pity She's a Whore*) which he had translated under
the title *Annabella*, and how the news of the Parisian performance had been given in the *New York World*.

THE CARROLLTON
981 MADISON AVE.
Oct. 5th 1903

My Dear Professor Phelps

Pardon my seeming rudeness—I only read your kind letter yesterday on my return from a six months trip in Europe. I saw
Mr. Maeterlinck in Paris and he quite agreed with you; what more
can a friendly critic say on the subject!

In action 'Monna Vanna' is much less suggestive of 'Luria' than
in the book. The beautiful—and for me the instructive—part of the

affair is Maeterlinck's modesty. I'm glad, however, you made us all acknowledge you are in the right, especially as you are!

Sincerely

W.L.Phelps Esq. JAMES HUNEKER

This certainly is a handsome letter and it gratified me; I was a little surprised two years later, to read in Mr. Huneker's book *Iconoclasts* (published 1905) on page 428 the following:

> Then I brought up Browning's Luria and the opinion of Professor Phelps of Yale that Maeterlinck had profited by reading the English poet when he composed Monna Vanna. M. Maeterlinck smiled.
>
> 'Naturally I read Browning; who does not?' he said, with the naive intonation that becomes him so well. '*Luria* I have known for a long time, but *Luria* is not a stage play'; which, coming from the author of *Les Aveugles*, I considered sublime. He is quite right—*Monna Vanna* and *Luria* have little in common except that the scenes of both are laid at Pisa, and that both Luria and Prinzivalle were treated badly by an ungrateful country. But then, so was Coriolanus and a host of other historical patriots.

During the term of 1901–2, I was lecturing to my class in American literature, and the subject for the day being Whittier, I remarked that the Quaker poet had never been married and so far as I knew, had never wished to be. One of the undergraduates, Charles C.Russ of Hartford, came to the desk at the close of the lecture and said, 'I dislike to contradict you, but Whittier proposed to my great-aunt.' I asked him for proof, and he said the family had the letter. In response to my request, young Mr. Russ brought me the letter of Whittier's in which he certainly did propose marriage to Miss Russ. The family kindly gave me permission to print it, and it appeared in *The Century Magazine*.

Mr. Samuel T.Pickard, the leading authority on Whittier, stated in the newspapers that he thought the letter was a forgery. I took the train to Boston, showed him the epistle, and he immediately declared it genuine.

On 12 November John Drinkwater, whose play *Abraham Lincoln* was then attracting universal attention, gave a lecture at Yale. Professor Tarbell told me he had never seen a man whose face exhibited more integrity, more nobility. He made a fine address on the encouragement of good feeling between Great Britain and the United States, and that evening told us about his terrific struggles with the Birmingham Repertory Theatre. At long last success had been attained; had he known what difficulties he was to encounter, he would not have undertaken the thing at all. I thought Drinkwater was not a natural dramatist, and that the play on Lincoln was a fluke; yet his light but charming comedy, *Bird in Hand*, ran for two years in London and in New York.

ON 9 January in New York I heard for the first time
Eleanora Duse, in D'Annunzio's *Francesca*. In order to
make money, the play was given in the Metropolitan Opera
House, unsuitable for spoken drama. I was bored. And
indeed I was never fortunate in hearing the great Duse.
During her last journey in America, I heard her in Ibsen's
Ghosts, and she must have been ill, for she was uninspired.

On 16 January I heard Edward H.Sothern give a commendable performance of *Hamlet* and after the play, John
Corbin and I had a pleasant supper with him at the rooms
of Miss Purdy. We talked till four o'clock, and Mr. Sothern was very agreeable. Next day we lunched with him at
his New York house; he showed us a MS. play by Percy
Mackaye, of which he spoke with enthusiasm. I have never
met a famous actor more modest and more unaffected than
Mr. Sothern. He seemed, however, to be impressed by a
book called *It was Marlowe*, which tried to prove that
Marlowe wrote Shakespeare's plays. He begged me to read
it, so I took it and read it and found it worthless.

On 5 February about ten members of the Yale Faculty
went to Bridgeport as guests of Professor Sam Sanford—
an elaborate dinner. When the champagne came on in
swaddling clothes and before it had been served, Professor Sanford, addressing President Arthur Hadley, said 'I'll
bet you can't tell what brand of champagne this is.' To
which the university President replied, 'I will tell you not
only the brand but the year.' When the wine reached him,

he took one sip and immediately gave correctly both brand and year. This seemed to me miraculous, and on the way home I asked the President if he had bluffed. 'Oh, no, I had no difficulty whatever in telling the brand; and I knew that Professor Sanford, being a rich man, would have the best year obtainable. The difficulty was that for this particular brand there were two best years. I admit that I did guess between the two and got it right.' This feat, which still seems to me amazing, was only one more instance of scores illustrating Dr. Hadley's astounding memory. He never forgot anything he had ever seen, heard, tasted, or read. He was the only man on the University Faculty who could have passed the entrance examinations to Yale.

Before the war, he was Roosevelt Exchange Professor at the University of Berlin; he spoke German fluently, having taught it at Yale in his younger days. One night at a state dinner given by the Kaiser, a high official asked Hadley if he could tell the brand of wine that was being served. 'No,' said Hadley, 'because I have never tasted it before.' 'How do you know that?' 'If I had ever tasted it, I should remember it. But although I have never tasted it, it seems to me as if it must have come from an area'—and then he gave a small area near the junction of the Rhine and the Moselle. The official was astounded. 'But that is exactly where it comes from, and the reason you have never tasted it before is because all the wine from that region is reserved for the Kaiser. It is never sold.'

The only allusion I have ever seen referring to any one's ability to discern by tasting it the locality whence came any particular wine is in Goethe's *Wilhelm Meister* (Chapter VIII of the *Travels*). In a letter from Lenardo to his aunt, 'By the wares I sent, you would see how and where I was. By the wines, I doubt not my uncle has tasted out my several places of abode.' (Book I, Chapter VI in German original.)

President Hadley's knowledge was as varied and voluminous as it was exact. He could have filled a professorship in half a dozen departments, though his speciality was Economics. He could pour out a stream of information on widely different subjects. Once, on a ship coming back from Europe, a lady was so fascinated by listening to his conversation with his friends, that she finally interrupted and said 'Sir, I have been listening to your instructive remarks for several days; and I should like to ask you one question. Of all the things you have studied and upon which you have reflected, what is the one thing in the world you think you know best?' Hadley considered this, and replied, 'I think I know best how to discard at piquet.'

President Hadley was justly proud of his skill at games. He was admirable at chess and at difficult card games like skat; he was an excellent lawn tennis player, and fair at billiards.

In the Spring of this year Sidney Lee gave several lectures at Yale and I had long walks and talks with him. He was pleased that I had bought both the *Dictionary of National Biography* and the Oxford Facsimile copy of the First Folio of Shakespeare, which he had edited the previous year. He had in 1891 succeeded Leslie Stephen as the Editor of the D.N.B. He told me interesting anecdotes of Carlyle, Browning, Jowett, and others. He was sometimes shocked by my American accent. As we were walking, he asked for the name of a certain building, and I said it was a physics laboratory. 'Why do you say labora*tory*?' 'Well,' I replied, 'I don't think I do; but we always accent two syllables of that word; what do you call it?' He said 'La*bor*atry.'

I gave a dinner in his honour, attended by President Hadley, Professor Lounsbury, and others. And on this visit a friendship began which lasted until his death.

In 1906 I sent him a copy of an article I had written in

the *Yale Courant* containing photographs of various pages of the MS. of Browning's *Dramatis Personae*, then the property of Dr. and Mrs. John Meigs, of the Hill School, in Pottstown, Pennsylvania. This complete manuscript, which Browning had sent to the publishers, and which bears the finger-marks of the type-setters (1864) is now in the Morgan Library in New York. It is interesting in many ways; *Rabbi Ben Ezra* has hardly any corrections; evidently a fair copy. The long poem *Mr. Sludge, the Medium* which infuriated poor Mr. Home so fiercely, is covered with corrections. It must be the only draft in existence; Browning never took the trouble to copy it.

LONDON, 26 DEC. 1906

DEAR PHELPS,

All good wishes for the New Year. I am very much obliged to you for your kindness in sending me the Yale Courant, with your most interesting and valuable article on 'Browning's Dramatis Personae.' It is of great service to know where the MS. is, and I congratulate the Head Master of the Hill School on his good fortune in acquiring it.

I am going through a troubled time. The illness and death of one of my most intimate friends W.J.Craig proved coincident with the falling-ill of my sister who is still in a serious condition. I am at work on some articles for Scribner's Magazine. With very kind regards and pleasant memories of Yale, I am Yours very sincerely,

SIDNEY LEE

In 1913 he was appointed Professor of English Literature in the East London College, and held that post until 1924. He had been knighted in 1911, and died 3 March 1926, at the age of sixty-six.

In the Spring of 1903 there were exciting meetings of the Yale College Faculty, when after long discussions, it was finally voted to give eight elective courses in Freshman Year from which could be chosen five. The bone of contention was whether or not Greek, Latin, and Mathematics should continue to be required studies. On 7 March we came to a vote, and I give it here because some of the men who took part were so well known. Affirmative: Dean Wright, W.G.Sumner, A.Wright, Charlton Lewis, Phelps, G.M.Duncan, Charles C.Torrey, Hanns Oertel, Gustav Gruener, James Pierpont, E.H.Sneath, Henry Lang, H.S.Williams, John C.Schwab, Charles F.Kent, C.H.Smith, George B.Adams, E.G.Bourne, F.A.Gooch, Henry A. Beers, Henry C.Emery, Irving Fisher—22. Negative: Willard Gibbs, Tracy Peck, Thomas D.Seymour, E.P.Morris, B.Perrin, Horatio Reynolds, Thomas D.Goodell, A.W.Phillips—8. All but Gibbs and Phillips were professors of Latin or Greek. This was one of the last appearances of the mathematical genius, Josiah Willard Gibbs, whom Einstein has called the greatest mind in American history. He died during the next month, on 28 April.

President Hadley used to say that Gibbs's knowledge of mathematics began where that of other specialists left off. I know nothing of what he knew, but I knew him; he was a quiet, modest sweet-tempered man, with a beautiful head and face. There is no other adjective to express it. He was never married, and lived alone with his brother-in-law, the Yale Librarian, Addison Van Name. He was born in New Haven, was a Yale graduate, and after some years of study in France and Germany, was made Professor of Mathematical Physics at Yale in 1871, and held that position till his death in 1903. He lived only a few doors from my house in New Haven, and I used to see him taking his solitary walks; and I thought what an exciting life he really must be leading, away out on the remote frontiers of speculative thought. For, as Henry James said, ' There are no adventures like intellectual ones.'

On Monday 13 April 1903, at nine o'clock in the evening, my mother died. Had she lived until November, she would have been eighty. Her death was the severest loss and most bitter grief I have ever felt. She had had a cold, but colds were common in the last years of her life and there seemed no occasion for alarm. My oldest brother Dryden was living in the house with us, and we also had her cousin Nellie Hubbard, to take care of her. So there seemed to be no reason why my wife and I should not go to Virginia for a few days when the college Easter vacation began on Wednesday 8 April. On Sunday we received a telegram that my mother had pneumonia. We took the night train and were in New Haven about ten the next morning, to receive the greatest shock of my life. My mother was dying; three physicians and two nurses were there, but I shall never know whether or not she recognized me, as she could not speak, even with the aid of the oxygen. I had never believed it possible that my mother, whom I had talked with in the most natural fashion on Wednesday, should in four days be so tragically changed. She died that same evening, and Doctor Walter Judson, whom she had known since he was a boy, said ' There dies the best friend I have ever had.' I could not forgive myself for being absent those last days; I could not forgive myself for a thousand other small things where I could have shown her more tenderness or more consideration. I was overwhelmed. Among the letters we received, the one I liked best was from a Yale undergraduate, Paul Ney. He wrote. ' Ten years ago my mother died; it is just as hard for me to bear now as it was then; and I am glad it is.'

On 8 May I lectured on ' The Novels of Thomas Hardy ' at Williams College. Among the undergraduate listeners was Stuart P. Sherman, though I did not know it. In later years he was Professor of English at the University of Illinois and still later, the Editor of the weekly *Books* of the *New York Tribune*. He was the author of many books of literary criticism, and he told Dr. Henry S. Canby that he was first inspired to a literary career by that lecture of mine at Williams.

42

FIRST SABBATICAL YEAR

(1903–1904)

GIVING college professors a free year at half-salary is good for all concerned. As a friend of mine expresses it, 'You can go abroad and acquire a few ideas, and with half of your salary the college can hire a better man to take your place.' In my own instance the college hired nobody to take my place and saved the money for some possibly more useful purpose. Upon reflexion, I found this wholesome. Had the garbage-collector taken even a month off, someone would immediately have been appointed to take his place; but when I went away for a year, it seemed that the college proceeded well enough without me. Thus the garbage-collector was more essential to the community than I.

On 20 June, having left our Irish setter Rufus with Fred Lockwood, our brother-in-law in Norwalk, and our grey cat Tiger Tuesday with our neighbours, Mr. and Mrs. Sloan, we sailed from New York on S.S.*Pretoria*, on our first Sabbatical, to be gone fifteen months. It was a slow, heavily-laden ship, twelve days to Cherbourg. We went directly to a pension at 117, rue Notre Dame des Champs, where we found our old friends, Professor and Mrs. Ralph Catterall of Chicago. At this same pension were also Professor and Mrs. McGiffert, and Dr. Philip Churchman, a Princeton graduate, now Professor of French at Clark University.

I used to wonder how it was possible for Americans to

live for months abroad and learn nothing of any European language. But on this Sabbatical year we discovered that it was not enough to live in France and to be with French people; a will of iron was necessary, if one wished to acquire the art of speaking French, for nearly all the foreigners one meets wish to learn English. We accordingly made a vow and kept it; we might not learn French and German, but we determined *not* to teach English. This involved eternal vigilance and frequent rudeness; but we explained to those foreigners who wished to talk English with us, that if they would travel to America, we should be glad to oblige them. Thus we never conversed in English with Frenchmen or Germans except on the rare occasions when they spoke our language with absolute ease. Professor Beljame, head of the English Department of the Sorbonne, was very kind to us, and spoke English like a native; when we took dinner in his Paris apartment and in his country house, it would have been ridiculous to converse in French. I asked him one day how it happened that he, a Frenchman, spoke English without an accent; the only foreigner I had ever heard with that accomplishment. He replied, 'It is because I have spoken English every day for forty years. It takes that long to master the pronunciation.' He forgot to add that his mother was an Englishwoman.

Some of the best friends we made at this pension were also eager to learn French; Mr. Hans Escher and his sister, German-Swiss from Zürich, and two German lieutenants, Schiemann (son of the Berlin professor) and Remmets. I suppose both these men were killed in the war. But when in 1914 I read that every German military officer was a degenerate brute, I could think only of these two young gentlemen, so kind, so considerate, so generous and affectionate.

With Remmets we made excursions to Fontainebleau

and elsewhere, and also to the theatres; and our efforts at conversation on trains and tramcars fascinated the passengers. Whenever we began to converse, they would go into convulsions of uncontrollable laughter; we did not mind; how indeed could they help it? Their facial expression seemed to say, 'Why on earth don't those people converse in their own language, instead of butchering ours?' But we couldn't. Remmets could not speak English, and we could not speak German; thus we afforded innocent delight to fifty million Frenchmen.

I remember our horrible disappointment when, along with the good Remmets, we first went to a matinée at the Théâtre Antoine, to see how much we could understand. We understood nothing; and I can still see the expression of despair on the face of Remmets, as he whispered to me, '*Je suis désolé.*' So were we.

I remember how amused a French lady sitting in front of us at the theatre one day was, when, after a long speech in some classical drama, I whispered, 'Je n'ai pas compris un mot; mais c'est superbe, *c'est épatant*!'

When I hear people say, as I have so often, that they cannot speak French but can understand it, I think they are lying. For the average person, it is more difficult to understand a foreign language than to speak it. The exceptions to this are of two varieties; those who have learned French thoroughly in their childhood, and have not spoken it for years—and those few individuals, usually women, who are content in any company to remain silent, but have cultivated the art of listening. I was glad to see in a book by Somerset Maugham the statement that his servant could not understand English though he spoke it easily.

Long after I could speak French and German fluently, I had difficulty in understanding it, except in a conversation where someone was speaking directly to me, or in a lecture, or on the stage where I had previously read the play. For, when I spoke, I knew what I said, and could rapidly make up correct sentences; but what was the other fellow saying? I have invariably found this to be true with foreign professors and lecturers in America; they speak English easily (except for pronunciation) but it is clear they have not the remotest idea what we are saying, if we speak as we should to another American.

Indeed, I am certain that Joseph Conrad, who wrote English as well as any contemporary English man of letters, did not easily understand English conversation. I have seen him at dinner, and in social groups, and it was quite clear he did not know what was being said. Of course he understood if you spoke to him directly and with clear enunciation.

One of the best gifts parents can give their children is to have them taught by governesses French and German in their childhood; then they learn these languages naturally and without drudgery; and if care is taken so that they do not cease to use them as they grow, the accomplishment will add enormously to their happiness.

Mademoiselle Desfaveries, who taught us French, told me there was a distinguished American professor who had employed her to teach him, and he was so humiliated by not being able to understand, that he would often pretend he did, by nods and becks and wreathed smiles and various grimaces. So she cured him of this hypocrisy one day by telling him an agonizing story of a little child run over in the street by an automobile; while she told it, she kept laughing, and he joined heartily in this laughter, as if he were enjoying a very funny story. When he found the laugh was on him, he was disconcerted.

An amusing pun was made by an American woman whose wit triumphed over her sufferings. A Parisian dentist was trying to extract one of her teeth, and broke it. He exclaimed, '*Quelle tragédie!*' To which she calmly replied, '*Une tragédie de Racine, n'est-ce pas?*'

Among the lost opportunities of my life which trouble me like Rossetti's spilt water in hell, is the failure to see Coquelin in *Cyrano de Bergerac*. During that month of July 1903, he was playing it every night; but we decided to postpone going until our ears were more attuned to spoken French. At the end of the month he departed, was away from Paris all the rest of the year, and died in 1909. I had heard him in New York in *Thermidor* and I often heard his brother, Coquelin Cadet, who died ten days after Constant, at the Comédie Française.

I heard Richard Mansfield play Howard Thayer Kingsbury's translation of *Cyrano* and Walter Hampden play Brian Hooker's translation; I heard it in Italian at Rome, and I heard Le Bargy play it in the original at the original theatre in Paris. I suppose the finest translation of it is in German and by Ludwig Fulda. It was Ludwig Fulda who told me that a schoolgirl wrote on her exam paper that Goethe, after winning Frederike's affections, suddenly left her 'and was never heard of again.'

In 1913, being in Biarritz, I wished very much to call and see M. Rostand at his home in Campo; accordingly, I wrote, asking for an interview, and his secretary called me up on the telephone, saying the dramatist had just returned from Paris, was weary from his work there and from travel, but that I could see him in a few days. A cordial letter came a few days later inviting me to call, but I had given it up, and was at the Puy de Dome. I had supposed I should have another opportunity but he died in 1918.

On the day the great Pope Leo XIII died, 20 July 1903, we were in the cathedral at Chartres. As we entered it, I heard a French tourist whisper *C'est écrasant!* The interior of Chartres is the most impressive of any church I have ever seen, but the plain tower, over which the architects and critics become ecstatic, seems to me no better and no worse than the average steeple on any Methodist church. I know well that such a remark means damnation; but I have looked at that tower in different seasons and under varied skies, and the wonder and beauty others feel are hidden from me.

At the end of July we went to the village of Carolles near Mont St. Michel, to 'escape the heat of Paris,' and we nearly froze; there was day after day of bitter wind, driving horizontal rain. However, we made pleasant French acquaintances, as we were the only foreigners in the little town. All the Frenchmen in those days, young and old, wore beards; and in church on the day of the Assumption, 15 August, a Frenchman behind us whispered 'That man is either an actor or an American—he has no beard.' It was the growth of lawn tennis and other outdoor sports, then almost unknown in France, that eliminated the silky French beards. To play tennis with a full beard is grotesque, and a serious handicap on a windy day.

To see Carolles a little way off with the ancient church surrounded by the cluster of houses, reminded me of Guy de Maupassant's remark that the church in every French village looks like a hen surrounded by her chickens.

Carolles and that whole Norman coast in the neighbourhood has an atrocious summer climate; no wonder the Normans are a dour, hard-bitten race. We made various excursions, to Coutances, to Avranches, and saw the place where the English King, Henry II, did penance in 1172 for the death of Thomas à Becket in 1170. We stayed over night at Madame Poulard's at Mont Saint Michel, and took the two-hour steamer journey on the charming river Rance from Dinan to Dinard; and at St. Malo across the mouth of the river, saw the scene immortalized by

Browning in *Hervé Riel*. Although the rain fell in torrents all day, there was a steady stream of pilgrims to the tomb of Chateaubriand; I was told this happened every day in the year.

We made a number of delightful acquaintances with French people. M. Boulay, a haberdasher from Paris, who had been a French soldier in Madagascar, was most agreeable. He and his wife hired a little donkey named Rigolette for the season, and took us on many an afternoon drive to abbeys and old churches. I amazed and delighted him by curing him instantly of a case of hiccoughs that had lasted two hours and had given him great alarm. We were far out in the country and I told him I should cure him as soon as we could secure a glass of water. He would not believe he was to be instantly cured. I told him to place his two thumbs tightly in his ears, closing the ears hermetically; and with the forefinger of each hand to close both nostrils; whereupon I held the glass of water to his lips, and told him to swallow once. He did so and the hiccoughs ceased immediately. I have never known this simple method to fail.

When the weather permitted, we walked on the shore of the sea; and I remember one September afternoon we watched the sun hanging low over the horizon and then saw it sink into the ocean; exactly as Browning describes it in *Saul*.

> Than by slow pallid sunsets in autumn, ye watch from the shore
> At their sad level gaze o'er the ocean—a sun's slow decline.

In the midst of September we decided to escape from this accursed climate; we had paid in advance for our rooms till the first of October, and we knew that if we told our teacher we were going, it would involve us in a long explanation, as the French people do not believe in wasting money. So we eloped. We disappeared early one morning and spent three heavenly days on the Island of Jersey; the weather was fair, the climate was mild, and the place more English than England. It seemed incredible that a few miles could make so complete a change. From there we went to the Loire and once more were favoured during the last ten days of that September by mellow, lovely weather.

We followed the Loire to its mouth on a Browning pilgrimage, spending two days at Pornic, the scene of *Gold Hair*, and visiting Le Croisic, the home of Hervé Riel. His statue was erected nine years later, in 1912 on the occasion of the hundredth anniversary of Browning's birth.

Then we spent three months in Paris, from the first of October to the last day of the year. Here we revelled in the theatres, going four or five times a week. The Ministry of Public Instruction gave me free admittance to the Comédie Française, the Odéon, the Opéra, and the Opéra Comique; and I received the same privilege at the Théâtre Antoine. On 14 October the King of Italy (then young) drove on the Champs Elysées with the Queen and with President Loubet whose black simplicity of dress contrasted dramatically with the gorgeous raiment of royalty, and as the equipage passed I shouted '*Vive le roi!*' A Frenchman asked me why I did that, since I was an American. 'That is just the reason; I have never had a chance before,' and I let out another whoop.

My friend Lewis Einstein was Secretary at the American Embassy and in October he took me on a three days' automobile journey to Meaux, Château-Thierry (to see where La Fontaine was born), to Reims, to Laon, the enormous military tower at Coucy (destroyed in the World War), and to Soissons. Near Soissons we saw that astounding façade of the great Abbey. The façade with its two towers stood up like a stage set; the walls of the nave had disappeared long ago. In the World War, the tip of one of these towers was knocked off by a shell. When we got to Reims, it was dark; the cathedral was closed; but the sacristan, after a little financial persuasion, unlocked one of the doors, gave us a single candle, and departed. We spent an hour in that vast interior, illumined only by the light of our little candle, amid grotesque and gigantic shadows.

Einstein had a fine automobile and an excellent French chauffeur; near Laon he 'let her out' and the car reached the dizzy speed of thirty-six miles per hour, which at that time seemed miraculous.

In the Paris theatres, we frequently heard the classic plays and the actors Mounet-Sully, Sarah Bernhardt, and Lucien Guitry at the dawn of his fame. However great was the excitement when *Hernani* was first produced, modern audiences were impressively unimpressed. During the long harangues of Mounet-Sully, there was a steady accompaniment of coughing accompanied by unrestrained guffaws.

On a November evening I spoke at the annual dinner of the Yale Alumni in Paris; the famous Yale rowing coach, Bob Cook, was present. He told me that when he was in college he asked Professor Packard what his mark in Greek was. The Professor replied 'I don't know.' 'You don't know, Professor? Why not?' 'Because I haven't got a microscope. Your standing is so low I can't see it with the naked eye.'

One day at the Sorbonne, I had an interesting conversation with Emile Faguet, one of the most prolific authors of modern times; he was very agreeable. I asked him about the vogue of English poets in France; he thought Browning was little read. Faguet gave regular lectures at the Sorbonne, was the drama critic for the daily *Journal des Débats* and produced several books every year.

An amusing incident that led to a long friendship began with a letter of enquiry in the Paris edition of the *New York*

Herald. 'Where is Professor Wm. Lyon Phelps?' The signer said he was a Princeton man, had heard that I was somewhere in Paris, and that it was most important for him to meet me. The address he gave was two houses from ours! I went to see him. He was a wealthy young American gentleman, recently graduated from Princeton; he said he had told his friends he was going abroad *to study*, which seemed to amuse them (indeed they went into peals of laughter) for he had not distinguished himself by enthusiasm for work. 'Well,' I said, 'and why do you wish to see me?' 'Because you can tell me how to get a doctor's degree in literature from the Sorbonne. Mind you, I don't care a damn about scholarship. The only reason I want a degree is to fool my friends. I will work day and night, I will do anything, but I am going to get that degree, and you can show me how.' Never had I seen an advanced degree pursued with that motive; but he had three things in his favour; he had time, money, and determination. I told him I was not able to give any supervision; but the thing for him to do was to take an Elizabethan play, make a correct and variorum text, write a sufficient amount of annotation, take a few courses in the Department of English at the Sorbonne, and he might come through. The next day he departed for London, bought up all the expensive early editions he could find, critical works on the author, old and recent, and returned to Paris with his spoils. I introduced him to Professor Beljame, and then I stepped down and out. In two years this indefatigable young man of fashion got his *Docteur ès Lettres* at the Sorbonne, and published his edition of the play. Professor Beljame said the candidate had a tough time at the oral exam, but they finally decided to let him through, as he had done a prodigious amount of work, and had established a text.

On 20 December with our friend Philip Churchman, we

set out on a few days' journey by train, arriving at Rouen that evening. The next day in a fog we took the train for Le Petit Couronne, and visited the house where Corneille and his brother lived many years. It is kept as a museum. Then after visiting Flaubert's grave in the cemetery, we took a tiny steamer for Croisset, to see the cottage where Flaubert wrote *Madame Bovary* and where Turgenev used to stay with him. The little inn adjoining was kept by M. et Mme Colange, formerly members of Flaubert's household; they told many anecdotes, and proudly exhibited the signed photograph he had given them. It was also appropriate, considering my own name, to see in Rouen the mediaeval gate *William Lyon*. That evening we took the train for Amiens, and the next day we called on Jules Verne. The maid said we should probably find him walking near the cathedral. And there he was, a kindly old gentleman with a white beard. We stopped him and paid our compliments; he was gracious; and showed to us individually that warmth of affection which he displayed so frequently to Americans in his romances. The next time we came to Amiens (1913) we found his statue.

At Beauvais we were filled with amazement at the colossal proportions of the choir, the only part ever completed. That architect had set out to build a cathedral that should dwarf every other one in the world. They never got farther than the choir, but he erected a tower 500 feet high, which stood at the junction of choir and future nave; it fell down.

During our stay at 110 rue Notre Dame des Champs, the news came of the death of Whistler on 11 July. The next week in the *Revue Bleue*, a French critic stated that Whistler was the greatest painter of the nineteenth century. On 28 December George Gissing died at St. Jean de Luz, and the French journals gave him more recognition than he received elsewhere.

Looking back over those months in the theatres at Paris,

nothing impressed us so much as the new play *Les Affaires sont les Affaires* by Octave Mirbeau, played at the Comédie Française by the incomparable Féraudy. We saw it three times and with increasing enthusiasm. It was the success of the year and the theatre had to repeat it often; it was translated into all the languages of Europe; we saw it in German at Munich. It was Mirbeau's only striking success. There are interesting anecdotes about the hard-bitten Mirbeau in Sacha Guitry's memoirs. He remarked that many men of letters met Mirbeau and said they did not like him; but the truth was the other way around; he did not like *them*. It was Mirbeau, so difficult to please, who first saluted Maeterlinck and made him famous in Paris. He called him 'the Belgian Shakespeare.'

While *Les Affaires* was the most dramatic of the new plays, the most beautiful performance we saw (also at the Comédie) was Alfred de Musset's *Les Caprices de Marianne*, with Madame Sorel. This was a flawless production; it was like lovely music; it was like a tranquil sunset, serene and unforgettable beauty.

On the last day of the old year, we said goodbye to our hosts at the pension, Pastor Fuster, his wife and daughter; it was sad to leave them. Down at the train to see us off were Martin Telleen, a former student at Yale, Philip Churchman, our Rumanian friend Orescu, who embraced me fervently, and the Scot Miss MacInnes, a fine French scholar. We took the noon train for Munich, 31 December 1903.

43

THE CITY OF MUNICH

1904

NEVER shall I forget our invasion of Munich on the first day of January 1904. We had spent three months in Paris, and most of the time in drizzling weather. When we stepped out of our train at Munich in the morning, the sky was cloudless, the air was sharp, with some snow on the ground. It was a holiday; military bands were playing, the people looked radiantly happy, and the keynote of the place seemed to be cheerful animation. We drove up the broad Ludwigstrasse, turned to the left near the University at Schellingstrasse, and at No. 3, found the Pension Nordland, where we were to remain for months. It was kept by two charming German ladies, Fräulein Lammers and Fräulein Junkers, who were never separated until the former's death in 1937. They showed us to our rooms, which faced the South, and which were flooded with sunshine; in the corner of each stood a stove taller than Grandfather's Clock.

We had not been there five minutes before we felt at home, and Munich has seemed to me ever since *eine deutsche Heimat.*

Many novelists have written out plans and specifications for a Utopia, the city of their dreams. But while the Munich before the war had its imperfections like everything else on earth, it seemed to me then and seems to me in retrospect to be nearer the ideal city than any other.

Munich is nearly as large as Boston and yet as quiet as a country village. Where the people are I don't know, but those who are familiar with Boylston and Tremont Streets in Boston will see nothing like that in Munich. The streets are calm, the sidewalks uncrowded, the highway uncongested by traffic; there is no Great White Way; there are no flaring lights; there is no hurly-burly. You can hear your own footsteps. My colleague, Professor Emery, arrived at Munich at nine o'clock in the evening, and observing the silence of the streets, asked his taxi driver to take him somewhere. The driver said, 'Isn't that rather indefinite?' 'You know what I mean—take me where there is a lot of noise and a lot of people.' The driver answered, 'What you want is the railway station.' And indeed that is the only place in Munich that fulfils those requirements.

There was everything in Munich to make a cultivated foreigner happy, cheerful, and content. I have never seen any town that has so much to give to the visitor. In the first place, everything one wants to see is within easy walking distance. If one rooms in a boarding-house on a side street off the Ludwigstrasse, one can walk in a few moments to the university, to the public library, to the concert halls, to the State Opera House, to the State Theatre, to the Play House, to the art galleries; and the English Garden, an enormous tract of land, is in the centre of the town and close to all of these other delectable places. In the English Garden in summer one may take long walks or one may sit down and hear music as one sips coffee or beer. In the winter one may skate on the frozen lake. Those who are fond of winter sports have the mountains close at hand. It is estimated that on Sunday mornings in winter 100,000 people take early trains to the mountains for skiing and other amusements. In the summer the environs of Munich are beautiful. There are lakes where one may take excursions in a little steamer or in a rowboat;

where one may visit famous old castles and see their treasures.

If one is fond of tennis, there are three or four tennis clubs in the heart of the city where one may become a visiting member at a nominal fee and find plenty of agreeable companions. The golf links are ten minutes by trolley, and there again the entrance fee is nominal. The only objection that I have to the golf links is that the magnificent mountains are so near that one is constantly tempted to lift up one's eyes to the hills, and however valuable it may be for one's spiritual development, it is fatal to one's efficiency.

Every night in Munich there is something interesting to hear at the opera, at the theatre, or at the concert hall. Every morning there was published a little paper devoted exclusively to theatrical and musical affairs. This paper gave every event that would take place in the city in the afternoon and evening, with the exact time of beginning, the exact time of closing, and a list of the actors, singers, and performers.

One of the chief attractions of the theatre and the operas in Munich is the fact that they began early. The opera began at six o'clock and was always over before ten, except in the case of a very long one. The plays began at seven-thirty and in nearly every instance were over at nine-thirty. In other words, the opera and theatres were not run for the benefit of members of a leisure class who do not have to get up the next morning, but for the ordinary citizen and his family who are obliged to rise early and go to work. In New York, in Paris, and in London theatre-going and opera-going are in the nature of a dissipation. The theatres in Paris do not close until midnight, and in New York and London one does not usually get to one's domicile before that. The result is that one is exhausted, and, 'There is nothing certain but the morning head.' To go to the theatre or opera four nights in succession in London, Paris, or New York—unless one is able to rise very late the next day—is an exhausting ordeal, but in Munich, during a period of seven months, we averaged five nights a week at the opera and theatre and never felt fatigue.

There is another advantage about beginning early. Instead of going to the opera or theatre stuffed with a soggy dinner and made somnolent by food, one takes tea before going and when the entertainment is over one goes into a cheerful café, has a hot supper in delightful company, and is in bed before eleven.

What does going to the theatre mean in New York, London, and Paris? It too often means something like this. One attends a dinner party where half the guests arrive late; one then has a long course dinner, hurried toward the end; the company is hustled into automobiles and arrives at the theatre or opera a half-hour after the performance has begun and in a condition that precludes mental concentration.

After we had spent two or three months in Munich, we fell in love with the place, with the temper of the town, and with the people. After we had spent four months there, we went in April to Italy. There we lived in sunshine and enjoyed the glory and beauty. But after a while we became homesick for Munich, and, although on the morning of our return it was raining and the weather in general was doing its worst, our hearts were singing, for we were home again.

New Year's Day in 1904 was Friday; on Sunday evening, with my former pupil Alfred Ernest Richards, who took his doctorate at the University of Munich and is now Professor of English at the University of New Hampshire, we heard at the *Hoftheater* a splendid performance of *Die Meistersinger,* which began at six and closed at eleven. My friend at Paris, the German Lieutenant Remmets, told us that if we wished to know the inner spirit of the German people, the true heart of Germany, we must hear two operas—*Die Meistersinger* and *Der Freischütz*. We were fortunate in being in Munich in 1904, for the opera was like New York's in the nineties, distinguished by a constellation of stars. Fräulein Morena, Herr Knote, Herr Feinhals, Herr Bender (all of whom sang later at the Metropolitan in New York), were in their prime; and the Wagner performances were magnificent.

Among Americans living in Munich in 1904 were Gertrude Atherton, Poultney Bigelow, Doctor Coit (formerly of St. Paul's School), Professor and Mrs. Homer Eaton Keyes of Dartmouth, and others; and although we avoided English-speaking people as a rule, we had good times with these congenial friends.

Among those studying at the pension were several young Polish gentlemen, students at the University—Count Zoltowski, Count Stadinicki, and Pan Glabisz; we became intimate friends, and although they spoke French and English fluently, they were kind enough to speak only German with us; this was a sacrifice we appreciated, for like all Poles in those days, they hated Germany, Austria, and Russia. They were the best of company, at the theatre, on country excursions, and later in lawn tennis.

Among Shakespeare's plays I had never heard before in any language, I heard at the Royal Theatres *King Lear*, *Measure for Measure*, and *Pericles*. The Intendant of the Royal Theatres was the famous Ernst von Possart, the idol of Germany, almost a legendary figure. He gave me the entrée to the three theatres of the kingdom. Exactly forty years before, he had made his début at Munich in Schiller's *Die Räuber*; accordingly on the night of the anniversary, he played it again; and after the performance University students took the horses from his carriage, and drew him in triumph to his house on the other side of the Isar, a mile away.

I took regular courses at the University, and became intimately acquainted with Schick, the professor of English, Muncker, the professor of German, who smiled when I showed him a volume of the magnificent complete edition of Lessing, which he had edited. He said that although he had edited it, he had never been rich enough to buy it. The *privatdozent* in English, later professor, Ernst Sieper, was a good friend. He was to be as truly one of the war casualties as if he had fallen in battle; for he had devoted his whole career to increasing the good feeling and understanding between Great Britain and Germany, and when the war came, it broke his heart, and he died.

I saw the great Professor Röntgen, who had discovered the X-rays, frequently at the University, but I never had an opportunity to meet him.

One of the most intimate friends of my life was and is Doctor Jules Simon, a Belgian, lecturer in French at the University. Wishing to keep up our practice in hearing and speaking French, we attended his lectures; and a friendship began which will last until death do us part. A few years later he was married to a young lady of Munich; and now Barbara and Jules are grand-parents. Our friendship is kept alive by continuous correspondence. It was at a dinner-party at their house that I made a terrific German pun. Someone was saying that an acquaintance had got a divorce; he begged his wife to let him go. He was a dentist; whereupon I said that if he was a dentist, he could with double emphasis in making such a request of his wife use the language of Tannhäuser to Venus:

O Königin! Göttin! lass mich *ziehen*!

We went frequently to the Münchener Schauspielhaus; at the house of the Director, Herr Stollberg, we met the actors and actresses of the company. This little theatre is attractive and comfortable; it was interesting to be there on first nights, because the German audiences were so sincere that no matter how popular the actors and actresses were, if the play did not please, the final curtain was greeted with such hissing and such a tumult of disapproval that the piece could not be repeated. I remember one night at the first performance of *Hans Sollenstössers Himmelfahrt*, there was both cheering and hissing; finally the cheering was drowned in loud, derisive laughter; whereupon a stately German gentleman rose in the middle of the audience and shouted 'Es ist eine Roheit zu lachen!'

This is the piece that had in other cities of Germany only a moderate success and much opposition; but when Mr. George Kaufman and his collaborator remade it for the American stage, calling it *Beggar on Horseback*, it had an enormous success. I saw both the original and the American version; and I hope the German author got something from the immense receipts in America, for the idea and the plot were certainly his own.

44

LITERARY PILGRIMAGE IN ITALY

ON 21 March 1904 we left Munich for Italy by way of the
St. Gothard Tunnel—deep snow giving way to sunshine;
after visiting the Lakes, and staying three days at Genoa
with our friends the American consul William Henry
Bishop and his wife, we visited Rome, Arezzo, Florence,
Milan, Asolo, and Venice. I have never understood what
Bishop Burnet meant by his comment on Milan cathedral
—'The cathedral hath nothing to recommend it in the way
of architecture.' We were in St. Peter's on Maundy Thursday, Good Friday, and Easter; and I can still feel the
warmth of the body of the stranger tourist jammed tightly
against me for hours as we stood up during the long service
on Easter Day. On Thursday the famous Cardinal Ram-
polla was under the baldachin; it is that baldachin that
gave me the feeling of immense space in the church. It is
90 feet high and yet seems no more out of place than a
writing-desk in a private library.

We were on a Browning pilgrimage, verifying the places
the poet so definitely describes; 'those lancet-windows'
jewelled miracle' in the cathedral at Arezzo, and Caponsacchi's church Santa Maria della Pieve; the house where
Petrarch was born 20 July 1304 we had all to ourselves.
But I wished I might have been there three months later,
when delegates came from all over the world to celebrate
the six-hundredth anniversary of his birth. My Yale colleague Professor Kenneth McKenzie was delivering his
address in fluent Tuscan, when the official souvenir post

card photograph was taken; a great day for Arezzo, Petrarch, Yale, and McKenzie!

In Florence I wished to repeat as definitely as possible Browning's experience when he found the *Old Yellow Book*, which was to produce such a tremendous impact on his mind and to give the world the incomparable *Ring and the Book*.

> I found this book,
> Gave a *lira* for it, eightpence English just,
> Across a Square in Florence, crammed with booths,
> Buzzing and blaze, noontide and market-time,
> Toward Baccio's marble,—ay, the basement-ledge
> O' the pedestal where sits and menaces
> John of the Black Bands with the upright spear,
> 'Twixt palace and church,—Riccardi where they lived,
> His race,—and San Lorenzo where they lie. . . .
> (June was the month, Lorenzo named the Square)
> I leaned a little and overlooked my prize
> By the low railing round the fountain-source
> Close to the statue, where a step descends:
> While clinked the cans of copper, as stooped and rose
> Thick-ankled girls who brimmed them, and made place
> For marketmen glad to pitch basket down,
> Dip a broad melon-leaf that holds the wet,
> And whisk their faded fresh.

Well, if one goes there on market-day—for on every other day of the week the Square is empty—one will find an exact reproduction of this scene. As the bells of Florence were striking noon on Thursday 7 April 1904, I entered the Square; I stood at the foot of the statue by the little fountain; and as I stood there, a marketman came up with a basket of vegetables, dipped a broad melon-leaf into the water, whisked his faded wares fresh, and went on his way; as if he had been rehearsed for a Browning pageant.

The only child of Robert and Elizabeth Barrett Browning, Robert Wiedemann Barrett Browning, was born at Florence, 9 March 1849, and died at Asolo, 8 July 1912.

When Nathaniel Hawthorne visited the Brownings at Casa Guidi, he said that Browning had an elfin wife and an elf child. 'I wonder whether he will ever grow up, whether it is desirable that he should.' On this occasion the little elf flitted about the room, merrily handing strawberries to his father and mother, Nathaniel Hawthorne, and William Cullen Bryant. He grew up, entered Balliol College, Oxford, but left without taking a degree, his chief interest being in art. In 1887 he was married to Fannie Coddington of New York, and for the rest of his life lived mainly in Italy. His paintings and sculptures were sometimes exhibited in London and on the Continent, and he might have reached a high reputation if he had not carried the burden of his parents' fame. When I visited the Palazzo Rezzonico in Venice, the house where his father died, the rooms on the top floor were filled with large paintings by the son, some of them beautiful and interesting, but without any striking originality. I saw there, too, the original pen-and-ink sketch of Tennyson reading *Maud*, made by Dante Rossetti on that memorable evening at London, in 1855, when the Tennysons, the Brownings, Dante and William Rossetti were gathered together in an upper room. Tennyson, with one leg curled under him on the sofa, chanted *Maud*, the tears running down his cheeks; and Browning read *Fra Lippo Lippi*, both poems published that year.

After Browning's death in 1889, his sister Sarianna went to live with her nephew. She died 22 April 1903, in her ninetieth year. Barrett Browning took devoted care of her, and seriously injured his health, and particularly his eyes, in doing so. Up to the last few months of her life, she had that extraordinary vitality and vivacity characteristic of her famous brother. Her nephew, with considerable pride and evident affection, showed me a photograph that he took of her. I saw an old face full of strength and intelligence.

It was on a beautiful day, the twelfth of April 1904, that I saw and talked with Barrett Browning. He had sent me a cordial invitation to visit him, and I took the tramway at Giotto's Campanile in Florence. After several miles of steep ascent, I reached the terminus, and entered the carriage that Mr. Browning had sent for me. A few more miles of stiff grade, and I came to La Torre all' Antella, his lovely and romantically situated home. Mr. Browning greeted me with unaffected and charming friendliness. He was a short man, like his father, rotund and red-faced, and the red veins traced patterns on his cheeks and brow. He spoke with what we Americans call the English accent, and when I said that he must feel like a native Italian, he quickly and vigorously replied, 'Oh, dear, no; I'm an Englishman.'

The expense of this home, and that of buying the place in Asolo, where, in accordance with his father's wishes, he had built 'Pippa's Tower,' supply reasons enough, I think, why he was later forced to sell the Palazzo Rezzonico in Venice. He had a strange collection of exotic birds, some of which he would hold in his hands, while they screamed with ear-splitting screeches, and kept their formidable beaks in what seemed dangerous proximity to his eyes. Over the tea-cups we talked of his father and mother, for I had frankly stated the object of my visit.

I lamented the fact that there was no adequate biography of Robert Browning; this was before Griffin and Minchin's scrupulous work had appeared. When I particularly condemned the *Life and Letters* by Mrs. Orr, he cried out, 'Oh, that is a very bad book!' 'None of the family liked it,' said he. After Browning's death, the question of an authorized biography was discussed by his sister and his son. Mr. Browning declined to write it, and as Mrs. Orr had known Browning intimately, and as her *Handbook* to his works was excellent—he glanced at me here, and I nodded emphatic approval—she was selected to perform the task.

She was supplied with all available material. She never showed her manuscript either to Mr. Browning or to his aunt Sarianna, but at last sent the proof. They were both bitterly disappointed and corrected the worst and most glaring mistakes, and made many suggestions. Mrs. Orr brusquely replied, 'I cannot change the proofs.'

Mr. Chesterton's book had recently appeared, and it was anything but pleasing to Mr. Browning. He said the work was filled with errors; the mistake that apparently perturbed him the most was the statement that Browning was in weak health and 'declining' in the last years. On the contrary, he insisted that Browning was tremendously vigorous up to the last; that no change had taken place in his appearance, manner, or habits. He had caught a bad cold walking on the Lido, but refused to take proper care of himself. Instead of staying in, he set out for long tramps with friends, constantly talking in the raw autumn air. While suffering with this heavy cold, he ran rapidly up flights of stairs, the son vainly trying to restrain him. The result was bronchitis with heart trouble, and he died at ten in the night of 12 December 1889. That very afternoon he had risen from bed and walked about the room. During the last few days he told many good stories and talked with the utmost vivacity. There was never any 'decline,' and the son seemed almost fiercely to resent Mr. Chesterton's statement.

Robert Browning inherited excellent health from his father, who died at the age of eighty-four, without ever having known a day's illness. Mr. Barrett Browning told me that until the last sickness he had never seen the poet in bed during the daytime. He had a truly wonderful digestion; it was his firm belief that one should eat only what one really enjoyed, desire being the infallible sign that the food was healthful. 'My father was a man of *bonne fourchette*; he was not very fond of meat, but liked all kinds of Italian dishes, especially with rich sauces. He always ate freely of rich and delicate things. He could make a whole meal off mayonnaise.' I reminded him that Emerson used to eat pie for breakfast. Both men were optimists.

Late in life he was very fond of swimming, though he did not learn early. The son taught him how to swim at Pornic, in Brittany, and he was venturesome for a man well on in years. He learned with great eagerness, and swam far out with boyish delight. The poet alludes to this in the prologue to *Fifine at the Fair*.

Browning's eyes were peculiar, one having a long focus, the other very short. He had the unusual accomplishment (try it and prove) of closing either eye without 'squinching,' and without any apparent effort, though sometimes in strong sunlight on the street his face would be a bit distorted. He did all his reading and writing with one eye, closing the long one as he sat down to his desk. He never wore glasses, and was proud of his 'microscopic' eye. He often wrote minutely, to show off his powers. When he left the house to go for a walk, he shut the short eye and opened the long one, with which he could see an immense distance. He never suffered with any pain in his eyes except once, as a young man, when, in imitation of Shelley, he was trying to be a vegetarian.

He was amazingly vivacious and impulsive, with a great flow of talk. He constantly acted on impulse, and was boyish and enthusiastic even in old age. If he liked anything, he spoke of it in the heartiest manner. He was very generous in his appreciation and praise of other men's work. He always tried to see what was good. Occasionally he was enraged at reading a particularly hostile criticism of himself, but generally stood abuse very well. He had not been soured by the long years of neglect and ridicule. A great admirer of Tennyson's poetry and of Tennyson's character—they were dear and intimate friends—he never liked the stock comparison. He had no jealousy, but he said,

'Tennyson and I are totally unlike.' The son admitted that perhaps the desire to be original and different from other writers sometimes led him into excesses and eccentricities in his poems.

What was said of Browning's impulsiveness is borne out by the general testimony of his friends, and particularly by a letter from Mrs. Browning to Mrs. Jameson. The manuscript of this letter was bought by an American in London and went down with the *Titanic*. An extract from it appeared in the bookseller's catalogue: 'You must learn Robert—he is made of moods—chequered like a chessboard; and the colour goes for too much—till you learn to treat it as a game. He was very tired that evening.'

In conversation he was perfectly normal. He loved to talk, but no one would ever have guessed that he was a poet. He was interested in multitudinous things, and never spoke of his poetry if he could avoid doing so.

In later years Browning hated to write! His work became so distasteful to him that he would rather do almost anything else. He rose early, before his son; they had coffee together; then the father was never visible till lunch. He did all his composition and letter-writing in the morning. After lunch, he would not touch a pen if he could help it, and seemed relieved to have the morning's work over. He gave the impression of liking many things in life much better than poetry or literature. 'Yes,' repeated Mr. Browning, after a moment's hesitation, 'he really hated to write.'

Contrary to the oft-repeated statement, Browning was not a really fine pianist. As a very young man, he used to play several instruments, and perhaps then he played the piano well. In Casa Guidi he taught his little son pianoplaying. 'Much to my regret,' said Mr. Browning. 'It took up a lot of time and did no good.' In later life Browning became ambitious to improve his own skill on this instrument, but it was of no use, for his fingers were clumsy and stiff. Still, when old, he rose at six, and practised finger-exercises for an hour!

He loved first-class music ardently, had a profound knowledge of it, and was a good judge. If the performance was fine, he was delighted, and would express his praise with the utmost enthusiasm; but bad work gave him intense pain. Sometimes at a concert he would put his fingers in his ears, his suffering apparently being uncontrollable.

Robert Browning often talked of *his* father, a wonderful man, with an extraordinary range of knowledge and culture, but without one particle of literary ambition. He wrote reams of poetry, which he destroyed. Browning said his father had amazing facility in verse composition—that he could compose much faster than he himself. Robert Browning's education was the elective system pushed to the extreme limit. His education depended absolutely and exclusively on his inclinations; he was allowed to study anything he wished. His father gave him perfect liberty, never sent him anywhere, and allowed him to do exactly as he chose. He provided competent instruction in whatever line the youth expressed any interest.

Mr. Barrett Browning told me that he remembered his mother, Elizabeth Barrett Browning, as clearly as though he had seen her yesterday. When she died in 1861, he was eleven years old. Her ill health, both before and after her marriage, had been greatly exaggerated. She *was* an invalid, but did not give the impression of being one. She was able to do many things, and had considerable endurance. One day in Florence she walked from her home out through the Porta Romana, clear up on the heights, and back to Casa Guidi. 'That was pretty good, wasn't it?' She was of course the idol of her household, everything revolving about her. She was intensely loved by all her friends. Her father was a 'very peculiar man,' who grew more stubborn with advancing years.

The origin of his own nickname, 'Pen,' had almost always been stated inaccurately. It came about in this way. When he was a child, he stuttered (he stuttered, indeed, in telling me about it), and in trying to pronounce 'Nini'— the name Italians give their children—he said, 'P-n-n-n-nini.' English visitors called it 'Pen-nini,' and this led to 'Pen.'

In later years, at London, he often saw Carlyle with his father. 'Carlyle was always exceedingly kind and thoughtful and sweet.' He took tactful interest in the pictures painted by the young man, and made a point of speaking often about them. The traditional surly side to Carlyle never appeared. Mrs. Carlyle was the 'terror' of that household. One day Robert Browning, while calling on the Carlyles, took up the tea-kettle while talking animatedly. Mrs. Carlyle cried shrilly, 'Put that down!' The poet obeyed, but unfortunately placed it on the carpet. After that she hated him.

With reference to his own publication of the love-letters that passed between Robert Browning and Elizabeth Barrett in 1845–6, Mr. Browning told me that he was in a difficult position, but had to make a decision, and did not dare postpone it. In 1887, when Browning moved from one house to another in London, he destroyed an enormous mass of correspondence. It is probable that the uproar occasioned by Froude's printing of the Carlyle letters was one reason why Browning was determined to leave as little material behind him as possible; but if he had not moved his household effects, it is certain that thousands of letters would have been preserved. Still, Browning did not like to have his personal letters read. He told his son to be sure to destroy every letter that he received from his father, and the son had faithfully done this. Now, the love-letters were the sole exception. He not only had not destroyed them, but had taken special pains to preserve them, had numbered every one in its chronological order, and had placed them in a receptacle specially prepared for the purpose. The son had to do one of two things; he must either destroy them, which seemed really impossible to do, since his father had preserved them with such loving care, or he must print them himself. To make no decision, simply to leave them alone, would be to run the risk of having someone in the future print them inaccurately, 'edit' them, or omit certain portions. Mr. Browning therefore took the responsibility. He would never have printed them had he not been able to print every word exactly as it was written. There was no alteration from the manuscript, not a word omitted. He had been loudly abused for having given them to the world, and he felt this hostile criticism keenly, but he believed the verdict would ultimately be in his favour. Perhaps it was already.

Mr. Browning told me that horses were his passion, and invited me to go with him to the races at Siena. How I wish I had been able to accept this kind invitation! I know nothing whatever about horses, but I should have been glad of the opportunity for further intimate talk. The time had come to say good-bye and Mr. Browning himself drove me three or four miles toward Florence. A smart pair of horses, hitched tandem, carried us along at high speed; they were spirited and skittish, but were beautifully handled by my host. I shall remember Mr. Browning not only because he was his father's son, but because he was an exceedingly kindly, courteous, hospitable Englishman. As Dr. Kenyon said, 'It is not only as the breaking of a link with the two great poets that his death will be regretted both in England and in Italy.'

Mr. Browning's charitable work for Asolo, a pious tribute to his father, should not be forgotten. When Browning visited Asolo for the last time, in the summer of 1889, the silk-mill where Pippa worked was still standing, containing the obsolete wooden machinery. Mr. Barrett Browning bought the building and tried to re-establish the silk industry. This proved to be impossible; he therefore changed the institution into a lace school, thus providing remunerative occupation for thirty Asolo girls of about Pippa's age. When I visited Asolo, the school was flourishing, and I obtained a specimen of the work. Mr. Browning also brought to life an old industry of the little town, the 'hand-loom weaving of linen.' He built 'Pippa's Tower,' and lived to see in Asolo the celebration of his father's centenary, when a new street was formally named for the poet, and all the inhabitants came out to honour the memory of Robert Browning and show their hearty affection for his kindly and generous son.

Friday night 8 April we were present at the début of Clara Clemens as a concert singer; she sang from *Semiramide* with glorious tones. In the audience was her father Mark Twain. I spoke to him and he said in mock solemnity, 'Yes, I am passing off the stage, and now my daughter is the famous member of the family.' I asked permission to call at his villa and he told me to come early on the following Thursday 14 April; so that we could talk together before his weekly reception of visitors, which began at four o'clock. His daughter Jean was with him. He was 68 years old, but looked older; his wife was desperately ill and indeed died in this villa Sunday 5 June. During this hour's interview, Mark smoked three cigars; there was a constant twitching in his right cheek and his right eye seemed inflamed. He was excited about the Russo-Japanese War, and was an intense partisan of the Japanese. I told him that Edith M. Thomas had published a poem calling on Americans to support the Russians because they were Christians and the Japanese heathens; and he replied, 'Edith doesn't know what she's talking about.' He pretended to believe the Russians had made a fatal error and shown lack of judgement in not sending a sufficient number of ikons with their soldiers. 'Why,' speaking with great emphasis, 'I read that they have sent out only eighty holy images with their troops! General Kuropatkin ought to have carried at least 800!'

The conversation changed to literature. I asked him which he thought the best of all his books. He said, 'What do *you* think?' and I replied '*Huckleberry Finn.*' He thought a moment, and then said, rather unwillingly, I thought, 'That is my best.' I felt as if he had yielded to popular opinion, and in his own mind he did not agree with it. Probably he thought *Joan of Arc* his masterpiece. Knowing how profound and complete was his pessimism, I ventured to say, 'Mr. Clemens, when you look back on your life and realize what you have made of yourself without any assistance and without any lucky accident, that entirely by your own genius you have risen from obscurity to a position where you are a desired and welcome guest in any royal court in the world and in any intellectual society, I should think you would feel some pleasure in it.' In his inimitable drawl, he replied very slowly, 'Well, I do look back upon my career with considerable satisfaction.'

In Munich on 27 July with about thirty Americans, we took the train to Wolfratshausen, and there we embarked on an enormous raft of logs, and came down to Munich on the Isar rolling rapidly, driven only by the current. No oars, no engine, no sails; one steersman. It was the very poetry of motion. We glided past lovely meadows, through villages, through deep woods; and sliding down the occasional waterfalls lent additional excitement.

About a month later at Bayreuth between the acts of *Tannhäuser* we saw Frau Cosima Wagner walking about and I had some interesting conversation with her son Siegfried Wagner, the conductor of the orchestra. He was most agreeable. The Wolfram was the American Whitehill.

Next day (*Parsifal*) we happened to sit at the restaurant next to Madame Nordica, who had come to see the interpretation of Kundry, as she was studying it. She did not want anyone to know she was there, but of course we recognized her and she was in high spirits. She was just 'one of the crowd' after the performance and would not allow me to get her a cab; I could not help thinking how different was her exit from this theatre, jostled by the throng, from what she was accustomed to. But she liked it! She said the man who sang Parsifal had dirty fingernails, which seemed to her unnecessary. At luncheon I asked her if she thought George Moore's novel *Evelyn Innes* contained valuable criticisms of Wagner and of music, to which she replied it was worthless—exactly the opposite of the opinion given me by Professor Horatio Parker.

Our stay at Weimar was interesting, as I have been a fanatical admirer of Goethe since I was eighteen. The Römisches Haus seemed full of memories and on the wall hung the Calendar for the year 1828! It was the last year of the life of Duke Karl August. In the garden at Jena I was deeply moved seeing the table where Goethe and Schiller talked, which bears the inscription, taken from the words spoken here by Goethe to Eckermann on 8 October 1827: 'Sie wissen wohl kaum, an welcher merkwürdigen Stelle wir uns eigentlich befinden. Hier hat Schiller gewohnt. In dieser Laube, auf diesen jetzt fast zusammengebrochenen Bänken haben wir oft an diesen alten Steintisch gesessen und manches gute und grosse Wort miteinander gewechselt. . . . Das geht alles hin und vorüber: ich bin auch nicht mehr der ich gewesen.'

At Berlin we saw the opening play of the season at the Deutsches Theater; it was Shakespeare's *Troilus and Cressida*, which I had never had an opportunity to see in English; it was extremely well done; the next evening we saw Ibsen's *Lady from the Sea* and on the next Oscar

Wilde's *Lady Windermere's Fan*. The Berlin audiences at all three of these plays seemed cold, after the enthusiasm of Munich.

On 17 September we sailed from Hamburg on the same steamer we had taken from New York about fifteen months before, the slow *Pretoria*. We stopped several hours at Boulogne, because one Frenchman had taken the boat to England thinking it was the ship's tender, and we had to wait until he returned. The most famous authority on whist in the world, Mr. Foster, was on board, and it was amusing to play with him, for he knew what cards I held better than I did myself. There was one diverting episode; I had been asked to make up a party of four but told them they had better get someone else, as I never played for money. At the moment they could not find a fourth man, so they agreed to play 'for fun,' although 'it would not be exciting.' On the first hand my partner (not Foster) accused one of his opponents (not Foster) of reneging. This enraged the other, and he said he would bet five hundred dollars he had not. The other man got out his pocket-book and they both began to count from huge rolls of bills. Foster finally succeeded in pacifying them; they put up their pocket-books, but my partner said 'You *did* renege.' The other shouted 'You are a —— —— liar!' and they began to fight; we had considerable difficulty in separating them; and we did not play any more. And this was a game 'for fun' that was not to be exciting. It nearly ended in bloodshed.

45

EVENTS IN THE THEATRE

On 2 January 1905 I wrote in my journal, 'I am 40 years old today. Hard to realize it—that I shall never see the thirties again. I have no regrets, however, am wholly content with life, and don't mind being 40.' Being content with life is quite different from being self-satisfied. It is perhaps more common for persons to be dissatisfied with everything except themselves, than it is for them to be content with life.

On 2 May of that year Richard Mansfield produced *The Merchant of Venice* in New Haven. The house was sold out and we waited expectantly for some twenty minutes, wondering why the curtain did not rise. Finally the local manager appeared and read a statement dictated by Mr. Mansfield that ran something like this: 'Owing to my incredible and unpardonable stupidity and negligence, the lights have not been properly arranged for the performance. Mr. Mansfield has finally consented to play, under protest, but he wishes the audience to understand that the bad lighting is my fault and not his.' The audience would have noticed nothing amiss if this statement had not been read. Between the acts I found out that Mr. Mansfield had insisted that no performance be given and that the money be refunded to the spectators. His own acting was of course very fine; I think his death some years later the greatest loss the American stage ever suffered. After the performance that evening, a few of us met him at dinner at the Graduates' Club and talked until three in the morning. I asked him if it were true that he had refused to play. 'Of course it is true, and I ought not to have played.' 'But, Mr. Mansfield, people had come from all over the state to see you; they would have been bitterly disappointed if there had been no performance.' 'I can't help that,' he said, 'no true artist should appear unless the conditions are right.' He spoke bitterly about Joseph Jefferson, saying Jefferson had refused to help him at a critical moment in his career. Mansfield was difficult to get along with, but he was a great actor. When he played Shaw for the first time in America, the Irishman wrote him how a certain passage should be spoken to bring out the love interest, and Mansfield cabled him, 'Love interest be damned.' And Shaw cabled, 'The same to you.' Mr. Shaw told me in 1935, that when Mansfield was playing *The Devil's Disciple* in New York, a lady said to the playwright in London, 'Mansfield ought to get down on his knees and thank God for such a play,' to which Mr. Shaw replied, 'Yes, but he wishes to God someone else had written it.'

I saw Mansfield in many plays; his *Richard III* was magnificent. On this evening in New Haven, although he was amiable and charming, he expressed peculiar views. I had always wondered why he did not play Hamlet; he said Hamlet was an ass, and that morally Shylock was the best character in *The Merchant of Venice*.

The centenary of Schiller's death was celebrated at Yale on 9 May. The German department asked me to make the address, for which I made careful preparation.

At a dinner at Professor Sanford's 19 June we had the pleasure of meeting Sir Edward Elgar and his lady. He had been overcome by the heat (American weather) but was gracious and affable.

On 27 October in New Haven came the first public performance in the world of Shaw's *Mrs. Warren's Profession*, with Arnold Daly, who made a speech. I wrote a favourable review for the local newspaper. But the next day, by order of the Mayor, the afternoon and evening performances were prohibited. This made a sensation, because the first presentation of the play in New York was to occur only two days later. After one night in the metropolis it was suppressed although some of us protested in print. It was soon produced in Russia and the audiences called it conventional and old-fashioned and Philistine!

On 15 March 1905 Herr Conried brought from the Irving Place Theatre in New York, his German company to Yale in *Kabale und Liebe*. At the banquet following, I read the following original poem. A few days later I received a poem from my colleague Professor Albert S. Cook, one from Professor Hanns Oertel, then Professor at Yale, now Professor Emeritus of Sanscrit at the University of Munich, and one from my colleague, Professor Henry W. Farnam.

KABALE UND LIEBE

New Haven, d.15. März 1905

I

Wir grüssen Sie, vortreffliche Schauspieler!
Sir waren heute Abend kolossal!
Den Geist des grossen Dichters, Friedrich Schiller
Sie haben mitgebracht in diesen Saal!

II

Die besten Künstler schmückten unsere Bühne,
Der Präsident, sein Ferdinand, der Wurm:
Und Lady Milford, mit der edlen Miene,
War wie ein Stern in einem wilden Sturm.

III

Wir sahen auch den rohen Geiger Miller
Mit seiner geizigen und dummen Frau:
Und alle beide sahen aus wie Schiller
Hat sie zuerst geschöpft, und ganz genau!

IV

Der Hofmarschall, mit seiner fremden Sprache
Hat uns gefallen, und wir lachten viel:
Obgleich wir weinen über Walters Rache,
Ein bischen Lachen hilft dem Trauerspiel.

V

Wir müssen auch die Sophie nicht vergessen,
Als Kammerjungfer war sie riesig gut:
Und auch, in diesem knappen Abendessen,
Ich möchte denken an Luises Mut.

VI

Zum ersten Male tritt sie auf die Bühne!
Ohne Verlegenheit die Rolle spielt:
Sie spielte nicht wie eine stumm' Maschine,
Sondern wie Menschenskind, das Liebe fühlt.

VII

Von ganzem Herzen danken wir Herrn Conried,
Dem guten Freund und auch dem grossen Mann:
Wie Wagner sonst, in seinem Hause Wahnfried,
Fangen wir hier die Lebensfreude an.

VIII

Wir müssen plaudern, lachen, singen, trinken,
Allezusammen sind wir fröhlich hier:
Und wie die Steine in dem Meere sinken,
So sinkt Frau Sorge in dem dunklen Bier.

KABALISTISCHE LIEBE

Wie wird man nach und nach zu einem Dichter?
Durch deutsche Biederkeit und deutsches Bier;
Aus ihnen sprudeln Geniefunken-Lichter!
Glaubt man es nicht, er 'mal, wie Phelps, probier'!

A.S.C.

New Haven, d.20. März. 1905.

Hurrah! Der Phelps besteigt das Ross
Dressed up wie ein ' Kuhjunge,'
Er schwingt sich auf den Pegasos
Schont weder Haut noch Lunge.

Es bocket das alte Musenpferd
Es kickt und schlägt gar munter;
Dochendlich wird es ja belehrt:
''s kriegt Wilhelm doch nicht "runter."''

Erstaunet stehn der Goethe da,
Der Lessing, Schiller, Heine:
' Nee, so wat war ja noch nich da!'
' Die Kraft in die zwee Beine!'

Der Dichter-Schar (glaub mir, o Freund,)
Von Neid erfüllt ist gelb se,
Der Phelps sitzt oben auf dem Pferd,
Das Pferd'st nicht auf dem Phelpse.

H.O.

Wilhelm dem Löwen, dem tüchtigen Dichter, ihm danken wir schön,
Schmeichelnde Reime, geschickt und gesellig, geschunden zu haben.
Kälber und Würmererringen das Lob des Königs der Tiere;
König der Dichter! Was du uns gebrüllet, Dir flüstern wir's nach.

Dem hoch geehrten Verskünstler

Wilhelm von Löwen-Fels, resp. Löwen Pelz (nicht zu verwechseln mit
dem Schafe mitten im Süden. im Löwenpelz).

H.W.F.

On 2 February 1906 Sarah Bernhardt came to New
Haven. The undergraduate President of the Yale Dramatic
Association was Chauncey McCormick of Chicago, now
the famous art critic, largely responsible for the magnificent art exhibition at the Century of Progress Exhibition
in Chicago in 1934. A group of students went with me to her
private car at the railway station, to pay our compliments

and invite her to take tea that afternoon at the University. McCormick entered and she said 'Your mother brought you up very well, you speak French so beautifully.' She was in ebullient spirits but the day was so bitterly cold, 12 above zero, with an icy wind, that she gave him a little manuscript note on her writing-paper with the engraved legend *Quand Même*, saying she could not go out. As it had been stated in the college paper that she would appear on the campus, one of the undergraduates dressed in woman's clothes, with an enormous hat and veil, and was driven about the college grounds, throngs of students reverently standing uncovered and cheering with tremendous enthusiasm. That night she appeared in *La Dame aux Camélias*. After the play, we went back stage and I introduced a score of students and professors to her, calling her 'la plus grande actrice de deux siècles,' which seemed to please her. When I presented to her Professor McKenzie (now at Princeton) she held his hand and said 'McKenzie! comme le nom est drôle!' I asked her if she would like to hear the college football 'yell.' She stood and beat time while we gave the 'long cheer.' The marvellous woman left on the train at three o'clock in the morning for Providence.

On 22 June 1906 we sailed for Europe, spending the summer in France, Germany, Switzerland, and England. At Lincoln cathedral we saw in the close Watts's colossal statue of Tennyson, only recently placed there. It represents him looking at the Flower he had just taken from the crannied wall, 'root and all.' A party of young American girls came up and asked me who it was. 'Tennyson.' 'Why is he here?' 'Because he was born in Lincolnshire.' 'Why is he looking at his watch?'

Of all the English cathedrals, Lincoln is my favourite; yet I shall not forget rowing in a little boat on the Wear, and looking up at the majestic fortress-cathedral of Durham. On 12 September we had a beautiful journey on the river Wye; an Englishman having told me it was the loveliest scenery in England. At Ross we entered a rowboat, and two sturdy English oarsmen, who had fought in the Boer War, and who said the war was a mistake, rowed us down the river all day. We passed Goodrich Castle, where Wordsworth saw the little child that inspired 'We Are Seven,' the royal Forest of Dean (*Geraint and Enid*), the Seven Sisters, Monmouth (*King Henry V*), and stayed overnight at Tintern, visiting the Abbey, after looking at it in the light of early dawn from the windows of our room. We sailed from Plymouth 17 September on the *Pennsylvania*, the same day, the same ship, the same port, of precisely six years before. And in the dining-room we found we had been assigned seats next to Professor Jacobi and family, another exact repetition!

In New Haven on 5 November arrived the English dramatist Henry Arthur Jones, who gave a lecture at Yale on the drama. Our friendship began then and remained unbroken and unclouded till his death.

This autumn Mrs. LeMoyne produced on the New York stage *Pippa Passes*, omitting only the scene between Luigi and his mother. Contrary to my expectation the Ottima-Sebald scene fell flat and the last scene with the corrupt ecclesiastic was overwhelmingly impressive. Miss Taliaferro made a charming Pippa.

I never saw Edward Dowden but we had an epistolary friendship and I felt as if I had seen him because Mahaffy, Æ., and others gave me many anecdotes of him.

HIGHFIELD HOUSE
HIGHFIELD ROAD, RATHGAR,
DUBLIN
July 9, 1906

MY DEAR SIR:

I am very grateful to you for giving me one of the 50 copies of your Introduction to Jane Austen's novels. It comes to a true lover and constant reader of the novels. And I find it agrees so closely with my own judgment that I cannot but think it as just as it is certainly interesting. Perhaps however as I read three or four of the novels, I think each, while reading it, the best.

Our late Provost of Trinity College, Dublin (eminent as a Mathematician and as a Biblical critic) was a devoted Austenite, and I think somewhere in Temple Bar lurks an article on some points in the Novels by him (George Salmon).

My own introduction to her was delightful. When we were very young and very ignorant my brother (now Bishop of Edinburgh) and I were walking in Co. Wicklow and by stress of weather were compelled to spend one long wet day in a little wayside Inn. But it was the shortest of days—for a copy, wanting the title and opening leaves, of Mansfield Park made the hours speed by. We had never heard of Mansfield Park in those old antediluvian days, and when we returned to Dublin we were eager to discover who this wonderful magician was. It was not long before we knew our Jane Austen better than most readers of nearly half a century ago. And how a torn copy of Mansfield Park ever came to a little Wicklow country Inn, I cannot imagine, unless some kind Angel, humourously dropped it in his flight, for our delectation. How much you must have enjoyed your pleasant task! I am glad you pull up the Dict. Nat. Biog. for its errors. It is, I fear, swarming with errors still unnoted.

With cordial thanks, I am

Sincerely yours

EDWARD DOWDEN

Every year—when I lecture my class—I am your debtor, and confess the fact.

One of the happiest occasions of this 1906 summer in Europe was our accidental meeting with our intimate friends Mr. and Mrs. George Nettleton of Yale. We went to St. Moritz and Ragaz together and played in the tennis tournaments. George won the open singles championship of the Engadine.

46

WILLIAM DE MORGAN

My wife and I had the pleasure of meeting Mr. and Mrs. William De Morgan a number of times in their home in Chelsea, London, and in their apartments in Florence, whither they went for many years in the winter. Mr. De Morgan had been a potter until he began to write novels at the age of sixty-five; his wife was a distinguished painter. He was tall, very thin, with a thin voice and a thin beard. It was a delight to talk with him as he was always in high good humour and had had interesting experiences. He began to write by accident when he was recovering from an attack of the flu; and I believe it was his wife who persuaded him to continue and finish the manuscript of *Joseph Vance*. He gave an impression of benevolence and kindness. He was deeply religious in his own way. He told me the only parts of the Apostles' Creed that he thoroughly believed were the first seven words and the last four words, but there was no man in the world, I think, who believed them with more sincerity or with more confidence. He not only believed in personal immortality or 'immortalism' as he called it, but also in a way that was partly quizzical, partly humorous, but yet somehow wholly sincere, he believed in ghosts. That is, he believed that spirits of the departed occasionally revisited the glimpses of the moon. His long story, one of the last he wrote, *When Ghost Meets Ghost*, represented an inner conviction.

Joseph Vance was published in 1906; the author was a man of sixty-five, with no popular reputation. His novel contained two hundred and eighty thousand words. He wrote it in longhand, and the MS. looked like a bale of cotton. It was of course refused by publishers. Then Mr. Lawrence, who said it was too long, but that he wished it were longer, took it to William Heinemann, and said: 'You have got to read it.' Mr. Heinemann replied: 'I'll be damned if I do!' But he did and published it, and it had an enormous sale. In spite of the fact that it is not now being read by many, I believe it will never die.

I announced as subject for the John Hubbard Curtis prize, open to Yale undergraduates, *The Novels of De Morgan*. The prize was won by H. D. Hammond of Tennessee. The successful essay was published in the *Yale Courant*, and a copy sent to the novelist.

Mr. De Morgan wrote to the young critic, 13 August 1909,

> I have scarcely an exception to take—What I have is to be found among some jotted comments on the margins of the Courant that I return to you—I daresay you will see that your irreverence (shall I call it?) for Dickens has occasioned some implication of cavil from me—But all you young men are tarred with the same feather nowadays—
>
> Your remark about the red cap in David Copperfield made me reread the chapter. I am obliged to confess that the red cap is absurd—a mere stage expedient! He would have seen the hair, like enough. But oh dear!—What a puny scribbler that rereading made me feel!

> CHELSEA
> September 5, 1909
>
> DEAR PROF. PHELPS,
> How I agree with you about this spelling craze! How could I else, holding as I do that to ask the way to Charing Cross is to make an *en*quiry, but that one makes an *in*quiry into the Nature of Things? My broad impression is that *en*quiries get answers, and *in*quiries don't. Please put this down to flu, if you see no meaning in it.
>
> But surely the Marshalsea in Dorrit is fine?—Oh yes—and the death of Merdle?

I shall expect your essay with true interest—egotistic of course, but that cannot be helped.

Always yours truly,

WM. DE MORGAN

JULY 15 1912
127, CHURCH STREET,
CHELSEA, S.W.

DEAR PROF. PHELPS

It was a pleasure to get your Italian article in the "Alumni"—What a capital idea the Browning pilgrimage was!

It makes me wish I had read "The Ring and the Book." A shocking thing for a writer to say! But its all past praying for now, for me. I refer to the study of the literae humaniores. I scarcely looked in a book, unless it was about pots or mechanisms, for forty long years. There's a confession!—a little exaggerated in form from chagrin at the truth of its spirit, but substantially true for all that.

So I am really a stranger to my Browning, not having read what so many think his greatest achievement. (That's so, isn't it?) My ignorance of this poem must be forgotten, please, in consideration of my admiration of his shorter poems, within my grasp, and especially of the fact that my enjoyment of "John Jones" has rather than otherwise enhanced that admiration. Even so a friend once told me he had never really enjoyed the "Appassionata" sonata until a man wrote, and played, a caricature of it. But how that caricaturist must have known his Beethoven! What a knowledge of Browning must Swinburne's have been!

The twenty-six letters of the alphabet are very powerful. If it were not for them the chief recollection of Britannia by the States would be the discomfiture of the former's butler by Uncle Sam a century and more ago. But the mere re-arrangement of those 26 makes Browning and Shakespeare possible—even if the latter was really somebody else.

Will the rearrangements to come last forever? They will last *us* out, anyhow—and even if only

I◇◇◇◇◇◇◇◇◇◇◇◇◇◇◇◇◇◇◇◇◇◇◇◇◇◇◇◇◇◇◇◇◇◇◇◇◇   ◇◇◇◇◇◇◇◇◇◇◇◇◇◇◇◇◇◇◇◇◇◇◇◇◇◇◇
(10)

books are possible, with original matter in them, we may expect Literature to last your undergraduates out, even at the present rate of publication. Of course the number of books is large—and there may be a sort of shoddy infinity about it if we call two books different because a word is spelled differently. But an infinity got at this way won't wash.

We called on your friend Ellsworth and he was having a music party—so we did not attempt to get in—have not experienced any result.

I'm afraid you are even warmer than we are. What with the heat, and what with Lloyd George, living is uphill work in these parts.

Our kindest regards to yourself and Mrs. Phelps.

Yours always truly,

Wm. De Morgan

Oct. 26 1914
127, Church Street,
Chelsea, s.w.

My Dear Prof. Phelps

I am sorry to say that I am barbarous by nature and catch myself gloating over slaughter—slaughter of Germans of course!—half of them men I should have liked—a tenth of them men I should have loved. It is sickening—but . . .

A friend has just left me who maintains that the Germans never do anything that is not in strict accordance with International Law. Then a devil may break loose, and yet comply with international law!

Good forecasts—good for us—are in the air tonight! I hope—but I have done some hoping to no purpose latterly. However the last rumour I heard professed to come direct from Sir John French.

We have left Florence altogether, so you will find our nest tenanted by other birds if you go there. I feel as if the World were ending up, to the sound of melinite! And yet, as Browning wrote "God never says one word."

Our very best regards to yourselves.

Yours ever

Wm. De Morgan

DEC. 20 1915
127, CHURCH STREET,
CHELSEA, S.W.

DEAR PROF. PHELPS:

I put aside my long novel, because, with Kultur in full swing, I felt I should spoil it. I took up an old beginning—sketched in immediately after Joe Vance—and have got about halfway through, with great difficulty. The train of the poison gas is over us all here, and I can only get poor comfort from thinking what a many submarines we have made permanently so. All the same, one of my favourite employments is thinking how to add to their number—a grisly committee—coffins full of men very like our own. For all seamen are noble, because they live face to face with Death.

Always yours

WM. DE MORGAN

He died 15 January 1917.

47

QUEER SOUNDS AND SIGHTS

On the night of 25 February 1906, with the exception of the maids on the top floor, I was alone in the house. I had not been well for many days, and felt particularly miserable when I went to bed. I had lain uneasily for some hours, and had finally lapsed into semi-consciousness. At half-past two I was startled by the loud ringing of the front doorbell. Accoutred as I was, I descended, and opened the door. There was no-one. For a few moments, like the man in Poe's poem, I stood, deep into the darkness peering. But the darkness gave no token, and wonderingly I shut the door. I had not got half-way up the stairs, when once again the doorbell rang with violence. It is easy enough to tell this lightly now, but then, alone in the house, and ill, it was worse than mysterious. I ran to the door, and flung it wide open. Not a soul in sight, the street silent and deserted. Then I thought it might after all not have been the doorbell, but the telephone. Accordingly I rang up Central, only to be informed that no-one had called my number. While I was considering this, the doorbell once more reverberated through the empty house. Again I opened the door. No-one.

I decided that someone with a deficient or perverted sense of humour was making me a victim. Accordingly I shut the front door, and crouched directly behind it, with the intention of leaping out and seizing the humorist as soon as he rang again. In a few moments the bell rang loudly; I jerked back the door and sprang outside. But

473

there was no-one, and no sound of retreating steps.

I stood outside the door, lost in amazement and fear, for I was terrified. I gazed wonderingly at the button, half-expecting to see some spirit-finger push it; when, to my utter dismay, the bell rang shriller and louder than ever.

If I had really believed in ghosts, that would have been sufficient evidence. As it is, I shall never forget my distress while the bell continued ringing and I was looking directly at the only means of making it ring. I closed the door, and had a bad night.

In the morning I consulted a specialist, not on nerves, but on doorbells. The explanation was simple. A mouse was enjoying the flavour of the paraffin in which the wires in the cellar were wrapped, and every time he gave a particularly fervent bite, the bell rang. I hope it scared him as much as it did me, but if so, his hunger triumphed over his fear, for he kept returning to the feast.

On another occasion I was out shooting in a desolate place in Michigan accompanied by my friend, A. K. Merritt, who will vouch for the truth of the story. Dusk was falling; there was no wind. We had wandered into a scene of stagnant desolation. Dead trees had fallen in rotten ruin across the trail, and the swampy pools were covered with a green mantle of decay. Merritt was walking in front and I close behind him. The gloom and depression of the scene in the deepening dusk had affected our spirits, so that we had not spoken for some time. Suddenly I thought of the scenery of Browning's poem, 'Childe Roland.' The lines of that masterpiece of horror would well describe this place, I thought; and I began to repeat them in my mind without saying a word aloud. Methought only one thing was needed to make the picture complete. That was the horrible horse, which in the poem stood alone and sinister in the gathering night. If that horse were here, I said to myself, this would indeed be the veritable country of Childe Roland. Something impelled me to look behind, and to my ineffable surprise and horror, I was looking directly into the tragic eyes of a forlorn old horse, at a distance of six inches. I let out a yell of uncontrollable terror.

Merritt was as startled by the yell as I had been by its cause. I asked him if the horse was really there. It was bad to have him there, but worse if he were not. Merritt reassured me on that point.

I suppose the poor old horse had been pensioned off by some farmer, and had silently followed us on the spongy ground, either because he was lonesome or because he wanted salt. But he gave me the shock of my life.

I have thought much about it since, and I am unable to determine whether the appearance of the horse at the precise moment when I was thinking of him was the coincidence—or was I all the time *subconsciously aware of his presence*? That is to say, did the nearness of the horse, even though I had no conscious knowledge of it, suggest to my subconscious mind the lines from the poem? I wish I knew.

> As for the grass, it grew as scant as hair
>   In leprosy: thin dry blades pricked the mud
>   Which underneath looked kneaded up with blood.
> One stiff blind horse, his every bone a-stare,
> Stood stupefied, however he came there:
>   Thrust out past service from the devil's stud!
>
> Alive? he might be dead for aught I know,
>   With that red gaunt and colloped neck a-strain,
>   And shut eyes underneath the rusty mane;
> Seldom went such grotesqueness with such woe;
> I never saw a brute I hated so;
>   He must be wicked to deserve such pain.

On 6 March 1906 I gave an address at the University in commemoration of the one hundredth anniversary of the birth of Mrs. Browning: the newspaper report said Browning had to live in Italy on 'account of his wife's frailty.' One reason for the erroneous dates of her birth so frequently printed was that Browning himself would not tell. One day a man met him and had the impertinence to enquire 'How old is your wife?' and Browning replied, 'I don't know, Sir; I never asked.'

While we were playing golf at Farmington 18 April, a man came running to us on the links, saying San Francisco was being destroyed by an earthquake and fire, the worst disaster that had ever happened to an American city. And unlike most sensational news, the reports the next few days showed that the situation was becoming worse and worse.

On 6 June we celebrated at the University the 300th anniversary of the birth of Corneille. The French Ambassador, J. J. Jusserand attended, and made an address, after which our students acted *Le Cid* in French. The leading actor, Francis Markoe, was an accomplished French scholar, but something went wrong with his costume. M. Jusserand did his best to control himself, but finally went into convulsions of mirth, in which the audience cordially joined. I do not believe Jusserand ever laughed more uproariously in his life.

48

VARIOUS NOTES

IN January 1907 I wrote an article for the *North American Review* on Mark Twain, in which I called him the greatest living American writer, which at that time seemed to many mere hyperbole.

On 12 February the Russian actress Alla Nazimova, who had just begun to act in English ('I have burnt my battles behind me') lunched at my house and gave an address to my students in Contemporary Drama. She said she enjoyed playing Ibsen more than Shakespeare because Shakespeare was statuesque (here she drew a statue in the air) and Ibsen was complex (she rolled her arms up dramatically). She declared that Norah would never return to her husband and as for her children, Norah would think more of her own life than of them. She was in the highest spirits and charmed the undergraduates. Shortly after this, she appeared in the theatre and after the play I took some of the students and one Princeton undergraduate to her dressing-room; and after the interview, the Princeton boy (bless his heart!) asked me, 'Is she married?' and when I told him I did not know, he said, 'Oh, Mr. Phelps, I do hope she isn't married.'

On 23 February I lectured at Hartford on Keats, and discovered after the lecture that a grand-daughter of George Keats was in the audience, accompanied by her two daughters. They were not enthusiastic over my emphasis on Keats's humble origin, which I had spoken of merely to accentuate the mystery of genius.

On 18 March I was Toastmaster at the Yale Phi Beta Kappa dinner; I lectured in Stamford that afternoon and my train returning was very late. Professor Barrett Wendell was to speak at the dinner and was staying at our house. After he dressed and came downstairs he found smoke and many firemen in the library. He called to my wife, 'I think the house is on fire, but I must go to the dinner.' Then my wife came down, and seeing the firemen she told them she was already late to a dinner and went out the front door. After that, I came tearing into the house and was surprised to find it full of firemen. 'Well, put it out as soon as you can, please; I can't wait a minute,' and I departed. They extinguished the flames, but they must have been amused at the casual manner in which all three of us took it. The chief guest at this dinner was William Howard Taft. I nominated him for President of the United States and then Professor Tracy Peck nominated him for the same office in Latin! This latter speech attracted much attention in the newspapers. The next year our guest of honour was Woodrow Wilson, the President of Princeton; who followed Taft as President of the U.S.A. After that, I gave up the Warwickian job of making Presidents by inviting them to the Phi Beta Kappa dinners, for fear I might eventually make a blunder.

At the Taft dinner Wendell whispered to me to notice how healthy the President of Yale looked and all the executive officers; whereas the Professors looked unhealthy and overworked. 'This is invariably true,' he said.

At the dinner where Wilson was present I told him a story of how two men were walking to Bridgeport and after they had gone ten miles they asked a stranger how far it was to Bridgeport and he said, 'Eight miles.' After another hour's walking they asked another, and he said, 'Eight miles.' They got the same response an hour later and then one of them said to the other, 'Well, cheer up!

It's not getting away from us; we're holding our own!' I had forgotten this, but in 1912, when the Democratic convention at Baltimore was balloting and a reporter asked Wilson what he thought his chances were, he replied, 'Well, two men were once walking to Bridgeport,' etc., and added, 'I'm holding my own.'

This Spring the undergraduates at Yale gave for the first time in the world in English, Ibsen's *Pretenders*; and William Archer the translator for the first time heard his own words spoken on the stage. And this was the beginning of my friendship with him, which gave me unalloyed pleasure for so many years. We had intimate conversations in America and in London; and once, staying at my house with his son who afterwards became a barrister in London, we took long walks. Alas, when Archer and I went together to see that disastrous first night of *Macbeth* (Lionel Barrymore) in New York, I asked 'How is your son getting along?' not knowing he had been killed in the war. 'I lost my boy.'

William Archer, professional drama critic for many years who always insisted he could not write a play, *dreamed* the plot of *The Green Goddess*. He invited Shaw to collaborate, and Shaw replied, 'When I want to write for the movies, I'll let you know.' This refusal was fortunate for Archer; he wrote the play; it made more money than he had earned during his life as critic. I went with him to its first night in New York and he was delighted with George Arliss and the enthusiasm of the audience.

In 1907, on a summer afternoon in Michigan, Emily Whitney, my wife, and I composed this vegetarian sonnet-parody; my friend Professor Irving Fisher had been writing articles about diet.

> The Meat is too much with us; late and soon,
> Guzzling and bolting, we lay waste our powers:
> Little we have in nature that is ours;

We have given our taste away, a sordid boon!
The wheat that bares her bosom to the moon:
The meals that should be eaten at fixed hours
Composed of varied vegetables and flours,
For these our stomachs now are out of tune,
They move us not. Fletcher! I'd rather be
A Pagan, suckled in some creed outworn:
So might I, standing on Lake Huron's lea,
Have a digestion somewhat less forlorn:
Have sight of PROTEID rising from the sea,
Or hear old Fisher blow his dinner horn.

At that time Mr. Fletcher had caused a sensation by re-commending very sparse diet, with an enormous amount of mastication; this was Horace Fletcher (1849–1919), from whom came the words fletcherism, fletcherite, fletcher-izing (now in American dictionaries).

I sent this sonnet also to my friend and former Yale pupil, Clarence Day. At that very moment he happened to be dieting himself in the sanatorium at Battle Creek, and sent me his original drawing. (See p.481.)

On 30 September with Baker of Harvard we dined in New York with Henry Arthur Jones and went with him to the opening night of his new play *The Evangelist*. This was a painful experience. Mr. Jones kept his eyes on the audience and never once looked at the stage. He reminded me of a man on trial for his life, gazing steadfastly at the jury for signs of mercy. I liked the play but it was clear that it was not a success. Walter Prichard Eaton, now a professor at Yale, was then drama critic on the *Sun*; he wrote a very fine review.

On a Whittier pilgrimage in November I met at the house of her parents, Mr. and Mrs. Charles Ingham, their little daughter Katharine, seven years old; one of the most bewitching children I ever saw. She is a well-known Ameri-can novelist today—Katharine Brush.

At Whittier's house in Amesbury I saw many curiosities;

B. DAY, JR. SECRETARY
5 WALL STREET, N. Y.

Battle Creek
XI. 9. '907

You irreverent brute!

the old bachelor poet evidently had had trouble keeping buttons on his shirt; therefore he had them all made without buttons; and every morning he pinned stiffly starched collars to the neckband; how he did this without blasphemy can be explained only by invincible piety. He never liked to see a high forehead on a woman; hence whenever the admiring ladies called on him, as they did nearly every day, he pulled their hair down nearly to their eyes. In his photograph album, containing scores of pictures given him by these fair admirers, whenever a high forehead was exposed, he had taken his pen and inked the hair down.

Henry Arthur Jones (1851–1929) celebrated a long run of *The Hypocrites* (1906–7) by giving a magnificent dinner on the evening of 28 June 1907 at the Claremont Restaurant in New York. The guests around the circular table were John Philip Sousa, Daniel Frohman, A.L.Erlanger, Samuel Harris, Henry Harris, Paul Armstrong, Charles Klein, Frederic Thompson, John Mead Howells, John Corbin, and a few others. Everyone was compelled to make at least one speech, and along toward dawn many were making speeches in unison. Paul Armstrong excitedly condemned the whole company for not praising the ' Master playwright of us all, William Gillette.' Mr. Howells made a beautiful, modest, and graceful tribute to his father, the novelist. This, and Dan Frohman's reminiscences were the only dignified speeches heard that night. Abraham Erlanger amazed us very late in the night by giving an accurate summary of every speech that had been made early in the evening by every individual present, accompanying this astounding feat of memory with an estimate of the personality and character of all speakers (only half of whom he had ever seen before) that would have been the envy of a professional psychoanalyst. Just as dawn was breaking John Philip Sousa conducted an oratorio—words and music extempore—in which we all took part. It was the only time I ever sang under his direction.

On New Year's Day 1908 we had a memorable experience in Detroit. Mr. Charles Lang Freer, the famous collector of Whistler's paintings and etchings, was kind enough to show us over his house, which had been built as a box for its treasures. There we saw the Peacock Room and many other works of art, an astonishing collection of Japanese screens, and his latest acquisition, the recently-discovered manuscript of the Gospels—which he valued for its uniqueness, but which gave him a text for one of his frequent onslaughts on religion. This was the only matter, however, which seemed to arouse his antagonism; he was most gracious, though it must have been a bore to him to exhibit his works of art over and over again to strangers. Mr. Freer had been an industrial and railway capitalist, who retired in 1900 in order to devote the rest of his life to collecting works of ancient and modern art, which on his death in 1919 he left to the Smithsonian Institution in Washington.

The story is told that when Mark Twain was introduced to Whistler, Mark went up to a painting not yet dry, and pretended to put his gloved finger on some object in the picture. Whistler cried out in horror; and Mark said, 'Don't worry; these gloves are old.'

On the evening of 3 January, at a dinner of the Society of Colonial Wars, in St. Paul, Minn., I gave a lecture on 'Jonathan Edwards and Benjamin Franklin,' and while I was reading Edwards's famous description of hell, the coloured waiters were in a state of absolute terror.

In the early evening of 17 January Professor Sanderson telephoned that he had found our Irish setter 'Lad,' lying unconscious on the pavement, evidently hit by an automobile. But when we arrived at the place, Sanderson was in bewilderment—the dog had disappeared while he was telephoning. In a state of semi-consciousness, Lad had walked a mile to a friend's house where my wife was having dinner. We got him home and expected he would die that night. The whole top of his head was so crushed that it felt like a bag of peanuts; there was a hole in the forehead bigger than a silver dollar; one eye was completely closed; and he lay in a state of coma. We did not expect to find him alive in the morning; but he was still breathing, though unconscious. We sent for the veterinary, who said a big operation was necessary; and while we were considering this, one of the greatest surgeons in Connecticut, Dr. Francis Bacon, who had retired from practice, and refused even the most importunate demands, came into the house. He had heard our dog had been injured and wished to see him. With his fingers he pulled three or four splinters of bone out of the hole in the head, and then said, 'Do absolutely nothing; don't touch the dog; leave him alone. Dogs sometimes get well of serious accidents if they are left alone.' The 'vet' remonstrated; said an operation was necessary or the dog would die. 'He may die anyway,' said Dr. Bacon; 'but his only chance is to be let alone.' Then Dr. Foster, our family physician, came in, and then Dr. Ring, the oculist, both of whom had heard of the accident. These regular physicians held a consultation (I had not sent for any of them) and agreed that the dog had a chance and that he might possibly recover the sight of the left eye; the right one was good. The next day, while we were at lunch, the dog came down stairs, although seemingly unconscious; and in a few weeks, he entirely recovered. The case attracted wide attention; the New York papers and the Paris *New York Herald* had long articles about it; and the oculist finally pronounced the left eye completely normal again, saying the recovery appeared miraculous. The big hole in the dog's head turfed over in a month or so, but until it did, he flatted his barks. He lived nine years after that and there was no mark or scar or unevenness of contour. It was an amazing demonstration of the recuperative forces of nature. A Japanese student at Yale, Mr. Okamoto, sent me a picture he had drawn of the dog in bed, with his head bandaged, dreaming of a man clad in a fur overcoat driving an automobile (just over him in the picture) and under it the Japanese artist had written, '*He calls me beast,*' *says Lad.*

On 27 March Madame Komisarzhevsky, a great Russian actress, took tea in one of the undergraduate rooms and in the evening gave the best interpretation of Norah in *A Doll's House* that I ever heard. Not long after this, having agreed to appear in some town in Russia, she insisted on keeping her engagement, although warned that smallpox was rampant; she played as advertised, caught the disease and died. She was not only a great actress; she gave the impression of being a Great Lady, a born aristocrat.

This year I gave a series of lectures on literature at the United States Military Academy at West Point. These expeditions are among the most pleasant memories of my life. I enjoyed the cadet audiences; and at the officers' mess and in other meetings, I shall always remember the remarkable conversations with Colonel and Mrs. Hugh Scott, the Astronomer-librarian E.S.Holden, Colonel and Mrs. C.W.Larned, Colonel and Mrs. Howze, and others. I have never found a more interesting group of people. At the conclusion of the course, I was offered the permanent position of Professor at the Academy, with the ultimate rank and pay of Colonel in the Army, with its perquisites. My devotion to Yale was all that kept me from accepting.

One very amusing incident took place at my last lecture in May. It was a warm and beautiful day and when the cadets had marched in with precision, the big doors at the end of the auditorium were left wide open. Being the only man in the room facing them, in the middle of the lecture

I observed two large setter dogs enter; and as I was the only face they could see and the only voice audible, I felt sure they would come to the platform, which of course was what happened. These big friendly setters came down the aisle, mounted the platform and placed their paws on my shoulders. The cadets wanted to laugh, but they were in the presence of their officers and the situation was strained. I petted the dogs and suddenly thought of the right thing to say then and there, instead of on the way home. I exclaimed 'Why, these are *setters*, and I had expected to see only West Pointers!' Then the whole audience roared with laughter and the situation was saved.

In 1908 Mrs. Humphry Ward lectured in America, but I could not possibly have accepted the invitation in the following letter. I wrote it would be impossible for me to praise her and what deplorable taste I should exhibit if I came and said what I thought. Gummere told me that Mrs. Ward's novels were filled with clever and brilliant people who never said anything clever or brilliant. Here is the letter:

HAVERFORD, 31 MARCH, 1908

My Dear Phelps:

We are very anxious to have you come on Monday night next, 6th April, and just talk for ten minutes as an American makeweight to Mrs. Humphry Ward, who addresses the Contemporary Club on the Peasant (it looked like peanut as I wrote it) in Literature and Fiction. It will be a turnout of all Philadelphia intellect, and we have had to take the largest room at the Bellevue-Stratford, the regular place for hoe-downs of the first magnitude Now of course the club will pay all your expenses and that sort of thing; but my concern is of another sort. I want somebody on our side of the water to speak who really knows the subject. It is pride, Sir, pride. Mrs. H. W. has an exaggerated reputation, to my mind, but they are all capping and cringing as if 'Old Leviticus himself' were back again. Can't you just throw your cap over the mill, cut Yale, and come? Weston, the Secretary, will write you about particulars; but I wish you would wire him, at his expense, what your decision may be, without waiting to hear from him:—S.Burns Weston, 1415 Locust St., Phila.—And make it 'Yes.' It will be a good occasion for you and Yale will not regret letting you go. Weir Mitchell will be on deck, and many another; but we want *you*.

Yours faithfully,

F. B. GUMMERE

When my book appeared, in which I attacked the novels of Mrs. Ward and praised those of William De Morgan, Gummere wrote me at some length. I still hold to my high regard for De Morgan's novels; but I wonder if the present neglect of them by the public is evidence that Gummere was right? I never believed De Morgan to be the equal of Dickens, only that he was more like him than any other writer of the twentieth century.

I wholly agree with Gummere about Norris, the neglect of whose novels is unfortunate. They are indeed 'never dull.' But despite the efforts of his fellow novelists to induce the public to read him, for the best craftsmen of his time saluted him as a peer, he is still largely unread. I met Norris in Paris and found him just as attractive as his books.

I agree with Gummere too in the implication in the sentence about Hancock, although Allen is not altogether forgotten. Professor Hancock I knew well and his early death was a severe loss to academic scholarship, however much he exaggerated the merits of *The Choir Invisible*.

20 JANUARY, 1910

DEAR PHELPS:

Your book reached me yesterday morning, and I read it last night,—all of it.

One can't dust a woman's jacket, as Macaulay put it about his fun with Croker; but whatever the feminine equivalent may be, you have achieved it with Mrs. Ward. I subscribe to every syllable. One crowlet I should pick with you is de Morgan. *Joseph Vance* through the initial stages,—and *praeterea nihil*, is my firm word. How can you range the man with Dickens? *Vance* was read aloud to me when my eyes were tied up; I took it steadily and all of it; and my roar of delight at the beginning changes to cries of pain for the rest.

To see what was wrong in *me*, I have just read *Somehow Good* once more; and with all the humbleness of my spirit,—for you don't talk in vain,—I could find nothing that makes for greatness in the whole extent. Get down your *Under the Greenwood Tree* and read how William Dewy and Reuben and the rest, with Leaf, visit Parson Maybold, in his study. Like the parson's own skin, that scene 'bursts out a'bleedin' afresh every time I think of it. Now go back to de Morgan,—can you draw such blood, any blood, from him? My good colleague Hancock once wrote for the *Outlook* an article 'On the Art of James Lane Allen.' And you, too, are a generous man.

Do you know that the best second-rate novelist in England is W. E. Norris? Do you like *Matrimony*? My dear old F. J. Child 'put me on' Norris, and I've read him all. Prolific, easy, mildly satiric, unexciting, but never dull. . . .

Cuss me for all this. The rest is admirable. The Hardy chapter I will swear to *jurare in verba magistri* with absolute emphasis on the magistracy.

Yours enviously,

F. B. Gummere

Francis B. Gummere was one of the most distinguished Professors of English Literature in America, both as scholar and teacher, and loved Haverford College so loyally that nothing would induce him to go elsewhere, though he had been offered a professorship at Harvard. His conversation was full of wit and sense; it was always a pleasure to be with him.

49

FIRST JOURNEY TO CALIFORNIA

Thirteen Thousand Miles in the West

In the year 1908 I was invited to lecture at the University of California in Berkeley, during the summer session. Accordingly we left New Haven on 9 June, and took the Santa Fé railway from Chicago. Near Kansas City we found enormous floods everywhere. For many miles the wheels were under water. It was a curious experience, to stand on the rear platform of the train, and to see the 'wake' made by our passage; no land visible for miles. On 14 June we saw for the first time the Grand Canyon of the Colorado. We stayed at a hotel there three days and saw the Canyon by sunlight, twilight, dawn, and moonlight; and took drives of many miles. The Canyon is the most sublime spectacle I have ever seen, and the only one of which a picture gives not even a faint representation or conception. It seems all the more astounding because the approach to it is so commonplace and tame. We walked through rough grass and scrubby, dwarfed trees, and then suddenly—But it is vain to attempt a description, either of the vast abyss or of one's impressions.

When we left the Canyon, taking the small junction-train to Williams, the fireman of the locomotive had a day off, and sat down in the train beside me. I said, 'The Canyon is the most sublime spectacle I have ever seen. You have to make three or four trips back and forth every day. Does it still seem to you wonderful? or is it just the end of the run?' He replied, 'You want to know how the canyon affects me? I can tell you best by quoting poetry.' Then he recited from memory the whole of Bryant's *Thanatopsis*. 'That's the way I feel about the Canyon and about scenes of natural beauty.'

That evening as we stopped out in the desert in the moonlight, the brakeman got off the rear platform and picked a bouquet of wild flowers. He said, 'I love flowers.' I do not know whether all the train-hands on the Santa Fé love natural scenery and flowers; these are the only two with whom I talked.

Among the travellers on this train was a German military officer, Major Steinbach. He had a German Baedeker of the United States, and was assiduously verifying everything he saw. In a conversation with him, I asked him about the German army and military life, and had the temerity to ask if he thought two famous recent plays which I had seen in Germany, *Rosenmontag* and *Zapfenstreich*, where the cruelty and hierarchy of the military officers were bitterly attacked, and the fact that both plays were popular and received with shouts of approval, had any significance. Did these plays represent anything evil or that needed correction or modification in German social life? In the emphatic manner characteristic of Germans in authority, he said 'There is nothing whatever in these attacks on German army life. The plays you mention were written by Jews. No Jew is allowed to be an officer, so they attack the army. That's all there is to it. And furthermore, something will have to be done about the Jews. They are cleverer and more unscrupulous in business affairs and in civic life than Christians. It is a great question what to do with them.' This was in 1908.

We reached Los Angeles on the morning of 17 June. My brother Arthur, who lived there, and my oldest brother Dryden, who was visiting him, welcomed us at the station.

We drove out through Pasadena, played golf, and that evening I spoke at a dinner of the Yale Alumni Association. The next afternoon I spoke to 1,700 pupils at the High School.

In San Francisco there were many evidences of the earthquake, or 'fire' as it was called there, but the city was making marvellous convalescent strides. Californian hospitality was all it was said to be. After our first evening, we were invited to dinner somewhere *every night for six weeks*. My first lecture was at eight in the morning, the second at ten daily. I gave a course on American literature at eight and on Tennyson and Browning at ten. The earnestness and enthusiasm of those students—many of whom were school-teachers from California, Oregon, and Nevada—was tremendous. It was a delight to speak to such eager and responsive students.

In the American literature class, I shall always remember two incidents. One day, quite unconscious of the sacrilege, I said, 'When I get back to America. . . .' A roar of laughter went up from the audience; that sentence was never finished.

The other incident was even more embarrassing at the time, though it resulted in a friendship. I was lecturing on Bret Harte, partly biographical, partly critical. In the latter part I spoke of the genius displayed in his early tales. In the early part, I made some derogatory remarks about his character. At the close of the lecture, a member of the California faculty whispered to me, 'Bret Harte's sister is in the audience, would you like to speak to her?' 'No, I should not like to, but I will.' A sweet-faced white-haired old lady was led up to the desk. She said, without waiting for any introductory formalities, 'Young man, every word you spoke of my brother's character is a lie!'

I replied that I earnestly hoped she was right, that I hated to believe what I had said, but supposed I had it on unimpeachable authority; that if she would give me the facts, I would not only correct what I had said, but would make a humble apology. We then found a place where we could talk together in seclusion, and the result was a warm friendship that lasted until her death. She told me that Frank, as she called him, was always kind to her and to his family, that he was noble and good in every way, and that the things said about his domestic and financial habits were slanders. The next day I began my lecture by saying that although I had been informed my statements were false, I was glad I had said them, because otherwise I might not have had the pleasure of meeting his sister, Mrs. Wyman, who had given me the facts.

Several times after that, I had conversation with her. 'I know how you adore the genius of Mark Twain. I want to give you this letter.'

It was a letter of inestimable value, yellow with age, that Mark had written to Harte on the day of the publication of *The Celebrated Jumping Frog*, 1 May 1867, a few days before his lecture in Cooper Union, and shortly before the voyage to the Holy Land that was to give him immortal fame. I included it in my *Essays on Books* (Macmillan 1914), now out of print.

WESTMINSTER HOTEL, MAY 1, 1867

DEAR BRET—

I take my pen in hand to inform you that I am well and hope these few line [*sic*] will find you enjoying the same God's blessing.

The book is out, and is handsome. It is full of damnable errors of grammar and deadly inconsistencies of spelling in the Frog sketch because I was away and did not read the proofs—but be a friend and say nothing about these things. When my hurry is over I will send you an autograph copy to pisen the children with.

I am to lecture in Cooper Union next Monday night. Pray for me.

We sail for the Holy Land June 8. Try and write me (at this hotel), and it will be forwarded to Paris, where we remain 10 to 15 days.

Regards and best wishes to Mrs Bret and the family.

Truly Yr Friend

MARK

The University of California deserves credit for what seems to have been forgotten. After Bret Harte had published *The Luck of Roaring Camp* in the *Overland Monthly* (1869) the University, then only a few years old, offered to make Harte *Professor of Recent Literature*, at a fine salary. Harte declined; but if he had accepted, California would have had the honour (if you like) of giving the first university course in the world on contemporary novels; that dubious honour was reserved for me in 1895 at Yale. But so far as I know, not any university has ever had a Professorship of Recent Literature. The formal vote of the trustees appointing Harte with that title is in the records.

The climate of Berkeley in the summer suited me perfectly. I was told that I would get sick of sunshine and long for clouds and rain; I never did. It was a blessing to know in advance that one could make any outdoor arrangements with confidence. Every morning we got up early; it was like a mild winter day; a fog covered the sky; if we had not known it couldn't rain, we should have thought it was going to rain in five minutes. We turned on the steam heat, and had breakfast in a well-heated dining room. Then I went to my first lecture at eight o'clock at the University, wearing an overcoat; when I came out of the lecture, the sun was shining bright, the temperature was eighty; another gorgeous summer day. After lunch we went out to play tennis or golf, carrying an overcoat although the temperature was about eighty-five. Along about four in the afternoon the sky became overcast, the fog rolled in at the Golden Gate, and during the rest of the day the temperature was about fifty. So we had four seasons of the year every day, with the one exception that it never rained or snowed.

Although it is next door, San Francisco is colder than Berkeley; the temperature during summer ranges usually from 52 to 60, and about four-thirty in the afternoon a cold fog rolls in with an icy wind from the ocean.

I had read Stevenson's descriptions of the beauty of the fog but did not realize what he meant until we ascended Mount Tamalpais. On 18 July Professor and Mrs. Osterhout took us on an early morning ferry to San Francisco, and on another ferry to Mill Valley. Then we took the train up the mountain. It was intensely hot up there until the middle of the afternoon, when we saw the fog rolling in at the Golden Gate; apparently a solid grey mass. It covered the cities of San Francisco, Berkeley and Oakland. Overhead was the blue sky and the brilliant sun; underneath was this infinite fog, glistering, dazzling white, rising and falling at various levels like a sea of silver, one of the most beautiful sights I have ever beheld. We came down the mountain on a 'gravity' car, that is a car equipped only with brakes. It was exciting. With this vehicle we reached Redwood Canyon; and saw the superb redwood trees, given to the United States by my Yale classmate William Kent. Among these trees we met the dramatist Percy Mackaye and his sister.

A few days later, at the Bohemian Club I met Kent and Gifford Pinchot, Yale 1889, afterwards Governor of Pennsylvania. On the same day at a meeting of the San Francisco Browning Society, I met Agnes Tobin, intimate friend of Joseph Conrad, William De Morgan, and many other contemporary British novelists. She gave me an amusing photograph of 'The Worship of William Heinemann.' In the picture, the publisher Heinemann is standing in mock solemn grandeur, and on their knees, imploring and worshipping him, are William De Morgan, Edmund Gosse, Agnes Tobin and another acolyte.

We spent a delightful week-end at the magnificent country home of Mrs. Phoebe Hearst, mother of William R. Hearst, whose two little children were there. Professor

Robert Herrick, the novelist, and his son Philip, were with us. Mrs. Hearst was then sixty-five; a rather small, slight figure, very clear-cut features, keenly intelligent face. She was kindness itself, showing us the treasures of the vast dwelling. A pure white building, standing entirely alone among rolling hills with mountains in the distance, no town or village in the neighbourhood, it seemed like a feudal castle, with its army of retainers. So it was; only far more comfortable.

Professor Thomas R. Bacon of the University of California, one of the most interesting men I ever knew, discussed past members of the Faculty. Every college president is called a liar by somebody. When I asked Bacon what he thought of the astronomer E. S. Holden, who at one time was President of the University of California, Bacon replied, 'He is a very able man; but the truth is not in him.' Later I met Holden at West Point, and asked him what he thought of Professor Bacon. 'Ah, don't you think he looks exactly like a hired assassin? Wouldn't you hate to meet him on a dark night?'

The familiar story illustrating the reputation for veracity attained by college presidents is generally told at the inauguration of every new one. When Dr. Canfield was inaugurated at Ohio State University, President Eliot of Harvard said to him, 'Well, Canfield, now you are President, and everybody will call you a liar.' 'Why, Dr. Eliot, did any one ever call *you* a liar?' 'Worse than that,' said Eliot, 'they proved it.'

The difficulty any President has in being regarded as truthful comes partly from his conversations with assistant professors who seek promotions or increases of salary. It is almost impossible for him to say anything without being misunderstood. The best story on this I ever read was by Robert Herrick, my colleague in California; but when I told him so, he said he had no recollection of ever having written or published such a tale. It appeared in the *Atlantic Monthly*.

Many English visitors to California, wishing to speak the vernacular, and please their hosts, call San Francisco 'Frisco.' As this is regarded everywhere among cultivated California people as the last word in disgusting vulgarity, it is better to speak of the city with its real name, giving the full value to every syllable.

It was in San Francisco that Stevenson had his first cocktail, sometimes regarded as America's most important contribution to civilization. Stevenson said, 'I took one sip and a streak of fire shot down my right leg. Thereafter I had the sensation as of a burning coal in the pit of the stomach, not altogether unpleasant.'

On the way West, I was sitting in tne smoking car one evening and a man sitting opposite kept looking at me. Finally he came over, took the seat next to mine and said, 'You *are* Lloyd Osbourne, aren't you?' I replied, 'You mean Stevenson's stepson?' He affirmed it. I told him I felt flattered but that I was not Mr. Osbourne and had never seen him. 'This won't do; you are Mr. Osbourne, and for some reason you are travelling *incog*.' Nothing that I could say convinced this gentleman. 'I don't see why you won't admit it, Mr. Osbourne; surely you must remember that night in Samoa when you and I sat out and talked together for hours.' Finally he went away sorrowful.

Some years later I met Isobel Strong, Osbourne's sister. I asked her if I looked like her brother. She scrutinized me closely and exclaimed, 'Why, yes, you do very much resemble Lloyd.' Not long after that I met Lloyd Osbourne at the Coffee House in New York and told him of the incident on the train.

I have sometimes played poker for fun, just to see which member of the party would first lose all his chips. I am the worst poker player in the world, having the opposite of a poker face. Everyone knows whether I have a big hand or whether I am bluffing.

I also have the misfortune to look guilty when I am innocent. Years ago when the Pullman fare from New Haven to New York was fifty cents, I caught the train just too late to buy a ticket. The Pullman conductor came through, and as he approached me, I remembered my total possessions were a ten dollar bill and a fifty cent piece. And I reflected that I needed to have that ten changed; but 'if I give it to him won't he ask me for something smaller and if I then produce the coin, won't he believe that the coin is bad and that he got it because he was asking for it?' All these reflexions passed through my mind as he drew near and all happened as rehearsed in my thought. I offered the ten. He asked if I had anything smaller. Looking like a crook, I produced the coin. He took it reluctantly and suspiciously, glaring at me. He tried to scratch it with his finger-nails. By now I had the appearance of a criminal. He looked at me sternly a long time. Then he went out on the vestibule of the train and I heard him bouncing the coin against metal. Every time he passed through the car he looked at me.

My last lectures in the Summer School at Berkeley were given on 31 July; it was painful to say farewell to such devoted students.

That night we took the train at Oakland for Portland. Many times I have taken a sleeper on warm evenings and felt cold in the hours before dawn. This experience was the opposite. The evening air at Oakland when we took the train was very cold; but as we went toward Sacramento in the night the temperature rose, and it was one of the hottest nights I have ever spent on a train. The next day was the hottest day, certainly. The temperature was 108 in the shade at every station and in the dining-car, with all the fans going, it was 98. Mount Shasta was a refreshing sight, an isolated peak, 14,000 feet, covered with snow. Arriving at Portland, Oregon, the second morning, there was a great change; it was refreshingly cool.

Wherever we went we met former Yale students and friends, who did everything possible to make our visits enjoyable.

We took the train up the Columbia River to the Dalles and returned to Portland by river steamer; I saw more splendid scenery that afternoon than on any other river in the world. Over and over again, looking at the innumerable lofty mountain cascades, I thought of Tennyson's lines in *The Lotos Eaters.*

> And like a downward smoke, the slender stream
> Along the cliff to fall and pause and fall did seem.
>
> A land of streams! some, like a downward smoke,
> Slow-dropping veils of thinnest lawn, did go;
> And some thro' wavering lights and shadows broke,
> Rolling a slumbrous sheet of foam below.
> They saw the gleaming river seaward flow
> From the inner land: far off, three mountain tops,
> Three silent pinnacles of aged snow,
> Stood sunset-flush'd: and, dew'd with showery drops,
> Up-clomb the shadowy pine above the woven copse.

After a visit to Seattle, we decided to make the round trip by railway from Vancouver to Banff and back to see the mountain scenery and Lake Louise. The scenery from the railway was superb; enormous canyons, rushing rivers, and mighty mountains. One westerner, being asked by a Boston lady if the scenery along the Canadian Pacific was good, replied 'Good? Good? Lady, on one side you can look up ten thousand feet; on the other side, you can spit twelve thousand.'

Yet this magnificent scenery was marred for me by a misfortune. During the day of 10 August I suffered more acute physical pain than in any other day of my life. It was an ulcerated tooth that finally gave me a temperature of 102; getting off the train at Banff, I found there was no dentist in the town. I telephoned to Calgary and made it clear to the dentist that he must on no account miss the train. I was sick in bed, in agony, quite unable to travel. At eight o'clock in the evening, after waiting for hours, word came from Calgary that the dentist had missed the train. We found a doctor in Banff who said he had occasionally pulled teeth for lumber-jacks. After a fearful struggle, he finally succeeded in getting mine out, unfortunately breaking the sound tooth next to it, for which I have found it difficult to forgive him. As he went out in the hall, I heard him say to a friend, 'It's a wonder I didn't break his damned jaw.'

At the dining-table in Vancouver, I met an Englishman, and I said 'You may be behind the times here in Vancouver, but why do you advertise the fact?' 'What on earth do you mean?' 'Well, look at the dinner-card. It says, *Vancouver, B.C.*' 'But it doesn't mean *that*, you know!'

We spent a day or so in Victoria, a garden-spot indeed, and more English than England. I wish we might have stayed there a long time.

On Tuesday 11 August it rained, the first rain we had seen since 14 June. To me it was not welcome.

From Seattle we took the excursion steamer *Spokane* to see the sights in Alaska, a fifteen-day trip, with marvellous scenery; the sea filled with bright blue icebergs, and tall mountains completely covered with snow rising from the sea. The boat takes the so-called inside route; one is in the open sea only four hours, in Queen Charlotte Sound, but during those four hours I saw more acute cases of seasickness than on any other voyage. There was an Australian gentleman who stood by the rail with a faraway look in his eyes, who erupted with such regularity that I called him *Old Faithful*. It was a fascinating spectacle, for it was possible to predict the exact moment of his next explosion. This was on a Monday afternoon and watching him, we counted back to the previous Thursday's luncheon, taking three meals for each day.

Besides this regularity, the like of which I have never seen, this Australian was a most interesting person. I told him all I knew about Australia was what I had read when a small boy in Charles Reade's novel, *It Is Never Too Late to Mend*. I asked him if he had ever read that book. He said the book had changed his life. 'I was born in Birmingham, England, and when I was nine years old I read that story. It took such a mighty hold on my imagination that I determined to see Australia. I ran away from home, grew up in Australia, was successful in business there, happily married, have two sons, and am now at the age of 45, for the first time returning to England to see my native city.'

At Skagway, our farthest north, nearly 60 degrees, I had the pleasure of meeting Mrs. Pullen, who lived there. A few months previously I had seen and talked with her son, an undergraduate at West Point. I told her she should be very proud of him. He was the fourth in his class in scholarship, Captain of the football team, respected and beloved by students and Faculty. She was quite overcome by emotion and thanked me with tears in her eyes. When we got back to the steamer, we found our stateroom filled with magnificent flowers, sent there by Mrs. Pullen.

On the way back east, we spent a week in Yellowstone Park, the most fantastic place in America; absolutely grotesque scenery. It seemed more like a comic opera than anything else, combining so much beauty, horror, and mirthful distortion. Everything is abnormal; one sees Paradise, one sees Hell, but nothing natural or human.

> Now blotches rankling, coloured gay and grim,
>   Now patches where some leanness of the soil's
>   Broke into moss or substances like boils;
> Then came some palsied oak, a cleft in him
> Like a distorted mouth that splits its rim
>   Gaping at death, and dies while it recoils

And now that I am quoting from Browning's 'Childe Roland,' readers will remember the stanza describing the unexpected river.

> A sudden little river crossed my path
>   As unexpected as a serpent comes.
>   No sluggish tide congenial to the glooms;
> This, as it frothed by, might have been a bath
> For the fiend's glowing hoof—to see the wrath
>   Of its black eddy bespate with flakes and spumes.

Stephen Philbin, who had been an undergraduate student of mine (1910), told me that he was a guest at a luncheon given by Ex-President Theodore Roosevelt, recently returned from his hunting expedition to Africa with his son Kermit. 'At twilight one evening, we were in a jungle where no white man had ever been before; when suddenly at our feet rushed a narrow stream, going at such speed that it startled us, for we had almost stepped into it. We paused and in the silence Kermit began to recite aloud the stanza from "Childe Roland." "Why, Kermit, I did not know that you knew that poem!" Then we repeated aloud together the three stanzas about the river.'

Browning wrote that poem in one day, 3 January 1852, in his apartment in Paris, to the accompaniment of vehicles on the Champs Elysées. In the next century two Americans recited parts of it aloud in a silent twilight in a remote desolation in Africa.

50

W. D. HOWELLS

ONE day in the late nineties I had the pleasure of a long conversation with Mr. Howells at his home in New York. He was extremely kind and made an indelible impression of sincerity and nobility. He expressed his dislike of romanticism in the strongest terms; his creed was realism. I never saw him or any one else laugh more unrestrainedly than he did while discussing romantic fiction; 'he drew himself up to his full height,' etc. He laughed till the tears ran down his face.

He gave a lecture in New Haven on 19 February 1900 and the next day he came to lunch at our house. Other guests were Professors T. R. Lounsbury, Henry A. Beers, Theodore S. Woolsey, Charlton M. Lewis. Mr. Howells was particularly agreeable, courteous, and kind to my mother. After luncheon, in my library, when he saw the Nathan Haskell Dole edition of Tolstoy in many volumes, he was enormously interested, as he had not known of its existence.

40 WEST 59TH STREET
March 25, 1900

My Dear Mr. Phelps:

Thank you for the book which you have sent me, and I will read it as soon as I get time, and write you again about it.

I have not been very well and I have been very busy; otherwise I should have acknowledged before this the great pleasure I enjoyed at your house, in meeting your family and friends. The cordial interest with which your Mother met me was especially gratifying and hereafter I shall write nothing without hoping that she will like it. I deeply felt the kindness of your whole household, and of all New Haven.

Yours sincerely,

W.D.HOWELLS

48 WEST 59TH STREET
May 24, 1902

MY DEAR MRS. PHELPS:

The books came yesterday, and I am very glad of them, and of the privilege of keeping them a little while. I hope to return them very early next month, after I have written my paper. They are just what I wanted.

We are greatly interested in this household by Mr. Phelps's Richardson enterprise; but I have not yet had time to read Mrs. Howells the *Clarissa* introduction. Do give him my best regards and wishes for his prompt and full recovery. I feel, rather selfishly, that he cannot be spared from the kind of work he is doing to be sick long. (Thank you for not saying he was 'ill.') I have not forgotten my delightful lunch with you. Will you kindly remember me to all under your roof, especially to Mrs. Phelps, sr.?

Yours sincerely,

W.D.HOWELLS

W.D.HOWELLS
KITTERY POINT, MAINE
July 28, 1907

MY DEAR MR. PHELPS:

Nothing ever gives me so much pleasure as praise of my son, and if the praise is from you! I am afraid, however, that since you speak of him as a young man, he may have acquired merit with you by his youthful appearance. He will be 39 in a fortnight, and he has had time to go through Harvard, get to be Diplomé of the French government at the Beaux Arts, and practice his profession twelve years in New York. I tell you all this that you may discount your favor as much as you think just. But he was as much pleased by your letter as if he deserved it every word.

I am slowly 'getting round' to your beautiful edition of the divine

Jane (I read your essay with great satisfaction) and hope to do a North Am. Rev. paper about it before the summer is over.

With regards to Mrs. Phelps and yourself,

Yours sincerely,

W.D.HOWELLS

W.D.HOWELLS, 130 WEST 57TH STREET
March 4, 1910

DEAR MR. PHELPS:

I ought to have written you before; now my wife is so very sick, I can hardly think what to say. But I felt the very great kindness and fairness of what you wrote about me; you have always been kind, and more than fair. I don't think Tolstoy has affected me aesthetically; my pace was set long before his giant strides overtook me; but his moral influence was like a 'religious experience' and I hope it will never end with me.

I liked your criticisms of other people as well as of myself; though I should have put Hardy above all the other living English. Stevenson is food for babes—boy babes—in his fiction, though he is a true, rare poet.

Yours sincerely,

W.D.HOWELLS

The doctor has just reported my wife a little better, and I am sorry I don't, won't, or can't praise R.L.S.

51

MAHAFFY AND JAPAN

On 7 January 1909 Professor J.P.Mahaffy of Trinity College, Dublin, whom I had not seen since we had had many talks together at Chautauqua in 1889, stayed a few days at our house and gave a lecture at Yale; I gave a formal dinner for him, inviting only the Professors of Latin and Greek, including Ex-President Dwight. I was shocked to see how old Mahaffy looked (he was only seventy), but he was as much of a Tory as ever. In 1889 he told me that he and Gladstone used to be intimate friends; they made many excursions together; 'but now,' said he, 'if I should meet him, I should refuse to recognize him; I would have nothing to do with him.' And in view of the disclosures about Mrs. O'Shea which startled the public and set back the cause of Home Rule in the very next year, 1890, it is interesting to recall what Mahaffy said to me in 1889. 'Parnell is one of the worst libertines in England; has many affairs.' I have no idea whether there is any truth in this or not; but nobody hated Gladstone and Parnell and Home Rule more than those in authority at Trinity College, Dublin.

This time, twenty years later, I went to the railway station in New Haven to meet him; he carried a huge rug, and seemed surprised I was able to recognize him! After dinner, the Japanese servant entered and placed some wood on the fire and then withdrew. 'I don't like that,' said Mahaffy, 'these Japanese are really spies; they are studying our resources.'

In the Irish rebellion of Easter 1916, Mahaffy directed the defence of the College. He was 77 years old.

In the collection of old portraits at Yale, Mahaffy was particularly interested in the contemporary painting of Bishop Berkeley and his family. He talked a good deal about him. His conversation was always interesting. He said when Oscar Wilde was an undergraduate and he had taken him with him on a journey to Italy, the young man's wit was as brilliant and as spontaneous as in later years. A wonderful travelling companion.

On 26 January we dined at the house of Professor and Mrs. John Berdan; as I bent to stroke their large cat, the animal bit me and drew blood. Our hosts were alarmed, but I said laughingly there was nothing to worry about so far as I was concerned; but that I feared for the cat, as I was sure I was full of poison. For several days thereafter, Berdan would open the door of my college room and ask 'How are you *now*?' I told him he was disappointed not to find me in convulsions, and again I said 'Do take care of your cat: give him an antidote.' Three days later he entered my room in a state of excitement. 'The cat died this morning!' I pretended not to be astonished.

On 11 February we heard Mischa Elman, 'a young Russian violinist,' give a recital in the theatre; he was unknown and only a few persons were present. But he was soon to be the reigning sensation in America and in Europe, until Jascha Heifetz appeared.

On 30 June at Yale Commencement, I officiated for the first time as Public Orator, in the temporary absence of Professor Perrin. On the platform, as one of the regular members of the Corporation, was the President of the United States, William Howard Taft; he told me that once he was introduced by a voluble chairman who said, 'The name of this man is known in every part of the world—Willian *Henry* Taft.'

The last person I presented for the degree was William Graham Sumner. The audience rose and he received such a tribute that the tears ran down his face. He had less than a year to live.

On 6 November the New Theatre opened in New York with a dress rehearsal of *Antony and Cleopatra*, with Edward Sothern and Julia Marlowe. It lasted till one a.m. I sat next to Thomas Edison, who could not hear a word, but who remained cheerfully till the end. In the afternoon we attended the public exercises held on the stage. J. Pierpont Morgan presided; addresses were made by Governor Charles Evans Hughes and Elihu Root. Forbes-Robertson gave Hamlet's address to the players. This theatre proved a financial failure, but it had a greater effect on the art of producing plays in America than anything else. Under the direction of Winthrop Ames, plays were produced with wonderful company-acting and with appropriate scenery. It was a turning-point in the history of the American stage. Some of their greatest successes were Galsworthy's *Strife*, Maeterlinck's *Blue Bird*, Besier's *Don*, and various plays of Shakespeare, notably *A Winter's Tale*.

52

JOURNEY TO THE SOUTH

On 5 January 1910 we moved from our old house at 44 High Street, which my father had built in 1868, to our new house at 110 Whitney Avenue, ground for which had been broken in November 1908. It is on the exact plot of ground where we first lived after our marriage in December 1892; just before breaking ground for the new house, we sold the old wooden one on the premises for fifty dollars! Our new house of Colonial style was very comfortable and for the first time in our lives we had electric light. Someone told me that as this was the first house we had built, we should only learn from it how to build another; that after we moved in, we should find many disappointments. The humble truth is that we were satisfied indoors and out on the first day we moved thither, and after nearly thirty years in it, we like it better than ever. On the day we moved the thermometer fell to zero; no mud or dust entered the house and the workmen had to move with speed.

Shortly after we were settled we were visited one evening by thirty of our neighbours who gave us a surprise party as a welcome. This was one of the happiest evenings of our lives.

On 18 June in the open air on the Yale campus the students gave a fine performance of *The Taming of the Shrew*—the feature being the admirable acting of Katherine by William C. Bullitt, Yale sophomore, who during the war was assistant in the Department of State and was sent abroad on various missions, and who was years later to become famous as American Ambassador to Russia and to France.

At Commencement John Burroughs received an honorary degree and stayed at our house; he said he had never owned a gown, so he did me the honour of wearing mine.

In December we saw Florida for the first time. We reached Jacksonville some four hours late, and transferred to the St. Augustine train. It had been raining heavily in the old Spanish town, and as we drove from the tracks to the hotel, the soft, balmy air was heavy with the scent of flowers. The two following days were superb; a real whiff from the tropics. We visited the old fort, the wonderful ocean beach, the slimy collection of crocodiles, and picked splendid oranges off the trees in a spacious grove.

At St. Augustine we saw two distinguished persons, and met one of them. We saw the great railway magnate Flagler, and had the pleasure of meeting Mr. Chatfield-Taylor of Chicago. He was writing a Life of Goldoni, and was interested to hear of the Yale performance of *The Fan*.

Wednesday, 21 December, is a day I have not yet forgotten, though I have made every effort to do so. We left Jacksonville early in the morning on a train that loafed across the longest width of Florida, with the palpably hypocritical pretence of ultimately reaching New Orleans. This train moved like a snail suffering from hookworm. The locomotive made a house to house canvass. However, we had a fine opportunity to become intimately acquainted with the hamlets strung along the line, as twenty minutes were assigned to each. At Tallahassee a large covey of girls flew aboard, and although it was pleasant to see how radiantly happy they were at the closing of school for the holidays, and although youth is always glorious, still, a pack of hyenas would have made less noise.

We entered New Orleans about eleven in the forenoon of 22 December, four hours late, and were gladdened by the sight of Stanhope Bayne-Jones, now Dean of the Yale School of Medicine. He was our guide and philosopher during the day, exhibiting the quaint French landmarks of the city, giving us a marvellous Gallic luncheon at Antoine's, taking us out to the wonderful parks, the great shell road, Tulane University, and the impressive dwellings of the dead, all buried above ground, in aristocratic miniature mansions of stone. That evening occurred the Yale Alumni dinner, arranged by LaCour, '04, and gracefully presided over by Stewart.

An additional pleasure in visiting New Orleans was that it was the birthplace and home of Lewis C. Everard of the Class of 1908. He had gone all the way from New Orleans to New Haven without any friends or influence or money, supported himself all through the four years, sent money home to help his parents, was elected to Phi Beta Kappa and became Champion Intercollegiate Gymnast. After graduation he became my Secretary, later a member of the Yale Faculty and afterwards entered the Government Service. In New Orleans I had the pleasure of meeting his proud parents. In the nineteen-thirties he had three sons at Yale.

We were taken to the French opera, one of the most interesting experiences of the whole expedition, and we saw Christmas arrive at midnight in the crowded cave of the Hotel Grunewald. Judge Godchaux, '96, and Leon Godchaux, '09, gave us a brilliant French luncheon, and the latter took us out Sunday afternoon to the great aviation meet, where I saw airplanes for the first time in my life. We witnessed several daring flights by Moisant, who was killed a few days later. On that evening, the last in New Orleans, I had the honour of being presented to Mr. James J. Corbett. He entered the dining room, and I remarked *sotto voce* 'That's Jim Corbett!' The waiter, misunderstanding my half-unconscious tribute to greatness, immediately brought him to my neighbourhood, and I apologetically explained the origin of the mistake. We shook hands, and then, instead of squaring off, parted in the most amicable fashion.

Sunday night we left New Orleans on a fine train over the Southern Pacific, which reached Houston (pronounced Hewston), Texas, exactly on time the next morning. We were greeted at the station by the Cleveland brothers, '94, and by Dillingham, '89, Sheff.

We spent an afternoon at Galveston, seeing the great sea wall and other wonders, and Tuesday 27 December was a red-letter day. The alumni at Houston met in the morning. We had luncheon together at the Club. In the afternoon a reception was given by the men and women of the city interested in university matters, and we had the opportunity of meeting the wives, mothers, sisters, and daughters of Yale. That evening came the Yale Alumni dinner, and I do not think I have ever heard more interesting speeches than those delivered on that occasion by the men of Texas representing Yale and other institutions. The speeches took the form of an animated discussion on such topics as whether a large university was better than a small college, whether a Southerner should go to his state institution or to Yale, and what education really means.

Wednesday, 28 December, we took the train for Abilene. The State Teachers Convention, which I had come to Abilene to address, was in full swing; there were nearly two thousand in attendance.

The next morning I took part in a heated discussion in the English group, where I found that they were just as 'hot and bothered' in Texas over the amount of time that should be given to English composition as we in the North.

There were evidences enough of a strong reaction against the terrible burden of theme-reading.

A paper was read by Mr. Wasson, of the *Dallas News*, a thoughtful and suggestive essay. The *Dallas News*, which Belo, '96, was directing at the time of his death, is one of the best newspapers in America. It is free from sensationalism, its editorials are admirable in matter and expression, and its reports accurate.

In the evening, 30 December, I made the closing address before the convention, speaking for an hour on the pleasures derived from education, taking as my text President Dwight's definition of happiness, that he gave to our Class in Senior year—'The happiest person is the person who thinks the most interesting thoughts.'

After leaving Abilene, we retraced our course in Texas travelling east and south to Austin, the State capital and seat of the University. I had good talk with Sidney Mezes the President and with William J. Battle, the Dean; both were intimate friends as we had been closely associated in the Harvard Graduate School twenty years before. John A. Lomax, the famous collector and interpreter of cowboy ballads, introduced me to many of the Faculty; one of the most interesting men was Professor Benedict, afterwards President of the University. His speciality, Mathematics, had sharpened his natural wits.

We visited Baylor University in Waco, where is now—under the care of Professor A. J. Armstrong—one of the finest collections of Browning memorabilia and manuscripts in the world.

I had heard wild stories of sudden changes in the weather in Texas; and after one experience, I did not feel they were greatly exaggerated. We spent New Year's Day, 1911, in Dallas; perfect summer it would have been in New York; seventy degrees all day long. That night we took the train *south* to San Antonio; before dawn the wind changed and blew a 'norther;' when we alighted at San Antonio, the temperature was exactly twelve degrees, a drop of 58 degrees in a few hours. I had been told of the man in Texas driving two oxen; one of them died of the heat; he went to the farm to get another; and when he returned, the survivor of the heat wave had frozen to death. I am now prepared to believe that.

53

SECOND SABBATICAL

On 16 February 1911 I persuaded Horace Howard Furness (1833–1912) the Shakespearean scholar and editor of the *Variorum*, to give a reading to the Yale undergraduates. This splendid old man, nearly eighty, was as deaf as Beethoven, and could not hear the applause of the students, which almost shook the building. As was his custom, he read from his own copy of the First Folio (1623). Every place in the hall including the aisles was filled with undergraduates, and how they did cheer! After he had read for nearly an hour, he announced a recess of ten minutes and withdrew to the room reserved for speakers. He told me there that he expected to see less than half of the original audience when he returned. Not a single man had left the room when he reappeared on the platform, and the enthusiasm was overwhelming. He read the famous passage in *King Henry V*, beginning

Once more unto the breach, dear friends!

Then he paused, and asked two questions. 'Just what did Shakespeare mean by that passage? But how can my puny mind comprehend the mind of William Shakespeare?'

There was proportionally not so much cheering on 19 November 1912, when I took Henry Arthur Jones, the English dramatist, to the annual football game between Yale and Harvard, the first and last he ever saw. He was disappointed when the result was a tie, neither side having scored. His emotions as a man of the theatre had been aroused by the hope of enjoying the enthusiasm caused by a touchdown and the cheering parade that follows a victory.

On 1 July 1911, we sailed for England on our Second Sabbatical. Our neighbours, Professor and Mrs. Russell Chittenden, were on the same steamer and we had a happy month together in western England. It was one of the exceptionally dry summers: we saw not a blade of green grass until we reached the Lake counties. One day on the top of a coach an English gentleman enquired of our friend, 'Are you any relation of the great Chittenden, the famous physiological chemist?' It was pleasant to see the stranger's enthusiasm when Chittenden modestly confessed.

I do not know whether the tiny corner of the planet where we live in New Haven has any special healthful atmosphere; but it is interesting that the two neighbours, whose gardens are next to ours, Judge John K. Beach and Dr. Chittenden, were both active after eighty. I played golf with Judge Beach when he was 82 and at this moment Chittenden, 82, is fishing in Maine. At the corner lived Professor Edward S. Dana who died in 1935 in his 86th year, while fifty yards from his house are living two brothers, Henry and Lewis English, both active and over eighty. In 1938 I attended a party given Henry on his birthday; he is 87. And at the next corner lived the late Henry L. Hotchkiss, also full of physical and mental activity well beyond eighty.

We said goodbye to the Chittendens in August and we proceeded to Copenhagen by way of Hamburg. The American Minister to Denmark was a distinguished man of letters, Maurice Francis Egan; he made our stay in the beautiful capital most agreeable, and in a few days we were at the same hotel with him in Christiania.

Although the University of Upsala in Sweden was founded in 1477, and the University of Copenhagen in 1479, the University of Christiania was not born till 1811. The hundredth birthday of this infant was celebrated with academic pomp and splendour during the week beginning 3 September, delegates from older institutions like Yale, Harvard, and Pennsylvania coming to pay homage. The weather, during every day of the *fest*, was like New Haven autumn weather, clear, bright, cool, tonic, reminding me keenly of the glorious sunshine of our Bicentennial.

We left Copenhagen at nine in the evening of Saturday, 2 September, passing through Elsinore two hours before the ghost of Hamlet's father was due on the platform. The next morning the train rolled along leisurely through Sweden and Norway among pine forests, slanting farms, lakes, and fjords. At one village we saw a little country church on the hillside, with a group of worshippers gossiping about the portal in the strong sunlight, exactly as Björnson pictures the scene in *Synnöve Solbakken*. We reached Christiania as the bells were knolling noon, and drove up the principal street of the city to the Grand Hotel, in the big café of which Ibsen spent so many hours of his later years.

It was Sunday in Christiania, not in London. The streets were crowded with people, spending the day in active uselessness, walking briskly, laughing and talking. Animation and gaiety were in the air and overhead was the Christiania sky, not drawn close like a tent-roof as it is in Paris, Berlin, and London, but unspeakably far aloft, with its radiant blue streaked here and there by long, thin clouds dazzling white, like snow-drifts. The sky in Christiania, at all hours of the day and night, is impressive.

The street, for a hundred yards in front of the University, was arched with bright flags and bunting. The handsome academic buildings stand a little back from the broad highway, with the big and dignified National Theatre directly opposite, and the palace of the King at the top of the hill.

During the afternoon, delegates from all parts of the earth began to arrive, and within twenty-four hours we had met many old, and made many new friends. Georgetown University had the honour of being represented by His Excellency the American Minister to Denmark. The University of Pennsylvania was there in the person of its distinguished head—Provost Smith. I had never seen him before, but it was worth a trip to Norway to know him, a specialist in chemistry, and an able executive, with the unshakable conviction that a college education which does not emphasize character and discipline is a poor thing. Harvard was represented by the American consul at Christiania, Mr. Gade, whom I was glad to see again, for he had been one of my pupils at Harvard. I wish I could believe I had helped to make him as I found him in 1911. Columbia's delegate was no less a person than its Dean, Professor Carpenter, experienced man of the world, as befits the Dean of an urban institution. These men were excellent company. My one regret was that Yale's delegate, Professor Charles Andrews (who lived across the street when we were boys in Hartford), and who would have represented Yale with such distinction, was prevented at the last moment from coming, by illness in the family. I was the regular delegate, not from Yale, but from the Connecticut Academy of Arts and Sciences, holding my commission from Governor Simeon Baldwin, the President, and George Eaton, the Secretary: on my arrival, I found a letter from Andrews, with his formal credentials, and a request that I should represent Yale in his place. I therefore stood for two groups, was obliged to mount the stage twice, and present two parchments.

At five in the afternoon of Monday, 4 September, the delegates met, and after an address from the Rector, each group held a separate conclave to elect its spokesman for the following day. This is a high honour, and when the

American University Group assembled, it appeared that two strong candidates were in the field. After a little skirmish, we elected Minister Egan. In the other group to which I belonged, Academies and Learned Societies, we elected Professor W.P.Ker, of England, a notable scholar in English Literature. That night an elaborate dinner was given to all the delegates at the Grand Hotel. We sat with a Norwegian Professor of Medicine, who spoke Norwegian fluently, but not French, German, or English. The conversation took the form of violent physical exercise, and at the end, while we were polite and even affectionate, we were exhausted.

The next morning, Tuesday, the first great public exercises took place in the National Theatre. The ceremony began at eleven o'clock, with the singing, by a large choir, of Björnson's ode, *Lyset* (light). This music was about five times too long—in fact, it was a colossal bore. Then the Rector made his formal address, setting forth the desirability and necessity of a World-university. He spoke in German. After this address, the various groups, eight in all, marched successively upon the stage, while the previously-elected spokesman presented the compliments of himself and colleagues to the Rector. Then each visitor's name and university or society were called out, each delegate shook hands with the Rector, presented his formal parchment, and went back to the auditorium. The spokesmen for the delegates usually made their brief address in the language of the country they represented. The Heidelberg professor spoke German, the Paris professor French, and Dr. Egan English. Mr. Ker, who represented the learned societies from various countries, quite properly spoke in Latin. A Czech professor from Prague delighted the audience by speaking Norwegian.

In the evening, the King and Queen entertained the delegates at dinner in the Royal Palace. This was the first time I had ever met a king, and I felt (like Franklin) the truth of the Scripture saying—'Seest thou a man diligent in his business? He shall stand before Kings.' This royal pair were democratic. They shook hands with each one of us (we were about six hundred, and Oh, the wild charge we made!) and actually talked with each delegate. The King asked me about the study of Scandinavian languages at Yale, and I was glad to be able to tell him of Professor Palmer's courses. As a compliment to the Americans, we were received first. Then we stood at the end of the hall and watched the others. Finally we all went in to dinner, and the King standing on the floor among the guests, cheek by jowl with the crowd, drank our health, to which we responded with a cheer. The delegates felt deeply grateful to the King and Queen for this royal invitation, and for the exceedingly friendly unceremonious manner of their Majesties.

The next morning we went to the University Aula, where the honorary degrees were to be distributed. After a brief spell of music, a general historical address was delivered in Norwegian by Professor Spang; but a French 'crib' had previously been handed to each delegate. Then the various Deans announced the list of honorary degrees. The names were read rapidly, and the recipients did not appear, as with us. The Dean of Theology came first, and delivered his remarks in German; then the Dean of Law, in English; then the Dean of Medicine, in English; then the Dean of Literature, in French; lastly the Dean of Science, in German. The last name on each list appeared to be the place of honour. Finally, to my great joy, the last name on the last list was Dr. Elkin! Then the delegate from Yale congratulated the delegate from the Connecticut Academy, and the delegate from the Academy congratulated the delegate from Yale.

That evening the Mayor and Commune of Christiania

gave a formal dinner in the Town Hall, where appropriate speeches were made between the courses. I found my entire Norwegian vocabulary, 'Skoal!' more than adequate.

The next day I went out to the beautiful cemetery to do homage at the graves of Ibsen and Björnson, who lie near together. Ibsen's monument is marked by a large hammer; Björnson had as yet no monument, no tomb, no stone; simply a mound of grass, grown over by wild flowers. A large fresh wreath lay upon it. . . . Before the theatre stand two colossal statues of Ibsen and Björnson, erected during the lifetime of these modern Norse gods. Ibsen's coat is buttoned tightly, and he is looking downward; Björnson's coat is flung wide open and his face looks defiantly up and out toward the world—for the personality of one was secretive, and the other just the contrary. The son of Ibsen married the daughter of Björnson, and their little boy often stood before the huge statues, and said proudly, 'These are my grandfathers!'

I heard an authentic anecdote in Christiania which I think had not been printed. When the statesmen of Norway were trying to arrange the separation from Sweden, Björnson, with his usual hot-headed and warm-hearted impetuosity, wrote a letter to the leading diplomat, volunteering his public services, and asking how he could most efficiently assist the cause. He received a telegram, 'Hold your tongue!'

Thursday evening the formal exercises were concluded by a gala performance in the National Theatre of Björnson's fine historical drama, *Maria Stuart*. This was particularly interesting to us, for only three weeks before we had stood in Holyrood Castle, Edinburgh. The acting and scenic effects were excellent, and the signal for beginning the play was the appearance of the King and Queen in the Royal Box, whereat the entire audience rose silently, and were rewarded by a gracious bow and smile from their Majesties.

The whole centenary was splendidly managed by patient, courteous, and efficient reception committees, every care was taken to see that each delegate enjoyed the occasion, and I am sure all the visitors were grateful to their kindly hosts.

54

JOURNEY TO RUSSIA

1911

IT is rather surprising that the short sea voyage from Stockholm to St. Petersburg is not better known in the western world. It is enchanting. We left Stockholm at six o'clock in the evening of a fine September day, and as we drew away, the sunset light over the fair city hung a new picture on the walls of my mind. It takes some five hours to reach the Baltic, five hours of constantly changing scenery, one view melting into another like a succession of dissolving panoramas. Hundreds of tiny wooded islands, dotted with châteaux and country houses; winking light-house towers: the grey sea and the long black land. Yes, and to my amazement and dismay, the yellow half-moon large and low! Every year I had told my Browning classes that the common interpretation of the famous poem, which places the visit at dusk, is incorrect; or else Browning's astronomy failed him. The half-moon is never low in the early evening in English or American latitudes. But here near the sixtieth parallel in September the half-moon leered at me just over the rim of a rocky hill. To be sure, it was not a precise half, something over, in fact, but close enough to be disquieting. Although it had no business to be there, it supplied the last touch of glory to the scene. We stood on the top deck, and beheld the spacious firmament on high, thick inlaid with patines of bright gold; while the long level light of the impossible moon fell across the darkening water and the myriad islands.

Some time in the night we crossed the Baltic, and early in the morning we entered the Gulf of Finland. The air was nipping and eager, but the sun shone from a cloudless sky. All day the steamerkin nosed her way through the blue sea, twisting and turning among the countless points of the earth's surface that were just able to keep their heads above water. A few of these were covered with green grass, and supported white farm buildings where laughing children ran out to see our transit, accompanied by dignified and serious dogs; but for the most part these elevations were bald rock, with a tall lighthouse as sole ornament. At five in the afternoon we reached Helsingfors, my farthest north, and stepped ashore to see the town, the boat not proceeding to St. Petersburg until late in the night. Here I obtained a clear notion of Finland's sentiment toward Russia. Prime Minister Stolypin had been shot the day before, and the evening paper reported him much better, on the road to recovery. A Finnish gentleman, highly educated, refined, tender-hearted, said to me with a smile, 'Yes, they say Stolypin is better: but we have our hopes.'

The passage across the gulf to Petersburg was rough, the clouded sky was low and harsh the next morning, and the sea was surly. Toward noon it cleared, and before two o'clock we saw the gilded domes and spires of Holy Russia. The approach to the great capital is immensely interesting, the boat moving through a long canal, passing interminable shipping. Finally, we docked, and after some delay with the passports—it was impossible to enter, leave, or visit any town in the empire without one—we drove across one of the bridges over the Neva to our hotel on a corner of the Nevski Prospect. Although it was September, the temperature was under fifty, and seemed colder. I had a severe cold, which had its origin in a bad chill which I had caught in rashly touching a piece of toast that a waiter brought me in a London hotel.

But I was right in style. Everybody in Petersburg had a cold. The coughing, sneezing, nose-blowing, and hawking reminded me grimly of Battell Chapel, where coughing drowned the parson's saw. Many of the people had their ears and mouths bandaged, while their feet were encased in huge boots—all seemed to be suffering from the foot and mouth disease. Never shall I forget the boots and overcoats on the Nevski Prospect. This question of leg-clothes would have interested the author of *Sartor Resartus*. In Edinburgh all the men and some of the suffragettes wore knickerbockers, with stockings that seemed an inch thick, made of material feathered like the legs of a setter. Scots of all ages and degrees donned the knickers. Tottering octogenarians, with wrinkled faces lost in a wealth of white whiskers, stumbled along Princes Street in motley knickerbockers, a world too wide for their shrunk shanks. In order to avoid the glare of publicity, I bought in Edinburgh a pair of these homespun garments myself, and tramped the city in them, much to the amusement of my comrade Professor Chittenden.

I tried them just once on the Nevski Prospect. Once was quite enough. Everyone stopped to stare. Had I worn a flowing scarlet robe, I should not have been so conspicuous. I was a mark for the populace. Officers gazed at me in cold amazement, as though I had the leprosy; while the more naïve inhabitants made audible comment, which was fortunately lost upon the victim. Then I tried the experiment of conventional clothing, but wore low shoes. Everyone gazed at my feet, some in wonder, some in admiration, some in apparent terror. I felt like a bold, bad man, but declined to fetter my legs in the enormous black knee-boots, which would have been as conspicuous elsewhere as the knickers were in Russia. Some twenty years ago, I walked the streets of Brussels with a curiously striped cap on my head. A gentleman looked at me earnestly, and then said in an almost reverent tone, and he said it three times, '*Nom de Dieu!*'

Americans at home show the same interest in strange clothing. Professor E.B.Wilson, then of the Yale Faculty, purchased a suit in Paris, which was 'just the thing' on the Avenue de l'Opéra. He wore it in America only once, and when I asked him why only once, he said that he tried it on Chapel Street. He got as far as Trinity Church, when a citizen of New Haven gazed at him steadfastly, and exclaimed, 'J——!'

Nearly every man on the Nevski seemed to be an officer or an official. There were an incredible number of uniforms, and as the overcoats, boots, and swords passed each other, the hand at the side rose to the cheek in a stiff salute, a salute that the projection of a half-inch would transform into the universal gesture of contempt, known and understood in all lands. One never forgets the Nevski. I see it as plainly in my mind's eye at this moment as I saw it in the grey Russian autumn. The broad avenue, crowded with the little Russian carriages, rolling with a dull sound over the wooden pavement, a pavement springy, as though the marsh lay just below; the almost total absence of automobiles, the roads outside the city being so bad that this vehicle was not useful; cathedrals, churches, and public buildings lining the sides of the street, with the needle gold spire of the Admiralty at the end; overhead the low, sombre sky, which often descended in a thick mist; the sidewalks always crowded with a moving mass of humanity, the conspicuous feature being the eternal overcoats and long boots.

The faces of the common people were sad to behold, both on the Nevski and in the churches alongside. Not only was there no hilarity, such as one sees in most cities;

the faces indicated an absence of illuminating ideas. They were blank, dull, apathetic, hopeless. Their religion seemed to be one of fear. I stood on the front platform of an electric tram-car, and every time we passed a church—which means every few moments—the motorman took off his cap three times. But his expression, while intensely serious, seemed to indicate that he did this to ward off bad luck, rather than from a principle of glad and active worship. Inside the churches, at any hour of the day, I saw wretched men on their knees. They would press their foreheads to the stone floor, then cross themselves, then down with the forehead again. In a corner by the altar stood a priest, holding a dirty cross: a constant procession of diseased and filthy folk trooped up, and kissed the cross. I accompanied my friend Gaylord '76, to the Russian Y.M.C.A., where a mass was held for the soul of Stolypin. Two priests chanted and swung incense, and we all got down on our knees and held lighted candles. Mr. and Mrs. Gaylord did a great work in St. Petersburg for young men, being careful to keep absolutely aloof from politics. Years ago, amid the greatest difficulties, they founded a Y.M.C.A., where religious exercises were held, lessons in modern languages and practical business and scientific work given, the building including an excellent gymnasium and reading room. Then the Gaylords went to Moscow to found a similar organization there. Today Franklin Gaylord at the age of 82 is full of vigour.

Armed with a French Baedeker (there was none in English) we saw the chief sights of the Russian capital. In the temporary absence of the Tsar, we visited the Winter Palace, the most interesting room being the study of Alexander II, with all his favourite things just as he left them before the assassination. We spent hours in the Hermitage, one of the finest art galleries in Europe—what stunning Murillos!

One afternoon I walked the entire length of the Nevski Prospect, no mean achievement in a heavy overcoat. I began at the banks of the restless, blustering Neva, to get a good running start: passed the extraordinary statue of Peter the Great, came through the garden by the statue of Gogol, and with the Admiralty at my back entered the long avenue. I followed the immense extension of the Nevski, clear to the cemetery, and stood reverently in front of the statue of Dostoevski. Here, in January 1881, the body of the great novelist was laid in the grave, forty thousand persons present as mourners. Then, in a corner of the enclosure, I found the tomb of the composer Tchaikovsky, whose harmonies will delight the world forever. I gazed on the grave of Glinka, father of modern Russian music, but I searched in vain for the earthly resting-place of Rubinstein, also buried here. On account of the marshy soil, the graves are above instead of below the ground, exactly as at New Orleans: it is really a city of the dead. I passed out of the cemetery, walked through the grounds of the convent, and came clear outside the city, on the edge of a blank gloomy wide plain.

In Moscow we stayed at a vast caravanserai, cold as Siberia. Everyone who still believes in war ought to spend an hour in the Tretiakov gallery, and see the pictures by Vereschagin. They are too horrible to describe, but not so horrible as war. I walked up the hill and took off my hat in front of the statue of Pushkin, remembering that when this statue was uncovered in 1880, Turgenev and Dostoevski made speeches to the innumerable throng, the address of Dostoevski, with its text of universal brotherhood, being as great a masterpiece as any of his books.

Twenty-four hours on the train between Moscow and Warsaw gave us only a faint notion of the Russian country. Immense forests of white birch trees, their slender silver boles contrasting exquisitely with the red and gold flames of the leaves, the autumn sunlight glorifying them all. Well are these feminine trees called the queens of the forest. Sometimes, on emerging from the woods, the train came out on a prodigious steppe, where nothing broke the view to the far horizon. Many villages were simply a few huts around a big church. Women were working in the fields, bent over double to the ground, as though looking into their graves.

In Warsaw, the Roman Catholic churches were as noticeable as the Greek. We walked through the lovely Saxon gardens, in the shade of mighty old trees. The statue of Copernicus stands not far away, and I thought as I looked at it, how much greater a miracle he had wrought than Joshua. Joshua commanded the sun to stand still, but only for a short time: Copernicus put it in its proper place, and it has not dared to move around the earth once since he finished with it. Strolling toward the hotel I almost ran into a squad of soldiers, that came briskly around the corner: at the same moment, a very stiff officer advanced; the men saluted, not with the legs, as in Germany, but with a loud unanimous shout. Something struck me as irresistibly ludicrous in all this, and I unintentionally caught the officer's eye, not six feet away. I burst into a quite irrepressible roar of laughter, even though I feared he would smite me with his sword for *lèse majesté*. But my guffaw hit him on the funny-bone. He roared too, and then all the soldiers joined in one spontaneous burst of mirth. Without speaking a word to each other, we all seemed to agree subconsciously that this military business was silly and out-of-date, but that one must still go through the forms. These men had only three or four years to live (1911–15).

55

GERHART HAUPTMANN

On Friday, 29 September 1911, we were in the Hotel
Adlon in Berlin. I took the elevator and at the third floor
I stepped directly into the arms of a man hurrying to
enter it. As soon as I released myself from the clinch, I
asked 'Aren't you Gerhart Hauptmann?' He replied with
a smile, '*Das ist mein Name.*' Then I told him I had the
honour of teaching his plays to undergraduates at Yale
University, and I should like very much to have ten minutes of conversation at his convenience. He said his wife
was in the hospital and he was on his way thither. Naturally I apologized for keeping him even for a moment. He
said if I would be in the office of the hotel the next morning at ten o'clock, he would be very glad to talk with me.
I was there of course, and he was accompanied by his son,
a pretty boy about ten years old, and dressed like Little
Lord Fauntleroy.

Herr Hauptmann was kind, considerate, charming. He
impressed me as an absolutely sincere man, modest, quiet,
with strong convictions—later, when I got to know John
Galsworthy, the two men seemed to me in their ideas and
in their manner very much alike. I asked Mr. Hauptmann,
'Which of your plays do you think is the best?' Without
any hesitation he said, '*Und Pippa Tanzt.*' This surprised
me. He added that he had never enjoyed writing a play
so much as he did *Fuhrmann Henschel*. He said the dramatist must never think of the box-office or of the possible
financial success of his work; he must write plays, as he

must write everything else, only to express himself. I believe he meant this; it was not a pose; certainly not an excuse; it was sincere. I asked him if the box-office failure of many of his plays disturbed him at all. 'Not in the least,' he affirmed emphatically, 'I write only to please myself. If the people like it, well and good; if they don't, I can't help it.' I asked, 'Do you express your own opinions in your plays? Does the character Loth in *Vor Sonnenaufgang*, for example, represent your opinions?' 'No, I do not express my opinions in my plays; but after reading five or six of my plays, anyone ought to know well enough what kind of a fellow I am.' He added that while no character, not even Loth, should express the playwright's opinions, the whole play should always express the author's personality. 'The play *Pippa* is very subjective; it came right out of my brain.'

He liked Berlin better than Munich. A better place for him to live in and work.

He said he was writing a novel, some of the scenes of which would be laid in America, indeed in Connecticut. I told him I had heard he had a brother living in Stamford, Connecticut. 'No, that is not true.' 'But you, Herr Hauptmann, you have been in Meriden?' 'That is true.' When this novel *Atlantis* appeared the next year (1912) I naturally read it with great interest. Many people thought the shipwreck in it was the *Titanic* which had gone down in April of that year; but it was the *Elbe*, which sank in the North Sea some years earlier. In *Atlantis* he also describes a journey on the railway from New York to Meriden, and he mentions the interesting old negro who for many years came on board at New Haven selling sandwiches.

He told me he intended to write both novels and dramas and in the many years since this interview, he has carried out that intention. Although his first play *Vor Sonnenaufgang* (1889) is starkly naturalistic, Hauptmann is at heart a thorough romantic and idealist, as is shown in most of his writing, and as was abundantly clear to me in this conversation.

I asked him to sign his name in my copy of his novel, *Der Narr in Christo*, which he did, and wrote under his name, '*Kunst ist Religion*' ('Art is Religion'), which interested me. Perhaps it would have been nearer to the exact truth if he had written *Kunst ist meine Religion*. Art and religion seem to me quite different.

As I was about to take my leave, he said, 'I want you to talk with my little boy over yonder; please don't say a single word in German to him; I have had him taught English, and I want you to see if he speaks it well.' Mr. Hauptmann and I had not uttered a word of English. The boy came up to me with charming grace. I spoke to him in English, and he answered in fluent and perfect English, without a trace of accent. The father listened to our conversation with an approving smile. He was evidently proud.

After that conversation, I did not wonder at the almost idolatrous admiration for Hauptmann everywhere evident in Germany. Although only a minority of his plays have been successful on the stage, there is a streak of genius in nearly all of them. And he himself is a sincere idealist—a poet at heart. In the early years of this century, some newspaper in Berlin sent out a questionnaire to many thousands of readers—'who are the ten Germans now living who are most important for Germany?' The first name was of course the German Emperor, but that was a complimentary vote. The second was Gerhart Hauptmann. Further down on the list were Koch and Roentgen, Koch who by his discoveries had saved the lives of millions, and Roentgen, who had made possible the use of the X-ray; yet Hauptmann, who had never done anything useful or a day's work, in the ordinary sense of that word, was regarded as more important than great physicians or men of science. For, while men cannot live without bread, they cannot live on bread alone.

In 1932, when Hauptmann was seventy years old, I saw in Munich the first performance of his new play, *Vor Sonnenuntergang*; it was not successful, yet it had, like all his work, that indefinable sense of latent power. The Director of the theatre told me he had to leave out an enormous part of it for the stage production; even after this amputation it was too long.

During the summer of 1911, we never heard any Englishman say a word about Germany or about the possibility of an approaching war; but when, late in August, we arrived in Hamburg, the German bellboy who showed us to our room asked if we were British or American. On hearing our answer, he said, 'Well, I want you to know that Germany can beat England in the war, and we're going to do it.' During that autumn in Germany, I heard similar talk from many Germans of varying degrees of education and social position. They all seemed to be eagerly looking forward to the war, and the hatred of England was intense and universal. When I ventured to suggest to a highly educated German that such a war would be the most disastrous calamity imaginable, he said, 'It is bound to come, and the sooner the better.' There seemed to be organized hostility to England felt by all classes of Germans. And when the war did come three years later, I do not believe any country has ever entered into a war with such united and such holy enthusiasm. It was like a release of long pent-up emotion. It is difficult to realize this now, because after the war Germany felt almost an affection for England, while her hatred was transferred to France; but there is no doubt that for the five or six years preceding the war, German public opinion was so inflamed with anti-British feeling, that one does not have to search far for the *immediate cause of the war*, whatever the remoter antecedents may have been. This hatred was like a swelling river that finally overflowed. I do not know whether anything could have been done to prevent it.

A strange thing happened that first night we spent in Germany in 1911. If we had been fanatical or suspicious, we should have believed that we had been deliberately poisoned, the Hamburg hotel waiters or cooks thinking we were British. I did not then and do not now believe it; but I know we came very near to death. We sat down to dinner and began with soup. I took one spoonful, and whispered to my wife, 'Don't touch another drop of this soup.' We had had only one table-spoonful apiece. To me there was a horrible taste in it. I called the waiter, and explained to him that there was something fatally wrong with the soup. He expressed surprise and scepticism, but I have always been glad I did not believe him. That night we were both taken ill, with every symptom of poisoning, and had to remain in bed, both with a temperature, and violent stomach disorder, for twenty-four hours. Indeed we should have stayed in bed three or four days, but we were anxious to leave that hotel. We went to Copenhagen, and got medical treatment. Although I believe it was an accident, I also believe that if we had taken half a dozen spoonfuls of that soup, we should both have died.

56

THE RIVIERA

1912

'ROUGH winds do shake the darling buds of May,' said the Englishman Shakespeare: I wonder what he would have said could he have seen the Riviera roses bending their pretty heads to the soft breath of February.

We left Munich early in the morning of the second day of February, in a blinding blizzard. All day long the snow fell, drawing an impenetrable curtain between us and the mountains as the train climbed and descended the Brenner pass. Verona was dressed in white, and the two gentlemen did not appear; when we reached Milan late in the evening, the city was buried in snow. Oh what a difference in the morning! At San Remo, the sky was a brilliant, cloudless blue, the dark-blue sea was trimmed with ermine: green grass, palms, orange and lemon trees everywhere, so that the whole place seemed to be full of gorgeous blue and green and gold. In spite of the high wind that sent tremendous waves crashing on the rocks, the air was gentle and pleasant: there were no teeth in the breeze.

We left the *train de luxe*, which like many luxurious people was six hours late, at Nice: and put up at a hotel which we could not put up with long. The food was excellent, and our rooms—it sounds impressive to use the plural—faced the splendid sea. But the table-manners of the 'guests' of that inn baffle description. I am no glass of fashion and mould of form, and do not pretend to be an

authority on etiquette. Yet, democratic as I am, I was
driven from that hotel at the point of the toothpick. Never
have I seen such a collection of sword-swallowers. There
was a dear old woman, who sat at a table close to ours: she
had a face that brought to mind the portraits of our New
England ancestors of the seventeenth century; her expression in repose was prim, austere, and yet not unkind. But
when she gathered, with infinite pains and astonishing
skill, a conglomerate mass of meat, gravy, and vegetables
on the long blade of her knife, and played the game right
up to the handle, I was fascinated: looking the other way,
with the hope of finding someone less expert, I saw worse
things. . . . A thesis should be written on 'The Decay of
the Toothpick.' In the days of Queen Elizabeth, it was the
height of fashion to parade the central aisle of St. Paul's,
bearing a toothpick in the mouth, and twisting it without
hands, as a politician worries his cigar: even a hundred
years ago, the toothpick was in great vogue, for in one of
Jane Austen's novels, I think it is *Sense and Sensibility*,
the young exquisite enters the expensive shop to buy a new
toothpick case. But things have changed. . . . The air in
this dining room was so full of toothpicks that it looked as
though Birnam wood had come to Dunsinane. Some kept
them in the mouth while eating and drinking: but the majority, after searching each remote orifice with scrupulous care,
and examining with loving interest the trophies of the chase,
used the weapon for purposes of emphasis and gesticulation.

No American accustomed to a comfortable house should
patronize a hotel on the Riviera where the furnace is not
taken seriously. How miserable it is to be colder indoors
than outside! I received an epistolary masterpiece from
my colleague Clarke, who was shivering in a hotel at
Cannes. 'They have central heating here,' he wrote, 'but
it is much more central than heating.' From the point of
view of physical comfort, I suppose one should visit Russia

in the winter, and Italy in the summer. A friend of mine, who had spent the winter in Stockholm, went to Italy in the spring, and was colder there in a week than he had been in three months in the frozen north. George Ade tried Venice in January; but declared that he would spend the next winter in Duluth, where he could keep warm.

Many French folk cannot bear to give out money for fuel. They think it a wicked waste. I remember with what horror our landlady in Paris watched me jovially heaving on to the fire the neat little lozenges of coal; she saw. the francs going right up the chimney. One mouse-poor student in Paris told me that he kept warm during the entire winter with one billet of wood. It seems he lived on the sixth floor. He hurled the stick out of the window, ran down six flights, retrieved it, and ran up again; this kept him warm fifteen minutes, when once more he threw the thing out of the window; by repeating this process every quarter of an hour, he got along famously.

I shall not soon forget the morning of Washington's Birthday. Our hotel at Mentone crowns a high hill, and we lived at the top of the house with a balcony commanding a marvellous view of mountains, terraces, orange-groves, gardens, town, and sea. I was awakened by the morning-star glaring directly into my left eye. The star stuck out of the sky so far I thought it was going to fall, and went out on the balcony to see it drop. There I beheld the great drama of the dawn, with the protagonist still invisible, but evidently waiting for his cue. He got it, and made a magnificent entrance. Straight out of the waves he rose in majesty, and came walking on the water, flooding the sea and the mountains with golden light.

> Full many a glorious morning have I seen
> Flatter the mountain tops with sovereign eye,
> Kissing with golden face the meadows green,
> Gilding pale streams with heavenly alchemy.

In 1911 Nice was a city with about the same population as New Haven, whereas Cannes and Mentone were like villages. We were in Nice during the heart of the Carnival, which I found not particularly interesting. It is too completely syndicated for the benefit of visitors. There was too much organized cheering and little spontaneous mirth. Even the far-heralded battle of flowers aroused no enthusiasm, because there was no gusto in it. A long and minute list of things that one must and that one must not do was carefully printed in the papers, and the zest went out of the parade. Many once quaint and beautiful customs and many charming places are now spoiled by being systematically financed and managed, before they meet the eye of the tourist. I remember even in that wonderful sea-village of Clovelly in England, much of the striking effect was lessened for me by seeing the old salts, clad in neat blue jerseys, standing about in attitudes that savoured of long and careful rehearsal. Instead of looking like those who go down to the sea in ships, they looked like a chorus in a musical comedy.

Mentone is more attractive than Nice, being situated on a little strip of land just between the ragged mountains and the blue sea. The twenty-mile drive over the hills from Nice is picturesque. And the view from the sea-front of Mentone of the long, winding, precipitous Italian coast is beautiful, and seems to change in colour every hour. One meets few Americans in this town; they are nearly all English. And although the English at this hotel are for the most part delightful companions, I overheard a conversation in the village between two sons of Albion that seemed insular. One was complaining to the other of the mistakes made by the Mentone compositors in a small bit of English printing he had ordered. 'You see they are all foreigners,' he remarked angrily. To speak of Frenchmen in a French town as foreigners, appeared to me to lack breadth of view.

The large number of English gentlemen who, from the American point of view, do nothing, is a never-ending source of wonder. In Ireland I met an English baronet at dinner. He said to me, 'I suppose you have always worked for a living, always had a regular occupation?' 'Certainly,' said I: 'I have supported myself since the summer I was graduated from college.' 'Ah,' said he, 'you are much happier than I. I have never done anything; my father, grandfather, and all my ancestors never did anything.' When I narrated this incident to an English lady at Mentone, she said, 'But most of the English gentlemen I know are very busy—busy all the time. They hunt, shoot, fish, play golf, polo, and tennis. They are not idle.' She enquired, 'You haven't any regular class of gentlemen in America, have you?' I replied, 'No, not in the sense in which you use the term.' 'But it seems strange that you have no recognized superior class. Doesn't the man who mows your lawn take off his hat to you?' 'No, he does not; and if he did, I should then take off mine.' 'How extraordinary!' said she.

The Secretary of Yale University, Anson Phelps Stokes, was staying at Cannes, and on Lincoln's Birthday took us for a superb motor excursion over the mountains. The road at first was so close to the sea that we were nearly splashed by the breakers; then we climbed the heights and far away saw the little town of Grasse, 'sown in a wrinkle of the monstrous hill, sparkling in the sunshine like a grain of salt,' as Tennyson says. Overhead the deep blue sky; below us the deep blue sea; and in the distance, tier on tier of snow-capped mountains. One afternoon Stokes and I went over to Monte Carlo, where every prospect pleases, and only man is vile. In the midst of that international crowd, an extraordinary collection of human curiosities, we appeared like Christian and Faithful at Vanity Fair. When I attempted to enter the famous gambling-rooms, I was

kindly but firmly shoved back; the guardian pointed eloquently to my *knee-breeches*, saying that no one was allowed near the tables unless properly clad. So I stood at
the portal and watched the aristocratic sansculottes pass
majestically by. My rejection seemed to amuse Stokes
prodigiously.

We had three Springs in 1912 instead of one: and it
would be difficult to say which was the most beautiful.
The roses on the Riviera in February, the bright fruit-
blossoms in Italy in April, and the magnificent horse-
chestnut trees on the Champs-Élysées in May, gave us four
months of the very pick of the season. We reached Florence
on 26 March, a day of cloudless, windless sunshine. There
we ran across one of the Honolulu Judds—may their tribe
increase—and proceeded to visit every spot in the city
associated with the Brownings. We gazed on the panorama
of the town from the height of San Miniato, and recited
the first two stanzas of 'Old Pictures in Florence.' We went
to the Square of San Lorenzo, where on a hot June noon,
Browning found the old yellow book, and we followed his
footsteps by the Strozzi, by the Pillar, by the Bridge, till
we reached his home in Casa Guidi. We grasped the iron
rings on the palace that casts the shadow, and in imagination saw Fra Lippo Lippi descending hand under hand,
and running after the girls. We regarded in another square
the bronze Duke—symbol of perpetual lack of motion—
gazing forever at the farthest window facing the east. Then
we went out to the lovely cemetery, and stood by the
graves of Elizabeth Barrett Browning, Landor, Clough,
Theodore Parker of Boston, and the American historian,
Richard Hildreth. When I was an undergraduate, i asked
Professor Sumner, 'What is the best history of America?'
Gruffly he grunted, 'Hildreth's!' So I read every word of
the six volumes, and have ever since had an enormous respect for this historian, whose sole object in writing was

to tell the truth. Twenty years after graduation, I told Mr. Sumner that I had done homage at the grave in Florence, and he was alertly interested. He was unaware of the location of Hildreth's dust, and I had the satisfaction, which came to very few, of telling Mr. Sumner something he had not already known. The tombstone is like the man it covers—simple and upright—marked only with the name and the date of his death.

We attracted some attention on these Florentine excursions, for besides Baedekers, we carried an even better guide, the Works of Browning. A pleasant result of this was that we made many converts; the booksellers straightway sold out all their Brownings, and wondering what on earth had happened, began to write to London for fresh supplies. We gathered accretions as we swept along. I remember the surprise and delight of an English lady, who annexed herself to us in front of Casa Guidi, when I pointed out to her the little terrace where Browning paced up and down in the night, thinking of Pompilia—and I read aloud the wonderful lines in which the poet describes this memorable experience. I think she had never heard them before, but she got out her notebook, and then made hot-foot for the nearest bookshop.

After ten golden days in Florence—I admire Rome for what it has been, I love Florence for what it is—we set out on the trail of Caponsacchi and Pompilia, as they fled through the gate of San Clemente in Arezzo in the solid black before the April dawn. Perugia is high up on the hill, with its twisted, narrow, sinuous streets wriggling over each other like a mess of worms—but in the midst of mediaeval memories we received a shock, for a huge placard near the Cathedral announced a great football match, 'Perugia vs. Ancona.' Here we left the railway, and drove southward in an open carriage on the same highway, where on another April morning, two hundred and fifteen years before, the young priest and the young wife rolled in mad haste toward Rome. The scenery has not changed; we saw the same miracle of the awakening year; fruit trees in blossom, green pastures, rich upturned earth with the peasants driving the white oxen; on our left, the bold mountains, carrying on their tops the last fragments of the defeated forces of winter.

We stopped some hours on the holy ground of Assisi, and visited the wonderful churches within the walls. Driving on again toward Foligno, we entered the great edifice that holds the first oratory of St. Francis, and pondered on the enormous changes in the world's history made by one lonely man. It was dark when Caponsacchi and Pompilia reached Foligno, but we passed through the gates an hour before sunset. Here we had a curious repetition of their experience on the way. The lady asked her friend

> How do you call that tree with the thick top
> That holds in all its leafy green and gold
> The sun now like an immense egg of fire?

(It was a million-leaved mimosa.)

Well, outside the walls we stood in front of an immense mimosa, and the bright sun just over the western horizon, shining directly through the thick mass of tiny leaves, seemed to be doing its very best to reproduce the picture that arrested the attention of Pompilia.

57

THE FANO CLUB

THE next day was Easter, glorious and cloudless, as Easter should be. We left for a time the Road to Rome, and carried out a project that had been in my mind for eight years. I had never met anyone of any nationality who had ever seen the little town of Fano, on the Adriatic, made immortal by Browning's splendid poem, 'The Guardian Angel.' We took the train to the beautiful city of Ancona, and then a branch road took us on the very edge of the blue sea to Fano. On the way we crossed the Metaurus, on whose banks was fought the battle that changed civilization, and in the course of an hour we came to the small city and realized our dreams.

In the Summer of 1848 Mr. and Mrs. Robert Browning left their house in Florence and travelled all night in the diligence over the Apennines to the east coast, their intention being to escape from the intolerable July heat of Florence and find solace in the cool sea air of Fano.

Fano is an old Roman town, with a Roman wall still in a fair state of preservation; by looking at the map of Italy you will see it is about thirty miles north of Ancona. It has a magnificent bathing beach, where people have enjoyed swimming for more than 2,000 years.

The Brownings found Fano even hotter than Florence; and, looking about the city for some shade, they happened by chance to enter the Church of San Agostino. There, in the chapel of the edifice, they were thrilled to discover a large painting, *The Guardian Angel* (*L'Angelo Custode*), by

a third-rate painter of the seventeenth century named
Guercino. For once in his life Guercino had achieved a
masterpiece; but it was unknown to the world. They were
so excited by the splendour and beauty of this painting
that they went to see it three times.

Then at Ancona, resting in the hotel, Browning wrote
one of the greatest of his poems, under the inspiration of
the picture. So far as I know, he had no copy of it with
him, but remembered the details.

The poem—'The Guardian Angel, A Picture at Fano'—
was first published in 1855 in the collection in two volumes
of *Men and Women.*

The picture represents death, birth, earth, and heaven.
On a large tomb stands a little child; the angel is teaching
the child to pray, holding its little hands pressed together;
the angel is looking out over the earth, perhaps for more
persons who need his protection; the child is looking up
past the angel's face into heaven.

In the poem Browning expresses the wish that he might
take the place of the child and receive the tender care of
the angel; and if this were granted, he would not look into
heaven, he would look into the angel's face. The last three
stanzas of the poem are a postscript; he sent it to his friend
Alfred Domett, then living in New Zealand.

This poem became so famous that it called the picture
out of the obscurity where it had reposed for so many years
and gave it a new lease of life. In many picture shops in
various parts of Italy I saw photographs of it, and in some
editions of Browning the picture was engraved.

But I wondered why no-one ever went to Fano to see the
original. The town is easy enough to visit. Every train
from Venice to Brindisi, running along the east coast of
Italy, stops at Fano. Ancona is an important seaport, and
there is a daily express train from Ancona to Rome. I
suppose the reason why no Americans ever went to Fano

was that it is off the beaten track. Americans, of course, see Florence and Venice and Rome. Many of them go to Milan and the Italian lakes; but Fano, never.

This ancient city was visited by Montaigne in his famous journey to Italy, 1580–1581, and I find in his diary the following entry (tr. E. J. Trechmann).

I forgot to say that at Ancona, in the church of San Ciriaco, there is a low tombstone of one *Antonia Rocamoro patre, matre Valetta, Galla, Aquitana, Paciotto, Urbanati, Lusitano nupta*, who has been buried ten or twelve years. We left there early in the morning, and followed the seacost by a very agreeable road. Near our dinner-time we crossed the river Metro, *Metaurus*, by a large wooden bridge, and dined at

FANO, fifteen miles, a little town in a pretty and very fertile plain adjoining the sea, rather badly built, very closed in. We were very well treated there as regards bread, wine and fish; the accommodation is not up to much. Fano has this advantage over the other towns on this coast, as Sinigaglia, Pesaro and others, that it has plenty of fresh water, many public fountains and private wells, whereas the others have to go as far as the mountains to fetch their water. We saw here a large ancient arch, on which there is an inscription under the name of Augustus, *qui muros dederat*. The town was formerly called Fanum, and was *Fanum Fortunae* (The Temple of Fortune).

Almost throughout Italy they boult their flour with wheels, by means of which the baker does more work in an hour than we in four.

In nearly all the hostelries you find rhymesters, who make rhymes on the spot, applicable to the people present. There is an instrument in every shop, even in those of the butchers at the street corners.

This town is renowned above all those in Italy for its handsome women: we saw none, but some very ugly ones; and when I questioned an honest man of the town, he told me that the age of them was past.

You pay on this route about 10 sous for the table, 20 sous a day per man; the horse, for hire and expenses, about 30 sous: which makes 50 sous.

This town belongs to the Church.

In 1900 I began to ask persons who had lived twenty years in Italy if they had ever seen Fano; no one had.

Sir Rennell Rodd, British Ambassador to Italy (1908–19), wrote a little poem about Fano, but that was the only reference I could discover from any contemporary.

Accordingly, on Easter Day 1912 we stood before the painting in the little church at Fano. There was a priest who had never seen an American; we were as fantastic figures to him as if we had been Eskimos or Kanakas. He walked around us, to get a front and rear view. Then he wished to show us the church; but I told him I was not interested in the ornate church, but only in the altarpiece in the chapel. He said no one had ever come there to see that. He, of course, had never heard of the existence of Browning. But when I told him of the great English poet, who had made this picture famous in all parts of the world, and that this year was the centenary of his birth, he became excited; I wrote in execrable Italian a one-page theme on Browning.

We scoured the city for picture postcards; we finally got about seventy-five, and sent them to various friends in America. These postcards never reached their destination. They are at the bottom of the Atlantic Ocean: all went down on the *Titanic*.

There in Fano on Easter Day we founded the Fano Club. Anyone could become a life member by doing three things. One must visit Fano. One must see the picture. One must send me a picture postcard postmarked Fano. When we returned home and were talking about this club, my colleague, Professor Alexander Evans, said this was the most exclusive club in the whole world; it had only two members. He immediately left for Italy and became the third member. Since that time the membership has steadily increased. Almost every month I receive a postcard from someone travelling in Italy who has just seen the picture. There are now over five hundred members. Many of these were brought in by my friend, Professor A.J.Armstrong of

Baylor University, Waco, Texas. He has taken parties of pilgrims there, and now on the wall of the church next to the picture is a tablet placed there by the Texas pilgrims.

In 1932—exactly twenty years after our first visit—we stood once more in Fano. But this time the picture was not in the church, though it is there now. Fano had been roused from its sleep of centuries by an earthquake, which had specialized on the church of San Agostino. The picture was shaken up; the wall on which it leaned was broken.

It took many months to make the necessary repairs; and in April 1932, we saw the picture, outside of its frame, leaning against the wall in a room in the city museum. Although it looks better in its natural setting as an altar-piece, still, there was one advantage in seeing it in the museum. The light was stronger. We sent an Italian painter from Florence, who made a life-size copy of the original, and now we have in New Haven what is probably the only copy of this picture that has ever been painted.

On this last visit I went to the largest postcard shop in Fano, and found hundreds of cards on sale. The proprietor asked me why it was that so many Americans had come to his shop in the last few years, asking for postcards of *The Guardian Angel*. And there was one thing that puzzled him still more. Many of these pilgrims talked about a *Fano Club*. Could I give him any information about that? 'Sir,' said I, 'I am its founder and president.' He did obeisance; he will never forget the day when the president of this famous organization entered his shop and deigned to talk with him.

One diverting by-product gave me much amusement. So much had been said about the Fano Club that notices of it appeared in Italian newspapers. I received a questionnaire. What is the Fano Club? For what purpose was it founded? What is discussed at its meetings? Who is the president?

I forget what I replied, but I suppose I gave assurance that the club had no political significance.

A number of my colleagues at Yale have followed the example set originally by Professor Evans. Professor Chauncey Brewster Tinker and his friend, the Rev. Dr. William Pitt McCune of New York, both of them former pupils of mine, arrived in Fano on a Sunday and could find only one picture postcard on sale, which was of a ramshackle bathing pavilion on the beach. Accordingly, they sent me this poem:

> To be in Italy and not see Fano?
> McCune and Tinker both cried, ' Ah, no!'
> For not to go, and here's the rub,
> Means missing Phelps's Fano Club.
> On Sunday at Fano shops close, all and each
> Save this poor place on the bathing beach.
> But even this we think, by Jiminy,
> Is better than a card from Rimini.

Many Yale students who had taken my course in Browning have visited Fano. At the annual dinners of the Fano Club on 7 May, Browning's birthday, we have received cables from high officials in the city of Fano, many telegrams, and delightful letters in Italian from Dean Wigmore of Northwestern University and many others. Sending Americans to Fano has been, I think, one of the major achievements of my life.

The Fano Club was also enriched by Henry T. Rowell, a Punditical member of the Senior class at Yale (now on the Faculty) and by two of Father McCune's New York parishioners, Constance A. Jones and Helena Paul Jones, who commemorated the fact that they followed their rector and Professor Tinker thither, in these stirring lines:

> To be in Italy and not see Fano?
> McCune and Tinker once cried, ' Ah, no!'
> So what could good Ignatians do
> But follow in their footsteps too?

And following, as you will see,
Our minds are filled with poesy.
And if the merest mortal dare
Her own poor efforts to compare,
We think we sing a better tune
Than either Tinker or McCune!

Some days after our Fano pilgrimage, we resumed our *Ring and the Book* journey; we visited the dreary little village near Rome, where the infuriated Guido came face to face with the runaways, Castelnuovo. We saw

The old tower, and the little white-walled clump
Of buildings and the cypress-tree or two,

and as we gazed on the windows of the wretched inn, the tragedy took on the air of reality.

Our hotel in Rome was close to the Piazza del Popolo, where Guido and his four accomplices were executed on the 22 February 1698. We followed the track of the condemned men as they were led from the prison cell by Castle Angelo, across the Tiber, through the Via Panico, Via Governo Vecchio, Via Pasquin, Piazza Navona, by the Pantheon, through the Piazza di Colonna, and down the full length of the Corso to the place of death. As Guido entered the Corso on his cart, he saw plainly in the distance the obelisk of the Square. What must have been his feelings during the last ten minutes of that journey, as he drew nearer and nearer to this ancient column?

We walked on other days through the Via Vittoria, the 'aspettable street' where Pompilia lived: entered the church of San Lorenzo in Lucina, looking on the lions at the door, that terrified her in childhood. This was the church where she was married, and where the bodies of her parents were exposed in front of Guido Reni's *Crucifixion*. Every detail of the church is still exactly as Browning describes it. And in the church of the Gesu, we saw the huge lump of lapis lazuli, mentioned by the dying delirious Bishop of St. Praxed's, as he gave instructions for his tomb.

On our way north again, we stopped at Chiusi, through which Guido rushed on his chase after the young pair. He took the shorter route to Rome and I have never understood why the fugitives took the longer one. But we remembered also that Chiusi used to be called Clusium, and in the railway station we shouted in chorus

> Lars Porsena of Clusium
> By the nine gods he swore

our enthusiasm arousing the officials on the platform.

At Siena, remembering that one of Browning's worst poems was written about old Pacchiarotto, we studied his curious work with some attention. Siena is probably the greatest cat town in the world. I counted nine cats in about nine paces. I stopped to caress each one. It is well to do this, for their owners immediately take a pleased interest in their furry possessions, and are sure to treat them with increased respect. I asked many Italians, 'How old is your cat?' and I never failed to receive immediately the precise number of years, showing that the animal is appreciated.

We reached London on the eve of Browning's one hundredth birthday, and the next morning—the seventh of May—I traversed the Southampton Street, across the river in Camberwell, where he was born on 7 May 1812. In the afternoon I attended the exercises in Westminster Abbey, which were devoted to his memory. Only a few feet from his grave, the choir sang a portion of his poem *Saul*, and some stanzas from Mrs. Browning's *He giveth his beloved sleep*. Then we went into the little College Hall, where interesting addresses were given by those who had known Browning personally. The son of Lord Houghton presided; a letter was read from Browning's son in Italy; the son of Tennyson was present, and the grandson of Coleridge.

58

HENRY JAMES

I FIRST saw Henry James in 1911 in New Haven. He had been staying with some friends in Farmington, Conn., and he seemed to enjoy motor trips more than anything else. Miss Pope, who brought him from Farmington in her motor car, said that if she asked him if he would like to meet some people at a luncheon, he would say No; but if she suggested a journey in an automobile, he gladly agreed to that, and never asked whither they were going. Accordingly on this day, 23 May 1911, she brought him from Farmington to New Haven, where he was the guest of honour at a luncheon given by Mr. and Mrs. Harry Day. Mrs. W.E.Hocking, Mrs. Kingsley Blake, and Mr. George Seymour were present.

I had supposed that Mr. James would be reserved and remote, difficult to talk with; on the contrary, he was absolutely charming. He made me feel immediately at ease, and as if we had been intimate friends. 'Come and sit here with me on the sofa,' he said, and put his arm affectionately around my shoulder. I had with me a copy of his book *The Turn of the Screw* and I told him that although his literary style had often been called obscure, there was something else in his work that was even more difficult to read. 'And what is that?' 'That is your handwriting.' He smiled and took pains to write his name very slowly and distinctly in my copy of his book. I told him I thought *The Turn of the Screw* was the most terrifying ghost story I had ever read; that I read it when it first appeared, late at night, and when I had finished it, I did not dare go down stairs and put out the hall light. However, as I did not wish to leave the gas burning all night, there was a struggle between my Yankee parsimony and my fear of the dark. Finally I got my wife to stand at the head of the staircase. 'Don't you go away for a moment! don't you take your eyes off me; for if you do, I'll never get this light out!' I extinguished it and raced upstairs as if the devil and all his angels were after me.

Mr. James expressed delight. 'Do you know, I wrote that story with the intention of terrifying every reader, and in the course of its composition, I thought it would be a total failure. I dictated every word of it to a Scot, who never from first to last betrayed the slightest emotion, nor did he ever make any comment. I might have been dictating statistics. I would dictate some phrase that I thought was blood-curdling; he would quietly take this down, look up at me and in a dry voice, say "What next?"'

It has been wittily said that Henry James conversed as if he were reading proof. This is really true. In desultory conversation on that day and on another occasion in England, he would stop in the middle of a sentence, feeling around in his mind for the right word; if he could not find it, he would abruptly change the subject, rather than use what he regarded as not quite the accurate or suitable word.

The next time I saw Henry James was on Saturday afternoon, 1 June 1912 in London, at a tea given by the English novelist, Mrs. W. K. Clifford; only Henry James and May Sinclair were present. The conversation turned on the novels of Thomas Hardy; and I expressed my feelings of many years before, when I read *Tess* for the first time. The events and persons in that story seemed so real to me, and the catastrophe so overwhelming, that for **days** after I had finished it, I could not shake off my depression. Miss Sinclair said that the same sense of reality impressed her in reading the novels of Mrs. Humphry Ward. This appalled Henry James, who said, '*May Sinclair, May Sinclair*, such a remark may do credit to your heart, but where does it leave your head?'

Drawn off into a corner of the room by Henry James, I spoke of testing a written style by reading it aloud; that I had found many passages in Browning which seemed obscure to the eye were transparently clear when I read them aloud. To my surprise, he became excited. With intense earnestness he whispered in my ear, 'I have never in my life written a sentence that I did not mean to be read aloud, that I did not specifically intend to meet that test; you try it and see. Only don't you tell.'

There are writers who have an immense public and no fame; and there are a few who have never had many readers yet are truly famous. It is interesting to see what has happened to many authors in the twenty years since Henry James's death. His fame is higher and greater now than it ever was; yet the number of his readers is still comparatively small. He himself would have been glad of a large constituency; it pained him that his books had so small sales; he suffered; but he would not change his method, or write in any manner except to satisfy himself.

He was appreciative of praise from individuals. I regard Henry James as perhaps the greatest literary critic America has ever produced. When his book *Notes on Novelists* appeared, I could not help writing and telling him of my enthusiasm; but I begged him not to acknowledge the letter; I told him I had the audacity to deliver a public lecture on his novels and I should advise my audience to read this latest critical work. He wrote me the following letter: and I have always been glad I had written him, because in the midst of his agony over the war—no unbereaved person suffered more—it evidently gave him a moment's gratification.

DECEMBER 15TH, 1914
21, CARLYLE MANSIONS,
CHEYNE WALK, S.W.

DEAR W.L.PHELPS.

But I *must* thank you for the pleasure given me by your generous lines about my "Notes"—letting you measure what that is by the fact that under this huge nightmare, the unprecedented oppression or obsession of our public consciousness here, pleasure (save of the grim sort that premonitions of Victory, terrifically paid for, bring) is very hard to take and very questionable even to desire. However, I rejoice without scruple in what you tell me of your so liberal appreciation of my book—and if I could only have been present in time—and in spirit—at your expounding lecture (it would have helped things even for your author), this would have represented, oh, such a blest break in the constant comprehensive ache of yours all faithfully.

HENRY JAMES

Lady Ritchie (Thackeray's daughter) told me a good story about Henry James. One day as she was entering Paddington Station and was carrying under her arm a copy of a novel by him, she had the good fortune to meet him. 'Look, Henry James, here I am carrying one of your works to read on the train, and I meet the author himself!' He simulated dismay. 'My dear Lady Ritchie, what bad luck for you! Don't you know that you have there a copy of the most expensive edition of that work, and a new edition has just been issued for six shillings?' 'Don't you worry about that, Henry James. I just bought this at a second-hand bookstall for *one* shilling.'

I coined a phrase to describe Henry James's style both in writing and in conversation—*verbose reticence*. He wrapped his meaning in layers of words, but he did not tell you much, and you had to dig it out for yourself. An incident told me by Sir James Barrie illustrates what I mean. Barrie said that one cold, dark autumn afternoon he and James went to a matinée to see a play. After the play was over, they stood on the pavement discussing it. James was describing how the play impressed him. Gradually it grew very dark; after an hour or so, it began to rain; Barrie finally suggested they enter a taxicab; the two men drove around for an hour or so, while James continued his criticism of the play; and finally, Barrie said he must leave him, as he had to dress for dinner. 'As I left him,' said Sir James, 'I gathered that he thought the play would do no harm.'

Mr. Robinson Smith tells me the following story. Henry James was saying that a bevy of young ladies had invited themselves to tea. 'Were they pretty?' asked Mr. Gosse. 'Pretty! Good Heavens! yet one of the wantons had something of a cadaverous grace!'

Mrs. Edith Wharton told me that once at a dinner-party where Henry James was among the guests, a message came from a newspaper asking her if she would verify a rumour. She read the message aloud to the assembled party—'are you and Henry James engaged to be married?' The silence was broken by Henry James, exclaiming 'And yet they say truth is stranger than fiction!'

Barrie told me that if he were in trouble, the first two men he would go to for assistance would be Bernard Shaw and Henry James. Everyone who knew Mr. James intimately had experience of his extraordinary kindness and marvellous tact. Miss Clare Benedict, in her books about Constance Fenimore Woolson and *The Benedicts Abroad*, describes the wonderful kindness of Henry James after the death of Constance. He gave up everything for six weeks, devoting himself to the bereaved family, taking on his own shoulders innumerable burdens of practical detail.

It would be difficult to imagine a more beautiful letter than the following which Mr. James wrote to Mrs. and

Miss Benedict, just before they took ship for Europe—beautiful in its sympathy and in its practical, definite assistance. He fulfilled the Scriptural admonition by really bearing their burden.

> Almost by this you will have heard from me that I will meet you at Genoa—be there when you arrive. I am sure Rome will be a very soothing, softening impression to you—that after a little . . . the horror of the weeks you have been living through will be lost in the simple assenting, participating tenderness with which (in regard to her memory and deep exemption now from everything that's hard in life) you will find yourselves thinking of her—till at last you will feel almost at peace in your acceptance. Meanwhile, only I live and think of living, from hour to hour, and day to day; it is perfect wisdom and it takes us through troubles that no other way can take us through . . . Have no plan whatever, in advance, about Venice . . . there is no need for any. The whole question will simplify itself, settle itself, facilitate itself, after you get to Italy . . . May you float down fast into kindly southern waters and meet the consoling, alleviating spring!

On 12 and 13 December 1915 Mrs. W. K. Clifford wrote me from London:

> I am so glad you remember that afternoon, dear Mr. Phelps, with beloved Henry James & one or two people here. This letter is so badly written I feel almost incoherent for I write it waiting for a telephone message from his illegible secretary (it is 10.30 on Sunday night) with the Dr.'s last report of him. He is very ill as the American papers I know have told you. We kept it out of the papers here till we heard it was in *The New York Times*. He had a slight stroke last Thursday week—a second one the next day, now an attack of pneumonia has developed and we fear the worst. Mrs. William James arrives at 3 p.m. tomorrow—we hope she may be in time. He is *very* dear to us. He has been so splendid too, ever since the war broke out, taking his part, & giving his share, & feeling it all intensely. He spent hours every week comforting the soldiers in Hospital—especially the French ones who were lonely in strange surroundings & found English difficult. It was in token of his love for the country he had lived in so long, & his sympathy with the allies—that he 'turned English' last summer. Not that he did not love his *own* country tho' after the

President's *first* note, which he thought fine and dignified, he has been disappointed in the attitude at Washington.

Monday 13th. I had to stop. He is better this morning but talking wildly. If he recovers we fear one side will be paralysed. Mrs. William James is expected anytime now. Her boat has been delayed by storms. All greetings to you both, . . .

Henry James died in his flat in Chelsea, 28 February 1916.

On 16 March 1916 Mrs. Clifford wrote me, and at the top of her letter she had written her name in full, with this note, 'I put my formal name thus for the benefit of the Censor. *Are* our letters to *you* opened? It is too funny or wd be if it were not sad.'

And at the end of the letter she wrote 'P.S. It is so strange. All our letters from America are opened by the Censor. Even those with the imprint of well-known names —I had one from the Century Co. & one from Harper's— both opened. Rather absurd?'

And here is the part of the letter concerning Henry James.

I do so want you to know that though it was too late to give the message in your letter to dear Henry James, I gave it to Mrs William James who was over here; and she seemed pleased and touched by it. Henry, as I think I told you, had two strokes before Christmas, and complications followed, and his head was never clear afterwards, or rather not clear for the present time; concerning things that had happened five-and-twenty years ago he was fairly lucid, but later things were all confused with him. It is a great loss. He was a great personality in London and everybody who knew him seemed to have felt his personal note, and of course in England we were so immensely touched at his becoming one of us in the darkest time our country has known for centuries. It was the most supreme proof he could give us of his sympathy and affection. But his *own* country must not for a moment think that he forgot it, for he didn't; and he left directions that his ashes, after cremation, were to be taken back to it. There was much talk of a service in Westminster Abbey; the Prime Minister approved of it and the Dean was quite willing there should be one, providing the Chapter consented (which was a matter of course). But Mrs. William James, very wisely I think, refused all idea of it. The simpler service in the little church not a stone's throw from his flat, was more in accord with his life, she said—better befitted the New Englander. So thus it was; and a most beautiful and dignified farewell took place in the little church that is now centuries old and will now forever be identified with him. I daresay you saw a letter about it from Edmund Gosse in The Times. The notices in the English and French papers have been wonderful and show how much he was thought of in Europe.

My acquaintance with Mrs. W. K. Clifford, which ripened into an intimate friendship, began in 1919. When I was an undergraduate editor of the *Yale Literary Magazine* in 1887, I reviewed Professor Clifford's book *Lectures and Essays*, which had been published after his death. Clifford was a brilliant mathematician and philosopher, who died in 1879, at the early age of thirty-four.

In 1891 I read a novel called *Love-Letters of a Worldly Woman*, by Mrs. W. K. Clifford. I enjoyed this story immensely: it made a permanent impression. I thought it would be interesting to know the author of such a book, though I never expected to meet her. In 1910 I published a book called *Essays on Modern Novelists*. To my surprise, I received a letter from her, in which she said that she supposed I had never heard of her or of her work, but that if only some critic would write about her as I had written of the novelists discussed in my book, how happy it would make her! I immediately wrote her expressing my delight in her novel read twenty years before, and also of the fact that I had reviewed her husband's book, so that she could not possibly appear to me as a stranger.

Two years later I saw her for the first time in her home near Paddington Station. A brave, gallant high-spirited woman, and almost any afternoon at her tea-parties one met some of the most interesting people in London. Sir Frederick Pollock, Dean Inge, Shaw, May Sinclair, and many others.

We enjoyed an amusing incident one night at the theatre. Mrs. Clifford had just written a vigorous letter to the *Times* asking if something could not be done to prevent people from coming late to the theatres; they climbed over people's ankles, interrupted the play, and were an unpardonable interruption. The night after this appeared, we were enjoying the first performance of a charming comedy called *Many Waters*, when, some twenty minutes after the play had begun, in came Mrs. Clifford and a friend, and climbed over a number of spectators to reach their seats, in the middle of the row, directly in front of us. She was recognized by many in the audience and there was general merriment. Between the acts she explained to us that she had quite forgotten the admirable London custom of beginning plays on first nights one half hour earlier, so that the critics would have a little more time to write their reviews.

At one of her afternoon teas I had an interesting conversation with Dean Inge, whom I found anything but 'gloomy.' He spoke with high admiration of the Quakers. When I asked him if he thought he really would enjoy their religious services as much as those of the Church of England—'wouldn't you miss the beautiful ritual?' 'No,' said he, 'for the Quakers have that in their faces.'

One afternoon in 1912 we went to the Coronet Theatre at Queen's Gate, where Miss Horniman's splendid company from Manchester were in repertory, to see Arnold Bennett's play *What the Public Wants*. In the course of the first act, Mr. Bennett accompanied by May Sinclair entered a box. In the intermission, he came down in the auditorium and took an empty seat next to mine. Interesting it was to be present at a play with its famous author beside me. I told him how much I enjoyed the comedy. He said he wished the public agreed with me, but it was not at all a box-office success. 'Do the people think it is too highbrow?' 'That is exactly what they think, and they will have nothing to do with it.' He looked seraphically happy, however, for at another theatre, his play *Milestones* was packing the house. I asked him if he had a good time at Yale during his recent visit to America. 'I had a terrible time there! I had just been at Harvard and had lost my digestion when I left for Yale. Those Harvard people gave me too much to eat. President Hadley gave me a luncheon, and oh, I was so sick, I couldn't play up to him at all, oh, not at all.' But he said he was certainly coming back to the States, as he wished to see many places and things he had missed. He never was able to carry out this plan.

Later they told me in New Haven that he was so ill at President Hadley's luncheon he could eat nothing, and asked for a cup of tea. Tea was brought to him, he took one sip, and exclaimed 'It isn't brewed!' The British can never understand why an American, handing them a cup of tea, will say, 'Will you have some tea? It's very weak.' Which in their thought is equivalent to saying, 'It's very bad.' The English novelist Miss E. M. Delafield (Mrs. Dashwood) wisely refused tea everywhere in America, although it was constantly offered her. She always took coffee. She knew that the Americans had the best coffee in the world and the English the worst, and that she could have plenty of tea at home. Arnold Bennett talked in conversation with me exactly as the author of his books ought to talk. He was simple, natural, unaffected, humorous, friendly, with the agreeable assurance that comes from success.

One of the most charming women we met in London in 1912 was Lady Ritchie. She pointed out various interesting things in the room. 'At that table Turgenev sat one day, waiting for me to come. Finally he gave it up, and wrote me a charming note, which I found when I came in.' As we walked around her room, looking at various wonders, she took a book off the shelf, and a little note, written in thick black ink, fell to the floor. I picked it up and she said, 'Read it aloud.' It ran like this: 'Dear Annie: be sure and be home tomorrow afternoon for I am coming around to walk with you. Alfred Tennyson.'

She showed me many of her father's novels, which were covered with pictures along the margins, which Thackeray had drawn to amuse his children. She was kind and gracious and looked exactly like the drawing of her by John Sargent.

She told me many things about Browning, whom she knew intimately. One evening at a large dinner-party, when the ladies had withdrawn, she mentioned a bit of gossip that she had heard, that Browning was to be married again. It seems that a day or two later, he heard this, and enquired who had said it and was told that it was said by Annie Thackeray. She did not know that it had reached his ears.

The next evening he was assigned to take her in to dinner. She came up to him with the usual intimate greeting, and to her amazement he would not look at her. She took his arm, and as they walked from where they were toward the dining-room, she attempted to speak to him, whereupon he spiked her with his elbow. They reached the table and during the entire meal he talked only with the lady on his left, not only saying nothing to Miss Thackeray, but not even replying to her questions. As soon as the ladies withdrew, she exclaimed 'Is Robert Browning crazy?' and described his behaviour. The others told her it was doubtless because he had heard that the rumour of a second marriage had come from her, and added cheerfully, 'He'll never forgive you.' During the rest of the season, although they met frequently at dinner-parties, he never spoke to her. But that summer, when he was spending a few weeks at a favourite resort in Normandy together with his friend the Frenchman Milsand, it so happened that

Anne Thackeray was at the other end of the village. One day Milsand said to Browning: 'You are behaving abominably. Miss Thackeray is heart-broken. She never intended to hurt your feelings and she is suffering tortures.' Browning, always impulsive, said, 'Why, is that so?' and he started on the run for her lodgings. She told me she was sitting lonely at a window in the second storey, when she saw Browning running toward her panting and puffing, but making good time. 'I ran down stairs, opened the front door, leaped into his arms, and had a wonderfully good time sobbing and weeping.' They were the best of friends again, and Browning dedicated his next long poem to her.

In 1889 when Browning, impulsively again, sent that terrible 'spitting' poem to the *Athenæum* on Edward Fitzgerald, he wrote a very long letter to Annie Thackeray explaining how he came to write such a poem and why he did it. She allowed me to read this letter through; it showed that Browning was suffering tortures, but he felt he was justified.

He had opened carelessly the newly published *Letters of Edward Fitzgerald* and had the bad luck to see the sentence 'Mrs. Browning is dead; thank God! we shall have no more Aurora Leighs.' Wild with rage, he sent in hot haste a poem to the *Athenæum* in which he said it would be difficult to think of an appropriate punishment for Old Fitz: kicking is the common lot of curs, and the only reason he could not spit on him was because he could not spit through lips that had been sanctified by hers.

It is unfortunate that this poem ever appeared in print. We know now that he tried in vain to recall it before it went into type. On page 378 of the *Letters of Robert Browning Collected by Thomas J. Wise*, we read:

Browning experienced a revulsion of feeling against the publication of these stanzas, and sent a telegram to Mr. MacColl, asking him to withhold the lines from publication. But, though there really was still time to excise them from the copy for the printer, Mr. MacColl so managed by talking to a friend before opening the telegram as to be able to inform Browning that it was too late to keep the stanzas from appearing.

In 1911 Thackeray's centenary had been celebrated at Yale; knowing of his daughter Lady Ritchie's intimate friendship with Turgenev, I sent her a copy of my *Essays on Russian Novelists*. This was before I had the pleasure of meeting her. Her admirable book *Blackstick Papers* had anecdotes of Turgenev. Having failed to keep an appointment, he came to her next day and held up his hands. 'Look at my thumbs! See how small they are! Such small thumbs mean that their owner is always being prevented from doing what he wants to do!' He laughed gaily and his manner was so charming she would have forgiven him anything. Furthermore, his resemblance to her father was uncanny.

The great Turgenev, in some respects my favourite novelist, was, I think, a pessimist from early youth; and his pessimism deepened as he descended into the vale of years. He said that he would give all his genius and all his fame if there were only one woman who cared whether or not he came home late to dinner. Although a giant in stature and very fond of outdoor sports, especially of shooting, he had attacks of the blackest melancholia. When these came upon him, he would remain motionless for two or three days neither eating nor sleeping. Although he was wholly without prejudices in contemplating the world of men and women, he had an active and extraordinarily sensitive conscience, both moral and artistic. This conscience forced him into various activities that he hated and fortunately for the world compelled him to write books. Once when asked his ideal of happiness, he replied 'Remorseless laziness.'

Some years ago there appeared in *Red Panorama*, a weekly Russian magazine published in Leningrad, a list of his replies to the same questionnaire, first in 1869 and the second in 1880. He died in 1883. The humour of the second list does not disguise its despair.

My friend Professor Petroff translated them for me.

Question	Answer in 1869	Answer in 1880
Your favourite virtue?	Sincerity.	Youth.
Your favourite quality in man?	Kindness.	Age of 25.
Your favourite quality in woman?	Kindness.	Age of 18.
Your favourite recreation?	Hunting.	To sniff tobacco.
Characteristic feature of your personality?	Laziness.	Laziness.
Your idea of happiness?	Excellent health.	To have nothing to do.
Your idea of unhappiness?	To be blind.	To work.
Your favourite colour?	Indigo.	Grey.
Your favourite flower?	Narcissus.	Cauliflower.
Your favourite writer?	Cervantes.	I do not read any more.
Your favourite poets?	Homer, Shakespeare, Goethe, Pushkin.	I do not read any more.
Your favourite artists and composers?	Rembrandt, Mozart, Schubert.	I do not go to concerts or exhibitions.
Your favourite heroes in history?	Washington, Pericles.	The man who discovered oysters.
Your favourite heroines?	Madame Roland.	Any dark complexioned maidens.
Your favourite heroes of romance?	King Lear, Prometheus.	Falstaff, Gargantua.
Your favourite dishes and drinks?	Meat, champagne.	What my stomach can digest.
Upon what vice do you look most leniently?	Drunkenness.	All.

Question	Answer in 1869	Answer in 1880
Your favourite motto?	None.	Good night.
If you were not what you are, what would you like to be?	My dog, Pegasus.	Nothing.

59

J.M.BARRIE

EVEN as there are elective affinities between men and women, and great friendships between men (I imagine that monks in mediaeval monasteries had friendships compared to which our best college friendships are thin and pale) so there are authors who especially appeal to certain individuals. It requires no effort and no peculiarity of taste to enjoy Shakespeare; it requires oddity not to admire him, which dislike was one of the many eccentricities of Tolstoy. But there are certain authors who affect us so profoundly that we suffer physical pain when we hear them disparaged or ridiculed.

Before Elizabeth Barrett had even the remotest idea of ever meeting Robert Browning, she said that attacks on his poetry affected her like the lashing of a whip on her skin.

Of all modern British authors, I am the most deeply affected by J.M.Barrie. My own attitude toward his writings has always been quite different from my admiration for some of his contemporaries; I admire their works; but for the creations of Barrie I feel something deeper than admiration. He touches something in me that instantly responds.

> Mon cœur est un luth suspendu:
> Sitôt qu'on le touche, il résonne.

I do not like to see the works of any authors misunderstood, misrepresented, undervalued; but when this hap-

pens with Barrie, I feel something more personal than disagreement. I have always felt this way, since I began to
read Barrie and since I first saw his plays on the stage.

In 1902 I began giving annually an elective course at
Yale confined to contemporary dramatists in Europe and
America. I think it was the first university course anywhere dealing *exclusively* with this theme; though there
were many courses in the history of the drama where some
modern playwrights were included. Among the foremost
living writers of plays in English, Barrie was the only one
who had published nothing. Accordingly in 1909 I sent
him the programme of my course, and begged him to make
his plays available for students and readers. I received the
following letter:

> LEINSTER CORNER,
> LANCASTER GATE, W.
> 15 May 1909

DEAR SIR,

I have been on the continent and hence delay in receiving and answering your very pleasant letter. I thank you for it heartily. Some
day I shall print 'What Every Woman Knows' and some others of
my plays, and it is an uncommon pleasure to me to think that at
Yale you may do them the honour you speak of.

Believe me

Yours sincerely,

J.M.BARRIE

As it turned out, the first play he consented to publish was
not *What Every Woman Knows*.

I felt more eager to see him than to see any other man of
genius. Being in London in May 1912, I wrote and asked
him for a brief interview. He immediately replied, asking
me to lunch; but I had promised to lunch that day with
some persons no more distinguished than myself; and I so
informed him. Then he asked me to come in the morning.

Accordingly, on the morning of 23 May 1912 I entered the lift in the building in Adelphi Terrace that took me up to his rooms. I was shown in by a servant who looked like the Admirable Crichton. A moment later, Barrie entered and greeted me cordially. A little man, very dark hair, tiny dark moustache, little hands, little feet, and with an expression on his face of profound sadness. I asked him if he were still smoking the Craven Mixture; no, he had given that up. 'But that was the Arcadia mixture that you made famous in *My Lady Nicotine*?' It was, and the book had made a fortune for the manufacturer. It appeared that he was now smoking John Cotton Number One. . . . 'Be sure and get Number One' (it was the mildest form of this tobacco). The next day I went to a tobacconist's on the Strand, and I could not remember the name of the mixture I was looking for. 'Have you the Ben Jonson smoking tobacco?' He immediately brought the desired John Cotton.

Barrie told me his work was entirely outside himself. No one could draw inferences from it about his own thoughts or opinions. Plays were harder to write than novels. At that time he had not published a single one of his plays. I besought him to print them, telling him he was the only important dramatist whose plays were not 'works.' He said that after he had written a play, and got it through the days and nights of rehearsals, and then through the final horror of the first night, he never wished to see it again, or even hear it mentioned. But I suggested that all he had to do was to give the manuscript to the publisher. 'Oh, no, there's an immense amount of work to be done. Think of the stage-directions!' I did not know what he meant by that remark, nor did I find out till his first plays were published, when it appeared that these stage-directions were in some ways the most original and striking passages (for the reader). If the reader have enough imagination to give him television, these stage directions will enable him to be present in the theatre, even while alone under the lamplight.

I kept on imploring him to print, no matter what the additional labour might be; and before I left the room he actually promised to do so. Of course it is improbable that my importunity could have changed his mind. But it is barely possible that I hastened the consummation.

For, shortly after (1914), two of his plays appeared in illustrated editions—*Quality Street* and *The Admirable Crichton*, illustrated by Hugh Thomson. Copies are now much sought after by collectors; at the time of their publication, Sinclair Lewis was working in a publisher's house in New York. He presented me with my copy of *Crichton*. Barrie then went on to publish all his other plays in small single volumes, although *Peter Pan* came much later. And finally he was induced to publish his collected plays in one tall tome.

In this same first interview, I asked him which of his plays he thought the best; without any hesitation, he answered *The Admirable Crichton*. Twenty years later I asked him the same question, and he said, 'Well, now I rather prefer *Dear Brutus*.'

He thought William Archer had done more for the elevation of the contemporary English stage than any other man.

At that time, Mr. and Mrs. Bernard Shaw lived next door in Adelphi Terrace, one storey lower. Barrie said that when he wished to talk with Shaw, he merely raised his window and called out. Sometimes, if Shaw's windows were lighted at two o'clock in the morning, both men leaned out of their windows and had long talks. If only one knew the time of these aerial conversations! they would have been well worth awaiting all night in the street below.

Once, he said, he could not attract Shaw's attention by calling; so he threw pieces of bread at Shaw's windows. It appeared that Mr. and Mrs. Shaw were giving a dinner-party. Mr. Shaw looked up at Barrie and wanted to know if he were contributing manna to the feast.

I told Barrie he ought to be the happiest man in the world; this remark caused astonishment. 'Why should I be happy?' 'Oh, I don't mean that you should be happy because you have given so much happiness to the hundreds of thousands who have seen your plays and read your novels, though that must be a source of considerable satisfaction. What I refer to is the fact that you, perhaps more than any other living writer, are able to embody your thoughts in words. Now the difficulty, even with the ablest creative writers, is to transfer the pictures in their imagination and the thoughts in their minds to the written page, without loss; even with most successful writers, there is a sad difference between conception and execution. But you sit at this desk and fantastic images and ideas come into your mind, so strange they must often surprise you and make you laugh aloud in solitude. Yet you have the divine gift of transferring them to paper so that we see them very much as they first appeared to you.'

He listened to this with polite attention, and made no comment.

Shortly after, I withdrew, feeling that he was all and more than I had hoped to find. He was the Man of his Works, and my admiration for them became almost idolatry toward him.

I had not been in my hotel more than fifteen minutes, when a messenger arrived, bringing Barrie's little book on George Meredith. On the flyleaf was written, 'W.L.Phelps, from his friend, J.M.Barrie.'

The next time I saw Barrie was in his London flat on 19 September 1924, when I had tea with him. His hair was just as black as in 1912, but he had grown stouter. He said that his short play which had aroused so much discussion, *Shall We Join the Ladies?* he originally had intended to write in four acts, as a full-length play, but now he would never finish it. He did not volunteer any information as to who was the murderer, although John Galsworthy told me it was the butler. I tried to draw him out a little about the significance of his play *Mary Rose*, but it seemed he did not wish to discuss this.

He told me that in this very flat on one evening during the war, there were gathered together sitting on the floor around one lighted candle, for on account of Zeppelin raids they were not allowed to show much light, Thomas Hardy, Bernard Shaw, Joseph Conrad, John Galsworthy, Arnold Bennett, and himself; when suddenly a tremendous bomb fell from the sky and exploded on the pavement very close to their apartment. Anyone may now verify this for himself. The bomb fell at the foot of the obelisk on the embankment, and while the pavement has since been repaired, the holes made in the base of the obelisk are as they were. It would have been a sad and sensational loss to English literature if the bomb had struck a few yards north.

We talked about Shaw's latest play, *Saint Joan*, which I had just seen. Barrie expressed the highest admiration for it, but when I told him I wished the epilogue had been omitted, he agreed with me. So did Mr. Galsworthy.

In 1928 we came over again.

ADELPHI TERRACE HOUSE,
STRAND, W.C.2
30 May 1928

DEAR MR. PHELPS,

Delighted to hear you are coming in July. This is 'As I like it,' and a warm welcome awaits you.

Yours sincerely

J.M.BARRIE

We reached London on 27 July and a telephone message greeted us at the hotel, asking my wife and me to come to dinner at his flat the following evening; that the only other guests would be Mr. and Mrs. Bernard Shaw and Mrs. Thomas Hardy.

If I had to describe the temperament of this famous Irishman in one word, I should use the word *happy*. He seemed the happiest man I had met, and I have met many cheerful individuals. He was seventy-two years old, but had the springy alertness of youth not only in his mind, which might be expected, but in his body. As Mr. Service expresses it, he had the mind of a savant in the body of a savage. He is over six feet, spare, active, and agile, so that his voluminous snowy beard seems incongruous, as though it were some histrionic mask. As a rule, beards, unless closely trimmed, look untidy; they are often discoloured in various sections, so that the general effect is unattractive. Mr. Shaw's beard, like his hair, is evenly white—it is the cleanest beard I ever saw. The whole effect of his clothes, beard, and general appearance is so clean as to look antiseptic, his only resemblance to the members of a profession he so often attacks. I observed that he ate no meat, drank no alcohol, and declined to smoke. Whatever may be true of others, he needs no wine to stimulate his dinner conversation or to elevate his spirit. He is the only person who has ever come anywhere near to converting me to vegetarianism. He is a magnificent advertisement of his dietary doctrines. If abstinence from meat, wine, and tobacco can make a man in the seventies so radiantly healthy, buoyant, and resilient, the experiment might be worth trying.

His keen blue eyes sparkled as he told one good story after another. He gave many good-humoured and diverting reminiscences of the actor Henry Irving. Irving's voice and articulation were not good; when he spoke slowly, he was clear enough, but when he increased in speed, his words turned into a series of grunts. Mr. Shaw gave a remarkable imitation. At this point the conversation turned on distinct enunciation and the correct pronunciation of English. Mr. Shaw is a member of a committee which determines the pronunciation of English for the professional broadcasters; for it is hoped that broadcasting may be used to standardize and improve the general pronunciation. He said that one difficulty arises from the fact that no two cultivated persons pronounce words exactly alike. For example, he was certain that no two persons, no matter how fastidious in their speech, would pronounce the word *Cross* in the same way. (Of course one of the most noticeable differences between American and British pronunciation is observable in the letter *o*. The average American pronounces 'motor' quite differently from the average Englishman.) The committee, which was very small, had, as I remember, one Irishman, one Scot, one Welshman, and only one Englishman.

Mr. Shaw was interested in the movietone, and spoke of it with animation and emphasis. When he was asked to appear in the movietone he took charge of the whole affair himself, directed it, managed it, used his voice according to his own judgement, and the result was a complete success. He described his method with abundant illustrations. 'I come forward through the shrubbery, blow my nose—' Mrs. Shaw enquired: 'And why, Bernard, did you blow your nose?' 'Because I wanted to give the effect of naturalness, informality.' Later we went to a London movietone, and it was immensely interesting to see him appear on the screen so soon after talking with him. He came forward in a golf suit, consulted his watch, blew his nose, and gave an entertaining monologue.

Mrs. Shaw is a charming Irishwoman, and she may accurately be described in the language Ibsen used when replying to an impertinent question concerning his wife. Ibsen said: 'She suits me exactly.'

We stepped outside on the balcony surrounding Barrie's flat, which looks out over the Embankment all along the river. This is holy ground to the lover of literature. In an adjoining street Rousseau came and lodged with David Hume. Just below us was the inn where the Pickwick Club started on their famous journey. Doctor Johnson and Boswell had many conversations in the house next door. Thomas Hardy worked in the same block for several years as an architect. A house in the next street, plainly visible, was the place where 'Milady' stayed on her famous visit to London in *The Three Musketeers*. On my expressing my unlimited enthusiasm for that series of tales, Sir James said: 'It is undoubtedly the best story ever written.'

He showed me some books owned by Thomas Hardy when Hardy was a small boy. One was a compendium of athletic games, a kind of sportsman's manual, containing also directions for fishing, the care of dogs, birds, etc. A short time ago someone gave Barrie a canary. He knew nothing about taking care of canaries, but he remembered Hardy's boy's book. Consulting it, he found complete directions for the diet and regimen of canaries. He had been following these directions, and the bird prospered. Another book, owned by Hardy when he was twenty-five, was a copy of the poems of Shelley. Hardy had marked page after page, underlining words that especially appealed to him.

I spoke of the unhappiness suffered by many writers when they see their vogue declining, and younger men taking their places, as Ibsen expressed it in *The Master Builder*, with the younger generation 'knocking at the door.' Barrie said he often felt that the love of money was not the root of all evil, but rather jealousy. That is, the jealousy felt by one artist toward another. He had seen the evil effects of it in many instances, where men, brooding over their fancied wrongs, had turned sour, and had therefore lost happiness and peace of mind. It is a vice that naturally accompanies ambition, distinction, and love of fame. He added that he had never known a man more completely free of anything like jealousy than Bernard Shaw. Even in the long years when Shaw, although writing steadily, was receiving no recognition, he was quite free from envy and jealousy. 'Shaw has a healthy mind.'

I reminded Barrie of a passage in one of the novels by Archibald Marshall, where it is said that possibly the happiest persons are those who live in the country on an income just sufficient for their needs and *who are without ambition*. 'Yes,' said Sir James, 'that may be true. But perhaps even in those instances their minds are filled with little jealousies, little grievances arising from local affairs.'

I asked Mr. Marshall himself if he would be willing to give up ambition, literary fame, and the arduous labor of writing in exchange for a mind free from all these things but filled with placid contentment. 'Not for all the world,' was his emphatic reply. He was living in London and steadily engaged in writing *Simple Stories*, a series of tales about children that had great success in England. Mr. Marshall knew his London very well indeed and we had some interesting pilgrimages together, visiting the old city churches.

On 26 July 1928 I had a long talk over the teacups with Barrie. He was gratified by the success of Helen Hayes in her revival of his play *What Every Woman Knows*. I told him of the excitement at the first night of *Dear Brutus* in New York when Helen Hayes and William Gillette appeared in the play. She was sixteen, and in that one night went from obscurity to a fame that has never diminished. Barrie spoke highly of the work that Eva Le Gallienne was doing in New York with the Civic Repertory Theatre, and I was pleased to see that it was probable he would give her permission to play *Peter Pan*. Her success in this play the following Christmas season was immense.

He talked about Henry Irving, saying there was something compelling about Irving's personality, so that when he was acting, it made no difference how many people there were on the stage, you saw only Irving.

The conversation turned on Daisy Ashford and the publication of the story written when she was a child, called *The Young Visiters*, for which he had written a preface. Many believed he had written the book himself; he said there was not the slightest foundation in fact for such a statement. He had never seen Daisy Ashford until after he had written the preface; though he had met and talked with her after the appearance of the book. My wife suggested that no adult could possibly have written the story, because it contains the expression, 'Mr. Salteena got down from his chair.' That is what a child has to do, whereas a man or woman gets up. 'No,' said Barrie, smiling, 'I could have thought of that expression, only I didn't.'

Barrie was deeply impressed with the new novel by Thornton Wilder, *The Bridge of San Luis Rey*. He said Americans should be proud of two things; first, that the author was an American, second, that over 200,000 copies of the book had been sold in the United States. 'He is a true literary artist. I am a writer, and I know what good writing is. That passage toward the end of the story "he leant against the flame,"—is abundant evidence of Mr. Wilder's great ability as a writer.' I told him Wilder was a school-teacher and that on long, lonely walks he could not only think of ideas and material for plots, but could actually compose pages of dialogue. 'I can understand that, and I think it is fortunate that Mr. Wilder is a professional teacher. It is better for a writer to have some regular occupation besides writing. I have often wished I had myself. But I am only a writer.'

ADELPHI TERRACE HOUSE,
STRAND, W.C.2.
26 May 1932

DEAR LYON PHELPS

Welcome to these shores. You probably just missed our summer week, but no matter. What matters is when you are coming in to see me. Can you come in to luncheon Wed—or Thursday next week? Both of you at 1.30. Just alone. Will fix something else if you are engaged.

Always Yours

J. M. BARRIE

Barrie was a true Scot and had the reserve and reticence characteristic of his nationality; but one could not help feeling that his sincerity was as marked in his personal friendships as in his art; and that his sympathy was as deep as it was unaffected He had a positive genius for friendship; he was one of the closest friends of George Meredith, and during the last twenty years of his life he was more intimate with Hardy than any other man of etters; he enjoyed the devoted affection of Henry James, and was a lifelong friend of Bernard Shaw.

Since I began reading the works of Barrie in 1891, I have never wavered in my faith in his genius; but I will add that every time I met him and talked with him, I felt that he himself was greater than everything he has written. And I believe there are no greater English dramas of the twentieth century than *Peter Pan*, *The Admirable Crichton*, and *Dear Brutus*.

We talked of Arnold Bennett's new play *The Return Journey*, which he had not yet seen. I said the first act was excellent; then the play declined and the last act was positively bad. I asked if it were not true that the greatest difficulty in play-writing was to make a good last act. 'There is no doubt of it; and in order to make sure of having a good last act, when I wrote *The Admirable Crichton*, I wrote the last act first.' 'Did you ever do that again?' 'No.'

On 6 June 1932, we lunched with Barrie in his flat. During the conversation, I mentioned his fine University Commencement addresses, *Courage* and —— neither of us could recall the exact title of the other. I knew the word was not *enchanting*, but like it. He thought for a few moments and said, 'Well, I can't remember it, either; but I know *enchanting* is not it.' Then the conversation turned on other themes, when all of a sudden Barrie exclaimed 'I've got it! The word is *entrancing*! *The Entrancing Life*.'

On 5 June 1935 I had tea with Barrie and we talked for more than two hours. He was in good health and exceedingly animated, laughing aloud several times—rather unusual for him. We talked about books we had read and enjoyed twenty years ago, and wondered if on reading them again we should feel equally enthusiastic. 'Usually not,' he said; 'but I have just read through Bennett's *The Old Wives Tale*. It is a very great novel. It seems to me greater than when I first read it.' Then we spoke of the tremendous rise in fame in the twentieth century of the novels of Dickens. 'He is next to Shakespeare.' Barrie had been reading Thornton Wilder's new novel. 'Perhaps it is not so good as *The Bridge*, but I enjoyed it very much indeed. It is full of humour. And remember this, even if he had never written *The Bridge*, even if *Heaven's My Destination* were his first novel, we should see right off that he was a remarkable writer. No one but a literary artist could have written it.'

I asked him about the new play he had made for the actress Elisabeth Bergner. I told him that a few months before, after her matinée performance in New York of the play *Escape me never*, I had talked with her in her dressing room. She said 'Barrie is the greatest living dramatist and his new play that he has written for me is a tremendous masterpiece.' I told her I agreed with her in the general statement and felt equally sure she was right in the particular one. 'Well,' said Barrie, 'I had not written a play for fifteen years, when I decided to write one for Miss Bergner. I had forgotten how to write plays, and wondered how I used to do it. Did I think of incidents and a plot first, or did I think of the characters? I had no idea. But the moment I sat down at my desk and took my pen, everything seemed natural and easy. It all came back.'

The death of Barrie on 19 June 1937 was felt as a personal loss by individuals in every part of the English-speaking world.

Barrie could never dictate, not even letters; and as he had never learned to use a typewriter, everything he wrote was in longhand. The result was that after many years he was afflicted with writer's cramp; he then learned gradually to write with his left hand, and perhaps the enforced slowness explains the increased legibility. For the letters he wrote me with his left hand are easier to read than the preceding ones.

Yale University several times offered Barrie an honorary degree and I naturally wrote him personal letters; in 1914 he replied

> ADELPHI TERRACE HOUSE,
> STRAND, W.C.
>
> DEAR PROF LYON PHELPS,
>   I wish I could have arranged it immensely but I had to write to the Secretary that circumstances made it impossible for me to get away. We shd have had a good time. It was very pleasing to me to be asked at any rate. Glad you liked 'Leonora,' and hoping to see you again on that side or this,
>
> Yours very sincerely,
>
> J.M.BARRIE

In 1918 I published a little book called *The Twentieth Century Theatre*.

2, ROBERT STREET,
ADELPHI, W.C.2.
20 Jan 1919

DEAR PROF. PHELPS,

My hearty thanks for the 'twentieth century theatre' which I have enjoyed much. Alas, for the nice things you say of my own efforts! But in my heart I am glad that you are so kind to them, I can do the headshaking myself. I dont know whether you have had such an out-pouring of war-plays as has deluged us. A V.C. to every leading actor, and I think that if the plays were to remain the record of the war future generations would decide that we had had no casualties. How many! And indeed we sometimes feel that all the best are gone. One seems to miss them more when the war is over, as if they should come back now.

I was nearly starting for America just now, had a pleasant invitation but could not get away. All hail and much happiness to you in 1919.

Yours Sincerely

J. M. BARRIE

In Barrie's own plays included in the volume *Echoes of the War* there were certainly casualties.

In 1927 appeared the following paragraph in *The New York Times*.

A UNIQUE HONOR FOR BARRIE

For the first time in the history of the Théâtre Français a play by a living British dramatist has been selected for performance on that classic stage. Sir JAMES MATTHEW BARRIE's "The Old Lady Shows Her Medals," as adapted by the French playwright NOZIERE, is to be produced in the coming season. If it is surprising for the Comédie Française to break through its traditions in the case of a contemporary foreigner, the work selected is equally puzzling, for it is in no sense Gallic in form or treatment, and does not even show its author in his real whimsical form. Perhaps the title adopted for the French version, "La Vieille Maman," should give a clew. The war is too recent and too serious for anything connected with it, however remotely, not to be taken seriously in the home of French comedy.

In 1928 I saw this at the *Comédie* and at its close the audience rose and cheered vociferously while the tears ran down their faces. As played in America by Beryl Mercer, the effect was overwhelming. In the last scene, as the Old Lady moved in absolute silence about the stage, uncontrollable sobs were heard all over the auditorium.

In 1921 Yale made one more effort to induce Barrie to come over and receive a degree.

ADELPHI TERRACE HOUSE,
STRAND, W.C.2.
2 April, 1921

DEAR MR LYON PHELPS,

I am much honoured by the action of the Yale University Corporation and am replying formally to the Secretary from whom I have heard also. Alas, there is I think no possibility of my being able to visit America at that time, but the pleasure you all give me is as great almost as if I could be among you. I look forward to the new book and hope to enjoy it as much as the last which I liked immensely. You will gradually get me to believe some at least of the nice things you say about me. I think you may have seen in papers that I meditated going to America to produce a Peter Pan film, but the only truth is that I said No to it. Yet it might have been worth while. It is the only thing of mine that I can see being dealt with satisfactorily in that bewildering medium.

My kindest regards to you, and I wish you would revisit these shores.

Yours Sincerely

J.M.BARRIE

The book he alludes to was one called *Essays on Modern Dramatists* published that same year.

I was in London in September 1924, and I hardly expected to have the good fortune to meet him there in that month. However, I sent him a line from my hotel.

ADELPHI TERRACE HOUSE,
STRAND, W.C.2.
17 Sep

DEAR MR PHELPS,

I have just arrived in London, obviously with the express purpose of seeing you again. Anyhow it is a sufficient reason. The prospect delights me, and I hope you can come in at tea time tomorrow (Thursday) about 5 o'clock. If there is anything not suiting you in this time, almost any other day would be right for me. My telephone (not in book) is Gerrard, 9764.

Yours

J.M.BARRIE

I had a good talk with him, and when the conversation fell on authors whose books were very popular and undistinguished, he said that in every best-seller there was always something good; the things that were good, not the things that were bad, caused the popularity. Later I had an interesting conversation on this same theme with Bernard Shaw, who said that best-sellers were never written down to the public, but in order to reach a huge sale, their authors must be sincere, no matter what the critics thought of their work.

In 1925 the American publishers, Charles Scribner's Sons, wished to issue a volume of selected plays by Barrie and when they wrote asking him whom he would choose to write the Introduction, he gave them my name. The book appeared in 1926.

ADELPHI TERRACE HOUSE,
STRAND, W.C.2.
27 Sep. 1925

DEAR LYON PHELPS,

I am very pleased that you are to write that introduction. I naturally thought of you at once when Scribners put me to the question, and your letter is delightful. I take off my hat to your course of lectures and wish we had something more like it here. I am however furious with you for saying you wish 'Leonora' was available, because I thought it was. Enquiry shows it isn't, and it must now be shrinking from observation in a bursting and loathsome cupboard. Or it has gone over-board in the night with some companions too. I am reminded of a stranger whom I sat beside in a railway carriage. We stopped at a small station where an elderly woman was sitting, and after gazing at her he said "I once asked that woman to marry me, and now I cant remember her name." My pretty dears, I cant remember all their names.

All kind regards

Yours

J.M.BARRIE

Whenever I wrote him, unless a reply was necessary, I begged him not to acknowledge the letter, as I knew how completely his time was taken. But against my urgence he wrote this note in response to a little paragraph I had printed about him.

ADELPHI TERRACE HOUSE,
STRAND, W.C.2.
15 Aug 1934

DEAR LYON PHELPS,

I enjoyed the fairy poem much and the kind thought that made you send the cutting also. You dont speak of being [sic] coming over this year but if such is in your head please see that you turn in at my door. Yours sincerely

J.M.BARRIE

On 23 June 1926 Barrie received an honorary degree from Oxford, the Public Orator, A.B.Poynton, whose citations delighted University audiences many years, presenting him. I had an interesting talk with Mr. Poynton at a luncheon given at University College, Oxford, by my friend and former pupil, Arthur Goodhart. Both Goodhart

G. K. Chesterton, William Lyon Phelps, and Æ. in my house in New Haven, 1931

The American Academy
William Lyon Phelps, Dr. Wilbur Cross, Robert Underwood
Johnson, Henry Van Dyke, Dr. Nicholas Murray Butler

Seven Gables, Huron City, Michigan
August 1938

Seven Gables, 1938

Saluting the Owl at Seven Gables, 1938
Shot by Mr. Phelps, 1933

W.L.P., Thornton Wilder, and the late Ellery Walter,
author of the book Around the World on One Leg, *New Haven*

Rowing on the Cam at Cambridge
England. 1900, *aged* 35

Telling a funny story. Rotary dinner, Philadelphia. On the left William K. Huff, director of the Forum, and on the right C. Arthur White, president of the Rotary Club

and Poynton are Fellows of that college. Mr. Poynton amazed me by saying that my citations as Public Orator at Yale were more difficult to write than his; to which I naturally replied that mine were in English whereas he had to write in Latin. 'Exactly,' said he; 'you have got to be witty, because all understand every word you say; whereas, mine being in Latin, the audience have no idea whether mine are any good or not.' However, he would certainly perform my task better than I should his. Here is what he said in presenting Barrie: (from the London *Times*, 24 June 1926).

SIR JAMES BARRIE

After allusions to *Quality Street*, *A Window in Thrums*, and other literary masterpieces of Sir James Barrie, Mr. Poynton continued: *ad insulam illam solitariam avolemus, ubi promus ille* κρείττων αὐτοῦ *naturae obsequens cuivis Stoico par regnat*. This inventor of *dulcissimae inanitatis* had a sure place in our hearts, *cum eorum memoria, quos infantes ita amavimus ut tamen "adultos esse" gaudeamus.*

Sir James, who received an ovation from the House, was welcomed by the Chancellor as *Vir dilectissime, qui personas tuo ingenio fictas ita ad vivum describis ut apud nos vivere videantur.*

The biographical part of my introduction I put into the first paragraph, as follows:

James Matthew Barrie was born on an island situated seven leagues west of the most western of the Islands of the Hebrides. It can be reached only by the right pair of boots. In ancestry he comes straight down in the authentic line of apostolic succession, there being two of the disciples in his name; a happy combination of works and faith. Although a mortal man, he is the father of immortal children, among whom may be mentioned Tommy, born in 1896; Crichton, born in 1902; Peter Pan, born in 1917; Mary Rose, born in 1920. So much for biography.

60

SINGING BIRDS

I SHALL have more to say of travelling in England, but I will content myself now by relating my long and finally triumphant pursuit of the nightingale. Many may think it is ridiculous to go abroad merely to hear a nightingale; but this is the most famous of song-birds; and when I remember how I had unsuccessfully chased the vocal fowl through many countries and for many years, the result is worth recording. All the great British poets for five centuries paid poetic homage to the famous bird, and it became essential to my happiness that I should hear him. Wherever I went, I found he had just left. For example, whenever I was in Florence, and went out to the Cascine or along the Arno, and listened to nothing, I was always informed that last week scores of them were in activity. Speaking of the moon in Florence, Browning said:

> Full she flared it, lamping Samminiato,
> Rounder twixt the cypresses and rounder,
> Perfect, till the nightingales applauded.

Well, many a night I walked along the Arno, and saw the moonlight on the façade of San Miniato, but heard no nightingale. It was the same way in Germany; Bremen is famous for its nightingales, but there were none for me. I asked my English golf-partner if he had ever heard a nightingale, and he replied, 'I wish I had a shilling for every bootjack I have thrown at them.' I never saw a bootjack, but it appears to be an implement used by Englishmen to throw at nocturnal soloists. I suppose every well-regulated British household has a collection of bootjacks, which are hurled at the voices of the night, are collected again during the day, and conveniently arranged for the midnight barrage.

In an interesting conversation with the English novelist, Alfred Ollivant, I mentioned my bad luck, and he declared that if I would come down to his house in Sussex on the following Saturday, he would produce a nightingale. Accordingly at the appointed time we took the train, and I was agreeably shocked to observe that the station where we got off was Horsham, the town where Shelley was born; of course there should be singing-birds. We drove in the twilight nine or ten miles; and after we had proceeded some distance, Mr. Ollivant remarked, 'Now, this is funny.' 'No,' said I, 'this is not funny at all; this is the same bad luck I have had for years.' 'Why, last Saturday night there were scores of them all along the road.' This time there were none. After dinner we sat in the garden till midnight; nothing. I gave it up, and went to my room; but just as I was getting into bed, there was an excited knock on the door and a hurry call. At the word, accoutred as I was, I sprang to the window. It was a very dark night, no moon, no stars; I made out three big blurs rising from the lawn—three tall trees. In each of the trees there was a nightingale, and the three birds were singing together. It was a concert worth all the years of waiting. As I listened in ecstasy, I thought of the long succession of British poets who had paid their tribute to the midnight minstrels, and the splendid stanza by Keats came into my mind,

> Thou wast not born for death, immortal Bird!

and ends

> . . . the same that oft-times hath
> Charmed magic casements, opening on the foam
> Of perilous seas, in faery lands forlorn.

Kipling, in his story, *Wireless*, referring to these lines, says: ' These are the pure Magic. These are the clear Vision. The rest is only poetry.'

How well repaid I was for my Sussex adventure! For the next morning as we walked across the fields on our way to church, we heard two other English soloists—the skylark and the cuckoo, so celebrated in British poetry. The larks rose almost vertically, as if trying for the altitude record; and after they had become invisible aloft, we could hear their voices—the poet calls it a 'sightless song.' The cuckoo I had never heard before; his song is a precise imitation of that abomination known as the cuckoo-clock, only of course you cannot train him to strike right. He is a ventriloquist; the powerful notes seemed to be directly behind my shoulder, whereas they came from a distance of about a thousand yards.

The most famous four birds in English literature are the nightingale, the blackbird, the cuckoo, and the skylark. All four are unknown in America. We have the yellow-bill and black-bill cuckoo, but they are quite unlike the English variety. As for the blackbird, I agree with Theodore Roosevelt and with Lord Grey that he is the finest singer in England. When I read many years ago Tennyson's poem to the blackbird, celebrating the beauty of his music, I could not imagine what caused the poet's enthusiasm; the word blackbird had for me a quite different connotation. Our red-winged blackbird, with the scarlet epaulets, has only a genial wheeze; while the so-called crow-blackbird sings as though he had tonsillitis, or as though his voice were adolescently changing. But the British and the continental blackbirds emit the most heavenly music. In spring dawns in Germany, they used to wake me up at four o'clock; I never thought of throwing bootjacks at them, for I was entranced. One February day, while standing in front of the University of Munich during a copious snowstorm, I saw a blackbird on the branch of a tree; he had his beak pointed toward the wind, and, while the snowflakes beat upon his little face, he poured out a stream of the loveliest music in the world.

61

DOROTHY CANFIELD

ONE day more than twenty years ago as I was at work in my library in New Haven, I was pleasantly interrupted by the advent of a distinguished-looking elderly gentleman accompanied by an extremely shy young girl. The man was the librarian of Columbia University, formerly president of Ohio State—how fortunate to be able to exchange the terrible job of college president for the agreeable position of librarian!—and the bashful girl was his daughter Dorothy. Dr. Canfield never wasted time or words on preliminaries.

' This is my daughter and she has got to write a thesis in Old French for her Ph.D. at Columbia.'

' God help her!'

' No, *you* help her!'

' But I don't know anything whatever about Old French. The only French that interests me is modern French.'

' Yes,' said he, ' but you once wrote a thesis in English and got a Ph.D.'

' That is quite true; and I made up my mind then that if the Lord would forgive me I would never write another.'

' Well, this thesis has got to be written, and we have come to New Haven to discuss the method of its production with you.'

I did my best to point out the way in which 'original work,' if it were to be valuable and important, must be done; what to include, what to emphasize, what to omit. Miss Canfield wrote her thesis with the customary bloody sweat, successfully met all the requirements, and has whatever rights and privileges go with the title of 'Doctor.'

In the summer vacation of the year 1912, as I was sitting in my house in Michigan after the diurnal eighteen holes, came the diurnal parcel of new books containing a novel by a woman unknown to fame. The novel was *The Squirrel Cage*; the name of the author, Dorothy Canfield. I did not connect this name in my mind with that of the former aspirant to the doctorate; but the title of the book was beguiling, and the first paragraph caught my attention. I read the book from beginning to end with steadily increasing admiration. Somewhere during its perusal I *heard* the timid, almost inaudible voice of that terror-stricken, thesis-haunted girl in New Haven. I wrote a letter to her in care of the publisher asking if it were really she. I received a reply from Mrs. J.R.Fisher in Arlington, Vermont, confessing everything. What a development in four years! The timid girl had become a Ph.D., a wife, and a novelist!

As I considered *The Squirrel Cage*, I thought how strange it was that this author had ever supposed her 'vocation' lay in Old French or in anything other than creative work. For although she has since written better novels, this particular specimen has intrinsic value. It contained unmistakable evidence that its author was a genuine, realistic writer—realistic without being sensational.

I dare say that the labour in Old French was not fruitless; the painstaking accuracy of that thesis was transferred to a wider and more interesting domain. Her education in France, where precision of language is thought to be important, was as valuable for her as for her older contemporaries, Anne Sedgwick and Edith Wharton. All three had a thorough knowledge of the French language and literature.

In her next novel, *The Bent Twig*, Dorothy Canfield produced the best story of undergraduate and faculty life in

America that I have read. She described a coeducational state institution, the kind of thing she knew as a child; for, as I mentioned before, her father had been president of Ohio State University.

During the war Mrs. Fisher went to France, where her accurate knowledge of the language and of the people made her presence of the highest value. Many women, and some elderly men, feeling that they ought to 'do their bit,' managed to cross the water, where they were in innumerable instances a nuisance. They could not speak or understand the language with facility, they fell sick and had to be taken care of; and when they were well, they had a genius for getting in the way of those who were useful. But Mrs. Fisher knew exactly what she could do, knew how to do it, and did it. She took care of blind soldiers and of their children. This would not be worth mentioning in an estimate of her literary art if it were not for the fact that it aided in producing some of her best writing.

One of our Yale professors, now no longer living, who was born in France, was so impatient with what he thought was the vulgarity of America that on a sabbatical year he went over to France thinking he would escape for a time from a distressing environment. I discovered him in a village in Brittany. He was desperately homesick for America. 'Why,' said he, 'I never thought such ignorance, stupidity, and vulgarity could exist as I have found in this French village. And the language of the old women when they speak angrily to each other!' He was unfortunately able to understand everything they said.

We know what Flaubert thought of small-town life in France. And Dostoevski said that in Russian villages the inhabitants spent so much time poking their noses into their neighbours' affairs that one would think they would all be great psychologists. 'On the contrary, they are nearly all idiots.'

Dorothy Canfield believes that a New England village contains an almost complete assortment of the various types of human nature; there one can study them better than in a large city. With her large, tolerant view of human nature, and her womanly sympathy, she gives us not a travesty, but a picture.

Of all her novels I like best *Her Son's Wife*. In the first place, her attention is concentrated on three characters; from multiplicity of characters arises a tendency to diffuseness. This book deals with a fight between two women for the possession of one man. When two men fight for a woman, the theme is not particularly interesting, both because it is so common and because there is a pact known as a gentleman's agreement—who ever heard of a lady's agreement? When two women fight for a man, the struggle is interesting because there are no rules. In this particular novel a mother, accustomed for many years to domination over her son, finds that he has married without consulting her; and has married a detestable female.

The mother is a school-teacher. On arriving home from her professional duties one afternoon she sees in the hall a woman's hat. Now just as a zoologist can from the sight of one bone reconstruct the entire animal, so a woman from the sight of one hat can visualize the form and character of its wearer. This hat is not reassuring; in fact, her worst fears are confirmed.

Some have wondered how this woman could have done her teaching when the hours before and after were filled with nerve-shattering misery. I say that it was her professional work that saved her life and her soul. For the daily round of teaching is like the work of a military captain in action. There are certain kinds of toil that can be done mechanically; the work goes on while the mind is otherwise employed. But the blessed thing about teaching is that it demands unrestricted attention. When the teacher is alone in the classroom with her pupils, no other person can help her, and she cannot think of anything else. Many teachers are doing brilliant and successful work in the classroom while suffering from ill health and financial worry. The loss of income is only one of the tragedies of unemployment.

I regard Dorothy Canfield's novels as a contribution to American literature. She has won a place in the first rank of American contemporary woman novelists, and there she stands with her compeers—Edith Wharton, Willa Cather, Pearl Buck, Anne Sedgwick, Edna Ferber, Zona Gale, Ellen Glasgow.

> WAITING-ROOM
> GRAND CENTRAL STATION
> NEW YORK CITY
> Aug. 3–1916

DEAR PROFESSOR PHELPS:

I've been trying desperately to find a moment in which I might write you, but packing and children, and getting our house ready to leave for the winter and saying good-byes have so more than filled every moment that it's only now, at five in the morning, as I arrive from Vermont on an early train, that I see a breathing-space, and feel I can write you the "report" I've been wanting so much to make to you. For, do you know, I feel that I owe you an accounting for what I do. That's one of the penalties you pay for your generous interest and sympathy! I really want you to know what I'm up to, for I'm counting on your help to make the most I can out of my life.

Sally Cleghorn—my very dear and close sister-friend—has written you that I am going to France, but she didn't tell you why, I believe. It's mainly for the very simple, elemental reason that my husband is there, and that we are the kind of husband-and-wife who find it almost intolerable to be separated. Life's too short to miss any of that perfect companionship! I'm not going into "relief work" (except what informal help I can give without interfering with my care for our children) I'm going to establish a quiet little French home in a suburb of Paris, near the American Ambulance in Neuilly where my husband will be, for the most part, in service, and just live there through the winter to come, instead of on our Vermont mountain side.

I'm not going to write, because I've written a great deal this last year, and I want to give myself time to do a lot of thinking and living before undertaking anything new. And I hope our two children will enjoy their French winter as much as a Vermont one. You must remember there is nothing new in this for me. I was half brought up in France, you know, and have established French homes and lived there at intervals all my life. It all seems quite simple and natural to me, my husband giving up a year of his life to France, and I going to live near my dear French friends in this very dark moment of their lives—like going to help out one's cousins in need. I think we'll both be happier all our lives to have done this. I hate war, I'm almost as much of a pacifist as Sally Cleghorn (though not quite!) but like nearly all of my generation I'm terribly, tragically bewildered by the complexity of the situation. And it will ease an aching heart to do the simple, obvious, human thing, even if it is not very deep or far-reaching, establish a home near my husband who is alleviating pain, and fill my house, small though it will be, with a succession of homeless Belgian and French children who can share in the mothering I give to my own. Perhaps I can think more clearly what it all means if I can stop the misery of feeling that I am doing nothing—not even the little I might do—to help out in the suffering.

I've written you all this as though you were my God-father, to whom indeed I have recently written very much such a letter. He has disapproved very much of our leaving our comfortable Vermont home, but now, I hope and believe, feels more reconciled to it. I hope you will, too. It makes a good deal of difference to me—what you think.

With every good wish

Faithfully yours,

DOROTHY CANFIELD FISHER

114 RUE DE BRANCAS
SEVRES
SEINE ET-OISE FRANCE
All Saints Day (1923)

MY DEAR PROFESSOR PHELPS:

Your note about "Raw Material" was the first news I had of it, and it has stayed almost the only news! The book came out in August, I imagine, and I suppose some copies were sent me as usual, but customs, or slow mails or something have delayed them. I still haven't

seen a copy. We were in Switzerland well on into September, and had
no word that the book was published. I felt as though I had dropped
it down a well. And then came your letter, . . . can you imagine the
effect? No you can't. I never had so vividly from any written communication the effect of a warm, actual handshake of encouragement. . . .

I watched some very carefully trained tennis players this summer
at Evian (where we were playing this season) with a rather alarmed
interest. They had had evidently the infinitely careful instruction
which is given to leisure-class folks over here, their form was simply
perfection, it was a delight to see them make one perfect stroke after
another, like an artistic creation. But along came a middle-aged Englishman, who had evidently struggled along by himself, had any
number of faulty habits, but who went right through their perfection
like tissue-paper, simply because he had about forty times their
motive-power. It made me think very hard about the art of writing
(everything makes me think hard about that).

Ever yours,

DOROTHY CANFIELD FISHER

114 RUE BRANCAS—SEVRES
April 2, 1924

DEAR PROFESSOR PHELPS:

I'm horrified by your writing that you once addressed "a Normal
School" at Sèvres! Don't you let Mlle. Amieux the Directrice, hear
you! It's as if a French man of letters said that he once spoke to "a
military school at West Point." We consider that this is *the* Normal
School of France, and indeed, so it is! I hope you'll meet and talk to
Mlle. Amieux when you're here. She's a credit to her race and sex.

Every sort of good wish to you for your year over here, and thanks
for your letter.

Affectionate greetings always

DOROTHY CANFIELD FISHER

62

CONVERSATIONS WITH PAUL HEYSE

PAUL HEYSE died on the second of April 1914, at his home in Munich, having reached the age of eighty-four years. His literary career began in 1850, and he wrote steadily to his last hour; his publications covered an immense range—novels, short stories, poems, plays, with a great number of essays in philosophy and criticism. The King of Bavaria in 1854 offered him a home in Munich, with a pension of five hundred dollars a year, so that nearly the whole active life of this Berliner was identified with the intellectual centre of South Germany. In 1910 he received the Nobel Prize.

When I was young, I came across an old paper-cover translation of Heyse's long novel, *The Children of the World*. I read it with such delight that I remember my first waking thoughts every day were full of happy anticipation. I lived with that group of characters, and whenever I open the book now, I find their charm as potent as ever. My hope of sometime seeing and talking with the man who had given me so much pleasure was satisfied in 1904.

It was Sunday, the fifth of June, and a bright, warm afternoon, when I walked along the Luisenstrasse in Munich, and stopped at Number 22. Almost before I knew it, I was talking intimately with the famous novelist. He was then seventy-four, but remarkably vigorous and fresh-faced, an abundant shower of dark hair falling on his neck and shoulders, and his full beard slightly grizzled. He was immensely interested in the criticisms of his play, *Maria von Magdala*, which Mrs. Fiske had been presenting with great success in America. He told me with ardent satisfaction of the large cash royalties that had steadily poured in from across the sea. He wished to know infinite detail about Mrs. Fiske. 'She is a most beautiful woman, is she not?' asked the old man, eagerly. 'On the contrary,' said I, 'she is decidedly lacking in physical charm, both in face and figure.' This seemed a cruel disappointment to him, as he had evidently pictured a superbly handsome creature as the incarnation of his work. I explained to him that so soon as Mrs. Fiske had spoken a dozen lines on the stage, no one knew or cared whether she were beautiful or not; her personality was so impressive, so compelling, that she drew irresistibly the most intense sympathy; that this seemed to me her greatest triumph, by sheer brains and art to produce the illusion of a lovely, suffering woman. But Heyse was not satisfied. '*Man hat mir gesagt, dass sie sehr schön ist.*' Several other visitors entered, and Heyse, forgetting he was a dramatist, and remembering only that he was a doctor of philosophy, plunged into an excited discussion about the work of Professor Justi, of the University of Bonn. Not being particularly interested, I have forgotten everything he said about this philosopher and art critic. I waited patiently for a change in the weather.

It came. The conversation suddenly shifted to American literature. 'Who is your greatest living writer?' I knew that Heyse was a grave, serious, melancholy man, but I boldly answered, 'Mark Twain.' Heyse shook his head, more in sorrow than in anger. 'I have always heard of Mark Twain's humour—that he was the funniest man on earth. I therefore read with the most conscientious attention every word of *Huckleberry Finn*. I never laughed once. I found absolutely not a funny thing in the book.'

Before going, I asked him to write his name in my copy of *Kinder der Welt*. He complied most graciously, though he was surprised, and not overpleased to learn of my enthusiasm for this particular novel. He gave me a really affectionate farewell, and asked me to come and see him whenever I should be in Munich.

On the twenty-first of January 1912, a glorious winter day, I went to see him again, and literally sat at his feet. He was over eighty years old; he occupied a huge carved chair in the centre of his library; the winter sunlight streamed through the windows, crowning his noble head with gold. The walls of the room were entirely lined with books, and he made such an impressive picture in these surroundings, that for a time I hardly heard a word he said, so absorbed was I by the dignity and beauty of the scene.

I took a little chair, directly in front of him, looking up reverently into his face. 'I have lived in this same house nearly sixty years. When I first came here, everyone said, "Why do you live in the country, so far from the city?" But you see the city has come to me, and now I am in the very heart of Munich. I love this house and this street, for I have known no other home since I came to Bavaria.' Once more I told him of my youthful enthusiasm for *The Children of the World*. He said, 'I never read any of my own works. I have forgotten practically everything in the book you admire. But I do remember that it does not express my real attitude towards life, only a certain viewpoint. Everyone who reads that story ought also to read my *Merlin*, as it supplies exactly the proper antidote. The fact is, I read no novels at all, and have not for years. My reading is entirely confined to works on philosophy and metaphysics, which have been the real passion of my life.' He mentioned, however, a number of the young poets, novelists, and dramatists of the day, without a jealous or disparaging word. 'I have not time to read much of these young fellows, but from all appearances, I think the outlook for German literature in the next generation exceed-

ingly bright. The air is full of signs of promise. For me—
ach, ich bin alter Herr!' He said this with indescribable
charm.

I reminded him that on the coming Wednesday night a
new play of his was to have its first performance at the
Residenz Theatre. I told him how keenly I enjoyed *Urauf-
führungen* in Munich, and remarked that of course he
would be present. '*Aber nein!* I never under any circumstances attend the first performances of my plays. It is too
painful. How can I be sure, no matter how intelligent the
actors may be, that they will interpret correctly my real
meaning in my characters and dialogue? And to be in the
least misinterpreted is as distressing to me as a typographical error in one of my printed works. When I take up a
new book of mine, fresh from the press, and find a single
typographical error, I lie awake all night.'

Then the conversation turned to religion. 'Now that
I am an old man, I have changed somewhat my views
about religion. I used to think that perhaps we could get
along without it. Now I know that humanity can never
exist without religion, and that there is absolutely no substitute for it. How are the poor and the sick to live without
the hope and comfort of faith in God? Suppose a poor
seamstress has consumption, who would wish to take away
from her the only hope she has—her belief in religion?
Science and Monism can never fill any place in the human
heart. Religion alone can satisfy human longings and
human aspiration.'

When I rose to go, he accompanied me to the door. I
was deeply affected, as he knew I should not see his face
again. He seemed to read my mind, for he said affectionately, but gravely, '*Wenn Sie in Amerika wieder sind,
denken Sie an mich.*'

63

FRANCE IN 1913

THE summer of 1913 my wife and I spent mainly in France, taking with us our nieces Carolyn Hubbard, aged 19 and Annabel, aged 15. We debarked at Boulogne, spent the whole afternoon in the cathedral and the next day proceeded to Amiens. In Paris we heard *Cyrano de Bergerac* with M. Le Bargy as the hero. On the afternoon of 27 June George Santayana came to tea with us, and was most agreeable. We had not seen him since he left America in 1911. This summer, without the slightest suspicion of its being the last time when France would seem normal, we visited Reims, and made a special pilgrimage to Château-Thierry because it was the birthplace of LaFontaine. We saw Soissons, Laon, Châlons-sur-Marne, Troyes, Langres, Dijon, where the Hôtel de la Cloche looked inside exactly as it did when I stopped there in 1890. We spent a few days at Lyons, and then took the train—I tried in vain to find a boat—for Avignon. Visited the graves of J.S. Mill and his wife; the inscription on her tomb, written by her husband, is filled with superlatives. One night in Avignon we went to a motion picture, and it turned out to be a Wild West American film, with cowboys shooting; the French peasants seemed to enjoy it immensely.

On the National holiday, 14 July, we attended a bull fight in the Roman amphitheatre at Nîmes. There were 20,000 people; it had been previously announced that it would be a mild fight, with no horses or bulls killed. We visited Marseilles and the lovely little university town of

Aix-en-Provence. Carcassonne was just as good as we thought it would be, and our expectations were high. We saw Toulouse, Pau, Biarritz and San Sebastian, the only time I have ever been in Spain.

We spent that night at Rennes: My colleague at Yale, Professor Albert Feuillerat, was for some years professor at the University of Rennes; his wife is the sister of Paul Bourget.

At Vitré we found a curious church, with a fine open-air pulpit on the south side, covered with gargoyles. We visited the Château des Rochers, the home of Madame de Sévigné, only four miles away. And then we had an interesting domestic experience. Our chauffeur was eager to have us visit the home of his parents, because he wanted us to meet them, and because his duties as chauffeur in Caen had prevented his seeing them for I don't know how long. So we motored to a remote village called Bourgon, and we met these peasant parents M. et Mme Odolant. We ate a big lunch in the house of their son-in-law; the loaf of bread was longer than a baseball bat. This father and mother had never been away from the village, had never seen a railway train. They were hospitable, and could not do enough for the friends of their son. One member of our party suspected the chauffeur, and thought that he was leading us into this remoteness in order to murder us. She therefore wrote messages to America, telling where we were going when last heard from. And at table, when the old peasant got out an enormous knife to cut the bread, she felt her worst fears confirmed.

In Paris I went to a rehearsal where only music critics were admitted; when I told the man at the door I was President of the New Haven Symphony Orchestra, which happened to be true, he showed me in with courtesy. The most curious feature of the afternoon's entertainment was a dramatic version of Poe's *The Tell Tale Heart*, called *Le*

Cœur Révélateur. The curtain rose on the scene in the *Raven*, with Poe himself seated in a flood of lamplight.

In September we were in Munich and saw Richard Strauss in the Residenz Theatre conducting his new opera, *Ariadne auf Naxos*.

On 22 April 1913 Sir William Osler came to Yale and at the Elizabethan Club gave a magnificent lecture on his favourite book, *The Anatomy of Melancholy*. After he had spoken for some time, he asked me if we could endure any more; and I told him I thought the undergraduates could sit as long as he could stand. He made, as he did everywhere and on everybody, an unforgettable impression of learning, wisdom, humour and kindliness.

On 8 May J. M. Dent, the London publisher, stayed overnight at our house; he astounded me by saying he had never refused to publish a manuscript which he thought deserved publication on its merits, without any regard to financial return. I told him I thought such a policy would result in bankrupty. 'On the contrary,' said he, 'I have found it profitable.' He told me the greatest undertaking of his life and the one nearest his heart was *Everyman's Library*. One often thinks of the idealistic author and the hard-headed publisher; but I have never seen any poet or novelist more idealistic than Mr. Dent. He seemed unworldly.

64

SOME EVENTS IN 1914

ON St. Patrick's Day the poet William Butler Yeats gave
a reading from his poems at the Yale Elizabethan Club.
At noon I had a long talk with him; he expressed hatred of
George Moore, and said a great many 'events' that Moore
described in his books, conversations with Yeats, etc.,
never happened.

Alfred Noyes and Gerald Stanley Lee were our guests on
30 March; they spoke at the annual banquet of the *Yale
Literary Magazine*. Mr. Noyes regretted the current depreciation of the genius of Tennyson and made a spirited
defence of his poetry.

On 19 April President Wilson gave Huerta of Mexico
until six o'clock that evening to promise to salute the
American flag. At six he had not saluted. War seemed
imminent; a huge crowd of students gathered in front of
my house, expecting a 'patriotic' speech; I ridiculed war
and said the U.S.A., if it really wished to fight had better
take a bigger opponent. I said a war with Mexico would be
silly and criminal. Rather to my surprise, the speech was
well received.

Three days later I presided at a peace meeting of the
students addressed by Norman Angell.

On 23 May at Cincinnati, I spoke with President Taft at
a Yale dinner. A jolly song was sung, written by Cole
Porter, of the class of 1913—a foretaste of the professional
success he was to enjoy in later years.

In this same month I had an unusual experience at a

girls' college in the South. The Commencement bacca-
laureate was given by the President; he read from manuscript but he had no arms and turned the pages with his
teeth. After my own address, he suggested that we go to
a ball game, three miles away; this seemed good to me, and
we hired a horse and buggy, fortunately taking along a
negro boy who crawled in behind. The horse was so enormous that I, an inexperienced driver, could hardly see over
his back. He looked like a dinosaur. On Main Street, amid
crowded traffic, the horse suddenly stood up on his hind
legs, waving his front feet in the air like an impassioned
evangelist. I had great difficulty in getting him into a
horizontal position. In about five minutes he again stood
upright and was so very perpendicular that I expected he
would fall over backwards, in which event I should not now
be describing the incident. The President, since he was defenceless, suggested that we both jump out; a large crowd
of persons had assembled, who seemed intensely amused by
our predicament. I sprang out and then caught the President in my arms. I gave the animal and buggy in charge of
the boy and we walked to the ball game.

What a driver should do when a horse insists on standing
upright and making sweeping gestures, I have not the
faintest idea. Shortly after my return home, I got a letter
from the President, saying 'I am in good health, and so, I
regret to say, is the horse. As soon as I hear of his death, I
will telegraph you.'

This was the last time I attempted to drive a horse.
Every horse I have attempted to ride or drive has endeavoured to murder me. Every horse knows instantly,
when I come near him, of my inexperience, and proceeds
to take advantage of it. I have sometimes been sitting
alongside a man driving a most conservative horse, seemingly destitute of spirit and originality. If my friend asks
me merely to hold the reins while he enters a shop for a

moment, the horse instantly begins to exhibit unsuspected depths of depravity. He will attempt to back the buggy onto the sidewalk and through the shop window. When I am asked if I am afraid of horses I say 'afraid' is too mild a term; I am in terror. When I go shooting in the South, I astonish my hosts by refusing to ride the 'most gentle' horses; I must have a wagon and a driver. I understand the man on horseback when a pedestrian asked, 'Where are you going?' and drew the reply, 'How should I know? ask the horse.'

On 3 August at our house in Michigan our friend and my former Harvard room-mate, Ralph Catterall, professor of history at Cornell, died from a stroke, after an illness of two days. With his son I accompanied the body to Ithaca; as the funeral was not to take place until late in the afternoon, Andrew D. White, who had been first President of Cornell, then Minister to Russia and later Ambassador to Germany, called and took me for a long drive over the beautiful countryside. He spoke mainly about the war which had just been declared in Europe. I remember his saying impressively, 'You will live to see the end of this war, but I shall not.' This prophecy was technically fulfilled. He was then over eighty, and he died on 4 November 1918, only a few days before the formal ending of the war; three days before his eighty-sixth birthday. His conversation in 1914, which lasted four hours, as he drove leisurely through the country roads, was most interesting. He thought that the Kaiser was personally responsible for the outbreak of the war, and hoped to gain dominion over Holland. White felt the war was a catastrophe whose evil results would be felt for a great many years. He gave interesting anecdotes of his residences in Europe. When he was in Russia, he often took walks with Tolstoy. No sooner did the great novelist appear on the street, than he was surrounded by a swarm of beggars, to whom he invariably gave money. Mr. White remonstrated with him, but Tolstoy replied, 'Jesus said Give to him that asketh of thee, and I have no choice in the matter.'

On 7 November we observed the Transit of Mercury, contact coming a little after 9 a.m. We went to the old observatory, collecting Professor Beebe, and the telescope would not work; then in desperation, I entered a room in the Sheffield Scientific School where Professor Farnham was giving a lecture. He consented to an immediate adjournment, found a surveyor's instrument and we had a fine view of the transit.

On 18 November at a reception given in New York to the National Institute by President Butler, we met Eugène Brieux, the French dramatist, who had come over to increase American sympathy for France in the war. He was agreeable and unaffected. He said prohibition must come after the war and it would be a good thing. It did come and was bad. He said the Parisian critics treated him rather condescendingly, calling him *l'honnête Brieux*. I told him how greatly I enjoyed seeing at the Comédie Française his play *Blanchette*; but he said that had little relevancy for America. 'On the contrary,' I told him, 'we have plenty of girls who have passed through our Normal Schools, receive the proper certificates showing they are qualified for teaching, but cannot get any jobs.' It was a pity that Brieux was known chiefly in America as the author of *Damaged Goods*; that gave him the wrong kind of reputation. I always liked particularly his comedy, *La Française*, meant as a rejoinder to *La Parisienne*, although there was a ridiculous American Harvard student, who spoke French much better than English. It is seldom that one sees English correctly given in foreign plays and novels. Brieux felt that an international movement should be started to make foreigners understand that the numerous French novels and plays on adultery did not correctly represent the standards of the French people.

On 27 November I went to Charlotte, North Carolina to address a convention of school teachers. I was asked if I should like to see the house where Mrs. Stonewall Jackson was living; I was amazed that she was living anywhere, because her distinguished husband was mortally wounded in action, in the very moment of victory, shot by mistake in the dusk by his own men, in 1863! This was 51 years later. His wife was living, but too ill to see any visitor. I stood uncovered before the house where there was a light in her room. Time seemed to go back a half-century. The death of Jackson was a fatal blow to the confederacy. When Lee heard he was wounded, he wrote him, 'I should have wished for the good of the country to be disabled in your stead.'

On 24 December we went with Henry Arthur Jones to the first night of his play *The Lie*; we shared a box with Mr. and Mrs. Joseph Choate, the dramatist Augustus Thomas, Professors Brander Matthews, George P. Baker, and the publisher George H. Doran. This was a pleasanter occasion than the first night of Jones's *The Evangelist*, for *The Lie* was a success. I had heard Mr. Choate quoted as having said in a public address, 'The happiest time of life is between seventy and eighty, and I advise everyone to hurry up and get there as soon as possible.' Knowing how happy he had been in the days of his greatest activities, I now asked him if he were correctly reported and if he definitely meant it. He replied that the report was correct and that he was sincere; after seventy he had been happier than ever before.

This autumn I contributed an article to the *North American Review*, called *War*, in which I took the ground that all wars were really civil wars and were contrary to religious teaching. This brought down on my head a good

many attacks, but nothing to what I was to receive in
1917.

On 25 November Edward H. Sothern and Julia Marlowe,
who were playing the entire week in New Haven, came
with me to the Elizabethan Club and there Julia Marlowe
read aloud to the undergraduates some of Shakespeare's
sonnets from the original edition of 1609.

65

WILLIAM HOWARD TAFT

MR. TAFT was the only man in American history to hold both the office of President and of Chief Justice of the Supreme Court; and in private and public life he was always the same, unselfish, modest, kindly, full of mirth and good-humour. His famous chuckle is remembered by all who saw him. He was graduated from Yale in the class of 1878; and although he had made an enormous number of friends in the course of his long professional and public career, I heard him say there were no friendships so strong as those formed in his college days. He was spiritually healthy; he was without jealousy or malevolence or envy. After his tragic quarrel with Theodore Roosevelt and long before they 'made it up' he told me Roosevelt was a man of genius, one of the greatest men he had ever known; and that he always spoke impulsively, without any regard as to possible consequences, as when he said to a group (I think of newspaper men) 'Root is worth all the rest of my Cabinet put together!' Taft enjoyed this all the more because he was included. Taft's two famous remarks about his own nominations are well known. 'I owe both my nominations to Theodore Roosevelt,' for he was willing to step aside in 1912 if Roosevelt would agree to do the same. The other statement concerned Bryan, for whom Taft, like everybody else, had strong personal affection. 'Bryan announced that I was elected President by a majority; but that I would be defeated unanimously. Now when he said that I thought it was one of Brother Bryan's numerous inaccurate prophecies; but I believe for once in his life he was very nearly right!' (Taft got the electoral votes of only Utah and Vermont.)

Taft read aloud to me an anonymous insulting letter he had received; when he had finished, he roared with laughter, and said 'Now think how happy that fellow was when he had got that out of his system!'

After his defeat for re-election in November 1912, he was elected Kent Professor of Law at Yale *College*, as he wished to teach undergraduates. He intended to take up his residence at New Haven as soon as his presidential term expired on 4 March 1913. In common I suppose with others, I wrote him a letter expressing my delight in the honour conferred on Yale by his joining the Faculty, to which I received the following reply:

THE WHITE HOUSE
WASHINGTON
January 7, 1913

MY DEAR PROFESSOR PHELPS:

I very much appreciate your kind letter of January 5th, and I thank you for taking the trouble to write it. The prospect of a closer association with my many friends at Yale is most attractive.

Sincerely yours,

WM. H. TAFT

He arrived in New Haven 1 April. All university lectures were cancelled and three thousand students greeted him at the railway station. When he first entered our Faculty-meeting as a new member, Dean Frederick S. Jones welcomed him as the retiring President of a young country to an old university. It appeared there was no chair in the room sufficiently large for his frame. Someone remembered that the Campus policeman, Jim Donnelley, who weighed nearly three hundred pounds, owned a colossal arm-chair. It was sent for, brought up on the elevator, and it appeared *adorned with the horns of a bull moose*! (Bull Moose was the name of the party headed by Roosevelt in opposition to Taft.) Everyone, including Mr. Taft, laughed aloud.

That Spring of 1913 I played golf very often with him; and he was the best of company, though always keen to win. One day, when he was playing in another foursome, he came into the locker-room, banged his clubs down on the floor, and gave a snort of rage. (He never swore.) I said, 'Why, you feel worse about being beaten at golf than you did on losing the Presidency!' He replied emphatically, 'Well, I do, *now*!'

Here are some letters he wrote:

POINTE-AU-PIC, P.Q., CANADA

MY DEAR BILL:

I have read your article in The Nation on "Sporting Blood" with a great deal of pleasure, and I am glad "to stand on your paper," as the Germans say. Whether what you say is true or not, it might have been true, and therefore the accuracy of history is preserved.

I hope you have been having a pleasant summer.

With affectionate regard both for yourself and your charming comrade, from Mrs. Taft and me, believe me, as always,

Faithfully yours,

WM. H. TAFT

No account of Mr. Taft's residence at Yale would approach completeness without mentioning the immense pleasure given to all Yale and New Haven by the presence of Mrs. Taft. She was so interesting, so charming, and had such a wide experience of people in Europe and America and the Far East, that the society of the University and of the city gained in every way by her residence.

I had sent him the outline of a plan by an American

poet who was deeply interested in educating children in the love and understanding of verse.

JANUARY 3RD, 1916

MY DEAR BILL:

I don't think that the proposition of Miss —— is a practical one. The objections to it are so many that I forbear to mention them. You cannot have a republic of children, because they don't know enough to run a republic, so that she will have to have somebody else run your government, and then when you have somebody else to run your government, who is to be that somebody else, and where are they to get the money, and who is going to be responsible? Bill, it is the result of poetic imagination, and has not a practical element in it. Now you send a diplomatic answer to her.

I reciprocate your good wishes, old man, and send to you and your good wife, from Mrs. Taft and me, our warmest and most affectionate New Year's greetings.

Sincerely yours,

WM. H. TAFT

SUPREME COURT OF THE UNITED STATES
WASHINGTON, D.C.

March 6, 1926

MY DEAR BILL:

I have yours of March 1st. It must have been forwarded to me at Augusta and returned here. I was only in Augusta six days. Nellie and I had a very good time. I had to avoid meetings, but I had the pleasure of seeing some dear old friends, especially Major Black, whom the President of the Hotel invited to come and spend the week at the hotel, so that I saw a good deal of him. An automobile struck him and injured his legs, so that I doubt if he ever walks again except on crutches, but in other respects he seems to be in excellent health and in very good spirits. He is a very white soul. I heard of you very much. Murray Butler was not there when we were there. Sir Robert Borden was. I had known him very pleasantly in Canada.

I have read what you have said, my dear Bill, and of course feel as grateful as I can be for your kindly words.

I hope that Annabel is well and that the old University is going on as it ought to go. It would gratify me much to have a chance to see you both and talk over matters, but I have to be very careful and stay close at home in order to do my work.

Affectionately yours,

WM. H. TAFT

SUPREME COURT OF THE UNITED STATES
WASHINGTON, D.C.

May 30, 1927

MY DEAR BILL:

It is a very great disappointment to me that I cannot be present at Commencement when Justice Van Devanter is presented for his degree. No man ever deserved a degree more, and I don't know but that you might wish a statement from me as to his standing, so that you might give more detail and more certainty as to what you have to say in presenting him. . . .

He is one of the ablest Judges in this country and one of the ablest Judges that we have ever had on the Court, but he is a very modest man and nobody knows the position he occupies on the Court but those who have to do with him in Conference. No one can appreciate his influence except through knowledge gained from the intimacy of the deliberations of the Court over opinions. He was an Indiana boy who went to Purdue University, but was obliged to give up because his father lost such money as he had, and so he did not graduate but went to the Cincinnati Law School. After that he went west and settled at Cheyenne, Wyoming, when Wyoming was a territory. He became District Attorney of the territory, and afterwards, when the Chief Justice had to be removed for something that looked very like graft, he was made Chief Justice, and when the territory came in I think he was still Chief Justice. Then he resigned and went back to the practice, and subsequently was appointed by McKinley to be Assistant Attorney General in charge of the Interior Department, which meant in charge of the land and Indian litigation of the Government. I suppose he is the most deeply versed in land and Indian litigation of all in the profession or on the Bench. He was appointed by Roosevelt to be a Circuit Judge in the 8th Circuit. The 8th Circuit is the largest Circuit in the United States geographically, and runs from the Mississippi west to the Rocky Mountains, and from Texas and Louisiana north to the Canadian border. He was there for seven or eight years, and then I made him a Supreme Court Judge, and he has been on the Supreme Court Bench now about seventeen years. He . . . does not write so many opinions, but they are all admirable when he writes them. I don't know how we could get along without him in Conference. I don't think the Bar realizes generally what a commanding figure he is on the Court. He never advertises and he never seeks publicity. He has not what some of our Judges have by reason of their relations to Law Schools—a claque who are continually sounding their praises, but when it comes to keeping the Court straight and consistent with itself, he is the man who does it, and his power of statement and his exactness and his immense memory for our cases makes him an antagonist in the Conference who generally wins against opposition. He is 68 years old, and he has two sons. One of them he sent to Yale, and he now represents the Guaranty Trust Company in Washington, and is Secretary of the Yale Association here. His wife, like yours, was born in Michigan, and like your wife a charming woman. I hope she will be able to go to the Commencement, but she is not in very good health.

In addition to all his qualities, Van is a fine fellow and a man of substance to whom you can tie. He has more familiarity with our rules than anyone on our Bench. Indeed he drafted the last set of rules himself, and he has had much to do with the legislation that has enabled the Court to reduce the arrears and to catch up with its docket. The truth is I think those who refer to the Court who are in the "know" think when they refer to the Court that they are referring to Van Devanter. Perhaps I do not need to send you a copy of the letter I wrote to the President, but I shall see if I can find it.

Affectionately yours,

WM. H. TAFT

SUPREME COURT OF THE UNITED STATES
WASHINGTON, D.C.

POINTE-AU-PIC, CANADA
July 15, 1927

MY DEAR BILL:

I have yours of July 9th and thank you for writing me. I was very much delighted to hear from Judge Van Devanter of your kindness to him and also of the high opinion that he manifested of your work as the public orator. What I wrote you about Van is entirely true, and the degree that Yale gave him was as deservedly conferred as any degree that the institution ever conferred. He is so modest that it is a real satisfaction to take part in honoring him.

You are very good to be interested in the interview that was published by the Associated Press. I did not revise the interview. Indeed I never saw it until it was published. The correspondent of the Associated Press that does the work of the Court for that institution came to me and said that they were anxious to say something about my becoming seventy. I had something that I was anxious to have them publish in respect to the work of the Court during the last year, and that was published at once. I dictated that. But this last was withheld for a month and there were some inaccuracies in it—one that I did not intend to retire in 1931 when my ten years would entitle me to a pension. If I am living in 1931, I don't know whether I shall retire or not, but certainly I did not intend to make any such announcement. While my health is better than it was last year, my heart is a defective heart, and I can only get along and discharge my duties by the exercise of the greatest care. Next year I am hoping, if I live, to attend our fifty years' anniversary. The boys are falling fast and we have to close up ranks too often.

I am very much disappointed that we did not complete the $20,000,000 fund, but hope that we shall rally to the cause and add something to our subscriptions and induce those who have been lax in the matter to make new subscriptions. No matter what we may have originally thought of the project, now is no time to have Yale fail.

I shall get "Barnum's Own Story" and read it.

Give Annabel Nellie's love and mine, keep a lot for yourself, and believe me, as always, my dear Bill,

Affectionately yours,

WM. H. TAFT

SUPREME COURT OF THE UNITED STATES
WASHINGTON, D.C.

Sept. 23rd, 1927

DEAR BILL:

Thank you for your demonstration that a man at seventy has many reasons for happiness if only he seeks and has the means of having interesting thoughts. . . .

I hope that dear wife of yours is well and is, as I know she is, contributing to your happiness as of yore.

I have been enjoying much the messages of good will that have come to me on the occasion of passing into old age. Judge Holmes denies that 70 is old age. He says that it is only the beginning of middle age. Others assure me that the decade between 70 and 80 is the best of life. Well, I do not wish to institute comparisons, but only to register my gratitude to God that I have been permitted to have had the happiness which has been mine and to be willing to accept whatever may come of sorrow still mindful of the goodness of God.

What a blessing is the affection of friends and family! How rich as compared with any other earthly boon!

With love to you both, in which Nellie joins me.

Affectionately yours,

BILL

SUPREME COURT OF THE UNITED STATES
WASHINGTON, D.C.

January 15, 1929

MY DEAR BILL:

I thank you for giving me a chance to breathe in again the atmosphere of Augusta. I miss what I used to enjoy there, but it makes me sad that Major Black has gone.

Thank you, too, for the revival of Augusta in my heart.

Nellie sends love to you both, as I do.

Affectionately yours,

WM. H. TAFT

SUPREME COURT OF THE UNITED STATES
WASHINGTON, D.C.

POINTE-AU-PIC, CANADA
August 14, 1929

MY DEAR BILL:

I am glad to hear, by your letter of August 9th, that you are in good condition, and that you are in a good work for the preservation of the good things which Nathan Straus has done for his fellowmen.

Nellie and I are delighted to hear from you and Annabel. I have been ill this summer, but I am hopeful now that I am pulling out. I have about half the vacation still to spend in regular vacation work until the first of October.

I see you write from Grindstone City, Michigan. I am delighted to see your signature and to have this evidence that you and Annabel are in good condition.

Affectionately yours,

WM. H. TAFT

Mr. Taft died 8 March 1930.

66

SOME EVENTS IN 1915–16

In New York on New Year's Day I attended the first meeting of the newly-formed American Association of University and College Professors. It was voted to exclude Presidents.

On 18 January for the first time I heard *King John*. It was played by Robert Mantell. I have never had an opportunity to hear it again, but it is effective on the stage even if it was the cause of wit in Mr. Huneker, who said Mantell played the King as if he was afraid someone else was going to play the ace.

Our niece Carolyn Hubbard stayed with us most of the winter and taught me to dance. I had never learned. It seemed strange to begin dancing at fifty, but for the next twenty years I enjoyed it.

On 6 February in Grand Rapids, Michigan, Mrs. Mary H. Gilbert gave me a copy of Anne Sedgwick's novel *The Encounter*, which I regard as one of her best. It is unfortunate that it appeared in England during the early weeks of the outbreak of the war, for in ordinary times it would certainly have attracted much attention. In this novel the character Sachs says, 'If only strength is good, yet it is still more true to say that only goodness is strong.'

Harley Granville-Barker came to New York in February to produce plays and I had many good talks with him; an amazingly interesting personality. On 26 February I saw his production of *Midsummer Night's Dream* with the 'gold heads.' I shall always remember this as the best of many productions of this play. In the next few days I saw his productions of *Androcles and the Lion* and *The Doctor's Dilemma,* both magnificent. He came to New Haven on 3 March and with Evert Wendell, Professor Jack Crawford, and a few others, we went out to the Yale Bowl (an amphitheatre holding 80,000) to test its acoustic properties. It was a bitter cold day with a howling wind; and although the Bowl had been built for spectacles and not for auditions, to our astonishment the acoustics were so perfect that spoken words were distinctly heard. As a result of this test, Granville-Barker decided to produce a Greek play here in the Spring. He and Wendell stayed overnight at our house, and I shall always remember our jolly breakfast party on 4 March. The winter sun flooded the room while our two guests kept up a flow of conversation that matched the sunlight in brilliance.

Granville-Barker gave a fine lecture at Yale and I had the pleasure of speaking at a public dinner held in his honour at New York. His visit had a definite effect on the art of American stage production.

My older colleague, Professor Thomas R. Lounsbury, died suddenly on 9 April; his funeral was held in the University Chapel on 13 April. I was one of the bearers; among the honorary bearers were Theodore Roosevelt and William H. Taft, who had not met or communicated since their unfortunate quarrel four years previously. I was standing by the coffin in the vestibule just before the obsequies, when the two men came up from opposite sides. Roosevelt gave no sign of recognition, whereupon Taft went up to him, said 'How are you, Theodore?' and extended his hand. Roosevelt shook hands silently without smiling; no further communication passed between them.

We celebrated May Day by giving a large luncheon party in honour of Mr. Adams (F.P.A.) of New York; in his Pepys's Diary column that week, he wrote, 'Up, and to New Haven, to Will Phelps's house, where was a brave luncheon; and so to the court, where C. Merz and I did play against Will Phelps and Jack Crawford, who beat us often, too. But this was chiefly Merz's fault.' This was Charles 'Doc' Merz, now the Editor of the *New York Times* and author of many books.

On 7 May (Browning's Birthday) I was Toastmaster at the dinner of the *Yale Literary Magazine*. John Kendrick Bangs was the guest of honour when, after I had reminded the assembly that this was the poet's birthday and that in his last poem he had asked all who remembered him after his death to greet him with a cheer, as he expected to be alive and happily developing, I called on the company to rise and give a cheer for Robert Browning. Mr. Bangs told me he had never been more deeply affected.

Greet the unseen with a cheer!

And on that very day Charles Frohman stood on the deck of the sinking *Lusitania* and made his famous remark that he had always considered death a great adventure.

On 15 May at the Yale Bowl in magnificent weather and before an audience of 10,000 Granville-Barker and Lillah McCarthy gave an impressive performance of Euripides' *Iphigenia in Tauris*. The appearance at the end of the play of the goddess Athene was thrilling.

An astounding solar spectacle happened on the morning of 20 May between 11.30 and noon. An undergraduate entered my classroom and excitedly urged me to come out. I immediately adjourned the class. There in a cloudless sky was the sun, a yellow ball in the midst of a huge solid black circle with a ring of fire on its circumference; from the sun (like the hub of a wheel) to the rim of fire (like a tire) all was solid black; the rest of the sky outside this circle bright blue. I have never seen anything like it before or since. On this very morning had come the news that Italy had decided to enter the war. There were 60,000 Italians living in New Haven; many of them were in terror, as they thought this spectacle was a portent. Who could blame them?

On 3 June the great surgeon Dr. William F. Verdi operated on my neck, removing something or other; I never found out what it was, but I had absolute confidence in Dr. Verdi. I was under ether three hours. Curiously enough, when I emerged, I could *hear* everything perfectly, every footstep and every word, but could see nothing. Sight came back later.

In this year I had two operations, on the outside and on the inside of my neck; the cure in both cases was permanent.

On 19 June in the open air on the Yale Campus occurred the world première of Tennyson's *Harold*, given effectively by the undergraduates. I agree with William Archer that it is Tennyson's best play, although he never saw it on the stage.

This autumn I gave the Lowell Lectures in Boston; six lectures on American literature. The audiences were so large that I was asked to repeat the course after Christmas; but I was not able to do this.

At a dinner party in connexion with these lectures, given by Dr. Sedgwick in Boston, I had the pleasure of meeting that remarkable woman, Mrs. Bell, the daughter of Rufus Choate. She was one of the best conversationalists I have ever known. She was 83, full of vigour and enthusiasm.

At the annual dinner of the Ends of the Earth Club in New York on 3 December, I had the pleasure of meeting the famous astronomer Percival Lowell. I asked, 'Aren't you the brother of President Lowell?' which was a *faux pas*. He replied with severity, 'He is my youngest brother.' I apologized with such fervour that we became the best of friends and on two subsequent occasions he sent me beautiful photographs of Saturn which he had taken at his observatory in Flagstaff, Arizona.

The American novelist Forman went down on the *Lusitania* four months after writing this letter.

CENTURY CLUB

NEW YORK

January 7/15

DEAR PROFESSOR PHELPS:

Certain good ladies of the committee of the "Lafayette" relief fund are asking university men to write a letter to their college undergraduate paper urging the mention of the fund. They have asked me to write a letter to the *Yale News* and I have said I would but it might be best, first, I think, to enquire from someone on the spot whether this would be an undesirable thing to do. So I turn, by your leave, to you. Do you know of any good reason why I, or another, should not write a brief and moderately expressed letter to the *News* suggesting that undergraduates could, through this fund, contribute about as effectively as possible to a very good and much needed work?

I am sorry to impose upon your time but in matters like this one need not apologize.

Drop me a single line, if you will, at your leisure.

With compliments and best wishes, I am

Very faithfully yours,

JUSTIN MILES FORMAN

On 6 December in New Haven we heard the first performance in America of Shaw's *Major Barbara*, with a distinguished cast. Louis Calvert, who created the role in England, was superb. Later I got to know him very well indeed. He was always agreeable, but off the stage he seemed in no way remarkable, either in appearance or in conversation; but the moment he appeared before the footlights, he was a genius. The art of impersonation is often entirely distinct from a man's personality, as perhaps it ought to be. Dr. Johnson said, 'Pritchard, in common life, was a vulgar idiot; she would talk of her *gownd*; but, when she appeared upon the stage, seemed to be inspired by gentility and understanding.'

Those who regard Johnson as elephantine should remember the graceful compliment he paid Mrs. Siddons; this was during the last year of his life, when he was ill. She came to see him and there was no chair for her. He said with a smile, 'Madam, you who so often occasion a want of seats to other people, will the more easily excuse the want of one yourself.'

On 27 December in New York we had a charming evening dining at the house of Mr. and Mrs. Otto Kahn; he was President of the Metropolitan Opera; they took us to *Martha*, which I do not remember to have heard since I heard Patti in it in 1892; Caruso was in splendid voice and high spirits, making it a great occasion.

On 14 January 1916 John Masefield gave his first American lecture at Yale. His deep cultivated voice added greatly to the charm of his reading. He told me of all his works he most enjoyed writing the play *Nan* and the poems *The Everlasting Mercy* and *The Widow in the Bye Street*. He said Dauber was a real person whom he knew and that he died in exactly the way described in the poem. After he had read for a while, he invited the audience to choose poems; whereupon *August 1914* was called for. After reciting four or five stanzas he broke down, overcome with emotion, and said he must read something else.

On 2 March in New Haven was given the first performance of Galsworthy's play *Justice* with John Barrymore. It was immensely successful and had a long run in New York. Many managers had refused it, thinking it could not possibly succeed. On the way out from the theatre a lady asked me if I did not find the play depressing. 'On the contrary, I find it exhilarating. Musical comedy I find depressing.'

As during the last few years (1930–38) we have been hearing so much about British propaganda and how the wily, wicked British lured America into the World War, I take pleasure in recording that the philosopher Lowes Dickinson of King's College, Cambridge, came to Yale on 12 April 1916 and gave an eloquent talk on peace; he was opposed to the war and to our having anything to do with it. I had a long talk with him.

On 8 and 9 December I lectured at Bowdoin College in Brunswick, Maine, on their two most famous graduates— Longfellow and Hawthorne—who were classmates but not intimate until long after graduation. On the early morning of the second day, in brilliant windless winter sunshine, I had a long walk with President Hyde in the Longfellow woods, which I shall never forget. Later in the church I entered Pew 25, where Mrs. Stowe conceived *Uncle Tom's Cabin*.

On 18 December at Yale we celebrated the two-hundredth anniversary of the birth of Gray. I read the *Elegy* in English and then Professor Robert Sanderson read his fine translation of it in French verse.

67

JOURNEY TO THE HAWAIIAN ISLANDS

IN 1916 I was invited by the Yale Alumni of Honolulu to
come and speak at their annual banquet, and with the
invitation came a cheque covering expenses from New
Haven to Honolulu and return, for us both. Before this,
the longest distance I had ever travelled for one Yale
dinner was in 1902, to Denver, Colorado; the Honolulu
journey established a record.

In the dining-car on the morning when we were due in
San Francisco, I glanced at the morning paper, just to
make sure that our steamer, the *Matsonia*, would leave on
time; and to my dismay, I found that on account of a
strike, her sailing was postponed. This was a tragedy as
the dinner was set for the night we were due at Honolulu.
Looking through the shipping-list, I saw there was a
steamer for Australia, the *Sierra*, due to leave the next
day, which would stop at Honolulu. I hurried to the office,
and found there was only one room unengaged—the Bridal
Chamber! We sailed at two o'clock the next afternoon; it
was bitterly cold, with fog and icy wind as we proceeded
through the Golden Gate. The first five nights were overcast, so that no stars could be seen. This made the sixth
and last night on board thrilling, for when I looked aloft,
I saw a sky new and strange. Indeed I think the change in
the constellations was the one thing that impressed me as
more 'different' than any other spectacle. There was the
Southern Cross, and the brilliant star Alpha Centauri
(why don't they have a name for that wonderful star?),

with many other stars I had never seen before; and the whole of Scorpio in all its magnificence. In the sea there was a wonderful exhibition of phosphorescent fish. At noon of that day, 18 June, for the only time in my life, I saw the Captain take the sun looking north.

When we drew up at the dock, there was a large group of Yale men, with a brass band, playing Queen Lil's national air, and we got a hearty welcome from J.R.Galt, '89, and representatives of the old Yale families of the islands— the Judds, the Cookes, the Alexanders, the Baldwins, with Chief Justice Frear and others. They gave a Yale cheer just before we landed, which brought tears to my eyes. We were taken to the beautiful home of Mr. and Mrs. Galt where we remained during our entire visit; and where the word hospitality took on new connotation; kindness, consideration, affection that never failed.

That night I spoke at the Yale Alumni Dinner; about thirty men were present. The following night I spoke at the seventy-fifth anniversary exercises of Oahu College, the oldest college in the United States west of the Mississippi.

On the following day in the open air the great historical pageant was given. In a conspicuous place sat the former Queen Lilioukuani; a most interesting, if tragic figure. Her face combined extreme intelligence with profound melancholy. As she reviewed the pageant, the procession came to a stop in front of her, and a Hawaiian made a long oration in the Hawaiian language, all of which was addressed directly and exclusively to her. I would have given much to know what he was saying. For it was a historical moment; and what were her thoughts as she saw this pageantry of her past glories, and listened to that intimate speech? After the exercises, we were presented to the Queen, and shook hands. She spoke a few words in English to us. In the procession of the pageant, the natives came first, then the missionaries, then the school-children. There were of course many floats, giving historical tableaux.

Many years before this, when King Kalakaua made his famous journey around the world, an important matter of royal etiquette in England was settled with characteristic, shrewd common sense and tact by the Prince of Wales, afterward King Edward VII. The question was as to who should go in to dinner after Queen Victoria; was this dark-skinned man from the Sandwich Islands a real king taking precedence over the Prince of Wales, or should he go in among the general nobility and diplomatic guests? The Prince said, 'Either this man is a king and must precede me, or he is a negro and should go in with a napkin over his arm.'

One day I had a grand experience riding the waves. I was not clever enough to ride a plank alone, and it was marvellous enough to see some of the natives do it. But a number of us, clad in bathing-suits, were taken out in a big outrigger three or four miles from shore. While we were waiting for the right kind of wave, I dived into the sea, which had exactly the same temperature as the air, swam around awhile, and when I climbed into the boat again, I was neither too cold nor too warm. All of a sudden one of the natives gave a sharp cry, the men paddled for shore desperately, and then, strangely enough, it was as if Neptune himself had lifted us high in the air. The thrill of that moment! Our big outrigger rose on the crest of an enormous wave; we were raised by a submarine power of irresistible, overwhelming might. Instantly the men put away their paddles and with one man to steer, we rode that one big wave two or three miles to shore,

> like Arion on the dolphin's back.

It was a marvellous experience. Strange it was to look around and see other boatloads of people at various places before and behind us, and all, like the figures on Keats's urn, remaining at precisely the same relative positions.

Honolulu is the only place I have ever seen where various races and nationalities live together in absolute harmony, with no self-consciousness. I visited the Kaiulani School, where, counting the different Hawaiian strains, there were among the children 58 distinct nationalities. The American flag was brought out, the pupils saluted it in the open air, and then recited Longfellow's *The Building of the Ship*. In one of the rooms I made an address to the children of the first grade—Chinese, Japanese, Portuguese, part-Hawaiian, all Hawaiian, and American.

It was a night's voyage to Hawaii, the biggest of the islands; Mr. Galt took us there, and in an automobile on the railroad tracks, we went through miles of sugar-cane; and at various points had views of the ocean, Rainbow Falls, and other splendours.

We went to the top of the plateau later, and spent the night at the Crater Hotel. In the twilight we walked three miles across a field of dead lava, feeling as if we were in an extinct world. Looking down into the horrible boiling crater Halemauman was like looking into hell; and there was such a horrible fascination about it, that I felt an almost overpowering impulse to hurl myself into the dreadful fiery pit.

In the distance we saw the two great mountains, Mauna Loa, largest volcano in the world, with a capacity of 120 Vesuviuses, and Mauna Kea, its summit covered with snow. Both are about 14,000 feet high. At sunset the double column of smoke rising from Mauna Loa was an impressive spectacle. On Hawaii it was very hot by day and very cold by night. In Honolulu it is pleasantly warm (not too oppressive) the year round, but the frequent daily showers are a nuisance. The inhabitants refuse to call them rain; the name is *liquid sunshine*. There are so many members of the Judd family there that my wife said that the rain falls on the Judds and on the Unjudds.

We sailed for California on the *Matsonia*, so heavily loaded with sugar that the odour overcame the salty smell of the ocean. As the ship was ready to depart, our necks were swathed with the flowers called *lei*.

Those who have been around the world tell me there are only two places that can be called Paradise; one is Ceylon and the other the Hawaiian Islands. I never saw Ceylon but the Islands fully deserve the name. Mark Twain suffered from nostalgia for them all the rest of his life; and his description of them in *Roughing It* (1872) is still the best account I have seen. Now they are a part of the United States; and while there, one must never speak of returning to America or to the United States, but use only the expression 'the mainland,' for they are just as much a part of the United States as Michigan or Ohio. I had the pleasure of a long talk with Mr. Dole, the only President of the Hawaiian Republic; for after the revolution that deposed the monarchy and before the annexation, there was a period of brief independence. It took tremendous courage to assume the responsibility of the Presidency; for if the Republic had failed, and it was a narrow thing, the President would have certainly been executed. Mr. Dole was a tall, splendid man with a huge snow-white beard. He spoke so softly and with such quiet, unassuming modesty, that it seemed strange to think of the turbulent scenes when he rode the whirlwind and directed the storm.

68

VACHEL LINDSAY

The American poet, Nicholas Vachel Lindsay, was the nearest approach to the mediaeval minstrel I ever saw. He walked from Florida to New Jersey, and later from Illinois to Arizona, carrying no luggage and no money. All that he carried was a package of his printed poems, called *Rhymes to be Traded for Bread*. He described his adventures in a charming book, *A Handy Guide for Beggars*. I regard his poetry, at its best, as original and imperishable. *General William Booth Enters into Heaven*, *The Congo*, *The Santa Fé Trail*, and many other poems, are truly great, both in their soaring imagination and in their felicity of diction. Edgar Lee Masters, who wrote the best biography of Lindsay, has said that if only Lindsay could have had an intimate friend, as Wordsworth had Coleridge, his life would have been happier and even more productive.

In 1916 I got Lindsay to lecture at Yale, the first of three or four of his appearances in New Haven.

On one evening, when he sat unrecognized in the audience, I lectured at the Brooklyn Institute on his poems and read them aloud. We returned together to Manhattan and sat up late talking. He thought I read *The Santa Fé Trail* better than he had, but I made a bad mess of the poem *1889* and we differed on the proper way to interpret *The Congo* to an audience.

Vachel Lindsay was a charming, affectionate, noble-minded idealist. He was also a man of genius.

603 SOUTH FIFTH STREET
SPRINGFIELD, ILLINOIS
October 31, 1916

MY DEAR WILLIAM LYON PHELPS:

Enclosed you will find some proof-sheets, which you need not acknowledge or return. The book will be out in a week or so, but I felt this special story might interest you.

Thank you indeed for putting my books into your courses. I hereby withdraw anything that sounded like a petition that you beat the drum on my behalf that I may have my books established among you. It seems that the drum has been beaten, the works put on the proper shelf and the war is over that I thought just begun, and I have a reasonable share of the spoils.

In your class of one hundred and twenty-five boys, twenty-five will be writing verses. I want them for my friends year by year and I am sure you can keep them for me, and that is all anyone should ask of any one institution. I am especially anxious for the five out of the twenty-five, they will be not only rhymers, but poets. I want them for nephews!

Very sincerely,

NICHOLAS VACHEL LINDSAY

603 SOUTH FIFTH STREET
SPRINGFIELD, ILLINOIS
August 8, 1917

Prof. William Lyon Phelps,
Seven Gables,
Grindstone City Michigan:

MY DEAR FRIEND: Thank you indeed for your letter. I never see your name in print, your work or an allusion in a review, but what I remember your exceedingly fraternal greeting at Yale, and am thoroughly grateful for such an ally among the wise of this generation. The war is so all-absorbing one would scarcely expect one friend to remember him, as you have remembered me in Michigan.

I make friends slowly, and am perfectly reconciled to that state of affairs, particularly when I am able to keep them. What more can a man ask in this world? To have one's writing seem a reality to even a few is a justification of one's existence. And many a worthy and painstaking writer goes through life not sure that anything he has ever done has ever been alive to anyone. I am satisfied that is the hard fate of many a good poet. And I am certainly dependent on the people who are willing to talk about my work occasionally, for more and more I see myself as a writer, and less as a public speaker. If I could get into one room the people like you who really cared, every year, I would be satisfied with about one recital, as I feel at present.

This Fall the Macmillan Company brings out *The Chinese Nightingale and Other Poems*, comprising all I have written and recited since the Congo collection. Next Spring they will bring out the book on which I have been working off and on for years: *The Golden Book of Springfield*, a prose work to which I expect to give all my time this summer and fall and all the time I am not in public in the winter. In brief it treats my home town in the same spirit in which I treat the road, in my prose books on the road. The actual Golden Book is a hypothetical book about Springfield to be written one hundred years hence. So my volume is a hypothetical review, showing what I hope that book will say, and what my intimates in this town hope it will say. Frankly the N.V.Lindsay the reviewers know came nearer existing twelve years ago, than today, my manuscripts are so far behind my notes. And a thing that has helped in this is that through changing publishers etc., my first book is my latest. If you want my ideas in order, assume the writer of the *Handy Guide for Beggars* is just out of college, of *Adventures While Preaching* beginning in the thirties, and *The Art of the Moving Picture* half way through the thirties. The Moving Picture book, in the last half embodies my main social ideas of two years ago. In mood and method, you will find *The Golden Book of Springfield* a direct descendant of the general social and religious philosophy which I crowded into the photoplay book whether it belonged there or not. I hope you will do me the favor and honor to set my work in this order in your mind, for many of my small public still think *A Handy Guide for Beggars* the keynote of my present work. But it was really my first wild dash. Well, well, it is midnight, therefore I am too silly to stop. . . .

If ever you mention my pictures, (which will of course be a favor) should you ever mount the rostrum on my behalf again, do not be too certain in an official way that they will ever come out in a book. This time next year is a long way off. But I would appreciate it if you would express toleration of such pictures as are in existence. My claim for them is that while labored and struggling in execution, they represent a study of Egyptian hieroglyphics and Japanese art, two most orthodox origins for art, and have no relation whatever to cubism, post-impressionism, or futurism. When I was in art school none of those movements were in existence, and frankly I have no patience with them. I mean they give me the fidgets. Of course I do not question the taste of the man who enjoys them. But his taste is not mine.

I have been very fond of Swinburne all my life, and I should say my drawing is nearer to his ornate mood than any of my writing has been. But that is a matter for your judgement.

I am spending my summer absolutely alone in an empty house, and it makes one communicative at midnight. The noise of the typewriter becomes actual conversation in a house as empty as this one.

Very sincerely,

NICHOLAS VACHEL LINDSAY

69

AMERICA IN THE WAR

WE woke up New Year's Day 1917 in Augusta, Georgia;
we had been there a few days and liked the place, the climate, and the people; and we liked them even more eight
years later! On our return North, we stopped 7 January
at Washington, where I called on Browning's daughter-in-
law, Fanny (Mrs. Pen Browning). She told me about the
poet's last days, how cheerful he was even up to the end,
how he lay in bed on that last day (12 December 1889)
turning over the leaves of his last book of poems, *Asolando*,
an advance copy of which had been sent him. She showed
me the very copy. He died at ten in the evening. He was
told that the book was published in London that day; the
evening papers contained complimentary reviews. 'That
is very gratifying' said he; and those were his last words.
She made me some presents so valuable that I was amazed;
an original etching by Rembrandt and a picture of the
Abbé Vogler, both of which had belonged to Browning; a
lock of his hair, a book of press cuttings and other treasures.

On 22 January and succeeding five days I gave lectures
at the Convocation of Bangor Theological Seminary in
Maine; weather ten below zero, air crisp and inspiring. I
had distinguished colleagues as speakers that week—
William H. Taft, Harry Emerson Fosdick, Ritchie Smith of
Princeton. Taft made a fine address on world peace, but it
was clear to him and to us all that we should soon be in the
war.

On 31 January in New Haven, after a magnificent recital by Josef Hofmann, I had the pleasure of meeting him
at supper with a few friends. He was full of fun. He had recently played a concerto somewhere, and when asked if
the orchestra had followed him well, he said, 'Yes, they
followed me about two bars behind.'

On 2 March in Detroit I heard the orchestra conducted
by a former Yale pupil of mine, Weston Gales; the piano
soloist was Ossip Gabrilowitsch, who played the *Emperor
Concerto* with genius; he was later to become conductor of
the Detroit orchestra.

On 7 March the English poet W.W.Gibson gave a curiously slow public reading of his works at Yale; later, in conversation with him, I told him that I had read aloud to
appreciative audiences some of his poems. 'I am sure you
read them better than I could,' he said modestly and truly.

On Wednesday, 4 April, at the instigation of President Wilson, the U.S.Senate voted for war, 82 to 6; and on
Good Friday, 6 April, the House followed suit, at 3.15 a.m.
with fifty negative votes. The President's signature followed the same afternoon and as we emerged from hearing
Parsifal in New York, the evening papers announced that
our country was at war. No more operas were sung in
German in New York for some time.

The American poet, Robert Frost, read from his works
at the Elizabethan Club on 16 May; he read as if composing. He said the sound of the voice should be heard in every
creative line.

On 25 October in Cambridge, Mass. I had the pleasure of
dining with Miss Grace Norton; she was about eighty years
old, and full of wit and intellectual energy.

In New Haven on 29 October I had the first opportunity
of my life to hear *King Lear* in English (Robert Mantell).

On 17 November for the first time I heard Percy
Grainger, the Australian composer, give a piano recital in

New York. He reminded me of a young tawny lion, bursting with vitality. I had good talk with him and his mother afterwards; that was the beginning of an intimate friendship.

Another memorable musical performance I heard in New York at the Punch and Judy theatre on 26 November —Bauer and Thibaud played three of Beethoven's sonatas for piano and violin; and once more I wondered at Tolstoy's impressions on hearing the *Kreutzer*; no music is more healthy and wholesome. Yet his strange novel, however falsely inspired, is a work of genius, though I wish he had never 'explained' it.

While suffering from a bad cold, I gave a lecture at Springfield, Ohio; at the conclusion a lady said to me with great earnestness, 'You have a very dangerous organic disease; I can tell it positively by looking into your eyes; my husband looked exactly that way; he died of it.' I thanked her for her warning, but told her I was sure she was mistaken. 'No,' she said, 'do not imagine it is only a cold. You have the disease.' The next day when I reached Indianapolis, I waited between trains at a club, where for five hours I read from beginning to end an early novel by Booth Tarkington, called *The Two Vanrevels*, and forgot my cold and my fatigue.

The Modern Language Association met this Christmas vacation in New Haven and I read a paper on *Robert Browning and Alfred Austin* containing entirely new material that I had discovered in the manuscripts at Balliol. Browning's Hogarthian attack on Austin does not appear in the MS. but is in the first edition of *Pacchiarotto*. I wonder what happened while he was reading the proof. And how amazed Austin would have been if he had known that year (1876) that Browning would be buried in Westminster Abbey and how even more amazed Browning would have been if he had known that Austin whom he regarded as a ridiculous mannikin would succeed Alfred Tennyson as Poet Laureate!

I do not know exactly when I began to hate war; as a boy, of course, I loved it and gloried in it. I read many histories of our Civil War and my heroes were Union generals and admirals. Early in 1898, however, the propaganda for war with Spain seemed to me silly and wicked. I could see no reason for war with Spain, and the slogan, *Remember the Maine*, left me quite cold. It seemed President McKinley did not want war, and that he was doing everything possible to prevent it. I was sad indeed when he finally yielded to the pressure of public opinion.

During that war, the leading scholar and teacher on the Yale Faculty, Professor W.G.Sumner, delivered a public lecture which he called 'The Conquest of the United States by Spain,' meaning that the results of our victory would be injurious to our peace, security, and prosperity. I admired him for his courage and independence, and as nothing happened except scattered protests from those who thought he was both mistaken and unpatriotic, I foolishly came to believe that even in war there would be freedom of speech, and that those who opposed a war in which their country was engaged would suffer nothing worse than social ostracism, which they ought to expect. This feeling of mine was strengthened by the experience of the English independent thinkers who publicly disapproved of the Boer War in 1900. If any one had told me then that free speech would be suppressed by force in a general European war, and that no country would be less free than my own, I should not have believed it.

I also remembered the public expression of hostility to the war with Mexico that had been so general and so outspoken in New England. I ardently admired Lowell's *Biglow Papers*.

Suppression of free speech is founded on fear; and I

should have remembered what happened to the Tories in the War of the Revolution and what happened to those who were called Copperheads in the Civil War. So long as a country is engaged in a small war and sure to win, those who oppose it are regarded merely as cranks, or perhaps sneered at as unpatriotic. But in an important war where the outcome is uncertain, those who oppose it are rightly or wrongly regarded as worse than the foreign enemy. I say rightly or wrongly, because it is not entirely clear to me whether a man should follow his conscience as a Christian and oppose any war, or whether he should co-operate with his fellow-countrymen after a war has actually begun. No man was ever a more complete pacifist than Benjamin Franklin; he did everything he could to prevent war with England. After America was victorious, he said there never was a good war or a bad peace. But during the war, he worked with all his genius for American victory.

'God's intimations fail in clearness rather than in energy,' said Browning; even when we feel a tremendous impulsion to do right, we are not always sure what is the right thing to do. No class of men has been more maligned by intransigent pacifists, communists, and atheists than Christian ministers who have supported their country in a war; but two things may be said in their defence.

First, ministers are naturally co-operative. They are not lazy or selfish or accustomed to isolation. They work and work hard with groups and organizations. When everyone is making sacrifices for what is believed to be the public welfare, it seems natural to them to support with zeal the common cause. They are not coldly critical of group enthusiasms; they are perhaps somewhat easily stirred by appeals to justice. And in wartime propaganda does its perfect work, and a majority of ministers in every country believe they are helping in a just and righteous cause.

Secondly, there were a great many more ministers who opposed the World War than there were men of science. All my life I had heard of the ardent love of truth displayed by scientific investigators; no matter whither the truth led, they followed. They were not swayed by sentiment, like clergymen; they did not suffer from wish-beliefs; no, they were dispassionate, uncompromising followers of the truth. Yet, when the war broke out, these men of science forgot truth and devoted all their abilities and energies to perfecting the means for a more extensive slaughter of the 'enemy.' How Haeckel used to ridicule sentimental believers in religion! Yet no old woman telling her beads was more sentimental in her faith than he was in his faith in Germany's cause; in his faith that she was fighting a noble, just war of defence.

Of all the thousands of scientific men in the world, I can think of only one who publicly opposed the war, Bertrand Russell. He went to prison for his opinions.

But many clergymen were jailed. When America entered the war in 1917, a Baptist minister in Vermont who expressed publicly his opinion that the war was wicked, was tried and condemned to a Federal prison for fifteen years. After the war was over, he was released by a presidential pardon.

Among all the 'conscientious objectors' who suffered for their love of truth, was there one distinguished scientist, except Russell? What is truth?

I mention these matters to explain the perplexity and agony of mind from which I suffered from 1914 till 1918. When the war broke out in 1914, I wrote an article for the *North American Review*, in which I took the position that all war was wrong, contrary to religion and reason and common sense; and that Christians should oppose it. This article brought down upon my head condemnation from many sources; but I had expected that, and did not mind.

I wrote other articles in behalf of peace, and made a number of public addresses. The feeling in America was so ardent that I was called pro-German; but I was not pro-German; I was pro-British. I wrote an article for the *New York Times* called *The Dance of Death*, in which I said I hoped Germany would lose the war, because I believed she was chiefly responsible for starting it; but I also said that we in America ought not to be angry with the Germans for their resentment against the United States for supplying Great Britain and the Allies with munitions. In our Civil War the American poet James Russell Lowell thus addressed Great Britain in his poem

JONATHAN TO JOHN

You wonder why we're hot, John?
Your mark was on the guns,
The *neutral* guns that shot, John,
Our brothers and our sons.

But I soon found that any appeal to reason in time of a great war was like attempting to stop a cyclone with one's breath or to check a locomotive by placing a feather in front of it.

In the months immediately preceding America's entrance into the war, David Starr Jordan, Ex-President of Stanford University in California, came to the Atlantic Seaboard to make public addresses against it. He was forcibly expelled from every college where he attempted to speak. He then wrote me from New York asking if he might speak at Yale. Although I had no authority to grant this permission officially, I thought it would be a good time to find out whether free speech was to be tolerated in our universities or not. I told him to come. Then I called on Anson Phelps-Stokes, the Secretary of the University, who conferred with President Hadley, and although they both disapproved of Doctor Jordan and hoped I would not agree to his coming, they did give me permission, which I have always thought was a fine and sportsmanlike action on their part. It must be remembered that Jordan had not been allowed to speak at any other Eastern university. It was natural that some outbreak was feared if he came to Yale.

Well, I felt that the question of free speech was more important than anything else. The feeling against Jordan was terrific. He came to Yale to make his speech on 29 March, and the United States entered the war the next week. I received threatening letters and many visits from persons either begging or demanding that I refuse Jordan permission. On the morning of the fateful day, a letter appeared in the *Yale News*, signed by two undergraduates, which gave me to understand that both Jordan and I would be ridden out of town on a rail. Most fortunately for me and for the cause, my large class in American Literature, over a hundred Seniors and Juniors, had its regular meeting that noon. I told them that I had read the letter in the *News*. That I had not asked Jordan to come and thus provoke a riot. But that President Jordan, a distinguished scholar, had written me asking permission to speak at Yale. I thought the honour of Yale was involved. I could not and would not tell Doctor Jordan that Yale did not allow public expression of unpopular opinions. I considered it my duty to comply with his request. I believed in the fairness of mind of the average Yale undergraduate.

I shall be grateful to these students as long as I live. They spent the afternoon arousing sentiment in the university in favour of the meeting. I met President Jordan at the train, took him to dinner at my house, and while this was going on, a member of the Faculty called and begged me not to hold the meeting. 'There is an organized group who are going to run you out of town!'

We went to the meeting, however, and were saved by the very size of the crowd; every place taken, and the aisles so jammed with men standing that the 'organized group' whom I saw near the doors could not get at us. The front seats were taken by undergraduates in the military uniform of the United States. As we came to the platform, there was some hissing in the rear of the room which was drowned by cheers. I began by saying 'I about to die salute you!' I said I was proud that Yale permitted free speech if other colleges did not, and introduced the speaker. After the speech had gone on for fifteen minutes there was organized shouting outside 'We want Woolsey Hall!' the largest hall in the University, holding three thousand. Doctor Jordan, thinking students outside were trying to break up the meeting, made an angry remonstrance. But I sprang up and said 'Doctor Jordan, this is a great compliment. The men outside want to hear you. They cannot get in. This meeting is now adjourned and we shall all go over to Woolsey Hall.' This was a dangerous experiment because we had to walk there. But the crowd was so eager to get seats they paid no attention to us, but left the hall as if it were on fire; by the time we reached the stage of Woolsey, the huge auditorium was crowded. Some students whispered to me, 'Do you mind if we have a patriotic parade with band, *after* this meeting, to show our own sentiments?' 'On the contrary,' I replied, 'you ought to show your sentiments just as Jordan and I are trying to show ours.' The speech went on for nearly an hour; then I heard the band getting ready in the street; and I suggested to Doctor Jordan that we adjourn, as we had won our fight.

I found out afterwards that we were saved from one possible rumpus by Jim Braden, an undergraduate friend of mine, member of the football team, who later saw service in France. Guy Nickalls, the English coach of the crew, was standing in the rear of the hall, wild with rage. He announced that he was going on the platform to break my neck. Whereupon Jim Braden said, 'The first move you make, I'll smash your face in!'

Although I suffered greatly from fear—downright physical cowardice—during the days preceding this meeting, and the meeting was a terrific nervous strain, now, looking back on it, I am more proud of that affair than of any one thing in my career. For once in my life, anyhow, I really stood by my convictions in the face of peril. For, if as seemed probable, I had been tarred and feathered, and ridden out of town on a rail, could I ever have recovered from that kind of public ridicule? I honestly did not mind being killed; what I feared was the disgusting, degrading— well, I was in a cold sweat of fear. How magnificent those undergraduates were! They were all eager to enlist; the only thing they were afraid of was that the war would be over before they could get to France; yet they not only saw this double peace-meeting through, but at the end of it, gave tremendous cheers. I wrote a letter to the *Yale News*, in which I said, 'The students did not agree with President Jordan before, or during, or after his address; but a great victory has been won for free speech, a victory that left no bitterness behind it.'

Thereafter and for the next six months, I received (not once from Yale, but from many places all over the country) insulting letters, some signed, some unsigned. One prominent Yale alumnus wrote me, 'I am ashamed of you and shall be ashamed of Yale if she does not expel you.' President Hadley and the Corporation were daily besought to expel me from my professorship, being told that instead of being on the Faculty, I ought to be in prison.

I shall always be grateful to President Hadley for standing by me, especially because he did not agree with me at all. He was subjected to tremendous pressure but he insisted that I had a right to do exactly what I had done. One of my best friends was Major Danforth, of the U.S. Army, who had been detailed as professor of military tactics at Yale. I had several talks with him. He tried to convince me that the U.S. was absolutely right in entering the war and that the war itself was wholly just, but he told me he had no feeling for me personally except respect and affection.

I don't like war, but I have never known a graduate of West Point or Annapolis, or any military or naval officer, whom I did not admire.

These exciting events happened in March; it was not until August that my attitude changed, and it was certainly not then because of any special thing. I could not stand it any longer to see all my friends working for their country, while I seemed to be in opposition. This was all the harder for me, because the majority of those who attacked me said I was pro-German. I could not reconcile my religious beliefs with war.

But late that summer I came around; I took part in 'drives' for Liberty bonds, etc., I made public addresses and did what I could. I shall never know for certain whether I made this change from sincere conviction or from fear. 'Know thyself' is an old saying; but who has ever known himself? Finally I came to believe that it was necessary, now that we were in the war, to win it; and the microscopic part due from me must be contributed. If one believes fifty-one per cent in a cause, I suppose one should give it one hundred per cent support.

Cowardice certainly was a contributing motive; and yet, I am convinced that had I been *sure* it was right and just to go on publicly opposing the war, I should have done so and gone to prison. I wasn't quite sure.

The only good thing I can say of my speeches in behalf of Liberty Bonds, etc. is that I never attempted to increase the hatred for Germans; indeed, I kept my friendship with my German friends, while I lost permanently my long and intimate friendship with a French professor. I have always regretted this. In a public address, I compared Kaiser Wilhelm with Napoleon, and said they had the same selfish ambition and that the German Emperor would fail, even as Napoleon had failed. My French friend (now dead) hated the Kaiser, but could not endure any adverse criticism of Napoleon. We never spoke to each other again.

One of the innumerable casualties of the war among those who remained at home was the famous philosopher Hugo Münsterberg, who dropped dead on the floor while lecturing to his class of girls at Radcliffe College, Cambridge, Mass., on 16 December 1916. He was born in Danzig, 1 June 1863, and went to Harvard in charge of the psychological laboratory in 1892. He was a notable addition to that brilliant department of Philosophy, and when the Phillips Brooks house was in process of construction, some wag suggested that they inscribe on its façade *Ein Münsterberg ist unser Gott.*

After the European War broke out in 1914, he quite naturally expressed pro-German sympathies; but the feeling against Germany was so strong in Boston and in Harvard that he suffered acutely. In an article I wrote for the *Yale Alumni Weekly* I used his name as an illustration of how famous scientific men, who had always maintained they must follow the truth no matter what it cost, forgot the truth whenever war occurred and every man became a sentimental follower of the Religion of Nationalism. The chief illustration I used was certainly Haeckel; but I mentioned Münsterberg, because I was writing for an American university group, and he was conspicuous.

He wrote me the following letter and I wrote him an explanatory apology, I am glad to say, for it cemented a strong friendship. But he was attacked so bitterly by many other people, called a German spy and other bad names, that his health gave way. I saw him in New York, meeting him by chance in an hotel only a few weeks before his death, and we had a most agreeable conversation. It was clear to me that he was nervously overwrought, though I had no suspicion that there was anything organically wrong. Here is the letter:

CAMBRIDGE, MASSACHUSETTS,
April 24, 1916

MY DEAR PROFESSOR PHELPS:

The Boston Herald of April 19th brought out a reprint of your article in the *Yale Alumni Weekly*. I agree with essential parts of it, but just therefore you may pardon me for insisting that your remarks about me seem to me mistaken. You single me out from all the Germans in this country as a man who can see only one side in this war. I take the liberty of sending you my book "The Peace and America" which appeared in the first year of the war, and I beg you to read the chapter "The Socalled Facts" and perhaps also the chapter "The Highest Values" and finally the last one "Tomorrow." You may then be less surprised if you discover that other critics of my literary activity during the war have claimed exactly the opposite, namely that I have done more justice to opposing standpoints than anybody else.

But your attack on me interests me still more from a theoretical point of view. You say that if I had been born in France I should scoff at everything that I now proclaim to be the truth and that my scientific education and my search for facts mean nothing at all to me, because Germany faces a crisis. You even say that like religious people whom I have ridiculed I believe what I want to believe. With regard to this expression of your views, I wish you would look not into my books about the war but into my philosophical books of the last twenty years. Then you would see that according to my conviction the statement that my utterances are ultimately based on belief is not a reproach but the acknowledgment of a necessity. About ten years ago I had the great honor to be invited by Yale University as representative of Harvard to give an address before the whole academic body. I did so and published my paper under the title "Science and Idealism." An essential aim of that paper was to say what I have expressed much more fully in my book "The Eternal Values" namely that the historical world does not belong to the sphere of the psycho-physical mechanisms which are the material for the scientist who seeks facts. Historical reality is formed not by objects but by subjects whose existence is will activity, which as such can never be grouped among facts which are to be described and explained, but which must be acknowledged and interpreted and valued. To enter into this world in which alone our values and our duties lie means to affirm or to deny the attitudes and propositions of other subjects. Far from ridiculing religious people and their belief, I firmly declared that there is no reality in the historical and normative world but that which is ultimately dependent upon belief. Of course, we can, and from a scientific standpoint we must, consider every historical process also as a psychophysical happening, but that is an artificial construction, while the immediate reality in which we live our historical political life precedes such reconstructed, intellectual schemes. Reality is purposive and only the constructed world of the scientist is causal, and if the metaphysicians finally ask what is the ultimate reality, the object or the subject, the answer must be that which Fichte gave a hundred years ago, namely that it depends upon the kind of man you are, that is, it depends upon your belief.

From these philosophical views of mine, for which I have stood a lifetime, you can deduce that I am not denying my scientific education and above all that I am not neglecting the demands of truth, if I speak in political discussions a teleological language and not a causal one. I affirm certain ideals, in this particular case the ideal of an over-individual state view as against an individualistic one. In affirming them, I move in a sphere in which the category of scientific truth has no meaning whatever. The one is not true and the other is not untrue, but the one is one teleologically involved in my fundamental life assertions, and I take it for granted that an opposite affirmation is established and demanded by the fundamental life decisions of men of other nationality. I therefore feel it as very unfair if a devotion to those ideals in which I believe is denounced as a denial of my search for truth, simply because I know that others fight for other ideals.

Very sincerely yours,

HUGO MÜNSTERBERG

Tom Stix was an undergraduate at Yale when America entered the World War; he was in my class in Browning.

In 1918 he wrote the following letter to me from back of the lines at Soissons where he was brigaded with the Gordon Highlanders as a liaison officer:

> I had a most extraordinary experience yesterday. Lieutenant Colonel McDonnough was taking me around and introducing me to some of the officers in the brigade. I came into a little dugout, and there sat Lieutenant Anderson, reading by the light of a candle stuck into a bottle; not an unusual picture, of course. Just after we had been introduced, Colonel McDonnough was called away, and I sat down to talk with Anderson for a little while. After we were through with the amenities he happened to remark in passing that he was a Cambridge man, and I said I was from Yale. He turned over the book that he was reading. It was a pocket edition of Browning.
>
> "You went to Yale?" he said. "Did you by any chance know William Lyon Phelps?"
>
> "Of course I knew Billy Phelps; everybody at Yale knows Billy Phelps." I told him that I had practically gone from one of Billy Phelps's classes and enlisted.
>
> He looked up at me with I think a little envy. "I'd like to know that man. He can explain poetry so that anybody can understand it."
>
> The campus didn't seem so far away.
>
> Always,
>
> Tom

Incidentally, Tom Stix told me what I think is the most affecting incident that I have either heard or read from the World War. A few years later he included it in his book, *The Sporting Gesture*; New York, 1934. John Henderson, whom he had known at Yale, took a year at Oxford after leaving Yale, enlisted in 1914, and came out as a private in Kitchener's First Hundred Thousand; and in 1915 when he was a captain of the Highlanders, they were holding the front line in the Somme. As dawn broke, John saw a German boy hanging on the barbed wire on the ground between the British and German trenches. His foot was shot off, and he was screaming. It is said that often men who are desperately wounded in the body are silent, whereas those who are shot in the hands or feet cannot help screaming. I now quote from Mr. Stix's book:

I have seen men wounded beyond recognition who could somehow control themselves, but I have never seen a man shot in the hand or foot who could. I don't know why. Perhaps there are more nerves in the hands and feet. The boy's face was beginning to gray. It was a horrible sight. A rat walked across the parapet, went up to the wounded Boche, and began to sniff. John stood it for as long as he could, which must have been all of five minutes. Then he climbed out over the parapet and tried to shake the youngster off the wire, but he was caught too tightly. So John stood up and lifted him off. No Man's Land was only forty yards wide, and the enemy could see what he was doing. Johnny put the boy on his shoulder and started back to our lines. Then something struck him—I don't know what. He must have realized that the boy was dying. He turned around and started across No Man's Land with his burden. They were standing up in the German trenches now, applauding, and in the English trenches too. He reached the enemy's line, climbed over the wires, handed his charge over and started back for his own side. When he had gone about ten yards, a voice called, "Herr Lieutenant!" John turned, and out of the Boche trenches came the captain of the Death's Head Hussars. When he was within five or six feet of the Englishman, he stopped, saluted and put out his hand. John took it. Then the German officer took off the iron cross he was wearing and pinned it on the other man. They shook hands a second time, and each returned to his own lines. What happened? I haven't the vaguest idea of what happened to the German captain, but John almost lost his commission. "Fraternizing with the enemy" they called it.

I don't know, but I've always imagined that an incident like that had just as good a chance of stopping the War as the Sarajevo incident had of starting it.

70

ALFRED NOYES AND OTHERS

THIS winter of 1917–18 was the coldest ever known in New England and on account of the war, coal was very difficult to obtain; that, and the feeling that the war was going to last four or five more years made this a depressing time.

Sunday 30 December 1917 the thermometer outside my window was 12 below zero, the lowest registration in New Haven I have ever seen. And the cold was almost continuous from early December till March. Many city thermometers showed 18 below.

On 8 January Walter Camp in New Haven gave a luncheon in honour of the famous actor John Drew; later in the afternoon I had a long talk with Mr. Drew at the Elizabethan Club. I urged him to write his autobiography. He told me many amusing anecdotes of his career. I had seen him as Orlando in *As You Like It*, when Charles the Wrestler was impersonated by Wm. Muldoon, the champion; who made a magnificent figure on the stage. Mr. Drew said it galled the big man to have to be thrown every night by himself and one night when Muldoon fell heavily in front of the footlights, he let out a profane ejaculation that was audible in most parts of the house, adding to the gaiety of the evening.

On 26 January I saw the new painting of President Wilson by John Sargent, which was to go to the National Art Gallery in Dublin. It is reported that when a lady asked the artist what part of the portrait he thought most characteristic of his own art, he said the eye-glasses.

The general gloom in this winter war-month was lightened for me on two occasions; on one I heard the Ninth Symphony, and on the other Sonata 111 played by Josef Hofmann. Many 'patriots' tried to prevent the playing of any German music; and many Victrola discs of Beethoven, Wagner, Bach, etc., were patriotically destroyed.

One of my students, Frederick S.Blackall, Jr., had won an ensign's commission in the Navy; while in the hospital with jaundice, he read *Pride and Prejudice* and was cured; I had myself been cured of tonsillitis by reading *Treasure Island*, so I had no difficulty in believing his story.

On 30 March clocks were pushed forward one hour in accordance with the new Federal Law. Benjamin Franklin had advocated this method of daylight saving but it took a world war over a century later to make us adopt it. He also advocated the substitution of arbitration for war; that will come, I think, in about a thousand years.

During the Autumn term at the University I taught European History to the students in the Naval reserve, and enjoyed it. My regular courses were also continued but students were few.

As the winter of 1917 was the coldest on record, the winter of 1918–19 was the mildest I have ever known. I mention this for two reasons: first, because the weather is interesting; second, as illustrating the very common determination of people to make themselves unhappy. After December had progressed three weeks and it was like May, I spoke of it with delight to many friends; invariably (and I mean invariably) the response was, 'Just wait; we'll catch it later' or pessimistic words in the same vein. But January was also mild, and I continued my comments, drawing always the same rejoinder; then in February I increased them, enjoying the invariable replies. It stayed mild the entire winter; and yet nine out of ten persons could not enjoy it, because they were so sure it would not last.

The English poet, Alfred Noyes, I met when he first came to lecture at Yale before the War. Of all the poets that I have heard read their own works he was the best. I heard him many times, and his work always gained by his public interpretation. He spent a year at Princeton University as visiting professor, lectured several times at Yale, was kind enough to be our guest of honour at the dinner of our undergraduate *Yale Literary Magazine,* and then, in the year 1935 in response to a cordial invitation from Mr. and Mrs. Noyes, my wife and I visited their beautiful place on the southern shore of the Isle of Wight. We stopped on the way to see the grave of Swinburne, and I deeply regret we were not able to stay over Sunday and take dinner, because Admiral and Mrs. Jellicoe, who were neighbours, were to be present. Mr. Noyes, like Chesterton, Baring, Sheila Kaye-Smith, and other distinguished British authors, became a devout member of the Roman Catholic church; his religious autobiography, *The Unknown God,* is impressive, both in its sincerity of thought and clarity of expression.

13, HANOVER TERRACE
REGENT'S PARK, N.W.1
LONDON, ENGLAND
March 28th, '34

DEAR BILLY:

I'm asking Sheed & Ward to send you my new book (in prose) which contains several references to Browning. It's a record of my own gropings towards a few definite religious beliefs, from boyhood, through agnosticism (and the days that I fed on Dante and Darwin) to my present views. It's called *The Unknown God,* and I hope it may be of a little use to a few in this bewildered time. It has taken me some years to write, and more to think out.

If you are ever on this side, (you and yours) *do* let us know. I miss my American friends greatly; and it would be an immense joy if you could come and stay with us in our Earthly Paradise in the Isle of Wight. Our garden is now ablaze with spring flowers and great banks of primroses; and I could motor you to many haunts of the poets on the island. *Do* come, if ever you can. We are there all April, and from the end of June till Xmas. The rest of the year here in town.

With very best remembrances from my wife and myself to you and Mrs. Phelps,

Yours always,

ALFRED NOYES

Inasmuch as a few years ago the American Association for the Advancement of Atheism held a dinner in New York in honour of Voltaire, I quote from the great Frenchman:

I tell you, without repetition, that I love quakers. Yes, if the sea did not disagree with me, it should be in thy bosom, O Pennsylvania! that I would finish the rest of my career; if there be any remaining. Thou art situated in the fortieth degree of latitude, in the softest and most favourable climate; thy houses commodiously built; thy inhabitants industrious; thy manufactures in repute. An eternal peace reigns among thy citizens; crimes are almost unknown; and there is but a single example of a man banished from the country. He deserved it very properly, being an Anglican priest who turning quaker, was unworthy of being so. This poor man was no doubt possessed of the devil, for he dared to preach intolerance; he was called George Keith, and they banished him. I know not where he went; but may all intolerants go with him.

In 1937 Alfred Noyes, the devout Catholic, wrote a biography of Voltaire, filled with glowing admiration.

On 6 January 1919 Theodore Roosevelt died and it seemed as if a sudden silence fell on the whole country. Professor Beers said it seemed as if a military band had stopped playing. Rudyard Kipling made an international impression by quoting the words of Mr. Valiant-for-Truth:

Then said he, I am going to my Fathers, and tho' with great Difficulty I am got hither, yet now I do not repent me of all the Trouble I have been at to arrive where I am. *My Sword*, I give to him that

shall succeed me in my Pilgrimage, and my *Courage* and *Skill*, to him
that can get it. . . . So he passed over, and all the Trumpets sounded
for him on the other side.

In February of this year I gave the L.P.Stone lectures at
the Princeton Theological Seminary, on the Bible. They
were published by Macmillan in a book called *Reading the
Bible*. I enjoyed this experience at the Seminary.

I was one of the speakers at a great dinner at the Lotos
Club in New York on 22 February to commemorate the
centenary of the birth of James Russell Lowell. The guest
of honour was John Galsworthy, who charmed the audience. Other speakers were Alfred Noyes, Robert Nichols,
Stephen Leacock, Sir Robert Falconer. This was the first
time I had seen young Robert Nichols, the English poet,
who was in his military uniform. I had a good talk with
him; he was enthusiastic about the poetry of Vachel Lindsay. Nichols was amusing in describing what the professors
made him do to get his degree at Oxford. 'They told me I
had to read St. Paul's Epistles in Greek; why the hell
should I read St. Paul's Epistles?'

On a later occasion I had the pleasure of entertaining
Nichols at my house; and I placed him in the great chair
that had belonged to Robert Browning. He sat down in it
and composed a poem before rising.

On 28 March, at a school convention in Carbondale,
Illinois, I asked Mr. Black, the Superintendent, how far
away was the Mississippi River. I told him I had seen it at
St. Paul, St. Louis, Memphis, and New Orleans; but I
wished to see it in its glory, with no towns in the neighbourhood. It was only twenty miles away. Accordingly on
that afternoon he and his daughter took me to its margin;
it was in open country, but owing to the levee, it was invisible until we came within a few feet of it. The mighty
river at that point was one mile wide, fifty feet deep, and
running silently at seven miles an hour. It came swinging

around a great bend a few miles to the North, and the trees on the Missouri side were in the living green of Spring. There were no towns in sight, not even a house; and we had the splendid river all to ourselves. In imagination I could see the raft coming along, bearing Huck and Jim.

On 9 May in Brooklyn I gave the address commemorating the centenary of the birth of Whitman. John Burroughs was on the stage but too feeble to speak to the audience. He thanked me with the tears running down his face. Never did a man have a more faithful disciple than old Walt had in John Burroughs.

Count Ilya Tolstoy, the son of the novelist, was in New Haven and I took him to the Elizabethan Club, and had a long talk with him. He shared his father's views on religion, morality, and art. He himself was a large man, very like his father in appearance. He said (with passion) '*Anna Karenina* is the worst book my father ever wrote; he wished he could destroy it and so do I.' I asked him, 'Didn't he like any of his novels?' '*War and Peace* and *Anna Karenina* he despised; but when he had finished the manuscript of *The Kreutzer Sonata* he gave it to the family to read, leaving the room as was his invariable custom, so that we could discuss it without embarrassment. After we had read it, I said "I think this is the best thing Father has done." A moment later he entered the room and said, "I have done something I never did before in all my life—I have been listening at the door. And I think Ilya is right. This is the best thing I have written." My father also was not ashamed of *Resurrection*, though as a rule he wished he had not written novels.'

Count Ilya put his hands on my rough homespun suit. 'Oh, I like these clothes! I have a suit exactly like yours in Russia, if the Bolsheviks haven't got it!'

His pocket bulged with a detective novel; he said he was **never** without one.

He described in detail how careful his father was in the boy's early training; when he was about twenty, his father asked him if he had had any sexual intercourse, and when Ilya replied in the negative, the great writer wept for joy and gave him his blessing.

71

MEA ORNAMENTA

THE highest ambition of every good teacher is to be excelled by his pupils. The one thing he wants more than anything else is that those whom he teaches will surpass him in every respect—in brains, character, achievement. As every normal father is prouder of his son's success than of his own, is made happier by his son's accomplishments than by his own independent work, so every normal teacher looks with happiness and pride on the success of those who were once his students.

I cannot claim to have been a vital factor in the later work of my pupils; all I can say is that they were exposed to my teaching. I follow the careers of my students after their graduation with a feeling akin to parental interest; it is a delight to meet their wives and their children; for even after the men have become grey or bald, they are always to me undergraduates—my students.

There is a fundamental difference between American and European students (not including English); American undergraduates, as a group, are the most conservative men in the world, and European the most radical. The majority of our undergraduates, except in the south, where special reasons prevail, are 'good' Republicans, believers in high tariff, 'untainted' by radicalism; their attitude toward anything like a popular uprising would be a burlesque, as years ago they burlesqued Coxey's army. A large group of Yale or Harvard undergraduates seriously leading a mob is unthinkable, despite the fact that the radical clubs in these institutions are more prominent than formerly. Whereas in Europe, whenever there is a political disturbance, an uprising, or a radical row, the university students are always in the forefront.

Again, when one talks with European college students, they seem at first sight to be more intellectually mature than our boys. I have talked often with German, Russian, Polish, French university youth; they discuss fluently philosophy, metaphysics, international affairs, the leading thinkers and writers of the world, in a manner that seems entirely beyond the tastes and the capacities of young Americans. I remember a time, many years ago, when I spent fifteen months on the Continent, and was daily amazed at the conversational capacity of foreign students; when I returned to America, it seemed almost as if our young men were simply boyishly healthy, well groomed and well bred.

But—after seven years I returned to these same places in Europe and met these same students—for they were still students; they were still discussing philosophy, politics, and international affairs. Yet in seven years many of those boyishly healthy Americans were holding positions of power and influence.

To a European professor travelling in America or lecturing at an American university, there is a tragic contrast in health, physical vigour, and personal charm between the aspect of his students at home and those he meets in the United States. An instructor from Belgium pointed out to me a group of Yale students, and said, 'Look at them! I did not believe there were anywhere in the world such magnificent specimens of young manhood. Our students at home are small in size, low in stature, underfed, poor, many of them unhealthy, even anaemic in appearance; your students are big, tall, clean, healthy, happy boys. I wonder if they have any idea of their good fortune. It is a delight to look at them, to teach them, to talk with them.'

There is another characteristic of American college youth. They are not unduly intellectual, but they are fired by an ambition to be of service in the world. Their aims are not selfish; and they take their places in various communities where they expect to aid in the advancement of civilization. Among my pupils I not only had boys who are now college deans, bishops, public-spirited clergymen, workers in city settlements and in foreign missions, but many who are devoting their wealth and their lives to the public welfare.

I taught university students 42 years. If you multiply forty-two by four hundred, you will get fairly near the actual number of students who have been in my classroom.

In travelling through England, France, Germany, in 1928, I found that apparently the best known of all living American writers was Sinclair Lewis. There was universal curiosity about him; any item of information had news value. I remember him well as a freshman at Yale. He came from Sauk Center, Minnesota, in 1903. His name was Harry S. Lewis. He was very tall, incredibly thin, and his head was crowned with a mass of fiery red hair. Very few of his classmates knew his Christian name; he was universally called 'Red' Lewis, both because of his hair and because of his radical opinions, which he took no pains to conceal. At that time he was a disciple of Upton Sinclair. He was not disliked in college, but was regarded with amiable tolerance as a freak. He took not the slightest interest in the idols of the place—athletics, societies, and so on; nor did he care to 'make' any of the positions in extracurricular activities that are rewarded with social distinction. He took no interest in these things and he did not pretend to. He was a complete and consistent individualist, going his own way, and talking only about things that interested him. We at once found a common bond of friendship in our admiration for a Minnesota poet, Arthur Upson, whom Lewis brought to my house. His brief life ended tragically, but he had written some beautiful verse. On that ground of intimacy, we had long discussions on literature, the real passion of Lewis. I liked and admired him, for although our views on many subjects were and are irreconcilable, it was a pleasure to me to see a lad who thought for himself. In his senior year he became an editor of the *Yale Literary Magazine*.

After graduating from college in 1907, he worked on newspapers as a reporter, and then in the houses of various publishers. His first novel appeared in 1914, *Our Mr. Wrenn*, a book I recommend to critics who wish to understand Mr. Lewis's art. All his subsequent methods are there in embryo. He then became a successful magazine writer, but finally, although having very little money, he staked everything on one throw. He retired in absolute seclusion and spent one year writing a novel which appeared in 1920 under the name of *Main Street*.

It fired the shot heard round the world. He awoke and found himself famous, a fame immensely increased by the publication of *Babbitt*, a name that has become universal. Mr. Lewis is the same man that I knew as an undergraduate; he has developed, but he has not changed. His satires are born of a passionate desire to make the world better, for if ever there was an evangelist, it is Sinclair Lewis.

In many ways, as is natural, he has mellowed. When we remember how he used to ridicule the Rotarians and other service clubs, we should read an article about them in an English periodical in which he says that the Rotarians and their fellows are the most efficient workers for world peace now existing, and that if war ever is abolished, it will be owing to these service clubs more than to any other one thing.

Three of my undergraduate students, who were in college

at the same time, and intimate friends, have now become famous through creative literary work. The playwright, Philip Barry, 1918; the poet, Stephen Vincent Benét, 1919; the novelist, Thornton Wilder, 1920. All three showed remarkable talent in college.

Philip Barry was an editor of the *Yale Literary Magazine*, and was so much interested in play-writing that after graduating he went to Harvard and studied under Professor George P. Baker, later head of the Department of Drama at Yale. His play (written in Mr. Baker's school) received the prize, was put on later on the New York professional stage, and ran a year. It was called *You and I*, and discerning judges saw at once the dawn of a real dramatist. Curiously enough, for a time Philip Barry had thought of a diplomatic career, and was associated with the Department of State at Washington, and for one year was attached to the American Embassy in London.

The success of his first play stimulated his ambition to write something better. Two plays of his, produced in New York, *In a Garden*, and *White Wings*, were really beyond the public appreciation of that time. Edna Ferber wrote an article for the New York *World*, expressing her indignation at the financial failure of *In a Garden*.

Since then, Philip Barry has combined excellence with popular success. *Paris Bound* and *Holiday* both 'clicked,' but have not satisfied their author. He is more than a popular playwright, and will never be content with merely box-office successes, pleasant as such things must be. His play, *Hotel Universe*, produced by the Theatre Guild, puzzled both critics and audiences, but it is a beautiful and original work of pure imagination, the kind of play one enjoys better at the second hearing. I am proud of Philip Barry.

Stephen Vincent Benét is the son of an army officer. His brother, William Rose Benét, now one of the editors of the *Saturday Review of Literature*, has published several volumes of poems; and Stephen is a born, foreordained poet. At the age of seventeen, and before entering Yale, he published a volume of original poems. During his under-graduate career he took three prizes for verse. He was universally popular, having a peculiarly lovable disposition. His gift for satire and irony was exercised in such a manner that it charmed his victims. He is one of the most sparkling conversationalists I have met. He was born in Bethlehem, Pennsylvania, and has lived in Augusta, Georgia. He has a combination of northern energy with southern relaxation that makes him irresistible.

Stephen Benét wished to write nothing but poetry, but he was forced to produce novels and short stories to keep the pot boiling. Then he received the Guggenheim Fellow-ship, and going to Paris, he there wrote an epic poem of the American Civil War, *John Brown's Body*, which attracted universal attention, and won the Pulitzer Prize.

I have known Thornton Niven Wilder since he was a child. His father, Amos Parker Wilder, was a senior at Yale when I was a freshman, and was even then known outside of academic walls for his brilliance as an orator. Later he became a journalist. In college Thornton showed remarkable versatility. He composed and played music on the piano, he wrote plays and short stories, he wrote professional dramatic criticisms for the newspapers.

After graduation, he studied for a year at the Graduate School in Princeton, was a housemaster at Lawrenceville School in New Jersey, where he taught French, and re-ceiving a fellowship, he lived for a year in Italy.

His first novel, *The Cabala*, displayed a literary style so full of grace and distinction that it attracted the attention of many critics; but it was too remote in matter for the popular taste. His second novel, *The Bridge of San Luis Rey*, was accepted by the publishers because they thought so fine a book ought to be printed; but they had no belief in its success with the public, and they have not yet recovered from the shock.

This novel is a masterpiece. It gave Thornton Wilder international fame (he is constantly discussed in the press of France, Italy, Spain, as well as in that of Great Britain and America), and it was to be hailed both by the critics and by some three hundred thousand readers as a notable work of art. His short novel, *The Woman of Andros*, is slighter in content but fully as distinguished in style. His next novel, *Heaven's My Destination*, is totally different from the preceding novels, being a story of contemporary American life and seeming to point toward the stage.

His first full-length play that appeared on the professional stage is *Our Town*, and the first night in February, 1938, it received enthusiastic comment from the critics and tumultuous applause from the audience. In May it was given the Pulitzer Prize, the highest honour in America, so that Thornton Wilder has twice received this Prize, for *The Bridge* in 1928 and exactly ten years later for *Our Town*. Thus he is a double winner in the field of the novel and of the drama. All three of these men—Barry, Benét, Wilder—were, in college, quiet, modest, attractive fellows, wholly free from conceit or even from pretentiousness, but all three were imbued with literary ambition.

Henry Seidel Canby, after graduating from the Sheffield Scientific School at Yale in 1899, entered the Graduate School, and I had the pleasure of being one of his teachers. He is today one of the most influential literary critics in America, and an authority on American literature. Every one of his books has added to his reputation.

Anson Phelps Stokes, former Secretary of Yale, and now Canon of Washington Cathedral, was a pupil of mine in the class of 1896. In his undergraduate days he won many prizes. Henry Sloane Coffin, the President of Union Theological Seminary, was a pupil of mine in 1897. Howard Chandler Robbins, one of the best preachers in America, was chiefly distinguished in college (1899) for his ability to write verse. Sherrill, of the class of 1911, is Bishop of Massachusetts. John Dallas (1904), is Bishop of New Hampshire. The Bishop of Southern Ohio, Henry Hobson, was one of my students in the class of 1914. Philemon Sturges was one of my pupils in the class of 1896. He is now dean of St. Paul's Cathedral in Boston. George Paull T. Sargent for some years was Dean of the Cathedral in Garden City and is now Rector of the great metropolitan church of St. Bartholomew. He was in the class of 1905.

Yale, like other New England colleges, was founded to train men for the Christian ministry; while the proportion of clergymen is not so great as it was a century ago, I submit that the quality is even higher.

Many Roman Catholics now enter Yale as undergraduates; and one of the most brilliant and learned priests in the church is Father T. Lawrason Riggs (1910), the Yale chaplain for all the Catholic students.

Eugene Meyer, a world authority on public finance, and an immense help to his country in the World War, was a pupil of mine in the class of 1895; and I could name other financiers and influential men of affairs, including Cabinet members.

One of the most promising young writers in America is Jesse Stuart. He comes from Scotch ancestry. He was brought up on a farm in Kentucky and some years ago published a collection of original sonnets called *Man with a Bulltongue Plow*. I first met him in Kentucky in 1936 where he was teaching school in the winter and working on the farm in the summer, and I told him that he would have to give up both teaching and farming for creative writing. He has since published two volumes of prose tales.

Shortly after my visit to Kentucky he wrote the following letter:

GREENUP COUNTY HIGH SCHOOL

MCKELL BUILDING
JESSE STUART, PRINCIPAL

FULLERTON, KENTUCKY

Sept. 22nd, 1936

DEAR WILLIAM LYON PHELPS:

I shall never forget the trip across Kentucky—how I left at 4 o'clock one morning to meet you at Eastern State Teacher's College, Richmond, Kentucky. I shall never forget the train you were supposed to arrive on and how I sent the porter through the coaches calling for you; about that time the train hit a truckload of pigs and we were all thrown out of our seats. Part of the pigs were killed—the better half of them took through the cornfields squealing. Several women on the train wished it had been the driver killed instead of the poor pigs since the train had whistled three times and the driver didn't pay any attention. When I got in Richmond there wasn't any Mr. Phelps and the people wondered until they got your telegram.

I shall never forget you and the talk you made, your ease of speaking, and your alert mind. I shall never forget the things you said about England. But that is a part of time past and only memory lingers, a very dear sweet memory. When I came back on the train I told a fellow my belief in immortality now was stout as an oak because I had seen a man who convinced me that man couldn't die. The fact was not in the words you said but because of you. I cannot see how any man of your type would be allowed to pass from the universe. I used to think a lot about such things and I've a story coming out in *Esquire* called "Resurrection" and I want you to read it.

May I thank you for the things you have said for me. Allow me to say that I am glad to have met you, have known you, talked to you, laughed with you, sat at the table and to have eaten with you and smoked with you. It was a pleasure and pleasant memory. I shall thank W. F. O'Donnell long as I live for inviting me over there.

Now that you are not conducting your section in *Scribner's* AS I LIKE IT, I must say that I regret it. I always read that section. . . .

My best regards to you ever William Lyon Phelps. I hope you write

your autobiography. I want a copy autographed. I'd gladly place my
order now for a first edition.

Always,

JESSE STUART

My relations with my colleagues in the Yale English
department have been more than cordial; we are devoted
friends. We have naturally differed occasionally on men
and measures, but no cloud has even momentarily obscured
the affection which has grown stronger by length of time
and intimacy of association. Most of them were my pupils,
and while I certainly do not claim credit for their achievements, it pleases me to remember the early days and our
relations in my classroom. George Nettleton, John Berdan,
John C. Adams, I have already mentioned; I am proud of
their work and of the scholarly achievements of Chauncey
Tinker, Samuel Hemingway, Robert French, Stanley
Williams, Frederick Pottle, William De Vane, all of whom
were my students.

Only two full professors of English came to Yale from
other universities; both of them have added distinction
to our department by their productions, and happiness by
their presence—Karl Young and Tucker Brooke. We are a
very happy family. The only reason I do not mention our
younger colleagues, so many of whom are brilliant scholars,
is their number. When I began teaching at Yale in 1892,
the English department consisted of Professors Lounsbury,
Beers, Albert S. Cook, E. T. McLaughlin; that was all. In
about thirty years, instead of five men teaching English,
we had fifty.

In 1894 Wilbur Cross was appointed Instructor. He rose
rapidly through the regular grades of promotion, for many
years was not only a Professor but Dean of the Graduate
School and Editor of the *Yale Review*. When he reached the
age of retirement in 1931, he was in a few days nominated

by the Democratic party for Governor of Connecticut, and has been reelected four times.

It is impossible to exaggerate the affection I have for these colleagues and for many who are teaching in other departments; I am inordinately proud to be their associate—*Meine gute Kameraden!*

72

JOHN GALSWORTHY

In the year 1906 two excellent novels appeared in England which gave their authors popularity and fame—*Joseph Vance*, by William De Morgan, and *The Man of Property*, by John Galsworthy. One of the first notable men in England to recognize the distinction of the latter book was the late Alfred Ollivant, author of the finest dog-story ever written—*Bob, Son of Battle*. He was a good friend of mine, and when I wrote to him urging him to read *Joseph Vance*, I received the following reply, written from Eastbourne, 18 August 1907.

I have not read *Joseph Vance* yet. Thank you for telling me about him. He has been well reviewed here in the considerable papers but I have not heard him talked about probably because I live a very secluded life, and know no literary folk. But curiously enough, two days after getting your letter I heard from Henry Jackson, the Regius Professor of Greek at Cambridge, and perhaps our biggest scholar now Jebb is dead, and he advised me to read the book as being notable. And I shall certainly do so.

The literary sensation here to my mind has been the publication of a book called *The Country House* by a man called Galsworthy. It is the truth to say that I had not read a page before I found myself saying, "Here is a new mind." And further reading confirmed my first impression. In the first place G. is a consummate artist—how rare for an Englishman. I have heard him compared to Flaubert. In the second place he is soaked in our great modern idea of Evolution. It is this last characteristic which puts him in a place by himself, and distinguishes him from his contemporaries, and from those who have gone before. I may say I have been waiting for his coming for years. He is the first big mind who has applied the vast resources thrown open to the gaze of the men of our generation by Science to literature—perhaps it would be more accurate to say the first big Anglo-Saxon mind. Some of his effects in this kind are marvellous. He has written several books, but only two of note, I fancy—*The Country House* and *The Man of Property*. The second is very strong, almost brutal. It is a purely critical book; there is no creative beauty about it; but G's genius is essentially critical. At the same time he is on our side, the side of the angels, right enough. And if he is brutal, it is with the brutality of the surgeon. He destroys to make alive. The other book has more poetry in it. Do get them and let me know what you think of them.

Mark Twain received a tremendous ovation from the undergraduates at Oxford when taking his degree there—far greater than Kipling.

I must have written him that I preferred *The Man of Property* rather than *The Country House* (as I did and do), for on 17 October 1907, he wrote

As to *The Country House* I think one reason I like it so much is that it deals with the life I know best. Then again I think you hardly do justice to Mrs. Pendyce and her charm. There is true beauty, true romance, about her. Moreover up and down the book there are passages of poetry which say all manner of mysterious things to me— the dying rabbit bit, the bits about the race-horse, bits here and there about flowers. They whisper to me of the Oneness of things. Galsworthy is the first novelist I have come across who really understands the Doctrine of Evolution; and for that alone, apart from his critical insight, his bitter humour, his philosophy, his work is for me remarkable.

I am quite sure that some readers will snort when they see Galsworthy called brutal—but in comparison with other novels published during the early years of this century, I can understand how *The Man of Property* seemed to Mr. Ollivant 'very strong.' And after all, it is stronger than many vociferous novels of these latter days —and seems to have enough virility and vitality to out-live more sensational works.

In 1909, 'Observer,' in the London *Daily Mail*, made the following comment:

> Of all quickly made reputations, that of Mr. John Galsworthy is one of the most remarkable. A few, a very few, years ago only the really initiated ever heard of such a person; today, it may be proclaimed, both as playwright and novelist, Mr. Galsworthy occupies the central chair in the Areopagus of English letters for all-round talent and brilliancy. The case is an unusual one. Not many men succeed in fiction and the drama. . . . Now Mr. Galsworthy has succeeded in both these arts. And more. Not only does he practice them both, but he practices them both at one and the same time. . . Yet another curious thing. He has had no failures, no positive stoppage or set back, and this is the more remarkable because he has never pandered to popular taste.

I first saw Mr. John Galsworthy at the dinner in New York on 20 February 1919, in honour of the centenary of the birth of James Russell Lowell. It was a British-American dinner given by the American Academy. Among the speakers were Elihu Root, Brander Matthews, the Canadian representative, and John Galsworthy. The following evening a gala performance of *Dear Brutus* was given, a letter from Barrie read by William Gillette, with Mr. Galsworthy sitting in a box, apparently enjoying the occasion.

On 5 March Mr. Galsworthy came to New Haven, and lunched at the house of Mr. and Mrs. Henry S. Canby. He said he thought there would be in the near future only two political parties in England, Labour and Tory. He was to lecture that afternoon at Yale, and I asked him if he would give an extempore talk on his early struggles as a writer, or on his work in the theatre. The cold sweat broke out all over his face; he was in such distress that I told him such a speech would not be necessary, that it was just a suggestion. He said he could not speak one sentence *extempore*; every word had to be written and read from manuscript, as indeed he had done at the New York dinner. I asked him if he could answer questions from the students. He smiled and said 'Will you stand by me and catch me when I faint?' I relieved his mind immediately by saying no questions would be allowed.

He read a very fine address called *Talking with Oneself*. He was paid two hundred dollars which he immediately presented to the Yale (undergraduate) University Dramatic Association.

That he enjoyed the occasion is clear from the following:

THE MANOR, ALBEMARLE PARK,
ASHEVILLE, N.C.

MY DEAR PROFESSOR PHELPS

Your letter of March 11th has only this evening reached me. It gave me the greatest possible pleasure—for I loved Yale & the whole atmosphere there; and I thought the students splendid fellows. It will be a bright spot for me always, & I'm only sorry my wife wasn't there to make your acquaintance & that of many other friends. And so is she.

With very warm remembrances I am

Sincerely yours

JOHN GALSWORTHY

HOTEL CHATHAM
48TH STREET & VANDERBILT AVE.
NEW YORK

March 30, 1921

MY DEAR PHELPS:

I have been reading your Essays on myself and the rest with the greatest pleasure. Thank you very much for sending me the volume, and for the sympathetic understanding which you have extended to my work.

There's one thing in your diagnosis which puzzles me. I am unable to correlate it with so much evidence tendered me by play-goers after seeing my plays. It's your dictum "he appeals to the mind almost exclusively." Surely it is not mental appeal which moves people strongly; and yet so very many have told me of the almost unbearable emotional effect my plays have had on them. Perhaps the answer is that the emotion starts in the mind, moved by some conception of contrast. Still it *is* emotion, not mere mental interest, such as I think is the ultimate sole appeal of Shaw.

By the way, I don't think travel very responsible for my 'view' of England. It was due to three other causes, 'The Boer War'; close acquaintanceship with the vagabond of whom Ferrand is the projection; and one other (the greatest) into which I will not enter.

I am wholly with you in admiration of Barrie's "Admirable Crichton," "Dear Brutus," and "The Twelve Pound Look," and "The Will"; but in his work at large I found so many little lapses from what one can only call "taste"—austerity of sentiment—so many little scrapes at one's epidermis—that I confess to listening to him often with great discomfort, and a feeling that he cannot be acquitted of too much eye on his audience.

Perhaps I lack the blessed gift of admiration; and yet I have it for certain writers (not many) without reserve.

Your diagnosis of "Leonora" struck me as singularly clear-sighted and admirable. Where I think he went technically a little wrong was in starting with too actual a first act, or rather in not hitting that 'dramatisation of thought and impulse' nail on the head from the start; because' though you're undoubtedly right, hardly any one saw what he was after, and that surely is not what he hoped for.

Well, we shall talk anon. In the meantime ever so many thanks again.

Sincerely yours,

JOHN GALSWORTHY

By the way, please don't
expect me to speechify at
dinner. I simply can't.
J.G.

In April 1921, he lectured again at Yale; his visit was preceded by the following letters.

Nov. 28, 1920

MY DEAR WILLIAM LYON PHELPS

It was a great delight to receive your letter, and to hear of your visit to my two plays.

We are now in California where I am writing, & both of us are revelling in sunshine.

If I do lecture at all this time which is more than doubtful, I would come to Yale with the alacrity of one who remembers with delight the welcome it gave me last time. But I think we English are over-lecturing, and I feel less fit than ever to tell anybody anything.

Please give our warm remembrances to Mrs. Phelps and all who were so good to me. We saw Mr. and Mrs. Canby in New York. I think his paper is jolly good. But am I really like that drawing? My wife says ' No,' but you never can tell, Sir, 'you never can tell.'

It is delicious here—such pepper trees!

With warm regards

I am Yours sincerely

JOHN GALSWORTHY

SAN ISIDEO RANCH
MONTECITO
SANTA BARBARA
CAL.
Dec. 30 (1920)

DEAR WILLIAM LYON PHELPS,

It is very good of you to want me to come, but I literally dare not make any hard & fast engagements; because my wife's health may necessitate our staying longer in a warm climate, and on the other hand, her health permitting, advices from England may take us back sooner than we expect. I can only tell you that I will let you know when our faces are actually set East, whether there is a possibility, and in that case, if you have a day still free I might be able to come. This would mean that you would not get more than a fortnight's notice at the outside.

With all good wishes to you in the New Year

J.G.

SAN MARCOS HOTEL
CHANDLER
ARIZONA
Feb. 7 (1921)

DEAR WILLIAM LYON PHELPS

I write this line to say that, barring accidents, we could come to Yale on Friday, April 1st., and I would discourse to the students for

50 minutes or so at some hour which would enable us to get back to New York that same night, if this were quite convenient. May I, however, beg that you will keep this arrangement, if you make it, dark for as long as ever you can, because it is breaking through my rule of not lecturing on this visit, and if known, will let me in for all sorts of invitations which it will be very difficult to refuse. In fact, it would be a boon if you didn't let the cat out of the bag till, say, a week beforehand.

We shall be here for some weeks longer; the place is very delightful, and is doing my wife good.

With very kind regards, I am

Cordially yours

JOHN GALSWORTHY

Oh! and by the way I would ask that *No Press* should be admitted.

J.G.

I was enthusiastic about Barrie's play *Mary Rose*; but Galsworthy did not like it; he told me that he thought Barrie had not dealt entirely fairly with his audience or with the theatre; although he was a great admirer of many of Barrie's plays.

It was a great pleasure to have Mrs. Galsworthy accompany him. He gave a lecture at Yale on Monday 4 April 1921, but the hall, holding eight hundred, was jammed ten minutes before the hour, and when I heard the roar of the crowd outside and saw through the windows the students climbing the fire escapes, I adjourned the lecture to the neighbouring Woolsey Hall, which holds three thousand. The transfer of the audience was a delirium, but in an astonishingly brief time the crowd flowed into the vast auditorium and filled it. At the close of the lecture, the immense stage was invaded by a throng of students, each one bringing a copy of one of his books for him to autograph. I tried to protect him; but when he heard a despairing voice on the outskirts crying 'I'll never reach him!' Mr. Galsworthy spoke up and said 'I will stay here until I have signed every book,' and he did.

My friend and former pupil, the literary scholar and bibliophile, Frank Altschul, sent me the following interesting letter he had received from his father.

C.ALTSCHUL
32 WEST 86TH ST.

NEW YORK, APRIL 9, 22

MY DEAR FRANK,

I have just read Mr. William Lyon Phelps' reviews of the *Forsyte Saga* in *The Literary Review* (*Evening Post*) of yesterday and in *The N.Y.Times Book Review* and *Magazine* of today, and have been exceedingly interested in them. As you know, I have admired the books comprising the *Saga* more than anything I have read of late years in English.

Mr. Phelps makes particular mention of the delight he experienced when Mr. Galsworthy returned to the Forsyte family in 1920. I wonder if he knows what induced Mr. Galsworthy to recall the creatures of his fancy already in 1918 when he wrote *The Indian Summer of a Forsyte*, which I am glad to notice Mr. Phelps evidently thinks as lovely as I do. If you think he might be interested, will you tell him that I have a copy of *The Man of Property* on the fly-leaf of which Mr. Galsworthy has inscribed the following:

Nov. 20, 1911

I have often been asked what became of Soames and of Irene. I have as often answered that I know no more than my questioners. In me, when the last scene of a book has been imagined and the last word written,—all is ended; and the creatures of my tale step out into darkness.

John Galsworthy

I confess I am very curious to know whether it was the repeated inquiry of correspondents, or whether anything definite is known regarding his drift of mind, in those days between 1911 and 1918, that would give a definite answer to the inquiry.

Your loving

DAD

Mr. Galsworthy told me, as he told many others, that when he finished *The Man of Property* (1906) he had no intention of ever using again any of its characters. Mr. Jesse H. Shera of New Haven on 3 January 1927 wrote to Mr. Galsworthy as follows:

The marital relations of Soames and Irene are suggestive of certain parallel elements in the somewhat similar situation of Helmer and Nora in Ibsen's *A Doll's House*, especially as presented in the final act of that play. In view of Ibsen's profound influence upon modern social thought, is it not reasonable to assume that his influence acted upon your work? If such an influence were present, to what extent were you conscious of it, and of how great importance do you consider it to be?

Secondly, at the time of the creation of *The Man of Property* did you foresee a possible future return to the theme? Does the *Salvation of a Forsyte* represent the dawning of the Forsyte conception, or was *The Man of Property* in preparation at the time, i.e. in 1900? Similarly, when was the change in Soames' character, as presented in *The Silver Spoon*, first conceived, and was this change the result of a determined plan, or was it an unconscious evolutionary growth?

Finally, from the standpoint of American jurisprudence the basis for the law suit in *The Silver Spoon*, would appear to be insufficient. How severe is the English law concerning slander and libel?

It was probably on the day he received Mr. Shera's letter than he answered it, as follows:

EN VOYAGE,
Feb. 13, 1927

DEAR SIR:

In answer to your queries of Jan. 3 which have found me out here—

(1) It might be reasonable but it is *not true* to assume that Ibsen had any influence on me. He has had none, neither in that particular matter nor in any other. I have always been a poor Ibsenite.

(2) I did not foresee any return to the theme when I wrote 'The Man of Property.'

(3) I do not see any particular change in Soames' character in 'The Silver Spoon,' as compared with his character in 'To Let'

and 'The White Monkey.' He mellows as he gets older, mainly through his love for Fleur. There has been no set plan about it.

(4) English law is pretty searching in the matter of libel and slander.

I expect this answer will come too late to be any good.

Very truly yours,

JOHN GALSWORTHY

On 18 September 1928 I spent the day with the Galsworthys at their beautiful country home at Pulborough. After eating a copious lunch, Mr. Galsworthy asked me if I would like to play some tennis doubles. I replied that I should like nothing better but that I had no clothes with me except those in which I was standing. Accordingly he lent me his shoes, socks, underclothes, trousers, shirt, and sweater, and everything from the soles of my feet to my neck fitted me exactly as if made for me. So in this humble way I am a replica of the great writer.

When the game was over, I was soaked in sweat and could not wait for tea as I had to take the train back to London. Accordingly, I took a hot bath, and Mr. Galsworthy put mustard into it, so that it was the first and last time I ever had a mustard bath. He said that it would keep me from getting cold, and apparently it did. I came down stairs and found the entire company, wrapped in sweaters and coats, having tea; I had time for one cup of the most delicious tea I ever tasted and then I was off to the train. It was the end of a perfect day.

I fell in love with their dogs, especially with a Dalmatian and an exquisite Irish setter; and as Mrs. Galsworthy said snapshots of their visit to Arizona had been taken, I begged for one. After we had returned from Europe in October that year (1928) I received the following letter from Mrs. Galsworthy:

MY DEAR FRIENDLY LYON:

Thank you for your two good letters and the clipping from your mangled article, which was natheless very interesting.

I have not been 'forgetting it'—that flattering request; but was 'laid by' (as Shakespeare says) with a baddish cold in Town, and unable to get at my snapshot negatives; but being now nearly rid of my disabilities (and I do hope your good lady is also), I have sent for some enlargements and among them that one you were pleased with, of J.G. and me squatting under a tree somewhere near the Grand Canyon. (I say *my* snapshots; but it's clear that I didn't take that one.)

We returned to Bury yesterday, and it is the most glamorous weather; too lovely for words. The dogs are handsomer than ever, Rex especially. Dickie is the ghost of beauty. I'm suffering *very* slightly from embonpoint. We have a small Scottie terrier at Grove Lodge, and yesterday acquired a lovely solemn black and white spaniel. So, the dog news is all alive. Cats are very well and charming, too. Uncle and nephew had a great set-to at tennis very soon after arriving and this morning before breakfast all, with dogs and horses, have been far & wide on Mose Downs against the sky.

Hoping soon to send that humble snapshot, and with our united affectionate greetings to you both,

Always cordially yours

ADA GALSWORTHY

The two enlarged Arizona pictures delighted us and I wrote expressing appreciation.

One of the things that most gratified Mr. Galsworthy happened while I was in London. I took up the morning paper, and there in headlines which had the appearance not of literary criticism or gossip about books, but rather seemed to belong to the news of the world, was

DEATH OF SOAMES FORSYTE

It would be impossible to have a more eloquent tribute to the reality of this character. I asked his creator if he were not pleased, and he laughed and said 'Very much.'

I have often wondered if men who have lost the Christian faith in which they were brought up, would not be happier if they could also lose their conscience. If they could have no conscience at all, like Sanin, or a robust conscience such as Ibsen seemed to admire. Mr. Galsworthy lost his religious faith; but I have never known anyone anywhere who was more conscientious, more absolutely upright. His conscience often made him unhappy.

At their home in Hampstead, London, 24 July 1928, we took luncheon with them, no-one else being present. He showed us a room filled with the manuscripts of his novels, all bound in asbestos. As he could not dictate, and had never learned to play the type-writer, his books had been written in longhand. I think he intended to give them to the British Museum. I had the privilege of examining some of these manuscripts; they were filled with corrections.

We talked about the legends and myths that accumulate about every person who becomes widely known. I reminded him of a statement recently published in many English and American papers, that he had taken farewell of the stage and would never write another play. 'There is absolutely no foundation for that announcement. I never made such a remark.'

Otis Guernsey, a famous undergraduate Yale athlete in 1916, wrote to Mr. Galsworthy about *Justice* and received the following reply:

WINGSTONE
MANATON
DEVON

MY DEAR SIR:

Your kind letter reached me yesterday. Falder killed himself because of the general over-wroughtness of his position. The knowledge that Ruth had not waited for him perhaps gave him the last squeeze;

but the idea of going back—a procession of going backs, was almost enough without. Suicide, I think, is generally an affair of an over-wrought *moment*. One may go about in a suicidal frame for weeks and not be given the last shove needful.

I'm so glad the play stirs people up.

With much appreciation of your letter, I am

Very faithfully yours

JOHN GALSWORTHY

In the Spring of 1930 I wrote him in response to an urgent request from a friend that I would ask him about the use of the 'double possessive' in one of his books. A characteristic letter came:

GROVE LODGE,
THE GROVE, HAMPSTEAD,
LONDON, N.W.3.
May 8, 1930.

MY DEAR WILLIAM LYON PHELPS

I hope you are in the most robust condition. We send you warmest greetings.

About that letter you 'respectfully refer' to me from —— Well, you see, as is very common with readers she (in the instance given) confuses the author with the character speaking. That double possessive is very common in current English speech. I should say people use about six of the single possessive to about half a dozen of the double possessive; and the example she quotes is a perfect specimen of the practice.

I'm not going to say however that I wouldn't be capable of using it myself; such is the force and attraction of corruptions, and I am, alas, the least precise of persons.

Bury is looking nice just now, and I wish I could once more place you within my integuments and defeat (ahem!) you at tennis.

Always yours

JOHN GALSWORTHY

That matron-mother of three,—with whom you played has not yet got over her delight at being told by you to 'run Child, run!'

His third and last visit to Yale was on 9 April 1931. This was preceded by the following letters.

GROVE LODGE,
THE GROVE, HAMPSTEAD,
LONDON, N.W.3.
Dec. 3, 1930

DEAR WILLIAM

Greetings! And thank you for the challenge. The onset will set us south as fast as we can leg it. The retreat will see us bobbing like peas on the knife with which, I believe, they should not be eaten. In other words—our souls will not be our own I guess, nor our bodies. If we can hop off the blade on the way to or from Boston in April 23 we will—to see you both *but not to speak*. I'm under an oath.

As to tennis. Think of my age, infirmity, & the condition I shall be in. You American youngsters of 65 have no mercy on us.

Again greetings and a Xmas blessing.

Yours,

J.G.

Address but not for dissemination
Hotel St. Moritz: 59th Street
New York

THE BELLEVUE-STRATFORD
PHILADELPHIA
April 2, 1931

MY DEAR 'BILLY'

Thank you for your note. I go to Boston on the 8th, and shall take the 9.30 a.m. back on the 9th which reaches New Haven at 1 p.m. It would be delightful if I might lunch with you and resume my journey at 4.17 p.m.—for I must be in New York for dinner that evening. But on your immortal soul you must swear that I don't have to make a speech of any kind. I don't believe I could play tennis so soon after lunch (as that would mean), so I must forego the pleasure of being beaten by you. Ada has had such a lot of travelling that I shall have to leave her behind—the train is no joke to her, poor dear. I look forward very much to seeing you both again.

Always yours,

J.G.

Ada joins me in best greetings to you both.

He arrived at one o'clock and I invited to meet him at my house a group of undergraduates called The Pundits. He was in high spirits and talked in an intimate, friendly fashion with the students. After they had left, I had an hour or two of good talk with him. The sensation of the year was Somerset Maugham's novel *Cakes and Ale* in which to everyone's amazement, the life of Thomas Hardy was apparently held up to ridicule. I have never found any explanation of this extraordinary book. A novel, written as a rejoinder, in which Somerset Maugham was made to appear in an unfavourable light, followed immediately. It was called *Gin and Bitters*, came out anonymously, and evidently Mr. Galsworthy thought the author was Hugh Walpole, for he said 'I have been reading on the train today Hugh Walpole's novel in which he attacks Maugham.' But the novel was not written by Mr. Walpole, but by Elinor Mordaunt (good name), an accomplished English novelist who has travelled all over the world.

Mr. Galsworthy could not understand why Mr. Maugham had written his story, and he would not express an opinion on the merits of *Gin and Bitters*.

It is interesting to see how one distinguished writer feels about experiments made by his contemporaries. No-one admired the genius and character of Henry James more than Barrie; yet Barrie told me he did not think that *The Turn of the Screw* should have been written. He seemed to feel it wasn't quite fair. In the same way, in this conversation with Mr. Galsworthy, although he admired Barrie immensely, he told me he thought *Mary Rose* was not quite a legitimate play; that the dramatist was not fair to his audience. However this may be, I am very glad both were written; for they are among the works of literary art that made an indelible impression.

The last time I saw Mr. Galsworthy was in 1932 in London. We lunched with them on 27 May at their house in Hampstead; he seemed in excellent health and spirits; there was no indication of sickness. He told me the Ivy Restaurant was his boothole. On first nights he could not be induced to make any appearance or speech; he would not even attend the performance, but waited doggo in the Ivy until news was brought concerning the reception of the play.

We drove with them down to the city in their car; and as I had to get out near Westminster, and was about to close the door of the car, he said 'Be sure it closes' and as I heard it latch, I said 'It clicks—just like your plays.' He laughed and seemed pleased.

He was greatly interested in a new gadget that had enabled him to smoke the pipe as often as he pleased without 'biting the tongue.' This was a system of paper cartridges filled with tobacco called 'Smoker's Circles; a Boon to Wet Smokers' each one just the size of the bowl of the pipe. You inserted it and then as the paper around the tobacco burned away, you could smoke to your heart's content. We tried it and he gave me a lot of the cartridges.

As we were leaving for America, I wrote him a note saying that the Senior class students of the Sheffield Scientific School at Yale had voted him their favourite novelist. The following is the last letter I received from him.

BURY HOUSE,
BURY AT PULBOROUGH,
SUSSEX.
June 9, 1932

DEAR WILLIAM

Thank you for that pleasing card. How strange & flattering are the tastes of the Science Students of Yale University!

I hope you will take home a suit case full of R.J.Smokers Circles. We had hoped to see you both again, but one thing and another have cropped up.

A good voyage to you! Our love to you both.

Always yours

J.G.

He was awarded the Nobel Prize that autumn of 1932; and I have often wondered if it indirectly hastened his death. Mr. and Mrs. Galsworthy often left England in the Autumn to go to Arizona or to some warm winter climate; this time naturally he waited, expecting to go to Stockholm in November. It would have been a fearful ordeal for him in any case, as his modesty and shyness would have made a public appearance agonizing; though he was of course gratified with the award. When the time came, he was not well enough to attend.

He died 31 January 1933.

In 1938 appeared Mrs. Galsworthy's admirable book, *Over the Hills and Far Away*. I wrote congratulating her not only on the book but because she showed in it that the *memory* of happiness was a source of happiness, and not of unavailing regret.

LONDON, MARCH 28, 1938

MY DEAR FRIEND,

Your kind letter gave me the very greatest pleasure, as you may easily imagine. Such generous praise from such a high authoritative source has seldom come my way and I thank you most heartily.

You are so right about happiness; of course it can be in the present, and the real. I have known times during mountain days of walking and climbing when I've nearly swooned with joy in the beauty, the joy, the happiness of it all. Old man Johnson had too suffering a body ever to have experienced such hours, and he ought not to have talked on the subject; there were so many other things that he *could* expound, explain, illuminate. But I am truly no great admirer of him, for he was a coward about some things, and cowardice casts a horrid dinginess on a character, as I see it.

I have been wintering in England, as an experiment, and it has proved very successful. I went to Torquay in early November with no great hopes of being able to bear either climate or surroundings, and there has been hardly a day when I felt cold or disinclined to go out of doors. It is a wonderful centre for motoring, for coast and inland are both lovely, and Dartmoor, quite near, provides an entirely different landscape and climate. I came home last Thursday, leaving mid-June weather behind me.

I must again thank you for that lovely letter, which I shall give myself the pleasure of re-reading when I am feeling too down-trodden; and hoping you and your dear Lady are very well and happy,

I am
Affectionately yours,

ADA GALSWORTHY

73

SECOND JOURNEY TO CALIFORNIA

In 1919 I accepted another invitation from the University
of California, this time to teach in the Summer School of
the Southern Branch of the University at Los Angeles. We
arrived on Sunday 29 June. That afternoon as we passed
through various towns in California, the heat was so intense that I wondered how we should be able to endure it.
I got off the train for a few moments at San Bernardino,
and on the platform I felt as if I were walking on a hot
stove; and it is not an exaggeration when I say that the
soles of my shoes were hot for half an hour after. But when
we arrived at the station in Los Angeles, I noticed that the
men on the street were not wearing Palm Beach suits; and
indeed there was a cool breeze blowing and the temperature
was below seventy. Such is the difference in summer between the cool coast and even a few miles in the interior.

The sessions of the University were held in the fine building of the State Normal School at Hollywood, not nearly so
famous then as in later years. We lived at Pasadena some
nine miles away, in an excellent boarding-house called La
Solana; and I reflected that after my death, if some curious
stranger should examine my extinct cheque-books and find
so many weekly stubs made out to La Solana, he would
make a natural but erroneous inference. Pasadena was hot
in the daytime, but it was a dry heat, not uncomfortable
even at a high temperature, and in afternoon came the
cool wind, so that every evening one had to wear an overcoat and then sleep under thick blankets—in other words

the perfect climate. The fine residences on Orange Grove Avenue were closed for Pasadena is a winter resort; but I prefer it in the summer, when the nights are always cool and there is no possibility of rain.

We saw the great Maurice McLoughlin and his partner Bundy play tennis, and the woman champion, Miss Mary Browne, and one of the famous Sutton sisters. McLoughlin was kind enough to ask me to play with him one day in doubles; I did, though my contribution to our victory was negligible. In talking with him it was easy to see why he was the most ardently beloved of all tennis-players; he had an irresistible charm. We accompanied him to the train when he left for the East to take part in the national championships. But alas! his great days were over.

In Hollywood I had the pleasure of meeting Miss Florence Sutton. I told her I had never been beaten by a woman, and being always on the lookout for new experiences, I asked her if she would do me the honour of playing three sets of singles. She beat me quite easily, as I could not get more than three games in a set. Later, in one day, with her as partner, I played eleven sets!

On one of the numerous links near Pasadena I played golf when the temperature was 104 in the shade; and made the best score I have ever made in my life on a full-length course, 75.

I found in my lectures at the Los Angeles branch of the University the same enthusiasm and devotion that impressed me so much at Berkeley in 1908; and from the people the same inexhaustible kindness and gracious hospitality. Mr. and Mrs. John Perrin put an automobile and a chauffeur at our disposal for the entire term of six weeks! When we finally had to take the train East, we found our drawing-room filled with flowers, and an immense group of people came to the station to say farewell.

We took the Santa Fé train at Pasadena. On arriving in

New York, we went to the delightful camp of our friends Mr. and Mrs. James R.Sheffield in the Adirondacks, and there I saw Mount Whiteface for the first time since I was nine years old, when I had seen the sunset from the summit and spent the night on the mountain.

The latter part of the vacation I spent in San Antonio, Texas, where I made three addresses a day at the convention of school-teachers. I was impressed by the courage of these men and women. Every day the temperature was well over ninety, and probably over a hundred. They were packed like sardines into the vast auditorium, and compelled to listen daily to many addresses. Yet they showed enthusiasm.

One of the most interesting hours for me was speaking to the coloured school-teachers, who had a daily assembly. The grateful appreciation of these devoted men and women was deeply affecting. One of them wrote me, 'When you were speaking, I forgot I was black.'

Every morning I had breakfast before sunrise on the roof of the hotel, and every evening I had dinner outdoors after sunset. Miss Sarah King, who celebrated in 1936 her fiftieth year as teacher, gave me a genuine Spanish dinner; every dish was new to me, and they all tasted good.

I visited the Spanish church, several centuries old, and the priest showed me a strange painting of the Trinity— three young men standing close together, dressed in the height of fashion of those days.

On my way north, I stopped at Little Rock, Arkansas, simply because of childish geographical memories. I fell in love with the town, though the heat was fierce. At a railway stall I bought a copy of *Tom Brown at Oxford*, which I had not read for many years. At Memphis I crossed the Mississippi.

74

SOME POETS AND NOVELISTS

LORD DUNSANY, the Irish dramatist, gave a lecture at Yale University on a particularly appropriate day—Hallowe'en, 1919. The thing that impressed the audience more than anything else was the enormous amount of water he drank during the lecture. The huge pitcher of water stood on the table; he preferred to give his lecture sitting down. He would constantly reach over, swallow an entire glass of water, and proceed with the lecture. This went along well enough until he was reading from one of his plays in which the following incident occurred. Two filled cups were offered to a certain character. One of them was harmless; the other was poisoned. The man had to drink, and it was an even chance. As Lord Dunsany came to this dramatic point in his reading, he poured another glass of water out, held it in front of him, and read, 'Shall I drink the poisoned cup?' without observing the situation. After the lecture was over, he said to me, 'I hope the water is good; I drank an awful lot of it, didn't I?'

Sara Teasdale (Filsinger), 1884–1933, the American lyrical poet who won the Pulitzer Prize in 1917, was a good friend of mine; and we both admired the poetry of Vachel Lindsay. The Poetry Society of America offered an annual award, and in 1919 Sara Teasdale, Richard Burton, and I were the Committee. We could not agree, and finally the prize was divided between Carl Sandburg and Stephen Vincent Benét. I had an agreeable afternoon with Sara Teasdale talking about poets and poetry. Considering the excellence of her own work, she was extremely modest, painfully sensitive to adverse criticism, and appreciative of praise. I had spoken highly of her work and she alludes to that in one of the two following letters. Richard Burton has been a lifelong intimate friend; we both grew up in Hartford.

In 1937 a volume of her verse was published (no editor's name given) called *The Collected Poems of Sara Teasdale*.

I WEST 81ST STREET
NEW YORK CITY
May 29, 1919

DEAR PROF. PHELPS:

We tried "at the hour of nine" as Romeo says, (or is it Juliet?) to reach you last night by long distance, and the combined efforts of Prof. Burton and S.T.F. were unavailing. . . .

I do wish you could have been here to argue with Burton. It would have been such fun. I liked B. ever so much. He came in all hot and excited at being half an hour late. We had a cocktail and hurried to the dining room where B. seemed to grow mightily in general good spirits.

Do you know, I've been in a state of extreme contrition ever since you were here that I didn't even offer you a glass of ginger ale? My plans for serving tea were upset at the last minute and I forgot all about three perfectly good bottles of ginger ale out in my husband's closet. Sometime when you're in town *do* come out and let me show you I'm not such a bad hostess after all. And I *did* want to dress up instead of slipping into the first thing that came to hand, all of which can be done next time, if you are so good as to make a next time.

I've been rolling the good things that you said about my poetry back and forth in my mind until I am very proud and very happy. I hope you really meant some of it. It would hearten me more than you know to be able to feel that say even three-eighths of it were truth telling. I don't know why I said three-eighths. It sounds so properly mathematical and I'm like you in mathematics, slow but not sure. Do you remember saying that in *The Advance of English Poetry*?

All good greetings, and don't forget to make a next time.

SARA TEASDALE FILSINGER

EL ENCANTO
HOTEL AND COTTAGES
SANTA BARBARA, CAL.
October 10, '19

DEAR PROF. PHELPS:

Haven't I travelled a long way since I wrote to you last? I wonder if you were in Santa Barbara when you were out here on the coast last summer? If you were, I know you liked it. I am way up on Mission Ridge in the most adorable little new hotel with a real fairy-tale garden. My husband had to go to South America and I came out here because I didn't feel up to going with him. I haven't forgotten the promise I made myself to give you one of my most precious possessions, a drawing by Vachel from the censers and the hearth series. I hope the whole series will be in his book of drawings when Macs. bring it out. I'm sure you won't mind having yours used if they ask for it.

With all good wishes for a fine autumn,

Sincerely,

SARA TEASDALE FILSINGER

JOSEPH HERGESHEIMER

Before Mr. Hergesheimer had produced anything of importance, some of his friends sent me (quite without his knowledge) his play in manuscript called *The Zenith* and a copy of his first published novel *The Lay Anthony*. I wrote to my correspondents that I thought the play had no merit and no promise. But while I did not write so disparagingly of the novel, I said I was not impressed by it. I ought to have perceived its latent power. Years later when Mr. Hergesheimer's position among contemporary novelists was very high, I wondered if I had missed what I ought to have seen in those two early works and in response to my letter he wrote as follows:

THE DOWER HOUSE
WEST CHESTER, PENNSYLVANIA

DEAR DR. PHELPS:

You are, of course, right about the crudeness of *The Zenith*; but I am unable to accompany you so far in that opinion of *The Lay Anthony*. As a first novel it had a decided right to any support. However, looking back now on about sixteen years of total isolation, an initial book that in its year sold perhaps eight hundred, a second the proceeds of which were stolen from me; remembering an imponderable academic frown, I am almost convinced that I had the best possible experience for a remote end.

I'd like to write to you convincingly about my work; but, in addition to an innate distrust of the mere discussion of creative literature —I mean for the creator—I am very unsettled in my comprehension of the conventional phrases necessary to any such proceeding. I am glad you like *Java Head*, it was solely written for liking, is the most direct and sincerest reply I can make to your generous appreciation.

Very faithfully,

JOSEPH HERGESHEIMER

April 14, 1919

Mr. Hergesheimer's career as a novelist was so brilliant and successful that it is surprising he did not continue. *The Three Black Pennys*, *Java Head*, and *Linda Condon* are distinguished, particularly in literary style. In later years he devoted himself more to biography, writing an admirable life of General Sheridan. He came to Yale to give a lecture in which he humorously but very positively attacked American women for what he regarded their bad opinion of American authors, and he told me afterwards that this lecture not only made it impossible for him to give any more lectures but almost stopped the sale of his books. I think he admires beautiful old furniture more than anything else in the world, and when he entered my house before we went to the lecture he viewed my eighteenth century family furniture with something very near adoration.

The intense loneliness of the novelist, for most of his time is spent not in observing life but in monastic solitary seclusion, was distasteful to Mr. Hergesheimer; in later years he produced books of travel in Europe, Cuba, and other places.

He could write an interesting autobiography. He told some of us at Yale of the years of severe labour he spent at the art of English composition, after he had decided to give up painting.

ZONA GALE

When we were in Pasadena in 1919, I received a letter from the novelist Zona Gale. She was somewhat disturbed by an adverse criticism of her work. I wrote her to pay no attention to it, especially not to think of replying to it. If a critic says (for example) that a certain writer is not a literary artist, there is no good in asserting the contrary. The only effective reply is a work of literary art.

> Meet Lutwyche, I—
> And save him from my statue meeting him?

The very next year she produced a masterpiece, *Miss Lulu Bett*, which gave her an unassailable position in the front rank of living American novelists. She turned this into a play which won the Pulitzer Prize.

This correspondence in 1919 (I had not then seen her) led to an intimate friendship. Here is a characteristic letter:

DEAR WILLIAM LYON PHELPS:

How good you were to "Papa LeFleur" and how greatly I appreciate it. Thank you so much for your letter.

Michigan seems so near. I wish sometime you would ferry across!

You will have received a copy of the short stories which I put together. I am going to write an article and send it to the Yale Review on what constitutes the sentimental. If in a story a girl says "I want to see my mother," that is sentimental. But if a nun says in a story, "I want to be a saint. O I hope I will get to be one. I have always thought it must be so wonderful to be a saint. That's what I want to be—a saint." Then that is an approved utterance. I suppose the point is that in any statement of aspiration or emotion in these days there must be a touch of mockery in order to make it the real and not the romantic. One wonders why. One wonders too why one need be swept into the current of these period reactions which herd and stamp all human utterance.

My love to you both,

Affectionately yours,

ZONA GALE

Portage, Wisconsin
October 14, 1933

EDWIN ARLINGTON ROBINSON

One December day in the year 1896 I received through the post a thin paper-covered booklet called

THE TORRENT
AND THE NIGHT BEFORE
BY EDWIN ARLINGTON
ROBINSON, GARDINER
MAINE, 1889–1896

On the title-page was printed a disarming ironical quotation from François Coppée—

Qui pourrais-je imiter pour être original?

and at the foot of the title-page, instead of a publisher's name was the statement

PRINTED FOR THE AUTHOR
MDCCCXCVI

and across the title-page was written in ink

W. L. Phelps,
with compliments of E. A. Robinson
9 December, 1896

The printed dedication of the tiny volume was humorously modest:

> This book is dedicated to any man,
> woman, or critic who will cut the
> edges of it.—I have done the top.

I have no recollection of reading this book, and none of acknowledging it; but I must have done both, for the next year (1897) I received a bound volume of 123 pages, called

THE CHILDREN OF THE NIGHT

A Book of Poems

By

Edwin Arlington Robinson

Boston

Richard G. Badger & Company

MDCCCXCVII

A publisher's note preceding the title page said

This first edition of The Children of the Night consists of Five Hundred Copies on Batchworth Laid Paper, and Fifty Copies on Imperial Japanese Vellum

and on the fly-leaf was written in ink

W. L. Phelps
from E. A. Robinson
4 December, 1897

I read every word of this volume, as is proved by a note I made at the end of it, only a few days after I received it.

For more than twenty years these two precious volumes disappeared from my sight; during that interval we moved twice. One day, somewhere in the nineteen-twenties, I found the two resting quietly among a lot of old papers, uninjured by their prolonged slumber.

I mention these facts, because the first of these books is now one of the most valuable to collectors in American Literature, and the second fetches an exalted price; the fact that they are both autograph copies adds to their value.

I never saw Robinson until Yale gave him the honorary degree of Doctor of Letters in 1922. He was quiet, reticent, modest, and produced an impression of absolute sincerity.

Edwin Arlington Robinson was born at Head Tide, Maine, 22 December 1869, and died in New York, 6 April 1935. He was never married. He was three times awarded the Pulitzer Prize in Poetry. He was elected a member of the Academy on 10 November 1927.

His fiftieth birthday, 22 December 1919, was celebrated all over the United States; one of the very few occasions in the history of our country, when the birthday of a poet had a nationwide commemoration during his lifetime. It is unnecessary to say that he took no part in it, nor made any public appearance.

The year after his death, 18 October 1936, a tablet to Robinson was unveiled at Gardiner, Maine, in the presence of a large assembly. The exercises were as simple as they were dignified. Hermann Hagedorn called him a beloved figure in the American Pantheon, 'the anchorite, outside space and time, conscious of an eternal eye upon him and upon the work of his hands.'

This tablet was presented to the city by Henry Richards, husband of Laura E. Richards, author of the little book giving all the information we have of Robinson's childhood and boyhood in Maine.

It is interesting, in view of the facilities for publicity in the twentieth century, that during his entire career Robinson did everything possible to avoid attracting attention. No one could secure a photograph of him or any biographical data from himself; he refused to appear in public, he did not read or discuss his poems before audiences, he remained solitary and inaccessible. Yet he was generally acknowledged as the foremost living American poet; raised to that eminence by the sheer merit of his verse.

When in the year 1928, he was awarded by the National Institute of Arts and Letters the Gold Medal for poetry, he wrote me this characteristic letter:

ROOM 411
30 IPSWICH STREET
BOSTON, NOVEMBER 18, 1929

DEAR PHELPS,

I am writing to you as President of the Institute of Arts and Letters to express my sincere thanks to all concerned in my receipt of the Gold Medal for Poetry this year. It is certainly a source of great pleasure and satisfaction to me. At the risk of appearing a little ungracious, may I ask if anything in the nature of a formal presentation may be omitted? As I grow older I find myself less inclined, if possible, to indulge in the luxuries of publicity. I am still human, however, and am glad to know that there are several people somewhere who like what I have done, or some of it.

Yours sincerely,

E. A. ROBINSON

His statement, 'As I grow older I find myself less inclined, if possible, to indulge in the luxuries of publicity,' has a humour all its own.

In this same year the Letters of Thomas Sergeant Perry were published, with an Introduction by Robinson. I wrote him again about the Medal and about these Letters, but I lamented the absence of an Index. He replied as follows:

30 IPSWICH STREET
BOSTON, NOVEMBER 20, 1929

DEAR PHELPS,

Thank you for your letter of the nineteenth regarding the award of the medal. Your consideration is much appreciated, and you have my gratitude.

Your approval of the Letters and the Introduction gives me great pleasure, as you know. The lack of an index has called down curses on my head, and with reason, as I have to admit.

Yours very sincerely,

E.A.ROBINSON

When Robinson began to publish his poetry in the late nineties, the times were not favourable; but the true poet should have genius for the inopportune. These two early volumes attracted very little attention; and apparently they were doomed to speedy and complete oblivion, the inescapable fate of ninety-nine books out of every hundred.

But about fifteen years later, in the revival of poetry in America, Robinson came into his own; and he deserved his fame, both for the excellence of his work and because he was one of the leaders in this renaissance. The dates are significant. *The Torrent*, 1896; *Children of the Night*, 1897; *Captain Craig*, 1902; *The Town Down the River*, 1910; *The Man Against the Sky*, 1916; and *Merlin*, 1917.

His original play *Van Zorn*, is not only very fine as drama and as literature but it exhibits a side of his talents usually unknown; it had the bad luck to appear in 1914.

I confess that I made two errors in estimating his work. I thought that when *Merlin* appeared, he was on the wrong track, that he had better let those legends alone. It seemed to me as if he were trying to dilute Tennyson; and to dilute Tennyson won't do at all. My second error was my belief that the value of Robinson's work was analytical and intellectual, rather than emotional. In 1918, I wrote,

It is of course possible that Mr. Robinson wished to try something in a romantic vein; but it is not his vein. He excels in the clear presentment of character; in pith; in sharp outline; in solid, masculine effort . . . He is an excellent draughtsman; everything that he has done has beauty of line; anything pretentious is to him abhorrent. He is more map-maker than painter.

Then, to my amazement and delight, he proved me wrong by producing in 1927 his masterpiece, *Tristram*. It not only is his best poem, it is the best poetic version of that immortal story that has ever appeared in English. It glows with passion and is radiant with beauty. And indeed, perhaps its closing lines about the other Isolde, Isolt of the White Hands, leaves on our minds the deepest impression. For here he rises from the particular to the universal.

> Isolt of the white hands,
> Isolt with her gray eyes and her white face,
> Still gazed across the water to the north
> But not now for a ship. Were ships to come,
> No fleet of them could hold a golden cargo
> That would be worth one agate that was hers—
> One toy that he had given her long ago,
> And long ago forgotten. Yet there she gazed
> Across the water, over the white waves,
> Upon a castle that she had never seen,
> And would not see, save as a phantom shape
> Against a phantom sky. He had been there,
> She thought, but not with her. He had died there,
> But not for her. He had not thought of her,
> Perhaps, and that was strange. He had been all,
> And would be always all there was for her,
> And he had not come back to her alive,
> Not even to go again. It was like that
> For women, sometimes, and might be so too often
> For women like her. She hoped there were not many
> Of them, or many of them to be, not knowing
> More about that than about waves and foam,
> And white birds everywhere, flying, and flying;
> Alone, with her white face and her gray eyes,
> She watched them there till even her thoughts were white,
> And there was nothing alive but white birds flying,
> Flying, and always flying, and still flying,
> And the white sunlight flashing on the sea.

75

A JOURNEY TO ANDOVER

(1919)

In June I went to Phillips Academy, Andover, Mass., to give the Commencement address. I took the night train from New Haven to Boston, and was eating breakfast in the Copley Plaza Hotel, when a young Yale graduate whom I had not seen since his senior year in 1913, came to my table. He asked if I were going to Andover; receiving an affirmative reply, he wished to know how I was going. 'Well, in about five minutes I shall drive to the North Station and take the train.' 'But won't you go with me? I have a taxi outside.' 'You mean you have a taxi to the North Station?' 'No, I have a taxi to Andover.' Now Andover is about forty miles from Boston. I remembered this young man very well. He had shown energy and heroism in 'working his way' through Yale only six years past; he had managed a boot-blacking and clothes-pressing establishment, had waited on table, had for four years done a vast amount of menial labour. And now he was inviting me to travel forty miles with him in a taxi. I was puzzled. 'Are you sure you have room?' 'Plenty.' So we went out, and there was a taxi, that had been steadily churning up money while we were at breakfast. We entered it and my young friend merely said to the driver, 'Andover,' and we started. He began the conversation by asking me to come to New York when I had leisure, as he would like to show me some of his pictures. I supposed he had some snapshots, and replied that I should be very glad to see them. He remarked that some of his pictures were really very good. 'I bought one last week for two hundred thousand dollars.' I looked at him. 'Yes, I have a collection of masterpieces and Italian primitives.' This seemed to me like a page out of the *Arabian Nights.* 'Look here, it's none of my business, of course, but didn't you work your way through Yale?' 'Indeed I did; but that was six years ago. My salary is now $200,000 a year, but that is the least part of my income.' We are all familiar with the millionaires who started with nothing and became fabulously rich at fifty; but here was a young man still under thirty. However, everything he told me was true; I felt as if I were in a dream, where, as Goethe says, one wonder fades into another, and the succeeding wonder takes us by surprise. I listened to one miracle after another as the taxi carried us to Andover.

It seemed to me that the record of this man was astounding, but in two hours I was to discover that he was a timid, shrinking violet in comparison with the stranger with whom I was to converse on the way back to Boston. After the Commencement exercises were over, and I was eating lunch at the Principal's house, a middle-aged man at the end of the table asked me when I was going. I told him I must take the train to Boston. 'But won't you go with me in my car?' I reflected that I had 'bummed' a ride on the way up, and I might as well repeat the act, only I thought to myself, it will be impossible to hear any such romantic tales as on the morning journey. After a polite skirmish, I agreed to go to Boston with this gentleman. He told his chauffeur to get into the back seat, as he intended to drive himself, so I sat with my host in front. He drove with ease and skill through the traffic and after we had gone two or three miles, he said casually, 'Of course if this car should break down, I can stop any

passing car and order them to take us to Boston.' Supposing
he had a mistaken sense of humour, I looked at him, and
found he was quite serious. Then he suddenly asked if I
had ever seen a man drive a car with his little finger, and
without waiting to discover whether I had or not, he
placed the little finger of his left hand on the steering-
wheel, stepped on the accelerator, and the indicator
showed we were travelling sixty miles an hour. Then,
while we were still whirling at this pace, he suddenly
threw his right arm around my neck, and forced my head
down on his shoulder. 'You see, at any moment I could
kill you. I might be driving and if my seatmate should
become offensive, I could choke him with one hand while
driving with the other. Or, I could draw a pistol with
one hand and shoot either him or any other enemy in a
pursuing car. It is really necessary for me to be able to
drive with one finger.' I saw and said nothing. What was
there to say?

I felt relieved when he took his right arm off my throat
and began to drive again in normal fashion. 'If we should
be late in reaching Boston I will telegraph and have the
train to New York stopped so that they will wait for us.'
I told him I thought that would not be wise. 'Or, I can
drive you right on to Providence and overtake the train.'
'No! whatever you do, don't do that!'

'I have three houses, one in Boston, one in Washington,
one in Maine. I keep them open with a staff of servants,
for at any moment I might have to stay in one of them.
I have a great deal to do. I went down to Washington and
talked with some of the Senators. I spoke to a few men
there who had made a profound study of a difficult subject
for years; but in talking with them only five minutes, I
understood the matter far better than any of them did,
and was able to give them valuable advice, just the
solution they needed. How do you account for my ability

to grasp a difficult subject in a moment?' I told him I thought it was genius. 'Ah, but that is nothing to my power over women. To women I am absolutely irresistible. I know five women now, who are happily married and living in contentment with their husbands. Yet, if I should go to any one of them and crook my finger, she would instantly leave her husband and come to me. How do you account for that, Professor?' and he looked at me earnestly. 'That,' I said frankly, 'is magnetism. That's what it is —just magnetism.'

He told me how he had gone to a sailing-ship lying at the port in Boston, and although he had never studied navigation, he took command of this vessel, and took it safely to the Azores. I quite agreed with him that such a thing was unusual.

But the cream was to come. After listening to a stream of talk of this kind, we entered Boston at last, and at a corner of one of the most crowded business streets, he drove our car into the middle of the cross-section, so that we held up the traffic both ways. Immediately the air resounded with the blowing of innumerable horns and curses were showered on us from every direction. The traffic policeman advanced toward us, and I knew that while some journeys end in lovers meeting, our journey's end would be the jail, where I fully expected to spend the night with my new friend.

As the policeman came alongside, my friend enquired pleasantly 'How are you, Officer?' and to my unspeakable amazement, the policeman answered smiling that he was very well. 'And Mrs. —— and your children, all quite well?' 'They are in fine shape, thank you, Mr. ——.' Around us pandemonium, horns, shrieks, curses filled the air. But the officer and my companion went on conversing with the *insouciance* of ladies at an afternoon tea. After this had lasted some time, my friend enquired, 'How long will you permit me to hold up the traffic, Officer?' 'The entire afternoon, if you wish.' And that was that.

We started at last, drove to a fine-looking house in a good residence section. He opened the door with a key, called aloud for a servant and a coloured man appeared. We had some light refreshment, my host showed me every courtesy, and I caught the three o'clock train for New Haven.

76

EVENTS IN 1920 AND 1921

On 3 January 1920 I was one of the speakers at a dinner in
New York given to Maeterlinck by the Lotos Club. I sat
next to him and had much good talk. He said he understood every word of my speech because I spoke English so
clearly. This dinner followed his disastrous lecture. He had
come over to undertake a long lecture tour through the
United States, and a tremendous crowd appeared at his
first address. He knew English well but could not speak it;
he had therefore hit upon the extraordinary plan of writing
English words with a phonetic French pronunciation. After
he had spoken some ten sentences, a woman stood up in
the audience and called out, ' Mr. Maeterlinck, we cannot
understand a word.' If he had spoken in French many
would have understood, or he could have had an interpreter on the stage, to translate for the audience after every
paragraph, as was the method adopted successfully by
Senor Benavente. But Maeterlinck's language was impossible, and the coast-to-coast lecture tour was abandoned
after that one attempt. In my speech I said that he had
paid Americans a remarkable and unique compliment. As
in the old days when toasts were given to royalty and the
glasses smashed so that they could not be used a second
time, M. Maeterlinck had used for our benefit a language
that had never been used before and certainly would never
be used again. I never heard anyone laugh more heartily
than he did during my speech. His projected tour was a
failure, thirty or forty dates cancelled, his nerves were

on edge, but my treating the matter in this way released his pent-up nervousness. It was an Aristotelian catharsis. He laughed and laughed till the tears ran down his cheeks.

After the formal dinner was over we adjourned to another room for drinking and intimate conversation. I had the good fortune to be placed at a small table with only two men, the British Admiral Lord Jellicoe and the famous American Charles M. Schwab. I had supposed that after the terrific years of responsibility in the war when by a disaster to the Grand Fleet Jellicoe might have 'lost the war in one afternoon' the Admiral would look worn and tragic; instead of that he was the picture of robust health and jollity; a weather-beaten sea-dog, full of mirth and high spirits. And I had thought with the tremendous undertakings by Mr. Schwab, he would show signs of the strain; he looked as happy as a schoolboy and both men talked and laughed as if they had never had a care in the world.

On the afternoon of 27 February in New York I saw Ervine's fine play *Jane Clegg*; Dudley Digges and Margaret Wycherley at their best. I went back stage to congratulate them and Miss Wycherley said, 'Ah, you are from Yale; in that university the drama is always taken seriously.'

On 18 March I introduced Sir Oliver Lodge who lectured to an enormous audience at Yale. He was absolutely confident of survival after death and said he had had communications. There was nothing sensational in his manner.

CARDINAL GIBBONS (1834–1921)

As it is sometimes stated that Catholics do not emphasize the study of the Bible, the following letter from one of the greatest of them is interesting.

CARDINAL'S RESIDENCE
408 N.CHARLES ST.
BALTIMORE
January 10, 1920

Mr. Wilbur Cross,
Editor, Yale Review,
New Haven, Conn.

MY DEAR MR. CROSS:—

I read with much interest the review of Mr. Maurice Egan, based upon the work of Mr. William Lyon Phelps, "Reading the Bible," and I am happy to see an interest taken in the Scriptures. Up to seventy-five years ago, the public men of our country seemed to have been saturated with the Bible. They were familiar with its contents and quoted freely text after text. Among many others, Mr. Webster seemed to have at his fingers end the words of this inspired book. I remember to have counted in the pleading of Mr. Webster, counsel in the Girard Will Case, no less than 14 quotations from or allusions to Scripture. Apart from its inspirational character, the Bible still remains the one means of culture.

Mr. Egan is well qualified to review this work of Mr. Phelps.
With best wishes,

Faithfully yours,

J.CARD. GIBBONS

I do not know whether the following story is true or not, but if it is not true, it ought to be. After he had returned from an interview with the Pope, some Gigadibs said to him, 'Cardinal Gibbons, I don't see how you or any reasonable man can believe in the infallibility of the Pope. Do you really believe the Pope is infallible?' To which the Cardinal smilingly replied, 'He called me "Jibbons."'

A BAPTIST AND ACTRESSES

The variety of my own interests and the widely divergent moods caused by them remind me of what happened on Palm Sunday 1921. I attended the Baptist Church in New

Haven in the morning, officiating during part of the service. Then I took the train to New York, to officiate as toastmaster at the great public dinner given in honour of David Belasco. On my way to church that morning I reflected that I should be in all probability not only the one member of the congregation who was to attend a dinner celebrating the theatre on the same evening but perhaps the only person in attendance at any evangelical Protestant Church on Palm Sunday who was to spend the evening in the way I had planned.

And that night in New York as I took my place as toastmaster at this dinner given by the Society of Playwrights with five hundred guests, I could not help thinking how astonished that particular audience would be if I began my remarks by telling them how I had spent the morning!

And yet to me there is nothing 'inconsistent' in these two congregations on the same day. I love the church and I love the theatre. Religion and Drama are two of my passions; thus I myself feel absolutely at home with Baptists, Methodists, Presbyterians in church and prayer-meeting and equally at home with actors and actresses, playwrights and theatre managers.

After preliminaries, I was told that I should escort to the table in the hotel ballroom 'the most beautiful woman in America,' and Mrs. Lionel Atwill certainly was beautiful. At the table David Belasco was on my right and shaking like a leaf at the thought of speaking. He was in terror. But on my left were two of his adorers, Jane Cowl and Frances Starr, and the three of us, working together, brought him into a semblance of calm before his zero hour. They both whispered to me during the dinner of the immense kindness always shown to them by the famous director. There were many speeches—I remember an animated one by W. A. Brady. A brilliant impromptu speech by Laurette Taylor received tremendous applause. She walked out in front of the head table and made delightful remarks on the appearance of the guests of honour. It so happened that the ascetic-looking Sir Philip Gibbs was sitting next to the lovely Mrs. Atwill. 'What do that pair remind you of?' called out Miss Taylor. 'They remind me of the temptation of St. Anthony.'

The next morning the *New York World* had a good account of the banquet, but objected strenuously to a part of my introductory speech. I said that whenever I made an after-dinner address, I always made four speeches at the same time, not one of which resembled any of the other three. 'First, there is the speech that I had carefully prepared beforehand; it was very good; but not at all like the one you are hearing; the second is the one I am now speaking, and it is the worst of the four; the third is the best of them all, brilliant, witty, and full of charm; it is the one I make on the way home from the banquet; and the fourth, entirely unlike any of the others, is the report of the speech in the papers the next morning.' This pleasantry troubled the *World* reporter.

On 15 June I received the honorary degree of Doctor of Literature at Brown University, the first of my honorary degrees. It was fitting that it should be the first as my father had been a graduate and Trustee of Brown, and my oldest brother Dryden was graduated there in 1877. On 21 June I received the same degree from Colgate University, which had also given my father the honorary degree of Doctor of Divinity.

On 12 November in New Haven Marshal Foch attended the football game between Yale and Princeton. He had never seen American football and followed the plays from scrimmage with binoculars. In the middle of the second half, one of his associates asked him if he did not wish to leave. 'Why, the game isn't over, is it? I certainly shall not leave until the end,' and indeed he seemed intensely interested.

I saw an impressive performance of *The Madras House*, by Granville-Barker, given at the Neighbourhood Playhouse in New York, directed by Miss Lewisohn. I had been unable to visualize this play in reading it; and I was amazed to find that on the stage it was one of the most interesting of all modern dramas. I wish it could be revived.

Shortly after the war, Mr. Hubert Sedgwick (Yale 1893) a New Haven journalist, brought me from the Rotary Club of New Haven an invitation to become a member. I have always been glad I accepted. Rotary is a powerful force for good, locally, nationally, and internationally. A number of my colleagues on the Yale Faculty are members and the close association with men in various other occupations and professions is both agreeable and valuable. Many warm friendships have resulted, in New Haven and in far-distant places in America and in Europe.

The Rotarian, the monthly magazine published in Chicago, has contributions from men in every country; leading statesmen, economists, scientists, and others. During the last few years I have contributed a monthly article on the new books.

One of the pleasant events coming to me from Rotary is an annual excursion every August from my summer home in Michigan to Port Huron, eighty miles away. Mr. Edgar A. Guest, whose summer cottage is only seven miles distant, the Rev. Herbert Hichens, who learned golf as a child in Cornwall, England, caddying for the professionals, Mr. William Pottinger, 'Mayor' of Huron City, and I make up the expeditionary force. We drive to Port Huron, Mr. Guest and I speak at an open meeting of Rotary at lunch, and then follow exciting golf matches. For more than a dozen years Mr. Guest and I have had as our

opponents two leading Rotarians of Port Huron, Mr.
Louis Weil, editor of the *Times-Herald*, one of the best daily
newspapers in America; and Mr. David MacTaggart, born
in Scotland, and owner of a large bookshop. Our friendship
with Mr. Weil and Mr. MacTaggart has added immensely
to my happiness; and the gracious hospitality of Mr. and
Mrs. Weil at the close of the afternoon heals the suffering
caused by my misfortunes on the links.

My Father in 1860.

General J.G. Harbord and I
about to go shooting in Georgia

My Father in 1888

My Mother in 1865

Mr. and Mrs. John Galsworthy
At the front porch of the Elizabethan Club
Yale University, 1921

Painting by Jere Wickwire, 1926

Mr. and Mrs. Phelps
On their front porch, 110 *Whitney Avenue, New Haven*

77

BRITISH DIALECT AND AMERICAN VOICES

DICKENS's novels are filled with talk where *w* and *v* are interchanged—*Samivel* and *wery*. I have never heard this, and most Englishmen from whom I have sought information have never heard it. But in 1927 I got a letter from an octogenarian in Toronto:

> Speaking of the English in some districts of England using W for V, I was born in a remote Essex village, and lived most of my days there until I was twenty-three. Our parish had 1,000 inhabitants and I verily believe at least 800 of them would have said a thing was "wery wexatious," "wery wexing," they would have "wisitors" and "weal and winegar" were commonly used; indeed my grandmother who was from Northampton used to say there was no letter "v" in the Essex alphabet.

The *w* and *v* are also interchanged in Bermuda.

Few books are more interesting to read than dictionaries; many years ago Henry A. Beers, Professor of English Literature at Yale, gave a regular college course in *Webster's Unabridged Dictionary*. But the most interesting dictionary I have ever seen is *A Dictionary of Modern English Usage*, by H. W. Fowler. It combines learning, wisdom, humour, common sense, and an almost infallible good taste. It appeared in the nineteen-twenties, and has become not only a popular reference work, but a classic of literature. After my review of it in *Scribners*, the following letter came from its distinguished maker.

HINTON ST. GEORGE
SOMERSET

31 December, 1926

DEAR SIR:

Your notice of *Modern English Usage* in Scribner, of which you
have been good enough to send me a copy, lays me under a deep
obligation. I was already aware, from some press cuttings in which
a lecture of yours was referred to, that you were doing much to give
the book a chance in America as well as here.

You of course praise it much more highly than it deserves; but it
takes a more virtuous person than myself to resent over-praise.

Books are not a commodity that you stand in need of. Nevertheless I am tempted by your remark about personality to send you an
anonymous booklet of mine in which I had occasion to talk on that
subject. It is only a set of lay sermons to big public school boys
and I will turn down the pages of the relevant ones.

With very many thanks for your help,

Yours very truly,

H.W.FOWLER

This letter led to a spirited correspondence; Fowler was
a 'rationalist' whose lay sermons to boys are not nearly so
well known as they deserve to be. In fact, the book he
sent me has become a rarity.

In *Scribners* for March 1927 I expressed dissent from
some pronunciations preferred by Fowler; and someone
informed him that I had 'attacked' his Dictionary. Inasmuch as I had praised it publicly and privately, he was
rather astonished and wrote me the following letter.

HINTON ST. GEORGE
SOMERSET

12 June, 1927

DEAR PROFESSOR PHELPS:

Many thanks for the cuttings from *Scribner*. I was rather alarmed
at the news that you "attacked" *Modern English Usage* in the March
Scribner, and, as I had not seen it, at once sent for a copy. When it
came, I was equally relieved to find the "attack" confined to my

pronunciation—a matter on which much chastisement has made me callous. In pronunciation I am neither on the side of the angels (university professors, that is) nor on the side of the devil (who is the nearest vulgarian), but take my stand with the ordinary (or lazy but civilized) human being.

Yours very truly,

H. W. FOWLER

Fowler's death, 26 December 1933, was a great loss to the world of scholarship and a sharp personal grief to me.

WASHINGTON'S ACCENT

There are questions that interest me, all the more perhaps because of the impossibility of getting an accurate answer. Why did Ben Jonson, with his tremendous size, set out to walk the 400 miles from London to Edinburgh? How much did Doctor Samuel Johnson weigh? Why did Shakespeare stop writing in the prime of life? What was the actual religious belief of the Rev. Robert Herrick and the Rev. Jonathan Swift? (I don't care about Sterne's.) What did Emily Brontë say to her dog Keeper on those long walks? On 27 September 1907 I received the following letter from Arnold Daly, the actor-manager, written from New York.

DEAR PROFESSOR:

I am going to ask a favor of you—another favor I should say, as I am your debtor in the past.

I am rehearsing a short play concerning George Washington, just before or at the time when he was lieutenant in the Virginia Militia, and I am anxious to know if he spoke with a Virginian accent. Did the Southerners have the peculiar soft accent in those days that they use now? I can't find any authority for or against it, and I shall be greatly obliged to you, if you know of any.

Hoping you will pardon me for troubling you, I am,

Very truly yours,

ARNOLD DALY

Thirty years later I wrote to Miss Eugenia Lee of Augusta, a student in Virginia. She gave me the information that Washington spoke like an English gentleman with a voice somewhat affected by the Virginia *patois*.

I have often wished that American women would ponder carefully on Lear's description of the voice of Cordelia. I am very glad to print this verse-letter sent me by an American living in Paris.

LINES INDITED BY A GROUCHY AMERICAN LIVING IN PARIS

A pretty mid-west maiden with a smile
As lovely as a flower, called today—
Niece of an oldtime friend—smart, charming, gay,
But oh, the voice! As rasping as a file!
And when she mentioned *aunt* and called her *ant*
My impulse was to kick her in the pant.

A very little thing you say? But, man,
It's little things that cause most irritation.
Why *should* we be so careless as a nation!
Why not Ameri- (not Amurri-) can?
We're fine! Just add a modulated voice
And gods and little fishes will rejoice.

A reasonable respect for spoken English
Won't make us climb a high pedantic steeple.
Our language has a glamour which our people
All seem to do their damnedest to extinguish.
Our slang's piquant as catsup; I decry it
Not as a condiment but an entire diet.

So having spent much vitriolic juice
I add a milk-and-water: What's the Use!

PETER NITWIT

It is said that the late Andrew Lang wrote so many books that he kept unfinished manuscripts in various rooms in his house, and then continued writing a book in the room that seemed at the moment to be most comfortable. Well, it might be a good idea to have a dictionary in every room. Shakespeare would have enjoyed reading dictionaries. He loved words as men love things of beauty and grandeur, and he loved words as men love children and pet animals. He loved to play with them, in every kind of fantastic pun, one word always suggesting another. It is interesting to read *Love's Labour's Lost* exclusively from that point of view.

78

ST. JOHN ERVINE

I FIRST had the pleasure of meeting Mr. St. John Ervine when he came to Yale to lecture in 1916. I had read a number of his novels, *Mrs. Martin's Man, Alice and Her Family,* and other books. He wrote one novel about the War and to please his mother said that he put no swearing into it.

It was a play by St. John Ervine that established the fame and fortune of the Theatre Guild in New York. This organization had high artistic aims and low funds, and its first performances were financial failures.

One day a gentleman walking around New York glanced at a window of Brentano's book shop, and there saw among other books *John Ferguson.* He remembered that he had met the author in England at some kind of debate, I think, and merely out of curiosity he went in and bought this printed play. There it lay for any manager in the world to use. He took it to the Theatre Guild. They decided to produce it; it was an enormous success. It ran steadily all that spring and through the hot summer and during most of the following season. They were fortunate in having Dudley Digges to act the part of Caesar, but the whole production was admirable, and I don't believe the play could have failed, even if it had been poorly produced and badly acted. It is one of the best plays of the Twentieth Century.

The Theatre Guild followed up this success by another play by Mr. Ervine, *Jane Clegg,* in which Dudley Digges and Margaret Wycherley took the leading parts. This was again both an artistic and a financial success. An amusing thing happened during the rehearsal of this piece. Somewhere in the course of the play one of the characters makes a remark to the effect that if a person has lost a leg he feels pain in the vanished member if bad weather approaches, and when in the rehearsal the character spoke that line, a voice from the darkened auditorium said, 'I know now this is not true.' For when Mr. Ervine wrote the play he had both legs, and when the play was produced he had lost one in the World War.

I asked him one day, 'Which would you rather have, the ability to write plays minus a leg, or to have both legs without that creative ability?' He replied without hesitation, 'Oh, I would much rather have one leg and be a dramatist; yet I do miss the other leg.'

When Mr. and Mrs. Ervine came to our house in New Haven on the occasion of the lecture he delivered at the University, our admiration ripened immediately into affection, and an unclouded, intimate friendship resulted.

We met occasionally, both in England and in America; in 1935 Mrs. Thomas Hardy was kind enough to take my wife and me by motor to the house of Mr. and Mrs. Ervine at Seaton in Devonshire. They had a magnificent cat which added to the pleasure of our visit. Mr. Ervine, greatly to my surprise, told me that he was writing a biography of William Booth, founder of the Salvation Army. When this book appeared, I found it one of the most thrilling, inspiring biographies I had ever read.

For one year Mr. Ervine came to New York and was drama critic on the *New York World*. That was the era of prohibition, and although Mr. Ervine is not a total abstainer, he announced that during his entire stay in the United States he would not touch liquor because to do so was against the law of the land. This was in such contrast to the habits and declarations of most visitors from Europe that it deserves to be recorded. As a drama critic

Mr. Ervine was severe. He aroused considerable hostility, but his judgements were invariably honest and sincere and based on a thorough knowledge of the history of drama and the necessities of society. A year after this, his own play *The First Mrs. Fraser* was produced in New York, and I think a number of persons who had been angered by his very frank criticisms hoped that the play might be a failure. It was, however, a prodigious success and ran a whole year to capacity houses.

Mr. Ervine's books and plays are all good, but he is even better than his writings. His personality has an extraordinary charm. I should like to travel around the world with him.

In an article in the London *Observer*, he lamented because there was no word to describe the citizens of the U.S.A. He thought Canadians objected to our being called Americans. I heard an Englishman addressing an audience in England; he said in his speech that he 'landed in Quebec, travelled in Canada for a while and then in America.' Our Ambassador in England is called the American Ambassador. The word American is convenient and carries no assumptions.

But if we consider that many Canadians and Mexicans and South Americans really object to the term Americans as descriptive of the people of the United States, and if we also remember that the British usually speak of our country as The States, why not call all inhabitants of the U.S.A. simply Statesmen?

9, ARCADE HOUSE,
TEMPLE FORTUNE,
N.W.4
31st July, 1920

My DEAR PHELPS:

Your letter of the 17th of July has just this moment come to hand, and as I am going off to Scotland on Tuesday for a month and have just completed my rewriting of "The Wonderful Visit" which John

Barrymore is to do, I feel like writing to my friends . . . the kind of writing I like above all others. It is good to know that you like The Foolish Lovers. I think myself that the first 100 pages of it are better than what follows. As a whole, the book is a disappointment to me because I had hoped it would be a much bigger one. It was begun in France, interrupted by the March, 1918, offensive and by my being wounded, and was written at odd intervals, between operations, in hospital and out of it, and then abandoned for a while and finished in a great hurry before going to America. That, you will see, is hardly the best way in which to write a book. I was afraid it would smell of ether and surgery, but I hope I have kept surgeon's mess out of it.

I do not take the London Mercury, though I saw the review of my book. It was sent to me by the clippings agency. The Mercury is a curious production. Jack Squire, who edits it, is a very able man and an accomplished writer, but his judgment of other writers is remarkably bad. He was literary editor of the New Statesman until recently and for a while edited a paper called Land and Water. His own contributions to these papers invariably were well-done and nearly always of great interest. . . .

He is a man of curious antipathies and also of very strong and steadfast friendships. In appearance, he is the last word in eccentricity and decadence, but in mind he is the last word in conservatism. I have not seen him for some years, but when I last saw him, one might have imagined him as the original of the comic cartoonist's picture of a Bolshevist. Yet in mind he is almost a reactionary. He is, however, devoted to his friends and is I think an exceedingly good comrade. . . .

Squire is really a meritable person, with a genuine love and knowledge of letters, and, as I say, with an immense capacity for devoted friendship.

What you say of the reference to Hardy and the Nobel Prize appeals particularly to me. I deeply resent the attitude of many of these whippersnappers whose behaviour to America is that of immensely superior persons to totally uninformed people. Most of them are people who have never been to America and are resentful of the fact that they have not been invited there to lecture. They are generally impertinent persons, given to showing-off, and are mentally and spiritually third-rate. Most of them, when they say "America" merely mean "Ezra Pound" and it is not very easy to like Ezra Pound. I think you may discount nine-tenths of the superior attitude to America on that ground . . . anti-Poundism . . . and the remaining tenth to pure pique or ignorance!

Israel Zangwill introduced me to Heifetz when he was here lately . . . a calm, immovable lad, whose face was the nearest approach to the mask which rejoices the heart of Gordon Craig which I have seen on any human being. Why don't you write to the Mercury in the sense of your letter to me, so far as Hardy and the musical criticism are concerned. Don't trouble about me. I can bear that sort of thing with ease, but the other matters are of importance. These infants do not realize the harm they do. I consider that any man who makes mischief between England and America is a criminal. I believe and always will believe that if the Anglo-Saxon peoples can keep the peace, they can make the rest of the world keep it.

I hope you are both well. I sent a copy of my novel to Mrs. Phelps about a fortnight or three weeks ago . . . to New Haven. I hope she has received it. Thank you for sending the cuttings. It was most kind of you. I look forward to seeing you again when I return to America. My wife sends her regards to you both.

Sincerely

St. John Ervine

I first saw Sir John Squire, or 'Jack,' as he is universally called, when he, accompanied by Mr. A.P.Herbert, paid a visit to New Haven, not to lecture but to see the University. Mr. Herbert, as everyone ought to know, has long been on the staff of *Punch*, has written many novels and other books, and is a Member of Parliament for Oxford University. In talking with him he said the thing that astonished him most in American universities was the terrific competition for editorial places on the college papers; for at Yale University the competition for the editorial board of the *Yale Daily News* is so severe that it is probable that the students trying for it will never work so hard again, no matter what may be their future careers. Mr. Herbert said that at Oxford University the greatest difficulty was to induce anyone to have anything to do with the University papers. He said that he went around in the various colleges

vainly attempting to find someone who would take the job.
After Mr. Herbert was elected to Parliament he published
an original, humorous, and scholarly little book called
What a Word. This is one of the most valuable books on
good English usage that I have ever seen; and everyone
who thinks he writes or speaks correct English will, in reading it, learn something to his disadvantage. In speaking of
the immense usefulness of Latin, Mr. Herbert called attention to an American newspaper heading

VETERANS' BONUS VETOED

reminding us that all three words are Latin. Everything
that Mr. Herbert says and writes is original; his murder-
stories are different from those written by anyone else.

I was a subscriber to the *London Mercury* during the entire administration of Squire; it pleased me to know that
there was one monthly magazine in the world devoted exclusively to literature and the fine arts, without a single
word on politics. Squire himself has written much good
poetry, amazingly clever parodies, and one of the most diverting autobiographies I have ever read. He is, as Mr. Ervine points out, an extraordinarily interesting personality.

MARINE COTTAGE,
BEER,
EAST DEVONSHIRE
24th February, 1921

MY DEAR PHELPS:
I came down here to recover from the fatigue of very long and
difficult rehearsals of "The Wonderful Visit" which has been a
failure over here. I have never seen such devastating notices of any
play as this one has had from the critics. However, that is all part
of the fortune of war, and I hope I can take my kicks with as much
fortitude as I try to bear my favours.
The Granville-Barkers live near us here—we are going there to
tea to-day with Mrs. H.G.Wells and Frank Swinnerton who are
staying with us. This cottage is not our own house, but we hope

some day to have a home of our own in the village which is the scene of the Devon parts of "Changing Winds." The trouble is that all who live here are afflicted with what seems to be an incurable longevity, and the houses for which we hanker are slow to become vacant.

I went to see Thomas Hardy at Dorchester ten days ago, and found him very serene. It is a wonderful thing to see an old man of eighty producing poetry of such quality that young men must sometimes feel dubious about the worth of youth.

Please give my good wishes to Mrs. Phelps and be assured yourself of my gratitude and friendship,

Yours sincerely,

ST. JOHN ERVINE

HONEY DITCHES, SEATON, DEVON
29th July, 1935

MY DEAR BILLY,

I need not tell you that your praise of *God's Soldier* is gratifying to me. If ever anybody wrote a book "for no reward," as the rebel says in Lady Gregory's *The Rising of the Moon*, I'm the man. I shall be lucky if it earns me what it cost me in research alone. But although I'm not indifferent to money—I've yet to meet the author who is!— I have the natural desire of every writer to produce something in total indifference to the profit it may make; and God's Soldier satisfies me in that respect at least. I *liked* writing it, and felt lonely when it was finished. I'd do it again, if there was the need, even if I were to be told that I'd lose money heavily. The conviction that impressed itself on my mind, while I was interviewing Army officers for the book, was that efficiency by itself is not enough. There must also be spirit. Spirit, indeed, is more important than efficiency; for the spiritually-minded man will make the best of a bad job, whereas the merely efficient man won't make anything of it: he will be too disgusted with its badness. What the S.A. badly needs is a young General—not an old woman of almost seventy—whose heart is a furnace. It has hundreds of highly efficient officers, all of them good men at desks, but it needs another William Booth, a man with the saint's concentration on essentials and indifference to mere irrelevances.

Opinions of the Epilogue vary considerably. To me it is the climax of Booth's work. If he had not run so often to lawyers, that awful deposition might never have occurred. He lost virtue in legality. Bramwell was badly abused in 1929, and treated as a mere placeholder and profit-seeker, a parent ambitious for his children, but he was a man convinced that his father's system was also his Father's system: that God had inspired William Booth and that any departure from William Booth's system must bring ruin in its trail. That is the point that is still elaborately ignored by those who, though they are now uneasy about the part they played in his deposition, are bemused with nonsense about democratic organisation. How can you democratise the Almighty?

My religious views are not orthodox. Far from it. I find that when I read the Apostle's Creed, I stop at "I believe in God!" That's as far as I can get without arguing or qualifying. I share Dean Inge's belief that Christianity is a life to be lived rather than a creed to be believed, and I think that it would be enough for all of us if we reduced our creeds to the Founder's assertion that we should love God and our neighbour as ourselves. Everything that is important is in that. All else is perplexity. You will scarcely believe me when I tell you that the town of Dornoch, in Scotland, at this moment is shaken to its core because a Provost gave a children's party at Christmas and little boys and girls were allowed to dance together. The elders of the Provost's Church have solemnly suspended the Provost! . . . If I were God, I'd dump the whole lot in hell. Don't these people ever read their Bible? Are they incapable of realising the geniality of Jesus, his mateiness, his ease in any company, the pleasure his mere presence in a house gave to its occupants, how quick he was to join in the fun? I mean, Billy, that the man who turned up at a wedding feast in Cana, and, finding his host in a jamb about wine, immediately got him out of it, was not the sort of man who would have turned sulky about a children's Christmas dance. Please don't suppose from this that I'm one of those flabby people who are tolerant of everything. I'm not. But when I'm intolerant, I try to be intolerant about something that matters and not about trifles or harmless things. As a small boy in Ulster, I could not bring myself to believe that God, who had made the Universe, would fly into a rage if he saw me playing marbles on Sunday, and I suspected that my elders who said he *would*, were attributing to him their own mean natures.

But I must not inflict any more of this stuff on you who know these things better than I do. Nora and I send our love to you both.

                    Yours ever,

                                        St. John Ervine

HONEY DITCHES,
SEATON,
DEVON
14th October 1935

MY DEAR BILLY,

An old play of mine, *Anthony and Anna* is in rehearsal at the moment and will be performed in London about the beginning of November. The bloody Government having heard of this, has announced its intention of holding a General Election which will do no play any good, but thank God the King has had the decency to arrange for his son's wedding to take place about the same time, so we shall have two rumpuses simultaneously instead of two separately, which would have about completed our ruin.

Yours ever,

ST. JOHN ERVINE

I had written asking him if the hymn *There are no flies on Jesus* was ever sung by the Salvation Army, as several persons said they had heard it. St. John Ervine is surely the only man not in the Army who had actually read every number of their periodical *The Warcry*.

MY DEAR BILLY,

I've never heard of that hymn, and I feel certain it exists only in somebody's imagination. The number of people who tell you that they know *positively* this, that or the other makes me wonder why Ananias was singled out for summary treatment. When a man assures me that he *knows for a fact* so-and-so, I say to myself, "Damned liar!! . . . ." At the risk of being called one myself, I want to say "I know for a fact you're telling lies!"

But supposing there had been such a hymn, what's wrong with it? Isn't "There are no flies on Jesus" merely a colloquial rendering of Galatians vi, 7: "Be not deceived; God is not mocked: for whatsoever a man soweth, that shall he also reap." There was a very popular padre in the War who once said to the Tommies, "Don't you chaps run away with the idea that God's a bloody fool!" A number of refined persons were extremely shocked, but the Tommies loved the man and instantly perceived his point. Supposing a simple preacher in a village in America said to a congregation of rustics, "You can't put anything over on God!" would anybody in his senses suppose him to be blasphemous or even vulgar. He would surely be talking to them in the language they understood, the language that most vividly conveyed to their minds the thought he was trying to express. Shaw's *Blanco Posnet* puts the argument, I think, with great force. We Protestants rejected Latin from our religious services, in spite of its manifold advantages, such as its universality, because we wished to have them rendered in language "understanded of the people." Well, there are varieties of ways of understanding language, and although a hymn, with "There are no flies on Jesus" is not likely to move you or me, there must be millions of people to whom it instantly and more vividly than any other form of words expresses what Paul said to the Galatians.

There is a passage in *God's Soldier* where I describe Booth's attitude towards those who charged his soldiers with calling for three cheers for Jesus Christ. They hadn't, in fact, done so, but Booth rightly retorted to their accusers, "Why shouldn't they call for cheers for Christ!" and thereafter, I have been told, he himself often invited a meeting to give them. That's what I call turning the enemy's guns against him.

I remember, when I was new to London, hearing a very delicate-minded High Anglican expressing horror because some Nonconformists, during a General Election in this country, sang a hymn which began with the words:

> Take my vote and let it be
> Consecrated, Lord, to Thee.

Wasn't it shocking? the genteel Anglican asked, and "No, it isn't," I replied. (As you know I am a coarse-grained fellow!) He practically called me a blasphemer when I said that this hymn seemed to me entirely religious. Here was a man humble and devout enough to ask God to show him how to cast his vote at an election, so that it should result in the greatest possible good. I saw nothing irreligious or vulgar in that. Indeed, I recommended the refined Anglican to take the hymn to heart.

The fact is, Billy, this is the sort of thing Jesus himself was always doing. *God's Soldier* was reviewed in *The New Statesman* by a most refined person, one Raymond Mortimer. He thought the book a dull one and found fault with Booth for his vulgarity. Jesus was never vulgar, he said. I wonder what Mortimer would have said about Him if he had been a contemporary of Jesus. I have a feeling he would have called him a low-class ranter who went about the country railing against the authorities and filling the minds of common people with sensational thoughts about the coming kingdom. He would certainly have found fault with Him and have called him a brawling cad for kicking up a row in the Temple. If I may judge what Mortimer's actions would have been then by what they are now, he would certainly have been on the side of the exquisites of the time, and more likely to be sharing the opinions of the Sanhedrim or the Romans than those of the Galilean . . . unless, of course, he was living in Jerusalem's Bloomsbury, when he would have canted in terms of Virginia Woolf.

I have just read an extraordinarily good book, called *Jesus*, by Professor Charles Guignebert, Professor of The History of Christianity in the Sorbonne, which has been translated into English by Professor S.H.Hooke, Professor of Old Testament Studies in the University of London. If you haven't read it, and it is not available to you in America, let me send it to you. I am under so many obligations to you, chiefly for your friendship, that I'd like to give the book to you for Christmas.

I've had a very busy time since we met. I have been appointed again Shute Lecturer in the Art of the Theatre at the University of Liverpool—I held the office twelve years ago—and I have composed the five lectures I am to deliver under the general title of "Present Time Tendencies in the Theatre." Then I am to give three lectures in November, under the title of "Adventures in Drama" to the Royal Institution, and another, entitled "Propaganda and the Playwright," as part of my duty as Professor of Dramatic Literature at the Royal Society of Literature. The lot are written. In addition to these lectures, I shall be dashing up and down the country, just like you, lecturing here, there and everywhere. Somehow, I must manage to write another Ulster play I have in my mind and get rid of ideas that have been forming in my head for a long time in a book to be called "Faith at Fifty." So the winter will be fierce.

Nora's name, by the way, is a contraction of her proper name, "Leonora," so the Irish version, "Norah," has no relation to her. She sends you both her love. So do I.

Yours ever,

ST. JOHN ERVINE

I have since been informed by the leading officers of the Salvation Army that the hymn *Flies* was never sung or used anywhere by the Army.

HONEY DITCHES, SEATON, DEVON
27th January 1936

MY DEAR BILLY,

I have two causes for gratitude to you: one, your note, which arrived this morning, with its extract from one to you written by Professor Carlton Wells; the other, your extraordinarily interesting article on Mark Twain in the last *Yale Review*—a very good number, by the way. Wilbur Cross amazingly keeps up the quality of the *Review*. I like a man who *edits* his paper. Wilbur Cross seems to do that. When I was in New York, all the editors seemed to edit their papers from their bedrooms. They telephoned all day long. Dial-fiends, I called them. The damned fellows didn't know or didn't do their jobs. They lay in bed all morning and telephoned. But Cross obviously works at his job. The result is a readable review—a rare thing these days. Your contribution to the Winter Number was as good an article on a writer as I have read for a long time. How odd that Twain should have thought little of Dickens! Meredith, I remember, made what seems to me a fatuous remark when he said that *Pickwick Papers* would not live, and gave as his reason, the fact that it is the essence of Cockneydom. I should have thought that a book which contained the essence of anything had a fair prospect of immortality. It must gall Meredith in heaven to hear that Dickens is always "out" of our public libraries, while *his* works are always "in," mouldering on the shelves. Men of genius appear less able than ordinary people to recognise genius. Tolstoy thought little of Shakespeare, Ibsen thought Tolstoy was a fool, and Strindberg foamed at the mouth every time Ibsen's name was mentioned! . . .

That, I suppose, is natural: the genius is so busy seeing his own point of view, that he either cannot see any other person's or is annoyed with it when he can. It is a comic reflection that one has to be an ordinary person to recognise variety of genius or see more than one point of view. But I should have thought that Twain would have loved Dickens. I shall break my heart if anybody tells me that Dickens could see nothing in Mark.

Has anybody, besides me, pointed out that the great American authors, Emerson, Walt Whitman, Mark Twain, Edgar Allan Poe and the rest, all belong to the period of your history when your people could be called homogeneous? Lincoln belonged to that homogeneous age. There hasn't been *greatness* in American literature since its people became heterogeneous, and there won't be until they become homogeneous again. Cleverness, yes, any amount of it—glimpses even, of genius—as in Sinclair Lewis, Susan Glaspell, Willa Cather, but genius itself, no. That woman, Emily Dickinson, had a hint of it, and I suspect that Edna St. Vincent Millay belongs to the great tradition, but I'm waiting, as I am sure you are, for the authentic genius. Eugene O'Neill looked at first as if he might be the man, but alas, alas! . . . All that dreary half-highbrow stuff about masks and psycho-analysis. I'd give the whole of *Strange Interlude* and *Mourning Becomes Electra* for the poetic spirit that suffused *Beyond the Horizon*. But I've not lost hope of O'Neill. The poet in him is not dead, but snoring. Why don't you wake him up?

Do you ever see Edna St. Vincent Millay? I met her once, on my first visit to America, but I remember her very vividly: a wispy, pale girl with a thin body, but a vigorous mind and an assured manner. John Drinkwater and she and I were to speak at one of those interminable dinners in which your countrymen delight: dinners that go on and on and on, with innumerable courses and terrible bouts of oratory. There were thirteen speakers that night, and the only comfort I had was that John Drinkwater was the thirteenth. I was the twelfth. My God, how bored I was. But in the middle of the orgy of speeches, Edna Millay rose up to speak, and she sauced everybody. My heart leaped within me. Thank heaven, I said to myself, somebody's being cheeky! She was wearing a white dress, and she looked pathetically young, but she talked well, *and she's a poet*. Hardy liked her work. I once heard him say so.

Professor Carlton Wells' reference to letter-writing interests me. I like writing letters, and I think the modern habit of scribbling notes is deplorable. We're cheating posterity when we send the barest lines to our friends for we are robbing those who come after us of all hope of intimacy with us. I suppose our letters are poor because we take for granted everybody's familiarity with ordinary events, through the newspaper and the radio (We call it the wireless). We do not say what we think of current events because we assume that current events are everybody's knowledge and there is no need, therefore, to mention them. But supposing all reference to King George's death were omitted from private correspondence on the ground that everybody knows he is dead, how little posterity would glean from newspapers of the private person's feelings about him. We loved our king. I can't hope to make you realise how much we loved him, how very dear that simple, sincere, unaffected English gentleman was to his people, but you'll have seen the newspaper reports of the way in which great crowds have stood in queues five miles long to pay their tribute of respect to his dead body. Queen Victoria was a venerable being, almost a legend to us; King Edward was a likeable, human person, but we weren't sure of ourselves with him; King George, however, commanded both our respect and our affection. We liked him and we admired him. Insensibly he grew into our love, and we never saw the old man without pleasure. I think his life is a remarkable proof of the way in which upright character prevails. His early manhood was overshadowed by the fact that he was not the heir; then when the Duke of Clarence died, he was in the shadow of the Queen and of his father. Edward VII was so popular that there seemed no hope of any popularity for George, and the facts of his reign, at the beginning, were not auspicious for him. The War might have wiped him out. After it was over, his son's popularity looked as if it were going to throw him into another and deeper shade. But somehow, nobody can tell exactly how, the King came through his oppressions and troubles to our inalienable love. There isn't a taint of insincerity in the demonstrations of that love at this moment. The King's death was a bitter blow to us. We did not believe that he was going to die, and the swiftness with which the end came was profoundly shocking.

Did I ever tell you the story of the little Elizabeth and her grandfather. He was very fond of the child, and had her to play with him while he was convalescing after that bad illness. One day she was naughty and refused to be good. "Very well," the King said to her, "if you won't behave properly I'll leave the room!" She made no sign of amendment, and the King walked away. He had scarcely gone when the child cried out, in an agitated voice, "Grandpa England! Grandpa England!" and the King came running back, fearing she had hurt herself. "You forgot to shut the door after you!" she said when he had returned.

King Edward the Eighth has started well. Everything he has done, however small, seems to have been right. I think he'll be a very fine king, entirely different from his father, but no less liked. The first thing he did after his father's death was to have all the clocks at Sandringham, hitherto kept half an hour fast, put right. I shall not be cowardly enough to refuse to see something symbolic in that act.

But talking about letters, I remember in the War asking to be allowed to censor the letters of the men in my battalion. I thought I should learn from them what the private soldiers thought about the War. They never mentioned it, except to wish it were over. All their references were to small domestic events. "So glad you went to Aunt Pollie's on Sunday and had a nice tea!" Things like that, much more important and much more enduring than war. I'd give the world—wouldn't you?—for a bundle of letters, not intended for publication, written by Anne Hathaway? Or a bundle from Shakespeare to his friends, to his wife, to his daughters and his son?

I didn't intend to burden you with this effusion when I started to write you, but I felt in the mood to write—one ought not to write letters unless one is in the mood—and your letters always provoke me to say something.

Our love to you both.

Yours ever,

St. John Ervine

P.S. A friend in Liverpool has just sent me a cutting from a newspaper published in that city. It seems that young women between 16 and 20, aspiring to be secretaries, had to sit for general knowledge examination. One of the questions asked was "Who is St. John Ervine?" Two of the answers were "one of the men who attempted to climb Mount Everest, but never returned," and "he lived a long time ago and was canonised by the Pope."

HONEY DITCHES, SEATON, DEVON
23 Septr. 1937

My dear Billy:

About six weeks ago, we both drove over to Dorchester to see Florence Hardy, and found her lying in a tent on the lawn, longing to die. She has extraordinary fortitude and is the calmest invalid I have ever seen. But she wants to die quickly, and is appalled by the thought of a long drawn death. She told me she had had a letter from you. We talked about Barrie, who had visited her in the London Nursing Home a few days before his death. She says she saw death in his face, but that he seemed to have no notion of anything much being the matter with him, and left her with promises to go to Dorchester to see her. About a week later, he was dead. The failure of *The Boy David* affected him profoundly: a bitter blow to his pride; and I feel that he fell under it and did not try to rise again.

Yes, I'd say I'm a Christian, but I doubt if many Christians would. I can enlist as a disciple of Jesus, the man, but I cannot offer any allegiance to Jesus, the god. The doctrine of his divinity withdraws him from human experience and puts him apart for ever. It was easy for a god to spend thirty years on earth, since that's no time at all in eternity, and anyhow he knew he'd rise again; but a young workman who conceived a great idea and tried to pass it on and was crucified for doing so, catches my love and enables me to believe that if I had enough will and strength I could do what he did or some of what he did. I haven't any hope of ever emulating the activities of an immortal and omnipotent deity.

I begin to feel as if I were the world's crock: one leg, one eye, lungs like bellows, and a periodical bout of lumbago. I went to Port Patrick in Scotland a fortnight ago, hoping that northern air would do me good. It did, and would probably have done more if I had not had the misfortune to travel in the same carriage with one of those female fresh air fiends whose first act on entering a train is to fling open all the windows and doors. She was a big woman, with a weatherbeaten face and excessive feet, and she spent almost the entire journey from London to Scotland in tabulating things in a sort of ledger. Obviously, a busy woman, always going to committees and conferences and reading agenda. I wished her in hell. For I landed at Port Patrick with a streaming cold which did my bronchitic-asthma no good. As I was recovering from the cold, my back decided to have its mid-term bout of lumbago. So I was in a bloody state. I have had singularly few illnesses in my life, nothing beyond infantile complaints and few of those, and I'm not accustomed to all this sickness. It looks as if the Almighty were trying to cram into one year of my life the illnesses that other people spread over a lifetime—Sorry for that bad blob!—but I can't say I like the experience much.

And now I must hop off to a rehearsal. Love to you both from us both.

Yours sincerely,

ST. JOHN ERVINE

HONEY DITCHES
31st May 1937

MY DEAR BILLY:

I've never known anybody so rebellious against old age as G.B.S. is, nor have I ever known anyone who fended it off so long and so successfully. But it is getting the better of him now. Mrs. Shaw, who is eighty, looks years younger than he is, although she is his junior only by about twelve months, and she is remarkably active and alert. So, indeed, is he, but because he has never shown any ageiness before, the few signs that are visible now surprise his friends far more than more numerous signs in other people.

I am interested to hear that you heard the Coronation service so clearly. Two things surprised me about it. One was the strength of the King's voice, a much more pleasing voice than Edward's, which was horridly Cockney. The other was how large a part the Archbishop of Canterbury played in the service. Scarcely anybody else had a word to say, the Queen, indeed, hadn't any lines at all. I think the King ought to have had "a bit of fat" as actors say, somewhere in the middle, a sort of Richard the Second declaration, "I'll be your leader," and the Queen really ought to have been allowed one line. It was Cosmo Gordon Lang's day out.

Why were you surprised at the failure of "Night Must Fall" in America? Apart from its eeriness and the skill with which it was acted, it did not stand examination. It ought to have ended in the second act. If that detective had been up to his job, he would have had the hat box opened—and then the murder would have been out. I'm working on a play at present, and I hope to finish it by the end of July. An old piece of mine, *Anthony and Anna*, has been running now for 646 performances, and seems likely to be good for at least 700. Yet I had a deuce of a job to get it produced.

The animals are all well, and Titus is flattered at being remembered by you. He sends you miaows in greeting. Our love to you both. What, by the way, is the meaning of this "emeritus" stuff? Don't tell me you, who seem to have solved the problem of perpetual motion and eternal youth, have been superannuated—for I won't believe it if you do. I can more readily believe in the old age of Bernard Shaw than I can in the old age of Billy Phelps.

Yours ever,

St. John Ervine

honey ditches,
seaton, devon
July 25th, 1938

Professor W.Lyon Phelps,
Grindstone City,
Michigan, U.S.A.

My dear Billy,

What a terrible name for a town: Grindstone City. Dickens must have invented it. It certainly does not sound like the name of any city in which you could live, though heaven knows you keep your nose to it, for I have never known so hard a worker as you are. I believe that the fiction of hardworking American men is entirely based on your activities, and that you are the only person in your country who really does a long day at anything. I used to watch the American business men wearing themselves to skin and bone in New York. They sat at lunch so long that I sometimes thought they must have been having all the day's meals at once. They played draughts (or checkers as we call them in Ulster) for an hour. At the end of that time they went to their offices and pretended to be whirlwinds for the rest of the day, and finally were carried home in a semi-comatose condition to their deluded wives who let themselves be humbugged into the belief that their spouses were—what do you call it?—worn to a frazzle and capable of appreciating only one of the less exacting movies. You have a lot to answer for: the deceiving of millions of innocent American women who still believe the terrific lie that their husbands every day exhaust themselves. If one of these trusting females begins to suspect the truth, her husband immediately says, "Why, look at William Lyon Phelps! He's a typical American, and never stops working even at golf!" On the day you die, Billy, the bluff will be called, and the disillusionment of the American woman will begin. The American man will then have to start doing some honest-to-God work or admit that he is one of the world's greatest loafers. The average Englishman does more work in a morning than the average American man does in a day.

I remember when I was in America, asking a publisher to send some books to that charming old lady, Mrs. Cadwallader Jones, the sister of Edith Wharton. Mrs. Cadwallader Jones lived only a few blocks away from the publisher's office, but the delivery of those books took the best part of a week: four days to be exact. I discovered that the parcel had to pass through many departments before it could be delivered, and as far as I could make out, each department had to hold a conference on it. When I returned to London, I asked a friend who is a publisher how long it would take his office to deliver the same number of books the same distance. He said he thought they might take twenty minutes over it! . . . I then told him how deliveries are hustled in New York. That was only one instance of about a dozen dilatory deliveries or incompetently performed jobs of which I had personal experience in New York; and now, when I hear people talking of American hustle and expedition, I just lie back and laugh. You, in fact, are the only American known to me who has ever hustled in his life, and if it had not been for you, the legend could never have been spread. Why, I once worked under an editor in New York who edited his paper from his bedroom!

We get along here. Alarums and excursions are reported every fifteen minutes. War is about to be declared; war has been declared; war has been postponed; war has been cancelled. But somehow we contrive not to take much notice of the sensationalists. All our pacificists have become aggressively militaristic—those of them, that is to say, who have safely passed the military age—and they go about boiling their blood all day long. That is *all* they do with their blood. Gentlemen who were conscientious objectors in 1914–18 are now howling in hordes for the effusion of other people's blood and getting themselves into quite a state because Chamberlain won't instantly consent to general slaughter. Why don't they show the rest of us a good example by going to Spain and shedding some of *their* blood? They might at least get it off the boil! . . . My own feeling is one of horror at the cruelty that seems to prevail in the world. Here we are in an age of what is solemnly called progress . . . and yet there is as much brutality in our lives as there was in the lives of our remotest ancestors, if, indeed, there is not more.

My conviction is that the next great fight mankind will have to make if it is to save itself from extinction will be against the State. Its tyranny steadily increases. We have even reached the stage at which young men who believe themselves to be high-minded, but are in reality degenerate, advocate the extinction of the individual and his entire submersion in the community. I have lately read one of those futile clever-clever books, in which assertion is assumed to be argument, called *A Short History of the Future* by John Langdon-Davies, in which the ant, which apparently has not altered itself in the slightest degree for ages and ages, is held up to human admiration. It is what a man should desire to be. The whole object of life should be to perpetuate ourselves. That object secured, there is nothing else for us to desire. There are to be specialised breeders on whom the rest of the community will wait. The Heap is what matters. The idea may seem fantastic and farfetched as New York, but I fear that a great many people may be brutally butchered in refuting it, if, indeed, its refutal is achieved. It does not appear to matter who triumphs, the Fascist or the Communist, the result will be the same, the exaltation of the State, which will not only be permitted, but encouraged, to commit acts for which individuals would very rightly be hanged. I cannot understand why it is wrong for me to steal or commit murder, but right for the State to commit one or the other.

Hitler, at this moment, is stealing the property of the Jews in Germany and Austria. If he were to steal it for his own profit, he would be run in by the police, but because he calls himself the State, he can steal it with impunity and amid resounding cheers from the young who, as always, are the stoutest upholders of oppression and brutal tyranny. (How did this legend get about that the young are generous-minded and full of high ideals? If it were not for the middle-aged and the old, liberty would long ago have died).

The tragically farcical fact about all this State worship is that what is called the State is only a gang of political thugs who have somehow contrived to seize authority and who call themselves the State. Hitler is the State; Mussolini is the State; Stalin is the State. In other words, individualism seems to have gone mad. One person, calling himself the community or the spirit of the people, arrogates to himself the right to do what he likes, which means, of course, that the rest of us have to do what he likes. And that is called the Community Spirit! . . . I have lived in England now for thirty-seven years, and I think that Job, in comparison with the English, was positively impatient. There are times when I think they are the world's fatheads, willing to put up with anything, even their own cooking; but those times do not last long, and the conviction returns to my mind that the British people are undoubtedly chosen of God. I would rather be poor in England than rich in America. The longer I live in England, the more certain I feel that it is the only country in the world that is fit to be inhabited. After that outburst, Billy, you will probably want to hit me on the nose.

I doubt if I shall go to America again. The idea of any travelling appeals to me less and less. We all rush about far too much, and I can't see that we are any the better for it. I believe more and more that Pascal was right when he said that all our troubles come from our inability to sit still in one room. I meet people who are perpetually flinging themselves about the earth, and all they gain from the performance is a fit of the jitters. The only thing that gets me really going is any attempt to interfere with the right of the individual to the utmost freedom of action and speech and thought that is compatible with the equal freedom of other people. I'll shed oceans of gore in defence of that.

We're very happy in this house. The garden has grown very lovely, though it is still a young one, and we have continual happiness in the thought that we made it, that everything it contains was put into it by us—even the grass; for it was a ploughed field when we bought it.

Titus continues his highly individual life—no dictator will ever subdue cats—but my dog, Jock, who was my constant companion, is dead. He was killed by a passing lorry. The inevitable blasted errand boy left the gate open, and Jock thought he would cross the road to savour the smells in a field opposite our house. Unluckily, two large dogs were in that field and they made a rush at Jock who hurriedly ran back to the road and collided with the lorry. That was the end of nine years of devotion. I used to sneer at dog lovers and was frightfully sarcastic over John Galsworthy who was devoted to his dogs; but I became as fond of Jock as the most infatuated dog lover could be, and his death was a blow to me. I could not have believed that I would feel the death of an animal so much as I felt his. He was a dear companion, and I still miss him though he has been dead since Easter. Isn't it extraordinary this friendship and affection between men and dogs? It is one of the most unaccountable things in life. Jock showed no distress when his Jill was killed. He sniffed at her once and then turned away, apparently unperturbed. Yet when I went to London and left him behind, he was full of resentment and lay about the house, brooding. There must be some good in human beings, since dogs like them so much, or is it that dogs have no sense?

Leonora sends you both her love. So do I.

Yours ever,

St. John Ervine

Bernard Shaw has been dangerously ill, but is now much better and seems likely to continue to improve.

79

'AS I LIKE IT'

ON 10 February 1922, Dr. Will Howe, of the firm of Charles Scribner's Sons in New York, came to New Haven, with the suggestion that I write a monthly article on books for *Scribner's Magazine*. I promised to consider this, and a few days later, meeting by appointment Mr. Charles Scribner and Mr. Howe at lunch at New York, I consented. I made only two conditions. I was to write anything I pleased, and nothing I wrote should be altered or 'edited' in the office of the magazine. Although the magazine was financed by the publishing firm of Scribners, I was not to consider that, but was to treat their books with no more consideration than those from other publishers. These two conditions were immediately accepted. I was asked to suggest a title for my articles, and I chose *As I Like It*.

Some years later on a school examination in New York, in reply to a question 'Who wrote *As You Like It*?' the candidate replied, William Lyon Phelps. I wish I had.

My articles began in the number of the magazine for September 1922, and appeared regularly in every monthly number, until September 1936, when the management and policy of the magazine were changed.

In my farewell in the number for September 1936, I said:

From September, 1922 to September, 1936, inclusive, I have never once been asked to review any book published by Scribners, nor has any written opinion of mine on any subject been altered in the office of the magazine. I suggested the title AS I LIKE IT, and it has been just that and nothing else. I appreciate more than I can say the courtesy and fairness consistently shown me by my. employers. I have served under two editors, Robert Bridges and his successor, Alfred Dashiell. With both of these men, and with their entire office staffs, my relations have been not only cordial, but ideal. I shall never forget the kindness with which I have been treated.

I wish to thank also those who have written me letters which have contributed so much to the value of my monthly articles; these letters have come from every part of the world; many of them have been written by distinguished authors, all have contained either valuable information or interesting suggestions. I am deeply grateful to my corrspondents.

I wish also to thank the thousands of readers who have done me the honour to read my monthly discussions; no writing that I have done has ever given me more pleasure, and this is largely owing to the immedeate and gratifying response from innumerable friends *Ave atque vale.*

It is true that I never enjoyed writing more than I enjoyed writing these *causeries* during the fourteen years. They attracted the attention of readers and authors in every corner of the world; and the letters from George Santayana, St. John Ervine, Charles Morgan, Sir James Barrie, and many others added immensely to my pleasure.

I made epistolary friendships in every state in the Union and in nearly all foreign countries; so that I look back on these fourteen years with unalloyed delight.

The news of the death of Arthur Nikisch on 23 January depressed me; he was expected to come to America the next season. I have heard all the great orchestra conductors of the last fifty years, and he seemed to me the best. I never saw him with his own orchestra in Leipzig, but I heard him many times in American cities; and in 1912 in conducting at Munich *Die Meistersinger* he revealed new wonders; he raised the orchestra, the singers, and the audience into a land of enchantment.

At Dartmouth College in June I gave a series of lectures on American literature; I had the honour of being associated in this enterprise with the famous American historian, Charles A. Beard. We both lectured every day for over a week. We left on 30 June and made an excursion to Montreal and Quebec, seeing Quebec for the first time. Our room in the Hotel Château-Frontenac overlooked the mighty river. It was interesting to walk about Quebec and find many residents who could not speak English.

On 3 August Mr. E. F. Hey, a piano-tuner from the county town of Bad Axe, came to inspect our Knabe piano, which had been left in our country home in Michigan for several winters. It had been condemned by professional musicians, as half the notes refused to strike. I had endeavoured to induce Mr. Hey to rent me a piano for the summer, but he insisted that if I had a Knabe, it would be a much better instrument than any I could hire from him. In spite of my assertions that my piano was worthless and that he would have the journey for his pains, he travelled 26 miles to look at it. He took out the entrails about ten in the morning, placed them outdoors in the strong sunshine, left them there until the middle of the afternoon, then replaced them in the piano, tuned the instrument, and to our amazement, it was as good as new and has been perfect ever since. I was so astounded by this miraculous resurrection, that I printed in *Scribner's Magazine* an account of what this village piano tuner, in a remote part of Michigan, had accomplished after the instrument had been professionally pronounced dead. I had the satisfaction of finding my account of it copied in journals in every country in Europe, in South Africa, Australia, and New Zealand!

On 7 November the novelist Hugh Walpole made his first visit to Yale and gave a fine lecture on *The Psychology of the Novel*. He stayed at our house and we had much good talk. Of all the British novelists who come to

America to lecture, he is the most accomplished as a public speaker.

In December we went for the first time to Miami, Florida, for the Christmas vacation. There the weather is eternal summer; on the very rare occasions when the thermometer drops to 55 degrees, the public schools close. It is the only place I have been where the fall of night produces no change in temperature; it comes down with velvet softness and without the semblance of chill. In subsequent years we made many visits to Miami, but finally chose Georgia as a more inspiring climate. Miami has summer in January and Georgia in the same month has autumn.

EUGENE O'NEILL

The foremost living American playwright has always allowed his plays to speak for themselves and for his art; he has so far as I know written no articles about the drama and has consistently refused to lecture; his excellent reasons are given in the following letter.

PEAKED HILL BAR
PROVINCETOWN, MASS.
Oct. 27, 1922

MY DEAR PROFESSOR PHELPS:

I am very grateful to you for the honor of your invitation but I have never lectured and don't believe I ever will. Frankly, there is a certain prejudice in my mind against it. It seems to me that authors should neither be seen nor heard outside of their work—(not this one, at any rate, for I'm quite certain my plays act better than I ever could—which is faint praise for them indeed!) So, both from the standpoint of personal discretion and of Christian charity toward the audience, I feel bound to decline.

But again, all gratitude to you for the honor of selecting me. I appreciate that immensely and regret that I cannot accept.

Faithfully yours,

EUGENE O'NEILL

I went with my friend, Tom Cushing, to the opening night of his play *La Gringa* 2 Feb. 1927. This play introduced to New York an actress who was in a few years to become universally known. She captivated the audience immediately. In reviewing the play for the papers I spoke in high terms of her beauty and intelligence and received the following letter.

115 WEST 73 STREET,
NEW YORK CITY

MY DEAR MR. PHELPS

A thousand thanks for your lovely note and your kindness at "Town Hall"—I can't tell you how happy I was—praise from you, is praise indeed!! In fact my head has been swelling visibly ever since!

"La Gringa"—alas—Requiescat in Pace—it is hard to please New York, isn't it? I am heartbroken for dear Tom Cushing—he is such a lamb and worked so hard over this.

I hope to have the pleasure of meeting you sometime—and please let me thank you once more. I was very very grateful.

Most sincerely,

CLAUDETTE COLBERT

Monday—the eleventh of February

80

A VISIBLE CHURCH IN AN INVISIBLE TOWN

Looking at a map of Lower Michigan, one will see it is shaped like a mitten on the left hand, with a distinctly marked Thumb. The Thumb-Nail is Huron County, the county town being Bad Axe, and the old railroad terminus being Grindstone; the nearness of the two places inspiring obvious pleasantries. Four miles east of Grindstone is Huron City, once a fairly large and prosperous lumbering village, and now so small that strangers drive through it without seeing it. Many have motored on ten miles in the vain endeavour to find it.

Seventy-five years ago pioneers from Connecticut were very busy there; as payment for making roads in the interior and building long piers into Lake Huron, they received grants of forest lands from the Federal Government. The entire Thumb was covered with superb pine trees, standing like columns in a vast cathedral. The founders of Huron City felled the tall timber, floated the logs down Willow Creek, sawed them in the Huron City sawmills, and loaded the boards on steamers at the Huron City Dock. Then came the devastating forest fire of 1871, which began on the same day as the Chicago conflagration. The prosperous town of Huron City was erased, and the lumbering business received a mortal blow. Still, the hardy men rebuilt the town and carried on as best they could. But the second forest fire of 1881 took the pine trees that were left, and everything in Huron City with them. Once more Huron City was rebuilt; but it soon became clear that the Thumb-Nail and the Thumb itself would be forced to go through the slow and difficult transition from lumbering to agriculture. Thus the people not only left Huron City, but literally took their houses with them. Today Huron City has no railroad, no postoffice, no telegraph—the only buildings are a country store, a Methodist church, a Community House, an unused skating rink, a school, and three or four dwellings. Situated directly on the shore of Lake Huron, with the finest summer climate in the world, neither sultry nor cold, it is an ideal place for a summer home. And as I have spent nearly every summer there for fifty-five years, I ought to know.

Mr. Langdon Hubbard, of Bloomfield, Conn., founded the town in the 'fifties, made roads through the forests, and built the first pier. Eighty years ago he made it possible to have regular religious services. For a long time the schoolhouse served this purpose, but in 1885 Mr. Hubbard made provision for a church edifice, which has been open since that date. The Methodist minister assigned to this 'charge' preaches in three places; in the morning at Redman, eight miles away, in the afternoon at Huron City, and in the evening at Port Hope, where he lives. In the days of horses, this was a serious undertaking; for the roads were never good, even in the best of summer weather, and for the rest of the year they were almost incredibly bad. But with the advent of the Ford Car, all this has been changed. Now we have excellent roads, and the Huron City Church is easily accessible to those who live within a radius of a hundred miles and more.

I wish the following account of a successful experiment might induce summer visitors from city to country elsewhere not to be content with merely taking rest and recreation, but to give as well as receive—to identify themselves with the life of rural communities, and if they have any talent for usefulness, to employ that in summer service. Browning says,

> God uses us to help each other so,
> Lending our minds out.

Many religious people dream of a genuine Christian Community Church, where devout people from various denominations and sects will worship together without any self-consciousness; that is, without being aware that they are doing anything unusual. What ought to be common is extremely rare. Of course there are Community Churches which are little more than Assembly Halls and Forums; it is comparatively easy to unite people on a negative platform; they come together because there is no definite Christian teaching. Many such churches do a vast amount of good in their consecration to social service, relief of the poor, and spiritual elevation. But the more difficult problem is, how are we to get earnest and devoted Presbyterians, Methodists, Baptists, Congregationalists, High and Low Episcopalians, Christian Scientists, and Catholics, to come together in the same building and listen to the Gospel?

Naturally, you say, they won't; it can't be done. It is a pretty dream, desirable in many ways, but beyond the bounds of possibility. Yet in our Huron City Church, to use Kipling's phrase, 'the thing that couldn't has occurred.' Representatives from all the churches mentioned above, together with many others, come cheerfully to Huron City every Sunday afternoon in July, August, and September.

About fifty years ago, at the request of the Methodist minister (for the Huron City Church is a Methodist church, under the control of the Methodists), I occasionally took the pulpit and preached an informal sermon. These substitutions increased in number year after year; and finally, in 1922, with the courteous permission of the Methodist pastor, I took entire charge in summer of the Huron City Church, preaching regularly at three o'clock in the afternoon for thirteen consecutive Sundays.

The automobile had made it unnecessary to seek a good or convenient location for a church; any location will do; if the services are interesting and beneficial, people will come. Ordinarily one might think that with the extensive secularization of Sunday, the most hopeless time to have a church service would be three o'clock. But we hold our services at that hour for two reasons; we do not wish to interfere with any other church whose services are held morning or evening; we take the one time in the day that no one else wants. Furthermore, this makes it possible for clergymen of all denominations to attend our church; we often have in the audience twenty ordained ministers of the gospel. It is interesting to see an Episcopal rector in full uniform sitting with a Baptist evangelist.

I have been asked, 'What do you preach to such a collection of sects? Do you give a literary lecture or a moral talk?' My answer is that I preach only the simple gospel and nothing else; and there being so many members of so many sects in the audience, I leave out non-essentials and dogmas peculiar to individual churches (winds of doctrine) and stick close to the central theme of the New Testament.

No subject is more interesting than religion; the trouble with many ministers is that they preach everything except religion, and wonder why their audiences diminish. I never mention politics and I never mention prohibition and I never discuss either Fundamentalism or Modernism. I remember an earnest Protestant pastor (now with God) who conceived it his duty during an entire Presidential campaign to preach against one of the candidates; the trouble with any minister who has only one idea is that his flock know what he is going to say; they lose interest and stay away. And this man kept it up; after the candidate whom he had opposed was elected, and he with other men at a club was listening to the election returns, he cried out in distress of mind, 'Oh, what shall I do now?' Professor Lounsbury remarked, 'There is only one thing, Doctor, for you to do now; and that is, to preach the gospel.'

In the year 1925, it became necessary to increase the size of our church, which, through the generosity of one man, was accomplished; again, during the winter of 1929–30, with the help of this man and others, we doubled again the size of the edifice. Now we have regular pews for eight hundred people, and by means of chairs, we increase the capacity to one thousand.

During the summer of 1930, by passing around cards once or twice for people to sign, it appeared that there were in our average congregation a score of Roman Catholics, seven or eight Christian Scientists, several hundreds respectively of Methodists, Presbyterians, and Episcopalians, a number of Baptists and Congregationalists, a few Mormons, Unitarians, Jews, and members of other religious denominations. Many motored a hundred miles and more to come to the church. But we are chiefly interested in reaching the resident farmers of the Thumb and their families, who come from every direction. In addition to the people who live and work in the Thumb the year round, there are in July and August 'resorters,' some of whom have cottages seventeen miles away at Harbor Beach and others seven miles away at Pointe aux Barques.

No member of the congregation enjoys this church more than I. As I go into the pulpit and look over that audience of hard-working farmers, their wives and babies, and know that they and many others have given up their Sunday afternoon and motored many miles to be present, I feel a thrill unspeakable.

In one respect our church is like a mediaeval parish church; after the service, the people are in no hurry to leave. They gather around the doors outside in the cool summer air, and exchange news and pleasant gossip. Often a family that used to live in the Thumb and has moved to Detroit, one hundred and thirty miles away, will meet and talk with their old friends and former neighbours. There is no formality about this church and there is no one to greet visitors with a professional smile and handclasp; people enter this building as they enter their own home, knowing there will be neither coldness nor officious effusiveness. Nor are they ever urged to come again; they will come again when they feel like it.

On one occasion immediately after the service, when nearly everyone had gone outside, an over-enthusiastic gentleman came up to the pulpit and said emphatically, 'I want you to know that I'm a Unitarian! I don't care one whoop for the damn dogmas you people believe; but I like this church; it's the first time I've been here; and I want to give fifty dollars to it; so long as you understand I am a Unitarian!' Although his excitement had an alcoholic foundation, he showed his interest in a practical way; for the collections taken during the summer support this church during the barren winter months. He wrote his cheque in a firm hand; I thanked him, and saw him no more. Before adding it to our contributions, however, I made enquiries to see if he could afford it, as I did not wish him to regret his good impulse after his zeal had cooled. I found that he was abundantly able to spare the fifty dollars. Then I sat down and wrote a letter to the most ardent Unitarian in America, Chief Justice William Howard Taft. 'There was a Unitarian in our Methodist Church last Sunday; he seemed abnormally excited, but he was a thorough gentleman, for he contributed fifty dollars.' I immediately received a reply: 'I am not surprised there was a Unitarian in your Methodist Church; and I am not very much surprised that he was excited;

but I am amazed that you got fifty dollars out of him. I never knew any Unitarian who was that much ahead.'

During the summer of 1930, our church received another compliment, equally charming and equally unexpected. As we were assembling a few minutes before three on a brilliantly clear Sunday afternoon, a message was handed to me from Port Austin, a town eight and a half miles distant. It seems that on that very afternoon a professional baseball game had been advertised to begin in Port Austin at the exact hour of our service, but, said the writer of the note, 'There are so many people in our town who want to attend service in the church at Huron City, we are going to postpone the game till a late hour in the afternoon; and won't you announce the fact?' Well, although I have no objection to outdoor games on Sunday, it is not my habit to make such announcements from the pulpit; but this seemed too interesting to pass over. I informed the audience that we had received a great compliment; there were so many persons in Port Austin who wished to come to our church that they thought it best to postpone the ball game; 'and so, you who sacrificed a ball game to come hither, may know that after this service is over, you will still have time to see part of the contest.'

I chronicle this because it is *News*. Talk about the man biting the dog! When summer afternoon church services are given up because too many people want outdoor recreation, that is not news. But to postpone a professional ball game, where some of the players had been brought from Detroit to play, and to postpone it because of a church service nearly nine miles away!

New Year's day 1923 dawned hot and sultry in Miami; temperature of the air at dawn was 77, and the ocean when we went swimming was 73. On returning to New Haven, we found deep snow.

On 13 January before dawn we watched the magnificent spectacle of the occultation of Venus by the moon—the first time it had occurred for forty years.

Having discovered that no public or university library in America possessed a copy of the first edition of Browning's *Pauline* (1833) and having secured one from Mr. Sessler's bookshop in Philadelphia for $1,000, a remarkably low price (one having sold for $17,000), I determined that this should be presented to the Yale University Library formally, with pomp and ceremony. Accordingly, on Browning's birthday, 7 May, at noon I led a procession of my Browning undergraduate students, about four hundred of them marching two by two. We advanced through the Yale Campus to the doors of the Library, where the Librarian, Andrew Keogh, in cap and gown, made an address in response to mine, and received the book amid tremendous cheering from the students. Those who came to scoff remained to cheer. The New York newspapers were highly amused because the students cheered for Browning as they were accustomed to do only at great games of football; and Heywood Broun, in his column, said this explained for the first time why Yale had not been so successful in athletics as in former years. 'They are cheering poetry instead of football.'

Margot Asquith lectured in New York and held the audience spellbound by telling how Clive, in India, told his opponent in a duel to go to hell. (She did not mention that she had got the story from Browning.) Heywood Broun, in his account of the lecture, said the story was the climax of the address and that it was new. He received scores of letters from my undergraduate students which proved that they were in the habit of reading both Browning and Mr. Broun's column—as they are still.

On 20 May I gave some lectures in Aberdeen, South Dakota. When the train entered this state and made its first stop, I sprang out, hurled some of the soil in the air and shouted *South Dakota*! much to the amusement of the crowd. I had been in every one of the forty-eight states of the Union except this.

I had some golf there and was interested by the printed notice on the score-card—'Ball rolling into gopher hole may be dropped without penalty.'

On 24 May I spoke at the dinner of the Connecticut Medical Society, being the only one present who was not a physician. The toastmaster, introducing me, pretended to find fault with something I had recently published, saying my punctuation was not perfect, that I had not properly used the comma. In reply I said it was better to have a wrong comma than to have a bad colon.

81

MRS. WHARTON; CONRAD; BENAVENTE

In 1923 Mrs. Wharton came from her home in France to New Haven in America to receive the honorary degree of Doctor of Letters from Yale. She has always hated hot weather and the heat on that June Commencement day was terrific; in giving out the degrees as Public Orator, I lost four pounds. She suffered even more, but made no complaint. In presenting her for the degree, I said

DOCTOR OF LETTERS

EDITH WHARTON

American novelist of international fame. Chevalier of the Legion of Honour in France. For nearly twenty-five years she has produced novels, some of the most notable being *The House of Mirth, Ethan Frome, The Age of Innocence*. Her books are marked by sincerity in art, beauty in construction, distinction in style. She writes short stories and full-length works with equal skill. She is a master in the creation of original and living characters, and her powers of ironical description are exerted to salutary ends. She is a realist in the best sense of the word; revealing the inner nature of men and women without resource to sensationalism and keeping ever within the boundaries of true art. She holds a universally recognized place in the front rank of the world's living novelists. She has elevated the level of American literature. We are proud that she is an American and especially proud to enroll her name among the daughters of Yale.

On 13 August 1928 we were in Paris and she very kindly invited us to lunch with her at her summer home, Villa Colombe, at St. Brice sous Forêt. It is a beautiful place, a fine old eighteenth century house, with magnificent gardens.

Her only physical exercise and her chief recreation were gardening; we walked about the gardens with her. She also commented on various French and English writers, speaking with great admiration and affection of the French dramatist Edouard Bourdet, an intimate friend of hers. We had just seen his brilliant comedy *Vient de Paraître,* which we enjoyed so much we saw it three times.

I asked Mrs. Wharton if she were writing another novel, and she smiled rather sadly, and said 'I am always writing!'

When her autobiography *A Backward Glance* appeared in 1934, I could not help telling her how much I admired it.

> PAVILLON COLOMBE
> July 21, 34

DEAR MR. PHELPS:

How very kind of you to snatch a moment from your holiday and tell me that you liked my book. I hoped you would, for I knew there were pages in it where our thoughts wd meet.

I'm glad you liked what I said of dear Clyde Fitch. My chance meeting with him is a very pleasant memory, and I am interested in knowing the name of the play with that delicious first act in the Vatican.

If you wd cure New York of having heat waves in June I shd come out to see you all; but even our temperate wavelet here this summer has sapped my activities—a bad thing at a time when we all have to be living in Grindstone City! (I admire the irony with which you have selected your holiday home & wish I knew why it was called so).

Well, I say a hopeful aurevoir soon, in one hemisphere or the other, & send, meanwhile, my best greetings to Mrs. Phelps & to you.

> Yrs ever sincerely,
>
> EDITH WHARTON

She died at her French home 11 August 1937.

I first saw Joseph Conrad on the evening of 10 May 1923 at the house of Mr. and Mrs. Arthur Curtiss James in New York. He looked like a sea-captain, with his pointed, grizzled beard, weather-tanned skin, and a far-horizon speculation in his eyes. He read aloud from his novel *Victory* and talked interestingly about the book. It is curious, considering that perhaps his chief claim to distinction was his mastery of English literary style, that he spoke the language so badly; not only with a very strong foreign accent, but with frequent mistakes in the pronunciation of words. Strange indeed to hear a man read from his own works and not be able to pronounce correctly the words and sentences he had written with such accuracy and beauty! But when we remember that he knew no English until he was twenty-one and thereafter for many years his speaking vocabulary was largely confined to the sea, that when he became a writer he spent most of his waking hours in solitary composition, and was reserved in company, it is not so remarkable.

He made a great impression on his audience, however, by his natural dignity, courtesy, and modesty.

The next day, 11 May, Mr. and Mrs. F.N.Doubleday kindly invited us to spend the night at their beautiful home on Long Island, where Mr. Conrad was staying. At an intimate family dinner that evening, he was absolutely charming. I had supposed, from the austerity of his mind and art, that he would be difficult to approach. Quite the contrary; he was not only affable; he was affectionate.

On Tuesday of the following week, 15 May, Mr. and Mrs. Doubleday brought him to our house in New Haven by motor; and he spent the night. We took him to see the Elizabethan Club and various college buildings, and the next morning I had a long intimate conversation with him. He was not at all well, suffering from gout, in constant physical pain; he uttered no word of complaint and was the incarnation of courtesy and kindness and consideration. In the course of conversation, he said, laughing, 'This is the difference between H.G.Wells and me. Wells does not love humanity but thinks he can improve it; I love humanity but I know it is unimprovable.' I spoke to him about Galsworthy; he exclaimed 'Isn't Jack a dear fellow!'

After luncheon, the Doubledays took him away to Springfield in their motor. I helped him on with his coat. He looked at me earnestly a moment and said, 'I know you like my books because you have said so in print; but I hope you like me myself a little?' I replied, 'Why, Mr. Conrad, I love you!' Immediately he started to kiss me and almost had his arms around my neck, when his British training suddenly seemed to get the better of his Polish blood, and with a gesture of apology, he refrained. I should, of course, have been pleased had he embraced me.

It was not in the least necessary for him to write, but the following letters are characteristic.

1st June '23

MY DEAR PROFESSOR,

Accept my warmest thanks for the more than friendly terms of your letter. I have in your house an unforgettably kind and charming reception and you gave me an impression of Yale Coll: which shall be treasured. I commend myself to Mrs. Phelps' and your memory, as your affectionate friend

J. CONRAD

HOTEL KIMBALL
SPRINGFIELD, MASSACHUSETTS
16.5.23

DEAR MRS. PHELPS

I do not know how to express to you my deep sense of your charming hospitality and friendly kindness. Pray take the will for the deed and believe that I am saying no more than the bare truth when I assure you I have found an unforgettable impression under your roof.

Will you kindly convey to the Professor my affectionate regards and allow me to subscribe myself your very grateful and most faithful servant

JOSEPH CONRAD

On Saturday 17 March 1923 Señor Benavente, the famous Spanish dramatist and winner of the Nobel Prize in Literature, gave a lecture at Yale University on the Francis Bergen Memorial Foundation. Professor Underhill of Columbia stood on the platform with him. Benavente spoke in five-minute intervals in Spanish, Mr. Underhill translated aloud in English, and thus the audience had the pleasure of hearing the beautiful Spanish language and of understanding what was said. We were all impressed by Mr. Underhill's skill in his accurate and fluent rendering in English, without the use of notes.

A great Spanish dinner was given to the distinguished guest that same evening at the Hotel Taft and on the following morning I gave a breakfast at my house. Señor Benavente sat in the chair that had formerly belonged to Robert Browning, presented to me by Yale undergraduate Pundits of the Class of 1914. It was not only one of Browning's chairs—it was *the* chair, the chair at his desk, in which he composed.

Benavente was thin and slight, but hardy and wiry in appearance. He eats and sleeps very little—hardly enough to keep alive, one would think; and he smokes a large number of cigars daily. He reminds me in these ways of my dear friend Daniel Frohman, who sleeps about four hours out of the twenty-four, eats almost no breakfast and no lunch at all, never drinks, and smokes about twenty-five quotidian cigars. Both men are not only vigorous, but full of cheerfulness and high spirits.

It may have been Spanish courtesy and charm, but Benavente seemed to enjoy his visit to Yale as much as we enjoyed having him—and he could not have enjoyed it more.

On one occasion—not at Yale—Benavente, discussing the interesting fact that theatre audiences are always on the side of virtue, always sympathize with self-sacrifice, nobility of soul, and upright behaviour, said that if these people in daily life exhibited one-tenth of the virtue which they evidently believe in and admire in the theatre, the millennium would be a reality.

82

AN AMERICAN IN ENGLAND

IF, instead of being human, I belonged to a breed of cattle or to any species of herb-eating beast, and could choose my country, I should choose England. It is the paradise for grazers. The climate is so moderate that the kine live outdoors, winter and summer, day and night; there is so much rain that the grass is ever dewy and lush; there are hardly any flies or biting insects; there is water, water everywhere, and all of it to drink; there are few vast lonely places—pleasant farms, hedgerows, and diversified scenery greet the eye. Furthermore, the men and women understand quadrupeds and treat them with respect.

It is only by studying maps that we realize the unimportance of size. A map that shows Siberia makes England look insignificant; but think of the comparative contributions of these two countries to history!

England has the same area as the State of Michigan or of North Carolina; but this area holds forty-five million people, the largest city in the world, and several other towns of over a million each; it contains an amazing variety of scenery, Roman remains, splendid mediaeval Gothic cathedrals, and the loveliest countryside in the world. Looking through the windows of the English train from Dover to London, one sees tidy villages, small farms divided by hedgerows, thousands of trees with star-proof foliage; the very atmosphere seems denser and more soft. I can only vaguely imagine the heartrending homesickness that must torture Englishmen under the pitiless glare of the sun in India and in Africa, when they remember the dewy freshness of their native land.

Late September is a bad time in London, for the interiors of all buildings, theatres, and trains are much too cold for comfort, and yet the calendar is not sufficiently advanced to obtain artificial heat. Everyone seems to follow the example of the terrible father of Eugénie Grandet, and lights no fires until a certain date, regardless of the temperature. I wore my overcoat throughout every performance I attended at the theatres; but something happened at the Royalty Theatre which is so surprising it ought to be recorded. The auditorium resembled the others in being admirably adapted for cold storage; but in addition, this had an icy draught that hit the back of the neck with precision. As soon as the first act was over I hastened to the box-office, complained of the draught, and the girl on duty replied that she would immediately telephone somebody or other and have it stopped. I thanked her, but did not expect anything; in a pair of minutes the draught ceased. It was almost the first time in my life when I have known a complaint to produce a favourable result.

An amusing incident happened at this play. We took my brother-in-law and his wife; it was his first appearance after an attack of flu, apparently rather a narrow escape from pneumonia. The play was by Arnold Bennett, and when the first curtain rose, it revealed a sick man with a thermometer in his mouth; the physician removed the instrument, looked at it and said '104!' Our companion left his seat and ran down the aisle and out.

The English trains are fast and for short distances—and most distances in England are short—they are incomparably superior to our 'cars.' The fact that the compartments all have doors opening on the station platform means that every train can be emptied of passengers and baggage in a few minutes, and you step from the platform into the compartment on the same level, and do not have either to hoist your travelling-bag, or fight your way with it down a long aisle. You do not have to wait at every station till every person and his luggage has left the train before you can enter it.

Furthermore, you do not have to smoke in a lavatory, an abomination that is taken as a matter of course on many American pullmans. Outside of the worst city slums there are few more odious spectacles than the lavatory of an American sleeping-car; especially when the men are dressing, shaving, and performing other necessities in the morning.

Then, English trains, being lighter than ours, and perhaps having engine-drivers who are more considerate of the passengers than some of ours are, start as gently and as silently as a bicycle; whereas ours, often starting in the night, rend soul and body asunder, and if you are in the dining-car you have to be an expert food-dodger.

The express trains from London to Edinburgh, about four hundred miles, run the entire distance without a single stop, the longest non-stop trains in the world. One of their cars is fitted up as a lounge, equipped with large revolving easy chairs, and has extra large windows. There is a dining-car, with seats of special design. Half of this car is fitted with three small compartments, in which meals can be served; and, if there are four passengers travelling together, they can enjoy their food in peaceful isolation. The three compartments have been differently designed, and are called respectively the Jacobean, the Grey, and the Chippendale rooms. Beneath the carpet is a heavy layer of felt to deaden outside sounds. There are full-length mirrors.

Yet for a person travelling alone for eight or ten hours, an American first-class train is the best in the world. I call no train first-class unless it has both a club-car and an observation-car. The individual is sure of his own pullman chair by a window, and if he wants a table the porter will bring him one.

But in England, especially for those of advanced years, the best way to see the country is to go to a city hotel, make that the base of operations, travel by train in baggageless delight whithersoever you wish, and return to the city hotel in the afternoon or evening. While travelling, one has a perfect, uninterrupted view of the incomparable English countryside.

For example. We wished to visit Somersby in Lincolnshire, the microscopic village where Tennyson was born. We left London in the morning and travelled to the city of Lincoln in three hours, the train running smoothly at tremendous speed. At Lincoln we hired a motor-car, which took us forty miles to Somersby. We visited the church where Tennyson's father preached and where the poet was baptized. The church, when crowded, would hold about thirty-seven people. The grave of the Rev. Mr. Tennyson is in the churchyard, in a sad state, with uncut grass. The rectory, where Tennyson was born, is almost directly opposite; a family is living there, and we could not enter. The famous brook—is anything so inexplicably immortal as a river?—goes bickering along, even as the poet described it. The seven elms (see Tennyson's *Ode to Memory*) are near the front door of the rectory, and one can hear the church-bells of four other villages, as Tennyson told us in *In Memoriam*. When the poet lived there the entire population of Somersby was sixty-two. And as the Rev. Mr. and Mrs. Tennyson had twelve children, the Tennysonian proportion was considerable. When Alfred's college friend, Arthur Henry Hallam, came there on a visit in the summer vacation from Cambridge, he said that one hundred years hence pilgrims would come from all over the world to see Tennyson's birthplace. That sounded like a monstrous hyperbole, but time has made it true.

We motored back to Lincoln, had lunch at the White Hart, spent an hour and a half looking over the giant cathedral—my favourite English church—took the train, and were back in London at half past five in the afternoon. The most comfortable way to see England.

A few persons among the millions who have walked on Fleet Street may remember that back from the street on the north side at St. Dunstan's church stood a grimy old statue of Queen Elizabeth. Thanks to the enterprise and generosity of Dame Millicent Fawcett and some other ladies, the statue has been cleaned and repainted; it was ceremoniously unveiled. *The Times* had an interesting editorial, called 'Gloriana in Fleet-street.'

It was made in 1586, when the Queen was fifty-three (but no artist nor courtier would dare to remember her age) and had been not far from thirty years on the throne; and it was made for Lud Gate, which in that year was rebuilt. Gloriana, ever fair and ever young, faced westward; and back to back with her, looking up Ludgate-hill to Paul's church, stood King Lud (who, as every one knows, had built the first gate long before the Christian era began) and his two sons. They wore Roman dress; and lucky is Fleet-street today that the sculptor, whoever he was, did not put the Queen in Roman dress too. When the inhabitants of the two Farringdons insisted that, Lud or no and Gloriana or no, Lud Gate must come down, the poor King and the princes were left in the parish bonehouse. The masterful Tudor woman, clinging to existence as firmly as ever, came westward to old St. Dunstan's Church, and survived yet another move to the new St. Dunstan's Church which men see today. And, all these years after, this statue, the only known contemporary statue of the great Queen, the only known relic of any of the City of London's gates (for Temple Bar was not technically a City gate), has been by generous women cleaned, painted, restored to notice and to respect. Painted she was originally; and very likely in colours much stronger than those which make her look so fresh and dapper today. Elizabethans, like men of the Middle Ages, could not think of a statue unpainted. "The statue is but newly fix'd, the colour's not dry," cries Paulina in alarm when Perdita is in too great a hurry to kiss the hand of her mother. Today Gloriana is new painted, a delightful spot of purity in a grubby region. Fleet-street will be proud of her; and the ghosts of old Templars and courtiers with whom she danced and jested will steal out to look upon her. Let us hope that among them will be some profitable ghost who will make it his business to keep the statue as clean as it is today.

On the south side of the river, near the Elephant and Castle, stands the old York Street Chapel, where Robert Browning was christened. Together with some adjoining buildings it is now used as the Robert Browning Settlement; the warden was the Rev. J.W.Graves, a graduate of the Yale Divinity School. I do not know of any more useful and important work among the poor than is being done here under the devoted leadership of the Warden, who is 'on the job' from seven in the morning until midnight. The children receive instruction in books, games, and general behaviour, free legal service is provided, an Old Man's Club has been formed—the place, in the heart of a district crowded with very poor people, is a centre of wise, efficient charity. I wish Americans might visit this institution on the Walworth Road and see for themselves the splendid work and realize the desperate need of it. You cannot give money to a better cause, though you will never be asked to give anything. Mr. Graves seemed to be working beyond human endurance; but he said he was in perfect health, and seemed in high spirits. I recalled the famous sonnet by Matthew Arnold describing his conversation with a preacher in the slums.

Not content with charitable work alone, Mr. Graves kept an upper room as a Browning museum. It is filled with interesting memorials of the poet, his manuscripts, account-books, and other precious things, which are gladly shown to visitors. Mr. Graves told me a remarkable story of an incident that happened during his American journey, when he was exhibiting the Browning memorials in a large city. Someone stole the most valuable manuscript. In de-

spair he went to the chief of police. The chief asked him
if he had tried every possible means to recover the treasure.
'Yes,' said Mr. Graves, and the officer asked: 'Have you
prayed about it?' Mr. Graves is a devout clergyman, but
he confessed that he had not yet prayed for this particular
thing. 'Well,' said the American police chief, 'whenever I
have a particularly perplexing problem, I go home, and
my wife and I pray earnestly for help and guidance. I advise you to do the same.' Mr. Graves took this advice, and
the next day the treasure was found; the thief confessed.

On the night I gave a lecture on 'The Life of Browning'
at this settlement, the gentleman who presided was none
other than Browning's personal friend, Mr. W.G. Kingsland, well past eighty. Mr. Kingsland was a printer who,
over fifty years ago, became inspired by Browning's poetry
and wrote a little book called *Browning the Chief Poet of
the Age*. Browning sent him a remarkable letter; the original is on exhibition among famous letters in a public room
at the British Museum.

England is full of contrasts.

Through the ineffable peace of its countryside run the
fast crowded express trains; the newspapers of London, with
a circulation far greater than any in New York, are, a few
hours after publication, within every town and village in
the country; one may sleep at night in a country village
that itself always seems asleep, and go to business in the
world's largest metropolis.

One of the noisiest street corners of the world is Charing
Cross, where the Strand empties into Trafalgar Square;
and only a few yards away is one of the quietest streets in
the world, Adelphi, a narrow way between Charing Cross
and the Thames Embankment.

The leading journalist in London is an American—
Ralph D. Blumenfeld, born in Wisconsin in 1864, but a
resident of London since 1894. He has been in newspaper

work all his life. In his youth he was a Chicago reporter and editor, correspondent of the United Press, general superintendent of the New York *Herald*; and it was under his direction that the sensational one-story building of the *Herald* was erected at the junction of Broadway and Sixth Avenue at Thirty-fifth Street. Then he went to London and became the editor of the London *Daily Express* and *The Evening Standard*. He has a genius not only for newspaper work, but for designing newspaper buildings. He took me from cellar to roof of the sensational new home of the *Daily Express*, on Fleet Street. It is built with front and sides entirely of glass, from pavement to top. There are no columns in the structure.

The United States of America is not so very young, as we have celebrated our one hundred and fiftieth anniversary; but to an American travelling in England, our own country seems an infant. I took dinner in a college hall in Oxford, and after dinner we went first to one room for this and that; and then to another. I asked my table companion, 'Have you always been coming to this room after dinner?' He replied, 'Oh, dear no! we have been doing this only since the seventeenth century.' He seemed to regard it as a questionable innovation.

Oxford and Cambridge illustrate, as do so many places in England, how age can take on dignity and honour.

One meets everywhere in England heroic fathers and mothers, and wives who lost their men in the war. In London I took tea one afternoon at Mrs. Alec Tweedie's, a painter and a writer. She told me that her husband died many years ago, leaving her with two baby boys. She brought them up carefully, gave them a splendid education, and just after they had been graduated from Cambridge, the war came, they enlisted and were killed. It was only her interest in the life of the mind that made it possible for her to carry on at all.

WILLIAM ARCHER AND THE AIR

Archer was a modest man with a fine sense of humour. He never took himself too seriously, but no man ever took his work as a critic more seriously, more conscientiously than he. He represented the highest standards of journalism, and was proud to be a newspaper man.

He described his own attitude as a drama critic as follows: 'The faculty for making the best of the actual without losing sight of the ideal.'

In 1894 he made this public statement:

> I was born with an instinctive, unreasoning, unreasonable love for the theatre, the place of light and sound, of mystery and magic, where, at the stroke of the prompter's bell, a new world is revealed to the delighted sense. That unreasoning love is still strong within me. If all the germs of progress were stamped out, and the stage declined entirely upon spectacle and buffoonery, I should still, I believe, find a melancholy fascination in the glare of the footlights. But close upon the heels of this mania for the theatre came another and still more absorbing passion—the passion for high thoughts and beautiful words, for things delicately seen, and subtly felt, and marvellously imagined—in short, for that divinest emanation of the human spirit which we call literature. These two things have I loved, sometimes blindly and foolishly, sometimes, I hope, with understanding; and it has been the instinctive, inevitable effort of my life to make these two one flesh.

This happy union Archer detected immediately when he saw on the English stage in 1895 Edmond Rostand's *La Princesse Lointaine*. This was two years before Rostand produced *Cyrano*. Archer wrote a long criticism of *La Princesse Lointaine*, in which he expressed his towering admiration for the comparatively unknown author; and the letter he received from Rostand must have been re-read many times by Archer in later years. Rostand said:

> Cette défense si fine et si spirituelle de ma pièce, ce commentaire délicat de mes plus secrètes intentions, cette analyse qui est assuré-

ment la plus complète qui ait été faite de mon œuvre, je la dois à un étranger? Comment avez vous fait, Anglais, pour comprendre des choses que tant de Français n'ont pas comprises?

Although Archer had something of the typical Scotsman's reserve, and was not given to superlatives, he took no pleasure in ironical or destructive criticism.

The worst sort of criticism is sterilizing criticism. I would rather see columns of fatuous gush about a foolish play than a brilliant but discouraging and sterilizing criticism of a play with any germs of good in it.

Such a remark is all the more interesting, coming from a man who never wrote or spoke a sentence that could be called gush.

The lifelong friendship between Shaw and Archer was marked by extreme frankness on both sides; the numerous letters back and forth are a commentary on the contemporary stage, and a revelation of the characters of both men. In 1921 Archer wrote to his friend:

I doubt if there is any case of a man so widely read, heard, seen, and known as yourself, who has produced so little practical effect on his generation. I am strongly under the impression (I may be wrong) that you have less of a following today than you had twenty years ago. . . . You have no serious competitor; but your public (small blame to them) declines to take you seriously.

Yet on 17 December 1924, just before he underwent the operation from which he did not recover (he died 27 December), he wrote to Shaw:

This episode gives me an excuse for saying, what I hope you don't doubt—namely, that though I may sometimes have played the part of the all-too-candid mentor, I have never wavered in my admiration and affection for you, or ceased to feel that the Fates had treated me kindly in making me your contemporary and friend. I thank you from my heart for forty years of good comradeship.

Shaw was deeply affected by this, and responded in a foreword to Archer's *Three Plays* (1927), as warm-hearted a tribute as Shaw ever wrote.

I am glad to see also in the admirable biography by his brother Lieut.-Col. Charles Archer, a good account of William's only son, Tom, who was killed in the war. He was a fine young man. One day in New Haven, Archer and his son and I took a long walk and I got to know Tom fairly well. As a child, he must have been irresistible; some of his conversations with his father are diverting. When he was six, the following dialogue took place:

T   What did King Lear die of, father?

W.   Well, you see, he was a very old man—and his daughters had been very cruel to him—and he had been out all night in a terrible storm—

T.   That's the worst of old people—the least thing upsets them!

We should remember Archer with gratitude, for he was a lifelong, devoted friend to America.

Never have I heard any one speak the English language more correctly, more clearly, and more winningly than he.

I shall always remember the last meal we had together, because it was only a few weeks before his death, in the autumn of 1924. He invited me to dinner at a London club, and tried in vain to persuade me not to take the airplane to Paris on the next day. He said there were many accidents. Then he told me the best play in Paris was *Knock*, and he was right. I never saw a man in better apparent health than Archer was on that evening.

Despite Archer's advice, the next day we *flew* from London to Paris. For the first time in my life I travelled in an airplane.

In about two weeks occurred the funeral of Anatole France. In Paris a distinguished man of letters is not merely admired; he is idolized. He is a super-hero. The populace regard him with the kind of reverential awe accorded in England and in America by schoolboys to a great football player. Anatole France died at Tours on 12 October 1924. His body was brought to Paris, and the coffin placed on exhibition in his home near the Bois de Boulogne on Friday, 17 October. At dusk I went thither to do homage. There was a dense crowd. We stood in line, entering the house and passing silently through the chamber of death. I asked a policeman if the procession of worshippers had been continuous all day, and he informed me that every moment it had been just as I saw it. Fifteen thousand people viewed the coffin that Friday, and we either left cards or signed our names in a big book. The next day, Saturday, there was a public funeral in front of the house on the *quai* where he was born; the coffin, fittingly enough, was placed in the shadow of the statue of Voltaire. There were funeral orations by men of letters and political radicals, and there were many thousands assembled to do him honour.

As a man of letters, Anatole France was an aristocrat; in politics, he was a radical. Thus his appeal was universal, and it was interesting to see all classes of people represented among the mourners.

Of the honours paid him, and they were innumerable and varied, one particularly impressed me. There was to have been a play at the *Comédie Française* on the afternoon of the funeral. Although the house had been sold out, the performance was cancelled, and the money returned to ticket-holders. For a state-theatre to give such recognition—involving a heavy financial loss—is a fact worth remembering. Men of genius are so few and so esteemed that even the usually unpardonable sin of political heresy is overlooked in the acclaim given to their literary ability.

French literature probably contains more first-rate prose

writers than the literature of any other land; Anatole France is among them. I cannot see that he contributed any constructive ideas to the world; he was not a thinker or a philosopher. But style is the best preservative. As a master of prose style, he belongs with Flaubert and the other immortals.

The day before his death he was conscious. He asked the physicians to tell him his exact condition, and they replied cheeringly that he must continue to hope, because there was no organic difficulty. Then he remarked, characteristically enough: '*Donnez-moi une petite maladie, par grâce, que j'en finisse!*'

It is affecting to recall that the last word he uttered was a cry of appeal to his mother to come and help him, for he was suffering; thus the dying octogenarian returned dreamingly to the days of his babyhood. When this last word was reported in the press, M.Hubert Morant, in the *Journal des Débats,* called public attention to the fact that the first book of Anatole France, published in 1859, bore the following dedication:

À UN PÈRE ET UNE MÈRE BIEN AIMÉS

Chers parents,
  Les premiers mots que prononce l'enfant sur la terre sont: "maman, papa!" S'il souffre, il crie: "Maman! s'il veut quelque chose, s'il a besoin d'aide, il dit: "maman."

The French people are grateful to artists and men of letters, and take care that their memories shall be cherished. Sunday 19 October was the seventy-fifth anniversary of the death of Chopin. Accordingly public exercises were held at his tomb, in Père Lachaise, with commemorative addresses.

This hero-worship must affect the boys and girls in the schools. The homage paid to men and women who have distinguished themselves in some form of art is a factor in the education of French youth. Everyone knows how much attention is given in French schools to literary composition and to every form of expression. And as the road to public success and distinction so often leads through the prize-competitions in various schools and institutions, all things work together toward one goal. The successful poet, dramatist, novelist, singer, actor, painter, architect, has a position universally envied.

That Parisians are not hostile to German art is abundantly proved by the fact that *Parsifal* and *Die Walküre* are given at the opera. Even more striking was the production in 1924 of that one hundred per cent German play, *Old Heidelberg*, which had a long run at the Porte Saint-Martin. I went to see this best of all college plays, and although it seemed strange to hear the German student songs sung in French, it was a competent and delightful performance. The house was packed, and everyone seemed to enjoy the glorification of the old German university town, and at the parting of Karl Heinz and Käthie (Charles Henri and Catherine) the good Frenchmen around me were weeping unrestrainedly. I did not see a German in the audience.

The most amusing French comedy running in Paris was *Knock* (pronounce the initial K), or, *Le Triomphe de la Médecine*, written by Jules Romains. This is a delightful satire on physicians, on patients, and on humanity. Young Doctor Knock is just the opposite of Monsieur Coué. Coué endeavoured to persuade sick people that they are well; Knock persuades well people that they are sick, an easier task. He enters a village where illness is unknown, but he soon has all the inhabitants in a sanatorium, by the simple process of beginning with free examinations.

83

EDNA FERBER

NEARLY all our distinguished American women novelists
of the twentieth century were either graduates of universities or, like Edith Wharton and Anne Sedgwick,
educated in Europe; Dorothy Canfield belonged to both
classes. But Edna Ferber from the age of seventeen has
been on her own. Born in Kalamazoo, she entered newspaper work on graduating from high school, and after
writing a number of magazine stories and popular novels,
she turned from the production of tales written for the
market to the creation of literature. She has interpreted
various sections of the United States. *So Big*, which I like
best of all her novels, although she does not, deals with
people and localities in and near Chicago. *Show Boat* is, I
suppose, the best novel ever written of the moving theatres of our great southern rivers. *Cimarron* is an interpretation of the opening and settling of Oklahoma; *American
Beauty*, of the invasion of Connecticut; *Come and Get It*
deals with the lumber magnates and lumberjacks of Wisconsin. She is an accomplished and successful playwright.

The first time I persuaded her to lecture at Yale she
came with Mrs. George Kaufman. After the lecture they
took dinner at our house, and I, as is my custom, said
grace. There was a moment's pause, and to cover what
might have been a slight embarrassment, my wife said to
me, 'I didn't hear a word you said,' to which I replied,
'I wasn't speaking to you.' This amused Miss Ferber so
much that she told it to Alexander Woollcott, who not only

printed it in his daily article in the New York *World*, but, I believe, broadcast it later. Miss Ferber some years after made a second visit, bringing her charming nieces with her.

FIFTY CENTRAL PARK WEST
September 20th
1926

DEAR MR. PHELPS:

There are, I should say, ten or twelve show boats now playing the rivers of the United States. Because of the dangers of the Mississippi they rarely play that river now. But they are well known on the Ohio, the Missouri, the smaller rivers of the middle west, and on the eastern rivers and the southern. The James Adams Floating Theatre, for example, plays Maryland and North Carolina. She's probably somewhere in Maryland now. They are much grander and larger than they used to be, of course. And they make a lot of money. You should see Mrs. Adams' diamond ear-drops, and Mr. Adams' Packard car!

I'm sorry you didn't like *Show Boat* as well as *So Big*. I like it better. But that you liked it at all is good news.

Sincerely,

EDNA FERBER

FIFTY CENTRAL PARK WEST
March 6th
1927

DEAR MR. PHELPS:—

I've had a change of heart about that 3,000 audience. For the sort of thing I do it's nonsense to shout at an audience of that size. I don't want to do it. I'd rather entertain, amuse, or interest 700 people than baffle, irritate, and fail to reach 3,000. I don't want to speak in the larger hall unless that hall is made for rather intimate speaking. Remember, I don't lecture. I have no MESSAGE. I refuse to shout.

Also, I'd like to have you believe me when I say I'm not trying to be snooty about autographing books, but I hate to do it. I don't know why. I just hate to.

I haven't any subject. I shall read 'The Gay Old Dog,' a short story, and talk informally for a few minutes before reading.

I hope none of these decisions will make you hate me.

EDNA FERBER

III EAST FIFTY-SIXTH STREET
March 25th
1930

DEAR WILLIAM LYON PHELPS:

My thanks to you for the letter asking me to become a member of the Town Hall Club. I hope you won't think I am thoroughly mad when I say that I have a sort of horror of joining—I belong to no organization except the Authors' League of America. I don't know any reasonable explanation for this feeling, but there it is.

I'm happy to learn that you like *Cimarron*. My experience with it, after publication, has been devastating. I mean that I wrote or thought I wrote—a book about one amazing phase of American life, colored with irony. Its whole intent was, for that matter, ironic.

It has been received as a straight romantic Western. I feel as though I were living in a nightmare. I hate Sabra Cravat, and I find her considered a fine flower of American womanhood (in the reviews).

Oh, well——

EDNA FERBER

THE LOMBARDY
III EAST FIFTY-SIXTH STREET
NEW YORK
October 23d
1931

DEAR WILLIAM LYON PHELPS:—

It's no good my trying to tell you what your letter did to me. I had been, as you may know, pretty well panned by many of the boys who write pieces for the papers. They had their Connecticut information straight from McGuffey's First Reader, which tells all about how the New Englanders loved the Serl, and how noble New England is, was, and always will be.

Then one of them . . . left me staring and open-mouthed with the statement that *American Beauty* obviously had been written for a possible motion picture sale. This quiet, tight and rather poisonous book which I had written with infinite pains, and because not writing it made me more uncomfortable than writing it.

So now and then I succumb, partially at least, to a series of these attacks. What weapon have I with which to reply to them? None that I feel justified in using. Then you come riding toward me. And if you think you don't look like a knight in shining armor—plumes, pennants, sword, white charger, velvet trappings and all—then you just don't know this romantic old girl.

EDNA FERBER

III EAST FIFTY-SIXTH STREET
November 30th
1931

My dear W.L.P. (I think I'll have to do something about shortening that. I'm sort of hoping this will turn into one of those Shaw-Terry correspondences). How about making it Wilp? No, that won't do. Anyway, dear William Lyon Phelps, your syndicate letter about AMERICAN BEAUTY is grand, and the things you know about me and my feelings are uncanny.

I am going to Washington on Thursday to dine with the Hoovers, much to my surprise. I have never met them, and I hope that Herb has long cherished a secret passion for me.

I shall be back by Friday or Saturday, but I suppose you'll take advantage of my absence from New York to sneak into town and be off before I can see you.

III EAST FIFTY-SIXTH STREET
January 5th
1932

Dear Wilp, I hope you got my wire.

I may bring with me a couple of nieces, so don't be surprised if I appear flanked by two beautiful misses with spangles in their eyes and delusion about Yale athletes being found in my audience. May I have some sort of high reading stand thing, for odds and ends of papers?

I'm sorry not to seem polite about signing books. It's a custom that I always have loathed

Yours,

E.F.

PEBBLES
SASCO HILL
SOUTHPORT
CONNECTICUT
September 6th
1934

If you think, Deceiver of Girlish Hearts, that I don't see through your devilish machinations and that I am unaware of the fiend that lurks behind your false smile and fair words, you simply do not know the Fighting Ferbers. Because, look, when the man I love dashes off to Michigan the minute I come to Connecticut, and comes zooming back to Connecticut the instant my face is turned toward Michigan, I need no crystal-gazer to tell me that all is over. This, Mr. P., is the end.

If I ever again visit Ironwood! As soon as the book comes out (I'm plugging away, day after day, and have been at it for a solid year and more) I never again can visit Ironwood. Slowly the United States is closing in on me like Poe's prison walls. CIMARRON shut me out of Oklahoma (and a good thing, too. What a hell-hole!) AMERICAN BEAUTY made my name synonymous with poison in New England. SHOW BOAT had the whole sunny south sueing me. SO BIG and THE GIRLS got me in bad in Chicago and the middle west. After this book, which is pretty much northern Wisconsin and some Michigan, I am going up with one of those stratosphere (that isn't spelled right but you know what I mean) boys and stay up until America freezes over.

I shall be here until October first. I've had a lovely though grinding summer.

FERBER

CONTE DI SAVOIA
March 10th
1935

Your letter, dear Wilp, came to me at Gibraltar, on my way home. How dear of you—how kind! Most of the reviews had been forwarded to me and I was feeling rather low in my mind, what with one thing and another. They seemed to me, with one or two exceptions, to be pretty bad. Curiously enough, I don't so much mind those reviewers who say, of any book of mine, "This is terrible." Or, "I don't like this stuff, or the writer, or the way it's written." The thing that infuriates me is when one of these lads says, sagely, "This will not endure." As though anyone ever wrote a book with the feeling of penning deathless prose. Holy God, I'm glad if I can just get it down on paper, groaning and sweating.

I remember when SO BIG was published Burton Rascoe came to interview me, and to do a review of the new book. In the review he said;

"This book is selling, and will sell more. But in one year it will be as dead as this interview, and as forgotten."

That was in 1924. SO BIG has sold, year after year, for eleven years, and this year has been brought out in a new edition. When I wrote it I wanted only to get it out of my system. Whether anyone ever would read it at all was something on which I never once reckoned. Oh, well.

I'm writing this propped up in bed at ten in the morning, and I should be out on deck looking at the Azores, which are just now going by. But I'd rather talk to you, my dear.

I've been reading Maurice Baring's SARAH BERNHARDT, and at the end the tears were streaming down my cheeks.

I'll be home March 15th. I should so love to see you. Can't we do a matinee together some time? I promise not to talk during the performance, or to tear bits of paper from my program, or rattle beads.

EDNA

791 PARK AVENUE
March 25th
1938

For once I don't agree with you, dear Wilp. I honestly don't believe that the critics are, as you say, out to get the old established writers. You named two or three books that had been badly received. Sonny, that book by Sinclair Lewis was a dud. Pearl Buck's is dull and the heroine is a prig. ACTION AT AQUILA is rejected by the human eye, and that's my story and I'll stick to it. And I suspect that if the boys didn't like my book it was because it wasn't very good, either. And there you are.

My love to you,

EDNA

84

THE CONVERSATION CLUB IN AUGUSTA

(1925-38)

SEVERAL Christmas vacations my wife and I spent in Miami, Fla., where we made many friends among the people and where I particularly admired the courage of the citizens in their united and successful efforts toward recovery after two great disasters, the cyclone-floods and the financial crash. We especially enjoyed the Christmas vacation of 1922-3 which we spent at the home of Mr. William J. Matheson in Coconut Grove. He was one of the most interesting men I have ever known.

But we have come to regard Augusta, Georgia, as our winter home. It has often been jocularly said that heaven has the climate and hell has the people, but Augusta has the best winter climate I have ever seen, and I have never found people more attractive than the permanent inhabitants. After two brief visits in 1910 and 1916 we arrived in Augusta on my sixtieth birthday, 2 January 1925, and remained nearly four months.

In those days there were at the hotel many interesting men; every morning the Conversation Club, consisting of some five and twenty, conversed for two hours. For three months there was no cessation of good talk. We had no President, but we had a King, the royal golfer Walter J. Travis. The Prime Minister was Sir Robert Borden, of Canada; Secretary of State, Nicholas Murray Butler, of New York; Treasurer, the Honourable Charles F. Brooker, of Ansonia. Then we had the four Georges: George Crocker, the Iron Man and hole-in-one specialist; George Clapp, of Boston; George M.Gray, of New York, crossword fiend, and George the Fourth was George Ade. The Manager was Daniel Frohman, who made a permanent impression not only on the Club, but on the city of Augusta, because he generously produced three plays in Augusta's Little Theatre Guild. Louis Cheney, of Connecticut, and Louis Coolidge, of Massachusetts, and Frank W.Hubbard, of Detroit, perhaps the youngest presidential elector, came in March. Baseball was represented by Judge K.M.Landis and John M.Ward and peaceful revolution by Harvey Firestone.

Cabot Morse, the son of the distinguished historian and biographer, John T.Morse, was with us three months. Ex-Governor Durbin of Indiana contributed political conversation, John V.Farwell, of the Yale Corporation, and Frank L.Babbott, president of the Brooklyn Institute; W.Orison Underwood headed all the lawyers supported by Sidney Miller and George J.Peet; bankers in James A.Blair and Jacob Farrand; railroads in Patrick Crowley; the trustees of the University of Pittsburgh were represented by David Gillespie; critics by Clayton Hamilton; McGill University, of Montreal, had a good exhibit in J.T.McCall; the courts of Ohio in Judge Henderson of Columbus; among the great athletes were Joshua Crane, of Massachusetts; Wesley Oler, Senior, of Connecticut; the Duke of Lancaster, from the Copley Plaza, and Mr. Justice Thompson, of Philadelphia. One of the most interesting members was Major Black, eighty-four years old, a Confederate veteran; and thereby hangs a tale.

One morning Major Black—the finest of Southern gentlemen—was asked if during the War he penetrated as far as Ohio. He remarked that he did get into Ohio, and became the guest of the Federal government, which escorted him to a prison on Johnson's Island, at Sandusky. This drew an exclamation from Daniel Frohman. He and his brother Charles were born in Sandusky, and when Daniel was a small boy, he used to go near Johnson's Island, and there 'cockasnook' at the Rebel prisoners. At that time he met Major Black and now met him again in the Conversation Club after an interval of sixty years!

Walter J. Travis was as interesting off the links as on the greens.

During February and March there was almost no rain and no wind. One stilly cloudless day after another. But in January we had five days' continuous rain, which brought the Savannah River to the almost unprecedented height of thirty-seven feet. Hundreds flocked to the bridge every day to see the mad flood. And had it not been for the efforts of one man, who sat at the table next to mine in the hotel, the city would have been under water, and the loss of property would have gone into millions. This gentleman was ex-Mayor Barrett, who, in the year 1912 persuaded the citizens, and only with the greatest difficulty, to erect a levee. In four years it was completed.

Naturally enough, during this river-elevation of 1925, Mr. Barrett became a hero. A statue is to be erected in his honour, though he cared for no memorial except the levee.

Among the many distinguished guests at the hotel in 1925, I became acquainted with two philanthropists, Nathan Straus and Adolph Lewisohn, both of whom were genial and full of ideas. As is well known, Mr. Straus for many years gave his wealth, his time, and himself to the pasteurization of milk, thereby saving the lives of thousands of children.

One day the all-star cast of *The Rivals* came to Augusta, and we met them at a luncheon, where speeches were made by Mr. Fiske, Thomas A.Wise, Chauncey Olcott, James T.Powers, Daniel Frohman, and others; all being the guests of the Little Theatre Guild of Augusta. We saw an excellent performance, which took me back to the year 1896.

	New Haven 8 May 1896	Augusta 1 April 1925
Sir Anthony Absolute	William H.Crane	Thomas A.Wise
Capt. Absolute	Robert Taber	Kenneth Thomson
Faulkland	Joseph Holland	Fred Eric
Acres	Joseph Jefferson	James T.Powers
Sir Lucius O'Trigger	Nat Goodwin	Chauncey Olcott
Fag	E.M.Holland	Gerald Rogers
David	Francis Wilson	George Tawde
Mrs. Malaprop	Mrs. John Drew	Mrs. Fiske
Lydia Languish	Julia Marlowe	Lola Fisher
Lucy	Fanny Rice	Marie Carroll
Thomas		Herbert Belmore
Julia Melville		Lotus Robb

The beautiful Lola Fisher was unable to appear at the luncheon; so I went behind the scenes after the first act, and she gave me two photographs of her wonderful cat, which had a face like a Cimabue madonna. Miss Fisher was even then suffering from tuberculosis and I think she knew the end was near.

The following correspondence needs no explanation.

To the President and Corporation of Yale University,

ESTEEMED AND RESPECTED SIRS:

We, the humble subscribers, addicted to the use of all manna that falls from Heaven, do hereby petition that Professor William Lyon Phelps be assigned to resident service as Missionary Bishop of Augusta, Ga., for the month of March of each year and given a full supply of comfortable rooms, conversation and golf balls.

And your petitioners will ever pray.

NICHOLAS MURRAY BUTLER, and others, listed above.

And the president's reply, significantly dated April first:

To Nicholas Murray Butler, Esq.,
And Twenty-five Other Petitioning Malefactors of Great Wealth.

SIRS:

The President and Fellows of Yale University are graciously pleased to take cognizance of your humble petition that one William Lyon Phelps, the same being sound in the faith of the Baptist Communion, be annually assigned during the month of March to resident service as Missionary Bishop of Georgia. Being firmly convinced of the deep spiritual need of our petitioners and of the pagan conditions among which they dwell, our hearts are moved to grant this request. But, be it well known to ye all and several that His Reverence must, at your expense, be well and fitly housed and fed, with golf balls of the newest breed liberally supplied, and that once at least upon each Sabbath Day ye are to gather and listen to his ministrations.

Given under our hand and seal this first day of April, Nineteen hundred and twenty-five.

SEAL   JAMES R. ANGELL

On the resignation of President Hadley, when the Corporation were considering various names, Otto Bannard asked me 'How would you feel if we should take a President who is not a Yale graduate?' I replied, 'I should feel exactly as a Catholic would feel if a Mohammedan were elected Pope.' But after Dr. Angell was chosen, I was loyal not only from a sense of duty, but very soon and permanently because of his ability and character. It is remarkable that he, coming from State Universities into perhaps the most traditionally conservative community in academic life, should have combined his great executive ability with such consummate tact.

In Augusta I have had the honour of playing golf with migratory champions, Glenna Collett, Maureen Orcutt and Helen Detweiler; their playing with me was an act of queenly condescension. And with Lansing Lee and other *inhabitants* I have had many a game of golf, shot innumerable quail, and had many conversations at midnight.

Augusta's foremost living citizen in 1938 is Dr. Eugene Murphey, who was born in Augusta and has never lived anywhere else although he has travelled extensively. He is a first-rate physician, in active practice; he reminds me of Sir William Osler in his love of literature, in his varied reading, and in his insatiable intellectual curiosity. Besides being very well informed, he is one of the foremost ornithologists in America. His conversation is illuminated by knowledge, wit and wisdom, and his home on Telfair Street, presided over by his charming wife ' Mis' Willie,' is a place where food, drink, and conversation are perfect.

In proportion to the population (60,000) Augusta has probably more first-class physicians than any other city in America. The University Hospital and the Medical School partly account for this; also amazingly good luck. When I was very ill, Dr. W.W.Battey, Jr., physician and surgeon, took such magnificent care of me that I owe my complete restoration to health entirely to his skill coupled with his friendship; Dr. Seidenstricker, Head of the University Hospital, Dr. Warren Coleman, heart specialist, and Dr. Peter Wright are absolutely first-class. These men, including, of course, Dr. Murphey, would be distinguished physicians in any city or in any medical school in the world, and they are not the only men of their class in Augusta.

One evening the famous and beloved American novelist, Mary Roberts Rinehart, arrived at our hotel in Augusta on a motor journey to Florida. She had the flu and a temperature of 102; but she was full of vivacity, talked about books and life with her customary vigour, and continued her travels with her son the next morning. Her autobiography, *My Story*, would be exciting reading if it were her only book. And indeed I find it more thrilling than her mystery stories, exciting as they are.

85

NOTES OF TRAVEL AND OTHER NOTES

ONE winter afternoon in 1927 I took the train from New York, expecting to reach Philadelphia about half-past five, which would give me plenty of time to change and dine and reach the Metropolitan Opera House at half-past eight. But a blizzard had been raging, the train was more than two hours late, and I had no time even to change. As soon as I reached the hotel, I entered a taxi, clad in my light tweeds and told the driver my destination. On one of those narrow streets choked with snow, the taxi came to a standstill, and all efforts to revive the engine were fruitless. 'Can't you make her go?' 'She's dead, boss.' I got out and stood in the middle of the narrow snowy thoroughfare, and when the first car came along, I raised my hands, believing it would not run over me. The driver stopped with a shrieking of brakes and some language. I explained my predicament. I was due in five minutes at the auditorium and it was a long distance. 'Get in!' He drove with terrific speed, running up on the sidewalks and around lamp-posts to avoid vehicles. We drew up on time in front of the vast building. I looked up at him out of the corner of my left eye, as I wondered whether he were a gentleman and would feel insulted or whether it would be safe to offer him money. I decided on the latter course and gave him a bill. He accepted it nonchalantly and said 'Just a moment. Let me give you my card.' 'Why?' I wondered. He handed me a card with his name and telephone number. Then he whispered, 'Any time you want any real good liquor, you call me up.' Those were the days of prohibition. The man was a bootlegger! I walked out on the platform in my daylight clothes and told the whole story to the audience before beginning the lecture. It is my custom to call for questions at the close of my lectures. Ushers collect written questions on literature from the audience, bring them to the platform and I answer them. That night seven of the cards brought to the desk had the same question: ' What was that telephone number?'

On 9 January 1928 at the Shubert Theatre in New Haven, under the direction of Winthrop Ames, Mr. George Arliss, for the first time in his life, appeared in a Shakespearean role. The play ran smoothly, the whole cast was adequate, Peggy Wood made a brilliant and charming Portia, neglecting the statuesque for the human; but naturally the chief interest centred on Mr. Arliss's interpretation of Shylock. I had seen in this role Edwin Booth, Henry Irving, Richard Mansfield, Walter Hampden, Edward Sothern, Ernst von Possart, David Warfield. Edwin Booth was the most impressive. The poorest was Henry Irving, for it seemed to me that in representing him as a sympathetic character he reversed the dynamics. Mr. Arliss made him sinister but human; he was a patrician; he had that air toward his Christian adversaries that comes from a sense of superiority; they wanted money and he had it. He spoke his lines quietly but with a suggestion of reserved power. Next to his Disraeli, I think Shylock is Mr. Arliss's best performance. The whole production showed the impeccable taste and intelligence characteristic of Winthrop Ames, whose death (1937) was a sad loss to the theatre and an intense personal grief to thousands of individuals.

Jan. 13, 1928

DEAR DR. PHELPS

Allow me to thank you for your splendid tribute to our production and to me. It has been a disappointment to me that I have not been able to spend any time with my friends of New Haven. We have practically lived in the theatre. I hope I may come later when I am not in the throes of a new production.

With kind regards,

GEORGE ARLISS

President Coolidge's famous utterance ' I do not choose to run' made the word *choose* so famous that for several years any repetition of it drew an audible response. When Portia said ' But this reasoning is not in the fashion to choose me a husband. O me, the word choose!' a ripple of mirth flowed over the audience.

When Stephen Benét's *John Brown's Body* appeared in 1928, it scored an instant success; it seems to belong to American literature. The following letter came from the locality where it was written:

36 RUE DE LONGCHAMP, NEUILLY-SUR-
SEINE, FRANCE

DEAR PROFESSOR PHELPS:

Thank you for your letter—I am glad if you liked the book. It was a long job and I was very much surprised—still am—at the reception it has had. Now I should like to get to work on something else—but this has been a vile winter over here and I am still dry as far as writing goes. However, they say the sun will emerge sometime, though it hasn't yet been authenticated.

With all best wishes

Sincerely

STEPHEN VINCENT BENÉT

220 EAST 69TH STREET
NEW YORK

DEAR BILLY:

I am having Doubleday send you a copy of Paul Engle's " American Song" because it seems to me the sort of thing you'd be particularly interested in. He's a young Iowan, now at Merton, on a Rhodes —and he is the first voice in poetry that I know of that represents the new, young generation just out of college—and it seems to me good speech. It's authentic, American, and it has a queer new idealism that ought to surprise a good many people—though not yourself, after the years at Yale. But I think you'll like it—and if you can do anything for it, that would be simply swell. You know what a row most young poets have to hoe—and this is a real one.

With all good wishes

STEVE BENÉT

In 1928 one curious repetition which I may have been the only one to witness should be recorded. On a certain Thursday afternoon I went to see *Interference* at the Lyceum Theatre in New York. In the middle of the second act the leading man was violently threatening a certain woman, who was intelligently presented by Miss McDonnell. At exactly the proper moment she fainted. Not a person in the audience suspected the truth until her threatener requested 'Sterling' to lower the curtain. Then a man came before the curtain and announced: 'Miss McDonnell has fainted. We must ask the kind indulgence of the audience to wait five minutes in order to see if she can proceed. If she is unable to do so, we must find her understudy.' In five minutes, and to great applause, Miss McDonnell did proceed. Well, exactly two weeks after this strange interlude, I was in the neighbouring Belasco Theatre, witnessing *The Bachelor Father*. In the course of the second act the curtain was rung down; a man came before it and said: 'Miss June Walker fainted at the close of the first act; we must ask the kind indulgence of the audience to wait five minutes to see if she will be able to continue. If she cannot, we must find her understudy.' In five minutes, and to great applause, Miss Walker did continue. Now then: is there a peculiar fatality attached to Thursday matineés, or did these actresses faint because I was in the audience?

On 7 June 1927 died one of the best columnists America has ever had—Keith Preston of Chicago. I agree with Harry Hansen that the following is one of Preston's most characteristic contributions:

THE LIBERATORS

Among our literary scenes,
Saddest this sight to me,
The graves of little magazines
That died to make verse free.

Among the men I met in June in a golfing expedition to Manchester, Vermont, was a certain gentleman who spoke of his favourite mixture for the pipe with such earnestness that his face took on a holy look. 'Why,' said I, 'you ought to be Professor of Nicotine.' 'Yes,' added Professor E. B. Reed, 'and then you could preach the tobacco-laureate sermon.'

During the season of 1926–7, Helen Hayes revived with immense success Barrie's *What Every Woman Knows*. When she reached New Haven, I took to the performance two undergraduates at Yale, one from Oxford, one from Cambridge, one a Scot and the other English. They had never seen this play and enjoyed the opportunity each had to laugh at the other. I took them to Miss Hayes's dressing-room after the play; she was amused at their coming together.

Helen Hayes made her first journey abroad a few weeks later.

GRAND HOTEL, NAPLES
JUNE 18, 1927

DEAR MR. PHELPS—
You were very kind to me in New Haven. I feel you were chiefly responsible for our splendid week there. The extent of my gratitude proven by my leaving Naples for five minutes to tell you of it. I

have never been so happy in my life as in this past week. We leave for Rome tomorrow. I hope I don't burst with the joy of that.

Many good wishes

Sincerely

HELEN HAYES

Elizabeth Haldane, sister of Lord Haldane, exhibited learning and common sense in all her books, which I read with enjoyment. I wrote how much I admired her book on George Eliot.

CLOAN, AUCHTERARDER,
PERTHSHIRE.
Aug. 6, 1927

MY DEAR SIR:

I am extremely gratified by hearing that my George Eliot meets with your approval & greatly pleased that you have noticed it in so important a journal as " Scribner's."

The study of this great woman gave me much pleasure & I only wish I could have done more justice to her. Her work seems to surpass most of the fiction of the day & I have great hope that there may be a revival of George Eliot as there has been (in this country at least) a revival of Trollope.

With warm thanks for your courtesy in writing, I am

Very truly yours,

ELIZABETH HALDANE

The name of your home brings such happy recollections of the reading of Hawthorne's masterpiece. [Seven Gables, our summer home in Michigan.]

Miss Haldane died in December 1937.

TWO TRAGIC WORDS BY SWIFT

In the course of my life I have seen hundreds of rare manuscripts and first editions; but I have never received a greater thrill than when Mrs. Prescott showed me her copy of a book by Jonathan Swift with his own manuscript annotations. The reason for this particular thrill is seen in two words. In his regular birthday poem for Stella, with the date 1724–5, called *Stella's Birthday*, and first published in the last volume of his *Miscellanies*, 1727, the last four lines of the poem express the hope that when Stella grows old she will ever appear young to him provided his *hearing* should be better than his *sight*. The four lines run as follows, in the edition of 1727:

> Thus you may still be young to me,
> While I can better *hear* than *see*;
> Oh, ne'er may Fortune shew her Spight,
> To make me *deaf*, and mend my *Sight*.

In Mrs. Prescott's copy I saw that, fifteen years after he had written the poem, Swift had underlined the word 'deaf' and then written in the margin 'now deaf—1740.'

That volume, apart from this 'tremendous trifle,' has had a curious history. I am glad I saw it when I did in Mrs. Prescott's house in Stamford, Conn., for it might have been my last opportunity. Some years later she told me she had exchanged it for something she wanted even more. In 1938 appeared Harold Williams's admirable edition of Swift's *Poems* (3 vols. Oxford) and in response to my enquiry, he was kind enough to write, 'I have seen the set of the Pope and Swift *Miscellanies* to which you refer several times, and both in Ireland and England. I never saw it while it was in America. For a long time it was in the library of Lord Powerscourt in Ireland. Then it passed to Mr. W. G. Panter, who lived near Dublin. After his death it found its way to . . . Mrs. Prescott. . . . It has now come back to England, and is in the possession of Lord Rothschild.'

Two New Haven women whom I knew well, in their lives illustrated the highest possibilities of nobleness and courage. Mrs. Virginia Curtis, who lost her husband early in life, had two sons in my class in college. Tom was the valedictorian and John the fourth in rank. Only a few years after graduation Tom died of a fever; and John, who was at a distant sanatorium after a nervous breakdown, committed suicide. She was informed of this by a newspaper reporter who woke her at two o'clock in the morning. She lost the major part of her fortune by a frost in Florida that destroyed her property. A highly educated woman, devoted to studies in various languages, she went to bed one night without any premonition of evil, and woke up in the morning incurably and totally blind. I often talked with her after these shattering disasters, and never heard her utter one word of complaint. She was always calm and always interested in contemporary books and events. Although she was a devout Christian, she never uttered a sanctimonious expression or any of the stock phrases of holiness. But once, when we were talking about religion, she remarked quietly that if religion were not true, life would be meaningless, a tragic farce.

Mrs. Henry P. Wright, the wife of the Dean of Yale College, also had two brilliant sons who were in the highest group of scholars. Alfred died of tuberculosis shortly after graduation; Henry became a Professor at Yale and exerted a widespread and inspiring influence on colleagues and students; he died suddenly in early middle age. Her only daughter, an admirable scholar and school-teacher, died of cancer in the thirties. Her husband died before the death of Henry and her daughter. Then Mrs. Wright became totally blind. Mrs. Curtis was serene and composed like a Stoic; Mrs. Wright was cheerful and *radiantly happy*. She told me once that she was so grateful for life. 'Grateful!' I exclaimed. 'Why, of course, why not? I have devoted friends, I am not ill, I have so many beautiful things to think about.' And indeed she was fortunate in the devoted care of Josephine, her son Henry's wife, who is a saint; and other more distant relations and friends were often with her. But *grateful*? These two women seemed to me like heroines of Greek tragedy; they suffered the worst disasters that can befall any one. They were living illustrations of the triumph of Christian faith.

There is no doubt that women have more courage than men. And there is a reason for it; they need it more. It takes courage just to be a woman.

> Tell me, are men unhappy, in some kind
> Of mere unhappiness at being men,
> As women suffer, being womanish?

86

GENE TUNNEY

On Thursday 22 December 1927, while we were staying at the house of Mr. William Matheson at Coconut Grove, Florida, I went over to Miami Beach and had a long talk with the champion heavy-weight boxer of the world, Joseph J.Tunney of New York, universally known as Gene Tunney. I knew he was fond of reading Shakespeare. I told him that I was teaching Shakespeare at Yale, and that during the coming Spring term I should be very glad to have him address my class. He immediately agreed.

When this was announced in the newspapers, I was called up on the telephone by a reporter and asked 'Can Tunney really talk in public on Shakespeare, or is this just part of the ballyhoo for the next fight?' I replied that if we should change places, Mr. Tunney would look much better lecturing on Shakespeare than I should in the ring with Jack Dempsey.

Mr. Matheson invited Tunney to meet the Bishop of Florida and Mrs. Mann, together with Ruth Bryan Owen, and several others, at lunch. Although Tunney is a big man and weighed two hundred pounds, his hands and feet are small. He stood beside Mrs. Owen, a tall woman, and we found her hands were longer, though not as broad as his. Tunney and the Bishop carried on a spirited conversation; and Tunney told us how he came to enjoy Shakespeare. It was when he was a private soldier in the World War. There was a comrade who was always talking about Shakespeare; and Tunney, becoming interested, made up his mind he would read him. He had the bad luck to begin with *Winter's Tale*. He read it through from beginning to end and it made no impression. I think most adventurers would have stopped there. Not so Tunney. *He read through Winter's Tale ten times.*

After the tenth reading, he felt he had mastered it. He then went on to read the other plays. In a similar manner, by concentrating his listening powers, he became a passionate lover of the best symphonic music and of the operas of Wagner.

On 23 April Tunney addressed my Shakespeare class. The large auditorium was jammed, with crowds standing up. Tunney used no notes. He spoke informally for three-quarters of an hour. He told the students they had had every educational advantage and he had had none. 'But when you are graduated and out in the world, then your case will be like mine. Your professors will not be able to help you; you will have to do it all for yourself. If you succeed, it will be because you have had the necessary will-power and perseverance.' He said perhaps his favourite play of Shakespeare was *Troilus and Cressida*. For it applied exactly to his own case. 'Why have I been invited to speak at Yale? Surely not because I have anything important to say about Shakespeare. I have been invited because I am the champion boxer of the world. I am that *now*, and there is great interest in everything I do and say. I am followed around by crowds. But how long do you suppose that will last? It will last just as long as I am heavyweight champion. Ten years from now nobody will care what I do or what I say. It is important for me therefore to make the most of the present moment, for the present moment is all I have.'

He said Shakespeare understood that situation perfectly. Hector was the heavy-weight champion of the Trojans and the only man among the Greeks who could stand up to him was Achilles. But Achilles would not fight. He sulked in his tent. And yet he was very angry when Ulysses and the other Greeks put up Ajax to fight Hector; and all their cheers were for Ajax. 'Now Ajax,' said Mr. Tunney, 'was a big powerful man without much brains, just like Jack Sharkey.'

The next day a reporter called up Sharkey at his training-camp and said 'Tunney says you are like Ajax.' It is possible that Mr. Sharkey thought Ajax was some kind of a disease, for he responded, 'You can tell Tunney there is nothing the matter with me at all.'

I believe every newspaper in the world contained some kind of report of Tunney's address. Press cuttings were sent me from India, New Zealand, Alaska, Japan—indeed from everywhere. For the moment, Tunney found himself more famous for having lectured at Yale than for having defeated Dempsey; and I found myself more famous for having invited him than for any book I had written or any professional work I had done.

From the *Münchener Neueste Nachrichten*:

SHAKESPEARE—KOLLEG DES BOXERS

Wie Professor Phelps, der den Lehrstuhl für englische Literatur an der amerikanischen Yale Universität innehat, mitteilt, hat er Gene Tunney, den Schwergewichtsboxmeister der Welt, eingeladen, an der Universität Vorlesungen über Shakespeare und seine Zeit zu halten. Tunney hat den ehrenvollen Auftrag auch angenommen, *Professor Phelps* traf den Boxmeister während seines Aufenthalts in Florida und spricht sich begeistert über die Sachkenntnis und das Urteil aus, das Tunney in der Unterhaltung mit ihm offenbarte.

About thirty years before this occasion, when on St. Patrick's Day, 1897, Jim Corbett fought Fitzsimmons at Carson City, Nevada, several prominent undergraduates at Yale had sent a small Yale flag for Corbett to place in his corner as a talisman during the fight. Although Corbett did not do this, the fact that the flag had been sent got into the newspapers, and the result was a scandal. Hundreds of persons insisted that these students be expelled, and I well remember that there was a long and exciting Faculty meeting, and that they were saved only by a close vote. One of the students was Payne Whitney.

Suppose the Faculty could have known that in thirty years the champion boxer of the world would lecture at Yale on Shakespeare!

That summer of 1928 Tunney was in the island of Brioni in the Mediterranean; there he was joined by the most famous literary man in the world and by the most famous musical composer—Bernard Shaw and Richard Strauss. The three men took long walks together. Mr. Shaw told me, 'The newspaper men kept coming over from the mainland; they cared nothing whatever for anything I said or that Strauss could say; our opinions did not interest them. But the moment Tunney opened his mouth the reporters took down every word. They wished to know his opinions on every subject.'

Some literary man, I have forgotten which, said he would rather be champion boxer of the world than a great poet. 'For how wonderful it must be to go to any city in the world and know that you can lick any man in that town.'

When one considers the number of strong fellows in every city, it seems incredible that any one man can feel certain of whipping them. I asked Tunney about that, and he replied 'Well, there is room for only one champion at a time. The place is free and open to any man who can take and hold it.' Then, after some reflexion, he said, 'There are five qualities necessary if one wishes to be champion of the world, and all five are seldom found in one man.'

The candidate for the championship must possess great strength; he must have a body far stronger than that of the average healthy young man. Of course there are thousands of whom this is true; there are any number of powerful young men. The second qualification is panther-like agility, speed, and nimbleness; this quality, when it is combined with immense weight and strength, is not so common. The man must be like an elephant in solid strength and like a leopard in ease and grace of movement. Still, while the combination is not so common as either quality taken singly, there are plenty of young men who are both strong and fast. The third quality is courage, the foundation of all virtues for any ambitious man, no matter where his ambition may lie. Many men are secretly afraid, no matter how confident their bearing, or how assured their speech. The successful fighter must either be without fear or succeed in overcoming it. Tunney told me (and without a shade of conceit) that he was not afraid of anybody or anything.

The fourth quality must be the ability to take punishment without becoming disabled. This is different from courage. Just as the bravest man may be seasick, or dizzy at a great height, so the bravest man in the ring may receive a blow either so powerful or so well directed that he cannot go on, and the fight is lost. This was the case with Corbett in his memorable contest with Fitzsimmons. He had courage, confidence, and will power; but when Fitzsimmons hit him in the solar plexus, he was like a man paralysed; he was through. If he had been able to endure that blow, he could have gone on and probably won. 'Now,' said Tunney, 'if I had received that particular blow, it would have hurt, I should have felt the terrible impact, but I should not have become disabled. In Chicago, Dempsey repeatedly hit me fearful blows; they were like the shock of a pile-driver; every one of those blows hurt; yet I was able to go on. One reason was that whether I am in training or not, I keep my body, by the proper

exercises every day, in such condition that it can successfully withstand almost any human blow.'

And he explained how, on rising from bed every morning, he sat down, put his feet under the radiator, and bent
over backward, keeping the abdominal muscles hard as
steel. Should the ordinary healthy man try that motion
just once, the result would be hernia.

The fifth, last, and by no means least of the qualifications is perfect control of the nerves; for strange as it may
seem in the case of professional boxers, all of whom are of
exceptional strength and bodily vigour, more men fail to
reach the championship through bad nerves than through
any other defect. Prizefighters suffer from insomnia even
more than brain workers, and it is easy to see why. The
ordinary prizefighter is not a man of many intellectual resources; he cannot divert his mind with a variety of things.
Thus, when he is in training for a contest and the day of
doom draws near, he becomes more and more nervous.
He cannot exercise every moment, and when he is not in
full bodily activity, he finds it difficult to relax and feel
cheerful, because he is thinking all the time of the great
day. Finally, when he steps into the ring, his nerves are
in a frazzle.

I envy Gene Tunney his nerve control more than his
strength or agility. On the day before his contests and on
the morning thereof, he was as calm and self-possessed as
if nothing unusual were going on.

He said something of value to every man and woman
without regard to the nature of their work. He regarded it
as fortunate that he loved good books and music, etc.,
quite apart from the intrinsic value of such things; because, during his weeks of active training, he could at any
moment divert his mind by reading a good book or listening to the piano. It is not healthy for any man or woman
to be obsessed by one thought; the mind becomes hag-

ridden, and the nerves go to pieces. The brain needs variety; thus the more avocations a man has outside of his work, the more efficiently he will do that work, and the fresher and healthier his mind will be.

Thus all the five qualities enumerated by Gene Tunney are very seldom found in any one man. 1. Strength. 2. Supple agility and speed. 3. Courage. 4. Ability to take punishment. 5. Complete control of the nerves.

The ideal element in Tunney's nature enabled him to see the goal long before he reached it, as one sees the towers and pinnacles of a city from afar. He has all along been aided by sensitiveness to beauty, which has found expression and which has brought him refreshment and inspiration in poetry and music. Stephen Phillips's poem, *Marpessa*, is one of his favourites, and he carried it everywhere. Another of his best-loved poets is Francis Thompson, original, imaginative, and spiritual. In music, the *études* of Chopin move him more deeply than anything else. Among novelists, his most intimate friend is Thornton Wilder.

Unlike many self-made men, he has allowed neither success nor flattery to turn his head. He is not conceited; yet in his ring contests and in his preparation for them he was filled with confidence. His nature illustrates the difference between confidence and conceit.

This cheerful confidence did not make him careless, either in the ring or out of it. He made his own training rules and never departed from them. And even when he was not in training, he kept himself in condition by neither smoking nor drinking, by being careful in diet, *and by not getting excited*. On the day he fought Dempsey at Chicago, he had a good dinner at three o'clock, then read Somerset Maugham's novel *Of Human Bondage* for an hour and a half, and actually forgot he was to fight that evening!

Confidence means two things; it means that one is certain of one's ability to perform the assigned task, certain of being equal to the situation; and secondly, it means that one enjoys the work in the assurance that one can do it well. The great surgeon goes to the hospital, not with fear and trembling, but with the certainty that he will perform the operation as it should be performed; so he is happy in his work.

87

JOURNEY TO EUROPE IN 1928

WE landed at Plymouth in a dense fog. At dinner a large and old yellow cat walked solemnly about the room. I picked him up and caressed him. Immediately a waiter came to me in horror. 'Do not hold the cat, sir; he is very dangerous; he does not allow anyone to touch him; and we have had some most unfortunate experiences.' Accordingly I put the cat down; but although he had not purred, he submitted to my endearments with no show of resentment.

Mr. and Mrs. Harley Granville-Barker were living at a beautiful old manor house at Netherton Hall, not far from Plymouth; a telephone message came inviting us to visit them. It was a magnificent place over three hundred years old. The weather was perfect and that afternoon I had eight sets of lawn tennis with our host and with Mrs. Dashwood (E. M. Delafield).

After dinner Mrs. Granville-Barker played beautifully on the clavichord. A genuine English breakfast was served the next morning and for the first time we became acquainted with 'back' bacon. The coffee was delicious; Mrs. Granville-Barker is an American.

NETHERTON HALL,
COLYTON, DEVON
24.7.28

MY DEAR "BILLY"

So glad you've had a good time. And why shouldn't you have? You bring the good time with you. We've even given you some summer weather. That I do take credit for—but only that. I made arrangements for it with the B.B.C.

Glad in particular that you met Hawkins and know his Memoirs—you knew him before, of course. There's no book I d rather have America read to learn what the English governing mind is like—and what the English voice is when you can hear it for the bawling of Beavermere and Rotherbrook.

Don't tell me to come back and 'produce.' One ploughs the sands lightheartedly when one is young: when the sun's past meridian one thinks of leaving some thing behind. As we've no theatre in England which lets one do that—we had a European war instead; you can't have *all* the pleasures of life—I've turned (but I always planned to) to the printed page.

Our kind thoughts to you both and a pleasant time abroad—as we call the mere continent and I hope you do, this not being 'abroad' for you. But come back to England and count always on a welcome not least from

Yrs

H.G.B.

This letter alludes to a delightful day we had spent with 'Anthony Hope' and Lady Hawkins. In the third paragraph Mr. Granville-Barker expressed an intention which during the following ten years was magnificently fulfilled.

One day we went out to Hampstead to call on my friend, the veteran dramatist Henry Arthur Jones. He was in poor health, weakened by several major operations, but his mind alert and keen as ever, deeply interested in contemporary life and letters. He lived with his daughter, Mrs. Doris Thorne, who is keeping up the family traditions. Mr. Jones showed me over his house, filled with furniture made by William Morris and tiles and pottery by William De Morgan.

One afternoon at Mrs. Clifford's house on Chilworth Street, I met my former pupil at Yale, Frederick Kaye, who became a distinguished scholar and Professor of

English literature at Northwestern University. His early death closed a brilliant career.

7 CHILWORTH STREET
LONDON, W.2

Nov., 1928

I was delighted to get your little letter, dear Billy, for your learned Professorship seems to wish me to call you that. But your word about Fred Kaye made me very sad. We have known him so well and had many happy hours with him. He is a curious and delightful combination of the real lover of work and student, and the simple hearted school boy. I think he has overworked his too subtle brain? We are haunted by the dread of hearing—it is what my husband did. *His* brain was always clear and eager, but the rest of him was not strong enough to bear the strain.

We think of you both so often—*what* a joy it was to see you two dear people and how kind you have been to me in Scribner and elsewhere—so much more than I deserve. I wish you had been here just a week earlier to meet those nice people who took themselves off too soon to the country. Still I love to think you had a good time and good weather. We have been having, so far in, a wonderful November—so mild and soft—just mitigated by one terrible gale last Friday. I lunched today with Lady Walston, the widow of Sir Charles Walston (*Waldstein* before the war). She would have so much liked to meet you. She was abroad. . . .

I wonder if you were satisfied with your Presidential Election? We all voted Hoover over here; we remember all he did (for the starving Belgians especially) in the war. Well? What next?

St. John Ervine's Theatre articles in the Observer are much read. He is alive—has fine qualities. Do you remember the play at the little "Ambassador Theatre"? You were both at the first night. It is still running and has emerged with a solid success. Is it done over there?

Now I must stop—with love to you both.

Yours as always,

LUCY C.

The play she mentions in the last paragraph was *Many Waters*, which had great success in London and not much in New York.

On 13 July I saw the grave of Hardy in Westminster Abbey; and once more verified the original inscription on the grave of Ben Jonson:

O RARE BEN JOHNSON

Yes, the *H* is in the name on the inscription, though it is often stated otherwise.

Mr. Leon M. Lion, the famous actor-manager, identified with the producing and acting of Galsworthy's plays, invited us to a matinée of *Justice*; we talked with him and with Michael Morton after the performance. During this conversation, a letter was brought from a man waiting in the street, saying he had served a term in prison, and wanted Mr. Lion to give him financial assistance. Ever since his first appearance in this play Mr. Lion said he had had requests from convicts every day; and that Mr. Galsworthy got even more.

On the next day at Hammersmith we heard a delightful performance of Bickerstaff's *Love in a Village* produced by Sir Nigel Playfair. That evening Mr. and Mrs. Charles Morgan gave us a dinner at the Garrick Club, where we met the Rev. Mr. Fry and his wife (Sheila Kaye-Smith), Mr. and Mrs. Ellis, and Mr. and Mrs. Brett Young.

I am glad Mr. Young refers in this letter to *My Brother Jonathan*, for I think it is one of his best.

CASTLE HOTEL,
HORNBY,
NEAR LANCASTER

DEAR WILLIAM LYON PHELPS,

When we dined with the Morgans at the Garrick you were so kind as to ask me if I would lecture at Yale when I came to America. We are sailing for New York on the Carmania, on October 27th, and shall be staying there with our headquarters at our old friends, the T. W. Lamonts (107 East 70th St.) until the New Year. I should love to talk to your young men, who must be one of the best audiences in the world, on THE IDEALS OF A NOVELIST. (Incidentally, I've tried to follow those ideals in my new book, MY BROTHER JONATHAN, which I asked Knopf to send you.) I also hope very much to see, for the first time in my life, the Yale-Harvard game in November. The only engagement I have booked at present—for, as you know, this is a pleasure-trip, not a lecture-tour, is a lunch in N.Y. on December 6th. Perhaps you will be good enough to let me know on my arrival at the Lamonts' if the idea of my subject appeals to you.

It will be a great delight for both of us to renew our acquaintance with Mrs. Phelps and your charming self. Our meeting at the Garrick was a delightful surprise; I had heard so much about you from Archie Marshall and other friends, including Hugh Walpole, with whom we spent last week-end at his Lakeland cottage. And I do hope you'll like MY BROTHER JONATHAN, because, if you don't, I'm afraid you'll never like anything else of mine, being positively convinced—quite apart from my natural predilection for the latest-born—that it's my very best.

Very sincerely yours,

FRANCIS BRETT YOUNG

On 16 July we lunched with Mr. and Mrs. Walter Payne and with Sir Nigel and Lady Playfair. During the conversation, both Sir Nigel and Mr. Payne said there were many good things about the censorship as practised in England. I was not quite sure whether they themselves were unreservedly in favour of it, but they said some theatre managers were; that when the Lord Chamberlain refused a licence, that ended the matter, and they were saved from expense. On the other hand, when he gave permission, that made it impossible for any crank or any organization to interfere with the play or to threaten its withdrawal. If a censorship is to be established, and on the whole I don't believe in it, the English method is the only good one. The Lord Chamberlain is a great personage. He is irresponsible, as he should be. He never has to explain or give any reason. He does or does not give permission and that's the end of the matter. In America, one judge will refuse, and after that is efficiently advertised, another judge per-

mits the show, thus assured of a sensational success, to
proceed.

Tuesday evening, 17 July, I lectured on Browning at
the Browning Settlement in South London; in the audience
were Thornton Wilder and his family.

Wednesday evening 18 July we went to the first performance of *Many Waters*. The leading woman's part was
admirably given by Marda Vanne. Later we were so fortunate as to come to know her well, both at her house in
London and at our own house in New Haven when she
came over to take this same part in New York.

On 19 July I dined with the novelist Archibald Marshall
and the famous journalist S. K. Ratcliffe, at Brooks's, and
then I took them and my colleague Professor Karl Young
to a concert at Queen's Hall given by the Yale University
Glee Club.

On a brilliant day in July 1928 we saw the cricket-match
between Eton and Harrow at Lord's, the English equivalent of a Yale-Harvard football game. Only as it is played
in the midst of summer, the thousands of men and women,
dressed in their absolute best, make a never-to-be-
forgotten spectacle. As we wandered about among the
throng only one element of tragedy marred the gay scene.
This was the almost complete absence of men between the
ages of thirty and forty. Old and middle-aged men, boys
and girls, but an entire generation was missing—the war
had taken them.

We were fortunate in being accompanied by the novelist
Archibald Marshall and by Gerald Campbell, sports writer
for the London *Times* and an old cricketer. They explained
to me the mysteries of the game and the significance of the
occasion.

Over a hundred years ago, when Eton beat Harrow as
she did on this day also, an Eton schoolboy-poet produced
the following poem.

> Ye silly boys of Harrow School,
> Of cricket ye've no knowledge.
> It was not cricket, but the fool,
> Ye played with Eton College.

Alas, there was a boy at Harrow named George Gordon, later Lord Byron. He instantly replied:

> If as you say we played the fool,
> No wonder we were beaten;
> For at that game no other School
> Could e'er compete with Eton.

One afternoon we went to Chelsea to take tea with Mr. and Mrs. Charles Morgan. Mr. Morgan was in Oxford when the war broke out. He immediately enlisted and when the war was over returned to the university, was graduated with high honours, and soon was appointed drama critic on the London *Times*, the blue ribbon of that profession. He told me that although he enjoyed writing criticisms his particular ambition was to be a novelist. A few years later he published *The Fountain*, which had enormous success in England and in America.

His next novel, *Sparkenbroke*, is a combination of philosophy and mysticism, as well as an exciting story, for although Mr. Morgan is a practical and sensible English critic, there is a deeply spiritual side to his nature which gives a poetical and elevating atmosphere to all his novels.

G. K. CHESTERTON

We went to take lunch with Mr. and Mrs. G. K. Chesterton in an old Tudor farmhouse in Beaconsfield. They had a lovely garden, and the whole place made an ideal setting for persons so thoroughly and traditionally English. And I highly enjoyed talking with Mrs. Chesterton's mother, eighty years old.

In 1890 I had bicycled by this place, on the high road

from London to Oxford. Mr. Chesterton was then sixteen years old. But a few yards from his garden I dismounted to read the inscription on the grave of the seventeenth-century poet, Edmund Waller, who, when past eighty, wrote:

> The soul's dark cottage, battered and decayed,
> Lets in new light through chinks that time has made
> Stronger by weakness, wiser men become
> As they draw near to their eternal home.

I hope that will be true of me if I succeed in living that long.

Mr. Chesterton was one of the busiest men in the world and never seemed to be in a hurry. During the Boer War, while he was making a speech, the mob got excited and somebody stole his watch. He never carried one again. 'Why, how do you manage without one?' He laughed. 'Oh, it doesn't really make any particular difference what time it is, and if I really want to know, I ask.' He edited, in addition to his poems, novels, religious works, essays, biographies, *G. K.'s Weekly*, a worse burden than the Old Man of the Sea. But its object was to promulgate ideas in which he believed.

When he was taken to see the great White Way in New York he made a remark that ought to live forever. He looked up at the amazing illumination and said: 'What a place this would be for a man who could not read!'

I asked him what impressed him as the chief difference between the aspect of England and America. He said: 'Your wooden houses.' I had never thought there was anything unusual about wooden houses, because we take them for granted. But a wooden house in England is a rare spectacle. It seems incredible that there can be enough stone in that small island to supply the demand.

Mr. Chesterton gave me a copy of the booklet containing his famous debate with Bernard Shaw. I would I had been present. It was not the clumsy contact of the irresistible force and the immovable object; it was a duel between two of the best swordsmen in England, each of whom had an affectionate admiration for his opponent's skill.

Mr. Chesterton not only gave the impression of thoroughly enjoying life; he had an extraordinary kindness, a certain gentleness, a consideration for others, that went well with his masculine vitality. He never lost what Browning called the 'faculty of wonder.' He never outgrew his zest for life. In *Saint Barbara*, he wrote

> When all my days are ending
> And I have no song to sing,
> I think I shall not be too old
> To stare at everything;
> As I stared once at a nursery door
> Or a tall tree and a swing.

I found this comment in a French newspaper, (I think *Figaro*) a few days after his death.

On a rapellé, ces jours, nombre de mots que G.K.Chesterton avait semé tout au long de sa vie et de son œuvre. Celui-ci est, croyons-nous, inédit.

Grand et fort, Chesterton se moquait volontiers de son obésité. Récemment, un de ses amis lui reprochait sa rudesse.

"Peut-être suis-je rude," dit-il, "mais du moins je suis toujours courtois. Ce matin, j'étais assis dans l'autobus, et bien, j'ai cédé ma place à trois femmes."—*Figaro* (?)

In an essay on American morals, G.K.C. made a pertinent and significant enquiry into certain conceptions, perhaps more common in America than elsewhere, of right and wrong. One reason for his poking fun at us on ethical questions arises from the fact, I believe, that Americans as a class are more *anxious to be right* than the people of any other country. That leads us no doubt into some absurdities. Here is what G.K.C. said about an American attitude toward smoking.

> . . . I remember once receiving two American interviewers on the same afternoon; there was a box of cigars in front of me and I offered one to each in turn. Their reaction (as they would probably call it) was very curious to watch. The first journalist stiffened suddenly and silently, and declined in a very cold voice. He could not have conveyed more plainly that I had attempted to corrupt an honourable man with a foul and infamous indulgence; as if I were the Old Man of the Mountain offering him the hashish that would turn him into an assassin. The second reaction was even more remarkable. The second journalist first looked doubtful; then looked sly; then seemed to glance about him nervously, as if wondering whether we were alone, and then said with a sort of crestfallen and covert smile: " Well, Mr. Chesterton, I'm afraid I have the habit."
>
> As I also have the habit, and have never been able to imagine how it could be connected with morality or immorality, I confess that I plunged with him deeply into an immoral life. In the course of our conversation, I found he was otherwise perfectly sane. He was quite intelligent about economics or architecture; but his moral sense seemed to have entirely disappeared. He really thought it was rather wicked to smoke.

Now it is just possible that these two men were misunderstood by G.K.C. They were in the presence of a great man; they had never seen him before; they were naturally awkward and embarrassed. I am certain that if Bernard Shaw should offer an American reporter a cigar—which he would not do—the stranger would be in some confusion.

But I agree with Mr. Chesterton that there is more often in America than in any other country a misconception of morals which has done a great deal of harm. Excessive smoking for the very young and for certain invalids is probably not hygienic; just as coffee is bad for people who suffer from heart disease. But that smoking in itself and for the average person should have a flavour of wickedness is unfortunate; it confuses standards of morals and actually makes some people who enjoy smoking feel that they are indulging in secret vice.

There should be no flavour about smoking except the flavour of tobacco; and yet I was brought up to believe that smoking was wrong, 'inconsistent with a Christian life.' While the daily consumption of even a moderate amount of alcohol is probably injurious to the majority of persons, and while we should probably be better off if no alcohol were obtainable, I am convinced that the idea that to taste wine or beer is a sin has wrought injury. If we could regard wine as it was regarded by the early Christians, indifferently, as we regard tea or coffee, that is, without a shade of wickedness, it would probably be better for the morals of the human race, and there would be fewer hip-pocket flasks and less swinish drinking.

I remember how shocked and bewildered I was when first reading *Tom Brown at Oxford* to find that the most serious and most spiritually minded men drank together as naturally as they ate. When the late Mr. James B. Reynolds went forty years ago to a certain town in Belgium to form a Y.M.C.A. among university students, their meeting was opened with prayer and beer.

In 1928 Thornton Wilder published his first successful book, *The Bridge of San Luis Rey*. This book attracted almost as much attention in Europe as in America; and, showing the diversity of views that it caused in the very same week, in the summer of 1928 I happened to read a French critic who said that Mr. Wilder's style reminded him of Prosper Mérimée and that he was in his attitude toward religion an ironical sceptic. Later in the week I was talking to G. K. Chesterton in England and he asked, 'Mr. Wilder is an ardent Roman Catholic, is he not?' and when I informed him that he was not, Mr. Chesterton said *The Bridge* sounded exactly as if it were written by a practising Catholic.

DAVIS HOUSE
LAWRENCEVILLE, NEW JERSEY

DEAR MR. PHELPS:

I was balanced for a long while over the League's invitation, but at last I decided not to dare. I simply never will be able to speak on my feet. In the spring of 1929 I am doing some readings for Lee Keedick (to take the place of the Davis House in an empty life) but reading my three-minute plays is a different matter. Speaking is so natural and so happy with you that you can scarcely imagine my dread of it; but it's very real. I have told Mr. Ely how proud and eager, from every other point of view, I would be to do it.

When I last saw you I hadn't the faintest notion what I would write about next. Now I know that it will be a curious novelization of Terence's *Andria*; a picture of life on an Aegean island, the pagan world shot through with intimations of Christianity.

In the meantime the Davis House goes on; it keeps me in the village and is full of detail, but very satisfying.

Many letters come to me from people who were introduced to the book by you, and full of beautiful references to yourself and the place you have made in the best part of their lives. I cannot imagine you ever tired or anything less than eager; if ever so, remember all this affection and remember mine

ever so

THORNTON

March 9, 1928

After reading Dickens and other novelists, I often wondered what it must be like to live in chambers in the Inns of Court. Well, I found out. I took tea with Maurice Baring in his rooms in Gray's Inn. Here we were, in the heart of London, only a few steps from Fleet Street, and we might have been in the country. Although the windows were open, it was so quiet we could have conversed in whispers. Major Baring is one of my favourite novelists. There is an original flavour in everything he writes, coming from a charming personality, enriched by years of experience in Russia and in remote parts of the earth.

I received from Percival Christopher Wren an autograph

copy of a special illustrated edition of *Beau Geste*, a novel I admire without reservations.

WESTWOOD HOUSE,
TALBOT WOODS,
BOURNEMOUTH
13th Dec. 1928

DEAR PROFESSOR LYON-PHELPS

Very many thanks for your letter of 3rd Dec. I am very gratified to learn that the copy of " Beau Geste " gave you so much pleasure.

I thank you for the generous compliment you pay me both in your allusion to " The Three Musketeers " and in your recommendation of my books in your public lectures.

I shall look forward to the pleasure of meeting you when you are again in England.

With the compliments of the Season

Yours very sincerely,

P. WREN

88

ANTHONY HOPE

On 20 July 1928 we motored to Epsom Downs not to see the Derby, but for a purpose more exciting. It was to take lunch with Sir Anthony and Lady Hawkins. Many years before I had heard Anthony Hope give a public reading in New Haven; and ever since the publication of *The Prisoner of Zenda* and *The Dolly Dialogues* in 1894, I had been eager to meet their author. My eagerness was strengthened by two quite different facts; one was the publication of his autobiography and the other was Lady Hawkins, not only because she was Lady Hawkins, but because she was a sister of Lewis Sheldon, a Yale pupil of mine in the class of 1896.

They lived in a beautiful old house with a charming garden close to the immense heath. They made the day memorable with their delightful hospitality and with stimulating conversation. They read aloud to us important letters from Barrie, Lord Charnwood, Thomas Hardy, and many other contemporaries.

I had reviewed his autobiography, expressing my admiration for the book and its author; but I said that as a public reader of his works he was ineffective. I had heard he had said that when he was reading aloud on the stage he was usually thinking of something else; to which I mentally added 'So is the audience.'

On this visit we discussed that matter with considerable earnestness; for he believed he read aloud very well, and Lady Hawkins assured me that everyone was delighted

with his readings from *The Dolly Dialogues*. It is probable
the night I heard him in New Haven was not a fair test; I
remember there was a tremendous blizzard and the audience was small. Certainly the brilliance and vivacity of his
conversation would indicate that he would read aloud extremely well.

He was so unpretentiously modest and unaffected it was
not easy to draw him out to discuss his own works; but he
was certainly gratified, as he had every reason to be, with
the success of his autobiography.

I told him I had enjoyed his novel *The Secret of the
Tower*, which I had read in 1919; he laughed aloud, and
said 'Ah, if you really like that book, I shall not have a
high opinion of your critical judgement.'

Like so many authors, he did not believe his most popular book was his best. He said he had written *The Prisoner
of Zenda* at tremendous speed, that he had been astonished
at its popularity, and that he had written much better
books on which he had spent more time and effort. I then
asked him which of all his works he thought was the finest;
and without hesitation he said *The King's Mirror*. He was
kind enough to give me an autograph copy of it. I read
it attentively and thought I saw why he regarded it so
highly.

The following letter shows that he had been mis-quoted.
I had sent him a proof-sheet of my review of his autobiography in *Scribners*.

28 April/28
HEATH FARM,
WALTON-ON-THE-HILL,
TADWORTH,
SURREY

DEAR PROFESSOR PHELPS,
   I am very grateful for your letter and for the Scribner "Proof"
which you have sent with it. I have read both with the greatest plea-

sure. I have little right to put forth a book of memories (even a small one!) at all and even less to have it published in America: indeed I am sure that the publishers undertook it more from kindness to me than from any chance of profit.

At any rate—so far as I am concerned—I am content with having pleased *you*,—even if I have not pleased—or reached—any other reader. But I think that, thanks to you, I shall reach some more—for your imprimatur is, I know, a powerful one.

I don't exactly "place" that melancholy reading of mine—in a blizzard and a void! Pretty bad, I daresay. But my remark to the interviewer is, as we used to say in the law, "not admitted"—which was different from being "denied." In fine—I am proud—as well as pleased—that you have written as you have about me—and send you thanks most cordial. I grow old, and shall probably do little more. And how little it all is! You know—I *am* right *once* in the little book—unless in the Arts, you are great, you are nothing!

Yours very truly

ANTHONY HOPE HAWKINS

HEATH FARM
WALTON-ON-THE-HILL
TADWORTH
SURREY
10th July/28

DEAR PROFESSOR PHELPS,

I have waited to answer your kind note of the 14th June till the time when you expect to be in London.

It would be a great pleasure to me to meet you. But I have now no house in town and come up there very seldom. My wife and I would be delighted if you and Mrs. Phelps could find time to run down here some day. We are less than 20 miles out by road. What about lunch next Saturday or Sunday, or any day next week? Or in the afternoon, if you can't manage lunch (but I hope you can!)? Our country here is really rather beautiful.

If you come by train (Tadworth Station—and look out for a possible change at Purley) we will meet you. But the road is better,— via Sutton to Welton Heath Golf Club (which very likely your driver will know). The London side of the club building is a lane, go up it to the top—where stands a horribly ugly village "hall," and I stand exactly opposite. Do let us hear that you can come. Call up my wife. I am deaf on the telephone.

As for your enclosure—I think I stand mid-way in opinion between you and the lady! I think I read the "romantic" stuff very badly, but the "Dollies" rather well.

Yours very truly

ANTHONY H. HAWKINS

Sir Anthony told me about a great public dinner he had attended in London in honour of Mark Twain, when most of those present were hearing him for the first time. There was intense curiosity when he rose to speak. He, the Master of the Pause, stood for some seconds in silence. Then, very slowly, and with pauses, he drawled 'Homer is dead—Shakespeare is dead—and I am far from well.' The typical American humour of exaggeration was given to an audience whose conception of humour was understatement. But his manner and his expression were so droll that the dinner-guests roared with laughter and Mark Twain came into his kingdom.

At another time a dinner was given in honour of Sarah Bernhardt. On the same day the indomitable actress had given a matinée followed by an evening performance and now she had to attend this banquet. She seemed the incarnation of vigour and energy.

During that summer of 1928 I had the good fortune to meet not only a large number of remarkable men and women, but also extraordinary animals. I should have liked to take home with me a beautiful Irish setter, Rex, a member of the Galsworthy household; and to annex two literary cats, one of whom belonged to Thomas Hardy while the other lived with the famous novelist, Sheila Kaye-Smith. Both of these cats were magnificent Persians. There is a well-known picture of Sheila Kaye-Smith and her cat, so that in a way I felt acquainted before the actual meeting took place. This is a Supercat. He had an expression on his austere and majestic countenance that would do credit to the President of the League of Nations. His gracious owner told me many interesting facts about him that displayed his intelligence. It is more than possible that he inspired the second noun in her novel *Iron and Smoke*.

We had the pleasure of hearing an excellent sermon preached by her husband in his London church on Gloucester Road. The Reverend T.P.Fry is a remarkably interesting personality, and was then an Anglo-Catholic. I had supposed that *The End of the House of Alard*, my favourite among the works of Sheila Kaye-Smith, was written after she had become engaged to Mr. Fry; was perhaps a tribute to his influence. She said that it was written before, and that it represented her own independent view; though she is too fine an artist to make this book or any other a medium of opinion.

Both of them subsequently became Roman Catholics.

89

GEORGE MOORE

In July and again in September of 1928 I had good talk
with George Moore at his house in Ebury Street. His published conversations with the late Edmund Gosse and
others have made this 'long, unlovely street' distinguished,
for Mr. Moore was one of the very few who could write
profound and penetrating literary criticism in the manner
of informal talk. Being a genuine literary aristocrat, he
had the unaffected affability of his class, a combination of
ease and elegance. He wasted not a moment on the weather,
but immediately began to say things worth remembering.
I am unfortunately no Boswell, but I can give the substance of what he said, though not altogether as he said it.
He was in the serene seventies, physically weak from a
recent operation, and a major one drawing nearer; but
there was no sign of illness in his face or in his voice. Unlike many sufferers, he showed no inclination to talk of his
ailments, of his medicines or physicians, or of his operations; the main interest of his life was art, and he was as
keenly interested in it as he had been fifty years before.

Two other subjects seemed to arouse his excitement; the
only two I did not care to hear him discuss. One was the
utter worthlessness of the writing of Thomas Hardy,
worthless in thought ('The man never could think—he had
no mind') worthless in style ('he never wrote well') worthless in construction ('he knew nothing of the art of fiction').

The other was sex. He would repeatedly draw the conversation around to that. He was kind enough to give me a

copy of his *Daphnis and Chloe* and he read aloud a certain passage with immense gusto. He said 'Adultery? adultery? everybody commits adultery.' I said with a laugh, 'Not everybody; I know someone who has never committed adultery.' '*What?*' he shouted in amazement. If I had told him of some miracle, he could not have been more astounded.

'I am writing a novel of Greek life in the time of Pericles, and I need in my mind's eye a picture of the coast of the island of Euboea. To write a good novel of men and women, one should go far back in time. Human nature has never changed and the intellectual capacity of the human mind has increased not at all. Our age is so fuddled with machinery, physical luxuries, conveniences of every kind, that personality is being swamped. Men and women as they really are interest me; it is necessary for me to isolate individuals for purposes of study and analysis; hence I must go back in time, when people lived as men and women, not as standardized machines.

'The fact that the majority of persons in ancient times had no formal education does not mean they lacked intelligence or determination or passion. Today we have an immense diffusion of culture, which is far from being a universal blessing, for true culture is an individual affair, and can be acquired only by persistent individual effort. The difficulty nowadays is that thousands of young men and women who go to colleges and universities have culture spread over them; they are buttered with it. But that does not mean they are truly educated, for they have mastered nothing for themselves. They live social, communal lives, like cogs in some vast machine, but they do not live personally and individually, as men and women used to do.'

He wished to know what had first occasioned my interest in his work, and I told him of a course in literature I had given as a young teacher at Yale in 1895. I had included a book recently published, *Esther Waters*. 'Oh, I have since written many books better than that,' he said with emphasis. 'Yes,' I replied, 'that may be true, but *Esther Waters* is the novel that made your name known all over the world. One of the best things in it is the description of Derby Day, an amazingly vivid picture. I have never seen the Derby, and I shall not have to see it, because your account of it is absolutely real.' He smiled and said, 'Ah, you are right. That is really good. I made a success of that chapter. The Derby I did very well, very well indeed.'

Then I spoke of *Evelyn Innes* and of its sequel, *Sister Teresa*. He shuddered with horror. 'Oh, that is a bad novel, very bad. I rewrote it and rewrote it in the vain endeavour to improve it. But it was hopeless. I could make nothing of it. Just as I believe the worst of all sins is bad writing, so I believe the highest virtue is found in corrections, in an author's revisions. If you wish to estimate the true value of an author's art, study his revisions. But no amount of correction could save that book.' I reminded him of two striking passages, the one where it is written 'You never see poplar trees except at evening,' which he had quite forgotten, and the other where Evelyn plays the *Lohengrin Vorspiel* to the nun, who had never heard such music. She asked the nun for her impressions, and the nun gave a picture of mountains before dawn, exactly what she saw and felt while the music was being played. Mr. Moore was aroused. 'Why, you have hit upon the only good thing in the entire novel. That *is* good, and it may have been what Wagner himself had in mind while composing that passage.' I then turned the conversation to his recent book *Avowals*, and told him I thought the best thing in it was the criticism of Rudyard Kipling. 'Look here, how is it that you pick out the best pages in every one of my books?

The remarks on Kipling are certainly the best I wrote in that volume.' Perhaps it was a good time to stop; I made no further selections.

In the room where we sat there were some admirable oil paintings, including some excellent likenesses of himself, and on the table were some French translations of his works, and, as might be expected, a copy of *Mademoiselle de Maupin*. I looked around for the cat, because George Moore is a cat lover, and once wrote a famous description of a cat, and of its quiet dignity in the hour of death. The absence of his contemporary cat was explained by the presence of a canary which someone had recently given him, and the cat was banished to the kitchen. 'This is a very stupid cat,' said he, 'and you would not care to make his acquaintance. But I had a cat who used to spring from the floor to my shoulder, and often when I was writing he would leap on the desk and take the pen from my fingers, urging me to stop work and play with him. Cats wish to be entertained as much as dogs.' I reminded him of the passage in Montaigne where it is suggested that the cat is perhaps as much amused by us as we are by the cat. 'Ah, Montaigne is an inexplicable writer. I cannot understand him at all. I can make nothing of him.'

Mr. Moore read aloud to me from the manuscript a short story he had recently composed. He read it extremely well. When he finished he said, ' Turgenev would take off his hat to this.' The conversations in the story harmonized perfectly with the descriptions of nature. I told him it was like a solo violin accompanied by the orchestra. 'But that is exactly the effect I wished to produce. You are a musician.' 'No, I am not a musician, but I love music, and have cultivated the art of listening.' While he was reading, the canary began singing, furnishing an exquisite *obbligato*. The pale September sunlight filtered into the room, no sound from the windless street was heard, and the memory of

George Moore in his armchair reading aloud beautiful English prose, while the canary was singing, abides with me.

On another occasion, I asked him about his early life. The early years in Paris nearly made a Frenchman out of him. 'Had I stayed in Paris another year I should have become quite French, and should have written all my books in French, which would have been a pity, because one cannot write satisfactorily in any language but one's own.' He by no means shared the general admiration for Conrad's style. 'The man could not write good English to save his life. He did not know good English, and those who praise him do not know what they are talking about.' I made some reservations here, but did not care to start a controversy, because I wanted him to go on talking about his early years.

'I left France for England with only one purpose, to write the aesthetic novel. The artistic novel in Victorian days did not exist in England. Thackeray, Dickens, and George Eliot wrote novels about various classes of people, but they were all afflicted with a conscience; they had a moral bias, fatal to art. Nearly all Englishmen are cursed with a conscience—it is a bad thing to have. In the ordinary sense of those words, I have no religion and no morality. The Victorians never wrote exclusively from the standpoint of pure art, to tell the truth about men and women as they really are, with no regard to conventions. I did this. I founded the artistic novel in England, and after a long struggle, won my battle. It has been my whole life's work. When I published *A Mummer's Wife*, I accomplished something original and new. *Esther Waters* had an immense success, but it is far from being my best book.' I asked him about his earlier attempts, *Mike Fletcher*, for example. 'Oh, that is no good at all. I was trying myself out, taking the first steps. In later years I accomplished

what I was aiming at in *The Lake*, but you have not seen
the genuine version of *The Lake* any more than you have
seen the correct edition of *Memoirs of My Dead Life*.' I
told him I was sure I had, because nothing could possibly
have been expurgated from the copies I read.

I reminded him of one of his novels which seems to have
escaped public attention—*Spring Days*. I was impressed
by his description there of the greenery of early spring,
which he called a 'shrill' green. 'Ah, but you know that
early green is really not green at all. It is yellow.' That is
what I have always thought and never dared to say, thinking it must be some form of colour-blindness. But if
George Moore, he who said an accurate sense of colour
was more important than a sense of right and wrong, can
say it. . . .

Alas, the conversation turned on Thomas Hardy.
Mr. Moore was a great critic, but like all great critics, he
had his perversities. His contempt for the novels of Hardy
was an obsession. 'Hardy could not write English. *Tess*
is a ridiculous book,' and he began to point out what he
regarded as absurdities, Angel Clare carrying Tess, a heavy
woman, and so on. I asked him how he accounted for the
almost unanimous praise by critics. 'Oh, they were personal friends of Hardy.' I regard Hardy as one of the
greatest writers of modern times, a great artist and a great
man. I ventured to say something about the artistic structure of his books, but he would not listen. It was impossible to discuss this question. I cannot make out why he
was so strenuous about it, unless he felt that public opinion
was so mistaken about Hardy that it was his duty to take
the opposite view.

There is no reason why a sharp difference of opinion
should interfere with friendship or with mutual respect.
But Mr. Moore's attacks on Hardy, inopportune as they
were, cost him the friendship and esteem of some of his

contemporaries. And this was only one of many controversies in which he was engaged. No writer took less pains
to preserve the affection of his friends. I wondered at this,
and I asked him if the things he said so publicly of prominent persons never caused him worry. I could not see how
he could involve himself in so many quarrels and indiscretions and preserve peace of mind. 'Is it because you are an
Irishman?' 'Irish?' he replied, 'Irish? I am no more Irish
than you are. My people have been in Ireland only three
hundred years. That does not make me an Irishman.'
Yet I ventured to remark that just for his own contentment and tranquillity he might have found it better
not to involve himself in so many controversies. 'It does
not worry me in the least. I say exactly what I think.
The only thing that worries me is when I have not written
well.'

If I could not applaud his discretion or his amenity, I
certainly admired his courage. Here he was, alone in the
world, an old man, with a terrible operation facing him,
without a grain of religion, but apparently also without a
grain of remorse. His Credo, like that of Dudebat in *The
Doctor's Dilemma*, was Art. This is the only thing he ever
believed in, and old age, solitude, and illness changed his
mind not one iota.

On another occasion, we talked of American literature,
and I rejoiced greatly when he said Nathaniel Hawthorne
was by all odds the foremost of American writers. He especially admired the first half of *The House of the Seven
Gables*. He dwelt on the incidents of this story with the
keenest admiration. 'Hawthorne was an artist of the first
rank. I have never read *The Scarlet Letter* because I know
I should find it too painful. I should not be able to endure
it.' He was undoubtedly right in his surmise. *The Scarlet
Letter* is Hawthorne's masterpiece, but the tragedy is
founded on a conception of sin so alien to the pagan mind

of George Moore that it would not only have been distressing, it would have been incomprehensible.

He went on to speak of some of his visitors. 'One day an American novelist called on me. His name is Drooser, Dowzer, what is it?' I suggested Theodore Dreiser. 'That's the man. And a good fellow he is. We had an interesting talk. I never have read anything by him, but I enjoyed talking with him. We have the same American publisher, Horace Liveright. Dreiser gave me a really wonderful description of Liveright, as he appears in the morning, afternoon, and night, and he did it so vividly that I felt I was present in Liveright's room.'

We talked of Victor Hugo, whom he does not admire. 'Hugo had great facility in writing platitudes.' I asked him wonderingly if he did not admire Hugo as a lyrical poet. I called attention to the songs in *Les Burgraves*. Mr. Moore was deeply interested in the art of translation, as in every fine art, or in anything relating to excellence in composition. I thought Rossetti had made wonderful versetranslations of the songs in *Les Burgraves*, and as Mr. Moore did not remember them, I recited them. He was excited. 'They are splendid! recite them again.'

Those who imagine that conversation is a lost art ought to have talked with George Moore. Though everything he said was worth listening to, he did not deliver himself of solemn pronouncements, declamation, or long monologues. He treated his visitor with natural and unaffected courtesy, and made him feel that he was sharing in the conversation on a plane of equality, which is the secret of the art of conversation.

Although Mr. Moore was entirely without fear in his attacks on his contemporaries, there are incidents that incontrovertibly prove that Mr. Moore did have some regard for the feelings of the men of genius whom he admired. I learn from a bookseller's catalogue that in October 1930 Moore wrote to Shaw saying that in a newspaper interview he was quoted as speaking contemptuously of Shaw; and that he assured Shaw he had said nothing of the kind.

Shaw wrote back to Moore on the blank space in Moore's letter to show Moore that he would not even preserve anything that looked like an apology. He wrote, addressing him as 'My dear George,' said there could not be any cause for offence and that the difficulty was that the journalists had every prominent man classified. The journalist evidently believed Moore was contemptuous, Shaw satirical, Oliver Lodge superstitious, the Archbishop of Canterbury pious, etc. Shaw said he knew the game only too well, having frequently suffered from it himself. Then he went on to say he was delighted that Moore had escaped with his life from the surgeons, for he had been horrified to learn that Moore had fallen into their hands. He signed the letter 'Ever the best of friends, G.B.S.'

At the same time Moore wrote to Barrie, whom he had also been represented as attacking. Barrie replied that he had retained and increased his admiration for the work of Moore. He followed this the next month with a second letter beginning 'My dear Moore' in which he says he is glad the newspaper did publish such an interview because it gave him an opportunity to renew his friendship. He said he was living like a hermit, but asked Moore to dinner; no one else would be present. He added that when he had previously observed that Moore was turning playwright, he had come near writing him and offering him suggestions from his own experience that might be useful.

Extracts from those letters were printed in the catalogue of Bertram Rota, which offered for sale all four manuscripts. Moore told his correspondents he had written to the newspaper correcting the statements ascribed to him.

121 EBURY STREET
THURSDAY NIGHT

DEAR MR. PHELPS,

I know of no day or time more agreeable for aesthetic talk than Sunday morning and shall expect you about eleven o'clock if I do not hear that after consideration one of the other days you mention will suit you better.

Very sincerely yours,

GEORGE MOORE

Even as Æ. was beloved and respected both by Irish Republicans and Irish Unionists, so was he by Yeats the poet and George Moore the novelist, who certainly had no liking for each other. It may be that in those three remarkable volumes *Ave*, *Salve*, *Vale*, which purport to be accurate narrations of events, Moore was more of a novelist than in the books he called novels. Certainly as literature they are far greater than *The Brook Kerith*, which I was never able to finish.

Although Æ. was full of humour and his comments awakened irresistible mirth, I never heard him laugh; I cannot even imagine Yeats laughing; but Moore laughed loud and often, usually *at* somebody or something, especially when he was pointing out what he thought were the absurdities in the novels of Thomas Hardy. Despite Moore's anti-Hardy obsession, where I could not follow him at all, he was, like Henry James, a truly great literary critic.

90

Æ.

ON 9 February 1928 Æ. (George W. Russell) spent the day
in New Haven. He attended my undergraduate class in
Browning at eleven, stayed with me at my house until
five, when he lectured at the University and then came
back with me for dinner and the evening. He said 'I am
and always have been a pacifist; but what am I to believe
now? Although I have always condemned violence, we got
nothing in Ireland by peaceful means. Yes, all the freedom
the Irish have attained has been won by fighting, violence
and bloodshed.'

I have been fortunate enough to know some of the
leading writers that Ireland has given to the world in the
twentieth century—Bernard Shaw, W.B.Yeats, St. John
Ervine, George Moore, Lady Gregory, Lennox Robinson,
Padraic and Mary Colum, Æ., and others; but while Shaw
and Ervine are greater dramatists, Moore a greater novelist, Mary Colum a more accomplished literary critic, Yeats
a greater poet, the greatest personality in Ireland was Æ.
He was a poet, a novelist, a painter, an agriculturist, a
journalist, a statesman, a farmer, and many other things;
but his chief distinction was as a conversationalist. Toward
the end of his life, he was successful as a public speaker.

Johnson said if one wished to find out whether or
not a man had a first-rate mind, one must come
close to him in intimate conversation. Well, everyone
who knew Æ. recognized his unique powers; never have
I heard talk that combined so much learning, intelligence

and charm. 'The air seems bright with his past presence yet.'

Bernard Shaw says Americans have an athletic pronunciation. It is well said. Our voices are often too penetrating to be agreeable; perhaps what they lack in melody they make up for in audibility. Æ.'s voice was of a triple softness. It was an Irish voice, that seemed to come through the fogs and mists of his native land. This softness was further softened by his copious beard; the voice came sifting through the whiskers. It was further softened by clouds of tobacco smoke, for he was a chronic pipe-smoker; hour after hour this soft dreamy Irish voice came through the whiskers and through the smoke, so that I felt as if I were listening to the Delphic oracle, which I am sure never uttered such continuous wisdom.

On this ninth day of February 1928 he talked to me for ten hours; and I could have heard him till his voice gave out. Now nothing is more exhausting than to listen to a steady stream of gabble; and it happens that the specific gravity of talk is often in inverse proportion to its volume. The astonishing thing is that every sentence he spoke with such fluent ease was worth hearing. Every word was interesting. In one respect Oscar Wilde (another genius in conversation) would not have approved of Æ., for Wilde said he disliked people who were not serious about their meals. Well, Æ. was not serious about his meals; but in some way he contrived to eat plentifully without even checking the flow of talk. After he had been talking from twelve till one, I suggested lunch; we went into the dining-room and he ate everything set before him without looking at it; he was braver in this respect than Benjamin Franklin, who invented bi-focal glasses so that he could look at his food and at beautiful women.

After lunch he went on talking till five, when I reminded him of the hall filled with people at the University awaiting his appearance. We went there, he spoke easily and magnificently for an hour on the platform; then we returned home, conversing on the way. At seven we again entered the dining-room where he performed in an even more impressive manner the miracle of lunch. Then I listened with enchantment to his talk until ten o'clock.

He said that narrative poetry no matter how good was always second-rate, because it was on one plane. The highest form of poetry was always the poetry of transfiguration. I immediately asked him to read one of his poems, which he did, chanting it with a rhythm that will be remembered by thousands of people; for whether on platform or in an armchair, he had only one way of repeating verse; it would have been monotonous from any other man. This is the poem he chanted:

DUST

> I heard them in their sadness say
> " The earth rebukes the thought of God;
> We are but embers wrapped in clay,
> A little nobler than the sod."
>
> But I have touched the lips of clay;
> Mother, thy rudest sod to me
> Is thrilled with fire of hidden day
> And haunted by all mystery.

It is amazing that he remembered every line of verse he had written. John Eglinton says that Æ. remarked of Yeats, that if he had written a poem in the morning and you asked him to repeat it in the evening, he would have to read it from the manuscript. Æ. could have dictated without hesitation every page from memory in every volume of poems he had ever published!

He did not give any illustrations of transfiguration in poetry except the one that I asked him to repeat; he went on to talk of something else. But I believe a perfect illustration of what he meant is the short piece *Overtones* by the American poet, William Alexander Percy.

> I heard a bird at break of day
>   Sing in the autumn trees
> A song so mystical, so calm,
>   So full of certainties,
> No man, I think, could listen long
>   Except upon his knees:
> Yet this was but a simple bird,
>   Alone, among dead trees.

Even if Æ. had never published anything, he would not be forgotten; he had a rich personality. Everyone reads *Robinson Crusoe*, but only a minority remember even the name of the author; very few indeed read the works of Sir Philip Sidney, but his personality is not forgotten.

The universal respect and affection given to Æ. are an imperishable tribute to his mind and character; George Moore, who treated his enemies and his friends so often with insults, gave the world an artistic portrait of Æ., for whom he had affection, and what was unique with Moore, reverence. That great Pagan, who said his 'only recreation was Religion,' was awestruck by Æ., and his reverence was not diminished by a long friendship.

After I had printed in *Scribner's Magazine* an account of his ten hours' talk, he wrote to me

84 MERRION SQUARE,
DUBLIN
6–12–28

DEAR PHELPS,

I have read with consternation the paragraph about me in Scribners. Did I go on talking like that? I always supposed I was a silent man! I think I am, but my shyness must have burst when I was in your country and without my being aware of it. The desperately shy man goes on talking desperately. Please put it down to that. I am accustomed to sit silently when really good talkers like Yeats,

James Stephens, Stephen MacKenna, Oliver Gogarty or George
Moore start talking. They were prodigally endowed by nature with
eloquence or wit. I would never break in on any of these once they
got started. If I could induce Oliver Gogarty to go to America it
would hear really good talk flashing out in every sentence. When
George Moore wondered whether our round towers were Christian
or unchristian, Oliver settled the question in ten words: "Pre Christian, of course! no parish priest could get through the doorway."
Perhaps this sounds irreverant to you. I hesitate to repeat his philo-
sophic reflection after he said that. "You know when the Word
incarnates in Ireland it suffers from fatty degeneration of the heart."
I am afraid his conversation would be censored in your country.
Most such conversation would be. Our Government is making a
beginning not with the spoken but with censoring of the written
word. Any literature "calculated to excite sexual passion" is prohibited as "indecent." Romeo and Juliet would go out and Shelley's
"I arise from dreams of thee." I see our literature getting more and
more Puritan and our conversation getting more and more Restoration. Come here five years after the censorship and you will find
the country publicly pure and privately abandoned. And the conversation will probably make your hair stand up. But I must not
ramble on or you will say once I begin writing I never stop with the
pen any more than I do with the tongue. Forgive its ten hours of
wagging.

Yours sincerely,

A.E.

84 MERRION SQUARE,
DUBLIN
10.6.29

MY DEAR PHELPS.

I forgive you but I doubt whether Oliver will forgive you or myself
for raking up the irreverent wit of his boyhood. He could not go to
the United States now. Your countrymen would have been better
pleased if they had known the precautions he took to avoid the danger
of knighthood. He wrote to Lloyds the insurance brokers to get a
quotation on the premium he must pay to insure himself against
the risk. He told them it was customary in his city when a doctor
had attained a certain degree of eminence in his profession that he
should be offered a knighthood. "This," said Oliver, "is a very

serious matter for me. Half my clients are nationalists; the other half imperialists. If I accept this knighthood which shall be offered to me I shall lose my nationalist clients. If I refuse it I shall lose my imperialist clients." Dublin in pre-treaty days was locally known as "the City of Dreadful Knights" and you can understand why a poet should try to insure himself against the risk. Oliver's surname was ——— I will not tell you the right name as he may desire sometime to go to the States and the story cannot be brought up against him.

Yours ever,

A.E.

152 EAST FORTIETH STREET
May 5, 1931

DEAR BILLY:

I find everybody refers to you by this familiar title so I am adopting it as I am going back to Ireland and you cannot cast on me a frown of professorial dignity in rebuke of my familiarity.

I would come with pleasure to talk to your class only I am fixed up on my last day here with many engagements and I start off on the 7th to Montreal.

I would have been very glad to see you—you are a most companionable person—and to have initiated you further into the mystery of commingled tobacco and coltsfoot. I am so afraid you will not get the proper blend.

Sincerely yours,

"A.E."

20
9
——
31

17 Rathgar Avenue
Dublin
Ireland

DEAR BILLY. May I trespass on your good nature. A Mrs. ——— wrote to me saying she was writing something about me in the Yale Review and asked some questions. I answered her and mislaid her letter afterwards. Now she writes again and I cannot make out her address except that it is in "Conn" and she has some strange hieroglyph before that of which below is a faithful copy

"Westville"

This is unintelligible. As you are at Yale I surmise a relation of some sort or knowledge of the Yale Review—that the Yale Review has probably some knowledge of Mrs. — —. Therefore on all these suppositions I am daring to send you a letter addressed by name to her in the hope that from the Yale Review it might get to her. I have no U.S.A. stamps but I let you into the secret of increasing the enjoyment from your life by telling you about Coltsfoot. That is worth the two cents you must pay on the letter. If you boggle at this send it unstamped to her c/o Yale Review. She deserves the punishment for writing so badly.

With best wishes and apologies,

A.E.

P.S. I enclose her last note. You knowing all geography of the land about might be able to interpret the hieroglyphics.

A.E.

Mrs. George Russell was a self-effacing, unselfish woman. When she was slowly dying of cancer, a friend called upon her. She said 'Do go into the next room and tell my husband how much you like his new book. It will cheer him immensely and take his mind off, for a time from his grief about my illness.'

If there were such a thing as an epidemic of cancer (and my friend the great specialist Doctor Francis Wood says there is not), one might believe that these three persons, so closely united, were sufferers from a common cause; for Susan Mitchell the Secretary, Mrs. Russell, and Æ. himself, all died from cancer within a few years. When I mentioned this to Dr. Wood, he said 'No, there is no common cause and no pathological significance because three persons closely associated every day for years died of cancer; it was just a shake of the dice; it just happened.'

In 1928 Æ. had just returned from his lecturing tour in America, when he was offered an honorary degree of Doctor of Literature from Yale. He immediately returned to receive this academic honour. As I was the Public Orator, I had the pleasure of presenting him for the degree which I did with the following words:

GEORGE WILLIAM RUSSELL, LITT.D.

The foremost citizen of Ireland. He is the very genius of the unexpected, an Irishman who loves peace. He is a patriotic internationalist who loves all nations including his own. His versatility is remarkable; he has attained distinction in widely different fields of human effort. He is a mystic and a farmer; a poet and a practical statesman; a journalist and a painter; with a character of such nobility and unselfishness that even George Moore treats him with respect. Absolutely independent, with a courage that abhors compromise, he is admired and trusted by all political parties in Ireland, including Ulster and Cork, Protestants and Catholics, Republicans and Tories. The best thing that could happen to that country would be to make him Dictator for Life. He is an authority on poetry and public finance; he is both spiritual and shrewd, this combination giving to his imaginative work the element of transfiguration, for in his own words, it takes two currents to make the electric light. Perhaps of all the arts which he has mastered, he is greatest in the fine art of conversation; he should have a Boswell. He is in a double sense a man of letters, for he has given special and lasting significance to the two letters A.E.

91

CAPTAIN LIDDELL HART AND GENERAL
J.G.HARBORD

CAPTAIN LIDDELL HART, the military historian of the London *Times* and author of many books ranging from war to contemporary masters of the game of lawn tennis, began his career at an early age. He was born 31 October 1895, so that when the War broke out he was only 19. He was at that time a student at Corpus Christi, Cambridge. He served in the European War and was wounded. His publications began when he was 22 years old with *New Methods of Infantry Training*, and his career since then is well known. When he published in 1928 his *Ten Years After*, I wrote to my friend, Major General J.G.Harbord, and asked his opinion about it. And considering the great reputation of both experts, the following letters should be of interest.

General Harbord is one of the finest men I have ever known. He is as modest as he is able, and there is no better companion anywhere. I have been shooting with him; I have played innumerable games of golf with him, and my respect for his ability is equalled only by my affection for him.

233 BROADWAY, NEW YORK
ROOM 1856
March 17, 1928

DEAR BILLIE:
Your letter of March 14th, about Liddell-Hart's book on the Generals, has been received and would have been answered sooner but

that I wanted to take another look at the two articles on the Americans,—Pershing and Liggett. I read the Pershing article in the Atlantic when it came out early in the winter, but wanted to take another look at it. I found last night, which was the evening I had reserved for this purpose, that Emma had sent the book over to her Father, in Washington, to read and it has not yet been returned, so I am unable to freshen my memory.

My impression is that the book is fair and unprejudiced, and is a very correct estimate of what I believe the place in history of those several gentlemen will be. I had a personal acquaintance with Lord Haig, with Joffre, Foch and Petain. My actual acquaintance was perhaps closer with Marshal Petain and Lord Haig than with the others named. I think the estimate of General Haig was a very fair one, so too with the estimate of Petain whom I, myself, have always rated higher as a General than I rate Foch. The choice of the latter as Commander-in-Chief of the Allies seemed to me to be more or less of a political accident. He had, of course, an excellent reputation after the first Battle of the Marne, but in the spring of 1917, after the Nivelle Offensive, the French Government evidently rated Petain higher than Foch because they selected him for the Command of the French Armies when the two Generals were equally available for selection. Foch then drifted on for another year as Chief of Staff at the War Office but exercising authority as such only in theatres of war other than the Western Front. As I have understood it, he exercised no control over Petain and the French Armies in France during that period. When the disaster at Caporetto occurred there was a strong feeling, probably groping toward unity of command, which crystallized in the form of the Supreme War Council at Versailles where each Prime Minister of the Allied countries was to be a member, each with a Military Adviser. Our General Bliss, who had been retired for age from the position of Chief of Staff of our Army, was made the American member. There was a quarrel among the British which resulted in the relief of Sir William Robertson as Chief of the Imperial General Staff and the substitution of Sir Henry Wilson, in my judgment a less able man; and Foch, and Clemenceau, were the French representation. This Supreme War Council, naturally, began to aggrandize itself and seek power. The first apparent move in this direction was to attempt to form an Allied Reserve by contributions of troops from each of the Allied Armies on the Western Front. This determined upon, it was evident, even to a bunch of Prime Ministers, that such a formed Reserve could not be commanded by a committee which was really what the Supreme War Council was, so the natural act was to take the most experienced and Senior Officer connected with the Supreme War Council and give him the job,— that meant Foch. Due to the inability of Haig and Petain, however, to spare their quota of troops for this Allied Reserve, it had not been formed when the German Offensive of March 21st was undertaken which resulted in the practical destruction of the British Fifth Army and created a situation which forced the unity of command, and Foch again, naturally, was agreed upon for Commander-in-Chief. That, itself, was accomplished in two bites. He was first, still acting apparently for the Supreme War Council, appointed to coordinate the action of the Allied Armies. Coordination, without authority to command, is an unworkable situation, and the next step was to make him Commander-in-Chief. Petain who, as I said above I regard as a better General, had by his contempt for politicians made himself persona non grata with the high civil authorities in France while, in the meantime, Foch had been more and more in contact with them and had won their esteem.

As I said above, I have not read the article on Pershing since November or December, when it came out in the Atlantic, but there were two things, which I seem to recall as having attracted my attention at that time, which were wrong. One was that in General Pershing's pressure for open warfare, or war of movement as they sometimes call it, instead of the continuation of trench warfare, he was not fully aware of the effect of machine guns which, of course, had been developed in the War to an extent never before known. That is not the case. General Pershing was fully aware of the potentialities of all the weapons that were being used in the War but he found in France the opposing forces glaring at each other from trenches, in some cases only a few yards apart and some of which had been occupied for four years. He realized that in order to win the War somebody on one side or the other must crawl out of his trenches and move forward, taking all the risks that pertain to such a movement. The professional training of American Officers, as was of course true of our Allies before the outbreak of the War, had been in open warfare and had never contemplated a stalemate in permanent trenches. These considerations led General Pershing to insist on a different character of warfare than that which he found on arrival. It seems to me, too, that the article on Pershing criticized the great loss of Officers, particularly of Company rank, as compared to the enlisted casualties, which the Allies were accustomed to attribute to our inexperience in warfare. The truth is that there are certain things in war which every nation has to learn for itself. The losses of Officers in the American Expeditionary Forces corresponded very closely with the losses of the Allies and of the enemy in the first year and a half of the War. We could not profit by their experience in that particular case. Those losses did not result principally from inexperience. At the beginning of a war Officers, indeed the officer class generally, have to demonstrate their mettle and their capacity for leadership before their men including the willingness to take risks. The less trained the men are and the less unprepared the nation, the more certain it is that the officer class are obliged to demonstrate their capacity for personal leadership. It always results in an undue proportion of losses among the class which the nation can least afford to lose. This is exactly why the Allies lost heavily of Officers in 1914 and 1915 and why we lost heavily in 1918, and it also explains why we could not benefit by their experience and thus avoid such losses ourselves. It is particularly true of a democracy, where officers are selected from the same level as the enlisted men, that they get no more than scant official respect from their men until they demonstrate physical courage.

This has grown to be a very long letter and sounds a little diffuse. I thought, however, from your inquiry as to my opinion, that perhaps it was not out of order to mention these matters. Liddell-Hart appears to me to be a very able writer on military subjects. I understand he fills the place on the London Times which was so ably filled for many years by the late Colonel Repington. I have an idea that, ten years after the War, he has pretty correctly stated what will be the ultimate verdict of history on the men of whom he writes.

FROM CAPTAIN LIDDELL HART

I always read with keen interest as well as most appreciatively your comments on my writings. And in this case I am the more interested because of the quotation of the letter from General Harbord, a man for whom no student of the war can help feeling great admiration. Indeed it was because of my impression of Gen. Harbord in the light of what I heard of him from all quarters that in "appreciating" Pershing I attached special weight to Gen. Harbord's own comments. For in writing upon Pershing I was more handicapped than in other cases, having less intimate evidence and knowledge than when dealing with the leaders of the European armies. As regards Gen. Harbord's two points of criticism of my essay I would say that my suggestion was that he underestimated the paralysing power of machine-guns rather than "he was not fully aware of the effect." My opinion was based not merely on the results in the Meuse-Argonne but on the frequent reiteration of the view among his associates and himself that grenade and trench-warfare had paralysed the offensive spirit of the French and British, without qualifying reference to or suggestion of the part that machine-guns had played as the primary cause.

I feel that the method adopted in the U.S. Army to counteract this paralysis would have failed against the Germans of 1916, and I see Gen. Liggett rather endorses such a view, and even against the Germany of early 1918. If . . . November 1918 partially justified this training doctrine it was, at the least, tending to extreme optimism to base a training doctrine on the hypothesis that the fighting morale of the Germans—half-starved, stricken by sickness, and bombarded by wailing letters from home,—would sink so rapidly as it did between July and September 1918. As regards the second criticism, this is evidently based on a lapse of memory—as Gen. Harbord suggests may have occurred owing to a lapse of time since he read the *Atlantic* article. I nowhere criticised the excessive loss of officers compared with enlisted casualties. Indeed, I specially refrained from doing so. For I agree most emphatically with the penetrating comments which Gen. Harbord makes in this connection. An excessive toll of officers is an inevitable price which must be paid for unpreparedness and for democracy.

I hope that these observations may interest and not bore you. Once more with warm thanks, and cordial regards, I remain

Yours very truly,

B. H. LIDDELL HART

In 1929 appeared Captain Liddell Hart's biography of General Sherman; an admirable book.

92

EVENTS IN 1929-30

AMONG living American novelists none has a higher standing than Willa Cather. Her art like her nature has mellowed with maturity; there is a spiritual advance from irony to sympathy; with this growth in grace there is an added literary distinction. The rather venomous acidity of *A Lost Lady*, *My Mortal Enemy*, and *The Professor's House* changed into the profound insight (born of love) into the characters of obscure people shown in *Death Comes for the Archbishop*, *Shadows on the Rock*, *Obscure Destinies*, *Lucy Gayheart*. When I read *My Mortal Enemy*, I could not tell which was the enemy, the husband or the wife. One day my friend the novelist Lee Dodd told me he had asked her and she had told him; whereupon he told me and I have forgotten.

In June 1929 at the Yale Commencement it was with unusual pleasure that, as Public Orator, I had the honour of presenting her for the degree of Doctor of Letters:

Born in Virginia, a graduate of the University of Nebraska, for some years a Pittsburgh journalist, Willa Cather is today one of the leading English-writing novelists of the world. Her worst novel *One of Ours* received the Pulitzer Prize because in that year her worst novel was better than everybody else's masterpiece. It is impossible to classify her work; she has attained eminence in such different fields of literary art. *The Professor's House* is a dynamic and terrifying story; *Death Comes for the Archbishop* is a static and tranquil book, written without emphasis, and full of beauty. It is impossible to say what the nature of her next book will be, but we know that it will make an impression on competent critics. Miss Cather has given honour to American literature, and we are proud today to include her among the daughters of Yale.

On 25 October 1929 appeared in New Haven the British actor Leslie Howard, for the première of that magnificent play *Berkeley Square*. At about five o'clock I went over to the theatre and found Leslie and the whole company in a state of feverish excitement. I invited him to take dinner with me and the undergraduate Pundits at six o'clock. One of the actresses exclaimed, 'Oh, Mr. Phelps, do take him! It will do him good. He is not needed here any more and it will refresh him before he goes on the stage.' In the presence of the undergraduates he seemed to forget the imminent ordeal. He was a delightful dinner companion and so captivated the students that they elected him an honorary Pundit.

We went from the dinner to the theatre; the play had an enormous success and ran for a year in New York. I particularly enjoy fourth dimension plays like this and *Outward Bound* and *Hotel Universe* and *Lost Horizons*.

In 1930 the famous American actress Minnie Maddern Fiske came to play in New Haven, and I asked her to address my class in Contemporary Drama. She did so, but on that day she was so excited by the news that there was to be a bull-fight in New Jersey, that she devoted her remarks exclusively to denouncing the wickedness of such barbarism and asked the students to promise that they would write letters of protest. 'Those who will promise to write a letter today, please raise your hands!'

DEAR PROFESSOR PHELPS:

I shall be delighted to speak a few words to the students tomorrow before the matinee. And now comes the great favor! I am going to ask you if I may speak to the boys upon the subject that is occupying me today? It has nothing to do with the theatre but it is a critical moment in another department of life and I want and need the help of the students. *I shall be grateful beyond words for their help.*

With warmest good wishes,

M.M.FISKE

The fiery speech she made to the students was as dramatic and as effective as many of her professional impersonations in the theatre.

On 10 June, as the guest of Mrs. Benjamin Stern of New York, a charming and cultivated woman, we had the honour of meeting the great *prima donna* Lucrezia Bori. She was as attractive personally as she was on the stage. She told me she was born one Christmas Eve in Spain, in a carriage.

Lucrezia Bori was not only a great singer and actress, she showed executive ability of a high order, with energy as powerful as it was productive, when the campaigns were made for the continued support of the Metropolitan Opera House in the years of depression.

On 16 October at my house in New Haven, I gave a dinner in honour of Sir Edmund Chambers, the famous Elizabethan scholar. That evening he spoke on Shakespeare at the Elizabethan Club. Thinking he might be impressed by the things we had there, I showed him the oil painting of Elizabeth, for which she sat to Zucchero. His only comment was, 'Zucchero was always painting her, wasn't he?' I still think the picture is valuable.

I was amazed at the appearance of Chambers; as he has been all his life a research scholar, I expected to see a frail, pale, bookish-looking man. But he looked more like an Elizabethan soldier of fortune, big, aggressive, and although he was 64 years old, his abundant hair was coalblack.

If there is any man alive who is absolutely satisfied with his career, that man should be Chambers. He never wanted to teach. He wanted to be a research scholar, devoting himself to the early religious drama, and the Elizabethan, and to writing the most complete biography of Shakespeare. He has done and done magnificently everything that in his youth he wanted to do. *Finis coronat opus.*

And was there ever a more typically British scholar? If one judged him only by his preface to *The Mediaeval Stage*, one would almost think he had carelessly written the book whilst resting his body between important sets of tennis. It is in reality a work of monumental research and of permanent value.

In this year of 1929 for the first time in my life I acquired asthma. On the advice of Lafayette Mendel, my distinguished Yale colleague (physiological chemistry) whose death was such a loss to science, and of Dr. Henry Swain, who knew my throat and nose as Mark Twain knew the Mississippi Channel, I consulted Dr. Bret Ratner in New York and was greatly impressed by his ability and personality. Following his instructions I gave away my four cats and a parrot and sent the dog into the country. In a few months the asthma vanished.

On 1 November at the house of Professor and Mrs. Ross Harrison of Yale, I had the pleasure of meeting Julian Huxley, tall, black-haired, spectacled, charming, unaffected. He told me his brother Aldous's bitter, ironical way of looking at life was largely caused by the fact that when the war broke out in 1914 and he was anxious to serve in the army, his eyes were so bad that he feared he was going blind and had to spend many months in a dark room. Julian showed intense pride and affection in Aldous, and seemed to think Americans might get a false impression of his character. However, he is greatly admired and highly valued by Americans. I dislike his books, but I am in a hopeless minority.

On 5 November it was announced that Sinclair Lewis had received the Nobel Prize, the first American to be so honoured. When his wife Dorothy Thompson informed him over the telephone he laughed, not dreaming that she meant it.

In order to attend the farewell dinner given to him in New York by various writers, I had to take the train from New Haven at 6.20, reach New York at 8.15, hurry to the dinner, make my speech, leave the dinner, and take the ten o'clock train home; for that morning I had had three lectures at the University, a public address at a luncheon, and a public lecture at four o'clock. At the dinner I sat with Mrs. Corinne Roosevelt Robinson, Fannie Hurst, and Mrs. Alice Duer Miller.

Corinne Robinson, the sister of Theodore Roosevelt, adored her brother and was very like him; filled with gusto and the joy of living, and with invincible courage. I liked her immensely; and our acquaintance began with her forgiveness. She wrote asking me to come to some gathering in New York, where her brother would be present. It was early in the War. I wrote thanking her but declining to come, saying that if Mr. Roosevelt knew my views about the War, he would refuse to shake hands with me. To my surprise and pleasure, she wrote me a charming letter in reply, and after that, I met her often. Fannie Hurst is always the best of company; and so is Alice Duer Miller.

In this year 1930 I received from the University of Syracuse the honorary degree of Doctor of Sacred Theology, D.S.T., which some of my friends thought was *Daylight Saving Time*, of which I have always been an advocate.

93

EDISON

THURSDAY 20 February 1930 was the hottest 20 February in the records of the New York weather bureau. Nearly seventy degrees. That night I attended a dinner at the Harvard Club given by Thomas B. Wells in honour of H.M. Tomlinson of England. Hugh Walpole, Harry Hansen, William Bolitho, Professor Samuel Morison, Sava Botzaris, Cass Canfield, Eugene Saxton, Leo Hartman were present. Wells told me that Tomlinson was more like Jesus Christ than any man he had ever known. Tomlinson impressed us by his modesty, sincerity, and unaffected *goodness*.

When I came out at midnight, it was difficult to believe it was February; the air was balmy.

Next morning my wife and I entrained for Winter Park, Florida; it was fearfully hot on the train and during the few days we spent at Winter Park, the temperature reached 96 every day.

I was to receive the Honorary degree of Doctor of Laws from Rollins College; but the great event was the appearance of Thomas Edison, who broke his almost invariable custom of refusing degrees, and was made Doctor of Science. He was 83 years old, and I was amazed to see him reading without glasses the fine print of the programme. After the ceremonies were over, I asked him if he always read without glasses. He laughed and took from his pocket a pair of spectacles. 'I can read well enough without them, but I use them when I feel like it.'

We all had lunch at the house of President and Mrs. Hamilton Holt with Mr. and Mrs. Edison. Edison sat at the head of the table and seemed to me the happiest man I had ever met. He was smiling, cheerful, with an expression of extraordinary kindness and benevolence. He allowed us to write questions which he read and answered; he was stone deaf. For nearly an hour we passed questions up to him, and he read them aloud and answered them.

The scientific matter that most interested him at the moment was the question of making rubber in his laboratory, so that the United States would not have to import it for the next war. I do not know whether he succeeded in this or not; but he was certain that there would be another big war in which our country would be engaged, and that the most patriotic thing he could do would be to supply rubber.

I then asked him if the story of his first opportunity in life, as a newsboy on a train in Michigan was true; I heard it first from his friend Irving Bacheller; he said it was, and repeated it substantially as follows:

When he was a small boy, he sold papers every day on the train running between Port Huron and Detroit, a two-hour journey. He wanted to devote his time to mastering telegraphy; but he had no resources, and the daily earnings from the sale of papers were small. One day, as he entered one of the cars, there sat a gentleman who was gorgeously drunk. Alcohol had made him generous, so that he wanted to give away the whole world. He was accompanied by a manservant, whose name I cannot remember, but it was Biblical, so suppose I call him Obadiah.

The affluent gentleman looked at young Edison and asked, 'How many papers have you got there, boy?' and on being told, he said, 'Obadiah, take all these newspapers and throw them out of the window.' This was done and paid for. Then the boy went back to the baggage car and brought out his entire supply of magazines. 'How many magazines you got there, boy?' They were carefully counted and their current value computed. 'Obadiah, take all those magazines and throw them out of the window. Done and paid for. Young Edison went back to the baggage car, and soon returned staggering under the load of his complete stock of books. The gentleman was even more interested. It took some time to count them and appraise the value of each. It was a large sum of money. 'Obadiah, take all those volumes and throw them out of the window.' The railway tracks must have looked as if a circulating library had been visited by a cyclone. This time the boy became a capitalist, and determined on the spot to leave the newspaper business and devote himself to telegraphy and electricity.

He remembered his now empty iron trunk. He returned to the baggage car, and came back dragging the metallic receptacle. 'Boy, what do you charge for that trunk?' Edison named his price. 'Obadiah, take that trunk to the platform and push it off.'

This was Edison's first start in life. It was fortunate for him that this gentleman happened to be on the train that particular morning, and that his fancy took that quixotic turn.

I attended some of the classes at Rollins College where the usual system of instruction is reversed. The teacher asks no questions. He sits in a room with the boy and girl undergraduates who are studying; then any one who so desires asks the teacher questions. I do not know whether this system would work in other colleges or not. But it is only fair to say that in response to many questions I put to individual students and members of the Faculty, I invariably received enthusiastic affirmations of its success.

94

NATHAN STRAUS AND THE GRAND DUCHESS

On Sunday morning 11 January 1931 the family of the great philanthropist Nathan Straus called me by telephone from New York, saying that Mr. Straus had died at four o'clock that morning, and it was the unanimous request of the family that I make the address at his public funeral, to take place on Tuesday.

Early Tuesday morning I took the train to New York and at the station entered a taxi to be taken to the beautiful Temple Emanu-El for the funeral exercises. When I gave that address to the taxi driver, he said 'Then you are going to the funeral of one of the best men who ever lived.'

The magnificent auditorium was filled; the bearers were prominent citizens of New York, headed by Mayor Walker. Three Rabbis read Psalms and offered prayer, and I was the only non-Jewish person in the pulpit and the only speaker. Mr. Straus had told his sons that no long oration must be made and that he must not be praised; that they should ask me to make the address, and that I must confine myself to a brief account of the facts in his life. Accordingly I did so; but I quoted the remark made to me by the taxi driver.

The most conspicuous object in the temple was the coffin, a plain, unpainted pine box. Here he set an example which ought to be followed, but which will not. Mr. Straus thought it was contrary to ethics to spend a great sum on a coffin when the money could be put to so much better use in charity.

Not many days before his death I had a remarkable conversation with Nathan Straus. He was on his deathbed and he knew it; yet as I bent close to his face, he whispered 'I am one of the happiest men in the world, for although I am weak and hopelessly ill, I know that I have done the right thing with my wealth, in giving so much of it away while I was alive and well. I know many rich men who are laying up for themselves a miserably unhappy old age. They will not give away large sums of money, which they ought to do, if they wish to be at peace when they come to be where I am now. John D. Rockefeller has been so wise in this respect. He is a man of the noblest and finest character. He has shown us all what to do with our wealth.'

I took pains to speak very clearly as he seemed so desperately ill. He said, 'Don't try to raise your voice; I can't make a sound above a whisper but I hear perfectly.'

He then once more repeated to me his favourite quotation 'Money given in health is gold; money given in sickness is silver; money given at death is lead.'

I first saw Mr. and Mrs. Nathan Straus at the Bon Air Vanderbilt Hotel in Augusta, Georgia, in January 1925. We became close friends; after that time, I saw them often at their home in New York City, and at Mamaroneck.

Both of them were devout and deeply religious Jews; their charity and love for mankind knew no racial or theological boundaries.

On 24 March 1931 the Grand Duchess Marie of Russia was to give a lecture at Derby, Conn., about twelve miles from New Haven. I was asked to introduce her, and had a little talk with her beforehand. She was gracious and charming. I told her I had to leave before her lecture would be over, because I was due to give a lecture on her book in New Haven, later that same afternoon!

I took out my pen to write something for her, and she exclaimed, 'Oh, you use a stylographic pen! It is the only

kind I can write with, and I cannot find one in America.'
I begged her to accept mine.

She spoke English with absolute accuracy, only it was
almost too precise; it was faultily faultless. I asked her how
she learned various European languages at the same time
in her infancy; how it was possible to learn English, for
example, and not lose what she had learned of German. She
said she was not taught Russian until she had learned English, French, and German. That she was given a governess
in each of those languages. That they were forbidden to
speak to her in any language other than their own; that she
was forbidden to speak to them in any other. That if she
asked for anything in a language not their own, they were
forbidden to give it her.

A few days later I gave a public lecture at the Town Hall
in New York; the Grand Duchess was in the audience and
I had lunch with her afterwards. She complimented me on
my pronunciation of Russian proper names, saying I pronounced them like a native. English-speaking people usually pronounce erroneously the vowel *u* in Rasputin.

On Monday 13 April the Grand Duchess, accompanied
by her Secretary, Miss Tobias, came to Yale and delivered
a lecture on the Francis Bergen Memorial Foundation.
We gave a dinner at our house that evening and she spent
the night with us. At this dinner-party she amused everyone by her descriptions of her lecture tour in the West.

She then began to talk about the author of *San Michele*,
the book which at the moment was running neck and neck
with her own, in the list of best-sellers. There was nothing
bad enough she could say about him.

We told her when she went to bed that night that we
would send up breakfast to her room the next morning at
any hour she preferred; as it was the first time we had ever
entertained a Grand Duchess, we wondered what she
would like to eat. 'Ham and eggs,' she said.

When she came downstairs, she insisted on attending my regular undergraduate class in Browning. 'I want you to teach the class exactly as if I were not in the room.' I told her no women were ever allowed in undergraduate courses at Yale, but that I was sure an exception could be made. A curious thing about this visit of the Grand Duchess's was that it gave my wife an opportunity to hear me teach, something that had never happened before. We had been married nearly forty years and I had been teaching the same length of time; but on account of the rule forbidding women, she had never seen me in action. Accordingly, as the Duchess was to be admitted, my wife accompanied her and Miss Tobias. They took seats in a row of undergraduates; and I went ahead with the Browning lesson, calling on the students to recite. Then, about fifteen minutes before the close of the hour, I said, 'Gentlemen, we are honoured by the presence of the Grand Duchess Marie of Russia; and I am sure you would enjoy hearing her say a few words.' All the students rose, and the Grand Duchess sat down at the teacher's desk, an unusual spectacle in a Yale classroom. She said 'May I smoke?' I replied, 'Smoking is forbidden in classrooms, but as we have broken one rule already, we shall be glad to break another,' and I gave her a light.

She spoke informally and easily about her life in Russia, showing no bitterness against the Bolsheviks. Then the students asked questions, to which she made frank and definite answers.

After the class, she wished to see the Yale Library, and accompanied by a bodyguard of students, we walked across to the great building. In a half-hour she had to take the train to New York; she said she had enjoyed every moment of her Yale visit, and kissed my wife affectionately.

On her next return from Europe, she was obliged by an immigration law to have a certificate of character, and asked me to furnish her with it, which I was very glad to do.

She made a most agreeable impression, both on the lecture audience and on the students, and indeed on every one she met at Yale. There was not a trace either of shyness or of condescension. Perfect ease of manner.

On May 18 the twenty millionth Ford car arrived in New Haven on its festal journey through the cities of the United States. I was asked to appear in it with the Mayor in the procession. We did this, and Mayor Tully and I signed the book in front of the City Hall.

On 23 May in New Haven, on the front wall of the house at 40 Trumbull Street, where the famous composer Ethelbert Nevin had lived, a tablet was unveiled in his memory. Mrs. Nevin was present and I made the address. My wife and I had lived in the same block, at 44 Trumbull Street, from 1894 to 1898.

On 3 June 1931 I received a most valuable gift. Michael Phipps of the Senior Class, who had just finished his course with me in Tennyson and Browning, brought me as a present from his father the copy of Tennyson's Poems that *belonged to Browning*, with Robert Browning's signature on the title-page.

On Saturday afternoon 24 October 1931, I saw for the first time at a matinée in the Lyceum Theatre, New York, the (now) famous English actor, Charles Laughton. He had not been known in America at all before this autumn. He appeared in a play called *Payment Deferred*, and made a tremendous impression. Not long after that, I went to hear it again, also at a matinée, and went back to speak to him; he was walking up and down gesticulating wildly and cursing. 'The ——! the damned ——!' He explained, as soon as he became coherent, that during the whole performance, some ladies in the second row were conversing with apparent indifference both to the actors and to their neighbours in the audience. I do not blame him.

Since that time, Mr. Laughton has become universally

known both on the legitimate stage and on the screen. I admire his art in everything except in the film of *The Barrets of Wimpole Street*, where I think he was miscast.

On 12 November I was formally admitted to the American Academy of Arts and Letters, my new colleague being the sculptor Adolph Alexander Weinman.

On 22 December in California, my brother Dryden William died. He was 77 years old and was never married. He was buried in Grove Street cemetery, New Haven, on 29 December.

In 1920 Mr. Cox was the Democratic candidate for the Presidency against Mr. Warren Harding, the Republican. Although I knew Mr. Cox would be defeated, I voted for him for two reasons. First, I believed in the League of Nations. Second, I could not digest Harding. There were three respects in which Harding and I were exactly alike. We were born in the same year; we were brought up as Baptists; and we were both unfitted to be President of the United States.

MIAMI, FLORIDA, MAY 16, 1931

MY DEAR DR. PHELPS:

It has been a long time since Easter when your greetings came and well wishes in my sickness. However, this is the first opportunity I have had to make acknowledgment.

The affair of the appendix didn't amount to much, but I picked up a couple of annoying things which have kept me on my back and I am just getting a peep over the trenches. Life looks very interesting again. It does a crusty old cuss good to be thrown on his back and discover that there is a great deal more sweetness in the world than he knew anything about.

This is the first sickness I have ever had. My average of good health is still high and if I were anything but thankful in making the final appraisal, somehow I feel I would be irreverent.

It was gracious and thoughtful of you to think of me. Please be assured of my appreciation.

Sincerely,

JAMES M. COX

One of the things I regret most in the age of mass production is the obsolescence of the skilled artisan. From childhood to middle age I was intimately acquainted with shoemakers in New Haven, Providence, and Hartford— every one of them was an interesting personality. When I was a boy I never had more than one pair of shoes at a time; so when repairs became necessary I went to the tiny shop of the shoemaker and sat there for two hours in my stockinged feet, whilst he soled and heeled the shoes. He was always glad to talk and I was glad to listen; so whilst he worked the shoemaker talked of politics, theology and life in general. When I was grown up and there were still individual shoemakers in business for themselves and none other, such men as Otto Heinz and Millspaugh in New Haven made my athletic shoes to order and I loved to talk with them on many themes. I have not seen an individual shoemaker for thirty years.

Mass production has not yet extinguished barbers. The barber during the last forty thousand years is an individualist and invariably a conversationalist. I have never known a silent barber and almost invariably their remarks are interesting.

On 16 July 1931 I had the pleasure of conducting a merry celebration in the town of Harbor Beach in Michigan, seventeen miles from my summer home. A few years previously I had discovered that two barbers in that village, James Lytle and Abner Lee had been nearly forty years in partnership in the same business in the same place. I asked them if they had ever had a quarrel. Never. 'Have your wives ever quarrelled?' The same number of times.

Accordingly I told them something should be done to commemorate them and their work. On 16 July 1931 we held a public celebration in their honour. All shops and banks in the town were closed from twelve to two. Frank Murphy, then Mayor of Detroit (later Governor of Michigan), who was born in Harbor Beach, arrived by airplane from Detroit. Edgar A. Guest read an original poem. About three hundred men, the capacity of the hall, were present; the only women allowed were the wives of the two heroes.

One of the most interesting characters in New Haven is George Miller, the professional barber at the Graduates Club. When I discovered in 1936 that he had practised his profession for exactly fifty years in the same town, New Haven, and with no pause, I decided that the occasion called for a public celebration. Accordingly, we organized a dinner at the Graduates Club in his honour. This dinner was attended by the Governor of the State of Connecticut, Wilbur L. Cross, by Dr. Harvey Cushing, and by a number of other distinguished members of the Yale faculty. Hundreds of letters were sent in to Mr. Miller from his present and former clients. Mr. Miller is not only a philosopher, as many barbers are, but is also a wit. He said, 'It's curious that people go to fortune-tellers for knowledge of the future when they should come to me, for in my profession I can always see a head.'

95

HENRY FORD

Now that Edison has gone into the world of light, there is only one American left who is known in every corner of the world. The name Henry Ford is a label of the man; he might just as well have been called John Doe or Richard Doe, John Smith or Henry Ford; and yet this name expresses his character and habits more accurately than a spectacular appellation. For, apart from his genius and the wealth it created, he is an average American; sensible, practical, honest and honourable, faithful to his ideals.

In 1931 Henry Ford made my family and me a magnificent present. *He gave us one entire day.* It often happens, especially in America, that the richer a man is in money, the poorer he is in time. I know prominent men who literally have not one hour to spare; they cannot afford it. Well, Mr. and Mrs. Henry Ford sent word to us that they would set aside for our pleasure one whole day; and it happened to be perfect autumn weather.

About nine o'clock we all met in a suburb of Detroit at the house where Henry Ford was born. This modest structure of wood he has preserved and kept in perfect condition. Outside a dazzling white, inside spotless order. Kitchen, bedrooms, parlour, and workroom are exactly in the condition that they were in 1863. Stoves, lamps, candles, wallpaper, pictures, all correct. We saw the room where he was born; and the first lathe he used, the first watches which he had taken apart and repaired. From earliest childhood he loved to see the 'wheels go round.'

The difference between him and other boys who like to take machines to pieces is that he never destroyed or wasted anything. When he took a sick watch apart, and performed a major operation on its entrails, he restored it to perfect health.

His wife was born in an almost similar house in the vicinity, but they did not meet until they were in their 'teens. They became acquainted at a church social, were married, and lived happily forever after—a perfect union.

From the birthplace we motored to Dearborn, one of the most interesting small towns in the world. The change from the unpretentious farmhouse to the magnificent estate where Mr. Ford lives today, represents the change in fortune; although there has never been any change in his simplicity and unassuming manners. The great house is filled with treasures brought from Europe.

In the commodious garage, among the Lincolns, is the first car invented and driven by Henry Ford. In the second story of the building is an immense workshop, with scores of watches in various states of repair.

Then we went to the model village, where one lives in the past. As Mephistopheles, by a wave of magic, restored the aged Faust to his vigorous youth, so our American magician has enabled us to live and move and have our being in the environment of a hundred years ago.

We travelled in an old-fashioned high carriage, drawn by a pair of horses, driven by a coachman in appropriate costume, with two coach-dogs running close to the horses' hoofs. These dogs, who look as if they had swallowed huckleberry pies which were showing through, are as devoted to the horses as the horses are to them.

As we drove about the village, we saw a yoke of oxen drawing a load. A bell sounded in the old-fashioned schoolhouse; the children came out on the village green to play football; and Henry Ford and I played with them. We entered the beautiful Colonial church, with its severely lovely interior. The organist was playing, and we listened to the music, as he played Mr. Ford's favourite pieces. We visited the old-fashioned inn, which might have stood anywhere on the English countryside, with its quaint rooms and cheerful bar-parlour. The handbills and advertisements on the walls made us believe we were living in history.

The country store and post office are combined in one humble building. I love the smell of a general store; a combination of chewing tobacco, leather, spices, coffee, gingersnaps, sugar, candy, whips, hardware, and everything else.

In a small shanty, heated by an old-fashioned stove, we had our tintypes taken; and no one seemed to enjoy this more than the Ford family.

But the most remarkable feature of this remarkable village is the complete stone house, brought from England. Mr. Ford went to Gloucestershire to a little town called Chedworth, not far from the attractive town of Broadway, and selected an ancient Cotswold cottage. This he bought. The house was taken down, every stone numbered, brought across the ocean, transported to Dearborn, and erected exactly as it had stood for centuries in England, with original furniture of the period.

Here we were joined by the son, Edsel Ford, and his wife Eleanor; they have four children. Edsel and his wife are as natural and simple in appearance, manner, and conversation as if they were average members of a village community.

The food was cooked in a vast open fireplace in the kitchen (hanging of the crane, spit, and everything complete) and was served to us on a narrow refectory table centuries old.

If one enters the enormous museum at the great centre portal, the first thing to attract the eye is a memorial to

Henry Ford's most intimate friend, Thomas Edison. In an enclosure there is a large square of cement which, before it hardened, was autographed in huge written letters by Edison; so that his gigantic signature will remain there forever. Not only the signature of his hand, but the mark of his foot is preserved.

Just as the personality of a creative artist in literature or architecture is sometimes as interesting as his productive work, so the personality of Henry Ford appeals to me with more force than any of his numerous inventions.

I had had the pleasure of meeting and talking with him on many occasions. I had always been impressed by his placid demeanour; I had never seen him look worried or anxious, had never heard him raise his voice. He possessed the secret of equanimity.

But not until this day had I enjoyed the pleasure of spending a whole day with him and his family amid the things he had created and collected; so I had not realized the delightful boyish side of his disposition. All day long he was exuberant, ebullient, laughing and joking. His wife, his son, his daughter-in-law had the same infectious high spirits; so our whole party was in a gay and carefree mood.

It may be that Mr. Ford's habit of life contributes something to his cheerfulness. He is almost an ascetic in eating; he eats what he likes but he does not like to eat much. He never drinks or smokes. He is so thin that he seems almost transparent. No wonder he loves the old dances; he is as light on his feet as an adolescent.

In some manner, which I wish I understood (excellent digestion may have something to do with it), he can change the gear of his mind as easily as that of his car. At any moment, when he wishes to rest, he can turn off responsibilities or cares, shift the gear, and relax.

In the summer-time, he gets up at six o'clock or even earlier, goes out of doors and runs about a mile at a dogtrot. Then he is ready for work. I queried him: 'How about breakfast?' for, with me, breakfast is important. I am happy before breakfast because I am going to have it; I am happy during breakfast, because I enjoy it; I am happy after breakfast, because I feel its inspiration.

But Mr. Ford eats nothing till one o'clock. Having important things to consider, his mind is clearer and works with more precision if his stomach is empty.

His interests are in the future and in the past. As an inventor and as an executive, no one is ahead of him. He is always looking forward to see what is going to happen and is ready to meet coming conditions. Then of late years he has taken an increasing interest in the reconstruction of the past. His Wayside Inn at Sudbury, his village at Dearborn, his collections of antiques, his passion for old music and old-fashioned dancing illustrate this.

And indeed he himself is a combination of past and future; more so than any other person I know. He practises the old-fashioned virtues of purity, abstinence, regularity, honesty, industry, self-reliance; in business his methods are always a little ahead of everybody else.

He is an amazing combination of shrewd practical common sense with extreme idealism. I wish he might live five hundred years on this planet, for his life is a multitudinous blessing.

There is one more characteristic which not every one realizes—humour. In the famous days of the Peace Ship, one of its passengers returned to America and announced that he was through with the project because the company was made up of cranks and fools. A reporter called up Mr. Ford and said that the Reverend Doctor Blank had quit, because he said the company was made up of cranks and fools. 'Have you anything to say?'

Mr. Ford replied 'Apparently the situation is being improved by resignation.'

96

JOURNEY TO ATHENS

THE year 1932 was one of the happiest years in my happy life and made especially memorable because I saw for the first time two things I had always longed to see—Athens and a total eclipse of the sun.

On 19 February we sailed for Greece on the *Saturnia*. We had two reasons for taking this ship: one, that it sailed to Greece; the other, that we were informed it would stop at the Azores, Lisbon, Gibraltar, Cannes, Naples and give the passengers a fine opportunity to see these historic places.

Our first stop was Boston, which I had never before approached from the sea; I had had no idea of the picturesque beauty of the harbour. We were late in arriving, and very late in leaving.

On 25 February we reached the Azores, after dark, so we could see nothing. Some passengers who lived there left the ship, and a few got on board; we supposed we should wait till daylight and then have an opportunity to land. But the Captain said that was impossible; we thus moved on in the night. On 27 February we entered the Tagus and saw Lisbon after dark. The best scenery was in the sky. Over the city hung the three brightest stars in the universe, Venus and Jupiter and Sirius.

I had always wanted to see Lisbon, both for its own sake and because Henry Fielding is buried there, and I wished to do homage at his tomb. With his usual bad luck, he died there in 1754; if he could have hung on for one more year, he might have enjoyed a more exciting death in the earthquake. In Lisbon they still call it an earthquake—one does not have to remember to say 'fire.' The harbour is superb; an entire fleet of battleships could perform manoeuvres in the enclosure.

Many passengers were reading Lawton Mackall's witty and charming book, *Portugal for Two*. And we were all expecting to see the great city, and the little town of Belem, and beautiful Sintry by the light of day. It was not to be. We came like a thief in the night, with a cargo of two million dollars in gold, taken off the ship by Portuguese soldiers. We drove around the old city in the dark and saw the magnificent fifteenth century cathedral by *matchlight*.

The February night was clear and mild, and we walked about the streets; the cafés at midnight were crowded by men engaged in eager conversation, who apparently had no thought of sleep. Not a woman was to be seen in any of these spacious halls, and our ladies aroused considerable interest. The broad boulevards were also densely populated.

We finally went into a small shop with tables, something like an American drug store, and there we had some port wine and I smoked a Brazilian cigar, cheap and excellent. At the top of a steep, precipitous hill, which rose out of the midst of the town, we had a splendid view of the city with its illuminated streets. Lisbon seemed to me so beautiful and so interesting, that I wish we had been allowed to see it by day.

Our ship left sometime after midnight, and we were eager to see the straits of Gibraltar and the massive cliffs. But we arrived at Gibraltar after dark, and no one was allowed to land except those who were not to return. It was dark, it was foggy, it was rainy; but for about six seconds I saw a great hill or mountain on the African side, the only time I have seen Africa.

I had hoped to compare the Gibraltar cliff with its likeness in the Prudential Insurance Company's advertisement, but we saw nothing; a few days later, we had equally bad luck with Aetna's; so the only insurance advertisement we verified was the Travelers'.

At Cannes, our next stop, which we reached in the night, no one was allowed to land except those who intended to stay, and no visitors were permitted to come on board. Thus, an old friend of mine the scholar Robinson Smith, who had travelled from Nice to meet me there for a half-hour's conversation, had his journey for his pains. It was just as cold at Cannes as it had been in Boston. A lady who embarked there told me she had sat on a stove for six weeks in a vain endeavour to be warm.

Our next stop was at Naples. I have seen many pictures of the beautiful bay of Naples, but in my visits to Italy, I had never been south of Rome. We reached Naples about ten o'clock in the evening, and drove around the city in the night; our ship proceeded on its way about two in the morning.

At about eleven o'clock that morning, I was standing on deck looking at Stromboli and saying to myself that anyhow here was one object we had seen by daylight, when the deck steward came up, and said, 'You know, sir, Stromboli is much more beautiful if seen in the night.' I lay down in a deckchair and laughed helplessly; he does not yet know why.

On the early morning of Friday 4 March we looked out of our cabin window and there was Greece! Wild and sombre, romantic and mysterious, the austere mountains covered with snow. We landed at Patras, and the moment I stepped on shore, I knelt and kissed the ground.

Greek railways need a publicity agent. No one speaks well of them. When we were told it would take eight hours for our train to cover the 135 miles between Patras and

Athens, we were not exhilarated. But once started on that journey, I should not have cared if it had taken twenty hours. We came to Greece solely because of its literary associations; but if no book had ever been written there, it would be well worth a visit because of the splendour of the scenery.

From the windows of the train, the waters of the Corinthian Gulf, the grey-green olive trees, the dark green pines and cypresses, with the mighty barrier of snow-clad mountains, make an indelible impression. And the journey began and ended with Byron, the most potent foreign name in the country; he is adored by the Greeks. Close to Patras is Missolonghi, where he died; and near Athens is Sunium, with the pillar of the temple whereon he carved his name.

We went to the Acropolis with no teacher and no guide. The March air was suave; the intense blue of the sky was stainless. We *lived* in the Parthenon, in the Erechtheum, in the Wingless Victory. These buildings were not erected for architects, any more than Euripides wrote for professors; they were for us; common people who love beauty. They were as perfect in grace as in sublimity. Their massivities were as free from vulgarity as their tenuities. The Parthenon is overwhelming in its solid and severe austerity, in its colossal grandeur; while the tiny Niké and the Caryatides on the Erechtheum are as lovely as a perfect miniature. Those Greek architects played with stone as Beethoven played with an orchestra; they could make stone look as immovable as the eternal cliffs and as fluid as running water. The only thing they could not do was to be pretentious or insincere or ugly.

It is well to look at the buildings on the Acropolis without any verbal accompaniment; as it is well to listen to music without trying to explain what it means. Let Beauty have her chance—there is a whole education in that. As the poet Flecker said, 'The business of poetry (or art) is not to save men's souls, but to make them worth saving.'

We arrived in Athens on a Friday. On the next day, thanks to my friend Professor Samuel Bassett of the American school, I had the privilege of seeing and hearing the foremost Greek citizen of the twentieth century, Veniselos. And it was a great occasion, one of the most important in many years. Parliament convened at half-past four. The Royalists, few in number, sat at the extreme right, the Socialists and Communists at the left, and the Liberal majority in the centre. In front of the front row, the only persons to have desks, sat the Cabinet with Veniselos the Prime Minister, and the President of the Council. The Presiding Officer rang a bell; the minutes of the last meeting were read; a few speeches were made by various members during which reading, writing, and general conversation went on freely. But the moment Veniselos was called to the Tribune, and began his address, there was silence.

For many days it had been understood that the Premier would on this occasion make a general statement of the financial policy of the Government, and deliver an ultimatum. I could feel the tense interest, the suppressed excitement, as he began to speak. He had a natural, unaffected dignity and sincerity that should and did impress every one. The whiteness of his beard was accentuated by a black skullcap, which, when the heat of the room became almost unbearable, he would remove to wipe his brow, head, and neck. As Casca remarked, his speech was all Greek to me; but I was filled with admiration for his manner. Rhetorical flourishes, declamatory gestures, shoutings, tricks of oratory, were absent. He made this highly important address to a crowded Parliament and galleries as if he were speaking to a board of bank directors. His tones were quiet, matter-of-fact, the essence of plain, practical common sense. I did not wonder at his commanding influence.

That there is a yellow press in Greece and that many were afraid of it would appear from a speech made by Veniselos in the Senate.

> Everybody here is in terror of the press; for the immunity of the press, which we are trying to remedy by a law recently voted, makes everybody shudder at the thought that a newspaper may penetrate into private and family affairs, and display in publicity not dirty linen but clean linen made dirty. From the most obscure citizen up to a member of Parliament, up to a minister, up to a party leader, everybody is afraid of the newspaper. For my part, I do not pretend to be better than others. I certainly have my faults, but they are compensated for by one characteristic; I am one of those rare Greek politicians who have never been afraid of the press.

In addition to the American, British, and other schools of classical studies at Athens, there is the admirable institution known as Athens College, not far outside the city limits, where several hundred Greek youths have a liberal education under the direction of Homer W. Davis, assisted by an able American faculty. With the exception of one course given in Greek, the curriculum is in English and I have the best of reasons for believing that our language is efficiently taught. The students have tremendous enthusiasm for the study of the English language and literature. I gave a lecture there to three or four hundred Greek boys. They seemed to understand everything I said and were quick in seizing every point. Before the lecture they sang the school song in English, written by Mr. Darbishire, one of the teachers; after the lecture they sang *My Country, 'tis of Thee* followed by the Greek national anthem in their native tongue. Then came a graceful compliment to Yale, with an episode in Yale's history new to me. One of the teachers had discovered it. President Davis, in a felicitous speech gave the facts; then one of the Greek students, in excellent English, handed me a large volume, *Modern Greek-English Dictionary*, by A. Kyriakides, inscribed

> The students of Athens College present this Dictionary to the students of Yale University in grateful recognition of the aid given to the cause of Greek independence by students of Yale in 1823.

And here are the accompanying documents:

(FROM THE *National Gazette* [PHILADELPHIA] 18 DECEMBER 1823)

I

YALE COLLEGE
DEC. 13, 1823

SIR:

We enclose the sum of $800 collected in the College for the use of the Greeks. We request you to receive it, and forward it, with other collections for this purpose, or appropriate it, in such other way as will most benefit the cause. We subjoin the Resolutions adopted at our meeting, and with the most ardent wishes for your success in this work of national benevolence, have the honor to be, Sir, your most obed't servants.

In behalf of the Committee
To Wm. Bayard,
Chairman of the Greek Com. H.Y.

II

NEW HAVEN COMMITTEE
18 DEC. 1823

A meeting of the citizens of N.H. was held on the 17 inst. to concert measures to aid the Greeks. Noah Webster was called to the Chair, and Charles H. Pond, appointed Secretary. A committee consisting of the following gentlemen was appointed to prepare resolutions to be presented at a future meeting:

Noah Webster
David Daggett
David C. DeForest
Charles Dennison
Chauncey A. Goodrich
Charles H. Pond
Roger S. Baldwin.

III

(FROM THE *American Daily Advertiser* [PHILADELPHIA], 26 DEC. 1823)
The editor of the *Connecticut Mirror*, speaking of the patriotic donation to the Greeks from the students at Yale College, says: 'We hope that when the Greeks obtain their freedom, and have a chance to reward their benefactors they will send out, to show their gratitude, an explanation of certain hard words and dubious expressions, which are now and then to be found in Lucian's Dialogues and Demosthenes' Orations, with a glossary of expletives, heteroclites, etc. which if they should arrive in middle college, of a hot afternoon, just before the bell rings for recitation, would to many be peculiarly acceptable.'

And here they are, in this Dictionary, which I took back to Yale. No gift could have pleased me more than this tribute to the University which I had the honour to represent.

It is interesting to watch the excavations in Athens. At the Agora, under the direction of Mr. and Mrs. Shear, we saw an amphora in perfect condition taken out of the ground where it had lain since 1000 B.C. They have made many valuable and exciting discoveries.

On the Acropolis we had the good fortune to meet the veteran savant Professor Belanos, who is in charge of the restoration of the Parthenon. He took us over the vast structure, explaining the new work.

Most fortunately for us, among our travelling companions on the ship were Professor and Mrs. Edward Capps of Princeton. More than forty years ago Mr. Capps and I were graduate students at Yale. For many years he has been one of the foremost classical scholars in America; and his services in connexion with the Loeb Classical Library—an undertaking of immense and permanent value, so dear to the heart of that great London publisher, William Heinemann—have been important. But it was not until we entered Athens together that I realized how great was his reputation among native Athenians and the resident foreign scholars. Their respect for his learning is equalled by their affection for the man.

We were invited to a state dinner by Mr. and Mrs. Veniselos for Wednesday evening, 15 March. My wife was sick in bed. I woke up Monday morning with a high fever and a bad case of tonsillitis. I sent for Doctor Dorando, an admirable Greek physician who speaks English. I told him he must cure us both in 48 hours, because we were going to the dinner on Wednesday night. He shook his head gravely and said he would do his best. He gave me sixteen grains of quinine and on Tuesday the following day, sixteen more. On Wednesday night, though rather shaky, we went to the state dinner in the Veniselos mansion at nine o'clock. The guests of honour were Professor and Mrs. Capps, and others were Professor and Mrs. Carpenter, Mr. and Mrs. Adossides, Professor and Mrs. Davis, the Police Commissioner, and some foreign diplomats.

Although Mr. Veniselos had had an exhausting day with constant committee meetings and a full dress debate in Parliament, he gave no sign of it; he was full of gaiety and made every one feel at ease. My wife sat on his left and as he spoke English only with difficulty, they conversed in French. She asked him about the political situation in Greece, which relieved her from the necessity of saying anything at all. I sat on the left of Mrs. Veniselos, who speaks English fluently. She was in gay spirits and we had a good time discussing American and English detective stories, her favourite reading. A few years later, when she was recovering from several gunshot wounds meant for her husband, we sent her many of these thrillers, which she devoured with delight.

Suddenly there was a pause in the dinner-talk, one of those pauses supposed to occur every twenty minutes on such occasions. I took advantage of it and addressed the

Prime Minister. I told him that Yale University was the only American university that had, and had had for fifty years, a Greek *yell*. I had to explain what was meant by a yell; even then he did not see why we yelled, and I told him I could not explain it myself, but we yelled. This yell, I told him, was shouted in unison at all football games; and as it came from the *Frogs* of Aristophanes, one of the classics of his native land, I thought he ought to hear it, if only from patriotic motives. I therefore gave the Greek yell of Yale:

Brekekekex! koax! koax!

Brekekekex! koax! koax!

O, wop! O, wop!

Parabolou!

YALE!

He and the others were so pleased that I suggested we all shout it together. This was done several times by the entire company and with great enthusiasm.

41 AVENUE DE KIFISSIA

ATHENES

July 2nd 33

MY DEAR PROFESSOR PHELPS,

Thank you for your kind sympathetic cable & for the books you are so kind as to send me. I hope I will receive them before my departure on July 8th. We sail for Paris (22 rue Beaujon).

I am happy to say that I have entirely recovered from my bullet wounds & am feeling very well & fit. Fortunately these were not in any vital part.

Mr. Veniselos is today contesting the election of Salonika & writes to say that never in his whole political life has such a wonderful reception been awarded him.

Thank God his "charmed" life has been saved. Please remember me to Mrs. Phelps & with kindest regards, Believe me,

Yours v sincerely

HELENA VENISELOS

Several attempts had been made during his long career to assassinate Veniselos; on this latest occasion, he and his wife were in an automobile, when a number of shots were fired at him. None hit him, but three or four wounded his wife.

HALEPA, CANEA, CRETE
8th January 35

MY DEAR PROFESSOR PHELPS,

With the advent of the New Year let me wish you & Mrs. Phelps every possible happiness & above all health. I have received a few days ago the two books you were so kind as to send me & for which please accept my thanks. It is indeed kind of you to remember me & I am deeply touched by your kind thought.

Mr. Veniselos is, I am happy to say, in the best of health & spirits, and joins me in sending you & Mrs. Phelps our warmest greetings.

Yours v sincerely,

HELENA VENISELOS

The books alluded to in these letters were English and American detective novels.

On Friday 18 March I attended the regular weekly luncheon of the Rotary Club. The meetings of Rotary are unlike those to which I am accustomed in America. At home luncheon is usually served promptly at quarter past twelve; the speaker of the day talks from one to half-past one, when the meeting is over.

There are about forty-five members of the Athenian Rotary Club; they meet every Friday at the Petit Palais; the only other American present on this occasion was Professor Alexis of the University of Nebraska. He and I arrived about noon; the members dropped in casually, as if time were of no importance, and finally we sat down about half-past one, and the meeting lasted until half-past four. It was necessary to converse in French, for Greece is one of the few countries in the world where French, and not English, is the second language. If one enters Athenian society or wishes to meet Athenians in business, French is necessary. A daily paper is printed in French; and there are French movies.

But the thing that impressed me about this Rotary Club was that nearly every resident member was a distinguished scholar. I was presented to ten or eleven men in succession, and every one was a Professor. Finally, when I met a rotund, jolly-looking individual, I asked 'Are you also a Professor?' 'No, thank God, I am a wholesale wine merchant.'

Finally, it was time for the address of the day, delivered by a Rotary member. He was the Head of the School of Architecture, and the designer of the magnificent tomb of the Unknown Soldier, unveiled while we were in Athens. His address was in Greek, and appeared to be extremely technical. But the moment he had finished, at least a dozen members asked him questions in turn, and some of them seemed to be heckling him. The discussion was animated.

That was the most highbrow Rotary Club meeting I have ever attended.

Some weeks later I attended the Rotary Club in Florence, which was much like an American meeting. The address was by Sig. Salvini, a charming gentleman, son of the great Tommaso Salvini. I told him I had heard his father play Othello, on his last tour of the United States in 1889. Also that several times I had heard his brother as Romeo in the company headed by Margaret Mather. 'Ah, my brother! I so seldom hear about him now. He died many years ago, when he was still very young.'

Looking out of our hotel window in Athens one morning, I saw theatre advertisements on various posts.

AGAMEMNON BY AESCHYLUS

Inasmuch as that play was written and played at Athens in the fifth century before Christ, it was exciting to see such a playbill.

On Sunday, 20 March, the National Theatre opened with *Agamemnon*; it was played of course in modern Greek, but to hear it in the city of its birth was thrilling. The acting was very fine; especially that of the two women, who played Clytemnestra and Cassandra.

It is not merely in age that Athens is venerable; it is because in the fifth century before Christ, about the year 450, the citizens of Athens—that is to say, the voting population—reached a higher level of intellectual excellence than those of any other city before or since. Those citizens more than two thousand years ago breathed a purer and a nobler air; they knew a spiritual exaltation compared to which our finest American cities of the twentieth century are as a primary school to a university.

As Goethe has said, we should praise individuals who have illuminated the world and also praise the communities that produced such men and gave to them not only the necessary stimulation, but the indispensable appreciative audience. In that far-away century in Athens there was an intellectual ferment, a passion for the finest works of art; so that the average Athenian citizen was as competent a critic of drama, architecture, sculpture, as the average American citizen is of professional baseball.

Athens *today* is not superior in culture to New York; quite the contrary. New Yorkers have many theatres of high excellence, one of the finest opera companies in the world (even if it must rely mainly on foreign singers), innumerable opportunities to hear symphony orchestras, and great museums of art. It is the Athens of 438 B.C., rather than the Athens of 1938 A.D., which can teach us. But it is worth remembering that Athens today, in the throes of a financial crisis and with the country facing bankruptcy, saw fit, after a complete renovation, to reopen the National Theatre, subsidized by the government, and reopened with the *Agamemnon* of Aeschylus.

As I looked around on gatherings of modern Athenians, I was impressed by the triumph of the British face. Among priests, old men, and country farmers, the full beard is still in evidence; but nearly all the Athenians under fifty are smooth-shaven, and many wear the single eye-glass. The ancient Greek profile so familiar in pictures and copies of statues and coins, with the straight line from the tip of the forehead to the tip of the nose, has almost disappeared; there are more such profiles among American undergraduates than will be seen in Athens.

Thirty years ago, in our boarding-house in Munich, was a young Greek who was studying law; his name was Pericles Karapanos. I remembered him and his name perfectly; and I gave him a tremendous surprise by entering his busy law office one day. He is a very prominent man now, one of the leading lawyers in Greece, a Senator and public speaker, universally loved.

I wondered whether my digestion would last, during our stay. Owing to the fact that most of the year it is warm, Athenians have the habit of dining very late, and having two short sleeps like the old-fashioned deep-water sailor. Many go to bed at two or three in the morning, get up at seven, and go to bed again at two in the afternoon. Even in the cooler season, it is impossible to get dinner at the hotel before half-past eight, and the dining room is not fully occupied until after nine. Hundreds of men sit up nearly all night and talk.

Street life is even more animated than in Paris. When we remember that in most cities in America the sidewalks are being pared down to give more space for the parking of automobiles, it is interesting to see what an enormous place in social life here is filled by the sidewalk. Whether on the big boulevards or in the mean and narrow streets of the old town, tables and chairs are set out on the sidewalk, with many men conversing.

The New Testament, when it described the Athenians as being ever eager to see or discuss something new, might have been describing the Athenians of today. Many newspapers are hawked on the streets morning and afternoon; these are eagerly bought and read for the Greeks are a nation of newspaper readers. One of my friends asked the soldiers why, in their hours of liberty, they did not play football and other games.

'Oh,' was the reply, 'there is no time for that. Our soldiers would much rather spend their free hours in conversation. There is so much to talk about.'

And indeed they need no other athletic exercise; for their conversation is gymnastic; every part of the body is employed.

On 21 March we motored to Marathon, coming out from the olive trees toward the plain and the sea. I climbed to the top of the mound and shouted the two words spoken by the first Marathon runner, Pheidippides.

Χαίρετε, νικῶμεν!
Rejoice, we conquer!

On 24 March, in company with Professor Bassett, we took an early morning train on our way to Delphi. In Athens it was like a heavenly day in summer; when we reached Delphi, in the afternoon, it was like mid-winter, deep snow everywhere and bitter cold. The train went near the lake at Marathon, and we had a glorious view in the distance of a marvellous snowy mountain in Euboea. We saw Aulis and Thebes, and the battlefields of Epaminondas. Then the country became hilly, with thousands of sheep and millions of olive trees. The olive trees seemed to flow into every valley and every depression among hills. At Bralo, the last railway station, we engaged a motor-car and drove up the mountain through snow and along the edge of mighty precipices. We reached Delphi at half-past four; it was snowing hard. The inn was primitive; but we were glad of its shelter, and made no attempt to see Delphi until the next morning.

We rose early; the ground was covered with snow and the sky overcast. The scenery is sublime; and I do not wonder that the Greeks went there to receive messages from the Gods. We saw the Shining Rocks, the Castalian Spring (with a large cigarette advertisement), and the lovely little Doric Temple put up by the Athenians after the Battle of Marathon. And we saw the theatre.

Then I consulted the Oracle and was informed that it was safe to return by the automobile. It was fortunate that I had taken the trouble to do this; for our chauffeur flatly refused to make the return journey, saying we must wait for the snow to melt. But when I told him that I had consulted the Oracle, and got not only permission but a definite command to set off as soon as possible, he made no further objection.

After we had started, I did not wonder at his reluctance. The road along the edge of the terrible precipice was hub-deep in snow; and the wild, desolate grandeur of the scene added to our feeling of loneliness and helplessness. But even in the snow, we met flocks of sheep conducted by fierce-looking dogs; and I saw one big brilliant woodpecker, something like the American pileated woodpecker.

It was a relief to reach level ground, where we caught the Orient express from Paris; and long before our arrival, the snow changed into rain and we saw green fields.

That day in Athens had been a four-fold holiday—Lady Day, Good Friday, Independence Day, and the unveiling of the tomb of the Unknown Soldier. The streets were filled with parades.

Two days later, Easter Day, we sailed from Athens on the cruise of the Hellenic Society from London. There were about 250 people on board, all English except about ten Americans. The ship sailed from Piraeus at eight in the evening, and we saw the Acropolis illumined by floodlight.

Lord and Lady Conway were on the boat and made us feel as if we were intimate friends; and indeed we became so. Lady Conway was an American and after we had reached England, we spent a day at their house—Allington Castle in Kent, an interesting place, part Roman, with magnificent gardens. Lord Conway was a great mountain-climber. He had written many books on mountain climbing in Asia, Europe, and South America; and having seen the most remote wonders of the earth, in 1936 he published his book describing his adventures in the spiritual world—*A Pilgrim's Quest for the Divine*, a beautiful mystical work.

Another passenger was the distinguished historian, H.A.L.Fisher, Warden of New College, Oxford. There were many dons from Oxford and Cambridge, with their families. The whole expedition was composed of members of the Hellenic Society, under the direction of Sir Henry Lunn. Four voyages are made in the Mediterranean every year. I do not see how any expedition could be more admirably managed than this. It was cheap, yet the passengers had every comfort. At our frequent landings, motor-cars or special trains were invariably ready and never crowded; everything was provided, including tips. Lectures were given on board the ship twice a day and Canon Wigram was the scholarly guide on shore.

We sailed to Constantinople, spending two days there, sleeping on the ship. The American Ambassador, Mr. Grew, had just left for his new post at Paris, but hearing that we were coming, had placed the Embassy motor-car at our disposal. General Charles H.Sherrill, the new Ambassador, and an old Yale college-mate, had not arrived.

On Thursday 31 March, a lifelong dream was realized. We stood on the ringing plains of windy Troy. When I was a boy at the Hartford High School, our teacher Dr. Martin, said 'Dr. Schliemann has been digging there,' which led me to read the book *Troja*.

This was the first time we had ever been in Asia. The ship stopped at Chanak. It was bitterly cold, with an icy wind. Drawn up close to the dock were many battered old Ford cars; their drivers had been told they must not race. But their Oriental passion for competition was soon aroused, and each driver had the fierce light of battle in his eyes. It was about twenty-five miles to Troy, and the road was horrible, which made the race more exciting. Only three of our cars were upset, and miraculously there were no injuries.

The thing that impressed me most at Troy was the *wind*—windy Troy. It blew as steadily as the trades, never in gusts, but just the steady rushing of a mighty wind, as it no doubt blew in the sweaty face of Hector, as he ran from Achilles. Next to the impression made by the wind, was the topography of the Trojan plain. Troy itself was simply a mound; and I suppose the city, even in the days of Priam, was not so large as the Grand Central Station in New York. But there lay the unchanged plain, with the rivers Scamander and Simois. The sea was near by, with snowy mountains in the distance.

The excavations showed nine different cities, from the bronze age to the Roman, but not very clearly. Remains of walls and mounds and loose stones.

On the way down the Hellespont, we passed Gallipoli; all the passengers stood at attention with uncovered heads; yet the terrible losses at that place have never affected me as deeply as the death of Hector, or as the Athenian expedition to Syracuse.

In the Trojan War I am pro-Troy; in the Peloponnesian War I am pro-Athens; both times on the losing side.

The weather changed with the calendar; that last day of

March at Troy was like mid-winter. The next day, the first of April, we landed on Delos. It was clear, windless, mid-summer. Then we sailed to Crete, where they had a civilization before Homer. With the exception of Egypt and Mesopotamia, I suppose it was the oldest civilization in the world. The houses had conveniences not always found elsewhere today; hot and cold water laid on, bathrooms, and water-closets.

One of the high spots of the trip was Mycenae, and the house of Agamemnon, made even more vivid for me by the play I had seen in Athens. At Olympia it was intensely hot, and so dusty that I wondered if the contestants in the games could have been clearly discerned by the spectators.

Up along the Dalmatian coast we sailed, stopping at Ragusa, now called Dubrovnik. Sending a telegram in the post office there, I found I was one cent short; when a voice behind me said with a laugh, 'I'll lend you the cent.' It was Philip Guedalla, and when I met him again at a luncheon in London in 1935 I reminded him I had borrowed a cent from him three years before, and he said I was to remember the accumulated interest.

We reached Venice on a heavenly morning in April. At Asolo, which we had last visited 28 years before, we saw the street now named Via Roberto Browning and the grave of Eleonora Duse. She was buried close to the grave of Browning's son, but his coffin had been removed— nothing but the cavity remained. At that moment a funeral came to the place, the catafalque followed by many men on foot. After the ceremony was over, I asked Monsignor what had become of the body of Browning's son; and he said it had been moved to Florence. But I think it was really taken to Rome.

97

THE POPE

On 16 April 1932 we had an audience with the Pope. The audience was for one o'clock, and a large crowd, half of whom were Americans, assembled at the appointed hour, but the Pope kept us waiting until half-past two. I didn't understand this at the time, but when I read in William Teeling's *Life of Pope Pius XI* that he always finished what he was doing, no matter who might be waiting for him, I understood. At last the Pope appeared, clad in white, looking at us benevolently through his spectacles, and it was interesting to think that this same man, years before, had made first ascents in the Alps and several times had spent an entire night on their summits. He blessed us and walked around the room, offering us his ring finger to kiss as we knelt. He looked stoutish, healthy, and rugged. But the ceremony was one which was so often enforced upon him that both his actions and voice were mechanical.

98

MUNICH IN 1932

EARLIER in this book I have spoken of my love for Munich and its people, where we spent seven months in 1904, four months in 1911–12, and which always seems like home. In Paris I say with the Psalmist, 'By the rivers of Babylon I sit down and weep when I remember Zion.' But I am never homesick in Munich.

In the Spring of 1932 I met there my old University friends, Professor Schick (now Emeritus), Jules Simon, Hanns Oertel, formerly my colleague at Yale, and Professor Max Förster, my colleague to be; in addition to these and other friends and our beloved 'Eltern' at the Pension Nordland, there were two of my younger Yale colleagues in the English Department, Professors Robert D. French and Rudolph Willard. The University formally began its semester on a May morning; but as Professor Max Förster informed me, 'the informal opening of the university will take place at the Hofbräu this evening.'

He and Willard and I went down a narrow, dark street, left our hats and coats in a cloak-room, opened a door; we were in a vast room where about eight hundred men and women were seated at long tables, drinking the fresh beer of spring. In the gallery a band was playing, and the huge crowd were singing student songs. There was good fellowship—but no drunkenness, no disorder. Peasants, workers, students, servants, scholars, professors, business men, political magnates, officials, musicians mingled together with freedom. Such a thing as an 'introduction' to a neighbour would have been absurd. Although we had never seen our tablemates before, in three minutes we were old friends.

A strange thing happened. Four university students came up to the German professor with me, and he gave them three marks—seventy-five cents. They overwhelmed him with grateful appreciation. They were young gentlemen, well-dressed, with excellent manners.

I asked: 'Is it possible that you can tip students? In America a professor will sometimes help a poor student, but it has to be done secretly.'

'Ah,' the professor replied, 'most of these boys are desperately poor. They have no spending money whatever. They cannot even buy a glass of beer.'

'Well,' I asked, 'is it all right for me to contribute a little?' For at that moment four or five other students came up.

He said, 'Call it a donation to their society, and it is all right.' So I handed out three marks to the newcomers.

They immediately cheered lustily for America and for the 'American professor.' I meditated on the strange fact that only a few years ago we were at war with these people, for wherever I had gone in Munich I had found the most popular of all visitors were the Americans. When it was time to go, a group of students formed a bodyguard, and we walked clear through the hall to the exit, the students singing and cheering, while the crowds through which we passed raised their beer mugs.

While we were sitting there, I thought how impossible such a scene would be in England; there no one would speak to anyone else unless he knew him, and then hardly above a whisper. But my German professor said it would be equally impossible in North Germany. It was only in Munich that such informality reigned, that it was perfectly understood, and taken for granted.

I thought too how fortunate it was that such friendliness could exist. Several thousand students come to a great university for the first time, many of them lonely and homesick; an evening like this starts off the semester, and they have friends.

And in spite of the tremendous noise made by the band, the singing, the shouting, cheering, and laughing, there was not a single unpleasant sight.

I remarked to a student on the general good-fellowship of the assemblage. He replied, 'Munich is simply one whole family.'

It seemed to me (and this is my contributory thought to disarmament and world peace) that it would be a good idea to abandon Geneva as a meeting-place and have all sessions of international delegates in the Hofbräu Haus at Munich. (Munich was chosen in 1938.) Frenchmen, Germans, Italians, British, Russians, Japanese, Chinese, Americans all would lose their animosities after associating two or three evenings in this genial atmosphere.

The English department of the university asked me to give a lecture there on English Romanticism of the eighteenth century. There is such keen interest in English literature and the English language among the students that the regular lecture-room proved inadequate and we had to move to the largest hall in the building. I spoke slowly, and as distinctly as possible, and most of the students seemed to understand.

In spite of the general financial distress, the Germans in Munich are *theatre-minded*; they know that operas and plays are not luxuries, but necessities; thus at every performance I attended—and during two weeks I went to twelve—the house appeared to be sold out. But the Germans do not waste money on taxicabs; when the big audiences flowed out of the theatres at the close, there would be only three taxis waiting, and I never had any trouble in getting one.

The foremost living writer in Germany, Gerhart Hauptmann, began his career with a naturalistic play *Before Sunrise* (*Vor Sonnenaufgang*) which attracted the attention of the police. In 1932 he wrote *Before Sunset* (*Vor Sonnenuntergang*), a play dealing with a love affair between a widower of seventy and a young girl, with a naturally tragic conclusion. This was well given at the Playhouse. I also saw there a translation of St. John Ervine's clever comedy, *The First Mrs. Fraser*, which is called *Die Erste Mrs. Selby*. It was greeted with tremendous enthusiasm. I talked with the leading young actress of the company and she said to appear in several different plays every week while rehearsing others was exhausting; but when I told her that in New York every new play was expected to run for months with the actors learning nothing else, she said, 'But how destructive that must be for their art!'

99

AN AMERICAN IN PARIS

AN American woman in Paris is like a duck in water; it is her natural element. It takes about two seconds for the city by the Seine to hypnotize her. She loves it in her youth, she revisits it in maturity, she is homesick for it in her old age.

American women, who are as expert in shopping as Oriental rug-dealers, and whose audacity in entering expensive shops makes men breathless, are often called extravagant. But it should be remembered that they can make a few dollars last out a whole afternoon of visits to various shops; and that, unlike men, they never buy anything of which they do not approve. Any mediocre clerk can persuade a man that shoes fit him when he knows they do not; he buys in haste and repents at leisure.

If men were not so uncomfortable in shops, it would pay them to see the expression on the face of a Parisian salesman when he begins to show goods to some American woman whom he recognizes as a foe worthy of his steel. He is an expert seller and she is an expert buyer; it is a duel worth watching; and the amount eventually paid by the American husband or father should be regarded as the price he has paid for a ringside seat.

No man can feel toward Paris as a woman does; for Paris is itself a woman. Many men love it, but only women understand it. Paris is the most beautiful city I have ever seen; but I never feel at home there, though I have spent many months within its fair domain. I never fully analysed my sensations until an American scholar expressed them for me—'In Paris I feel as if I were surrounded by polite foes.' The French have a terrific family instinct; every housewife and mother seems to be on guard. If you speak to a woman on some proposition that may concern her purse, her home, or her offspring, her face assumes the expression of an American business man when asked for a loan.

Paris is the most beautiful city in the world; but it should not be forgotten that Paris is northern. The epithet 'sunny France' does not apply to Paris, where the climate is about the same as that of London; very, very bad. The clouds return after the rain. Anatole France in his entertaining novel, *The Crime of Sylvestre Bonnard*, describing his heroine's eyes, says, 'her eyes were grey; the grey of the Paris sky.' A typical day in Paris has a low-hung, impenetrable sky, slimy pavements, and a thin drizzle in the air.

Yet, while I do not think that in heaven I shall ever be homesick for Paris, it is, in addition to being beautiful, somewhat like the New Jerusalem:

> And the nations of them which are saved shall walk in the light of it; and the kings of the earth do bring their glory and honour into it.
>
> And the gates of it shall not be shut at all by day; for there shall be no night there.
>
> And they shall bring the glory and honour of the nations into it.

Paris draws distinguished men from every corner of France; and writers and painters from every country.

Furthermore, these poets and dramatists and novelists and sculptors and painters are national heroes; even small boys look upon them with awe. Streets and avenues and squares bear the names of great writers; and statues—not to warriors, but to novelists and sculptors—form a large portion of the stationary population.

Although France is in its feelings more self-sufficient than any other nation (one meets few Frenchmen outside of France), she is becoming more and more hospitable to foreign works of art.

If the national genius of England is represented by the English Bible and by Shakespeare, the national genius of France is represented by Racine and Voltaire. Religious ideals and romantic poetry for one; classic severity and a mocking smile for the other. Until Voltaire, French critics regarded Shakespeare as a barbarian; while the early performances of Wagner and of their own Victor Hugo turned into free fights.

Well, Shakespeare is coming into his own, even in Paris. In 1932 he was the most popular playwright in the French capital. One of the national theatres, the *Odéon*, had to give a vast number of performances of *King Lear* to satisfy the demand; and the other, the *Comédie Française*, repeated *Hamlet* over and over again, selling out the house every time. When I remember that an excellent performance of *Hamlet* had failed in New York the previous season, it did me good to sit in a French theatre and hear Shakespeare's masterpiece in French played to a house jammed to the last inch of space, and greeted with enthusiasm.

Some French writers think the passion for outdoor sport has been destructive to the French intellect; that it has killed the theatre, injured the book trade, and turned French boys and girls into healthy animals. However this may be, there is no doubt the British idea of sport has conquered young France; and a good thing it is for their health and presumably for their morals. The boys are playing football, tennis, golf; the expert boxer is a god; the girls have gone in or 'all out,' as the English say, for tennis. Sport has become a national passion, and the most acceptable present you can give to a French boy or girl is a tennis racket. The effect of sport is so far-reaching and for the most part so excellent that we should rejoice. It means health, vigour, courage, respect for an opponent, self-reliance, ability to take victory without conceit and defeat without excuse, good fellowship, and many other fine qualities.

One of the most spectacular sights in Paris is a funeral. Two hundred years ago Jonathan Swift said with his accustomed acidity, that the happiest looking people in the world are those who are attending a funeral. After one has recovered from the shock of this statement, and given it due reflexion, one will find in it some truth. The 'guests' are going to the cemetery, but they are coming back. I suppose it is for the same reason that people at funerals eat so tremendously; subconsciously they wish to stay alive. The Americans, most luxurious people in the world, make even a funeral comfortable; going and coming in motor cars. But the French, however they may actually feel, look at a funeral as they ought to look—solemn; because they follow the hearse *through the streets on foot.* I happened to be on a walk one day on the Boulevard Montparnasse when I heard funeral band music. I waited. The procession came along and I walked with it. It was the funeral of a general; the catafalque was spectacular and was followed by a long line of men and women. A military band in front of the hearse played in succession the three great funeral marches—Chopin's, Beethoven's, and Wagner's.

There is another custom in French funerals that might well be imitated elsewhere. Whenever a funeral procession passes, no matter how meagre or humble, every passer-by takes off his hat. I asked a Frenchman if this custom had a religious origin. 'Oh, no,' he replied, 'we are simply saying goodbye.'

One of the advantages of being in Paris is that we are near the finest works of architecture—the Gothic cathedrals of northern France. No buildings in the world are so beautiful as the cathedrals of Chartres, Mont Saint Michel, Rouen, Amiens, Reims, Laon, Bourges, Le Mans, Notre Dame of Paris. It is impossible to enter the cathedral of Chartres and be just the same person afterwards. The population of the world may be divided into two classes—those who have seen Chartres and those who have not.

The most characteristic quality of Parisian art and of Parisian people is grace. They hate ugliness and they hate awkwardness. French gardens, French meals, French people are graceful. They serve food in a dainty and attractive way. They wear their clothes as if they were a part of their personality. Books that are immoral are not vulgar; their plays have the same characteristic.

It is amusing to see how the Parisian will not admit that anything he manages is ugly. A woman in Paris who kept a boarding-house was showing me rooms. We came to one so small that I would not use it for a dog-kennel. I said it was impossibly small. She said, ' It is *mignonne, très mignonne*!'

PIRANDELLO, BERNSTEIN, DAUDET

In 1932 the famous Italian dramatist Luigi Pirandello was living in Paris in a pleasant flat on the top floor of a building near the Arch of Triumph. But as revealing either the narrow limits of fame or the suspicious nature of French females, when I reached the penultimate height, rang and asked the trim housemaid if M.Pirandello lived there, I received an emphatic negative '*Mais non.*' Nobody can say 'no' quite so negatively as a French woman. It means not only 'no,' it means 'get out of here as soon as possible, I don't know who you are and don't want to know, there is nothing in this house that concerns you, you mind your business and I'll mind mine;' all that is expressed in the word *non* and yet it was not spoken rudely or vulgarly; merely decisively. Such an attitude, instead of making me angry or embarrassed, amuses me. I asked if M.Pirandello lived on another floor of the same building; she did not know; she had never heard of him. I walked a few steps up to the next floor, rang, and M.Pirandello himself came to the door.

A short, solid, healthy-looking man, with grey hair and goatee. Very kind he was and cordial. Although he had on his desk the English translation of one of his books (American edition), he apparently did not speak English; we carried on in the language of the country where we were. Frenchmen say he speaks French with a decided accent; he certainly spoke it well enough for me. I understand French more easily when it is spoken by a foreigner than by a native.

I expressed my delight in the performance of *As You Desire Me* on the New York stage; and of my good fortune in seeing *Henry IV* at the Little Theatre in New Haven, directed by Jack Crawford. I asked him if it were not true that the key to the 'mistaken identity' in so many of his plays lies in what we *believe* rather than in what may be called fact. If the husband in *As You Desire Me* had gladly and confidently embraced his returning wife, instead of seeking proofs of her identity, she then *would have been* his wife. 'Most certainly! all my plays deal with spiritual realities; the reality in the mind is more real than reality in fact.'

I asked him which he preferred—the writing of novels or plays. He had no doubt about this; plays were nearer his heart.

His personality revealed quiet dignity, simplicity, sincerity.

The next afternoon I had a delightful conversation with Henry Bernstein, the most successful of living French playwrights. His house, filled with magnificent paintings and other works of art, was temporarily closed; and he was staying in a hotel. Mr. Bernstein is a tall and powerful man, built like a good Number Five in a University crew; his height seemed accentuated by a long dressing-gown. He has vitality, is cordial, and speaks with vivacity. He apologized for his English; unnecessarily, for he spoke it with fluency. He loves America and the Americans, and believed that our financial depression was only temporary. 'The Americans are too great and resourceful a people to stay down.' He had an original theory to account for part of our troubles. 'You make things altogether too well; your machines are made with such skill and such excellent material they don't wear out; one never has to buy anything new. My automobile is American, and it will last for many years.'

He thought our greatest writer was Ernest Hemingway. I remonstrated. 'Ah, of course he has faults, but what vigour, what power, what originality!' Like so many Parisians, he does not admire Rostand; 'our really great French mind was Ernest Renan.' He naturally prefers irony, the keen, sceptical, pure intelligence, to romance. I was not surprised. But when I asked him what he thought of the lyrical genius of Victor Hugo, he laughed and quoted André Gide, who on being asked who was the greatest of all French poets, said 'Victor Hugo—hélas!'

On my saying that only a Frenchman could really appreciate Racine and *enjoy* the golden age of the seventeenth century, he said, 'Oh, the seventeenth century is overrated.'

Late on the same afternoon, accompanied by my friend and former pupil, Hudson (Boz) Hawley, of the Associated Press in Paris, I went to see Léon Daudet in his office as Editor-in-Chief of the daily Royalist paper, *L'Action Française.*

Léon Daudet, son of the great Alphonse Daudet, although a Parisian born and bred, has the warm-hearted, passionate, expansive, temperament of the South, whence his father came. He is roly-poly in shape, keenly intelligent, with a remarkable flow of conversation. Everything he says is interesting. Although he must know English well, no English was spoken during the hour we spent together. Remembering how busy the writer of a daily paper is, I rose, after we had been there some twenty minutes, and he asked '*Comment? vous êtes pressé?*' and I gladly sat down again.

He is a good enthusiast and a good hater. His book *Reminiscences* (translated by Arthur K. Griggs) is vitriolic; but he has a genius for friendship, and absolute reverence for the memory of his father. He belongs to the Goncourt Academy and told us with much pleasure that the ten members, on a secret ballot to determine the greatest French novel of the nineteenth century, put Flaubert's *l' Education Sentimentale* first and Alphonse Daudet's *Le Nabab* second. In the history of French literature, he regarded the sixteenth as greater than the seventeenth century, because it contained Rabelais and Montaigne.

M. Daudet had the previous week attended the performance of *Hamlet* in French at the *Comédie*, and I quote from his interesting review.

La première, c'est que Shakespeare peignait, sous forme de dramatisation de chroniques anciennes et le folklore, des événements et allusions à des événements tragiques de la Cour de la reine Elisabeth, comme Racine peignait, sous des masques antiques, des figures passionnées de la Cour du Grand Roi. . . .

Ma seconde remarque est d'une portée plus générale. Ce qui donne au drame shakespearien en général, et à Hamlet en particulier, cette envolée extraordinaire, c'est qu'il est baigné de surnaturel, mieux, de divin; mieux encore, de divin chrétien. . . . Il est à la chrétienté ce que les grands tragiques grecs sont au paganisme; et toutes ses finales, après tant de crimes et d'épouvantes, sont baignées de pardon, de sérénité, d'espérance, de sacrifice consenti, en somme: de libération. . . .

Notre temps, si tragique, emporté par plusieurs tempêtes vers des récifs inconnus ou barbares, convient au déploiement en nous de Shakespeare. Sa gloire rencontre nos horreurs, nos pitiés, nos amours, nos remords, jusqu'à nos songes. Les vibrations de son tocsin s'accordent aux vibrations du nôtre. Ses gouffres, nous les avons sous nos yeux. Toutes les larmes incluses en ses tragédies ont été versées pendant quatre ans. Tous les cris de ses héros mourants ont été poussés pendant quatre ans. Mais le chemin qui monte de ses profondeurs est manifestement—pour qui s'est imprégné de lui et a vécu de lui, Shakespeare—celui de la Croix.

Conversation with M. Daudet is enlivening because he possesses such strong convictions in art, politics, and religion; he has none of the indifference, polite scepticism, and irony characteristic of many writers.

He told us stories and anecdotes of his father; and as I

took leave, he kissed me affectionately on both cheeks. During this embrace, Hawley, who had never seen his professor thus saluted, stood petrified like Lot's wife—and the story by this time has lost nothing in his telling of it.

Léon Daudet is an illustration of one of my favourite theories, that one cannot be unhappy so long as one remains profoundly interested in life. The world has not gone as M. Daudet would like to have it; in religion and in politics, he is in a minority. But he gave the impression not only of being genial, but of being happy. It is difficult to say how many Christians today would go to the stake rather than renounce their faith. I feel certain, that if such an emergency arose, Léon Daudet would stand singing in the flames.

I had stimulating conversations in Paris with my friends Padraic and Mary Colum. Wonderful talkers are they both! Mr. and Mrs. Colum have a charm all their own; they are not like anybody else. He has an imaginative quality as shown in his poems and fairy tales; and she is a profound and penetrating literary critic. They look out on the world without prejudice. In some strange fashion they combine the mellowing of experience with the candour of a child.

101

HELEN WILLS MOODY

WHOEVER reaches the top in any department of intellectual, artistic, or athletic competition has some interesting personal qualities. It is impossible for one to reach lonely eminence without them.

Of course the world loves a champion, and crowds follow him about; there is intense curiosity to see him. But I mean something quite different from the adoration of success. Also something quite different from the excitement over athletic sports.

The father of Helen Wills brought her up to be a tennis champion. She did not take to the game naturally as a child; she preferred to play Indians and what not. But she has left it on record that her father aroused both her interest and her ambition.

At the age of fifteen, she won the national junior championship for girls. The next year she was ranked third among the women players of the United States, and the year following she was Champion. The rest is history. At her first appearance in Wimbledon in 1926 for the British championships, she was beaten by Kitty McKane, after having the match apparently safe in her hands. Never again was she to come so close to winning, and lose.

The question that will always be discussed by those interested in tennis is this: Granted that Suzanne Lenglen was the greatest of all European women players and Helen Wills the greatest of all American women players, which of these two was better than the other at her prime? It is impossible to answer this accurately. Suzanne won her first British championship in 1919 and, with the exception of one match with Mrs. Mallory in America, was never defeated. She met Helen only once, on the Riviera in 1926. Suzanne won, 6–3, 8–6. After the match, Helen was asked to comment on her opponent, and she said, 'Suzanne is just as good as I thought she was.'

Now, this one match—the only time the two girls ever met in singles—does not answer the question given in the preceding paragraph. On that day, and in her own country, Suzanne won. But she was in the plenitude of her powers and Helen had not reached her own pinnacle. Furthermore, it must be remembered that in order to be a world champion, *one should be successful not only at home, but abroad, and under varying conditions.* Although the majority of experts say that Suzanne was a greater player at her best than Helen became, I venture to disagree. And for the following reason.

Suzanne won all her matches either in France or in neighbouring countries. Helen had to travel six thousand miles to play in Europe. Even if one granted that Suzanne at her best was better than Helen's best *in France*, it does not follow that she could have beaten Helen in a home-and-home match.

I am certain, if the two girls had been contemporary, and had reached their peaks, say, in 1930, that in seven matches, three to be played in France, three in America, and one whose locality should be chosen by lot, Helen would have won.

Perhaps she never was quite so brilliant as Suzanne. Certainly not so spectacular, so theatrical, so sensational. But she was stronger physically, had more endurance, and better match temperament. And in 1938, by winning for the eighth time at Wimbledon, she made a record no man or woman has ever equalled.

When she began to appear in tournaments, she was called

on both sides of the Atlantic 'Little Poker Face.' No matter whether she were playing well or badly, whether she lost or won, whether the linesmen gave favourable or abominable decisions, no one could read her thoughts. She never said a word, she never made a gesture, she never tried to wilt a linesman by giving him the evil eye. From beginning to end of a match, her expression was without expression. And this did not mean she was grim, or tense; it meant she was calm. I was certain, merely by what I had read about her, that this magnificent calm on the field of battle, did not come from stolidity, but from self-control. No one is stolid who is ambitious; she was afire with ambition.

This opinion of mine was confirmed by the article she wrote for a book *On the Meaning of Life*, compiled by Will Durant, and published in 1932. Some chapters are taken up by contributions from writers, H.L.Mencken, Sinclair Lewis, Theodore Dreiser, Charles A.Beard, Will Rogers, et cetera. Her contribution not only reveals a clear intelligence: but in describing herself she repeated several times the phrase 'My restless heart.' Her chief characteristic is restlessness. She *must* be active. She is driven by a demon of ambition that will not let her rest.

Her greatest conquests are those over her own temperament. She is naturally excitable, hungry for fame; yet in action, her face never betrays emotion. She achieves self-domination.

Some years ago, Stanley Doust, a member of the Australian Davis Cup team in 1913, writing about Helen Wills Moody in the London press said she was a model not only in her playing but in her behaviour on the courts; and suggested that every aspirant should imitate her.

The glacial calm of Mrs. Moody in action is as impressive as the dynamic romantic exuberance of Borotra or Suzanne Lenglen. Bunny Austin in the London *Evening News* after the tournament in 1938 expressed it perfectly. 'Mrs.Moody

is a tennis goddess. . . . I cannot believe that she is made of
the common clay of ordinary mortals, but of a substance
more rarefied, more goddess-like, a substance such as Jupiter might have donned when, seeking to fulfill his desires,
he descended from his Olympian heights. . . . that goddess-
like quality is still hers; spectators and players alike are
still enmeshed in the web of her beauty; the hall mark of
the champion is still upon her; win or lose, we are grateful
to her for her reappearance.'

In addition to the adverse criticism that came from certain
persons on the occasion of her default to Helen Jacobs in the
American championship, Mrs. Moody had to suffer again in
1938. She had fought her way to the finals in the Wimbledon
tournament and the stage was set for a tense drama—once
more the two Americans faced each other across the net. Toward the end of the first set, Helen Jacobs had an accident
which palpably made her continuance in the contest hopeless. However she went on. Many of the spectators felt
that Helen Wills should have gone up affectionately to her
rival, and shown sympathetic concern or have suggested
a pause or anyhow suggested something. Mrs. Moody
went ahead and finished the match as soon as possible.

Now whilst the two girls are not enemies, the newspapers
have played up their rivalry to such a pitch as to make
every contest between them full of tension. It seems to me
that Mrs. Moody did exactly the right thing; not merely
technically, but in harmony with the best traditions of
sport. If the two girls had had the same intimate friendship like that existing between Budge and Mako, then
Mrs. Moody would of course have stopped playing and run
over to her friend. But with the conditions as they were,
the final insult to Miss Jacobs would have been sympathy
and pity (publicly exhibited) by her rival.

I remember a match at golf where there was great tension. The players were in general equally able; but one of

them missed three short putts in successive holes. When he missed the third one, his opponent said, 'That's too bad!' to which came the immediate response, 'Damn you, don't you pity me!'

Mrs. Moody is a painter, an etcher, a writer. Her own books, *Tennis* and *Fifteen-Thirty*, are not only well written; they are illustrated by portraits from her own hand. She has given exhibitions of her paintings and drawings in Paris, London, and New York. During the French championship tournament in 1932, she gave a public exhibition of her work with the pencil.

The best tennis I ever saw her play was at Paris in May 1932; and not in the tournament, which she won. While I was watching the progress of this tournament, I happened to see her and Sidney Wood slip out of the stand. I followed them, and saw them play two long deuce sets. I had not realized it was possible for any woman to reach such excellence. As it was only a practice match, she did not care whether she won or lost; hence she made miraculous drives and returns. Of course the best man will beat the best woman. I have been told that Suzanne never forgave Tilden for beating her two love sets.

In a long and interesting conversation I had with Helen Wills Moody in New York, she was kind enough to speak freely of her work. Tennis was not her life ambition; she wants to achieve success in some field of effort where she can steadily develop.

She told me one thing which answered a question I have always put to myself. Why is it, when our players travel so much in foreign countries that so few of them become proficient in foreign languages? I had thought they were not only neglecting a great opportunity, but that they would actually play better if they could divert their minds by hard study. She told me that study, even reading, could not accompany tournament play. If she is to play in the afternoon, she never reads in the morning. Reading takes a little off the keenness of perception. The eyes must be clear.

As to whether tournament players enjoy the game more than duffers, that is open to doubt. But it is certain that Helen enjoys her competitive matches, partly because of her ambition. Off the courts she is an admirable conversationalist, and it would be a pleasure to talk with her even if she had never seen a tennis ball.

March 9, 1936

DEAR MR. PHELPS,

I have just finished *The Last Puritan*, which was given me by Maxwell Perkins in Scribners—he said it was going to be another "best-seller." This isn't what I wanted to tell you.

It is this, and for no special reason—I mean I have no right really, because the subject is so far removed and does not concern me— except because of the fact that the name, Santayana, has been in my mind for such a long time.

It was you, as I remember, who gave me a letter some years ago to him, which I never delivered because I was so busy with the tennis. Even had I been able I should have so hesitated that I don't think ever I could have presented it.

Do you remember that the reason we met was because in 1931 you read a little thing I had written for Will Durant which was called "On the Meaning of Life"? I always have thought that this was a very happy stroke of fortune for me that you did happen to see it. In this little article which was sincerely written then, but not an expression for me now of what I think "of life," I was surprised the other day, when going over some papers, to find something which I think is true—and I wonder how I recognized it then. I said of Santayana: "He is seeking something, something which will explain beauty and perfection. He derives his joy from the ceaseless activity that goes with the quest."

It is poorly expressed, but is it not true of him?

I had no idea that Santayana liked sport either. But having instinctively admired him, and having never forgotten him after college days, even though I was hardly prepared to understand what he wrote, I am in quite an inexpressible way touched by the book, *The Last Puritan*. It does not seem the least strange to me that the people in the book speak in such an unlifelike way. They seem the more real because of it. Is it true that it is a quite extraordinary way of achieving realness? And at the end where he says or rather questions (which is unnecessary, since he has proved it to be a fact) "what realities might the spirit call its own unhurt illusion save . . . those very illusions which have made up our story." He would not need to point out that this truth belonged to this particular story, rather it belongs to "life," which is what he really means.

It is obviously the business of books to awaken our interest, and one that does not can't be worth much. On the other hand, do books often do what *The Last Puritan* does? Santayana has always fascinated me—even his name, before I read anything by him—because it made me think of yellow butterflies on a crimson background.

If I could only once see him—to speak to him would not be necessary. But he is quite old, and I shall travel less, so that it is probably not possible.

I am really painting, and have finished four canvases of a requested twenty—so have sixteen to go! Like practically every person who considers himself an artist I believe I have just discovered a "way" of painting, a plan or formula—so that now all I have to do is "practise" every day, because I know my direction. Youthful confidence is pathetic in a way because it is so sure of itself—but if we could borrow from Santayana some joy in the activity of the doing, there is perhaps recompense enough.

I must not bore you.

I adored seeing New Haven, as I told you, but couldn't have been more stupid in choosing a week end when you were away. The X's were very kind, and the Carpenter boy delighted, as was I, about the tennis in the gymnasium. What a marvellous place it is!

I feel I should ask you to forgive my long letter, since it is only based upon an idea, which came as a surprise to me upon reading a book, but which I felt in some way was related to you, because of the little circle of the Will Durant article, your letter to Santayana that you gave me, and what I found in *The Last Puritan*. He should have taught philosophy in only this way—but perhaps it has taken this many years to know that. Every conclusion takes a certain amount of time, and in this particular field, it may be that the best conclusions follow a lifetime. I wonder if they do.

With love,

HELEN

This letter appeared in her book, *Fifteen-Thirty* (1938, Scribners).

102

LITERARY AND CELESTIAL EVENTS

In 1932 I saw for the first time a total eclipse of the sun. On 3 August I took a night train from Michigan to Montreal; it was ninety-four in the shade, and the weather predictions for the next day were *cloudy*. Early the next morning, eating breakfast at the Ritz-Carlton in Montreal on the terrace underneath a gun-metal sky, I pondered whether I should go to Magog, eighty-seven miles away, or to Sorel, about sixty. Both towns were in the centre of the line of totality, and in both the sun was to be eclipsed for the longest period on this occasion, one hundred seconds. I had made up my mind to go to Magog, because the Canadian astronomers had gone thither, accompanied by astronomers from Great Britain and South Africa; whereas apparently no scientific gentry had considered Sorel.

After breakfast I telephoned Mr. J.G.McConnell, an undergraduate of Corpus Christi, Cambridge, whom I had met on the voyage of the Hellenic Society in the spring; as he and I had both seen Troy together, why not the eclipse? His father is the owner of *The Montreal Star*, and lives on a magnificent estate ten miles out of the city. Young Mr. McConnell came immediately to the hotel and we planned an expedition to the eclipse. As he was not able to leave Montreal until one o'clock, and as the totality began at the mystic moment of 3.22, we reluctantly abandoned the attack on Magog, and decided to advance on Sorel. On the way out, the sky, which had been cloudy all the morning, became even more so; no sign of shine, no streak of blue. But before our arrival the sun suddenly appeared, a small corner of it already bit off. By the time we reached Sorel, the sky around the sun was stainless; but a sinister cloudbank was rapidly approaching and it was a question whether the eclipse would take place before the clouds reached their mark, or whether we should see a total eclipse of both sun and moon at the same moment, which, although an unusual spectacle, is nothing to write home about. I have watched many exciting races; but never one more thrilling than this. The sun won; we had a perfect view of the eclipse; and a few minutes after totality, the clouds covered the thin melon-slice, and the sky remained overcast until nightfall.

After our return to Montreal we found that none of the million inhabitants had seen anything; at Magog the sky was cloudy so the astronomers saw nothing; and indeed Sorel was one of the very few spots where the eclipse had been visible.

It is impossible to describe a total eclipse of the sun or to convey anything of the impression it makes on the beholder. Talking one day with the famous engineer Charles Augustus Stone, who had been all over the world, I asked him if the Grand Canyon of the Colorado were not the most sublime spectacle he had ever seen; 'Yes, with one exception—a total eclipse.' He had, I believe, seen seven total eclipses. At this eclipse in 1932 the beginning of totality was a supreme moment in my life. I saw the prominences, the corona, Bailey's beads; and the sudden darkness was made even more impressive by the planet Jupiter.

Through illness I had missed the eclipse of 1925; it was a terrible disappointment; and yet there are educated people who care nothing for eclipses. Some otherwise intelligent friends of mine left New York the day before that eclipse, when they could easily have waited. And another friend told me that as he and his brother (a Harvard graduate) were in exactly the right position to see it, his brother, one minute before the eclipse, said 'Well, this is my regular time for going to the bathroom,' and went indoors. Hundreds of busy men travel six thousand miles on the mere chance of seeing what this university graduate thought quite unimportant.

On 7 November 1932 Richard Harrison, the Negro actor who became famous in every part of the United States for his amazing impersonation of God in the play *The Green Pastures*, was kind enough to speak to my Yale class in Contemporary Drama. He gave a fine address, and I had a long talk with him afterwards. He told me he had been a waiter in the Hotel Pontchartrain in Detroit and that in his spare time he had learned many passages from Shakespeare by heart. At social meetings with other waiters, he was often called upon to declaim passages from Shakespeare or from other authors, so that although he had no professional experience when he came to take the leading part in the play, he felt at home on the stage. He was very modest and natural and altogether a charming person.

On the evening of 14 December in New Haven I saw a moon-rainbow for the first time in my life. Browning's striking description of a moon-rainbow in *Christmas Eve* had made me hope that some day I might see one for myself. They are in most latitudes extremely rare. In New Haven there had not been one in twenty-two years, when I saw this in 1932. It was not a particularly good moon-rainbow at that.

ANZIA YEZIERSKA

A good friend of mine is Anzia Yezierska, who, born in Russia, came to America as an immigrant in 1901, knowing no English. She worked in sweatshops, in factories, as domestic servant, and stole time from sleep to learn our language. At one time in the course of these terrible struggles for bread, she applied at one of the New York hotels for a job as scrubwoman; but her clothes were so poor and her appearance so devastated by hunger, that she was rejected. Five or six years later she returned to that same hotel as a famous American novelist, the guest of honour at a fashionable luncheon. She wrote novels and short stories about the poor in New York; in 1932, when her book *All I Could Never Be* appeared, I received from her the following letter.

ARLINGTON, VT.
Oct. 20, '32

MY DEAR PROF. PHELPS,

It was so kind of you to send me your encouraging few words about *All I Could Never Be.*

I thought it might interest you to know how the book came to be written. During the war, when rich and poor, educated and ignorant, native-born and newly-naturalized citizens were thrown together into a common cause, I happened to come in contact with a group of educators who were making a research study of the Poles. A wealthy American who lived in one of the large eastern cities, thickly settled with Poles wanted to know what kept those Poles isolated islands of foreignness, untouched by the American life about them. The men chosen to carry on the study were Ph.D. professors in sociology and education. I, working for them as their Polish interpreter was the only unschooled person among them.

The "scientific approach" of these sociology professors seemed to me so unreal, so lacking in heart and feeling. But I was too inarticulate to formulate a better way. At the end of the study, it seemed to me they knew less about the Poles than when they began. When they started out, they knew they didn't know, but after a few months investigation they had cut up the Poles into little sections, which they pigeon-holed and tabulated into sociological terms. They began turning out reports that seemed to bring out to me the deep, unutterable gulf between the professors who were analyzing the Poles and the Poles who were being analyzed.

At the end of the study, everyone was asked to write a report. I was the only one who could not write it. And this failure to write the report preyed upon me and tormented. I was a prisoner of an experience from which I could not escape till I saw Browning's lines: "All I could never be, All men ignored in me, That I was worth to 'God. . . ."

This novel ends the cycle of my experiences as an immigrant. I have started something entirely new. A play. And I know about as much of the technique of play writing as I knew about the writing of novels. I feel like a person who has set out in an air-ship across unknown seas—how—where will I come out in this new venture? God only knows. But Ah—the thrill of wrestling with dreams forever beyond us.

ANZIA YEZIERSKA

103

EMERITUS

THE rules of Yale University governing the Faculty require that on the Commencement following one's sixty-eighth birthday one must retire from active teaching. This is just and beneficent; even if a professor at that age shows no diminution in vigour, there are younger men in his department who have a right to look forward to promotion. Accordingly at the close of lectures in the Spring term of 1933, my forty-one years of active teaching at Yale came to an end. I do not like farewells; when I met my class in Browning for the last time, I conducted it exactly as if I were going to meet them the next day. But the students would not have it so, and made a demonstration I shall always remember.

My last Academic Year, October 1932–June 1933, began and ended with two magnificent gifts, both in their intrinsic value and in the spirit of the givers.

I received from my brilliant colleague Chauncey Brewster Tinker a testimonial of affection in the form of a gift of such extraordinary value that when I found it on my desk I was completely overcome. It was the *original manuscript* of Walter Savage Landor's poem on Browning which gave Browning and his fiancée such delight in November 1845. The gift was accompanied by the following letter:

1293 DAVENPORT COLLEGE
NEW HAVEN
October 1st, 1932

DEAR BILLY:

I was a member of your first class in Browning—only, in those first days, it was 'Chaucer and Browning.' By way of explaining this somewhat unusual conjunction, you expatiated on points in which the two poets resembled each other, and you recited Landor's Sonnet on Browning with its fine reference to Chaucer. I heard of that Sonnet for the first time in your class, and therefore, as you begin your last course in Browning, I am asking you to accept the manuscript of the poem as a slight expression of my indebtedness to you during my student days and for thirty long years of cloudless association as members of one department.

Yours affectionately,

C.B.TINKER

On 18 June 1933 I received another stunning surprise. I was asked to take dinner with some friends at the New Haven Lawn Club. Expecting to meet a little group, I found over eighty members of the Yale Pundits, graduates and undergraduates. The Reverend Father T.L.Riggs, 1910, presided, and I was presented with a large collection of manuscript letters by Browning which had never been printed. They were enclosed in a beautiful case suitably inscribed.

104

OTHER EVENTS IN 1933

A LITERARY FEAST

THE dinner at the Hotel Plaza in New York, on 4 May 1933 of the Friends of the Princeton Library, was a notable gathering of literary folk. Five hundred and fifty people were present; at the head table sat Burton Hendrick, Michael Pupin, Emory Holloway, T.S.Stribling, Margaret Ayer Barnes, Hamlin Garland, Leonora Speyer, Ernest Poole, J.Harlin O'Connell, Owen Davis, Marquis James, Frank D.Fackenthal, Elmer Rice, Robert Frost, Pearl S. Buck, James Truslow Adams, Nicholas Murray Butler, General Pershing, Philip Ashton Rollins, Edward D.Duffield, Willa Cather, Governor Wilbur Cross, Henry James, Charles Edward Russell, Morrie Ryskind, Oliver La Farge II, Bernadotte E.Schmitt, Hatcher Hughes, Herbert Putnam, Charles Warren, William Cabell Bruce, Henry F.Pringle, Maud Howe Elliott, Charles Howard McIlwain, Allan Nevins, Ira Gershwin. Mr. Rollins, as Chairman of the Friends of the Princeton Library, proposed a silent toast to John Galsworthy, and then introduced President Duffield, J.Harlin O'Connell, and finally me, the new toastmaster. At that moment we went on the air, and I felt like a traffic policeman at a king's garden party; never have I had to hustle along so many distinguished people, in order that they might all be heard over the radio within one hour.

Mr. Henry James spoke on biography, Willa Cather on

the novel, Mr. Adams on history, Elmer Rice on the theatre, Robert Frost on poetry, Mr. Putnam on libraries, and General Pershing, who had come all the way from Arizona to attend the dinner, gave a delightful talk and said it was a pleasure to meet so many distinguished persons whose books he had not read. He also remarked that when he was an instructor in mathematics at the University of Nebraska, one of his pupils was Willa Cather, and she gave no promise of distinction. When, years later, he heard her name, he said, 'That can't be the same Willa Cather; the girl I taught didn't seem to know anything.' Then Mr. Fackenthal, Provost of Columbia University, announced the new winners of the Pulitzer Prizes in letters. T.S.Stribling in fiction for his novel *The Store*, Allan Nevins in biography for *Grover Cleveland*, Archibald MacLeish in poetry for *Conquistador*, Maxwell Anderson in drama for *Both Your Houses*, the late Frederick J.Turner in history for *The Significance of Sections in American History*.

Mr. Stribling and Mr. Nevins spoke for the prize-winners, and the exercises closed with a graceful address by President Butler.

On 11 January 1933 Miss Sackville-West, the British novelist, came to New Haven to give a lecture and spent part of the afternoon at our house. She is a tall, healthy, black-haired woman, natural, talking easily and freely on contemporary affairs.

On 16 January the poet-laureate of England, John Masefield, lectured at Yale, and I had the honour of introducing him. I could not help thinking how much more at home he appeared to be on the platform than in 1916; now speaking informally and reading from his poems in his deep-sea voice. He was much interested in the beauty of Harkness Tower, and he insisted on getting out of the automobile and walking over in the darkness of the Quadrangle where he could see it outlined against the night sky.

On 17 March 1933 I met Pearl Buck, who was travelling in America for the first time in many years. Her novel, *The Good Earth*, was such a success that there was widespread curiosity in America to meet the author. There was nothing exotic about her appearance or accent. She was an American woman of fashion, very attractive, and wholly unaffected. She told me, however, that whenever she had to prepare any formal address, which she did not like to do, if it were in English she read it from manuscript. If it were in Chinese, she delivered it *extempore*. I told her that when I read *The Good Earth*, if I had not known the author was a woman, I should not have been able to tell whether it was a man or a woman, a Presbyterian or an atheist, a conservative or a communist; that I had never read an American novel so wholly objective. She told me she would rather have me say that than make any other comment.

I felt certain, although she was soon returning to China, that she would not stay there. After making such a success and meeting the men and women of letters in New York, I did not believe she could ever permanently separate herself from American life, and in a few years my belief was confirmed.

3 PING TSANG HSIANG, NANKING, CHINA
November 13, 1933

DEAR DR. PHELPS:

Here I sit by my own fireside in Nanking, remembering last year in America, and one of the pleasantest memories is you. I am so glad I had the pleasure of meeting you, of being in your delightful home and of meeting Mrs. Phelps. It was an honor to receive the citation from you in June, an honor to walk with you in the procession. I forget none of it, nor shall I. I hope I can see you again next summer.

I discover, now that I am back in this country, that I am more American than I knew I was. I felt myself growing American last year, loving the country more and more, and loving its people. I wasn't sure, however, until I came back here, whether or not I could live there. Now, having come back to this well known and very well loved environment, I find my feeling toward America does not change. I could live there quite happily.

These days here, nevertheless, are crowded with beauty. In my garden are chrysanthemums and roses, each doing their last best before the frosts come. And the hills are most beautifully ruddy in the sunshine. They are not wooded as so many American hills are, but are bare against the sky. Now upon their long slopes the peasants are cutting their supply of winter fuel. The dull blue of their garments is lovely against the reddened grass. China is so variable a country for beauty. At such times as these I think it the most beautiful country I have ever seen. But at other times it can be ugly and sordid and evil looking. One never feels the land is free of men, as American countryside is—Here the land seems man-possessed, utilized by both living and dead until the very contours of the landscape have a strangely human look. I cannot explain what I mean; perhaps it is as any very old country looks.

Meanwhile, *Shui Hu* is being lived once again. A few weeks ago a large bandit horde ravaged villages only twenty miles from here. But within this great city wall, built before Columbus discovered America, we live, snug and secure. I wish you might visit me. And yet, you are so American, I think of you as so essentially American, I wonder if you'd like us here? At any rate, we would like you!

Always gratefully yours,

PEARL S. BUCK

On 23 February I gave lunch to T. S. Eliot in New Haven, when he came to lecture at Yale. We talked a good deal about Paul Elmer More, whom we both admired. Mr. Eliot gives one the same impression in conversation that one receives in reading him—intense sincerity. We met again a few months later when we both received the honorary degree of Doctor of Letters from Columbia University in New York.

On 2 April I had the pleasure in New York of hearing Toscanini conduct two symphonies of Beethoven; and of dining with him afterwards at the home of Mr. and Mrs. Muschenheim. Toscanini was most kind and gracious, but was evidently greatly disturbed over the newspaper discussion concerning his invitation to conduct the following summer at Bayreuth. He finally decided not to go.

On 29 April I saw Lillian Gish at her very best in a play called *Nine Pine Street* dealing with the murder supposedly committed by Lizzie Borden. Lillian always had a *succès de beauté* but in this melodrama she displayed great histrionic ability. I talked with her afterwards in her dressing-room; and we both regretted the play had been put on so late in the season.

On 11 May the Royal Scot train, brought over from Scotland to be exhibited at the Fair at Chicago, appeared in New Haven. I received an invitation from the management of the New Haven Railroad. Accordingly I took a train to Providence, and after five minutes returned to New Haven on the Royal Scot. Outside of the British and American officials, there were only two or three invited guests. It was a fine train, but I was surprised there were no screens in the windows.

On 15 May I gave a lecture in Richmond, Virginia, and was invited to lunch by the famous novelist Ellen Glasgow, where I also met Mr. and Mrs. James Branch Cabell and the American Ambassador to the Argentine. It was a happy occasion. A month later I wrote to Miss Glasgow, and received the following letter from Baltimore.

June 18th, 1933

DEAR DOCTOR PHELPS,

What a friend you are! I feel as if I had known you always, and well.

For four weeks, in all this intolerable weather, I have been held here by an illness that required, it appears, Baltimore doctors. Your letter came like a ray of Maine sunshine.

Richmond is lovely in October or November—why not make your next visit, the one with Mrs. Phelps, in the autumn?

Sincerely yours—and Affectionately,

ELLEN GLASGOW

The weather that May day in Richmond had been fearfully hot; yet with that discomfort and with the journey to the Baltimore physicians imminent, Miss Glasgow had exhibited true Southern hospitality—warm-hearted, gracious and sincere.

I was astonished that Mr. Cabell attended my lecture; for I am sure that most men of letters never attend any lectures except their own, and who can blame them?

105

VARIOUS NOTES IN 1934-5

On 11 January 1934 I had luncheon with Emma Eames and took her to see Eugene O'Neill's religious play, *Days Without End*; its failure was partly attributable to poor casting but Robert Lorraine was magnificent. When the leading actors were recalled, Emma Eames shouted his name with immense enthusiasm. He was evidently astonished and looked in our direction appreciatively. But he was even more pleased when, a few days later, at the Coffee House, I told him who it was who had saluted him.

On 4 May at a dinner of the Round Table in New York, President Nicholas Murray Butler presiding, I met for the first time H.G. Wells. He was in high spirits, in spite of the fact that he predicted a world war in 1940. I reminded him that the Chancellor of the Exchequer had recently said in Parliament, 'We have gone from Bleak House to Great Expectations.' 'Yes,' said Wells, 'but in Great Expectations they didn't get the money.' He laughed when I told him the story of the undergraduate's question in zoology. The Professor had mentioned some bug and remarked 'A single bug of this kind will produce in one year eighty thousand offspring.' He then asked if there were any questions, and a youth asked, 'If a single bug can produce eighty thousand, how many will a married bug produce?'

In the Autumn of 1934 the D'Oyly Carte Gilbert and Sullivan Opera Company came to New York and took the city by storm; they were equally triumphant in other cities in America and on visits in subsequent years. These artists

916

have done more to increase and to cement good-fellowship between the British and American people than almost any other agency. They did not know when they planned their first invasion whether it would be successful or not; they knew our country was the home of jazz and its relations; they could not be certain that light operas more than fifty years old, given without changes or concessions, would be received with enthusiasm. But their productions were the most successful theatrical events of the season. The result is that these British singers love Americans as never before; and Americans are so enchanted by the presentation of these operatic masterpieces that we have an affection for these singers and musicians that cannot be diminished by time.

It is an error also to suppose because this music is 'light' that it is unimportant; Arthur Sullivan is the greatest musical composer in the history of the British Isles.

On 22 November at a New York luncheon I met the world-famous Mary Pickford and had a long talk. She was unaffected but intensely serious, interested over the reception to her first book, *Why not try God?*

On 7 December at a New York dinner I had the pleasure of meeting John Buchan, subsequently Lord Tweeds-muir and Governor General of Canada. He said the horsemanship displayed in coach-driving in his latest novel *The Free Fishers* was absolutely accurate. I wondered at the variety of important work he seemed to accomplish with ease.

On 20 June 1934, as Public Orator of Yale University, at the Commencement Exercises, I had given out all the degrees except the two for the President of Harvard and the President of the United States. Suddenly the Governor of Connecticut, from his place among the members of the Corporation, rose, and addressed the President of Yale. I was taken aback for the moment, but naturally believing that the Corporation had decided it would be more fitting for Roosevelt to receive his degree from the Governor, I hurried to my place and sat down. Professor Nettleton whispered to me 'Get up! get up!' I whispered back, 'He's going to give the degree to the President!' 'No, no! he's giving it to you!' I was flabbergasted—fortunately I could turn my back on the audience to receive the degree; fortunately also there was so much applause when I received it that I had time to recover myself before proceeding, for I think it was the most stunning surprise of my life.

It was the only instance where an honorary degree was given without preliminary notice to the recipient; the reason is as follows. One year before this Commencement, I called on the Secretary, Carl Lohmann, and told him that while in all probability I should not be considered for a degree, I wished to save Corporation time by saying flatly and positively that I should not under any circumstances accept it. I felt that Yale had many scholars on her Faculty of the highest merit, whose work could not attract public attention; that I had received degrees from other universities and some other professor must be chosen instead of me. I left no doubt in the mind of the Secretary that I should refuse it if offered, and then I dismissed the subject from my thoughts.

What happened was this. Several months before Commencement the Secretary called on my wife when I was away. She kept this secret from me for four months, so that I had no suspicion whatever. We had gone to our summer home in Michigan, and when the time came for me to prepare to go to New Haven, she expressed a desire to accompany me. I was surprised, but had no suspicion of the reason; she said she wished to be present when the President of the United States received his degree, for it had happened only twice before, the instances being George Washington and Rutherford B. Hayes. This seemed a satisfactory reason for making the journey.

After Commencement was over, a friend asked me if I had had any intimation; and on my negative reply, he said that after he had witnessed the affair, he made up his mind either that it had come as a complete surprise or that I was the best actor that had ever appeared on any stage.

I shall not forget the expression on the face of Dr. Conant, the President of Harvard, when I was pronouncing the citation for his degree. After appropriate praise, I said 'In his whole career he has made only one serious mistake' and paused; his face suddenly darkened and as suddenly lightened when I added 'and that is now about to be rectified.'

I have always taken delight in the performances of magicians; and after the late Howard Thurston's amazing miracles at the Paramount Theatre in New Haven, I went back and had a long talk with him.

> THURSTON THE MAGICIAN
> 7 OAK ST.
> WEEHAWKEN, N.J.
> January 10, 1935

DEAR DOCTOR PHELPS:

Thanks for your nice letter. From the sixty million people I have entertained and the countless thousands I have met, you are one of the few outstanding individuals that will cling to my memory.

With sincere esteem,

HOWARD THURSTON

SUNDAE

Crossing the ocean in the steamer *Bremen* in 1935, the German head steward asked me for the origin of the word 'sundae.' I could not give him any accurate information but when I made a comment on this in *Scribner's Magazine*, I got letters from every section of America. One of the most interesting is from the distinguished owner, publisher and editor of the *Tulsa Tribune* in Tulsa, Oklahoma, Mr. Richard Lloyd Jones.

Dear Dr. Phelps:

Words are full of romance. I too enjoy the history of words, so was I attracted to your references in October Scribner's to the delectable 'sundae.' Perhaps the dictionary makers did not know what I think I know about the origin of that term. And perhaps I do not know the truth.

I grew up as a Chicago kid who did the things that most city boys do. I chased the fire engines all over Chicago and early was as much a patron of the soda fountains as my purse would permit. I remember when the sundae first appeared over the marble fountain counter and I remember the soda jerkers of that time relating the story of the origin which was something like this:

Evanston, Chicago's Godly neighbor, "Heavenston" as the good Frances E. Willard used to call it, was in those days at least rather Methodist minded. The piety of the town resented the dissipating influences of the soda fountain on Sunday and the good town fathers, yielding to this churchly influence, passed an ordinance prohibiting the retailing of ice cream sodas on Sunday.

Some ingenious confectioners and drug store operators, in 'Heavenston,' obeying the law, served ice cream with the syrup of your choice without the soda. Thereby complying with the law. They did not serve ice cream sodas. They served sodas without soda on Sunday. This sodaless soda was the Sunday soda. It proved palatable and popular and orders for Sundays began to cross the counters on Mondays.

Objection then was made to christening a dish after the Sabbath. So the spelling of 'sunday' was changed. It became an established dish and an established word and finally the Heavenston 'sundae' appeared even in Congregational Connecticut.

I do not vouch for this as being totally accurate history, but it is the history of the word which was common gossip in my boyhood at the time the 'sunday' appeared at the soda counters which I patronised.

If this story may not be known to you, I just thought it might interest you. So with my warmest personal greetings, as always, I drop it in the mail shute for you.

Always cordially yours,

RICHARD LLOYD JONES

Miss Rachel Crothers, the foremost woman American playwright, and in 1937 particularly distinguished by her play *Susan and God*, consented some years ago to give a lecture at Yale, which delighted the huge audience.

125 EAST 57TH STREET

My Dear Professor Phelps—

I accept all your charming invitations with great pleasure—with the exception of staying till the next day—which will not be possible.

As to the lecture—which will be nothing after all but a most informal talk—I think I had better stick to what I know most about—and that is the actual production of a play from the minute the idea comes to the fatal raising of the curtain.

So will you call it that please—The Production of a Play?

You know the audience and I do not—but I find in my brief experience at this thing that all sorts of audiences enjoy hearing an act of a play read—so I suggest that I talk for about half an hour and finish with the first act of Expressing Willie.

Looking forward with great pleasure to being with you and Mrs. Phelps—

Most cordially—

RACHEL CROTHERS

106

EMMA EAMES AND MUSIC

IN *The Ring and the Book* Browning unconsciously described this great prima donna in the phrase 'the good girl with the velvet in her voice.' In my chapter describing my bicycle trip in Europe in 1890 I have mentioned the first time I saw Emma Eames singing 'Marguerite' in Paris. The next time I heard her was in Boston in 1892 when she sang with Jean and Edouard deReszké. She was the best Marguerite and the best Elsa I have ever heard or seen. I heard her many times in the Metropolitan Opera House until her retirement which took place in the plenitude of her powers. Born in Maine, she was a Yankee with an inflexible will; and when she made up her mind to retire, she retired. In those days I worshipped from afar, but in 1924 when my wife and I were in Paris, we called upon her at her hotel in the Place Vendôme. In the course of general conversation I happened to remark that inopportune intruders and jovial back-slappers were as well-known and as unwelcome in Bible days as they are now. When she asked me to illustrate, I quoted from the Book of Proverbs: 'He that blesseth his friend with a loud voice, rising early in the morning, it shall be counted a curse to him.' She laughed and asked me if I could prove that was in the Bible. I said there would be no difficulty if she would provide a copy, which she immediately did, and I wondered then how many great prima donnas carry a Bible with them. This meeting in Paris led to many meetings later both in Paris and in New York, and I had the honour of writing a preface to her autobiography called *Memories and Reflections.*

A matter that has always troubled me is this: How do singers ever learn to sing the most ravishingly affecting passages with *emotional* control? It is essential that they sing not only on the pitch and with perfect emission of tone, but that they sing with passion. Yet the singer must himself never be overcome by the beauty of the song. Nothing is more distressing than to see an orator or a singer more excited than his audience.

Now we know that Dr. Johnson never could repeat aloud the stanza from *Dies Irae* beginning

Jesu, me sedisti lassus,

because he always burst out crying. And the austere Housman has left it on record that there are passages that he was never able to read aloud. When Hawthorne read aloud to his wife the manuscript of *The Scarlet Letter*, during the last scene on the scaffold, his voice rose and fell as uncontrollably as the waves of the sea. (She fainted.)

This question is entirely different from the controversial question of the feelings of an actor on the stage, which used to be discussed with such acrimony during the career of the great Coquelin. He insisted that the actor should himself never be moved in the slightest; that he should be cold as ice; that it would be as fatal for him to *feel* the words as it would be for a surgeon to be overcome by sympathy during an operation. There were many actors who disagreed with Coquelin; who said that if they did not themselves feel as deeply as if they were indeed those whom they were impersonating, they could not act effectively.

No, what I am discussing is quite different from that. When we in the audience are so moved—as I always am by Elsa's dream and Lohengrin's farewell to the swan—how can the singers have such control that they sing with absolute accuracy? Some have told me that the answer to this question is *Double Personality*. If they were alone practising, they would indeed often be overcome by emotion; but on the stage and before the public, their own personality disappears—they are not themselves but are the persons they are representing.

Of course if the danger of emotional breakdown were overcome by anxiety not to wander from the pitch or not to produce clear tones, that would result in extreme self-consciousness; this would be worse than emotional surrender, as if the singer were more interested in himself and his performance than in the part.

In response to my request, Madame Emma Eames was kind enough to write to me:

30 SUTTON PLACE
March 23, 1938

DEAR BILLY

What a difficult letter to answer is yours just received! To make "very clear" to the average mind what you ask me is very different from making it clear to you.

I begin by saying how entirely I agree with Robert Louis Stevenson when he says "Until the excitable amateur is dead the artist is not born." To convince the hearer, however, one must conceive a role in passion but until the human passion has been mastered and the expression of it translated into a higher sphere, one cannot convince one's audience. The generation of artists to which I belonged sought calm—the calm of *self possession* which with a sure technique, animated by the invocation of the original emotion enabled one to carry and compel the audience to one's own emotion and vision. Emotion like fire and water is a good servant but a bad master. Though the public is often moved by one who has animal magnetism and simply "blows off steam" it is *obliged* to come under the spell of the real and sincere artist with elevated standards of art and convictions.

I quite understand why you are overcome by emotion when reading aloud for you have not been able to take the time to analyse your emotion and possess it. When I studied Sieglinde in Die Walküre I had to wait 2 years before I could trust myself to master my emotion and not to choke over certain phrases and even then I had to adjust my mind to the shock in order to avoid choking.

There are certain things which I read aloud that I always shall choke over—it does not matter and even in your case it does not for being in personal and intimate contact with your hearers they share even more your emotion. My "job" asked for something quite different. As I was completely possessed and obsessed by my own work I do not know much about the approach of many other singers to theirs. Calm was preached to me from the first by all teachers Gounod and Jean de Reszké included and glad am I of it as otherwise my emotions would have run away with me. Which, even in an argument gets the better of it? The one, who keeps calm and coolheaded! I feel as though I had not half answered, or answered well, your letter but I hope this may *do*.

Ever your truly affectionate friend

EMMA

CLARA CLEMENS

Although I first saw Clara when she was hardly more than a baby, my acquaintance with her began in April 1904, when she made her début as a concert singer in Florence, and a few days later I met her in her parents' villa outside the town. This led later to an intimate friendship not only with her but with her husband, Ossip Gabrilowitsch. We first met him with his wife in Munich when he was preparing for his American career. Mr. Gabrilowitsch became not only one of the best concert pianists in the world but one of the most distinguished of orchestra conductors. I have never known a man of higher integrity, or of greater sincerity. I had great respect for him and profound affection. He was kind enough to *give* a piano recital at Yale and for a few hours preceding it we had a long talk. He asked me then, 'What was the name of the Hartford physician who was responsible for the first use of anesthetic?' And I said, 'I can't remember.' Then he burst out laughing and said, 'Neither can I,' to which he added,

'How strange it is! We both know the names of most of the famous military men of the world, and we can't remember the name of one of the greatest benefactors of mankind.' Mr. Gabrilowitsch hated vulgarity in every form. and he could not bear any display of it in connexion with religion. I told him that a certain American editor asked a clergyman to write a Life of Christ that would be adapted to the ordinary reader. When the editor received the manuscript, he wrote to the clergyman, 'This won't do at all. What I want is a snappy Life of Christ.'

Clara Clemens's life of her father which followed her admirable public lecture about him is one of the best books on Mark Twain ever written, for she herself has inherited a good deal of her father's literary skill, his humour, and his sincerity. I have always thought that if she had cared to do so, she could have become a remarkable actress, as she had great skill in impersonation.

The death of Vladimir de Pachmann on 6 January 1933 brought back to me a host of recollections. I heard him a good many times when he was in his prime and also when he was so old, feeble and shaken that he went through his concert performance like a somnambulist. And even when I spoke to him after a concert he didn't seem to be fully conscious. But I first heard him at Chickering Hall, Boston, in 1892. He played, as was his custom, an all-Chopin programme including the B-flat Minor Sonata containing the Funeral March. In those days he wore a full black beard and continually talked to the audience in his broken English, saying, 'Wasn't dat nice?' and similar remarks. Often he would pretend to play fortissimo, bringing down both his hands with a tremendous crash and then just brushing the keys and playing pianissimo. Yet these monkey tricks (Huneker called him a Chopinzee) really didn't interfere with the beauty of his interpretation and his miraculous finger technique. The day after that concert, Philip Hale wrote a column in which he said that the effect of such playing was like an old woman looking at her bridal dress through eyes filled with tears. I have heard all the great pianists of the world, but I have not heard anything quite like De Pachmann playing Chopin.

On 10 March 1923 the Russian singer Chaliapin gave a concert in Woolsey Hall, Yale University, and Mr. Rudolph Steinert, whose guest he was, kindly invited me to join a small party of four of five persons at supper after the recital. Chaliapin (I greatly prefer the correct English spelling Shaliapin instead of this French form, but only Rosa Newmarch and I have ever dared to do it) was in the highest spirits, laughing aloud constantly and pretending to boast of his various wickednesses. He seemed like a great, healthy, overgrown boy. The only bad thing about him that evening was his English, which was as bad as his French was good.

At my request, Mr. Steinert was kind enough to write out his own recollections.

We invited a few guests to meet him at Ceriani's, a small Italian restaurant in New Haven where Rosa Ponselle had been entertainer before her days of glory.

During the early part of the evening he spoke hardly a word, giving all his attention to a large sirloin steak which he devoured. He next concentrated on mixing a salad in a huge bowl with much deliberation and ceremony. After steak and salad had been washed down by a bottle of Chianti and the inner man was at last satisfied he pushed back his chair, at peace with the world. His spirits rising, he crossed the room to a small upright piano, sat down and sang one song after another, accompanying himself and keeping us in roars of laughter as he brought out the humor of the songs by acting and grimacing.

This mood passed. He came back to the table and talked seriously of bygone days. He was saddened by conditions in Russia and by the loss of his personal properties through confiscation.

Among his anecdotes that evening was the tale of a concert in a small Russian community where people had gathered from far and near to hear him. While he was singing a pianissimo passage and the house was hushed to listen, he noticed a disturbance in one corner of the hall. Later he learned, to his amazement, that a child had been born. He always felt that this was a tribute to his art. He loved especially to sing to these Russian peasants, having been one of them himself. With the new regime all this was changed.

In a more confidential vein, he turned to me and told me a tale of another evening. This time he was to give a concert in a great city. In the lobby of his hotel he was introduced to a very charming woman. Conversation with her made him forget time and place. Suddenly he pulled out his watch, saw that it was nine o'clock and realized that he was already half an hour late for his concert. He rushed to the theatre to find the auditorium completely dark and the audience dispersed. Next day the newspapers flaunted headlines, "Chaliapin Drunk. Did not appear at Concert." "All this," said he, "made me feel very badly. But," he ended, "She was a BEAUTIFUL lady."

Chaliapin returned again and again to the little broken down piano and he sang with such gusto that it seemed the roof must surely fly off that small shabby room. It was three or four in the morning before the party broke up.

Chaliapin died in April 1938.

It is interesting that the three greatest bassos I have ever heard were all giants—Edouard de Reszké, Pol Plançon, and Chaliapin. All three I heard as Mephistopheles in *Faust*; and Plançon and Chaliapin I heard singing (many years between the recitals) *The Two Grenadiers*. The first time I heard Plançon was in 1890; and the last time I heard Chaliapin was about forty years later.

Our beloved Walter Damrosch used to play and conduct before cheering thousands; now over the radio he has audiences of many millions.

September 29, 1930

MY DEAR FRIEND:

What a charming little book on music you have been kind enough to send me! It is just what one would expect from your pen, for it expresses what seems to be the very keynote of your character—a power to feel and to enjoy intensely the beautiful things in life. Goethe says, " Wenn ihr's nicht fühlt, so könnt ihr's nicht verstehen." I read with so much interest how the "feeling" for music came to you only gradually and then the understanding followed as a matter of course.

With cordial greetings to you and your wife,

Always sincerely yours,

WALTER DAMROSCH

107

ENGLAND IN 1935

IF James Russell Lowell had been living in England in 1935, as he was in the eighties, he would probably amend one of his most famous verses so that it would read

> What is so rare as a fine day in June?

We arrived in London 29 May and sailed for home from Southampton on 22 June. Beginning with the first of these dates, it rained every day with the exception of the last. I don't mean that every day it rained all day; but it rained a good deal every day, and there were only two mornings when, on rising, we saw any bit of blue sky.

The majority of intelligent persons would probably say that no matter what we profess, we do in truth always seek our own happiness. I have never subscribed to this creed; and my recent two months in Europe have strengthened my convictions. So far as happiness is concerned, I believe the average intelligent Englishman is happier in England than he is in America or in Germany, France, or Italy. I believe the average person of any country is happier in his native land than anywhere else. Why, then, does anyone travel?

The British novelist, J.B.Priestley, once remarked that he would rather live in his suburb of London than in Florence; I understand that remark and I approve of it.

I am certainly happier in the United States than I am in any foreign land; I know, when I deliberately plan a journey to Europe, that I should be happier if I remained at home.

The poet Bryant made seven journeys to Europe, was always homesick there, and yet always went back. I have no difficulty in understanding that. There are two reasons: first, the best part of any journey is after it is over; second, we go abroad, not to seek happiness, but to acquire a few ideas.

I used to wonder why the poet and novelist Oliver Wendell Holmes, after making one journey to Europe, did not go again for fifty years; the answer is that he preferred his personal comfort and happiness. Furthermore, what with the Harvard Medical School, and literary work, he was a busy man. Incidentally, living in Boston, he wrote a poem called *Homesick in Heaven*.

I do not think what I am saying is inconsistent with the definition of happiness that I am always quoting—the happiest person is the person who thinks the most interesting thoughts. One should travel abroad to add to one's stock of interesting thoughts. One is aware of this increase after one's return.

I remember reading in Mark Twain, of the meeting of two Americans in Europe. 'Are you homesick?' 'Hell, yes!'

London in the rain is not enchantingly beautiful; but it is more interesting than America in the sunshine. Sitting in the window of our hotel in London, I could see Westminster Abbey, the Houses of Parliament, nine bridges, and the ever-exciting river itself, with its twice-a-day tide, and its eternal activity. Two thousand years of history are on the surface of that river. The Connecticut River cannot in such matters compare with it; *but how I love Connecticut*! The south shore of England has a more varied view of the sea than my home in Michigan has of Lake Huron; *but how I love Michigan*!

My beloved colleague, the late Professor Perrin, who

spent his life teaching Greek, went to Athens for a sabbatical year; after he had been there three days, he wrote me from the Acropolis, saying, 'If you can get me any job at Yale, say being janitor of one of the dormitories, cable me at once!'

I go abroad and hope to go again, because my mind needs the stimulation of Europe; because it is well for one's mental and spiritual development to live for a time in other countries; and because I have friends in Germany, France, England, and everywhere else; and it does me good to see them.

Certainly our stay in London was never more interesting, never more mentally profitable than in this June of 1935; we renewed old friendships, made many new ones, and stored up memories that will enliven our minds and warm our hearts for the rest of our lives.

We spent a glorious day with Alfred Noyes and his family at their beautiful home on the south shore of the Isle of Wight. There the sun shone bravely. At Oxford, Arthur Goodhart gave a luncheon to me and some of my former Yale students. He has had an extraordinary career; a graduate of Yale in the class of 1912, he became Fellow of Corpus Christi, Cambridge, then Fellow of University College, Oxford, and Professor of Law. At Cambridge I saw for the first time the bumping races on the Cam, after lunch with Robert Lassiter (Yale 1934) in his rooms in Clare College. Then, with some other Yale men, we walked out to Grantchester, immortalized by Rupert Brooke; we saw the river, the old church, and the vicarage; I had the pleasure of seeing Mary Ellen Chase, who was spending a sabbatical year in a beautiful English cottage, writing a novel.

The English novelist, Mrs. Belloc-Lowndes, sister of Hilaire Belloc, was kind enough to let me read remarkable manuscript letters by Dante Gabriel Rossetti, by the father of Charles Dickens (recommending his son for a position), by members of Shelley's family, and others. At her house we had the delight of meeting the painter Sir William Rothenstein and Lady Rothenstein; his autobiography is one of the best. And no wonder; he was an intimate friend of Whistler, Sargent, Oscar Wilde; all the painters, poets, novelists, dramatists, and wits of the nineties. He told me Oscar Wilde was the best talker, the best conversationalist he had ever known; that his flashes of wit and humour were absolutely spontaneous. Like everyone else who knows Rothenstein, he has immense admiration for the genius and for the character of Max Beerbohm. I asked Sir William a good many questions about the late George Calderon, who was killed in the war. His translation of two plays by Chekhov was accompanied by an introduction, the most penetrating piece of literary criticism I have ever read on the Russian dramatist.

I spent a memorable afternoon with Sir James Barrie in his lofty flat overlooking the river. Since the property roundabout once belonged to the Duke of Buckingham, there are five streets in that district named separately after these five words: *George Villiers Duke of Buckingham*. I found George Street, Villiers Street, Duke Street, and Buckingham Street; Sir James told me they were a little puzzled what to do with the word *of*; finally they named a little passage there, a tiny by-street *Of Alley*.

All Americans everywhere should be proud of R.D.Blumenfeld. I call him the Uncrowned King of Fleet Street. But he has been crowned as well; for he was chosen Master of the Ancient and Worshipful Company of Stationers and Newspaper Makers, the highest honour any newspaper man can receive. This company goes back long before the invention of printing. In his book *R.D.B.'s Procession*, you see Mr. Blumenfeld in the insignia of office, along with the Prince of Wales, the titular Master. As he looks back to his boyhood in Wisconsin, and the long march upward, he should be satisfied.

On the Thursday in June before we sailed, he gave me a luncheon at the *new* Stationers Hall in the City, built shortly after the fire of 1666; and a beautiful hall it is. About twenty men were present, all writers and publishers, with the one exception of Mr. Selfridge, who, like his host, came from Wisconsin, and became the merchant prince of London; we three Americans sat at the head of the table. Then on my right was Bernard Shaw, on his right Philip Guedalla, across the table Bruce Lockhart, Ralph Straus, Gilbert Frankau, Christopher Stone, Ivor Nicholson, Sir Denison Ross, and Lord Strabolgi. Mr. Shaw seemed the personification of health and vigour and high spirits.

I wonder how many persons would have enjoyed taking my place. I was suddenly called on to make a speech! While it is probable that making a speech causes me less distress than most men seem to feel (a friend said of me, 'it rests him to open his mouth'), imagine having to make an original address, with Bernard Shaw at a distance of three feet!

The London *Evening News* asked me to write an article on *The Paradox of the English*, which I did with alacrity. Fleet Street is exciting; and I was glad officially to belong to it, if only for one day. Accordingly I wrote an article on the difference between the English temperament and English poetry, and in a few hours I received from Rottingdean in Sussex the following telegram, which gave me great pleasure.

AN ENGLISH POET SENDS YOU HIS WARM THANKS FOR YOUR
SPLENDIDLY GENEROUS ARTICLE TODAY

SIR WILLIAM WATSON

Watson is surely 'among the English poets,' though I had mentioned no names in my article.

One day we went out to a distant suburb of London to take tea with the author of *Goodbye, Mr. Chips*. Mr. and Mrs. James Hilton lived by choice in a quiet corner, in order to have peace and leisure wherein to work. He was just what you would expect from reading his novels; what more can I say? The success of *Lost Horizon* and of *Mr. Chips* did not turn his head. I was glad to have a chance to talk with him, for I am interested in the career of a man who produced thirteen novels, reaching success only with the thirteenth.

At a luncheon given by Lady Harcourt, we met the Spanish Ambassador to Great Britain, and Madame Perez de Ayala. They are charming. Sir William Max Müller, the former Minister to Warsaw, was present. His father was the famous Max Müller, the Oxford philologist, whose translation of Kant's *Critique of Pure Reason* gave me two years of hard study under the late Professor Ladd at Yale. I was particularly interested in meeting at this luncheon Lord and Lady Gainford. Lord Gainford was formerly the Right Honourable Joseph Pease, and held various high offices in the cabinets of the Liberal Governments of 1905–16. He is a Quaker, as were all the Pease family in the old days, and at one time he was Chief Whip of the Liberal Party. I had an interesting conversation with him about British politics. I asked him many questions about John Morley; when he was a young man, he was Morley's secretary.

On this visit to England I had the pleasure of doing what I had wanted to do for forty years—I took tea on the terrace of the Houses of Parliament. I had read of this in many novels, and the terrace had looked so attractive from the river that I had hoped some day I might have this privilege. Well, on an afternoon between showers, having been invited by Lord Iddesleigh, this wish was realized. Lord Iddesleigh is the son-in-law of Mrs. Belloc-Lowndes, and is a member of the famous publishing firm of Eyre and Spottiswoode.

Early in the afternoon I was invited by Sir Arnold Wilson, member of the House of Commons, and Editor of *The Nineteenth Century*, to attend the session of the House; Sir Arnold, by the way, in addition to other accomplishments, speaks Latin fluently. At this session I heard the Prime Minister, Mr. Baldwin, and the Chancellor of the Exchequer, Mr. Chamberlain, make a few remarks; but most of the time was taken up by a Socialist who wished the taxes on the rich to be increased. At about half-past four, I went with Lord Iddesleigh to the terrace, where we were joined by my friend Lord Conway. About half-past five, I attended the session of the House of Lords, where an important debate was going on, the subject being India.

English people are rather surprised and often, I think, quietly amused by my zeal in visiting places in England of literary interest. Well, here is something I *dreamed*, and I think for a dream my answer was rather good. In my dream I was conversing with an English man of letters, and told him I was about to visit the place where a great writer had lived centuries ago; he said 'You will waste your time. There is nothing left there for you to see.' And in my dream I replied, 'His spirit is still there!'

ANNE SEDGWICK

The death of Anne Sedgwick (Mrs. Basil de Selincourt) in 1935 was a severe loss to American literature. I was often asked in public lectures why I called her an American; the majority of people believed she was English. I always replied that I called her an American because her father and mother were Americans and she was born in Englewood N.J. She was taken to France when hardly more than a child, educated in Europe, and married to an English gentleman. I had the pleasure of seeing her several times, both in London and in her beautiful home near Oxford. Her work was not only distinguished, there was a spiritual quality in it unusual in contemporary fiction. I have always believed that if her novel, *The Encounter*, had not been published in August 1914, it would have produced a profound impression. After her death her letters were collected by her husband. Everyone who read her books and everyone who met her personally had the highest intellectual respect for her art and for her character.

Although several of her novels had deservedly an immense circulation, notably *Tante* and *The Little French Girl*, I regard *The Encounter* as her masterpiece. Its appearance just after war was declared prevented its merits from being generally known. And yet there was something prophetic in her contrasting the powerful man who worshipped Force with the cripple Conrad who believed only in Goodness. In reply to my letter about this, she wrote me that I was entirely right in believing that Conrad represented the inner philosophy of the book. I had written to her that in the general wreckage of the world he seemed to me the rescuing sail on the horizon. 'I am so glad that you felt he *was* the rescuing sail; I did, of course.'

The most memorable event in my life in 1937 was the fiftieth reunion of my class at Yale. When I was an undergraduate, men who had been out ten years seemed rather elderly; those who had been graduated twenty-five years seemed venerable; those of the vintage of fifty years were curiosities.

But when our class met in June 1937, and marched around the baseball field, we felt like undergraduates. Our Class Secretary, Professor Robert Nelson Corwin, is wonderfully efficient and his annual reports at our meetings are literary masterpieces. He holds the class together. Some men returned who had never been back; the most conspicuous being John Calhoun Simonds of South Carolina, a grandson of Yale's greatest statesman John C. Calhoun, valedictorian of the class of 1804. We were delighted to have Simonds with us and he was interested in seeing our Calhoun College and meeting the Master, Arnold Whitridge, a grandson of Matthew Arnold. Our class presented Secretary and Mrs. Corwin with a fine gift. Our classmate Ira Copley, former Congressman and now owner of a chain of newspapers, took us to the boat race at New London in his yacht.

In 1912 and again in 1932 '87 presented me with the *long distance cup*, for although I live in New Haven, on both these occasions I returned from Europe simply to be with my beloved classmates.

One of the greatest events in 1938 happened on the last Sunday in March. I arrived at St. Louis early in the morning, and was met at the station by Edward Hidden, '85 and Bill Haverstick, '34, representing old and young Yale and both intimate friends. This was the last time I saw Ned as he died some months later. They asked me what I should like to do, as my lecture was not to take place till the afternoon. I said 'All my life I have wanted to see the junction of the two mighty rivers, the Mississippi and the Missouri.' They had lived in St. Louis all their lives and had never seen it. Bill Haverstick drove the car; the junction was seventeen miles north of St. Louis; and it was at a desolate plain so that we walked the last mile. This utter desolation added immensely to the unspeakable grandeur of the scene. The wide blue Mississippi came down from the north and the wide brown Missouri came out of the west; and at their union I descended to the shore, dropped some of the water solemnly on my head, and then stretched out my arms in a salutation. Bill took a fine photograph of the scene. I have always been awestruck by great rivers and these two historic waterways uniting gave me one of the supreme moments of my life.

108

RADIO

I BECAME a radio speaker late in life; at first I did not enjoy it, because having been accustomed to look into the faces of an audience while addressing them, I felt when speaking into the microphone as if I were soliloquizing in the dark. But as soon as letters began to arrive from several thousand miles away, saying my voice had come into their houses as clearly as if I had been there, the experience became exciting and has remained so. Even if there is an audience in the studio where I am talking on the air, I do not really see or feel them as I do the invisible audience sitting under vine and fig tree. Every radio speaker receives what is known as 'fan mail'; some of these letters are especially appealing. A former student of mine at Yale, who had not been back at the University for thirty years, and was living on the top of a mountain in Utah, turned on the radio not knowing what was on the air, and he said it was as if he were back in the classroom. Another, living in Paris, returned home with his wife at one o'clock in the morning, thought they would turn on the radio for a half-hour before going to bed, and were greeted by my familiar voice. Captain Alan Villiers, commanding the sailing-ship *Joseph Conrad* was somewhere south of the Azores, turned on his radio, with a similar result. After I had spoken between the acts of the opera at the Metropolitan Opera House, New York, I received letters from friends in Honolulu and then from Egypt, saying it was exactly as if I had been talking with them!

Tom Stix, who was an undergraduate at Yale when the war broke out, was the first to persuade me to speak over the microphone; I gave an address on good reading, and then a Commencement address to the youth of America on Courage. This was followed by a regular engagement lasting thirteen weeks. The year after that, another former student, Herschel Williams, got me an engagement for twenty-eight weeks on the 'Swift Hour' (1934–5), with Sigmund Romberg conducting the orchestra and playing original and classical music. I enjoyed this experience as much as any I have had. Even now, after three years, I am constantly spoken to by strangers, who hear my voice on the train or on the golf course, and ask me if I am not, etc. Not only are these experiences agreeable because of the number of invisible friends one collects, but I have always intensely enjoyed the radio hour in the studio with my singing or playing or performing colleagues. It has always been like a happy family engaged in a fascinating game.

Another kind of work I took up late in life was writing for newspaper syndicates; first once a week and later every day. My employer was George Matthew Adams; I enjoyed the work and I enjoyed working for him and for those in his office.

109

CITY OR COUNTRY

By birth I belong to the city. I was born in New Haven in the centre of the town. My first recollection of the country —as distinguished from nearby Connecticut villages—was a summer outing in the Adirondacks.

In the Adirondacks, I was a citified boy in a strange land. Everything was different—the splendid mountains, the wide open places (so unlike the wide open places in the city), the keen, cold air of August evenings, and the absolute silence of the nights—broken only by the musical sound of 'streams inaudible by day.' The native folks seemed different from city people. They were just naturally friendly. Accustomed as I was to pass strangers on city streets without a word or a look of greeting or recognition, it seemed pleasant and sociable to salute everybody with a 'good morning' or a remark about the weather. These people also seemed more self-reliant. In the city every man had only one job, which is one more than many of them have now. Every woman went through a weekly round of familiar duties or social affairs. Every boy went to school and played games the rest of the time.

In the country every man seemed to be able to take care of himself in a dozen different ways; one felt that if he were cast ashore on a desert island, he could get along somehow. Every woman was 'capable.' Each one did every kind of housework, indoors and out, incidentally preparing the next meal and the next baby. The small boys were useful, whether they wished to be or not; their multitudinous tasks

were covered by a word that I heard for the first time—
chores. My own range of knowledge and accomplishments
seemed narrow and trivial; these boys knew instinctively
everything I wanted to know. This knowledge and this
capability they took as a matter of course. They seemed to
me like people of another race.

I dimly perceived then, what in maturity I realized—
city people are consumers and country folks are producers.
We in the city live off the earth, and they live on it. Talk
about the daily productive capacity of a city factory—
what is that to the thin crust of the round old earth,
whence comes every single thing we use for food, shelter,
and clothing. No wonder that in America everybody thinks
everybody else ought to be a farmer!

In smart metropolitan newspapers and so-called comic
periodicals, no one is perhaps more often an object of ridicule than the rural visitor. He is represented as a country
bumpkin, with mouth ajar; he comes from the 'sticks' and
is an easy prey to sharpers. Even if this caricature were
an accurate portrait, I am not entirely sure that the joke
would be on the countryman; the reason he is so easily
swindled is that he is not accustomed to swindlers, whereas
in the city they excite no comment.

Inasmuch as no comic papers are published in the countryside, the city visitor to the country has never become
a typical subject for caricature. But a group of city people,
left stranded in the country by a broken automobile, often
give the country folks something to laugh about (among
themselves) for months to come. The rustic may make a
curious appearance on a city street; and the newsboys
may laugh at him. Yet he can usually take care of himself, and if he cannot always find his way about, he can at
all events find his way home. But the city person, stranded
in the country, is a helpless object. He is not only more
grotesquely out of place than the countryman in a big

town; his inability to take care of himself makes him not only ridiculous, but pitiable.

We often think that business men in the city indulge in more exciting, that is to say, more speculative enterprises, than men in the country have ever heard of; brokers, investors and theatre managers play for high stakes. Success means a fortune, and failure means not only no gain, but the loss of the investment. Yet in a certain sense there is no enterprise more speculative than farming; for its success depends on an element beyond human control—the weather.

Even the most capable farmers stand the chance of losing the hard work of a whole year by an evil change in the weather. I have known many who have suffered in this way, and I am amazed at their courage and patience. No poker-face gambler takes his losses with more outward serenity than the average farmer. I know a great many farmers intimately. I have seen them lose an entire crop by too much heat or too much rain, or by one catastrophic storm. I have never heard one whine about this, nor have I seen any of them completely cast down.

For many years I have lived during the winter in a sizable city, and very near the city of New York. For many years I have spent a quarter of my life—July, August, September—in the country; that is to say, in a place in Michigan on the shore of Lake Huron, where there is no town, no railway station, no post office. In this agricultural county, I know the resident farmers and their families; and I know their parents and their grandparents. Thus, although I was born and brought up in the city, I have actually lived what, in total, amounts to fifteen years in the country; have lived, not as a migratory summer visitor, but as one of the folks.

I like people as individuals, not as representatives. I do not like Americans because they are Americans or dislike foreigners because they are foreigners. I do not like people because they live in New York or like them less because they don't.

I have perhaps been unusually fortunate in meeting charming and attractive men and women all over the world, and among all races and classes. I mean simply that I have met so many young and old people who are so much better than I am, that I have never been able to attain to the state of mental and moral superiority that is necessary to the denouncer, the fault-finder. It is impossible for me to say whether the people who live in the cities or the people who live in the country are superior; I have known men and women of beautiful character who live in New York and London, and I have known men and women equally admirable who live in country places.

The most obvious differences between city people and country folks are, I think, superficial. Emerson said: 'Cities force growth, and make men talkative and entertaining, but they make them artificial.' Another writer said: 'Men, by associating in large masses, as in camps and cities, improve their talents, but impair their virtues; and strengthen their minds, but weaken their morals.'

These two statements mean that in every city there are more opportunities both for intellectual development and for demoralization than in the country; but character may shine out as brightly in one as in the other.

So far as the financial advantages of living in city and country are concerned, the law of compensation seems to arrange that. In times of prosperity, people in the city are perhaps better off. There is plenty of work and the pay is good. But in times of depression, the farmer is relatively better off. He has his home, with all that it implies, he has his food. Then the streets of every American city (and America is better off than Europe, and Europe better off than Asia) contain men who are looking not only for work, but for food and shelter.

When the famous scholar and foreign ambassador, Andrew D. White, was over eighty, he said to me, 'I wish you could do something to induce Americans to live in the country. The moment an Englishman makes a little money, he secures a place in the country; but the moment an American makes money, he goes to the city.'

It is true that the average Englishman loves to have a home in the country; but the conditions of life are different in England.

Henry Ford has done more than any other individual to make it possible for Americans to live in the country the year round. Every one remembers how those who could afford it used to have a country home ten or twenty miles from the city, where the wife and children spent the summer, and where the man came for the week-end. Now in innumerable instances this is the only home they have. More than ever before the countryside is becoming the dormitory for the city. But these people who live in the country in the night and on Sundays are not the genuine country folks.

It is possible that in the future we shall see more, and not less, of these men and women. I have lived long enough to observe, even in fairly prosperous times, many—especially of the younger generation—leaving the farms and going to the city 'for good;' and after a few months or a few years, I have seen them gladly returning to the farm. To their dismay, they found that in the city they had to pay money for food that they had always obtained for themselves; with every other thing proportionally expensive.

The chief thing about an American farmer is his independence. At work there is nothing over him but the sky; he acknowledges no superior but God. He has his home and his land. Furthermore, he is nothing like so lonely or isolated as he used to be. Civilization depends on communication. I can well remember, in this very country where I am now writing, the times when folks in remote farmhouses saw no one outside of their family for weeks. The roads were bad in summer, terrible in spring, and impassable in winter. Now there are good roads throughout this country, and every farmer's family has an automobile. In his house is a phonograph, a telephone, and a radio. The whole world is becoming one community. Just as there is now really one city along the Atlantic coast from Portland, Maine, to Norfolk, Virginia, so the time will come when the distinction between city and country will be slight.

But even if I live to see the time when country and town are one geographically, I shall never forget the splendid men and women I have known, who, in the lonely days of isolation, cleared the land, tilled the soil, and brought up their children. Heroes and heroines are like wild flowers; you find them in remote places.

INFORMALITY

In a lecture at Harvard in the early nineties by Professor R.G. Moulton, comparing modern times with the Elizabethan, he called our age *The Age of Anti-Conspicuousness*. In reading Dekker's *Gull's Hornbook* it was clear that the Elizabethan swells tried in clothes, manner, and appearance to attract as much attention as possible; whereas Englishmen and Americans three hundred years later dressed in the fashion not to attract attention but to avoid it. With this endeavour at protective colouring naturally came a growth in informality; one wonders now in 1938 whether it is possible to become more informal than the majority of men and women are at present.

Many people today, especially those of the older generation, observing everywhere the lack of formality in dress, social relations, and speech, believe that good manners have vanished—that young men and women are rude to their elders, rude to those in authority, and rude to each other.

We must be careful not to confuse the absence of elaborate formalities with bad manners. In comparing our age with that of fifty years ago, the most apparent social change is the decrease of formality. In those days American college undergraduates wore whiskers, tall silk hats, and frock coats; yet they were young, and probably more generally given to dissipation than college undergraduates are now. College professors in those days wore broadcloth coats with tails, and exposed a vast expanse of gleaming shirt-bosom. But a large proportion of their time was given neither to teaching nor to research in scholarship, but to the enforcement of discipline. Every college instructor was a policeman.

Today in many college enclosures the students are by no means formally arrayed, and it is not an unusual sight to see a professor in sport clothes. But the relations between students and members of the faculty are very often on the basis of intimate friendship. The absence of formality on the surface is accompanied with real respect on both sides, and with sincere affection. This is certainly an improvement.

Whether it is the growth of athletics, with its natural release for the superabundant vitality of youth, or whether it is a general advance in civilization, I cannot say; but it is certain that the decrease of formality in dress and speech has been accompanied with an improvement in academic manners. Seventy-five and even fifty years ago, the classrooms in American colleges were frequently scenes of turbulent disorder.

The social life of American colleges to a large extent runs parallel to that of the world outside; and I believe that what is true of academic manners is largely true of city and village life in general. The lack of formality is balanced by an increase of considerateness.

This whole question of formality is interesting. It is not at all surprising today, when we meet a gentleman who seems to have plenty of time for courtesy, that we call him a 'gentleman of the old school.' Quite so; but fifty years ago, when one met that kind of a man, one *then* called him a 'gentleman of the old school.' And I suspect that one hundred and perhaps two hundred years ago, the same object inspired the same description.

What does this mean? Except in clothes, is there after all such a tremendous difference? We are certainly informal in 1938; but in 1838 were they always as formal as we think? When we attempt to reconstruct in our minds the image of a long-past time, it is difficult to imagine the people in their more intimate aspects. It is easier to imagine Demosthenes delivering a public oration than it is to imagine him in his house after supper, roaring with laughter at a funny story. Yet the Greeks and the Romans spent more of their time in natural, intimate relations than they did in any official capacity. In the reconstruction of history, we must not make the mistake that children make, of being unable to realize a human being when he is enveloped in a uniform.

Or, on the other hand, has the whole world been steadily growing more informal from the very beginning to this moment? Even though Adam and Eve wore only their skin, did she address him something like this: 'The evening meal is prepared, and it merely awaits your lordship's convenience?' And did he reply: 'Ah, my queen, one moment, while I regard the last rays of the dying sunlight on the broad bosom of the Euphrates, and then I shall be ready to allay the pangs of hunger?'

And if they did talk in that elaborate fashion, they did not love each other any more than if she had said, 'Come along, Charley—everything will get cold.'

Among the best detective stories are those by the late Earl Derr Biggers, dealing with the Chinese sleuth, Chan. He speaks to all and sundry with the prolonged and involved phraseology of self-abasement characteristic of oriental politeness. 'Will you deign to make use of my contemptible intellect, or perhaps first condescend to enter my wretched hovel and partake of abominable food?' But this elaborate formality deceived the guest no more than the speaker. Chan is satisfied with his house, better satisfied with his food, and most of all satisfied with himself.

It may be that the decrease in formality through the ages is owing partly to the increasing preciousness of time. In the eighteenth century, before they had any time-saving devices, everybody apparently had leisure—leisure to write letters, leisure for conversation, leisure for prolonged politeness. Now everybody who amounts to anything is busy. We are impatient with superfluous preliminaries and embroideries, and wish, as the saying is, to get down to brass tacks. For the modern American is shockingly poor in time. He never seems to have any.

To support the proposition that the lack of superficial courtesy is a sign of the growth of civilization rather than the reverse, several things can be said. I heard an elderly pessimist, shaking his silver head sadly, make the following contribution to modern thought:

'The young people of today have no manners at all: if this goes on, we shall relapse into barbarism.'

But was not elaborate and formal courtesy one of the chief characteristics of barbarism? Read what Benjamin Franklin said about the courtesy of the Indian savages of North America; and what did Sam Houston think of their manners in comparison with those of white men? When the Indians discussed anything, they had infinite time. They sat in solemn conclave, passed the meditative pipe slowly around, and when one spoke, nobody any more thought of interrupting him than we think of interrupting the preacher in church. And even the silliest propositions were listened to with grave courtesy. Compare a modern meeting of bank directors with a committee of Indian braves.

Turning from savages to so-called civilized persons—the elaborate courtesy of the age of chivalry was only a thin veneer, barely concealing a cynical contempt. We know the rules of that game. The knight must professedly adore fair ladies, and be ready at any moment to risk his life for a damosel in distress. Her slightest whim is his law: he must be prepared to go upon a difficult, distant, and dangerous quest to satisfy her caprice. But although knights greeted ladies with formal respect, as if the ladies were of some superior race, we know today that if the Knights of the Round Table were functioning, nearly every one of them would be in jail. Underneath that studied devotion, there was little respect for women and little reason for it.

The formal courtesy of man to woman has been replaced in the twentieth century by comradeship.

Perhaps the most striking proof that extremes in elaborate courtesy bear no real relation to warmth of heart is seen in the old-fashioned custom of the duel. When one man sent a challenge to another with the intention of murdering him, nothing could exceed the courtesy with which the whole matter was arranged.

And now that the duel has disappeared from many places, the extreme courtesy which characterized it has been transferred to the duels between nations, to the apparatus of murder on a gigantic scale. When the ambassador of one nation takes his leave because the two countries are about to engage in wholesale slaughter, the formalities on both sides are without spot or blemish.

On the other hand, the surest sign of intimacy is the absence of formality. If a man is walking on the street, overtakes a woman, and they walk along together, it is (almost) certain they have met before. Intimate friends never have to make conversation unless they feel like it. William Dean Howells left it on record that on one occasion he and Mark Twain travelled side by side in the train from Hartford to New York, three hours; neither read anything, neither said a word.

And the most intimate of all relations, that of marriage, is characterized by the annihilation of formality, the obliteration of reserve.

The growth of real courtesy, as distinguished from the

enamel of formality, is shown, I think, in the increasing good nature and tolerance of crowds—with two notable exceptions: an infuriated mob, which is less intelligent and more cruel than any collection of wild beasts; and the crowded conditions of modern transportation. A visitor from Mars who should obtain his first impression of ladies and gentlemen in the New York subway at the rush hour would hardly believe that the human race had ever produced anyone like Jane Addams or Nathan Straus.

But in general, the crowds on their way to a football game, at a circus, listening in the night to election returns, or merely the crowds of human beings in densely populated thoroughfares, seem to me on the whole to be good-humoured, tolerant, and even kind.

The growth in genuine courtesy and good manners characteristic of this present time is born not only of increased consideration for others, but of increased sincerity. The relations between boys and girls, between men and women, between children and parents, between pupils and teachers, between the younger and the older generation, may seem to some easily shockable persons to be lacking in good manners; but in many ways there is an improvement, and the improvement comes from increased sincerity.

The chief difference between the manners of today and those of fifty years ago is that then Age and Authority and Females received as a matter of course a certain lip service which had nothing to do with the individual. Today there is an increasing impatience with rendering homage except when the individual by his own mind or character deserves it; and when he does deserve it, he receives it in its most gratifying form.

Some years ago, when a member of a congregation argued (outside the church) very candidly with the minister, the latter's wife said to me, 'Do you believe that is the way anybody should address a clergyman?'

But today we believe that depends on the individual clergyman, rather than on the office.

But perhaps the most striking and genuine improvement in good manners shown by this generation in comparison with former times is concerned with business—buying and selling, everything pertaining to commercial life. Surely there has never been any period in history where courtesy was so universally regarded as an asset. You might raise the objection that this form of courtesy is no more sincere than the traditional politeness of chivalry. But if, in every department of commercial affairs, courtesy today is regarded as part of the essential equipment of a successful man, it is a tribute to its value.

For courtesy is now the rule rather than the exception, a very different state of affairs from that which I can remember. Many years ago railway ticket-sellers, tellers in banks, clerks in shops, were often studiously disagreeable except to the very rich. That method of behaviour has gone forever.

REFLEXIONS IN THE NINETEEN–THIRTIES

WHEN Andrew D. White published his famous book, *A History of the Warfare of Science with Theology in Christendom*, he quite naturally supposed there was no doubt as to the victor. He was a good man and loved truth, and freedom in searching it. He thought theology had waged a steadily losing battle all along the line; and its defeat, if not so immediate, was as certain as that of King Canute. Religion had lost one position after another; Science, always opposed and hindered and delayed by the struggle with theology, had nevertheless advanced, because the Truth was on its side. Furthermore, this conquest of religion by science was something that all reasonable men should greet with joy; it meant the removing of shackles of superstition, a free field for independent individual investigators. This was to be at last a brave new world, where men and women, released from all theological or governmental restraint, were to live in the clear and bracing atmosphere of truth.

Very good: very good indeed: we are now living in this Paradise which the former men of science saw afar off. Except in certain localities, there is no restraint on scientific investigation and scientific experiment; the modern hero is the man of science, regarded with universal respect and admiration; and perhaps with some mystical wonder, like the mysterious priests of old. For just as ignorant people believed that the priests had access to sources of knowledge beyond the range of the crowd and that they lived in a world of their own—so today, the vast majority of mankind, being ignorant of science, have almost a superstitious reverence for those who live in laboratories and commune there with occult forces.

Why then is our modern world so full of despair? Why have not mental 'enlightenment' and mechanical resources brought more happiness? Why this bankruptcy of hope? For if hope deferred maketh the heart sick, hope destroyed maketh the heart dead.

My own ignorance of science is so abysmal that any remark of mine on any particular science would be an impertinence. But I am sensitive to mental temperatures; I can tell the direction in which certain scientific pronouncements would lead us.

I heard a justly famous scientific man make an elaborate statement by which we were asked to believe that man had not only no soul, but no mind; that is to say, man was exclusively a physical creature. This seemed to me a vicious circle. Here was a man using the splendid powers of a splendid mind to prove that he had no mind.

After the lecture, I asked another scientific man who was apparently in agreement with the speaker's opinions, 'Are you ever dubious about the value of your researches? Does it ever occur to you that the results of all your efforts to reduce man to a collection of particles of matter might have a tragic aspect?' I asked the question because the lecturer seemed to be in such high spirits; he believed not only that everything he said was true, but that it was a truth in which we should rejoice. 'If we do really amount to nothing, aren't you ever in the least disturbed by the results of your investigations?' And he replied, 'Ah, but we have such a good time in making the investigations!'

In the realm of applied science, its experts have been of incalculable benefit to mankind. The enormous decrease in infant mortality, and annihilation of many diseases like yellow fever, the saving of physical agony in modern surgery, the all but incredible aids to the preservation of human life and the prolongation of its activities; the overcoming of difficulties in transportation, the resources now furnished to the crippled, the deaf, and the blind, one could go on for hundreds of pages, and not even begin to exhaust the blessings given to humanity by scientific men; and it would take still more pages for me adequately to express my grateful appreciation.

But just as many men are sceptical as to the value of religion, so I am sceptical as to the indiscriminate attitude of reverence to all applied science. An individual poisoner is regarded with detestation, and if caught, is in some danger of execution. Is it a cause of rejoicing that all over the world there are distinguished men of science who employ their intelligence and their knowledge and their energy to the invention and improvement of poisons that in the next war will destroy thousands of innocent women and children? Should our attitude to such inventions be one of unalloyed reverence? Was it beneficial to mankind that the revolver and the automatic and the 'silencer' were invented? When the next war comes, its wholesale methods of torture and destruction will have had their origin in laboratories.

And it is interesting to observe that, although individuals are restrained now in the production of food and other useful and valuable articles, there is no restraint whatever placed on the amount or the efficiency of production of the means of torture and death. Here the accepted principle is still *laissez-faire*.

I hope that these queries will not make any reader imagine that I am 'opposed to science.' I might just as well be opposed to gravitation. I am inordinately proud of being a member of the American Philosophical Society, one of whose objects, in the language of its founder, Benjamin Franklin, is to 'promote useful knowledge.' I am merely asking one general question, which can be compressed into one word, WHITHER?

Modern novelists are as a rule more cheerful than the books they write; on the other hand, I wonder if modern scientists are always in their hearts as cheerful as they look. I wonder if they ever have secret misgivings as to the ultimate value to humanity of their contributions. Browning's Pope asked himself this serious question:

> The sum up of what gain or loss to God
> Came of His one more Vicar in the world.

And as all the culture, knowledge, philosophy of the ancient world resulted in a general mental and moral bankruptcy, and were not only powerless to save the world, but left it hopeless, would it be strange if the net results of the prodigious advance of modern science should bring about another collapse? My own attitude toward science is one of respectful agnosticism; I am not sure that its services to the world are wholly beneficial. And I refuse to regard either the mental attitude that it so often encourages, or the engines of destruction that it invents and improves, with enthusiasm. Before accepting every statement sent out by 'science' I want to be certain that it has been definitely and permanently proved to be true.

In the meanwhile there is a possibility that science, after taking away the last hope of mankind, will supply the only possible remedy by inventions so powerful that mankind will be destroyed. A possibility only, not a probability. Hope in the end always triumphs over despair; and religious truth is indestructible.

I shall certainly not commit intellectual suicide by refusing to accept anything proved; having spent a large part of my time on earth searching for truth, I am not going to resist it whenever or wherever I find it. But I cannot help wondering as to ultimate values.

AUTUMNAL REFLEXIONS

It is Saturday the twenty-second of October 1938, and the hour is eight in the morning. I shall see Yale play the University of Michigan at football this afternoon; then I shall be in a state of excitement unfavourable to thought. But this morning alone in my study under the roof of my house at 110 Whitney Avenue, New Haven, with the sunlight flooding the room, surrounded by my books, I am looking backward over my life. As soon as this book is finished and indeed it will be soon, I hope never to look back again. *Prospice!*

Well, as this is the last time, I should like to recall some of my experiences of sheer delight. I shall mention only a few, for there are hundreds of days when I have been filled with happiness. Omitting religion and family life, the two greatest sources of happiness I know, which need no explanation to those familiar with them, and which no language could explain to others, I must honestly say I have found life good. I would not have missed it for anything. There have of course been misfortunes, illnesses, periods of mental depression, failures, loss of friends, and the general sense of frustration that afflicts every candid mind. But these are shadows, and my life has mainly been passed in sunshine.

Of course I should like to be an immortal poet or an immortal something-or-other; to feel the steadfast assurance that one had left on earth some enduring work that would remain as a permanent memorial. But although one knows, as I do, that everything one has done will be speedily forgotten, I do not see why that should make one miserable. Why spend one's life or even one's last moments in crying for the moon? Why not make the best of the good old world?

My life has been divided into four parts—Work, Play, Development, Social Pleasures. Work is man's greatest blessing. Whenever it is in any way possible, every boy and girl should choose as his life work some congenial occupation. It has always been necessary for me to work, but if at any time during the last twenty years some eccentric person had left me a million dollars, I should have gone right on working at my chosen profession, teaching, writing, and public speaking. I enjoy all three. I enjoy them so much that I have no hesitation in saying that I enjoy them more than vacations.

I have also had an enormous amount of fun out of play. I like all kinds of games, except alley-bowling, just as I like all famous music except that by Meyerbeer. In every game I have never succeeded in rising above mediocrity; but here again I doubt if the great players (whom I nevertheless envy) have enjoyed playing football, baseball, hockey, tennis, golf, billiards, pool, duplicate whist more than I. If I were now given the opportunity to spend every day for the next five hundred years in an invariable programme of work all the morning, golf all the afternoon, and social enjoyment all the evening, I should accept with alacrity, making only one stipulation—that at the end of the five hundred years I should have the privilege of renewal. And that's that.

In cultural development, by which I mean the enrichment of the mind by Nature and Art, I have had unspeakable delight. Yet I am neither a naturalist nor an artist. I don't know anything about flowers, and very little about animals. I cannot draw or paint, or make anything with my hands.

But no one loves the scenes of nature more than I. The first sunset that I remember with enjoyment occurred when I was ten years old; and how many I have seen since then! I have seen the Matterhorn from the Gorner Grat, Mont Blanc from Chamonix, and the divine flush on the summit of the Jungfrau.

Fifty years ago I heard for the first time the Ninth Symphony; and while I have heard it often since then, the most memorable occasion was in May 1912 when I heard it at Paris, played by a magnificent orchestra, conducted by Felix Weingartner; I have heard *Die Meistersinger* in Munich, conducted by Arthur Nikisch, my favourite among all orchestra conductors. I have heard the *Emperor Concerto*, with Ossip Gabrilowitsch at the piano; I have heard *Tod und Verklärung* with Stokowski and the Philadelphia Orchestra, I have heard Toscanini conducting the Seventh Symphony; I have heard De Pachmann (in his prime) play Chopin's B flat minor sonata, Paderewski play Liszt's Hungarian Rhapsody No. 2, Josef Hofmann play Beethoven's Sonata III. I have heard *Carmen* sung by Emma Calvé, Emma Eames, Jean de Reszké and Lasalle; *Tristan und Isolde* sung by Jean de Reszké and Lilli Lehmann; *Faust* sung by Jean and Edouard de Reszké, Emma Eames, Maurel, and Scalchi; *Mignon* sung by Mme Lucrezia Bori; I have repeatedly heard the three greatest bassos of modern time, Edouard de Reszké, Pol Plançon, and Chaliapin.

In the theatre I have seen Edwin Booth as Shylock, Mansfield as Richard III, Irving in *The Lyons Mail*, Possart as Mephistopheles, Sarah Bernhardt as La Tosca, Duse as Francesca, Salvini as Othello, Maurice Evans in the unabridged *Hamlet*, and twice have I seen the Passion Play at Oberammergau. All these are memorable experiences. But if I should attempt to recall all the glorious things I have seen in nature and in art, I should have no time for fresh experiences that await me.

As for social pleasures, one of the highest enjoyments is

agreeable company for good conversation; and I especially like men, women, and children.

One of the chief sources of happiness in my life has been my family associations. My cousins who have always lived in New Haven are descended from that same Colonel William Lyon, my great-grandfather. Judge William Lyon Bennett is now ninety years old; his mind is clear and vigorous and his conversation always interesting. His brother the late Thomas Bennet was a member of the Yale Corporation; he married Jennie Winchester, the daughter of the famous arms inventor, O. F. Winchester. Their son, Winchester Bennett, now living in New Haven, married Susan Silliman Wright, a daughter of Professor Wright of Yale; and their daughter Mollie married Mr. Trevelyan, a son of the famous historian, Sir George M. Trevelyan, O. M., professor at Cambridge. Harriet Bennett, now living in New Haven, has published many poems, and Ethel, daughter of William Lyon, is an artist. My Bennett cousins and their parents and grandparents have always been associated with Yale.

My wife's brother and my most intimate friend, Frank Hubbard, was married a few months after my own marriage, to Miss Elizabeth Lockwood daughter of St. John Lockwood, a graduate of Yale; their two daughters married Yale graduates. My brother Arthur's boy is a Yale graduate and his son is named William Lyon Phelps. My personal associations with all of my own relations and of those of my wife have been and are ideal in affectionate intimacy. I mention these things because they have added to my happiness; and because they are uncommon.

I know of no greater fallacy or one more widely believed than the statement that youth is the happiest time of life. The foundation of this statement—the assumption on which it rests—is false. The assumption is that men and women are merely animals; but the differences between human beings and animals are greater and more important than the resemblances. The mind is more important than the body.

We are like animals in our physical sensations; we have hunger, thirst, lust, love of warmth and shelter; we suffer from physical injuries. But we have something they have not, something that literally makes all the difference in the world. We have the *power of development.*

We have the marvellous, boundless, incomparable gifts of observation, thought, and imagination.

Walt Whitman expressed it both concretely and poetically in his poem *To the Man-of-War Bird,* where, after showing the enormous superiority of the bird's flight over land and sea in comparison with the slow and limited motion of man, he concluded

> In them, in thy experiences, hadst thou my soul,
> What joys! what joys were thine!

And now the airplane gives man the experiences.

I am considering only this present life, this life on earth; and if this is all we have, we are still more fortunate than the animals, because ideas are more interesting than food. But I think our capacity for development supplies an intelligent reason for believing in a future life. If my clever and attractive dog should live to be one hundred or one thousand, he would be no further along than he is now. Whereas every child has potentialities for which eternity is not too long. This is what makes teaching so exciting—it is more exciting to teach boys and girls than it is to train horses and dogs.

To see the first awakening of intellectual interest in a young man gives a thrill; for it is a sign of life, of growth, an awakening of dormant powers.

Education means drawing forth from the mind latent powers and developing them, so that in mature years one may apply these powers not merely to success in one's occupation, but to success in the greatest of all arts—the art of living.

If one is fortunate enough to have attended a good school and a high-grade college, that is well. But it is better to have really educated oneself without these advantages than to have had the advantages and missed the opportunities.

It is with some misgiving that I see today evidences of a desire to get-rich-quick in ideas, even as so many have found disaster in the attempt to get-rich-quick in money; and the latter is certainly easier than the former. There is no short cut to the riches of thought. Acceleration is not upward, but downward. Merely because an ambitious and industrious student might learn of assigned lessons in two years at college what an average undergraduate would learn in four, does not mean that the former has got out of college life the enrichment of the latter. Oxford and Cambridge mean more than the mere curriculum.

I have no doubt the average person enjoys excitement more than comfort; although comfort means the absence of difficulties, and excitement means an increase of them. Now it is well to remember that many comfortable persons are unhappy, whereas nobody in a state of excitement is wholly unhappy. Melancholy visits the empty mind and settles there; the mind full of interesting or exciting ideas cannot be invaded by depression.

As we advance in years from childhood to youth, from youth to middle age, from middle age to old age, we really grow happier, if we live intelligently. The universe is spectacular, and it is a free show. Increase of difficulties and responsibilities strengthens and enriches the mind, and adds to the variety of life.

> The noble soul by age grows lustier:
> Her appetite and her digestion mend

To live abundantly is like climbing a mountain or a tower. Why is it that men every year pay money for the privilege of leaving the comfortable plains and highways, in order to climb through appalling difficulties and obstacles to the top of a mountain? Someone asked one of the adventurous heroes who tried to climb Mount Everest, 'Why do you want to climb it?' He answered, 'Because it is *there*.' (And now he is there.)

It was not the mere love of fame, though possibly that had something to do with it; it was because, in his quiet and safe lodgings in London, surrounded with comforts and luxuries, the mountain was *calling him*!

> Hark to it calling, calling clear
> Calling until you cannot stay
> From dearer things than your own most dear
> Over the hills and far away.

To climb the highest mountains is not for the average man; it is only for those especially gifted in body and mind, and for few of those.

I have myself climbed more towers than mountains; for although the works of nature exceed the works of man in beauty and grandeur, I have found the works of man more interesting. To me nature is not so interesting as human nature.

It is a pity that the great humorist, Mark Twain, was such a pessimist; yet it is true that excess of humour is often accompanied with excess of melancholy. The most terrible and consistent pessimist in English literature was Jonathan Swift, who was also one of the greatest humorists of all time. I suppose there is some balance, some compensation, in such a temperament. Then it is true that mere laughter and demonstrative gaiety are not the highest forms of happiness. The love of a man for a maid, though it may reach ecstatic happiness, is without humour. One

touch of humour might be fatal to it. In other deepest enjoyments there is no humour. The delight we take in
music and in painting and in sunsets is humourless. In
The Merchant of Venice Jessica said to her lover,

> I am never merry when I hear sweet music.

Mark Twain said life would be infinitely happier if we
could only be born at the age of eighty, and gradually
approach eighteen. This would mean we should gradually
lose our intelligence, our experience, our ideas, our work,
our personality, even our manhood. We should exchange
profound happiness for animal spirits.

To say that youth is happier than maturity is like saying
that the view from the bottom of a tower is better than the
view from the top. As we ascend the spiral staircase,
and glance from time to time through the narrow slits in
the stone, the range of our view widens immensely; the
horizon is pushed farther away. Finally as we reach the
summit it is as if we had the world at our feet.

St. Simeon Stylites, who spent sixty years on top of a
tower, was better off than a hermit in a cell.

The pursuit of knowledge, the advance of thought, the
gain in experience, the growth of a man or a woman from
youth upwards, are like the struggle up a height. Lessing
said he would choose the pursuit of truth rather than the
knowledge of truth, if he had to choose between the two.
The very problems of life, the meaning of life itself, become more interesting as we grow older. John Donne wrote

> On a huge hill
> Cragged and steep, Truth stands, and he that will
> Reach her, about must, and about must go;
> And what the hill's suddenness resists, win so.

Unhappiness comes from thinking about oneself, rather
than of something outside of oneself. The reason we are so

unhappy when we have a toothache is because we cannot think of anything except the ache. A toothache is importunate; it will not be denied. Shakespeare said that not even a philosopher could endure a toothache patiently. Children are made unhappy by physical aches and pains or by their inability to get what they want; and they are without resources, as helpless as a disappointed dog. Young people suffer from self-consciousness, the curse of adolescence. But as we grow older, we have more things to do and more things to think about. There is no comparison at all between the vague happiness of an irresponsible youth, and the real happiness of a busy man or woman, with a home and an occupation, whose work, ideas, and opinions count for something.

The ideas that come from one's work, from reading, from thought, from music, from art, and from mere observation of the world of men and women, are, curiously enough, both a refuge and an inspiration. They refresh and they stimulate. The best insurance against old age and disability is an interesting mind; and such a mind gives a stimulus to more enjoyment.

> This world's no blot for us,
> Nor blank; it means intensely, and means good;
> To find its meaning is my meat and drink.

I have seen persons in absolute agony; it seems incredible then, that the time will ever come when they will find a newspaper interesting, or that they will enjoy unconsciously simple pleasures like eating or drinking, or the air of an October morning. But the moment when that dull look of grief in the eyes is replaced by even a flicker of interest, they are on the way to recovery.

The art of living can be cultivated; the more we stock our minds with interesting thoughts, the richer we are. And these riches remain; they cannot be lost. They add to the happiness and to the excitement of daily living.

In my life of professional teaching, I have never endeavoured to make young men more efficient; I have tried to make them more interesting. If one is interested, one is usually interesting. The business of the teacher is not to supply information, it is to raise a thirst. I like to hang pictures on the walls of the mind, I like to make it possible for a man to live with himself, so that he will not be bored with himself. For my own part, *I live every day as if this were the first day I had ever seen and the last I were going to see.*

The Book of Proverbs, speaking of the ideal woman, says she can laugh at her approaching old age. It would be well if all women (and men) would remember that the cultivation of the mind is the best insurance, not against death, but against life. Those marvellous old people in the French aristocracy of the eighteenth century, were as sought after in society as if they had been fair to see. Their wit indeed defied both life and death. King Stanislas, who had received from his daughter, the Queen of France, a wadded dressing-gown, got his death from it, when one day it caught fire. An old woman, endeavouring to help him, was severely burned, and in the midst of his agony, he said 'How strange that at our ages you and I should both burn with the same flame!' He was eighty-eight. After two weeks of suffering, he died, and in his last hours dictated a letter to his daughter about the gown. 'You gave it me to keep me warm; it has kept me too warm.'

Wit is a great preservative. Age acted on the old ladies of the *salons* like a whetstone. They feared not the loss of grace and youth; they had the happy assurance that comes from the knowledge of being *wanted*. They had faults; but they never bored any one. They were beloved by contemporaries and envied by the young. There is never much trouble in any family where the children hope some day to resemble their parents.

Perhaps nothing nowadays is a more common target for ridicule than the hustler and booster, whether he boosts as an individual or as a member of a service organization. The man whose motto is 'bigger and better business,' a bigger town, with a bigger population and bigger buildings, is laughed at for his enthusiasm and for his perspiring efforts. Much of this laughter is merely the cynical adverse criticism of men who have never done anything themselves, never will do anything, and so pretend to be faintly and superciliously amused by the optimistic exertions of others. We may dismiss these unproductive and complacent occupiers of the seats of the scornful, for they are comparatively few in number and their opinions are of no moment. But the rational basis for laughter at the booster is that the hustler and the booster often have a false standard of excellence.

When a noisy man roars in your face that the population of his particular town has doubled in ten years we have a right to enquire, what of it? Is it a cause for rejoicing? When you climb into a trolley car on a rainy day you do not rejoice because the population of the trolley car doubles in three minutes. A mere increase in the number of persons at a given spot does not necessarily mean that collectively or individually they are any better off. What we wish to know is something quite different from the word 'more.' Is the community growing in intelligence? Are there better schools, better theatres, better art museums, better churches, better orchestras—are the individual inhabitants growing?

Strangely enough, some of the professional men of science, who are often the first to laugh at the booster because he applies the quantitative rather than the qualitative standard of measurement, are themselves guilty of the same fault on a larger scale. They do not apply standards of size to a growing business or a growing village; they apply these standards to the universe.

Some astronomers have recently been fond of reminding us that our sun itself is only a tiny star—one out of many billions—and that our earth is but the tiniest speck. They are fond of drawing diagrams showing the comparative size of our sun and that of other globes in the starry skies, and the earth dwindles to a mere point. 'Therefore,' say these scientists, 'how unimportant is man and how ridiculous that he should consider either himself or his earthly abode a matter of any importance to God or to space or time or gravitation;' the conclusion following that religion and morals are matters of small consequence and we need not bother our heads about them.

Now it seems to me that expressions of this kind are as fallacious and as injurious as any booster's standard of mere quantity; for what are these gentlemen trying to say except that as the earth is so tiny in comparison with other stars it must necessarily follow that man himself is a very unimportant factor in the universe? I believe the earth to be the most important spot in the entire creation and that the most precious thing on the earth is man—men, women, and children.

When I was a graduate student at Yale, I studied the complete works of the German philosopher Lotze, with not so much success as the late Lord Haldane, but with assiduity and enthusiasm. Lotze gave the best definition of existence. 'To be is to be in relations.' It is an accurate definition of life. A dead body, no matter where the soul or mind or spirit may be, has no relations with anything. It doesn't know its latitude or longitude, it doesn't know whether it is winter or summer, it doesn't know whether it is raining or the sun is shining, it doesn't know what is going on in the world of politics. Guy de Maupassant described a cemetery: 'The people in there are not reading the newspapers.'

Well, if a dead body is dead because it has no relations

with anything, it would seem to follow that the more relations we have the more life we have. If a man is interested only in his business, then so far as the worlds of music and art and science and foreign politics are concerned, he is dead. They do not exist for him any more than if he were in the grave. But if in addition to his business he is also interested in music or in playing games or in foreign politics he is just that much more alive. People of tremendous mental vitality are intensely interested in a variety of things. The late Theodore Roosevelt was interested in everything from a bumble-bee to a battleship, and I have never known a man more bursting with vitality.

I am interested in everything in the world except the higher mathematics; and I should be interested in that branch of study if I had sufficient intelligence. A very simple test that one can apply to oneself to discover a range of interest is to take up the daily newspaper and see if there is something on every page of interest: foreign news, national news, local news, athletics, the theatre, music, books, stock exchange, etc., and if there is something on every page that interests a man, he is very much alive.

Not only does this mean richness and abundance of life and a continually enlarging curiosity, but it is the best form of insurance against 'grey ultimate decrepitude' and against all troubles, disasters, sorrows, and heartbreak that everyone must pass through. For when one is despondent, one cannot recover by will power. One cannot say, 'I am feeling miserable, but I will be cheerful,' for the more will power he uses, the worse he feels. It is like sinking in a quicksand where every effort sends one deeper. But if one is alert and has an active mind continually interested in a variety of subjects, sooner or later his mind will be diverted from himself and from his sorrows to something quite different; and at that moment convalescence and recovery set in. Even if one is unhappy, one may find life interesting.

The world itself in this year of grace 1938 is in a much worse condition than it was thirty years ago, but it is more interesting.

I am filled with wonder and admiration whenever I think of the poem *Remembrance*, written by Emily Brontë when she was about twenty-five. It is one of the greatest love poems in literature; but we can account for that by the miracle of genius as we can account for great pieces of music being written by people with little experience. But where did Emily learn the secret that even great philosophers have sought in vain? Where did she learn not only in the midst of unhappiness but without the slightest hope of ever having any happiness, that life could not only be endurable but exciting? This is the stanza of her poem that gives me such respect not only for her courage but for the quality of her mind.

> But when the days of golden dreams had perished,
> And even Despair was powerless to destroy,
> Then did I learn how existence could be cherished,
> Strengthened and fed, without the aid of joy.

Her mind was so rich in thought, so alert and vigorous in intelligence, that looking forward to a future barren of happiness she still found life supremely worth living. And this was not the defiant, stoical courage of despair; there was no resignation in it.

The whole question of optimism and pessimism is interesting. There are many more consistent Christians than there are consistent pessimists. People who call themselves optimists are usually thought to be rather shallow, whereas people who call themselves pessimists are thought to be profound. Yet we nearly all of us congratulate others on their birthdays, and if we do that sincerely we are optimists. That does not mean that we think this the best of all possible worlds or that we think life a succession of beautiful experiences. But it does mean that we consider life as an asset and that we consider it good fortune to have been born. For a shallow optimism I have no respect whatever. But if optimism means one believes that in the long run truth will survive error and good will triumph over evil and that life is an experience for which one is grateful, then I am most certainly an optimist. There are few genuine pessimists, and although I do not share their beliefs, I respect them. The great Jonathan Swift was an absolute pessimist. He invariably celebrated his birthday by wearing black and by fasting, because he was so sorry he had been born. To the average man such an attitude is comic. In one of Strindberg's plays a question is asked, 'How is your wife?' 'She is almost blind.' And after an exclamation of sorrow, 'No, she says there is nothing worth seeing and she hopes she will soon be deaf because there is nothing worth hearing, and she says the best thing about being old is that you are almost through.' Such pessimism is genuine but seems almost absurd, so contrary is it to the deepest instincts of humanity. Like the remark of the gentleman from North Carolina—'The moment you're born, you're done for.'

INDEX

JOHN MARSHALL
From the portrait by Chester Harding

THE LIFE
OF
JOHN MARSHALL

BY
ALBERT J. BEVERIDGE

VOLUMES III AND IV
1800–1835

BOSTON AND NEW YORK
HOUGHTON MIFFLIN COMPANY
The Riverside Press Cambridge

The Riverside Press
CAMBRIDGE · MASSACHUSETTS
PRINTED IN THE U.S.A.

THE LIFE OF JOHN MARSHALL

VOLUME III
Conflict and Construction
1800–1815

PREFACE

MARSHALL'S great Constitutional opinions grew out of, or were addressed to, serious public conditions, national in extent. In these volumes the effort is made to relate the circumstances that required him to give to the country those marvelous state papers: for Marshall's opinions were nothing less than state papers and of the first rank. In order to understand the full meaning of his deliverances and to estimate the just value of his labors, it is necessary to know the historical sources of his foremost expositions of the Constitution, and the historical purposes they were intended to accomplish. Without such knowledge, Marshall's finest pronouncements become mere legal utterances, important, to be sure, but colorless and unattractive.

It is worthy of repetition, even in a preface, that the history of the times is a part of his greatest opinions; and that, in the treatment of them a résumé of the events that produced them must be given. For example, the decision of Marbury *vs.* Madison, at the time and in the manner it was rendered, was compelled by the political situation then existing, unless the principle of judicial supremacy over legislation was to be abandoned. The Judiciary Debate of 1802 in Congress — one of the most brilliant as well as most important legislative engagements in parliamentary history — can no more be overlooked by the student of American Constitutional development, than the opinion of Marshall in Marbury *vs.* Madison can be disregarded.

Again, in Cohens *vs.* Virginia, the Chief Justice rises to heights of exalted — almost emotional — eloquenc . Yet the case itself was hardly more than a police court controversy. If the trivial fine of itinerant peddlars of lottery tickets were alone involved, Marshall's splendid passages become unnecessary and, indeed, pompous rhetoric. But when the curtains of history are raised, we see the heroic part that Marshall played and realize the meaning of his powerful language. While Marshall's opinion in M'Culloch *vs.* Maryland, even taken by itself, is a major treatise on constitutional government, it becomes a fascinating chapter in an engaging story, when read in connection with an account of the situation which compelled that outgiving.

The same thing is true of his other historic utterances. Indeed, it may be said that his weightiest opinions were interlocking parts of one great drama.

Much space has been given to the conspiracy and trials of Aaron Burr. The combined story of that adventure and of those prosecutions has not hitherto been told. In the conduct of the Burr trials, Marshall appears in a more intimate and personal fashion than in any other phase of his judicial career; the entire series of events that make up that page of our history is a striking example of the manipulation of public opinion by astute politicians, and is, therefore, useful for the self-guidance of American democracy. Most important of all, the culminating result of this dramatic episode was the definitive establishment of the American law of treason.

In narrating the work of a jurist, the temptation is very strong to engage in legal discussion, and to cite and comment upon the decisions of other courts and the opinions of other judges. This, however, would be the very negation of biography; nor would it add anything of interest or enlightenment to the reader. Such information and analysis are given fully in the various books on Constitutional law and history, in the annotated reports, and in the encyclopædias of law upon the shelves of every lawyer. Care, therefore, has been taken to avoid making any part of the *Life of John Marshall* a legal treatise.

The manuscript of these volumes has been read by Professor Edward Channing of Harvard; Professor Max Farrand of Yale; Professor Edward S. Corwin of Princeton; Professor William E. Dodd of Chicago University; Professor Clarence W. Alvord of the University of Illinois; Professor James A. Woodburn of Indiana University; Professor Charles H. Ambler of the University of West Virginia; Professor Archibald Henderson of the University of North Carolina; Professor D. R. Anderson of Richmond (Va.) College; and Dr. H. J. Eckenrode of Richmond, Virginia. The manuscript of the third volume has been read by Professor Charles A. Beard of New York; Dr. Samuel Eliot Morison of Harvard; and Mr. Harold J. Laski of Harvard. The manuscript of both the third and fourth volumes has been read, from

the lawyer's point of view, by Mr. Arthur Lord of
Boston, President of the Massachusetts Bar Association, and by Mr. Charles Martindale of Indianapolis.

The chapters on the Burr conspiracy and trials
have been read by Professor Walter Flavius McCaleb
of New York; Professor Isaac Joslin Cox of the University of Cincinnati; and Mr. Samuel H. Wandell
of New York. Chapter Three of Volume Three (Marbury *vs.* Madison) has been read by the Honorable
Oliver Wendell Holmes, Associate Justice of the Supreme Court of the United States; by the Honorable Philander Chase Knox, United States Senator;
and by Mr. James M. Beck of New York. Other
special chapters have been read by the Honorable
Henry Cabot Lodge, United States Senator; by
Professor J. Franklin Jameson of the Department
of Historical Research of the Carnegie Institution
of Washington; by Professor Charles H. Haskins of
Harvard; by Dr. William Draper Lewis of Philadelphia, former Dean of the Law School of the University of Pennsylvania; and by Mr. W. B. Bryan of
Washington.

All of these gentlemen have made valuable suggestions of which I have availed myself, and I gratefully
acknowledge my indebtedness to them. The responsibility for everything in these volumes, however, is,
of course, exclusively mine; and, in stating my appreciation of the comment and criticism with which
I have been favored, I do not wish to be relieved of
my burden by allowing the inference that any part
of it should be assigned to others.

I also owe it to myself again to express my heavy

obligation to Mr. Worthington Chauncey Ford, Editor of the Massachusetts Historical Society. As was the case in the preparation of the first two volumes of this work, Mr. Ford has extended to me the resources of his ripe scholarship; while his wise counsel, steady encouragement, and unselfish assistance, have been invaluable in the prosecution of a long and exacting task.

I also again acknowledge my indebtedness to Mr. Lindsay Swift, Editor of the Boston Public Library, who has read with critical care not only the many drafts of the manuscript, but also the proofs of the entire work. Mr. Swift has given, unstintedly, his rare literary taste and critical accomplishment to the examination of these pages.

I also tender my hearty thanks to Dr. Gardner Weld Allen of Boston, who has generously directed the preparation of the bibliography and personally revised it.

Mr. David Maydole Matteson of Cambridge, Massachusetts, has made the index of these volumes as he made that of the first two volumes, and has combined both indexes into one. In rendering this service, Mr. Matteson has also searched for points where text and notes could be made more accurate; and I wish to express my appreciation of his kindness.

My thanks are also owing to the staff of The Riverside Press, and particularly to Mr. Lanius D. Evans, to whose keen interest and watchful care in the production of this work I am indebted for much of whatever exactitude it may possess.

The manuscript sources have been acknowledged, in all instances, in the footnotes where references to them have been made, except in the case of the letters of Marshall to his relatives, for which I again thank those descendants and connections of the Chief Justice named in the preface to Volumes One and Two. The Hopkinson manuscripts are in the possession of Mr. Edward Hopkinson of Philadelphia, to whom I am indebted for the privilege of inspecting this valuable source and for furnishing me with copies of important letters.

In preparing these volumes, Mr. A. P. C. Griffin, Assistant Librarian, and Mr. John Clement Fitzpatrick, of the Manuscript Division of the Library of Congress, have been even more obliging, if possible, than they were in the preparation of the first part of this work. The officers and their assistants of the Boston Public Library, the Boston Athenæum, the Massachusetts State Library, the Massachusetts Historical Society, the Pennsylvania Historical Society, the Virginia State Library, the Indiana State Library, and the Indianapolis City Library, have assisted whole-heartedly in the performance of my labors; and I am glad of the opportunity to thank all of them for their interest and help.

ALBERT J. BEVERIDGE

CONTENTS

CONTENTS

ments of counsel — Weakness of the House managers — They are overwhelmed by counsel for Chase — Joseph Hopkinson's brilliant appeal — He captivates the Senate — Nicholson's fatal admission — Rodney's absurd speech — Luther Martin's great argument — Randolph closes for the managers — He apostrophizes Marshall — His pathetic breakdown — The Senate votes — Tense excitement in the Chamber — Chase acquitted — A determinative event in American history — Independence of the National Judiciary saved — Marshall for the first time secure in the office of Chief Justice.

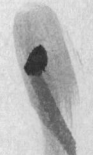

The people receive him cordially — He is given remarkable ovation at Nashville — Andrew Jackson's ardent friendship — Burr enthusiastically welcomed at New Orleans — War with Spain seemingly inevitable — Burr plans to lead attack upon Mexico when hostilities begin — Spanish agents start rumors against him — Eastern papers print sensational stories — Burr returns to the Capital — Universal demand for war with Spain — Burr intrigues in Washington — He again starts for the West — He sends his famous cipher dispatch to Wilkinson — Blennerhassett joins Burr — They purchase four hundred thousand acres of land on the Washita River — Plan to settle this land if war not declared — Wilkinson's eagerness for war — Burr arraigned in the Kentucky courts — He is discharged — Cheered by the people — Wilkinson determines to betray Burr — He writes mysterious letters to the President — Jefferson issues his Proclamation — Wilkinson's reign of military lawlessness in New Orleans — Arrest of Burr's agents, Bollmann and Swartwout — Arrest of Adair — Prisoners sent under guard by ship to Washington — The capital filled with wild rumors — Jefferson's slight mention of the Burr conspiracy in his Annual Message — Congress demands explanation — Jefferson sends Special Message denouncing Burr: his "guilt is placed beyond question" — Effect upon the public mind — Burr already convicted in popular opinion.

Bollmann and Swartwout arrive at Washington and are imprisoned — Adair and Alexander released by the court at Baltimore for want of proof — Eaton's affidavit against Burr — Bollmann and Swartwout apply to Supreme Court for writ of habeas corpus — Senate passes bill suspending the privilege of that writ — The House indignantly rejects the Senate Bill — Marshall delivers the first of his series of opinions on treason — No evidence against Bollmann and Swartwout, and Marshall discharges them — Violent debate in the House — Burr, ignorant of all, starts down the Cumberland and Mississippi with nine boats and a hundred men — First learns in Mississippi of the proceedings against him — Voluntarily surrenders to the civil authorities — The Mississippi grand jury refuses to indict Burr, asserting that he is guilty of no offense — Court refuses to discharge him — Wilkinson's frantic efforts to seize or kill him — He goes into hiding — Court forfeits his bond — He escapes — He is captured in Alabama and confined to Fort Stoddert — Becomes popular with both officers and men — Taken under military guard for a thousand miles through the wilderness — Arrives at Richmond — Marshall issues warrant for his delivery to the civil authorities — The first hearing before the Chief Justice — Shall Burr be committed for treason — The argument — Marshall's opinion — Probable cause to suspect Burr guilty of attempt to attack Mexico; no evidence upon which to commit Burr for treason — Marshall indirectly criticizes Jefferson — Burr's letters to his daughter — Popular demand for Burr's con-

lessly assail Marshall and the Supreme Court — The fight for the passage of a bill to relieve the New England investors is renewed — Marshall's opinion and the decision of the court influential in securing the final passage of the measure.

APPENDIX

LIST OF ABBREVIATED TITLES MOST FREQUENTLY CITED

All references here are to the List of Authorities at the end of this volume

Adams: *U.S.* *See* Adams, Henry. History of the United States.

Ames. *See* Ames, Fisher. Works.

Channing: *Jeff. System.* *See* Channing, Edward. Jeffersonian System, 1801–11.

Channing: *U.S.* *See* Channing, Edward. History of the United States.

Chase Trial. *See* Chase, Samuel. Trial.

Corwin. *See* Corwin, Edward Samuel. Doctrine of Judicial Review.

Cutler. *See* Cutler, William Parker, and Julia Perkins. Life, Journals, and Correspondence of Manasseh Cutler.

Dillon. *See* Marshall, John. Life, Character, and Judicial Services. Edited by John Forrest Dillon.

Eaton: Prentiss. *See* Eaton, William. Life.

Jay: Johnston. *See* Jay, John. Correspondence and Public Papers.

Jefferson Writings: Washington. *See* Jefferson, Thomas, Writings. Edited by Henry Augustine Washington.

King. *See* King, Rufus. Life and Correspondence.

McCaleb. *See* McCaleb, Walter Flavius. Aaron Burr Conspiracy.

McMaster: *U.S.* *See* McMaster, John Bach. History of the People of the United States.

Marshall. *See* Marshall, John. Life of George Washington.

Memoirs, J.Q.A.: Adams. *See* Adams, John Quincy. Memoirs.

Morris. *See* Morris, Gouverneur. Diary and Letters.

N.E. Federalism: Adams. *See* New-England Federalism, 1800–1815, Documents relating to. Edited by Henry Adams.

Plumer. *See* Plumer, William. Life.

Priv. Corres.: Colton. *See* Clay, Henry. Private Correspondence. Edited by Calvin Colton.

Records Fed. Conv.: Farrand. *See* Records of the Federal Convention of 1787.

Story. *See* Story, Joseph. Life and Letters.

Trials of Smith and Ogden. *See* Smith, William Steuben, and Ogden, Samuel Gouverneur. Trials for Misdemeanors.

Wharton: *Social Life.* *See* Wharton, Anne Hollingsworth. Social Life in the Early Republic.

Wharton: *State Trials.* *See* Wharton, Francis. State Trials of the United States during the Administrations of Washington and Adams.

Wilkinson: *Memoirs.* *See* Wilkinson, James. Memoirs of My Own Times.

Works: Colton. *See* Clay, Henry. Works.

Works: Ford. *See* Jefferson, Thomas. Works. Federal Edition. Edited by Paul Leicester Ford.

Writings, J. Q. A.: Ford. *See* Adams, John Quincy. Writings. Edited by Worthington Chauncey Ford.

THE LIFE OF JOHN MARSHALL

THE LIFE OF JOHN MARSHALL

CHAPTER I

DEMOCRACY: JUDICIARY

Rigorous law is often rigorous injustice. (Terence.)

The Federalists have retired into the Judiciary as a stronghold, and from that battery all the works of republicanism are to be battered down.
                                                                    (Jefferson.)

There will be neither justice nor stability in any system, if some material parts of it are not independent of popular control. (George Cabot.)

A STRANGE sight met the eye of the traveler who, aboard one of the little river sailboats of the time, reached the stretches of the sleepy Potomac separating Alexandria and Georgetown. A wide swamp extended inland from a modest hill on the east to a still lower elevation of land about a mile to the west.[1] Between the river and morass a long flat tract bore clumps of great trees, mostly tulip poplars, giving, when seen from a distance, the appearance of "a fine park." [2]

Upon the hill stood a partly constructed white stone building, mammoth in plan. The slight elevation north of the wide slough was the site of an apparently finished edifice of the same material, noble in its dimensions and with beautiful, simple lines,[3] but "surrounded with a rough rail fence 5 or 6 feet high unfit for a decent barnyard." [4] From the river

[1] Gallatin to his wife, Jan. 15, 1801, Adams: *Life of Albert Gallatin,* 252; also Bryan: *History of the National Capital,* I, 357–58.

[2] *First Forty Years of Washington Society:* Hunt, 11.

[3] *Ib.*; and see Wolcott to his wife, July 4, 1800, Gibbs: *Administrations of Washington and John Adams,* II, 377.

[4] Plumer to Thompson, Jan. 1, 1803, Plumer MSS. Lib. Cong.

nothing could be seen beyond the groves near the banks of the stream except the two great buildings and the splendid trees which thickened into a seemingly dense forest upon the higher ground to the northward.[1]

On landing and making one's way through the underbrush to the foot of the eastern hill, and up the gullies that seamed its sides thick with trees and tangled wild grapevines,[2] one finally reached the immense unfinished structure that attracted attention from the river. Upon its walls laborers were languidly at work.

Clustered around it were fifteen or sixteen wooden houses. Seven or eight of these were boarding-houses, each having as many as ten or a dozen rooms all told. The others were little affairs of rough lumber, some of them hardly better than shanties. One was a tailor shop; in another a shoemaker plied his trade; a third contained a printer with his hand press and types, while a washerwoman occupied another; and in the others there was a grocery shop, a pamphlets-and-stationery shop, a little dry-goods shop, and an oyster shop. No other human habitation of any kind appeared for three quarters of a mile.[3]

A broad and perfectly straight clearing had been made across the swamp between the eastern hill and the big white house more than a mile away to the westward. In the middle of this long opening ran a roadway, full of stumps, broken by deep mud holes in the rainy season, and almost equally deep with

---

[1] Gallatin to his wife, Jan. 15, 1801, Adams: *Gallatin*, 252–53.
[2] Hunt, 10.   [3] Gallatin to his wife, *supra*.

dust when the days were dry. On either border was a path or "walk" made firm at places by pieces of stone; though even this "extended but a little way." Alder bushes grew in the unused spaces of this thoroughfare, and in the depressions stagnant water stood in malarial pools, breeding myriads of mosquitoes. A sluggish stream meandered across this avenue and broadened into the marsh.[1]

A few small houses, some of brick and some of wood, stood on the edge of this long, broad embryo street. Near the large stone building at its western end were four or five structures of red brick, looking much like ungainly warehouses. Farther westward on the Potomac hills was a small but pretentious town with its many capacious brick and stone residences, some of them excellent in their architecture and erected solidly by skilled workmen.[2]

Other openings in the forest had been cut at various places in the wide area east of the main highway that connected the two principal structures already described. Along these forest avenues were scattered houses of various materials, some finished and some in the process of erection.[3] Here and there unsightly gravel pits and an occasional brick kiln added to the raw unloveliness of the whole.

Such was the City of Washington, with Georgetown near by, when Thomas Jefferson became President and John Marshall Chief Justice of the United States — the Capitol, Pennsylvania Avenue, the

---

[1] Bryan, I, 357–58.

[2] A few of these are still standing and occupied.

[3] Gallatin to his wife, *supra;* also Wharton: *Social Life in the Early Republic*, 58–59.

"Executive Mansion" or "President's Palace," the department buildings near it, the residences, shops, hostelries, and streets. It was a picture of sprawling aimlessness, confusion, inconvenience, and utter discomfort.

When considering the events that took place in the National Capital as narrated in these volumes, — the debates in Congress, the proclamations of Presidents, the opinions of judges, the intrigues of politicians, — when witnessing the scenes in which Marshall and Jefferson and Randolph and Burr and Pinkney and Webster were actors, we must think of Washington as a dismal place, where few and unattractive houses were scattered along muddy openings in the forests.

There was on paper a harmonious plan of a splendid city, but the realization of that plan had scarcely begun. As a situation for living, the Capital of the new Nation was, declared Gallatin, a "hateful place." [1] Most of the houses were "small miserable huts" which, as Wolcott informed his wife, "present an awful contrast to the public buildings." [2]

Aside from an increase in the number of residences and shops, the "Federal City" remained in this state for many years. "The *Chuck* holes were not *bad*," wrote Otis of a journey out of Washington in 1815; "that is to say they were none of them much deeper than the Hubs of the hinder wheels. They were however exceedingly frequent." [3] Pennsylvania

---

[1] Gallatin to his wife, Aug. 17, 1802, Adams: *Gallatin*, 304.

[2] Wolcott to his wife, July 4, 1800, Gibbs, ii, 377.

[3] Otis to his wife, Feb. 28, 1815, Morison: *Life and Letters of Harrison Gray Otis*, ii, 170–71. This letter is accurately descriptive

Avenue was, at this time, merely a stretch of "yellow, tenacious mud," [1] or dust so deep and fine that,
when stirred by the wind, it made near-by objects
invisible.[2] And so this street remained for decades. Long after the National Government was
removed to Washington, the carriage of a diplomat
became mired up to the axles in the sticky clay
within four blocks of the President's residence and
its occupant had to abandon the vehicle.

John Quincy Adams records in his diary, April 4,
1818, that on returning from a dinner the street was
in such condition that "our carriage in coming for us
. . was overset, the harness broken. We got home
with difficulty, twice being on the point of oversetting, and at the Treasury Office corner we were both
obliged to get out . . in the mud. . . It was a mercy
that we all got home with whole bones." [3]

of travel from the National Capital to Baltimore as late as 1815 and
many years afterward.

"The Bladensburg *run, before we came to the bridge,* was happily in
no one place *above* the Horses bellies. — As we passed thro', the driver
pointed out to us the spot, right under our wheels, where all the stage
horses last year were drowned, but then he consoled us by shewing the
tree, on which all the Passengers *but one,* were saved. Whether that
one was gouty or not, I did not enquire. . .

"We . . arriv'd safe at our first stage, Ross's, having gone at a rate
rather exceeding two miles & an half per hour. . . In case of a *break
Down* or other accident, . . I should be sorry to stick and freeze in
over night (*as I have seen happen to twenty waggons*) for without an
extraordinary thaw I could not be dug out in any reasonable dinner-
time the next day."

Of course conditions were much worse in all parts of the country,
except the longest and most thickly settled sections.

[1] Parton: *Life of Thomas Jefferson,* 622.
[2] Plumer to his wife, Jan. 25, 1807, Plumer MSS. Lib. Cong.
[3] *Memoirs of John Quincy Adams:* Adams, IV, 74; and see Quincy:
Life of Josiah Quincy, 186.

Bayard wrote to Rodney: "four months [in Washington] almost

Fever and other malarial ills were universal at certain seasons of the year.[1] "No one, from the North or from the high country of the South, can pass the months of August and September there without intermittent or bilious fever," records King in 1803.[2] Provisions were scarce and Alexandria, across the river, was the principal source of supplies.[3] "My God! What have I done to reside in such a city," exclaimed a French diplomat.[4] Some months after the Chase impeachment[5] Senator Plumer described Washington as "a little village in the midst of the woods."[6] " Here I am in the wilderness of Washington," wrote Joseph Story in 1808.[7]

Except a small Catholic chapel there was only one church building in the entire city, and this tiny wooden sanctuary was attended by a congregation which seldom exceeded twenty persons.[8] This absence of churches was entirely in keeping with the

killed me." (Bayard to Rodney, Feb. 24, 1804, N. Y. Library Bulletin, IV, 230.)

[1] Margaret Smith to Susan Smith, Dec. 26, 1802, Hunt, 33; also Mrs. Smith to her husband, July 8, 1803, *ib.* 41; and Gallatin to his wife, Aug. 17, 1802, Adams: *Gallatin*, 304–05.

[2] King to Gore, Aug. 20, 1803, *Life and Correspondence of Rufus King:* King, IV, 294; and see Adams: *History of the United States*, IV, 31.

[3] Gallatin to his wife, Jan. 15, 1801, Adams: *Gallatin*, 253.

[4] Wharton: *Social Life*, 60.   [5] See *infra*, chap. IV.

[6] Plumer to Lowndes, Dec. 30, 1805, Plumer: *Life of William Plumer*, 244.

"The wilderness, alias the federal city." (Plumer to Tracy, May 2, 1805, Plumer MSS. Lib. Cong.)

[7] Story to Fay, Feb. 16, 1808, *Life and Letters of Joseph Story:* Story, I, 161.

[8] This was a little Presbyterian church building, which was abandoned after 1800. (Bryan, I, 232; and see Hunt, 13–14.)

inclination of people of fashion. The first Republican administration came, testifies Winfield Scott, in "the spring tide of infidelity. . . At school and college, most bright boys, of that day, affected to regard religion as base superstition or gross hypocricy." [1]

Most of the Senators and Representatives of the early Congresses were crowded into the boarding-houses adjacent to the Capitol, two and sometimes more men sharing the same bedroom. At Conrad and McMunn's boarding-house, where Gallatin lived when he was in the House, and where Jefferson boarded up to the time of his inauguration, the charge was fifteen dollars a week, which included service, "wood, candles and liquors." [2] Board at the Indian Queen cost one dollar and fifty cents a day, "brandy and whisky being free." [3] In some such inn the new Chief Justice of the United States, John Marshall, at first, found lodging.

Everybody ate at one long table. At Conrad and McMunn's more than thirty men would sit down at the same time, and Jefferson, who lived there while he was Vice-President, had the coldest and lowest place at the table; nor was a better seat offered him

[1] *Memoirs of Lieut.-General Scott*, 9–10. Among the masses of the people, however, a profound religious movement was beginning. (See Semple: *History of the Rise and Progress of the Baptists in Virginia;* and Cleveland: *Great Revival in the West.*)

A year or two later, religious services were held every Sunday afternoon in the hall of the House of Representatives, which always was crowded on these occasions. The throng did not come to worship, it appears; seemingly, the legislative hall was considered to be a convenient meeting-place for gossip, flirtation, and social gayety. The plan was soon abandoned and the hall left entirely to profane usages. (Bryan, I, 606–07.)

[2] Gallatin to his wife, Jan. 15, 1801, Adams: *Gallatin*, 253.

[3] Wharton: *Social Life*, 72.

on the day when he took the oath of office as Chief
Magistrate of the Republic.[1] Those who had to rent
houses and maintain establishments were in distressing case.[2] So lacking were the most ordinary
conveniences of life that a proposal was made in
Congress, toward the close of Jefferson's first administration, to remove the Capital to Baltimore.[3]
An alternative suggestion was that the White House
should be occupied by Congress and a cheaper building erected for the Presidential residence.[4]

More than three thousand people drawn hither by
the establishment of the seat of government managed to exist in "this desert city."[5] One fifth of
these were negro slaves.[6] The population was made
up of people from distant States and foreign countries [7] — the adventurous, the curious, the restless,
the improvident. The "city" had more than the
usual proportion of the poor and vagrant who, "so
far as I can judge," said Wolcott, "live like fishes

[1] Hunt, 12.

[2] See Merry to Hammond, Dec. 7, 1803, as quoted in Adams:
U.S. ii, 362.

Public men seldom brought their wives to Washington because of
the absence of decent accommodations. (Mrs. Smith to Mrs. Kirkpatrick, Dec. 6, 1805, Hunt, 48.)

"I do not perceive how the members of Congress can possibly secure lodgings, unless they will consent to live like scholars in a college
or monks in a monastery, crowded ten or twenty in a house; and utterly excluded from society." (Wolcott to his wife, July 4, 1800,
Gibbs, ii, 377.)

[3] Plumer to Thompson, March 19, 1804, Plumer MSS. Lib. Cong.
And see *Annals*, 8th Cong. 1st Sess. 282–88. The debate is instructive.
The bill was lost by 9 yeas to 19 nays.

[4] Hildreth: *History of the United States*, v, 516–17.

[5] Plumer to Lowndes, Dec. 30, 1805, Plumer, 337.

[6] Channing: *History of the United States*, iv, 245.

[7] Bryan, i, 438.

by eating each other." [1] The sight of Washington filled Thomas Moore, the British poet, with contempt.

"This embryo capital, where Fancy sees
 Squares in morasses, obelisks in trees;
 Where second-sighted seers, even now, adorn
 With shrines unbuilt and heroes yet unborn,
 Though nought but woods and Jefferson they see,
 Where streets should run and sages *ought* to be." [2]

Yet some officials managed to distill pleasure from materials which one would not expect to find in so crude a situation. Champagne, it appears, was plentiful. When Jefferson became President, that connoisseur of liquid delights [3] took good care that the "Executive Mansion" was well supplied with the choicest brands of this and many other wines. [4] Senator Plumer testifies that, at one of Jefferson's dinners, "the wine was the best I ever drank, particularly the champagne which was indeed delicious." [5] In fact, repasts where champagne was served seem to have been a favorite source of enjoyment and relaxation. [6]

[1] Wolcott to his wife, July 4, 1800, Gibbs, II, 377.
"The workmen are the refuse of that class and, nevertheless very high in their demands." (La Rochefoucauld-Liancourt: *Travels Through the United States of North America*, III, 650.)

[2] "To Thomas Hume, Esq., M.D.," Moore: *Poetical Works*, II, 83.

[3] See Jefferson to Short, Sept. 6, 1790, *Works of Thomas Jefferson*: Ford, VI, 146; same to Mrs. Adams, July 7, 1785, *ib.* IV, 432–33; same to Peters, June 30, 1791, *ib.* VI, 276; same to Short, April 24, 1792, *ib.* 483; same to Monroe, May 26, 1795, *ib.* VIII, 179; same to Jay, Oct. 8, 1787, *Memoir, Correspondence, and Miscellanies, from the Papers of Thomas Jefferson*: Randolph, II, 249; also see Chastellux: *Travels in North America in the Years 1780–81–82*, 299.

[4] See Singleton: *Story of the White House*, I, 42–43.

[5] Plumer to his wife, Dec. 25, 1802, Plumer, 246.

[3] "Mr. Granger [Jefferson's Postmaster-General] .. after a few

Scattered, unformed, uncouth as Washington was, and unhappy and intolerable as were the conditions of living there, the government of the city was torn by warring interests. One would have thought that the very difficulties of their situation would have compelled some harmony of action to bring about needed improvements. Instead of this, each little section of the city fought for itself and was antagonistic to the others. That part which lay near the White House [1] strove exclusively for its own advantage. The same was true of those who lived or owned property about Capitol Hill. There was, too, an "Alexandria interest" and a "Georgetown interest." These were constantly quarreling and each was irreconcilable with the other.[2]

In all respects the Capital during the first decades of the nineteenth century was a representation in miniature of the embryo Nation itself. Physical conditions throughout the country were practically the same as at the time of the adoption of the Constitution; and popular knowledge and habits of thought had improved but slightly.[3]

A greater number of newspapers, however, had profoundly affected public sentiment, and demo-

bottles of champagne were emptied, on the observation of Mr. Madison that it was the most delightful wine when drank in moderation, but that more than a few glasses always produced a headache the next day, remarked with point that this was the very time to try the experiment, as the next day being Sunday would allow time for a recovery from its effects. The point was not lost upon the host and bottle after bottle came in." (S. H. Smith to his wife, April 26, 1803 Hunt, 36.)

[1] At that time it was called "The Executive Mansion" or "The President's Palace."

[2] Bryan, i, 44; also see La Rochefoucauld-Liancourt, iii, 642–51.

[3] See vol. i, chaps. vi and vii, of this work.

cratic views and conduct had become riotously dominant. The defeated and despairing Federalists viewed the situation with anger and foreboding. Of all Federalists John Marshall and George Cabot were the calmest and wisest. Yet even they looked with gloom upon the future. "There are some appearances which surprize me," wrote Marshall on the morning of Jefferson's inauguration to his intimate friend, Charles Cotesworth Pinckney.

"I wish, however, more than I hope that the public prosperity & happiness will sustain no diminution under Democratic guidance. The Democrats are divided into speculative theorists & absolute terrorists. With the latter I am disposed to class Mr. Jefferson. If he ranges himself with them it is not difficult to foresee that much difficulty is in store for our country — if he does not, they will soon become his enemies and calumniators." [1]

After Jefferson had been President for four months, Cabot thus interpreted the Republican victory of 1800: "We are doomed to suffer all the evils of *excessive* democracy through the United States. . . Maratists and Robespierrians everywhere raise their heads. . . There will be neither justice nor stability in any system, if some material parts of it are not independent of popular control" [2] — an opinion

[1] Marshall to Pinckney, March 4, 1801, MS. furnished by Dr. W. S. Thayer of Baltimore.

[2] Cabot to Wolcott, Aug. 3, 1801, Lodge: *Life and Letters of George Cabot*, 322.

George Cabot was the ablest, most moderate and far-seeing of the New England Federalists. He feared and detested what he called "excessive democracy" as much as did Ames, or Pickering, or Dwight, but, unlike his brother partisans, did not run to the opposite extreme himself and never failed to assert the indispensability of the democratic

which Marshall, speaking for the Supreme Court of
the Nation, was soon to announce.

Joseph Hale wrote to King that Jefferson's election meant the triumph of "the wild principles of uproar & misrule" which would produce "anarchy." [1]
Sedgwick advised our Minister at London: "The
aristocracy of virtue is destroyed." [2] In the course
of a characteristic Federalist speech Theodore
Dwight exclaimed: "The great object of Jacobinism
is . . to force mankind back into a savage state. . .
We have a country governed by blockheads and
knaves; our wives and daughters are thrown into the
stews. . . Can the imagination paint anything more
dreadful this side of hell." [3]

The keen-eyed and thoughtful John Quincy
Adams was of the opinion that "the basis of it all is
democratic popularity. . . There never was a system
of measures [Federalist] more completely and irrevocably abandoned and rejected by the popular
voice. . . Its restoration would be as absurd as to
undertake the resurrection of a carcass seven years in
its grave." [4] A Federalist in the *Commercial Gazette*
of Boston,[5] in an article entitled "Calm Reflections,"
mildly stated that "democracy teems with fanati-

element in government. Cabot was utterly without personal ambition
and was very indolent; otherwise he surely would have occupied a
place in history equal to that of men like Madison, Gallatin, Hamilton,
and Marshall.

[1] Hale to King, Dec. 19, 1801, King, iv, 39.

[2] Sedgwick to King, Dec. 14, 1801, *ib.* 34–35.

[3] Dwight's oration as quoted in Adams: *U.S.* i, 225.

[4] J. Q. Adams to King, Oct. 8, 1802, *Writings of John Quincy Adams:*
Ford, iii, 8–9. Within six years Adams abandoned a party which offered
such feeble hope to aspiring ambition. (See *infra*, chap. ix.)

[5] J. Russell's *Gazette-Commercial and Political*, January 28, 1799.

cism." Democrats "love liberty . . and, like other lovers, they try their utmost to debauch . . their mistress."

There was among the people a sort of diffused ego-tism which appears to have been the one character-istic common to Americans of that period. The most ignorant and degraded American felt himself far superior to the most enlightened European. "Be-hold the universe," wrote the chronicler of Congress in 1802. "See its four quarters filled with savages or slaves. Out of nine hundred millions of human be-ings but four millions [Americans] are free." [1]

William Wirt describes the contrast of fact to pre-tension: "Here and there a stately aristocratick palace, with all its appurtenances, strikes the view: while all around for many miles, no other buildings are to be seen but the little smoky huts and log cabins of poor, laborious, ignorant tenants. And what is very ridiculous, these tenants, while they approach *the great house*, cap in hand, with all the fearful trembling submission of the lowest feudal vassals, boast in their court-yards, with obstreper-ous exultation, that they live in a land of freemen, a land of equal liberty and equal rights." [2]

[1] *History of the Last Session of Congress Which Commenced 7th Dec. 1801* (taken from the *National Intelligencer*). Yet at that time in America manhood suffrage did not exist excepting in three States, a large part of the people could not read or write, imprisonment for debt was universal, convicted persons were sentenced to be whipped in public and subjected to other cruel and disgraceful punishments. Hardly a protest against slavery was made, and human rights as we now know them were in embryo, so far as the practice of them was concerned.

[2] Wirt: *Letters of the British Spy*, 10–11.

These brilliant articles, written by Wirt when he was about thirty

Conservatives believed that the youthful Republic was doomed; they could see only confusion, destruction, and decline. Nor did any nation of the Old World at that particular time present an example of composure and constructive organization. All Europe was in a state of strained suspense during the interval of the artificial peace so soon to end. "I consider the whole civilized world as metal thrown back into the furnace to be melted over again," wrote Fisher Ames after the inevitable resumption of the war between France and Great Britain.[1] "Tremendous times in Europe!" exclaimed Jefferson when cannon again were thundering in every country of the Old World. "How mighty this battle of lions & tygers! With what sensations should the common herd of cattle look upon it? With no partialities, certainly!"[2]

Jefferson interpreted the black forebodings of the defeated conservatives as those of men who had been thwarted in the prosecution of evil designs: "The

years old, were published in the Richmond *Argus* during 1803. So well did they deceive the people that many in Gloucester and Norfolk declared that they had seen the British Spy. (Kennedy: *Memoirs of the Life of William Wirt*, i, 111, 113.)

[1] Ames to Pickering, Feb. 4, 1807, Pickering MSS. Mass. Hist. Soc.

[2] Jefferson to Rush, Oct. 4, 1803, *Works:* Ford, x, 32.

Immediately after his inauguration, Jefferson restated the American foreign policy announced by Washington. It was the only doctrine on which he agreed with Marshall.

"It ought to be the very first object of our pursuits to have nothing to do with European interests and politics. Let them be free or slaves at will, navigators or agricultural, swallowed into one government or divided into a thousand, we have nothing to fear from them in any form. . . To take part in their conflicts would be to divert our energies from creation to destruction." (Jefferson to Logan, March 21, 1801, *Works:* Ford, ix, 219–20.)

clergy, who have missed their union with the State, the Anglo men, who have missed their union with England, the political adventurers who have lost the chance of swindling & plunder in the waste of public money, will never cease to bawl, on the breaking up of their sanctuary." [1]

Of all the leading Federalists, John Marshall was the only one who refused to "bawl," at least in the public ear; and yet, as we have seen and shall again find, he entertained the gloomy views of his political associates. Also, he held more firmly than any prominent man in America to the old-time Federalist principle of Nationalism — a principle which with despair he watched his party abandon. [2] His whole being was fixed immovably upon the maintenance of order and constitutional authority. Except for his letter to Pinckney, Marshall was silent amidst the clamor. All that now went forward passed before his regretful vision, and much of it he was making ready to meet and overcome with the affirmative opinions of constructive judicial statesmanship.

Meanwhile he discharged his duties — then very light — as Chief Justice. But in doing so, he quietly began to strengthen the Supreme Court. He did

[1] Jefferson to Postmaster-General (Gideon Granger), May 3, 1801, *Works:* Ford, ix, 249.

The democratic revolution that overthrew Federalism was the beginning of the movement that finally arrived at the abolition of imprisonment for debt, the bestowal of universal manhood suffrage, and in general, the more direct participation in every way of the masses of the people in their own government. But in the first years of Republican power there was a pandering to the crudest popular tastes and passions which, to conservative men, argued a descent to the sansculottism of France.

[2] See *infra*, chaps. iii and vi; also vol. iv, chap. i.

this by one of those acts of audacity that later
marked the assumptions of power which rendered his
career historic. For the first time the Chief Justice
disregarded the custom of the delivery of opinions by
the Justices *seriatim*, and, instead, calmly assumed
the function of announcing, himself, the views of
that tribunal. Thus Marshall took the first step in
impressing the country with the unity of the highest court of the Nation. He began this practice in
Talbot *vs.* Seeman, familiarly known as the case of
the Amelia,[1] the first decided by the Supreme Court
after he became Chief Justice.

During our naval war with France an armed
merchant ship, the Amelia, owned by one Chapeau
Rouge of Hamburg, while homeward bound from
Calcutta, was taken by the French corvette, La
Diligente. The Amelia's papers, officers, and crew
were removed to the French vessel, a French crew
placed in charge, and the captured ship was sent to
St. Domingo as a prize. On the way to that French
port, she was recaptured by the American frigate,
Constitution, Captain Silas Talbot, and ordered to
New York for adjudication. The owner demanded
ship and cargo without payment of the salvage
claimed by Talbot for his rescue. The case finally
reached the Supreme Court.

In the course of a long and careful opinion the
Chief Justice held that, although there had been no
formal declaration of war on France, yet particular
acts of Congress had authorized American warships
to capture certain French vessels and had provided

[1] 1 Cranch, 1 *et seq.*

for the payment of salvage to the captors. Virtually,
then, we were at war with France. While the Amelia ·was not a French craft, she was, when captured
by Captain Talbot, "an armed vessel commanded
and manned by Frenchmen," and there was "probable cause to believe" that she was French. So her
capture was lawful.

Still, the Amelia was not, in fact, a French vessel,
but the property of a neutral; and in taking her
from the French, Talbot had, in reality, rescued the
ship and rendered a benefit to her owners for which
he was entitled to salvage. For a decree of the
French Republic made it "extremely probable"
that the Amelia would be condemned by the French
courts in St. Domingo; and that decree, having been
"promulgated" by the American Government,
must be considered by American courts "as an
authenticated copy of a public law of France interesting to all nations." This, said Marshall, was "the
real and only question in the case." The first opinion
delivered by Marshall as Chief Justice announced,
therefore, an important rule of international law and
is of permanent value.

Marshall's next case [1] involved complicated questions concerning lands in Kentucky. Like nearly all
of his opinions, the one in this case is of no historical
importance except that in it he announced for the
second time the views of the court. In United
States *vs.* Schooner Peggy,[2] Marshall declared that,
since the Constitution makes a treaty a "supreme
law of the land," courts are as much bound by it as

[1] Wilson *vs.* Mason, 1 Cranch, 45–101.   [2] 1 Cranch, 102–10.

by an act of Congress. This was the first time that principle was stated by the Supreme Court. Another case [1] concerned the law of practice and of evidence. This was the last case in which Marshall delivered an opinion before the Republican assault on the Judiciary was made — the causes of which assault we are now to examine.

At the time of his inauguration, Jefferson apparently meant to carry out the bargain [2] by which his election was made possible. "We are all Republicans, we are all Federalists," were the reassuring words with which he sought to quiet those who already were beginning to regret that they had yielded to his promises.[3] Even Marshall was almost favorably impressed by the inaugural address. "I have administered the oath to the Presdt.," he writes Pinckney immediately after Jefferson had been inducted into office. "His inauguration speech . . is in general well judged and conciliatory. It is in direct terms giving the lie to the violent party declamation which has elected him, but it is strongly characteristic of the general cast of this political theory." [4]

It is likely that, for the moment, the President intended to keep faith with the Federalist leaders. But the Republican multitude demanded the spoils of victory; and the Republican leaders were not slow or soft-spoken in telling their chieftain that he must take those measures, the assurance of which

---

[1] Turner *vs.* Fendall, 1 Cranch, 115–30.

[2] See vol. II, 531–47, of this work.

[3] See Adams: *U.S.* I, chaps. IX and X, for account of the revolutionary measures which the Republicans proposed to take.

[4] Marshall to Pinckney, March 4, 1801, "four o'clock," MS.

had captivated the popular heart and given "the party of the people" a majority in both House and Senate.

Thus the Republican programme of demolition was begun. Federalist taxes were, of course, to be abolished; the Federalist mint dismantled; the Federalist army disbanded; the Federalist navy beached. Above all, the Federalist system of National courts was to be altered, the newly appointed Federalist National judges ousted and their places given to Republicans; and if this could not be accomplished, at least the National Judiciary must be humbled and cowed. Yet every step must be taken with circumspection — the cautious politician at the head of the Government would see to that. No atom of party popularity [1] must be jeopardized; on the contrary, Republican strength must be increased at any cost, even at the temporary sacrifice of principle.[2] Unless these facts are borne in mind, the curious blending of fury and moderation — of violent attack and sudden quiescence — in the Re-

---

[1] "It is the sole object of the Administration to acquire popularity." (Wolcott to Cabot, Aug. 28, 1802, Lodge: *Cabot*, 325.)

"The President has . . the itch for popularity." (J. Q. Adams to his father, November, 1804, *Writings, J. Q. A.*: Ford, III, 81.)

" The mischiefs of which his immoderate thirst for . . popularity are laying the foundation, are not immediately perceived." (Adams to Quincy, Dec. 4, 1804, Quincy, 64.)

"It seems to be a great primary object with him never to pursue a measure if it becomes unpopular." (Plumer's Diary, March 4, 1805, Plumer MSS. Lib. Cong.)

" In dress, conversation, and demeanor he studiously sought and displayed the arts of a low demagogue seeking the gratification of the democracy on whose voices and votes he laid the foundation of his power." (Quincy's Diary, Jan. 1806, Quincy, 93.)

[2] Ames to Gore, Dec. 13, 1802, *Works of Fisher Ames:* Ames, I. 309.

publican tactics during the first years of Jefferson's Administration are inexplicable.

Jefferson determined to strike first at the National Judiciary. He hated it more than any other of the "abominations" of Federalism. It was the only department of the Government not yet under his control. His early distrust of executive authority, his suspicion of legislative power when his political opponents held it, were now combined against the National courts which he did not control.

Impotent and little respected as the Supreme Court had been and still was, Jefferson nevertheless entertained an especial fear of it; and this feeling had been made personal by the thwarting of his cherished plan of appointing his lieutenant, Spencer Roane of Virginia, Chief Justice of the United States.[1] The elevation of his particular aversion, John Marshall, to that office, had, he felt, wickedly robbed him of the opportunity to make the new régime harmonious; and, what was far worse, it had placed in that station of potential, if as yet undeveloped, power, one who, as Jefferson had finally come to think, might make the high court of the Nation a mighty force in the Government, retard fundamental Republican reforms, and even bring to naught measures dear to the Republican heart.

It seems probable that, at this time, Jefferson was the only man who had taken Marshall's measure correctly. His gentle manner, his friendliness and conviviality, no longer concealed from Jefferson the

[1] Dodd in *American Historical Review*, XII, 776; and see next chapter.

courage and determination of his great relative; and
Jefferson doubtless saw that Marshall, with his universally conceded ability, would find means to vitalize the National Judiciary, and with his fearlessness,
would employ those means.

"The Federalists," wrote Jefferson, "have retired
into the judiciary as a stronghold . . and from that
battery all the works of republicanism are to be
beaten down and erased." [1] Therefore that stronghold must be taken. Never was a military plan more
carefully devised than was the Republican method
of capturing it. Jefferson would forthwith remove
all Federalist United States marshals and attorneys; [2] he would get rid of the National judges whom
Adams had appointed under the Judiciary Act of
1801. [3] If this did not make those who remained on
the National Bench sufficiently tractable, the sword
of impeachment would be held over their obstinate
heads until terror of removal and disgrace should
render them pliable to the dominant political will.

[1] Jefferson to Dickinson, Dec. 19, 1801, *Writings of Thomas Jefferson:* Washington, IV, 424.

[2] "The only shield for our Republican citizens against the federalism of the courts is to have the attorneys & Marshals republicans."
(Jefferson to Stuart, April 8, 1801, *Works:* Ford, IX, 248.)

[3] "The judge of course stands until the law [Judiciary Act of 1801]
shall be repealed which we trust will be at the next Congress." (Jefferson to Stuart, April 8, 1801, *Works:* Ford, IX, 247.) For two weeks
Jefferson appears to have been confused as to the possibility of
repealing the Judiciary Act of 1801. A fortnight before he informed
Stuart that this course would be taken, he wrote Giles that "the
courts being so decidedly federal and irremovable," it was "indispensably necessary" to appoint "republican attorneys and marshals." (Jefferson to Giles, March 23, 1801, MSS. Lib. Cong. as
quoted by Carpenter in *American Political Science Review,* IX, 522.)

But the repeal had been determined upon within six weeks after
Jefferson's inauguration as his letter to Stuart shows.

Thus by progressive stages the Supreme Court would be brought beneath the blade of the executioner and the obnoxious Marshall decapitated or compelled to submit.

To this agreeable course, so well adapted to his purposes, the President was hotly urged by the foremost leaders of his party. Within two weeks after Jefferson's inauguration, the able and determined William Branch Giles of Virginia, faithfully interpreting the general Republican sentiment, demanded "the removal of all its [the Judiciary's] executive officers indiscriminately." This would get rid of the Federalist marshals and clerks of the National courts; they had been and were, avowed Giles, "the humble echoes" of the "vicious schemes" of the National judges, who had been "the most unblushing violators of constitutional restrictions." [1] Again Giles expressed the will of his party: "The revolution [Republican success in 1800] is incomplete so long as that strong fortress [the Judiciary] is in possession of the enemy." He therefore insisted upon "the absolute repeal of the whole judiciary system." [2]

The Federalist leaders quickly divined the first part of the Republican purpose: "There is nothing which the [Republican] party more anxiously wish than the destruction of the judicial arrangements made during the last session," wrote Sedgwick. [3] And Hale, with dreary sarcasm, observed that "the independence of our Judiciary is to be confirmed

[1] Giles to Jefferson, March 16, 1801, Anderson: *William Branch Giles — A Study in the Politics of Virginia 1790–1830*, 77.

[2] Same to same, June 1, 1801, *ib.* 80.

[3] Sedgwick to King, Dec. 14, 1801, King, IV, 36.

by being made wholly subservient to the will of the legislature & the caprice of Executive visions." [1]

The judges themselves had invited the attack so soon to be made upon them. [2] Immediately after the Government was established under the Constitution, they took a position which disturbed a large part of the general public, and also awakened apprehensions in many serious minds. Persons were haled before the National courts charged with offenses unknown to the National statutes and unnamed in the Constitution; nevertheless, the National judges held that these were indictable and punishable under the common law of England. [3]

This was a substantial assumption of power. The Judiciary avowed its right to pick and choose among the myriad of precedents which made up the common law, and to enforce such of them as, in the opinion of the National judges, ought to govern American citizens. In a manner that touched directly the lives and liberties of the people, therefore, the judges

[1] Hale to King, Dec. 19, 1801, King, iv, 39.

[2] It must be carefully kept in mind that from the beginning of the Revolution most of the people were antagonistic to courts of any kind, and bitterly hostile to lawyers. (See vol. i, 297–99, of this work.)

Braintree, Mass., in 1786, in a town meeting, denounced lawyers and demanded by formal resolution the enactment of "such laws . . as may crush or, at least, put a proper check of restraint" upon them.

Dedham, Mass., instructed its members of the Legislature to secure the passage of laws that would "check" attorneys; and if this were not practicable, then "you are to endeavor [to pass a bill declaring] that the order of Lawyers be totally abolished." (Warren: *History of the American Bar*, 215.) All this, of course, was the result of the bitter hardships of debtors.

[3] For an able defense of the adoption by the National courts of the British common law, see *Works of the Honourable James Wilson:* Wilson, iii, 384.

became law-givers as well as law-expounders. Not without reason did the Republicans of Boston drink with loud cheers this toast: "The Common Law of England! May wholesome statutes soon root out this engine of oppression from America." [1]

The occasions that called forth this exercise of judicial authority were the violation of Washington's Neutrality Proclamation, the violation of the Treaty of Peace with Great Britain, and the numberless threats to disregard both. From a strictly legal point of view, these indeed furnished the National courts with plausible reasons for the position they took. Certainly the judges were earnestly patriotic and sincere in their belief that, although Congress had not authorized it, nevertheless, that accumulation of British decisions, usages, and customs called "the common law" was a part of American National jurisprudence; and that, of a surety, the assertion of it in the National tribunals was indispensable to the suppression of crimes against the United States. In charging the National grand jury at Richmond, May 22, 1793, Chief Justice John Jay first announced this doctrine, although not specifically naming the common law. [2] Two months later, Justice James Wilson claimed the same inclusive power in his address to the grand jury at Philadelphia. [3]

In 1793, Joseph Ravara, consul for Genoa, was in-

---

[1] *Columbian Centinel*, July 11, 1801, as quoted in Warren, 225–27.

[2] *Correspondence and Public Papers of John Jay:* Johnston, III, 478–85.

[3] Wharton: *State Trials of the U.S. during the Administrations of Washington and Adams*, 60 *et seq.*; and see Wilson's law lecture on the subject, Wilson, III, 384.

dicted in the United States District Court of Pennsylvania for sending an anonymous and threatening letter to the British Minister and to other persons in order to extort money from them. There was not a word in any act of Congress that referred even indirectly to such a misdemeanor, yet Justices Wilson and Iredell of the Supreme Court, with Judge Peters of the District Court, held that the court had jurisdiction,[1] and at the trial Chief Justice Jay and District Judge Peters held that the rash Genoese could be tried and punished under the common law of England.[2]

Three months later Gideon Henfield was brought to trial for the violation of the Neutrality Proclamation. The accused, a sailor from Salem, Massachusetts, had enlisted at Charleston, South Carolina, on a French privateer and was given a commission as an officer of the French Republic. As such he preyed upon the vessels of the enemies of France. One morning in May, 1793, Captain Henfield sailed into the port of Philadelphia in charge of a British prize captured by the French privateer which he commanded.

Upon demand of the British Minister, Henfield was seized, indicted, and tried in the United States Circuit Court for the District of Pennsylvania.[3] In the absence of any National legislation covering the

[1] 2 Dallas, 297–99.

[2] *Ib.* Ravara was tried and convicted by the jury under the instructions of the bench, "but he was afterward pardoned on condition that he surrender his commission and Exequatur." (Wharton: *State Trials*, 90–92.)

[3] For the documents preceding the arrest and prosecution of Henfield, see Wharton: *State Trials*, footnotes to 49–52.

subject, Justice Wilson instructed the grand jury that Henfield could, and should, be indicted and punished under British precedents.[1] When the case was heard the charge of the court to the trial jury was to the same effect.[2]

The jury refused to convict.[3] The verdict was "celebrated with extravagant marks of joy and exultation," records Marshall in his account of this memorable trial. "It was universally asked," he says, "what law had been offended, and under what statute was the indictment supported? Were the American people already prepared to give to a proclamation the force of a legislative act, and to subject themselves to the will of the executive? But if they were already sunk to such a state of degradation, were they to be punished for violating a proclamation which had not been published when the offense was committed, if indeed it could be termed an offense to engage with France, combating for liberty against the combined despots of Europe?"[4]

In this wise, political passions were made to strengthen the general protest against riveting the common law of England upon the American people by judicial fiat and without authorization by the National Legislature.

Isaac Williams was indicted and tried in 1799, in the United States Circuit Court for the District of

[1] See Wilson's charge, Wharton: *State Trials*, 59–66.

[2] See Wharton's summary of Wilson's second charge, *ib.* footnote to 85.

[3] *Ib.* 88.

[4] Marshall: *Life of George Washington*, 2d ed. ii, 273–74. After the Henfield and Ravara cases, Congress passed a law applicable to such offenses. (See Wharton: *State Trials*, 93–101.)

Connecticut, for violating our treaty with Great
Britain by serving as a French naval officer. Williams proved that he had for years been a citizen of
France, having been "duly naturalized" in France,
"renouncing his allegiance to all other countries,
particularly to America, and taking an oath of allegiance to the Republic of France." Although these
facts were admitted by counsel for the Government,
and although Congress had not passed any statute
covering such cases, Chief Justice Oliver Ellsworth
practically instructed the jury that under the British common law Williams must be found guilty.

No American could cease to be a citizen of his
own country and become a citizen or subject of another country, he said, "without the consent . . of
the community." [1] The Chief Justice announced as
American law the doctrine then enforced by European nations — "born a subject, always a subject." [2]
So the defendant was convicted and sentenced "to
pay a fine of a thousand dollars and to suffer four
months imprisonment." [3]

These are examples of the application by the National courts of the common law of England in cases

[1] Wharton: *State Trials*, 653–54.

[2] This was the British defense for impressment of seamen on
American ships. It was one of the chief points in dispute in the War of
1812. The adherence of Federalists to this doctrine was one of the
many causes of the overthrow of that once great party. (See *infra*,
vol. IV, chap. I, of this work.)

[3] Wharton: *State Trials*, 654. Upon another indictment for having
captured a British ship and crew, Williams, with no other defense
than that offered on his trial under the first indictment, pleaded
guilty, and was sentenced to an additional fine of a thousand dollars, and to further imprisonment of four months. (*Ib.*; see also vol.
II, 495, of this work.)

where Congress had failed or refused to act. Crime must be punished, said the judges; if Congress would not make the necessary laws, the courts would act without statutory authority. Until 1812, when the Supreme Court put an end to this doctrine,[1] the National courts, with one exception,[2] continued to apply the common law to crimes and offenses which Congress had refused to recognize as such, and for which American statutes made no provision.

Practically all of the National and many of the State judges were highly learned in the law, and, of course, drew their inspiration from British precedents and the British bench. Indeed, some of them were more British than they were American.[3] "Let a stranger go into our courts,' wrote Tyler, "and he

[1] U.S. *vs.* Hudson, 7 Cranch, 32–34. "Although this question is brought up now for the first time to be decided by this court, we consider it as having been long since settled in public opinion... The legislative authority of the Union must first make an act a crime, affix a punishment to it and declare the court that shall have jurisdiction of the offense." (Justice William Johnson delivering the opinion of the majority of the court, *ib.*)

Joseph Story was frantic because the National judges could not apply the common law during the War of 1812. (See his passionate letters on the subject, vol. IV, chap. I, of this work; and see his argument for the common law, Story, I, 297–300; see also Peters to Pickering, Dec. 5, 1807, March 30, and April 14, 1816, Pickering MSS. Mass. Hist. Soc.)

[2] The opinion of Justice Chase, of the Supreme Court of Philadelphia, sitting with Peters, District Judge, in the case of the United States *vs.* Robert Worral, indicted under the common law for attempting to bribe a United States officer. Justice Chase held that English common law was not a part of the jurisprudence of the United States as a Nation. (Wharton: *State Trials,* 189–99.)

[3] This was notably true of Justice James Wilson, of the Supreme Court, and Alexander Addison, President Judge of the Fifth Pennsylvania (State) Circuit, both of whom were born and educated in the United Kingdom. They were two of the ablest and most learned men on the bench at that period.

would almost believe himself in the Court of the King's Bench." [1]

This conduct of the National Judiciary furnished Jefferson with another of those "issues" of which that astute politician knew how to make such effective use. He quickly seized upon it, and with characteristic fervency of phrase used it as a powerful weapon against the Federalist Party. All the evil things accomplished by that organization of "monocrats," "aristocrats," and "monarchists" — the bank, the treaty, the Sedition Act, even the army and the navy — "have been solitary, inconsequential, timid things," avowed Jefferson, "in comparison with the audacious, barefaced and sweeping pretension to a system of law for the U.S. without the adoption of their legislature, and so infinitely beyond their power to adopt." [2]

But if the National judges had caused alarm by treating the common law as though it were a statute of the United States without waiting for an act of Congress to make it so, their manners and methods in the enforcement of the Sedition Act [3] aroused against them an ever-increasing hostility.

Stories of their performances on the bench in such cases — their tones when speaking to counsel, to accused persons, and even to witnesses, their immoderate language, their sympathy with one of the European nations then at war and their animosity

[1] Message of Governor John Tyler, Dec. 3, 1810, Tyler: *Letters and Times of the Tylers*, I, 261; and see Tyler to Monroe, Dec. 4, 1809, *ib.* 232.

[2] Jefferson to Randolph, Aug. 18, 1799, *Works*: Ford, IX, 73.

[3] See vol. II, chaps. X and XI, of this work.

toward the other, their partisanship in cases on trial before them — tales made up from such material flew from mouth to mouth, until finally the very name and sight of National judges became obnoxious to most Americans. In short, the assaults upon the National Judiciary were made possible chiefly by the conduct of the National judges themselves.[1]

The first man convicted under the Sedition Law was a Representative in Congress, the notorious Matthew Lyon of Vermont. He had charged President Adams with a "continual grasp for power . . an unbounded thirst for ridiculous pomp, foolish adulation and selfish avarice." Also, Lyon had permitted the publication of a letter to him from Joel Barlow, in which the President's address to the Senate and the Senate's response [2] were referred to as "the bullying speech of your President" and "the stupid answer of your Senate"; and expressed wonder "that the answer of both Houses had not

[1] The National judges, in their charges to grand juries, lectured and preached on religion, on morality, on partisan politics.

"On Monday last the Circuit Court of the United States was opened in this town. The Hon. Judge Patterson . . delivered a most elegant and appropriate charge.

"The *Law* was laid down in a masterly manner: *Politics* were set in their true light by holding up the Jacobins [Republicans] as the disorganizers of our happy country, and the only instruments of introducing discontent and dissatisfaction among the well meaning part of the community. *Religion & Morality* were pleasingly inculcated and enforced as being necessary to good government, good order, and good laws; for 'when the righteous [Federalists] are in authority, the people rejoice.' . .

"After the charge was delivered the Rev. Mr. Alden addressed the Throne of Grace in an excellent and well adapted prayer." (*United States Oracle of the Day*, May 24, 1800, as quoted by Hackett, in *Green Bag*, II, 264.)

[2] Adams's War Speech of 1798; see vol. II, 351, of this work.

been an order to send him [Adams] to the mad house." [1]

Lyon was indicted under the accusation that he had tried "to stir up sedition and to bring the President and Government of the United States into contempt." He declared that the jury was selected from his enemies. [2] Under the charge of Justice Paterson of the Supreme Court he was convicted. The court sentenced him to four months in jail and the payment of a fine of one thousand dollars. [3]

In the execution of the sentence, United States Marshal Jabez G. Fitch used the prisoner cruelly. On the way to the jail at Vergennes, Vermont, he was repeatedly insulted. He was finally thrown into a filthy, stench-filled cell without a fireplace and with nothing "but the iron bars to keep the cold out." It was "the common receptacle for horse-thieves . . runaway negroes, or any kind of felons." He was subjected to the same kind of treatment that was accorded in those days to the lowest criminals. [4] The people were deeply stirred by the fate of Matthew Lyon. Quick to realize and respond to public feeling, Jefferson wrote: "I know not which mortifies me most, that I should fear to write what I think, or my country bear such a state of things." [5]

One Anthony Haswell, editor of the *Vermont Ga-*

---

[1] Wharton: *State Trials*, 333–34.   [2] *Ib.* 339.

[3] *Ib.* 337. Paterson sat with District Judge Hitchcock and delivered the charge in this case. Luther Martin in the trial of Justice Chase (see *infra*, chap. IV) said that Paterson was "mild and amiable," and noted for his "suavity of manners." (*Trial of the Hon. Samuel Chase:* Evans, stenographer, 187–88.)

[4] See Lyon to Mason, Oct. 14, 1798, Wharton: *State Trials*, 339–41.

[5] Jefferson to Taylor, Nov. 26, 1798, Jefferson MSS. Lib. Cong.

zette published at Bennington, printed an advertisement of a lottery by which friends of Lyon, who was
a poor man, hoped to raise enough money to pay his
fine. This advertisement was addressed "to the enemies of political persecutions in the western district
of Vermont." It was asserted that Lyon "is holden
by the oppressive hand of usurped power in a loathsome prison, deprived almost of the right of reason,
and suffering all the indignities which can be heaped
upon him by a hard-hearted savage, who has, to the
disgrace of Federalism, been elevated to a station
where he can satiate his barbarity on the misery of
his victims." [1] The "savage" referred to was United
States Marshal Fitch. In the same paper an excerpt
was reprinted from the *Aurora* which declared that
"the administration publically notified that Tories
.. were worthy of the confidence of the government." [2]

Haswell was indicted for sedition. In defense he
established the brutality with which Lyon had been
treated and proposed to prove by two witnesses
not then present (General James Drake of Virginia,
and James McHenry, President Adams's Secretary
of War) that the Government favored the occasional
appointment of Tories to office. Justice Paterson
ruled that such evidence was inadmissible, and
charged the jury that if Haswell's intent was de-
famatory, he should be found guilty. Thereupon
he was convicted and sentenced to two months'
imprisonment and the payment of a fine of two
hundred dollars. [3]

[1] Wharton: *State Trials*, 684.   [2] *Ib.* 685.   [3] *Ib.* 685–86.

Dr. Thomas Cooper, editor of the *Sunbury and Northumberland Gazette* in Pennsylvania, in the course of a political controversy declared in his paper that when, in the beginning of Adams's Administration, he had asked the President for an office, Adams "was hardly in the infancy of political mistake; even those who doubted his capacity thought well of his intentions. . . Nor were we yet saddled with the expense of a permanent navy, or threatened . . with the existence of a standing army. . . Mr. Adams . . had not yet interfered . . to influence the decisions of a court of justice." [1]

For this "attack" upon the President, Cooper was indicted under the Sedition Law. Conducting his own defense, he pointed out the issues that divided the two great parties, and insisted upon the propriety of such political criticism as that for which he had been indicted.

Cooper was himself learned in the law,[2] and during the trial he applied for a subpœna *duces tecum* to compel President Adams to attend as a witness, bringing with him certain documents which Cooper alleged to be necessary to his defense. In a rage Justice Samuel Chase of the Supreme Court, before whom, with Judge Richard Peters of the District Court, the case was tried, refused to issue the writ. For this he was denounced by the Republicans. In the trial of Aaron Burr, Marshall was to issue this very writ to President Thomas Jefferson and, for doing so, to be rebuked, denounced, and abused by the very parti-

---

[1] Wharton: *State Trials*, 661–62. Cooper was referring to the case of Jonathan Robins. (See vol. II, 458–75, of this work.)

[2] Cooper afterward became a State judge.

sans who now assailed Justice Chase for refusing to grant it.[1]

Justice Chase charged the jury at intolerable length: "If a man attempts to destroy the confidence of the people in their officers . . he effectually saps the foundation of the government." It was plain that Cooper "intended to provoke" the Administration, for had he not admitted that, although he did not arraign the motives, he did mean "to censure the conduct of the President"? The offending editor's statement that "our credit is so low that we are obliged to borrow money at 8 per cent. in time of peace," especially irritated the Justice. "I cannot," he cried, "suppress my feelings at this gross attack upon the President." Chase then told the jury that the conduct of France had "rendered a loan necessary"; that undoubtedly Cooper had intended "to mislead the ignorant . . and to influence their votes on the next election."

So Cooper was convicted and sentenced "to pay a fine of four hundred dollars, to be imprisoned for six months, and at the end of that period to find surety for his good behavior himself in a thousand, and two sureties in five hundred dollars each."[2]

"Almost every other country" had been "convulsed with . . war," desolated by "every species of vice and disorder" which left innocence without protection and encouraged "the basest crimes." Only in America there was no "grievance to complain of." Yet our Government had been "as

[1] See *infra*, chap. VIII.

[2] Wharton: *State Trials*, 679. Stephen Girard paid Cooper's fine. (McMaster: *Life and Times of Stephen Girard*, I, 397–98.)

grossly abused as if it had been guilty of the vilest tyranny" — as if real "republicanism" could "only be found in the happy soil of France" where "Liberty, like the religion of Mahomet, is propagated by the sword." In the "bosom" of that nation "a dagger was concealed." [1] In these terms spoke James Iredell, Associate Justice of the Supreme Court, in addressing the grand jury for the District of Pennsylvania. He was delivering the charge that resulted in the indictment for treason of John Fries and others who had resisted the Federalist land tax.[2]

The triumph of France had, of course, nothing whatever to do with the forcible protest of the Pennsylvania farmers against what they felt to be Federalist extortion; nevertheless upon the charge of Justice Iredell as to the law of treason, they were indicted and convicted for that gravest of all offenses. A new trial was granted because one of the jury, John Rhoad, "had declared a prejudice against the prisoner after he was summoned as a juror." [3] On April 29, 1800, the second trial was held. This time Justice Chase presided. The facts were agreed to by counsel. Before the jury had been sworn, Chase threw on the table three papers in writing and announced that these contained the opinion of the judges upon the law of treason — one copy was for the counsel for the Government, one for the defendant's counsel, and one for the jury.

William Lewis, leading attorney for Fries, and one

[1] Wharton: *State Trials*, 466–69.
[2] See vol. II, 429 *et seq.* of this work.
[3] Wharton: *State Trials*, 598–609.

of the ablest members of the Philadelphia bar,[1] was enraged. He looked upon the paper, flung it from him,
declaring that "his hand never should be polluted
by a prejudicated opinion," and withdrew from the
case, although Chase tried to persuade him to "go
on in any manner he liked." Alexander J. Dallas,
the other counsel for Fries, also withdrew, and the
terrified prisoner was left to defend himself. The
court told him that the judges, personally, would see
that justice was done him. Again Fries and his accomplices were convicted under the charge of the court.
"In an aweful and affecting manner"[2] Chase pronounced the sentence, which was that the condemned
men should be "hanged by the neck *until dead*." [3]

The Republicans furiously assailed this conviction
and sentence. President Adams pardoned Fries and
his associates, to the disgust and resentment of the
Federalist leaders.[4] On both sides the entire proceeding was made a political issue.

On the heels of this "repetition of outrage," as the
Republicans promptly labeled the condemnation of
Fries, trod the trial of James Thompson Callender
for sedition, over which it was again the fate of
the unlucky Chase to preside. *The Prospect Before
Us*, written by Callender under the encouragement
of Jefferson,[5] contained a characteristically vicious

---

[1] For sketch of Lewis see Wharton: *State Trials*, 32–33.
[2] *Independent Chronicle*, Boston, May 12, 1800.
[3] Wharton: *State Trials*, 641 *et seq*.
[4] See vol. II, 429 *et seq*. of this work.
[5] Jefferson to Mason, Oct. 11, 1798, *Works:* Ford, VIII, 449–50;
same to Callender, Sept. 6, 1799, *ib*. IX, 81–82; same to same, Oct. 6,
1799, *ib*. 83–84; Pickering to Higginson, Jan. 6, 1804, Pickering MSS.
Mass. Hist. Soc.

screed against Adams. His Administration had been "a tempest of malignant passions"; his system had been "a French war, an American navy, a large standing army, an additional load of taxes." He "was a professed aristocrat and he had proved faithful and serviceable to the British interest" by sending Marshall and his associates to France. In the President's speech to Congress,[1] "this hoary headed incendiary . . bawls to arms! then to arms!"

Callender was indicted for libel under the Sedition Law.

Before Judge Chase started for Virginia, Luther Martin had given him a copy of Callender's pamphlet, with the offensive passages underscored. During a session of the National court at Annapolis, Chase, in a "jocular conversation," had said that he would take Callender's book with him to Richmond, and that, "if Virginia was not too depraved" to furnish a jury of respectable men, he would certainly punish Callender. He would teach the lawyers of Virginia the difference between the liberty and the licentiousness of the press.[2] On the road to Richmond, James Triplett boarded the stage that carried the avenging Justice of the Supreme Court. He told Chase that Callender had once been arrested in Virginia as a vagrant. "It is a pity," replied Chase, "that they had not hanged the rascal."[3]

[1] War speech of Adams to Congress in 1798, see vol. II, 351, of this work.

[2] Testimony of James Winchester (*Annals*, 8th Cong. 2d Sess. 246–47); of Luther Martin (*ib.* 245–46); and of John T. Mason (*ib.* 216); see also *Chase Trial*, 63.

[3] Testimony of James Triplett, *Chase Trial*, 44–45, and see *Annals*, 8th Cong. 2d Sess. 217–19.

But the people of Virginia, because of their hatred
of the Sedition Law, were ardent champions of Callender. Richmond lawyers were hostile to Chase
and were the bitter enemies of the statute which
they knew he would enforce. Jefferson was anxious
that Callender "should be substantially defended,
whether in the first stages by public interference or
private contributors." [1]

One ambitious young attorney, George Hay, who
seven years later was to act as prosecutor in the
greatest trial at which John Marshall ever presided, [2]
volunteered to defend Callender, animated to this
course by devotion to "the cause of the Constitution," in spite of the fact that he "despised" his
adopted client. [3] William Wirt was also inspired to
offer his services in the interest of free speech. These
Virginia attorneys would show this tyrant of the
National Judiciary that the Virginia bar could not
be borne down. [4] Of all this the hot-spirited Chase

[1] Jefferson to Monroe, May 26, 1800, *Works:* Ford, IX, 136. By
"public interference" Jefferson meant an appropriation by the Virginia Legislature. (*Ib.* 137.)

[2] The trial of Aaron Burr, see *infra*, chaps. VI, VII, VIII, and IX.

[3] See testimony of George Hay, *Annals*, 8th Cong. 2d Sess. 203;
and see especially Luther Martin's comments thereon, *infra*, chap. IV.

[4] The public mind was well prepared for just such appeals as those
that Hay and Wirt planned to make. For instance, the citizens of
Caroline County subscribed more than one hundred dollars for Callender's use.

The subscription paper, probably drawn by Colonel John Taylor,
in whose hands the money was placed, declared that Callender "has
a cause closely allied to the preservation of the Constitution, and to
the freedom of public opinion; and that he ought to be comforted
in his bonds."

Callender was "a sufferer for those principles." Therefore, and
"because also he is poor and has three infant children who live by his
daily labor" the contributors freely gave the money "to be applied

was advised; and he resolved to forestall the passionate young defenders of liberty. He was as witty as he was fearless, and throughout the trial brought down on Hay and Wirt the laughter of the spectators.

But in the court-room there was one spectator who did not laugh. John Marshall, then Secretary of State, witnessed the proceedings [1] with grave misgivings.

Chase frequently interrupted the defendant's counsel. "What," said he, "must there be a departure from common sense to find out a construction favorable" to Callender? The Justice declared that a legal point which Hay attempted to make was "a wild notion." [2] When a juror said that he had never seen the indictment or heard it read, Chase declared that of course he could not have formed or delivered an opinion on the charges; and then denied the request that the indictment be read for the information of the juror. Chase would not permit that eminent patriot and publicist, Colonel John Taylor of Caroline, to testify that part of Callender's statement was true; "No evidence is admissible," said the Justice, "that does not . . justify the whole charge." [3]

William Wirt, in addressing the jury, was arguing that if the jury believed the Sedition Act to be unconstitutional, and yet found Callender guilty, they

to the use of James T. Callender, and if he should die in prison, to the use of his children." (*Independent Chronicle*, Boston, July 10, 1800.)

[1] See *infra*, chap. IV.

[2] Wharton: *State Trials*, 692.

[3] *Ib.* 696–98; and see testimony of Taylor, *Chase Trial*, 38–39.

"would violate their oath." Chase ordered him to sit down. The jury had no right to pass upon the constitutionality of the law — "such a power would be extremely dangerous. Hear my words, I wish the world to know them." The Justice then read a long and very able opinion which he had carefully prepared in anticipation that this point would be raised by the defense.[1] After another interruption, in which Chase referred to Wirt as " the *young gentleman* " in a manner that vastly amused the audience, the discomfited lawyer, covered with confusion, abandoned the case.

When Hay, in his turn, was addressing the jury, Chase twice interrupted him, asserting that the beardless attorney was not stating the law correctly. The reporter notes that thereupon "Mr. Hay folded up and put away his papers . . and refused to proceed." The Justice begged him to go on, but Hay indignantly stalked from the room.

Acting under the instructions of Chase, Callender was convicted. The court sentenced him to imprisonment for nine months, and to pay a fine of two hundred dollars.[2]

The proceedings at this trial were widely published. The growing indignation of the people at the courts rose to a dangerous point. The force of popu-

---

[1] Wharton: *State Trials*, 717–18. Chase's charge to the jury was an argument that the constitutionality of a law could not be determined by a jury, but belonged exclusively to the Judicial Department. For a brief *précis* of this opinion see chap. III of this volume. Chase advanced most of the arguments used by Marshall in Marbury *vs* Madison.

[2] *Ib.* 718. When Jefferson became President he immediately pardoned Callender. (See next chapter.)

lar wrath was increased by the alarm of the bar, which generally had been the stanch supporter of the bench.[1]

Hastening from Richmond to New Castle, Delaware, Justice Chase emphasized the opinion now current that he was an American Jeffreys and typical of the spirit of the whole National Judiciary. Upon opening court, he said that he had heard that there was a seditious newspaper in the State. He directed the United States Attorney to search the files of all the papers that could be found, and to report any abusive language discovered. It was the haying season, and the grand jury, most of whom were farmers, asked to be discharged, since there was no business for them to transact., Chase refused and held them until the next day, in order to have them return indictments against any printer that might have criticized the Administration.[2] But the prosecutor's investigation discovered nothing "treasonable" except a brief and unpleasant reference to Chase himself. So ended the Delaware visit of the ferret of the National Judiciary.

Thus a popular conviction grew up that no man was safe who assumed to criticize National officials. The persecution of Matthew Lyon was recalled, and the punishment of other citizens in cases less widely known [3] became the subject of common talk, — all

[1] Wharton: *State Trials*, footnote to 718.

[2] See testimonies of Gunning Bedford, Nicholas Vandyke, Archibald Hamilton, John Hall, and Samuel P. Moore, *Chase Trial*, 98–101.

[3] For example, one Charles Holt, publisher of a newspaper, *The Bee*, of New London, Connecticut, had commented on the uselessness of enlisting in the army, and reflected upon the wisdom of the Admin-

adding to the growing popular wrath against the whole National Judiciary. The people regarded those brought under the lash of justice as martyrs to the cause of free speech; and so, indeed, they were.

The method of securing indictments and convictions also met with public condemnation. In many States the United States Marshals selected what persons they pleased as members of the grand juries and trial juries. These officers of the National courts were, without exception, Federalists; in many cases Federalist politicians. When making up juries they selected only persons of the same manner of thinking as that of the marshals and judges themselves.[1] So it was that the juries were nothing more than machines that registered the will, opinion, or even inclination of the National judges and the United States District Attorneys. In short, in these prose-

istration's policy; for this he was indicted, convicted, and sentenced to three months' imprisonment, and the payment of a fine of two hundred dollars. (Randall: *Life of Thomas Jefferson*, II, 418.)

When President Adams passed through Newark, New Jersey, the local artillery company fired a salute. One of the observers, a man named Baldwin, idly remarked that "he wished the wadding from the cannon had been lodged in the President's backside." For this seditious remark Baldwin was fined one hundred dollars. (Hammond: *History of Political Parties in the State of New York*, I, 130–31.)

One Jedediah Peck, Assemblyman from Otsego County, N.Y., circulated among his neighbors a petition to Congress to repeal the Alien and Sedition Laws. This shocking act of sedition was taken up by the United States District Attorney for New York, who procured the indictment of Peck; and upon bench warrant, the offender was arrested and taken to New York for trial. It seems that such were the demonstrations of the people, wherever Peck appeared in custody of the officer, that the case was dropped. (Randall, II, 420.)

[1] They were supposed to select juries according to the laws of the States where the courts were held. As a matter of fact they called the men they wished to serve.

cutions, trial by jury in any real sense was not to be had.[1]

Certain State judges of the rabid Federalist type, apostles of "the wise, the rich, and the good" political religion, were as insulting in their bearing, as immoderate in their speech, and as intolerant in their conduct as some of the National judges; and prosecutions in some State courts were as bad as the worst of those in the National tribunals.

In Boston, when the Legislature of Massachusetts was considering the Kentucky and Virginia Resolutions, John Bacon of Berkshire, a Republican State Senator, and Dr. Aaron Hill of Cambridge, the leader of the Republicans in the House, resisted the proposed answer of the Federalist majority. Both maintained the ground upon which Republicans everywhere now stood — that any State might disregard an act of Congress which it deemed unconstitutional.[2] Bacon and Hill were supported by the solid Republican membership of the Massachusetts Legislature, which the *Columbian Centinel* of Boston, a Federalist organ, called a "contemptible minority," every member of which was "worse than an infidel."[3]

The *Independent Chronicle*, the Republican newspaper of Boston, observed that "It is difficult for the

[1] McMaster: *History of the People of the United States*, II, 473; and see speech of Charles Pinckney in the Senate, March 5, 1800, *Annals*, 6th Cong. 1st and 2d Sess. 97.

[2] See speech of Bacon in the *Independent Chronicle*, Feb. 11–14, 1799; and of Hill, *ib.* Feb. 25, 1799.

[3] *Columbian Centinel*, Feb. 16, 1799; also see issue of Jan. 23, 1799. For condensed account of this incident see Anderson in *Am. Hist. Rev.* v, 60–62, quoting the *Centinel* as cited. A Federalist mob stoned the house of Dr. Hill the night after he made this speech. (*Ib.*) See also *infra*, chap. III.

common capacities to conceive of a sovereignty so situated that the *Sovereign shall have no right to decide on any invasion of his constitutional powers.*" Bacon's speech, said the *Chronicle*, "has been read with delight by all true Republicans, and will always stand as a monument of his firmness, patriotism, and integrity. . . The name of an *American* Bacon will be handed down to the latest generations of freemen with high respect and gratitude, while the names of such as have aimed a *death wound* to the Constitution of the United States will rot *above ground* and be unsavoury to the nostrils of every lover of Republican freedom." [1]

The *Massachusetts Mercury* of February 22, 1799, reports that "On Tuesday last . . Chief Justice Dana . . commented on the contents of the *Independent Chronicle* of the preceding day. He properly stated to the Jury that though he was not a subscriber to the paper, he obtained *that one* by accident, that if he was, his conscience would charge him with assisting to support a traitorous enmity to the Government of his Country."

Thereupon Thomas Adams, the publisher, and Abijah Adams, a younger brother employed in the office, were indicted under the common law for attempting "to bring the government into disrespect, hatred, and contempt," and for encouraging sedition. Thomas Adams was fatally ill and Abijah only was brought to trial. Under the instructions of the court he was convicted. In pronouncing sentence Chief Justice Dana delivered a political lecture.

[1] *Independent Chronicle*, Feb. 18, 1799.

The Virginia and Kentucky Resolutions, he said, had attempted "to establish the monstrous position" that the individual States had the right to pass upon the constitutionality of acts of Congress. He then gave a résumé of the reply of the majority of the Massachusetts Legislature to the Virginia Resolutions. This reply asserted that the decisions of all questions arising under the Constitution and laws of the United States "are exclusively vested in the Judicial Courts of the United States," and that the Sedition Act was "wise and necessary, as an audacious and unprincipled spirit of falsehood and abuse had been too long unremittingly exerted for the purpose of *perverting* public opinion, and threatened to undermine the whole fabric of government." The irate judge declared that the *Chronicle's* criticism of this action of the majority of the Legislature and its praise of the Republican minority of that body was an "indecent and outrageous calumny."

"Censurable as the libel may be in itself," Dana continued, the principles stated by Adams's counsel in conducting his defense were equally "dangerous to public tranquility." These daring lawyers had actually maintained the principle of the liberty of the press. They had denied that an American citizen could be punished under the common law of England. "Novel and disorganizing doctrines," exclaimed Dana in the midst of a long argument to prove that the common law was operative in the United States.[1]

---

[1] *Columbian Centinel*, March 30, 1799. The attorneys for Adams also advanced the doctrines of the Kentucky and Virginia Resolutions.

In view of the fact that Abijah Adams was not the author of the libel, nor even the publisher or editor of the *Chronicle*, but was "the only person to whom the public can look for retribution," the court graciously sentenced him to only one month's imprisonment, but required him to find sureties for his good behavior for a year, and to pay the costs of the trial.[1]

Alexander Addison, the presiding judge of one of the Pennsylvania State courts, was another Federalist State judge whose judicial conduct and assaults from the bench upon democracy had helped to bring courts into disrepute. Some of his charges to grand juries were nothing but denunciations of Republican principles.[2]

His manner on the bench was imperious; he bul-

so far, at least, as to assert that any State ought to protest against and resist any act of Congress that the Commonwealth believed to be in violation of the National Constitution. (Anderson, in *Am. Hist. Rev.* v, 226–27.)

[1] *Columbian Centinel*, March 27, 1799.

Another instance of intolerant and partisan prosecutions in State courts was the case of Duane and others, indicted and tried for getting signatures to a petition in Congress against the Alien and Sedition Laws. They were acquitted, however. (Wharton: *State Trials*, 345–89.)

[2] These charges of Judge Addison were, in reality, political pamphlets. They had not the least reference to any business before the court, and were no more appropriate than sermons. They were, however, written with uncommon ability. It is doubtful whether any arguments more weighty have since been produced against what George Cabot called "excessive democracy." These grand jury charges of Addison were entitled: "Causes and Error of Complaints and Jealousy of the Administration of the Government"; "Charges to the Grand Juries of the County Court of the Fifth Circuit of the State of Pennsylvania, at December Session, 1798"; "The Liberty of Speech and of the Press"; "Charge to Grand Juries, 1798"; "Rise and Progress of Revolution," and "A Charge to the Grand Juries of the State of Pennsylvania, at December Session, 1800."

lied counsel, browbeat witnesses, governed his associate judges, ruled juries. In one case,[1] Addison forbade the Associate Judge to address the jury, and prevented him from doing so.[2]

Nor did the judges stop with lecturing everybody from the bench. Carrying with them the authority of their exalted positions, more than one of them, notably Justice Chase and Judge Addison, took the stump in political campaigns and made partisan speeches.[3]

So it fell out that the manners, language, and conduct of the judges themselves, together with their use of the bench as a political rostrum, their partisanship as to the European belligerents, their merciless enforcement of the common law — aroused that public fear and hatred of the courts which gave Jefferson and the Republicans their opportunity. The questions which lay at the root of the Republican assault upon the Judiciary would not of themselves, and without the human and dramatic incidents of which the cases mentioned are examples, have wrought up among citizens that fighting spirit essential to a successful onslaught upon the

[1] Coulter *vs.* Moore, for defamation. Coulter, a justice of the peace, sued Moore for having declared, in effect, that Coulter "kept a house of ill fame." (*Trial of Alexander Addison, Esq.*: Lloyd, stenographer, 38; also Wharton: *State Trials*, 32 *et seq.*)

[2] This judge was John C. B. Lucas. He was a Frenchman speaking broken English, and, judging from the record, was a person of very inferior ability. There seems to be no doubt that he was the mere tool of another judge, Hugh H. Brackenridge, who hated Addison virulently. From a study of the case, one cannot be surprised that the able and erudite Addison held in greatest contempt the fussy and ignorant Lucas.

[3] Wharton: *State Trials*, 45; Carson: *Supreme Court of the United States, Its History*, i, 193.

National system of justice, which the Federalists
had made so completely their own.[1]

Those basic questions thus brought theatrically
before the people's eyes, had been created by the
Alien and Sedition Laws, and by the Virginia and
Kentucky Resolutions which those undemocratic
statutes called forth. Freedom of speech on the one
hand and Nationalism on the other hand, the crushing of "sedition" as against that license which Localism permitted — such were the issues which the
imprudence and hot-headedness of the Federalist
judges had brought up for settlement. Thus, un-
happily, democracy marched arm in arm with State
Rights, while Nationalism found itself the intimate
companion of a narrow, bigoted, and retrograde
conservatism.

Had not the Federalists, arrogant with power and
frantic with hatred of France and fast becoming
zealots in their championship of Great Britain,
passed the drastic laws against liberty of the press
and freedom of speech; had not the Republican
protest against these statutes taken the form of the
assertion that individual States might declare uncon-

[1] The uprising against the Judiciary naturally began in Pennsyl
vania where the extravagance of the judges had been carried to the
most picturesque as well as obnoxious extremes. For a faithful narrative of these see McMaster: *U.S.* iii, 153–55.

On the other hand, wherever Republicans occupied judicial positions, the voice from the bench, while contrary to that of the Federalist judges, was no less harsh and absolute.

For instance, the judges of the Supreme Court of New Hampshire
refused to listen to the reading of British law reports, because they
were from "musty, old, worm-eaten books." One of the judges declared that "not Common Law — not the quirks of Coke and Blackstone — but common sense" controlled American judges. (Warren,
227.)

stitutional and disregard the acts of the National
Legislature; and finally, had not National tribunals
and some judges of State courts been so harsh and
insolent, the Republican assault upon the National
Judiciary,[1] the echoes of which loudly sound in our
ears even to the present day, probably never would
have been made.

But for these things, Marbury *vs*. Madison [2] might
never have been written; the Supreme Court might
have remained nothing more than the comparatively
powerless institution that ultimate appellate judicial
establishments are in other countries; and the career
of John Marshall might have been no more notable
and distinguished than that of the many ghostly
figures in the shadowy procession of our judicial history. But the Republican condemnations of the severe punishment that the Federalists inflicted upon
anybody who criticized the Government, raised fundamental issues and created conditions that forced
action on those issues.

[1] See next chapter.
[2] See *infra*, chap. III, for a résumé of the conditions that forced
Marshall to pronounce his famous opinion in the case of Marbury *vs*.
Madison, as well as for a full discussion of that controversy

CHAPTER II

THE ASSAULT ON THE JUDICIARY

The angels of destruction are making haste. Our judges are to be as independent as spaniels. (Fisher Ames.)

The power which has the right of passing, without appeal, on the validity of your laws, is your sovereign. (John Randolph.)

ON January 6, 1802, an atmosphere of intense but suppressed excitement pervaded the little semicircular room where the Senate of the United States was in session.[1] The Republican assault upon the Judiciary was about to begin and the Federalists in Congress had nerved themselves for their last great fight. The impending debate was to prove one of the permanently notable engagements in American legislative history and was to create a situation which, in a few months, forced John Marshall to pronounce the first of those fundamental opinions which have helped to shape and which still influence the destiny of the American Nation.

The decision of Marbury *vs.* Madison was to be made inevitable by the great controversy to which we are now to listen. Marshall's course, and, indeed, his opinion in this famous case, cannot be understood without a thorough knowledge of the notable debate in Congress which immediately preceded it.[2]

Never was the effect of the long years of party

[1] The Senate then met in the chamber now occupied by the Supreme Court.

[2] See *infra*, chap. III.

training which Jefferson had given the Republicans better manifested than now. There was unsparing party discipline, perfect harmony of party plan. The President himself gave the signal for attack, but with such skill that while his lieutenants in House and Senate understood their orders and were eager to execute them, the rank and file of the Federalist voters, whom Jefferson hoped to win to the Republican cause in the years to come, were soothed rather than irritated by the seeming moderation and reasonableness of the President's words.

"The Judiciary system . . and especially that portion of it recently enacted, will, of course, present itself to the contemplation of Congress," was the almost casual reference in the President's first Message to the Republican purpose to subjugate the National Judiciary. To assist Senators and Representatives in determining "the proportion which the institution bears to the business it has to perform" Jefferson had "procured from the several states . . an exact statement of all the causes decided since the first establishment of the courts and of the causes which were pending when additional courts and judges were brought to their aid." This summary he transmitted to the law-making body.

In a seeming spirit of impartiality, almost of indifference, the President suggested Congressional inquiry as to whether jury trials had not been withheld in many cases, and advised the investigation of the manner of impaneling juries.[1]

---

[1] Jefferson to Congress, Dec. 8, 1801, *Works:* Ford, IX, 321 *et seq.*; also *Messages and Papers of the Presidents:* Richardson, I, 331.

Thus far and no farther went the comments on the National Judiciary which the President laid before Congress. The status of the courts — a question that filled the minds of all, both Federalists and Republicans — was not referred to. But the thought of it thrilled Jefferson, and only his caution restrained him from avowing it. Indeed, he had actually written into the message words as daring as those of his cherished Kentucky Resolutions; had boldly declared that the right existed in each department "to decide on the validity of an act according to its own judgment and uncontrolled by the opinions of any other department"; had asserted that he himself, as President, had the authority and power to decide the constitutionality of National laws; and had, as President, actually pronounced, in official form, the Sedition Act to be 'in palpable and unqualified contradiction to the Constitution." [1]

This was not merely a part of a first rough draft of this Presidential document, nor was it lightly cast aside. It was the most important paragraph of the completed Message. Jefferson had signed it on December 8, 1801, and it was ready for transmission to the National Legislature. But just before sending the Message to the Capitol, he struck out this passage,[2] and thus notes on the margin of the draft his reason for doing so: "This whole paragraph was omitted as capable of being chicaned, and furnishing something to the opposition to make a handle of.

[1] Jefferson, Jefferson MSS. Lib. Cong., partly quoted in Beard: *Economic Origins of Jeffersonian Democracy*, 454–55.

[2] For full text of this exposition of Constitutional law by Jefferson see Appendix A.

It was thought better that the message should be clear of everything which the public might be made to misunderstand."

Although Jefferson's programme, as stated in the altered message which he finally sent to Congress, did not arouse the rank and file of Federalist voters, it did alarm and anger the Federalist chieftains, who saw the real purpose back of the President's colorless words. Fisher Ames, that delightful reactionary, thus interpreted it: "The message announces the downfall of the late revision of the Judiciary; economy, the patriotism of the shallow and the trick of the ambitious. . . The U. S. Gov't . . is to be dismantled like an old ship. . . The state gov'ts are to be exhibited as alone safe and salutary." [1]

The Judiciary Law of 1801, which the Federalist majority enacted before their power over legislation passed forever from their hands, was one of the best considered and ablest measures ever devised by that constructive party.[2] Almost from the time of the organization of the National Judiciary the National judges had complained of the inadequacy and positive evils of the law under which they performed their duties. The famous Judiciary Act of 1789, which has received so much undeserved praise, did not entirely satisfy anybody except its author, Oliver Ellsworth. "It is a child of his and he defends

[1] Ames to King, Dec. 20, 1801, King, IV, 40.

Like most eminent Federalists, except Marshall, Hamilton, and Cabot, Fisher Ames was soon to abandon his Nationalism and become one of the leaders of the secession movement in New England. (See vol. IV, chap. I, of this work.)

[2] See vol. II, 531, 547–48, 550–52, of this work.

it . . with wrath and anger," wrote Maclay in his diary.[1]

In the first Congress opposition to the Ellsworth Act had been sharp and determined. Elbridge Gerry denounced the proposed National Judiciary as "a tyranny." [2] Samuel Livermore of New Hampshire called it "this new fangled system" which "would . . swallow up the State Courts." [3] James Jackson of Georgia declared that National courts would cruelly harass "the poor man." [4] Thomas Sumter of South Carolina saw in the Judiciary Bill "the iron hand of power." [5] Maclay feared that it would be "the gunpowder plot of the Constitution." [6]

When the Ellsworth Bill had become a law, Senator William Grayson of Virginia advised Patrick Henry that it "wears so monstrous an appearance that I think it will be *felo-de-se* in the execution. . . Whenever the Federal Judiciary comes into operation, . . the pride of the states . . will in the end procure its destruction" [7] — a prediction that came near fulfillment and probably would have been realized but for the courage of John Marshall.

While Grayson's eager prophecy did not come to pass, the Judiciary Act of 1789 worked so badly that it was a source of discontent to bench, bar, and people. William R. Davie of North Carolina, a member of the Convention that framed the Constitution and one of the most eminent lawyers of his time, condemned the Ellsworth Act as "so defective

---

[1] *Journal of Samuel Maclay:* Meginness, 90.
[2] *Annals*, 1st Cong. 1st Sess. 862.   [3] *Ib.* 852.
[4] *Ib.* 833–34.   [5] *Ib.* 864–65.   [6] *Maclay's Journal*, 98.
[7] Grayson to Henry, Sept. 29, 1789, Tyler, I, 170–71.

. . that . . it would disgrace the composition of the meanest legislature of the States." [1]

It was, as we have seen,[2] because of the deficiencies of the original Judiciary Law that Jay refused reappointment as Chief Justice. "I left the bench," he wrote Adams, "perfectly convinced that under a system so defective it would not obtain the energy, weight, and dignity which are essential to its affording due support to the national government, nor acquire the public confidence and respect which, as the last resort of the justice of the nation, it should possess." [3]

The six Justices of the Supreme Court were required to hold circuit courts in pairs, together with the judge of the district in which the court was held. Each circuit was to be thus served twice every year, and the Supreme Court was to hold two sessions annually in Washington.[4] So great were the distances between places where courts were held, so laborious, slow, and dangerous was all travel,[5] that

[1] Davie to Iredell, Aug. 2, 1791, *Life and Correspondence of James Iredell:* McRee, II, 335.

[2] Vol. II, 552–53, of this work.

[3] Jay to Adams, Jan. 2, 1801, *Jay:* Johnston, IV, 285.

[4] *Annals*, 1st Cong. 2d and 3d Sess. 2239.

[5] See vol. I, chap. VI, of this work. The conditions of travel are well illustrated by the experiences of six members of Congress, when journeying to Philadelphia in 1790. "Burke was shipwrecked off the Capes; Jackson and Mathews with great difficulty landed at Cape May and traveled one hundred and sixty miles in a wagon to the city; Burke got here in the same way. Gerry and Partridge were overset in the stage; the first had his head broke, . . the other had his ribs sadly bruised. . . Tucker had a dreadful passage of sixteen days with perpetual storms." (Letter of William Smith, as quoted by Johnson: *Union and Democracy*, 105–06.)

On his way to Washington from Amelia County in 1805, Senator Giles was thrown from a carriage, his leg fractured and his knee badly injured. (Anderson, 101.)

the Justices — men of ripe age and studious habits — spent a large part of each year upon the road.[1] Sometimes a storm would delay them, and litigants with their assembled lawyers and witnesses would have to postpone the trial for another year or await, at the expense of time and money, the arrival of the belated Justices.[2]

A graver defect of the act was that the Justices, sitting together as the Supreme Court, heard on appeal the same causes which they had decided on the Circuit Bench. Thus, in effect, they were trial and appellate judges in identical controversies. Moreover, by the rotation in riding circuits different judges frequently heard the same causes in their various stages, so that uniformity of practice, and even of decisions, was made impossible.

The admirable Judiciary Act, passed by the Federalists in 1801, corrected these defects. The membership of the Supreme Court was reduced to five after the next vacancy, the Justices were relieved of the heavy burden of holding circuit courts, and their duties were confined exclusively to the Supreme Bench. The country was divided into sixteen circuits, and the office of circuit judge was created for

[1] This arrangement proved to be so difficult and vexatious that in 1792 Congress corrected it to the extent of requiring only one Justice of the Supreme Court to hold circuit court with the District Judge; but this slight relief did not reach the serious shortcomings of the law. (*Annals*, 2d Cong. 1st and 2d Sess. 1447.)

See Adams: *U.S.* I, 274 *et seq.*, for good summary of the defects of the original Judiciary Act, and of the improvements made by the Federalist Law of 1801.

[2] See statement of Ogden, *Annals*, 7th Cong. 1st Sess. 172; of Chipman, *ib.* 123; of Tracy, *ib.* 52; of Griswold, *ib.* 768; of Huger, *ib.* 672.

each of these. The Circuit Judge, sitting with the District Judge, was to hold circuit court, as the Justices of the Supreme Court had formerly done. Thus the prompt and regular sessions of the circuit courts were assured. The appeal from decisions rendered by the Supreme Court Justices, sitting as circuit judges, to the same men sitting as appellate judges, was done away with.[1]

In establishing these new circuits and creating these circuit judges, this excellent Federalist law gave Adams the opportunity to fill the offices thus created with stanch Federalist partisans. Indeed, this was one motive for the enactment of the law. The salaries of the new circuit judges, together with other necessary expenses of the remodeled system, amounted to more than fifty thousand dollars every year — a sum which the Republicans exaggerated in their appeals to the people and even in their arguments in Congress.[2]

Chiefly on the pretext of this alleged extravagance, but in reality to oust the newly appointed Federalist judges and intimidate the entire National Judiciary, the Republicans, led by Jefferson, determined to re-

---

[1] Of course, to some extent this evil still continued in the appeals to the Circuit Bench; but the ultimate appeal was before judges who had taken no part in the cause.

The soundness of the Federalist Judiciary Act of 1801 was demonstrated almost a century later, in 1891–95, when Congress reënacted every essential feature of it. (See " Act to establish circuit courts of appeals and to define and regulate in certain cases the jurisdiction of the courts of the United States, and for other purposes," March 3, 1891, chap. 517, amended Feb. 18, 1895, chap. 96.)

[2] For example, Senator Cocke of Tennessee asserted the expense to be $137,000. (*Annals*, 7th Cong. 1st. Sess. 30.) See especially Prof. Farrand's conclusive article in *Am. Hist. Rev.* v, 682–86.

peal the Federalist Judiciary Act of 1801, upon the
faith in the passage of which John Marshall, with
misgiving, had accepted the office of Chief Justice.

On January 6, 1802, Senator John Breckenridge
of Kentucky pulled the lanyard that fired the opening gun.[1] He was the personification of anti-Nation-
alism and aggressive democracy. He moved the
repeal of the Federalist National Judiciary Act of
1801.[2] Every member of Senate and House — Republican and Federalist — was uplifted or depressed
by the vital importance of the issue thus brought to
a head; and in the debate which followed no words
were too extreme to express their consciousness of
the gravity of the occasion.[3]

In opening the debate, Senator Breckenridge confined himself closely to the point that the new Federalist judges were superfluous. "Could it be necessary," he challenged the Federalists, "to *increase*
courts when suits were *decreasing?* . . to multiply

[1] It was to Breckenridge that Jefferson had entrusted the introduction of the Kentucky Resolutions of 1798 into the Legislature of
that State. It was Breckenridge who had led the fight for them. At
the time of the judiciary debate he was Jefferson's spokesman in the
Senate; and later, at the President's earnest request, resigned as
Senator to become Attorney-General.

[2] Breckenridge's constituents insisted that the law be repealed, because they feared that the newly established National courts would
conflict with the system of State courts which the Legislature of Kentucky had just established. (See Carpenter, *Am. Pol. Sci. Rev.* ix, 523.)

Although the repeal had been determined upon by Jefferson almost
immediately after his inauguration (see Jefferson to Stuart, April 8,
1801; *Works:* Ford, ix, 247), Breckenridge relied upon that most
fruitful of Republican intellects, John Taylor "of Caroline," the originator of the Kentucky Resolutions (see vol. ii, 397, of this work) for
his arguments. See Taylor to Breckenridge, Dec. 22, 1801, *infra*,
Appendix B.

[3] *Annals*, 7th Cong. 1st Sess. 31–46, 51–52, 58, 513, 530.

judges, when their duties were diminishing?" No!
"The time never will arrive when America will stand
in need of thirty-eight Federal Judges." [1] The Federalist Judiciary Law was "a wanton waste of the
public treasure." [2] Moreover, the fathers never intended to commit to National judges "subjects of
litigation which . . could be left to State Courts."
Answering the Federalist contention that the Constitution guaranteed to National judges tenure of
office during "good behavior" and that, therefore,
the offices once established could not be destroyed
by Congress, the Kentucky Senator observed that
"sinecure offices, . . are not permitted by our laws
or Constitution." [3]

James Monroe, then in Richmond, hastened to inform Breckenridge that "your argument . . is highly
approved here." But, anxiously inquired that foggy
Republican, "Do you mean to admit that the legislature [Congress] has not a right to repeal the law
organizing the supreme court for the express purpose of dismissing the judges when they cease to possess the public confidence?" If so, "the people have
no check whatever on them . . but impeachment."
Monroe hoped that "the period is not distant" when
any opposition to "the sovereignty of the people"
by the courts, such as "the application of the principles of the English common law to our constitution," would be considered "good cause for impeachment." [4] Thus early was expressed the Republican
plan to impeach and remove Marshall and the entire

[1] *Annals*, 7th Cong. 1st Sess. 26.   [2] *Ib.* 25.   [3] *Ib.* 28.
[4] Monroe to Breckenridge, Jan. 15, 1802, Breckenridge MSS. Lib.
Cong.

Federal membership of the Supreme Court so soon to be attempted.[1]

In reply to Breckenridge, Senator Jonathan Mason of Massachusetts, an accomplished Boston lawyer, promptly brought forward the question in the minds of Congress and the country. "This," said he, "was one of the most important questions that ever came before a Legislature." Why had the Judiciary been made "as independent of the Legislature as of the Executive?" Because it was their duty "to expound not only the laws, but the Constitution also; in which is involved the power of checking the Legislature in case it should pass any laws in violation of the Constitution."[2]

The old system which the Republicans would now revive was intolerable, declared Senator Gouverneur Morris of New York. "Cast an eye over the extent of our country" and reflect that the President, "in selecting a character for the bench, must seek less the learning of a judge than the agility of a post boy." Moreover, to repeal the Federal Judiciary Law would be "a declaration to the remaining judges that they hold their offices subject to your [Congress's] will and pleasure." Thus "the check established by the Constitution is destroyed."

Morris expounded the conservative Federalist philosophy thus: "Governments are made to provide against the follies and vices of men. . . Hence, checks are required in the distribution of power among those who are to exercise it for the benefit of

---

[1] See *infra*, chaps. III and IV.
[2] *Annals*, 7th Cong. 1st Sess. 31-32.

the people." The most efficient of these checks was
the power given the National Judiciary — "a check
of the first necessity, to prevent an invasion of the
Constitution by unconstitutional laws — a check
which might prevent any faction from intimidating
or annihilating the tribunals themselves." [1]

Let the Republican Senators consider where their
course would end, he warned. "What has been the
ruin of every Republic? The vile love of popularity.
*Why are we here? To save the people from their most
dangerous enemy; to save them from themselves.*" [2] Do
not, he besought, "commit the fate of America to
the mercy of time and chance." [3]

"Good God!" exclaimed Senator James Jackson
of Georgia, "is it possible that I have heard such a
sentiment in this body? Rather should I have expected to have heard it sounded from the despots of
Turkey, or the deserts of Siberia.[4] . . I am more
afraid of an army of judges, . . than of an army of
soldiers. . . Have we not seen sedition laws?" The
Georgia Senator "thanked God" that the terrorism
of the National Judiciary was, at last, overthrown.
"That we are not under dread of the patronage of
judges, is manifest, from their attack on the Secretary of State." [5]

---

[1] *Annals*, 7th Cong. 1st Sess. 38.

[2] This unfortunate declaration of Morris gave the Republicans an
opportunity of unlimited demagogic appeal. See *infra.* (Italics the
author's.)

[3] *Annals*, 7th Cong. 1st Sess. 40–41.

Morris spoke for an hour. There was a "large audience, which is
not common for that House." He prepared his speech for the press.
(*Diary and Letters of Gouverneur Morris:* Morris, ii, 417.)

[4] *Annals*, 7th Cong. 1st Sess. 49.

[5] *Ib.* 47–48. Senator Jackson here refers to the case of Marbury *vs.*

Senator Uriah Tracy of Connecticut was so con-
:erned that he spoke in spite of serious illness.
"What security is there to an individual," he asked,
if the Legislature of the Union or any particular
State, should pass an *ex post facto* law? "None in
the world" but revolution or "an appeal to the Judiciary of the United States, where he will obtain a
decision that the law itself is unconstitutional and
void." [1]

That typical Virginian, Senator Stevens Thompson Mason, able, bold, and impetuous, now took up
Gouverneur Morris's gage of battle. He was one of
the most fearless and capable men in the Republican Party, and was as impressive in physical appearance as he was dominant in character. He was

Madison, then pending before the Supreme Court. (See *infra*, chap.
III.) This case was mentioned several times during the debate. It is
plain that the Republicans expected Marshall to award the mandamus,
and if he did, to charge this as another act of judicial aggression for
which, if the plans already decided upon did not miscarry, they
would make the new Chief Justice suffer removal from his office by
impeachment. (See *infra*, chap. IV.)

[1] *Annals*, 7th Cong. 1st Sess. 58. Tracy's speech performed the
miracle of making one convert. After he closed he was standing before
the glowing fireplace, "half dead with his exertions." Senator Colhoun
of South Carolina came to Tracy, and giving him his hand, said: "You
are a stranger to me, sir, but by —— you have made me your friend."
Colhoun said that he "had been told a thousand lies" about the Federalist Judiciary Act, particularly the manner of passing it, and he had,
therefore, been in favor of repealing it. But Tracy had convinced
him, and Colhoun declared: "I shall be with you on the question."
"May we depend upon you?" asked Tracy, wringing the South Carolina Senator's hand. "By —— you may," was the response. (Morison: *Life of the Hon. Jeremiah Smith*, footnote to 147.) Colhoun
kept his word and voted with the Federalists against his party's pet
measure. (*Annals*, 7th Cong. 1st Sess. 185.)

The correct spelling of this South Carolina Senator's name is *Colhoun*, and not *Calhoun*, as given in so many biographical sketches
of him. (See *South Carolina Magazine* for July, 1906.)

just under six feet in height, yet heavy with fat; he had extraordinarily large eyes, gray in color, a wide mouth with lips sternly compressed, high, broad forehead, and dark hair, thrown back from his brow. Mason had "wonderful powers of sarcasm" which he employed to the utmost in this debate.[1]

It was true, he said, in beginning his address, that the Judiciary should be independent, but not "independent of the nation itself." Certainly the Judiciary had not Constitutional authority "to control the other departments of the Government."[2] Mason hotly attacked the Federalist position that a National judge, once appointed, was in office permanently; and thus, for the second time, Marbury *vs.* Madison was brought into the debate. "Have we not heard this doctrine supported in the memorable case of the mandamus, lately[3] before the Supreme Court? Was it not there said [in argument of counsel] that, though the law had a right to establish the office of a justice of the peace, yet it had not a right to abridge its duration to five years?"[4]

---

[1] See Grigsby: *Virginia Convention of 1788*, ii, 260–262.

This was the same Senator who, in violation of the rules of the Senate, gave to the press a copy of the Jay Treaty which the Senate was then considering. The publication of the treaty raised a storm of public wrath against that compact. (See vol. ii, 115, of this work.) Senator Mason's action was the first occurrence in our history of a treaty thus divulged.

[2] *Annals*, 7th Cong. 1st Sess. 59.

[3] In that case Marshall had issued a rule to the Secretary of State to show cause why a writ of mandamus should not be issued by the court ordering him to deliver to Marbury and his associates commissions as justices of the peace, to which offices President Adams had appointed them. (See *infra*, chap. iii.)

[4] *Annals*, 7th Cong. 1st Sess. 61.

The true principle, Mason declared, was that judicial offices like all others "are made for the good of the people and not for that of the individual who administers them." Even Judges of the Supreme Court should do something to earn their salaries; but under the Federalist Judiciary Act of 1801 "what have they got to do? To try ten suits, [annually] for such is the number now on their docket."

Mason now departed slightly from the Republican programme of ignoring the favorite Federalist theory that the Judiciary has the power to decide the con-stitutionality of statutes. He fears that the Justices of the Supreme Court "will be induced, from want of employment, to do that which they ought not to do. . . They may . . hold the Constitution in one hand, and the law in the other, and say to the departments of Government, so far shall you go and no farther." He is alarmed lest "this independence of the Judiciary" shall become "something like su-premacy." [1]

Seldom in parliamentary contests has sarcasm, always a doubtful weapon, been employed with finer art than it was by Mason against Morris at this time. The Federalists, in the enactment of the Judiciary Act of 1801, had abolished two district courts — the very thing for which the Republicans were now assailed by the Federalists as destroyers of the Constitution. Where was Morris, asked Mason, when his friends had committed that sacrilege? "Where was the *Ajax Telamon* of his party" at that hour of fate? "Where was the hero with his seven-

[1] *Annals*, 7th Cong. 1st Sess. 63.

fold shield — not of bull's hide, but of brass — prepared to prevent or to punish this Trojan rape?" [1]

Morris replied lamely. He had been criticized, he complained, for pointing out "the dangers to which popular governments are exposed, from the influence of designing demagogues upon popular passion." Yet "'t is for these purposes that all our Constitutional checks are devised." Otherwise "the Constitution is all nonsense." He enumerated the Constitutional limitations and exclaimed, "Why all these multiplied precautions, unless to check and control that impetuous spirit . . which has swept away every popular Government that ever existed?" [2]

Should all else fail, "the Constitution has given us . . an independent judiciary" which, if "you trench upon the rights of your fellow citizens, by passing an unconstitutional law . . will stop you short." Preserve the Judiciary in its vigor, and in great controversies where the passions of the multitude are aroused, "instead of a resort to arms, there will be a happier appeal to argument." [3]

Answering Mason's fears that the Supreme Court, "having little else to do, would do mischief," Morris avowed that he should "rejoice in that mischief," if it checked "the Legislative or Executive departments in any wanton invasion of our rights. . . I know this doctrine is unpleasant; I know it is more popular to appeal to public opinion — that equivocal, transient being, which exists nowhere and every-

---

[1] *Annals*, 7th Cong. 1st Sess. 66. The eloquence of the Virginia Senator elicited the admiration of even the rabidly Federalist *Columbian Centinel* of Boston. See issue of February 6, 1802.

[2] *Ib*. 77.   [3] *Ib*. 83.

where. But if ever the occasion calls for it, I trust the Supreme Court will not neglect doing the great mischief of saving this Constitution." [1]

His emotions wrought to the point of oratorical ecstasy, Morris now made an appeal to "the good sense, patriotism, and . . virtue" of the Republic, in the course of which he became badly entangled in his metaphors. "Do not," he pleaded, "rely on that popular will, which has brought us frail beings into political existence. That opinion is but a changeable thing. It will soon change. This very measure will change it. You will be deceived. Do not . . commit the dignity, the harmony, the existence of our nation to the wild wind. Trust not your treasure to the waves. Throw not your compass and your charts into the ocean. Do not believe that its billows will waft you into port. Indeed, indeed, you will be deceived.

"Cast not away this only anchor of our safety. I have seen its progress. I know the difficulties through which it was obtained. I stand in the presence of Almighty God, and of the world; and I declare to you, that if you lose this charter, never, no, never will you get another! We are now, perhaps, arrived at the parting point. Here, even here, we stand on the brink of fate. Pause — Pause! For Heaven's sake, pause!" [2]

Senator Breckenridge would not "pause." The "progress" of Senator Morris's "anchor," indeed, dragged him again to "the brink of fate." The Senate had "wandered long enough" with the Federal-

---

[1] *Annals,* 7th Cong. 1st Sess. 89.   [2] *Ib.* 91–92.

ist Senators "in those regions of fancy and of terror, to which they [have] led us." He now insisted that the Senate return to the real subject, and in a speech which is a model of compact reasoning, sharpened by sarcasm, discussed all the points raised by the Federalist Senators except their favorite one of the power of the National Judiciary to declare acts of Congress unconstitutional. This he carefully avoided.[1]

On January 15, 1802, the new Vice-President of the United States, Aaron Burr, first took the chair as presiding officer of the Senate.[2] Within two weeks [3] an incident happened which, though seemingly trivial, was powerfully and dramatically to affect the course of political events that finally encompassed the ruin of the reputation, career, and fortune of many men.

Senator Jonathan Dayton of New Jersey, in order, as he claimed, to make the measure less objectionable, moved that "the bill be referred to a select committee, with instructions to consider and report the alterations which may be proper in the judiciary system of the United States."[4] On this motion the Senate tied; and Vice-President Burr, by his deciding vote, referred the bill to the select committee. In doing this he explained that he believed the Federalists sincere in their wish "to ameliorate the provisions of the bill, that it might be rendered more

---

[1] *Annals*, 7th Cong. 1st Sess. 99.

[2] Morris notes in his diary that, on the same day, the Senate resolved "to admit a short-hand writer to their floor. This is the beginning of mischief." (Morris, II, 416–17.)

[3] January 27, 1802.   [4] *Annals*, 7th Cong. 1st Sess. 149.

acceptable to the Senate." But he was careful to warn them that he would "discountenance, by his vote, any attempt, if any such should be made, that might, in an indirect way, go to defeat the bill." [1]

Five days later, one more Republican Senator, being present, and one Federalist Senator, being absent, the committee was discharged on motion of Senator Breckenridge; and the debate continued, the Federalists constantly accusing the Republicans of a purpose to destroy the independence of the National Judiciary, and asserting that National judges must be kept beyond the reach of either Congress or President in order to decide fearlessly upon the constitutionality of laws.

At last the steady but spirited Breckenridge was so irritated that he broke away from the Republican plan to ignore this principal article of Federalist faith. He did not intend to rise again, he said, but "an argument had been so much pressed" that he felt it must be answered. "I did not expect, sir, to find the doctrine of the power of the courts to annul the laws of Congress as unconstitutional, so seriously insisted on. . . I would ask where they got that

---

[1] *Annals*, 7th Cong. 1st Sess. 150.

Burr's action was perfectly correct. As an impartial presiding officer, he could not well have done anything else. Alexander J. Dallas, Republican Attorney-General of Pennsylvania, wrote the Vice-President a letter approving his action. (Dallas to Burr, Feb. 3, 1802, Davis: *Memoirs of Aaron Burr*, II, 82.) Nathaniel Niles, a rampant Republican, sent Burr a letter thanking him for his vote. As a Republican, he wanted his party to be fair, he said. (Niles to Burr, Feb. 17, 1802, *ib.* 83–84.) Nevertheless, Burr's vote was seized upon by his enemies as the occasion for beginning those attacks upon him which led to his overthrow and disgrace. (See chaps. VI, VII, VIII, and IX of this volume.)

power, and who checks the courts when they violate the Constitution?"

The theory that courts may annul legislation would give them "the absolute direction of the Government." For, "to whom are they responsible?" He wished to have pointed out the clause which grants to the National Judiciary the power to overthrow legislation. "Is it not extraordinary," said he, "that if this high power was intended, it should nowhere appear? . . Never were such high and transcendant powers in any Government (much less in one like ours, composed of powers specially given and defined) claimed or exercised by construction only." [1]

Breckenridge frankly stated the Republican philosophy, repeating sometimes word for word the passage which Jefferson at the last moment had deleted from his Message to Congress. [2] "The Constitution," he declared, "intended a separation of the powers vested in the three great departments, giving to each exclusive authority on the subjects committed to it. . . Those who made the laws are presumed to have an equal attachment to, and interest in the Constitution; are equally bound by oath to support it, and have an equal right to give a construction to it. . . The construction of one department of the powers vested in it, is of higher authority than the construction of any other department.

"The Legislature," he continued, "have the exclusive right to interpret the Constitution, in what

---

[1] *Annals*, 7th Cong. 1st Sess. 178–79.
[2] See Appendix A to this volume.

regards the law-making power, and the judges are
bound to execute the laws they make. For the Legislature would have at least an equal right to annul
the decisions of the courts, founded on their construction of the Constitution, as the courts would
have to annul the acts of the Legislature, founded on
their construction.[1] . . In case the courts were to
declare your revenue, impost and appropriation laws
unconstitutional, would they thereby be blotted out
of your statute book, and the operations of Government arrested? . . Let gentlemen consider well before
they insist on a power in the Judiciary which places
the Legislature at their feet." [2]

The candles [3] now dimly illuminating the little
Senate Chamber shed scarcely more light than radiated from the broad, round, florid face of Gouverneur Morris. Getting to his feet as quickly as his
wooden leg would permit, his features beaming with
triumph, the New York Senator congratulated "this
House, and all America, that we have at length got
our adversaries upon the ground where we can fairly
meet." [4]

The power of courts to declare legislation invalid
is derived from "authority higher than this Constitution . . from the constitution of man, from the
nature of things, from the necessary progress of
human affairs," [5] he asserted. In a cause on trial
before them, it becomes necessary for the judges to

[1] *Annals*, 7th Cong. 1st Sess. 179.   [2] *Ib.* 180.
[3] It was five o'clock (*ib.* 178) when Senator Breckenridge began to
speak; it must have been well after six when Senator Morris rose
to answer him.
[4] *Ib.* 180.   [5] *Ib.* 180.

"declare what the law is. They must, of course, determine whether that which is produced and relied on, has indeed the binding force of law."

Suppose, said Morris, that Congress should pass an act forbidden by the Constitution — for instance, one laying "a duty on exports," and "the citizen refuses to pay." If the Republicans were right, the courts would enforce a collection. In vain would the injured citizen appeal to the Supreme Court; for Congress would "defeat the appeal, and render final the judgment of inferior tribunals, subjected to their absolute control." According to the Republican doctrine, "the moment the Legislature . . declare themselves supreme, they become so . . and the Constitution is whatever they choose to make it." [1] This time Morris made a great impression. The Federalists were in high feather; even the Republicans were moved to admiration. Troup reported to King that "the democratical paper at Washington pronounced his speech to be the greatest display of eloquence ever exhibited in a deliberative assembly!" [2]

Nevertheless, the Federalist politicians were worried by the apparent indifference of the rank and file of their party. "I am surprized," wrote Bayard, "at the public apathy upon the subject. Why do not those who are opposed to the project, express in the public papers or by petitions their disapprobation? . . It is likely that a public movement would have great effect." [3] But, thanks to the former conduct of

[1] *Annals*, 7th Cong. 1st Sess. 181.
[2] Troup to King, April 9, 1802, King, IV, 103.
[3] Bayard to Bassett, Jan. 25, 1802, *Papers of James A. Bayard: Donnan*, 146–47.

the judges themselves, no "public movement" developed. Conservative citizens were apprehensive; but, as usual, they were lethargic.

On February 3, 1802, the Senate, by a strictly party vote[1] of 16 to 15, passed the bill to repeal the Federalist Judiciary Act of 1801.[2]

When the bill came up in the House, the Federalist leader in that body, James A. Bayard of Delaware, moved to postpone its consideration to the third Monday in March, in order, as he said, to test public opinion, because "few occasions have occurred so important as this."[3] But in vain did the Federalists plead and threaten. Postponement was refused by a vote of 61 to 35.[4] Another plea for delay was denied by a vote of 58 to 34.[5] Thus the solid Republican majority, in rigid pursuance of the party plan, forced the consideration of the bill.

The Federalist organ in Washington, which Marshall two years earlier was supposed to influence and to which he probably contributed,[6] saw little hope of successful resistance. "What will eventually be the issue of the present high-handed, overbearing proceedings of Congress it is impossible to determine," but fear was expressed by this paper that condition

[1] Except Colhoun of South Carolina, converted by Tracy. See *supra*, 62.

[2] *Annals*, 7th Cong. 1st Sess. 183.

[3] *Ib.* 510. A correspondent of the *Columbian Centinel*, reporting the event, declared that "the stand which the Federal Senators have made to preserve the Constitution, has been manly and glorious. They have immortalized their names, while those of their opposers will be execrated as the assassins of the Constitution." (*Columbian Centinel*, Feb. 17, 1802.)

[4] *Annals*, 7th Cong. 1st Sess. 518–19.   [5] *Ib.* 521–22.

[6] See vol. ii, 532, 541.

would be created "which impartial, unbiased and reflecting men consider as immediately preceding the total destruction of our government and the introduction of disunion, anarchy and civil war." [1]

This threat of secession and armed resistance, already made in the Senate, was to be repeated three times in the debate in the House which was opened for the Federalists by Archibald Henderson of North Carolina, whom Marshall pronounced to be "unquestionably among the ablest lawyers of his day" and "one of the great lawyers of the Nation." [2] "The monstrous and unheard of doctrine . . lately advanced, that the judges have not the right of declaring unconstitutional laws void," was, declared Henderson, "the very definition of tyranny, and wherever you find it, the people are slaves, whether they call their Government a Monarchy, Republic, or Democracy." If the Republican theory of the Constitution should prevail, "better at once to bury it with all our hopes." [3]

Robert Williams of the same State, an extreme but unskillful Republican, now uncovered his party's scheme to oust Federalist judges, which thus far had carefully been concealed: [4] "Agreeably to our Constitution a judge may be impeached," said he, but this punishment would be minimized if judges could declare an act of Congress unconstitutional. "However he may err, he commits no crime; how, then, can he be impeached?" [5]

[1] *Washington Federalist*, Feb. 13, 1802.
[2] Henderson in *North Carolina Booklet*, xvii, 66.
[3] *Annals*, 7th Cong. 1st Sess. 529–30.
[4] See *infra*, chap. iv.   [5] *Annals*, 7th Cong. 1st Sess. 531.

Philip R. Thompson of Virginia, a Republican, was moved to the depths of his being: "Give the Judiciary this check upon the Legislature, allow them the power to declare your laws null and void, .. and in vain have the people placed you upon this floor to legislate.[1] .. This is the tree where despotism lies concealed. .. Nurture it with your treasure, stop not its ramifications, and .. your atmosphere will be contaminated with its poisonous effluvia, and your soaring eagle will fall dead at its root."[2]

Thomas T. Davis of Kentucky, deeply stirred by this picture, declared that the Federalists said to the people, you are "incapable" of protecting yourselves; "in the Judiciary alone you find a safe deposit for your liberties." The Kentucky Representative "trembled" at such ideas. "The sooner we put men out of power, who [sic] we find determined to act in this manner, the better; by doing so we preserve the power of the Legislature, and save our nation from the ravages of an uncontrolled Judiciary."[3] Thus again was revealed the Republican purpose of dragging from the National Bench all judges who dared assert the right, and to exercise the power to declare an act of Congress unconstitutional.[4]

The contending forces became ever more earnest as the struggle continued. All the cases then known in which courts directly or by inference had held legislative acts invalid were cited;[5] and all the argu-

---

[1] *Annals*, 7th Cong. 1st Sess. 552–53.   [2] *Ib.* 554.

[3] *Ib.* 558.   [4] See *infra*, chap. IV.

[5] See, for example, the speeches of Thomas Morris of New York (*Annals*, 7th Cong. 1st Sess. 565–68); Calvin Goddard of Connecticut (*ib.* 727–34); John Stanley of North Carolina (*ib.* 569–78); Roger Griswold of Connecticut (*ib.* 768–69).

ments that ever had been advanced in favor of the
principle of the judicial power to annul legislation
were made over and over again.

All the reasons for the opinion which John Marshall, exactly one year later, pronounced in Marbury
vs. Madison were given during this debate. Indeed,
the legislative struggle now in progress and the result of it, created conditions which forced Marshall
to execute that judicial *coup d'état.* It should be repeated that an understanding of Marbury *vs.* Madison is impossible without a thorough knowledge of
the debate in Congress which preceded and largely
caused that epochal decision.

The alarm that the repeal was but the beginning of Republican havoc was sounded by every
Federalist member. "This measure," said John
Stanley of North Carolina, "will be the first link
in that chain of measures which will add the name
of America to the melancholy catalogue of fallen
Republics."[1]

William Branch Giles, who for the next five years
bore so vital a part in the stirring events of Marshall's life, now took the floor and made one of the
ablest addresses of his tempestuous career.[2] He was
Jefferson's lieutenant in the House.[3] When the Federalists tried to postpone the consideration of the
bill,[4] Giles admitted that it presented a question
"more important than any that ever came before

---

[1] *Annals,* 7th Cong. 1st Sess. 579.

[2] Anderson, 83. Grigsby says that "Mr. Jefferson pronounced
him (Giles) the ablest debater of the age." His speech on the Repeal Act, Grigsby declares to have been "by far his most brilliant
display." (Grigsby: *Virginia Convention of 1829–30,* 23, 29.)

[3] Anderson, 76–82.   [4] See *supra,* 72.

this house." [1] But there was no excuse for delay,
because the press had been full of it for more than
a year and the public was thoroughly informed
upon it. [2]

Giles was a large, robust, "handsome" Virginian,
whose lightest word always compelled the attention
of the House. He had a very dark complexion, black
hair worn long, and intense, "retreating" brown
eyes. His dress was "remarkably plain, and in the
style of Virginia carelessness." His voice was "clear
and nervous," his language "powerfully condensed." [3]

This Republican gladiator came boldly to combat.
How had the Federalists contrived to gain their
ends? Chiefly by "the breaking out of a tremendous
and unprecedented war in Europe," which had
worked upon "the feelings and sympathies of the
people of the United States" till they had neglected their own affairs. So it was, he said, that the
Federalists had been able to load upon the people an
expensive army, a powerful navy, intolerable taxes,

[1] This statement, coming from the Virginia radical, reveals the
profound concern of the Republicans, for Giles thus declared that the
Judiciary debate was of greater consequence than those historic controversies over Assumption, the Whiskey Rebellion, the Bank, Neutrality, the Jay Treaty, the French complication, the army, and other
vital subjects. In most of those encounters Giles had taken a leading
and sometimes violent part.

[2] *Annals*, 7th Cong. 1st Sess. 512.

[3] Story's description of Giles six years later: Story to Fay, Feb. 13.
1808, Story, I, 158–59. Also see Anderson, frontispiece and 238.

Giles was thirty-nine years of age. He had been elected to the House
in 1790, and from the day he entered Congress had exasperated the
Federalists. It is an interesting though trivial incident that Giles bore
to Madison a letter of introduction from Marshall. Evidently the
circumspect Richmond attorney was not well impressed with Giles,
for the letter is cautious in the extreme. (See Anderson, 10; also
Annals, 7th Cong. 1st Sess. 581.)

and the despotic Alien and Sedition Laws. But at last, when, as the result of their maladministration, the Federalists saw their doom approaching, they began to "look out for some department of the government in which they could entrench themselves . . and continue to support those favorite principles of irresponsibility which they could never consent to abandon."

For this purpose they had selected the Judiciary Department: "Not only because it was already filled" with rabid Federalists, "but because they held their offices by indefinite tenures, and of course were further removed from any responsibility to the people than either of the other departments." Thus came the Federalist Judiciary Act of 1801 which the Republicans were about to repeal.

Giles could not resist a sneer at Marshall. Referring to the European war, to which "the feelings and sympathies of the people of the United States were so strongly attracted . . that they considered their own internal concerns in a secondary point of view," Giles swiftly portrayed those measures used by the Federalists as a pretext. They had, jeered the sharp-tongued Virginia Republican, "pushed forward the people to the X, Y, Z, of their political alphabet, before they had well learned . . the A, B, C, of the principles of the [Federalist] Administration." [1]

But now, when blood was no longer flowing on European battle-fields, the interests of the American people in that "tremendous and unprecedented" combat of nations "no longer turn their attention

[1] *Annals*, 7th Cong. 1st Sess. 580–81.

from their internal concerns; arguments of the highest consideration for the safety of the Constitution and the liberty of the citizens, no longer receive the short reply, French partisans! Jacobins! Disorganizers!"[1] So "the American people and their Congress, in their real persons, and original American characters" were at last "engaged in the transaction of American concerns."[2]

Federalist despotism lay prostrate, thank Heaven, beneath the conquering Republican heel. Should it rise again? Never! Giles taunted the Federalists with the conduct of Federalist judges in the sedition cases,[3] and denounced the attempt to fasten British law on the American Nation — a law "unlimited in its object, and indefinite in its character," covering "every object of legislation."

Think, too, of what Marshall and the Supreme Court have done! "They have sent a . . process leading to a mandamus, into the Executive cabinet, to examine its concerns."[4] The real issue between Federalists and Republicans, declared Giles, was "the doctrine of irresponsibility against the doctrine of responsibility. . . The doctrine of despotism in opposition to the representative system." The Federalist theory was "an express avowal that the people were incompetent to govern themselves."

A handsome, florid, fashionably attired man of thirty-five now took the floor and began his reply to the powerful speech of the tempestuous Virginian.

---

[1] *Annals*, 7th Cong. 1st Sess. 582. [2] *Ib.* 583.
[3] See *supra*, chap. i.
[4] Marbury *vs.* Madison (see *infra*, chap. iii). For Giles's great speech see *Annals*, 7th Cong. 1st Sess. 579–602.

His complexion and stoutness indicated the generous manner in which all public men of the time lived, and his polished elocution and lofty scorn for all things Republican marked him as the equal of Gouverneur Morris in oratorical finish and Federalist distrust of the people.[1] It was James A. Bayard, the Federalist leader of the House.

He asserted that the Republican "designs [were] hostile to the powers of this government"; that they flowed from "state pride [which] extinguishes a national sentiment"; that while the Federalists were in charge of the National Administration they struggled "to maintain the Constitutional powers of the Executive" because "the wild principles of French liberty were scattered through the country. We had our Jacobins and disorganizers, who saw no difference between a King and a President; and, as the people of France had put down their King, they thought the people of America ought to put down their President.

"They [Federalists] who considered the Constitution as securing all the principles of rational and practicable liberty, who were unwilling to embark upon the tempestuous sea of revolution, in pursuit of visionary schemes, were denounced as monarchists. A line was drawn between the Government

[1] Bayard is "a fine, personable man . . of strong mental powers. . . Nature has been liberal to him. . . He has, in himself, vast resources . . a lawyer of high repute . . and a man of integrity and honor. . . He is very fond of pleasure . . a married man but fond of wine, women and cards. He drinks more than a bottle of wine each day. . . He lives too fast to live long. . . He is very attentive to dress and person." (Senator William Plumer's description of James A. Bayard, March 10, 1803, "Repository," Plumer MSS. Lib. Cong.)

and the people, and the friends of the Govern‚
ment [Federalists] were marked as the enemies of
the people." [1] This was the spirit that was now
triumphant; to what lengths was it to carry the
Republicans? Did they include the downfall of the
Judiciary in their plans of general destruction? Did
they propose to make judges the mere creatures of
Congress? [2]

Bayard skillfully turned the gibe at Marshall into
a tribute to the Chief Justice. What did Giles mean
by his cryptic X. Y. Z. reference? "Did he mean
that the dispatches . . were impostures?" Though
Giles "felt no respect" for Marshall or Pinckney —
"two characters as pure, as honorable, and exalted,
as any the country can boast of" — yet, exclaimed
Bayard, "I should have expected that he would have
felt some tenderness for Mr. Gerry." [3]

The Republicans had contaminated the country
with falsehoods against the Federalist Administrations; and now the target of their "poisoned ar-
rows" was the National Judiciary. "If . . they
[the judges] have offended against the Constitution
or laws of the country, why are they not impeached?
The gentleman now holds the sword of justice. The
judges are not a privileged order; they have no
shelter but their innocence." [4]

In detail Bayard explained the facts in the case
of Marbury *vs*. Madison. That the Supreme Court
had been "hardy enough to send their mandate into
the Executive cabinet" [5] was, said he, "a strong proof

---

[1] *Annals*, 7th Cong. 1st Sess. 605.   [2] *Ib*. 606.
[3] *Ib*. 609.   [4] *Ib*. 611.   [5] *Ib*. 614.

of the value of that Constitutional provision which makes them independent. They are not terrified by the frowns of Executive power, and dare to judge between the rights of a citizen and the pretensions of a President." [1]

Contrast the defects of the Judiciary Act of 1789 with the perfection of the Federalist law supplanting it. Could any man deny the superiority of the latter? [2] The truth was that the Republicans were "to give notice to the judges of the Supreme Court of their fate, and to bid them to prepare for their end." [3] In these words Bayard charged the Republicans with their settled but unavowed purpose to unseat Marshall and his Federalist associates. [4]

Bayard hotly denied the Republican accusation that President Adams had appointed to the bench Federalist members of Congress as a reward for their party services; but, retorted he, Jefferson had done that very thing. [5] He then spoke at great length on

[1] *Annals*, 7th Cong. 1st Sess. 615.

[2] Bayard's summary of the shortcomings of the Ellsworth Act of 1789 and the excellence of the Judiciary Act of 1801 (*Annals*, 7th Cong. 1st Sess. 616–27) was the best made at that time or since.

[3] *Ib.* 632.   [4] See *infra*, chap. IV.

[5] Bayard pointed out that Charles Pinckney of South Carolina, whose "zeal and industry" decided the Presidential vote of his State, had been appointed Minister to Spain; that Claiborne of Tennessee held the vote of that State and cast it for Jefferson, and that Jefferson had conferred upon him "the high degree of Governor of the Mississippi Territory"; that Mr. Linn of New Jersey, upon whom both parties depended, finally cast his deciding vote in favor of Jefferson and "Mr. Linn has since had the profitable office of supervisor of his district conferred upon him"; and that Mr. Lyon of Vermont neutralized the vote of his State, but since "his character was low . . Mr. Lyon's son has been handsomely provided for in one of the Executive offices." (*Annals*, 7th Cong. 1st Sess. 640.) Bayard named other men who had influenced the vote in the House and who had thereafter been rewarded by Jefferson.

the nature of the American Judiciary as distinguished from that of British courts, gave a vivid account of the passage of the Federalist Judiciary Act under attack, and finally swung back to the subject which more and more was coming to dominate the struggle — the power of the Supreme Court to annul acts of Congress.

Again and again Bayard restated, and with power and eloquence, all the arguments to support the supervisory power of courts over legislation.[1] At last he threatened armed resistance if the Republicans dared to carry out their plans against the National Judiciary. "There are many now willing to spill their blood to defend that Constitution. Are gentlemen disposed to risk the consequences? . . Let them consider their wives and children, their neighbors and their friends." Destroy the independence of the National Judiciary and "the moment is not far when this fair country is to be desolated by civil war."[2]

Bayard's speech aroused great enthusiasm among the leaders of his party. John Adams wrote: "Yours is the most comprehensive masterly and compleat argument that has been published in either house and will have, indeed . . has already had more effect and influence on the public mind than all other publications on the subject."[3] The *Washington Federalist* pronounced Bayard's performance to be "far superior, not only to . . the speeches of Mr. Morris

[1] *Annals*, 7th Cong. 1st Sess. 645–48.

[2] *Ib.* 648–50. This was the second open expression in Congress of the spirit that led the New England Federalist leaders into their futile secession movement. (See *infra*, chaps. III and VI; also vol. IV, chap. I, of this work.)

[3] Adams to Bayard, April 10, 1802; *Bayard Papers:* Donnan, 152.

and Mr. Tracy in the Senate, but to any speech of a Demosthenes, a Cicero, or a Chatham." [1]

Hardly was Bayard's last word spoken when the man who at that time was the Republican master of the House, and, indeed, of the Senate also, was upon his feet. Of medium stature, thin as a sword, his straight black hair, in which gray already was beginning to appear, suggesting the Indian blood in his veins, his intense black eyes flaming with the passion of combat, his high and shrilling voice suggesting the scream of an eagle, John Randolph of Roanoke — that haughty, passionate, eccentric genius — personified the aggressive and ruthless Republicanism of the hour. He was clad in riding-coat and breeches, wore long riding-boots, and if the hat of the Virginia planter was not on his head, it was because in his nervousness he had removed it; [2] while, if his riding-whip was not in his hand, it was on his desk where he had cast it, the visible and fitting emblem of this strange man's mastery over his partisan followers. [3]

[1] *Washington Federalist*, Feb. 20, 1802.

[2] Members of Congress wore their hats during the sessions of House and Senate until 1828. For a description of Randolph in the House, see Tyler, I, 291. Senator Plumer pictured him as "a pale, meagre, ghostly man," with "more popular and effective talents than any other member of his party." (Plumer to Emery, Plumer, 248.) See also Plumer's letter to his son, Feb. 22, 1803, in which the New Hampshire Senator says that "Randolph goes to the House booted and spurred, with his whip in his hand, in imitation, it is said, of members of the British Parliament. He is a very slight man, but of the common stature." At a distance he looks young, but "upon a nearer approach you perceive his wrinkles and grey hairs. He is, I believe, about thirty." (*Ib.* 256.)

[3] The personal domination which John Randolph of Roanoke wielded over his party in Congress, until he broke with Jefferson (see *infra*, chaps. IV and X), is difficult to realize at the present day. Nothing like it has since been experienced, excepting only the merci-

"He did not rise," he said, his voice quivering and body trembling,[1] "for the purpose of assuming the gauntlet which had been so proudly thrown by the Goliah of the adverse party; not but that he believed even his feeble powers, armed with the simple weapon of truth, a sling and a stone, capable of prostrating on the floor that gigantic boaster, armed cap-a-pie as he was." Randolph sneered, as only he could sneer, at the unctuous claims of the Federalists, that they had "nobly sacrificed their political existence on the altar of the general welfare"; he refused "to revere in them the self-immolated victims at the shrine of patriotism." [2]

As to the Federalist assertion that "the common law of England is the law of the United States in their confederate capacity," Randolph observed that the meaning of such terms as "court," "jury," and the like must, of course, be settled by reference to common-law definitions, but "does it follow that that indefinite and undefinable body of law is the irrepealable law of the land? The sense of a most important phrase, 'direct tax,' as used in the Constitution, has been . . settled by the acceptation of Adam Smith; an acceptation, too, peculiar to himself. Does the Wealth of Nations, therefore, form a part of the Constitution of the United States?"

And would the Federalists inform the House what phase of the common law they proposed to adopt for the United States? Was it that "of the reign of less rule of Thaddeus Stevens of Pennsylvania from 1862 until 1868. (See Woodburn: *Life of Thaddeus Stevens*, 247 *et seq.*)

[1] *Washington Federalist*, Feb. 22, 1802.
[2] *Annals*, 7th Cong. 1st Sess. 650–51.

Elizabeth and James the first; or . . that of the time of George the Second?" Was it that "of Sir Walter Raleigh and Captain Smith, or that which was imported by Governor Oglethorpe?" Or was it that of some intermediate period? "I wish especially to know," asked Randolph, "whether the common law of libels which attaches to this Constitution, be the doctrine laid down by Lord Mansfield, or that which has immortalized Mr. Fox?" Let the Federalists reflect on the persecution for libel that had been made under the common law, as well as under the Sedition Act.[1]

Proper restraint upon Congress, said Randolph, was not found in a pretended power of the Judiciary to veto legislation, but in the people themselves, who at the ballot box could "apply the Constitutional corrective. That is the true check; every other is at variance with the principle that a free people are capable of self-government." Then the imperious Virginian boldly charged that the Federalists intended to have John Marshall and his associates on the Supreme Bench annul the Republican repeal of the Federalist Judiciary Act.

"Sir," cried Randolph, "if you pass the law, the judges are to put their veto upon it by declaring it unconstitutional. Here is a new power of a dangerous and uncontrollable nature. . . The decision of a Constitutional question must rest somewhere. Shall it be confided to men immediately responsible to the people, or to those who are irresponsible? . . From whom is a corrupt decision most to be feared? . .

[1] *Annals*, 7th Cong. 1st Sess. 652.

The power which has the right of passing, without appeal, on the validity of your laws, is your sovereign. . . Are we not as deeply interested in the true exposition of the Constitution as the judges can be?" inquired Randolph. "Is not Congress as capable of forming a correct opinion as they are? Are not its members acting under a responsibility to public opinion which can and will check their aberrations from duty?"

Randolph referred to the case of Marbury *vs*. Madison and then recalled the prosecution of Thomas Cooper in which the National court refused "to a man under criminal prosecution . . a subpœna to be served on the President, as a witness on the part of the prisoner.[1] . . This court, which it seems, has lately become the guardian of the feeble and oppressed, against the strong arm of power, found itself destitute of all power to issue the writ. . .

"No, sir, you may invade the press; the courts will support you, will outstrip you in zeal to further this great object; your citizens may be imprisoned and amerced, the courts will take care to see it executed; the helpless foreigner may, contrary to the express letter of your Constitution, be deprived of compulsory process for obtaining witnesses in his defense; the courts in their extreme humility cannot find authority for granting it."

Again Marbury *vs*. Madison came into the de-

---

[1] See *supra*, chap. I, 33; also *infra*, chap. IX, where Marshall, during the trial of Aaron Burr, actually issued such a subpœna. Randolph was now denouncing the National court before which Cooper was tried, because it refused to grant the very writ for the issuing of which Marshall in a few years was so rancorously assailed by Jefferson personally, and by nearly all Republicans as a party.

bate:[1] "In their inquisitorial capacity," the Supreme Court, according to Marshall's ruling in that case, could force the President himself to discharge his executive functions "in what mode" the omnipotent judges might choose to direct. And Congress! "For the amusement of the public, we shall retain the right of debating but not of voting."[2] The judges could forestall legislation by "inflammatory pamphlets," as they had done.[3]

As the debate wore on, little that was new was adduced. Calvin Goddard of Connecticut reviewed the cases in which judges of various courts had asserted the Federalist doctrine of the judicial power to decide statutes unconstitutional,[4] and quoted from Marshall's speech on the Judiciary in the Virginia Convention of 1788.[5]

John Rutledge, Jr., of South Carolina, then delivered one of the most distinguished addresses of this notable discussion. Suppose, he said, that Congress were to pass any of the laws which the Constitution forbids, "who are to decide between the Constitution and the acts of Congress? . . If the people . . [are] not shielded by some Constitutional checks" their liberties will be "destroyed . . by demagogues, who filch the confidence of the people by pretending

[1] At the time Marshall issued the rule against Madison he apparently had no idea that Section 13 of the Ellsworth Judiciary Act was unconstitutional. (See next chapter.)

[2] *Annals*, 7th Cong. 1st Sess. 662–63.

[3] The Federalist organ tried, by ridicule, to minimize Randolph's really strong speech. "The speech of Mr. Randolph was a jumble of disconnected declamation. . . He was horribly tiresome to the ear and disgusting to the taste." (*Washington Federalist*, Feb. 22, 1802.)

[4] *Annals*, 7th Cong. 1st Sess. 727.

[5] *Ib.* 737. See also vol. I, 452, of this work.

to be their friends; . . demagogues who carry daggers in their hearts, and seductive smiles in their hypocritical faces." [1]

Rutledge was affected by the prevailing Federalist pessimism. "This bill," said he, "is an egg which will produce a brood of mortal consequences. . . It will soon prostrate public confidence; it will immediately depreciate the value of public property. Who will buy your lands? Who will open your Western forests? Who will build upon the hills and cultivate the valleys which here surround us?" The financial adventurer who would take such risks "must be a speculator indeed, and his purse must overflow . . if there be no independent tribunals where the validity of your titles will be confirmed.[2] . .

"Have we not seen a State [Georgia] sell its Western lands, and afterwards declare the law under which they were sold made null and void? Their nullifying law would have been declared void, had they had an independent Judiciary." [3]   Here Rutledge anticipated by eight years the opinion delivered by Marshall in Fletcher vs. Peck.[4]

"Whenever in any country judges are dependent, property is insecure." What had happened in France? "Frenchmen received their constitution as the followers of Mahomet did their Koran, as though it came to them from Heaven. They swore on their standards and their sabres never to abandon it. But, sir, this constitution has vanished; the swords which were to have formed a rampart around it, are now

---

[1] *Annals*, 7th Cong. 1st Sess. 747–55.   [2] *Ib*. 759.
[3] *Ib*. 760.   [4] See *infra*, chap. x.

worn by the Consular janissaries, and the Republican standards are among the trophies which decorate the vaulted roof of the Consul's palace.[1] Indeed . . [the] subject," avowed Rutledge with passionate earnestness, "is perhaps as awful a one as any on this side of the grave. This attack upon our Constitution will form a great epoch in the history of our Government."[2]

Forcible resistance, if the Republican assault on the Judiciary succeeded, had twice been intimated during the debate. As yet, however, actual secession of the Northern and Eastern States had not been openly suggested, although it was common talk among the Federalists;[3] but now one of the boldest and frankest of their number broadly hinted it to be the Federalist purpose, should the Republicans persist in carrying out their purpose of demolishing the National courts.[4] In closing a long, intensely partisan and wearisome speech, Roger Griswold of Connecticut exclaimed: "There are states in this Union who will never consent and are not doomed to become the humble provinces of Virginia.'

Joseph H. Nicholson of Maryland, Republican, was hardly less prolix than Griswold. He asked whether the people had ever approved the adoption of the common law by the Judiciary. "Have they ever sanctioned the principle that the judges should make laws for them instead of their Representatives?"[6] Tiresome as he was, he made a conclusive

---

[1] *Annals*, 7th Cong. 1st Sess. 760.   [2] *Ib.* 760.
[3] See *infra*, chaps. III and VI.
[4] *Annals*, 7th Cong. 1st Sess. 767–94.
[5] *Ib.* 793.   [6] *Ib.* 805–06.

argument against the Federalist position that the National Judiciary might apply the common law in cases not provided for by acts of Congress.

The debate ran into the month of March.[1] Every possible phase of the subject was gone over time and again. All authorities which the ardent and tireless industry of the contending partisans could discover were brought to light. The pending case of Marbury *vs.* Madison was in the minds of all; and it was repeatedly dragged into the discussion. Samuel W. Dana of Connecticut examined it minutely, citing the action of the Supreme Court in the case of the application for a mandamus to the Secretary of War upon which the court acted February 14, 1794: "There does not appear to have been any question respecting the general power of the Supreme Court, to issue a mandamus to the Secretary of War, or any other subordinate officer." That was "a regular mode for obtaining a decision of the Supreme Court. . . When such has been the unquestioned usage heretofore, is it not extraordinary that there has not been prudence enough to say less about the case of Marbury against the Secretary of State?"[2]

---

[1] In sour disgust Morris notes in his diary: "The House of Representatives have talked themselves out of self-respect, and at headquarters [White House] there is such an abandonment of manner and such a pruriency of conversation as would reduce even greatness to the level of vulgarity." (March 10, 1802, Morris, II, 421.)

[2] *Annals*, 7th Cong. 1st Sess. 904.

Dana's statement is of first importance and should be carefully noted. It was at the time the universally accepted view of the power of the Supreme Court to issue writs of mandamus. Neither Federalists nor Republicans had ever questioned the Constitutional right of the Supreme Court to entertain original jurisdiction of mandamus proceedings in proper cases. Yet just this was what Marshall was so soon to deny in Marbury *vs.* Madison. (See *infra*, chap. III.)

Dana then touched upon the general expectation that Marshall would declare void the Repeal Act. Because of this very apprehension, the Republicans, a few days later, suspended for more than a year the sessions of the Supreme Court. So Dana threatened that if the Republicans should pass the bill, the Supreme Court would annul it; for, said he, the Judiciary were sworn to support the Constitution, and when they find that instrument on one side and an act of Congress on the other, "what is their duty? Are they not to obey their oath, and judge accordingly? If so, they necessarily decide, that your act is of no force; for they are sworn to support the Constitution. This is a doctrine coeval with the existence of our Government, and has been the uniform principle of all the constituted authorities." [1] And he cited the position taken by National judges in 1792 in the matter of the pension commission. [2]

John Bacon, that stanch Massachusetts Republican, [3] asserted that "the Judiciary have no more right to prescribe, direct or control the acts of the other departments of the Government, than the other departments of the Government have to prescribe or direct those of the Judiciary." [4]

The Republicans determined to permit no further delay; for the first time in its history the House was kept in session until midnight. [5] At twelve o'clock, March 3, 1802, the vote was taken on the final passage of the bill, the thirty-two Federalists voting against and the fifty-nine Republicans for the meas-

---

[1] *Annals*, 7th Cong. 1st Sess. 920.   [2] *Ib*. 923–26.
[3] See *supra*, chap. I, 43.
[4] *Annals*, 7th Cong. 1st Sess. 983.   [5] Hildreth, v, 441.

ure.[1] "Thus ended this gigantic debate," chronicles
the historian of that event.[2] No discussion in Congress had hitherto been so widely reported in the
press or excited such general comment. By the great
majority of the people the repeal was received with
enthusiasm, although some Republicans believed
that their party had gone too far.[3] Republican papers, however, hailed the repeal as the breaking of
one of those judicial fetters which shackled the people, while Federalist journals bemoaned it as the beginning of the annihilation of all that was sane and
worthy in American institutions.

"The fatal bill has passed; our Constitution is no
more," exclaimed the *Washington Federalist* in an
editorial entitled

"FAREWELL, A LONG FAREWELL, TO ALL OUR
GREATNESS."

The paper despaired of the Republic — nobody
could tell "what other acts, urged by the intoxication of power and the fury of party rage" would be
put through. But it announced that the Federalist
judges would disregard the infamous Republican
law: "The judges will continue to hold their courts
as if the bill had not passed. 'T is their solemn duty
to do it; their country, all that is dear and valuable,
call upon them to do it. By the judges this bill will
be declared null and void. . . And we now ask the

[1] Bayard to Bassett, March 3, 1802, *Bayard Papers :* Donnan, 150;
and see *Annals,* 7th Cong. 1st Sess. 982. One Republican, Dr. William
Eustis of Boston, voted with the Federalists.

[2] *Hist. Last Sess. Cong. Which Commenced 7th Dec. 1801* (taken
from the *National Intelligencer*), 71.

[3] Tucker: *Life of Thomas Jefferson,* II, 114.

mighty victors, what is your triumph? . . What is the triumph of the President? He has gratified his malice towards the judges, but he has drawn a tear into the eye of every thoughtful patriot . . and laid the foundation of infinite mischief." The Federalist organ declared that the Republican purpose was to force a "dissolution of the Union," and that this was likely to happen.

This significant editorial ended by a consideration of the Republican purpose to destroy the Supreme Court: "Should Mr. Breckenridge now bring forward a resolution to repeal the law establishing the Supreme Court of the United States, we should only consider it a part of the system to be pursued. . . We sincerely expect it will be done next session. . . Such is democracy." [1]

Senator Plumer declared, before the final vote, that the passage of the Republican Repeal Bill and of other Republican measures meant "anarchy." [2]

The ultra-Federalist *Palladium* of Boston lamented: "Our army is to be less and our navy nothing: Our Secretaries are to be aliens and our Judges as independent as spaniels. In this way we are to save everything, but our reputation and our rights.[3] . . Has Liberty any citadel or fortress, has mob despotism any impediments?" [4]

---

[1] *Washington Federalist*, March 3, 1802. Too much importance cannot be attached to this editorial. It undoubtedly expressed accurately the views of Federalist public men in the Capital, including Marshall, whose partisan views and feelings were intense. It should not be forgotten that his relations with this newspaper were believed to be intimate. (See vol. II, 532, 541, of this work.)

[2] Plumer to Upham, March 1, 1802, Plumer MSS. Lib. Cong.

[3] March 12, 1802.   [4] March 23, 1802.

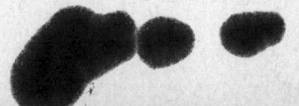

The *Independent Chronicle*, on the other hand, "congratulated the public on the final triumph of *Republicanism*, in the repeal of the late obnoxious judiciary law." [1] The Republicans of Boston and Cambridge celebrated the event with discharges of artillery.

Vans Murray reported to King that "the principle of . . disorganizing . . goes on with a destructive zeal. Internal Taxes — Judicial Sanctity — all are to be overset." [2] Sedgwick was sure that no defense was left against "legislative usurpation." [3] "The angels of destruction . . are making haste," moaned Fisher Ames. [4]

"The angels of destruction" lost no time in striking their next blow. On March 18, two weeks after the threat of the *Washington Federalist* that the Supreme Court would declare unconstitutional the Republican Repeal Act, a Senate committee was appointed to examine further the National Judiciary establishment and report a bill for any improvements considered necessary. [5] Within a week the committee laid the measure before the Senate, [6] and on April 8 it was passed [7] without debate.

When it reached the House, however, the Federalists had taken alarm. The Federalist Judiciary Act of 1801 had fixed the terms of the Supreme Court in December and June instead of February and August. This new bill, plainly an afterthought, abolished the

---

[1] March 15, 1802.
[2] Vans Murray to King, April 5, 1802, King, IV, 95.
[3] Sedgwick to King, Feb. 20, 1802, *ib.* 73.
[4] Ames to Dwight, April 16, 1802, Ames, I, 297.
[5] *Annals*, 7th Cong. 1st Sess. 201.   [6] *Ib.* 205.   [7] *Ib.* 257.

June session of the Supreme Court, directed that, thereafter, that tribunal should convene but once each year, and fixed the second Monday of February as the time of this annual session.

Thus did the Republicans plan to take away from the Supreme Court the opportunity to pass upon the repeal of the Federalist Judiciary Act of 1801 until the old and defective system of 1789, which it restored, was again in full operation. Meanwhile, the wrath of the new National judges, whom the repeal left without offices, would wear itself down, and they would accept the situation as an accomplished fact.[1] John Marshall should have no early opportunity to overturn the Repeal Act, as the Republicans believed he would do if given the chance. Neither should he proceed further with the case of Marbury vs. Madison for many months to come.[2]

Bayard moved that the bill should not go into effect until July 1, thus permitting the Supreme Court to hold its June session; but, said Nicholson, that was just what the Republicans intended to prevent. Was a June session of the Supreme Court "a source of alarm?" asked Bayard. "The effect of the present bill will be, to have no court for fourteen months. . . Are gentlemen afraid of the judges? Are they afraid that they will pronounce the repealing law void?"[3]

Nicholson did not care whether the Supreme

[1] They never occupied the bench under the Federalist Act of 1801. They were appointed, but the swift action of Jefferson and the Republicans prevented them from entering upon the discharge of their duties.

[2] This case was before the Supreme Court in December, 1801, and, ordinarily, would have been decided at the next term, June, 1802.

[3] *Annals*, 7th Cong. 1st Sess. 1228–29.

Court "pronounced the repealing law unconstitutional or not." The Republican postponement of the session for more than a year "does not arise from any design . . to prevent the exercise of power by the judges." But what of the Federalists' solicitude for an early sitting of the court? "We have as good a right to suppose gentlemen on the other side are as anxious for a session in June, that this power may be exercised, as they have to suppose we wish to avoid it, to prevent the exercise." [1]

Griswold could not credit the Republicans with so base a purpose: "I know that it has been said, out of doors, that this is the great object of the bill. I know there have been slanders of this kind; but they are too disgraceful to ascribe to this body. The slander cannot, ought not to be admitted." So Griswold hoped that Republicans would permit the Supreme Court to hold its summer session. He frankly avowed a wish for an early decision that the Repeal Act was void. "I think the speedier it [usurpation] is checked the better." [2]

Bayard at last flatly charged the Republicans with the purpose of preventing the Supreme Court from holding the Repeal Act unconstitutional. "This act is not designed to amend the Judicial system," he asserted; "that is but pretense. . . It is to prevent that court from expressing their opinion upon the validity of the act lately passed . . until the act has gone into full execution, and the excitement of the public mind is abated. . . Could a less motive induce gentlemen to agree to suspend

---

[1] *Annals,* 7th Cong. 1st Sess. 1229.   [2] *Ib.* 1229–30.

the sessions of the Supreme Court for fourteen months ?" [1]

But neither the pleading nor the denunciation of the Federalists moved the Republicans. On Friday, April 23, 1802, the bill passed and the Supreme Court of the United States was practically abolished for fourteen months.[2]

At that moment began the movement that finally developed into the plan for the secession of the New England States from the Union. It is, perhaps, more accurate to say that the idea of secession had never been entirely out of the minds of the extreme New England Federalist leaders from the time Theodore Sedgwick threatened it in the debate over the Assumption Bill.[3]

Hints of withdrawing from the Union if Virginia should become dominant crop out in their correspondence. The Republican repeal of the Judiciary Act immediately called forth many expressions in Federalist papers such as this from the Boston *Palladium* of March 2, 1802: "Whether the rights and interests of the Eastern States would be perfectly safe when Virginia rules the nation is a problem easy to solve but terrible to contemplate. . . As ambitious *Virginia* will not be just, let valiant *Massachusetts* be zealous."

Fisher Ames declared that "the federalists must entrench themselves in the State governments, and endeavor to make State justice and State power a

[1] *Annals*, 7th Cong. 1st Sess. 1235–36.
[2] *Ib*. 1236. See also Channing, *U.S.* iv, 280–81.
[3] See vol. ii, 62, of this work.

shelter of the wise, and good, and rich, from the wild destroying rage of the southern Jacobins." [1] He thought the Federalists had neglected the press. "It is practicable," said he, "to rouse our sleeping patriotism — sleeping, like a drunkard in the snow. . . The newspapers have been left to the lazy or the ill-informed, or to those who undertook singly work enough for six." [2]

Pickering, the truculent, brave, and persistent, anticipated "a new confederacy. . . There will be — and our children at farthest will see it — a separation. . . The British Provinces, even with the assent of Britain, will become members of the Northern Confederacy." [3]

The more moderate George Cabot, on the contrary, thought that the strong defense made by the Federalists in Congress would induce the Republicans to cease their attacks on the National courts. "The very able discussions of the Judiciary Question," he wrote, "& great superiority of the Federalists in all the debates & public writings have manifestly checked the career of the *Revolutionists*." [4] But for once Cabot was wrong; the Republicans were jubilant and hastened to press their assault more vigorously than ever.

[1] Ames to Gore, Dec. 13, 1802, Ames, I, 310.

[2] *Ib*. Here is another characteristic passage from Ames, who accurately expressed New England Federalist sentiment: "The second French and first American Revolution is now commencing. . . The extinction of Federalism would be followed by the ruin of the wise, rich, and good." (Ames to Smith, Dec. 14, 1802, *ib*. 313–16.)

[3] Pickering to Peters, Dec. 24, 1803, *New-England Federalism*: Adams, 338.

[4] Cabot to King, March 27, 1802, King, IV, 94.

The Federalist newspapers teemed with long arguments against the repeal and laboriously strove, in dull and heavy fashion, to whip their readers into fighting humor. These articles were little more than turgid repetitions of the Federalist speeches in Congress, with a passage here and there of the usual Federalist denunciation. For instance, the *Columbian Centinel*, after restating the argument against the Repeal Act, thought that this "refutes all the absurd doctrines of the Jacobins upon that subject, . . and it will be sooner or later declared by the people, in a tone terrible to the present disorganizing party, to be the true construction of their constitution, and the only one compatible with their safety and happiness." [1]

The *Independent Chronicle*, on the other hand, was exultant. After denouncing "the impudence and scurrility of the Federal faction," a correspondent of that paper proceeded in this fashion: "The Judiciary! The Judiciary! like a wreck on Cape Cod is dashing at every wave"; but, thank Heaven, "instead of the 'Essex Junto's' Judiciary we are sailing by the grace of God in the Washington *Frigate* — our judges are as at first and Mr. Jefferson has thought fit to practice the old navigation and steer with the same compass by which *Admiral Washington* regulated his log book. The Essex Junto may be afraid to trust themselves on board but every true Washington American will step on board in full confidence of a prosperous voyage. Huzza for the *Washington Judiciary* — no windows

[1] *Columbian Centinel*, April 7, 1802.

broke — no doors burst in — free from leak — tight and dry." [1]

Destiny was soon again to call John Marshall to the performance of an imperative duty.

[1] "Bowling" in the *Independent Chronicle* of April 26, 1802. An example of Jefferson's amazing skill in directing public opinion is found in the fact that the people were made to feel that the President was following in Washington's footsteps.

CHAPTER III

MARBURY VERSUS MADISON

To consider the judges as the ultimate arbiters of all constitutional questions would place us under the despotism of an oligarchy. (Jefferson.)

The constitution is either a superior paramount law, unchangeable by ordinary means, or it is on a level with ordinary legislative acts alterable when the legislature shall please to alter it. It is emphatically the province and duty of the judicial department to say what the law is. This is the very essence of judicial duty. (Marshall.)

To have inscribed this vast truth of conservatism upon the public mind, so that no demagogue not in the last stages of intoxication denies it — this is an achievement of statesmanship which a thousand years may not exhaust or reveal all that is good. (Rufus Choate.)

"RAWLEIGH, Jany 2^d 1803

"MY DEAREST POLLY

"You will laugh at my vexation when you hear the various calamaties that have befallen me. In the first place when I came to review my funds, I had the mortification to discover that I had lost 15 silver dollars out of my waist coat pocket. They had worn through the various mendings the pocket had sustained & sought their liberty in the sands of Carolina.

"I determined not to vex myself with what coud not be remedied & orderd Peter to take out my cloaths that I might dress for court when to my astonishment & grief after fumbling several minutes in the portmanteau, staring at vacancy, & sweating most profusely he turned to me with the doleful tidings that I had no pair of breeches. You may be sure this piece of inteligence was not very graciously receivd; however, after a little scolding I determined to make the best of my situation & immediately set out to get a pair made.

"I thought I should be a sans culotte only one day & that for the residue of the term I might be well enough dressd for the appearance on the first day to be forgotten. But, the greatest of evils, I found, was followed by still greater! Not a taylor in town coud be prevaild on to work for me. They were all so busy that it was impossible to attend to my wants however pressing they might be, & I have the extreme mortification to pass the whole time without that important article of dress I have mentiond. I have no alleviation for this misfortune but the hope that I shall be enabled in four or five days to commence my journey homeward & that I shall have the pleasure of seeing you & our dear children in eight or nine days after this reaches you.

"In the meantime I flatter myself that you are well & happy.

"Adieu my dearest Polly

I am your ever affectionate

J MARSHALL." [1]

With the same unfailing light-heartedness which, nearly a quarter of a century before, had cheered his comrades at Valley Forge, John Marshall, Chief Justice of the United States, thus went about his duties and bore his troubles. Making his circuit in a battered gig or sulky, which he himself usually drove, absent-minded and laughing at himself for the mishaps that his forgetfulness and negligence

---

[1] Marshall to his wife, Jan. 2, 1803, MS.

continually brought upon him, he was seemingly
unperturbed in the midst of the political upheaval.

Yet he was not at ease. Rufus King, still the
American Minister to Great Britain, had finally
settled the controversy over the British debts, upon
the very basis laid down by Marshall when Secretary of State.[1] But Jefferson's Administration now
did not hesitate to assert that this removal of one
cause of conflict with Great Britain was the triumph
of Republican diplomacy. Marshall, with unreserve
so unlike him, reveals to King his disgust and sense
of injury, and in doing so portrays the development
of political conditions.

"The advocates of the present administration
ascribe to it great praise," wrote Marshall to our
Minister in London, "for having, with so much dex-
terity & so little loss, extricated our country from
a debt of twenty-four million of dollars in which a
former administration had involved it. . . The mor-
tifying reflection obtrudes itself, that the reputation
of the most wise & skilful conduct depends, in this
our capricious world, so much on accident. Had
Mr. Adams been reelected President of the United
States, or had his successor been [a Federalist] . . a
very different reception . . would have been given
to the same measure.

"The payment of a specific sum would then have
been pronounced, by those who now take merit to
themselves for it, a humiliating national degradation, an abandonment of national interest, a free
will offering of millions to Britain for her grace &

[1] See vol. II, 502–05, of this work.

favor, by those who sought to engage in a war with
France, rather than repay, in part, by a small loan
to that republic, the immense debt of gratitude we
owe her."

So speaks with bitter sarcasm the new Chief Justice, and pessimistically continues: "Such is, & such
I fear will ever be human justice!" He tells King
that the Federalist "disposition to coalesce" with
the Republicans, which seemed to be developing
during the first few months after Jefferson's inauguration, had disappeared; "but," he adds, "the minority [Federalist Party] is only recovering its strength
& firmness. It acquires nothing." Then, with the
characteristic misgivings of a Federalist, he prophesies: "Our political tempests will long, very long,
exist, after those who are now toss'd about by them
shall be at rest." [1]

For more than five years [2] Marshall had foreseen
the complicated and dangerous situation in which
the country now found itself; and for more than a
year [3] he had, in his ample, leisurely, simple manner
of thinking, been framing the constructive answer
which he was at last forced to give to the grave
question: Who shall say with final authority what is
and what is not law throughout the Republic? In
his opinion in the case of Marbury *vs.* Madison, to
which this chapter is devoted, we shall see how John
Marshall answered this vital question.

[1] Marshall to King, May 5, 1802, King, IV, 116–18.
[2] Since the adoption of the Kentucky and Virginia Resolutions in
1798. (See vol. II, chaps. X, XI, XII, of this work.)
[3] Since the Republican repeal of the Federalist Judiciary Act was
proposed. See *supra*, 51.

The philosophy of the Virginia and Kentucky Resolutions had now become the ruling doctrine of the Republican Party. The writer of the creed of State Rights sat in the Executive chair, while in House and Senate Virginia and her daughter Kentucky .ruled the Republican majority. The two States that had declared the right and power of any member of the Union to pronounce a National law unconstitutional, and that had actually asserted a National statute to be null and void, had become the dominant force in the National Government.

The Federalist majority in the legislatures of ten States,[1] it is true, had passed resolutions denouncing that anti-National theory, and had vigorously asserted that the National Judiciary alone had the power to invalidate acts of Congress.[2] *But in none of*

[1] Maryland, Pennsylvania, New Jersey, Delaware, New York, Vermont, New Hampshire, Massachusetts, Connecticut, Rhode Island.

[2] The Federalist majority in Vermont resolved that: "It belongs not to *State Legislatures* to decide on the constitutionality of laws made by the general government; this power being exclusively vested in the *Judiciary Courts of the Union.*" (*Records of Governor and Council of Vermont*, iv, 529.)

The Federalist majority in the Maryland Legislature asserted that "no state government . . is competent to declare an act of the federal government unconstitutional, . . that jurisdiction . . is exclusively vested in the courts of the United States." (Anderson, in *Am. Hist. Rev.* v, 248.)

The New York Federalists were slow to act, but finally resolved "that the right of deciding on the constitutionality of all laws passed by Congress . . appertains to the judiciary department." (*Ib.* 248–49.)

Connecticut Federalists declared that the Kentucky and Virginia plan was "hostile to the existence of our national Union." (*Ib.* 247.)

In Delaware the then dominant party decided that the Kentucky and Virginia Resolutions were "not a fit subject" for their consideration. (*Ib.* 246.)

The Pennsylvania Federalist majority resolved that the people

these States had the Republican minority concurred.
In all of them the Republicans had vigorously fought
the Federalist denial of the right and power of the
States to nullify National laws, and had especially
resisted the Federalist assertion that this power was
in the National Judiciary.

In the New York Legislature, forty-three Republicans voted solidly against the Federalist reply to
Virginia and Kentucky, while the Federalists were
able to muster but fifty votes in its favor. In Massachusetts, Pennsylvania, and Maryland, the Republican opposition was determined and outspoken.

The thirty-three Republicans of the Vermont
Legislature cited, in their protest, the position
which Marshall had taken on the Sedition Law in his
campaign for Congress: [1] "We have ever been of an
opinion, with that much and deservedly respected
statesman, Mr. Marshall, (whose abilities and in-

"have committed to the supreme judiciary of the nation the high authority of ultimately and conclusively deciding the constitutionality
of all legislative acts." (Anderson, in *Am. Hist. Rev.* v, 245.)

On February 8, 1799, Massachusetts replied to the Virginia Resolutions that: "This legislature are persuaded that the decision of all
cases in law or equity, arising under the Constitution of the United
States, and the construction of all laws made in pursuance thereof,
are exclusively vested by the people in the Judicial Courts of the
U. States." (*Mass. Senate Journal, 1798–99,* XIX, 238, MS. volume
Mass. State Library.)

Such was the general tenor of the Federalists' pronouncements upon
this grave problem. But because the people believed the Sedition
Law to be directed against free speech, the Federalist supremacy in
many of the States that insisted upon these sound Nationalist principles was soon overthrown.

The resolutions of the Republican minorities in the Legislatures of
the Federalist States were emphatic assertions that any State might
declare an act of Congress unconstitutional and disregard it, and *that
the National Judiciary did not have supervisory power over legislation.*

[1] See vol. II, 387–89, of this work.

tegrity have been doubted by no party, and whose spirited and patriotic defence of his country's rights, has been universally admired) [1] that 'it was calculated to create *unnecessarily*, discontents and jealousies, at a time, when our very existence as a nation may depend on our union.'" [2]

In Southern States, where the Federalists were dominant when Kentucky and Virginia adopted their famous Resolutions, the Republicans were, nevertheless, so strong that the Federalist majority in the Legislatures of those States dared not attempt to deny formally the new Republican gospel. [3]

So stood the formal record; but, since it had been written, the Jeffersonian propaganda had drawn scores of thousands of voters into the Republican ranks. The whole South had now decisively repudiated Federalism. Maryland had been captured; Pennsylvania had become as emphatically Republican as Virginia herself; New York had joined her forces to the Republican legions. The Federalists still held New England and the States of Delaware and New Jersey, but even there the incessant Republican assaults, delivered with ever-increasing strength, were weakening the Federalist power. Nothing was plainer than that, if the Kentucky and Virginia Resolutions had been submitted to the Legislatures of the various States in 1801–1803, most of them would have enthusiastically endorsed them.

Thus the one subject most discussed, from the campaign of 1800 to the time when Marshall deliv-

[1] Referring to Marshall's conduct in the French Mission. (See vol. II, chaps. VII, VIII, IX, of this work.)

[2] Anderson, in *Am. Hist. Rev.* v, 249.   [3] *Ib.* 235–37.

ered his opinion in Marbury *vs.* Madison, was the all-important question as to what power, if any, could annul acts of Congress.[1] During these years popular opinion became ever stronger that the Judiciary could not do so, that Congress had a free hand so far as courts were concerned, and that the individual States might ignore National laws whenever those States deemed them to be infractions of the Constitution. As we have seen, the Republican vote in Senate and House, by which the Judiciary Act of 1801 was repealed, was also a vote against the theory of the supervisory power of the National Judiciary over National legislation.

Should this conclusion go unchallenged? If so, it would have the sanction of acquiescence and soon acquire the strength of custom. What then would become the condition of the country? Congress might pass a law which some States would oppose and which they would refuse to obey, but which other States would favor and of which they would demand the enforcement. What would this entail? At the very least it would provoke a relapse into the chaos of the Confederation and more probably civil war. Or a President might take it upon himself to pronounce null and void a law of Congress, as Jefferson had already done in the matter of the Sedition Law,[2] and if House and Senate were of a hostile political party, Congress might insist upon

---

[1] The questions raised by the Kentucky and Virginia Resolutions were principal themes of debate in State Legislatures, in the press, in Congressional campaigns, and in the Presidential contest of 1800. The Judiciary debate of 1802 was, in part, a continuance of these popular discussions.

[2] See *supra*, 52.

the observance of its legislation; but such a course would seriously damage the whole machinery of the National Government.

The fundamental question as to what power could definitely pass upon the validity of legislation must be answered without delay. Some of Marshall's associates on the Supreme Bench were becoming old and feeble, and death, or resignation enforced by illness, was likely at any moment to break the Nationalist solidarity of the Supreme Court; [1] and the appointing power had fallen into the hands of the man who held the subjugation of the National Judiciary as one of his chief purposes.

Only second in importance to these reasons for Marshall's determination to meet the issue was the absolute necessity of asserting that there was one department of the Government that could not be influenced by temporary public opinion. The value to a democracy of a steadying force was not then so well understood as it is at present, but the Chief Justice fully appreciated it and determined at all hazards to make the National Judiciary the stabilizing power that it has since become. It should be said, however, that Marshall no longer "idolized democracy," as he declared he did when as a young man he addressed the Virginia Convention of 1788. [2] On the contrary, he had come to distrust popular rule as much as did most Federalists.

[1] Within a year after Marbury vs. Madison was decided, Albert Moore, one of the Federalist Associate Justices of the Supreme Court, resigned because of ill health and his place was filled by William Johnson, a Republican of South Carolina.

[2] See vol. I, 410, of this work.

A case was then pending before the Supreme
Court the decision of which might, by boldness and
ingenuity, be made to serve as the occasion for that
tribunal's assertion of its right and power to invalidate acts of Congress and also for the laying-down
of rules for the guidance of all departments of the
Government. This was the case of Marbury *vs.*
Madison.

Just before his term expired,[1] President Adams
had appointed forty-two persons to be justices of
the peace for the Counties of Washington and Alexandria in the District of Columbia.[2] The Federalist Senate had confirmed these nominations,[3] and
the commissions had been signed and sealed, but
had not been delivered. When Jefferson was inaugurated he directed Madison, as Secretary of State, to
issue commissions to twenty-five of the persons appointed by Adams, but to withhold the commissions
from the other seventeen.[4]

Among the latter were William Marbury, Dennis
Ramsay, Robert Townsend Hooe, and William Harper. These four men applied to the Supreme Court
for a writ of mandamus compelling Madison to
deliver their commissions. The other thirteen did
not join in the suit, apparently considering the office
of justice of the peace too insignificant to be worth
the expense of litigation. Indeed, these offices were
deemed so trifling that one of Adams's appointees to

---

[1] March 2, 1801.

[2] *Journal of the Executive Proceedings of the Senate*, i, 388.

[3] *Ib.* 390.

[4] *Ib.* 404. Jefferson did this because, as he said, the appointees of
Adams were too numerous.

whom Madison delivered a commission resigned, and five others refused to qualify.[1]

When the application of Marbury and his associates came before Marshall he assumed jurisdiction, and in December, 1801, issued the usual rule to Madison ordering him to show cause at the next term of the Supreme Court why the writ of mandamus should not be awarded against him. Soon afterward, as we have seen, Congress abolished the June session of the Supreme Court;[2] thus, when the court again convened in February, 1803, the case of Marbury *vs*. Madison was still pending.

Marshall resolved to make use of this unimportant litigation to assert, at the critical hour when such a pronouncement was essential, the power of the Supreme Court to declare invalid acts of Congress that violate the Constitution.

Considering the fact that Marshall was an experienced politician, was intimately familiar with the political methods of Jefferson and the Republican leaders, and was advised of their purposes, he could not have failed to realize the probable consequences to himself of the bold course he now determined to take. As the crawling months of 1802 wore on, no signs appeared that the Republican programme for overthrowing the independence of the Judiciary would be relinquished or modified. On the contrary, the coming of the new year (1803) found the second phase of the Republican assault determined upon.

At the beginning of the session of 1803 the House impeached John Pickering, Judge of the United

[1] *Journal, Exec. Proc. Senate*, I, 417.   [2] See *supra*, 94–97.

States District Court for the District of New Hampshire. In Pennsylvania, the recently elected Republican House had impeached Judge Alexander Addison, and his conviction by a partisan vote was assured. Already the Republican determination to remove Samuel Chase from the Supreme Bench was frankly avowed.[1]

Moreover, the Republicans openly threatened to oust Marshall and his Federalist associates in case the court decided Marbury *vs.* Madison as the Republicans expected it would. They did not anticipate that Marshall would declare unconstitutional that section of the old Federalist Judiciary Act of 1789 under which the suit had been brought. Indeed, nobody imagined that the court would do that.

Everybody apparently, except Marshall and the Associate Justices, thought that the case would be decided in Marbury's favor and that Madison would be ordered to deliver the withheld commissions. It was upon this supposition that the Republican threats of impeachment were made. The Republicans considered Marbury's suit as a Federalist partisan maneuver and believed that the court's decision and Marshall's opinion would be inspired by motives of Federalist partisanship.[2]

[1] See *infra*, chap. IV.

[2] This belief is strikingly shown by the comment of the Republican press. For example, just before Marshall delivered his opinion, a correspondent of the *Independent Chronicle* of Boston sent from Washington this article:

"The efforts of *federalism* to exalt the Judiciary over the Executive and Legislature, and to give that favorite department a political character & influence, may operate for a time to come, as it has already, to the promotion of one party and the depression of the other; but

There was a particular and powerful reason for Marshall to fear impeachment and removal from office; for, should he be deposed, it was certain that Jefferson would appoint Spencer Roane of Virginia to be Chief Justice of the United States. It was well known that Jefferson had intended to appoint Roane upon the death of Chief Justice Ellsworth.[1] But Ellsworth had resigned in time to permit Adams to appoint Marshall as his successor and thus thwart Jefferson's purpose. If now Marshall were removed, Roane would be given his place.

Should he be succeeded by Roane, Marshall knew that the great principles of Nationalism, to the car-

will probably terminate in the degradation and disgrace of the Judiciary.

"Politics are more improper and dangerous in a Court of Justice, if possible, than in the pulpit. Political charges, prosecutions, and similar modes of official influence, ought never to have been resorted to by any party. The fountains of justice should be unpolluted by party passions and prejudices.

"The *attempt* of the Supreme Court of the United States, by a mandamus, to control the Executive functions, is a new experiment. It seems to be no less than a commencement of war between the constituted departments.

"The Court must be defeated and retreat from the attack; or march on, till they incur an impeachment and removal from office. But our *Republican* frame of Government is so firm and solid, that there is reason to hope it will remain unshaken by the assaults of opposition, & the conflicts of interfering departments.

"The will of the nation, deliberately and constitutionally expressed, must and will prevail, the predictions and exertions of *federal* monarchists and aristocrats to the contrary notwithstanding." (*Independent Chronicle*, March 10, 1803.)

Marshall's opinion was delivered February 24. It took two weeks of fast traveling to go from Washington to Boston. Ordinary mail required a few days longer. The article in the *Chronicle* was probably sent while Marbury *vs.* Madison was being argued.

[1] Dodd, in *Am. Hist. Rev.* xii, 776. Under the law Marshall's successor must come from Virginia or North Carolina.

rying-out of which his life was devoted, would never
be asserted by the National Judiciary. On the contrary, the Supreme Court would become an engine
for the destruction of every theory of government
which Marshall held dear; for a bolder, abler, and
more persistent antagonist of those principles than
Spencer Roane did not exist.[1] Had he become Chief
Justice those cases in which Marshall delivered opinions that vitalized the Constitution would have been
decided in direct opposition to Marshall's views.[2]

But despite the peril, Marshall resolved to act.
Better to meet the issue now, come what might, than
to evade it. If he succeeded, orderly government
would be assured, the National Judiciary lifted to
its high and true place, and one element of National
disintegration suppressed, perhaps destroyed. If he
failed, the country would be in no worse case than
that to which it was rapidly tending.

No words in the Constitution gave the Judiciary
the power to annul legislation. The subject had
been discussed in the Convention, but the brief and
scattering debate had arisen upon the proposition to
make the President and Justices of the Supreme

[1] As President of the Court of Appeals of Virginia he later challenged Marshall and brought about the first serious conflict between
the courts of a State and the supreme tribunal of the Nation; and as
a pamphleteer he assailed Marshall and his principles of Nationalism
with unsparing rigor. (See vol. IV, chaps. III, and VI, of this work.)

[2] For example, in Fletcher vs. Peck, Roane would have held that
the National Courts could not annul a State statute; in Martin vs.
Hunter's Lessees and in Cohen vs. Virginia, that the Supreme Court
could not review the judgment of a State court; in McCulloch vs.
Maryland, that Congress could not exercise implied powers, but only
those expressly granted by the specific terms of the Constitution, etc.
All this we know positively from Roane's own writings. (See vol. IV,
chaps. III, VI, and VII, of this work.)

Court members of a Council of Revision with power to negative acts of Congress. No direct resolution was ever offered to the effect that the Judiciary should be given power to declare acts of Congress unconstitutional. In the discussion of the proposed Council of Revision there were sharp differences of opinion on the collateral question of the right and wisdom of judicial control of legislative acts.[1] But,

---

[1] It seems probable, however, that it was generally understood by the leading men of the Convention that the Judiciary was to exercise the power of invalidating unconstitutional acts of Congress. (See Corwin: *Doctrine of Judicial Review*, 10–11; Beard: *Supreme Court and the Constitution*, 16–18; McLaughlin: *The Courts, the Constitution and Parties*, 32–35.)

In the Constitutional Convention, Elbridge Gerry of Massachusetts asserted that the judicial function of expounding statutes "involved a power of deciding on their Constitutionality." (*Records of the Federal Convention of 1787:* Farrand, I, 97.) Rufus King of Massachusetts — later of New York — was of the same opinion. (*Ib.* 109.)

On the other hand, Franklin declared that "it would be improper to put it in the power of any Man to negative a Law passed by the Legislature because it would give him the controul of the Legislature." (*Ib.*)

Madison felt "that no Man would be so daring as to place a veto on a Law that had passed with the assent of the Legislature." (*Ib.*) Later in the debate, Madison modified his first opinion and declared that "a law violating a constitution established by the people themselves, would be considered by the Judges null & void." (*Ib.* II, 93.)

George Mason of Virginia said that the Judiciary "could declare an unconstitutional law void. . . He wished the further use to be made of the Judges of giving aid in preventing every improper law." (*Ib.* 78.)

Gouverneur Morris of Pennsylvania — afterwards of New York — dreaded "legislative usurpations" and felt that "encroachments of the popular branch . . ought to be guarded agst." (*Ib.* 299.)

Gunning Bedford, Jr., of Delaware was against any "check on the Legislative" with two branches. (*Ib.* I, 100–01.)

James Wilson of Pennsylvania insisted that power in the Judiciary to declare laws unconstitutional "did not go far enough" — the judges should also have "Revisionary power" to pass on bills in the process of enactment. (*Ib.* II, 73.)

Luther Martin of Maryland had no doubt that the Judiciary had "a negative" on unconstitutional laws. (*Ib.* 76.)

John Francis Mercer of Maryland "disapproved of the Doctrine

in the end, nothing was done and the whole subject was dropped.

Such was the record of the Constitutional Convention when, by his opinion in Marbury *vs.* Madison, Marshall made the principle of judicial supremacy over legislation as much a part of our fundamental law as if the Constitution contained these specific words: the Supreme Court shall have the power to declare invalid any act of Congress which, in the opinion of the court, is unconstitutional.

In establishing this principle Marshall was to contribute nothing new to the thought upon the subject. All the arguments on both sides of the question had been made over and over again since the Kentucky and Virginia Resolutions had startled the land, and had been freshly stated in the Judiciary debate in the preceding Congress. Members of the Federalist majority in most of the State Legislatures had expressed, in highly colored partisan rhetoric, every sound reason for the theory that the National Judiciary should be the ultimate interpreter of the Constitution. Both Federalist and Republican newspapers had printed scores of essays for and against that doctrine.

In the Virginia Convention of 1788 Marshall had announced as a fundamental principle that if Con-

that the Judges as expositors of the Constitution should have authority to declare a law void." (*Records, Fed. Conv.*: Farrand, 298.)

John Dickinson of Delaware "thought no such power ought to exist," but was "at a loss what expedient to substitute." (*Ib.* 299.)

Charles Pinckney of South Carolina "opposed the interference of the Judges in the Legislative business." (*Ib.* 298.)

The above is a condensed *précis* of all that was said in the Constitutional Convention on this vital matter.

गgress should pass an unconstitutional law the courts
would declare it void,[1] and in his reply to the address
of the majority of the Virginia Legislature [2] he had
elaborately, though with much caution and some
mistiness, set forth his views.[3] Chief Justice Jay and
his associates had complained that the Judiciary
Act of 1789 was unconstitutional, but they had not
had the courage to announce that opinion from the
Bench.[4] Justices Iredell and Paterson, sitting as
circuit judges, had claimed for the National Judiciary the exclusive right to determine the constitutionality of laws. Chief Justice Jay in charging a
grand jury, and Associate Justice Wilson in a carefully prepared law lecture, had announced the same
conclusion.

Various State judges of the Federalist faith,
among them Dana of Massachusetts and Addison of
Pennsylvania, had spoken to like effect. At the trial
of Callender [5] Marshall had heard Chase deliver the
opinion that the National Judiciary had the exclusive power to declare acts of Congress unconstitutional.[6] Jefferson himself had written Meusnier, the
year before the National Constitution was framed,
that the Virginia Legislature had passed unconstitutional laws,[7] adding: "I have not heard that in
the other states they have ever infringed their con-

---

[1] See vol. i, 452, of this work.   [2] The Virginia Resolutions.
[3] Address of the Minority, Jan. 22, 1799, *Journal of the House of
Delegates of Virginia, 1798–99*, 90–95.
[4] Jay to Iredell, Sept. 15, 1790, enclosing statement to President
Washington, *Iredell:* McRee, 293–96; and see letter of Jay to Washington, Aug. 8, 1793, *Jay:* Johnston, iii, 488–89.
[5] See *supra*, 40, footnote 1.   [6] Wharton: *State Trials*, 715–18.
[7] Jefferson to Meusnier, Jan. 24, 1786, *Works:* Ford, v, 31–32.

stitution; . . *as the judges would consider any law as void* which was contrary to the constitution." [1]

Just as Jefferson, in writing the Declaration of Independence, put on paper not a single new or original idea, but merely set down in clear and compact form what had been said many times before,[2] so Marshall, in his opinion in Marbury *vs*. Madison, did nothing more than restate that which had previously been declared by hundreds of men. Thomas Jefferson and John Marshall as private citizens in Charlottesville and Richmond might have written Declarations and Opinions all their lives, and to-day none but the curious student would know that such men had ever lived. It was the authoritative position which these two great Americans happened to occupy and the compelling emergency for the announcement of the principles they expressed, as well as the soundness of those principles, that have given immortality to their enunciations.

Learned men have made exhaustive research for legal decisions by which Marshall's footsteps may have been guided, or which, at least, would justify his conclusion in Marbury *vs*. Madison.[3] The cases thus discovered are curious and interesting, but it is

---

[1] Jefferson to Meusnier, Jan. 24, 1786, *Works:* Ford, v, 14–15. (Italics the author's.)

[2] For instance, the Legislature of Rhode Island formally declared Independence almost two months before Congress adopted the pronouncement penned by Jefferson, and Jefferson used many of the very words of the tiny colony's defiance. In her Declaration of Independence in May, 1776, Virginia set forth most of the reasons stated by Jefferson a few weeks later in similar language.

[3] For these cases and references to studies of the question of judicial supremacy over legislation, see Appendix C.

probable that Marshall had not heard of many of them. At any rate, he does not cite one of them in the course of this opinion, although no case ever was decided in which a judge needed so much the support of judicial precedents. Neither did he know anything whatever of what was said on the subject in the Constitutional Convention, unless by hearsay, for its sessions were secret [1] and the Journals were not made public until 1819 — thirty years after the Government was established, and sixteen years after Marbury *vs.* Madison was decided.[2] Nor was Marshall informed of the discussions of the subject in the State Conventions that ratified the Constitution, except of those that took place in the Virginia Convention.[3]

On the other hand, he surely had read the Judiciary debate in Congress, for he was in the Capital when that controversy took place and the speeches were fully reported in the Washington press. Marshall probably was present in the Senate and the House when the most notable arguments were made.[4] More important, however, than written decisions or printed debates in influencing Marshall's mind was *The Federalist*, which we know he read carefully. In number seventy-eight of that work, Hamilton stated the principle of judicial supremacy which Marshall whole-heartedly adopted in Marbury *vs.* Madison.

[1] See vol. i, 323, of this work.

[2] See *Records Fed. Conv.*: Farrand, i, Introduction, xii.

[3] Elliot's *Debates* were not published until 1827–30.

[4] Until very recently Justices of the Supreme Court often came to the Senate to listen to debates in which they were particularly interested.

"The interpretation of the laws," wrote Hamilton, "is the proper and peculiar province of the courts. A constitution is, in fact, and must be regarded by the judges, as a fundamental law. It therefore belongs to them to ascertain its meaning, as well as the meaning of any particular act proceeding from the legislative body. If there should happen to be an irreconcilable variance between the two, . . the Constitution ought to be preferred to the statute, the intention of the people to the intention of their agents." [1]

In this passage Hamilton merely stated the general understanding of nearly all the important framers of the Constitution. Beyond question, Marshall considered that principle to have been woven into the very fiber of the Nation's fundamental law.

In executing his carefully determined purpose to have the Supreme Court formally announce the exclusive power of that tribunal as the authority of last resort to interpret the Constitution and determine the validity of laws by the test of that instrument, Marshall faced two practical and baffling difficulties, in addition to those larger and more forbidding ones which we have already considered.

The first of these was the condition of the Supreme Court itself and the low place it held in the public esteem; from the beginning it had not, as a body, impressed the public mind with its wisdom, dignity, or force.[2] The second obstacle was techni-

---

[1] *The Federalist:* Lodge, 485–86. Madison also upheld the same doctrine. Later he opposed it, but toward the end of his life returned to his first position. (See vol. IV, chap. X, of this work.)

[2] John Jay had declined reappointment as Chief Justice because.

cal and immediate. Just how should Marshall declare the Supreme Court to be the ultimate arbiter of conflicts between statutes and the Constitution? What occasion could he find to justify, and seemingly to require, the pronouncement as the judgment of the Supreme Court of that opinion now imperatively demanded, and which he had resolved at all hazards to deliver?

among other things, he was "perfectly convinced" that the National Judiciary was hopelessly weak. (See *supra*, 55.) The first Chief Justice of the United States at no moment, during his occupancy of that office, felt sure of himself or of the powers of the court. (See Jay to his wife, *Jay:* Johnston, I.I, 420.) Jay had hesitated to accept the office as Chief Justice when Washington tendered it to him in 1789, and he had resigned it gladly in 1795 to become the Federalist candidate for Governor of New York.

Washington offered the place to Patrick Henry, who refused it. (See Henry: *Patrick Henry — Life, Correspondence and Speeches*, II, 562–63; also Tyler, I, 183.) The office was submitted to William Cushing, an Associate Justice of the Supreme Court, and he also refused to consider it. (Wharton: *State Trials*, 33.) So little was a place on the Supreme Bench esteemed that John Rutledge resigned as Associate Justice to accept the office of Chief Justice of the Supreme Court of South Carolina. (*Ib.* 35.)

Jefferson considered that the government of New Orleans was "the second office in the United States in importance." (Randal, III, 202.) For that matter, no National office in Washington, except the Presidency, was prized at this period. Senator Bailey of New York actually resigned his seat in the Senate in order to accept the office of Postmaster at New York City. (*Memoirs, J. Q. A.*: Adams, I, 290.) Edmund Randolph, when Attorney-General, deplored the weakening of the Supreme Court, and looked forward to the time when it should be strengthened. (Randolph to Washington, Aug. 5, 1792, *Writings of George Washington:* Sparks, X, 513.)

The weakness of the Supreme Court, before Marshall became Chief Justice, is forcibly illustrated by the fact that in designing and building the National Capitol that tribunal was entirely forgotten and no chamber provided for it. (See Hosea Morrill Knowlton in *John Marshall — Life, Character and Judicial Services:* Dillon, I, 198–99.) When the seat of government was transferred to Washington, the court crept into an humble apartment in the basement beneath the Senate Chamber.

When the Republicans repealed the Federalist Judiciary Act of 1801, Marshall had actually proposed to his associates upon the Supreme Bench that they refuse to sit as circuit judges, and "risk the consequences." By the Constitution, he said, they were Judges of the Supreme Court only; their commissions proved that they were appointed solely to those offices; the section requiring them to sit in inferior courts was unconstitutional. The other members of the Supreme Court, however, had not the courage to adopt the heroic course Marshall recommended. They agreed that his views were sound, but insisted that, because the Ellsworth Judiciary Act had been acquiesced in since the adoption of the Constitution, the validity of that act must now be considered as established.[1] So Marshall reluctantly abandoned his bold plan, and in the autumn of 1802 held court at Richmond as circuit judge. To the end of his life, however, he held firmly to the opinion that in so far as the Republican Judiciary Repeal Act of 1802 deprived National judges of their offices and salaries, that legislation was unconstitutional.[2]

Had the circuit judges, whose offices had just been taken from them, resisted in the courts, Marshall might, and probably would, have seized upon the issue thus presented to declare invalid the act by which the Republicans had overturned the new Federalist Judiciary system. Just this, as we have

[1] *New York Review*, III, 347. The article on Chief Justice Marshall in this periodical was written by Chancellor James Kent, although his name does not appear.

[2] See vol. IV, chap. IX.

seen, the Republicans had expected him to do, and therefore had so changed the sessions of the Supreme Court that it could not render any decision for more than a year after the new Federalist courts were abolished.

Certain of the deposed National judges had, indeed, taken steps to bring the "revolutionary" Republican measure before the Supreme Court,[1] but their energies flagged, their hearts failed, and their only action was a futile and foolish protest to the very Congress that had wrested their judicial seats from under them.[2] Marshall was thus deprived of that opportunity at the only time he could have availed himself of it.

A year afterward, when Marbury *vs.* Madison came up for decision, the entire National Judiciary had submitted to the Republican repeal and was holding court under the Act of 1789.[3] This case,

[1] See Tilghman to Smith, May 22, 1802, Morison: *Smith*, 148–49.

"A general arrangement [for action on behalf of the deposed judges] will be attempted before we separate. It is not descrete to say more at present." (Bayard to Bassett, April 19, 1802, *Bayard Papers:* Donnan, 153.)

[2] See "Protest of Judges," *American State Papers, Miscellaneous*, I, 340.

Writing to Wolcott, now one of the displaced National circuit judges (Wolcott's appointment was secured by Marshall; see vol. II, 559, of this work), concerning "the outrage committed by Congress on the Constitution" (Cabot to Wolcott, Dec. 20, 1802, Lodge: *Cabot*, 328), Cabot said: " I cannot but approve the intention of your judicial corps to unite in a memorial or remonstrance to Congress." He considered this to be "a manifest duty" of the judges, and gave Wolcott the arguments for their action. (Cabot to Wolcott, Oct. 21, 1802, *ib.* 327–28.)

A proposition to submit to the Supreme Court the constitutionality of the Repeal Act was rejected January 27, 1803. (*Annals*, 7th Cong. 2d Sess. 439.)

[3] See *infra*, 130, 131.

then, alone remained as the only possible occasion for announcing, at that critical time, the supervisory power of the Judiciary over legislation.

Marshall was Secretary of State when President Adams tardily appointed, and the Federalist Senate confirmed, the forty-two justices of the peace for the District of Columbia,[1] and it was Marshall who had failed to deliver the commissions to the appointees. Instead, he had, with his customary negligence of details, left them on his desk. Scarcely had he arrived at Richmond, after Jefferson's inauguration, when his brother, James M. Marshall, wrote him of the plight in which the newly appointed justices of the peace found themselves as the result of Marshall's oversight.

The Chief Justice replied: "I learn with infinite chagrin the 'development of principle' mentioned in yours of the 12th," — sarcastically referring to the Administration's conduct toward the Judiciary, — "& I cannot help regreting it the more as I fear some blame may be imputed to me. . .

"I did not send out the commissions because I apprehended such as were for a fixed time to be completed when signed & sealed & such as depended on the will of the President might at any time be revoked. To withhold the commission of the Marshal is equal to displacing him which the President, I presume, has the power to do, but to withhold the commissions of the Justices is an act of which I entertaind no suspicion. I should however have sent out the commissions which had been signed & sealed

[1] See *supra*, 110.

but for the extreme hurry of the time & the absence
of Mr. Wagner [Clerk of the State Department]
who had been called on by the President to act as his
private secretary." [1]

Marshall, it thus appears, was thoroughly familiar
with the matter when the application of Marbury
and his three associates came before the Supreme
Court, and took in it a keen and personal interest.
By the time [2] the case came on for final disposition
the term had almost half expired for which Marbury
and his associates had been appointed. The other
justices of the peace to whom Madison had delivered commissions were then transacting all the business that required the attention of such officials.
It was certain, moreover, that the Administration
would not recognize Marbury and his associates, no
matter what Marshall might decide. In fact, these
appointees must have lost all interest in the contest
for offices of such slight dignity and such insignificant emoluments.

So far, then, as practical results were concerned,
the case of Marbury *vs.* Madison had now come to
the point where it was of no consequence whatever
to any one. It presented only theoretical questions,
and, on the face of the record, even these were as
simple as they were unimportant. This controversy,
in fact, had degenerated into little more than "a moot
case," as Jefferson termed it twenty years later.[3]

At the hearing it was proved that the commissions

---

[1] Marshall to James M. Marshall, March 18, 1801, MS.

[2] February, 1803.

[3] Jefferson to Johnson, June 12, 1823, *Works:* Ford, xii, footnote to
256.

had been signed and sealed. One witness was Marshall's brother, James M. Marshall. Jefferson's Attorney-General, Levi Lincoln, was excused from testifying as to what finally became of them. Madison refused to show cause and denied, by utterly ignoring, the jurisdiction of the Supreme Court to direct or control him in his administration of the office of Secretary of State.[1]

Charles Lee, former Attorney-General, counsel for the applicants, argued the questions which he and everybody else thought were involved. He maintained that a mandamus was the proper remedy, made so not only by the nature of the relation of the Supreme Court to inferior courts and ministerial officers, but by positive enactment of Congress in the Judiciary Law of 1789. Lee pointed out that the Supreme Court had acted on this authority in two previous cases.

Apparently the court could do one or the other of two things: it could disavow its power over any branch of the Executive Department and dismiss the application, or it could assert this power in cases like the one before it and command Madison to deliver the withheld commissions. It was the latter course that the Republicans expected Marshall to take.

If the Chief Justice should do this, Madison undoubtedly would ignore the writ and decline to obey the court's mandate. Thus the Executive and Judicial Departments would have been brought into direct conflict, with every practical advantage in the hands of the Administration. The court had no

[1] See 1 Cranch, 137–80.

physical means to compel the execution of its order. Jefferson would have denounced the illegality of such a decision and laughed at the court's predicament. In short, had the writ to Madison been issued, the court would have been powerless to enforce obedience to its own mandate.

If, on the contrary, the court dismissed the case, the Republican doctrines that the National courts could not direct executives to obey the laws, and that the Judiciary could not invalidate acts of Congress, would by acquiescence have been admitted.

No matter which horn of the dilemma Marshall selected, it was hard to see how his views could escape impalement. He chose neither. Instead of allowing his cherished purpose of establishing the principle of supervisory power of the Judiciary over legislation to be thus wounded and perhaps fatally injured, he made the decision of this insignificant case — about which the applicants themselves no longer cared — the occasion for asserting that principle. And he did assert that principle — asserted it so impressively that for more than a century his conclusion has easily withstood repeated assaults upon it, which still continue.

Marshall accomplished his purpose by convincing the Associate Justices of the unconstitutionality of that section of the Ellsworth Judiciary Act of 1789 [1]

[1] Section 13 provided, among other things, that "the Supreme Court . . shall have power to issue writs of prohibition to the district courts . . and writs of *mandamus*, in cases warranted by the principles and usages of law, to any courts appointed, or persons holding office, under the authority of the United States." (*U.S. Statutes at Large*, i, 73; *Annals*, 1st Cong. 2d Sess. 2245.)

which expressly conferred upon the Supreme Court the power to issue writs of mandamus and prohibition, and in persuading them to allow him to announce that conclusion as the opinion of the court. When we consider that, while all the Justices agreed with Marshall that the provision of the Ellsworth Judiciary Law requiring them to sit as circuit judges was unconstitutional, and yet refused to act upon that belief as Marshall wanted them to act, we can realize the measure of his triumph in inducing the same men to hold unconstitutional another provision of the same act — a provision, too, even less open to objection than the one they had sustained.

The theory of the Chief Justice that Section 13 of the old Judiciary Law was unconstitutional was absolutely new, and it was as daring as it was novel. It was the only original idea that Marshall contributed to the entire controversy. Nobody ever had questioned the validity of that section of the statute which Marshall now challenged. Ellsworth, who preceded Marshall as Chief Justice, had drawn the act when he was Senator in the First Congress; [1] he was one of the greatest lawyers of his time and an influential member of the Constitutional Convention.

One of Marshall's associates on the Supreme Bench at that very moment, William Paterson, had also been, with Ellsworth, a member of the Senate Committee that reported the Judiciary Act of 1789, and he, too, had been a member of the Constitutional Convention. Senators Gouverneur Morris of

[1] See *supra*, 53–54.

New York, William S. Johnson of Connecticut,
Robert Morris of Pennsylvania, William Few of
Georgia, George Read and Richard Bassett of Delaware, and Caleb Strong of Massachusetts supported
the Ellsworth Law when the Senate passed it; and
in the House James Madison and George Wythe of
Virginia, Abraham Baldwin of Georgia, and Roger
Sherman of Connecticut heartily favored and voted
for the act. Most of these men were thorough lawyers, and every one of them had also helped to draft
the National Constitution. Here were twelve men,
many of them highly learned in the law, makers of
the Constitution, draftsmen or advocates and supporters of the Ellsworth Judiciary Act of 1789, not
one of whom had ever dreamed that an important
section of that law was unconstitutional.[1]

Furthermore, from the organization of the Supreme Court to that moment, the bench and bar had
accepted it, and the Justices of the Supreme Court,
sitting with National district judges, had recognized
its authority when called upon to take action in a
particular controversy brought directly under it.[2]
The Supreme Court itself had held that it had jurisdiction, under Section 13, to issue a mandamus in a
proper case,[3] and had granted a writ of prohibition
by authority of the same section.[4] In two other
cases this section had come before the Supreme

[1] See Dougherty: *Power of the Federal Judiciary over Legislation*, 82.
Professor Corwin says that not many years later Marshall concurred
in an opinion of the Supreme Court which, by analogy, recognized the
validity of it. (Corwin, 8–9.)

[2] U.S. *vs*. Ravara, 2 Dallas, 297.

[3] U.S. *vs*. Lawrence, 3 Dallas, 42.   [4] U.S. *vs*. Peters, *ib.* 121.

Court, and no one had even intimated that it was unconstitutional.[1]

When, to his great disgust, Marshall was forced to sit as a circuit judge at Richmond in the winter of 1802, a case came before him that involved both the validity of the Republican Repeal Act and also the constitutionality of that provision of the Ellsworth Judiciary Law requiring justices of the Supreme Court to sit as circuit judges. This was the case of Stuart vs. Laird. Marshall held merely that the plea which raised these questions was insufficient, and the case was taken to the Supreme Court on a writ of error. After extended argument Justice Paterson delivered the opinion of the court, Marshall declining to participate in the decision because he had "tried the cause in the court below." [2]

At the same term, then, at which Marbury vs. Madison was decided, and immediately after Marshall's opinion in that case was delivered, all the justices of the Supreme Court except the Chief Justice, held "that practice and acquiescence under it [the Judiciary Act of 1789] for a period of several years, commencing with the organization of the

[1] In the argument of Marbury vs. Madison, Charles Lee called Marshall's attention to the case of U.S. vs. Hopkins, in the February term, 1794, in which a motion was made for a mandamus to Hopkins as loan officer for the District of Virginia, and to the case of one John Chandler of Connecticut, also in February, 1794, in which a motion was made in behalf of Chandler for a mandamus to the Secretary of War. These cases do not seem to have been reported, and Lee must have referred to manuscript records of them. (See 1 Cranch, 148–49.)

Samuel W. Dana of Connecticut also referred to the Chandler case during the Judiciary debate in the House, March, 1802. (See *Annals*, 7th Cong. 1st Sess. 903–04.)

[2] 1 Cranch, 308.

judicial system . . has fixed the construction. It is a contemporary interpretation of the most forcible nature. This practical exposition is too strong and obstinate to be shaken or controlled. Of course, the question is at rest, and ought not now to be disturbed." [1]

But the exigency disclosed in this chapter required immediate action, notwithstanding the obstacles above set forth. The issue raised by the Republicans — the free hand of Congress, unrestrained by courts — must be settled at that time or be abandoned perhaps forever. The fundamental consideration involved must have a prompt, firm, and, if possible, final answer. Were such an answer not then given, it was not certain that it could ever be made. As it turned out, but for Marbury *vs.* Madison, the power of the Supreme Court to annul acts of Congress probably would not have been insisted upon thereafter. For, during the thirty-two years that Marshall remained on the Supreme Bench after the decision of that case, and for twenty years after his death, no case came before the court where an act of Congress was overthrown; and none had been invalidated from the adoption of the Constitution to the day when Marshall delivered his epochal opinion. So that, as a matter of historical significance, had he not then taken this stand, nearly seventy years would have passed without any question arising as to the omnipotence of Congress. [2] After so long a period of judicial acquiescence

[1] Stuart *vs.* Laird, 1 Cranch, 309.

[2] The next case in which the Supreme Court overthrew an act of

in Congressional supremacy it seems likely that opposition to it would have been futile.

For the reasons stated, Marshall resolved to take that step which, for courage, statesmanlike foresight, and, indeed, for perfectly calculated audacity, has few parallels in judicial history. In order to assert that in the Judiciary rested the exclusive power [1] to declare any statute unconstitutional, and to announce that the Supreme Court was the ultimate arbiter as to what is and what is not law under the Constitution, Marshall determined to annul Section 13 of the Ellsworth Judiciary Act of 1789. In taking such a step the Chief Justice made up his mind that he would sum up in final and conclusive form the reasoning that sustained that principle.

Marshall resolved to go still further. He would announce from the Supreme Bench rules of procedure which the Executive branch of the Government must observe. This was indispensable, he correctly thought, if the departments were to be harmonious branches of a single and National Government, rather than warring factions whose dissensions must in the end paralyze the administration of the Nation's affairs. [2]

Congress was that of Scott *vs.* Sandford — the famous Dred Scott case, decided in 1857. In this case the Supreme Court held that Congress had no power to prohibit slavery in the territory purchased from France in 1803 (the Louisiana Purchase), and that the Act of March 6, 1820, known as the Missouri Compromise, was unconstitutional, null, and void. (See Scott *vs.* Sandford, 19 Howard, 393 *et seq.*)

[1] The President can veto a bill, of course, on the ground of unconstitutionality; but, by a two thirds vote, Congress can pass it over the Executive's disapproval.

[2] Carson, i, 203; and see especially Adams: *U.S.* i, 192.

It was not, then, Marshall's declaring an act of Congress to be unconstitutional that was innovating or revolutionary. The extraordinary thing was the pretext he devised for rendering that opinion — a pretext which, it cannot be too often recalled, had been unheard of and unsuspected hitherto. Nothing but the emergency compelling the insistence, at this particular time, that the Supreme Court has such a power, can fully and satisfactorily explain the action of Marshall in holding this section void.

In his opinion the Chief Justice spoke of "the peculiar delicacy of this case, the novelty of some of its circumstances, and the real difficulty attending the points which occur in it." [1] He would follow, he said, the points of counsel in the order in which they had been made.[2] Did the applicants have a right to the commissions? This depended, he said, on whether Marbury had been appointed to office. If so, he was entitled to the commission which was merely the formal evidence of the appointment. The President had nominated him to the Senate, the Senate had confirmed the nomination, the President had signed the commission, and, in the manner directed by act of Congress, the Secretary of State had affixed to it the seal of the United States.[3]

The President could not recall his appointment if "the officer is not removable." Delivery of the commission was not necessary to the consummation of the appointment which had already been effected;

[1] 1 Cranch, 154.
[2] This seems to have been inaccurate. Compare Lee's argument with Marshall's opinion.
[3] 1 Cranch, 158.

otherwise "negligence, . . fraud, fire or theft, might deprive an individual of his office." But the truth was that "a copy from the record . . would be, to every intent and purpose, equal to the original." [1] The appointment of Marbury "vested in the officer legal rights . . of his country," and "to withhold his commission is an act . . not warranted by law, but violative of a vested legal right. . ."[2]

"The very essence of civil liberty," continues Marshall, "certainly consists in the right of every individual to claim the protection of the laws, whenever he receives an injury. One of the first duties of government is to afford that protection." Ours has been "emphatically termed a government of laws, and not of men. It will certainly cease to deserve this high appellation, if the laws furnish no remedy for the violation of a vested legal right. . ."[3]

"The act of delivering or withholding a commission" is not "a mere political act, belonging to the executive department alone," but a ministerial act, the performance of which is directed by statute. Congress had ordered the Secretary of War to place the names of certain persons on the pension rolls; suppose that he should refuse to do so? "Would the wounded veteran be without remedy? . . Is it to be contended that the heads of departments are not amenable to the laws of their country?"[4]

Would any person whatever attempt to maintain that a purchaser of public lands could be deprived of his property because a Secretary of State withheld his patent?[5] To be sure, the President had certain

[1] 1 Cranch, 160.   [2] *Ib.* 162.   [3] *Ib.* 163.   [4] *Ib.* 164.   [5] *Ib.* 165.

political powers and could appoint agents to aid him in the exercise of them. The courts had no authority to interfere in this sphere of Executive action. For example, the conduct of foreign affairs by the Secretary of State, as the representative of the President, can never be examinable by the courts. But the delivery of a commission to an office or a patent to land was a different matter.

When Congress by statute peremptorily directs the Secretary of State or any other officer to perform specific duties on which "the rights of individuals are dependent . . he cannot at his discretion sport away the vested rights of others." If he attempts to do so he is answerable to the courts. "The question whether a right has vested or not, is, in its nature, judicial, and must be tried by the judicial authority." The court therefore was empowered to decide the point; and held that Madison's refusal to deliver Marbury's commission was "a plain violation of that right, for which the laws of his country afford him a remedy." [1]

But was this remedy the writ of mandamus for which Marbury had applied? It was, said Marshall; but could such an order be directed to the Secretary of State? This was a task "peculiarly irksome, as well as delicate," [2] for, he observed, there were those who would at first consider it "as an attempt to intrude into the cabinet, and to intermeddle with the prerogatives of the executive." Far be it from John Marshall to do such a thing. He need hardly "disclaim all pretensions to such jurisdiction." Not

---

[1] 1 Cranch, 166–68.   [2] *Ib.* 169.

"for a moment" would he entertain "an extravagance so absurd and excessive. . . Questions in their nature political, . . can never be made in this court." But if the case before him presented only questions concerning legal rights of an individual, "what is there in the exalted station" of the Secretary of State which "exempts him from . . being compelled to obey the judgment of the law"? The only remaining question, therefore, was whether a mandamus could issue from the Supreme Court.[1]

In such manner Marshall finally arrived at the examination of the constitutionality of Section 13, which, he said, fitted the present case "precisely"; and "if this court is not authorized to issue a writ of mandamus" to Madison, "it must be because the law is unconstitutional, and therefore absolutely incapable of conferring the authority."[2] In reaching this point Marshall employs almost seven thousand words. Fifteen hundred more words are used before he takes up the principle of judicial supremacy over legislation.

The fundamental law of the Nation, Marshall explained, expressly defined the original jurisdiction of the Supreme Court and carefully limited its authority. It could take original cognizance only of specific cases. In all others, the court was given nothing but "appellate jurisdiction." But he omitted the words that immediately follow in the same sentence — "with such exceptions . . as the Congress shall make." Yet this language had, for fourteen years, apparently been considered by the whole bench and

[1] 1 Cranch, 170.   [2] *Ib.* 173.

bar as meaning, among other things, that while Congress could *not take from* the Supreme Court original jurisdiction in the cases specifically named in Article Three of the Constitution, Congress *could add* other cases to the original jurisdiction of the Supreme Court.

Marshall was quite conscious of all this, it would seem. In the argument, counsel had insisted that since "the clause, assigning original jurisdiction to the Supreme Court, contains no negative or restrictive words, the power remains to the legislature, to assign original jurisdiction to that court in other cases than those specified." [1] But, reasons Marshall, in answer to this contention, if Congress could thus enlarge the original jurisdiction of the Supreme Court, "the subsequent part of the section [2] is mere surplusage, is entirely without meaning, . . is form without substance. . . Affirmative words are often . . negative of other objects than those affirmed; and in this case, a negative or exclusive sense must be given to them, *or they have no operation at all*." [3]

That is to say, when the Constitution conferred upon the Supreme Court original jurisdiction in specified cases, it thereby excluded all others — denied to Congress the power to add to the jurisdiction thus affirmatively granted. And yet, let it be repeated, by giving original jurisdiction in cases specifically named, the Constitution put it beyond the power of Congress to interfere with the Supreme

[1] 1 Cranch, 174.

[2] In all "other cases . . the Supreme Court shall have appellate jurisdiction . . with such exceptions . . as the Congress shall make."

[3] *Ib.* 174. (Italics the author's.)

Court in those cases; but Marshall asserted that
the specific grant of jurisdiction has "*no operation
at all*" unless "a negative or exclusive sense" be
given it.[1]

Marshall boldly held, therefore, that Section 13 of
the Ellsworth Judiciary Act was "not warranted by
the Constitution." Such being the case, ought the
Supreme Court to act under this unconstitutional
section? As the Chief Justice stated the question,
could "an act, repugnant to the constitution . . become the law of the land"? After writing nearly
nine thousand words, he now reached the commanding question: Can the Supreme Court of the United
States invalidate an act which Congress has passed
and the President has approved?

Marshall avowed that the Supreme Court can
and must do that very thing, and in so doing made
Marbury *vs.* Madison historic. In this, the vital
part of his opinion, the Chief Justice is direct, clear,
simple, and convincing. The people, he said, have
an elemental right to establish such principles for
"their future government, as . . shall most conduce
to their own happiness." This was "the basis on
which the whole American fabric had been erected."
These " permanent" and "fundamental" principles,
in the instance of the American Government, were
those limiting the powers of the various departments: "That those limits may not be mistaken,
or forgotten, the constitution is written. To what
purpose are powers limited . . if these limits may,

[1] 1 Cranch, 176. This particular part of the text adopts Professor
Edward S. Corwin's careful and accurate analysis of Marshall's opinion
on this point. (See Corwin, 4–10.)

at any time, be passed by those intended to be restrained?"[1]

If Congress or any other department of the Government can ignore the limitations of the Constitution, all distinction between government of "limited and unlimited powers" is done away with. To say that "acts prohibited and acts allowed are of equal obligation" is to deny the very purpose for which our fundamental law was adopted. "The constitution controls any legislative act repugnant to it." Congress cannot alter it by legislation.[2] All this, said Marshall, was too clear to admit of discussion, but he proceeded, nevertheless, to discuss the subject at great length.

There is "no middle ground." The Constitution is either "a superior paramount law" not to be changed by legislative enactment, or else "it is on a level with the ordinary legislative acts" and, as such, "alterable" at the will of Congress. If the Constitution is supreme, then an act of Congress violative of it is not law; if the Constitution is not supreme, then "written constitutions are absurd attempts, on the part of the people, to limit a power in its own nature illimitable." Three times in a short space Marshall insists that, for Congress to ignore the limitations which the Constitution places upon it, is to deny the whole theory of government under written constitutions.

Although the contention that the Judiciary must consider unconstitutional legislation to be valid was "an absurdity too gross to be insisted on," Marshall

[1] 1 Cranch, 176.   [2] *Ib.* 176–77.

would, nevertheless, patiently examine it.[1] This he did by reasoning so simple and so logical that the dullest citizen could not fail to understand it nor the most astute intellect escape it. But in the process he was tiresomely repetitious, though not to so irritating an extent as he at times became.

If two laws conflict, the courts must decide between them. Where the Constitution and an act of Congress apply to a case, "the court must determine which . . governs [it]. This is of the very essence of judicial duty. . . If, then, . . the constitution is superior to any ordinary act of the legislature," the Judiciary must prefer it to a mere statute. Otherwise "courts must close their eyes on the constitution," and see only the legislative enactment.[2]

But to do this "would subvert the very foundation of all written constitutions." It would be to "declare that an act which . . is entirely void, is yet . . completely obligatory," and that Congress may do "what is expressly forbidden." This would give to the legislature "a practical and real omnipotence, with the same breath which professes to restrict their powers within narrow limits." It would be "prescribing limits, and declaring that those limits may be passed at pleasure." This "reduces to nothing" both the letter and the theory of the Constitution.

That instrument expressly extends the judicial power to cases "arising under the constitution." Must the courts decide such a case "without examining the instrument under which it arises?" If the

[1] 1 Cranch, 177.   [2] Ib. 178.

courts must look into the Constitution at all, as assuredly they must do in some cases, "what part of it are they forbidden to read or to obey?"

Marshall cites hypothetical examples of legislation in direct conflict with the fundamental law. Suppose that Congress should place an export duty on cotton, tobacco, flour, and that the Government should bring suit to recover the tax. "Ought judgment to be rendered in such a case?" Or if a bill of attainder should be passed and citizens prosecuted under it, "must the court condemn to death those victims whom the constitution endeavors to preserve?"

Take, for example, the crime of treason: the Constitution emphatically prescribes that nobody can be convicted of this offense "unless on the testimony of two witnesses to the same overt act, or on confession in open court." The Judiciary particularly are addressed — "it prescribes, directly for them, a rule of evidence not to be departed from." Suppose that Congress should enact a law providing that a citizen might be convicted of treason upon the testimony of one witness or by a confession out of court? Which must the court obey — the Constitution or the act altering that instrument?

Did not these illustrations and many others that might be given prove that the Constitution must govern courts as well as Congress? If not, why does the Constitution require judges "to take an oath to support it"? That solemn obligation "applies in an especial manner to their conduct in their official character." How "immoral" to direct them to take this oath "if they were to be used as the instruments, and the knowing instruments, for violating what they swear to support!" Such contradictions and confusions would make the ceremony of taking the oath of judicial office "a solemn mockery" and even "a crime."

There is, then, said Marshall, no escape from the conclusion "that a law repugnant to the constitution is void," and that the judicial as well as other departments are bound by the Constitution.[1] The application of Marbury and others must therefore be dismissed.

Thus, by a coup as bold in design and as daring in execution as that by which the Constitution had been framed,[2] John Marshall set up a landmark in American history so high that all the future could take bearings from it, so enduring that all the shocks the Nation was to endure could not overturn it. Such a decision was a great event in American history. State courts, as well as National tribunals, thereafter fearlessly applied the principle that Marshall announced, and the supremacy of written constitutions over legislative acts was firmly established.

This principle is wholly and exclusively American. It is America's original contribution to the science of law.[3] The assertion of it, under the conditions related in this chapter, was the deed of a great man. One of narrower vision and smaller courage never

---

[1] 1 Cranch, 178–80.   [2] See vol. i, 323, of this work.

[3] It must be borne in mind that the American Constitution declares that, in and of itself, it is law — the supreme law of the land; and that no other written constitution makes any such assertion.

would have done what Marshall did. In his management and decision of this case, at the time and under
the circumstances, Marshall's acts and words were
those of a statesman of the first rank.

His opinion gave fresh strength to the purpose
of the Republican leaders to subdue the Federalist
Judiciary. It furnished Jefferson and his radical
followers a new and concrete reason for ousting
from the National Bench, and especially from the
Supreme Court, all judges who would thus override
the will of Congress. Against himself, in particular,
Marshall had newly whetted the edge of Republican
wrath, already over-keen.

The trial of John Pickering, Judge of the United
States Court for the District of New Hampshire,
brought by the House before the bar of the Senate,
was now pushed with cold venomousness to what
Henry Adams calls "an infamous and certainly an
illegal conviction"; and then Marshall's associate
on the Supreme Bench, Justice Samuel Chase, was
quickly impeached for high crimes and misdemeanors. If the Republican organization could force from
its partisans in the Senate a verdict of "guilty" in
Chase's case also, Marshall's official head would be
the next to fall.[1]

Concerning Marshall's assertion of the power of
the National Judiciary to annul acts of Congress
and to direct administrative officers in the discharge
of their legal duties, Jefferson himself said nothing
at the time. But the opinion of the Chief Justice
was another ingredient thrown into the caldron of

[1] See *infra*, chap. IV.

Jefferson's heart, where a hatred was brewed that poisoned the great politician to his latest day.

Many months after the decision in the Marbury case, Jefferson first broke his silence. "Nothing in the Constitution has given them [the Supreme Court] a right to decide for the Executive, more than to the Executive to decide for them," he wrote. "The opinion which gives to the judges the right to decide what laws are constitutional, and what not, not only for themselves in their own sphere of action, but for the Legislature & Executive also, in their spheres, would make the judiciary a despotic branch." [1]

Again, during the trial of Aaron Burr,[2] Jefferson denounced Marshall for his opinion in Marbury *vs.* Madison; and toward the close of his life he returned again and again with corroding words to the subject regarding which, at the moment it arose, he concealed, so far as written words were concerned, his virulent resentment. For instance, seventeen years later Jefferson wrote that "to consider the judges as the ultimate arbiters of all constitutional questions . . would place us under the despotism of an oligarchy." [3]

But for the time being, Jefferson was quiescent.

[1] Jefferson to Mrs. Adams, Sept. 11, 1804, *Works:* Ford, x, footnote to 89.

[2] See *infra*, chap. VIII.

[3] Jefferson to Jarvis, Sept. 28, 1820, *Works:* Ford, XII, 162. Yet, at the time when he was founding the Republican Party, Jefferson had written to a friend that "the laws of the land, administered by upright judges, would protect you from any exercise of power unauthorized by the Constitution of the United States." (Jefferson to Rowan, Sept. 26, 1798, *ib.* VIII, 448.)

His subtle mind knew how, in political controversies, to control his tongue and pen. It could do no good for him, personally, to make an outcry now; and it might do harm. The doctrine which Marshall announced had, Jefferson knew, a strong hold on all Federalists, and, indeed, on many Northern Republicans; the bar, especially, upheld it generally.

The Presidential campaign was drawing near, and for the President openly to attack Marshall's position would create a political issue which could win none to the Republican cause not already fighting for it, and might keep recruits from joining the Republican colors. Jefferson was infinitely concerned about his reëlection and was giving practical attention to the strengthening of his party for the approaching contest.

"I am decidedly in favor of making all the banks Republican, by sharing deposits among them in proportion to the [political] dispositions they show," he wrote to his Secretary of the Treasury three months after Marshall's bold assertion of the dignity and power of the National courts. "It is," he continued, "material to the safety of Republicanism to detach the mercantile interests from its enemies and incorporate them into the body of its friends." [1]

Furthermore, Jefferson was, at that particular moment, profoundly troubled by intimate personal

---

[1] Jefferson to Gallatin, July 12, 1803, *Works:* Ford, x, 15–16. It should be remembered that most of the banks and the financial and commercial interests generally were determined opponents of Jefferson and Republicanism. As a sheer matter of "practical politics," the President cannot be fairly criticized for thus trying to weaken his remorseless foes.

matters and vast National complications. He had
been trying, unsuccessfully, to adjust our dispute
with France; the radical West was becoming clamorous for a forward and even a militant policy concerning the control of the Mississippi River, and especially of New Orleans, which commanded the mouth
of that commercial waterway; while the Federalists,
insisting upon bold measures, had a fair prospect of
winning from Jefferson's support those aggressive
and predatory frontiersmen who, until now, had
stanchly upheld the Republican standard.

Spain had ceded Louisiana to France upon the
condition that the territory never should be transferred to any other government; but neither New
Orleans nor any part of Louisiana had actually been
surrendered by the Spanish authorities. Great
Britain informed the American Government that
she would not consent to the occupation by the
French of any part of Spain's possessions on the
American continent.

Hating and distrusting the British, but also in
terror of Napoleon, Jefferson, who was as weak in
the conduct of foreign affairs as he was dexterous
in the management of political parties, thought to
escape the predicament by purchasing the island of
Orleans and perhaps a strip on the east side of the
Mississippi River.[1]

A series of events swiftly followed the decision of
Marbury *vs.* Madison which enthralled the eager
attention of the whole people and changed the destiny of the Republic. Three months after Marshall

[1] See Channing: *U.S.* IV, 313–14.

delivered his opinion, Napoleon, yielding to "the empire of circumstances," as Talleyrand phrased it,[1] offered, and Livingston and Monroe accepted, the whole of Louisiana for less than fifteen million dollars. Of course France had no title to sell — Louisiana was still legally owned and actually occupied by Spain. The United States bought nothing more than a pretension; and, by force of propinquity and power, made it a fact.[2]

The President was amazed when the news reached him. He did not want Louisiana [3] — nothing was further from his mind than the purchase of it.[4] The immorality of the acquisition affected him not at all; but the inconvenience did. He did not know what to do with Louisiana. Worse still, the treaty of cession required that the people living in that territory should be admitted into the Union, "according to the principles of the Federal Constitution."

So, to his infinite disgust, Jefferson was forced to deal with the Louisiana Purchase by methods as vigorous as any ever advocated by the abhorred Hamilton — methods more autocratic than those which, when done by others, he had savagely denounced as unconstitutional and destructive of liberty.[5] The President doubted whether, under the Constitution, we could acquire, and was sure that we

---

[1] Talleyrand to Decrès, May 24, 1803, as quoted in Adams: *U.S.* II, 55.

[2] Morison: *Otis*, I, 262; see also Adams: *U.S.* II, 56.

[3] See instructions to Livingston and Monroe, *Am. State Papers, Foreign Relations*, II, 540.

[4] Adams: *U.S.* I, 442–43.   [5] *Ib.* II, 120–28.

could not govern, Louisiana, and he actually prepared amendments authorizing the incorporation
into the Republic of the purchased territory.[1] No
such legal mistiness dimmed the eyes of John Marshall who, in time, was to announce as the decision
of the Supreme Court that the Republic could acquire territory with as much right as any monarchical government.[2]

To add to his perturbations, the high priest of
popular rights found himself compelled to abandon
his adored phrase, "the consent of the governed,"
upon which he had so carefully erected the structure
of his popularity, and to drive through Congress a
form of government over the people of Louisiana
without consulting their wishes in the least.[3]

The Jeffersonian doctrine had been that the Union
was merely a compact between sovereign States, and
that new territory and alien peoples could not be
added to it without the consent of all the partners.
The Federalists now took their stand upon this
indefensible ground,[4] and openly threatened the
secession at which they had hinted when the Federalist Judiciary Act was repealed.

[1] *Works:* Ford, x, 3–12.

[2] American Insurance Company *et al. vs.* Canter, 1 Peters, 511–46
and see vol. IV, chap. III, of this work.

[3] See *U.S. Statutes at Large,* II, 283; and *Annals,* 8th Cong. 2d
Sess. 1597.

[4] For instance, Senator Plumer, two years later, thus stated the old
Republican doctrine which the Federalists, in defiance of their party's
creed and traditions, had now adopted as their own: "We cannot admit a new partner into the Union, from without the original limits
of the United States, without the consent, first obtained, of each of
the partners composing the firm." (Plumer to Smith, Feb. 7, 1805,
Plumer, 328.)

Jefferson was alive to the danger: "Whatever Congress shall think it necessary to do [about Louisiana]," he cautioned one of the Republican House leaders, "should be done with as little debate as possible." [1] A month earlier he wrote: "The Constitution has made no provision for our holding foreign territory, still less for incorporating foreign nations into our Union. The Executive . . have done an act beyond the Constitution." [2]

Therefore, he declared, "the less we say about constitutional difficulties respecting Louisiana the better. . . What is necessary for surmounting them must be done sub-silentio." [3] The great radical favored publicity in affairs of state only when such a course was helpful to his political plans. On other occasions no autocrat was ever more secretive than Thomas Jefferson.[4] Seemingly, however, the President was concerned only with his influence on the destiny of the world.[5]

At first the Federalist leaders were too dazed to do more than grumble. "The cession of Louisiana . . is like selling us a Ship after she is surrounded by a

[1] Jefferson to Nicholas, Sept. 7, 1803, *Works:* Ford, x, 10.

[2] Jefferson to Breckenridge, Aug. 12, 1803, *ib.* 7.

[3] Jefferson to Madison, Aug. 18, 1803, *ib.* 8.

[4] "The medicine for that State [North Carolina] must be very mild & secretly administered." (Jefferson to Nicholas, April 7, 1800, *ib.* ix, 129; and see Adams: *U.S.* iii, 147.)

[5] "The millenium was to usher in upon us as the irresistible consequence of the goodness of heart, integrity of mind, and correctness of disposition of Mr. Jefferson. All nations, even pirates and savages, were to be moved by the influence of his persuasive virtue and masterly skill in diplomacy." (Eaton's account of a call on President Jefferson, 1803, *Life of the Late Gen. William Eaton:* Prentiss, 263; also quoted in Adams: *U.S.* ii, 431.)

British Fleet," shrewdly observed George Cabot, when the news was published in Boston.[1] Fisher Ames, of course, thought that "the acquiring of territory by money is mean and despicable," especially when done by Republicans. "The less of it [territory] the better. . . By adding an unmeasured world beyond that river [Mississippi], we rush like a comet into infinite space." [2]

Soon, however, their dissatisfaction blew into flame the embers of secession which never had become cold in their bosoms. "I am convinced," wrote Uriah Tracy, "that the accession of Louisiana will accelerate a division of these States; whose whenabouts is uncertain, but somewhen is inevitable." [3] Senator Plumer thought that the Eastern States should form a new nation: "Adopt this western world into the Union," he said, "and you destroy at once the weight and importance of the Eastern States, and compel them to establish a separate and independent empire." [4] A few days' reflection brought Ames to the conclusion that "our country is too big for union, too sordid for patriotism, too democratic for liberty." [5] Tapping Reeve of Connecticut made careful inquiry among the Federalists in his vicinity and informed Tracy that "all . .

---

[1] Cabot to King, July 1, 1803, King, iv, 279. The Louisiana Purchase was first publicly announced through the press by the *Independent Chronicle* of Boston, June 30, 1803. (Adams: *U.S.* ii, 82–83.)

[2] Ames to Gore, Oct. 3, 1803, Ames, i, 323–24.

[3] Tracy to McHenry, Oct. 19, 1803, Steiner: *Life and Correspondence of James McHenry*, 522.

[4] Oct. 20, 1803, Plumer, 285.

[5] Ames to Dwight, Oct. 26, 1803, Ames i, 328.

believe that we must separate, and that this is the most favorable moment." [1]

Louisiana, however, was not the only motive of the foremost New England Federalists for their scheme of breaking up the Republic. As we have seen, the threat of secession was repeatedly made during the Republican assault on the Judiciary; and now, as a fundamental cause for disunion, the Northern Federalists speedily harked back to Jefferson's purpose of subverting the National courts. The Republicans were ruling the Nation, Virginia was ruling the Republicans, Jefferson was ruling all. Louisiana would permanently turn the balance against the Northern and Eastern States, already outweighed in the National scales; and the conquest of the National Judiciary would remove from that section its last protection against the pillaging hands of the Huns and Vandals of Republicanism. So reasoned the Federalists.

What could be done to save the rights and the property of "the wise, the rich and the good"? By what pathway could the chosen escape their doom? "The principles of our Revolution point to the remedy," declared the soured and flint-hearted Pickering. "The independence of the judges is now directly assailed. . . I am not willing to be sacrificed by such popular tyrants. . . I do not believe in the practicability of a long-continued union." [2]

---

[1] Reeve to Tracy, Feb. 7, 1804, *N.E. Federalism:* Adams, 342; and see Adams: *U.S.* ii, 160.

Members of Congress among the Federalists and Republicans became so estranged that they boarded in different houses and refused to associate with one another. (Plumer, 245, 336.)

[2] Pickering to Cabot, Jan. 29, 1804, Lodge: *Cabot,* 338.

For the same reasons, Roger Griswold of Connecticut avowed that "there can be no safety to the Northern States *without a separation from the confederacy*." [1] The Reverend Jedediah Morse of New Hampshire wrote Senator Plumer that "our empire . . must . . break in pieces. Some think the sooner the better." [2] And the New Hampshire Senator replied: "I hope the time is not far distant when . . the sound part will separate from the corrupt." [3]

With the exception of John Adams, only one eminent New England Federalist kept his head steady and his patriotism undefiled: George Cabot, while sympathizing with his ancient party friends, frankly opposed their mad project. Holding that secession was impracticable, he declared: "I am not satisfied that the thing itself is to be desired. My habitual opinions have been always strongly against it." [4]

But the expressions of such men as Pickering, Ames, and Griswold indicated the current of New England Federalist thought and comment. Their secession sentiment, however, did not appeal to the young men, who hailed with joy the opportunity to occupy these new, strange lands which accident, or Providence, or Jefferson had opened to them. Knowledge of this was indeed one cause of the anger of some Federalist managers who owned immense tracts in New England and in the Ohio Valley and wanted them purchased and settled by those now

---

[1] Griswold to Wolcott, March 11, 1804, *N.E. Federalism:* Adams, 356.

[2] Morse to Plumer, Feb. 3, 1804, Plumer, 289.

[3] Plumer to Morse, March 10, 1804, *ib.*

[4] Cabot to King, March 17, 1804, Lodge: *Cabot*, 345.

turning their eyes to the alluring farther western
country.[1] They saw with something like fury the
shifting of political power to the South and West.

The management of the unwelcome Louisiana
windfall, the conduct of the National campaign, the
alarming reports from New England, left Jefferson
no time to rail at Marshall or to attack that "subtle
corps of sappers and miners" who were then beginning "to undermine . . our confederated fabric," as
Jefferson declared seventeen years later.[2] For the
present the great public duty of exposing Marshall's
decision in Marbury *vs.* Madison must be deferred.

But the mills of democracy were grinding, and
after he was reëlected certain impeachments would
be found in the grist that would make all right.
The defiant Marshall would at least be humbled,
perhaps — probably — removed from office. But all
in good time! For the present Jefferson had other
work to do. He himself must now exercise powers
which, according to his philosophy and declarations,
were far beyond those conferred upon him by the
Constitution.

So it came about that the first of Marshall's great
Constitutional opinions received scant notice at the
time of its delivery. The newspapers had little to
say about it. Even the bench and the bar of the
country, at least in the sections remote from Washington, appear not to have heard of it,[3] or, if they

---

[1] See Morison: *Otis*, I, 262.

[2] Jefferson to Ritchie, Dec. 25, 1820, *Works:* Ford, XII, 177.

[3] For instance, in 1808, the United States District Court of Massachusetts, in the decision of a case requiring all possible precedents like
that of Marbury *vs.* Madison, did not so much as refer to Marshall's

had, to have forgotten it amid the thrilling events that filled the times.

Because popular interest had veered toward and was concentrated upon the Louisiana Purchase and the renewal of war in Europe, Republican newspapers, until then so alert to discover and eager to attack every judicial "usurpation," had almost nothing to say of Marshall's daring assertion of judicial supremacy which later was execrated as the very parent of Constitutional evil. An empire had been won under Jefferson; therefore Jefferson had won it — another proof of the far-seeing statesmanship of "The Man of the People." Of consequence

opinion, although every other case that could be found was cited. Marbury *vs*. Madison, long afterwards, was added in a footnote to the printed report. (McLaughlin, 30, citing *Am. Law Journal*, old series, II, 255–64.)

Marshall's opinion in Marbury *vs*. Madison was first referred to by counsel in a legal controversy in *Ex Parte* Burford, 1806 (3 Cranch, 448). Robert Goodloe Harper next cited it in his argument for Bollmann (4 Cranch, 86; and see *infra*, chap. VII). Marshall referred to it in his opinion in that case, and Justice William Johnson commented upon it at some length.

A year later Marshall's opinion in Marbury *vs*. Madison was cited by Jefferson's Attorney-General, Cæsar A. Rodney. In the case *Ex Parte* Gilchrist *et al. vs*. The Collector of the Port of Charleston, S.C. (5 Hughes, 1), the United States Court for that circuit, consisting of Johnson, Associate Justice of the Supreme Court, and the Judge of the District Court, granted a mandamus under the section of the Judiciary Act which Marshall and the entire court had, five years before, declared to be unconstitutional, so far as it conferred original jurisdiction upon the Supreme Court in applications for mandamus.

Rodney wrote to the President a letter of earnest protest, pointing out the fact that the court's action in the Gilchrist case was in direct antagonism to the opinion in Marbury *vs*. Madison. But Jefferson was then so savagely attacking Marshall's rulings in the Burr trial (see *infra*, chaps. VII, VIII, IX) that he was, at last, giving public expression of his disapproval of the opinion of the Chief Justice in Marbury *vs.* Madison. He did not even answer Rodney's letter.

he must be reëlected. Such was the popular logic; and reëlected Jefferson was — triumphantly, almost unanimously.

Circumstances which had shackled his hands now suddenly freed them. Henceforth the President could do as he liked, both personally and politically. No longer should John Marshall, the abominated head of the National Judiciary, rest easy on the bench which his audacity had elevated above President and Congress. The opinion of the "usurping" Chief Justice in Marbury *vs.* Madison should have answer at last. So on with the impeachment trial of Samuel Chase! Let him be deposed, and then, if Marshall would not bend the knee, that obdurate judicial defender of Nationalism should follow Chase into desuetude and disgrace.

The incessant clamor of the Federalist past-statesmen, unheard by the popular ear, had nevertheless done some good — all the good it ought to have done. It had aroused misgivings in the minds of certain Northern Republican Senators as to the expediency, wisdom, and justice of the Republican plan to shackle or overthrow the National Judiciary. This hesitation was, however, unknown to the masters of the Republican organization in Congress. The Federalists themselves were totally unaware of it. Only Jefferson, with his abnormal sensibility, had an indistinct impression that somewhere, in the apparently perfect alignment of the Republican forces, there was potential weakness.

Marshall was gifted with no such divination. He knew only the fate that had been prepared for him.

A crisis was reached in his career and a determinative phase of American history entered upon. His place as Chief Justice was to be made secure and the stability of American institutions saved by as narrow a margin as that by which the National Constitution had been established.

CHAPTER IV

IMPEACHMENT

The judges of the Supreme Court must fall. Our affairs approach an important crisis. (William Plumer.)

These articles contained in themselves a virtual impeachment of not only Mr. Chase but of all the Judges of the Supreme Court.
(John Quincy Adams.)

We shall bring forward such a specimen of judicial tyranny, as, I trust in God, will never be again exhibited in our country. (John Randolph.)

We appear for an ancient and infirm man whose better days have been worn out in the service of that country which now degrades him.
(Joseph Hopkinson.)

Our property, our liberty, our lives can only be protected by independent judges. (Luther Martin.)

"WE *want your offices*, for the purpose of giving them to men who will fill them better." In these frank words, Senator William Branch Giles [1] of Virginia stated one of the purposes of the Republicans in their determined attack on the National Judiciary. He was speaking to the recently elected young Federalist Senator from Massachusetts, John Quincy Adams.[2]

They were sitting before the blazing logs in the wide fireplace that warmed the Senate Chamber. John Randolph, the Republican leader of the House, and Israel Smith, a Republican Senator from Vermont, were also in the group. The talk was of the

[1] Giles was appointed Senator August 11, 1804, by the Governor to fill the unexpired term of Abraham Venable who resigned in order that Giles might be sent to the Senate. In December the Legislature elected him for the full term. Upon taking his seat Giles immediately became the Republican leader of the Senate. (See Anderson, 93.)

[2] Dec. 21, 1804, *Memoirs, J. Q. A.*: Adams, I, 322–23.

approaching trial of Samuel Chase, Associate Justice of the Supreme Court of the United States, whom the House had impeached for high crimes and misdemeanors. Giles and Randolph were, "with excessive earnestness," trying to convince the doubting Vermont Senator of the wisdom and justice of the Republican method of ousting from the National Bench those judges who did not agree with the views of the Republican Party.

Giles scorned the idea of "an *independent* judiciary!" The independence claimed by the National judges was "nothing more nor less than an attempt to establish an aristocratic despotism in themselves." The power of the House to impeach, and of the Senate to try, any public officer was unlimited.

"If," continued Giles, "the Judges of the Supreme Court should dare, *as they had done*, to declare acts of Congress unconstitutional, or to send a mandamus to the Secretary of State, *as they had done*, it was the undoubted right of the House to impeach them, and of the Senate to remove them for giving such opinions, however honest or sincere they may have been in entertaining them." He held that the Senate, when trying an impeached officer, did not act as a court. "Removal by impeachment was nothing more than a declaration by Congress to this effect: You hold dangerous opinions, and if you are suffered to carry them into effect you will work the destruction of the Nation." [1]

Thus Giles made plain the Republican objective.

[1] Dec. 21, 1804, *Memoirs, J. Q. A.*: Adams I, 322-23.

Judges were to be removed for any cause that a dominant political party considered to be sufficient.[1] The National Judiciary was, in this manner, to be made responsive to the popular will and responsible to the representatives of the people in the House and of the States in the Senate.[2]

Giles, who was now Jefferson's personal representative in the Senate,[3] as he had been in the House, bore down upon his mild but reluctant fellow partisan from Vermont in a "manner dogmatical and peremptory." Not only must the aggressive and irritating Chase be stripped of his robes, but the same fate must fall upon "all other Judges of the Supreme Court except the one last appointed," [4] who, being a Republican, was secure.[5] Adams rightly concluded that the plan was

---

[1] Plumer, 274–75; and see especially Plumer, Jan. 5, 1804, "Congress," Plumer MSS. Lib. Cong.

[2] The powerful Republican organ, the *Aurora*, of Philadelphia, thus indicted the National Judiciary: Because judges could not be removed, "many wrongs are daily done by the courts to humble, obscure, or poor suitors. . . It is a prodigious monster in a free government to see a class of men set apart, not simply to administer the laws, but who exercise a legislative and even an executive power, directly in defiance and contempt of the Constitution." (*Aurora*, Jan. 28, 1805, as quoted in Corwin, 41.) Professor Corwin says that this utterance was approved by Jefferson.

[3] "Mr. Giles from Virginia . . is the Ministerial leader in the Senate." (Plumer to Thompson, Dec. 23, 1804, Plumer MSS. Lib. Cong.)
"I considered Mr. Giles as the ablest *practical* politician of the whole party enlisted under Mr. Jefferson's banners." (Pickering to Marshall, Jan. 24, 1826, Pickering MSS. Mass. Hist. Soc.)

[4] William Johnson of South Carolina, appointed March 26, 1804, vice William Moore, resigned. Johnson was a stanch Jeffersonian when appointed. He was thirty-three years old at the time he was made Associate Justice.

[5] It is impossible to put too much emphasis on Giles's avowal. His statement is the key to the Chase impeachment.

to "have swept the supreme judicial bench clean at a stroke." [1]

For a long time everybody had understood that the impeachment of Chase was only the first step in the execution of the Republican plan to replace with Republicans Marshall and the four Federalist Associate Justices. "The judges of the Supreme Court are all Federalists," wrote Pickering six weeks before Johnson's appointment. "They stand in the way of the ruling power. . . The Judges therefore, are, if possible, to be removed," by impeachment. [2]

Nearly two years before, Senator William Plumer of New Hampshire had accurately divined the Republican plan: "The judges of the Supreme Court must fall," he informed Jeremiah Mason. "They are *denounced* by the Executive, as well as the House. They must be removed; they are obnoxious unyielding men; & why should they remain to awe & embarrass the administration? Men of more flexible nerves can be found to succeed them. Our affairs seem to approach an important crisis." [3] The Federalists rightly believed that Jefferson was the directing mind in planning and effecting the subjugation of the National Judiciary. That, said Bayard, "has been an object on which Mr. Jefferson has long been resolved, at least ever since he has been in office." [4]

[1] Adams to his father, March 8, 1805, *Writings, J. Q. A.*: Ford, III, 108.

[2] Pickering to Lyman, Feb. 11, 1804, *N.E. Federalism*: Adams, 344; Lodge: *Cabot*, 444; also see Plumer, 275.

[3] Plumer to Mason, Jan. 14, 1803, Plumer MSS. Lib. Cong.

[4] Bayard to Bassett, Feb. 12, 1802, *Bayard Papers*: Donnan, 148.

John Marshall especially must be overthrown.[1]
He had done all the things of which Giles and the
Republicans complained. He had "dared to declare
an act of Congress unconstitutional," had "dared"
to order Madison to show cause why he should not
be compelled to do his legal duty. Everybody was
at last awake to the fact that Marshall had become
the controlling spirit of the Supreme Court and of
the whole National Judiciary.

Every one knew, too, that he was the most determined Nationalist in the entire country, and that
Jefferson and the Republican Party had no more
unyielding enemy than the Chief Justice. And he
had shown by his management of the Supreme
Court and by his opinion in Marbury *vs.* Madison,
how powerful that tribunal could be made. The
downfall of Samuel Chase was a matter of small
importance compared with the removal of John
Marshall.

"They hate Marshall, Paterson, etc. worse than
they hate Chase because they are men of better
character," asserted Judge Jeremiah Smith of New
Hampshire. "To be safe in these times good men
must not only resign their offices but they must
resign their good names. . . They will be obnoxious
as long as they retain *either*. If they will neither die
nor resign they give Mr J the trouble of correcting
the *procedure*. . . Tell me what the judges say —
are they frightened?" he anxiously inquired of
Plumer.[2] Frightened they were — and very badly

---

[1] Channing: *Jeffersonian System*, 119–20; Adams: *U.S.* ii, 225–27,
235; Anderson, 93, 95.

[2] Smith to Plumer, Feb. 11, 1804, Plumer MSS. Lib. Cong.

frightened. Even John Marshall, hitherto imperturbable and dauntless, was shaken.[1]

In addition to his "heretical" opinion in Marbury vs. Madison, Marshall had given the Republicans, and Jefferson especially, another cause for complaint. A year after the decision of that case, he had again gone out of his way to announce from the Supreme Bench the fallacy of Jefferson's Constitutional views and the soundness of the Nationalist theory. During the February term of the Supreme Court for the year 1804, that tribunal, in the case of the United States vs. Fisher,[2] was called upon to decide whether the United States was a preferred creditor of an insolvent, under the Bankruptcy Act of 1800, which Marshall had helped to draw.[3] Among other objections, it was suggested by counsel for Fisher, the insolvent, that the Bankruptcy Law was unconstitutional and that the priority which that act gave the Nation over other creditors of the bankrupt would prevent the States from making similar laws for their own protection.

But, said Marshall, this is "the necessary consequence of the supremacy of the laws of the United States on all subjects to which the legislative power of the United States extends. . . The Constitution did not prohibit Congress" from enacting a bankruptcy law and giving the Nation preference as a creditor. On the contrary, Congress was expressly authorized "to make all laws which shall be necessary and proper to carry into execution the powers

[1] See *infra*, 176–77, 196.   [2] 2 Cranch, 358–405.
[3] See vol. ii, 481–82, of this work.

vested by the Constitution in the National Government." To say that "no law was authorized which was not indispensably necessary . . would produce endless difficulties. . . Congress must possess the choice of means and must be empowered to use any means which are, in fact, conducive to the exercise of a power granted by the Constitution."

This was an emphatic denial of Jefferson's famous opinion on the power of Congress to charter a bank, and an outright assertion of the views of Hamilton on that celebrated question.[1] The case could have been decided without such an expression from the court, but it presented an opportunity for a judicial statement of liberal construction which might not soon come again,[2] and Marshall availed himself of it.

For two years no part of the Republican plans against the Judiciary had miscarried. Close upon the very day when John Breckenridge in the Senate had moved to repeal the National Judiciary Act of 1801, a petition signed by the enraged Republicans of Alleghany County, Pennsylvania, had been sent to the Legislature of that State, demanding the impeachment of Alexander Addison; and almost simultaneously with the passage of the Judiciary Repeal Act of Congress, the Pennsylvania House of Representatives transmitted to the State Senate articles charging the able but arrogant Federalist judge with high crimes and misdemeanors.

[1] See vol. II, 71–74, of this work.

[2] Fifteen years passed before a critical occasion called for another assertion by Marshall of the doctrine of implied powers; and that occasion produced one of Marshall's greatest opinions — in the judgment of many, the greatest of all his writings. (See McCulloch vs. Maryland, vol. IV, chap. VI, of this work.)

Addison's trial speedily followed; and while the evidence against him, viewed through the perspective of history, seems trivial, the Republican Pennsylvania Senate pronounced judgment against him and deposed him from the bench. With notable ability, Addison conducted his own defense. He made a powerful speech which is a classic of conservative philosophy.[1] But his argument was unavailing. The Republican theory, that a judge might be deposed from office for any conduct or opinion of which the Legislature disapproved, was ruthlessly carried out.[2]

Almost as soon as Congress convened after the overthrow of the obnoxious Pennsylvania Federalist judge, the Republicans in the National House, upon representations from Jefferson, took steps to impeach John Pickering, Judge of the United States Court for the District of New Hampshire.[3] This

[1] Addison's address is historically important; it perfectly shows the distrust of democracy which all Federalist leaders then felt. Among other things, he pleaded for the independence of the Judiciary, asserted that it was their exclusive province to decide upon the constitutionality of laws, and stoutly maintained that no judge could be impeached except for an offense for which he also could be indicted. (*Addison Trial*, 101–43.)

[2] The petition praying for the impeachment of Addison was sent to the Pennsylvania House of Representatives on January 11, 1802. On March 23, 1802, that body transmitted articles of impeachment to the State Senate. The trial was held in early January, 1803. Addison was convicted January 26, 1803. (*Ib.*)

[3] Jefferson's Message was transmitted to the House, February 4, 1803, nine days after the conviction of Addison. It enclosed a "letter and affidavits" setting forth Pickering's conduct on the bench in the case of the ship Eliza, and suggested that "the Constitution has confided [to the House] a power of instituting proceedings of redress." (*Annals*, 7th Cong. 2d Sess. 460.)

On March 2 the committee reported a resolution for Pickering's impeachment because of the commission by him of "high crimes and misdemeanors," and, though a few Federalists tried to postpone a vote, the resolution was adopted immediately.

judge had been hopelessly insane for at least three years and, as one result of his mental and nervous malady, had become an incurable drunkard.[1] In this condition he had refused to hear witnesses for the Government in the case of the ship Eliza, seized for violation of the revenue laws. He peremptorily ordered the vessel returned to its captain, and finally declined to allow an appeal from his decree. All this had been done with ravings, cursings, and crazed incoherences.[2]

That he was wholly incapacitated for office and unable to perform any act requiring intelligence was conceded by all. But the Constitution provided no method of removing an officer who had become insane.[3] This defect, however, gave the Republicans an ideal opportunity to put into practice their theory that impeachment was unrestricted and might be applied to any officer whom, for any reason, two thirds of the Senate deemed undesirable. "If the facts of his denying an appeal & of his intoxication, as stated in the impeachment, are proven, that will be sufficient cause for removal without further enquiry," asserted Jefferson when assured that Pickering was insane, and when asked "whether

[1] Depositions of Samuel Tenney, Ammi R. Cutter, Joshua Brackett, Edward St. Loe Livermore. (*Annals*, 8th Cong. 1st Sess. 334–42.)

[2] Testimony of John S. Sherburne, Thomas Chadbourne, and Jonathan Steele. (*Ib.* 351–56.)

[3] The wise and comprehensive Federalist Judiciary Act of 1801 covered just such cases. It provided that when a National judge was unable to discharge the duties of his office, the circuit judges should name one of their members to fill his place. (See *Annals*, 6th Cong. 2d Sess. 1545.) This very thing had been done in the case of Judge Pickering (see McMaster: *U.S.* iii, 166). It is curious that, in the debate, the Republicans did not denounce this as unconstitutional.

insanity was good cause for impeachment & removal from office." [1]

The demented judge did not, of course, appear at his trial. Instead, a petition by his son was presented, alleging the madness of his father, and praying that evidence to that effect be received by the Senate.[2] This plea was stoutly resisted, and for two days the question was debated. "The most persevering and determined opposition is made against having evidence and counsel to prove the man insane," records John Quincy Adams, "only from the fear, that if insanity should be proved, he cannot be convicted of *high crimes and misdemeanors* by acts of decisive madness." [3] Finally the determined Republicans proceeded to the trial of the insane judge for high crimes and misdemeanors, evidence of his dethroned reason to be received "in mitigation." [4] In immense disgust the House managers withdrew, because "the Senate had determined *to hear evidence*" that the accused person was insane. Before they returned, they publicly denounced the Senators for their leniency; and thus Republican discipline was restored.[5]

Jefferson was impatient. "It will take two years to try this impeachment," he complained to Senator Plumer. "The Constitution ought to be altered,"

[1] Plumer, Jan. 5, 1804, "Congress," Plumer MSS. Lib. Cong.

[2] *Annals*, 8th Cong. 1st Sess. 328–30.

[3] *Memoirs, J. Q. A.*: Adams, I, 299–300.

[4] "This," records Adams, "had evidently been settled .. out of court. And this is the way in which these men administer justice." (*Ib.*)

[5] "In the House .. speeches are making every day to dictate to the Senate how they are to proceed; and the next morning they proceed accordingly." (*Ib.* 301–02.)

he continued, "so that the President should be authorized to remove a Judge from office, on the address of the two Houses." [1] But the exasperated Republicans hastened the proceedings; and the trial did not consume two weeks all told.

If an insane man should be condemned, "it will not hereafter be necessary," declared Senator Samuel Smith of Maryland, "that a man should be guilty of high crimes and misdemeanors," the commission of which was the only Constitutional ground for impeachment. Senator Jonathan Dayton of New Jersey denounced the whole proceeding as "a mere mockery of a trial." [2] Senator John Quincy Adams, in the flurry of debate, asserted that he should "speak until [his] mouth was stopped by force." [3] Senator Nicholas of Virginia shouted "Order! order! order!" when Samuel White of Delaware was speaking. So furious became the altercation that a duel seemed possible.[4] No delay was permitted and, on March 12, 1804, the demented Pickering was, by a strictly partisan vote of 19 to 7,[5] adjudged guilty of high crimes and misdemeanors.

An incident happened which was prophetic of a

[1] Feb. 18, 1803, Plumer, 253.

[2] *Annals*, 8th Cong. 1st Sess. 365.

[3] See *Memoirs, J. Q. A.*; Adams, i, 302–04, for a vivid account of the whole incident.

[4] Plumer, March 10, 1804, "Congress," Plumer MSS. Lib. Cong.

[5] *Annals*, 8th Cong. 1st Sess. 367. "The independence of our judiciary is no more. . . I hope the time is not far distant when the people east of the North river *will manage their own affairs in their own way;* . . and that the *sound* part will separate from the *corrupt*." (Plumer to Morse, March 10, 1804, Plumer MSS. Lib. Cong.) On the unconstitutional and revolutionary conduct of the Republicans in the Pickering impeachment trial see Adams: *U.S.* ii, 158.

decline in the marvelous party discipline that had
kept the Republicans in Senate and House in solid
support of the plans of the leaders. Three Republican Senators left the Chamber in order to avoid
the balloting.[1] They would not adjudge an insane
man to be guilty of high crimes and misdemeanors,
but they were not yet independent enough to vote
against their party.[2] This, however, did not alarm
the Republican managers. They instantly struck

[1] Senators John Armstrong of New York, Stephen R. Bradley of
Vermont, and David Stone of North Carolina. Jonathan Dayton of
New Jersey and Samuel White of Delaware, Federalists, also with-
drew. (*Annals*, 8th Cong. 1st Sess. 366.) And see *Memoirs, J. Q. A..*
Adams, I, 308–09; J. Q. Adams to his father, March 8, 1805, *Writings,
J. Q. A.*: Ford, III, 110; Plumer to Park, March 13, 1804, Plumer MSS.
Lib. Cong.

Senator John Brown of Kentucky, a Republican, "could not be induced to join the majority, but, unwilling to offend them, he obtained
& has taken a leave of absence." (Plumer to Morse, March 10, 1804,
Plumer MSS. Lib. Cong.) Senator Brown had been elected President
pro tem. of the Senate, January 23, 1804.

Burr "abruptly left the Senate" to attend to his candidacy for the
governorship of New York. (Plumer, March 10, 1804, "Congress,"
Plumer MSS. Lib. Cong.) Senator Franklin of North Carolina was
then chosen President *pro tem.* and presided during the trial of Pickering. But Burr returned in time to arrange for, and preside over, the
trial of Justice Chase.

[2] The Republicans even refused to allow the report of the proceedings to be "printed in the Appendix to the Journals of the Session."
(*Memoirs, J. Q. A.*: Adams, I, 311.)

The conviction and removal of Pickering alarmed the older Feder-
alists almost as much as did the repeal of the Judiciary Act. "The
demon of party governed the decision. All who condemned were
Jeffersonians, and all who pronounced the accused not guilty were
Federalists." (Pickering to Lyman, March 4, 1804, *N.E. Federalism:*
Adams, 358–59; Lodge: *Cabot,* 450.)

"I really wish those in New England who are boasting of the independence of our Judiciary would reflect on what a slender tenure
Judges hold their offices whose political sentiments are at variance
with the dominant party." (Plumer to Park, March 13, 1804, Plumer
MSS. Lib. Cong.)

the next blow upon which they had determined more than two years before. Within an hour after John Pickering was convicted the House voted to impeach Samuel Chase.

Marshall's irascible associate on the Supreme Bench had given the Republicans a new and serious cause for hostilities against him. In less than two months after Marshall had delivered the unanimous opinion of the Supreme Court in Marbury *vs.* Madison, Justice Chase, in charging the grand jury at Baltimore, denounced Republican principles and mercilessly assailed Republican acts and purposes.

This judicial critic of democracy told the grand jury that "the bulk of mankind are governed by their passions, and not by reason. . . The late alteration of the federal judiciary . . and the recent change in our state constitution, by the establishing of universal suffrage, . . will . . take away all security for property and personal liberty . . and our republican constitution will sink into a mobocracy, the worst of all popular governments."

Chase condemned "the modern doctrines by our late reformers, that all men, in a state of society, are entitled to enjoy equal liberty and equal rights, [which] have brought this mighty mischief upon us"; — a mischief which he feared "will rapidly progress, until peace and order, freedom and property, shall be destroyed. . . Will justice be impartially administered by judges dependent on the legislature for their . . suport? Will liberty or property be protected or secured, by laws made by representatives chosen by electors, who have no property in, or a common interest with, or attachment to, the community?" [1]

Burning with anger, a young Republican member of the Maryland Legislature, John Montgomery, who had listened to this judicial tirade, forthwith savagely denounced Chase in the *Baltimore American*.[2] He demanded that the Justice be impeached and removed from the bench.[3] Montgomery hastened to send to the President [4] a copy of the paper.

Jefferson promptly wrote Nicholson: "Ought this seditious and official attack on the principles of our Constitution, and on the proceedings of a State, go unpunished? And, to whom so pointedly as yourself will the public look for the necessary measures?"

But Jefferson was not willing to appear openly. With that uncanny power of divining political currents to which coarser or simpler minds were oblivious, he was conscious of the uneasiness of Northern Republicans over ruthless impeachment and decided not to become personally responsible. "For myself," he cautioned Nicholson, "it is better that I should not interfere." [5]

Upon the advice of Nathaniel Macon,[6] Republican Speaker of the House, Nicholson concluded that it

---

[1] Exhibit VIII, *Chase Trial*, Appendix, 61–62; also see *Annals*, 8th Cong. 2d Sess. 675–76.

[2] June 13, 1803.   [3] See *Chase Trial*, 101 *et seq.*

[4] See McMaster: *U.S.* III, 162–70.

[5] Jefferson to Nicholson, May 13, 1803, *Jefferson Writings:* Washington, IV, 484.

[6] Macon to Nicholson, Aug. 6, 1803, Dodd: *Life of Nathaniel Macon*, 187–88. Macon seriously doubted the expediency and legality of the impeachment of Chase. However, he voted with his party.

would be more prudent for another to take the lead. It was well understood that he was to have Chase's place on the Supreme Bench,[1] and this fact would put him at a disadvantage if he became the central figure in the fight against the aged Justice. The procurement of the impeachment was, therefore, placed in the eager hands of John Randolph, that "unusual Phenomenon," as John Adams called him,[2] whose lust for conspicuous leadership was insatiable.

The Republican managers had carefully moulded public opinion into the belief that Chase was guilty of some monstrous crime. Months before articles of impeachment were presented to the House, *ex parte* statements against him were collected, published in pamphlet form, and scattered throughout the country. To assure wider publicity all this "evidence" was printed in the Republican organ at Washington. The accused Justice had, therefore, been tried and convicted by the people before the charges against him were even offered in the House.[3]

This preparation of the popular mind accomplished, Chase was finally impeached. Eight articles setting forth the Republican accusations were laid before the Senate. Chase was accused of everything

---

[1] Dodd, 187–88.

[2] Adams to Rush, June 22, 1806, *Old Family Letters*, 100.

[3] Chase "is very obnoxious to the *powers that be* & must be *denounced*, but articles will not be exhibited agt him this session. The Accusers have collected a volume of exparte evidence against him, printed & published it in pamphlets, & now it is publishing in the Court gazette to be diffused in every direction. . . If a party to a suit at law, . . was to practice in this manner he would merit punishment." (Plumer to Smith, March 11, 1804, Plumer MSS. Lib. Cong.)

of which anybody had complained since his appoint‑
ment to the Supreme Bench. His conduct at the
trials of Fries and Callender was set forth with te‑
dious particularity: in Delaware he had stooped "to
the level of an informer"; his charge to the grand
jury at Baltimore was an "intemperate and inflam‑
atory political harangue"; he had prostituted his
"high judicial character . . to the low purpose of an
electioneering partizan"; his purpose was "to
excite . . odium . . against the government." [1]

This curious scramble of fault-finding, which was
to turn out so fatally for the prosecution, was the
work of Randolph. When the conglomerate indict‑
ment was drawn, no one, except perhaps Jefferson,
had the faintest idea that the Republican plan would
miscarry; Randolph's multifarious charges pleased
those in Virginia, Pennsylvania, Delaware, and
Maryland who had first made them; they were so
drawn as to lay a foundation for the assault which
was to follow immediately. "These articles," wrote
John Quincy Adams, "contained in themselves a
virtual impeachment not only of Mr. Chase, but of

[1] See *supra*, chap. i. For the articles of impeachment see *Annals*,
8th Cong. 2d Sess. 85–88; *Chase Trial*, 10–11.

The Republicans, for a time, contemplated the impeachment of
Richard Peters, Judge of the United States Court for the District of
Pennsylvania, who sat with Chase during the trial of Fries. (*Annals*,
8th Cong. 1st Sess. 823–24, 850, 873–74.) But his name was dropped
because he had not "so acted in his judiciary capacity as to require
the interposition of the Constitutional powers of this House." (*Ib.*
1171.)

Peters was terrified and turned upon his fellow judge. He showered
Pickering and other friends with letters, complaining of the conduct
of his judicial associate. "If I am to be immolated let it be with some
other Victim — or for my own Sins." (Peters to Pickering, Jan. 26,
1804, Pickering MSS. Mass. Hist. Soc.)

all the Judges of the Supreme Court from the first establishment of the national judiciary." [1]

In an extended and carefully prepared speech, Senator Giles, who had drawn the rules governing the conduct of the trial in the Senate, announced the Republican view of impeachment which, he said, "is nothing more than an enquiry, by the two Houses of Congress, whether the office of any public man might not be better filled by another." Adams was convinced that "this is undoubtedly the source and object of Mr. Chase's impeachment, and on the same principle any officer may easily be removed at any time." [2]

From the time the House took action against Chase, the Federalists were in despair. "I think the Judge will be removed from Office," was Senator Plumer's opinion. [3] "The event of the impeachment is already determined," wrote Bayard before the trial began. [4] Pickering was certain that Chase would be condemned — so would any man that the House might impeach; such "measures . . are made questions of *party*, and therefore at all events to be carried into effect according to the wishes of the prime mover [Jefferson]." [5]

As the day of the arraignment of the impeached Justice approached, his friends were not comforted

---

[1] J. Q. Adams to his father, March 14, 1805, *Writings, J. Q. A.*: Ford, III, 116.

[2] Dec. 20, 1804, *Memoirs, J. Q. A.*: Adams, I, 321.

[3] Plumer to Cogswell, Jan. 4, 1805, Plumer MSS. Lib. Cong.; and see Plumer to Sheafe, Jan. 9, 1805, Plumer MSS. *loc. cit.*

[4] Bayard to Harper, Jan. 30, 1804, *Bayard Papers:* Donnan, 160.

[5] Pickering to Lyman, March 14, 1804, Lodge: *Cabot*, 450; also *N.E. Federalism:* Adams, 359.

by their estimate of the public temper. "Our public
. . will be as tame as Mr. Randolph can desire,"
lamented Ames. "You may broil Judge Chase and
eat him, or eat him raw; it shall stir up less anger
or pity, than the Six Nations would show, if Corn-
planter or Red Jacket were refused a belt of wam-
pum." [1]

When finally Chase appeared before the bar of the
Senate, he begged that the trial should be postponed
until next session, in order that he might have time
to prepare his defense. His appeal fell on remorseless
ears; the Republicans gave him only a month. But
this scant four weeks proved fatal to their purpose.
Jefferson's wise adjustment of the greatest financial
scandal in American history [2] came before the House
during this interval; and fearless, honest, but impolitic John Randolph attacked the Administration's
compromise of the Yazoo fraud with a ferocity all
but insane in its violence. Literally screaming with
rage, he assailed Jefferson's Postmaster-General
who was lobbying on the floor of the House for
the passage of the President's Yazoo plan, and delivered continuous philippics against that polluted
transaction out of which later came the third of
John Marshall's most notable opinions. [3]

In this frame of mind, nervously exhausted, physically overwrought and troubled, the most brilliant

[1] Ames to Dwight, Jan. 20, 1805, Ames, i, 338.
[2] The Yazoo fraud. No other financial scandal in our history
equaled this, if one considers the comparative wealth and population
of the country at the times other various great frauds were perpetrated.
For an account of it, see *infra*, chap. x.
[3] For Randolph's frantic speech on the Yazoo fraud and Marshall's
opinion in Fletcher *vs.* Peck, see *infra*, chap. x.

and effective Congressional partisan leader of our early history came to the trial. Moreover, Randolph had broken with the Administration and challenged Jefferson's hitherto undisputed partisan autocracy. This was the first public manifestation of that schism in the Republican Party which was never entirely healed.

Such was the situation on the 4th of February, 1805, when the Senate convened to hear and determine the case of Samuel Chase, impeached by the House for high crimes and misdemeanors, to settle by the judgment it should render the fate of John Marshall as Chief Justice of the United States, and to fix forever the place of the National Judiciary in the scheme of American government.

"Oyez! Oyez! Oyez! — All persons are commanded to keep silence on pain of imprisonment, while the grand inquest of the nation is exhibiting to the Senate of the United States, sitting as a Court of Impeachments, articles of impeachment against Samuel Chase, Associate Justice of the Supreme Court of the United States." [1]

So cried the Sergeant-at-Arms of the National Senate when, in the Chase trial, John Marshall, the Supreme Court, and the whole National Judiciary were called to judgment by Thomas Jefferson, on the bleak winter day in dismal, scattered, and quarreling Washington. An audience crowded the Senate Chamber almost to the point of suffocation. There were present not only the members of Senate

---

[1] This form was adopted in the trial of Judge Pickering. See *Annals*, 8th Cong. 1st Sess. 319.

and House, the officers of the Executive departments, and the men and women of the Capital's limited society, but also scores of eminent persons from distant parts of the country.[1]

Among the spectators were John Marshall and the Associate Justices of the Supreme Court, thoroughly conscious that they, and the institution of which they were the highest representatives, were on trial almost as much as their imprudent, rough, and outspoken fellow member of the Bench. It is not improbable that they were helping to direct the defense of Chase,[2] in which, as officials, they were personally interested, and in which, too, all their convictions as citizens and jurists were involved.

Marshall, aroused, angered, and frightened by the articles of the impeachment, had written his brother ι year before the Chase trial that they are "sufficient to alarm the friends of a pure, and, of course, an independent Judiciary, if, among those who rule our land there be any of that description."[3] At the beginning of the proceedings Chase had asked Marshall, who was then in Richmond, to write an account of what occurred at the trial of Callender, and Marshall promptly responded: "I instantly applied to my brother[4] & to Mr. Wickham[5] to state their recollection of the circumstances under which Colo. Taylors testimony was rejected.[6] They both declared that they remembred them very im-

[1] See Plumer, 323.   [2] Channing: *U.S.* IV, 287.
[3] Marshall to James M. Marshall, April 1, 1804, MS.
[4] William Marshall. See *infra*, 191–92.
[5] John Wickham, leader of the Richmond bar and one of Marshall's intimate friends.
[6] See *supra*, chap. I; and *infra*.

perfectly but that they woud endeavor to recollect what passed & commit it to writing. I shall bring it with me to Washington in february." Marshall also promised to bring other documents.

"Admitting it to be true," continues Marshall, "that on legal principles Colo. Taylors testimony was admissible, it certainly constitutes a very extraordinary ground for an impeachment. According to the antient doctrine a jury finding a verdict against the law of the case was liable to an attaint; & the amount of the present doctrine seems to be that a Judge giving a legal opinion contrary to the opinion of the legislature is liable to impeachment.

"As, for convenience & humanity the old doctrine of attaint has yielded to the silent, moderate but not less operative influence of new trials, I think the modern doctrine of impeachment should yield to an appellate jurisdiction in the legislature. A reversal of those legal opinions deemed unsound by the legislature would certainly better comport with the mildness of our character than [would] a removal of the Judge who has rendered them unknowing of his fault.

"The other charges except the 1st & 4th which I suppose to be altogether unfounded, seem still less to furnish cause for impeachment. But the little finger of [blotted out — probably "democracy"] is heavier than the loins of ———.[1]

"Farewell — With much respect and esteem. . .

"J. MARSHALL."[2]

---

[1] See 1 Kings, xii, 10.
[2] Marshall to Chase, Jan. 23, 1804, Etting MSS. Pa. Hist. Soc.

Marshall thus suggested the most radical method for correcting judicial decisions ever advanced, before or since, by any man of the first class. Appeals from the Supreme Court to Congress! Senators and Representatives to be the final judges of any judicial decision with which a majority of the House was dissatisfied! Had we not the evidence of Marshall's signature to a letter written in his well-known hand, it could not be credited that he ever entertained such sentiments. They were in direct contradiction to his reasoning in Marbury *vs.* Madison, utterly destructive of the Federalist philosophy of judicial control of legislation.

The explanation is that Marshall was seriously alarmed. By his own pen he reveals to us his state of mind before and on that dismal February day when he beheld Samuel Chase arraigned at the bar of the Senate of the United States. During the trial Marshall's bearing as a witness [1] again exhibited his trepidation. And, as we have seen, he had good cause for sharp anxiety.[2]

The avowed Republican purpose to remove him and his Federalist associates from the Supreme Bench, the settled and well-known intention of Jefferson to appoint Spencer Roane as Chief Justice when Marshall was ousted, and the certainty that this would be fatal to the execution of those fundamental principles of government to which Marshall was so passionately devoted — these important considerations fully warranted the apprehension which the Chief Justice felt and now displayed.

[1] See *infra*, 192–96.   [2] See *supra*, chap. III, 113.

Had he been indifferent to the peril that confronted him and the whole National Judiciary, he would have exhibited a woeful lack of sense and feeling. He was more than justified in resorting to any honorable expedient to save the great office he held from occupancy by a resolute and resourceful foe of those Constitutional theories, the application of which, Marshall firmly believed, was indispensable to the sound development of the American Nation.

The arrangements for the trial were as dramatic as the event itself was momentous.[1] The scenes of the impeachment prosecution of Warren Hastings were still vivid in the minds of all, and in imitation of that spectacle, the Senate Chamber was now bedecked with impressive splendor. It was aglow with theatrical color, and the placing of the various seats was as if a tragic play were to be performed.

To the right and left of the President's chair were two rows of benches with desks, the whole covered with crimson cloth. Here sat the thirty-four Senators of the United States. Three rows of benches, arranged in tiers, extended from the wall toward the center of the room; these were covered with green cloth and were occupied by the members of the House of Representatives. Upon their right an enclosure had been constructed, and in it were the members of Jefferson's Cabinet.

Beneath the permanent gallery to which the general public was admitted, a temporary gallery, supported by pillars, ran along the wall, and faced

---

[1] "Mr Burr had the sole power of making the arrangements . . for the trial." (Plumer to Sheafe, Jan. 9, 1805, Plumer MSS. Lib. Cong.)

the crimson-covered places of the Senators. At either end of it were boxes. Comfortable seats had been provided in this enclosure; and these were covered with green cloth, which also was draped over the balustrade.

This sub-gallery and the boxes were filled with ladies dressed in the height of fashion. A passage-way was left from the President's chair to the door-way. On either side of this aisle were two stalls covered with blue cloth, as were also the chairs within them. They were occupied by the managers of the House of Representatives and by the lawyers who conducted the defense.[1]

A short, slender, elegantly formed man, with pallid face and steady black eyes, presided over this Senatorial Court. He was carefully dressed, and his manners and deportment were meticulously correct. Aaron Burr, fresh from his duel with Hamilton, and under indictment in two States, had resumed his duties as Vice-President. Nothing in the bearing of this playwright character indicated in the smallest degree that anything out of the ordinary had hap-pened to him. The circumstance of his presence, however, dismayed even the most liberal of the New England Federalists. "We are indeed fallen on evil times," wrote Senator Plumer. "The high office of President is filled by an *infidel*, that of Vice-President by a *murderer*." [2]

For the first time since the Republican victory of 1800, which, but for his skill, courage, and energy in

---

[1] *Annals*, 8th Cong. 2d Sess. 100; *Chase Trial*, 2–5.
[2] Plumer to Norris, Nov. 7, 1804, Plumer, 329.

New York, would not have been achieved,[1] Burr now found himself in favor with the Administration and the Republican chieftains.[2]   Jefferson determined that Aaron Burr must be captured — at least conciliated. He could not be displaced as the presiding officer at the Chase impeachment trial; his rulings would be influential, perhaps decisive; the personal friendship and admiration of several Senators for him were well known; the emergency of the Republican Party was acute. Chase must be convicted at all hazards; and while nobody but Jefferson then doubted that this would be the result, no chances were to be taken, no precaution overlooked.

The President had rewarded the three principal witnesses against Pickering with important and lucrative offices [3] after the insane judge had been removed from the bench. Indeed he had given the vacated judgeship to one of these witnesses. But such an example Jefferson well knew would have no effect upon Burr; even promises would avail nothing with the man who for nearly three years had suffered indignity and opposition from an Administration which he, more than any one man except Jefferson himself, had placed in power.

[1] See *infra*, chap. VI.

[2] See J. Q. Adams to his father, Jan. 5, 1805, *Writings, J. Q. A.*: Ford, III, 104.

[3] Plumer, 274. "John S. Sherburne, Jonathan Steele, Michael McCleary and Richard Cutts Shannon were the principal witnesses against Pickering. Sherburne was appointed Judge [in Pickering's place]; Steele, District Attorney; McCleary, Marshal; and Shannon, Clerk of the Court. . . Steele, expecting to have been Judge refused to accept his appointment, assigning as the reason his agency in the removal of Pickering."

So it came about that Vice-President Aaron Burr, with only four weeks of official life left him, with the whole North clamorous against him because of his killing of Hamilton and an indictment of murder hanging over him in New Jersey, now found himself showered with favors by those who owed him so much and who, for nearly four years, had so grossly insulted him.

Burr's stepson, his brother-in-law, his most intimate friend, were forthwith appointed to the three most valuable and commanding offices in the new government of the Louisiana Territory, at the attractive city of New Orleans.[1] The members of the Cabinet became attentive to Burr. The President himself exercised his personal charm upon the fallen politician. Time after time Burr was now invited to dine with Jefferson at the Executive Mansion.

Nor were Presidential dinners, the bestowal of patronage hitherto offensively refused, and attentions of the Cabinet, the limit of the efforts to win the coöperation of the man who was to preside over the trial of Samuel Chase. Senator Giles drew a petition to the Governor of New Jersey begging that the prosecution of Burr for murder be dropped, and to this paper he secured the signature of nearly all the Republican Senators.[2]

Burr accepted these advances with grave and

[1] Plumer, 329-30; and see Adams: *U.S.* II, 220.

[2] Nov. 26, 1804, *Memoirs, J. Q. A.*: Adams, I, 317-18; and Adams, *U.S.* II, 220-22.

"Burr is flattered and feared by the administration." (Plumer to Thompson, Dec. 23, 1804, Plumer MSS. Lib. Cong.; and Plumer to Wilson, Dec. 7, 1804, Plumer MSS. *loc. cit.*)

reserved dignity; but he understood the purpose that inspired them, did not commit himself, and remained uninfluenced and impartial. Throughout the momentous trial the Vice-President was a model presiding officer. "He conducted with the dignity and impartiality of an angel, but with the rigor of a devil," records a Washington newspaper that was bitterly hostile to Burr personally and politically.[1]

When Chase took his place in the box, the Sergeant-at-Arms brought him a chair; but Burr, adhering to the English custom, which required

---

[1] Davis, II, 360; also Adams: *U.S.* 218-44.

"It must be acknowledged that Burr has displayed much ability, and since the first day I have seen nothing of partiality." (Cutler to Torrey, March 1, 1805, Cutler: *Life, Journals and Correspondence of Manasseh Cutler*, II, 193.)

At the beginning of the trial, however, Burr's rigor irritated the Senate: "Mr. Burr is remarkably testy — he acts more of the tyrant — is impatient, passionate — scolds — he is in a rage because we do not sit longer." (Plumer, Feb. 8, 1805, "Diary," Plumer MSS. Lib. Cong.)

"Just as the time for adjourning to morrow was to be put . . Mr. Burr said he wished to inform the Senate of some irregularities that he had observed in the Court.

"Some of the Senators as he said during the trial & while a witness was under examination walked between him & the Managers — others eat apples — & some eat cake in their seats.

"Mr. Pickering said he eat an apple — but it was at a time when the President had retired from the chair. Burr replied he did not mean him — he did not see him.

"Mr. Wright said he eat cake — he had a just right to do so — he was faint — but he disturbed nobody — He never would submit to be schooled & catechised in this manner.

"At this instance a motion was made by Bradley, who also had eaten cake, for an adjournment. Burr told Wright he was not in order — sit down. The Senate adjourned — & I left Burr and Wright scolding.

"Really, *Master Burr*, you need a ferule, or birch to enforce your lectures on polite behavior!" (*Ib.* Feb. 12, 1805; also *ib.* Jan. 2, 1805.) Burr was sharply criticized by the *Washington Federalist*, January 8, for his rude conduct at the beginning of the trial.

prisoners to stand when on trial in court, ordered it to be taken away.[1] Upon the request of the elderly Justice, however, Burr quickly relented and the desired seat was provided.[2]

Chase was, in appearance, the opposite of the diminutive and graceful Vice-President. More than six feet tall, with thick, broad, burly shoulders, he was a picture of rugged and powerful physical manhood, marred by an accumulation of fat which his generous manner of living had produced. Also he was afflicted with an agonizing gout, with which it seems so many of "the fathers" were cursed. His face was broad and massive, his complexion a brownish red.[3] "Bacon face" was a nickname applied to him by the Maryland bar.[4] His head was large, his brow wide, and his hair was thick and white with the snows of his sixty-four winters.[5]

---

[1] Plumer to Sheafe, Jan. 1805, Plumer, 330–31.

[2] *Annals*, 8th Cong. 2d Sess. 92; *Chase Trial*, 4.

[3] Dwight: *Signers of the Declaration of Independence*, 245–52.

[4] Hudson: *Journalism in the United States, 1690–1872*, 214; and see Story to Bramble, June 10, 1807, Story, i, 154.

[5] "In person, in manners, in unwieldy strength, in severity of reproof, in real tenderness of heart; and above all in intellect," he was "the living, I had almost said the exact, image of Samuel Johnson." (Story to Fay, Feb. 25, 1808, Story, i, 168.)

Chase's career had been stirring and important. Carefully educated by his father, an Episcopal clergyman, and thoroughly grounded in the law, he became eminent at the Maryland bar at a very early age. From the first his aggressive character asserted itself. He was rudely independent and, as a member of the Maryland House of Burgesses, treated the royal governor and his Tory partisans with contemptuous defiance. When the British attempted to enforce the Stamp Act, he joined a band of high-spirited young patriots who called themselves "The Sons of Liberty," and led them in their raids upon public offices, which they broke open, seizing and destroying the stamps and burning in effigy the stamp distributor.

His violent and fearless opposition to British rule and officials

The counsel that surrounded the impeached Justice were brilliant and learned.[1] They were Joseph Hopkinson, who six years before, upon Marshall's return from France, had written "Hail Columbia; or, The President's March"; Philip Barton Key, brother of the author of "The Star-Spangled Banner";[2] Robert Goodloe Harper, one of the Federalist leaders in Congress during the ascendancy of that party; and Charles Lee, Attorney-General under President Adams when Marshall was Secretary of State, and one of Marshall's most devoted friends.[3]

But in the chair next to Chase sat a man who, single-handed and alone, was more than a match for

made young Chase so popular that he was elected as one of the five Maryland delegates to the first Continental Congress that assembled during the winter of 1774. He was reëlected the following year, and was foremost in urging the measures of armed defense that ended in the appointment of Washington as Commander-in-Chief of the American forces. Disregarding the instructions of his State, Chase hotly championed the adoption of the Declaration of Independence, and was one of the signers of that document.

On the floor of Congress he denounced a member as a traitor --- one Zubly, a Georgia parson — who in terror fled the country. Chase continued in the Continental Congress until 1778 and was appointed a member of almost every important committee of that body. He became the leader of his profession in Maryland, was appointed Chief Justice of the Criminal Court of Baltimore, and elected a member of the Maryland Convention, called to ratify the National Constitution. Thereafter, he was made Chief Justice of the Supreme Court of the State. In 1796, President Washington appointed Chase as Associate Justice of the National Supreme Court of which he was conceded to be one of the ablest members. (Dwight, 245–52.)

[1] See Plumer to his brother, Feb. 25, 1805, Plumer MSS. Lib. Cong.

[2] *Maryland Historical Society Fund-Publication No. 24*, p. 20. Burr told Key that "he must not appear as counsel with his loose coat on." (Plumer, Feb. 11, 1805, "Diary," Plumer MSS. Lib. Cong.)

[3] Adams: *U.S.* ii, 227–28. Bayard strongly urged Chase to have no counsel, but to defend himself. (Bayard to Harper, Jan. 30, 1804, *Bayard Papers*: Donnan, 159–60.)

all the managers of the House put together. Luther Martin of Maryland — of medium height, broad-shouldered, near-sighted, absent-minded, shabbily attired, harsh of voice, now sixty-one years old, with gray hair beginning to grow thin and a face crimsoned by the brandy which he continually imbibed — was the dominating figure of this historic contest.[1]

---

[1] See Story's description of Martin three years later, Story to Fay, Feb. 16, 1808, Story, I, 163–64.

Luther Martin well illustrates the fleeting nature of the fame of even the greatest lawyers. For two generations he was "an acknowledged leader of the American bar," and his preëminence in that noble profession was brightened by fine public service. Yet within a few years after his death, he was totally forgotten, and to-day few except historical students know that such a man ever lived.

Martin began his practice of the law when twenty-three years of age and his success was immediate and tremendous. His legal learning was prodigious — his memory phenomenal.

Apparently, Martin was the heaviest drinker of that period of heavy drinking men. The inexplicable feature of his continuous excesses was that his mighty drinking seldom appeared to affect his professional efficiency. Only once in his long and active career did intoxication interfere with his work in court. (See *infra*, 586.)

Passionate in his loves and hates, he abhorred Jefferson with all the ardor of his violent nature; and his favorite denunciation of any bad man was, "Sir! he is as great a scoundrel as Thomas Jefferson."

For thirty years Martin was the Attorney-General of Maryland. He was the most powerful member of his State in the Convention that framed the National Constitution which he refused to sign, opposing the ratification of it in arguments of such signal ability that forty years afterward John C. Calhoun quarried from them the material for his famous Nullification speeches.

When, however, the Constitution was ratified and became the supreme law of the land, Martin, with characteristic wholeheartedness, supported it loyally and championed the Administrations of Washington and Adams.

He was the lifelong friend of the impeached justice, to whom he owed his first appointment as Attorney-General of Maryland as well as great assistance and encouragement in the beginning of his career. Chase and he were also boon companions, each filled with admiration for the talents and attainments of the other, and strikingly similar in

Weary and harried as he was, Randolph opened the trial with a speech of some skill. He contrasted the conduct of Chase in the trial of Callender with that of Marshall in a trial in Richmond in 1804 at which Marshall had presided. "Sir," said Randolph, "in the famous case of Logwood,[1] whereat the Chief Justice of the United States presided, I was present, being one of the grand jury who found a true bill against him. . . The government was as deeply interested in arresting the career of this dangerous and atrocious criminal, who had aimed his blow against the property of every man in society, as it could be in bringing to punishment a weak and worthless scribbler [Callender]."

But how had Marshall acted in the conduct of that trial? "Although," continued Randolph, "much testimony was offered by the prisoner, which did by no means go to his entire exculpation, although

their courage and fidelity to friends and principles. So the lawyer threw himself into the fight for the persecuted judge with all his astonishing strength.

When, in his old age, he was stricken with paralysis, the Maryland Legislature placed a tax of five dollars annually on all lawyers for his support. After Martin's death the bench and bar of Baltimore passed a resolution that "we will wear mourning for the space of thirty days." (*American Law Review*, I, 279.)

No biography of Martin has ever been written; but there are two excellent sketches of his life, one by Ashley M. Gould in *Great American Lawyers*: Lewis, II, 3–46; and the other by Henry P. Goddard in the *Md. Hist. Soc. Fund. Pub. No. 24.*

[1] *Annals*, 8th Cong. 2d Sess. 160–61. The case to which Randolph refers was that of the United States *vs.* Thomas Logwood, indicted in April, 1801, for counterfeiting. Logwood was tried in the United States Circuit Court at Richmond during June, 1804. Marshall, sitting with District Judge Cyrus Griffin, presided. Notwithstanding Marshall's liberality, Logwood was convicted and Marshall sentenced him to ten years' imprisonment at hard labor. (Order Book No. 4, 464, Records, U.S. Circuit Court, Richmond.)

much of that testimony was of a very questionable nature, none of it was declared *inadmissable.*" Marshall suffered it "to go to the jury, who were left to judge of its weight and credibility"; nor had he required "any interrogatories to the witnesses . . to be reduced to writing," — such a thing never had been done in Virginia before the tyrannical ruling of Chase in the trial of Callender.

"No, Sir!" he cried. "The enlightened man who presided in Logwood's case knew that, although the basest and vilest of criminals, he was entitled to *justice*, equally with the most honorable member of society." Marshall "did not avail himself of the previous and great discoveries in criminal law, of this respondent [Chase]"; Marshall "admitted the prisoner's testimony to go to the jury"; Marshall "never thought it *his right* or *his duty* to require questions to be reduced to writing"; Marshall "gave the accused *a fair trial* according to law and usage, without any innovation or departure from the established rules of criminal jurisprudence in his country."

Marshall's gentle manner and large-minded, soft-spoken rulings as a trial judge were thus adroitly made to serve as an argument for the condemnation of his associate, and for his own undoing if Chase should be convicted. Randolph denounced "the monstrous pretension that an act to be impeachable must be indictable. Where? In the Federal Courts? There, not even robbery and murder are indictable."

A judge could not, under the National law, be indicted for conducting a National court while drunk, and perhaps not in all State courts. "It is indictable nowhere for him to omit to do his duty, to refuse to hold a court. But who can doubt that both are impeachable offenses, and ought to subject the offender to removal from office?"

The autocrat of Congress then boldly announced to the Republican Senators that the House managers "confidently expect on his [Chase's] conviction. . . We shall bring forward . . such a specimen of judicial tyranny, as, I trust in God, will never be again exhibited in our country."[1]

Fifty-two witnesses were examined. It was established that, in the trial of Fries, Chase had written the opinion of the court upon the law before the jury was sworn, solely in order to save time; had withdrawn the paper and destroyed it when he found Fries's counsel resented the court's precipitate action; and, finally, had repeatedly urged them to proceed with the defense without restriction. Chase's inquisitorial conduct in Delaware was proved, and several witnesses testified to the matter and manner of his charge to the Baltimore grand jury.[2]

Every incident in the trial of Callender[3] was described by numerous witnesses.[4] George Hay,

---

[1] *Annals*, 8th Cong. 2d Sess. 163–65; *Chase Trial*, 18. Randolph disgusted the Federalists. "This speech is the most feeble — the most incorrect that I ever heard him make." (Plumer, Feb. 9, 1805, "Diary," Plumer MSS. Lib. Cong.)

[2] Two witnesses to the Baltimore incident, George Reed and John Montgomery, committed their testimony to memory as much "as ever a Presbyterian clergyman did his sermon — or an Episcopalian his prayer." (Plumer, Feb. 14, 1805, "Diary," Plumer MSS. Lib. Cong.)

[3] See *supra*, chap. I.

[4] Annals, 8th Cong. 2d Sess. 203–05; *Chase Trial*, 36–37.

who had been the most aggressive of Callender's counsel, was so anxious to help the managers that he made a bad impression on the Senate by his eagerness.[1] It developed that the whole attitude of Chase had been one of sarcastic contempt; and that Callender's counsel were more piqued by the laughter of the spectators which the witty sallies and humorous manner of the Justice excited, than they were outraged by any violence on Chase's part, or even by what they considered the illegal and oppressive nature of his rulings.

When, in defending Callender, Hay had insisted upon "a literal recital of the parts [of *The Prospect Before Us*] charged as libellous," Chase, looking around the court-room, said with an ironical smile: "It is contended . . that the book ought to be copied *verbatim et literatim*, I wonder, . . that *they* do not contend for *punctuatim* too." [2] The audience laughed. Chase's interruption of Wirt [3] by calling the young lawyer's "syllogistical" conclusion a "*non sequitur*, sir," was accompanied by an inimitable "bow" that greatly amused the listeners.

In short, the interruptions of the sardonic old Justice were, as John Taylor of Caroline testified, in "a very high degree imperative, satirical, and witty . . [and] extremely well calculated to abash and disconcert counsel." [4]

---

[1] Plumer, Feb. 11, 1805, "Diary," Plumer MSS. Lib. Cong.

[2] *Annals*, 8th Cong. 2d Sess. 200; *Chase Trial*, 35.

[3] See *supra*, chap. i.

[4] *Annals*, 8th Cong. 2d Sess. 207. John Quincy Adams's description of all of the evidence is important and entertaining:

"Not only the casual expressions dropped in private conversations among friends and intimates, as well as strangers and adversaries, in

Among the witnesses was Marshall's brother William, whom President Adams had appointed clerk of the United States Court at Richmond.[1] His testimony was important on one point. One John Heath, a Richmond attorney and a perfect stranger to Chase, had sworn that Chase, in his presence, had asked the United States Marshal, David M. Randolph, "if he had any of those creatures or people called democrats on the panel of the jury to try Callender"; that when the Marshal replied that he had "made no discrimination," the

the recess of a bed-chamber as well as at public taverns and in stage coaches, had been carefully and malignantly laid up and preserved for testimony on this prosecution; not only more witnesses examined to points of *opinion*, and called upon for discrimination to such a degree as to say whether the deportment of the Judge was *imperative* or *imperious*, but hours of interrogation and answer were consumed in evidence to *looks*, to *bows*, to tones of voice and modes of speech — to prove the insufferable grievance that Mr. Chase had more than once raised a laugh at the expense of Callender's counsel, and to ascertain the tremendous fact that he had accosted the ATTORNEY GENERAL *of Virginia* by the appellation of *Young Gentleman!!*

"If by thumbscrews, the memory of a witness trace back for a period of five years the features of the Judge's face, it could be darkened with a frown, it was to be construed into rude and contumelious treatment of the Virginia bar; if it was found lightened with a smile, 'tyrants in all ages had been notorious for their pleasantry.'

"In short, sir, Gravity himself could not keep his countenance at the nauseating littlenesses which were resorted to for proof of atrocious criminality, and indignation melted into ridicule at the puerile perseverance with which *nothings* were accumulated, with the hope of making *something* by their multitude.

"All this, however, was received because Judge Chase would not suffer his counsel to object against it. He indulged his accusers with the utmost licence of investigation which they ever derived [*sic*], and contented himself with observing to the court that he expected to be judged upon the *legal* evidence in the case." (J. Q. Adams to his father, March 8, 1805, *Writings*, *J. Q. A.*: Ford, III, 112–13.)

[1] This was the fourth member of the Marshall family upon whom offices were bestowed while Marshall was Secretary of State. (See vol. II, 560, of this work.)

Judge told him "to look over the panel and if there were any of that description, strike them off."

William Marshall, on the contrary, made oath that Chase told him that he hoped even Giles would serve on the jury — "Nay, he wished that Callender might be tried by a jury of his own politics." David M. Randolph then testified that he had never seen Heath in the Judge's chambers, that Chase "never at any time or place" said anything to him about striking any names from the jury panel, and that he never received "any instructions, verbal, or by letter, from Judge Chase in relation to the grand jury." [1]

John Marshall himself was then called to the stand and sworn. Friendly eye-witnesses record that the Chief Justice appeared to be frightened. He testified that Colonel Harvie, with whom he "was intimately acquainted," [2] had asked him to get the Marshal to excuse Harvie from serving on the jury because "his mind was completely made up . . and whatever the evidence might be, he should find the traverser not guilty." When Marshall told this to the court official, the latter said that Harvie must

---

[1] *Annals*, 8th Cong. 2d Sess. 251–62; *Chase Trial*, 65–69. "I was unable to give credence to his [Heath's] testimony." (Plumer, Feb. 12, 1805, "Diary," Plumer MSS. Lib. Cong.) Although Heath's story was entirely false, it has, nevertheless, found a place in serious history.

Marshall's brother made an excellent impression on the Senate. "His answers were both prompt & lucid — There was a frankness, a fairness & I will add a firmness that did him much credit. His testimony was [on certain points] . . a complete defense of the accused." (*Ib.* Feb. 15, 1805.)

[2] Harvie's son, Jacquelin B. Harvie, married Marshall's daughter Mary. (Paxton: *Marshall Family*, 100.)

apply to the Judge, because he "was watched," and
"to prevent any charge of improper conduct" he
would not discharge any of the jury whom he had
summoned. Marshall then induced Chase to release
Harvie "upon the ground of his being sheriff of
Henrico County and that his attendance was necessary" at the county court then in session.

Marshall said that he was in court during a part
of the Callender trial and that "there were several
circumstances that took place . . on the part both
of the bar and the bench which do not always occur
at trials. . . The counsel appeared . . to wish to
argue to the jury that the Sedition Law was unconstitutional. Mr. Chase said that that was not a
proper question to go to the jury"; and that whenever Callender's attorneys began to argue to the
contrary the court stopped them.

The Chief Justice further testified that George
Hay had addressed the court to the effect that in
this ruling Chase was "not correct in point of law,"
and again the Judge "stopped him"; that "Mr. Hay
still went on and made some political observations;
Judge Chase stopped him again and the collision
ended by Mr. Hay sitting down and folding up his
papers as if he meant to retire."

Marshall did not recollect "precisely," although
it appeared to him that "whenever Judge Chase
thought the counsel incorrect in their points, he
immediately told them so and stopped them short."
This "began early in the proceedings and increased.
On the part of the judge it seemed to be a disgust
with regard to the mode adopted by the traverser's

counsel, at least . . as to the part which Mr. Hay took in the trial."

Randolph asked Marshall whether it was the practice for courts to hear counsel argue against the correctness of rulings; and Marshall replied that "if counsel have not been already heard, it is usual to hear them in order that they may change or confirm the opinion of the court, when there is any doubt entertained." But there was "no positive rule on the subject and the course pursued by the court will depend upon circumstances: Where the judge believes that the point is perfectly clear and settled he will scarcely permit the question to be agitated. However, it is considered as decorous on the part of the judge to listen while the counsel abstain from urging unimportant arguments."

Marshall was questioned closely as to points of practice. His answers were not favorable to his Associate Justice. Did it appear to him that "the conduct of Judge Chase was mild and conciliatory" during the trial of Callender? Marshall replied that he ought to be asked what Chase's conduct was and not what he thought of it. Senator William Cocke of Tennessee said the question was improper, and Randolph offered to withdraw it. "No!" exclaimed Chase's counsel, "we are willing to abide in this trial by the opinion of the Chief Justice." Marshall declared that, except in the Callender trial, he never heard a court refuse to admit the testimony of a witness because it went only to a part and not to the whole of a charge.

Burr asked Marshall: "Do you recollect whether

the conduct of the judge at this trial was tyrannical, overbearing and oppressive?" "I will state the facts," cautiously answered the Chief Justice. "Callender's counsel persisted in arguing the question of the constitutionality of the Sedition Law, in which they were constantly repressed by Judge Chase. Judge Chase checked Mr. Hay whenever he came to that point, and after having resisted repeated checks, Mr. Hay appeared to be determined to abandon the cause, when he was desired by the judge to proceed with his argument and informed that he should not be interrupted thereafter.

"If," continued Marshall, "this is not considered tyrannical, oppressive and overbearing, I know nothing else that was so." It was usual for courts to hear counsel upon the validity of rulings "not solemnly pronounced," and "by no means usual in Virginia to try a man for an offense at the same term at which he is presented"; although, said Marshall, "my practice, while I was at the bar was very limited in criminal cases."

"Did you ever hear Judge Chase apply any unusual epithets — such as 'young men' or 'young gentlemen' — to counsel?" inquired Randolph. "I have heard it so frequently spoken of since the trial that I cannot possibly tell whether my recollection of the term is derived from expressions used in court, or from the frequent mention since made of them." But, remarked Marshall, having thus adroitly placed the burden on the irresponsible shoulders of gossip, "I am rather inclined to think that I did hear them from the judge." Randolph then drew from Marshall the startling and important fact that William Wirt was "about thirty years of age and a widower." [1]

Senator Plumer, with evident reluctance, sets down in his diary a description from which it would appear that Marshall's manner affected the Senate most unfavorably. "John Marshall is the Chief Justice of the Supreme Court of the United States. I was much better pleased with the manner in which his brother testified than with him.

"The Chief Justice really discovered too much caution — too much fear — too much cunning — He ought to have been more bold — frank & explicit than he was.

"There was in his manner an evident disposition to accommodate the Managers. That dignified frankness which his high office required did not appear. A cunning man ought never to discover the arts of the *trimmer* in his testimony." [2]

Plainly Marshall was still fearful of the outcome of the Republican impeachment plans, not only as to Chase, but as to the entire Federalist membership of the Supreme Court. His understanding of the Republican purpose, his letter to Chase, and his manner on the stand at the trial leave no doubt as to his state of mind. A Republican Supreme Court, with Spencer Roane as Chief Justice, loomed forbiddingly before him.

Chase was suffering such agony from the gout

---

[1] *Annals*, 8th Cong. 2d Sess. 262–67; *Chase Trial*, 71.

[2] Plumer, Feb. 16, 1805, "Diary," Plumer MSS. Lib. Cong.

that, when the testimony was all in, he asked to
be released from further attendance.[1] Six days before the evidence was closed, the election returns
were read and counted, and Aaron Burr "declared
Thomas Jefferson and George Clinton to be duly
elected to the respective offices of President and
Vice-President of the United States." [2] For the
first time in our history this was done publicly; on
former occasions the galleries were cleared and the
doors closed.[3]

Throughout the trial Randolph and Giles were in
frequent conference — judge and prosecutor working together for the success of the party plan.[4] On
February 20 the arguments began. Peter Early of
Georgia spoke first. His remarks were "chiefly
declamatory." [5] He said that the conduct of Chase
exhibited that species of oppression which puts
accused citizens "at the mercy of *arbitrary and
overbearing judges.*" For an hour and a half he
reviewed the charges,[6] but he spoke so badly that
"most of the members of the other House left the
chamber & a large portion of the spectators the
gallery." [7]

---

[1] Feb. 19, 1805, *Memoirs, J. Q. A.*: Adams, I, 354.

Chase did not leave Washington, and was in court when some of the
arguments were made. (See Chase to Hopkinson, March 10, 1805;
Hopkinson MSS. in possession of Edward P. Hopkinson, Phila.)

[2] Feb. 13, 1805, *Memoirs, J. Q. A.*: Adams, I, 351.

[3] *Ib.* The motion to admit the public was carried by one vote only.
(Plumer, Feb. 13, 1805, "Diary," Plumer MSS. Lib. Cong.)

[4] Feb. 13, 1805, *Memoirs, J. Q. A.*: Adams, I, 353.

[5] Feb. 20, 1805, *ib.* 355.

[6] Cutler, II, 183; also *Annals*, 8th Cong. 2d Sess. 313–29; *Chase
Trial*, 101–07.

[7] Plumer, Feb. 20, 1805, " Diary," Plumer MSS. Lib. Cong.

George Washington Campbell of Tennessee argued "long and tedious[ly]" [1] for the Jeffersonian
idea of impeachment which he held to be "a kind
of an inquest into the conduct of an officer . . and the
effects that his conduct . . may have on society."
He analyzed the official deeds of Chase by which
"the whole community seemed shocked. . . Future
generations are interested in the event." [2] He spoke
for parts of two days, having to suspend midway in
the argument because of exhaustion.[3] Like Early,
Campbell emptied the galleries and drove the members of the House, in disgust, from the floor.[4]

Joseph Hopkinson then opened for the defense.
Although but thirty-four years old, his argument
was not surpassed,[5] even by that of Martin — in
fact, it was far more orderly and logical than that
of Maryland's great attorney-general. "We appear,"
began Hopkinson, "for an ancient and infirm man,
whose better days have been worn out in the service of that country which now degrades him." The
case was "of infinite importance," truly declared
the youthful attorney. "The faithful, the scrutiniz-
ing historian, . . without fear or favor" will render
the final judgment. The House managers were following the British precedent in the impeachment of
Warren Hastings; but that celebrated prosecution
had not been instituted, as had that of Chase, on

[1] Cutler, II, 183.
[2] *Annals*, 8th Cong. 2d Sess. 329–53; *Chase Trial*, 107 *et seq.*
[3] *Memoirs, J. Q. A.*: Adams, I, 355–56.
[4] Plumer, Feb. 21, 1805, "Diary," Plumer MSS. Lib. Cong.
[5] Adams: *U.S.* II, 231. Even Randolph praised him. (*Annals*, 8th
Cong. 2d Sess. 640.)

"a petty catalogue of frivolous occurrences, more calculated to excite ridicule than apprehension, but for the alleged murder of princes and plunder of empires"; yet Hastings had been acquitted.

In England only two judges had been impeached in half a century, while in the United States "seven judges have been prosecuted criminally in about two years." Could a National judge be impeached merely for "error, mistake, or indiscretion"? Absurd! Such action could be taken only for "an indictable offense." Thus Hopkinson stated the master question of the case. In a clear, closely woven argument, the youthful advocate maintained his ground.

The power of impeachment by the House was not left entirely to the "opinion, whim, or caprice" of its members, but was limited by other provisions of the fundamental law. Chase was not charged with treason, bribery, or corruption. Had any other "high crimes and misdemeanors" been proved or even stated against him? He could not be impeached for ordinary offenses, but only for "high crimes and high misdemeanors." Those were legal and technical terms, "well understood and defined in law. . . A misdemeanor or a crime . . is an act committed or omitted, in violation of a *public* law either forbidding or commanding it. By this test, let the respondent . . stand justified or condemned."

The very nature of the Senatorial Court indicated "the grade of offenses intended for its jurisdiction. . . Was such a court created . . to scan and punish paltry errors and indiscretions, too insignificant to have a name in the penal code, too paltry for the notice of a court of quarter sessions? This is indeed employing an elephant to remove an atom too minute for the grasp of an insect."

Had Chase transgressed any State or National statute? Had he violated the common law? Nobody claimed that he had. Could any judge be firm, unbiased, and independent if he might at any time be impeached "on the mere suggestions of caprice . . condemned by the mere voice of prejudice"? No! "If his nerves are of iron, they must tremble in so perilous a situation."

Hopkinson dwelt upon the true function of the Judiciary under free institutions. "All governments require, in order to give them firmness, stability, and character, some permanent principle, some settled establishment. The want of this is the great deficiency in republican institutions." In the American Government an independent, permanent Judiciary supplied this vital need. Without it "nothing can be relied on; no faith can be given either at home or abroad." It was also "a security from oppression."

All history proved that republics could be as tyrannical as despotisms; not systematically, it was true, but as the result of "sudden gust of passion or prejudice. . . If we have read of the death of a Seneca under the ferocity of a Nero, we have read too of the murder of a Socrates under the delusion of a Republic. An independent and firm Judiciary, protected and protecting by the laws, would have snatched the one from the fury of a despot, and preserved the other from the madness of a people." [1] So

[1] *Annals*, 8th Cong. 2d Sess. 354–94; *Chase Trial*, 116–49.

spoke Joseph Hopkinson for three hours,[1] made brief and brilliant by his eloquence, logic, and learning.

Philip Barton Key of Washington, younger even than Hopkinson, next addressed the Senatorial Court. He had been ill the day before [2] and was still indisposed, but made an able speech. He analyzed, with painstaking minuteness, the complaints against his client, and cleverly turned to Chase's advantage the conduct of Marshall in the Logwood case.[3] Charles Lee then spoke for the defense; but what he said was so technical, applying merely to Virginia legal practice of the time, that it is of no historical moment.[4]

When, on the next day, February 23, Luther Martin rose, the Senate Chamber could not contain even a small part of the throng that sought the Capitol to hear the celebrated lawyer. If he "*only* appeared in defense of a friend," said Martin, he would not be so gravely concerned; but the case was plainly of highest possible importance, not only to all Americans then living, but to "posterity." It would "establish a most important precedent as to future cases of impeachment." An error now would be fatal.

For what did the Constitution authorize the

[1] Feb. 21, 1805, *Memoirs, J. Q. A.*: Adams, I, 356.
"The effect on the auditory [was] prodigiously great." (Cutler, II, 184.)
"His argument . . was one of the most able . . I ever heard." (Plumer, Feb. 21, 1805, "Diary," Plumer MSS. Lib. Cong.)
[2] Feb. 22, 1805, *Memoirs, J. Q. A.*: Adams, I, 356.
[3] *Annals*, 8th Cong. 2d Sess. 394–413; see also *Chase Trial*, 149–62; and Cutler, II, 184.
[4] *Annals*, 8th Cong. 2d Sess. 413–29; *Chase Trial*, 162–72.

House to impeach and the Senate to try an officer of the National Government? asked Martin. Only for "an indictable offense." Treason and bribery, specifically named in the Constitution as impeachable offenses, were also indictable. It was the same with "other high crimes and misdemeanors," the only additional acts for which impeachment was provided. To be sure, a judge might do deeds for which he could be indicted that would not justify his impeachment, as, for instance, physical assault "provoked by insolence." But let the House managers name one act for which a judge could be impeached that did not also subject him to indictment.

Congress could pass a law making an act criminal which had not been so before; but such a law applied only to deeds committed after, and not to those done before, its passage. Yet if an officer might, years after the event, be impeached, convicted, and punished for conduct perfectly legal at the time, "could the officers of Government ever know how to proceed?" Establish such a principle and "you leave your judges, and all your other officers, at the mercy of the prevailing party."

Had Chase "used *unusual*, rude and *contemptuous* expressions towards the prisoner's counsel" in the Callender case, as the articles of impeachment charged? Even so, this was "rather a violation of the principles of politeness, than the principles of law; rather the want of decorum, than the commission of a *high crime and misdemeanor*." Was a judge to be impeached and removed from office because his deportment was not elegant?

The truth was that Callender's counsel had not acted in his interest and had cared nothing about him; they had wished only "to hold up the prosecution as oppressive" in order to "excite public indignation against the court and the Government." Had not Hay just testified that he entertained "no hopes of convincing the court, and scarcely the faintest expectation of inducing the jury to believe that the sedition law was unconstitutional"; but that he had wished to make an "impression upon the public mind. . . What barefaced, what unequalled hypocrisy doth he admit that he practiced on that occasion! What egregious trifling with the court!" exclaimed Martin.

When Chase had observed that Wirt's syllogism was a "*non sequitur*," the Judge, it seems, had "bowed." Monstrous! But "as *bows*, sir, according to the manner they are *made*, may . . convey very different meanings," why had not the witness who told of it, "given us a *fac simile* of it?" The Senate then could have judged of "the propriety" of the bow. "But it seems this *bow*, together with the '*non sequitur*' entirely discomfitted poor Mr. Wirt, and down he sat 'and never word spake more!'" By all means let Chase be convicted and removed from the bench — it would never do to permit National judges to make bows in any such manner!

But alas for Chase! He had committed another grave offense — he had called William Wirt "*young* gentleman" in spite of the fact that Wirt was actually thirty years old and a widower. Perhaps Chase did not know "of these circumstances"; still, "if he had, considering that Mr. Wirt was a widower, he certainly erred on the right side . . in calling *him* a *young* gentleman." [1]

When the laughter of the Senate had subsided, Martin, dropping his sarcasm, once more emphasized the vital necessity of the independence of the Judiciary. "We boast" that ours is a "government of laws. But how can it be such, unless the laws, while they exist, are sacredly and impartially, without regard to popularity, carried into execution?" Only independent judges can do this. "Our property, our liberty, our lives, can only be protected and secured by such judges. With this honorable Court it remains, whether we shall have such judges!" [2]

Martin spoke until five o'clock without food or any sustenance, "except two glasses of wine and water"; he said he had not even breakfasted that morning, and asked permission to finish his argument next day.

When he resumed, he dwelt on the liberty of the press which Chase's application of the Sedition Law to Callender's libel was said to have violated. "My honorable client with many other respectable characters . . considered it [that law] as a wholesome and necessary restraint" upon the licentiousness of the press. [3] Martin then quoted with telling effect from Franklin's denunciation of newspapers. [4] "Franklin, himself a printer," had been "as great an advocate

[1] *Annals*, 8th Cong. 2d Sess. 429–82; *Chase Trial*, 173 *et seq.*

[2] *Annals*, 8th Cong. 2d Sess. 483.   [3] *Ib.* 484–87.

[4] See résumé of Franklin's indictment of the press in vol. i, 268–69, of this work.

for the liberty of the press, as any reasonable man ought to be"; yet he had "declared that unless the slander and calumny of the press is restrained by some other law, it will be restrained by club law." Was not that true?

If men cannot be protected by the courts against "base calumniators, they will become their own avengers. And to the bludgeon, the sword or the pistol, they will resort for that purpose." Yet Chase stood impeached for having, as a judge, enforced the law against the author of "one of the most flagitious libels ever published in America." [1]

Throughout his address Martin mingled humor with logic, eloquence with learning.[2] Granted, he said, that Chase had used the word "damned" in his desultory conversation with Triplett during their journey in a stage. "However it may sound elsewhere in the United States, I cannot apprehend it will be considered *very* offensive, *even* from the mouth of a judge on this side of the Susquehanna; — to the southward of that river it is in familiar use . . supplying frequently the place of the word 'very' . . connected with subjects the most pleasing; thus we say indiscriminately a very good or a damned good bottle of wine, a damned good dinner, or a damned clever fellow." [3]

Martin's great speech deeply impressed the Senate with the ideas that Chase was a wronged

[1] *Annals*, 8th Cong. 2d Sess. 488; *Chase Trial*, *223.
[2] "Mr. Martin really possesses much legal information & a great fund of good humour, keen satire & poignant wit . . he certainly has talents." (Plumer, Feb. 23, 1805, "Diary," Plumer MSS. Lib. Cong.)
[3] *Annals*, 8th Cong. 2d Sess. 489; *Chase Trial*, *224.

man, that the integrity of the whole National Judicial establishment was in peril, and that impeachment was being used as a partisan method of placing the National Bench under the rod of a political party. And all this was true.

Robert Goodloe Harper closed for the defense. He was intolerably verbose, but made a good argument, well supported by precedents. In citing the example which Randolph had given as a good cause for impeachment — the refusal of a judge to hold court — Harper came near, however, making a fatal admission. This, said Harper, would justify impeachment, although perhaps not an indictment. Most of his speech was a repetition of points already made by Hopkinson, Key, and Martin. But Harper's remarks on Chase's charge to the Baltimore grand jury were new, that article having been left to him.

"Is it not lawful," he asked, "for an aged patriot of the Revolution to warn his fellow-citizens of dangers, by which he supposes their liberties and happiness to be threatened?" That was all that Chase's speech from the bench in Baltimore amounted to. Did his office take from a judge "the liberty of speech which belongs to every citizen"? Judges often made political speeches on the stump — "What law forbids [them] to exercise these rights by a charge from the bench?" That practice had "been sanctioned by the custom of this country from the beginning of the Revolution to this day."

Harper cited many instances of the delivery by

judges of political charges to grand juries, beginning with the famous appeal to the people to fight for independence from British rule, made in a charge to a South Carolina grand jury in 1776.[1]

The blows of Chase's strong counsel, falling in unbroken succession, had shaken the nerve of the House managers. One of these, Joseph H. Nicholson of Maryland, now replied. Posterity would indeed be the final judge of Samuel Chase. Warren Hastings had been acquitted; "but is there any who hears me, that believes he was innocent?" The judgment of the Senate involved infinitely more than the fortunes of Chase; by it "must ultimately be determined whether justice shall hereafter be impartially administered or whether the rights of the citizen are to be prostrated at the feet of overbearing and tyrannical judges."

Nicholson denied that the House managers had "resorted to the forlorn hope of contending that an impeachment was not a criminal prosecution, but a mere inquest of office. . . If declarations of this kind have been made, in the name of the Managers, I here disclaim them. We do contend that this is a criminal prosecution, for offenses committed in the discharge of high official duties." [2]

The Senate was dumbfounded, the friends of Chase startled with joyful surprise; a gasp of amazement ran through the overcrowded Chamber! Nicholson had abandoned the Republican position — and at a moment when Harper had all but admitted it to be

---

[1] *Annals*, 8th Cong. 2d Sess. 556; *Chase Trial*, *205-44.
[2] *Annals*, 8th Cong. 2d Sess. 560-62; *Chase Trial*, 237 *et seq.*

sound. What could this mean but that the mighty
onslaughts of Martin and Hopkinson had disconcerted the managers, or that Republican Senators
were showing to the leaders signs of weakening in
support of the party doctrine.

At any rate, Nicholson's admission was an irre-
trievable blunder. He should have stoutly championed his party's theory upon which Chase had
been impeached and thus far tried, ignored the
subject entirely, or remained silent. Sadly confused, he finally reversed his argument and swung
back to the original Republican theory.

He cited many hypothetical cases where an officer
could not be haled before a criminal court, but could
be impeached. One of these must have furnished
cause for secret mirth to many a Senator: "It is possible," said Nicholson, "that the day may arrive
when a President of the United States . . may endeavor to influence [Congress] by holding out threats
or inducements to them. . . The hope of an office
may be held out to a Senator; and I think it cannot
be doubted, that for this the President would be
liable to impeachment, although there is no positive
law forbidding it."

Lucky for Nicholson that Martin had spoken before him and could not reply; fortunate for Jefferson that the "impudent Federal Bulldog," [1] as the
President afterward styled Martin, could not now be
heard. For his words would have burned the paper
on which the reporters transcribed them. Every
Senator knew how patronage and all forms of

---

[1] See Jefferson to Hay, *infra*, chap. VIII.

Executive inducement and coercion had been used by the Administration in the passage of most important measures — the Judiciary repeal, the Pickering impeachment, the Yazoo compromise, the trial of Chase. From the floor of the House John Randolph had just denounced, with blazing wrath, Jefferson's Postmaster-General for offering Government contracts to secure votes for the Yazoo compromise.[1]

For two hours and a half Nicholson continued,[2] devoting himself mainly to the conduct of Chase during the trial of Fries. He closed by pointing out the inducements to a National judge to act as a tyrannical tool of a partisan administration — the offices with which he could be bribed, the promotions by which he could be rewarded. The influence of the British Ministry over the judges has been "too flagrant to be mistaken." For example, in Ireland "an overruling influence has crumbled [an independent judiciary] into ruins. The demon of destruction has entered their courts of justice, and spread desolation over the land. Execution has followed execution, until the oppressed, degraded and insulted nation has been made to tremble through every nerve, and to bleed at every pore."

The fate of Ireland would be that of America, if an uncontrolled Judiciary were allowed to carry out, without fear of impeachment, the will of a high-handed President, in order to win the preferments he had to offer. Already "some of our judges have

[1] See *infra*, chap. x.
[2] *Memoirs, J. Q. A.*: Adams, I, 358.

been elevated to places of high political importance. . . Let us nip the evil in the bud, or it may
grow to an enormous tree, bearing destruction upon
every branch." [1]

Cæsar A. Rodney of Delaware strove to repair
the havoc Nicholson had wrought; he made it worse.
The trial was, he said, "a spectacle truly solemn and
impressive . . a trial of the first importance, because
of the first impression; . . a trial . . whose novelty
and magnitude have excited so much interest . . that
it seems to have superseded for the moment, not only
every other grave object or pursuit, but every other
fashionable amusement or dissipation." [2]

Rodney flattered Burr, whose conduct of the
trial had been "an example worthy of imitation."
He cajoled the Senators, whose attitude he had "observed with heartfelt pleasure and honest pride";
and he warned them not to take as a precedent
the case of Warren Hastings, "that destroyer of the
people of Asia, that devastator of the East," —
murderer of men, violator of *zenanas*, destroyer of
sacred treaties, but yet acquitted by the British
House of Lords.

Counsel for Chase had spoken with "the fascinating voice of eloquence and the deluding tongue of
ingenuity"; but Rodney would avoid "everything

---

[1] *Annals*, 8th Cong. 2d Sess. 582; *Chase Trial*, 237–43.

[2] *Annals*, 8th Cong. 2d Sess. 583.

This was an under-statement of the facts; for the first time the celebration of Washington's birthday was abandoned in the National
Capital. (Plumer, 326.) Plumer says that this was done because the
celebration might hurt Chase, "for there are senators who for the veri-
est trifles may be brought to vote against him." (Feb. 22, 1805, "Congress," Plumer MSS. Lib. Cong.)

like declamation" and speak "in the temperate language of reason." [1] He was sure that "the weeping voice of history will be heard to deplore the oppressive acts and criminal excesses [of Samuel Chase]. . . In the dark catalogue of criminal enormities, perhaps few are to be found of deeper dye" than those named in the articles of impeachment. "The independence of the Judiciary, the political tocsin of the day, and *the alarm bell of the night*, has been rung through every change in our ears. . . The poor hobby has been literally rode to death." Rodney was for a "rational independence of the Judiciary," but not for the "inviolability of judges more than of Kings.[2] In this country I am afraid the doctrine has been carried to such an extravagant length, that the Judiciary may be considered like a spoiled child."

An independent Judiciary, indeed! "We all know that an associate justice may sigh for promotion, and may be created a Chief Justice,[3] while . . more than one Chief Justice has been appointed a Minister Plenipotentiary." [4] With what result? Had judges stood aloof from politics — or had they "united in the *Io triumphe* which the votaries and idolators of power have sung to those who were seated in the car of Government? Have they made no offerings at the shrine of party; have they not

---

[1] *Annals*, 8th Cong. 2d Sess. 583–84; *Chase Trial*, 243–56.

[2] *Annals*, 8th Cong. 2d Sess. 585–87.

[3] Rodney here refers to the Republican allegation that Chase tried to secure appointment as Chief Justice by flattering Adams through charges to juries, rulings in court, and speeches on the stump.

[4] John Jay to England and Oliver Ellsworth to France. (See vol. II, 113, 502, of this work.)

preached political sermons from the bench, in which they have joined chorus with the anonymous scribblers of the day and the infuriate instruments of faction?"[1]

In this fashion Rodney began a song of praise of Jefferson, for the beneficence of whose Administration "the lamentable annals of mankind afford no example." After passing through many "citadels" and "Scean gates," and other forms of rhetorical architecture, he finally discovered Chase "seated in a curricle of passion" which the Justice had "driven on, Phæton-like, . . with destruction, persecution, and oppression" following.

At last the orator attempted to discuss the law of the impeachment, taking the double ground that an officer could be removed for any act that two thirds of the Senate believed to be not "good behavior," and that the Chase impeachment was "a criminal prosecution." For parts of two days [2] Rodney examined every phase of the charges in a distracting mixture of high-flown language, scattered learning, extravagant metaphor, and jumbled logic.[3] His speech was a wretched performance, so cluttered with tawdry rhetoric and disjointed argument that it would have been poor even as a stump speech.

In an address that enraged the New England Federalists, Randolph closed for the House managers.[4] He was late in arriving at the Senate Cham-

[1] *Annals*, 8th Cong. 2d Sess. 587–89.
[2] *Memoirs, J. Q. A.*: Adams, I, 359.
[3] *Annals*, 8th Cong. 2d Sess. 583–641; *Chase Trial*, 243–56.
[4] Cutler announced it as "an outrageous, infuriated declamation.

ber. He had been so ill the day before that Nicholson, because of Randolph's "habitual indisposition," had asked the Senate to meet two hours later than the usual time.[1] Sick as he was, without his notes (which he had lost), Randolph nevertheless made the best argument for the prosecution. Wasting no time, he took up the theory of impeachment upon which, he said, "the wildest opinions have been advanced" — for instance, "that an offense, to be impeachable, must be indictable." Why, then, had the article on impeachment been placed in the Constitution at all? Why "not have said, at once, that any . . officer . . convicted on indictment should (*ipso facto*) be removed from office? This would be coming at the thing by a short and obvious way." [2]

Suppose a President should veto every act of Congress "indiscriminately"; it was his Constitutional right to do so; he could not be indicted, but would anybody say he could not be impeached? Or if, at a short session, the President should keep back until the last moment all bills passed within the previous ten days, as the Constitution authorized him to do, so that it would be a physical impossibility for the two Houses to pass the rejected measures over the President's veto, he could not be indicted for this abuse of power; but surely "he could be impeached, removed and disqualified." [3]

which might have done honor to Marat, or Robespierre." (Cutler, II, 184.)

[1] *Memoirs, J. Q. A.*: Adams, I, 359.
[2] *Annals*, 8th Cong. 2d Sess. 642; *Chase Trial*, 256.
[3] *Annals*, 8th Cong. 2d Sess. 644; *Chase Trial*, 257.

Randolph's Virginia soul was deeply stirred by
what he considered Chase's alternate effrontery
and cowardice. Is such a character "fit to preside
in a court of justice? . . Today, haughty, violent,
imperious; tomorrow, humble, penitent and submissive. . . . Is this a character to dispense law and
justice to this nation? No, Sir!" Randolph then
drew an admirable picture of the ideal judge: "firm,
indeed, but temperate, mild though unyielding,
neither a blustering bravo, nor a timid poltroon." [1]

As far as he could go without naming him, Randolph described John Marshall. Not without result
had the politically experienced Chief Justice conciliated the House managers in the manner that had so
exasperated the Federalist Senators. He would not
thereafter be impeached if John Randolph could
prevent.

With keen pleasure at the annoyance he knew
his words would give to Jefferson,[2] Randolph continued to praise Marshall. The rejection of Colonel
Taylor's testimony at the Callender trial was contrary to "the universal practice of our courts."
On this point "what said the Chief Justice of the
United States,' on whose evidence Randolph said
he specially relied? "He never knew such a case [to]
occur before. He never heard a similar objection
advanced by any court, until that instance. And
this is the cautious and guarded language of a man
placed in the delicate situation of being compelled
to give testimony against a brother judge."

[1] *Annals*, 8th Cong. 2d Sess. 644–45; *Chase Trial*, 258.
[2] See *infra*, chap. x.

With an air of triumph Randolph asked: "Can anyone doubt Mr. Marshall's thorough acquaintance with our laws? Can it be pretended that any man is better versed in their theory and practice? And yet in all his extensive reading, his long and extensive practice, in the many trials of which he has been spectator, and the yet greater number at which he has assisted, he had never witnessed such a case." Chase alone had discovered "this fatal novelty, this new and horrible doctrine that threatens at one blow all that is valuable in our criminal jurisprudence."

Had Martin shown that Chase was right in requiring questions to be reduced to writing? "Here again," declared Randolph, "I bottom myself upon the testimony of the same great man, yet more illustrious for his abilities than for the high station that he fills, eminent as it is." And he recited the substance of Marshall's testimony on this point. Consider his description of the bearing of Chase toward counsel! "I again ask you, what said the Chief Justice? . . And what did he *look?* [1] He felt all the delicacy of his situation, and, as he could not approve, he declined giving any opinion on the demeanor of his associate." [2] In such manner Randolph extolled Marshall.

Again he apostrophized the Chief Justice. If Fries and Callender "had had fair trials, our lips would have been closed in eternal silence. Look at the case of Logwood: The able and excellent judge whose

[1] See *supra*, 196.
[2] *Annals*, 8th Cong. 2d Sess. 651–52; *Chase Trial*, 266.

worth was never fully known until he was raised to
the bench . . uttered not one syllable that could
prejudice the defense of the prisoner." Once more
he contrasted the judicial manners and rulings of
Marshall with those of Chase: "The Chief Justice
knew that, sooner or later, the law was an over-
match for the dishonest, and . . he disdained to
descend from his great elevation to the low level of
a public prosecutor."

The sick man spoke for two hours and a half, his
face often distorted and his body writhing with pain.
Finally his tense nerves gave way. Only public duty
had kept him to his task, he said. "In a little time
and I will dismiss you to the suggestions of your
own consciences. My weakness and want of ability
prevent me from urging my cause as I could wish,
but" — here the overwrought and exhausted man
broke into tears — "it is the last day of my sufferings and of yours."

Mastering his indisposition, however, Randolph
closed in a passage of genuine power: "We adjure
you, on behalf of the House of Representatives and
of all the people of the United States, to exorcise
from our Courts the baleful spirit of party, to give
an awful memento to our judges. In the name of the
nation, I demand at your hands the award of justice
and of law." [1]

---

[1] *Annals*, 8th Cong. 2d Sess. 641–62. John Quincy Adams notes
in his diary that Randolph spoke for more than two hours "with as
little relation to the subject matter as possible — without order, connection, or argument; consisting altogether of the most hackneyed
commonplaces of popular declamation." Throughout, records Adams,
there was "much distortion of face and contortion of body, tears,
groans and sobs." (*Memoirs, J. Q. A.*: Adams, I, 359.)

So ended this unequal forensic contest in one of the most fateful trials in American history. The whole country eagerly awaited tidings of the judgment to be rendered by the Senatorial tribunal. The fate of the Supreme Court, the character of the National Judiciary, the career of John Marshall, depended upon it. Even union or disunion was involved; for if Chase should be convicted, another and perhaps final impulse would be given to the secessionist movement in New England, which had been growing since the Republican attack on the National Judiciary in 1802.[1]

When the Senate convened at half-past twelve on March 1, 1805, a dense mass of auditors filled every inch of space in the Senate Chamber.[2] Down the narrow passageway men were seen bearing a couch on which lay Senator Uriah Tracy of Connecticut, pale and sunken from sickness. Feebly he rose and took one of the red-covered seats of the Senatorial judges.[3]

"The Sergeants-at-Arms will face the spectators and seize and commit to prison the first person who

---

"His speech . . was devoid of argument, method or consistency — but was replete with invective & even vulgarity. . . I never heard him deliver such a weak feeble & deranged harangue." (Plumer to his wife, Feb. 28, 1805, Plumer MSS. Lib. Cong.)

"After he sat down — he threw his feet upon the table — distorted his features & assumed an appearance as disgusting as his harangue." (Plumer, Feb. 27, 1805, "Diary," Plumer MSS. Lib. Cong.)

[1] See *supra*, chaps. II and III; *infra*, chap. VI, and vol. IV, chap. I.

[2] "There was a vast concourse of people . . and great solemnity." (Cutler to Torrey, March 1, 1805, Cutler, II, 193.) "The galleries were crowded — many ladies. I never witnessed so general & so deep an anxiety." (Plumer to his wife, March 1, 1805, Plumer MSS. Lib. Cong.)

[3] Plumer, 323.

makes the smallest noise or disturbance," sternly ordered Aaron Burr.

"The secretary will read the first article of impeachment," he directed.

"Senator Adams of Massachusetts! How say you? Is Samuel Chase, the respondent, guilty of high crimes and misdemeanors as charged in the article just read?"

"Not guilty!" responded John Quincy Adams.

When the name of Stephen R. Bradley, Republican Senator from Vermont, was reached, he rose in his place and voted against conviction. The auditors were breathless, the Chamber filled with the atmosphere of suspense. It was the first open break in the Republican ranks. Two more such votes and the carefully planned battle would be lost to Jefferson and his party.

"Not guilty!" answered John Gaillard, Republican Senator from South Carolina.

Another Republican defection and all would be over. It came from the very next Senator whose name Aaron Burr pronounced, and from one whose answer will forever remain an enigma.

"Senator Giles of Virginia! How say you? Is Samuel Chase guilty of the high crimes and misdemeanors as charged in the articles just read?"

"Not guilty!"

Only sixteen Senators voted to impeach on the first article, nine Republicans aligning themselves with the nine Federalists.

The vote on the other articles showed varying results; on the fourth, fourteen Senators responded

"Guilty!"; on the fifth, the Senate was unanimous for Chase.

Upon the eighth article — Chase's political charge to the Baltimore grand jury — the desperate Republicans tried to recover, Giles now leading them. Indeed, it may be for this that he cast his first vote with his party brethren from the North — he may have thought thus to influence them on the one really strong charge against the accused Justice. If so, his stratagem was futile. The five Northern Republicans (Bradley and Smith of Vermont, Mitchell and Smith of New York, and John Smith of Ohio) stood firm for acquittal as did the obstinate John Gaillard of South Carolina.[1]

The punctilious Burr ordered the names of Senators and their recorded answers to be read for verification.[2] He then announced the result: "It appears that there is not a constitutional majority of votes finding Samuel Chase, Esq. guilty of any one article. It therefore becomes my duty to declare that Samuel Chase, Esq. stands acquitted of all the articles exhibited by the House of Representatives against him."[3]

The fight was over. There were thirty-four Senators, nine of them Federalists, twenty-five Republi-

---

[1] *Annals*, 8th Cong. 2d Sess. 665–69; *Memoirs, J. Q. A.*: Adams, I, 362–63.　　　　　　　[2] *Ib.* 363.

[3] *Annals*, 8th Cong. 2d Sess. 669. By this time Burr had changed to admiration the disapproval with which the Federalist Senators had, at first, regarded his conduct of the trial. "Mr. Burr has certainly, on the whole, done himself, the Senate, and the Nation honor by the dignified manner in which he has presided over this high and numerous court," testifies Senator Plumer, notwithstanding his deep prejudice against Burr. (Plumer, March 1, 1805, "Diary," Plumer MSS. Lib. Cong.)

cans. Twenty-two votes were necessary to convict. At their strongest the Republicans had been able to muster less than four fifths of their entire strength. Six of their number — the New York and Vermont Senators, together with John Gaillard of South Carolina and John Smith of Ohio — had answered "not guilty" on every article.

For the first time since his appointment, John Marshall was secure as the head of the Supreme Bench.[1] For the first time since Jefferson's election, the National Judiciary was, for a period, rendered independent. For the first time in five years, the Federalist members of the Nation's highest tribunal could go about their duties without fear that upon them would fall the avenging blade of impeachment which had for half a decade hung over them. One of the few really great crises in American history had passed.[2]

"The greatest and most important trial ever held in this nation has terminated justly," wrote Senator Plumer to his son. "The venerable judge whose head bears the frost of seventy winters,[3] is honorably acquitted. I never witnessed, in any place, such a display of learning as the counsel for the accused exhibited." [4]

Chagrin, anger, humiliation, raged in Randolph's heart. His long legs could not stride as fast as his

[1] See Adams: *U.S.* II, 243.

[2] See Plumer, 324; *Memoirs, J. Q. A.* : Adams, I, 371; Adams: *John Randolph*, 131–32, 152; Channing: *Jeff. System*, 120; Adams: *U.S.* II, 243.

[3] Plumer here adds six years to Chase's age — an unusual inaccuracy in the diary of that born newspaper reporter.

[4] Plumer to his son, March 3, 1805, Plumer. 325.

frenzy, when, rushing from the scene of defeat, he flew to the floor of the House. There he offered an amendment to the Constitution providing that the President might remove National judges on the joint address of both Houses of Congress.[1] "Tempest in the House," records Cutler.[2]

Nicholson was almost as frantic with wrath, and quickly followed with a proposal so to amend the Constitution that State Legislatures might, at will, recall Senators.[3]

Republicans now began to complain to their party foes of one another. Over a "rubber of whist" with John Quincy Adams, Senator Jackson of Georgia, even before the trial, had spoken "slightingly both of Mr. John Randolph and of Mr. Nicholson";[4] and this criticism of Republicans *inter se* now increased.

Jefferson's feelings were balanced between grief and glee; his mourning over the untoward result of his cherished programme of judicial reform was ameliorated by his pleasure at the overthrow of the unruly Randolph,[5] who had presumed to dissent from the President's Georgia land policy.[6] The great politician's cup of disappointment, which the acquittal of Chase had filled, was also sweetened by the knowledge that Republican restlessness in the Northern States would be quieted; the Federalists who were ready, on other grounds, to come to his

[1] *Annals*, 8th Cong. 2d Sess. 1213; and see *Annual Report, Am. Hist. Assn. 1896*, II, 64; also Adams: *U.S.* II, 240.

[2] Cutler, II, 185.

[3] *Annals*, 8th Cong. 2d Sess. 1213; and see J. Q. Adams to his father, March 14, 1805, *Writings, J. Q. A.*: Ford, III, 117.

[4] Jan. 30, 1805, *Memoirs, J. Q. A.*: Adams, I, 341.

[5] See Adams: *U.S.* II, 243.   [6] See *infra*, chap. X.

standard would be encouraged to do so; and the New England secession propaganda would be deprived of a strong argument. He confided to the gossipy William Plumer, the Federalist New Hampshire Senator, that "impeachment is a farce which will not be tried again." [1]

The Chief Justice of the United States, his peril over, was silent and again serene, his wonted composure returned, his courage restored. He calmly awaited the hour when the wisdom of events should call upon him to render another and immortal service to the American Nation. That hour was not to be long delayed.

[1] Plumer, 325. Jefferson soon took Plumer into the Republican fold.

CHAPTER V

BIOGRAPHER

Marshall has written libels on one side. (Jefferson.)

What seemed to him to pass for dignity, will, by his reader, be pronounced dullness. (Edinburgh Review.)

That work was hurried into the world with too much precipitation. It is one of the most desirable objects I have in this life to publish a corrected edition. (Marshall.)

ALTHOUGH the collapse of the Chase impeachment made it certain that Marshall would not be removed from office, and he was thus relieved from one source of sharp anxiety, two other causes of worry served to make this period of his life harried and laborious. His heavy indebtedness to Denny Fairfax [1] continuously troubled him; and, worse still for his peace of mind, he was experiencing the agonies of the literary composer temperamentally unfitted for the task, wholly unskilled in the art, and dealing with a subject sure to arouse the resentment of Jefferson and all his followers. Marshall was writing the "Life of Washington."

In a sense it is fortunate for us that he did so, since his long and tiresome letters to his publishers afford us an intimate view of the great Chief Justice and reveal him as very human. But the biography itself was to prove the least satisfactory of all the labors of Marshall's life.

Not long after the death of Washington, his nephew, Bushrod Washington, had induced Marshall

[1] See vol. II, 210–12, of this work.

to become the biographer of "the Father of his
Country." Washington's public and private papers
were in the possession of his nephew. Although it
was advertised that these priceless original materials were to be used in this work exclusively, many
of Washington's writings had already been used by
other authors.

Marshall needed little urging to undertake this
monumental labor. Totally unfamiliar with the
exhausting toil required of the historian, he deemed
it no great matter to write the achievements of his
idolized leader. Moreover, he was in pressing need
of money with which to pay the remaining $31,500 [1]
which his brother and he still owed on the Fairfax
purchase, as well as the smaller but yet annoying
sum due their brother-in-law, Rawleigh Colston, for
his share of the estate which the Marshall brothers
had bought of him.[2] To discharge these obligations,
Marshall had nothing but his salary and the income
from his lands, which were wholly insufficient to
meet the demands upon him. Some of his plantations, in fact, were "productive only of expense &
vexation." [3]

Marshall and Bushrod Washington made extravagant estimates of the prospective sales of the
biography and of the money they would receive.
Everybody, they thought, would be eager to buy the
true story of the life of America's "hero and sage."
Perhaps the multitude could not afford volumes so
expensive as those Marshall was to write, but there

[1] See *infra;* also vol. II, 211, of this work.
[2] Marshall to James M. Marshall, April 1, 1804, MS.
[3] Marshall to Peters, Oct. 12, 1815, Peters MSS. Pa Hist. Soc.

would be tens of thousands of prosperous Federalists who could be depended upon to purchase at a generous price a definitive biography of George Washington.[1]

Nor was the color taken from these rosy expectations by the enthusiasm of those who wished to publish the biography. When it became known that the book was to be produced, many printers applied to Bushrod Washington "to purchase the copyright,"[2] among them C. P. Wayne, a successful publisher of Philadelphia, who made two propositions to bring out the work. After a consultation with Marshall, Bushrod Washington wrote Wayne: "Being ignorant of such matters . . we shall therefore decline any negotiation upon the subject for the present."[3]

After nearly two years of negotiation, Marshall and his associate decided that the biography would require four or five volumes, and arrived at the modest opinion that there would be "30,000 subscribers in America. . . Less than a dollar a volume cannot be thought of," and this price should yield to the author and his partner "$150,000, supposing there to be five volumes. This . . would content us, whilst it would leave a very large profit" to the publisher. But, since the number of subscribers could not be foretold with exactness, Marshall and Bushrod Washington decided to "consent to receive

[1] Several persons were ambitious to write the life of Washington. David Ramsay and Mason Locke Weems had already done so. Noah Webster was especially keen to undertake the task, and it was unfortunate that he was not chosen to do it.

[2] Washington to Wayne, April 11, 1800, Dreer MSS. Pa. Hist. Soc.

[3] *Ib.*

$100,000 for the copyright in the United States";
and they sternly announced that, "less than this sum
we will not take." [1]

Wayne sought to reduce the optimism of Marshall and Washington by informing them that "the
greatest number of subscribers ever obtained for
any one publication in this country was . . 2000 and
the highest sum ever paid in for the copyright of
any one work . . was 30,000 Dollars." Wayne thinks
that Marshall's work may sell better, but is sure
that more than ten thousand sets cannot be disposed
of for many years. He gives warning that, if the
biography should contain anything objectionable
to the British Government, the sale of it would be
prevented in England, as was the case with David
Ramsay's "History of the Revolution." [2]

Marshall and Washington also "rec^d propositions
for the purchase of the right to sell in G^t Britain,"
and so informed Wayne, calling upon him to "say
so" if he wished to acquire British, as well as American rights, "knowing the grounds upon which we
calculate the value in the United States." [3]

So we find Marshall counting on fifty thousand
dollars [4] at the very least from his adventure in the
field of letters. His financial reckoning was expansive; but his idea of the time within which he could
write so important a history was grotesque. At first

[1] Bushrod Washington to Wayne, Dec. 11, 1801, Dreer MSS.
loc. cit.
[2] Wayne to Bushrod Washington, Dec. 10, 1801, Dreer MSS.
loc. cit.
[3] Bushrod Washington to Wayne, Dec. 11, 1801, Dreer MSS.
loc. cit.
[4] The division was to be equal between Marshall and Washington.

he counted on producing "4 or 5 volumes in octavos of from 4 to 500 pages each" in less than one year, provided "the present order of the Courts be not disturbed or very materially changed." [1]

It thus appears that Marshall expected the Federalist Judiciary Act of 1801 to stand; that he would not be called upon to ride the long, tiresome, time-consuming Southern circuit; and that, with no great number of cases to be disposed of by the Supreme Court, he would have plenty of leisure to write several large volumes of history in a single year.

But the Republican repeal of the act gave the disgusted Chief Justice "duties to perform," as John Randolph expressed it. Marshall was forthwith sent upon his circuit riding, and his fondly anticipated relief from official labors vanished. Although he had engaged to write the biography during the winter following Washington's death, not one line of it had he penned at the time the contract for publication was made in the autumn of 1802. He had, of course, done some reading of the various histories of the period; but he had not even begun the examination of Washington's papers, the subsequent study of which proved so irksome to him.

After almost two years of bartering, a contract was made with Wayne to print and sell the biography. This agreement, executed September 22, 1802, gave to the publisher the copyright in the United States and all rights of the authors "in any part of North and South America and in the West India

---

[1] Bushrod Washington to Wayne, Dec. 11, 1801, Dreer MSS. *loc. cit.*

Islands." The probable extent of the work was to be "four or five volumes in Octavo, from four to five hundred pages" each; and it was "supposed" that these would "be compleated in less than two years" — Marshall's original estimate of time having now been doubled.

Wayne engaged to pay "one dollar for every volume of the aforesaid work which may be subscribed for or which may be sold and paid for." It was further covenanted that the publisher should "not demand" of the public "a higher price than three dollars per volume in boards."[1] This disappointed Marshall, who had insisted that the volumes must be sold for four dollars each, a price which Wayne declared the people would not pay.[2]

It would seem that for a long time Marshall tried to conceal the fact that he was to be the author; and, when the first volume was about to be issued, strenuously objected to the use of his name on the title-page. However, Jefferson soon got wind of the project. The alert politician took swift alarm and promptly suggested measures to counteract the political poison with which he was sure Marshall's pen would infect public opinion. He consulted Madison, and the two picked out the brilliant and versatile Joel Barlow, then living in Paris, as the best man to offset the evil labor in which Marshall was engaged.

---

[1] "Articles of Agreement" between C. P. Wayne and Bushrod Washington, Sept. 22, 1802. (Dreer MSS. *loc. cit.*) Marshall's name does not appear in the contract, Washington having attended to all purely business details of the transaction.

[2] Wayne to Bushrod Washington, May 16, 1802, Dreer MSS *loc. cit.*

"Mr. Madison and myself have cut out a piece of work for you," Jefferson wrote Barlow, "which is to write the history of the United States, from the close of the War downwards. We are rich ourselves in materials, and can open all the public archives to you; but your residence here is essential, because a great deal of the knowledge of things is not on paper, but only within ourselves for verbal communication."

Then Jefferson states the reason for the "piece of work" which he and Madison had "cut out" for Barlow: "John Marshall is writing the life of Gen. Washington from his papers. It is intended to come out just in time to influence the next presidential election." The imagination of the party manager pictured Marshall's work as nothing but a political pamphlet. "It is written therefore," Jefferson continues, "principally with a view to electioneering purposes; but it will consequently be out in time to aid you with information as well as to point out the perversions of truth necessary to be rectified." [1]

Thus Marshall's book was condemned before a word of it had been written, and many months before the contract with Wayne was signed — a circumstance that was seriously to interfere with subscriptions to the biography. Jefferson's abnormal sensitiveness to even moderate criticism finally led him to the preparation of the most interesting and untrustworthy of all his voluminous papers, as a reply to Marshall's "Washington." [2]

---

[1] Jefferson to Barlow, May 3, 1802, *Works: Ford*, IX, 372.
[2] The "Anas," *Works: Ford*, I, 163–430, see *infra*. The "Anas" was

News was sent to Republicans all over the country that Marshall's book was to be an attack upon their party. Wayne tells Marshall and Washington of the danger, but Washington testily assures the nervous publisher that he need have no fear: "The democrats may say what they please and I have expected they would say a great deal, but this is at least not intended to be a party work nor will any candid man have cause to make this charge." [1]

The contract signed, Wayne quickly put in motion the machinery to procure subscribers. Of this mechanism, the most important part should have been the postmasters, of whom Wayne expected to make profitable use. There were twelve hundred of them, "each acquainted with all the gentlemen of their respective neighborhoods . . and their neighbors would subscribe at request, when they would not to a stranger. . . All letters to and from these men go free of postage," Wayne advised Marshall, while assuring the anxious author that "every Post Master in the United States holds a subscription paper." [2] But, thanks to Jefferson, the postmasters were to prove poor salesmen of the product of Marshall's pen.

Other solicitors, however, were also put to work:

Jefferson's posthumous defense. It was arranged for publication as early as 1818, but was not given to the public until after his death. It first appeared in the edition of Jefferson's works edited by his grandson, Thomas Jefferson Randolph. "It is the most precious mélange of all sorts of scandals you ever read." (Story to Fay, Feb. 5, 1830, Story, II, 33.)

[1] Bushrod Washington to Wayne, Nov. 19, 1802, Dreer MSS. loc. cit.

[2] Wayne to Marshall, Feb. 17, 1803, Dreer MSS. loc. cit.

among them the picturesque Mason Locke Weems,
part Whitefield, part Villon, a delightful mingling
of evangelist and vagabond, lecturer and politician,
writer and musician.[1] Weems had himself written a
"Life of Washington" which had already sold extensively among the common people.[2] He had long

[1] Weems is one of the most entertaining characters in American
history. He was born in Maryland, and was one of a family of nineteen children. He was educated in London as a physician, but abandoned medicine for the Church, and served for several years as rector
of two or three little Episcopal churches in Maryland and ministered
occasionally at Pohick Church, in Truro Parish (sometimes called
Mount Vernon Parish), Virginia. In this devout occupation he could
not earn enough to support his very large family. So he became a
professional book agent — the greatest, perhaps, of that useful fra-
ternity.

On horseback he went wherever it seemed possible to sell a book,
his samples in his saddlebags. He was a natural orator, a born entertainer, an expert violinist; and these gifts he turned to good account
in his book-selling activities.

If a political meeting was to be held near any place he happened
upon, Weems would hurry to it, make a speech, and advertise his
wares. A religious gathering was his joy; there he would preach and
exhort — and sell books. Did young people assemble for merrymak-
ing, Weems was in his element, and played the fiddle for the dancing. If he arrived at the capital of a State when the Legislature
was in session, he would contrive to be invited to address the Solons
— and procure their subscriptions.

[2] Weems probably knew more of the real life of the country, from
Pennsylvania southward, than any other one man; and he thoroughly
understood American tastes and characteristics. To this is due the
unparalleled success of his *Life of Washington*. In addition to this
absurd but engaging book, Weems wrote the *Life of Gen. Francis
Marion* (1805); the *Life of Benjamin Franklin* (1817); and the *Life
of William Penn* (1819). He was also the author of several temperance pamphlets, the most popular of which was the *Drunkard's
Looking Glass*. Weems died in 1825.

Weems's *Life of Washington* still enjoys a good sale. It has been one
of the most widely purchased and read books in our history, and has
profoundly influenced the American conception of Washington. To
it we owe the grotesque and wholly imaginary stories of young Washington and the cherry tree, the planting of lettuce by his father to
prove to the boy the designs of Providence, and other anecdotes that

been a professional book agent with every trick of
the trade at his fingers' ends, and was perfectly acquainted with the popular taste.

First, the parson-subscription agent hied himself
to Baltimore. "I average 12 subs pr day. *Thank
God for that*," he wrote to his employer. He is on
fire with enthusiasm: "If the Work be done handsomely, you will sell at least 20,000," he brightly
prophesies. Within a week Weems attacks the postmasters and insists that he be allowed to secure
sub-agents from among the gentry: "The Mass of
Riches and of Population in America lie in the
Country. There is the wealthy Yeomanry; and
there the ready Thousands who wd. instantly second
you were they but duly stimulated." [1]

Almost immediately Weems discovered a popular
distrust of Marshall's forthcoming volumes: "The
People are very fearful that it will be prostituted to
party purposes," he informs Wayne. "*For Heaven's
Sake, drop now and then a cautionary Hint to John
Marshall Esq.* Your all is at stake with respect to
this work. If it be done in a generally acceptable
manner you will make your fortune. Otherwise the
work will fall an Abortion from the press." [2]

Weems's apprehension grew. Wayne had written
that the cities would yield more subscribers than
the country. "For a moment, admit it," argues
Weems: "Does it follow that the Country is a mere

make that intensely human founder of the American Nation an impossible and intolerable prig.

The only biography of Weems is *Parson Weems*, by Lawrence C.
Wroth, a mere sketch, but trustworthy and entertaining.

[1] Weems to Wayne, Dec. 10, 1802, Dreer MSS. *loc. cit.*
[2] Same to same, Dec. 14, 1802, Dreer MSS. *loc. cit.*

blank, a cypher not worth your notice? Because there are 30,000 wealthy families in the City and but 20,000 in the Country, must nothing be tried to enlist 5000, at least of these 20,000??? *If the Fed^s sh^d be disappointed*, and the Demo^s disgusted with Gen$^{l.}$ Marshals performance, will it not be very convenient to have 4 to 5000 good Rustic Blades to lighten your shelves & to shovel in the Dol$.$" [1]

The dean of book agents evidently was having a hard time, but his resourcefulness kept pace with his discouragement: "Patriotic Orations — Gazetter Puffs — Washingtonian Anecdotes, Sentimental, Moral Military and Wonderful — All sh^d be Tried," he advises Wayne.[2] Again, he notes the failure of the postmasters to sell Marshall's now much-talked-of book. "In six months," he writes from Martinsburg, Virginia, "the P. Master here got 1. In $\frac{1}{2}$ day. *I thank God*, I've got 13 sub^s." [3]

The outlook for subscriptions was even worse in New England. Throughout the whole land, there was, it seems, an amazing indifference to Washington's services to the Nation. "I am sorry to inform you," Wayne advised Marshall and his associate, "that the Prospect of an extensive Subscription is gloomy in N. England, particularly they argue it is too Expensive and wait for a cheaper Edition — 'tis like Americans, Mr. Wolcott and Mr. Pickering say they are loud in their professions, but attempt to touch their purses and they shut them in a moment." [4]

[1] Weems to Wayne, Dec. 17, 1802, Dreer MSS. *loc. cit.*
[2] Same to same, Dec. 22, 1802, Dreer MSS. *loc. cit.*
[3] Same to same, April 2, 1803, Dreer MSS. *loc. cit.*
[4] Wayne to Bushrod Washington, Jan. 23, 1803, Dreer MSS. *loc. cit*

Writing from Fredericksburg, Virginia, Weems at last mingles cheer with warning: "Don't indulge a fear — let no sigh of thine arise. Give *Old Washington fair play* and all will be well. Let but the *Interior* of the Work be Liberal & the *Exterior Elegant*, and a Town House & a Country House, a Coach and Sideboard and Massy Plate shall be thine." Still, he declared, "I sicken when I think how much may be marr^d." [1]

A week later found the reverend solicitor at Carlisle, Pennsylvania, and here the influence of politics on the success of Marshall's undertaking again crops out: "The place had been represented to me," records Weems, "as a Nest of Anti Washingtonian Hornets who w^d draw their Stings at mention of his name — and the Fed [torn] Lawyers are all gone to York– However, I dash^d in among them and *thank God* have obtain^d already 17 good names." [2]

By now even the slow-thinking Bushrod Washington had become suspicious of Jefferson's postmasters: "The postmasters being (I believe) Democrats.[3] Are you sure they will feel a disposition to advance the work?"[4] Later he writes: "I would not give one honest soliciting agent for 1250 quiescent postmasters." [5]

---

[1] Weems to Wayne, April 8, 1803, Dreer MSS. *loc. cit.*

[2] Same to same, April 18, 1803, Dreer MSS. *loc. cit.*

[3] Bushrod Washington, like the other Federalists, would not call his political opponents by their true party name, Republicans: he styled them "democrats," the most opprobrious term the Federalists could then think of, excepting only the word "Jacobins." (See **vol. II**, 439, of this work.)

[4] Washington to Wayne, March 1, 1803, Dreer MSS. *loc. cit.*

[5] Same to same, March 23, 1803, Dreer MSS. *loc. cit.*

A year passed after the first subscriptions were made, and not even the first volume had appeared. Indeed, no part of the manuscript had been finished and sent to the publisher. Wayne was exasperated. "I am extremely anxious on this subject," he complains to Bushrod Washington, "as the Public evince dissatisfaction at the delay. Each hour I am questioned either verbally or by letter relative to it & its procrastination. The subscription seems to have received a check in consequence of an opinion that it is uncertain when the work will go to press. *Twelve thousand* dollars is the Total Cash yet rece^d — not quite 4,000 subscribers." [1]

By November, 1803, many disgusted subscribers are demanding a refund of the money, and Wayne wants the contract changed to the payment of a lump sum. The "Public [are] exclaiming against the price of 3 Doll^s per vol.," and his sanguine expectations have evaporated: "I did hope that I should realize *half* the number of subscribers you contemplated, *thirty thousand;* . . but altho' *two active*, and twelve hundred other agents have been employed 12 months, the list of names *does* not amount to *one seventh* of the contemplated number." [2]

[1] Wayne to Washington, Oct. 23, 1803, Dreer MSS. *loc. cit.*

An interesting sidelight on the commercial methods of the times is displayed by a circular which Wayne sent to his agents calling for money from subscribers to Marshall's *Life of Washington:* "The remittance may be made through the Post Office, and should any danger be apprehended, you can cut a Bank note in two parts and send each by separate mails." (Wayne's Circular, Feb. 17, 1803, Dreer MSS. *loc. cit.*)

[2] This list was published in the first edition. It is a good directory of the most prominent Federalists and of the leading Republican politicians of the time. "T. Jefferson, P.U.S." and each member of

Wayne insists on purchasing the copyright "for a *moderate, specifick* sum" so that he can save himself from loss and "that the Publick disgust may be removed." He has heard, he says, and quite directly, that the British rights have been sold "at two thousand doll^s!!!" — and this in spite of the fact that, only the previous year, Marshall and Washington "expected *Seventy* Thousand." [1]

At last, more than three years after Marshall had decided to embark upon the uncertain sea of authorship, he finished the first of the five volumes. And such a mass of manuscript! "It will make *at least* Eight hundred pages!!!!" moaned the distraught publisher. At that rate, considering the small number of subscribers and the greatly increased cost of paper and labor,[2] Wayne would be ruined. No title-page had been sent, and Marshall's son, who had brought the manuscript to Philadelphia, "astonished" Wayne by telling him "that his father's name was not to appear in the Title." [3]

When Marshall learned that the publisher demanded a title-page bearing his name, he insisted

his Cabinet subscribed; Marshall himself was a subscriber for his own book, and John C. Calhoun, a student at Yale College at the time, was another. In the cities most of the lawyers took Marshall's book.

[1] Wayne to Bushrod Washington, Nov. 3, 1803, Dreer MSS. *loc. cit.*

It would seem from this letter that Marshall and Washington had reduced their lump cash price from $100,000 to $70,000. In stating his expenses, Wayne says that the painter "Gilbert Stuart demanded a handsome sum for the privilege of Engraving from his Original" portrait of Washington.

[2] See letter last cited.

[3] Wayne to Bushrod Washington, Dec. 16, 1803, Dreer MSS. *loc. cit.*

that this was unnecessary and not required by the copyright law. "I am unwilling," he hastened to write Wayne, "to be named in the book or in the clerk's office as the author of it, if it be avoidable." He cannot tell how many volumes there will be, or even examine, before some time in May, 1804, Washington's papers relating to the period of his two administrations. The first volume he wants "denominated *an introduction*." It is too long, he admits, and authorizes Wayne to split it, putting all after "the peace of 1763" into the second volume.[1]

Marshall objects again to appearing as the author: "My repugnance to permitting my name to appear in the title still continues, but it shall yield to your right to make the best use you can of the copy." He does not think that "the name of the author being given or withheld can produce any difference in the number of subscribers"; but, since he does not wish to leave Wayne "in the Opinion that a real injury has been sustained," he would "submit scruples" to Wayne and Washington, "only requesting that [his] name may not be given but on mature consideration and conviction of its propriety." In any case, Marshall declares: "I wish not my title in the judiciary of the United States to be annexed to it."

He writes at great length about punctuation, paragraphing, capital letters, and spelling, giving minute directions, but leaves much to Wayne's judgment. As to spelling: "In any doubtful case I wou^d de-

[1] Marshall to Wayne, Dec. 23, 1803, Dreer MSS. *loc. cit.*

cidedly prefer to follow Johnson." [1] Two other long
letters about details of printing the first volume
followed. By the end of March, 1804, his second
volume was ready. [2]

He now becomes worried about "the inaccuracies
. . the many and great defects in composition" of
the first two volumes; but "the hurried manner in
which it is press^d forward renders this inevitable."
He begs Bushrod Washington to "censure and alter
freely. . . You mistake me very much if you think
I rank the corrections of a friend with the bitter
sarcasms of a foe, or that I shou^d feel either wounded
or chagrined at my inattentions being pointed out
by another." [3]

Once more the troubled author writes his associate, this time about the spelling of "Chesapeak"
and "enterprise," the size of the second volume, and
as to "the prospects of subscribers." [4] Not until
June, 1804, did Marshall give the proof-sheets of
the first volume even "a hasty reading" because
of "the pressure of . . official business." [5] Totally
forgotten was the agreed plan to publish maps in
a separate volume, although it was thus "stated in
the prospectus." [6] He blandly informs the exasperated publisher that he must wait a long time after
publishing the volumes describing the Revolution
and those on the Presidency of Washington before

---

[1] Marshall to Wayne, Jan. 10, 1804, Dreer MSS. *loc. cit.*
[2] Marshall to Bushrod Washington, March 25, 1804, Dreer MSS.
loc. cit.
[3] Same to same, April, 1804, Dreer MSS. *loc. cit.*
[4] Same to same, April 29, 1804, Dreer MSS. *loc. cit.*
[5] Marshall to Wayne, June 1, 1804, Dreer MSS. *loc. cit.*
[6] Same to same, June 6, 1804, Dreer MSS. *loc. cit.*

the manuscript of the last volume can be sent to press — this when many subscribers were clamoring for the return of the money they had paid, and the public was fast losing interest in the book. Large events had meanwhile filled the heavens of popular interest, and George Washington's heroic figure was already becoming dim and indistinct.

The proof-sheets of the second volume were now in Marshall's hands; but the toil of writing, "superintending the copying," and various other avocations "absolutely disabled" him, he insists, from giving them any proper examination. He had no idea that he had been so careless in his writing and is anxious to revise the work for a second edition. He complains of his health and says he must spend the summer in the mountains, where, of course, he "cannot take the papers with [him] to prosecute the work." He will, however, read the pages of the first two volumes while on his vacation.

The manuscript of the third he had finished and sent to Bushrod Washington.[1] When Wayne saw the length of it, his Quaker blood was heated to wrath. Did Marshall's prolixity know no limit? The first two volumes had already cost the publisher far more than the estimate — would not Washington persuade Marshall to be more concise?[2]

By midsummer of 1804 the first two volumes appeared. They were a dismal performance. Nevertheless, one or two Federalist papers praised them,

[1] Marshall to Wayne, June 10, July 5, July 8, 1804, Dreer MSS. *loc. cit.*

[2] Wayne to Bushrod Washington, Aug. 20, 1804, Dreer MSS. *loc. cit.*

and Marshall was as pleased as any youthful writer
by a first compliment. He thanks Wayne for sending the reviews and comments on one of them: "The
very handsome critique in the 'Political and Commercial Register' was new to me." He modestly
admits: "I cou^d only regret that there was in it more
of panuegyric than was merited. The editor . . manifests himself to be master of a style of a very superior
order and to be, of course, a very correct judge of the
composition of Others."

Marshall is somewhat mollified that his parentage
of the biography has been revealed: "Having,
Heaven knows how reluctantly, consented against
my judgement to be known as the author of the work
in question I cannot be insensible to the opinions
entertained of it. But, I am much more solicitous
to hear the strictures upon it" — than commendation of it — because, he says, these would point
out defects to be corrected. He asks Wayne, therefore, to send to him at Front Royal, Virginia, "every
condemnatory criticism. . . I shall not attempt to
polish every sentence; that wou^d require repeated
readings & a long course of time; but I wish to correct obvious imperfections & the animadversions of
others wou^d aid me very much in doing so." [1]

Within three weeks Marshall had read his first
volume in the form in which it had been delivered to
subscribers, and was "mortified beyond measure
to find that it [had] been so carelessly written." He
had not supposed that so many "inelegancies . . cou^d
have appeared in it," and regrets that he must re-

[1] Marshall to Wayne, July 20, 1804, Dreer MSS. *loc. cit.*

quire Wayne to reset the matter "so materially."
He informs his publisher, nevertheless, that he is
starting on his vacation in the Alleghanies; and he
promises that when he returns he "will . . review
the corrections" he has made in the first volume,
although he would "not have time to reperuse the
whole volume." [1]

Not for long was the soul of the perturbed author
to be soothed with praise. He had asked for "strictures"; he soon got them. Wayne promptly sent him
a "Magazine [2] containing a piece condemnatory of
the work." Furthermore, the books were not going
well; not a copy could the publisher sell that had
not been ordered before publication. "I have all
those on hand which I printed over the number
of subscribers," Wayne sourly informs the author.

In response to Marshall's request for time for revision, Wayne is now willing that he shall take all he
wishes, since "present prospects would not induce
[him] to republish," but he cautions Marshall to "let
the idea of a 2d edit. revised and corrected remain
a secret"; if the public should get wind of such a
purpose the stacks of volumes in Wayne's printing
house would never be sold. He must have the
manuscript of the "*fourth* vol. by the last of September at furthest. . . Can I have it? — or must I dismiss my people."

At the same time he begs Marshall to control
his redundancy: "The first and second vols. have

[1] Marshall to Wayne, Aug. 10, 1804, Dreer MSS. *loc. cit.*

[2] *Literary Magazine and American Register of Philadelphia*, July,
1804. The reviewer makes many of the criticisms that appeared on
the completion of the biography. (See *infra*, 261–79.)

cost me (1500) fifteen hundred dollars more than calculated! " [1]

It was small wonder that Marshall's first two bulky books, published in the early summer of 1804, were not hailed with enthusiasm. In volume one the name of Washington was mentioned on only two minor occasions described toward the end.[2] The reader had to make his way through more than one hundred thousand words without arriving even at the cradle of the hero. The voyages of discovery, the settlements and explorations of America, and the history of the Colonies until the Treaty of Paris in 1763, two years before the Stamp Act of 1765, were treated in dull and heavy fashion.

The author defends his plan in the preface: No one connected narrative tells the story of all the Colonies and "few would . . search through the minute details"; yet this he held to be necessary to an understanding of the great events of Washington's life. So Marshall had gathered the accounts of the various authorities[3] in parts of the country and in England, and from them made a continuous history. If there were defects in the book it was due to "the impatience . . of subscribers" which had so hastened him.

The volume is poorly done; parts are inaccurate.[4]

[1] Wayne to Marshall, Aug. 20, 1804, Dreer MSS. *loc. cit.*

[2] The affair at Little Meadows and the defeat of Braddock. (Marshall: *Life of George Washington*, 1st ed. I, 356–58, 368–71.)

[3] These were: Belknap, Belsham, Chalmers, Dodsley, Entick or Entinck, Gordon, Hutchinson, Minot, Ramsay, Raynal, Robertson, Russell, Smith, Stedman, Stith, Trumbull.

[4] For example, Marshall's description of Sir William Berkeley, who was, the reader is informed, "distinguished . . by the mildness of

To Bacon's Rebellion are given only four pages.[1]
The story of the Pilgrims is fairly well told.[2] A page
is devoted to Roger Williams and six sympathetic
lines tell of his principles of liberty and toleration.[3]
The Salem witchcraft madness is well treated.[4] The
descriptions of military movements constitute the
least disappointing parts of the volume. The beginnings of colonial opposition to British rule are tiresomely set out; and thus at last, the reader arrives
within twelve years of Bunker Hill.

Marshall admits that every event of the Revolutionary War has been told by others who had examined Washington's "immensely voluminous correspondence," and that he had copied these authors,
sometimes using their very language. Still, he promises the reader "a particular account of his [Wash-
ington's] own life." [5]

One page and three lines at the beginning of the
second volume are all that Marshall gives of the ancestry, birth, environment, upbringing, education,
and experiences of George Washington, up to the
nineteenth year of his age. On the second page the
hero, fully uniformed and accoutred, is plunged
into the French and Indian Wars. Braddock's defeat, already described in the first volume, is repeated and elaborated.[6] Six lines, closing the first
chapter, disposes of Washington in marriage and
describes the bride.[7]

his temper, the gentleness of his manners and . . popular virtues."
(Marshall, 1st ed. I, 72.)
  [1] *Ib.* 188–92; and see vol. I, 6, of this work.
  [2] *Ib.* 1st ed. I, 86–89. [3] *Ib.* 111–12.   [4] *Ib.*; see Notes, 9–18.
  [5] *Ib.* x.   [6] *Ib.* 1st ed. II, 14–20.   [7] *Ib.* 67.

About three pages are devoted to the Stamp Act speeches in the British Parliament; while but one short paragraph is given to the immortal resolutions of Patrick Henry and the passage of them by the Virginia House of Burgesses. Not a word describes the "most bloody" debate over them, and Henry's time-surviving speech is not even referred to.[1] All mention of the fact that Washington was a fellow member with Henry and voted for the resolutions is omitted. Henry's second epoch-making speech at the outbreak of the Revolution is not so much as hinted at, nor is any place found for the Virginia Resolutions for Arming and Defense, which his unrivaled eloquence carried.

The name of the supreme orator of the Revolution is mentioned for the second time in describing the uprising against Lord Dunmore,[2] and then Marshall adds this footnote: "The same gentleman who had introduced into the assembly of Virginia the original resolution against the stamp act."[3]

Marshall's account of the development of the idea of independence is scattered.[4] He gives with unnecessary completeness certain local resolutions favoring it,[5] while to the great Declaration less than two pages[6] are assigned. It is termed "this important paper"; and a footnote disposes of the fact that "Mr. Jefferson, Mr. John Adams, Mr. Franklin, Mr. Sherman, and Mr. R. R. Livingston, were appointed to prepare this declaration; and the draft reported by the committee has been generally at-

[1] Marshall, 1st ed. II, 82–83; and see vol. I, 66, of this work.
[2] See vol. I, 74–79, of this work.   [3] Marshall, 1st ed. II, 193.
[4] Ib. 160–69.   [5] Ib. 374–75.   [6] Ib. 377–78.

tributed to Mr. Jefferson." [1] A report of the talk between Washington and Colonel Paterson of the British Army, concerning the title by which Washington insisted upon being addressed,[2] is given one and one third times the space that is bestowed upon the Declaration of Independence.

Marshall is satisfactory only when dealing with military operations. He draws a faithful picture of the condition of the army; [3] quotes Washington's remorseless condemnations of the militia,[4] short enlistments, and the democratic spirit among men and officers.[5] When writing upon such topics, Marshall is spirited; his pages are those of the soldier that, by nature, he was.

The earliest objection to Marshall's first two volumes came from American Tories, who complained of the use of the word "enemy" as applied to the British military forces. Wayne reluctantly calls Marshall's attention to this. Marshall replies: "You need make no apology for mentioning to me the criticism of the word 'enemy.' I will endeavor to avoid it where it can be avoided." [6]

Unoffended by such demands, Marshall was deeply chagrined by other and entirely just criticisms. Why, he asks, had not some one pointed out to him "some of those objections . . to the plan of the work" before he wrote any part of it? He wishes "very sincerely" that this had been done. He "should very readily have relinquished [his own]

---

[1] Marshall, 1st ed. II, 377.   [2] Ib. 386–89.   [3] Ib. 390–94.
[4] Ib. 417–18, 445–46; and see vol. I, 83–86, of this work.
[5] Marshall, 1st ed. II, 259–61.
[6] Marshall to Wayne, Aug. 10, 1804, Dreer MSS. *loc. cit.*

opinion . . if [he] had perceiv^d that the public taste required a different course." Thus, by implication, he blames Wayne or Bushrod Washington, for his own error of judgment.

Marshall also reproaches himself, but in doing so he saddles on the public most of the burden of his complaints: "I ought, indeed, to have foreseen that the same impatience which precipitated the publication wou^d require that the life and transactions of Mr. Washington should be immediately entered upon." Even if he had stuck to his original plans, still, he "ought to have departed from them so far as to have composed the introductory volume at leizure after the principal work was finished."

Marshall's "mortification" is, he says, also "increased on account of the careless manner in which the work has been executed." For the first time in his life he had been driven to sustained and arduous mental labor, and he found, to his surprise, that he "had to learn that under the pressure of constant application, the spring of the mind loses its elasticity. . . But regrets for the past are unavailing," he sighs. "There will be great difficulty in retrieving the reputation of the first volume. . . I have therefore some doubts whether it may not be as well to drop the first volume for the present — that is not to speak of a republication of it."

He assures Wayne that he need have no fears that he will mention a revised edition, and regrets that the third volume is also too long; his pen has run away with him. He would shorten it if he had the copy once more; but since that cannot be, perhaps

Wayne might omit the last chapter. Brooding over the "strictures" he had so confidently asked for, he grows irritable. "Whatever might have been the execution, the work wou^d have experienced unmerited censure. We must endeavor to rescue what remains to be done from such [criticism] as is deserved. I wish you to consult Mr. Washington." [1]

Another very long letter from Front Royal quickly follows. Marshall again authorizes the publisher himself to cut the bulk of the third volume, in the hope that it "will not be so defective. . . It shall be my care to render the 4th more fit for the public eye." He promises Wayne that, in case of a second edition,[2] he will shorten his interminable pages which shall also "receive very material corrections." But a corrected and improved edition! "On this subject . . I remain silent. . . Perhaps a free expression of my thoughts . . may add to the current which seems to set against it." Let the public take the first printing "before a second is spoken of." [3]

Washington drew on the publisher [4] and wrote Wayne that "the disappointment will be very great if it is not paid." In December, 1804, Wayne sent the first royalty. It amounted to five thousand dollars.[5]

---

[1] Marshall to Wayne from Front Royal, Virginia, Sept. 3, 1804, Dreer MSS. *loc. cit.*

[2] Marshall spent many years preparing this second edition of his *Washington*, which appeared in 1832, three years before Marshall's death. See *infra*, 272–73.

[3] Marshall to Wayne, Sept. 8, 1804, Dreer MSS. *loc. cit.*

[4] The amount of this draft is not stated.

[5] This would seem to indicate that Wayne had been able to collect payment on the first two volumes, from only two thousand five hundred subscribers, since, by the contract, Marshall and Washington together were to receive one dollar for each book sold.

Our author needed money badly. "I do not wish to press you upon the subject of further remittances but they will be highly acceptable," Washington tells Wayne, "particularly to Mr. Marshall, whose arrangements I know are bottomed upon the expectation of the money he is to receive from you." [1] In January, 1805, Wayne sent Washington another thousand dollars — "which I have paid," says Washington, "to Mr. Marshall as I shall also do of the next thousand you remit." [2] Thus pressed, Wayne sends more money, and by January 1, 1805, Marshall and Washington have received the total sum of eight thousand seven hundred and sixty dollars.[3]

Toward the end of February, 1805, Marshall completed the manuscript of the fourth volume. He was then in Washington, and sent two copies from there to Philadelphia by Joseph Hopkinson, who had just finished his notable work in the Chase impeachment trial. "They are both in a rough state; too rough to be sent . . but it was impossible to have them recopied," Marshall writes Wayne. He admits they are full of errors in capitalization, punctuation, and spelling, but adds, "it has absolutely been impossible to make corrections in these respects." [4] This he "fears will produce considerable difficulty." Small wonder, with the Chase trial absorbing his every thought and depressing him with heavy anxiety.

Marshall's relief from the danger of impeachment

---

[1] Washington to Wayne, Dec. 25, 1804, Dreer MSS. *loc. cit.*
[2] Same to same, Jan. 15, 1805, Dreer MSS *loc. cit.*
[3] Same to same, Dec. 30, 1804, Dreer MSS. *loc. cit.*
[4] Marshall to Wayne, Feb. 27, 1805, Dreer MSS. *loc. cit.*

is at once reflected in his correspondence with Wayne. Two weeks after the acquittal of Chase, he placidly informs his publisher that the fifth volume will not be ready until the spring of 1806 at the earliest. It is "not yet commenced," he says, "but I shall however set about it in a few days." He explains that there will be little time to work on the biography. "For the ensuing twelve months I shall scarcely have it in my power to be five in Richmond."[1] Three months later he informs Wayne that it will be "absolutely impossible" to complete the final volume by the time mentioned. "I regret this very seriously but it is a calamity for which there is no remedy."

The cause of this irremediable calamity was "a tour of the mountains" — a journey to be made "for [his] own health and that of [his] family" from which he "cannot return till October." He still "laments sincerely that an introductory volume was written because [he] finds it almost impossible to compress the civil administration into a single volume. In doing it," he adds, "I shall be compelled to omit several interesting transactions & to mutilate others."[2]

At last Marshall's eyes are fully opened to what should have been plain to him from the first. Nobody wanted a tedious history of the discovery and settlement of America and of colonial development, certainly not from his pen. The subject had been dealt with by more competent authors.

But the terrible years following the war, the Con-

[1] Marshall to Wayne, March 16, 1805, Dreer MSS. *loc. cit.*
[2] Same to same, June 29, 1805, Dreer MSS. *loc. cit.*

stitutional period, the Administrations of Washington and the first half of that of Adams, the decisive part played by Washington throughout this critical time of founding and constructing — all these were virgin fields. They constituted, too, as vital an epoch in American history as the Revolution itself. Marshall's own life had been an important part of it, and he was not unequipped to give it adequate treatment.

Had Marshall written of these years, it is probable that the well-to-do Federalists alone would have purchased the thirty thousand sets that Marshall originally counted on to be sold. He would have made all the money he had expected, done a real public service, and achieved a solid literary fame. His "Life of Washington" might have been the great social, economic, political, and Constitutional history of the foundation processes of the Government of the American Nation. His entire five volumes would not have been too many for such a work.

But all this matter relating to the formative years of the Nation must now be crowded between two covers and offered to an indifferent, if not hostile, public — a public already "disgusted," as the publisher truly declared, by the unattractive rehash of what had already been better told.

Wayne again presses for a change in the contract; he wants to buy outright Marshall's and Washington's interests, and end the bankrupting royalty he is paying them: "If you were willing to take 70000$ for 30000 Sub^s I thought it would not be deemed

illiberal in offering twenty thousand dollars for four
thousand subscribers — this was two-sevenths of
the original sum for less than *one-seventh* of the subscribers contemplated." Wayne asks Marshall and
Washington to "state the lowest sum" they will
take. Subscriptions have stopped, and in three
years he has sold only "*two* copies . . to non-sub-
scribers." But the harried publisher sends two
thousand dollars more of royalty.[1]

In the autumn of 1805, upon returning from his
annual vacation, Marshall is anxious to get to work,
and he must have the *Aurora* and *Freneau's Gazette*
quickly. His "official duties recommence . . on the
22^d of November from which time they continue 'till
the middle of March." Repeating his now favorite
phrase, he says, "It is absolutely impossible to get
the residue of the work completed in the short time
which remains this fall." He has been sorely vexed
and is a cruelly overworked man: "The unavoidable
delays which have been experienced, the immense
researches among volumes of manuscript, & chests
of letters & gazettes which I am compelled to make
will impede my progress so much that it is absolutely
impossible" to finish the book at any early date.[2]

Want of money continually embarrasses Marshall:
"What payments my good Sir, will it be in your
power to make us in the course of this & the next
month?" Bushrod Washington asks Wayne. "I
am particularly anxious," he explains, "on account
of Mr. M. . . His principal dependence is upon this

---

[1] Wayne to Washington, July 4, 1804, Dreer MSS. *loc. cit.*
[2] Marshall to Wayne, Oct. 5, 1805, Dreer MSS. *loc. cit.*

fund." [1] Marshall now gets down to earnest and continuous labor and by July, 1806, actually finishes the fifth and only important volume of the biography. [2]

During all these years the indefatigable Weems continued his engaging career as book agent, and, like the subscribers he had ensnared, became first the victim of hope deferred and then of unrealized expectations. The delay in the publication of Marshall's first volumes and the disfavor with which the public received them when finally they appeared, had, it seems, cooled the ardor of the horseback-and-saddlebag distributer of literary treasures. At all events, he ceases to write his employer about Marshall's "Life of Washington," but is eager for other books. [3] Twice only, in an interval of two years, he

[1] Washington to Wayne, April 1, 1806, Dreer MSS. *loc. cit.* It was in this year that the final payments for the Fairfax estate were made and the deed executed to John and James M. Marshall and their brother-in-law Rawleigh Colston. See vol. II, footnote to 211, and vol. IV, chap. III, of this work.

[2] Same to same, July 14, 1806, Dreer MSS. *loc. cit.*

[3] Weems's orders for books are trustworthy first-hand information concerning the literary tastes of the American people at that time, and the extent of education among the wealthy. Writing from Savannah, Georgia, August, 1806, he asks for "Rippons hymns, Watts D$^{\circ}$, Newton's D$^{\circ}$, Methodist D$^{\circ}$, Davies Sermons, Massillons D$^{\circ}$, Villiage D$^{\circ}$, Whitfields D$^{\circ}$, Fuller [the eminent Baptist divine,] Works, viz. His Gospel its own evidence, Gospel Worthy of all Acceptation, Pilgrim's progress, Baxter's Sts Rest, Call to the Unconverted, Alarm, by Allein, Hervey's Works, Rushe's Medical Works; All manner of School Books, Novels by the cart load, particularly Charlotte Temple .. 2 or 300 of Charlotte Temple .. Tom Paines Political Works, Johnson's Poets boun^{d} in green or in any handsome garb, particularly Miltons Paradise lost, Tompsons Seasons, Young's N. Thoughts wou'd do well." (Weems to Wayne, Aug. 1806, Dreer MSS. *loc. cit.*)

Another order calls for all the above and also for "Websters Spell^{g} book, Universal D$^{\circ}$, Fullers Backslider, Booths reign of Grace, Looking Glass for the mind, Blossoms of Morality, Columbian Orator,

mentions Marshall's biography, but without spirit or enthusiasm.[1] In the autumn of 1806, he querulously refers to Marshall and Washington: "I did not call on *you* [Wayne] for increase of Diurnal Salary. I spoke to Judge W. I hope and expect that he and Gen. M.[2] will do me something."

Marshall's third volume, which had now appeared, is an improvement on the first two. In it he continues his narrative of the Revolutionary War until 1779, and his statement of economic and financial conditions [3] is excellent. The account of the battles of Brandywine and Germantown, in both of which he had taken part,[4] is satisfactory,[5] and his picture of the army in retreat is vivid.[6] He faithfully relates the British sentiment among the people.[7] Curiously enough, he is not comprehensive or stirring in his story of Valley Forge.[8] His descriptions of Lafayette and Baron von Steuben are worthy.[9] Again and again he attacks the militia,[10] and is merciless in his criticism of the slip-shod, happy-go-

Enticks Dictionary, Murrays Grammar, Enfield's Speaker, Best Books on Surveying, D⁰ on Navigation, Misses Magazine, Vicar of Wakefield, Robinson Crusoe, Divine Songs for Children, Pamela Small." In this letter forty-four different titles are called for.

[1] Weems to Wayne, Jan. 28, 1804, and Aug. 25, 1806, Dreer MSS. *loc. cit.*

[2] Same to same, Sept. 20, 1806, Wayne MSS. *loc. cit.* This letter is written from Augusta, Georgia. Among other books ordered in it, Weems names twelve copies each of "Sallust, Corderius, Eutropius, Nepos, Caesar's Commentaries, Virgil Delph., Horace Delphini, Cicero D⁰, Ovid D⁰"; and nine copies each of "Greek Grammar, D⁰ Testament, Lucian, Xenophon."

[3] Marshall, III, 28–42. [4] See vol. I, 93–98, 102, of this work.
[5] Marshall, III, chaps. III and IV.
[6] See vol. I, 98–101, of this work. [7] Marshall, III, 43–48, 52
[8] *Ib.* 319, 330, 341–50; and see vol. I, 110–32, of this work.
[9] Marshall, III, 345, 347–49. [10] *Ib.* 50–53, 62.

lucky American military system. These shortcomings were offset, he says, only by the conduct of the enemy.[1] The treatment of American prisoners is set forth in somber words,[2] and he gives almost a half-page of text [3] and two and a half pages of appendix [4] to the murder of Miss McCrea.

The story of the battle of Monmouth in which Marshall took part is told with spirit.[5] Nineteen pages [6] are devoted to the history of the alliance with the French monarch, and no better résumé of that event, so fruitful of historic results, ever has been given. The last chapter describes the arrival of the British Commission of Conciliation, the propositions made by them, the American answer, the British attempts to bribe Congress,[7] followed by the Indian atrocities of which the appalling massacres at Kingston and Wyoming were the worst.

The long years of writing, the neglect and crudity of his first efforts, and the self-reproval he underwent, had their effect upon Marshall's literary craftsmanship. This is noticeable in his fourth volume, which is less defective than those that preceded it. His delight in verbiage, so justly ridiculed by Cal-

---

[1] Marshall, III, 59. "No species of licentiousness was unpracticed. The plunder and destruction of property was among the least offensive of the injuries sustained." The result "could not fail to equal the most sanguine hopes of the friends of the revolution. A sense of personal wrongs produced a temper, which national considerations had been found too weak to excite. . . The great body of the people flew to arms."

[2] *Ib.* 20, 22, 24, 27, 386. See also vol. I, 115–16, of this work, and authorities there cited.

[3] Marshall, III, 246–47.   [4] *Ib.* Notes, 4–6.

[5] *Ib.* chap. 8; and see vol. I, 134–38, of this work.

[5] Marshall, III, 366–85.   [7] *Ib.* 486–96.

lender in 1799,[1] is a little subdued, and his sense of
proportion is somewhat improved. He again criticizes the American military system and traces its
defects to local regulations.[2] The unhappy results of
the conflict of State and Nation are well presented.[3]

The most energetic narrative in the volume is that
of the treason of Benedict Arnold. In telling this
story, Marshall cannot curb the expression of his
intense feeling against this "traitor, a sordid traitor,
first the slave of his rage, then purchased with
gold." Marshall does not economize space in detail-
ing this historic betrayal of America,[4] imperative as
the saving of every line had become.

He relates clearly the circumstances that caused
the famous compact between Denmark, Sweden,
and Russia known as "The Armed Neutrality,"
formed in order to check Great Britain's power on
the seas. This was the first formidable assertion
of the principle of equality among nations on the
ocean. Great Britain's declaration of war upon Holland, because that country was about to join "The
Armed Neutrality," and because Holland appeared
to be looking with favor upon a commercial treaty
which the United States wished to conclude with
her, is told with dispassionate lucidity.[5]

Marshall gives a compact and accurate analysis
— by far the best work he has done in the whole four
volumes — of the party beginnings discernible when
the clouds of the Revolutionary War began to break.
He had now written more than half a million words,

---

[1] See vol. ii, 405, of this work.　[2] Marshall, iv, 114–15.　[3] Ib. 188.
[4] Ib. 247–65; see vol. i, 143–44, of this work.　[5] Marshall, iv, 284–88.

and this description was the first part of his work
that could be resented by the Republicans. The
political division was at bottom economic, says
Marshall — those who advocated honest payment
of public debts were opposed by those who favored
repudiation; and the latter were also against military establishments and abhorred the idea of any
National Government.[1]

The fourth volume ends with the mutiny of part
of the troops, the suppression of it, Washington's
farewell to his officers, and his retirement when
peace was concluded.

Marshall's final volume was ready for subscribers
and the public in the autumn of 1807, just one year
before the Federalist campaign for the election of
Jefferson's successor — four years later than Jefferson had anticipated.[2] It was the only political part
of Marshall's volumes, but it had not the smallest
effect upon the voters in the Presidential contest.

Neither human events nor Thomas Jefferson had
waited upon the convenience of John Marshall. The
Federalist Party was being reduced to a grumbling
company of out-of-date gentlemen, leaders in a
bygone day, together with a scattered following
who, from force of party habit, plodded along after
them, occasionally encouraged by some local circumstance or fleeting event in which they imagined an
"issue" might be found. They had become anti-
National, and, in their ardor for Great Britain, had
all but ceased to be American. They had repudiated
democracy and assumed an attitude of insolent

[1] Marshall, IV, 530–31.   [2] See Jefferson's letter to Barlow, *supra*.

superiority, mournful of a glorious past, despairing of a worthy future.[1]

Marshall could not hope to revive the fast weakening Federalist organization. The most that he could do was to state the principles upon which opposing parties had been founded, and the determinative conflicts that had marked the evolution of them and the development of the American Nation. He could only set forth, in plain and simple terms, those antagonistic ideas which had created party divisions; and although the party to which one group of those ideas had given life was now moribund, they were ideas, nevertheless, which would inevitably create other parties in the future.

The author's task was, therefore, to deal not only with the years that had gone; but, through his treatment of the past, with the years that were to come. He must expound the philosophy of Nationalism as opposed to that of Localism, and must enrich his exposition by the unwritten history of the period between the achievement of American Independence and the vindication of it in our conflict with France.

Marshall was infinitely careful that every statement in his last volume should be accurate; and, to make sure of this, he wrote many letters to those who had first-hand knowledge of the period. Among others he wrote to John Adams, requesting permission to use his letters to Washington. Adams readily agreed, although he says, "they were written under great agitation of mind at a time when a

---

[1] See *supra*, chap. III, and *infra*, chap. VI; and see especially vol. IV, chap. I, of this work.

cruel necessity compelled me to take measures which I was very apprehensive would produce the evils which have followed from them. If you have detailed the events of the last years of General Washington's Life, you must have run the Gauntlet between two infuriated factions, armed with scorpions. . . It is a period which must however be investigated, but I am very confident will never be well understood." [1]

Because of his lack of a sense of proportion in planning his "Life of Washington," and the voluminousness of the minor parts of it, Marshall had to compress the vital remainder. Seldom has a serious author been called upon to execute an undertaking more difficult. Marshall accomplished the feat in creditable fashion. Moreover, his fairness, restraint, and moderation, even in the treatment of subjects regarding which his own feelings were most ardent, give to his pages not only the atmosphere of justice, but also something of the artist's touch.

[1] Adams to Marshall, July 17, 1806, MS.

This letter is most important. Adams pictures his situation when President: "A first Magistrate of a great Republick with a General officer under him, a Commander in Chief of the Army, who had ten thousand times as much Influence Popularity and Power as himself, and that Commander in Chief so much under the influence of his Second in command [Hamilton], . . the most treacherous, malicious, insolent and revengeful enemy of the first Magistrate is a Picture which may be very delicate and dangerous to draw. But it must be drawn. . .

"There is one fact . . which it will be difficult for posterity to believe, and that is that the measures taken by Senators, Members of the House, some of the heads of departments, and some officers of the Army to force me to appoint General Washington . . proceeded not from any regard to him . . but merely from an intention to employ him as an engine to elevate Hamilton to the head of affairs civil as well as military."

Washington's Nationalism is promptly and skill-fully brought into the foreground.[1] An excellent ac-count of the Society of the Cincinnati contains the first covert reflection on Jefferson.[2] But the state of the country under the Articles of Confederation is passed over with exasperating brevity — only a few lines are given to this basic subject.[3]

The foundation of political parties is stated once more and far better — "The one . . contemplated America as a nation," while "the other attached itself to state authorities." The first of these was made up of "men of enlarged and liberal minds . . who felt the full value of national honour, and the full obligation of national faith; and who were persuaded of the insecurity of both, if resting for their preservation on the concurrence of thirteen distinct sovereignties"; and with these far-seeing and upright persons were united the "officers of the army" whose experience in war had weakened "local prejudices."[4]

Thus, by mentioning the excellence of the mem-bers of one party, and by being silent upon the short-comings of those of the other party, Marshall imputes to the latter the reverse of those qualities which he praises — a method practiced throughout the book, and one which offended Jefferson and his followers more than a direct attack could have done.

He succinctly reviews the attempts at union,[5] and the disputes between America and Great Britain

---

[1] He was "accustomed to contemplate America as his country, and to consider . . the interests of the whole." (Marshall, v, 10.)

[2] *Ib.* 24–30. [3] *Ib.* 31–32. [4] *Ib.* 33–34. [5] *Ib.* 45–47.

over the Treaty of Peace; [1] he quickly swings back to the evolution of political parties and, for the third time, reiterates his analysis of debtor and Localist as against creditor and Nationalist.

"The one [party] struggled . . for the exact observance of public and private engagements"; to them "the faith of a nation, or of a private man was deemed a sacred pledge." These men believed that "the distresses of individuals" could be relieved only by work and faith, "not by a relaxation of the laws, or by a sacrifice of the rights of others." They thought that "the imprudent and idle could not be protected by the legislature from the consequences of their indiscretion; but should be restrained from involving themselves in difficulties, by the conviction that a rigid compliance with contracts would be enforced." Men holding these views "by a natural association of ideas" were "in favour of enlarging the powers of the federal government, and of enabling it to protect the dignity and character of the nation abroad, and its interests at home." [2]

With these principles Marshall sharply contrasts those of the other party: "Viewing with extreme tenderness the case of the debtor, their efforts were unceasingly directed to his relief"; they were against "a faithful compliance with contracts" — such a measure they thought "too harsh to be insisted on . . and one which the people would not bear." Therefore, they favored "relaxing . . justice," suspending the collection of debts, remitting taxes. These men resisted every attempt to transfer from their own

[1] Marshall, v, 65.   [2] *Ib.* 85–86.

hands into those of Congress all powers that were, in reality, National. Those who held to such "lax notions of honor," were, in many States, "a decided majority of the people," and were very powerful throughout the country. Wherever they secured control, paper money, delay of justice, suspended taxes "were the fruits of their rule"; and where they were in the minority, they fought at every election for the possession of the State Governments.

In this fashion Marshall again states those antipodal philosophies from which sprang the first two American political parties. With something like skill he emphasizes the conservative and National idea thus: "No principle had been introduced [in the State Governments] which could resist the wild projects of the moment, give the people an opportunity to reflect, and allow the good sense of the nation time for exertion." The result of "this instability in principles which ought if possible to be rendered immutable, produced a long train of ills." [1] The twin spirits of repudiation and Localism on one side, contending for the mastery against the companion spirits of faith-keeping and Nationalism on the other, were from the very first, says Marshall, the source of public ill-being or well-being, as one or the other side prevailed.

Then follows a review of the unhappy economic situation which, as Marshall leaves the reader to infer, was due exclusively to the operation of the principles which he condemns by the mere statement of them. [2] So comes the Philadelphia Convention

[1] Marshall, v, 85–87.   [2] *Ib.* 88–89.

of 1787 that was deemed by many "an illegitimate meeting." [1]

Although Washington presided over, and was the most powerful influence in, the Constitutional Convention, Marshall allots only one short paragraph to that fact.[2] He enumerates the elements that prepared to resist the Constitution; and brings out clearly the essential fact that the proposed government of the Nation was, by those who opposed it, considered to be "foreign." He condenses into less than two pages his narrative of the conflict over ratification, and almost half of these few lines is devoted to comment upon "The Federalist."

Marshall writes not one line or word of Washington's power and activities at this critical moment. He merely observes, concerning ratification, that "the intrinsic merits of the instrument would not have secured" the adoption of the Constitution, and that even in some of the States that accepted it "a majority of the people were in the opposition." [3]

He tells of the pressure on Washington to accept the Presidency. To these appeals and Washington's replies, he actually gives ten times more space than he takes to describe the formation, submission, and ratification of the Constitution itself.[4] After briefly telling of Washington's election to the Presidency, Marshall employs twenty pages in describing his journey to New York and his inauguration.

Then, with quick, bold strokes, he lays the final

---

[1] Marshall, v, 105. Marshall's account of the causes and objects of Shays's Rebellion is given wholly from the ultra-conservative view of that important event. (*Ib.* 123.)

[2] *Ib.* 128–29.   [3] *Ib.* 132.   [4] *Ib.* 133–50.

color on his picture of the state of the country before the new government was established, and darkens the tints of his portrayal of those who were opposing the Constitution and were still its enemies. In swift contrast he paints the beginnings of better times, produced by the establishment of the new National Government: "The new course of thinking which had been inspired by the adoption of a constitution that was understood to prohibit all laws impairing the obligation of contracts, had in a great measure restored that confidence which is essential to the internal prosperity of nations." [1]

He sets out adequately the debates over the first laws passed by Congress,[2] and is generous in his description of the characters and careers of both Jefferson and Hamilton when they accepted places in Washington's first Cabinet.[3] He joyfully quotes Washington's second speech to Congress, in which he declares that "to be prepared for war is one of the most effectual means of preserving peace"; and in which the people are adjured "to discriminate the spirit of liberty from that of licentiousness." [4]

An analysis of Hamilton's First Report on the

[1] Marshall, v, 178–79. Thus Marshall, writing in 1806, states one of the central principles of the Constitution as he interpreted it from the Bench years later in three of the most important of American judicial opinions — Fletcher vs. Peck, Sturgis vs. Crowninshield, and the Dartmouth College case. (See infra, chap. x; also vol. iv, chaps. iv and v, of this work.)

[2] Marshall, v, 198–210.

[3] Ib. 210–13. At this point Marshall is conspicuously, almost ostentatiously impartial, as between Jefferson and Hamilton. His description of the great radical is in terms of praise, almost laudation; the same is true of his analysis of Hamilton's work and character. But he gives free play to his admiration of John Adams. (Ib. 219–20.)

[4] Ib. 230–32.

Public Credit follows. The measures flowing from it "originated the first regular and systematic oppo-sition to the principles on which the affairs of the union were administered." [1] In condensing the momentous debate over the establishment of the American financial system, Marshall gives an excellent summary of the arguments on both sides of that controversy. He states those of the Nationalists, however, more fully than the arguments of those who opposed Hamilton's plan. [2]

While attributing to Hamilton's financial measures most of the credit for improved conditions, Marshall frankly admits that other causes contributed to the new-found prosperity: By "progressive industry, . . the influence of the constitution on habits of thinking and acting," and especially by "depriving the states of the power to impair the obligation of contracts, or to make any thing but gold and silver a tender in payment of debts, the conviction was impressed on that portion of society which had looked to the government for relief from embarrassment, that personal exertions alone could free them from difficulties; and an increased degree of industry and economy was the natural consequence." [3]

Perhaps the most colorful pages of Marshall's entire work are those in which he describes the effect of the French Revolution on America, and the popular hostility to Washington's Proclamation of Neutrality [4]

[1] Marshall, v, 241.   [2] Ib. 243–58.   [3] Ib. 271.

[4] "That system to which the American government afterwards inflexibly adhered, and to which much of the national prosperity is to be ascribed." (Ib. 408.)

and to the treaty with Great Britain negotiated by John Jay.[1]

In his treatment of these subjects he reveals some of the sources of his distrust of the people. The rupture between the United States and the French Republic is summarized most inadequately. The greatest of Washington's state papers, the immortal "Farewell Address,"[2] is reproduced in full. The account of the X. Y. Z. mission is provokingly incomplete; that of American preparations for war with France is less disappointing. Washington's illness and death are described with feeling, though in stilted language; and Marshall closes his literary labors with the conventional analysis of Washington's character which the world has since accepted.[3]

Marshall's fifth volume was received with delight by the disgruntled Federalist leaders. A letter of Chancellor James Kent is typical of their comments. "I have just finished . . the last Vol. of Washington's Life and it is worth all the rest. It is an excellent History of the Government and Parties in this country from Vol. 3 to the death of the General."[4]

Although it had appeared too late to do them any harm at the election of 1804, the Republicans and Jefferson felt outraged by Marshall's history of the foundation period of the Government. Jefferson said nothing for a time, but the matter was seldom out of his thoughts. Barlow, it seems, had been laggard in writing a history from the Republican point of view, as Jefferson had urged him to do.

---

[1] See vol. II, chaps. I to IV, of this work.
[2] Marshall, v, 685–709.   [3] *Ib.* 773.
[4] James Kent to Moss Kent, July 14, 1807, Kent MSS. Lib. Cong.

Three years had passed since the request had been made, and Barlow was leaving for Paris upon his diplomatic mission. Jefferson writes his congratulations, "yet . . not unmixed with regret. What is to become of our past revolutionary history? Of the antidotes of truth to the misrepresentations of Marshall?" [1]

Time did not lessen Jefferson's bitterness: "Marshall has written libels on one side," [2] he writes Adams, with whom a correspondence is opening, the approach of old age having begun to restore good relations between these former enemies. Jefferson's mind dwells on Marshall's work with increasing anxiety: "On the subject of the history of the American Revolution . . who can write it?" he asks. He speaks of Botta's "History," [3] criticizing its defects; but he concludes that "the work is nevertheless a good one, more judicious, more chaste, more classical, and more true than the party diatribe of Marshall. Its greatest fault is in having taken too much from him." [4]

Marshall's "party diatribe" clung like a burr in Jefferson's mind and increased his irritation with the passing of the years. Fourteen years after Marshall's last volume appeared, Justice William Johnson of the Supreme Court published an account of the

---

[1] Jefferson to Barlow, April 16, 1811, *Works:* Ford, XI, 205.

[2] Jefferson to Adams, June 15, 1813, *ib.* 296.

[3] Botta: *History of the War of the Independence of the United States of America.* This work, published in Italian in 1809, was not translated into English until 1820; but in 1812–13 a French edition was brought out, and that is probably the one Jefferson had read.

[4] Jefferson to Adams, Aug. 10, 1815, *Works:* Ford, XI, 485.

period [1] covered by Marshall's work, and it was
severely criticized in the *North American Review*.
Jefferson cheers the despondent author and praises
his "inestimable" history: "Let me . . implore you,
dear Sir, to finish your history of parties. . . We
have been too careless of our future reputation, while
our tories will omit nothing to place us in the wrong."
For example, Marshall's "Washington," that "five-
volumed libel, . . represents us as struggling for
office, and not at all to prevent our government
from being administered into a monarchy." [2]

In his long introduction to the "Anas," Jefferson
explains that he would not have thought many of
his notes "worth preserving but for their testimony
against the only history of that period which pretends to have been compiled from authentic and
unpublished documents." Had Washington himself
written a narrative of his times from the materials
he possessed, it would, of course, have been truthful:
"But the party feeling of his biographer, to whom
after his death the collection was confided, has
culled from it a composition as different from what
Genl. Washington would have offered, as was the
candor of the two characters during the period of
the war.

" The partiality of this pen is displayed in lavish-
ments of praise on certain military characters, who
had done nothing military, but who afterwards, &

---

[1] Johnson: *Sketches of the Life and Correspondence of General Nathanael Greene*. This biography was even a greater failure than Marshall's *Washington*. During this period literary ventures by judges
seem to have been doomed.

[2] Jefferson to Johnson, March 4, 1823, *Works:* Ford, xii, 277–78.

before he wrote, had become heroes in party, altho' not in war; and in his reserve on the merits of
others, who rendered signal services indeed, but did
not earn his praise by apostatising in peace from the
republican principles for which they had fought in
war."

Marshall's frigidity toward liberty "shews itself
too," Jefferson continues, "in the cold indifference
with which a struggle for the most animating of
human objects is narrated. No act of heroism ever
kindles in the mind of this writer a single aspiration
in favor of the holy cause which inspired the bosom,
& nerved the arm of the patriot warrior. No gloom
of events, no lowering of prospects ever excites a
fear for the issue of a contest which was to change
the condition of man over the civilized globe.

" The sufferings inflicted on endeavors to vindicate
the rights of humanity are related with all the frigid
insensibility with which a monk would have contemplated the victims of an *auto da fé*. Let no man
believe that Gen. Washington ever intended that
his papers should be used for the suicide of the cause,
for which he had lived, and for which there never
was a moment in which he would not have died."

Marshall's "abuse of these materials," Jefferson
charges, "is chiefly however manifested in the history of the period immediately following the establishment of the present constitution; and nearly
with that my memorandums [the "Anas"] begin.
Were a reader of this period to form his idea of it
from this history alone, he would suppose the republican party (who were in truth endeavoring to

keep the government within the line of the Constitution, and prevent it's being monarchised in
practice) were a mere set of grumblers, and disor-
ganisers, satisfied with no government, without fixed
principles of any, and, like a British parliamentary
opposition, gaping after loaves and fishes, and ready
to change principles, as well as position, at any time,
with their adversaries." [1]

Jefferson denounces Hamilton and his followers as
"monarchists," "corruptionists," and other favorite
Jeffersonian epithets, and Marshall is again assailed:
"The horrors of the French revolution, then raging,
aided them mainly, and using that as a raw head and
bloody bones they were enabled by their stratagems
of X. Y. Z. in which this historian was a leading
mountebank, their tales of tub-plots, Ocean massacres, bloody buoys, and pulpit lyings, and slander-
ings, and maniacal ravings of their Gardiners, their
Osgoods and Parishes, to spread alarm into all but
the firmest breasts.' [2]

Criticisms of Marshall's "Life of Washington"
were not, however, confined to Jefferson and the
Republicans. Plumer thought the plan of the work
"preposterous." [3] The Reverend Samuel Cooper
Thatcher of Boston reviewed the biography through
three numbers of the *Monthly Anthology*.[4] "Every

---

[1] *Works:* Ford, i, 165–67.   [2] *Ib*. 181–82.

[3] Plumer, March 11, 1808, "Diary," Plumer MSS. Lib. Cong.

[4] May, June, and August numbers, 1808, *Monthly Anthology and
Boston Review*, v, 259, 322, 434. It appears from the minutes of the
Anthology Society, publishers of this periodical, that they had a hard
time in finding a person willing to review Marshall's five volumes.
Three persons were asked to write the critique and declined. Finally,
Mr. Thatcher reluctantly agreed to do the work.

reader is surprized to find," writes Mr. Thatcher, "the history of North America, instead of the life of an individual. . . He [Washington] is always presented . . in the pomp of the military or civil costume, and never in the ease and undress of private life." However, he considers Marshall's fifth volume excellent. "We have not heard of a single denial of his fidelity. . . In this respect . . his work [is] *unique* in the annals of political history."

Thatcher concludes that Marshall's just and balanced treatment of his subject is not due to a care for his own reputation: "We are all so full of agitation and effervescence on political topicks, that a man, who keeps his temper, can hardly gain a hearing." Indeed, he complains of Marshall's fairness: he writes as a spectator, instead of as "one, who has himself descended into the arena . . and is yet red with the wounds which he gave, and smarting with those which his enemies inflicted in return"; but the reviewer charges that these volumes are full of "barbarisms" and "grammatical impurities," "newspaper slang," and "unmeaning verbiage."

The Reverend Timothy Flint thought that Marshall's work displayed more intellect and labor than "eloquence and interest." [1] George Bancroft, reviewing Sparks's " Washington," declared that "all that is contained in Marshall is meagre and incomplete in comparison." [2] Even the British critics were not so harsh as the *New York Evening Post*, which pronounced the judgment that if the biography "bears

---

[1] Flint, in London *Athenæum* for 1835, 803.
[2] *North American Review*, XLVI, 483.

any traces of its author's uncommon powers of mind, it is in the depths of dulness which he explored." [1]

The British critics were, of course, unsparing. The *Edinburgh Review* called Marshall's work "unpardonably deficient in all that constitutes the soul and charm of biography. . . We look in vain, through these stiff and countless pages, for any sketch or anecdote that might fix a distinguishing feature of private character in the memory. . . What seemed to pass with him for dignity, will, by his reader, be pronounced dullness and frigidity." [2] *Blackwood's Magazine* asserted that Marshall's "Life of Washington" was "a great, heavy book. . . One gets tired and sick of the very name of Washington before he gets half through these . . prodigious . . octavos." [3]

Marshall was somewhat compensated for the criticisms of his work by an event which soon followed the publication of his last volume. On August 29, 1809, he was elected a corresponding member of the Massachusetts Historical Society. In a singularly graceful letter to John Eliot, corresponding secretary of the Society at that time, Marshall expresses his thanks and appreciation. [4]

As long as he lived, Marshall worried over his biography of Washington. When anybody praised it,

---

[1] *New York Evening Post*, as quoted in Allibone: *Dictionary of English Literature and British and American Authors*, II, 1227.

[2] *Edinburgh Review*, Oct. 1808, as quoted in Randall, II, footnote to 40.

[3] *Blackwood's Edinburgh Magazine*, XVII, 179.

[4] Marshall to Eliot, Sept. 20, 1809, MSS. of the Mass. Hist. Soc.

he was as appreciative as a child. In 1827, Archibald D. Murphey eulogized Marshall's volumes in an oration, a copy of which he sent to the Chief Justice, who thanks Murphey, and adds: "That work was hurried into a world with too much precipitation, but I have lately given it a careful examination and correction. Should another edition appear, it will be less fatiguing, and more worthy of the character which the biographer of Washington ought to sustain." [1]

Toilsomely he kept at his self-imposed task of revision. In 1816, Bushrod Washington wrote Wayne to send Marshall "the last three volumes in sheets (the two first he has) that he may devote this winter to their correction." [2]

When, five years later, the Chief Justice learned that Wayne was actually considering the risk of bringing out a new edition, Marshall's delight was unbounded. "It is one of the most desirable objects I have in this life to publish a corrected edition of that work. I would not on any terms, could I prevent it, consent that one other set of the first edition should be published." [3]

Finally, in 1832, the revised biography was published. Marshall clung to the first volume, which was issued separately under the title "History of the American Colonies." The remaining four volumes were, seemingly, reduced to two; but they were so closely printed and in such comparatively small

[1] Marshall to Murphey, Oct. 6, 1827, *Papers of Archibald D. Murphey:* Hoyt, I, 365–66.

[2] Washington to Wayne, Nov. 26, 1816, Dreer MSS. *loc. cit.*

[3] Marshall to Washington, Dec. 27, 1821, MS.

type that the real condensation was far less than it appeared to be. The work was greatly improved, however, and is to this day the fullest and most trustworthy treatment of that period, from the conservative point of view.[1]

Fortunately for Marshall, the work required of him on the Bench gave him ample leisure to devote to his literary venture. During the years he consumed in writing his "Life of Washington" he wrote fifty-six opinions in cases decided in the Circuit Court at Richmond, and in twenty-seven cases determined by the Supreme Court. Only four of them [2] are of more than casual interest, and but three of them [3] are of any historical consequence. All the others deal with commercial law, practice, rules of evidence, and other familiar legal questions. In only one case, that of Marbury *vs*. Madison, was he called upon to deliver an opinion that affected the institutions and development of the Nation.

[1] So popular did this second edition become that, three years after Marshall's death, a little volume, *The Life of Washington*, was published for school-children. The publisher, James Crissy of Philadelphia, states that this small volume is "printed from the author's own manuscript," thus intimating that Marshall had prepared it. (See Marshall, school ed.)

[2] Talbot *vs*. Seeman, United States *vs*. Schooner Peggy, Marbury *vs*. Madison, and Little *vs*. Barreme.

[3] The first three in above note.

CHAPTER VI

THE BURR CONSPIRACY

My views are such as every man of honor and every good citizen must approve. (Aaron Burr.)

His guilt is placed beyond question. (Jefferson.)

I never believed him to be a Fool. But he must be an Idiot or a Lunatic if he has really planned and attempted to execute such a Project as is imputed to him. But if his guilt is as clear as the Noonday Sun, the first Magistrate ought not to have pronounced it so before a Jury had tryed him. (John Adams.)

On March 2, 1805, not long after the hour of noon, every Senator of the United States was in his seat in the Senate Chamber. All of them were emotionally affected — some were weeping.[1] Aaron Burr had just finished his brief extemporaneous address [2] of farewell. He had spoken with that grave earnestness so characteristic of him.[3] His remarks produced a

---

[1] "We were all deeply affected, and many shed tears." (Plumer to his wife, March 2, 1805, Plumer, 331; and see *Memoirs, J. Q. A.*: Adams, I, 367.)

"Tears did flow abundantly." (Burr to his daughter, March 13, 1805, Davis, II, 360.)

[2] "There was nothing written or prepared. . . It was the solemnity, the anxiety, the expectation, and the interest which I saw strongly painted in the countenances of the auditors, that inspired whatever was said." (*Ib.* 360.)

[3] The speech, records the *Washington Federalist*, which had been extremely abusive of Burr, "was said to be the most dignified, sublime and impressive that ever was uttered."

"His address . . was delivered with great force and propriety." (Plumer to his wife, March 2, 1805, Plumer, 331.)

"His speech . . was delivered with great dignity. . . It was listened to with the most earnest and universal attention." (*Memoirs, J. Q. A.*: Adams, I, 367.) Burr made a profound impression on John Quincy Adams. "There was not a member present but felt the force of this solemn appeal to his sense of duty." (J. Q. Adams to his father, March 14, 1805, *Writings, J. Q. A.*: Ford, III, 119.)

The franking privilege was given Burr for life, a courtesy never before

curious impression upon the seasoned politicians and statesmen, over whose deliberations he had presided for four years. The explanation is found in Burr's personality quite as much as in the substance of his speech. From the unprecedented scene in the Senate Chamber when the Vice-President closed, a stranger would have judged that this gifted personage held in his hands the certainty of a great and brilliant career. Yet from the moment he left the Capital, Aaron Burr marched steadily toward his doom.

An understanding of the trial of Aaron Burr and of the proceedings against his agents, Bollmann and Swartwout, is impossible without a knowledge of the events that led up to them; while the opinions and rulings of Chief Justice Marshall in those memorable controversies are robbed of their color and much of their meaning when considered apart from the picturesque circumstances that produced them. This chapter, therefore, is an attempt to narrate and condense the facts of the Burr conspiracy in the light of present knowledge of them.

Although in a biography of John Marshall it seems a far cry to give so much space to that episode, the import of the greatest criminal trial in American history is not to be fully grasped without a summary of the events preceding it. Moreover, the fact that in the Burr trial Marshall destroyed the law of "constructive treason" requires that the circumstances of the Burr adventure, as they appeared to Marshall, be here set forth.

extended except to a President of the United States and Mrs. Washington. (See Hillhouse's speech, *Annals*, 10th Cong. 1st Sess. 272.)

A strong, brave man who, until then, had served his country well, Aaron Burr was in desperate plight when on the afternoon of March 2 he walked along the muddy Washington streets toward his lodging. He was a ruined man, financially, politically, and in reputation. Fourteen years of politics had destroyed his once extensive law practice and plunged him hopelessly into debt. The very men whose political victory he had secured had combined to drive him from the Republican Party.

The result of his encounter with Hamilton had been as fatal to his standing with the Federalists, who had but recently fawned upon him, as it was to the physical being of his antagonist. What now followed was as if Aaron Burr had been the predestined victim of some sinister astrology, so utterly did the destruction of his fortunes appear to be the purpose of a malign fate.

His fine ancestry now counted for nothing with the reigning politicians of either party. None of them cared that he came of a family which, on both sides, was among the worthiest in all the country.[1] His superb education went for naught. His brilliant services as one of the youngest Revolutionary offi cers were no longer considered — his heroism at Quebec, his resourcefulness on Putnam's staff, his valor at Monmouth, his daring and tireless efficiency at West Point and on the Westchester lines, were, to these men, as if no such record had ever been written.

Nor, with those then in power, did Burr's notable

---

[1] His father was the President of Princeton. His maternal grandfather was Jonathan Edwards.

public services in civil life weigh so much as a feather
in his behalf. They no longer remembered that only
a few years earlier he had been the leader of his
party in the National Senate, and that his appointment to the then critically important post of Minister to France had been urged by the unanimous
caucus of his political associates in Congress. None
of the notable honors that admirers had asserted
to be his due, nor yet his effective work for his party,
were now recalled. The years of provocation [1] which

[1] Hamilton's pursuit of Burr was lifelong and increasingly venomous. It seems incredible that a man so transcendently great as Hamilton — easily the foremost creative mind in American statesmanship
— should have succumbed to personal animosities such as he displayed toward John Adams, and toward Aaron Burr.

The rivalry of Hamilton and Burr began as young attorneys at the
New York bar, where Burr was the only lawyer considered the equal
of Hamilton. Hamilton's open hostility, however, first showed itself
when Burr, then but thirty-five years of age, defeated Hamilton's
father-in-law, Philip Schuyler, for the United States Senate. The
very next year Hamilton prevented Burr from being nominated and
elected Governor of New York. Then Burr was seriously considered
for Vice-President, but Hamilton also thwarted this project.

When Burr was in the Senate, the anti-Federalists in Congress unanimously recommended him for the French Mission; and Madison and
Monroe, on behalf of their colleagues, twice formally urged Burr's
appointment. Hamilton used his influence against it, and the appointment was not made. At the expiration of Burr's term in the Senate,
Hamilton saw to it that he should not be chosen again and Hamilton's
father-in-law this time succeeded.

President Adams, in 1798, earnestly desired to appoint Burr to the
office of Brigadier-General under Washington in the provisional army
raised for the expected war with France. Hamilton objected so strenuously that the President was forced to give up his design. (See
Adams to Rush, Aug. 25, 1805, *Old Family Letters*, 77; and same to
same, June 23, 1807, *ib.* 150.)

In the Presidential contest in the House in 1801 (see vol. II, 533–38,
of this work), Burr, notwithstanding his refusal to do anything in his
own behalf (*ib.* 539–47), would probably have been elected instead of
Jefferson, had not Hamilton savagely opposed him. (*Ib.*)

When, in 1804, Burr ran for Governor of New York, Hamilton

had led, in an age of dueling,[1] to a challenge of his remorseless personal, professional, and political enemy were now unconsidered in the hue and cry raised when his shot, instead of that of his foe, proved mortal.

Yet his spirit was not broken. His personal friends stood true; his strange charm was as potent as ever over most of those whom he met face to face; and throughout the country there were thousands who still admired and believed in Aaron Burr. Particularly in the West and in the South the general sentiment was cordial to him; many Western Senators were strongly attached to him; and most of his brother officers of the Revolution who had settled beyond the Alleghanies were his friends.[2] Also, he was still in vigorous middle life, and though delicate of frame and slight of stature, was capable of greater physical exertion than most men of fewer years.

What now should the dethroned political leader do? Events answered that question for him, and,

again attacked him. It was for one of Hamilton's assaults upon him during this campaign that Burr challenged him. (See Parton: *Life and Times of Aaron Burr*, 339 *et seq.*; also Adams: *U.S.* II, 185 *et seq.*; and *Private Journal of Aaron Burr*, reprinted from manuscript in the library of W. K. Bixby, Introduction, iv–vi.) So prevalent was dueling that, but for Hamilton's incalculable services in founding the Nation and the lack of similar constructive work by Burr, the hatred of Burr's political enemies and the fatal result of the duel, there certainly would have been no greater outcry over the encounter than over any of the similar meetings between public men during that period.

[1] Dueling continued for more than half a century. Many of the most eminent of Americans, such as Clay, Randolph, Jackson, and Benton, fought on "the field of honor." In 1820 a resolution against dueling, offered in the Senate by Senator Morrill of New Hampshire, was laid on the table. (*Annals*, 16th Cong. 1st Sess. 630, 636.)

McCaleb: *Aaron Burr Conspiracy*, 19; Parton: *Burr*, 382.

beckoned forward by an untimely ambition, he followed the path that ended amid dramatic scenes in
Richmond, Virginia, where John Marshall presided
over the Circuit Court of the United States.

Although at the time Jefferson had praised what
he called Burr's "honorable and decisive conduct"[1]
during the Presidential contest in the House in February of 1801, he had never forgiven his associate
for having received the votes of the Federalists,
nor for having missed, by the merest chance, election as Chief Magistrate.[2] Notwithstanding that
Burr's course as Vice-President had won the admiration even of enemies,[3] his political fall was decreed
from the moment he cast his vote on the Judiciary
Bill in disregard of the rigid party discipline that
Jefferson and the Republican leaders then exacted.[4]

Even before this, the constantly increasing frigidity of the President toward him, and the refusal of
the Administration to recognize by appointment any
cne recommended by him for office in New York,[5]
had made it plain to all that the most Burr could
expect was Jefferson's passive hostility. Under these
circumstances, and soon after his judiciary vote, the
spirited Vice-President committed another impru-

---

[1] Vol. ii, 545, of this work.   [2] Adams: *U.S.* i, 331.

[3] "His official conduct in the Senate . . has fully met my approbation," testifies the super-critical Plumer in a letter to his wife March 2,
1805. (Plumer, 331.)

[4] "Burr is completely an insulated man." (Sedgwick to King, Feb.
20, 1802, King, iv, 74.)

"Burr has lost ground very much with Jefferson's sect during the
present session of Congress. . . He has been not a little abused . . in the
democratic prints." (Troup to King, April 9, 1802, King, iv, 103.)

Also see *supra*, chap. ii; Adams: *U.S.* i, 280; and Parton: *Burr*, 309.

[5] Adams: *U.S.* i, 230–33; Channing: *Jeff. System*, 17–19.

dence. He attended a banquet given by the Federalists in honor of Washington's birthday. There he proposed this impolitic toast: "To the union of all honest men." Everybody considered this a blow at Jefferson. It was even more offensive to the Administration than his judiciary vote had been.[1]

From that moment all those peculiar weapons which politicians so well know how to use for the ruin of an opponent were employed for the destruction of Aaron Burr. Moreover, Jefferson had decided not only that Burr should not again be Vice-President, but that his bitterest enemy from his own State, George Clinton, should be the Republican candidate for that office; and, in view of Burr's strength and resourcefulness, this made necessary the latter's political annihilation.[2] "Never in the history of the United States did so powerful a combination of rival politicians unite to break down a single man as that which arrayed itself against Burr."[3]

Nevertheless, Burr, who "was not a vindictive man,"[4] did not retaliate for a long time.[5] But at last

[1] "Burr is a gone man; . . Jefferson is really in the dust in point of character, but notwithstanding this, he is looked up to . . as the Gog and Magog of his party." (Troup to King, Dec. 12, 1802, King, IV, 192–93.) See also Adams: U.S. I, 282.

[2] Channing: *Jeff. System*, 18–19.   [3] Adams: *U.S.* I, 332.

[4] Adams: *U.S.* II, 185.

"He was accused of this and that, through all of which he maintained a resolute silence. It was a characteristic of his never to refute charges against his name. . . It is not shown that Burr ever lamented or grieved over the course of things, however severely and painfully it pressed upon him." (McCaleb, 19.) See also Parton: *Burr*, 336.

[5] "Burr . . is acting a little and skulking part. Although Jefferson hates him as much as one demagogue can possibly hate another who is aiming to rival him, yet Burr does not come forward in an open and manly way agt. him. . . Burr is ruined in politics as well as in fortune." (Troup to King, Aug. 24, 1802, King, IV, 160.)

to retrieve himself,[1] he determined to appeal to the
people — at whose hands he had never suffered defeat — and, in 1804, he became a candidate for the
office of Governor of New York. The New York
Federalists, now reduced to a little more than a
strong faction, wished to support him, and were
urged to do so by many Federalist leaders of other
States. Undoubtedly Burr would have been elected
but for the attacks of Hamilton.

At this period the idea of secession was stirring in
the minds of the New England Federalist leaders.
Such men as Timothy Pickering, Roger Griswold,
Uriah Tracy, and James Hillhouse had even avowed
separation from the Union to be desirable and certain; and talk of it was general.[2] All these men were
warm and insistent in their support of Burr for
Governor, and at least two of them, Pickering and
Griswold, had a conference with him in New York
while the campaign was in progress.

Plumer notes in his diary that during the winter
of 1804, at a dinner given in Washington attended
by himself, Pickering, Hillhouse, Burr, and other
public men, Hillhouse "unequivocally declared that
. . the United States would soon form two distinct
and separate governments."[3] More than nine
months before, certain of the most distinguished
New England Federalists had gone to the extreme
length of laying their object of national dismemberment before the British Minister, Anthony Merry,

---

[1] Davis, II, 89 *et seq.*; Adams: *U.S.* I, 332–33; McCaleb, 20; Parton:
Burr, 327 *et seq.*

[2] See *supra*, 150–52, and vol. IV, chap. I, of this work.

[3] Plumer, 295.

and had asked and received his promise to aid them
in their project of secession.[1]

There was nothing new in the idea of dismembering the Union. Indeed, no one subject was more
familiar to all parts of the country. Since before the
adoption of the Constitution, it had been rife in the
settlements west of the Alleghanies.[2] The very year
the National Government was organized under the
Constitution, the settlers beyond the Alleghanies
were much inclined to withdraw from the Union because the Mississippi River had not been secured to
them.[3] For many years this disunion sentiment grew
in strength. When, however, the Louisiana Purchase
gave the pioneers on the Ohio and the Mississippi a

[1] It appears that some of the New England Federalists urged upon
the British Minister the rejection of the articles of the Boundary
Treaty in retaliation for the Senate's striking out one article of that
Convention. They did this, records the British Minister, because, as
they urged, such action by the British Government "would prove to be
a great exciting cause to them [the New England Secessionists] to go
forward rapidly in the steps which they have already commenced toward a separation from the Southern part of the Union.

"The [Federalist] members of the Senate," continues Merry, "have
availed themselves of the opportunity of their being collected here to
hold private meetings on this subject, and . . their plans and calculations respecting the event have been long seriously resolved. . . They
naturally look forward to Great Britain for support and assistance
whenever the occasion shall arrive." (Merry to Hawkesbury, March
1, 1804, as quoted in Adams: *U.S.* ii, 392.)

[2] As early as 1784, Washington declared that he feared the effect on
the Western people "if the Spaniards on their right, and Great Britain
on their left, instead of throwing impediments in their way as they
now do, should hold out lures for their trade and alliance. . . The
western settlers (I speak now from my own observations) stand as it
were, upon a pivot. The touch of a feather would turn them any way.
. . It is by the cement of interest alone we can be held together."
(Washington to the Governor of Virginia, 1784, as quoted in Marshall, v, 15–16.)

[3] Marshall, v, 179.

free water-way to the Gulf and the markets of the world, the Western secessionist tendency disappeared. But after the happy accident that bestowed upon us most of the great West as well as the mouth of the Mississippi, there was in the Eastern States a widely accepted opinion that this very fact made necessary the partitioning of the Republic.

Even Jefferson, as late as 1803, did not think that outcome unlikely, and he was prepared to accept it with his blessing: "If they see their interest in separation, why should we take sides with our Atlantic rather than our Mississippi descendants? It is the elder and the younger brother differing. God bless them both, and keep them in union, if it be for their good, but separate them, if it be better." [1]

Neither Spain nor Great Britain had ever given over the hope of dividing the young Republic and of acquiring for themselves portions of its territory. The Spanish especially had been active and unceasing in their intrigues to this end, their efforts being directed, of course, to the acquisition of the lands adjacent to them and bordering on the Mississippi and the Ohio.[2] In this work more than one American was in their pay. Chief of these Spanish agents was James Wilkinson, who had been a pensioner of Spain from 1787,[3] and so continued until at least 1807, the bribe money coming into his hands for several years

[1] Jefferson to Breckenridge, Aug. 12, 1803, *Works:* Ford, x, footnotes to 5–6.

[2] See Shepherd in *Am. Hist. Rev.* VIII, 501 *et seq.*; also *ib.* IX, 748 *et seq.*

[3] Clark: *Proofs of the Corruption of Gen. James Wilkinson*, 11–12, 16, 18–24, and documents therein referred to and printed in the appendix to Clark's volume.

after he had been placed in command of the armies of the United States.[1]

None of these plots influenced the pioneers to wish to become Spanish subjects; the most that they ever desired, even at the height of their dissatisfaction with the American Government, was independence from what they felt to be the domination of the East. In 1796 this feeling reached its climax in the Kentucky secession movement, one of its most active leaders being Wilkinson, who declared his purpose of becoming "the Washington of the West."[2]

By 1805, however, the allegiance of the pioneers to the Nation was as firm as that of any other part of the Republic. They had become exasperated to the point of violence against Spanish officials, Spanish soldiers, and the Spanish Government. They regarded the Spanish provinces of the Floridas and of Mexico as mere satrapies of a hated foreign autocracy; and this indeed was the case. Everywhere west of the Alleghanies the feeling was universal

[1] "Wilkinson is entirely devoted to us. He enjoys a considerable pension from the King." (Casa Yrujo, Spanish Minister, to Cevallos, Jan. 28, 1807, as quoted in Adams: *U.S.* iii, 342.) And see affidavits of Mercier and Derbigny, *Blennerhassett Papers:* Safford, footnotes to 429, 432.

"He [Wilkinson] had acted conformably as suited the true interests of Spain, and so I assured him for his satisfaction." (Folch, Spanish Governor of Florida, to the Governor-General of Cuba, June 25, 1807, as quoted by Cox in *Am. Hist. Rev.* x, 839.)

[2] Parton: *Burr*, 383; see also McCaleb, 4–9.

It should be borne in mind that this was the same Wilkinson who took so unworthy a part in the "Conway Cabal" against Washington during the Revolution. (See vol. i, 121–23, of this work.)

For further treatment of the Spanish intrigue, see Cox in *Am. Hist. Rev.* xix, 794–812; also Cox in *Southwestern Historical Quarterly*, xvii, 140–87.

that these lands on the south and southwest, held in subjection by an ancient despotism, should be "revolutionized" and "liberated"; and this feeling was shared by great numbers of people of the Eastern States.

Moreover, that spirit of expansion — of taking and occupying the unused and misused lands upon our borders — which has been so marked through American history, was then burning fiercely in every Western breast. The depredations of the Spaniards had finally lashed almost to a frenzy the resentment which had for years been increasing in the States bordering upon the Mississippi. All were anxious to descend with fire and sword upon the offending Spaniards.

Indeed, all over the Nation the conviction was strong that war with Spain was inevitable. Even the ultra-pacific Jefferson was driven to this conclusion; and, in less than ten months after Aaron Burr ceased to be Vice-President, and while he was making his first journey through the West and Southwest, the President, in two Messages to Congress, scathingly arraigned Spanish misdeeds and all but avowed that a state of war actually existed.[1]

Such, in broad outline, was the general state of things when Aaron Burr, his political and personal fortunes wrecked, cast about for a place to go and for work to do. He could not return to his practice in New York; there his enemies were in absolute control and he was under indictment for having chal-

---

[1] Annual Message, Dec. 3, 1805, and Special Message, Dec. 6, 1805. Richardson, I, 384-85, 388-89.

lenged Hamilton. The coroner's jury also returned
an inquest of murder against Burr and two of his
friends, and warrants for their arrest were issued. In
New Jersey, too, an indictment for murder hung
over him.[1]

Only in the fresh and undeveloped West did a new
life and a new career seem possible. Many projects
filled his mind — everything was possible in that inviting region beyond the mountains. He thought of
forming a company to dig a canal around the falls
of the Ohio and to build a bridge over that river,
connecting Louisville with the Indiana shore. He
considered settling lands in the vast dominions beyond the Mississippi which the Nation had newly
acquired from Spain. A return to public life as
Representative in Congress from Tennessee passed
through his mind.

But one plan in particular fitted the situation
which the apparently certain war with Spain created. Nearly ten years earlier,[2] Hamilton had
conceived the idea of the conquest of the Spanish
possessions adjacent to us, and he had sought to
enlist the Government in support of the project of
Miranda to revolutionize Venezuela.[3] Aaron Burr
had proposed the invasion and capture of the
Floridas, Louisiana, and Mexico two years before

[1] See *Memoirs, J. Q. A.*: Adams, I, 314–15.

Burr wrote: "In New-York I am to be disfranchised, and in New-
Jersey hanged" but "you will not . . conclude that I have become
disposed to submit tamely to the machinations of a banditti." Burr
to his son-in-law, March 22, 1805, Davis, II, 365.

[2] 1797–98.

[3] Lodge: *Alexander Hamilton*, 212–15; and see Turner in *Am. Hist.
Rev.* x, 276.

Hamilton embraced the project,[1] and the desire to carry out the plan continued strong within him. Circumstances seemed to make the accomplishment of it feasible. At all events, a journey through the West would enlighten him, as well as make clearer the practicability of his other schemes.

Now occurred the most unfortunate and disgraceful incident of Burr's life. In order to get money for his Mexican adventure, Burr played upon the British Minister's hostile feelings toward America and, in doing so, used downright falsehood. Although it was unknown at the time and not out of keeping with the unwritten rules of the game called diplomacy as then played, and although it had no effect upon the thrilling events that brought Burr before Marshall, so inextricably has this shameful circumstance been woven into the story of the Burr conspiracy, that mention of it must be made. It was the first thoroughly dishonorable act of Burr's tempestuous career.[2]

[1] Davis, II, 376–79.

[2] Only one previous incident in Burr's public life can even be faintly criticized from the point of view of honesty. In 1799 there were in New York City but two banking institutions, and both were controlled by Federalists. These banks aided business men of the Federalist Party and refused accommodation to Republican business men. The Federalists controlled the Legislature and no State charter for another bank in New York could be had.

Burr, as a member of the State Senate, secured from the Legislature a charter for the Manhattan Company to supply pure water to the city; but this charter authorized the use by the company of its surplus capital in any lawful way it pleased. Thus was established a new bank where Republican business men could get loans. Burr, in committee, frankly declared that the surplus was to establish a bank, and Governor Jay signed the bill. Although the whole project appears to have been open and aboveboard as far as Burr was concerned, yet when the bank began business, a violent attack was made on him. (Parton: Burr, 237–40.) For charter see Laws of New York (Webster and Skinner's edition), 1799, chap. 84.

Five months after Pickering, Griswold, and other New England Federalists had approached Anthony Merry with their plan to divide the Union, Burr prepared to follow their example. He first sounded that diplomat through a British officer, one Colonel Charles Williamson. The object of the New England Senators and Representatives had been to separate their own and other Northern States from the Union; the proposition that Williamson now made to the British Minister was that Burr might do the same thing for the Western States.[1] It was well known that the break-up of the Republic was expected and hoped for by the British Government, as well as by the Spaniards, and Williamson was not surprised when he found Merry as favorably disposed toward a scheme for separation of the States beyond the Alleghanies as he had been hospitable to the plan for the secession of New England.

Of the results of this conference Burr was advised; and when he had finished his preparations for his journey down the Ohio, he personally called upon Merry. This time a part of his real purpose was revealed; it was to secure funds.[2] Burr asked that half a million dollars be supplied him[3] for the revolutionizing of the Western States, but he did not tell of his dream about Mexico, for the realization of which the money was probably to be employed. In short, Burr lied; and in order to persuade Merry to

[1] Merry to Harrowby, Aug. 6, 1804, as quoted in Adams: *U.S.* ii, 395.

[2] McCaleb, viii–ix, 20–23.

[3] Merry to Harrowby (No. 15), "most secret," March 29, 1805, as quoted in Adams: *U.S.* ii, 403.

secure for him financial aid he proposed to commit treason. Henry Adams declares that, so far as the proposal of treason was concerned, there was no difference between the moral delinquency of Pickering, Griswold, Hillhouse, and other Federalists and that of Aaron Burr.[1]

The eager and credulous British diplomat promised to do his best and sent Colonel Williamson on a special mission to London to induce Pitt's Ministry to make the investment.[2] It should be repeated that Burr's consultations with the shallow and easily deceived Merry were not known at the time. Indeed, they never were fully revealed until more than three quarters of a century afterward.[3] Moreover, it has been demonstrated that they had little or no bearing upon the adventure which Burr finally tried to carry out.[4] He was, as has been said, audaciously and dishonestly playing upon Merry's well-known hostility to this country in order to extract money from the British Treasury.[5] This attempt and the later one upon the Spanish Minister, who was equally antagonistic to the United States, were revolting exhibitions of that base cunning and du-

[1] Adams: *U.S.* ii, 394.   [2] Davis, ii, 381; also Parton: *Burr*, 412.

[3] Henry Adams, in his researches in the British and Spanish archives, discovered and for the first time made public, in 1890, the dispatches of the British, Spanish, and French Ministers to their Governments. (See Adams: *U.S.* iii, chaps. xiii and xiv.)

[4] Professor Walter Flavius McCaleb has exploded the myth as to Burr's treasonable purposes, which hitherto has been accepted as history. His book, the *Aaron Burr Conspiracy*, may be said to be the last word on the subject. The lines which Professor McCaleb has therein so firmly established have been followed in this chapter.

[5] Pitt died and Burr did not get any money from the British. (See Davis, ii, 381.)

plicity which, at that period, formed so large a part of secret international intrigue.[1]

On April 10, 1805, Burr left Philadelphia on horseback for Pittsburgh, where he arrived after a nineteen days' journey. Before starting he had talked over his plans with several friends, among them former Senator Jonathan Dayton of New Jersey, who thereafter was a partner and fellow "conspirator."[2]

Another man with whom Burr had conferred was General James Wilkinson. Burr expected to meet him at Pittsburgh, but the General was delayed and the meeting was deferred. Wilkinson had just been appointed Governor of Upper Louisiana — one of the favors granted Burr during the Chase impeachment — and was the intimate associate of the fallen politician in his Mexican plan until, in a welter of falsehood and corruption, he betrayed him. Indeed, it was Wilkinson who, during the winter of 1804–05, when Burr was considering his future, proposed to him the invasion of Mexico and thus gave new life to Burr's old but never abandoned hope.[3]

On May 2, Burr started down the Ohio. When he

[1] "Burr's intrigue with Merry and Casa Yrujo was but a consummate piece of imposture." (McCaleb, viii.)

[2] Up to this time Dayton had had an honorable career. He had been a gallant officer of the Revolution; a member of the New Jersey Legislature for several years and finally Speaker of the House; a delegate to the Constitutional Convention; a Representative in Congress for four terms, during the last two of which he was chosen Speaker of that body; and finally Senator of the United States. He came of a distinguished family, was a graduate of Princeton, and a man of high standing politically and socially.

[3] See Cox in *Am. Hist. Rev.* xix, 801; also in *Southwestern Hist. Quarterly*, xvii, 174.

reached Marietta, Ohio, he was heartily welcomed. He next stopped at an island owned by Harman Blennerhassett, who happened to be away. While inspecting the grounds Burr was invited by Mrs. Blennerhassett to remain for dinner. Thus did chance lay the foundations for that acquaintance which, later, led to a partnership in the enterprise that was ended so disastrously for both.

At Cincinnati, then a town of some fifteen hundred inhabitants, the attentions of the leading citizens were markedly cordial. There Burr was the guest of John Smith, then a Senator from Ohio, who had become attached to Burr while the latter was Vice-President, and who was now one of his associates in the plans under consideration. At Smith's house he met Dayton, and with these friends and partners he held a long conversation on the various schemes they were developing.[1]

A week later found him at the "unhealthy and inconsiderable village"[2] of Louisville and from there he traveled by horseback to Frankfort and Lexington. While in Kentucky he conferred with General John Adair, then a member of the National Senate,

[1] That Burr, Dayton, and others seriously thought of building a canal around the falls of the Ohio on the Indiana side, is proved by an act passed by the Legislature of Indiana Territory in August, 1805, and approved by Governor William Henry Harrison on the 24th of that month. The act — entitled "An Act to Incorporate the Indiana Canal Company" — is very elaborate, authorizes a capital of one million dollars, and names as directors George Rogers Clark, John Brown, Jonathan Dayton, Aaron Burr, Benjamin Hovey, Davis Floyd, and six others. (See *Laws of the Indiana Territory, 1801–1806*, 94–108.) The author is indebted to Hon. Merrill Moores, M.C., of Indianapolis, for the reference to this statute.

[2] Hildreth, v. 597.

who, like Smith and Dayton, had in Washington formed a strong friendship for Burr, and was his confidant.[1] Another eminent man with whom he consulted was John Brown, then a member of the United States Senate from Kentucky, also an admirer of Burr.

It would appear that the wanderer was then seriously considering the proposal, previously made by Matthew Lyon, now a Representative in Congress from Kentucky, that Burr should try to go to the National House from Tennessee,[2] for Burr asked and received from Senator Brown letters to friends in that State who could help to accomplish that design. But not one word did Burr speak to General Adair, to Senator Brown, or to any one else of his purpose to dismember the Nation.

Burr arrived at Nashville at the end of the month. The popular greeting had grown warmer with each stage of his journey, and at the Tennessee Capital it rose to noisy enthusiasm. Andrew Jackson, then Major-General of the State Militia, was especially fervent and entertained Burr at his great log house. A "magnificent parade" was organized in his honor. From miles around the pioneers thronged into the

---

[1] Adair had been a soldier in the Revolutionary War, an Indian fighter in the West, a member of the Kentucky Constitutional Convention, Speaker of the House of Representatives of that State, Registrar of the United States Land Office, and was one of the ablest, most trusted, and best beloved of Kentuckians.

Adair afterward declared that "the intentions of Colonel Burr . . were to prepare and lead an expedition into Mexico, predicated on a war" between Spain and the United States; "without a war he knew he could do nothing." If war did not come he expected to settle the Washita lands. (Davis, II, 380.)

[2] See McCaleb, 25; Parton: *Burr*, 385–86.

frontier Capital. Flags waved, fifes shrilled, drums
rolled, cannon thundered. A great feast was spread
and Burr addressed the picturesque gathering.[1]
Never in the brightest days of his political success
had he been so acclaimed. Jackson, nine years before, when pleading with Congress to admit Tennessee into the Union, had met and liked Burr, who
had then advocated statehood for that vigorous and
aggressive Southern Territory. Jackson's gratitude
for Burr's services to the State in championing its
admission,[2] together with his admiration for the
man, now ripened into an ardent friendship.

His support of Burr well reflected that of the
people among whom the latter now found himself.
Accounts of Burr's conduct as presiding officer at
the trial of Chase had crept through the wilderness;
the frontier newspapers were just printing Burr's
farewell speech to the Senate, and descriptions of
the effect of it upon the great men in Washington
were passing from tongue to tongue. All this gilded
the story of Burr's encounter with Hamilton, which,
from the beginning, had been applauded by the
people of the West and South.

Burr was now in a land of fighting men, where
dueling was considered a matter of honor rather than
disgrace. He was in a rugged democracy which regarded as a badge of distinction, instead of shame,
the killing in fair fight of the man it had been taught
to believe to be democracy's greatest foe. Here, said
these sturdy frontiersmen, was the captain so long

[1] McCaleb, 26; Parton: *Life of Andrew Jackson*, I, 307-10.
[2] Parton: *Jackson*, I, 309.

sought for, who could lead them in the winning of
Texas and Mexico for America; and this Burr now
declared himself ready to do — a purpose which
added the final influence toward the conquest of the
mind and heart of Andrew Jackson.

Floating down the Cumberland River in a boat
provided by Jackson, Burr encountered nothing but
friendliness and encouragement. At Fort Massac he
was the guest of Wilkinson, with whom he remained
for four days, talking over the Mexican project. Soon
afterward he was on his way down the Mississippi
from St. Louis in a larger boat with colored sails,
manned by six soldiers — all furnished by Wilkinson. After Burr's departure Wilkinson wrote to
Adair, with whom he had served in the Indian
wars, that "we must have a peep at the unknown
world beyond me."

On June 25, 1805, Burr landed at New Orleans,
then the largest city west of the Alleghanies. There
the ovation to the "hero" surpassed even the demonstration at Nashville. Again came dinners, balls,
fêtes, and every form of public and private favor.
So perfervid was the welcome to him that the Sisters
of the largest nunnery in Louisiana invited Burr to
visit their convent, and this he did, under the conduct of the bishop.[1] Wilkinson had given him a
letter of introduction to Daniel Clark, the leading
merchant of the city and the most influential man
in Louisiana. The letter contained this cryptic sentence: "To him [Burr] I refer you for many things

[1] Burr to his daughter, May 23, 1805. This letter is delightful. "I
will ask Saint A. to pray for thee too. I believe much in the efficacy
of her prayers." (Davis, II, 372.)

improper to letter, and which he will not say to any other." [1]

The notables of the city were eager to befriend Burr and to enter into his plans. Among them were John Watkins, Mayor of New Orleans, and James Workman, Judge of the Court of Orleans County. These men were also the leading members of the Mexican Association, a body of three hundred Americans devoted to effecting the "liberation" of Mexico — a design in which they accurately expressed the general sentiment of Louisiana. The invasion of Mexico had become Burr's overmastering purpose, and it gathered strength the farther he journeyed among the people of the West and South. To effect it, definite plans were now made. [2]

The Catholic authorities of New Orleans approved Burr's project, and appointed three priests to act as agents for the revolutionists in Mexico. [3] Burr's vision of Spanish conquest seemed likely of realization. The invasion of Mexico was in every heart, on every tongue. All that was yet lacking to make it certain was war between Spain and the United States, and every Western or Southern man believed that war was at hand.

Late in July, Burr, with justifiably high hope, left New Orleans by the overland route for Nashville, riding on horses supplied by Daniel Clark. Everywhere he found the pioneers eager for hostilities. At Natchez the people were demonstrative. By August 6, Burr was again with Andrew Jackson, having

---

[1] McCaleb, 27; Parton: *Burr*, 393.   [2] McCaleb, 29.

[3] Davies, Parton, and McCaleb state that the Catholic Bishop appointed three Jesuits, but there was no bishop in New Orleans at that time and the Jesuits had been suppressed.

ridden over Indian trails four hundred and fifty miles through the swampy wilderness.[1]

The citizens of Nashville surpassed even their first welcome. At the largest public dinner ever given in the West up to that time, Burr entered the hall on Jackson's arm and was received with cheers. Men and women vied with one another in doing him honor. The news Burr brought from New Orleans of the headway that was being made regarding the projected descent upon the Spanish possessions, thrilled Jackson; and his devotion to the man whom all Westerners and Southerners had now come to look upon as their leader knew no bounds.[2] For days Jackson and Burr talked of the war with Spain which the bellicose Tennessee militia general passionately desired, and of the invasion of Mexico which Burr would lead when hostilities began.[3] At Lexington, at Frankfort, everywhere, Burr was received in similar fashion. While in Kentucky he met Henry Clay, who at once yielded to his fascination.

But soon strange, dark rumors, starting from Natchez, were sent flying over the route Burr had just traveled with such acclaim. They were set on foot by an American, one Stephen Minor, who was a paid spy of Spain.[4] Burr, it was said, was about to raise the standard of revolution in the Western and Southern States. Daniel Clark wished to advise Burr of these reports and of the origin of them, but

[1] Burr to his daughter, May 23, 1805, Davis, ii, 372.

[2] "No one equalled Andrew Jackson in warmth of devotion to Colonel Burr." (Adams: *U.S.* iii, 221.)

[3] Parton: *Jackson*, i, 311–12; and McCaleb, 81.

[4] McCaleb, 32–33. Minor was probably directed to do this by Casa Yrujo himself. (See Cox: *West Florida Controversy*, 189.)

did not know where to reach him. So he hastened
to write Wilkinson that Burr might be informed
of the Spanish canard: "Kentucky, Tennessee, the
State of Ohio, . . with part of Georgia and Carolina,
are to be bribed with the plunder of the Spanish
countries west of us, to separate from the Union."
And Clark added: "Amuse Mr. Burr with an account of it." [1]

Wilkinson himself had long contemplated the idea
of dismembering the Nation; he had even sounded
some of his officers upon that subject.[2] As we have
seen, he had been the leader of the secession movement in Kentucky in 1796. But if Burr ever really
considered, as a practical matter, the separation of
the Western country from the Union, his intimate contact with the people of that region had driven such a
scheme from his mind and had renewed and strengthened his long-cherished wish to invade Mexico. For
throughout his travels he had heard loud demands
for the expulsion of Spanish rule from America; but
never, except perhaps at New Orleans, a hint of secession. And if, during his journey, Burr so much as
intimated to anybody the dismemberment of the Republic, no evidence of it ever has been produced.[3]

Ignorant of the sinister reports now on their way
behind him, Burr reached the little frontier town of
St. Louis early in September and again conferred
with Wilkinson, assuring him that the whole South

[1] Clark to Wilkinson, Sept. 7, 1805, Wilkinson: *Memoirs of My
Own Times*, II, Appendix XXXIII.

[2] Testimony of Major James Bruff, *Annals*, 10th Cong. 1st Sess.
589–609, 616–22.

[3] Except, of course, Wilkinson's story that Burr urged Western
revolution, during the conference of these two men at St. Louis.

ànd West were impatient to attack the Spaniards, and that in a short time an army could be raised to invade Mexico.[1] According to the story which the General told nearly two years afterward, Burr informed him that the South and West were ripe for secession, and that Wilkinson responded that Burr was sadly mistaken because "the Western people . . are bigoted to Jefferson and democracy."[2]

Whatever the truth of this may be, it is certain that the rumors put forth by his fellow Spanish agent had shaken Wilkinson's nerve for proceeding further with the enterprise which he himself had suggested to Burr. Also, as we shall see, the avaricious General had begun to doubt the financial wisdom of giving up his profitable connection with the Spanish Government. At all events, he there and then began to lay plans to desert his associate. Accordingly, he gave Burr a letter of introduction to William Henry Harrison, Governor of Indiana Territory, in which he urged Harrison to have Burr sent to Congress from Indiana, since upon this "perhaps . . the Union may much depend."[3]

Mythical accounts of Burr's doings and intentions had now sprung up in the East. The universally known wish of New England Federalist leaders for a division of the country, the common talk east of the Alleghanies that this was inevitable, the vivid memory of a like sentiment formerly prevailing in Kentucky, and the belief in the seaboard States that it still continued — all rendered probable, to those liv-

[1] McCaleb, 34.
[2] Wilkinson's testimony, *Annals*, 10th Cong. 1st Sess. 611.
[3] McCaleb, 35; Parton: *Burr*, 401.

ing in that section, the schemes now attributed to Burr.

Of these tales the Eastern newspapers made sensations. A separate government, they said, was to be set up by Burr in the Western States; the public lands were to be taken over and divided among Burr's followers; bounties, in the form of broad acres, were to be offered as inducements for young men to leave the Atlantic section of the country for the land of promise toward the sunset; Burr's new government was to repudiate its share of the public debt; with the aid of British ships and gold Burr was to conquer Mexico and establish a vast empire by uniting that imperial domain to the revolutionized Western and Southern States.[1] The Western press truthfully denied that any secession sentiment now existed among the pioneers.

The rumors from the South and West met those from the North and East midway; but Burr having departed for Washington, they subsided for the time being. The brushwood, however, had been gathered — to burst into a raging conflagration a year later, when lighted by the torch of Executive authority in the hands of Thomas Jefferson.

During these months the Spanish officials in Mexico and in the Floridas, who had long known of the hostility of American feeling toward them, learned of Burr's plan to seize the Spanish possessions, and magnified the accounts they received of the preparations he was making.[2]

The British Minister in Washington was also in

[1] McCaleb, 36–37.   [2] Cox, 190; and McCaleb, 39.

spasms of nervous anxiety.[1] When Burr reached
the Capital he at once called on that slow-witted
diplomat and repeated his overtures. But Pitt had
died; the prospect of British financial assistance had
ended; [2] and Burr sent Dayton to the Spanish Minister with a weird tale [3] in order to induce that diplomat to furnish money.

Almost at the same time the South American
adventurer, Miranda, again arrived in America, his
zeal more fiery than ever, for the "liberation" of
Venezuela. He was welcomed by the Administration, and Secretary of State Madison gave him a
dinner. Jefferson himself invited the revolutionist
to dine at the Executive Mansion. Burr's hopes
were strengthened, since he intended doing in
Mexico precisely what Miranda was setting out to
do in Venezuela.

[1] McCaleb, 38.

[2] Pitt died January 6, 1806. The news reached America late in the
winter and Wilkinson learned of it some time in the spring. This fed
his alarm, first awakened by the rumors set afloat by Spanish agents
of which Clark had advised him. According to Davis and Parton,
Wilkinson's resolve to sacrifice Burr was now taken. (See Davis, II,
381–82; also Parton: *Burr*, 412.)

[3] This was that Burr with his desperadoes would seize the President
and other officers of the National Government, together with the public money, arsenals, and ships. If, thereafter, he could not reconcile
the States to the new arrangement, the bandit chief and his followers
would sail for New Orleans and proclaim the independence of Louisiana.

Professor McCaleb says that this tale was a ruse to throw Casa Yrujo
off his guard as to the now widespread reports in Florida and Texas, as
well as America, of Burr's intended descent upon Mexico. (See Mc-
Caleb, 54–58.) It should be repeated that the proposals of Burr and
Dayton to Merry and Casa Yrujo were not publicly known for many
years afterward.

Wilkinson had coached Dayton and Burr in the art of getting money
by falsehood and intrigue. (*Ib.* 54.)

In February, 1806, Miranda sailed from New York upon his Venezuelan undertaking. His openly avowed purpose of forcibly expelling the Spanish Government from that country had been explained to Jefferson and Madison by the revolutionist personally. Before his departure, the Spanish filibuster wrote to Madison, cautioning him to keep "in the deepest secret" the "important matters" which he (Miranda) had laid before him.[1] The object of his expedition was a matter of public notoriety. In New York, in the full light of day, he had bought arms and provisions and had enlisted men for his enterprise.

Excepting for Burr's failure to secure funds from the British Government, events seemed propitious for the execution of his grand design. He had written to Blennerhassett a polite and suggestive letter, not inviting him, however, to engage in the adventure;[2] the eager Irishman promptly responded, begging to be admitted as a partner in Burr's enterprises, and pledging the services of himself and his friends.[3] Burr, to his surprise, was cordially received by Jefferson at the White House where he had a private conference of two hours with the President.

The West openly demanded war with Spain; the whole country was aroused; in the House, Randolph offered a resolution to declare hostilities; everywhere the President was denounced for weakness and delay.[4] If only Jefferson would act — if only the people's earnest desire for war with Spain were granted —

[1] Adams: *U.S.* III, 189–91.   [2] *Blennerhassett Papers:* Safford, 115.
[3] Blennerhassett to Burr, Dec. 21, 1805, *ib.* 118; and see Davis, II, 392.
[4] McCaleb, 50–53.

Burr could go forward. But the President would make no hostile move — instead, he proposed to buy the Floridas. Burr, lacking funds, thought for a moment of abandoning his plans against Mexico, and actually asked Jefferson for a diplomatic appointment, which was, of course, refused.[1]

The rumor had reached Spain that the Americans had actually begun war. On the other hand, the report now came to Washington that the Spaniards had invaded American soil. The Secretary of War ordered General Wilkinson to drive the Spaniards back. The demand for war throughout the country grew louder. If ever Burr's plan of Mexican conquest was to be carried out, the moment had come to strike the blow. His confederate, Wilkinson, in command of the American Army and in direct contact with the Spaniards, had only to act.

The swirl of intrigue continued. Burr tried to get the support of men disaffected toward the Administration. Among them were Commodore Truxtun, Commodore Stephen Decatur, and "General"[2] William Eaton. Truxtun and Decatur were writhing under that shameful treatment by which each of these heroes had been separated, in effect removed, from the Navy. Eaton was cursing the Administration for deserting him in his African exploits, and even more for refusing to pay several thousand dollars which he claimed to have expended in his Barbary transactions.[3]

[1] Plumer, 348; Parton: *Burr*, 403–04.

[2] Eaton assumed this title during his African career. He had no legal right to it.

[3] Eaton had done good work as American Consul to Algiers, a post

Truxtun and Burr were intimate friends, and the Commodore was fully told of the design to invade Mexico in the event of war with Spain; should that not come to pass, Burr advised Truxtun that he meant to settle lands he had arranged to purchase beyond the Mississippi. He tried to induce Truxtun to join him, suggesting that he would be put in command of a naval force to capture Havana, Vera Cruz, and Cartagena. When Burr "positively" informed him that the President was not a party to his enterprise, Truxtun declined to associate himself with it. Not an intimation did Burr give Truxtun of any purpose hostile to the United States. The two agreed in their contemptuous opinion of Jefferson and his Administration.[1] To Commodore Decatur, Burr talked in similar fashion, using substantially the same language.

But to "General" Eaton, whom he had never be-

to which he was appointed by President Adams. In 1804, Jefferson appointed him United States Naval Agent to the Barbary States. With the approval of the Administration, Eaton undertook to overthrow the reigning Pasha of Tripoli and restore to the throne the Pasha's brother, whom the former had deposed. In executing this project Eaton showed a resourcefulness, persistence, and courage as striking as the means he adopted were bizarre and the adventure itself fantastic. (Allen: *Our Navy and the Barbary Corsairs*, 227 *et seq.*)

Eaton charged that the enterprise failed because the American fleet did not properly coöperate with him, and because Tobias Lear, American Consul-General to Algiers, compromised the dispute with the reigning Bey whom Eaton's nondescript "army" was then heroically fighting. (Eaton to the Secretary of the Navy, Aug. 9, 1805, *Eaton:* Prentiss, 376.)

Full of wrath he returned to the United States, openly denouncing all whom he considered in any way responsible for the African *débâcle*, and demanding payment of large sums which he alleged had been paid by him in advancing American interests in Africa. (*Ib.* 393, 406; also see Allen, 265.)

[1] See Truxtun's testimony, *infra*, 459–60.

fore met, Burr unfolded plans more far-reaching and bloody, according to the Barbary hero's account of the revelations.[1] At first Burr had made to Eaton the same statements he had detailed to Truxtun and Decatur, with the notable difference that he had assured Eaton that the proposed expedition was "under the authority of the general government." Notwithstanding his familiarity with intrigue, the suddenly guileless Eaton agreed to lead a division of the invading army under Wilkinson who, Burr assured him, would be "Chief in Command."

But after a while Eaton's sleeping perception was aroused. Becoming as sly as a detective, he resolved to "draw Burr out," and "listened with seeming acquiescence" while the villain "unveiled himself" by confidences which grew ever wilder and more irrational: Burr would establish an empire in Mexico and divide the Union; he even "meditated overthrowing the present Government" — if he could secure Truxtun, Decatur, and others, he *"would turn Congress neck and heels out of doors, assassinate the President, seize the treasury and Navy; and declare himself the protector of an energetic government."*

Eaton at last was "shocked" and "dropped the mask," declaring that the one word, *"Usurper,* would destroy" Burr. Thereupon Eaton went to Jefferson and urged the President to appoint Burr American Minister to some European government and thus get him out of the country, declaring that " if *Burr were not in some way disposed of we should*

---

[1] The talks between Burr and Eaton took place at the house of Sergeant-at-Arms Wheaton, where Burr boarded. (*Annals*, 10th Cong. 1st Sess. 510.)

*within eighteen months have an insurrection if not a
revolution on the waters of the Mississippi.*" The
President was not perturbed — he had too much
confidence in the Western people, he said, "to admit
an *apprehension* of that kind." But of the horrid
details of the murderous and treasonable villain's
plans, never a word said Eaton to Jefferson.[1]

However, the African hero did "detail the whole
projects of Mr. Burr" to certain members of Congress.[2] "They believed Col. Burr capable of anything — and agreed that *the fellow ought to be
hanged*"; but they refused to be alarmed — Burr's
schemes were "too chimerical and his circumstances
too desperate to . . merit of serious consideration." [3]
So for twelve long months Eaton said nothing more
about Burr's proposed deviltry. During this time
he continued alternately to belabor Congress and the
Administration for the payment of the expenses of
his Barbary exploits.[4]

Andrew Jackson, while entertaining Burr on his

[1] See Eaton's deposition, *Eaton:* Prentiss, 396–403; 4 Cranch, 462–
67. (Italics are Eaton's.)

[2] Samuel Dana and John Cotton Smith. (See Eaton's testimony,
Annals, 10th Cong. 1st Sess. 512; and *Eaton:* Prentiss, 396–403.)

That part of Eaton's account of Burr's conversation which differs
from those with Truxtun and Decatur is simply unaccountable. That
Burr was capable of anything may be granted; but his mind was
highly practical and he was uncommonly reserved in speech. Undoubtedly Eaton had heard the common talk about the timidity and
supineness of the Government under Jefferson and had himself used
language such as he ascribed to Burr.

Whichever way one turns, no path out of the confusion appears.
But for Burr's abstemious habits (he was the most temperate of all
the leading men of that period) an explanation might be that he and
Eaton were very drunk — Burr recklessly so — if he indulged in this
uncharacteristic outburst of loquacity.

[3] *Eaton:* Prentiss, 402.   [4] McCaleb, 62.

first Western journey, had become the most promising, in practical support, of all who avowed themselves ready to follow Burr's invading standard into
Mexico; and with Jackson he had freely consulted
about that adventure. From Washington, Burr
now wrote the Tennessee leader of the beclouding
of their mutually cherished prospects of war with
Spain.

But hope of war was not dead, wrote Burr —
indeed, Miranda's armed expedition "composed of
American citizens, and openly fitted out in an American port," made it probable. Jackson ought to be
attending to something more than his militia offices,
Burr admonished him: "Your country is full of fine
materials for an army, and I have often said a brigade could be raised in West Tennessee which would
drive double their number of Frenchmen off the
earth." From such men let Jackson make out and
send to Burr "a list of officers from colonel down to
ensign for one or two regiments, composed of fellows
fit for business, and with whom you would trust your
life and your honor." Burr himself would, "in case
troops should be called for, recommend it to the
Department of War"; he had "reason to believe that
on such an occasion" that department would listen
to his advice.[1]

[1] Burr to Jackson, March 24, 1806, Parton: *Jackson*, i, 313–14.
Burr also told Jackson of John Randolph's denunciation of Jefferson's "duplicity and imbecility," and of small politics receiving "more
of public attention than all our collisions with foreign powers, or than
all the great events on the theatre of Europe." He closed with the
statement, then so common, that such "things begin to make reflecting men think, many good patriots to doubt, and some to despond."
(See McCaleb, 51.)

At last Burr, oblivious to the danger that Eaton might disclose the deadly secrets which he had so imprudently confided to a dissipated stranger, resolved to act and set out on his fateful journey. Before doing so, he sent two copies of a cipher letter to Wilkinson. This was in answer to a letter which Burr had just received from Wilkinson, dated May 13, 1806, the contents of which never have been revealed. Burr chose, as the messenger to carry overland one of the copies, Samuel Swartwout, a youth then twenty-two years of age, and brother of Colonel John Swartwout whom Jefferson had removed from the office of United States Marshal for the District of New York largely because of the Colonel's lifelong friendship for Burr. The other copy was sent by sea to New Orleans by Dr. Justus Erich Bollmann.[1]

No thought had Burr that Wilkinson, his ancient army friend and the arch conspirator of the whole plot, would reveal his dispatch. He and Wilkinson were united too deeply in the adventure for that to be thinkable. Moreover, the imminence of war appeared to make it certain that when the General received Burr's cipher, the two men would be comrades in arms against Spain in a war which, it cannot

[1] This man, then thirty-five years of age, and "engaging in . . appearance" (*Blennerhassett Papers:* Safford, 434), had had a picturesque career. A graduate of Göttingen, he lived in Paris during the Revolution, went to London for a time, and from there to Vienna, where he practiced medicine as a cover for his real design, which was to discover the prison where Lafayette was confined and to rescue him from it. This he succeeded in doing, but both were taken soon afterward. Bollmann was imprisoned for many months, and then released on condition that he leave Austria forever. He came to the United States and entered into Burr's enterprise with unbounded enthusiasm. His name often appears as "Erick Bolman" in American records.

be too often repeated, it was believed Wilkinson could bring on at any moment.

Nevertheless, Burr and Dayton had misgivings that the timorous General might not attack the Spaniards. They bolstered him up by hopeful letters, appealing to his cupidity, his ambition, his vanity, his fear. Dayton wrote that Jefferson was about to displace him and appoint another head of the army; let Wilkinson, therefore, precipitate hostilities — "You know the rest. . . Are you ready? Are your numerous associates ready? Wealth and glory! Louisiana and Mexico!" [1]

In his cipher dispatch to Wilkinson, Burr went to even greater lengths and with reason, for the impatient General had written him another letter, urging him to hurry: "I fancy Miranda has taken the bread out of your mouth; and I shall be ready for the grand expedition before you are." [2] Burr then assured Wilkinson that he was not only ready but on his way, and tried to strengthen the resolution of the shifty General by falsehood. He told of tremendous aid secured in far-off Washington and New York, and intimated that England would help. He was coming himself with money and men, and details were given. Bombastic sentences — entirely unlike any language appearing in Burr's voluminous correspondence and papers — were well chosen for their effect on Wilkinson's vainglorious mind: "The gods invite us to glory and fortune; it remains to be seen whether we deserve the boon. . . Burr guarantees

[1] Dayton to Wilkinson, July 24, 1806, *Annals*, 10th Cong. 1st sess. 560.

[2] See testimony of Littleton W. Tazewell, John Brokenbrough, and Joseph C. Cabell. (*Annals*, 10th Cong. 1st Sess. 630, 675, 676).

the result with his life and honor, with the lives and honor and the fortunes of hundreds, the best blood of our country." [1]

Fatal error! The sending of that dispatch was to give Wilkinson his opportunity to save himself by assuming the disguise of patriotism and of fealty to Jefferson, and, clad in these habiliments, to denounce his associates in the Mexican adventure as traitors to America. Soon, very soon, Wilkinson was to use Burr's letter in a fashion to bring his friend and many honest men to the very edge of execution — a fate from which only the fearlessness and penetrating mind of John Marshall was to save them.

But this black future Burr could not foresee. Certain, as were most men, that war with Spain could not be delayed much longer, and knowing that Wilkinson could precipitate it at any moment, Burr's mind was at rest. At the beginning of August, 1806, he once more journeyed down the Ohio. On the way he stopped at a settlement on the Monongahela, not far from Pittsburgh, where he visited one Colonel George Morgan. This man afterward declared that Burr talked mysteriously — the Administration was contemptible, two hundred men could drive the Government into the Potomac, five hundred could take New York; and, Burr added laughingly, even the Western States could be detached from the Union. Most of this was said "in the presence of a considerable company." [2]

[1] For Burr's cipher dispatch see Appendix D.
[2] *Annals*, 10th Cong. 1st sess. 424–28 and see McCaleb, 77.
Professor McCaleb evidently doubts the disinterestedness of Morgan and his sons. He shows that they had been in questionable land

The elder Morgan, who was aged and garrulous,[1] pieced together his inferences from Burr's meaning looks, jocular innuendoes, and mysterious statements,[2] and detected a purpose to divide the Nation. Deeply moved, he laid his deductions before the Chief Justice of Pennsylvania and two other gentlemen from Pittsburgh, a town close at hand; and a letter was written to Jefferson, advising him of the threatened danger.[3]

From Pittsburgh, Burr for the second time landed on the island of Harman Blennerhassett, who was eager for any adventure that would restore his declining fortunes. If war with Spain should, after all, not come to pass, Burr's other plan was the purchase of the enormous Bastrop land grant on the Washita River. Blennerhassett avidly seized upon both projects.[4] From that moment forward, the settlement of this rich and extensive domain in the then untouched and almost unexplored West became the alternative purpose of Aaron Burr in case the

transactions and, at this moment, were asking Congress to grant them a doubtful land claim. (See McCaleb, footnote to 77.)

[1] Testimony of Morgan's son, *Annals*, 10th Cong. 1st Sess. 424.

[2] "Colonel Burr, on this occasion as on others, comported himself precisely as a man having 'treasonable' designs would *not* comport himself, unless he were mad or intoxicated." (Parton: *Burr*, 415.) Professor McCaleb's analysis of the Morgan incident is thorough and convincing. (See McCaleb, 76–78.)

[3] Nevill and Roberts to Jefferson, Oct. 7, 1806, "Letters in Relation to Burr Conspiracy," MSS. Lib. Cong. This important letter set out that "to give a correct written statement of those [Burr's] conversations [with the Morgans] . . would be difficult . . and indeed, according to our informant, much more was to be collected, from the *manner* in which certain things were said, and hints given than from words used."

[4] McCaleb, 78–79; Parton: *Burr*, 411.

desire of his heart, the seizure of Mexico, should fail.[1]

Unfortunately Blennerhassett who, as his friends declared, "had all kinds of sense, except common sense," [2] now wrote a series of letters for an Ohio country newspaper in answer to the articles appearing in the Kentucky organ of Daveiss and Humphrey Marshall, the *Western World*. The Irish enthusiast tried to show that a separation of the Western States from "Eastern domination" would be a good thing. These foolish communications were merely repetitions of similar articles then appearing in the Federalist press of New England, and of effusions printed in Southern newspapers a few years before. Nobody, it seems, paid much attention to these vagaries of Blennerhassett. It is possible that Burr knew of them, but proof of this was never adduced. When the explosion came, however, Blennerhassett's maunderings were recalled, and they became another one of those evidences of Burr's guilt which, to the public mind, were "confirmation strong as proofs of holy writ."

Burr and his newly made partner contracted for the building of fifteen boats, to be delivered in four months; and pork, meal, and other provisions were purchased. The island became the center of operations. Soon a few young men from Pittsburgh joined the enterprise, some of them sons of Revolutionary officers, and all of them of undoubted loyalty

[1] McCaleb, 83–84; Parton: *Burr*, 412–13.

At this time Burr also wrote to William Wilkins and B. H. Latrobe calling their attention to his Bastrop speculation. (Miscellaneous MSS. N.Y. Pub. Lib.)

[2] See testimony of Dudley Woodbridge, *infra*, 489.

to the Nation. To each of these one hundred acres of land on the Washita were promised, as part of their compensation for participating in the expedition, the entire purpose of which was not then explained to them.[1]

Burr again visited Marietta, where the local militia were assembled for their annual drill, and put these rural soldiers through their evolutions, again fascinating the whole community.[2] At Cincinnati, Burr held another long conference with his partner, Senator John Smith, who was a contractor and general storekeeper. The place which the Washita land speculation had already come to hold in his mind is shown by the conversation — Burr talked as much of that project as he did of war with Spain and his great ambition to invade Mexico;[3] but of secession, not a syllable.

Next Burr hurried to Nashville and once more became the honored guest of Andrew Jackson, whom he frankly told of the modification of his plans. His immediate purpose, Burr said, now was to settle the Washita lands. Of course, if war should break out he would lead a force into Texas and Mexico. Burr kept back only the part Wilkinson was to play in precipitating hostilities; and he said nothing of his efforts to bolster up that frail warrior's resolution.[4]

In Tennessee and Kentucky the talk was again of war with Spain. Indeed, it was now the only talk.[5]

---

[1] McCaleb, 80.   [2] Parton: *Burr*, 415–16.   [3] McCaleb, 81.
[4] *Ib.*; and see Parton: *Jackson*, i, 318.
[5] "There were not a thousand persons in the United States who did not think war with Spain inevitable, impending, begun!" (Parton: *Burr*, 407; McCaleb, 110.)

For the third time in the Tennessee Capital a public
banquet was given to the hero by whom the people
expected to be led against the enemy. Soon afterward Jackson issued his proclamation to the Tennessee militia calling them to arms against the hated
Spaniards, and volunteered his services to the National Government. Jefferson answered in a letter
provoking in its vagueness.[1]

At Lexington, Kentucky, Burr and Blennerhassett now purchased from Colonel Charles Lynch,
the owner of the Bastrop grant, several hundred
thousand acres on the Washita River in Northern
Louisiana.[2]

To many to whom Burr had spoken of his scheme
to invade Mexico he gave the impression that his
designs had the approval of the Administration; to
some he actually stated this to be the fact. In case
war was declared, the Administration, of course,
would necessarily support Burr's attack upon the
enemy; if hostilities did not occur, the "Government might overlook the preparations as in the case
of Miranda." [3] It is hard to determine whether the
project to invade Mexico — of which Burr did not
inform them, but which they knew to be his purpose — or the plan to settle the Washita lands, was
the more attractive to the young men who wished
to join him. Certainly, the Bastrop grant was so

[1] See Jefferson to Jackson, Dec. 3, 1806, as quoted in McCaleb, 82.
[2] See testimony of Colonel Charles Lynch, *Annals*, 10th Cong.
1st Sess. 656–58; and that of Thomas Bodley, Clerk of the Circuit
Court, *ib.* 655–56. The statements of these men are also very important as showing Burr's plans and preparations at this time.
[3] McCaleb, 84–85.

placed as to afford every possible lure to the youthful, enterprising, and adventurous.[1]

At this moment Wilkinson, apparently recovered from the panic into which Clark's letter had thrown him a year before, seemed resolved at last to strike. He even wrote with enthusiasm to General John Adair: "The time long looked for by many & wished for by more has now arrived, for subverting the Spanish government in Mexico — be ready & join me; we will want little more than light armed troops. . . More will be done by marching than by fighting. . . We cannot fail of success.[2] Your military talents are requisite. Unless you fear to join a Spanish intriguer [Wilkinson] come immediately — without your aid I can do nothing."[3] In reply Adair wrote Wilkinson that "the United States had not declared war against Spain and he did not believe they would." If not, Adair would not violate the law by joining Wilkinson's projected attack on Spain.[4]

By the same post Wilkinson wrote to Senator John Smith a letter bristling with italics: "I shall assuredly push them [the Spaniards] over the Sabine . . as that you are alive. . . *You must speedily send me a force* to

[1] The Bastrop grant was accessible to the markets of New Orleans; it was surrounded by Indian tribes whose trade was valuable; its forests were wholly unexplored; it was on the Spanish border, and therefore an admirable point for foray or retreat. (See McCaleb, 83; and Cox in *Southwestern Hist. Quarterly*, XVII, 150.)

[2] Wilkinson to Adair, Sept. 28, 1806, as quoted in open letter of Adair to the *Orleans Gazette*, May 16, 1807, "Letters in Relation," MSS. Lib. Cong.

[3] Wilkinson to Adair, Sept. 28, 1806, as quoted by Plumer, Feb. 20, 1807, "Register," Plumer MSS. Lib. Cong.

[4] Adair to Wilkinson, Oct. or Nov. 1806, as quoted by Plumer Feb. 20, 1807, "Register," Plumer MSS. Lib. Cong.

support our pretensions . . 5000 *mounted infantry . . may suffice to carry us forward as far as Grand River* [the Rio Grande], *there we shall require* 5000 *more to conduct us to Mount el Rey . . after which from* 20 *to* 30,000 *will be necessary to carry our conquests to California* and the *Isthmus of Darien. I write in haste, freely* and *confidentially*, being ever your friend." [1]

In Kentucky once more the rumors sprang up that Burr meant to dismember the Union, and these were now put forward as definite charges. For months Joseph Hamilton Daveiss, a brother-in-law of John Marshall — appointed at the latter's instance by President Adams as United States Attorney for the District of Kentucky [2] — had been writing Jefferson exciting letters about some kind of conspiracy in which he was sure Burr was engaged. The President considered lightly these tales written him by one of his bitterest enemies.

With the idea of embarrassing the Republican President, by connecting him, through the Administration's seeming acquiescence in Burr's projects as in the case of the Miranda expedition, Daveiss and his relative, former Senator Humphrey Marshall — both leaders of the few Federalists now remaining in Kentucky — welded together the rumors of Burr's Mexican designs and those of his treasonable plot to separate the Western States from the Union. These they published in a newspaper which they controlled at Frankfort. [3]

---

[1] Wilkinson to Smith, Sept. 28, 1806, "Letters in Relation," MSS. Lib. Cong.

[2] See vol. II, 560, of this work.

[3] The *Western World*, edited by the notorious John Wood, author of

The moss was removed from the ancient Spanish intrigues; Wilkinson was truthfully denounced as a pensioner of Spain; but the plot, it was charged, had veered from a union of the West with the Spanish dominions, to the establishment, by force of arms, of an independent trans-Alleghany Government.[1] The Federalist organs in the East adopted the stories related in the *Western World*, and laid especial emphasis on the disloyalty of the Western States, particularly of Kentucky.

The rumors had so aroused the people living near Blennerhassett's island that Mrs. Blennerhassett sent a messenger to warn Burr that he could not, in safety, appear there again. Learning this from the bearer of these tidings, Burr's partner, Senator John Smith, demanded of his associate an explanation. Burr promptly answered that he was "greatly surprised and really hurt" by Smith's letter. "If," said Burr, "there exists any design to separate the Western from the Eastern States, I am totally ignorant of it. I never harbored or expressed any such intention to any one, nor did any person ever intimate such design to me."[2]

---

the *History of the Administration of John Adams*, which was suppressed by Burr. (See vol. II, 380, of this work.) Wood was of the same type of irresponsible pamphleteer and newspaper hack as Callender and Cheetham. His so-called "history" was a dull, untruthful, scandalous diatribe; and it is to Burr's credit that he bought the plates and suppressed the book. Yet this action was one of the reasons given for the remorseless pursuit of him, after it had been determined to destroy him.

[1] McCaleb, 172–75.

[2] Adams: *U.S.* III, 276. This was a falsehood, since Burr had proposed Western secession to the British Minister. But he knew that no one else could have knowledge of his plot with Merry. It is both

Daveiss and Humphrey Marshall now resolved to stay the progress of the plot at which they were convinced that the Republican Administration was winking. If Jefferson was complacent, Daveiss would act and act officially; thus the President, by contrast, would be fatally embarrassed. Another motive, personal in its nature, inspired Daveiss. He was an able, fearless, passionate man, and he hated Burr violently for having killed Hamilton whom Daveiss had all but worshiped.[1]

Early in November the District Attorney moved the United States Court at Frankfort to issue compulsory process for Burr's apprehension and for the attendance of witnesses. Burr heard of this at Lexington and sent word that he would appear voluntarily. This he did, and, the court having denied Daveiss's motion because of the irregularity of it, the accused demanded that a public and official investigation be made of his plans and activities. Accordingly, the grand jury was summoned and Daveiss given time to secure witnesses.

On the day appointed Burr was in court. By his side was his attorney, a tall, slender, sandy-haired

interesting and important that to the end of his life Burr steadily maintained that he never harbored a thought of dismembering the Nation.

[1] (Clay to Pindell, Oct. 15, 1828, *Works of Henry Clay:* Colton, IV, 206; also *Private Correspondence of Henry Clay:* Colton, 206–08.)

So strong was his devotion to Hamilton, that "after he had attained full age," Daveiss adopted the name of his hero as part of his own, thereafter signing himself Joseph Hamilton Daveiss and requiring everybody so to address him. "Chiefly moved . . by his admiration of Colonel Hamilton and his hatred of Colonel Burr," testifies Henry Clay, Daveiss took the first step in the series of prosecutions that ended in the trial of Burr for treason. (*Ib.*)

young man of twenty-nine who had just been appointed to the National Senate. Thus Henry Clay entered the drama. Daveiss failed to produce a single witness, and Burr, "after a dignified and grave harangue," was discharged, to the tumultuous delight of the people.[1]

Two weeks later the discomfited but persistent and undaunted District Attorney again demanded of Judge Innes the apprehension of the "traitor." Clay requested of Burr a written denial of the charges so incessantly made against him. This Burr promptly furnished.[2] Clay was so convinced of Burr's integrity that he declared in court that he "could pledge

[1] Adams: *U.S.* III, 278.

[2] "I have no design, nor have I taken any measure to promote a dissolution of the Union, or a separation of any one or more States from the residue. I have neither published a line on this subject nor has any one, through my agency, or with my knowledge. I have no design to intermeddle with the Government or to disturb the tranquillity of the United States, or of its territories, or any part of them.

"I have neither issued, nor signed, nor promised a commission to any person for any purpose. I do not own a musket nor a bayonet, nor any single article of military stores, nor does any person for me, by my authority or with my knowledge.

"My views have been fully explained to, and approved by, several of the principal officers of Government, and, I believe, are well understood by the administration and seen by it with complacency. They are such as every man of honor and every good citizen must approve." (Burr to Clay, Dec. 1, 1806, *Priv. Corres.*: Colton, 13–14.)

Parton says that this was substantially true: "Jefferson and his cabinet undoubtedly knew . . that he was going to settle in the western country, and that if the expected war should break out, he would head an onslaught upon the Dons.

"His *ulterior* views may have been known to one, or even two, members of Jefferson's cabinet, for anything that can *now* be ascertained. The moment the tide really turned against this fated man, a surprising ignorance overspread many minds that had before been extremely well-informed respecting his plans." (Parton: *Burr*, 422–23; see also McCaleb, 191.)

his own honor and innocence" for those of his client. Once more no witnesses were produced; once more the grand jury could not return an indictment; once more Burr was discharged. The crowd that packed the court-room burst into cheers.[1] That night a ball, given in Burr's honor, crowned this second of his triumphs in the United States Court.[2]

Thereafter Burr continued his preparations as if nothing had happened. To all he calmly stated the propriety of his enterprise. To his fellow adventurer, Senator John Smith, he was again particularly explicit and clear: "If there should be a war between the United States and Spain, I shall head a corps of volunteers and be the first to march into the Mexican provinces. If peace should be proffered, which I do not expect, I shall settle my Washita lands, and make society as pleasant as possible. . . I have been persecuted, shamefully persecuted."[3] As to dividing the Union, Burr told Smith that "if Bonaparte with all his army were in the western country with the object . . he would never see salt water again."[4]

While Burr was writing this letter, Jefferson was signing a document that, when sent forth, as it immediately was, ignited all the rumors, reports, accusations, and suspicions that had been accumulating.

---

[1] "When the grand jury returned the bill of indictment not true, a scene was presented in the Court-room which I had never before witnessed in Kentucky. There were shouts of applause from an audience, not one of whom . . would have hesitated to level a rifle against Colonel Burr, if he believed that he aimed to dismember the Union, or sought to violate its peace, or overturn its Constitution." (Clay to Pindell, Oct. 15, 1828, *Priv. Corres.*: Colton, 207.)

[2] Adams: *U.S.* III, 282–83; McCaleb, 192–93; Parton: *Burr*, 418–22.

[3] Burr to Smith, as quoted in McCaleb, 183.   [4] Parton: *Burr*, 423.

and set the country on fire with wrath against the disturber of our national bliss.

When Wilkinson received Burr's cipher dispatch, he took time to consider the best methods for saving himself, filling his purse, and brightening his tarnished reputation.[1] The faithful and unsuspecting young Swartwout, Burr's messenger, was persuaded to remain in Wilkinson's camp for a week after the delivery of the fatal letter. He was treated with marked friendliness, and from him the General afterward pretended to have extracted frightful details of Burr's undertaking.[2]

[1] The Spanish Minister accurately explained to his home Government the motives that now animated the commander of the American Army:

"Wilkinson is entirely devoted to us. He enjoys a considerable pension from the King. . . He anticipated . . the failure of an expedition of this nature [Burr's invasion of Mexico]. Doubtless he foresaw from the first that the improbability of success in case of making the attempt would leave him like the dog in the fable with the piece of meat in his mouth; that is, that he would lose [both] the honorable employment . . [as American Commander] and the generous pension he enjoys from the King. These considerations, secret in their nature, he could not explain to Burr; and when the latter persisted in an idea so fatal to Wilkinson's interests, nothing remained but to take the course adopted.

"By this means he assures his pension; and will allege his conduct on this occasion as an extraordinary service, either for getting it increased, or for some generous compensation.

"On the other hand this proceeding secures his distinguished rank in the military service of the United States, and covers him with a popularity which may perhaps result in pecuniary advantages, and in any case will flatter his vanity.

"In such an alternative he has acted as was to be expected; that is, he has sacrificed Burr in order to obtain, on the ruins of Burr's reputation, the advantages I have pointed out." (Casa Yrujo to Cevallos, Jan. 28, 1807, as quoted in Adams: *U.S.* iii, 342–43.)

[2] Swartwout, under oath, denied that he had told Wilkinson this story. Swartwout's affidavit is important. He swears that he never heard of the revolutionizing of "the N[ew] O[rleans] Territory" until

Seven more days passed, and at last, two weeks after he had received Burr's cipher dispatch, Wilkinson wrote Jefferson that "a Numerous and powerful Association, extending from New York to . . the Mississippi had been formed to levy & rendezvous eight or Ten Thousand Men in New Orleans . . & from thence . . to carry an Expedition against Vera Cruz." Wilkinson gave details — dates and places of assembling troops, methods of invasion, etc., and added: "It is unknown under what Authority this Enterprize has been projected, from where the means of its support are derived, or what may be the intentions of its leaders in relation to the Territory of Orleans." [1]

Surprising as this was, the General supported it by a "confidential" and personal letter to Jefferson [2] still more mysterious and disquieting: "The mag-

Wilkinson mentioned it — "I first heard of such a project from Wilkinson"; that Burr never had spoken of attacking Mexico except "in case of war with Spain"; that if there were no war, Burr intended to settle the Washita lands. (See Henshaw in *Quarterly Pub. Hist. and Phil. Soc. Ohio*, IX, Nos. 1 and 2, 53–54.)

This young man made a deep impression of honesty and straightforwardness on all who came in contact with him. (See testimony of Tazewell, Cabell, and Brokenbrough, *Annals*, 10th Cong. 1st Sess. 633.) "Swartwout is a fine genteel intelligible young man." (Plumer to Mason, Jan. 30, 1807, Plumer MSS. Lib. Cong.)

Notwithstanding his frank and engaging manner, Swartwout was at heart a basely dishonest person. Thirty years later, when Collector of the Port of New York, he embezzled a million and a quarter dollars of the public funds. (Bassett: *Life of Andrew Jackson*, II, 452–53.)

[1] Wilkinson's dispatch, Oct. 20, 1806, "Letters in Relation," MSS. Lib. Cong. Wilkinson's dispatch to Jefferson was based on the revelations which he pretended to have drawn from Swartwout.

[2] The dispatch would go on file in the War Department; the "personal and confidential" communication to Jefferson would remain in the President's hands.

nitude of the Enterprize, the desperation of the Place, and the stupendous consequences with which it seems pregnant, stagger my belief & excite doubts of the reality, against the conviction of my Senses; & it is for this reason I shall forbear to commit Names. . . I have never in my whole Life found myself in such circumstances of perplexity and Embarrassment as at present; for I am not only uninformed of the prime mover and Ultimate Objects of this daring Enterprize, but am ignorant of the foundation on which it rests."

Wilkinson went on to say that, as an inducement for him to take part in it, he had been told that "you [Jefferson] connive at the combination and that our country will justify it." If this were not true, "then I have no doubt the revolt of this Territory will be made an auxiliary step to the main design of attacking Mexico." So he thought he ought to compromise with the Spaniards and throw himself with his "little Band into New Orleans, to be ready to defend that Capitol against Usurpation and violence."

He wrote more to the same effect, and added this postscript: "Should Spain be disposed to War seriously with us, might not some plan be adopted to correct the delirium of the associates, and by a pitiable appeal to their patriotism to engage them in the service of their Country. I merely offer the suggestion as a possible expedient to prevent the Horrors of a civil contest, and I do believe that, with competent authority I could accomplish the object." [1]

[1] Wilkinson to Jefferson, Oct. 21, 1806, "Letters in Relation," MSS. Lib. Cong.

This was the letter which a few months later caused Chief Justice John Marshall to issue a subpœna *duces tecum* directed to President Thomas Jefferson in order to have it produced in court.[1]

Jefferson had known of the rumors about Burr — George Morgan, Joseph H. Daveiss, and William Eaton had put him on the track of the "traitor." Others had told of the American Catiline's treasonable plans; and the newspapers, of which he was a studious reader, had advised the President of every sensation that had appeared. Jefferson and his Cabinet had nervously debated the situation, decided on plans to forestall the conspiracy, and then hurriedly abandoned them;[2] evidently they had no faith in the lurid stories of Burr's treasonable purposes and preparations.

Letters to Jefferson from the West, arriving October 24, 1806, bore out the disbelief of the President and his Cabinet in Burr's lawless activities; for these advices from the President's friends who, on the ground, were closely watching Burr, contained "not one word . . of any movements by Colonel Burr. This total silence of the officers of the Government, of the members of Congress, of the newspapers, proves he is committing no overt act against law," Jefferson wrote in his Cabinet Memorandum.[3] So the President and his Cabinet decided to do nothing further at that time than to order John Graham, while on his way to assume the office of

[1] See *infra*, chap. VIII.

[2] Jefferson's Cabinet Memorandum, Oct. 22, 1806, as quoted in Adams: *U.S.* III, 278–80.

[3] *Ib.* Oct. 25, 1806, as quoted in Adams: *U.S.* III, 281.

Secretary of the Orleans Territory, to investigate Burr's activities.

But when the mysterious warnings from Wilkinson reached Jefferson, he again called his Cabinet into consultation and precipitate action was taken. Orders were dispatched to military commanders to take measures against Burr's expedition; Wilkinson was directed to withdraw his troops confronting the Spaniards and dispose of them for the defense of New Orleans and other endangered points.

Most important of all, a Presidential Proclamation was issued to all officials and citizens, declaring that a conspiracy had been discovered, warning all persons engaged in it to withdraw, and directing the ferreting out and seizure of the conspirators' "vessels, arms and military stores." [1] Graham preceded the Proclamation and induced Governor Tiffin and the Ohio Legislature to take action for the seizure of Burr's boats and supplies at Marietta; and this was done.

On December 10, 1806, Comfort Tyler of Onondaga County, New York, one of the minor leaders of the Burr expedition,[2] arrived at Blennerhassett's island with a few boats and some twenty young men who had joined the adventure. There were a half-

---

[1] Jefferson's Proclamation, Nov. 27, 1806, *Works*, Ford, x, 301–02; Wilkinson: *Memoirs*, ii, Appendix xcvi.

[2] Tyler had been in the New York Legislature with Burr and there became strongly attached to him. (See Clark: *Onondaga*.) He went to Beaver, Pennsylvania, in the interests of Burr's enterprise, and from there made his way to Blennerhassett's island. Tyler always maintained that the sole object of the expedition was to settle the Washita lands. (See his pathetic letter asserting this to Lieutenant Horatio Stark, Jan. 23, 1807, "Letters in Relation," MSS. Lib. Cong.)

dozen rifles among them, and a few fowling pieces. With these the youths went hunting in the Ohio forests. Blennerhassett, too, had his pistols. This was the whole of the warlike equipment of that militant throng — all that constituted that "overt act of treason by levying war against the United States" which soon brought Burr within the shadow of the gallows.

Jefferson's Proclamation had now reached Western Virginia, and it so kindled the patriotism of the militia of Wood County, within the boundaries of which the island lay, that that heroic host ' resolved to descend in its armed might upon the embattled "traitors," capture and deliver them to the vengeance of the law. The Wood County men, unlike those of Ohio, needed no act of legislature to set their loyalty in motion. The Presidential Proclamation, and the sight of the enemies of the Nation gathered in such threatening and formidable array on Blennerhassett's island, were more than enough to cause them to spring to arms in behalf of their imperiled country.

Badly frightened, Blennerhassett and Tyler, leaving Mrs. Blennerhassett behind, fled down the river with thirty men in six half-equipped boats. They passed the sentries of the Wood County militia only because those ministers of vigilance had got thoroughly drunk and were sound asleep. Next day, however, the militia invaded the deserted island and, finding the generously stocked wine cellar, restored their strength by drinking all the wine and whiskey on the place. They then demonstrated their abhorrence of treason by breaking the windows, demolishing the furniture, tearing the pictures, trampling the flower-beds, burning the fences, and insulting Mrs. Blennerhassett.[1]

Graham procured the authorities of Kentucky to take action similar to that adopted in Ohio. Burr, still ignorant of Jefferson's Proclamation, proceeded to Nashville, there to embark in the boats Jackson was building for him, to go on the last river voyage of his adventure.

Jackson, like Smith and Clay, had been made uneasy by the rumors of Burr's treasonable designs. He had written Governor Claiborne at New Orleans a letter of warning, particularly against Wilkinson, and not mentioning Burr by name.[2] When Burr arrived at the Tennessee Capital, Jackson, his manner now cold, demanded an explanation. Burr, "with his usual dignified courtesy, instantly complied." [3] It would seem that Jackson was satisfied by his reassurance, in spite of the President's Proclamation which reached Nashville three days before Burr's departure; [4] for not only did Jackson permit him to proceed, but, when the adventurer started down the Cumberland in two of the six boats which he had built on Burr's previous orders, consented that a nephew of his wife should make one of the ten or fifteen young men who accompanied the expedi-

---

[1] Hildreth, v, 619; Parton: *Burr*, 436–38.

[2] Jackson to Claiborne, Nov. 12, 1806, Parton: *Jackson*, i, 319; and see McCaleb, 253.

[3] Adams: *U.S.* iii, 287; Parton: *Jackson*, i, 320–21.

[4] Parton inaccurately says that the Proclamation reached Nashville after Burr's departure. (Parton: *Jackson*, i, 322.)

tion. He even gave the boy a letter of introduction
to Governor Claiborne at New Orleans.[1]

After the people had recovered from the shock of
astonishment that Jefferson's Proclamation gave
them, the change in them was instantaneous and
extreme.[2] The President, to be sure, had not mentioned Burr's name or so much as hinted at treason;
all that Jefferson charged was a conspiracy to attack
the hated Spaniards, and this was the hope and
desire of every Westerner. Nevertheless, the public
intelligence penetrated what it believed to be the
terrible meaning behind the President's cautious
words; the atrocious purpose to dismember the
Union, reports of which had pursued Burr since a
Spanish agent had first set the rumor afoot a year
before, was established in the minds of the people.

Surely the President would not hunt down an
American seeking to overthrow Spanish power in
North America, when a Spanish "liberator" had
been permitted to fit out in the United States an
expedition to do the same thing in South America.
Surely Jefferson would not visit his wrath on one
whose only crime was the gathering of men to strike
at Spain with which power, up to that very moment,
everybody supposed war to be impending and, indeed, almost begun. This was unthinkable. Burr
must be guilty of a greater crime — the greatest of

[1] Adams: *U.S.* III, 288; Parton: *Jackson*, I, 321.

[2] For instance, at Nashville, Burr was burnt in effigy in the public
square. (Parton: *Jackson*, I, 322.) At Cincinnati an amusing panic
occurred: three merchant scows loaded with dry goods were believed
to be a part of Burr's flotilla of war vessels about to attack the town.
The militia was called out, citizens organized for defense, the adjacent country was appealed to for aid. (See McCaleb, 248–49.)

crimes. In such fashion was public opinion made ready to demand the execution of the "traitor" who had so outrageously deceived the people; and that popular outcry began for the blood of Aaron Burr by which John Marshall was assailed while presiding over the court to which the accused was finally taken.

From the moment that Wilkinson decided to denounce Burr to the President, his language became that of a Bombastes Furioso, his actions those of a military ruffian, his secret movements matched the cunning of a bribe-taking criminal. By swiftest dispatch another message was sent to Jefferson. "My doubts have ceased," wrote Wilkinson, concerning "this deep, dark, wicked, and wide-spread conspiracy, embracing the young and the old, the democrat and the federalist, the native and the foreigner, the patriot of '76 and the exotic of yesterday, the opulent and the needy, the ins and the outs."

Wilkinson assured Jefferson, however, that he would meet the awful emergency with "indefatigable industry, incessant vigilance and hardy courage"; indeed, declared he, "I shall glory to give my life" to defeat the devilish plot. But the numbers of the desperadoes were so great that, unless Jefferson heavily reinforced him with men and ships, he and the American army under his command would probably perish.[1]

As the horse bearing the messenger to Jefferson disappeared in the forests, another, upon which rode

[1] Wilkinson to Jefferson, Nov. 12, 1806, Wilkinson: *Memoirs*, II. Appendix c.

a very different agent, left Wilkinson's camp and galloped toward the Southwest. The latter agent was Walter Burling, a corrupt factotum of Wilkinson's, whom that martial patriot sent to the Spanish Viceroy at Mexico City to advise him of Wilkinson's latest service to Spain in thwarting Burr's attack upon the royal possessions, and in averting war between the United States and His Catholic Majesty. For these noble performances Wilkinson demanded of the Spanish Viceroy more than one hundred and ten thousand dollars in cash, together with other sums which "he [had] been obliged to spend in order to sustain the cause of good government, order and humanity." [1]

Wilkinson had asked the Viceroy to destroy the letter and this was accordingly done in Burling's presence. The Royal representative then told Burling that he knew all about Burr's plans to invade Mexico, and had long been ready to repel a much larger force than Wilkinson stated Burr to be leading. "I thanked him for his martial zeal and insinuated that I wished him happiness in the pursuit of his righteous intentions," wrote the disgusted and sarcastic Viceroy in his report to the Government at

---

[1] Iturrigaray to Cevallos, March 12, 1807, as quoted in McCaleb, 169; and see Shepherd in *Am. Hist. Rev.* IX, 533 *et seq.*

The thrifty General furnished Burling with a passport through the posts he must pass. ("Letters in Relation," as quoted in McCaleb, 166.)

Credentials to the Spanish official were also given Burling by one of Wilkinson's friends, Stephen Minor of Natchez, the man who had first set on foot the rumor of Burr's secession intentions. He was also in the pay of Spain. (*Ib.* 166–67.)

The Spaniards aided Burling on his journey in every way possible. (Herrera to Cordero, Dec. 1, 1806, as quoted in *ib.* 167–68.)

Madrid.[1] With this Wilkinson had to be content, for
the Viceroy refused to pay him a peso.

Upon Burling's return, the vigilant American
Commander-in-Chief forwarded to Jefferson a report of conditions in Mexico, as represented by
Burling, together with a request for fifteen hundred dollars to pay that investigator's expenses.[2]
The sole object of Burling's journey was, Wilkinson
informed the President, to observe and report upon
the situation in the great Spanish Vice-royalty as
recent events had affected it, with respect to the
interests of the United States; and Jefferson was assured by the General that his agent was the soundest and most devoted of patriots.[3]

To back up the character he was now playing,
Wilkinson showered warnings upon the officers of
the Army and upon government officials in New
Orleans. "The plot thickens. . . My God! what a
situation has our country reached. Let us save it if
we can. . . On the 15th of this month [November],
Burr's declaration is to be made in Tennessee and
Kentucky; hurry, hurry after me, and, if necessary,
let us be buried together, in the ruins of the place we
shall defend." This was a typical message to Colonel
Cushing.[4]

Wilkinson dispatched orders to Colonel Freeman
at New Orleans to repair the defenses of the city;
but "be you as silent as the grave. . . You are sur-

[1] Iturrigaray to Cevallos, March 12, 1807, as quoted in McCaleb,
168–69.   [2] *Ib*. 171.
[3] Wilkinson to Jefferson, March 12, 1807, "Letters in Relation,"
MSS. Lib. Cong.
[4] Wilkinson to Cushing, Nov. 7, 1806, Wilkinson: *Memoirs*, II,
Appendix XCIX.

rounded by secret agents." [1] He informed Governor
Claiborne that "the storm will probably burst in
New Orleans, where I shall meet it and triumph or
perish." [2] Otherwise "the fair fabric of our inde-
pendence . . will be prostrated, and the Goddess of
Liberty will take her flight from the globe forever."
Again and again, Wilkinson sounded the alarm.
"Burr with rebellious bands may soon be at hand."
Therefore, "civil institutions must . . yield to the
strong arm of military law." [3] But Claiborne must
"not breathe or even hint" that catastrophe was
approaching.

At last, however, Wilkinson unbosomed himself to
the merchants of New Orleans whom he assembled
for that purpose. Agents of the bandit chief were all
around them, he said — he would have arrested
them long since had he possessed the power. The
desperadoes were in larger force than he had at first
believed — "by all advices the enemy, at least 2000
strong," would soon reach Natchez. They meant,
first, to sack New Orleans and then to attack Mexico
by land and sea. If successful in that invasion, "the
Western States were then to be separated from the
Union." But Wilkinson would "pledge his life in the
defense of the city and his country." [4]

At that moment Burr had not even started down
the Mississippi with his nine boats manned by sixty
young men.

[1] Wilkinson to Freeman, Wilkinson: *Memoirs*, II, Appendix XCIX.
[2] Wilkinson to Claiborne, Nov. 12, 1806, *ib.* 328.
[3] Wilkinson to Claiborne, Dec. 6 and 7, 1806, as quoted in McCaleb,
205–06.
[4] *Ib.* 209–10.

For a time the city was thrown into a panic.[1] But Wilkinson had overblustered. The people, recovered from their fright, began to laugh. Thousands of fierce Vandals, brandishing their arms, on their way to take New Orleans, capture Mexico, destroy the Union! And this mighty force not now far away! How could that be and no tidings of it except from Wilkinson? That hero witnessed with dismay this turn of public sentiment. Ruthless action, then, or all his complicated performances would go for naught. Ridicule would be fatal to his plans.

So General James Wilkinson, as head of the Army of the United States, began a reign of lawless violence that has no parallel in American history. To such base uses can authority be put — with such peril to life and liberty is it invested — when unchecked by Constitutional limitation enforced by fearless and unprejudiced judges! Men were arrested and thrown into prison on Wilkinson's orders, wholly without warrant of law. The first thus to be seized were Samuel Swartwout and Dr. Justus Erich Bollmann. Their papers were confiscated; they were refused counsel, were even denied access to the courts. Soldiers carried them to a warship in the river which at once set sail with orders from Wilkinson for the delivery of the prisoners to the President at Washington.[2]

---

[1] Wilkinson to Clark, Dec. 10, 1806, Clark: *Proofs*, 150; also McCaleb, 212; and see Wilkinson to Claiborne, Dec. 15, 1806, as quoted in McCaleb, 213–14.

[2] Swartwout was treated in a manner peculiarly outrageous. Before his arrest Wilkinson had borrowed his gold watch, and afterward refused to return it. When the soldiers seized Swartwout they "hurried"

Another man similarly arrested was Peter V. Ogden of New York, nephew of Jonathan Dayton, who had been the companion of Swartwout in his long overland journey in quest of Wilkinson. Public-spirited lawyers swore out writs of habeas corpus for these three men. Not a syllable of evidence was adduced against Ogden, who by some mischance had not been transported with Bollmann and Swartwout, and the court discharged him.

In response to the order of the court to produce the bodies of Bollmann and Swartwout, Wilkinson sent his aide with the General's return to the process. As the "Commander of the Army of the United States," he said, he took on himself "all responsibility . . resulting from the arrest of Erick Bollmann, who is accused of being guilty of the crime of treason against the government and the laws of the United States," and he had "taken opportune measures to warrant his safe delivery into the hands of the President."

This had been done, avowed Wilkinson, solely in

him across the river, lodged him "for several days & nights in a poor inhospitable shed — & deprived of the necessaries of life."

Finally, when ordered to march with his guard — and being refused any information as to where he was to be taken — the prisoner declared that he was to be murdered and leapt into the river, crying, "I had as well die here as in the woods," whereupon "the L^t drew up his file of six men & ordered them to shoot him. The soldiers directed their guns at him & snapt them, but owing to the great rain, 3 of the guns flashed in the pan, & the other's would not take fire. The men pursued & took him. But for the wetness of the powder this unfortunate young man must have be[en] murdered in very deed."

Swartwout was not permitted to take his clothing with him on the ship that carried him to Baltimore; and the officer in charge of him was under orders from Wilkinson to put his prisoner in chains during the voyage. (Plumer, Feb. 21, 1807, "Register," Plumer MSS. Lib. Cong.)

order "to secure the nation which is menaced to its foundations by a band of traitors associated with Aaron Burr." To that end he would, he defiantly informed the court, "arrest, without respect to class or station, all those against whom [he had] positive proof of being accomplices in the machinations against the state."[1] This defiance of the courts was accompanied by a copy of Wilkinson's version of Burr's cipher letter and some memoranda by Bollmann, together with Wilkinson's assertion that he had certain evidence which he would not, at that time, disclose.

Jefferson had long demanded of Wilkinson a copy of the incriminating Burr letter, and this was now forwarded, together with the General's account of the arrest of Bollmann, Swartwout, and Ogden. In his report to the President, Wilkinson accused the judge who had released Ogden of being an associate of Burr in his "treasonable combinations," and characteristically added that he would "look to our country for protection" in case suit for damages was brought against him by Bollmann and Swartwout.[2]

While Bollmann and Swartwout, in close confinement on the warship, were tossing on the winter seas, the saturnalia of defiance of the law continued in New Orleans. Ogden was again seized and incarcerated. So was his friend, James Alexander of New

[1] Wilkinson's return reported in the *Orleans Gazette*, Dec. 18, 1806, as quoted in McCaleb, 217. It does not appear what return was made in the matter of the application for a writ of habeas corpus in favor of Swartwout.

[2] Wilkinson to Jefferson, printed in *National Intelligencer*, Jan. 23. 1807, as quoted in McCaleb, 218.

York, who had displeased Wilkinson by suing out
the writs of habeas corpus. Both were shortly taken
to a military prison. Judges, leading lawyers, prominent citizens — all protested in vain. New writs of
habeas corpus were issued and ignored. Edward
Livingston sued out a writ of attachment [1] against
Wilkinson. It was defied. The civil governor was
appealed to; he was cowed and declined to act in
this "delicate as well as dangerous" state of things.
In despair and disgust Judge James Workman adjourned the Orleans County Court *sine die* and resigned from the Bench; [2] he too was seized by Wilkinson's soldiers, and recovered his liberty only by
the return of the Judge of the United States District
Court, who dared the wrath of the military tyrant
in order to release his imprisoned fellow judge. [3]

In the midst of this debauch of military lawlessness, General John Adair, late one afternoon, rode
into New Orleans. He had come on business, having
sent three thousand gallons of whiskey and two boatloads of provisions to be sold in the city, and expecting also to collect a debt of fifteen hundred dollars
due him at that place; he had also intended to make
some land deals.

The moment Wilkinson heard of the arrival of his
old friend and comrade, the General ordered "a captain and one hundred soldiers" to seize Adair. This
was done so peremptorily that he was not allowed to
dine, "altho the provision was ready on the table";

[1] This was one cause of Jefferson's hatred of Livingston. For the
celebrated litigation between these men and the effect of it on Marshall and Jefferson, see vol. IV, chap. II, of this work.

[2] McCaleb, 219–21.   [3] Hildreth, v, 613.

he was denied medicine, which on account of illness
he wished to take with him; he was refused extra
clothing and was not even allowed "to give directions respecting his horses which· cost him $700 in
Kentucky." Then the bewildered Adair was hurried
on board a schooner and taken "down the river 25
miles, landed on the other side . . and placed under
a tent in a swamp."

After he had been kept six days under guard
in this situation, Adair "was shipped aboard the
schooner Thatcher for Baltimore . . in the custody
of Lt. Luckett." Wilkinson ordered the lieutenant to
keep Adair in close confinement and to resist "with
force and arms" any civil officer who might attempt
to take Adair "by a writ of habeas corpus." [1]

The reason for this particular atrocity was that
Wilkinson had written Adair the letters quoted
above, and unless his correspondent were discredited and disgraced, he could convict Wilkinson of
the very conspiracy with which Burr was being
charged.[2] During his reign of terror to put down

[1] Plumer's résumé of a letter from Adair to Clay. (Feb. 20, 1807,
"Register," Plumer MSS. Lib. Cong.)

For this outrage Adair, within a year, brought suit against Wilkinson for false imprisonment. This was bitterly fought for ten years, but
finally Adair secured judgment for $2500, "against which Wilkinson
was indemnified by Congress." (Hildreth, v, 627.)

For three or four years Adair continued in public disfavor solely
because of his supposed criminal connection with Burr, of which his
arrest by Wilkinson convinced the inflamed public mind. He slowly
recovered, however, rendered excellent service as an officer in the War
of 1812, and under Jackson commanded the Kentucky troops at the
battle of New Orleans with distinguished gallantry. In 1820 the old
veteran was elected Governor of Kentucky. Afterward he was chosen
Representative in Congress from his district.

[2] Plumer's résumé of Adair's letter to Clay, supra, note 1. Every

"treason," the General was in secret communication with the Spaniards, earning the bribe money
which he was, and long had been, receiving from
them.[1]

While Wilkinson at New Orleans was thus openly
playing despot and secretly serving Spain, the President's Annual Message was read to Congress.

In this document Jefferson informed the National
Legislature of the advance of the Spaniards toward
American territory, the alarming posture of affairs,
the quick response of the pioneers to the call of the
Government for volunteers. "Having received information," he said, "that, in another part of the
United States, a great number of private individuals
were combining together, arming and organizing
themselves contrary to law, to carry on a military
expedition against the territories of Spain [he]
thought it necessary to take measures . . for suppressing this enterprise . . and bringing to justice

word of Adair's startling account of his arrest was true. It was never
even denied. John Watkins told Wilkinson of a conversation with
Adair immediately after the latter's arrival which showed that nobody had reason to fear Burr: "He [Adair] observed . . that the bubble would soon burst & signified that the claims were without foundation & that he had seen nothing like an armament or preparations for
a warlike expedition." (Watkins to Wilkinson, Jan. 14, 1807, Wilkinson MSS. Chicago Hist. Soc.)

Professor Cox has suggested to the author that Wilkinson's summary arrest of Adair was to prevent the further circulation of his
statement.

[1] "During the disturbances of Burr the aforesaid general [Wilkin-
son] has, by means of a person in his confidence, constantly maintained a correspondence with me, in which he has laid before me not
only the information which he acquired, but also his intentions for the
various exigencies in which he might find himself." (Folch to the Governor-General of Cuba, June 25, 1807, as quoted by Cox in *Am. Hist.
Rev.* x, 839.)

its authors and abettors." [1] Such was the slight reference made to the Burr "conspiracy." Thanks to the President's Proclamation, the "treasonable" plot of Aaron Burr was already on every tongue; but here, indeed, was an anti-climax.

The Senate referred the brief paragraph of the President's Message relating to the conspiracy to a special committee. The committee took no action. Everybody was in suspense. What were the facts? Nobody knew. But the air was thick with surmise, rumor, conjecture, and strange fancies — none of them bearing the color of truth. [2] Marshall was then

[1] Jefferson's Message, Dec. 2, 1806, *Annals*, 9th Cong. 2d Sess. 12; Richardson, I, 406.

[2] "We have been, & still are, both amused & perplexed with the rumours, reports, & conjectures respecting Aaron Burr. They are numerous, various, & contradictory. . . I must have plenary evidence before I believe him capable of committing the hundredth part of the absurd & foolish things that are ascribed to him. . . The president of the United States, a day or two since, informed me that he knew of no evidence sufficient to convict him of either high crimes or misdemeanors." (Plumer to Jeremiah Mason, Jan. 4, 1807, Plumer MSS. Lib. Cong.) See also Plumer to Langdon, Dec. 1806, and to Livermore, Jan. 19, 1807, Plumer MSS. *loc. cit.*

These letters of Plumer's are most important. They state the general opinion of public men, especially Federalists, as expressed in their private conversations.

"I never believed him to be a Fool," wrote John Adams to his most intimate friend. "But he must be an Idiot or a Lunatick if he has really planned and attempted to execute such a Project as is imputed to him." Politicians have "no more regard to Truth than the Devil. . . I suspect that this Lying Spirit has been at Work concerning Burr. . . But if his guilt is as clear as the Noon day Sun, the first Magistrate ought not to have pronounced it so before a Jury had tryed him." (Adams to Rush, Feb. 2, 1807, *Old Family Letters*, 128–29.) See also Adams to Pickering, Jan. 1, 1807, Pickering MSS. Mass. Hist. Soc.; and Peters to Pickering, Feb. 1807, Pickering MSS. *loc. cit.*

Marshall undoubtedly shared the common judgment, as his conduct at Burr's trial abundantly shows.

in Washington and must have heard all these tales which were on every tongue.

In two weeks from the time Jefferson's Message was read to Congress, John Randolph rose in his place in the House, and in a speech of sharp criticism both of Spain and of the President, demanded that the President lay before Congress any information in his possession concerning the conspiracy and the measures taken to suppress it.[1]

A heated debate followed. Jefferson's personal supporters opposed the resolution. It was, however, generally agreed, as stated by George W. Campbell of Tennessee, that "this conspiracy has been painted in stronger colors than there is reason to think it deserves." There was no real evidence, said Campbell; nothing but "newspaper evidence."[2] Finally that part of the resolution calling for the facts as to the conspiracy was passed by a vote of 109 yeas to 14 nays; while the clause demanding information as to the measures Jefferson had taken was carried by 67 yeas to 52 nays.[3]

A week later the President responded in a Special Message. His information as to the conspiracy was, he said, a "voluminous mass," but there was in it "little to constitute legal evidence." It was "chiefly in the form of letters, often containing such a mixture of rumors, conjectures, and suspicions, as renders it difficult to sift out the real facts." On November 25, said Jefferson, he had received Wilkinson's letter exposing Burr's evil designs which the General, "with the honor of a soldier and fidelity of a

[1] *Annals*, 9th Cong. 2d Sess. 336.   [2] *Ib.* 347.   [3] *Ib.* 357–58.

good citizén," had sent him, and which, "when brought together" with some other information, "developed Burr's general designs." [1]

The President assured Congress that "one of these was the severance of the Union of these States beyond the Alleghany mountains; the other, an attack on Mexico. A third object was provided . . the settlement of a pretended purchase of a tract of country on the Washita." But "this was merely a pretext." Burr had soon found that the Western settlers were not to be seduced into secession; and thereupon, said Jefferson, the desperado "determined to seize upon New Orleans, plunder the bank there, possess himself of the military and naval stores, and proceed on his expedition to Mexico." For this purpose Burr had "collected . . all the ardent, restless, desperate, and disaffected persons" within his reach.

Therefore the President made his Proclamation of November 27, which had thwarted Burr's purposes. In New Orleans, however, General Wilkinson had been forced to take extreme measures for the defense of the country against the oncoming plunderers. Among these was the seizure of Bollmann and Swartwout who were "particularly employed in the endeavor to corrupt the General and the Army of the United States," and who had been sent oversea by Wilkinson for "ports in the Atlantic states, probably on the consideration that an impartial trial could not be expected . . in New

---

[1] *Annals*, 9th Cong. 2d Sess. 39–41. Jefferson's Message, Jan. 22, 1807, Richardson, i, 412–17.

Orleans, and that the city was not as yet a safe place of confinement." [1]

As to Burr, Jefferson assured Congress that his *"guilt is placed beyond question."* [2]

With this amazing Message the President sent an affidavit of Wilkinson's, as well as two letters from that veracious officer,[3] and a copy of Wilkinson's version of Burr's letter to him from which the General had carefully omitted the fact that the imprudent message was in answer to a dispatch from himself. But Jefferson did not transmit to Congress the letter, dated October 21, 1806, which he had received from Wilkinson.

Thoughtful men, who had personally studied Burr for years and who were unfriendly to him, doubted the accuracy of Wilkinson's version of the Burr dispatch: "It sounds more like Wilkinson's letter than Burr's," Senator Plumer records in his diary. "There are . . some things in it quite irrelevant. . . Burr's habits have been never to trust himself on paper, if he could avoid it — when he wrote, it was with great caution. . .Wilkinson is not an accurate correct man." [4]

No such doubts, however, assailed the eager multitude. The awful charge of treason had now been

[1] *Annals*, 9th Cong. 2d Sess. 43; Richardson, I, 416.

[2] *Annals*, 9th Cong. 2d Sess. 40. (Italics the author's.)

[3] "Wilkinson's letter is a curiosity. . . Tis Don Adriano de Armado the second." (J. Q. Adams to L. C. Adams, Dec. 8, 1806, *Writings, J. Q. A.*: Ford, III, footnote to 157.)

[4] Plumer, Jan. 22, 1807, "Diary," Plumer MSS. Lib. Cong.

Senator Plumer wrote his son, concerning Wilkinson's account of Burr's letter: "I am satisfied he has not accurately decyphered it. There is more of Wilkinsonism than of Burrism in it." (Plumer to his son, Jan. 24, 1807, Plumer MSS. Lib. Cong.)

formally made against Burr by the President of the United States. This, the most sensational part of Jefferson's Message, at once caught and held the attention of the public, which took for granted the truth of it. From that moment the popular mind was made up, and the popular voice demanded the life of Aaron Burr. No mere trial in court, no adherence to rules of evidence, no such insignificant fact as the American Constitution, must be permitted to stand between the people's aroused loyalty and the miscreant whom the Chief Executive of the Nation had pronounced guilty of treason.

CHAPTER VII

THE CAPTURE AND ARRAIGNMENT

It was President Jefferson who directed and animated the prosecution.
(Winfield Scott.)

The President's popularity is unbounded and his will is that of the nation.
(Joseph Nicholson.)

The press from one end of the continent to the other has been enlisted to excite prejudices against Colonel Burr.   (John Wickham.)

Two thirds of our speeches have been addressed to the people.   (George Hay.)

It would be difficult or dangerous for a jury to acquit Burr, however innocent they might think him.   (Marshall.)

WHILE Washington was still agitated by the President's Special Message, the long winter voyage of Bollmann and Swartwout ended at Baltimore, and Burr's dazed dispatch-bearers were brought by military guards to the National Capital. There, on the evening of January 22, they were thrown into the military prison at the Marine Barracks, and "guarded, night and day, by an officer & 15 soldiers of the Marine Corps." [1]

The ship bearing James Alexander had made a swift passage. On its arrival, friends of this prisoner applied to Joseph F. Nicholson, now United States Judge at Baltimore, for a writ of habeas corpus. Alexander was at once set free, there being not the slightest evidence to justify his detention. [2]

[1] Plumer, Jan. 30, 1807, "Diary," Plumer MSS. Lib. Cong. Senator Plumer adds: "The government are apprehensive that the arts & address of *Bollman*, who effected the liberation of the Marquis de Lafayette from the strong prison of Magdeburge, may now find means to liberate himself."

[2] Clay to Prentiss, Feb. 15, 1807, *Priv. Corres.*: Colton, 15; also *Works:* Colton, IV, 14.

A week or two later the schooner Thatcher, on
board which was the disconsolate and dumbfounded
General Adair — Wilkinson's fourth prisoner to be
sent to Jefferson — tied up to its dock at Baltimore
and he was delivered "over to the commander of
the fort at that city." But a passenger on the vessel,
"a stranger . . of his own accord . . assured [Adair]
he would procure a writ of Habeas Corpus for him."
Adair also was "immediately liberated, . . there being
no evidence against him." [1]

After the incarceration of Bollmann and Swartwout in Washington, attorneys were secured for
them and an application was made to Judge William
Cranch, United States Judge for the District of Columbia, for a writ of habeas corpus in their behalf,
directed to Colonel Wharton, who was in command
at Washington. Wharton brought the luckless prisoners into court and stated that "he held them
under the orders of his superior officer. They were
then taken upon a bench warrant charging them
with treason which superseded the writ. A motion
was made by the prisoners council . . that they be
discharged. The Court required evidence of their
probable guilt." [2]

Jefferson now took a hand in the prosecution.
He considered Wilkinson's affidavit insufficient [3] to
hold Bollmann and Swartwout, and, in order to

[1] Plumer, Feb. 20, 1807, "Register," Plumer MSS. Lib. Cong.
[2] Plumer to Mason, Jan. 30, 1807, Plumer MSS. Lib. Cong.
Plumer's account of the proceedings is trustworthy. He was an
eminent lawyer himself, was deeply interested in the case, and was
writing to Jeremiah Mason, then the leader of the New England bar.
[3] *Eaton:* Prentiss, 396.

strengthen the case against them, secured from Eaton an affidavit stating the dire revelations which Eaton alleged Burr had made to him a year before.[1] Eaton's theatrical story was thus given to the press,[2] and not only fortified the public conviction that a conspiracy to destroy the Union had been under way, but also horrified the country by the account of Burr's intention to assassinate Jefferson.

The Attorney-General and the United States District Attorney, representing the Government, demanded that Bollmann and Swartwout be held; Charles Lee, Robert Goodloe Harper, and Francis S. Key, attorneys for the prisoners, insisted that they be released. Long was the argument and "vast" the crowd that heard it; "collected & firm" was the appearance of the accused men.[3] So universal was

---

[1] See *supra*, 303–05.

Three days before he made oath to the truth of this story, Eaton's claim against the Government was referred to a committee of the House (see *Annals*, 9th Cong. 2d Sess. 383), and within a month from the time the historic affidavit was made, a bill was passed, without debate, "authorizing the settlement of the accounts between the United States and William Eaton."

John Randolph was suspicious: "He believed the bill had passed by surprise. It was not so much a bill to settle the accounts of William Eaton, as to rip up the settled forms of the Treasury, and to transfer the accountable duties of the Treasury to the Department of State. It would be a stain upon the Statute Book." (*Ib.* 622.)

The very next week after the passage of this measure, Eaton received ten thousand dollars from the Government. (See testimony of William Eaton, *Trials of Colonel Aaron Burr:* Robertson, stenographer, i, 483.)

[2] "Eaton's story . . has now been served up in all the newspapers. . . The amount of his narrative is, that he advised the President to send Burr upon an important embassy, BECAUSE!!! he had discovered the said Burr to be a *Traitor to his country.*" (J. Q. Adams to L. C. Adams, Dec. 8, 1806, *Writings, J. Q. A.:* Ford, iii, footnote to 157.)

[3] Plumer, Jan. 30, 1807, "Diary," Plumer MSS. Lib. Cong.

the curiosity, says John Quincy Adams, that the
Senate was "scarcely able here to form a quorum . .
and the House . . actually adjourned." [1] The court
decided that Bollmann and Swartwout should be
sent back to prison "for trial without bail or main-
prize." For the first time in our history a National
court divided on political grounds. Judge Cranch,
a Federalist first appointed by President Adams,[2]
thought that the prisoners should be discharged,
but was overruled by his associates, Judges Nicholas Fitzhugh and Allen Bowie Duckett, Republicans
appointed by Jefferson.[3]

But John Marshall and the Supreme Court had
yet to be reckoned with. Counsel for the reimpris-
oned men at once applied to that tribunal for a writ
of habeas corpus, and Marshall directed process to
the jailer to show cause why the writ should not
issue.

An extreme and violent step was now taken to
end the proceedings in court. On Friday, January
23, 1807, the day after the President's Special Message denouncing Burr had been read in the Senate,
Senator Giles, who, it should be repeated, was Jefferson's personal representative in that body, actually
moved the appointment of a committee to draft a
bill "to suspend the privilege of the writ of habeas

---

[1] J. Q. Adams to his father, Jan. 30, 1807, *Writings, J. Q. A.*: Ford,
III, 159.

[2] Feb. 28, 1801, *Journal Exec. Proc. Senate*, I, 387. Cranch was
so excellent a judge that, Federalist though he was, Jefferson reappointed him February 21, 1806. (*Ib.* II, 21.)

[3] Jefferson appointed Nicholas Fitzhugh of Virginia, November 22,
1803 (*ib.* I, 458), and Allen Bowie Duckett of Maryland, February 28,
1806 (*ib.* II, 25).

corpus." Quickly Giles himself reported the measure, the Senate suspended its rules, and the bill was hurriedly passed, only Bayard of Delaware voting against it.[1]   More astounding still, Giles recommended, and the Senate adopted, a special message to the House, stating the Senate's action "which they think expedient to communicate to you in confidence," and asking the popular branch of Congress to pass the Senate bill without delay.[2]

Immediately after the House convened on Monday, January 26,[3] Senator Samuel Smith of Maryland appeared on the floor and delivered this "confidential message," together with the Senate bill, which provided that "in all cases, where any person or persons, charged on oath with treason, misprision of treason, or other high crime or misdemeanor . . shall be arrested or imprisoned . . the privilege of the writ of habeas corpus shall be . . suspended, for and during the term of three months."[4]

The House was astounded. Party discipline was, for the moment, wrathfully repudiated. Mr. Philip R. Thompson of Virginia instantly moved that the "message and the bill received from the Senate ought not to be kept secret and that the doors be opened." Thompson's motion was adopted by 123 yeas to 3 nays.

Then came a motion to reject the bill, followed by a brief and almost one-sided debate, which was little

[1] J. Q. Adams to his father, Jan. 27, 1807, *Writings, J. Q. A.*: Ford, III, 158.

[2] *Annals*, 9th Cong. 2d Sess. 44.

[3] On Friday afternoon the House adjourned till Monday morning.

[4] *Annals*, 9th Cong. 2d Sess. 402.

more than the angry protest of the representatives
of the people against the proposed overthrow of this
last defense of liberty. William A. Burwell of Virginia asked whether there was any danger "to justify this suspension of this most important right of
the citizen. . . He could judge from what he had
already seen that men, who are perfectly innocent,
would be doomed to . . undergo the infamy of the
dungeon." [1] "Never," exclaimed John W. Eppes
of the same State, "under this Government, has
personal liberty been held at the will of a single
individual." [2]

On the other hand, Joseph B. Varnum of Massachusetts said that Burr's "insurrection" was the
worst in all history.[3] James Sloan of New Jersey
made a similar statement.[4] But the House promptly
rejected the Senate bill by 113 yeas to 19 nays. The
shameful attempt to prevent John Marshall from
deciding whether Bollmann and Swartwout were entitled to the benefit of the most sacred writ known to
the law was thereby defeated and the Chief Justice
was left free to grant or reject it, as justice might
require.

The order of the court of the District of Columbia
was that Bollmann and Swartwout "be committed to
prison of this court, to take their trial for treason
against the United States, by levying war against
them."[5] In the Supreme Court the prisoners and the
Government were represented by the same counsel
who had argued the case below, and Luther Martin

[1] *Annals*, 9th Cong. 2d Sess. 404–05.
[2] *Ib.* 410. Eppes was Jefferson's son-in-law.
[3] *Ib.* 412.   [4] *Ib.* 414–15.   [5] 4 Cranch, 76.

also appeared in behalf of the men whose long-contin-ued and, as he believed, wholly illegal suffering had aroused the sympathies of that admirable lawyer.

The Supreme Court first decided that it had juris-diction. The application for the writs of habeas cor-pus was, in effect, an appeal from the decision of the District Court. On this point Justice Johnson de-livered a dissenting opinion, observing, as an aside, that the argument for the prisoners had shown "an unnecessary display of energy and pathos."[1] The affidavit of General Wilkinson and his version of the Burr letter, concerning which "the court had diffi-culty," were admitted by a vote of the majority of the Justices. At noon on the twenty-first day of February, 1807, Marshall delivered the opinion of the majority of the court upon the main question,[2] "whether the accused shall be discharged or held to trial."

The specific charge was that of "treason in levy-ing war against the United States." This, declared Marshall, was the most serious offense of which any man can be accused: "As there is no crime which can more excite and agitate the passions of men than treason, no charge demands more from the tribunal before which it is made a deliberate and temperate inquiry. Whether this inquiry be directed to the fact or to the law, none can be more solemn, none more

[1] 4 Cranch, 107. Justice Chase, who was absent because of ill-ness, concurred with Johnson. (Clay to Prentiss, Feb. 15, 1807, *Priv. Corres.*: Colton, 15; also *Works:* Colton, IV, 15.)

Cæsar A. Rodney, Jefferson's Attorney-General, declined to argue the question of jurisdiction.

[2] 4 Cranch, 125-37.

important to the citizen or to the government; none can more affect the safety of both."

In order that it should never be possible to extend treason "to offenses of minor importance," the Constitution "has given a rule on the subject both to the legislatures and the courts of America, which neither can be permitted to transcend." Marshall then read, with solemn impressiveness, these words from the Constitution of the United States: "Treason against the United States shall consist only in levying war against them, or in adhering to their enemies, giving them aid and comfort."

To support the charge against Bollmann and Swartwout, said Marshall, "war must be actually levied. . . To conspire to levy war, and actually to levy war, are distinct offenses. The first must be brought into open action by the assemblage of men for a purpose treasonable in itself, or the fact of levying war cannot have been committed." It was not necessary for the commission of this crime that a man should actually "appear in arms against his country. . . If a body of men be actually assembled for the purpose of effecting by force a treasonable purpose; all those who perform any part, however minute, or however remote from the scene of the action, and who are actually leagued in the general conspiracy, are to be considered as traitors." [1] This passage was soon to cause Marshall great embarrassment when he was confronted with it in the trial of Aaron Burr at Richmond.

Did this mean that men who go to the very edge

[1] 4 Cranch, 125–26.

of legal boundaries — who stop just short of committing treason — must go scathless? By no means! Such offenses could be and must be provided for by statute. They were not, like treason, Constitutional crimes. "The framers of our Constitution . . must have conceived it more safe that punishment in such cases should be ordained by general laws, formed upon deliberation, under the influence of no resentments, and without knowing on whom they were to operate, than that it should be inflicted under the influence of those passions which the occasion seldom fails to excite, and which a flexible definition of the crime, or a construction which would render it flexible, might bring into operation."

This was a direct rebuke to Jefferson. There can be no doubt that Marshall was referring to the recent attempt to deprive Bollmann and Swartwout of the protection of the courts by suspending the writ of habeas corpus. "It is, therefore, more safe," continued Marshall, "as well as more consonant to the principles of our constitution, that the crime of treason should not be extended by construction to doubtful cases; and that crimes not clearly within the constitutional definition should receive such punishment as the legislature in its wisdom may provide."

What do the words "levying war" mean? To complete that crime, Marshall repeated, "there must be an actual assemblage of men for the purpose of executing a treasonable design . . but no conspiracy for this object, no enlisting of men to effect it, would be an actual levying of war."[1] He then

[1] 4 Cranch, 127.

applied these principles to the testimony. First he took up the deposition of Eaton [1] which, he said, indicated that the invasion of Mexico "was the immediate object" [2] that Burr had in mind.

But, asked the Chief Justice, what had this to do with Bollmann and Swartwout? The prosecution connected the prisoners with the statements made in Eaton's deposition by offering the affidavit of General Wilkinson, which included his version of Burr's celebrated letter. Marshall then overruled the "great and serious objections made" to the admission of Wilkinson's affidavit. One of these objections was to that part which purported to set out the Wilkinson translation of the Burr cipher, the original letter not having been presented. Marshall announced that "a division of opinion has taken place in the court," two of the Judges believing such testimony totally inadmissible and two others holding that it was proper to consider it "at this incipient stage of the prosecution."

Thereupon Marshall analyzed Wilkinson's version of Burr's confidential cipher dispatch. [3] It was so vague, said the Chief Justice, that it "furnishes no distinct view of the design of the writer." But the "coöperation" which Burr stated had been secured "points strongly to some expedition against the territories of Spain."

---

[1] See *supra*, 303–05.   [2] 4 Cranch, 128–29.

[3] See Appendix D.

In his translation Wilkinson carefully omitted the first sentence of Burr's dispatch: "Yours, post-marked 13th of May, is received." (Parton: *Burr*, 427.) This was not disclosed until the fact was extorted from Wilkinson at the Burr trial. (See *infra*, chap. VIII.)

Marshall then quoted these words of Burr's famous message: "'Burr's plan of operations is to move down rapidly from the falls on the 15th of November, with the first 500 or 1,000 men in the light boats now constructing for that purpose, to be at Natchez between the 5th and 15th of December, there to meet Wilkinson; then to determine whether it will be expedient in the first instance to seize on, or to pass by, Baton Rouge. The people of the country to which we are going are prepared to receive us. Their agents now with Burr say that if we will protect their religion, and will not subject them to a foreign power, in three weeks all will be settled.'"

This language was, said Marshall, "rather more explicit." But "there is no expression in these sentences which would justify a suspicion that any territory of the United States was the object of the expedition. For what purpose seize on Baton Rouge? Why engage Spain against this enterprise, if it was designed against the United States?" [1]

Burr's statement that "the people of the country to which we are going are prepared to receive us," was, said Marshall, "peculiarly appropriate to a foreign country." And what was the meaning of the statement: "Their agents now with Burr say, that if we will protect their religion, and will not subject them to a foreign power, in three weeks all will be settled"? It was not probable that this referred to American citizens; but it perfectly fitted the Mexicans. "There certainly is not in the letter delivered to General Wilkinson . . one syllable which has a

[1] 4 Cranch, 131–32.

necessary or a natural reference to an enterprise against the territory of the United States."

According to Wilkinson's affidavit, Swartwout knew the contents of the dispatch he was carrying; Wilkinson had deposed that Burr's messenger had frankly said so. Without stating that, in his long journey from New York through the Western States and Territories in quest of Wilkinson, he had "performed on his route any act whatever which was connected with the enterprise," Swartwout had declared "their object to be 'to carry an expedition to the Mexican provinces.'" [1] This, said Marshall, was "explanatory of the letter of Col. Burr, if the expressions of that letter could be thought ambiguous."

But Wilkinson declared in his affidavit that Swartwout had also told him that "this territory would be revolutionized where the people were ready to join them, and that there would be some seizing, he supposed at New Orleans." [2] If this meant that

---

[1] 4 Cranch, 132–33.

[2] Wilkinson declared in his affidavit that he "drew" from Swartwout the following disclosures: "Colonel Burr, with the support of a powerful association, extending from New York to New Orleans, was levying an armed body of seven thousand men from the state of New York and the Western states and Territories" to invade Mexico which "would be revolutionized, where the people were ready to join them."

"There would be some seizing, he supposed at New Orleans"; he "knew full well" that "there were several millions of dollars in the bank of this place," but that Burr's party only "meant to borrow and would return it — they must equip themselves at New Orleans, etc., etc." (*Annals*, 9th Cong. 2d Sess. 1014–15.)

Swartwout made oath that he told Wilkinson nothing of the kind. The high character which this young man then bore, together with the firm impression of truthfulness he made on everybody at that time and during the distracting months that followed, would seem to suggest the conclusion that Wilkinson's story was only another of the brood of falsehoods of which that fecund liar was so prolific.

the Government in any American territory was to be revolutionized by force, "although merely as a . . means of executing some greater projects, the design was unquestionably treasonable," said Marshall; "and any assemblage of men for that purpose would amount to a levying of war." It was, then, of first importance to discover the true meaning of the youthful and indiscreet messenger.

For the third time the court divided. "Some of the judges," Marshall explained, suppose that these words of Swartwout "refer to the territory against which the expedition was intended; others to that in which the conversation was held. Some consider the words, if even applicable to a territory of the United States, as alluding to a revolution to be effected by the people, rather than by the party conducted by Col. Burr."

Swartwout's statement, as given in Wilkinson's affidavit, that Burr was assembling thousands of armed men to attack Mexico, did not prove that Burr had gathered an army to make war on the United States.[1] If the latter were Burr's purpose, it was not necessary that the entire host should have met at one spot; if detachments had actually formed and were marching to the place of rendezvous, treason had been committed. Following his tedious habit of repeating over and over again, often in identical language, statements already clearly made, Marshall for the fourth time asserted that there must be "unequivocal evidence" of "an actual assemblage."

[1] 4 Cranch, 133–34.

The mere fact that Burr "was enlisting men in his service . . would not amount to levying war." That Swartwout meant only this, said Marshall, was "sufficiently apparent." If seven thousand men had actually come together in one body, every one would know about it; and surely, observed Marshall, "some evidence of such an assembling would have been laid before the court."

Burr's intention to do certain "seizing at New Orleans" did not amount to levying war from anything that could be inferred from Swartwout's statement. It only "indicated a design to rob." Having thus examined all the testimony before the court, Marshall announced the opinion of the majority of the Justices that there was not "sufficient evidence of his [Swartwout's] levying war against the United States to justify his commitment on the charge of treason." [1]

The testimony against Bollmann was, if possible, still weaker. There was, indeed, "no evidence to support a charge of treason" against him. Whoever believed the assertions in Wilkinson's affidavit could not doubt that both Bollmann and Swartwout "were engaged in a most culpable enterprise against the dominions of a power at peace with the United States"; but it was apparent that "no part of this crime was committed in the District of Columbia." They could not, therefore, be tried in that District.

Upon that point the court was at last unanimous. The accused men could have been tried in New Orleans — "there existed a tribunal in that city,"

[1] 4 Cranch, 135.

sarcastically observed Marshall; but to say that citizens might be seized by military power in the jurisdiction where the alleged crime was committed and thereafter tried "in any place which the general might select, and to which he might direct them to be carried," was not to be thought of — such a thing "would be extremely dangerous." So the long-suffering Bollmann and Swartwout were discharged.[1]

Thus, by three different courts, five of the "conspirators" had successively been released. In the case of Ogden, there was no proof; of Alexander, no proof; of Adair, no proof; of Bollmann and Swartwout, no proof. And the Judges had dared to set free the accused men — had refused to consign them to prison, despite public opinion and the desire of the Administration. Could anything be more undemocratic, more reprehensible? The Supreme Court, especially, should be rebuked.

On learning of that tribunal's action, Giles adjourned the meeting of his committee on the treason bill in order to secure immediately a copy of Marshall's opinion. In a true Virginian rage, Giles threatened to offer an amendment to the Constitution "taking away all jurisdiction of the Supreme Court in criminal cases." There was talk of impeaching every occupant of the Supreme Bench.[2]

More news had now reached Washington concerning the outrages committed at New Orleans; and on the day that the attorneys for Bollmann and Swart-

[1] 4 Cranch, 136.
[2] Feb. 21, 1807, *Memoirs, J. Q. A.*: Adams, I, 459.

wout applied to the Supreme Court for writs of habeas corpus, James M. Broom of Delaware rose in the House, and introduced a resolution "to make further provision for securing the privilege of the writ of habeas corpus to persons in custody under or by color of the authority of the United States." [1] While the cases were being argued in the Supreme Court and the divided Judges were wrangling over the disputed points, a violent debate sprang up in the House over Broom's resolution. "If, upon every alarm of conspiracy," said Broom, "our rights of personal liberty are to be entrusted to the keeping of a military commander, we may prepare to take our leave of them forever." [2] All day the debate continued; on the next day, February 18, while Marshall was delivering his opinion that the Supreme Court had jurisdiction of the application of Bollmann and Swartwout, the controversy in the House was renewed.

James Elliot of Vermont said that "most of the privileges intended to be secured" by the Fourth, Fifth, and Sixth Amendments [3] "have recently been

---

[1] *Annals*, 9th Cong. 2d Sess. 472.   [2] *Ib.* 506.

[3] They are: "Article IV. The right of the people to be secure in their persons, houses, papers and effects, against unreasonable searches and seizures, shall not be violated, and no warrants shall issue but upon probable cause, supported by oath or affirmation, and particularly describing the place to be searched, and the persons or things to be seized.

"Article V. No person shall be held to answer for a capital or otherwise infamous crime, unless on a presentment or indictment of a grand jury, except in cases arising in the land or naval forces, or in the militia when in actual service in time of war or public danger; nor shall any person be subject for the same offence to be twice put in jeopardy of life or limb; nor shall be compelled, in any criminal case, to be witness against himself, nor be deprived of life, liberty, or prop-

denied .. at the point of the bayonet, and under
circumstances of peculiar violence." He read Wilkinson's impertinent return to the Orleans County
Court. This, said Elliot, was "not obedience to
the laws .. but .. defiance... What necessity could
exist for seizing one or two wandering conspirators,
and transporting them fifteen hundred or two thousand miles from the Constitutional scene of inquisition and trial, to place them particularly under the
eye of the National Government"? [1] Not only was
the swish of the party whip heard in the House,
he asserted, but members who would not desert
the fundamentals of liberty must "be prepared for
the insinuation that we countenance treason, and
sympathize with traitors." [2]

The shrill voice of John Randolph was heard.
Almost his first sentence was a blow at Jefferson. If
the President and his party "ever quit the ground of
trial by jury, the liberty of the press, and the subordination of the military to the civil authority, they
must expect that their enemies will perceive the desertion and avail themselves of the advantage." [3]
Randolph assailed the recent attempt to suspend
the writ of habeas corpus which, he said, "was in-

erty, without due process of law; nor shall private property be taken
for public use without just compensation.

"Article VI. In all criminal prosecutions the accused shall enjoy
the right to a speedy and public trial, by an impartial jury of the
state and district wherein the crime shall have been committed,
which district shall have been previously ascertained by law, and to
be informed of the nature and cause of the accusation; to be confronted with the witnesses against him; to have compulsory process
for obtaining witnesses in his favour, and to have the assistance of
counsel for his defence."

[1] *Annals*, 9th Cong. 2d Sess. 531.   [2] *Ib.* 532–33.   [3] *Ib.* 535.

tended . . to cover with a mantle the most daring
usurpation which ever did, will, or can happen, in
this or any country. There was exactly as much
right to shoot the persons in question as to do what
has been done." [1] The Declaration of Independence
had assigned wrongs of precisely the kind suffered by
Bollmann and Swartwout "as one of the grievances
imposed by the British Government on the colonies.
Now, it is done under the Constitution," exclaimed
Randolph, "and under a republican administration,
and men are transported without the color of law,
nearly as far as across the Atlantic." [2]

Again and again angry speakers denounced the
strenuous attempts of the Administration's supporters to influence Republican votes on partisan
grounds. Only by the most desperate efforts was
Jefferson saved from the rebuke and humiliation of
the passage of the resolution. But his escape was
narrow. Indefinite postponement was voted by the
dangerous majority of 2 out of a total of 118 members.[3]

While Burr's messengers were on the high seas,
prisoners of war, and Wilkinson at New Orleans
was saving the Republic by rending its laws, Burr
himself, ignorant of all, was placidly making his way
down the Ohio and Mississippi with his nine boats
and sixty adventurers, mostly youths, many only
boys. He had left Jackson at Nashville on December 22, and floating down the Cumberland in two
unarmed boats, had joined the remainder of the
little expedition.

[1] *Annals*, 9th Cong. 2d Sess. 536.   [2] *Ib.* 537–38.   [3] *Ib.* 589

He then met for the first time the young adventurers whom Blennerhassett, Comfort Tyler of
Syracuse, New York, and Davis Floyd of the tiny
settlement of New Albany, Indiana Territory, had
induced to join the expedition. On a cold, rainy December morning they were drawn up in a semi-circle
on a little island at the mouth of the Cumberland
River, and Burr was introduced to each of them.
Greeting them with his customary reserved friendliness, he told them that the objects of the expedition
not already disclosed to them would be revealed at
a more opportune time.[1]

Such was the second "overt act" of the gathering
of an armed host to "levy war" on the United
States for which Jefferson later fastened the charge
of treason upon Aaron Burr.

As it floated down the Ohio and Mississippi, the
little flotilla[2] stopped at the forts upon the river
bluffs, and the officers proffered Burr all the courtesies at their command. Seven days after Burr had
left Fort Massac, Captain Bissel, in answer to a letter of inquiry from Andrew Jackson, assured him
that "there has nothing the least alarming appeared"; Burr had passed with a few boats "having
nothing on board that would even suffer a conjecture, more than a man bound to market."[3] John

---

[1] Nearly all the men had been told that they were to settle the
Washita lands; and this was true, as far as it went. (See testimony of
Stephen S. Welch, Samuel Moxley, Chandler Lindsley, John Mulhol-
lan, Hugh Allen, and others, *Annals*, 10th Cong. 1st Sess. 463 *et seq*.)

[2] The boats were very comfortable. They were roofed and had compartments for cooking, eating, and sleeping. They were much like the
modern house boat.

[3] Bissel to Jackson, Jan. 5, 1807, *Annals*, 9th Cong. 2d Sess. 1017-18.

Murrell of Tennessee, sent on a secret mission of investigation, reported to Jackson that, pursuant to instructions, he had closely followed and examined Burr's movements on the Cumberland; that he had heard reports that Burr "had gone down the river with one thousand armed men"; but Murrell had found the fact to be that there were but ten boats with only "sixty men on board," and "no appearance of arms." [1]

During the week when John Randolph, in the House, was demanding information of the President, and Wilkinson, in New Orleans, was making his second series of arrests, Burr, with his little group of boats and small company of men — totally unequipped for anything but the settlement of the Washita lands, and poorly supplied even for that — serenely drew up to the landing at the small post of Bayou Pierre in the Territory of Mississippi. He was still uninformed of what was going forward at New Orleans and at Washington — still unconscious of the storm of hatred and denunciation that had been blown up against him.

At the little settlement, Burr learned for the first time of the fate prepared for him. Bloody and violent were the measures he then adopted! He wrote a letter to Cowles Mead, Acting Governor of the Territory, stating that rumors he had just heard were untrue; that "his object is agriculture and his boats are the vehicles of immigration." But he "hinted at resistance to any attempt to coerce him." [2]

[1] Murrell to Jackson, Jan. 8, 1807, *Annals*, 9th Cong. 2d Sess. 1017.
[2] Mead to the Secretary of War, Jan. 13, 1807, *ib.* 1018.

What followed was related by Mead himself. As directed by the War Department, he had prorogued the Legislature, put the Territory in a state of defense, and called out the militia. When Burr's letter came, Mead ordered these frontier soldiers to "rendezvous at certain points. . . With the promptitude of Spartans, our fellow-citizens shouldered their firelocks, and in twenty-four hours I had the honor to review three hundred and seventy-five men at Natches, prepared to defend their country." Mead sent two aides to Burr, "who tendered his respects to the civil authority." The Acting Governor himself then saw Burr, whereupon the desperado actually "offered to surrender himself to the civil authority of the Territory, and to suffer his boats to be searched." This was done by "four gentlemen of unquestionable respectability, with a detachment of thirty men." Burr readily went into court and awaited trial.

"Thus, sir," concludes Governor Mead, "this mighty alarm, with all its exaggeration, has eventuated in nine boats and one hundred men,[1] and the major part of these are boys, or young men just from school," wholly unaware of Burr's evil designs.[2]

The Legislature of the Territory of Orleans had just convened. Governor Claiborne recommended that a law be passed suspending the writ of habeas corpus. Behind closed doors the Representatives

[1] Burr had picked up forty men on his voyage down the Mississippi.

[2] Mead to the War Department, Jan. 19, 1807, *Annals*, 9th Cong. 2d Sess. 1019.

were harangued by Wilkinson on the subject of the
great conspiracy. All the old horrors were again
paraded to induce the legislators to support Wilkinson in his lawless acts. Instead, that body denied the
existence of treason in Louisiana, expressed alarm at
the "late privation" of the rights of American citizens, and determined to investigate the "measures
and motives" of Wilkinson. A memorial to Congress
was adopted, denouncing "the acts of high-handed
military power .. too notorious to be denied, too
illegal to be justified, too wanton to be excused," by
which "the temple of justice" had been "sacrile-
giously rifled." [1]

In Mississippi, Burr calmly awaited his trial before the United States Court of that Territory. Bail
in the sum of five thousand dollars had been furnished by Colonel Benijah Osmun and Lyman Harding, two Revolutionary comrades of Burr, who years
before had emigrated to Mississippi and developed
into wealthy planters. Colonel Osmun invited Burr
to be his guest. Having seen the ogre and talked with
him, the people of the neighborhood became Burr's
enthusiastic friends.

Soon the grand jury was impaneled to investigate
Burr's "crimes" and indict him for them if a true
bill could be found. This body outdid the performance of the Kentucky grand jury nine weeks earlier.
The grand jurors asserted that, after examining the

---

[1] McCaleb, 233–36. For the discussion over this resolution see
*Debate in the House of Representatives of the Territory of Orleans, on a
Memorial to Congress, respecting the illegal conduct of General Wilkinson.* Both sides of the question were fully represented. See also Cox,
194, 200, 206–08.

evidence, they were "of the opinion that Aaron
Burr has not been guilty of any crime or misdemeanor against the laws of the United States or of
this Territory or given any just alarm or inquietude
to the good people of this Territory." Worse still
followed — the grand jury formally presented as "a
grievance" the march of the militia against Burr,
since there had been no prior resistance by him to
the civil authorities. Nor did the grand jurors stop
there. They also presented "as a grievance, destructive of personal liberty," Wilkinson's military outrages in New Orleans.[1]

When the grand jury was dismissed, Burr asked to
be discharged and his sureties released from his
bond. The judge was Thomas Rodney, the father
of Cæsar A. Rodney whom Jefferson soon afterward
appointed Attorney-General. Judge Rodney out-
Wilkinsoned Wilkinson; he denied Burr's request
and ordered him to renew his bond or go to jail. This
was done despite the facts that the grand jury had
refused to indict Burr and that there was no legal
charge whatever before the court.

Wilkinson was frantic lest Burr escape him. Every
effort was made to seize him; officers in disguise
were sent to capture him,[2] and men "armed with
Dirks & Pistolls" were dispatched to assassinate
him.[3] Burr consulted Colonel Osmun and other

[1] Return of the Mississippi Grand Jury, Feb. 3, reported in the
Orleans Gazette, Feb. 20, 1807, as quoted in McCaleb, 272–73.

[2] *Annals*, 10th Cong. 1st Sess. 528–29, 536, 658–61.

[3] Deposition of George Peter, Sept. 10, 1807, *Am. State Papers*,
Misc. I, 566; and see *Quarterly Pub. Hist. and Phil. Soc. of Ohio*, IX,
Nos. 1 and 2, 35–38; McCaleb, 274–75; Cox, 200–08.

friends, who advised him to keep out of sight for a time. So he went into hiding, but wrote the Governor that he would again come before the court when he could be assured of being dealt with legally.

Thereupon the bond of five thousand dollars, which Judge Rodney had compelled Burr to give, was declared forfeited and a reward of two thousand dollars was offered for his apprehension. From his place of retreat the harried man protested by letter. The Governor would not relent. Wilkinson was raging in New Orleans. Illegal imprisonment, probably death, was certain for Burr if he should be taken. His friends counseled flight, and he acted on their judgment.[1]

But he would not go until he had seen his disconsolate followers once more. Stealthily visiting his now unguarded flotilla, he told his men to take for themselves the boats and provisions, and, if they desired, to proceed to the Washita lands, settle there, and keep as much as they wanted. He had stood his trial, he said, and had been acquitted; but now he was to be taken by unlawful violence, and the only thing left for him to do was to "flee from oppression." [2]

Colonel Osmun gave him the best horse in his stables. Clad "in an old blanket-coat begirt with a leathern strap, to which a tin cup was suspended on the left and a scalping knife on the right," Aaron Burr rode away into the wilderness.

At ten o'clock of a rainy night, on the very day when Marshall delivered his first opinion in the case

---

[1] McCaleb, 277.　　　　[2] *Ib.*

of Bollmann and Swartwout, Burr was recognized at a forest tavern in Washington County,[1] where he had stopped to inquire the way to the house of Colonel Hinson, whom he had met at Natchez on his first Western journey and who had invited Burr to be his guest if he ever came to that part of the Territory. "Major" Nicholas Perkins, a burly backwoods lawyer from Tennessee, penetrated the disguise,[2] because of Burr's fine eyes and erect carriage.

Perkins hurried to the cabin of Theodore Brightwell, sheriff of the county, and the two men rode after Burr, overtaking him at the residence of Colonel Hinson, who was away from home and whose wife had prepared supper for the wanderer. Brightwell went inside while Perkins remained in the downpour watching the house from the bushes.

Burr so won the hearts of both hostess and sheriff that, instead of arresting him, the officer proposed to guide the escaping criminal on his way the next morning.[3] The drenched and shivering Perkins, feeling that all was not right inside the cabin, hastened by horse and canoe to Fort Stoddert and told Captain Edward P. Gaines of Burr's whereabouts. With a file of soldiers the captain and the lawyer set off to find and take the fugitive. They soon met him with the sheriff, who was telling Burr the roads to follow.

Exclusively upon the authority of Jefferson's Proc-

---

[1] In that part of the Territory which is now the State of Alabama.

[2] Perkins had read and studied the description of Burr in one of the Proclamations which the Governor of Mississippi had issued. A large reward for the capture of Burr was also offered, and on this the mind of Perkins was now fastened.

[3] Pickett: *History of Alabama*, 218–31.

lamation, Burr was arrested and confined in the fort.
With quiet dignity, the "traitor" merely protested
and asked to be delivered to the civil courts. His
arrest was wholly illegal, he correctly said; let a
judge and jury again pass on his conduct. But seizure and incarceration by military force, utterly without warrant of law, were a denial of fundamental
rights — rights which could not be refused to the
poorest citizen or the most abandoned criminal.[1]

Two weeks passed before Burr was sent northward. During this period all within the stockades
became his friends. The brother of Captain Gaines
fell ill and Burr, who among other accomplishments knew much about medicine, treated the sick
man and cheered him with gay conversation. The
soldiers liked Burr; the officers liked him; their
wives liked him. Everybody yielded to his strange
attractiveness.

Two weeks after Marshall discharged Bollmann
and Swartwout at Washington, Burr was delivered
by Captain Gaines to a guard of nine men organized
by Perkins; and, preceded and followed by them, he
began the thousand-mile journey to Washington.
For days torrential rains fell; streams were swollen;
the soil was a quagmire. For hundreds of miles the
only road was an Indian trail; wolves filled the forest; savage Indians were all about.[2] At night the

[1] Yet, five months afterward, Jefferson actually wrote Captain
Gaines: "That the arrest of Colo. B. was military has been disproved;
but had it been so, every honest man & good citizen is bound, by any
means in his power, to arrest the author of projects so daring & dangerous." (Jefferson to Gaines, July 23, 1807, *Works:* Ford, x, 473.)

[2] Pickett, 224-25.

party, drenched and chilled, slept on the sodden earth. Burr never complained.

After ten days the first white settlements appeared. In two days more, South Carolina was reached. The cautious Perkins avoided the larger settlements, for Burr was popular in that State and his captor would run no risks of a rescue. As the prisoner and his convoy were passing through a village, a number of men were standing before a tavern. Burr suddenly threw himself from his horse and cried: "I am Aaron Burr, under military arrest, and claim the protection of the civil authorities."

Before any one could move, Perkins sprang to Burr's side, a pistol in each hand, and ordered him to remount. Burr refused; and the gigantic frontier lawyer lifted the slight, delicate prisoner in his hands, threw him into his saddle, and the sorry cavalcade rode on, guards now on either side, as well as before and behind their charge. Then, for the first and last time in his life, Burr lost his composure, but only for a moment; tears filled his eyes, but instantly recovering his self-possession, he finished the remainder of that harrowing trip as courteous, dignified, and serene as ever.[1]

At Fredericksburg, Virginia, Perkins received orders from the Government to take his prisoner to Richmond instead of to Washington. John Randolph describes the cavalcade: "Colonel Burr . . passed by my door the day before yesterday under a strong guard. . . To guard against enquiry as

---

[1] For the account of Burr's arrest and transfer from Alabama to Richmond, see Pickett, 218–31. Parton adopts Pickett's narrative, adding only one or two incidents; see Parton: *Burr*, 444–52.

much as possible he was accoutred in a shabby suit of homespun with an old white hat flopped over his face, the dress in which he was apprehended." [1]

In such fashion, when the candles were being lighted on the evening of Thursday, March 26, 1807, Aaron Burr was brought into the Virginia Capital, where, before a judge who could be neither frightened nor cajoled, he was to make final answer to the charge of treason.

Burr remained under military guard until the arrival of Marshall at Richmond. The Chief Justice at once wrote out,[2] signed, and issued a warrant by virtue of which the desperate yet composed prisoner was at last surrendered to the civil authorities, before whom he had so long demanded to be taken.

During the noon hour on Monday, March 30, Marshall went to "a retired room" in the Eagle Tavern. In this hostelry Burr was confined. Curious citizens thronged the big public room of the inn and were "awfully silent and attentive" as the pale and worn conspirator was taken by Major Joseph Scott, the United States Marshal, and two deputies through the quiet but hostile assemblage to the apartment where the Chief Justice awaited him. To the disappointment of the crowd, the door was closed and Aaron Burr stood before John Marshall.[3]

George Hay, the United States District Attorney, had objected to holding even the beginning of the preliminary hearing at the hotel, because the great

[1] Randolph to Nicholson, March 25, 1807, Adams: *Randolph*, 220.

[2] The warrant was written by Marshall himself. (MS. Archives of the United States Court, Richmond, Va.)

[3] *Burr Trials*, I, 1.

number of eager and antagonistic spectators could
not be present. Upon the sentiment of these, as will
be seen, Hay relied, even more than upon the law
and the evidence, to secure the conviction of the
accused man. He yielded, however, on condition
that, if any discussion arose among counsel, the
proceedings should be adjourned to the Capitol.[1]

It would be difficult to imagine two men more
unlike in appearance, manner, attire, and characteristics, than the prisoner and the judge who now
confronted each other; yet, in many respects, they
were similar. Marshall, towering, ramshackle, bony,
loose-jointed, negligently dressed, simple and un-
conventional of manner; Burr, undersized and erect,
his apparel scrupulously neat,[2] his deportment that
of the most punctilious society. Outwardly, the two
men resembled each other in only a single particular: their eyes were as much alike as their persons
were in contrast.[3] Burr was fifty years of age, and
Marshall was less than six months older.

Both were calm, admirably poised and self-possessed; and from the personality of each radiated a
strange power of which no one who came near either
of them could fail to be conscious. Intellectually,
also, there were points of remarkable similarity.
Clear, cold logic was the outstanding element of
their minds.

[1] *Burr Trials,* I, 1.

[2] The first thing that Burr did upon his arrival at Richmond was to
put aside his dirty, tattered clothing and secure decent attire.

[3] Marshall's eyes were "the finest ever seen, except Burr's, large,
black and brilliant beyond description. It was often remarked during
the trial, that two such pairs of eyes had never looked into one another before." (Parton: *Burr,* 459.)

The two men had the gift of lucid statement, although Marshall indulged in tiresome repetition while Burr never restated a point or an argument. Neither ever employed imagery or used any kind of rhetorical display. Notwithstanding the rigidity of their logic, both were subtle and astute; it was all but impossible to catch either off his guard. But Marshall gave the impression of great frankness; while about every act and word of Burr there was the air of mystery. The feeling which Burr's actions inspired, that he was obreptitious, was overcome by the fascination of the man when one was under his personal influence; yet the impression of indirectness and duplicity which he caused generally, together with his indifference to slander and calumny,[1] made it possible for his enemies, before his Western venture, to build up about his name a structure of public suspicion, and even hatred, wholly unjustified by the facts.

The United States District Attorney laid before Marshall the record in the case of Bollmann and Swartwout in the Supreme Court, and Perkins proudly described how he had captured Burr and brought him to Richmond. Hay promptly moved to commit the accused man to jail on the charges of treason and misdemeanor. The attorneys on both sides agreed that on this motion there must be argument. Marshall admitted Burr to bail in the sum of five thousand dollars for his appearance the next day at the court-room in the Capitol.

When Marshall opened court the following morn-

[1] It was a rule of Burr's life to ignore attacks upon him. (See *supra*, 280.)

ing, the room was crowded with spectators, while hundreds could not find admittance. Hay asked that the court adjourn to the House of Delegates, in order that as many as possible of the throng might hear the proceedings. Marshall complied, and the eager multitude hurried pell-mell to the big ugly hall, where thenceforth court was held throughout the tedious, exasperating months of this historic legal conflict.

Hay began the argument. Burr's cipher letter to Wilkinson proved that he was on his way to attack Mexico at the time his villainy was thwarted by the patriotic measures of the true-hearted commander of the American Army. Hay insisted that Burr had intended to take New Orleans and "make it the capital of his empire." The zealous young District Attorney "went minutely into . . the evidence." The prisoner's stealthy "flight from justice" showed that he was guilty.

John Wickham, one of Burr's counsel, answered Hay. There was no testimony to show an overt act of treason. The alleged Mexican project was not only "innocent, but meritorious"; for everybody knew that we were "in an intermediate state between war and peace" with Spain. Let Marshall recall Jefferson's Message to Congress on that point. If war did not break out, Burr's expedition was perfectly suitable to another and a wholly peaceful enterprise, and one which the President himself had "recommended" — namely, "strong settlements beyond the Mississippi." [1]

---

[1] *Burr Trials*, I, 5.

Burr himself addressed the court, not, he said, "to remedy any omission of his counsel, who had done great justice to the subject," but "to repel some observations of a personal nature." Treason meant deeds, yet he was being persecuted on "mere con- jecture." The whole country had been unjustly aroused against him. Wilkinson had frightened the President, and Jefferson, in turn, had alarmed the people.

Had he acted like a guilty man, he asked? Briefly and modestly he told of his conduct before the courts and grand juries in Kentucky and Mississippi, and the result of those investigations. The people among whom he journeyed saw nothing hostile or treason- able in his expedition.

His "flight"? That had occurred only when he was denied the protection of the laws and when armed men, under illegal orders of an autocratic military authority, were seeking to seize him vio- lently. Then, and only then, acting upon the advice of friends and upon his own judgment, had he "abandoned a country where the laws ceased to be the sovereign power." Why had the guards who brought him from Alabama to Richmond "avoided every magistrate on the way"? Why had he been refused the use of pen, ink, and paper — denied even the privilege of writing to his daughter? It was true that when, in South Carolina, the soldiers chanced upon three civilians, he did indeed "de- mand the interposition of the civil authority." Was that criminal? Was it not his right to seek to be de- livered from "military despotism, from the tyranny

of a military escort," and to be subjected only to
" the operation of the laws of his country"? [1]

On Wednesday, April 1, Marshall delivered the
second of that series of opinions which established
the boundaries of the American law of treason and
rendered the trial of Aaron Burr as notable for the
number and the importance of decisions made from
the bench during the progress of it, as it was famous
among legal duels in the learning, power, and eloquence of counsel, in the influences brought to bear
upon court and jury, and in the dramatic setting
and the picturesque incidents of the proceedings.

Marshall had carefully written his opinion. At
the close of court on the preceding day, he had announced that he would do this in order "to prevent
any misrepresentations of expressions that might
fall on him." He had also assured Hay that, in case
he decided to commit Burr, the District Attorney
should be heard at any length he desired on the
question of bail.

Thus, at the very beginning, Marshall showed
that patience, consideration, and prudence so characteristic of him, and so indispensable to the conduct of this trial, if dangerous collisions with the
prevailing mob spirit were to be avoided. He had in
mind, too, the haughty and peremptory conduct of
Chase, Addison, and other judges which had given
Jefferson his excuse for attacking the Judiciary, and
which had all but placed that branch of the Government in the absolute control of that great practical
genius of political manipulation. By the gentleness

[1] *Burr Trials*, I, 6-8.

of his voice and manner, Marshall lessened the excuse which Jefferson was eagerly seeking in order again to inflame the passions of the people against the Judiciary.

Proof strong enough to convict "on a trial in chief," or even to convince the judge himself of Burr's guilt, was not, said Marshall, necessary to justify the court in holding him for the action of the grand jury; but there must be enough testimony "to furnish good reason to believe" that Burr had actually committed the crimes with which he stood charged.

Marshall quoted Blackstone to the effect that a prisoner could be discharged only when it appeared that the suspicion against him was "wholly groundless," but this did not mean that "the hand of malignity may grasp any individual against whom its hate may be directed or whom it may capriciously seize, charge him with some secret crime and put him on the proof of his innocence."

Precisely that "hand of malignity," however, Burr was feeling by orders of Jefferson. The partisans of the President instantly took alarm at this passage of Marshall's opinion. Here was this insolent Federalist Chief Justice, at the very outset of the investigation, presuming to reflect upon their idol. Such was the indignant comment that ran among the Republicans who packed the hall; and reflect upon the President, Marshall certainly did, and intended to do.

The softly spoken but biting words of the Chief Justice were unnecessary to the decision of the question before him; they accurately described the conduct of the Administration, and they could have been uttered only as a rebuke to Jefferson or as an attempt to cool the public rage that the President had aroused. Perhaps both motives inspired Marshall's pen when he wrote that statesmanlike sentence.[1]

On the whole, said Marshall, probable cause to suspect Burr guilty of an attempt to attack the Spanish possessions appeared from Wilkinson's affidavit; but the charge of treason was quite another matter. "As this is the most atrocious offence which can be committed against the political body, so it is the charge which is most capable of being employed as the instrument of those malignant and vindictive passions which may rage in the bosoms of contending parties struggling for power." Treason is the only crime specifically mentioned in the Constitution — the definition of all others is left to Congress. But the Constitution itself carefully and plainly describes treason and prescribes just how it must be proved.

Did the testimony show probable grounds for believing that Burr had committed treason? Marshall analyzed the affidavits of Eaton and Wilkinson, which constituted all of the "evidence" against Burr; and although the whole matter had been ex-

[1] At the noon hour "a friend" told the Chief Justice of the impression produced, and Marshall hastened to forestall the use that he knew Jefferson would make of it. Calling the reporters about him, he "explicitly stated" that this passage in his opinion "had no allusion to the conduct of the government in the case before him." It was, he assured the representatives of the press, "only an elucidation of Blackstone." (*Burr Trials*, I, footnote to 11.)

amined by the Supreme Court in the case of Bollmann and Swartwout, he nevertheless went over the
same ground again. No impatience, no hasty or
autocratic action, no rudeness of manner, no harshness of speech on his part should give politicians a
weapon with which once more to strike at judges
and courts.

Where, asked Marshall, was the evidence that
Burr had assembled an army to levy war on the
United States? Not before the court, certainly.
Mere "suspicion" was not to be ignored when means
of proving the suspected facts were not yet secured;
but where the truth could easily have been established, if it existed, and yet no proof of it had been
brought forward, everybody "must admit that the
ministers of justice at least ought not officially to
entertain" unsupported conjectures or assertions.

"The fact to be proved . . is an act of public notoriety. It must exist in the view of the world, or it
cannot exist at all. . . Months have elapsed since the
fact did occur, if it ever occurred. More than five
weeks have elapsed since the . . supreme court has
declared the necessity of proving the fact, if it exists.
Why is it not proved?" It is, said Marshall, the
duty of the Executive Department to prosecute
crimes. "It would be easy" for the Government
"to procure affidavits" that Burr had assembled
troops five months ago. Certainly the court "ought
not to believe that there had been any remissness"
on the part of the Administration; and since no
evidence had been presented that Burr had gathered
soldiers, "the suspicion, which in the first instance

might have been created, ought not to be continued, unless this want of proof can be in some manner accounted for."

Marshall would, therefore, commit Burr for high misdemeanor, but not for treason, and must, of consequence, admit the prisoner to bail. The Chief Justice suggested the sum of ten thousand dollars as being "about right." [1] Hay protested that the amount was too small. Burr "is here among strangers," replied Wickham. He has fewer acquaintances in Richmond than anywhere in the country. To be sure, two humane men had saved the prisoner "from the horrors of the dungeon" when he arrived; but the first bail was only for two days, while the present bail was for an indefinite period. "Besides," asserted Wickham, "I have heard several gentlemen of great respectability, who did not doubt that colonel Burr would keep his recognisance, express an unwillingness to appear as bail for him, lest it might be supposed they were enemies to their country." [2]

Thus were cleverly brought into public and official view the conditions under which this trial, so vital to American liberty, was to be held. Burr was a "traitor," asserted Jefferson. "Burr a traitor!" echoed the general voice. That all who befriended Burr were, therefore, also "traitors at heart," was the conclusion of popular logic. Who dared brave the wrath of that blind and merciless god, Public Prejudice? From the very beginning the prosecution invoked the power of this avenging and re-

[1] *Burr Trials,* I, 11–18.   [2] *Ib.* 19.

morseless deity, while the defense sought to break that despotic spell and arouse the spirit of opposition to the tyranny of it. These facts explain the legal strategy of the famous controversy — a controversy that continued throughout the sweltering months of the summer and far into the autumn of 1807.

Hay declared that he had been "well informed that Colonel Burr could give bail in the sum of one hundred thousand dollars." Gravely Burr answered that there was serious doubt whether bail in any sum could be procured; "gentlemen are unwilling to expose themselves to animadversions" which would be the result of their giving bail for him. He averred that he had no financial resources. "It is pretty well known that the government has ordered my property seized, and that the order has been executed." He had thus lost "upwards of forty thousand dollars," and his "credit had consequently been much impaired." [1]

Marshall, unmoved by the appeals of either side, fixed the bail at ten thousand dollars and adjourned court until three o'clock to enable Burr to procure sureties for that amount. At the appointed hour the prisoner came into court with five men of property who gave their bond for his appearance at the next term of the United States Circuit Court, to be held at Richmond on May 22.

For three precious weeks at least Aaron Burr was free. He made the best of his time, although he

---

[1] *Burr Trials*, I, 20. His "property," however, represented borrowed money.

could do little more than perfect the plans for his defense. His adored Theodosia was in alternate rage and despair, and Burr strove to cheer and steady her as best he might. Some of "your letters," he writes, "indicate a sort of stupor"; in others "you rise into phrenzy." He bids her come "back to reason. . . Such things happen in all democratic governments." Consider the "vindictive and unrelenting persecution" of men of "virtue, . . independence and . . talents in Greece and Rome." Let Theodosia "amuse" herself by collecting instances of the kind and writing an essay on the subject "with reflections, comments and applications." The perusal of it, he says, will give him "great pleasure" if he gets it by the time court opens in May.[1]

Burr learned the names of those who were to compose the grand jury that was to investigate his misdeeds. Among them were "twenty democrats and four federalists," he informs his daughter. One of "the former is W. C. Nicholas my vindictive . . personal enemy — the most so that could be found in this state. The most indefatigable industry is used by the agents of government, and they have money at command without stint. If I were possessed of the same means, I could not only foil the prosecutors, but render them ridiculous and infamous. The democratic papers teem with abuse of me and my counsel, and even against the chief justice. Nothing is left undone or unsaid which can tend to prejudice the public mind, and produce a conviction without evidence. The machinations of

[1] Burr to his daughter, May 15, 1807, Davis, II, 405–06.

this description which were used against Moreau in
France were treated in this country with indignation.
They are practiced against me in a still more impudent degree, not only with impunity, but with
applause; and the authors and abettors suppose,
with reason, that they are acquiring favour with the
administration." [1]

Every word of this was true. The Republican
press blazed with denunciation of "the traitor."
The people, who had been led to believe that the
destruction of their "liberties" had been the object
at which Burr ultimately aimed, were intent on the
death of their would-be despoiler. Republican politicians were nervously apprehensive lest, through
Marshall's application of the law, Burr might escape
and the Administration and the entire Republican
Party thereby be convicted of persecuting an innocent man. They feared, even more, the effect on
their political fortunes of being made ridiculous.

Giles was characteristically alert to the danger.
Soon after Marshall had declined to commit Burr
for treason and had released him under bail to appear on the charge of misdemeanor only, the Republican leader of the Senate, then in Virginia, wrote
Jefferson of the situation.

The preliminary hearing of Burr had, Giles stated,
greatly excited the people of Virginia and probably
would "have the same effect in all parts of the
United States." He urged the President to take
"all measures necessary for effecting . . a full and
fair judicial investigation." The enemies of the Ad-

[1] Burr to his daughter, May 15, 1807, Davis, II, 405–06.

ministration had gone so far as to "suggest doubts" as to the "measures heretofore pursued in relation to Burr," and had dared to "intimate that the executive are not possessed of evidence to justify those measures" — or, if there was such evidence, that the prosecution had been "extremely delinquent in not producing it at the examination." Nay, more! "It is even said that General Wilkinson will not be ordered to attend the trial." That would never do; the absence of that militant patriot "would implicate the character of the administration, more than they can be apprised of." [1]

But Jefferson was sufficiently alarmed without any sounding of the tocsin by his Senatorial agent. "He had so frightened the country . . that to escape being overwhelmed by ridicule, he must get his prisoner convicted of the fell designs which he had publically attributed to him." [2] It is true that Jefferson did not believe Burr had committed treason; [3] but he had formally declared to Congress and the country

[1] Giles to Jefferson, April 6, 1807, Anderson, 110. The date is given in Jefferson to Giles, April 20, 1807, *Works:* Ford, x, 383.

[2] Parton: *Burr*, 455.

[3] "Altho' at first he proposed a separation of the Western country, . . yet he very early saw that the fidelity of the Western country was not to be shaken and turned himself wholly towards Mexico and so popular is an enterprize on that country in this, that we had only to be still, & he could have had followers enough to have been in the city of Mexico in 6. weeks." (Jefferson to James Bowdoin, U.S. Minister to Spain, April 2, 1807, *Works:* Ford, x, 381–82.)

In this same letter Jefferson makes this amazing statement: "If we have kept our hands off her [Spain] till now, it has been purely out of respect for France. . . We expect therefore from the friendship of the emperor [Napoleon] that he will either compel Spain to do us justice, or abandon her to us. We ask but one month to be in . . the city of Mexico."

that Burr's "guilt is placed beyond question," and, at any cost, he must now make good that charge.[1]

From the moment that he received the news of Marshall's decision to hold Burr for misdemeanor and to accept bail upon that charge, the prosecution of his former associate became Jefferson's ruling thought and purpose. It occupied his mind even more than the Nation's foreign affairs, which were then in the most dangerous state.[2] Champion though he was of equal rights for all men, yet any opposition to his personal or political desires or interests appeared to madden him.[3] A personal antagonism, once formed, became with Thomas Jefferson a public policy.

He could see neither merit nor honesty in any act or word that appeared to him to favor Burr. Anybody who intimated doubt of his guilt did so, in Jefferson's opinion, for partisan or equally unworthy reasons. "The fact is that the Federalists make Burr's cause their own, and exert their whole influence to shield him," he asserted two days after Marshall had admitted Burr to bail.[4] His hatred of the National Judiciary was rekindled if, indeed, its fires ever had died down. "It is unfortunate that federalism is still predominant in our judiciary department, which is consequently in opposition to the legislative & Executive branches & is able to

[1] McCaleb, 325.

[2] See *infra*, 476–77; also vol. IV, chap. I, of this work.

[3] See Nicholson to Monroe, April 12, 1807, Adams: *Randolph*, 216–18. Plumer notes "the rancor of his personal and political animosities." (Plumer, 356.)

[4] Jefferson to James Bowdoin, U.S. Minister to Spain, April 2 1807, *Works:* Ford, x, 382.

baffle their measures often," he averred at the same time, and with reference to Marshall's rulings thus far in the Burr case.

He pours out his feelings with true Jeffersonian bitterness and passion in his answer to Giles's letter. No wonder, he writes, that "anxiety and doubt" had arisen "in the public mind in the present defective state of the proof." This tendency had "been sedulously encouraged by the tricks of the judges to force trials before it is possible to collect the evidence dispersed through a line of two thousand miles from Maine to Orleans."

The Federalists too were helping Burr! These miscreants were "mortified only that he did not separate the Union and overturn the government." The truth was, declares Jefferson, that the Federalists would have joined Burr in order to establish "their favorite monarchy" and rid themselves of "this hated republic," if only the traitor had had "a little dawn of success." Consider the inconsistent attitude of these Federalists. Their first "complaint was the supine inattention of the administration to a treason stalking through the land in the open light of day; the present one, that they [the Administration] have crushed it before it was ripe for execution, so that no overt acts can be proved."

Jefferson confides to Giles that the Government may not be able to establish the commission of overt acts; in fact, he says, "we do not know of a certainty yet what will be proved." But the Administration is already doing its very best: "We have set on foot an inquiry through the whole of the country which has been the scene of these transactions to be able to prove to the courts, if they will give time, or to the public by way of communication to Congress, what the real facts have been" — this three months after Jefferson had asserted, in his Special Message on the conspiracy, that Burr's "guilt is placed beyond question."

In this universal quest for "the facts," the Government had no help from the National courts, complains the President: "Aided by no process or facilities from Federal Courts,[1] but frowned on by their new-born zeal for the liberty of those whom we would not permit to overthrow the liberties of their country, we can expect no revealments from the accomplices of the chief offender." But witnesses would be produced who would "satisfy the world if not the judges" of Burr's treason. Jefferson enumerates the "overt acts" which the Administration expected to prove.[2]

Marshall, of course, stood in the way, for it was

[1] This was flatly untrue. No process to obtain evidence or to aid the prosecution in any way was ever denied the Administration. This statement of the President was, however, a well-merited reflection on the tyrannical conduct of the National judges in the trials of men for offenses under the Sedition Law and even under the common law. (See *supra*, chap. i.) But, on the one hand, Marshall had not then been appointed to the bench and was himself against the Sedition Law (see vol. ii, chap. xi, of this work); and, on the other hand, Jefferson had now become as ruthless a prosecutor as Chase or Addison ever was.

[2] These were: "1. The enlistment of men in a regular way; 2. the regular mounting of guard round Blennerhassett's island; . . 3. the rendezvous of Burr with his men at the mouth of the Cumberland; 4. his letter to the acting Governor of Mississippi, holding up the prospect of civil war; 5. his capitulation, regularly signed, with the aides of the Governor, as between two independent and hostile commanders."

plain that "the evidence cannot be collected under 4 months, probably 5." Jefferson had directed his Attorney-General, "unofficially," but "expressly," to "inform the Chief Justice of this." With what result? "Mr. Marshall says, 'more than 5 weeks have elapsed since the opinion of the Supreme Court has declared the necessity of proving the overt acts if they exist. Why are they not proved?' In what terms of decency," growls Jefferson, "can we speak of this? As if an express could go to Natchez or the mouth of the Cumberland and return in 5 weeks, to do which has never taken less than twelve."

Jefferson cannot sufficiently criticize Marshall's opinion: "If, in Nov. or Dec. last, a body of troops had assembled on the Ohio, it is impossible to suppose the affidavits establishing the fact could not have been obtained by the last of March," he quotes from Marshall's ruling. "I ask the judge where they [the affidavits] should have been lodged? At Frankfort? at Cincinnati? at Nashville? St. Louis? . . New Orleans? . . Where? At Richmond he certainly meant, or meant only to throw dust in the eyes of his audience." [1]

As his pen flew over the burning page, Jefferson's

[1] The affidavits in regard to what happened on Blennerhassett's island would necessarily be lodged in Richmond, since the island was in Virginia and the United States Court for the District of that State alone had jurisdiction to try anybody for a crime committed within its borders.

Even had there been any doubt as to where the trial would take place, the Attorney-General would have held the affidavits pending the settlement of that point; and when the place of trial was determined upon, promptly dispatched the documents to the proper district attorney.

anger grew. Marshall's love of monarchy was at the bottom of his decision: "All the principles of law are to be perverted which would bear on the favorite offenders who endeavor to overrun this odious Republic."

Marshall's refinements as to proof required to establish probable cause to believe Burr guilty, particularly irritated Jefferson. "As to the overt acts, were not the bundle of letters of information in Mr. Rodney's hands, the letters and facts published in the local newspapers, Burr's flight, & the universal belief or rumor of his guilt, probable ground for presuming the facts . . so as to put him on trial? Is there a candid man in the U S who does not believe some one, if not all, of these overt acts to have taken place?"

How dare Marshall require legal evidence when "letters, newspapers and rumors" condemned Burr! How dare he, as a judge, not heed "the universal belief," especially when that general public opinion had been crystallized by Jefferson himself!

That Marshall was influenced by politics and was of a kidney with the whole breed of National judges up to that time, Jefferson had not the slightest doubt. "If there ever had been an instance in this or the preceding administrations, of federal judges so applying principles of law as to condemn a federal or acquit a republican offender, I should have judged them in the present case with more charity."

But the conduct of the Chief Justice will be the final outrage which will compel a great reform. "The nation will judge both the offender & judges

for themselves . . the people . . will see . . & amend
the error in our Constitution, which makes any
branch independent of the nation. . . One of the
great co-ordinate branches of the government, setting itself in opposition to the other two, and to the
common sense of the nation, proclaims impunity to
that class of offenders which endeavors to overturn
the Constitution, and are themselves protected in
it by the Constitution itself; for impeachment is
a farce which will not be tried again."

Thus Jefferson extracts some comfort from Marshall's refusal to obey popular clamor and condemn
on "rumor." If Marshall's "protection of Burr produces this amendment,[1] it will do more good than
his condemnation would have done. Against Burr,
personally," audaciously adds Jefferson, "I never
had one hostile sentiment." [2]

Such was the state of the President's mind when
he learned of Marshall's ruling on the Government's
motion to commit Burr to jail upon the charges of
treason and high misdemeanor. Jefferson felt that
he himself was on trial; he knew that he must make
good his charges or suffer a decline in the popularity
which he prized above all else in life. He proposed
that, at the very least, the public should be on
his side, and he resolved to exert the utmost efforts
of the National Government to bend Marshall to
his will.

[1] The reference is to the amendment to the Constitution urged by
Jefferson, and offered by Randolph in the House, providing that a
judge should be removed by the President on the address of both
Houses of Congress. (See *supra*, chap. IV, 221.)

[2] Jefferson to Giles, April 20, 1807, *Works:* Ford, x, 383–88.

Thus the President of the United States became the leading counsel in the prosecution of Aaron Burr, as well as the director-general of a propaganda planned to confirm public opinion of Burr's treason, and to discredit Marshall should his decisions from the bench result in the prisoner's escape from the gallows.[1] Jefferson ordered his Attorney-General, Cæsar A. Rodney, to direct justices of the peace throughout the country to examine everybody supposed to have any knowledge of Burr, his plans, movements, or conversations. Long lists of questions, designed to elicit replies that would convict Burr, were sent to these officials on printed forms. A vast drag-net was spread over almost the whole of the United States and drawn swiftly and remorselessly to Washington.

The programme for the prosecution became the subject of anxious Cabinet meetings, and the resources of every department of the Executive branch of the Government were employed to overwhelm the accused man. Jefferson directed Madison as Secretary of State "to take the necessary measures," including the advance of money for their expenses, to bring to Richmond witnesses "from great distances."

Five thousand dollars, in a single warrant, was given to the Attorney-General for use in supporting

---

[1] See Parton: *Burr*, 456–57. "The real prosecutor of Aaron Burr, throughout this business, was Thomas Jefferson, President of the United States, who was made President of the United States by Aaron Burr's tact and vigilance, and who was able therefore to wield against Aaron Burr the power and resources of the United States." (*Ib.* 457.) And see McCaleb, 361.

the Administration's case.[1] The total amount of the public money expended by Jefferson's orders to secure Burr's conviction was $11,721.11, not a dollar of which had been appropriated for that purpose. "All lawful expenses in the prosecution of Burr were audited, and paid in full," under a law which provided for the conduct of criminal cases; the sums spent by direction of the President were in addition to the money dispensed by authority of that law.[2]

When Bollmann had been brought to Washington, he had read with rage and amazement the newspaper accounts that Burr had led two thousand armed men in a violent and treasonable attack upon the United States. Accordingly, after Marshall released him from imprisonment, he hastened to Jefferson and tried to correct what he declared to be "false impressions" concerning Burr's treason. Bollmann also wished to convince the President that war with Spain was desirable, and to get his support of Burr's expedition. Jefferson, having taken the precaution to have the Secretary of State present at the interview, listened with apparent sympathy. The following day he requested Bollmann to write out and deliver to him his verbal statements, "Thomas Jefferson giving him *his word of honour* that they should never be used against himself [Bollmann] and *that the paper shall never go out of his* [Jefferson's] *hand.*"[3]

[1] Jefferson to the Secretary of State, April 14, 1807, *Works:* Ford, x, 383.
[2] Jenkinson: *Aaron Burr*, 282–83.
[3] Jefferson to "Bollman," Jan. 25, 1807, Davis, ii, 388.

The confiding Bollmann did as the President requested, his whole paper going "to disprove treason,
and to show the expediency of war." Because of unfamiliarity with the English language "one or two
expressions" may have been "improperly used." [1]
Bollmann's statement Jefferson now transmitted to
the District Attorney at Richmond, in order, said
the President, "that you may know how to examine
him and draw everything from him."

Jefferson ordered Hay to show the paper only to
his associate counsel; but, if Bollmann "should pre-
varicate," the President adds, "ask him whether he
did not say so and so to Mr. Madison and myself."
The President assures Hay that "in order to let
him [Bollmann] see that his prevarication will be
marked, Mr. Madison will forward [Hay] a pardon
for him, which we mean should be delivered previously." Jefferson fears that Bollmann may not
appear as a witness and directs Hay to "take effectual measures to have him immediately taken into
custody."

Nor was this all. Three months earlier, Wilkinson had suggested to Jefferson the base expedient
of offering pardons to Burr's associates, in order to
induce them to betray him and thus make certain
his conviction.[2] Apparently this crafty and sinister
advice now recurred to Jefferson's mind — at least
he followed it. He enclosed a sheaf of pardons and
directed Hay to fill them out "at [his] discretion, if
[he] should find a defect of evidence, & believe that
this would supply it, by avoiding to give them to

[1] Bollmann's narrative, Davis, ii, 389.   [2] McCaleb, 331.

the gross offenders, unless it be visible that the principal will otherwise escape." [1]

In the same letter Jefferson also sent to Hay the
affidavit of one Jacob Dunbaugh, containing a mass
of bizarre falsehoods, as was made plain during
the trial. Dunbaugh was a sergeant who had been
arrested for desertion and had been pardoned by
Wilkinson on condition that he would give suitable
testimony against Burr. "If," continues Jefferson,
"General Wilkinson gets on in time,[2] I expect he
will bring Dunbaugh with him. At any rate it
[Dunbaugh's affidavit] may be a ground for an arrest
& committment for treason."

Vividly alive to the forces at work to doom him,
Burr nevertheless was not dismayed. As a part of
his preparation for defense he exercised on all whom
he met the full power of his wonderful charm; and
if ever a human being needed friends, Aaron Burr
needed them in the Virginia Capital. As usual, most
of those who conversed with him and looked into his
deep, calm eyes became his partisans. Gradually,
a circle of men and women of the leading families
of Richmond gathered about him, supporting and
comforting him throughout his desperate ordeal.

Burr's attorneys were no longer merely his
counsel performing their professional duty; even
before the preliminary hearing was over, they had

[1] Jefferson to the United States District Attorney for Virginia, May
20, 1807, *Works:* Ford, x, 394–401.

Bollmann, in open court, scornfully declined to accept the pardon.
(See *infra*, 452.)

[2] Wilkinson was then *en route* by sea to testify against Burr before
the grand jury.

become his personal friends and ardent champions. They were ready and eager to go into court and fight for their client with that aggressiveness and enthusiasm which comes only from affection for a man and a faith in his cause. Every one of them not only had developed a great fondness for Burr, but earnestly believed that his enterprise was praiseworthy rather than treasonable.

One of them, John Wickham, was a commanding figure in the society of Richmond, as well as the leader of the Virginia bar at that time.[1] He was a close friend of Marshall and lived in an imposing house near him. It was to Wickham that Marshall had left the conduct of his cases in court when he went to France on the X. Y. Z. mission.

Dinners were then the principal form of social intercourse in Richmond, and were constantly given. The more prominent lawyers were particularly devoted to this pleasing method of cheer and relaxation. This custom kept the brilliant bar of Richmond sweet and wholesome, and nourished among its members a mutual regard, while discouraging resentments and animosities. Much of that courtesy and deference shown to one another by the lawyers of that city, even in the most spirited encounters in court, was due to that esteem and fellowship which their practice of dining together created.

Of the dispensers of such hospitality, Marshall and Wickham were the most notable and popular. The "lawyer dinners" given by Marshall were famous; and the tradition of them still casts a

[1] Mordecai: *Richmond in By-Gone Days*, 68.

warm and exhilarating glow. The dinners, too, of John Wickham were quite as alluring. The food was as plentiful and as well prepared, the wines as varied, select, and of as ancient vintage, the brandy as old and "sound," the juleps as fragrant and seductive; and the wit was as sparkling, the table talk as informing, the good humor as heartening. Nobody ever thought of declining an invitation to the house of John Wickham.

All these circumstances combined to create a situation for which Marshall was promptly denounced with that thoughtlessness and passion so characteristic of partisanship — a situation that has furnished a handle for malignant criticism of him to this day. During the interval between the preliminary hearing and the convening of court in May, Wickham gave one of his frequent and much-desired dinners. As a matter of course, Wickham's intimate friend and next-door neighbor was present — no dinner in Richmond ever was complete without the gentle-mannered, laughter-loving John Marshall, with his gift for making everybody happy and at ease. But Aaron Burr was also a guest.

Aaron Burr, "the traitor," held to make answer to charges for his infamous crimes, and John Marshall, the judge before whom the miscreant was to be tried, dining together! And at the house of Burr's chief counsel! Here was an event more valuable to the prosecution than any evidence or argument, in the effect it would have, if rightly employed, on public opinion, before which Burr had been and was arraigned far more than before the court of justice.

Full use was made of the incident. The Republican organ, the Richmond *Enquirer*, promptly exposed and denounced it. This was done by means of two letters signed "A Stranger from the Country," who "never had any, the least confidence in the political principles of the chief justice" — none in "that noble candor" and "those splendid . . even god-like talents which many of all parties ascribe to him." Base as in reality he was, Marshall might have "spared his country" the "wanton insult" of having "feasted at the same convivial board with Aaron Burr." What excuse was there for "conduct so grossly indecent"? To what motive should Marshall's action be ascribed? "Is this charity, hypocracy, or federalism?" Doubtless he "was not actuated by any corrupt motive," and "was unapprised of the invitation of B." [1] However, the fact is, that the judge, the accused, and his attorney, were fellow guests at this "treason rejoicing dinner." [2]

---

[1] According to a story, told more than a century after the incident occurred, Marshall did not know, when he accepted Wickham's invitation, that Burr was to be a guest, but heard of that fact before the dinner. His wife, thereupon, advised him not to go, but, out of regard for Wickham, he attended. (Thayer: *John Marshall*, 80–81.)

This tale is almost certainly a myth. Professor Thayer, to whom it was told by an unnamed descendant of Marshall, indicates plainly that he had little faith in it.

The facts that, at the time, even the *Enquirer* acquitted Marshall of any knowledge that Burr was to be present; that the prudence of the Chief Justice was admitted by his bitterest enemies; that so gross an indiscretion would have been obvious to the most reckless; that Marshall, of all men, would not have embarrassed himself in such fashion, particularly at a time when public suspicion was so keen and excitement so intense — render it most improbable that he knew that Burr was to be at the Wickham dinner.

[2] *Enquirer*, April 10 and 28, 1807.

Thus the great opinions of John Marshall, delivered during the trial of Aaron Burr, were condemned before they were rendered or even formed. With that lack of consideration which even democracies sometimes display, the facts were not taken into account. That Marshall never knew, until he was among them, who his fellow guests were to be; that Wickham's dinner, except in the presence of Burr, differed in no respect from those constantly given in Richmond; that Marshall, having arrived, could do nothing except to leave and thus make the situation worse; — none of these simple and obvious facts seemed to have occurred to the eager critics of the Chief Justice.

That Marshall was keenly aware of his predicament there can be no doubt. He was too good a politician and understood too well public whimsies and the devices by which they are manipulated, not to see the consequences of the innocent but unfortunate evening at Wickham's house. But he did not explain; he uttered not a syllable of apology. With good-natured contempt for the maneuvers of the politicians and the rage of the public, yet carefully and coolly weighing every element of the situation, John Marshall, when the appointed day of May came around, was ready to take his seat upon the bench and to conduct the historic trial of Aaron Burr with that kindly forbearance which never deserted him, that canny understanding of men and motives which served him better than learning, and that placid fortitude that could not be shaken.

CHAPTER VIII

ADMINISTRATION VERSUS COURT

In substance Jefferson said that if Marshall should suffer Burr to escape, Marshall himself should be removed from office. (Henry Adams.)

It becomes our duty to lay the evidence before the public. Go into any expense necessary for this purpose. (Jefferson.)

The President has let slip the dogs of war, the hell-hounds of persecution, to hunt down my friend. (Luther Martin.)

If you cannot exorcise the demon of prejudice, you can chain him down to law and reason. (Edmund Randolph.)

On May 22, 1807, the hall of the House of Delegates at Richmond was densely crowded long before the hour of half-past twelve, when John Marshall took his seat upon the bench and opened court. So occupied was every foot of space that it was with difficulty that a passage was opened through which the tall, awkwardly moving, and negligently clad Chief Justice could make his way. By Marshall's side sat Cyrus Griffin, Judge of the District Court, who throughout the proceedings was negligible.

The closely packed spectators accurately portrayed the dress, manners, and trend of thought of the American people of that period. Gentlemen in elegant attire — hair powdered and queues tied in silk, knee breeches and silver buckles, long rich cloth coats cut half away at the waist, ruffled shirts and high stocks — were conspicuous against the background of the majority of the auditors, whose apparel, however, was no less picturesque.

This audience was largely made up of men from the smaller plantations, men from the mountains,

men from the backwoods, men from the frontiers.
Red woolen shirts; rough homespun or corduroy
trousers, held up by "galluses"; fringed deerskin
coats and "leggings" of the same material kept in
place by leather belts; hair sometimes tied by strings
in uncouth queues, but more often hanging long and
unconfined — in such garb appeared the greater
part of the attendance at the trial of Aaron Burr.
In forty years there had been but little change in
the general appearance of Virginians [1] except that
fewer wore the old dignified and becoming attire of
well-dressed men.

Nearly all of them were Republicans, plain men,
devoted to Jefferson as the exponent of democracy
and the heaven-sent leader of the people. Among
these Jeffersonians, however, were several who, quite
as much as the stiffest Federalists, prided themselves
upon membership in the "upper classes."

Nearly all of the Republicans present, whether of
the commonalty or the gentry, were against Aaron
Burr. Scattered here and there were a few Federalists — men who were convinced that democracy
meant the ruin of the Republic, and who profoundly
believed that Jefferson was nothing more than an
intriguing, malicious demagogue — most of whom
looked upon Burr with an indulgent eye. So did
an occasional Republican, as now and then a lone
Federalist denounced Burr's villainy.

The good-sized square boxes filled with sand that
were placed at infrequent intervals upon the floor
of the improvised court-room were too few to receive

[1] See vol. I, 201, of this work.

the tobacco juice that filled the mouths of most of the spectators before it was squirted freely upon the floor and wall. Those who did not chew the weed either smoked big cigars and fat pipes or contented themselves with taking snuff.[1] Upon recess or adjournment of court, all, regularly and without loss of time, repaired to the nearest saloons or taverns and strengthened themselves, with generous draughts of whiskey or brandy, taken "straight," for a firmer, clearer grasp of the points made by counsel.

Never, in its history, had Richmond been so crowded with strangers. Nearly five thousand people now dwelt in the Virginia Capital, the site of which was still "untamed and broken" by "inaccessible heights and deep ravines."[2] Thousands of visitors had come from all over the country to witness the prosecution of that fallen angel whose dark deeds, they had been made to believe, had been in a fair way to destroy the Nation. The inns could shelter but an insignificant fraction of them, and few were the private houses that did not take in men whom the taverns could not accommodate. Hundreds brought covered wagons or tents and camped under the trees or on the river-banks near the city. Correspondents of the press of the larger cities were present, among them the youthful[3] Washington Irving, who wrote one or two articles for a New York paper.

---

[1] Tobacco chewing and smoking in court-rooms continued in most American communities in the South and West down to a very recent period.

[2] Address of John Tyler on "Richmond and its Memories," Tyler, I, 219.

[3] Irving was twenty-four years old when he reported the Burr trial.

In the concourse thus drawn to Richmond, few there were who were not certain that Burr had planned and attempted to assassinate Jefferson, overthrow the Government, shatter the Nation, and destroy American "liberty"; and so vocal and belligerent was this patriotic majority that men who at first held opinions contrary to the prevailing sentiment, or who entertained doubts of Burr's guilt, kept discreetly silent. So aggressively hostile was public feeling that, weeks later, when the bearing and manners of Burr, and the devotion, skill, and boldness of his counsel had softened popular asperity, Marshall declared that, even then, "it would be difficult or dangerous for a jury to venture to acquit Burr, however innocent they might think him." [1] The prosecution of Aaron Burr occurred when a tempest of popular prejudice and intolerance was blowing its hardest.

The provision concerning treason had been written into the American Constitution "to protect the people against that horrible and dangerous doctrine of constructive treason which had stained the English records with blood and filled the English valleys with innocent graves." [2]

The punishment for treason in all countries had been brutal and savage in the extreme. In Eng-

[1] *Blennerhassett Papers:* Safford, 465. Marshall made this avowal to Luther Martin, who personally told Blennerhassett of it.

[2] Judge Francis M. Finch, in Dillon, i, 402.

"The men who framed that instrument [Constitution] remembered the crimes that had been perpetrated under the pretence of justice; for the most part they had been traitors themselves, and having risked their necks under the law they feared despotism and arbitrary power more than they feared treason." (Adams: *U.S.* iii, 468.)

land, that crime had not perhaps been treated with
such severity as elsewhere. Yet, even in England,
so harsh had been the rulings of the courts against
those charged with treason, so inhuman the execution of judgments upon persons found guilty under
these rulings, so slight the pretexts that sent innocent men and women to their death,[1] that the
framers of our fundamental law had been careful
to define treason with utmost clearness, and to declare that proof of it could only be made by two
witnesses to the same overt act or by confession of
the accused in open court.[2]

That was one subject upon which the quarreling
members of the Constitutional Convention of 1787
had been in accord, and their solution of the question had been the one and the only provision of
which no complaint had been made during the struggle over ratification.

Every member of that Convention — every officer
and soldier of the Revolution from Washington down
to private, every man or woman who had given

[1] A favorite order from the bench for the execution of the condemned was that the culprit should be drawn prostrate at the tails of
horses through the jagged and filthy streets from the court-room to
the place of execution; the legs, arms, nose, and ears there cut off; the
intestines ripped out and burned "before the eyes" of the victim;
and finally the head cut off. Details still more shocking were frequently added. See sentences upon William, Lord Russell, July 14,
1683 (*State Trials Richard II to George I*, vol. 3, 660); upon Algernon
Sidney, November 26, 1683 (*ib.* 738); upon William, Viscount Stafford,
December 7, 1680 (*ib.* 214); upon William Stayley, November 21,
1678 (*ib.* vol. 2, 656); and upon other men condemned for treason.

[2] Even in Philadelphia, after the British evacuation of that place
during the Revolution, hundreds were tried for treason. Lewis alone,
although then a very young lawyer, defended one hundred and fifty-
two persons. (See *Chase Trial*, 21.)

succor or supplies to a member of the patriot army, everybody who had advocated American independence — all such persons could have been prosecuted and might have been convicted as "traitors" under the British law of constructive treason.[1] "None," said Justice James Iredell in 1792, "can so highly . . prize these provisions [of the Constitution] as those who are best acquainted with the abuses which have been practised in other countries in prosecutions for this offence. . . We . . hope that the page of American history will never be stained with prosecutions for treason, begun without cause, conducted without decency, and ending in iniquitous convictions, without the slightest feelings of remorse." [2]

Yet, six years later, Iredell avowed his belief in the doctrine of constructive treason.[3] And in less than seventeen years from the time our National Government was established, the reasons for writing into the Constitution the rigid provision concerning treason were forgotten by the now thoroughly partisanized multitude, if, indeed, the people ever knew those reasons.

Moreover, every National judge who had passed upon the subject, with the exception of John Mar-

[1] "In the English law . . the rule . . had been that enough heads must be cut off to glut the vengeance of the Crown." (Isaac N. Phillips, in Dillon, II, 394.)

[2] Iredell's charge to the Georgia Grand Jury, April 26, 1792, *Iredell:* McRee, II, 349; and see Iredell's charge to the Massachusetts Grand Jury, Oct. 12, 1792, *ib.* 365.

[3] See his concurrence with Judge Peters's charge in the Fries case, Wharton: *State Trials,* 587–91; and Peters's opinion, *ib.* 586; also see Chase's charge at the second trial of Fries, *ib.* 636.

shall, had asserted the British doctrine of constructive treason. Most of the small number who realized
the cause and real meaning of the American Constitutional provision as to treason were overawed by
the public frenzy; and brave indeed was he who
defied the popular passion of the hour or questioned
the opinion of Thomas Jefferson, then at the summit
of his popularity.[1]

One such dauntless man, however, there was
among the surging throng that filled the Capitol
Square at Richmond after the adjournment of court
on May 22, and he was a vigorous Republican, too.
"A tall, lank, uncouth-looking personage, with long
locks of hair hanging over his face, and a queue
down his back tied in an eel-skin, his dress singular,
his manners and deportment that of a rough back-
woodsman,"[2] mounted the steps of a corner grocery and harangued the glowering assemblage that
gathered in front of him.[3]   His daring, and an unmistakable air that advertised danger to any who
disputed him, prevented that violent interruption
certain to have been visited upon one less bold and
formidable. He praised Burr as a brave man and a
patriot who would have led Americans against the
hated Spanish; he denounced Jefferson as a perse-
cutor who sought the ruin of one he hated. Thus
Andrew Jackson of Tennessee braved and cowed
the hostile mob that was demanding and impatiently
awaiting the condemnation and execution of the

---

[1] "The President's popularity is unbounded, and his will is that of
the nation. . . Such is our present infatuation." (Nicholson to Randolph, April 12, 1807, Adams: *Randolph*, 216–17.)

[2] Hildreth, IV, 692.   [3] Parton: *Burr*, 458.

one who, for the moment, had been made the object of the country's execration.[1]

Jackson had recovered from his brief distrust of Burr, and the reaction had carried his tempestuous nature into extreme championship of his friend. "I am more convinced than ever," he wrote during the trial, "that treason was never intended by Burr." [2] Throughout the extended and acrimonious contest, Jackson's conviction grew stronger that Burr was a wronged man, hounded by betrayers, and the victim of a political conspiracy to take his life and destroy his reputation. And Jackson firmly believed that the leader of this cabal was Thomas Jefferson. "I am sorry to say," he wrote, "that this thing [the Burr trial] has . . assumed the shape of a political persecution." [3]

The Administration retaliated by branding Andrew Jackson a "malcontent"; and Madison, because of Jackson's attitude, prevented as long as possible the military advancement of the refractory Tennesseean during the War of 1812.[4] On the other hand, Burr never ceased to be grateful to his frontiersman adherent, and years later was one of those who set in motion the forces which made Andrew Jackson President of the United States.[5]

Nor was Jackson the only Republican who considered Jefferson as the contriving and energizing hand of the scheme to convict Burr. Almost riotous

[1] Parton: *Jackson*, I, 333.

[2] Jackson to Anderson, June 16, 1807, *ib.* 334.

[3] *Ib.* 335.   [4] *Ib.* 334–36.

[5] Parton: *Burr*, 606–08; see also Parton: *Jackson*, II, 258–59, 351–54; and Davis, II, 433–36.

were the efforts to get into the hall where the trial was held, though it was situated on a steep hill and "the ascent to the building was painfully laborious." [1] Old and eminent lawyers of Richmond could not reach the bar of the court, so dense was the throng.

One youthful attorney, tall and powerful, "the most magnificent youth in Virginia," determined to witness the proceedings, shouldered his way within and "stood on the massive lock of the great door" of the chamber. [2] Thus Winfield Scott got his first view of that striking scene, and beheld the man whose plans to invade Mexico he himself, more than a generation afterward, was to carry out as Commander of the American Army. Scott, there and then, arrived at conclusions which a lifetime of thought and experiences confirmed. "It was President Jefferson who directed and animated the prosecution," he declares in his "Memoirs." Scott records the political alignment that resulted: "Hence every Republican clamored for execution. Of course, the Federalists . . compacted themselves on the other side." [3]

Of all within the Hall of Delegates, and, indeed, among the thousands then in Richmond, only two persons appeared to be perfectly at ease. One of them was John Marshall, the other was Aaron Burr. Winfield Scott tells us of the manner of the imperiled man as he appeared in court on that sultry midday of May: "There he stood, in the hands of power, on the brink of danger, as composed, as immovable,

[1] Address of John Tyler, "Richmond and its Memories," Tyler, I, 219.
[2] Parton: *Burr*, 459.   [3] *Memoirs of Lieut.-General Scott*, I, 13.

as one of Canova's living marbles." But, says Scott, "Marshall was the master spirit of the scene." [1]

Gathered about Burr were four of his counsel, the fifth and most powerful of his defenders, Luther Martin, not yet having arrived. The now elderly Edmund Randolph, bearing himself with "overawing dignity"; John Wickham, whose commanding presence corresponded well with his distinguished talents and extensive learning; Benjamin Botts, a very young lawyer, but of conceded ability and noted for a courage, physical and moral, that nothing could shake; and another young attorney, John Baker, a cripple, as well known for his wit as Botts for his fearlessness — this was the group of men that appeared for the defense.

For the prosecution came Jefferson's United States District Attorney, George Hay — eager, nervous, and not supremely equipped either in mind or attainments; William Wirt — as handsome and attractive as he was eloquent and accomplished, his extreme dissipation [2] now abandoned, and who, by his brilliant gifts of intellect and character, was beginning to lay the solid foundations of his notable career; and Alexander MacRae, then Lieutenant-Governor of Virginia — a sour-tempered, aggressive, well-informed, and alert old Scotchman, pitiless in his use of sarcasm, caring not the least whom he

---

[1] *Memoirs of Lieut.-General Scott*, i, 13, 16.

[2] See *Great American Lawyers:* Lewis, ii, 268–75.

Kennedy says that the stories of Wirt's habits of intoxication were often exaggerated (Kennedy, i, 68); but see his description of the bar of that period and his apologetic reference to Wirt's conviviality (*ib.* 66–67).

offended if he thought that his affronts might help
the cause for which he fought. David Robertson,
the stenographer who reported the trial, was a
scholar speaking five or six languages.[1]

With all these men Marshall was intimately acquainted, and he was well assured that, in making
up his mind in any question which arose, he would
have that assistance upon which he so much relied
— exhaustive argument and complete exposition of
all the learning on the subject to be decided.

Marshall was liked and admired by the lawyers
on both sides, except George Hay, who took Jefferson's view of the Chief Justice. Indeed, the ardent
young Republican District Attorney passionately
espoused any opinion the President expressed. The
whole bar understood the strength and limitations
of the Chief Justice, the power of his intellect no
less than his unfamiliarity with precedents and the
learning of the law. From these circumstances, and
from Marshall's political wisdom in giving the lawyers a free hand, resulted a series of forensic encounters seldom witnessed or even tolerated in a
court of justice.

The first step in the proceedings was the examination by the grand jury of the Government's witnesses, and its return, or refusal to return, bills of
indictment against Burr. When the clerk had called
the names of those summoned on the grand jury,
Burr arose and addressed the court. Clad in black
silk, hair powdered and queue tied in perfect fashion,
the extreme pallor of his face in striking contrast to

[1] *Blennerhassett Papers:* Safford, 426.

his large black eyes, he made a rare picture of elegance and distinction in the uncouth surroundings of that democratic assemblage.

The accused man spoke with a quiet dignity and an "impressive distinctness" which, throughout the trial, so wrought upon the minds of the auditors that, fifty years afterward, some of those who heard him could repeat sentences spoken by him.[1] Burr now objected to the panel of the grand jury. The law, he said, required the marshal to summon twenty-four freeholders; if any of these had been struck off and others summoned, the act was illegal, and he demanded to know whether this had been done.[2]

For an hour or more the opposing counsel wrangled over this point. Randolph hints at the strategy of the defense: "There never was such a torrent of prejudice excited against any man, before a court of justice, as against colonel Burr, and by means which we shall presently unfold." Marshall sustained Burr's exception: undoubtedly the marshal had acted "with the most scrupulous regard to what he believed to be the law," but, if he had changed the original panel, he had transcended his authority.[3] It was then developed that the panel had been changed, and the persons thus illegally placed on the grand jury were dismissed.[4]

"With regret," Burr demanded the right to challenge the remainder of the grand jury "for favour."[5] Hay conceded the point, and Burr challenged Sena-

---

[1] Parton: *Burr*, 461.   [2] *Burr Trials*, I, 31–32.   [3] *Ib.* 37.   [4] *Ib.* 38.
[5] Meaning the partiality of the persons challenged, such as animosity toward the accused, conduct showing bias against him, and the like. See *Bouvier's Law Dictionary:* Rawle, 3d revision, II, 1191.

tor William Branch Giles. Merely upon the documents in Jefferson's Special Message to Congress,
Giles had advocated that the writ of habeas corpus
be suspended, and this, argued Burr, he could have
done only if he supposed "that there was a rebellion
or insurrection, and a public danger, of no common
kind." This action of Giles was a matter of record;
moreover, he had publicly made statements to the
same effect.[1]

Senator Giles admitted that he had acted and
spoken as Burr charged; and while denying that
he held any "personal resentments against the accused," and asserting that he could act fairly as
a grand juror, he graciously offered to withdraw.
Marshall mildly observed that "if any gentleman
has made up and declared his mind, it would be best
for him to withdraw." With superb courtesy, Burr
disavowed any reflection on Giles; it was merely
above "human nature" that he should not be prejudiced. "So far from having any animosity against
him, he would have been one of those whom I should
have ranked among my personal friends."

Burr then challenged Colonel Wilson Cary Nicholas,[2] who spiritedly demanded the objections to him.
Nicholas "entertained a bitterly personal animosity" against him, replied Burr. He would not, however, insist upon "further inquiry" if Nicholas would
withdraw as Giles had done. Nicholas then addressed the court. He had been a member of the
National House, he said, "when the attempt was
made to elect colonel Burr president," and every-

---

[1] *Burr Trials*, I, 38–39.   [2] *Ib.* 41–42.

body knew how he felt about that incident. He had
been in the Senate for three years "while colonel
Burr was president of that body," and had done all
he could to nominate Clinton in Burr's stead.

His suspicions had been "very much excited"
when Burr made his Western journey, and he had
openly stated his "uncommon anxiety" concerning
"not only the prosperity, but the union of the
states." Therefore, he had not desired to serve on
the grand jury and had asked the marshal to excuse
him. He had finally consented solely from his delicate sense of public duty. Also, said Nicholas, he
had been threatened with the publication of one of
the "most severe pieces" against him if he served
on the grand jury; and this inclined him to "defy
[his] enemies [rather] than to ask their mercy or
forbearance."

His friends had advised him not to make mention
of this incident in court; but, although he was "not
scrupulous of acquiring, in this way, a reputation of
scrupulous delicacy," and had determined to heed
the counsel of his friends, still, he now found himself
so confused that he did not know just what he ought
to do. On the whole, however, he thought he would
follow the example of Senator Giles and withdraw.[1]

At that very moment, Nicholas was a Republican
candidate for Congress and, next to Giles, Jefferson's
principal political agent in Virginia. Four days after
Burr had been brought to Richmond, Jefferson had
written Nicholas a letter of fulsome flattery "be-
seeching" him to return to the National House in

[1] *Burr Trials*, I, 41–42.

the place of the President's son-in-law, Thomas
Mann Randolph, who had determined to retire, and
assuring him of the Republican leadership if he
would do so.[1]

Thus, for a moment, was revealed a thread of
that web of intrigue and indirect influence which,
throughout the trial, was woven to enmesh judge,
jury, and public. Burr was instantly upon his feet
denouncing in his quiet but authoritative manner
the "attempt to intimidate" Nicholas as "a contrivance of some of [his] enemies for the purpose of
irritating" the hot-blooded Republican politician
"and increasing the public prejudice against [Burr];
since it was calculated to throw suspicion on [his]
cause." Neither he nor his friends had ever "sanctioned" such an act; they were wholly ignorant of
it, and viewed it "with indignation." [2]

Mr. Joseph Eggleston, another of the grand jurors,
now asked to be excused because he had declared his
belief of Burr's guilt; but he admitted, in answer to
Marshall's questions, that he could act justly in the
impending investigation. Burr said that he would
not object to Eggleston: "the industry which has
been used through this country [Virginia] to prejudice
my cause, leaves me very little chance, indeed, of
an impartial jury." Eggleston's "candour . . in
excepting to himself" caused Burr to hope that he
would "endeavour to be impartial." But let Marshall decide — Burr would be "perfectly passive." [3]
The scrupulous grand juror was retained.

---

[1] Jefferson to Nicholas, Feb. 28, 1807, *Works:* Ford, x, 370–71.
[2] *Burr Trials*, i, 43.   [3] *Ib.* 44.

John Randolph and Dr. William Foushee were then added to the grand jury panel and Marshall appointed Randolph foreman.[1] He promptly asked to be excused because of his "strong prepossession." "Really," observed Burr, "I am afraid we shall not be able to find any man without this prepossession." Marshall again stated "that a man must not only have formed but declared an opinion in order to excuse him from serving on the jury." So Randolph was sworn as foreman, the oath administered to all, and at last the grand jury was formed.[2]

Marshall then instructed the jury, the substance of his charge being to the same effect as his opinion in the case of Bollmann and Swartwout. Burr asked the Chief Justice also to advise the men who were to decide the question of his indictment "as to the admissability of certain evidence" which he supposed Hay would lay before them. The District Attorney objected to any favor being shown Burr, "who," he declared, "stood on the same footing with every other man charged with crime."

For once Burr unleashed his deep but sternly

---

[1] In view of the hatred which Marshall knew Randolph felt toward Jefferson, it is hard to reconcile his appointment with the fairness which Marshall tried so hard to display throughout the trial. However, several of Jefferson's most earnest personal friends were on the grand jury, and some of them were very powerful men. Also fourteen of the grand jury were Republicans and only two were Federalists.

[2] *Burr Trials*, I, 45-46. This grand jury included some of the foremost citizens of Virginia. The sixteen men who composed this body were: John Randolph, Jr., Joseph Eggleston, Joseph C. Cabell, Littleton W. Tazewell, Robert Taylor, James Pleasants, John Brockenbrough, William Daniel, James M. Garnett, John Mercer, Edward Pegram, Munford Beverly, John Ambler, Thomas Harrison, Alexander Shephard, and James Barbour.

repressed feeling: "Would to God," he cried, his voice vibrant with emotion, "that I did stand on the same ground with every other man. This is the first time [since the military seizure] that I have been permitted to enjoy the rights of a citizen. How have I been brought hither?" Marshall checked this passionate outburst: it was not proper, he admonished both Hay and Burr, to "go into these digressions."

His composure restored, Burr insisted that he should be accorded "the same privileges and rights which belonged to every other citizen." He would not now urge his objections to Marshall's opinion in the Bollmann-Swartwout case;[1] but he pointed out "the best informed juryman might be ignorant of many points . . relating to testimony, . . for instance, as to the article of papers," and he wished Marshall to inform the jury on these matters of law.

A brief, sharp debate sprang up, during which Burr's counsel spoke of the "host of prejudices raised against [their] client," taunted Hay with his admission "that there was no man who had not formed an opinion," and denounced "the activity of the Government."[2] Upon Hay's pledging himself that he would submit no testimony to the grand jury "without notice being first given to Colonel Burr and his counsel," Marshall adjourned the court that the attorneys might prepare for "further

[1] Marshall's error in this opinion, or perhaps the misunderstanding of a certain passage of it (see *supra*, 350), caused him infinite perplexity during the trial; and he was put to his utmost ingenuity to extricate himself. The misconstruction by the grand jury of the true meaning of Marshall's charge was one determining cause of the grand jury's decision to indict Burr. (See *infra*, 466.)

[2] *Burr Trials*, I, 47–48.

discussion." The Government was not ready to present any testimony on either the following day or on Monday because its principal witness, General Wilkinson, had not arrived.

Hay now sent Jefferson his first report of the progress of the case. Burr had steadily been making friends, and this irritated the District Attorney more than the legal difficulties before him. "I am surprised, and afflicted, when I see how much, and by how many, this man has been patronised and supported." Hay assured Jefferson, however, that he would "this day move to commit him for treason."[1] Accordingly, he announced in the presence of the grand jury that he would again ask the court to imprison Burr on that accusation. In order, he said, that the impropriety of mentioning the subject in their presence might be made plain, Burr moved that the grand jury be withdrawn. Marshall sustained the motion; and after the grand jury had retired, Hay formally moved the court to order Burr's incarceration upon the charge of treason.[2]

Burr's counsel, surprised and angered, loudly complained that no notice had been given them. With a great show of generosity, Hay offered to delay his motion until the next day. "Not a moment's postponement," shouted Botts, his fighting nature thoroughly aroused. Hay's "extraordinary application," he said, was to place upon the court the functions of the grand jury. Burr wanted no delay. His dearest wish was to "satisfy his country . . and even

[1] Hay to Jefferson, May 25, 1807, Jefferson MSS. Lib. Cong.
[2] *Burr Trials*, I, 48–51.

his prosecutors, that he is innocent." Was ever a
man so pursued? He had been made the victim of
unparalleled military despotism; his legal rights
had been ignored; his person and papers unlawfully
seized. The public had been excited to anger.
Through newspaper threats and "popular clamor"
attempts had been made to intimidate every officer
of the court. Consider "the multitude around us"
— they must not be further infected "with the
poison already too plentifully infused."

Did Hay mean to "open the case more fully?"
inquired Marshall. No, answered Hay; but Wilkinson's arrival in Virginia might be announced before
he reached Richmond. Who could tell the effect
on Burr of such dread tidings? The culprit might
escape; he must be safely held.[1] "The bets were
against Burr that he would abscond, should W. come
to Richmond." [2]

If Wilkinson is so important a witness, "why is
he not here?" demanded Wickham. Everybody
knew that "a set of busy people . . are laboring to
ruin" Burr. "The press, from one end of the continent to the other, has been enlisted . . to excite
prejudices" against him. Let the case be decided
upon "the evidence of sworn witnesses" instead of
"the floating rumours of the day."

Did the Government's counsel wish that "the
multitude around us should be prejudiced by garbled
evidences?" Wickham avowed that he could not
understand Hay's motives, but of this he was sure —

[1] *Burr Trials*, I, 53–54.
[2] Irving to Paulding, June 22, 1807, *Life and Letters of Washington Irving:* Irving, I, 145.

that if, thereafter, the Government wished to oppress any citizen, drag him by military force over the country, prejudice the people against him, it would "pursue the very same course which has now been taken against colonel Burr." The prosecution admitted that it had not enough evidence to lay before the grand jury, yet they asked to parade what they had before the court. Why? — "to nourish and keep alive" the old prejudices now growing stale.[1]

Wirt answered at great length. He understood Wickham's purpose, he said. It was to "divert the public attention from Aaron Burr," and "shift the popular displeasure . . to another quarter." Wickham's speech was not meant for the court, exclaimed Wirt, but for "the people who surround us," and so, of course, Marshall would not heed it. Burr's counsel "would convert this judicial inquiry into a political question . . between Thomas Jefferson and Aaron Burr."

Not to be outdone by his gifted associate, Hay poured forth a stream of words: "Why does he [Burr] turn from defending himself to attack the administration?" he asked. He did not answer his own question, but Edmund Randolph did: "An order has been given to treat colonel Burr as an outlaw, and to burn and destroy him and his property." Jefferson, when requested, had furnished the House information; — "would to God he had stopped here, as an executive officer ought to have done!" But instead he had also pronounced Burr guilty — an opinion calculated to affect courts, juries, the people.

[1] *Burr Trials*, i, 57–58.

Wickham detailed the treatment of Burr, "the only man in the nation whose rights are not secure from violation." [1]

Burr himself closed this unexpected debate, so suddenly thrust upon his counsel and himself. His speech is a model of that simple, perspicuous, and condensed statement of which he was so perfectly the master. He presented the law, and then, turning to Hay, said that two months previous the District Attorney had declared that he had enough evidence to justify the commitment, and surely he must have it now. Nearly half a year had elapsed since Jefferson had "declared that there was a crime," and yet, even now, the Government was not ready. Nevertheless, the court was again asked to imprison him for an alleged offense for which the prosecution admitted it had not so much as the slight evidence required to secure his indictment by the grand jury.

Were the Government and he "on equal terms?" Far from it. "The United States [could] have compulsory process" to obtain affidavits against him but he had "no such advantage." So the prosecution demanded his imprisonment on *ex parte* evidence which would be contradicted by his own evidence if he could adduce it. Worse still! The Government affidavits against him "are put into the newspapers, and they fall into the hands of the grand jury." Meanwhile, he was helpless. And now the opinion of the court was also to be added to the forces working to undo him.

[1] *Burr Trials*, I, 58–76.

Wirt and Hay had charged his counsel "with declamation against the government." Certainly nobody could attribute "declamation" to him; but, said Burr, his restrained voice tense with suppressed emotion, "no government is so high as to be beyond the reach of criticism" — that was a fundamental principle of liberty. This was especially true when the Government prosecuted a citizen, because of "the vast disproportion of means which exists between it and the accused." And "if ever there was a case which justified this vigilance, it is certainly the present one"; let Marshall consider the "uncommon activity" of the Administration.

Burr would, he said, "merely state a few" of the instances of "harrassing, . . contrary to law" to which he had been subjected. His "friends had been every where seized by the military authority," dragged before "particular tribunals," and forced to give testimony; his papers taken; orders to kill him issued; post-offices broken open and robbed — "nothing seemed too extravagant to be forgiven by the amiable morality of this government." Yet it was for milder conduct that Americans rightly condemned "European despotisms."

The President was a great lawyer; surely "he ought to know what constitutes war. Six months ago he proclaimed that there was a civil war. And yet, for six months they have been hunting for it and cannot find one spot where it existed. There was, to be sure, a most terrible war in the newspapers; but no where else." He had been haled before the court in Kentucky — and no proof; in Mississippi — and no proof. The Spaniards actually invaded American territory — even then there was no war.

Thus early the record itself discloses the dramatic, and, for Marshall, perilous, conditions under which this peculiar trial was to be conducted. The record makes clear, also, the plan of defense which Burr and his counsel were forced to adopt. They must dull the edge of public opinion sharpened to a biting keenness by Jefferson. They must appeal to the people's hatred of oppression, fear of military rule, love of justice. To do this they must attack, attack, always attack.

They must also utilize every technical weapon of the law. At another time and place they could have waived, to Burr's advantage, all legal rights, insisted upon his indictment, and gone to trial, relying only upon the evidence. But not in the Virginia of 1807, with the mob spirit striving to overawe jury and court, and ready to break out in violent action — not at the moment when the reign of Thomas Jefferson had reached the highest degree of popular idolatry.

Just as Hay, Wirt, and MacRae generally spoke to the spectators far more than to the Bench, so did Wickham, Randolph, Botts, and Martin.[1] Both sides so addressed the audience that their hearers were able to repeat to the thousands who could not get into the hall what had been said by the advocates.

---

[1] "I . . contented myself . . with . . declaring to the Audience (for two thirds of our speeches have been addressed to the people) that I was prepared to give the most direct contradiction to the injurious Statements." (Hay to Jefferson, June 14, 1807, giving the President an account of the trial, Jefferson MSS. Lib. Cong.)

From the very first the celebrated trial of Aaron
Burr was a contest for the momentary favor of public opinion; and, in addition, on the part of Burr, an
invoking of the law to shield him from that popular wrath which the best efforts of his defenders
could not wholly appease.

Marshall faced a problem of uncommon difficulty.
It was no small matter to come between the populace and its prey — no light adventure to brave the
vengeance of Thomas Jefferson. Not only his public
repute [1] — perhaps even his personal safety [2] and
his official life [3] — but also the now increasing influence and prestige of the National Judiciary were
in peril. However, he must do justice no matter
what befell — he must, at all hazards, pronounce
the law truly and enforce it bravely, but with elas-
tic method. He must be not only a just, but also
an understanding, judge.

When court opened next morning, Marshall was
ready with a written opinion. Concisely he stated
the questions to be decided: Had the court the power
to commit Burr, and, if so, ought the circumstances
to restrain the exercise of it? Neither side had made
the first point, and Marshall mentioned it only
"to show that it [had] been considered." Briefly he
demonstrated that the court was clothed with authority to grant Hay's motion. Should that power,

[1] He was hanged in effigy soon after the trial. (See *infra*, 539.)

[2] It must be remembered that Marshall himself declared, in the
very midst of the contest, that it would be dangerous for a jury to
acquit Burr. (See *supra*, 401.)

[3] He had narrowly escaped impeachment (see *supra*, chap. IV), and
during the trial he was openly threatened with that ordeal (see *infra*,
500).

then, be exerted? Marshall thought that it should. The Government had the right to ask Burr's incarceration at any time, and it was the duty of the court to hear such a motion.

Thus far spoke Marshall the judge. In the closing sentences the voice of the politician was heard: "The court perceives and regrets that the result of this motion may be publications unfavourable to the justice, and to the right decision of the case "; but this must be remedied "by other means than by refusing to hear the motion." Every honest and intelligent man extremely deplored "any attempt . . to prejudice the public judgment, and to try any person," not by the law and the evidence, but "by public feelings which may be and often are artificially excited against the innocent, as well as the guilty, . . a practice not less dangerous than it is criminal." Nevertheless he could not "suppress motions, which either party may have a legal right to make." So, if Hay persisted, he might "open his testimony." [1]

While Marshall, in Richmond, was reading this opinion, Jefferson, in Washington, was writing directions to Hay. He was furious at "the criminal and voluntary retirement" of Giles and Nicholas from the grand jury "with the permission of the court." The opening of the prosecution had certainly begun "under very inauspicious circumstances." One thing was clear: "It becomes our duty to provide that full testimony shall be laid before the Legislature, and through them the public."

[1] *Burr Trials*, I, 79–81.

If the grand jury should indict Burr, then Hay must furnish Jefferson with all the evidence, "taken as verbatim as possible." Should Burr not be indicted, and no trial held and no witnesses questioned in court, then Hay must "have every man privately examined by way of affidavit," and send Jefferson "the whole testimony" in that form. "This should be done before they receive their compensation, that they may not evade examination. Go into any expense necessary for this purpose,[1] & meet it from the funds provided to the Attorney general for the other expenses."[2]

Marshall's decision perplexed Hay. It interfered with his campaign of publicity. If only Marshall had denied his motion, how effectively could that incident have been used on public sentiment! But now the Republican press could not exclaim against Marshall's "leniency" to "traitors" as it had done. The people were deprived of fresh fuel for their patriotic indignation. Jefferson would be at a loss for a new pretext to arouse them against the encroachments of the courts upon their "liberties."

Hay strove to retrieve the Government from this disheartening situation. He was "struck," he said, with Marshall's reference to "publications." To avoid such newspaper notoriety, he would try to arrange with Burr's counsel for the prisoner's appearance under additional bail, thus avoiding insistence upon the Government's request for the imprisonment of the accused. Would Marshall adjourn

---

[1] See *supra*, 390–91.

[2] Jefferson to Hay, May 26, 1807, *Works:* Ford, x, footnote to 394–95.

court that this amicable arrangement might be brought about? Marshall would and did.

But next day found Hay unrelieved; Burr's counsel had refused, in writing, to furnish a single dollar of additional bail. To his intense regret, Hay lamented that he was thus forced to examine his witnesses. Driven to this unpleasant duty, he would follow the "chronological order — first the depositions of the witnesses who were absent, and afterwards those who were present." [1]

The alert Wickham demanded "strict legal order." The Government must establish two points: the perpetration of an overt act, and "that colonel Burr was concerned in it." [2] Hay floundered — there was one great plot, he said, the two parts of it "intimately blended"; the projected attack on Spain and the plot to divide the Union were inseparable — he must have a free hand if he were to prove this wedded iniquity. Was Burr afraid to trust the court?

Far from it, cried Wickham, "but we do fear to prejudicate the mind of the grand jury. . . All propriety and decorum have been set at naught; every idle tale which is set afloat has been eagerly caught at. The people here are interested by them; and they circulate all over the country." [3] Marshall interrupted: "No evidence certainly has any bearing . . unless the overt act be proved." Hay might, however, "pursue his own course."

A long altercation followed. Botts made an extended speech, in the course of which he discredited

---

[1] *Burr Trials*, i, 81–82.   [2] *Ib.* 82.   [3] *Ib.* 84–85.

the Government's witnesses before they were introduced. They were from all over the country, he
said, their "names, faces and characters, are alike
unknown to colonel Burr." To what were they to
testify? Burr did not know — could not possibly
ascertain. "His character has long been upon public torture; and wherever that happens . . the impulses to false testimony are numerous. Sometimes
men emerge from the sinks of vice and obscurity
into patronage and distinction by circulating interesting tales, as all those of the marvelous kind are.
Others, from expectation of office and reward, volunteer; while timidity, in a third class, seeks to
guard against the apprehended danger, by magnifying trifling stories of alarm. . . When they are afterwards called to give testimony, perjury will not ap-
pal them, if it be necessary to save their reputations." Therefore, reasoned Botts — and most justly
— strict rules of evidence were necessary.[1]

Hay insisted that Wilkinson's affidavit demonstrated Burr's intentions. That "goes for nothing,"
said Marshall, "if there was no other evidence to
prove the overt act." Therefore, "no part of it [was]
admissible at this time."[2] Thrice Marshall patiently reminded Government counsel that they
charged an overt act of treason and must prove it.[3]

Hay called Peter Taylor, Blennerhassett's former
gardener, and Jacob Allbright, once a laborer on
the eccentric Irishman's now famous island. Both
were illiterate and in utter terror of the Government. Allbright was a Dutchman who spoke Eng-

---

[1] *Burr Trials*, I, 91.   [2] *Ib.* 94.   [3] *Ib.* 95–96.

lish poorly; Taylor was an Englishman; and they told stories equally fantastic. Taylor related that Mrs. Blennerhassett had sent him to Kentucky with a letter to Burr warning him not to return to the island; that Burr was surprised at the people's hostility; that Blennerhassett, who was also in Kentucky, confided they were going to take Mexico and make Burr king, and Theodosia queen when her father died; also that Burr, Blennerhassett, and their friends had bought "eight hundred thousand acres of land" and "wanted young men to settle it," and that any of these who should prove refractory, he [Blennerhassett] said, "by God, . . I will stab"; that Blennerhassett had also said it would be a fine thing to divide the Union, but Burr and himself could not do it alone.

Taylor further testified that Blennerhassett once sent him with a letter to a Dr. Bennett, who lived in Ohio, proposing to buy arms in his charge belonging to the United States — if Bennett could not sell, he was to tell where they were, and Blennerhassett "would steal them away in the night"; that his employer charged him "to get [the letter] back and burn it, for it contained high treason"; and that the faithful Taylor had done this in Bennett's presence.

Taylor narrated the scene on the island when Blennerhassett and thirty men in four boats fled in the night: some of the men had guns and there was some powder and lead.[1]

Jacob Allbright told a tale still more marvelous.

[1] *Burr Trials*, i. 492-97.

Soon after his employment, Mrs. Blennerhassett had come to this dull and ignorant laborer, while he was working on a kiln for drying corn, and confided to him that Burr and her husband "were going to lay in provisions for an army for a year"; that Blennerhassett himself had asked Allbright to join the expedition which was going "to settle a new country." Two men whom the Dutch laborer met in the woods hunting had revealed to him that they were "Burr's men," and had disclosed that "they were going to take a silver mine from the Spanish"; that when the party was ready to leave the island, General Tupper of Ohio had "laid his hands upon Blennerhassett and said, 'your body is in my hands in the name of the commonwealth,'" whereupon "seven or eight muskets [were] levelled" at the General; that Tupper then observed he hoped they would not shoot, and one of the desperadoes replied, "I'd as lieve as not"; and that Tupper then "changed his speech," wished them "to escape safe," and bade them Godspeed.

Allbright and Taylor were two of the hundreds to whom the Government's printed questions had been previously put by agents of the Administration. In his answers to these, Allbright had said that the muskets were pointed at Tupper as a joke.[1] Both Taylor and he swore that Burr was not on the island when Blennerhassett's men assembled there and stealthily departed in hasty flight.

To the reading of the deposition of Jacob Dunbaugh, Burr's counsel strenuously objected. It was

[1] *Burr Trials*, I, 509–14.

not shown that Dunbaugh himself could not be produced; the certification of the justice of the peace, before whom the deposition was taken, was defective. For the remainder of the day the opposing lawyers wrangled over these points. Marshall adjourned court and "took time to consider the subject till the next day"; when, in a long and painfully technical opinion, he ruled that Dunbaugh's affidavit could not be admitted because it was not properly authenticated.[1]

May 28, when the court again convened, was made notable by an event other than the reading of the unnecessarily long opinion which Marshall had written during the night: the crimson-faced, bellicose superman of the law, Luther Martin, appeared as one of Burr's counsel.[2] The great lawyer had formed an ardent admiration and warm friendship for Burr during the trial of the Chase impeachment,[3] and this had been intensified when he met Theodosia, with whom he became infatuated.[4] He had voluntarily come to his friend's assistance, and soon threw himself into the defense of Burr with all the passion of his tempestuous nature and all the power and learning of his phenomenal intellect.

After vexatious contendings by counsel as to whether Burr should give additional bail,[5] Marshall declared that "as very improper effects on the public mind [might] be produced," he wished that no opinion would be required of him previous to the action of

[1] *Burr Trials*, i, 97–101.　　[2] *Ib.* 97.
[3] *Md. Hist. Soc. Fund-Pub. No. 24*, 22.
[4] *Blennerhassett Papers:* Safford, 468–69.
[5] *Burr Trials*, i, 101–04.

the grand jury; and that the "appearance of colonel
Burr could be secured without . . proceeding in this
inquiry." Burr denied the right of the court to hold
him on bail, but said that if Marshall was "embarrassed," he voluntarily would furnish additional bail,
"provided it should be understood that no opinion
on the question even of probable cause was pronounced by the court." [1] Marshall agreed; and Burr
with four sureties, among whom was Luther Martin,
gave bond for ten thousand dollars more.[2]

Day after day, court, grand jury, counsel, and
spectators awaited the coming of Wilkinson. The
Government refused to present any testimony to
the grand jury until he arrived, although scores of
witnesses were present. Andrew Jackson was very
much in town, as we have seen. So was Commodore
Truxtun. And "General" William Eaton was also
on hand, spending his time, when court was not in
session, in the bar-rooms of Richmond.

Wearing a "tremendous hat," clad in gay colored coat and trousers, with a flaming Turkish belt
around his waist, Eaton was already beginning to
weaken the local hatred of Burr by his loud blustering against the quiet, courteous, dignified prisoner.[3]
Also, at gambling-tables, and by bets that Burr
would be convicted, the African hero was making
free with the ten thousand dollars paid him by the
Government soon after he made the bloodcurdling

---

[1] *Burr Trials*, i, 105.

[2] The men who went on this second bail bond for Burr were: William Langburn, Thomas Taylor, John G. Gamble, and Luther Martin.
(*Ib.* 106.)

[3] *Blennerhassett Papers*: Safford, 315–16.

affidavit [1] with which Jefferson had so startled Congress and the country.

While proceedings lagged, Marshall enjoyed the dinners and parties that, more than ever, were given by Richmond society. On one of these occasions that eminent and ardent Republican jurist, St. George Tucker, was present, and between him and Marshall an animated discussion grew out of the charge that Burr had plotted to cause the secession of the Western States; it was a forecast of the tremendous debate that was to end only at Appomattox. "Judge Tucker, though a violent Democrat," records Blennerhassett, "seriously contended .. with Judge Marshall .. that any State in the Union is at any time competent to recede from the same, though Marshall strongly opposed this doctrine." [2]

Hay wrote Jefferson of the slow progress of the case, and the President "hastened" to instruct his district attorney: If the grand jury should refuse to indict Burr, Hay must not deliver the pardon to Bollmann; otherwise, "his evidence is deemed entirely essential, & .. his pardon is to be produced before he goes to the book." Jefferson had become more severe as he thought of Bollmann, and now actually directed Hay to show, in open court, to this new object of Presidential displeasure, the "sacredly confidential" statement given Jefferson under pledge of the latter's "word of honor" that it should never leave his hand. Hay was directed to ask Bollmann whether "it was not his handwriting." [3]

---

[1] *Eaton:* Prentiss, 396–403; 4 Cranch, 463–66.
[2] *Blennerhassett Papers:* Safford, 425.
[3] Jefferson to Hay, May 28, 1807, *Works:* Ford, x, 395–96.

With the same ink on his pen the President wrote his son-in-law that he had heard only of the first day of the trial, but was convinced that Marshall meant to do all he could for Burr. Marshall's partiality showed, insisted Jefferson, "the original error of establishing a judiciary independent of the nation, and which, from the citadel of the law can turn it's guns on those they were meant to defend, & controul & fashion their proceedings to it's own will." [1]

Hay quickly answered Jefferson: The trial had "indeed commenced under inauspicious circumstances," and doubtless these would continue to be unfavorable. Nobody could predict the outcome. Hay was so exhausted and in such a state of mind that he could not describe "the very extraordinary occurrences in this very extraordinary examination." Burr's "partizans" were gloating over the failure of Wilkinson to arrive. Bollmann would neither accept nor reject the pardon; he was "as unprincipled as his leader." Marshall's refusal to admit Dunbaugh's affidavit was plainly illegal — "his eyes [were] almost closed" to justice. [2]

Jefferson now showered Hay with orders. The reference in argument to Marshall's opinion in Marbury vs. Madison greatly angered him: "Stop . . citing that case as authority, and have it denied to be law," he directed Hay, and gave him the arguments to be used against it. An entire letter is devoted to this one subject: "I have long wished for a proper occasion to have the gratuitous opinion in Marbury

[1] Jefferson to Eppes, May 28, 1807, *Works:* Ford, x, 412-13.
[2] Hay to Jefferson, May 31, 1807, Jefferson MSS. Lib. Cong.

v. Madison brought before the public, & denounced as not law; & I think the present a fortunate one, because it occupies such a place in the public attention."

Hay was openly to declare that the President rejected Marshall's opinion in that case as having been "given extra-judicially & against law," and that the reverse of it would be Jefferson's "rule of action." If necessary, Hay might state that the President himself had said this.[1]

Back and forth went letters from Hay to Jefferson and from Jefferson to Hay,[2] the one asking for instructions and the other eagerly supplying them. To others, however, the President explained that he could take no part in any judicial proceeding, since to do so would subject him to "just censure."[3]

In spite of the abundance of Government witnesses available, the prosecution refused to go on until the redoubtable savior of his country had arrived from New Orleans. Twice the grand jury had to be dismissed for several days, in order, merrily wrote Washington Irving, "that they might go home, see their wives, get their clothes washed, and flog their negroes."[4] A crowd of men ready to testify was held. The swarms of spectators waited with angry impatience. "If the great hero of the South does not arrive, it is a chance if we have any trial this term,"[5] commented Irving.

---

[1] Jefferson to Hay, June 2, 1807, *Works: Ford*, x, 396–97.

[2] Same to same, June 5, 1807, *ib.* 397–98; Hay to Jefferson, same date, Jefferson MSS. Lib. Cong.; and others cited, *infra*.

[3] Jefferson to Dayton, Aug. 17, 1807, *Works: Ford*, x, 478.

[4] Irving to Mrs. Hoffman, June 4, 1807, Irving, I, 142.   [5] *Ib.*

During this period of inaction and suspense, suddenly arose one of the most important and exciting
questions of the entire trial. On June 9, while counsel and court were aimlessly discussing Wilkinson's
journey to Richmond, Burr arose and said that he
had a "proposition to submit" to the court. The
President in his Message to Congress had made
mention of the letter and other papers dated October 21, which he had received from Wilkinson. It
had now become material that this letter should be
produced in court.

Moreover, since the Government had "attempted
to infer certain intentions on [his] part, from certain
transactions," such as his flight from Mississippi,
it had become necessary to prove the conditions
that forced him to attempt that escape. Vital
among these were orders of the Government to the
army and navy "to destroy" Burr's "person and
property." He had seen these orders in print,[1] and
an officer had assured him that such instructions had
actually been issued. It was indispensable that this
be established. The Secretary of the Navy had refused to allow him or his counsel to inspect these
orders. "Hence," maintained Burr, "I feel it necessary . . to call upon [the court] to issue a subpœna
to the President of the United States, with a clause,
requiring him to produce certain papers; or in
other words, to issue the subpœna *duces tecum.*" If
Hay would agree to produce these documents, the
motion would not be made.[2]

---

[1] Burr had seen the order in the *Natchez Gazette.* It was widely
published.

[2] *Burr Trials*, i, 113-14.

Hay was sadly confused. He would try to get all the papers wanted if Marshall would say that they were material. How, asked Marshall, could the court decide that question without inspecting the papers? "Why . . issue a subpœna to the President?" inquired Hay. Because, responded Marshall, "in case of a refusal to send the papers, the officer himself may be present to show cause. This subpœna is issued only where fears of this sort are entertained."

Counsel on both sides became angry. Hay denied the authority of the court to issue such a writ. Marshall called for argument, because, he said, "I am not prepared to give an opinion on this point." [1] Thus arose the bitter forensic struggle that preceded Marshall's historic order to Jefferson to come into court with the papers demanded, or to show cause why he should not do so.

Hay instantly dispatched the news to Jefferson; he hoped the papers would be "forwarded without delay," because "detention of them will afford [Burr] pretext for clamor." Besides, "L. Martin has been here a long time, perfectly inactive"; he was yearning to attack Jefferson and this would "furnish a topic." [2]

The President responded with dignified caution: "Reserving the necessary right of the President of the U S to decide, independently of all other authority, what papers, coming to him as President, the public interests permit to be communicated, & to whom, I assure you of my readiness under that

---

[1] *Burr Trials*, I, 115–18.
[2] Hay to Jefferson, June 9, 1807, Jefferson MSS. Lib. Cong.

restriction, voluntarily to furnish on all occasions, whatever the purposes of justice may require." He had given the Wilkinson letter, he said, to the Attorney-General, together with all other documents relating to Burr, and had directed the Secretary of War to search the files so that he (Jefferson) could "judge what can & ought to be done" about sending any order of the Department to Richmond.[1]

When Marshall opened court on June 10, Burr made affidavit that the letters and orders might be material to his defense. Hay announced that he had written Jefferson to send the desired papers and expected to receive them within five days. They could not, however, be material, and he did not wish to discuss them. Martin insisted that the papers be produced. Wickham asked what Hay was trying to do — probably trying to gain time to send to Washington for instructions as to how the prosecution should now act.

Was not "an accused man . . to obtain witnesses in his behalf?" Never had the denial of such a right been heard of "since the declaration of American Independence." The despotic treatment of Burr called aloud not only for the court's protection of the persecuted man, but "to the protection of every citizen in the country as well." [2] So it seemed to that discerning fledgling author, Washington Irving. "I am very much mistaken," he wrote, "if the most underhand . . measures have not been observed toward him. He, however, retains his serenity." [3]

[1] Jefferson to Hay, June 12, 1807, *Works:* Ford, x, 398–99.
[2] *Burr Trials*, i, 124–25.
[3] Irving to Mrs. Hoffman, June 4, 1807, Irving, i, 143.

Luther Martin now took the lead: Was Jefferson "a kind of sovereign?" No! "He is no more than a servant of the people." Yet who could tell what he would do? In this case his Cabinet members, "under presidential influence," had refused copies of official orders. In another case "the officers of the government screened themselves . . under the sanction of the president's name." [1] The same might be done again; for this reason Burr applied "directly to the president." The choleric legal giant from

[1] Martin here refers to what he branded as "the farcical trials of Ogden and Smith." In June and July, 1806, William S. Smith and Samuel G. Ogden of New York were tried in the United States Court for that district upon indictments charging them with having aided Miranda in his attack on Caracas, Venezuela. They made affidavit that the testimony of James Madison, Secretary of State, Henry Dearborn, Secretary of War, Robert Smith, Secretary of the Navy, and three clerks of the State Department, was necessary to their defense. Accordingly these officials were summoned to appear in court. They refused, but on July 8, 1806, wrote to the Judges — William Paterson of the Supreme Court and Matthias B. Talmadge, District Judge — that the President "has specially signified to us that our official duties cannot . . be at this juncture dispensed with." (*Trials of Smith and Ogden:* Lloyd, stenographer, 6–7.)

The motion for an attachment to bring the secretaries and their clerks into court was argued for three days. The court disagreed, and no action therefore was taken. (*Ib.* 7–90.) One judge (undoubtedly Paterson) was "of opinion, that the absent witnesses should be laid under a rule to show cause, why an attachment should not be issued against them"; the other (Talmadge) held "that neither an attachment in the first instance, nor a rule to show cause ought to be granted." (*Ib.* 89.)

Talmadge was a Republican, appointed by Jefferson, and charged heavily against the defendants (*ib.* 236–42, 287); but they were acquitted.

The case was regarded as a political prosecution, and the refusal of Cabinet officers and department clerks to obey the summons of the court, together with Judge Talmadge's disagreement with Justice Paterson — who in disgust immediately left the bench under plea of ill-health (*ib.* 90) — and the subsequent conduct of the trial judge, were commented upon unfavorably. These facts led to Martin's reference during the Burr trial.

Maryland could no longer restrain his wrath: "This is a peculiar case," he shouted. "The president has undertaken to prejudice my client by declaring, that 'of his guilt there can be no doubt.' He has assumed to himself the knowledge of the Supreme Being himself, and pretended to search the heart of my highly respected friend. He has proclaimed him a traitor in the 'face of that country, which has rewarded him. He has let slip the dogs of war, the hell-hounds of persecution, to hunt down my friend."

"And would this president of the United States, who has raised all this absurd clamor, pretend to keep back the papers which are wanted for this trial, where life itself is at stake?" That was a denial of "a sacred principle. Whoever withholds, wilfully, information that would save the life of a person, charged with a capital offence, is substantially a murderer, and so recorded in the register of heaven." Did Jefferson want Burr convicted? Impossible thought! "Would the president of the United States give his enemies . . the proud opportunity of saying that colonel Burr is the victim of anger, jealousy and hatred?" Interspersed with these outbursts of vitriolic eloquence, Martin cited legal authorities. Never, since the days of Patrick Henry, had Richmond heard such a defiance of power.[1]

Alexander MacRae did his best to break the force of Martin's impetuous attack. The present question was "whether this court has the right to issue a subpœna *duces tecum*, addressed to the president of

[1] *Burr Trials*, I, 127–28.

the United States." MacRae admitted that "a
subpœna may issue against him as well as against
any other man." Still, the President was not bound
to disclose "confidential communications." Had not
Marshall himself so ruled on that point in the matter
of Attorney-General Lincoln at the hearing in Marbury *vs.* Madison? [1]

Botts came into the fray with his keen-edged sarcasm. Hay and Wirt and MacRae had "reprobated"
the action of Chase when, in the trial of Cooper, that
judge had refused to issue the writ now asked for;
yet now they relied on that very precedent. "I congratulate them upon their dereliction of the old
democratic opinions." [2]

Wirt argued long and brilliantly. What were the
"orders," military and naval, which had been described so thrillingly? Merely to "apprehend Aaron
Burr, and *if . . necessary . . to destroy his boats.*" Even
the "sanguinary and despotic" orders depicted
by Burr and his counsel would have been a "great
and glorious virtue" if Burr "was aiming a blow at
the vitals of our government and liberty." Martin's
"fervid language" had not been inspired merely by
devotion to "his honourable friend," said Wirt. It
was the continued pursuit of a "policy settled . . before Mr. Martin came to Richmond." Burr's counsel,
on the slightest pretext, "flew off at a tangent . .
to launch into declamations against the government,
exhibiting the prisoner continually as a persecuted
patriot: a Russell or a Sidney, bleeding under the
scourge of a despot, and dying for virtue's sake!"

[1] *Burr Trials,* I 130–33.   [2] *Ib.* 134–35.

He wished to know "what gentlemen can intend, expect, or hope, from these perpetual philippics against the government? Do they flatter themselves that this court feel political prejudices which will supply the place of argument and of innocence on the part of the prisoner? Their conduct amounts to an insinuation of the sort." What would a foreigner "infer from hearing . . the judiciary told that the administration are 'blood hounds,' hunting this man with a keen and savage thirst for blood," and witnessing the court receive this language "with all complacency?" Surely no conclusion could be made very "honourable to the court. It would only be inferred, while they are thus suffered to roll and luxuriate in these gross invectives against the administration, that they are furnishing the joys of a Mahomitan paradise to the court as well as to their client." [1]

Here was as bold a challenge to Marshall as ever Erskine flung in the face of judicial arrogance; and it had effect. Before adjourning court, Marshall addressed counsel and auditors: he had not interfered with assertions of counsel, made "in the heat of debate," although he had not approved of them. But now that Wirt had made "a pointed appeal" to the court, and the Judges "had been called upon to support their own dignity, by preventing the government from being abused," he would express his opinion. "Gentlemen on both sides had acted improperly in the style and spirit of their remarks; they had been to blame in endeavoring to excite the prejudices

[1] *Burr Trials*, I, 137–45.

of the people; and had repeatedly accused each other of doing what they forget they have done themselves." Marshall therefore "expressed a wish that counsel . . would confine themselves on every occasion to the point really before the court; that their own good sense and regard for their characters required them to follow such a course." He "hoped that they would not hereafter deviate from it." [1]

His gentle admonition was scarcely heeded by the enraged lawyers. Wickham's very "tone of voice," exclaimed Hay, was "calculated to excite irritation, and intended for the multitude." Of course, Jefferson *could* be subpœnaed as a witness; that was in the discretion of the court. But Marshall ought not to grant the writ unless justice required it. The letter might be "of a private nature"; if so, it ought not to be produced. Martin's statement that Burr had a right to resist was a "monstrous . . doctrine which would have been abhorred even in the most turbulent period of the French revolution, by the jacobins of 1794!"

Suppose, said Hay, that Jefferson had been "misled," and that "Burr was peaceably engaged in the project of settling his Washita lands!" Did that give him "a right to resist the president's orders to stop him?" Never! "This would be treason." The assertion of the right to disobey the President was the offspring of "a new-born zeal of some of the gentlemen, in defence of the rights of man." [2]

Why await the arrival of Wilkinson? asked Edmund Randolph. What was expected of "that great

---

[1] *Burr Trials*, I, 147–48.   [2] *Ib.* 148–52.

accomplisher of all things?" Apparently this: "He is to support . . the *sing-song* and the ballads of treason and conspiracy, which we have heard delivered from one extremity of the continent to the other. The funeral pile of the prosecution is already prepared by the hands of the public attorney, and nothing is wanting to kindle the fatal blaze but the torch of James Wilkinson," who "is to officiate as the high priest of this human sacrifice. . . Wilkinson will do many things rather than disappoint the wonder-seizing appetite of America, which for months together he has been gratifying by the most miraculous actions." If Burr were found guilty, Wilkinson would stand acquitted; if not, then "the character, the reputation, every thing . . will be gone for ever from general Wilkinson."

Randolph's speech was a masterpiece of invective. "The President testifies, that Wilkinson has testified to him fully against Burr; then let that letter be produced. The President's declaration of Burr's guilt is unconstitutional." It was not the business of the President "to give opinions concerning the guilt or innocence of any person." Directly addressing Marshall, Randolph continued: "With respect to your exhortation," that Burr's appeal was to the court alone, "we demand justice only, and if you cannot exorcise the demon of prejudice, you can chain him down to law and reason, and then we shall have nothing to fear." [1]

The audacious Martin respected Marshall's appeal to counsel even less than Hay and Randolph had

[1] *Burr Trials*, I, 153–64.

done. The prosecution had objected to the production of Wilkinson's mysterious letter to Jefferson because it might contain confidential statements. "What, sir," he shouted, "shall the cabinet of the United States be converted into a lion's mouth of Venice, or into a *repertorium* of the inquisition? Shall envy, hatred, and all the malignant passions pour their poison into that cabinet against the character and life of a fellow citizen, and yet that cabinet not be examined in vindication of that character and to protect that life?"

Genuine fury shook Martin. "Is the life of a man, lately in high public esteem . . to be endangered for the sake of punctilio to the president?" Obey illegal orders! "If every order, however arbitrary and unjust, is to be obeyed, we are slaves as much as the inhabitants of Turkey. If the presidential edicts are to be the supreme law, and the officers of the government have but to register them, as formerly in France, . . we are as subject to despotism, as . . the subjects of the former 'Grands Monarques.'"[1]

Now occurred as strange a mingling of acrimony and learning as ever enlightened and enlivened a court. Burr's counsel demanded that Marshall deliver a supplementary charge to the grand jury. Marshall was magnificently cautious. He would, he said, instruct the jury as confused questions arose. On further reflection and argument — Marshall's dearly beloved argument — he wrote additional instructions,[2] but would not at present announce them. There must be an actual "levying of war"; the overt

[1] *Burr Trials*, I, 164–67.   [2] *Ib.* 173–76.

act must be established; no matter what suspicions were entertained, what plans had been formed, what enterprises had been projected, there could be "no treason without an overt act." [1]

In such would-and-would-not fashion Marshall contrived to waive this issue for the time being. Then he delivered that opinion which proved his courage, divided Republicans, stirred all America, and furnished a theme of disputation that remains fresh to the present day. He decided to grant Burr's demand that Jefferson be called into court with the papers asked for.

The purpose of the motion was, said Marshall, to produce copies of the army and navy orders for the seizure of Burr, the original of Wilkinson's letter to Jefferson, and the President's answer. To accomplish this object legally, Burr had applied for the well-known subpœna *duces tecum* directed to the President of the United States.

The objection that until the grand jury had indicted Burr, no process could issue to aid him to obtain testimony, was, Marshall would not say new elsewhere, but certainly it had never before been heard of in Virginia. "So far back as any knowledge of our jurisprudence is possessed, the uniform practice of this country [Virginia] has been, to permit any individual . . charged with any crime, to prepare for his defence and to obtain the process of the court, for the purpose of enabling him so to do." An accused person must expect indictment, and has a right to compel the attendance of witnesses to meet it. It

[1] *Burr Trials*, i, 177.

was perhaps his duty to exercise that right: "The genius and character of our laws and usages are friendly, not to condemnation at all events, but to a fair and impartial trial."

In all criminal prosecutions the Constitution, Marshall pointed out, guarantees to the prisoner "a speedy and public trial, and to compulsory process for obtaining witnesses in his favour." The courts must hold this "sacred," must construe it "to be something more than a dead letter." Moreover, the act of Congress undoubtedly contemplated "that, in all capital cases, the accused shall be entitled to process before indictment found." Thus "immemorial usage," the language of the Constitution, the National statute, all combined to give "any person, charged with a crime in the courts of the United States, . . a right, before, as well as after indictment, to the process of the court to compel the attendance of his witnesses."

But could "a subpœna *duces tecum* be directed to the president of the United States?" If it could, ought it to be "in this case"? Neither in the Constitution nor in an act of Congress is there any exception whatever to the right given all persons charged with crime to compel the attendance of witnesses. "No person could claim an exemption." True, in Great Britain it was considered "to be incompatible with his dignity" for the King "to appear under the process of the court." But did this apply to the President of the United States? Marshall stated the many differences between the status of the British King and that of the American President.

The only possible ground for exempting the President "from the general provisions of the constitution" would be, of course, that "his duties . . demand his whole time for national objects. But," continued Marshall, "it is apparent, that this demand is not unremitting" — a statement at which Jefferson took particular offense.[1] Should the President be so occupied when his presence in court is required, "it would be sworn on the return of the subpœna, and would rather constitute a reason for not obeying the process of the court, than a reason against its being issued."

To be sure, any court would "much more cheerfully" dispense with the duty of issuing a subpœna to the President than to perform that duty; "but, if it be a duty, the court can have no choice" but to perform it.

If, "as is admitted by counsel for the United States," the President may be "summoned to give his personal attendance to testify," was that power nullified because "his testimony depends on a paper in his possession, not on facts which have come to his knowledge otherwise than by writing?" Such a distinction is "too much attenuated to be countenanced in the tribunals of a just and humane nation." [2] The character of the paper desired as evidence, and not "the character of the person who holds it," determines "the propriety of introducing any paper . . as testimony."

It followed, then, that "a subpœna *duces tecum* may issue to any person to whom an ordinary subpœna

[1] See *infra*, 455–56.   [2] *Burr Trials*, I, 181–83.

may issue." The only difference between the two
writs is that one requires only the attendance of the
witness, while the other directs also "bringing with
him a paper in his custody."

In many States the process of subpœna *duces
tecum* issues of course, and without any action of the
judge. In Virginia, however, leave of the court is
required; but "no case exists . . in which the motion . . has been denied or in which it has been
opposed," when "founded on an affidavit."

The Chief Justice declared that he would not issue
the writ if it were apparent that the object of the
accused in applying for it was "not really in his own
defence, but for purposes which the court ought to
discountenance. The court would not lend its aid to
motions obviously designed to manifest disrespect to
the government; but the court has no right to refuse
its aid to motions for papers to which the accused
may be entitled, and which may be material in his
defence." If this was true in the matter of Burr's
application, "would it not be a blot in the page,
which records the judicial proceedings of this country, if, in a case of such serious import as this, the
accused should be denied the use" of papers on
which his life might depend?

Marshall carefully examined a case cited by the
Government[1] in which Justice Paterson had presided, at the same time paying to the memory of
the deceased jurist a tribute of esteem and affection.
He answered with tedious particularity the objections to the production of Wilkinson's letter to Jeffer-

[1] United States *vs.* Smith and Ogden. (See *supra*, 436, foot-note.)

son, and then referred to the "disrespect" which the Government counsel had asserted would be shown to the President if Marshall should order him to appear in court with the letters and orders.

"This court feels many, perhaps peculiar motives, for manifesting as guarded respect for the chief magistrate of the Union as is compatible with its official duties." But, declared Marshall, "to go beyond these . . would deserve some other appellation than the term respect."

If the prosecution should end, "*as is expected*" by the Government, those who withheld from Burr any paper necessary to his defense would, of course, bitterly regret their conduct. "I will not say, that this circumstance would . . tarnish the reputation of the Government; but I will say, that it would justly tarnish the reputation of the court, which had given its sanction to its being withheld."

With all that impressiveness of voice and manner which, on occasion, so transformed Marshall, he exclaimed: "Might I be permitted to utter one sentiment, with respect to myself, it would be to deplore, most earnestly, the occasion which should compel me to look back on any part of my official conduct with so much self-reproach as I should feel, could I declare, on the information now possessed, that the accused is not entitled to the letter in question, if it should be really important to him."

Let a subpœna *duces tecum*, therefore ruled the Chief Justice, be issued, directed to Thomas Jefferson, President of the United States.[1]

[1] *Burr Trials*, I, 187–88.

Nothing that Marshall had before said or done so highly excited counsel for the prosecution as his assertion that they "expected" Burr's conviction. The auditors were almost as deeply stirred. Considering the peculiarly mild nature of the man and his habitual self-restraint, Marshall's language was a pointed rebuke, not only to the Government's attorneys, but to the Administration itself. Even Marshall's friends thought that he had gone too far.

Instantly MacRae was on his feet. He resented Marshall's phrase, and denied that the Government or its counsel "wished" the conviction of Burr — such a desire was "completely abhorrent to [their] feelings." MacRae hoped that Marshall did not express such an opinion deliberately, but that it had "accidentally fallen from the pen of [his] honor."

Marshall answered that he did not intend to charge the Administration or its attorneys with a desire to convict Burr "whether he was guilty or innocent"; but, he added dryly, "gentlemen had so often, and so uniformly asserted, that colonel Burr was guilty, and they had so often repeated it before the testimony was perceived, on which that guilt could alone be substantiated, that it appeared to him probable, that they were not indifferent on the subject." [1]

Hay, in his report to Jefferson, gave more space to this incident than he did to all other features of the case. He told the President that Marshall had issued the dreaded process and then quoted the offensive sentence. "This expression," he relates,

[1] *Burr Trials*, I, 189.

"produced a very strong & very general sensation. The friends of the Judge, both personal & political, Condemned it. Alex. McRae rose as soon as he had finished, and in terms mild yet determined, demanded an explanation of it. The Judge actually blushed." And, triumphantly continues the District Attorney, "he did attempt an explanation. . . I observed, with an indifference which was not assumed, that I had endeavored to do my duty, according to my own judgment and feelings, that I regretted nothing that I had said or done, that I should pursue the same Course throughout, and that it was a truth, that I cared not what *any man* said or thought about it."

Marshall himself was perturbed. "About three hours afterwards," Hay tells Jefferson, "when the Crowd was thinned, the Judge acknowledged the impropriety of the expression objected to, & informed us from the Bench that he had erased it." The Chief Justice even apologized to the wrathful Hay: "After he had adjourned the Court, he descended from the Bench, and told me that he regretted the remark, and then by way of apology said, that he had been so pressed for time, that he had never read the opinion, after he had written it." Hay loftily adds: "An observation from me that I did not perceive any connection between my declarations & his remark, or how the former could regularly be the Cause of the latter, closed the Conversation." [1]

Hay despondently goes on to say that "there never was such a trial from the beginning of the

---

[1] Hay to Jefferson, June 14, 1807, Jefferson MSS. Lib. Cong.

world to this day." And what should he do about Bollmann? That wretch "resolutely refuses his pardon & is determined not to utter a word, if he can avoid it. The pardon lies on the clerks table. The Court are to decide whether he is really pardoned or not. Martin says he is not pardoned. Such are the questions, with which we are worried. If the Judge says that he is not pardoned, I will take the pardon back. What shall I then do with him?"

The immediate effect of Marshall's ruling was the one Jefferson most dreaded. For the first time, most Republicans approved of the opinion of John Marshall. In the fanatical politics of the time there was enough of honest adherence to the American ideal, that all men are equal in the eyes of the law, to justify the calling of a President, even Thomas Jefferson, before a court of justice.

Such a militant Republican and devotee of Jefferson as Thomas Ritchie, editor of the Richmond *Enquirer*, the party organ in Virginia, did not criticize Marshall, nor did a single adverse comment on Marshall appear in that paper during the remainder of the trial. Not till the final verdict was rendered did Ritchie condemn him.[1]

Before he learned of Marshall's ruling, Jefferson had once more written the District Attorney giving him well-stated arguments against the issuance of the dreaded subpœna.[2] When he did receive the doleful tidings, Jefferson's anger blazed — but this time chiefly at Luther Martin, who was, he wrote,

[1] Ambler: *Thomas Ritchie —A Study in Virginia Politics*, 40–41
[2] Jefferson to Hay, June 17, 1807, *Works:* Ford, x, 400–01.

an "unprincipled & impudent federal bull-dog."
But there was a way open to dispose of him: Martin
had known all about Burr's criminal enterprise.
Jefferson had received a letter from Baltimore stating that this had been believed generally in that city
"for more than a twelve-mouth." Let Hay subpœna as a witness the writer of this letter — one
Greybell.

Something must be done to "put down" the
troublesome "bull-dog": "Shall L M be summoned
as a witness against Burr?" Or "shall we move to
commit L M as *particeps criminis* with Burr? Greybell will fix upon him misprision of treason at least
. . and add another proof that the most clamorous
defenders of Burr are all his accomplices."

As for Bollmann! "If [he] finally rejects his pardon, & the Judge decides it to have no effect . .
move to commit him immediately for treason or
misdemeanor." [1] But Bollmann, in open court, had
refused Jefferson's pardon six days before the President's vindictively emotional letter was written.

After Marshall delivered his opinion on the question of the subpœna to Jefferson, Burr insisted, in
an argument as convincing as it was brief, that the
Chief Justice should now deliver the supplementary
charge to the grand jury as to what evidence it could
legally consider. Marshall announced that he would
do so on the following Monday. [2]

Several witnesses for the Government were sworn,
among them Commodore Thomas Truxtun, Com-

[1] Jefferson to Hay, June 19, 1807, *Works:* Ford, x, 402–03.
[2] *Burr Trials*, I, 190.

modore Stephen Decatur, and "General" William
Eaton. When Dr. Erich Bollmann was called to the
book, Hay stopped the administration of the oath.
Bollmann had told the Government all about Burr's
"plans, designs and views," said the District Attorney; "as these communications might criminate
doctor Bollman before the grand jury, the president has communicated to me this pardon" — and
Hay held out the shameful document. He had already offered it to Bollmann, he informed Marshall,
but that incomprehensible person would neither
accept nor reject it. His evidence was "extremely
material"; the pardon would "completely exonerate
him from all the penalties of the law." And so, exclaimed Hay, "in the presence of this court, I offer
this pardon to him, and if he refuses, I shall deposit
it with the clerk for his use." Then turning to Bollmann, Hay dramatically asked:

"Will you accept this pardon?"

"No, I will not, sir," firmly answered Bollmann.

Then, said Hay, the witness must be sent to the
grand jury "with an intimation, that he has been
pardoned."

"It has always been doctor Bollman's intention
to refuse this pardon," broke in Luther Martin.
He had not done so before only "because he wished
to have this opportunity of publicly rejecting it."

Witness after witness was sworn and sent to the
grand jury, Hay and Martin quarreling over the
effect of Jefferson's pardon of Bollmann. Marshall
said that it would be better "to settle . . the validity
of the pardon before he was sent to the grand jury."

Again Hay offered Bollmann the offensive guarantee of immunity; again it was refused; again Martin protested.

"Are you then willing to hear doctor Bollman indicted?" asked Hay, white with anger. "Take care," he theatrically cried to Martin, "in what an awful condition you are placing this gentleman."

Bollmann could not be frightened, retorted Martin: "He is a man of too much honour to trust his reputation to the course which you prescribe for him."

Marshall "would perceive," volunteered the nonplussed and exasperated Hay, "that doctor Bollman now possessed so much zeal, as even to encounter the risk of an indictment for treason."

The Chief Justice announced that he could not, "at present, declare, whether he be really pardoned or not." He must, he said, "take time to deliberate."

Hay persisted: "Categorically then I ask you, Mr. Bollman, do you accept your pardon?"

"I have already answered that question several times. I say no," responded Bollmann. "I repeat, that I would have refused it before, but that I wished this opportunity of publicly declaring it." [1]

Bollmann was represented by an attorney of his own, a Mr. Williams, who now cited an immense array of authorities on the various questions involved. Counsel on both sides entered into the discussion. One "reason why doctor Bollman has refused this pardon" was, said Martin, "that it would

[1] *Burr Trials*, I, 191–93.

be considered as an admission of guilt." But "doctor Bollman does not admit that he has been guilty. He does not consider a pardon as necessary for an innocent man. Doctor Bollman, sir, knows what he has to fear from the persecution of an angry government; but he will brave it all."

Yes! cried Martin, with immense effect on the excited spectators, "the man, who did so much to rescue the marquis la Fayette from his imprisonment, and who has been known at so many courts, bears too great a regard for his reputation, to wish to have it sounded throughout Europe, that he was compelled to abandon his honour through a fear of unjust persecution." Finally the true-hearted and defiant Bollmann was sent to the grand jury without having accepted the pardon, and without the legal effect of its offer having been decided.[1]

When the Richmond *Enquirer*, containing Marshall's opinion on the issuance of the subpœna *duces tecum*, reached Washington, the President wrote to Hay an answer of great ability, in which Jefferson the lawyer shines brilliantly forth: "As is usual where an opinion is to be supported, right or wrong, he [Marshall] dwells much on smaller objections, and passes over those which are solid. . . He admits no exception" to the rule "that all persons owe obedience to subpœnas . . unless it can be produced in his law books."

"But," argues Jefferson, "if the Constitution enjoins on a particular officer to be always engaged in a particular set of duties imposed on him, does not

---

[1] *Burr Trials*, i, 193–96.

this supersede the general law, subjecting him to minor duties inconsistent with these? The Constitution enjoins his [the President's] constant agency in the concerns of 6. millions of people. Is the law paramount to this, which calls on him on behalf of a single one?"

Let Marshall smoke his own tobacco: suppose the Sheriff of Henrico County should summon the Chief Justice to help " quell a riot " ? Under the "general law" he is "a part of the *posse* of the State sheriff"; yet, "would the Judge abandon major duties to perform lesser ones?" Or, imagine that a court in the most distant territory of the United States "commands, by subpœnas, the attendance of all the judges of the Supreme Court. Would they abandon their posts as judges, and the interests of millions committed to them, to serve the purposes of a single individual?"

The Judiciary was incessantly proclaiming its "independence," and asserting that "the leading principle of our Constitution is the independence of the Legislature, executive and judiciary of each other." But where would be such independence, if the President "were subject to the *commands* of the latter, & to imprisonment for disobedience; if the several courts could bandy him from pillar to post, keep him constantly trudging from north to south & east to west, and withdraw him entirely from his constitutional duties?"

Jefferson vigorously resented Marshall's personal reference to him. "If he alludes to our annual retirement from the seat of government, during the

sickly season," Hay ought to tell Marshall that
Jefferson carried on his Executive duties at Monticello.[1]

Crowded with sensations as the proceedings had
been from the first, they now reached a stage of thrilling movement and high color. The long-awaited and
much-discussed Wilkinson had at last arrived "with
ten witnesses, eight of them Burr's select men," as
Hay gleefully reported to Jefferson.[2] Fully attired
in the showy uniform of the period, to the last item
of martial decoration, the fat, pompous Commanding General of the American armies strode through
the crowded streets of Richmond and made his way
among the awed and gaping throng to his seat by
the side of the Government's attorneys.

Washington Irving reports that "Wilkinson strutted into the Court, and . . stood for a moment
swelling like a turkey cock." Burr ignored him
until Marshall "directed the clerk to swear General
Wilkinson; at the mention of the name Burr turned
his head, looked him full in the face with one of his
piercing regards, swept his eye over his whole person
from head to foot, as if to scan its dimensions, and

[1] Jefferson to Hay, June 20, 1807, *Works:* Ford, x, 403–05.

[2] Hay to Jefferson, June 11, 1807, Jefferson MSS. Lib. Cong. This
letter announced Wilkinson's landing at Hampton Roads.

Wilkinson reached Richmond by stage on Saturday, June 13. He
was accompanied by John Graham and Captain Gaines, the ordinary
witnesses having been sent ahead on a pilot boat. (Graham to Madison, May 11, 1807, "Letters in Relation," MSS. Lib. Cong.) Graham
incorrectly dated his letter May 11 instead of June 11. He had left
New Orleans in May, and in the excitement of landing had evidently
forgotten that a new month had come.

Wilkinson was "too much fatigued" to come into court. (*Burr
Trials*, I, 196.) By Monday, however, he was sufficiently restored to
present himself before Marshall.

then coolly . . went on conversing with his counsel as tranquilly as ever." [1]

Wilkinson delighted Jefferson with a different description: "I saluted the Bench & in spite of myself my Eyes darted a flash of indignation at the little Traitor, on whom they continued fixed until I was called to the Book– here Sir I found my expectations verified– This Lyon hearted Eagle Eyed Hero, sinking under the weight of conscious guilt, with haggard Eye, made an Effort to meet the indignant salutation of outraged Honor, but it was in vain, his audacity failed Him, He averted his face, grew pale & affected passion to conceal his perturbation." [2]

But the countenance of a thin, long-faced, roughly garbed man sitting among the waiting witnesses was not composed when Wilkinson appeared. For three weeks Andrew Jackson to all whom he met had been expressing his opinion of Wilkinson in the unrestrained language of the fighting frontiersman; [3] and he now fiercely gazed upon the creature whom he regarded as a triple traitor, his own face furious with scorn and loathing.

Within the bar also sat that brave and noble

[1] Irving to Paulding, June 22, 1807, Irving, i, 145.

[2] Wilkinson to Jefferson, June 17, 1807, "Letters in Relation," MSS. Lib. Cong.

The court reporter impartially states that Wilkinson was "calm, dignified, and commanding," and that Burr glanced at him with "haughty contempt." (*Burr Trials*, i, footnote to 197.)

[3] "Gen: Jackson of Tennessee has been here ever since the 22ᵈ [of May] denouncing Wilkinson in the coarsest terms in every company." (Hay to Jefferson, June 14, 1807, Jefferson MSS. Lib. Cong.)

Hay had not the courage to tell the President that Jackson had been as savagely unsparing in his attacks on Jefferson as in his thoroughly justified condemnation of Wilkinson.

man whose career of unbroken victories had made
the most brilliant and honorable page thus far in
the record of the American Navy — Commodore
Thomas Truxtun. He was dressed in civilian attire.[1]
By his side, clad as a man of business, sat a brother
naval hero of the old days, Commodore Stephen Decatur.[2] A third of the group was Benjamin Stoddert,
the Secretary of the Navy under President Adams.[3]

[1] Truxtun left the Navy in 1802, and, at the time of the Burr trial,
was living on a farm in New Jersey. No officer in any navy ever made
a better record for gallantry, seamanship, and whole-hearted devotion
to his country. The list of his successful engagements is amazing. He
was as high-spirited as he was fearless and honorable.

In 1802, when in command of the squadron that was being equipped
for our war with Tripoli, Truxtun most properly asked that a captain
be appointed to command the flagship. The Navy was in great disfavor with Jefferson and the whole Republican Party, and naval affairs
were sadly mismanaged or neglected. Truxtun's reasonable request
was refused by the Administration, and he wrote a letter of indignant
protest to the Secretary of the Navy. To the surprise and dismay of
the experienced and competent officer, Jefferson and his Cabinet construed his spirited letter as a resignation from the service, and, against
Truxtun's wishes, accepted it as such. Thus the American Navy
lost one of its ablest officers at the very height of his powers. Truxtun
at the time was fifty-two years old. No single act of Jefferson's
Administration is more discreditable than this untimely ending of a
great career.

[2] This man was the elder Decatur, father of the more famous officer
of the same name. He had had a career in the American Navy as
honorable but not so distinguished as that of Truxtun; and his service
had been ended by an unhappy circumstance, but one less humiliating
than that which severed Truxtun's connection with the Navy.

The unworthiest act of the expiring Federalist Congress of 1801,
and one which all Republicans eagerly supported, was that authorizing most of the ships of the Navy to be sold or laid up and most of the
naval officers discharged. (Act of March 3, 1801, *Annals*, 6th Cong.
1st and 2d Sess. 1557–59.) Among the men whose life profession was
thus cut off, and whose notable services to their country were thus
rewarded, was Commodore Stephen Decatur, who thereafter engaged in business in Philadelphia.

[3] It was under Stoddert's administration of the Navy Department
that the American Navy was really created. Both Truxtun and
Decatur won their greatest sea battles in our naval war with France.

In striking contrast with the dignified appearance and modest deportment of these gray-haired friends was the gaudily appareled, aggressive mannered Eaton, his restlessness and his complexion advertising those excesses which were already disgusting even the hard-drinking men then gathered in Richmond. Dozens of inconspicuous witnesses found humbler places in the audience, among them Sergeant Jacob Dunbaugh, bearing himself with mingled bravado, insolence, and humility, the stripes on the sleeve of his uniform designating the position to which Wilkinson had restored him.

Dunbaugh had gone before the grand jury on Saturday, as had Bollmann; and now, one by one, Truxtun, Decatur, Eaton, and others were sent to testify before that body.

Eaton told the grand jury the same tale related in his now famous affidavit.[1]

Commodore Truxtun testified to facts as different from the statements made by "the hero of Derne"[2] as though Burr had been two utterly contrasted persons. During the same period that Burr had seen Eaton, he had also conversed with him, said Truxtun. Burr mentioned a great Western land speculation, the digging of a canal, and the building of a bridge. Later on Burr had told him that "in the event of a

while Stoddert was Secretary. The three men were close friends and all of them warmly resented the demolition of the Navy and highly disapproved of Jefferson, both as an individual and as a statesman. They belonged to the old school of Federalists. Three more upright men did not live.

[1] See *supra*, 304–05.

[2] A popular designation of Eaton after his picturesque and heroic Moroccan exploit.

war with Spain, which he thought inevitable, . . he contemplated an expedition to Mexico," and had asked Truxtun "if the Havanna could be easily taken . . and what would be the best mode of attacking Carthagena and La Vera Cruz by land and sea." The Commodore had given Burr his opinion "very freely," part of it being that "it would require a naval force." Burr had answered that "*that* might be obtained," and had frankly asked Truxtun if he "would take the command of a naval expedition."

"I asked him," testified Truxtun, "if the executive of the United States were privy to, or concerned in the project? He answered *emphatically* that he was not: . . I told Mr. Burr that I would have nothing to do with it. . . . He observed to me, that in the event of a war [with Spain], he intended to establish an independent government in Mexico; that Wilkinson, the army, and many officers of the navy would join. . . Wilkinson had projected the expedition, and he had matured it; that many greater men than Wilkinson would join, and that thousands to the westward would join."

In some of the conversations "Burr mentioned to me that the government was weak," testified Truxtun, "and he wished me to get the navy of the United States out of my head; [1] . . and not to think more of those men at Washington; that he wished to *see* or

[1] Truxtun at the time of his conversations with Burr was in the thick of that despair over his cruel and unjustifiable separation from the Navy, which clouded his whole after life. The longing to be once more on the quarter-deck of an American warship never left his heart.

make me, (I do not recollect which of those two terms he used) an Admiral."

Burr wished Truxtun to write to Wilkinson, to whom he was about to dispatch couriers, but Truxtun declined, as he "had no subject to write about." Again Burr urged Truxtun to join the enterprise — "several officers would be pleased at being put under my command. . . The expedition could not fail — the Mexicans were ripe for revolt." Burr "was sanguine there would be war," but "if he was disappointed as to the event of war, he was about to complete a contract for a large quantity of land on the Washita; that he intended to invite his friends to settle it; that in one year he would have a thousand families of respectable and fashionable people, and some of them of considerable property; that it was a fine country, and that they would have a charming society, and in two years he would have doubled the number of settlers; and being on the frontier, he would be ready to move whenever a war took place. . .

"All his conversations respecting military and naval subjects, and the Mexican expedition, were in the event of a war with Spain." Truxtun testified that he and Burr were "very intimate"; that Burr talked to him with "no reserve"; and that he "never heard [Burr] speak of a division of the union."

Burr had shown Truxtun the plan of a "kind of boat that plies between Paulus-Hook and New-York," and had asked whether such craft would do for the Mississippi River and its tributaries, especially on voyages upstream. Truxtun had said they would. Burr had asked him to give the plans to "a naval constructor to make several copies," and Truxtun had done so. Burr explained that "he intended those boats for the conveyance of agricultural products to market at New-Orleans, and in the event of war [with Spain], for transports."

The Commodore testified that Burr made no proposition to invade Mexico "whether there was war [with Spain] or not." He was so sure that Burr meant to settle the Washita lands that he was "astonished" at the newspaper accounts of Burr's treasonable designs after he had gone to the Western country for the second time.

Truxtun had freely complained of what amounted to his discharge from the Navy, being "pretty full" himself of "resentment against the Government," and Burr "joined [him] in opinion" on the Administration.[1]

Jacob Dunbaugh told a weird tale. At Fort Massac he had been under Captain Bissel and in touch with Burr. His superior officer had granted him a furlough to accompany Burr for twenty days. Before leaving, Captain Bissel had "sent for [Dunbaugh] to his quarters," told him to keep "any secrets" Burr had confided to him, and "advised" him "never to forsake Col. Burr"; and "at the same time he made [Dunbaugh] a present of a silver breast plate."

After Dunbaugh had joined the expedition, Burr had tried to persuade him to get "ten or twelve

---

[1] *Burr Trials*, I, 486–91. This abstract is from the testimony given by Commodore Truxtun before the trial jury, which was substantially the same as that before the grand jury.

of the best men" among his nineteen fellow soldiers then at Chickasaw Bluffs to desert and join
the expedition; but the virtuous sergeant had refused. Then Burr had asked him to "steal from the
garrison arms such as muskets, fusees and rifles,"
but Dunbaugh had also declined this reasonable
request. As soon as Burr learned of Wilkinson's
action, he told Dunbaugh to come ashore with him
armed "with a rifle," and to "conceal a bayonet under
[his] clothes. . . He told me he was going to tell me
something I must never relate again, . . that General Wilkinson had betrayed him . . that he had
played the devil with him, and had proved the
greatest traitor on the earth."

Just before the militia broke up the expedition,
Burr and Wylie, his secretary, got "an axe, auger
and saw," and "went into Colonel Burr's private
room and began to chop," Burr first having "ordered no person to go out." Dunbaugh did go out,
however, and "got on the top of the boat." When
the chopping ceased, he saw that "a Mr. Pryor and
a Mr. Tooly got out of the window," and "saw two
bundles of arms tied up with cords, and sunk by
cords going through the holes at the gunwales of
Colonel Burr's boat." The vigilant Dunbaugh also
saw "about forty or forty-three stands [of arms],
besides pistols, swords, blunderbusses, fusees, and
tomahawks"; and there were bayonets too.[1]

Next Wilkinson detailed to the grand jury the
revelations he had made to Jefferson. He produced
Burr's cipher letter to him, and was forced to admit

[1] *Annals*, 10th Cong. 1st Sess. 452–63. See note 1, next page.

that he had left out the opening sentence of it —
"Yours, postmarked 13th of May, is received" —
and that he had erased some words of it and substituted others. He recounted the alarming disclosures
he had so cunningly extracted from Burr's messenger, and enlarged upon the heroic measures he had
taken to crush treason and capture traitors. For
four days [1] Wilkinson held forth, and himself escaped indictment by the narrow margin of 7 to 9 of
the sixteen grand jurymen. All the jurymen, however, appear to have believed him to be a scoundrel.[2]

"The mammoth of iniquity escaped," wrote John
Randolph in acrid disgust, "not that any man pretended to think him innocent, but upon certain wire-
drawn distinctions that I will not pester you with.
Wilkinson is the only man I ever saw who was from
the bark to the very core a villain. . . Perhaps you
never saw human nature in so degraded a situation
as in the person of Wilkinson before the grand jury,
and yet this man stands on the very summit and
pinnacle of executive favor."[3]

---

[1] Wilkinson's testimony on the trial for misdemeanor (*Annals*,
10th Cong. 1st Sess, 520–22) was the same as before the grand jury.
"Wilkinson is now before the grand jury, and has such a mighty
mass of *words* to deliver himself of, that he claims at least two days
more to discharge the wondrous cargo." (Irving to Paulding, June 22,
1807, Irving, i, 145.)

[2] See McCaleb, 335. Politics alone saved Wilkinson. The trial was
universally considered a party matter, Jefferson's prestige, especially,
being at stake. Yet seven out of the sixteen members of the grand
jury voted to indict Wilkinson. Fourteen of the jury were Republicans, and two were Federalists.

[3] Randolph to Nicholson, June 25, 1807, Adams: *Randolph*, 221–
22. Speaking of political conditions at that time, Randolph observed:
"Politics have usurped the place of law, and the scenes of 1798 [re-
ferring to the Alien and Sedition laws] are again revived."

less "the extremity of circumstances might impel him to such a conduct." He could not, for the moment, decide; but that "unless it were extorted from him by law" he could not even "deliberate on the proposition to deliver up any thing which had been confided to his honour."

Marshall announced that there was no "objection to the grand jury calling before them and examining any man . . who laid under an indictment." Martin agreed "there could be no objection."

The grand jury did not want Burr as a witness, said John Randolph. They asked only for the letter. If they should wish Burr's presence at all, it would be only for the purpose of identifying it. So the grand jury withdrew.[1]

Hay was swift to tell his superior all about it, although he trembled between gratification and alarm. "If every trial were to be like that, I am doubtful whether my patience will sustain me while I am wading thro' this abyss of human depravity."

Dutifully he informed the President that he feared that "the Gr: Jury had not dismissed all their suspicions of Wilkinson," for John Randolph had asked for his cipher letter to Burr. Then he described to Jefferson the intolerable prisoner's conduct: "Burr rose immediately, & declared that no consideration, no calamity, no desperation, should induce *him* to betray a letter confidentially written. He could not even allow himself to deliberate on a point, where his conduct was prescribed by the clearest principles of honor &c. &c. &c."

[1] *Burr Trials*, I, 327–28.

Hay then related what Marshall and John Ran=
dolph had said, underscoring the statement that
"the Gr: Jury *did not want A. B. as a witness.*" Hay
did full credit, however, to Burr's appearance of
candor: "The attitude & tone assumed by Burr
struck everybody. There was an appearance of
honor and magnanimity which brightened the countenances of the phalanx who daily attend, for his
encouragement & support." [1]

Day after day was consumed in argument on
points of evidence, while the grand jury were examining witnesses. Marshall delivered a long written opinion upon the question as to whether a witness could be forced to give testimony which he
believed might criminate himself. The District
Attorney read Jefferson's two letters upon the subject of the subpœna *duces tecum.* No pretext was
too fragile to be seized by one side or the other, as
the occasion for argument upon it demanded —
for instance, whether or not the District Attorney
might send interrogatories to the grand jury. Always the lawyers spoke to the crowd as well as to
the court, and their passages at arms became ever
sharper.[2]

Wilkinson is "an honest man and a patriot" —
no! he is a liar and a thief; Louisiana is a "poor,
unfortunate, enslaved country"; letters had been
seized by "foulness and violence"; the arguments
of Burr's attorneys are "mere declamations"; the
Government's agents are striving to prevent Burr

---

[1] Hay to Jefferson, June 25, 1807, Jefferson MSS. Lib. Cong.
[2] *Burr Trials,* i, 197–357.

from having "a fair trial . . the newspapers and party writers are employed to *cry* and *write* him down; his counsel are denounced for daring to defend him; the passions of the grand jury are endeavored to be excited against him, at all events";[1] Hay's mind is "harder than Ajax's seven fold shield of bull's hide"; Edmund Randolph came into court "with mysterious looks of awe and terror . . as if he had something to communicate which was too horrible to be told"; Hay is always "on his heroics"; he "hopped up like a parched pea"; the object of Burr's counsel is "to prejudice the surrounding multitude against General Wilkinson"; one newspaper tale is "as impudent a falsehood as ever malignity had uttered" — such was the language with which the arguments were adorned. They were, however, well sprinkled with citations of authority.[2]

---

[1] This was one of Luther Martin's characteristic outbursts. Every word of it, however, was true.

[2] *Burr Trials*, I, 197–357.

CHAPTER IX

WHAT IS TREASON?

No person shall be convicted of Treason unless on the Testimony of two Witnesses to the same overt Act, or on Confession in open Court.
(Constitution, Article III, Section 3.)

Such are the jealous provisions of our laws in favor of the accused that I question if he can be convicted. (Jefferson.)

The scenes which have passed and those about to be transacted will hereafter be deemed fables, unless attested by very high authority. (Aaron Burr.)

That this court dares not usurp power is most true. That this court dares not shrink from its duty is no less true. (Marshall.)

WHILE the grand jury had been examining witnesses, interesting things had taken place in Richmond. Burr's friends increased in number and devotion. Many of them accompanied him to and from court each day.[1] Dinners were given in his honor, and Burr returned these courtesies, sometimes entertaining at his board a score of men and women of the leading families of the city.[2] Fashionable Richmond was rapidly becoming Burr-partisan. In society, as at the bar, the Government had been maneuvered into defense. Throughout the country, indeed, Burr's numerous adherents had proved stanchly loyal to him.

"I believe," notes Senator Plumer in his diary, "even at this period, that no man in this country, has more personal friends or who are more firmly attached to his interests — or would make greater

---

[1] *Blennerhassett Papers:* Safford, 298.
Blennerhassett wrote this comment when the trial was nearly over. He said that two hundred men acted as a bodyguard to Burr on his way to court each day.

[2] Parton: *Burr*, 481.

sacrifices to aid him than this man." [1] But this availed Burr nothing as against the opinion of the multitude, which Jefferson manipulated as he chose. Indeed, save in Richmond, this very fidelity of Burr's friends served rather to increase the public animosity; for many of these friends were persons of standing, and this fact did not appeal favorably to the rank and file of the rampant democracy of the period.

In Richmond, however, Burr's presence and visible peril animated his followers to aggressive action. On the streets, in the taverns and drinking-places, his adherents grew bolder. Young Swartwout chanced to meet the bulky, epauletted Wilkinson on the sidewalk. Flying into "a paroxysm of disgust and rage," Burr's youthful follower [2] shouldered the burly general "into the middle of the street." Wilkinson swallowed the insult. On learning of the incident Jackson "was wild with delight." [3] Burr's enemies were as furious with anger. To spirited Virginians, only treason itself was worse than the refusal of Wilkinson, thus insulted, to fight.

Swartwout, perhaps inspired by Jackson, later confirmed this public impression of Wilkinson's cowardice. He challenged the General to a duel; the hero refused — "he held no correspondence with traitors or conspirators," he loftily observed; [4] whereupon the young "conspirator and traitor" denounced, in the public press, the commander of the American armies as guilty of treachery, perjury,

[1] April 1, 1807, "Register," Plumer MSS. Lib. Cong.
[2] Swartwout was then twenty-four years old.
[3] Parton: *Jackson*, I, 335.
[4] Swartwout challenged Wilkinson after the trial was over.

forgery, and cowardice.[1] The highest officer in the
American military establishment "posted for cow-
ardice" by a mere stripling! More than ever was
Swartwout endeared to Jackson.

Soon after his arrival at Richmond, and a week
before Burr was indicted, Wilkinson perceived, to
his dismay, the current of public favor that was beginning to run toward Burr; and he wrote to Jefferson in unctuous horror: "I had anticipated that a
deluge of Testimony would have been poured forth
from all quarters, to overwhelm Him [Burr] with
guilt & dishonour – . . To my Astonishment I found
the Traitor vindicated & myself condemned by a
Mass of Wealth Character-influence & Talents–
merciful God what a Spectacle did I behold– Integrity & Truth perverted & trampled under foot
by turpitude & Guilt, Patriotism appaled & Usurpation triumphant."[2]

Wilkinson was plainly weakening, and Jefferson
hastened to comfort his chief witness: "No one is
more sensible than myself of the injustice which has
been aimed at you. Accept I pray, my salutations
and assurances of respect and esteem."[3]

[1] See brief account of this incident, including Swartwout's open letter to Wilkinson, in *Blennerhassett Papers:* Safford, footnote to 459–60.

[2] Wilkinson to Jefferson, June 17, 1807, "Letters in Relation,"
MSS. Lib. Cong.

[3] Jefferson to Wilkinson, June 21, 1807, Wilkinson: *Memoirs*, ii,
Appendix xxx. Jefferson's letter also contains the following: "You
have, indeed, had a fiery trial at New Orleans, but it was soon apparent that the clamorous were only the criminal, endeavouring to turn
the public attention from themselves, and their leader, upon any other
object. . . Your enemies have filled the public ear with slanders, and
your mind with trouble, on that account. The establishment of their
guilt, will . . place you on higher ground in the public estimate, and
public confidence."

Before the grand jury had indicted Burr and Blennerhassett, Wilkinson suffered another humiliation. On the very day that the General sent his wailing cry of outraged virtue to the President, Burr gave notice that he would move that an attachment should issue against Jefferson's hero for "contempt in obstructing the administration of justice" by rifling the mails, imprisoning witnesses, and extorting testimony by torture.[1] The following day was consumed in argument upon the motion that did not rise far above bickering. Marshall ruled that witnesses should be heard in support of Burr's application, and that Wilkinson ought to be present.[2] Accordingly, the General was ordered to come into court.

James Knox, one of the young men who had accompanied Burr on his disastrous expedition, had been brought from New Orleans as a witness for the Government. He told a straightforward story of brutality inflicted upon him because he could not readily answer the printed questions sent out by Jefferson's Attorney-General.[3] By other witnesses it appeared that letters had been improperly taken from the post-office in New Orleans.[4] An argument followed in which counsel on both sides distinguished themselves by the learning and eloquence they displayed.[5]

It was while Botts was speaking on this motion to attach Wilkinson, that the grand jury returned the bills of indictment.[6] So came the dramatic climax.

[1] *Burr Trials*, I, 227–53.
[2] *Ib.* 257–67. Wilkinson was then giving his testimony before the grand jury.
[3] *Ib.* 268–72. [4] *Ib.* 276–77. [5] *Ib.* 277–305. [6] See *supra*, 455–56.

Instantly the argument over the attachment of Wilkinson was suspended. Burr said that he would "prove that the indictment against him had been obtained by perjury"; and that this was a reason for the court to exercise its discretion in his favor and to accept bail instead of imprisoning him.[1] Marshall asked Martin whether he had "any precedent, where a court has bailed for treason, after the finding of a grand jury," when "the testimony . . had been impeached for perjury," or new testimony had been presented to the court.[2] For once in his life, Martin could not answer immediately and offhand. So that night Aaron Burr slept in the common jail at Richmond.

"The cup of bitterness has been administered to him with unsparing hand," wrote Washington Irving.[3] But he did not quail. He was released next morning upon a writ of habeas corpus;[4] the argument on the request for the attachment of Wilkinson was resumed, and for three days counsel attacked and counter-attacked.[5] On June 26, Burr's attorneys made oath that confinement in the city jail was endangering his health; also that they could not, under such conditions, properly consult with him about the conduct of his case. Accordingly, Marshall ordered Burr removed to the house occupied by Luther Martin; and to be confined to the front room, with the window shutters secured by bars, the door by a padlock, and the building guarded by seven men. Burr pleaded not guilty to the indictments

---

[1] *Burr Trials*, I, 306. [2] *Ib*. 308.
[3] Irving to Miss Fairlie, July 7, 1807, Irving, I, 152.
[4] *Burr Trials*, I, 312. [5] *Ib*. 313–50.

against him, and orders were given for summoning the jury to try him.[1]

Finally, Marshall delivered his written opinion upon the motion to attach Wilkinson. It was unimportant, and held that Wilkinson had not been shown to have influenced the judge who ordered Knox imprisoned or to have violated the laws intentionally. The Chief Justice ordered the marshal to summon, in addition to the general panel, fortyeight men to appear on August 3 from Wood County, in which Blennerhassett's island was located, and where the indictment charged that the crime had been committed.[2]

Five days before Marshall adjourned court in order that jurymen might be summoned and both prosecution and defense enabled to prepare for trial, an event occurred which proved, as nothing else could have done, how intent were the people on the prosecution of Burr, how unshakable the tenacity with which Jefferson pursued him.

On June 22, 1807, the British warship, the Leopard, halted the American frigate, the Chesapeake, as the latter was putting out to sea from Norfolk. The British officers demanded of Commodore James Barron to search the American ship for British deserters and to take them if found. Barron refused. Thereupon the Leopard, having drawn alongside the American vessel, without warning poured broadsides into her until her masts were shot away, her rigging destroyed, three sailors killed and eighteen wounded. The Chesapeake had not been fitted out, was unable

---

[1] *Burr Trials.* I, 350–54.   [2] *Ib.* 354–57.

to reply, and finally was forced to strike her colors. The British officers then came on board and seized the men they claimed as deserters, all but one of whom were American-born citizens.[1]

The whole country, except New England, roared with anger when the news reached the widely separated sections of it; but the tempest soon spent its fury. Quickly the popular clamor returned to the "traitor" awaiting trial at Richmond. Nor did this "enormity," as Jefferson called the attack on the Chesapeake,[2] committed by a foreign power in American waters, weaken for a moment the President's determination to punish the native disturber of our domestic felicity.

The news of the Chesapeake outrage arrived at Richmond on June 25, and John Randolph supposed that, of course, Jefferson would immediately call Congress in special session.[3] The President did nothing of the kind. Wilkinson, as Commander of the Army, advised him against armed retaliation. The "late outrage by the British," wrote the General, "has produced . . a degree of Emotion bordering on rage– I revere the Honourable impulse but fear its Effects– . . The present is no moment for precipitancy or a stretch of power– on the contrary the British being prepared for War & we not, a sudden appeal to hostilities will give them a great advantage– . . The efforts made here [Richmond] by a band of depraved Citizens, in conjunction with an

[1] See Adams: *U.S.* ii, chap. i; Channing: *Jeff. System*, 189–94; Hildreth, iii, 402; and see vol. iv, chap. i, of this work.

[2] Jefferson's Proclamation, July 2, 1807, *Works*: Ford, x, 434.

[3] Randolph to Nicholson, June 25, 1807, Adams: *John Randolph*, 222.

audacious phalanx of insolent exotics, to save Burr,
will have an ultimate good Effect, for the national
Character of the *Ancient dominion* is in display, and
the honest impulses of true patriotism will soon
silence the advocates of usurpation without & conspiracy within."

Wilkinson tells Jefferson that he is coming to
Washington forthwith to pay his "respects," and
concludes: "You are doubtless well advised of proceedings here in the case of Burr— to me they are
incomprehensible as I am no Jurist— The Grand
Jury actually made an attempt to present me for
Misprision of Treason—.. I feel myself between
'Scylla and Carybdis' the Jury would Dishonor me
for failing of my Duty, and Burr & his Conspirators
for performing it—" [1]

Not until five weeks after the Chesapeake affair
did the President call Congress to convene in special
session on October 26 — more than four months
after the occurrence of the crisis it was summoned to
consider.[2] But in the meantime Jefferson had sent a
messenger to advise the American Minister in London to tell the British Government what had happened, and to demand a disavowal and an apology.

Meanwhile, the Administration vigorously pushed
the prosecution of the imprisoned "traitor" at
Richmond.[3] Hay was dissatisfied that Burr should

---

[1] Wilkinson to Jefferson, June 29, 1807, "Letters in Relation,"
MSS. Lib. Cong.

[2] Jefferson to Congress, *Annals*, 10th Cong. 1st Sess. 9.

[3] At this time Jefferson wrote curious letters, apparently to explain,
by inference, to his friends in France his want of energy in the Chesapeake affair and the vigor he displayed in the prosecution of Burr.
"Burr's conspiracy has been one of the most flagitious of which his-

remain in Martin's house, even under guard and
with windows barred and door locked; and he obtained from the Executive Council of Virginia a
tender to the court of "apartments on the third
floor" of the State Penitentiary for the incarceration
of the prisoner. Burr's counsel strenuously objected, but Marshall ordered that he be confined
there until August 2, at which time he should be
returned to the barred and padlocked room in
Martin's house.[1]

In the penitentiary, "situated in a solitary place
among the hills" a mile and a half from Richmond,[2]
Burr remained for five weeks. Three large rooms
were given him in the third story; the jailer was considerate and kind; his friends called on him every
day;[3] and servants constantly "arrived with messages, notes, and inquiries, bringing oranges, lemons, pineapples, raspberries, apricots, cream, butter,
ice and some ordinary articles."[4]

tory will ever furnish an example. . . Yet altho' there is not a man in
the U S who is not satisfied of the depth of his guilt, such are the jealous provisions of our laws in favor of the accused, . . that I question
if he can be convicted." (Jefferson to Du Pont de Nemours, July 14,
1807, *Works:* Ford, x, 461; also see same to Lafayette, same date, *ib.*
463.) It will be observed that in these letters Jefferson condemns the
laxity of American laws instead of blaming Marshall.

[1] *Burr Trials*, I, 357–59.

[2] Irving to Miss Fairlie, July 7, 1807, Irving, I, 153. "The only reason given for immuring him in this abode of thieves, cut-throats, and
incendiaries," says Irving, "was that it would save the United States
a couple of hundred dollars (the charge of guarding him at his lodgings), and it would insure the security of his person."

[3] "Burr lives in great style, and sees much company within his
gratings, where it is as difficult to get an audience as if he really were
an Emperor." (*Blennerhassett Papers:* Safford, 324.) At first, however, his treatment was very severe. (See Irving to Miss Fairlie, July
7, 1807, Irving, I, 153.)

[4] Burr to his daughter, July 3, 1807, Davis, II, 409.

Burr wrote Theodosia of his many visitors, women as well as men: "It is well that I have an ante-chamber, or I should often be *gêné* with visiters." If Theodosia should come on for the trial, he playfully admonishes her that there must be "no agitations, no complaints, no fears or anxieties on the road, or I renounce thee." [1]

Finally Burr asked his daughter to come to him: "I want an independent and discerning witness to my conduct and that of the government. The scenes which have passed and those about to be transacted will exceed all reasonable credibility, and will hereafter be deemed fables, unless attested by very high authority. . . I should never invite any one, much less those so dear to me, to witness my disgrace. I may be immured in dungeons, chained, murdered in legal form, but I cannot be humiliated or disgraced. If absent, you will suffer great solicitude. In my presence you will feel none, whatever be the *malice* or the *power* of my enemies, and in both they abound." [2]

Theodosia was soon with her father. Her husband, Joseph Alston, now Governor of South Carolina, accompanied her; and she brought her little son, who, almost as much as his beautiful mother, was the delight of Burr's heart.

During these 'torrid weeks the public temper throughout the country rose with the thermometer. [3]

---

[1] Burr to his daughter, July 6, 1807, Davis, II, 410.

[2] Same to same, July 24, 1807, *ib.* 410.

[3] At a Fourth of July celebration in Cecil County, Maryland, toasts were proposed wishing for the grand jury "a crown of immortal glory" for "their zeal and patriotism in the cause of liberty"; hoping that

The popular distrust of Marshall grew into open hostility. A report of the proceedings, down to the time when Burr was indicted for treason, was published in a thick pamphlet and sold all over Virginia and neighboring States. The impression which the people thus acquired was that Marshall was protecting Burr; for had he not refused to imprison him until the grand jury indicted the "traitor"?

The Chief Justice estimated the situation accurately. He knew, moreover, that prosecutions for treason might be instituted thereafter in other parts of the country, particularly in New England. The Federalist leaders in that section had already spoken and written sentiments as disloyal, essentially, as those now attributed to Burr; and, at that very time, when the outcry against Burr was loudest, they were beginning to revive their project of seceding from the Union.[1] To so excellent a politician and so far-seeing a statesman as Marshall, it must have seemed probable that his party friends in New England might be brought before the courts to answer to the same charge as that against Aaron Burr.

At all events, he took, at this time, a wise and characteristically prudent step. Four days after the news of the Chesapeake affair reached Richmond, the Chief Justice asked his associates on the Supreme Bench for their opinion on the law of treason as pre-

---

Martin would receive "an honorable coat of tar, and a plumage of feathers" as a reward for "his exertions to preserve the Catiline of America"; and praying that Burr's treachery to his country might "exalt him to the scaffold, and hemp be his escort to the republic of dust and ashes." (Parton: *Burr*, 478.)

[1] See vol. IV, chap. I, of this work. Also *supra*, chap. III.

sented in the case of Aaron Burr. "I am aware," he wrote, "of the unwillingness with which a judge will commit himself by an opinion on a case not before him, and on which he has heard no argument. Could this case be readily carried before the Supreme Court, I would not ask an opinion in its present stage. But these questions must be decided by the judges separately on their respective circuits, and I am sure that there would be a strong and general repugnance to giving contradictory decisions on the same points. Such a circumstance would be disreputable to the judges themselves as well as to our judicial system. This suggestion suggests the propriety of a consultation on new and different subjects and will, I trust, apologize for this letter." [1]

Whether a consultation was held during the five weeks that the Burr trial was suspended is not known. But if the members of the Supreme Court did not meet the Chief Justice, it would appear to be certain that they wrote him their views of the American law of treason; and that, in the crucial opinion which Marshall delivered on that subject more than two months after he had written to his associates, he stated their mature judgments as well as his own.

It was, therefore, with a composure, unwonted even for him, that Marshall again opened court on August 3, 1807. The crowd was, if possible, greater than ever. Burr entered the hall with his son-in-law, Governor Alston. [2] Not until a week later was coun-

[1] Marshall to the Associate Justices of the Supreme Court, June 29, 1807, as quoted by Horace Gray, Associate Justice of the Supreme Court, in Dillon, i, 72.

[2] Parton: *Burr*, 483.

sel for the Government ready to proceed. When at
last the men summoned to serve on the petit jury
were examined as to their qualifications, it was all
but impossible to find one impartial man among
them — utterly impossible to secure one who had
not formed opinions from what, for months, had
been printed in the newspapers.

Marshall described with fairness the indispensable qualifications of a juror.[1] Men were rejected as
fast as they were questioned — all had read the stories and editorial opinions that had filled the press,
and had accepted the deliberate judgment of Jefferson and the editors; also, they had been impressed
by the public clamor thus created, and believed
Burr guilty of treason. Out of forty-eight men examined during the first day, only four could be
accepted.[2]

While the examination of jurors was in progress,
one of the most brilliant debates of the entire trial
sprang up, as to the nature and extent of opinions
formed which would exclude a man from serving on
a jury.[3]

When Marshall was ready to deliver his opinion,
he had heard all the reasoning that great lawyers
could give on the subject, and had listened to acute
analyses of all the authorities. His statement of the
law was the ablest opinion he had yet delivered during the proceedings, and is an admirable example of
his best logical method. It appears, however, to have
been unnecessary, and was doubtless delivered as a
part of Marshall's carefully considered plan to go to

---

[1] *Burr Trials*, I, 369–70.   [2] *Ib.* 370–85.   [3] *Ib.* 385–414.

the extreme throughout the trial in the hearing and examination of every subject.[1]

For nearly two weeks the efforts to select a jury continued. Not until August 15 were twelve men secured, and most of these avowed that they had formed opinions that Burr was a traitor. They were accepted only because impartial men could not be found.

When Marshall finished the reading of his opinion, Hay promptly advised Jefferson that "the [bi]as of Judge Marshall is as obvious, as if it was [stam]ped upon his forehead. . . [He is] endeavoring to work himself up to a state of [f]eeling which will enable [him] to aid Burr throughout the trial, without appearing to be conscious of doing wrong. He [Marshall] seems to think that his reputation is irretrievably gone, and that he has now nothing to lose by doing as he pleases. — His concern for Burr is wonderful. He told me many years ago, when Burr was rising in the estimation of the republican party, that he was as profligate in principle, as he was desperate in fortune. I remember his words. They astonished me.

"Yet," complained Hay, "when the Gr: Jury brought in their bill the Chief Justice gazed at him, for a long time, without appearing conscious that he was doing so, with an expression of sympathy & sorrow as strong, as the human countenance can exhibit without *palpable* emotion. If Mr. Burr has any feeling left, yesterday must have been a day of agonizing humiliation," because the answers of the

[1] *Burr Trials,* I, 414–20.

jurors had been uniformly against him; and Hay gleefully relates specimens of them.

"There is but one chance for the accused," he continued, "and that is a good one because it rests with the Chief Justice. It is already hinted, but not by himself [that] the decision of the Supreme Court will no[t be] deemed binding. If the assembly of men on [Blennerhassett's is]land, can be pronounced 'not an overt act' [it will] be so pronounced." [1]

Hay's opening statement to the jury was his best performance of the entire proceedings. He described Burr's purpose in almost the very words of Jefferson's Special Message. The gathering on Blennerhassett's island was, he said, the overt act; Burr, it was true, was not there at the time, but his presence was not necessary. Had not Marshall, in the Bollmann and Swartwout case, said that "if war be actually levied, . . *all those who perform any part, however minute, or however remote from the scene of action,* and who are actually *leagued in the general conspiracy, are to be considered* as *traitors*"? [2]

The examination of the Government's witnesses began. Eaton took the stand; but Burr insisted that the overt act must be proved before collateral testimony could be admitted. So came the first crossing of swords over the point that was to save the life of Aaron Burr. The arguments of counsel were brilliant; but neither side forgot the public. They must thrill the audience as well as convince the court. "There had been a great deal of war in the news-

[1] Hay to Jefferson, Aug. 11, 1807, Jefferson MSS. Lib. Cong.
[2] *Burr Trials,* I, 433-51.

papers," said Wickham, but everybody knew "that there had been no war in fact." Wirt insisted on "unfolding events as they occurred"; that was "the lucid order of nature and reason." Martin pointed out that Eaton's testimony did not "relate to any *acts* committed any where, but to mere declarations out of the district." [1] Let the evidence be pertinent. The indictment charged a specific act, and it must be proved as charged. No man could be expected suddenly to answer for every act of his life. If Burr had planned to free Mexico and had succeeded, "he would have merited the applause of the friends of liberty and of posterity; . . but his friends may now pray that he may not meet the fate that Washington himself would have met, if the revolution had not been established."

A mass of decisions, English as well as American, were cited by both Wirt and Martin; [2] and when, that night, Marshall began to write his opinion on whether the overt act must be proved before other testimony could be received, all authorities had been reviewed, all arguments made.

Must the overt act be proved before hearing collateral testimony? The question, said Marshall, was precisely the same as that raised and decided on the motion to commit Burr. But it came up now under different circumstances — an indictment had been found "specifying a charge which is to be proved," and thus "an issue made up which presents a point to which all the testimony must apply." So Mar-

---

[1] Hay had announced that Eaton's testimony would be to the same effect as his deposition.

[2] *Burr Trials*, I, 452–69.

shall could now "determine, with some accuracy, on the relevancy of the testimony."

The prosecution contended that the crime consisted of "the fact and the intention," and that the Government might first prove either of these; the defense insisted that the overt act must be shown before any testimony, explanatory or confirmatory of that fact, can be received. To prove first the fact charged was certainly "the most useful . . and . . natural order of testimony"; but no fixed rule of evidence required it, and no case had been cited in which any court had ever "forced" it on counsel for the prosecution.

The different impressions made upon the minds of the jury by the order of testimony was important, said Marshall: "Although human laws punish actions, the human mind spontaneously attaches guilt to intentions." When testimony had prepared the mind to look upon the prisoner's designs as criminal, a jury would consider a fact in a different light than if it had been proved before guilty intentions had been shown. However, since no rule prevented the prosecution from first proving either, "no alteration of that arrangement . . will now be directed."

But, continued Marshall, "the intention which is . . relevant in this stage of the inquiry is the intention which composes a part of the crime, the intention with which the overt act itself was committed; not a general evil disposition, or an intention to commit a distinct [different] fact." Testimony as to such intentions, "if admissible at all, is received as corroborative or confirmatory testimony," and could not precede "that which it is to corroborate or confirm."

Apply this rule to Eaton's testimony: it would be admissible only "so far as his testimony relate[d] to the fact charged in the indictment, . . to levying war on Blennerhassett's island," and the "design to seize on New-Orleans, or to separate by force, the western from the Atlantic states"; but "so far as it respect[ed] other plans to be executed in the city of Washington, or elsewhere," Eaton's story would be at best merely "corroborative testimony," and, "if admissible at any time," could be received only "after hearing that which it is to confirm."

So let Hay "proceed according to his own judgment." Marshall would not exclude any testimony except that which appeared to be irrelevant, and upon this he would decide when it was offered.[1]

Again Eaton was called to the stand. Before he began his tale, he wished to explain "the motives" of his "own conduct." Marshall blandly suggested that the witness stick to Burr's revelations to him. Then, said Eaton, "concerning any overt act, which goes to prove Aaron Burr guilty of treason I know nothing. . . But concerning Colonel Burr's expressions of treasonable intentions, I know much."

Notwithstanding Marshall's intimation that Eaton must confine his testimony to Burr, "the hero of Derne" was not to be denied his self-vindication; not even the Chief Justice should check his recital of his patriotism, his glories, his wrongs. Burr had good reasons for supposing him "disaffected toward

[1] *Burr Trials*, I, 469–72.

the Government"; he then related at length his services in Africa, the lack of appreciation of his ability and heroism, the preferment of unworthy men to the neglect of himself. Finally, Eaton, who "strutted more in buskin than usual," to the amusement of "the whole court,"[1] delivered his testimony, and once more related what he had said in his deposition. Since Marshall had "decided it to be irrelevant," Eaton omitted the details about Burr's plans to murder Jefferson, turn Congress out of the Capitol, seize the Navy, and make himself ruler of America at one bold and bloody stroke.[2]

Commodore Truxtun then gave the simple and direct account, already related, of Burr's conversation with him;[3] Peter Taylor and Jacob Allbright once more told their strange tales; and the three Morgans again narrated the incidents of Burr's incredible acts and statements while visiting the elder Morgan at Morganza.[4]

William Love, an Englishman, formerly Blennerhassett's servant — a dull, ignorant, and timorous creature — testified to the gathering of "*about betwixt* twenty and twenty-five" men at his employer's island, some of whom went "out a gunning." He saw no other arms except those belonging to his

---

[1] *Blennerhassett Papers:* Safford, 343.

[2] It was this farrago, published in every newspaper, that had influenced the country only less than Jefferson's Special Message to Congress.

[3] Commodore Decatur's testimony was almost identical with that of Truxtun. More convincing still, General Adair, writing before the trial began, told substantially the same story. (Adair's statement, March, 1807, as quoted in Parton: *Burr*, footnote to 493.)

[4] For the full Morgan testimony, see *Burr Trials*, I, 497–506.

master, nor did he "see any guns presented," as Allbright had described. Blennerhassett told him that
if he would go with him to the Washita, he should
have "a piece of land." Love "understood the object of the expedition was to settle Washita lands." [1]

Dudley Woodbridge, once a partner of Blennerhassett, told of Burr's purchase from his firm of a
hundred barrels of pork and fifteen boats, paid by
a draft on Ogden of New York; of Blennerhassett's
short conversation with Woodbridge about the enterprise, from which he inferred that "the object
was Mexico"; of his settlement with Blennerhassett
of their partnership accounts; of Blennerhassett's
financial resources; and of the characteristics of the
man — "very nearsighted," ignorant of military
affairs, a literary person, a chemist and musician,
with the reputation of having "every kind of sense
but common sense."

The witness related his observation of the seizure
at Marietta of Burr's few boats and provisions by
the Ohio militia, and the sale of them by the Government; of the assemblage of the twenty or thirty
men on Blennerhassett's island; of their quiet, orderly conduct; of Comfort Tyler's declaration "that
he would not resist the constituted authorities, but
that he would not be stopped by a mob"; of Mrs.
Blennerhassett's taking part of her husband's library with her when she followed him, after the flight
of the terrified little band from the island; and of the
sale of the remainder of the cultivated visionary's
books. [2]

---

[1] *Burr Trials*, I, 514–18.　　　　[2] *Ib.* 518–26.

Simeon Poole, who had been sent by Governor Tiffin of Ohio to arrest Blennerhassett, said that he was not on the island, but from dusk until ten o'clock watched from a concealed place on the Ohio shore. He saw a few men walking about, who during the night kindled a fire, by the light of which it seemed to Poole that some of them were "armed." He could not be sure from where he watched, but they "looked like sentinels." However, Poole "could not say whether the persons . . were not merely loitering around the fire." There were some boats, he said, both big and little. Also, when anybody wanted to cross from the Ohio side, the acute Poole thought that "a watchword" was given. The night was cold, the rural sleuth admitted, and it was customary to build fires on the river-bank. He observed, however, another suspicious circumstance — "lanterns were passing . . between the house and boats. . . Most of the people were without guns," he admitted; but, although he could not see clearly, he "apprehended that some of them had guns." [1]

Morris P. Belknap, an Ohio business man, testified that he had hailed a boat and been taken to the island on the night when the gathering and flight took place.[2] He saw perhaps twenty men in the house; "two or three . . near the door, had rifles, and appeared to be cleaning them. These were all the arms I saw." He also observed two or three boats.[3]

[1] *Burr Trials*, i, 527–28.
[2] Belknap was undoubtedly one of those whom Poole saw cross the stream. Woodbridge and Dana were the others.
[3] *Burr Trials*, i, 529.

Edmund P. Dana testified that, with two other young men, he had gone in a skiff to the island on that war-levying night.[1] In the hall he saw about "fifteen or sixteen" men — "one of them was running some bullets." Dana was shown to another room where he met "colonel Tyler, Blennerhassett, Mr. Smith of New-York . . and three or four other gentlemen." He had met Tyler the day before, and was now "introduced to Mr. Smith and Doctor M'Castle [2] who had his lady . . there." The men in the hall "did not appear to be alarmed" when Dana and his companions came in. Dana "never saw colonel Burr on the island." [3]

The Government's counsel admitted that **Burr** was in Kentucky at that time.[4]

Such was the testimony, and the whole of it, adduced to support the charge that Burr had, at Blennerhassett's island, on December 13, 1806, levied war against the United States. Such was the entire proof of that overt act as laid in the indictment when Marshall was called upon to make that momentous decision upon which the fate of Aaron Burr depended.

The defense moved that, since no overt act was proved as charged, collateral testimony as to what had been said and done elsewhere should not be received. Wickham opened the argument in an address worthy of that historic occasion. For nearly two days this superb lawyer spoke. Burr's counsel would, he said, have preferred to go on, for they

---

[1] These young men were thinking of joining the expedition.
[2] The physician who accompanied the party.
[3] *Burr Trials*, i, 528–29. [4] *Ib.* 529.

could "adduce . . conclusive testimony" as to Burr's innocence. But only seven witnesses out of "about one hundred and forty" summoned by the Government had been examined, and it was admitted that these seven had given all the testimony in existence to prove the overt act.

If that overt act had not been established and yet the more than one hundred and thirty remaining witnesses were to be examined, it was manifest that "weeks, perhaps months," would elapse before the Government completed its case. It was the unhealthy season, and it was most probable that one or more jurors would become ill. If so, said Wickham, "the cause must lie over and our client, innocent, may be subjected to a prolongation of that confinement which is in itself . . punishment." Yet, after all this suffering, expense, and delay, the result must be the same as if the evidence were arrested now, since there was no testimony to the overt act other than that already given.

Did that testimony, then, prove the overt act of levying war on the United States? Those who wrote the Constitution "well knew the dreadful punishments inflicted and the grievous oppressions produced by [the doctrine of] constructive treasons in other countries." For this reason, truly declared Wickham, the American Constitution explicitly defined that crime and prescribed the only way it could be proved. This could not be modified by the common law, since the United States, as a Nation, had not adopted it; and the purpose of the Constitution was to destroy, as far as America was concerned, the British theory of treason. The Constitution "explains itself," said Wickham; under it treason is a newly created offense against a newly created government. Even the Government's counsel "will not contend that the words [in the Constitution concerning treason] used in their natural sense," can embrace the case of a person who never committed an act of hostility against the United States and was not even present when one was committed;[1] otherwise what horrible cruelties any Administration could inflict on any American citizen.

The Supreme Court, in the case of Bollmann and Swartwout, had, indeed, pronounced a "*dictum*" to the contrary, said Wickham, but that had been in a mere case of commitment; the present point did not then come before the court; it was not argued by counsel. So Marshall's objectionable language in that case was not authority.[2]

It was only by the doctrine of constructive treason that Burr could be said to be at Blennerhassett's island at the time charged — the doctrine that "in treason all are principals," and that, by "construction of law," he was present, although in reality he was hundreds of miles away. But this was the very doctrine which the Constitution prohibited from ever being applied in America.

If Burr "conspired to levy war against the United States, and . . the war was carried on by others in his absence, his offense can only be punished by *a special indictment charging the facts as they existed.*" The prosecution "should at once withdraw their

[1] *Burr Trials*, i, 533–34. [2] *Ib.* 555–56.

indictment as it does not contain a specification that can be supported by the evidence." [1]

Edmund Randolph followed Wickham, but added nothing to his rich and solid argument. Addressing Marshall personally, Randolph exclaimed: "Amidst all the difficulties of the trial, I congratulate Your Honour on having the opportunity of fixing the law, relative to this peculiar crime, on grounds which will not deceive, and with such regard for human rights, that we shall bless the day on which the sentence was given, to prevent the fate of Stafford." [2]

When Randolph closed, on Friday, August 21, Hay asked Marshall to postpone further discussion until Monday, that counsel for the Government might prepare their arguments. [3] Burr's attorneys stoutly objected, but Marshall wisely granted Hay's request. [4] "Did you not do an unprecedented thing," a friend asked Marshall, "in suspending a criminal prosecution and granting two days, in the midst of the argument on a point then under discussion, for counsel to get ready to speak upon it?" "Yes," replied the Chief Justice, "I did and I knew it. But if I had not done so I should have been reproached with not being *disposed* to give the prosecutors an opportunity to answer." [5]

Saturday and Sunday were more than time enough to light the fires of MacRae's Scotch wrath. His anger dominated him to such an extent that he became almost incoherent. [6] Burr not a principal! "Let all who are in any manner concerned in treason

---

[1] *Burr Trials*, I, 557.   [2] *Ib.* II, 3–12.   [3] *Ib.* 25.   [4] *Ib.* 26–27.
[5] *Blennerhassett Papers:* Safford, 354–55.
[6] Alston's description in *ib.* 360.

be principals," and treason will be suppressed.[1] Mac-
Rae, speaking the language of Jeffreys, had, in his
rage, forgotten that he had immigrated to America.

On Tuesday, August 25, although the court
opened at nine o'clock,[2] the heat was so oppressive
that nothing but the public interest — now reaching
the point of hysteria — could have kept the densely
packed audience in the stifling hall.[3] But the spectators soon forgot their discomfort. The youthful,
handsome William Wirt enraptured them with an
eloquence which has lived for a century. It is impossible to give a faithful condensation of this
charming and powerful address, the mingled courtesy and boldness of it, the apt phrase, the effective
imagery, the firm logic, the wealth of learning. Only
examples can be presented; and these do scant justice to the young lawyer's speech.

"When we speak of treason, we must call it treason. . . Why then are gentlemen so sensitive . . as if
instead of a hall of justice, we were in a drawing-
room with colonel Burr, and were barbarously violating towards him every principle of decorum and
humanity? [4] This motion [to arrest the testimony]
is a bold and original stroke in the noble science of
defence," made to prevent the hearing of the evidence. But he knew that Marshall would not "sacrifice public justice, committed to [his] charge, by
aiding this stratagem to elude the sentence of the
law." [5]

---

[1] *Burr Trials*, II, 42.   [2] *Blennerhassett Papers:* Safford, 360.
[3] The temperature was very high throughout the trial. One night
Blennerhassett was overcome by it. (*Ib.* 319.)
[4] *Burr Trials*, II, 57.   [5] *Ib.* 57–59.

Why had Wickham said so little of American and so much of British precedents, vanishing "like a spirit from American ground and . . resurging by a kind of intellectual magic in the middle of the 16th century, complaining most dolefully of my lord Coke's bowels." It was to get as far as possible away from Marshall's decision in the case of Bollmann and Swartwout. If Marshall's opinion had been favorable, Wickham "would not have . . deserted a rock so broad and solid, to walk upon the waves of the Atlantic." Wirt made the most of Marshall's careless language.[1]

The youthful advocate was impressing Marshall as well as jury and auditors. "Do you mean to say," asked the Chief Justice, "that it is not necessary to state in the indictment in what manner the accused, who it is admitted was absent, became connected with the acts on Blennerhassett's island?" In reply Wirt condensed the theory of the prosecution: "I mean to say, that the *count* is *general* in modern cases; that we are endeavoring to make the accused a traitor by connection, by stating the act which was done, and which act, from his conduct in the transaction, he made his own; that it is sufficient to make this charge generally, not only because it is authorized by the constitutional definition, but because it is conformable to modern cases, in which the indictments are pruned of all needless luxuriances." [2]

Burr's presence at the island necessary! If so, a man might devise and set in motion "the whole mechanism" of treason, "go a hundred miles" away,

---

[1] *Burr Trials*, ii, 61–65. [2] *Ib.* 92.

let it be operated by his agents, "and he is innocent, . . while those whom he has deluded are to suffer the death of traitors." How infamous! Burr only the accessory and Blennerhassett the principal! "Will any man believe that Burr who is a soldier bold, ardent, restless and aspiring, the great actor whose brain conceived and whose hand brought the plot into operation, should sink down into an accessory and Blennerhassett be elevated into a principal!"

Here Wirt delivered that passage which for nearly a hundred years was to be printed in American schoolbooks, declaimed by American youth, and to become second only to Jefferson's Proclamation, Messages, and letters, in fixing, perhaps irremovably, public opinion as to Aaron Burr and Harman Blennerhassett.[1] But his speech was not all rhetoric. Indeed, no advocate on either side, except John Wickham and Luther Martin, approached him in analyses of authorities and closeness of reasoning.[2]

"I cannot promise you, sir, a speech manufactured out of tropes and figures," remarked Botts in beginning his reply. No man better could have been found to break the force of the address of his young brother of the bar. Wirt had defaced his otherwise well-nigh perfect address by the occasional use of extravagant rhetoric, some of which, it appears, was

---

[1] See *Burr Trials*, ii, 96–98.

For this famous passage of Wirt's speech, see Appendix E.

Burr was vastly amused by it and it became "a standing joke with him for the rest of his life." (See Parton: *Burr*, 506.) But it was no "joke" — standing or otherwise — to the people. They believed Wirt's imagery to be a statement of the facts.

[2] "Wirt raised his reputation yesterday, as high as MacRae sunk his the day before." (*Blennerhassett Papers*: Safford, 366.)

not reported. Botts availed himself of one such display to make Wirt's argument seem absurd and trivial: "Instead of the introduction of a sleeping Venus with all the luxury of voluptuous and wanton nakedness to charm the reason through the refined medium of sensuality, and to convince us that the law of treason is with the prosecution by leading our imaginations to the fascinating richness . . of heaving bosom and luscious waist, I am compelled to plod heavily and meekly through the dull doctrines of Hale and Foster." Botts continued, with daring but brilliant satire, to ridicule Wirt's unhappy rhetoric.[1] Soon spectators, witnesses, jury, were in laughter. The older lawyers were vastly amused. Even Marshall openly enjoyed the humor.

His purpose thus accomplished, Botts now addressed himself to the evidence, to analyze which he had been assigned. And a perfect job he made of it. He spoke with impetuous rapidity.[2] He reviewed the events at Blennerhassett's island: "There *was war*, when there was confessedly no war; and it happened although it was prevented!" As to arms: "No arms were necessary . . they might make war with their fingers." Yes, yes, "a most bloody war indeed — and ten or twelve boats." Referring to the flight from Blennerhassett's island, the sarcastic lawyer observed: "If I run away and hide to avoid a beating I am guilty and may be convicted of assault and battery!" What "simpletons" the people of Kentucky and Mississippi had been! "They hunted but

[1] *Burr Trials*, ii, 123–24.

[2] See Hay's complaint that Botts talked so fast that he could not make notes on his points. (*Ib.* 194.)

could not find the war," although there it was, right among them![1]

What was the moving force back of the prosecution? It was, charged Botts, the rescue of the prestige of Jefferson's Administration. "It has not only been said here but published in all the newspapers throughout the United States, that if Aaron Burr should be acquitted it will be the severest satire on the government; and that the people are called upon to support the government by the conviction of colonel Burr; . . even jurymen have been taught by the common example to insult him."

No lie was too contemptible to be published about him. For instance, "when the grand jury returned a true bill, he was firm, serene, unmoved, composed — no change of countenance. . . Yet the next day they announced in the newspapers," declared Botts, "that he was in a state of indescribable consternation and dismay." Worse still, "every man who dares to look at the accused with a smile or present him the hand of friendship" is "denounced as a traitor."[2]

Black but faithful was the picture the fearless lawyer drew of the Government's conduct.[3] He dwelt on the devices resorted to for inflaming the people against Burr, and after they had been

[1] *Burr Trials*, ii, 128-35.

[2] *Ib.* 168. Another story "propagated through the crowd" was that Burr had, by his "emissaries," attempted to poison with laudanum one of the Government's witnesses — this although the particular witness had been brought to Richmond to testify only that Wilkinson was not in the pay of Spain. (*Blennerhassett Papers: Safford,* 367.)

[3] *Burr Trials*, ii, 164-73.

aroused, the demand that public sentiment be heeded and the accused convicted. Was that the method of justice! If so, where was the boasted beneficence of democracies? Where the righteousness and wisdom of the people? What did history tell us of the justice or mercy of the people? It was the people who forced Socrates to drink hemlock, banished Aristides, compelled the execution of Admiral Byng. "Jefferson was run down in 1780 [1] by the voice of the people." If the law of constructive treason were to be adopted in America and courts were to execute the will of the people, alas for any man, however upright and innocent, whom public opinion had been falsely led to condemn.[2]

Hay, who had been ill for several days [3] and was badly worn, spoke heavily for the greater part of two days.[4] His address, though dull, was creditable; but he added nothing in thought or authorities to Wirt's great speech. His principal point, which he repeated interminably, was that the jury must decide both law and fact. In making this contention he declared that Marshall was now asked by Burr's counsel to do the very thing for which Chase had been impeached.[5] Time and again the District Attorney insinuated that impeachment would be Marshall's fate if he did not permit the jury to hear all the testimony.[6]

Charles Lee, Attorney-General under President

---

[1] Botts here refers to the public outcry against Jefferson, while Governor during the Revolution, that nearly resulted in his impeachment. (See vol. i, 143–44, of this work.)

[2] *Burr Trials*, ii, 135–92. [3] *Ib.* 224.

[4] *Ib.* 192–236. [5] *Ib.* 193–94. [6] *Ib.* 200–19, 235.

Adams, and an intimate friend of Marshall,[1] had
joined Burr's legal forces some time before. In opening his otherwise dry argument, Lee called Marshall's attention to Hay's threat of impeachment.
The exhausted District Attorney finally denied that
he meant such a thing, and Marshall mildly observed: "I did not consider you as making any personal allusion, but as merely referring to the law." [2]
Thus, with his kindly tactfulness, Marshall put the
incident aside.

On August 28, Luther Martin closed the debate.
He had been drinking even more than usual throughout the proceedings;[3] but never was he in more
perfect command of all his wonderful powers. No
outline of his address will be attempted; but a few
quotations may be illustrative.

It was the admitted legal right and "indispensable duty" of Burr's counsel, began Martin, to make
the motion to arrest the testimony; yet for doing so
"we have been denounced throughout the United
States as attempting to suppress the truth." Our
act "has been held up to the public and to this jury
as conclusive proof of our guilt." Such, declared
the great lawyer, were the methods used to convict
Burr.[4] He had been in favor, he avowed, of waiving

---

[1] See vol. II, 201, 428, of this work.   [2] *Burr Trials*, II, 237-80.

[3] Blennerhassett, in his diary, makes frequent mention of Martin's
drinking: "Martin was both yesterday and to-day more in his cups
than usual, and though he spared neither his prudence nor his feelings,
he was happy in all his hits." (*Blennerhassett Papers:* Safford, 438.)

"I . . recommended our brandy . . placing a pint tumbler before
him. No ceremonies retarded the libation." (*Ib.* 377.)

"Luther Martin has just made his final immersion into the daily
bath of his faculties." (*Ib.* 463.)

[4] *Burr Trials*, II, 260.

"obvious and undeniable rights," and of going on
with the trial because he was convinced that all the
evidence would not only clear "his friend," but remove the groundless prejudices which had so wickedly been excited against Burr. But he had yielded
to the judgment of his associates that the plan
adopted was more conformable to law.

"I shall ever feel the sincerest gratitude to heaven,
that my life has been preserved to this time, and
that I am enabled to appear . . in his defense." And
if his fellow counsel and himself should be "successful in rescuing a gentleman, for whom I with pleasure
avow my friendship and esteem, from the fangs of
his persecutors . . what dear delight will my heart
enjoy!"[1] Martin thanked Heaven, too, for the boon
of being permitted to oppose the "destructive" doctrine of treason advanced by the Government. For
hours he analyzed the British decisions which he
"thanked God . . are not binding authority in this
country." He described the origin and growth of the
doctrine of constructive treason and defined it with
clearness and precision.[2] It was admitted that Burr
was not actually present at the time and place at
which the indictment charged him with having committed the crime; but, according to the Government,
he was "constructively" present.

With perfect fearlessness Martin attacked Marshall's objectionable language in the Bollmann and
Swartwout opinion from the Supreme Bench: "As
a binding judicial opinion," he accurately declared,
"it ought to have no more weight than the ballad of

---

[1] *Burr Trials*, ii, 262.   [2] *Ib.* 275–79; see also 339–42, 344–48.

Chevy Chase." [1] Deftly he impressed upon Marshall, Hay's threat of impeachment if the Chief Justice should presume to decide in Burr's favor.[2] Lamenting the popular hostility toward Burr, Martin defied it: "I have with pain heard it said [3] that such are the public prejudice against colonel Burr, that a jury, even should they be satisfied of his innocence, must have considerable firmness of mind to pronounce him *not guilty*. I have not heard it without horror.

"God of Heaven! have we already under our form of government (which we have so often been told is best calculated of all governments to secure all our rights) arrived at a period when a trial in a court of justice, where life is at stake, shall be but . . a mere idle . . ceremony to transfer innocence from the gaol to the gibbet, to gratify popular indignation excited by bloodthirsty enemies!"

Martin closed by a personal appeal to Marshall: "But if it require in such a situation firmness in a jury, so does it equally require fortitude in judges to perform their duty. . . If they do not and the prisoner fall a victim, they are guilty of murder in *foro cœli* whatever their guilt may be in *foro legis*. . . May that God who now looks down upon us, and who has in his infinite wisdom called you into existence and placed you in that seat to dispense justice to your fellow citizens, to preserve and protect innocence against persecution — may that God so illuminate your understandings that you may *know* what

---

[1] *Burr Trials*, ii, 334.   [2] *Ib*. 377.

[3] One of those who told Martin this was Marshall himself. See *supra*, 401.

is right; and may he nerve your souls with firmness and fortitude to *act* according to that knowledge." [1]

The last word of this notable debate had been spoken. [2] The fate of Aaron Burr and of American liberty, as affected by the law of treason, now rested in the hands of John Marshall.

On Monday morning, August 31, the Chief Justice read his opinion. All Richmond and the multitude of strangers within her gates knew that the proceedings, which for four months had enchained the attention of all America, had now reached their climax. Burr's friends were fearful, and hoped that the laudanum calumny [3] would "strengthen" Marshall to do his duty. [4] For the moment the passions of the throng were in abeyance while the breathless spectators listened to Marshall's calm voice as it pronounced the fateful words.

The opinion of the Chief Justice was one of the longest ever rendered by him, and the only one in which an extensive examination of authorities is made. Indeed, a greater number of decisions, treatises, and histories are referred to than in all the rest of Marshall's foremost Constitutional opinions. Like every one of these, the Burr opinion was a state paper of first importance and marked a critical phase in the development of the American Nation.

Marshall stated the points first to be decided: under the Constitution can a man be convicted of treason in levying war who was not present when

[1] *Burr Trials*, ii, 377–78.
[2] Randolph made another speech, but it was of no moment.
[3] See *supra*, footnote to 499.
[4] *Blennerhassett Papers:* Safford, 367.

the war was levied; and, if so, can testimony be received "to charge one man with the overt acts of others until those overt acts as laid in the indictment be proved to the satisfaction of the court"? He made clear the gravity of the Constitutional question: "In every point of view in which it can be contemplated, [it] is of infinite moment to the people of this country and their government." [1]

What was the meaning of the words, "'levying war'? . . Had their first application to treason been made by our constitution they would certainly have admitted of some latitude of construction." Even so it was obvious that the term "levying war" literally meant raising or creating and making war. "It would be affirming boldly to say that those only who actually constituted a portion of the military force appearing in arms could be considered as levying war."

Suppose the case of "a commissary of purchases" for an army raised to make war, who supplied it with provisions; would he not "levy war" as much as any other officer, although he may never have seen the army? The same was true of "a recruiting officer holding a commission in the rebel service, who, though never in camp, executed the particular duty assigned to him."

But levying war was not for the first time designated as treason by the American Constitution. "It is a technical term," borrowed from an ancient English statute [2] and used in the Constitution in the sense understood in that country and this at the time our fundamental law was framed.

[1] *Burr Trials*, II, 401; also in 4 Cranch, 470. [2] 25th, of Edward III.

Not only British decisions, but "those celebrated elementary writers" whose "books are in the hands of every student," and upon which "legal opinions are formed" that are "carried to the bar, the bench and the legislature" — all must be consulted in ascertaining the import of such terms.[1]

Marshall reviewed Coke, Hale, Foster, and Blackstone, and found them vague upon the question "whether persons not in arms, but taking part in a rebellion, could be said to levy war independent of that legal rule [of constructive treason] which attaches the guilt of the principal to an accessory." Nor were the British decisions more satisfactory: "If in adjudged cases this question [has] been . . directly decided, the court has not seen those cases."[2] To trace the origin of "the doctrine that in treason all are principals" was unimportant. However "spurious," it was the British principle settled for ages.

The American Constitution, however, "comprizes no question respecting principal and accessory"—the traitor must "truly and in fact levy war." He must "perform a part in the prosecution of the war."[3]

Marshall then gingerly takes up the challenge of his opinion in the case of Bollmann and Swartwout. Since it had been upon the understanding by the grand jury of his language in that opinion that Burr had been indicted for treason, and because the Government relied on it for conviction so far as the prosecution depended on the law, the Chief Justice took pains to make clear the disputed passages.

[1] *Burr Trials*, ii, 402–03; 4 Cranch, 470.
[2] *Burr Trials*, ii, 403; 4 Cranch, 471.
[3] *Burr Trials*, ii, 404–05; 4 Cranch, 472.

"Some gentlemen have argued as if the supreme court had adopted the whole doctrine of the English books on the subject of accessories to treason.[1] But certainly such is not the fact. Those only who perform a part, and who are leagued in the conspiracy, are declared to be traitors. To complete the definition *both* circumstances must occur. They must 'perform a part' which will furnish the overt act; and they must be 'leagued in the conspiracy.'"

Did the things proved to have happened on Blennerhassett's island amount to the overt act of levying war? He had heard, said Marshall, that his opinion in Bollmann and Swartwout was construed as meaning that "any assemblage whatever for a treasonable purpose, whether in force or not in force, whether in a condition to use violence or not in that condition, is a levying of war." That view of his former opinion had not, indeed, "been expressly advanced at the bar"; but Marshall understood, he said, that "it was adopted elsewhere."[2]

Relying exclusively on reason, all would agree, he continued, "that war could not be levied without the employment and exhibition of force. . . Intention to go to war may be proved by words," but the actual going to war must "be proved by open deed."[3]

---

[1] The doctrine that accessories are as guilty as principals.

[2] *Burr Trials*, ii, 406–08; 4 Cranch, 476. This reference is to Jefferson's explanation of Marshall's opinion in Bollmann and Swartwout, which Giles and other Republican leaders were proclaiming throughout Virginia. It had been adopted by the grand jury; and it was this construction of Marshall's language under which they returned the bills of indictment for treason. Had the grand jury understood the law to be as Marshall was now expounding it, Burr would not have been indicted for treason.

[3] *Burr Trials*, ii, 409; 4 Cranch, 476.

This natural and reasonable understanding of the term was supported by the authorities. Marshall then made specific reference to the opinions of a large number of British writers and judges, and of all American judges who had passed upon the question. In none of these, he asserted, had "the words 'levying war' .. received a technical different from their natural meaning" [1] — that is, "the employment and exhibition of force."

Had he overruled all these opinions in the Bollmann-Swartwout case? Had he, in addition, reversed the natural interpretation of the Constitution which reason dictated? Surely not! Yet this was what he was now charged with having done.

But, said Marshall, "an opinion which is to overrule all former precedents, and to establish a principle never before recognized, should be expressed in plain and explicit terms." A mere implication was not enough. Yet this was all there was to justify the erroneous construction of his opinion in the case of Bollmann and Swartwout — "the omission of the court to state that the assemblage which constitutes the fact of levying war ought to be in force." [2]

Marshall then went into an extended and minute analysis of his misunderstood opinion, and painfully labored to show that he then intended to say, as he now did say: that the act of levying war required "an assemblage in force," and not merely "a secret furtive assemblage without the appearance

[1] *Burr Trials*, II, 409–13; 4 Cranch, 477–80.
[2] *Burr Trials*, II, 415; 4 Cranch, 481.

of force." The gathering "must be such as to prove that [war] is its object." If it was not "a military assemblage in a condition to make war, it was not a levying of war." [1]

The indictment charged Burr with having levied war at a specific place and stated the exact manner in which the act had been done; this was necessary; otherwise the accused could not make adequate defense. So the indictment "must be proved as laid"; otherwise "the charge of an overt act would be a mischief instead of an advantage to the accused," and would lead him from the true cause and nature of the accusation instead of informing him respecting it. [2]

The Government insisted that, although Burr "had never been with the party . . on Blennerhassett's island, and was, at the time, at a great distance and in a different state, . . he was yet legally present, and therefore may properly be charged in the indictment as being present in fact." Thus, the question arose "whether in this case the doctrine of constructive presence can apply." In answering it, John Marshall ended the contention that so cruel a dogma can ever be applied in America. This achievement was one of his noblest services to the American people. [3]

Again an imposing array of precedents was examined. "The man, who incites, aids, or procures a treasonable act," is not, merely on that account,

---

[1] *Burr Trials*, ii, 415–23; 4 Cranch, 482–88.

[2] *Burr Trials*, ii, 425; 4 Cranch, 490.

[3] This part of Marshall's opinion (*Burr Trials*, ii, 425–34; 4 Cranch, 490–504) is reproduced in full in Appendix F.

"legally present when that act is committed." [1] Of
course, other facts might require that a man should
be considered to be present although really absent;
for example, if he were on the way there for the
purpose of taking part in the specific act charged,
or if he were stationed near in order to coöperate
with those who actually did the deed, he would be
of them and associated with them in the perpetration of that particular act. [2] But otherwise he could
not be said to be present.

If this were not so, then a man levying war in one
part of the country might be construed to be present
at and taking part in hostilities at the most distant
point of the Republic — a participator in "every
overt act performed anywhere"; and he would be
liable to trial and conviction "in any state on the
continent where any overt act has been committed"
by anybody. "He may be proved to be guilty of an
overt act laid in the indictment in which he had no
personal participation, by proving that he advised
it, or that he committed other acts." [3]

If Burr were guilty of treason in connection with
the assemblage on Blennerhassett's island, it was
only because Burr procured the men to meet for the
purpose of levying war against the United States.
But the fact that he did procure the treasonable
assemblage must be charged in the indictment and
proved by two witnesses, precisely as must actual
physical presence — since the procuring of the assemblage takes the place of presence at it. "If in

[1] *Burr Trials*, ii, 426; 4 Cranch, 492.
[2] *Burr Trials*, ii, 429; 4 Cranch, 494.
[3] *Burr Trials*, ii, 430; 4 Cranch, 495.

one case," declared Marshall, "the presence of the individual make the guilt of the assemblage his guilt, and in the other case the procurement by the individual make the guilt of the assemblage his guilt, then presence and procurement are equally component parts of the overt act, and equally require two witnesses." [1]

Neither presence nor procurement could, therefore, be proved by collateral testimony: "No presumptive evidence, no facts from which presence may be conjectured or inferred will satisfy the constitution and the law." And "if procurement take the place of presence and become part of the overt act, then no presumptive evidence, no facts from which the procurement may be conjectured, or inferred, can satisfy the constitution and the law.

"The mind is not to be led to the conclusion that the individual was present by a train of conjectures, of inferences, or of reasoning; the fact must be proved by two witnesses," as required by the Constitution. "Neither, where procurement supplies the want of presence, is the mind to be conducted to the conclusion that the accused procured the assembly, by a train of conjectures or inferences or of reasoning; the fact itself must be proved by two witnesses." [2]

To the objection that this could "scarcely ever" be done, since "the advising or procurement of treason is a secret transaction," the answer was,

[1] *Burr Trials*, II, 436; 4 Cranch, 500.
[2] *Burr Trials*, II, 436–37; 4 Cranch, 500. These paragraphs furnish a perfect example of Marshall's method of statement and logic — the exact antithesis plainly put, the repetition of precise words with only the resistless monosyllables, "if" and "then," between them.

said Marshall, "that the difficulty of proving a fact will not justify conviction without proof." And most "certainly it will not justify conviction without [one] direct and positive witness in a case where the constitution requires two." The true inference from "this circumstance" was "that the advising of the fact is not within the constitutional definition of the crime. To advise or procure a treason . . is not treason in itself." [1]

The testimony which the Government now proposed to offer was to "prove — what? the overt act laid in the indictment? that the prisoner was one of those who assembled at Blennerhassett's island? No!" But, instead, "evidence [of] subsequent transactions at a different place and in a different state." But such "testimony was not relevant." If it could be introduced at all, it would be "only in the character of corroborative or confirmatory testimony, after the overt act has been proved by two witnesses in such a manner that the question of fact ought to be left with the jury." [2]

Before closing, Marshall answered the threats of Hay and Wirt that, if he decided in favor of Burr, he would be impeached: "That this court dares not usurp power is most true. That this court dares not shrink from its duty is not less true. . . No man is desirous of becoming the peculiar subject of calumny. No man, might he let the bitter cup pass from him without self reproach, would drain it to the bottom. But if he have no choice in the case, if there

---

[1] *Burr Trials*, II, 437; 4 Cranch, 501.
[2] *Burr Trials*, II, 443; 4 Cranch, 506.

be no alternative presented to him but a dereliction of duty or the opprobrium of those who are denominated the world, he merits the contempt as well as the indignation of his country who can hesitate which to embrace." [1]

Let the jury apply the law as announced to the facts as proved and "find a verdict of guilty or not guilty as their own consciences shall direct."

The next morning the petit jury retired, but quickly returned. Marshall's brother-in-law, Colonel Edward Carrington, foreman, rose and informed the court that the jury had agreed upon a verdict.

"Let it be read," gravely ordered Marshall.

And Colonel Carrington read the words of that peculiar verdict:

"We of the jury say that Aaron Burr is not proved to be guilty under this indictment by any evidence submitted to us. We therefore find him not guilty." [2]

· Instantly Burr, Martin, Wickham, and Botts were on their feet protesting. This was no verdict, according to law. It was informal, irregular. In such cases, said Burr, the jury always was sent back to alter it or else the court itself corrected it; and he accurately stated the proper procedure.

Discussion followed. Hay insisted that the verdict be received and recorded as returned. "It was like the whole play," exclaimed Martin, "Much Ado About Nothing." Of course the verdict must be corrected. Did the jury mean to "censure . . the court for suppressing irrelevant testimony?" Un-

[1] *Burr Trials*, II, 444-45; 4 Cranch, 507.   [2] *Burr Trials*, II, 446.

thinkable! And if not, they ought to answer simply "Guilty" or "Not Guilty." [1]

Colonel Carrington informed the court that, among themselves, the jury had said that "they would alter the verdict if it was informal — it was in fact a verdict of acquittal." Richard E. Parker, also of the jury, said he never would agree to change the form — they knew what they were about when they adopted it. Parker was "a violent Jeffersonian partisan," and Burr's friends had reproved him for accepting such a man as a member of the jury. [2]

Soothingly Marshall directed that the verdict "stand on the bill" as the jury wished it; but, since it was "in effect a verdict of acquittal," let "an entry be made on the record of 'Not Guilty.'"

The Chief Justice "politely thanked the jury for their patient attention during the whole course of this long trial, and then discharged them." [3]

A week before Marshall delivered his opinion, an attempt was made to induce Blennerhassett to betray Burr. On August 23 William Duane, editor of the *Aurora*, and an intimate friend, supporter, and agent of Jefferson, approached Blennerhassett for that purpose, and offered to go to Washington, "now or at any time hereafter," in his behalf. Duane assured him that the Administration would refuse him (Duane) "nothing he should ask." But Blennerhassett repulsed Duane's advances. [4]

[1] *Burr Trials*, ii, 446–47. Martin was right; the verdict should have been either "guilty" or "not guilty."

[2] *Blennerhassett Papers:* Safford, 339.

[3] *Burr Trials*, ii, 447.

[4] *Blennerhassett Papers:* Safford, 356–58; and see Adams: *U.S.* iii,

Hay, angry and discomfited, entered a *nolle pro-sequi* to the indictments of Dayton, Blennerhassett, and the others for the same crime; but, in obedience to Jefferson's orders, demanded that all of them, Burr included, be still held under the charge of treason, that they might be sent for trial to some place where an overt act might have been committed.[1] Marshall, after enduring another long argument, gently put the application aside because all the conspirators were now to be tried upon the charge of misdemeanor under the second indictment.[2]

Marshall's motives were clearer than ever to Jefferson. "The event has been what was evidently intended from the beginning of the trial; . . not only to clear Burr, but to prevent the evidence from ever going before the world. But this latter case must not take place." Hay must see to it that "not a single witness be paid or permitted to depart until his testimony has been committed to writing. . . These whole proceedings will be laid before Congress, that they may . . provide the proper remedy."[3]

Jefferson ordered Hay to press for trial on the indictment for misdemeanor, not with the expectation of convicting Burr, but in the hope that some sort of

448, 464–65. Duane was known to have unbounded influence with Jefferson, who ascribed his election to the powerful support given him by the *Aurora*.

Government agents also tried to seduce Colonel de Pestre, another of Burr's friends, by insinuating "how handsomely the Col. might be provided for in the army, if his principles . . were not adverse to the administration." De Pestre's brother-in-law "had been turned out of his place as Clerk in the War Office, because he could not accuse the Col. of Burr-ism." (*Blennerhassett Papers:* Safford, 328–29.)

[1] *Burr Trials*, II, 448–49. [2] *Ib.* 455.

[3] Jefferson to Hay, Sept. 4, 1807, as quoted in Adams, *U.S.* III, 470: and see *Jefferson:* Randolph, IV, 102.

testimony would be brought out that would convict Marshall in the court of public opinion, and perhaps serve as a pretext for impeaching him. Thus, in the second trial of which we are now to be spectators, "the chief-justice was occupied in hearing testimony intended for use not against Burr, but against himself."[1] It was for this reason that Marshall, when the trial for misdemeanor began, threw open wide the doors to testimony.[2]

Burr's counsel, made unwise by victory, insisted that he should not be required to give bail, and Marshall, although the point had been decided and was not open to dispute, permitted and actually encouraged exasperatingly extended argument upon it.[3] Burr had submitted to give bail at the beginning, said Botts, not because it was "demandable of right," but because he and his counsel "had reason to apprehend danger . . from the violence and turbulence of the mob."[4]

Marshall was careful to deliver another long and, except for the political effect, wholly unnecessary opinion; nor was it directly on the matter at issue. Counsel floundered through a tangle of questions, Marshall exhibiting apparent indecision by manifesting great concern, even on the simplest points.

---

[1] Adams: *U.S.* III, 470. [2] See *infra*, 524.
[3] *Burr Trials*, II, 473-80.
[4] *Ib.* 480. This statement of Botts is of first importance. The whole proceeding on the part of the Government was conspicuously marked by a reliance upon public sentiment to influence court and jury through unceasing efforts to keep burning the fires of popular fear and hatred of Burr, first lighted by Jefferson's Proclamation and Message. Much repetition of this fact is essential, since the nature and meaning of the Burr trial rests upon it.

Finally, he ordered that Burr "be acquitted and discharged" as to the indictment for treason, but to be
held in five thousand dollars bail under the indictment for misdemeanor. Jonathan Dayton and William Langbourne offered themselves and were accepted as sureties; and on September 3, after nearly
nine weeks of imprisonment, Burr walked out of
court unhindered, no longer to be under lock and
bar and armed guard.[1]

Merry were the scenes in the houses of Richmond
society that night; hilarious the rejoicing about the
flowing board of Luther Martin; and, confused and
afflicted with a blurred anger, the patriotic multitude talked resentfully of Marshall's decision. On
one side it was said that justice had prevailed and
persecution had been defeated; on the other, that
justice had been mocked and treason protected. Hay,
Wirt, and MacRae were bitter and despondent;
Edmund Randolph, Botts, Martin, and Burr, jubilant and aggressive.

Many conflicting stories sprang up concerning
Marshall — his majestic bearing on the bench, his
servility, his courage, his timidity. One of these has
survived: "Why did you not tell Judge Marshall
that the people of America demanded a conviction?"
a disgusted Republican asked of Wirt. "Tell *him*
that!" exclaimed Wirt. "I would as soon have gone
to Herschel, and told him that the people of America
insisted that the moon had horns as a reason why he
should draw her with them." [2]

---

[1] *Burr Trials*, II, 481–503.
[2] Van Santvoord: *Sketches of the Lives and Judicial Services of the*

The captain of the "conspiracy" had never lost heart, and, save when angered by Marshall's seeming inconsistency and indecision, had continued to be cheery and buoyant. Steadily he had assured his friends that, when acquitted, he would again take up and put through his plans. This thought now dominated him. Blennerhassett, upon visiting his chief, found Burr "as gay as usual, and as busy in speculations on reorganizing his projects for action as if he had never suffered the least interruption," with better prospects for success than ever.[1]

Quick to press his advantage, Burr the next morning demanded the production of the letters called for in the subpœna *duces tecum* to Jefferson. These had not been forthcoming, and Burr asserted the President to be in contempt of court and subject to punishment therefor.[2] Once more altercation flared up in debate. Hay said he had one of the letters; that it had not "the most distant bearing on the subject," and that he might prefer "to be put in prison" rather than disclose its contents.[3]

Jefferson had become very nervous about Marshall's order and plainly feared that the Chief Justice might attempt to enforce it. The thought frightened him; he had no stomach for a direct encounter. At last he wished to compose the differences between himself and the obstinate and fearless, if gentle-mannered, Marshall. So the President directed his

Chief-Justices of the United States, 379. Yet popular sentiment was the burden of many of the speeches of Government counsel throughout the trial.

[1] *Blennerhassett Papers:* Safford, 402.
[2] *Burr Trials,* ii, 504.   [3] *Ib.* 511.

district attorney to tell the United States Marshal
to obey no order of the court and to intimate to
the Chief Justice the wisdom of deferring the vexed
question until the next session of Congress.

He wrote, said Jefferson, "in a spirit of conciliation and with the desire to avoid conflicts of authority between the high branches of the government
which would discredit equally at home and abroad."
Naturally Burr and his counsel would like "to convert this trial into a contest between the judiciary &
Exve Authorities"; but he had not "expected . .
that the Ch. Justice would lend himself to it."
Surely Marshall's "prudence and good sense" would
not "permit him to press it."

But if Marshall was determined to attack Jefferson and "issue any process which [would] involve
any act of force to be committed on the persons of
the Exve or heads of departs," Hay was to give
Jefferson "instant notice, and by express if you find
that can be done quicker than by post; and . . moreover . . advise the marshal on his conduct as he will
be critically placed between us."

The "safest way" for that officer to pursue "will
be to take no part in the exercise of any act of force
ordered in this case. The powers given the Exve by
the constn are sufficient to protect the other branches
from judiciary usurpation of pre-eminence, & every
individual also from judiciary vengeance, and the
marshal may be assured of it's effective exercise to
cover him."

Such was Jefferson's threat to use force against
the execution of the process of the National courts.

But the President went on: "I hope however that the discretion of the C. J. will suffer this question to lie over for the present, and at the ensuing session of the legislature [Congress] he may have means provided for giving individuals the benefit of the testimony of the Exve functionaries in proper cases, without breaking up the government. *Will not the associate judge* [Cyrus Griffin] *assume to divide his court and procure a truce at least in so critical a conjuncture?*"[1]

When Hay acknowledged that he had one of the letters from Wilkinson to Jefferson, a subpœna *duces tecum* was served on the District Attorney, notwithstanding his gallant declaration that he would not produce it even if he were sent to jail for not doing so. Hay then returned a copy of such parts of the letter as he thought "material for the purposes of justice," declining to give those passages which Jefferson deemed "confidential."[2] Burr insisted on the production of the entire letter.

Botts moved that the trial be postponed "till the letter shall be produced." Another of that unending series of arguments followed,[3] and still another of Marshall's cautious but convincing opinions came

[1] Jefferson to Hay, no date; but Paul Leicester Ford fixes it between August 7 and 20, 1807. It is, says Ford, "the mere draft of a letter . . which may never have been sent, but which is of the utmost importance." (*Works:* Ford, x, 406–07.) It would seem that Jefferson wrote either to Marshall or Judge Griffin personally, for the first words of his astounding letter to Hay were: "The *enclosed letter* is written in a spirit of conciliation," etc., etc. Whether or not the President actually posted the letter to Hay, the draft quoted in the text shows the impression which Marshall's order made on Jefferson. (Italics the author's.)

[2] *Burr Trials*, ii, 513–14.   [3] *Ib.* 514–33.

forth. Jefferson, he said, had not forbidden the production of the letter — the President, in response to the subpœna upon him, had sent the document to Hay, leaving to the discretion of the District Attorney the question as to what should be done with it. Of course if, for public reasons, Jefferson had declined to produce the letter, his "motives may [have been] such as to restrain the court" from compelling him to do so.[1] At least Burr might see the letter now; consideration of the other features of the controversy would be deferred.[2]

The distracted Hay, his sour temper made more acid by a "greatly aggravated influenza," wrote Jefferson of the Government's predicament; Marshall's remarks from the bench had not been explicit, he said, and "it is impossible to foresee what his opinion will be unless I could foresee what will be the state of his nerves. Wirt, who has hitherto advocated the *integrity* of the Chief Justice, now abandons him."

The District Attorney dolefully tells the President that he is "very decidedly of the opinion, that these prosecutions will terminate in nothing." He thinks the Government will be defeated on the trials for misdemeanor, and believes the indictments for that offense should be dismissed and motion made for the commitment of Burr, Blennerhassett, and Smith to be transferred to some spot where their crime

[1] This remark of Marshall would seem to indicate that Hay had tried to patch up "a truce" between the President and the Chief Justice, as Jefferson desired him to do. If so, it soon expired.

[2] *Burr Trials*, II, 533–37.

might be proved. "Instruct me," he begs Jefferson, "specially on this point." [1]

Jefferson, now on his vacation at Monticello, directed Hay to press at Richmond the trial of Burr for misdemeanor. "If defeated it will heap coals of fire on the head of the judge; if convicted, it will give them time to see whether a prosecution for treason can be instituted against him in any, and what court." A second subpœna *duces tecum* seems to have been issued against Jefferson, [2] and he defiantly refused to "sanction a proceeding so preposterous," by "any notice" of it. [3] And there this heated and dangerous controversy appears to have ended. [4]

Finally, the hearing of evidence began on the indictment against Burr for misdemeanor — for having conducted an attack upon Mexico. For seven weeks the struggle went on. The Government's attorneys showed the effects of the long and losing fight. Many witnesses were sent home unexamined or merely leaving their affidavits. Hay acted like the sick man he really was. The dour MacRae appeared "utterly chop-fallen; an object of disgust to his friends, and pity to his enemies." [5] Only Wirt, with his fine gallantry of spirit, bore himself manfully. Motions,

---

[1] Hay to Jefferson, Sept. 5, 1807, Jefferson MSS. Lib. Cong.

[2] The printed record does not show this, but Jefferson, in his letter to Hay, September 7, says: "I received, late last night, your favor of the day before, and now re-enclose you the subpœna."

[3] Jefferson to Hay, Sept. 7, 1807, *Works:* Ford, x, 408.

[4] For some reason the matter was not again pressed. Perhaps the favorable progress of the case relieved Burr's anxiety. It is possible that the "truce" so earnestly desired by Jefferson was arranged.

[5] *Blennerhassett Papers:* Safford, 394.

arguments, opinions continued. One of Marshall's rulings on the admissibility of evidence moved Blennerhassett to ecstasies.[1]

More than fifty witnesses were examined, the heavy preponderance of the evidence clearly showing that Burr's purpose and expectations had been to settle the Washita lands and, in case the United States went to war with Spain, and *only in that event*, to lead a force against the Spaniards. No testimony whatever was given tending to disclose any hostile plans against the United States, or even for an attack upon Mexico without war between America and Spain, except that of Wilkinson, Eaton, Taylor, Allbright, and the Morgans, as already set out. One witness also told of a wild and fanciful talk by the eccentric and imaginative Blennerhassett.[2]

The credibility of Dunbaugh was destroyed. Wilkinson was exposed in a despicable light,[3] and Eaton appeared more fantastic than ever; but both these heroes put on looks of lofty defiance. The warrior-diplomat of Algerian fame had now fallen so low in the public esteem that one disgusted Virginian had threatened to kick him out of a room.[4]

On September 15, 1807, the District Attorney, by

---

[1] "Today, the Chief Justice has delivered an able, full, and luminous opinion as ever did honor to a judge, which has put an end to the present prosecution." (*Blennerhassett Papers:* Safford, 403.)

[2] *Annals*, 10th Cong. 1st Sess. 416–19.

[3] This appears from the record itself. (See Wilkinson's testimony, *ib.* 512–44; also testimony of Major James Bruff, *ib.* 589–90.) Blennerhassett, who usually reported faithfully the general impression, notes in his diary: "The General exhibited the manner of a sergeant under a courtmartial, rather than the demeanor of an accusing officer confronted with his culprit." (*Blennerhassett Papers:* Safford, 422.)

[4] *Ib.* 418.

attempting to enter a *nolle prosequi* on the indictment of Burr for misdemeanor, tried to prevent
the jury from rendering a verdict.[1] One member
of the jury wanted that body to return a special
finding; but his associates would have none of it,
and in half an hour they reported a straight verdict
of "Not Guilty." [2]

Hay dismissed further proceedings against Smith
and Blennerhassett on the indictments for misdemeanor, and then moved to commit Burr and his
associates upon the charge of treason by "levying
war" within the jurisdiction of the United States
Court for the District of Ohio.[3] On this motion,
Marshall, as an examining magistrate, gave the
Government wide scope in the introduction of testimony, to the immense disgust of the triply accused
men. Blennerhassett thought that Marshall was
conciliating "public prejudice." [4] Burr told his
counsel that the Chief Justice "did not for two days
together understand either the questions or himself
. . and should in future be put right by strong language." So angered was he with Marshall's "wavering," that at times "Burr . . would not trust
himself to rise up to sum up and condense the forces
displayed by his counsel, into compact columns,
after the engagement, toward the close of the day,
as is generally his practice." [5]

Just at this time appeared a pamphlet [6] by Mar-

---

[1] Record, MSS. Archives U.S. Circuit Court, Richmond, Va.
[2] *Blennerhassett Papers:* Safford, 404.
[3] *Ib.* 409–10.   [4] *Ib.* 416.   [5] *Ib.* 412–13.
[6] Daveiss: "A View of the President's Conduct Concerning the
Conspiracy of 1806."

shall's brother-in-law, Joseph Hamilton Daveiss. Jefferson had removed him from the office of United States Attorney for the District of Kentucky because of Daveiss's failure in his attacks on Burr, and the revengeful Federalist lawyer and politician retaliated by abusing the President, Wilkinson, and Burr equally. Between Daveiss's pamphlet and Marshall's sudden admission of evidence, some saw a direct connection; the previous knowledge Marshall must have had of his brother-in-law's intended assault, inferred because of "the well-known spirit of clanship and co-operation with which the Marshalls and all their connections are so uniformly animated," showed, it was alleged, that the Chief Justice was working with his kinsman to bring down in indiscriminate ruin, Jefferson, Burr, and Wilkinson together.

The last volume of Marshall's "Life of Washington," that "five volumed libel," as Jefferson branded the biography, had recently appeared. Blennerhassett, who, in expressing his own opinions, usually reflected those of his associates, had "no doubt" that the President's perusal of Marshall's last volume and Daveiss's pamphlet "inspired Jefferson with a more deadly hatred of the Marshall faction than he has ever conceived of all the Burrites he ever heard of." [2]

The President's partisans in Virginia were prompt to stoke the furnace of his wrath. William Thompson of Petersburgh [3] wrote a brief "view" of the

[1] *Blennerhassett Papers:* Safford, 465–66.   [2] *Ib.* 502.
[3] The brother of John Thompson, author of "The Letters of Curtius" which attacked Marshall in 1798. (See vol. II, 395–96, of this work.)

Burr trial and sent "the first 72. pages" to Jefferson, who read them "with great satisfaction" and clamored for more.[1] Marshall's conduct should indeed fill everybody "with alarm," wrote Jefferson in reply. "We had supposed we possessed fixed laws to guard us equally against treason & oppression. But it now appears we have no law but the will of the judge. Never will chicanery have a more difficult task than has been now accomplished to warp the text of the law to the will of him who is to construe it. Our case too is the more desperate as to attempt to make the law plainer by amendment is only throwing out new materials for sophistry."[2]

The Federalists in Washington, fast dwindling in power and number, experienced as much relief as their chronic melancholia permitted them to enjoy. "Had the late vice president and two senators been convicted and executed for treason, it would in the opinion of Europe, have reflected disgrace upon our country," notes Senator Plumer in his diary.[3]

Hay, on the other hand, thought that "a correct and perspicuous legal history of this trial would be a valuable document in the hands of intelligent legislators," but that "among others it might perhaps do mischief. It might produce a sentiment toward all judicial system and law itself, the operation of which might perhaps be fatal to the tranquillity and good order of Society."[4]

---

[1] Thompson's "view" was published as a series of letters to Marshall immediately after the trial closed. (See *infra*, 533–35.)

[2] Jefferson to Thompson, September 26, 1807, *Works:* Ford, x, 501–02.

[3] Plumer, Aug. 15, 1807, "Diary," Plumer MSS. Lib. Cong.

[4] Hay to Jefferson, Oct. 15, 1807, Jefferson MSS. Lib. Cong.

On October 20, Marshall delivered his last opinion in the Burr trials. It was upon the Government's motion to commit Burr and his associates for treason and misdemeanor committed on the dismal island at the mouth of the Cumberland, where Burr had first greeted his little band of settlers and potential adventurers. He must grant the motion, Marshall said, "unless it was perfectly clear that the act was innocent." If there was any doubt, the accused must be held. The Chief Justice then carefully analyzed all the evidence.[1] He concluded that Burr's purposes were to settle the Washita lands and to invade Mexico if opportunity offered, perhaps, however, only in the event of war with Spain. But whether this was so ought to be left to the jury; Marshall would "make no comment upon it which might, the one way or the other, influence their judgment."[2] He therefore would commit Burr and Blennerhassett "for preparing and providing the means for a military expedition" against Spain.

"After all, this is a sort of drawn battle," Burr informed Theodosia. "This opinion was a matter of regret and surprise to the friends of the chief justice and of ridicule to his enemies — all believing that it was a sacrifice of principle to conciliate *Jack Cade*. Mr. Hay immediately said that he should advise the government to *desist from further prosecution*."[3]

[1] This statement is lucid, conspicuously fair, and, in the public mind, would have cleared Burr of any taint of treason, had not Jefferson already crystallized public sentiment into an irrevocable conviction that he was a traitor. (See *Annals*, 10th Cong. 1st Sess. 766–78.)

[2] *Ib.*

[3] Burr to his daughter, Oct. 23, 1807, Davis, II, 411–12.

If Marshall disappointed Burr, he infuriated Jefferson. In the closing words of his opinion the Chief Justice flung at the President this challenge: "If those whose province and duty it is to prosecute offenders against the laws of the United States shall be of the opinion that a crime of a deeper dye has been committed, it is at their choice to act in conformity with that opinion" — in short, let Jefferson now do his worst.

Marshall's final opinion and his commitment of Burr, under bail, to be tried in Ohio for possible misdemeanor at the mouth of the Cumberland should a grand jury indict him for that offense, disgusted Burr. Indeed he was so "exasperated" that "he was rude and insulting to the Judge."[1] Nor did Marshall's friends in Richmond feel differently. They "are as much dissatisfied," records Blennerhassett, "with his opinion yesterday as Government has been with all his former decisions. He is a good man, and an able lawyer, but timid and yielding under the fear of the multitude, led . . by the vindictive spirit of the party in power."[2]

Burr gave the bond of five thousand dollars required by Marshall, but in Ohio the Government declined to pursue the prosecution.[3] Burr put the

[1] Hay to Jefferson, Oct. 21, 1807, Jefferson MSS. Lib. Cong.

[2] *Blennerhassett Papers:* Safford, 301. If this were only the personal opinion of Burr's gifted but untrustworthy associate, it would not be weighty. But Blennerhassett's views while at Richmond, as recorded in his diary, were those of all of Burr's counsel and of the Richmond Federalists.

[3] No wonder the Government abandoned the case. Nearly all the depositions procured by Hay under Jefferson's orders demonstrated that Burr had not the faintest intention of separating the Western

whole matter out of his mind as a closed incident, left Richmond, and started anew upon the execution of his one great plan as though the interruption of it had never happened.

Marshall hurried away to the Blue Ridge. "The day after the commitment of Col°. Burr for a misdemeanor I galloped to the mountains," he tells Judge Peters. During the trial Peters had sent Marshall a volume of his admiralty decisions; and when he returned from his belated vacation, the Chief Justice acknowledged the courtesy: "I have as yet been able only to peep into the book. . . I received it while fatigued and occupied with the most unpleasant case which has ever been brought before a Judge in this or perhaps any other country, which affected to be governed by laws, since the decision of which I have been entirely from home. . . I only returned in time to perform my North Carolina Circuit which terminates just soon enough to enable me to be here to open the Court for the antient dominion. Thus you perceive I have sufficient bodily employment to prevent my mind from perplexing itself about the attentions paid me in Baltimore and elsewhere.[1]

"I wish I could have had as fair an opportunity to let the business go off as a jest here as you seem to have had in Pennsylvania: but it was most deplorably serious & I could not give the subject a different

States from the Union, or even of attacking Mexico unless war broke out between Spain and the United States. See particularly deposition of Benjamin Stoddert of Maryland, October 9, 1807 (*Quarterly Pub. Hist. and Phil. Soc. Ohio*, IX, nos. 1 and 2, 7–9); of General Edward Tupper of Ohio, September 7, 1807 (*ib.* 13–27); and of Paul H. M. Prevost of New Jersey, September 28, 1807 (*ib.* 28–30).

[1] See *infra*, 536.

aspect by treating it in any manner which was in my power. I might perhaps have made it less serious to my self by obeying the public will instead of the public law & throwing a little more of the sombre upon others." [1]

While Marshall was resting in the mountains, Jefferson was writing his reply to the last challenge of the Chief Justice.[2] In his Message to Congress which he prepared immediately after the Burr trials, he urged the House to impeach Marshall. He felt it to be his duty, he said, to transmit a record of the Burr trial. "*Truth & duty alone extort the observation that wherever the laws were appealed to in aid of the public safety, their operation was on behalf of those only against whom they were invoked.*" From the record "you will be enabled to judge whether the defect was in the testimony, or in the laws, or *whether there is not a radical defect* in the administration of the law? And wherever it shall be found the legislature alone can apply or originate the remedy.

"The framers of our constitution certainly supposed they had guarded, as well their government against destruction by treason, as their citizens against oppression under pretence of it: and if *the pliability of the law as construed in the case of Fries,*[3] *and it's wonderful refractoriness as construed in that of Burr, shew that neither end has been attained, and induce an awful doubt whether we all live under the*

---

[1] Marshall to Peters, Nov. 23, 1807, Peters MSS. Pa. Hist. Soc.

[2] Hay, for the moment mollified by Marshall's award of two thousand dollars as his fee, had made no further complaint for several days.

[3] See *supra*, chap. I, 35–36; also vol. II, 429–30, of this work.

same law. The right of the jury too to decide law as well as fact seems nugatory without the evidence pertinent to their sense of the law. If these ends are not attained it becomes worthy of enquiry by what means more effectual they may be secured?" [1]

On the advice of his Cabinet,[2] Jefferson struck out from the Message the sentences italicized above. But even with this strong language omitted, Congress was told to impeach Marshall in far more emphatic terms than those by which Jefferson had directed the impeachment of Pickering — in plainer words, indeed, than those privately written to Nicholson ordering the attack upon Chase. Jefferson's assault on Marshall was also inserted in a Message dealing with probable war against Great Britain and setting out the continuance of our unhappy relations with Spain, "to our former grounds of complaint" against which country had "been added a very serious one." [3]

Had these grave conditions not engaged the instant attention of Congress, had public sentiment — even with part of its fury drawn from Burr to Great Britain — been heeded at the National Capital,

[1] Jefferson's Seventh Annual Message, first draft, *Works:* Ford, x, 523–24.

[2] See notes of Gallatin and Rodney, *Works:* Ford, x, footnotes to 503–10.

[3] Jefferson's Seventh Annual Message, second draft, *Works:* Ford, x, 517. Blennerhassett, and probably Burr, would not have grieved had Marshall been impeached. It would be "penance for that timidity of conduct, which was probably as instrumental in keeping him from imbruing his hands in our blood as it was operative in inducing him to continue my vexations [the commitment of the conspirators to be tried in Ohio], to pacify the menaces and clamorous yells of the cerberus of Democracy with a sop which he would moisten, at least, with the tears of my family." (*Blennerhassett Papers:* Safford, 465.)

there can be little doubt that John Marshall would
have been impeached by the House that was now
all but unanimously Republican, and would have
been convicted by the overwhelmingly Jeffersonian
Senate.

Well for Marshall's peace of mind that he had
secluded himself in the solitudes of the Blue Ridge,
for never was an American judge subjected to abuse
so unsparing. The Jeffersonian press, particularly
the *Aurora* and the *Enquirer*, the two leading Republican papers, went to the limits of invective.
"Let the judge be impeached," said the *Enquirer;*
the Wickham dinner was recalled — why had Marshall attended it? His speech on the Jonathan
Robins case [1] — "the price of his seat on the bench"
— was "a lasting monument of his capacity to defend error."

Marshall's "wavering and irresolute spirit"
manifested throughout the trial had disgusted
everybody. His attempt to make his rulings
"palatable to all parties" had "so often wrapt them
in obscurity" that it was hard "to understand on
which side the court had decided." His conduct had
been inspired by "power illicitly obtained." And
think of his encouragement to Burr's counsel to
indulge in "unbounded . . slander and vilification"
of the President! Callender's libel on Adams was
insipid compared with Martin's vulgar billingsgate
toward Jefferson! But that "awful tribunal" — the
people — would try Marshall; before it "evidence

---

[1] See vol. II, 464–71, of this work.

will neither be perverted nor suppressed. . . The character of the Chief Justice awaits the issue." [1]

Another attack soon followed. Marshall's disgraceful conduct "has proved that the Judges are too independent of the people." Let them be made removable by the President on the address of Congress. The Chase trial had shown that impeachment could not be relied on to cleanse the bench of a judge no matter how "noxious," "ridiculous," "contemptible," or "immoral" he might be. But "shall an imposter be suffered to preside on the bench of justice? . . Are we to be eternally pestered with that most ridiculous and dangerous cant; that the people . . are incompetent to their own government: and that masters must be set over them and that barriers are to be raised up to protect those masters from the vengeance of the people?" [2]

Next came a series of "Letters to John Marshall," which appeared simultaneously in the *Aurora* and the *Enquirer*. They were written by William Thompson under the *nom de guerre* of "Lucius"; he undoubtedly was also the author of the earlier attacks on the Chief Justice in the *Enquirer*. They were widely copied in the Republican press of the country, and were a veracious expression of public sentiment.

"Your country, sir, owes you a debt of gratitude for former favors," which cannot be paid because

[1] "Portrait of the Chief Justice," in the Richmond *Enquirer*, Nov. 6, 1807. This article fills more than two closely printed columns. It discusses, and not without ability, the supposed errors in Marshall's opinions.

[2] *Enquirer*, Nov. 24, 1807.

"the whole stock of national indignation and con‑ tempt would be exhausted, before the half of your just claim could be discharged." Marshall had earned "infamy and detestation" by his efforts to erect "tyranny upon the tomb of freedom." His skill "in conducting the manouvres of a political party," his "crafty cunning" as a diplomat, had been perpetuated by the "genius" of John Thompson, whose "literary glory . . will shine when even the splendour of your talents and your crimes shall have faded forever. When your volumes of apology for British insolence and cruelty [1] shall be buried in oblivion, the 'Letters of Curtius' [2] will . . 'damn you to everlasting fame.'" Marshall's entire life, accord‑ ing to Lucius, had been that of a sly, bigoted politi‑ cian who had always worked against the people. He might have become "one of the boasted patri‑ ots of Virginia," but now he was "a disgrace to the bench of justice." He was a Jeffreys, a Bromley, a Mansfield. [3]

Quickly appeared a second letter to Marshall, accusing him of having "prostrated the dignity of the chief justice of the United States." Lucius goes into a lengthy analysis of Marshall's numerous opin‑ ions in the Burr trials. A just review of the proceed‑ ings, he said, demonstrates that the Chief Justice had "exhibited a culpable partiality towards the accused, and a shameless solicitude . . to implicate the government . . as negligent of their duty" —

---

[1] Marshall's *Life of Washington*.

[2] See vol. II, 395–96, of this work.

[3] "Letters to John Marshall, Chief Justice of the United States," in the *Aurora*, reprinted in the *Enquirer*, Dec. 1, 1807.

something that "a less malicious magistrate" never would have dared to display.[1] A third letter continued the castigation of Marshall and the defense of Jefferson. Closing an extended argument on this joint theme, Lucius addressed Marshall thus: "Common sense, and violated justice, cry aloud against such conduct; and demand against you the enforcement of these laws, which you refuse to administer."[2]

All these arraignments of Marshall had, as we have seen,[3] been submitted to Jefferson. They rose in the final letter to a climax of vituperation: "Could I be instrumental in removing you from the elevation which you have dishonored by . . your crimes, I would still trace you . . for screening a criminal and degrading a judge" by the "juggle of a judicial farce." Marshall and Burr were alike "morally guilty," alike "traitors in heart and in fact. . . Such a criminal and such a judge, few countries ever produced. . . You are forever doomed to blot the fair page of American history, to be held up, as examples of infamy and disgrace, of perverted talents and unpunished criminality, of foes to liberty and traitors to your country."[4]

Incited by similar attacks in the Republican press of Baltimore,[5] the more ardent patriots of that place resolved publicly to execute Marshall in effigy, along with Burr, Blennerhassett, and Martin. On the morning of November 3, satirical handbills,

---

[1] *Enquirer*, Dec. 4, 1807.
[2] *Ib.* Dec. 8, 1807.   [3] See *supra*, 525-26.
[4] *Enquirer*, Dec. 12, 1807.
[5] *Blennerhassett Papers:* Safford, 475.

announcing this act of public justice, were scattered over the city:

"AWFUL!!!

"The public are hereby notified that four 'choice spirits' are this afternoon, at 3 o'clock, to be marshaled for execution by the hangman, on Gallows Hill, in consequence of the sentence pronounced against them by the unanimous voice of every honest man in the community.

"The respective crimes for which they suffer are thus stated in the record:

"First, Chief Justice M. for a repetition of his X.Y.Z. tricks, which are said to be much aggravated by his *felonins* [*sic*] capers in open Court, on the plea of irrelevancy;

"Secondly, His Quid Majesty [Burr], charged with the trifling fault of wishing to divide the Union, and farm *Baron* Bastrop's grant;

"Thirdly, B[lennerhassett], the chemist, convicted of conspiracy to destroy the tone of the public Fiddle;

"Fourthly, and lastly, but not least, *Lawyer* Brandy-Bottle, for a false, scandalous, malicious Prophecy, that, before six months, 'Aaron Burr would divide the Union.'

"N.B. The execution of accomplices is postponed to a future day." [1]

Martin demanded of the Mayor the protection of the law. In response, police were sent to his house and to the Evans Hotel where Blennerhassett was

[1] *Blennerhassett Papers:* Safford, 477.

staying. Burr and the faithful Swartwout, who had accompanied his friend and leader, were escorted by a guard to the stage office, where they quickly left for Philadelphia.[1] Martin's law students and

[1] Gathering a few dollars from personal friends, Burr sailed for England, hoping to get from the British Government support for his plans to revolutionize Mexico. At first all went well. Men like Jeremy Bentham and Sir Walter Scott became his friends and admirers. But the hand of Jefferson followed him; and on representations of the American Minister, the British Government ordered him to leave the United Kingdom immediately.

Next he sought the ear of Napoleon; but again he was flouted and insulted by the American diplomatic and consular representatives — he was, they said, "a fugitive from justice." His last sou gone, ragged and often hungry, he managed at last, by the aid of one John Reeves, to secure passage for Boston, where he landed May 4, 1812. Then he journeyed to New York, where he arrived June 30 in abject poverty and utterly ruined. But still his spirit did not give way.

Soon, however, fate struck him the only blow that, until now, ever had brought this iron man to his knees. His passionately beloved little grandson, Aaron Burr Alston, died in June. In December, another and heavier stroke fell. His daughter sailed from Charleston, South Carolina, to join and comfort her father and be comforted by him. Her ship was lost in a storm, and Theodosia the beautiful, the accomplished, the adored, was drowned. Then, at last, the heart of Aaron Burr was broken.

Of the many ridiculous stories told of Burr and his daughter, one was that her ship was captured by pirates and she, ordered to walk the plank, did so with her child in her arms "without hesitation or visible tremor." This absurdity was given credit and currency by Harriet Martineau. (See Martineau: *Western Travels*, II, 291–92.) Theodosia's child had died six months before she sailed from Charleston to go to her father, and she embarked in a pilot boat, about which no pirate would have troubled himself.

The remainder of Burr's long life was given to the practice of his profession. His industry, legal learning, and ability, once more secured for him a good business. In 1824, Marshall ruled on an application to restore an attorney named Burr to the bar of the Circuit Court of the District of Columbia from which he had been suspended for unprofessional conduct. (*Ex parte* Burr, 9 Wheaton, 529–31.) It has often been erroneously supposed that this applicant was Aaron Burr: he was, however, one Levi Burr, a local practitioner, and not related to Aaron Burr.

It is characteristic of Burr that he remembered the great lawyer

other friends armed themselves to resist violence
to him.

A policeman named Goldsmith notified Blenner-

who voluntarily had hastened to defend him at Richmond, and Luther
Martin — aged, infirm, and almost deranged — was taken to the
home of Aaron Burr and tenderly cared for until he died. Burr's
marriage, at the age of seventy-eight, to Madame Jumel was, on his
part, inexplicable; it was the only regrettable but not unworthy incident of the latter years of his life. (See Shelton: *Jumel Mansion*,
170–74.)

Burr's New York friends were loyal to him to his very last day.
His political genius never grew dim. He early suggested and helped to
bring about the nomination of Andrew Jackson for the Presidency.
Thus did he pay the debt of gratitude for the loyalty with which the
rugged Tennesseean had championed his cause against public opinion and Administration alike.

During the summer of 1836 his last illness came upon him. When
his physician said that he could live but a few hours longer, a friend
at his bedside asked the supposedly expiring man "whether in the expedition to the Southwest he had designed a separation of the Union."
Believing himself to be dying, Burr replied: "No! I would as soon have
thought of taking possession of the moon and informing my friends
that I intended to divide it among them." To a man, his most intimate friends believed this statement to be true.

Finally, on September 14, 1836, Aaron Burr died and was buried
near his father at Princeton, New Jersey, where the parent had presided over, and the son had attended, that Alma Mater of so many
patriots, soldiers, and statesmen.

For two years his burial place was unmarked. Then, at night-time,
unknown friends erected over his grave a plain marble shaft, bearing
this inscription:

AARON BURR

Born Feb. 6, 1756
Died Sept. 14, 1836
Colonel in the Army of the Revolution
Vice-President of the United States from 1801 to 1805

(*Gulf States Historical Magazine*, ii, 379.)

Parton's *Life of Burr* is still the best story of this strange life. But
Parton must be read with great care, for he sometimes makes statements which are difficult of verification.

A brief, engaging, and trustworthy account of the Burr episode is
Aaron Burr, by Isaac Jenkinson. Until the appearance of Professor
McCaleb's book, *The Aaron Burr Conspiracy*, Mr. Jenkinson's little

hassett that a great mob was gathering, "had every-thing prepared for tarring and feathering and would, .. if disappointed or opposed, tear Martin [and Blennerhassett] to pieces." The manager of the hotel begged Blennerhassett to hide in the garret of the hostelry. This the forlorn Irishman did, and beheld from a window in the attic what passed below.

Shouting and huzzaing men poured by, headed by fifers and drummers playing the "Rogue's march." Midway in the riotous throng were drawn two carts containing effigies of Chief Justice Marshall and the other popularly condemned men "habited for execution. . . Two troops of cavalry patrolled the streets, not to disperse the mob, but to follow and behold their conduct." At Martin's house the crowd stopped for a moment, hurling threats and insults, jeering at and defying the armed defenders within and "the cavalry without."

Making "as much noise as if they were about to destroy the city," these devotees of justice and lib-erty proceeded to the place of public execution. There, amid roars of approval, the effigy of John Marshall, Chief Justice of the United States, was hanged by the neck until the executioner pronounced the stuffed figure to be dead. About him dangled from the gibbet the forms of the "traitors" — Aaron Burr and Harman Blennerhassett — and also that of Luther Martin, who had dared to defend them

volume was the best on that subject. Professor McCaleb's thorough and scholarly study is, however, the only exhaustive and reliable narrative of that ambitious plan and the disastrous outcome of the attempted execution of it.

and had thus incurred the malediction of Thomas Jefferson and " the people." [1]

In the Senate Giles reported a bill to punish as traitors persons who permitted or aided in the perpetration of certain acts, "although not personally present when any such act was done"; and he supported it in an argument of notable ability. He powerfully attacked Marshall, analyzed his opinions in the Burr case, contrasted them with those of other National judges, and pointed out the resulting confusion in the interpretation of the law. All this was spoken, however, with careful regard to the rules of parliamentary discussion. [2]

Legislation was necessary, said Giles; as matters stood, the decisions of judges on treason were like Congress "enacting our speeches, interspersed with our laws." With what result? No two judges have yet delivered the same opinion upon some of the most essential features of treason. Take for example the British doctrine that, in treason, accessories are principals. Were they in America? "Judge Chase and others say they are. Judge Marshall says he does not know whether they are or not, but his reasoning would go to show that they are not." [3]

Solely to gratify *vox populi*, the Senate next indulged in a doubtful performance. An attempt was made to expel Senator John Smith of Ohio. With

---

[1] *Blennerhassett Papers:* Safford, 480–82; also see *Baltimore American*, Nov. 4, 5, 6, 1807.

[2] *Annals*, 10th Cong. 1st Sess. 108–27.

[3] The bill passed the Senate, but foreign affairs, and exciting legislation resulting from these, forced it from the mind of the House. (See vol. IV, chap. I, of this work.)

only a partial examination, and without allowing
him to call a single witness in his own behalf beforehand, a special Senate Committee[1] presented a report concluding with a resolution to expel Smith
because of "his participation in the conspiracy of
Aaron Burr against the peace, union and liberties
of the people of the United States."[2] This surprising
document was the work of John Quincy Adams,[3]
who apparently adopted the ideas and almost the
language of Lucius.

Burr's conspiracy, wrote Adams, was so evil and
was "established by such a mass of concurring and
mutually corroborative testimony" that the "honor"
of the Senate and "the deepest interests of this

[1] John Quincy Adams of Massachusetts, Samuel Maclay of Pennsylvania, Jesse Franklin of North Carolina, Samuel Smith of Maryland, John Pope of Kentucky, Buckner Thruston of Kentucky, and
Joseph Anderson of Tennessee. (*Annals*, 10th Cong. 1st Sess. 42.)

[2] Smith had been indicted for treason and misdemeanor, but Hay
had entered a *nolle prosequi* on the bills of indictment after the failure
of the Burr prosecution. (*Memoirs, J. Q. A.*: Adams, i, 481.)

[3] Adams had been indulging in political maneuvers that indicated a
courtship of the Administration and a purpose to join the Republican
Party. His course had angered and disgusted most of his former Federalist friends and supporters, who felt that he had deserted his declining party in order to advance his political fortunes. If this were
true, his performance in writing the Committee report on the resolution to expel Smith was well calculated to endear him to Jefferson.
Adams expressed his own views thus: "On most of the great national
questions now under discussion, my sense of duty leads me to support
the administration, and I find myself of course in opposition to the
federalists in general. . . My political prospects are declining."
(*Memoirs, J. Q. A.*: Adams, i, 497–98.)

The Federalist Legislature of Massachusetts grossly insulted Adams
by electing his successor before Adams's term in the Senate had
expired. Adams resigned, and in March, 1809, President Madison
appointed him Minister to Russia, and later Minister to Great
Britain. President Monroe made the former Federalist his Secretary
of State. No Republican was more highly honored by these two
Republican Presidents than was John Quincy Adams.

nation" required that nobody connected with it should be a member of Congress. After an unctuous recitation of accepted generalities and a review of the expulsion of Senator Blount, together with an excellent statement of the law of parliamentary bodies in such cases, Adams got down to the business of destroying John Marshall.[1]

Marshall had "withheld from the jury . . a great part of the testimony which was essential to [Burr's] conviction. . . . In consequence of this suppression of evidence" the trial jury had not been allowed to find a verdict of guilty against the traitor. Marshall's "decisions, forming the basis of the issue upon the trials of Burr . . were the sole inducements upon which the counsel for the United States abandoned the prosecution against him" (Smith). An American grand jury had charged Senator Smith with being "an accomplice" of these diabolical plans, and the safety which Marshall's decisions in the Burr trial had thrown around Smith and other associates of the traitor "cannot, in the slightest degree, remove the imputation" which the indictment of Smith had brought to his door.

---

[1] Adams did not, of course, mention Marshall by name. His castigation of the Chief Justice, however, was the more severe because of the unmistakable designation of him. (See *Writings, J. Q. A.*: Ford, III, 173–84; also *Annals*, 10th Cong. 1st Sess. 56–63.)

It must be remembered, too, that this attack upon Marshall comes from the son of the man who, on January 20, 1801, appointed Marshall Chief Justice. (See vol. II, 552–53, of this work.) But John Quincy Adams soon came to be one of the stanchest supporters and most ardent admirers that Marshall ever had. It was peculiarly characteristic of Marshall that he did not resent the attack of Adams and, for the only time in his judicial career, actually interested himself in politics in behalf of Adams. (See vol. IV, chap. IX, of this work.)

"If," wrote Adams, "the daylight of evidence combining one vast complicated intention, with overt acts innumerable, be not excluded from the mind by the curtain of artificial rules, the simplest understanding cannot but see what the subtlest understanding cannot disguise, crimes before which ordinary treason whitens into virtue" and beyond "the ingenuity of a demon."

Adams continued: "Whether the transactions proved against Aaron Burr did or did not amount, in technical language, to an overt act of levying war, your committee have not a scruple of doubt .. that, but for the vigilance and energy of the government, and of faithful citizens under its directions .. in crushing his designs, they would .. have terminated not only in war, but in a war of the most horrible description, . . at once foreign and domestic."

To such lengths can popular demand, however unjust, drive even cold, unemotional, and upright men who are politically ambitious. Adams's Federalist confrères reacted quickly;[1] and the *New*

[1] Adams's colleague Senator Pickering was, of course, disgusted (see his letter to King, Jan. 2, 1808, King, v, 44), and in a pamphlet entitled "A Review of the Correspondence Between the Hon. John Adams and the late William Cunningham, Esq." which he published in 1824, Pickering wrote that the resolution "outraged .. every distinguished lawyer in America" (see p. 41 of pamphlet). King thought Adams "indiscreet" (see his letter to Pickering, Jan. 7, 1808, King, v, 50). Plumer declared that the report "had given mortal offence" in New Hampshire (see *Mass. Historical Society Proceedings*, xlv, 357). John Lowell asserted that "justice .. was to be dragged from her seat .. and the eager minister of presidential vengeance seemed to sigh after the mild mercies of the star chamber, and the rapid movements of the revolutionary tribunal" (see his "Remarks" as quoted in *Writings, J. Q. A.*: Ford, iii, footnote to 184).

York Evening Post sharply criticized him.[1] When the report came up in the Senate, James A. Bayard of Delaware, and James Hillhouse of Connecticut, attacked it and its author with "unusual virulence." Bayard was especially severe.[2] Thus assailed, Adams was cast into black depression: "It is indeed a fiery ordeal I have to go through. God speed me through it!" he wrote in his diary that night.[3]

William Branch Giles cast the deciding vote which defeated Adams's resolution — the Senate refusing to expel Smith by a vote of 19 yeas to 10 nays,[4] just one short of the necessary two thirds. The Virginia Republican Senator attacked the resolution with all his fiery eloquence, and compelled the admiration even of Adams himself.[5] "I shall vote against the resolution," Giles concluded, "solely from the conviction of the innocence of the accused."[6]

Herefrom one may judge the temper of the times and the perilous waters through which John Marshall had been compelled to pilot the craft of justice. If that "most deliberative legislative body" in our Government, and the one least affected by popular storms, was so worked upon, one can perceive the

[1] Jan. 28, 1808, *Memoirs, J. Q. A.*: Adams, I, 508; see also *Writings, J. Q. A.*: Ford, III, footnote to 184.

[2] "He poured himself forth in his two speeches to-day. . . It was all a phillipic upon me." (Jan. 7, 1808, *Memoirs, J. Q. A.*: Adams, I, 501.)

[3] *Ib.* 　　　　　　　　[4] *Annals*, 10th Cong. 1st Sess. 324.

[5] "Mr. Giles, in one of the most animated and eloquent speeches I ever heard him make, declared himself . . against the resolution for expulsion. He argued the case of Mr. Smith with all his eloquence, and returned to the charge with increasing warmth until the last moment." (April 9, 1808, *Memoirs, J. Q. A.*: Adams, I, 528.)

[6] *Annals*, 10th Cong. 1st Sess. 321–24.

conditions that surrounded the Chief Justice in overcrowded Richmond during the trial of Aaron Burr, and the real impending danger for Marshall, after the acquittal of the man whom Jefferson and the majority had branded with the most hideous infamy.

Fortunate, indeed, for the Chief Justice of the United States, and for the stability of American institutions, that the machinery of impeachment was, during these fateful months, locked because the President, Congress, and the Nation were forced to give their attention to the grave foreign situation which could no longer be ignored.

Going about his duties in Washington, or, at home, plodding out to the farm near Richmond, joking or gossiping with friends, and caring for his afflicted wife, Marshall heard the thunders of popular denunciation gradually swallowed up in the louder and ever-increasing reverberations that heralded approaching war with Great Britain. Before the clash of arms arrived, however, his level common sense and intelligent courage were again called upon to deal with another of those perplexing conditions which produced, one by one, opinions from the Supreme Bench that have become a part of the living, growing, yet stable and enduring Constitution of the American Nation.

CHAPTER X

FRAUD AND CONTRACT

If I were to characterize the United States, it should be by the appellation of the land of speculation. (William Priest.)

By the God of Heaven, if we go on in this way, our nation will sink into disgrace and slavery. (John Tyler.)

Millions of acres are easily digested by such stomachs. They buy and sell corruption in the gross. (John Randolph.)

When a law is in its nature a contract, when absolute rights have vested under that contract, a repeal of the law cannot divest those rights. The people can act only by their agents and, within the powers conferred upon them, their acts must be considered as the acts of the people. (Marshall.)

THE Honorable William Longstreet was an active and influential member of the Georgia Legislature during the winter of 1794–95. He was also a practical man. An important bill was then before that body, and Mr. Longstreet employed effective methods to forward its passage. The proposed legislation was to authorize the sale to four speculating land companies [1] of most of that territory which comprises the present States of Alabama and Mississippi.

"Why are you not in favor of selling the western lands?" frequently asked Representative Longstreet of his fellow member, Clem Lanier. "Because I do not think it right to sell to companies of speculators," was the answer. "Better vote for the bill," observed his seat mate, Representative Henry Gindrat, one day as they sat chatting before the Speaker of the House took the chair. "It will be worth your while. Senator Thomas Wylly says that he can have eight or ten likely negroes for his part."

[1] See *infra*, 550.

That afternoon Senator Wylly came to Lanier and began to talk of the land bill. A Mr. Dennison sauntered up. Wylly left, and the newcomer remarked that, of course, he advised no legislator how to vote, but he could not help noticing that all who favored the sale of the lands "were handsomely provided for." If Lanier should support the bill, he would be taken care of like the rest. He was buying, Dennison said, from members who wished to sell lands allotted to them for agreeing to support the measure.

Once more came Longstreet, who "presented a certificate entitling the bearer to two shares of twenty-five thousand acres each," as security that Lanier would be rewarded if he voted for the sale bill. The obdurate Representative, who wished to probe the depths of the plot, objected, and Longstreet assured him that he would immediately procure "another certificate . . for the same number of acres." But Lanier finally declined the bribe of seventy-five thousand acres of land.[1]

Representative Gindrat had offered to sell his shares for one thousand dollars, the price generally given; but, securing "a better market," declined that sum.[2] Representative Lachlan M'Intosh received six shares in one of the land companies, which he sold at a premium of two hundred and fifty dollars each.[3]

After the bill had passed, Senator Robert Thomas,

[1] Affidavit of Clem Lanier, *Am. State Papers, Public Lands*, I, 145.
[2] Affidavit of Peter L. Van Allen, *ib.*
[3] *Ib.* It would appear that one hundred and fifty thousand acres were allotted to the thrifty Scotch legislator. He sold them for $7500.

who had no means of acquiring ready cash,[1] brought two thousand dollars to the house where he boarded and asked Philip Clayton, the owner, to keep it for him. Clayton was curious — did Senator Thomas get the money for his share of the lands? he inquired. "It is nothing to you; take care of it," answered the suddenly affluent legislator, smiling.[2]

Representative Longstreet offered Representative John Shepperd one hundred thousand acres, but Shepperd was not interested; then Philip Clayton, the tavern-keeper, offered him seventy pounds to go home for the session.[3]

A saturnalia of corruption was in progress in the little village of Augusta, where the Legislature of Georgia was in session.[4] The leading men of that and neighboring States were on the ground urging the enactment of the law in which all were interested. Wade Hampton of South Carolina was on hand. State and National judges were present. James Wilson of Pennsylvania, Associate Justice of the Supreme Court of the United States, was there with twenty-five thousand dollars in bank bills.[5]

[1] Affidavit of John Thomas, Jr., *Am. State Papers, Public Lands*, I, 148.

[2] Affidavit of Philip Clayton, *ib*. 146.

[3] Affidavit of John Shepperd, *ib*.

[4] About sixty affidavits were made to show the venality of members of the Legislature. Of these, twenty-one are printed in *ib*. 144–49.

[5] Harris: *Georgia from the Invasion of De Soto to Recent Times*, 127–28; White: *Statistics of the State of Georgia*, 50; Chappell: *Miscellanies of Georgia*, 93–95.

These writers leave the unjust inference that Wilson was one of those who were corrupting the Legislature. This is almost certainly untrue. For a quarter of a century Wilson had been a heavy speculator in Indian lands, and it appears reasonable that he took this money to Augusta for the purpose of investment. When the deal was con-

William Smith, Judge of the Superior Court of Georgia, added his influence, receiving for his services as lobbyist thirteen thousand dollars. Nathaniel Pendleton, Judge of the United States Court for that district, urged the legislation and signed and issued the certificates for shares that were given to the members for their votes.[1] Directing all was General James Gunn, United States Senator from Georgia: his first term in the National Senate about to expire, he was now reëlected by this very Legislature.[2]

A majority of Georgia's lawmaking body thus became financially interested in the project, and the bill passed both houses. But Governor George Mathews vetoed the measure, because he thought the time not propitious for selling the lands, the price too low, the reservations for Georgians too small, and the principle of monopoly wrong.[3] Another bill was prepared to meet some of the Governor's objections. This was introduced as a supplement to a law just enacted to pay the State troops.[4] Again every possible influence was brought upon the Legislature to pass this bill with utmost dispatch.[5] Some mem-

summated, the Justice held shares to the amount of at least three quarters of a million of acres. (Chappell, 94.)

[1] *Ib.* 95.

[2] Gunn's reëlection was the first step in the conspiracy. Not until that was accomplished was a word said about the sale of the lands. Immediately after the Legislature had chosen Gunn for a second term in the National Senate, however, the bill was introduced and the campaign of intimidation and bribery launched, to force its passage. (*Ib.* 82–83.)

[3] See Mathews's reasons, as quoted in the Rescinding Act of 1796, *Am. State Papers, Public Lands,* i, 156.

[4] Chappell, 86.

[5] The claims of Spain to the territory had been a serious cloud on

bers, who would not support it, were induced to leave the tiny Georgia Capital; others, who were recalcitrant, were browbeaten and bullied.

Senator Gunn, the field marshal of this legislative campaign, strode about the village arrayed in broadcloth, top boots, and beaver hat, commending those who favored the bill, abusing those who opposed it. In his hand he carried a loaded whip, and with this the burly Senator actually menaced members who objected to the scheme.[1] In a little more than one week the bill was rushed through both houses. This time it received the reluctant approval of the Governor, and on January 7, 1795, became a law.

In such fashion was enacted the legislation which disposed of more than thirty-five million acres of fertile, well-watered, heavily wooded land at less than one and one half cents an acre.[2] The purchasers were four companies known as The Georgia Company, The Georgia Mississippi Company, The Tennessee Company, and The Upper Mississippi Company. The total purchase price was five hundred thousand dollars in specie or approved currency, one fifth to be deposited with the State Treasurer before the passage of the act, and the remainder to

the title. In October, 1795, the treaty with the Spanish Government, which removed this defect, was published. Senator James Gunn had knowledge that the treaty would be negotiated long before it was made known to the world or even concluded. This fact was one of the reasons for the mad haste with which the corrupt sale act was rushed through the Georgia Legislature. (See Chappell. 72–73.)

[1] Gunn was a perfect example of the corrupt, yet able, bold, and demagogical politician. He was a master of the arts alike of cajolery and intimidation. For a vivid account of this man see Chappell, 99–105.

[2] Haskins: *Yazoo Land Companies*, 24.

be paid on or before November 1, 1795. The Governor was directed to execute a deed in fee-simple to the men composing each company as tenants in common; and the deferred payments were secured by mortgages to the Governor, to be immediately foreclosed upon default of payment, and the one fifth already deposited to be forfeited to the State.

Two million acres were reserved for exclusive entry by citizens of Georgia, and the land companies were bound to form settlements within five years after the Indian titles had been extinguished. The lands were declared free of taxation until they should be so occupied that the settlers were represented in the Legislature.[1] Governor Mathews executed deeds in compliance with the law, and, the entire amount of the purchase money having been paid into the State Treasury before November 1, the mortgages were canceled and the transaction was closed in accordance with the provisions of the statute. So far as that legislation and the steps taken in pursuance of it could bring about such a result, the legal title to practically all of the domain stretching from the present western boundary of Georgia to the Mississippi River, and from the narrow strip of Spanish territory on the Gulf to the Tennessee line, was transferred to the men composing these four land companies. The greatest real estate deal in history was thus consummated.

But even while this bill was before the Legislature, popular opposition to it began. A young man of twenty-three was then teaching in a little school-

[1] *Am. State Papers, Public Lands*, i, 151–52.

house at Augusta, but he was destined to become United States Senator, Minister to France, Secretary of the Treasury, and candidate for President. Enraged at what he believed the despoiling of the people by a band of robbers using robbers' methods, young William H. Crawford hurried to his home in Columbia County, got up a petition to the Governor to reject the bill again, and hurried to the Capital where he presented it to the Chief Executive of the State.[1] But Governor Mathews, against whom no man, then or thereafter, charged corrupt motives, persisted in signing the measure.

And it must be said that the bill was not without merit. Georgia was but thinly populated, not more than fifty thousand human beings inhabiting its immense extent of savanna and forest. Most of these people were very poor[2] and unable to pay any public charges whatever. The State Treasury was empty; the State troops, who had been employed in the endless Indian troubles, were unpaid and clamoring for the money long due them; the State currency had so depreciated that it was almost without value. No commonwealth in the Union was in worse financial case.[3]

Moreover, the titles of the Indians, who occupied the country and who were its real owners, had not been extinguished. Under the Constitution, the National Government alone could deal with the tribes,

[1] Chappell, 87.

[2] "A small smoky cabin with a dirt floor was the home of most of them." (Smith: *Story of Georgia and the Georgia People*, 181.) For a good description of pioneer houses and manner of living, see Ramsey: *Annals of Tennessee to the End of the Eighteenth Century*, 715–16

[3] Smith, 170–71.

and it had long been urging Georgia to cede her
claims to the United States, as Virginia and Connecticut had done. Indeed, the State had once offered
to make this cession, but on such terms that Congress had refused to accept it. The purchasers now
took whatever title Georgia had, subject to these
burdens, the State to be saved from all annoyance
on account of them.

The tribes were powerful and brave, and they had
been prompt and bold in the defense of their lands.
The Creeks alone could put nearly six thousand
fighting men in the field, and the Choctaws had
more than four thousand trained warriors.[1] The
feeble and impoverished State had never been able
to subdue them, or to enforce in the slightest degree
the recognition of the State's title to the country
they inhabited. Georgia's right to their lands "depended on her power to dispossess the Indians; but
however good the title might be, the State would
have been fortunate to make it a free gift to any
authority strong enough to deal with the Creeks and
Cherokees alone."[2]

The sale of the territory was not a new or novel
project. Six years earlier the State had disposed of
twenty-five million five hundred thousand acres of
the same territory to four land companies on much
poorer terms.[3] Jefferson, then Secretary of State,
rendered a careful opinion on the right of Georgia to

---

[1] Morse's *American Gazetteer*, as quoted in Bishop: *Georgia Speculation Unveiled*, 3–4.

[2] Adams: *U.S.* i, 303.

[3] The South Carolina Yazoo Company, 10,000,000 acres for $66,964;
The Virginia Yazoo Company, 11,400,000 acres for $93,741; The Ten-
nessee Company, 4,000,000 acres for $46,875. (Haskins, 8.)

make the grant.[1] These purchasers had tendered payment in South Carolina and Continental scrip that was practically worthless; the Treasurer of Georgia had properly refused to accept it; and there ended the transaction as far as the State was concerned. A suit was later brought against Georgia by the grantees [2] to compel the performance of the contract; but the Eleventh Amendment of the Constitution thwarted that legal plan. So these speculators dropped the matter until the sale just described was made to the new companies six years later.

The most active promoters of the first purchasing companies, in 1789, were mere adventurers, although at first Patrick Henry and other men of honor and repute were interested in the speculation. Henry, however, soon withdrew.[3] The consummation of their deal with Georgia required the payment of sound money and *bona-fide* settlement by actual tillers of the soil. Also, the adventurers got into trouble with the Indians, became gravely involved in Spanish intrigue, and collided with the National Government;[4] so the enterprise lost, for a time, all attractiveness for these speculators.

The new land companies, on the other hand, were for the most part composed of men of excellent reputations.[5] At the head of the largest, The Georgia

---

[1] *Works:* Ford, VI, 55–57.

[2] Moultrie *vs.* Georgia, 1796, dismissed in 1798, *Am. State Papers, Public Lands,* I, 167; and see vol. II, 83–84, of this work.

[3] Chappell, 92–93.   [4] *Ib.* 67–68; Haskins, 13–15.

[5] "No men stood higher in Georgia than the men who composed these several companies and the members of the Legislature who made the sale." (Smith, 173.)

Company, were United States Senator James Gunn
and United States Attorney for the District of
Georgia, Mathew McAlister; associated with them,
in addition to Judges Stith and Pendleton, and Justice Wilson, were Robert Goodloe Harper, Representative in Congress from Maryland, Robert Morris,
the financier of the Revolution, and others of substance and position.[1] Also, as has been stated, they
paid for their lands in the money called for by the
act — the best money then circulating in America.
The first sales of Indian lands to which Georgia
claimed title were known as the "Yazoo" speculation, and this designation stuck to the second transaction.

In the six years that had intervened between the
sales to the irresponsible land-jobbers of 1789 and
the solvent investors of 1795, an event of world importance had occurred which doubled and trebled
the value of all cotton-bearing soil. Eli Whitney, a
Connecticut school-teacher twenty-seven years of
age, had gone to Georgia in 1792 to act as a private
tutor. Finding the position taken, he studied law
while the guest of the widow of General Nathanael
Greene. This discerning woman, perceiving that
the young man was gifted with inventive genius,
set him to work on a device for separating cotton
from the seed. The machine was built, and worked
perfectly. The news of it traveled with astonishing
rapidity throughout Georgia and the South. The
model was stolen; and so simple was the construction of it that everywhere in cotton-growing lands it

[1] See Haskins, 25, and sources there cited.

was freely reproduced by planters great and small.
The vast sweep of territory stretching from Georgia
to the Father of Waters, the best cotton land in the
world, thus rose in value as if the wand of a financial
deity had been waved over it. Settlers poured into
Georgia by the thousand, and Indian atrocities were
now as little feared as Indian rights were respected.[1]

The purchase of the unoccupied Georgia lands by
the *bona-fide*, if piratical, land companies of 1795
became, therefore, an adventure far more valuable
in possibilities for the investors, and incomparably
more attractive in the probability of political advantage to those who resisted it, than the innocuous and
unopposed sale to the Yazoo swindlers of six years
previous.

So it fell out that the mechanical genius of Eli
Whitney, in 1793, called into action, exactly eighteen
years afterward, the judicial genius of John Marshall.
His opinion in Fletcher *vs.* Peck was one of the first
steps toward the settling of the law of public contract in the riotous young Republic — one of the
earliest and strongest judicial assertions of the supremacy of Nationalism over Localism. And never
more than at that particular time did an established
rule on these vital subjects so need to be announced
by the highest judicial authority.

Since before the Revolution, all men had fixed
their eyes, hopes, and purposes upon land. Not the

---

[1] The effect of Whitney's invention is shown in striking fashion
by the increase of cotton exports. In 1791 only 189,500 pounds were
exported from the entire United States. Ten years later Georgia alone
exported 3,444,420 pounds. (Jones and Dutcher: *Memorial History
of Augusta, Georgia*, 165.)

humble and needy only, but the high-placed and opulent, had looked to the soil — the one as their chief source of livelihood, and the other as a means of profitable speculation. Indeed, dealing in land was the most notable economic fact in the early years of the American Nation. "Were I to characterize the *United States*," chronicles one of the most acute British travelers and observers of the time, "it should be by the appellation of the *land of speculation*." [1]

From the Nation's beginning, the States had lax notions as to the sacredness of public contracts, and often violated the obligations of them. [2] Private agreements stood on a somewhat firmer basis, but even these were looked upon with none too ardent favor. The most familiar forms of contract-breaking were the making legal tender of depreciated paper, and the substitution of property for money; but other devices were also resorted to. So it was that the provision, "no state shall pass any law impairing the obligation of contracts," was placed in the Constitution. [3] The effect of this on the public mind, as re-

---

[1] Priest: *Travels in the United States*, 132; and see Haskins, 3.

Otis speaks of the "land jobbing prospectors," and says that "money is the object here [Boston] with all ranks and degrees." (Otis to Harper, April 10, 1807, Morison: *Otis*, I, 283.)

The national character "is degenerated into a system of stock-jobbing, extortion and usury. . . By the God of Heaven, if we go on in this way, our nation will sink into disgrace and slavery." (Tyler to Madison, Jan. 15, 1810, Tyler, I, 235.)

[2] See vol. I, 428, of this work.

[3] It was, however, among the last items proposed to the Convention, which had been at work more than three months before the "contract clause" was suggested. Even then the proposal was only as to *new* States. The motion was made by Rufus King of New York on August 28. Gouverneur Morris objected. "This would be going

ported by conservatives like Marshall, is stated in the *Commercial Gazette* of Boston, January 28, 1799: "State laws protected debtors" when they "were citizens . . [and] the creditors foreigners. The federal constitution, prohibiting the states to clear off debts *without payment*, by exacting *justice*, seemed . . to establish *oppression*." The debtors, therefore, "pronounced . . the *equal* reign of law and debt-compelling justice, the beginning of an insidious attack on liberty and the erection of aristocracy."

too far," he said. George Mason of Virginia said the same thing. Madison thought "a negative on the State laws could alone secure the effect." James Wilson of Pennsylvania warmly supported King's motion. John Rutledge of South Carolina moved, as a substitute for King's proposition, that States should not pass "bills of attainder nor retrospective laws." (*Records, Fed. Conv.*: Farrand, II, 440.) This carried, and nothing more appears as to the contract clause until it was included by the Committee on Style in its report of September 12. (*Ib.* 596–97.) Elbridge Gerry of Massachusetts strongly favored it and even wanted Congress "to be laid under the like prohibitions." (*Ib.* 619.) The Convention refused to insert the word "previous" before "obligation." (*Ib.* 636.)

In this manner the provision that "no state shall pass any law impairing the obligation of contracts" was inserted in the Constitution. The framers of that instrument apparently had in mind, however, the danger of the violation of contracts through depreciated paper money rather than the invalidation of agreements by the direct action of State Legislatures. (See speech of William R. Davie in the North Carolina Convention, July 29, 1788, *ib.* III, 349–50; speech of James McHenry before the Maryland House of Delegates, Nov. 29, 1787, *ib.* 150; and speech of Luther Martin before same, same date, *ib.* 214; also see Madison to Ingersoll, Feb. 2, 1831, *ib.* 495.)

Madison best stated the reason for the adoption of the contract clause: "A violations [*sic*] of Contracts had become familiar in the form of depreciated paper made a legal tender, of property substituted for money, of Instalment laws, and of the occlusions of the Courts of Justice; although evident that all such interferences affected the rights of other States, relatively Creditor, as well as Citizens Creditors within the State." (*Ib.* 548.) Roger Sherman and Oliver Ellsworth explained briefly that the clause "was thought necessary as a security to commerce." (Letter to the Governor of Connecticut, Sept. 26, 1787, *ib.* 100.)

The "contract clause" of the Constitution was now to be formally challenged by a "sovereign" State for the first time since the establishment of the National Government. Georgia was to assert her "sovereignty" by the repudiation of her laws and the denial of contractual rights acquired under them. And this she was to do with every apparent consideration of morality and public justice to support her.

The tidings of the corruption attending the second "Yazoo" sale were carried over the State on the wings of fury. A transaction which six years before had met with general acquiescence,[1] now received deep-throated execration. The methods by which the sale was pushed through the Legislature maddened the people, and their wrath was increased by the knowledge that the invention of the Connecticut schoolmaster had tremendously enhanced the value of every acre of cotton-bearing soil.

Men who lived near Augusta assembled and marched on the Capital determined to lynch their legislative betrayers. Only the pleadings of members who had voted against the bill saved the lives of their guilty associates.[2] Meetings were held in every hamlet. Shaggy backwoodsmen met in "old-field" log schoolhouses and denounced "the steal." The burning in effigy of Senator Gunn became a favorite manifestation of popular wrath. The public indignation was strengthened by the exercise of it. Those responsible for the enactment of the law found it perilous to be seen in any crowd. One member left

---

[1] Chappell, 67. [2] Harris, 130.

the State. Another escaped hanging only by precipitate flight.[1] Scores of resolutions were passed by town, rural, and backwoods assemblages demanding that the fraudulent statute be rescinded. Petitions, circulated from the "mansion" of the wealthy planter to the squalid cabin of the poorest white man, were signed by high and low alike. The grand juries of every county in Georgia, except two, formally presented as a grievance the passage of the land sale act of 1795.

Among other things, the land sale act required the Senators and Representatives of Georgia in Congress to urge the National Government to speed the making of a treaty with the Indian tribes extinguishing their title to the lands which the State had sold. Upon receiving a copy of the nefarious law, Senator James Jackson of Georgia laid it before the Senate, together with a resolution declaring that that body would "advise and consent" to the President's concluding any arrangement that would divest the Indians of their claims.[2]

But although he had full knowledge of the methods by which the act was passed, the records do not show that Jackson then gave the slightest expression to that indignation which he so soon thereafter poured forth. Nor is there any evidence that he said a word on the subject when, on March 2, 1795, Georgia's title again came before the Senate.[3]

[1] Harris, 131.

[2] Feb. 27, 1795, *Annals*, 3d Cong. 1st and 2d Sess. 838–39.

[3] *Ib.* 844–45. The silence of Jackson at this time is all the more impressive because the report of the Attorney-General would surely be used by the land companies to encourage investors to buy. Both

Some time afterward, however, Senator Jackson
hurried home and put himself at the head of the
popular movement against the "Yazoo Frauds."
In every corner of the State, from seaport to remotest settlement, his fiery eloquence roused the
animosity of the people to still greater frenzy. In two
papers then published in Georgia, the *Savannah
Gazette* and the *Augusta Chronicle*, the Senator, under the *nom de guerre* of "Sicillius," published a series
of articles attacking with savage violence the sale
law and all connected with the enactment of it.[1]

It came out that every member of the Legislature
who had voted for the measure, except one,[2] had
shares of stock in the purchasing companies.[3] Stories of the extent of the territory thus bartered away
kept pace with tales of the venality by which the
fraud was effected. Bad as the plain facts were,
they became simply monstrous when magnified by
the imagination of the public.

Nearly every man elected[4] to the new Legislature
was pledged to vote for the undoing of the fraud in
any manner that might seem the most effective.
Senator Jackson had resigned from the National
Senate in order to become a member of the Georgia
House of Representatives; and to this office he
was overwhelmingly elected. When the Legislature

Jackson and Gunn were present when King offered his resolution.
(*Annals*, 3d Cong. 1st and 2d Sess. 846.) Jackson declined to vote
on the passage of a House bill "making provision for the purposes of
treaty" with the Indians occupying the Yazoo lands. (*Ib.* 849–50.)

[1] Smith, 174.   [2] Robert Watkins.

[3] See Report of the Commissioners, *Am. State Papers*, *Public
Lands*, I, 132–35.

[4] The "Yazoo men" carried two counties.

convened in the winter of 1795–96, it forthwith **went** about the task of destroying the corrupt work of its predecessor. Jackson was the undisputed leader;[1] his associates passed, almost unanimously, and Governor Irwin promptly approved, the measure which Jackson wrote.[2] Thus was produced that enactment by a "sovereign" State, the validity of which John Marshall was solemnly to deny from the Supreme Bench of the Nation.

Jackson's bill was a sprightly and engaging document. The preamble was nearly three times as long as the act itself, and abounded in interminable sentences. It denounced the land sale act as a violation of both State and National Constitutions, as the creation of a monopoly, as the dismemberment of Georgia, as the betrayal of the rights of man. In this fashion the "whereases" ran on for some thousands of words. On second thought the Legislature concluded that the law was worse than unconstitutional —it was, the "whereases" declared, a "usurped act." That part of the preamble dealing with the mingled questions of fraud and State sovereignty deserves quotation in full:

"And Whereas," ran this exposition of Constitutional law and of the nature of contracts, "divested

---

[1] Chappell, 126.

[2] The outgoing Governor, George Mathews, in his last message to the Legislature, stoutly defended his approval of the sale act. He attributed the attacks upon him to "base and malicious reports," inspired by "the blackest and the most persevering malice aided by disappointed avarice." The storm against the law was, he said, due to "popular clamour." (Message of Governor Mathews, Jan. 28, 1796, Harper: *Case of the Georgia Sales on the Mississippi Considered*, 92–93.)

of all fundamental and constitutional authority which the said usurped act might be declared by its advocates, and those who claim under it, to be founded on, fraud has been practised to obtain it and the grants under it; and it is a fundamental principle, both of law and equity, that there cannot be a wrong without a remedy, and the State and the citizens thereof have suffered a most grievous injury in the barter of their rights by the said usurped act and grants, and there is no court existing, if the dignity of the State would permit her entering one, for the trial of fraud and collusion of individuals, or to contest her sovereignty with them, whereby the remedy for so notorious an injury could be obtained; and it can no where better lie than with the representatives of the people chosen by them, after due promulgation by the grand juries of most of the counties of the State, of the means practised, and by the remonstrances of the people of the convention, held on the 10th day of May, in the year 1795, setting forth the atrocious peculation, corruption, and collusion, by which the usurped act and grants were obtained." [1]

At last the now highly enlightened Legislature enacted "that the said usurped act . . be declared null and void," and that all claims directly or indirectly arising therefrom be "annulled." The lands sold under the Act of 1795 were pronounced to be "the sole property of the State, subject only to the right of treaty of the United States, to enable the State to purchase, under its pre-emption right, the Indian title to the same." [2]

[1] *Am. State Papers, Public Lands*, I, 157.   [2] *Ib.* 158.

Such was the law which John Marshall was to declare invalid in one of the most far-reaching opinions ever delivered from the Supreme Bench.

The Legislature further enacted that the "usurped act" and all "records, documents, and deeds" connected with the Yazoo fraud, "shall be expunged from the face and indexes of the books of record of the State, and the enrolled law or usurped act shall then be publicly burnt, in order that no trace of so unconstitutional, vile, and fraudulent a transaction, other than the infamy attached to it by this law, shall remain in the public offices thereof." County officials were, under the severest of penalties for disobedience, directed to "obliterate" all records of deeds or other instruments connected with the anathematized grants, and courts were forbidden to receive any evidence of title of any kind whatever to lands from the grantees under the "usurped act." [1]

The Governor was directed to issue warrants for repayment to those who, in good faith, had deposited their purchase money, with this reservation, however: "Provided the same shall be now therein." [2] After six months all moneys not applied for were to become the property of Georgia. To prevent frauds upon individuals who might otherwise purchase lands from the pirate companies, the Governor was directed to promulgate this brief and simple act "throughout the United States."

[1] *Am. State Papers, Public Lands*, I, 158.
[2] The punctilious Legislature failed to explain that one hundred thousand dollars of the purchase money had already been appropriated and expended by the State. This sum they did not propose to restore.

A committee, appointed to devise a method for destroying the records, immediately reported that this should be done by cutting out of the books the leaves containing them. As to the enrolled bill containing the "usurped act," an elaborate performance was directed to be held: "A fire shall be made in front of the State House door, and a line formed by the members of both branches around the same. The Secretary of State [1] . . shall then produce the enrolled bill and usurped act from among the archives of the State and deliver the same to the President of the Senate, who shall examine the same, and shall then deliver the same to the Speaker of the House of Representatives for like examination; and the Speaker shall then deliver them to the Clerk of the House of Representatives, who shall read aloud the title to the same, and shall then deliver them to Messenger of the House, who shall then pronounce — 'GOD SAVE THE STATE!! AND LONG PRESERVE HER RIGHTS!! AND MAY EVERY ATTEMPT TO INJURE THEM PERISH AS THESE CORRUPT ACTS NOW DO!!!!'"[2]

Every detail of this play was carried out with all theatrical effect. Indeed, so highly wrought were the imaginations of actors and onlookers that, at the last moment, a final dash of color was added. Some one gifted with dramatic genius suggested that the funeral pyre of such unholy legislation should not be lighted by earthly hands, but by fire from Heaven. A sun-glass was produced; Senator Jackson held it

[1] "Or his deputy."

[2] Report of the joint committee, as quoted in Stevens: *History of Georgia from its First Discovery by Europeans to the Adoption of the Present Constitution in 1798*, II, 491–92.

above the fagots and the pile was kindled from "the burning rays of the lidless eye of justice." [1]

While the State was still in convulsions of anger, a talented young Virginian of impressionable temperament went to Georgia upon a visit to a college friend, Joseph Bryan, and was so profoundly moved by accounts of the attempt to plunder the State, that a hatred of the corrupt plot and of all connected with it became an obsession that lasted as long as he lived. [2] Thus was planted in the soul of John Randolph that determination which later, when a member of Congress, caused him to attack the Administration of Thomas Jefferson. [3]

Swift as was the action of the people and legislature of Georgia in attempting to recover the Yazoo lands, it was not so speedy as that of the speculators in disposing of them to purchasers in other States. Most of these investors bought in entire good faith and were "innocent purchasers." Some, however, must have been thoroughly familiar with the fraud. [4]

[1] Stevens, 492–93. Stevens says that there is no positive proof of this incident; but all other writers declare that it occurred. See Knight: *Georgia's Landmarks, Memorials and Legends*, I, 152–53; also Harris, 135.

[2] Adams: *Randolph*, 23; also Garland: *Life of John Randolph of Roanoke*, I, 64–68.

[3] See *infra*, 577–81; and *supra*, chap. IV.

[4] For instance, Wade Hampton immediately sold the entire holdings of The Upper Mississippi Company, millions of acres, to three South Carolina speculators, and it is quite impossible that they did not know of the corruption of the Georgia Legislature. Hampton acquired from his partners, John B. Scott and John C. Nightingale, all of their interests in the company's purchase. This was done on January 16 and 17, immediately after Governor Mathews had signed the deed from the State. Seven weeks later, March 6, 1795, Hampton conveyed all of this land to Adam Tunno, James Miller, and James Warrington. (*Am. State Papers, Public Lands*, I, 233.) Hampton was a member of Congress from South Carolina.

The most numerous sales were made in the Middle States and in New England. The land companies issued a prospectus,[1] setting out their title, which appeared to be, and indeed really was, legally perfect. Thousands of copies of this pamphlet were scattered among provident and moneyed people. Agents of the companies truthfully described the Yazoo country to be rich, the climate mild and healthful, and the land certain of large and rapid rise in value.

Three of the companies[2] opened an office in Boston, where the spirit of speculation was rampant. Then ensued an epidemic of investment. Throngs of purchasers gathered at the promoters' offices. Each day prices rose and the excitement increased. Buying and selling of land became the one absorbing business of those who had either money or credit. Some of the most prominent and responsible men in New England acquired large tracts.[3] The companies received payment partly in cash, but chiefly in notes which were speedily sold in the market for commercial paper. Sales were made in other Northern cities, and many foreigners became purchasers. The average price received was fourteen cents an acre.[4]

[1] *State of Facts, shewing the Right of Certain Companies to the Lands lately purchased by them from the State of Georgia.*

[2] The Georgia Mississippi Company, The Tennessee Company, and The Georgia Company. (See Haskins, 29.)

[3] Eleven million acres were purchased at eleven cents an acre by a few of the leading citizens of Boston. This one sale netted the Yazoo speculators almost a million dollars, while the fact that such eminent men invested in the Yazoo lands was a strong inducement to ordinary people to invest also. (See Chappell, 109.)

[4] See Chappell, 110–11.

Some New Englanders were suspicious. "The Georgia land speculation calls for vigor in Congress. Near fifty millions acres sold . . for a song," wrote Fisher Ames.[1] But such cautious men as Ames were few in number and most of them were silent. By the time reports reached Boston that the Legislature of Georgia was about to repeal the act under which the companies had bought the lands, numerous sales, great and small, had been made. In that city alone more than two millions of dollars had been invested, and this had been paid or pledged by "every class of men, even watch-makers, hair-dressers, and mechanics." The Georgia Company conveyed eleven million acres on the very day that the Legislature of Georgia passed the bill declaring the "usurped act" to be null and void and asserting the title of the whole territory still to be in the State.[2]

Three weeks later, the news of the enactment of the rescinding law was published in the New England metropolis. Anger and apprehension seized the investors. If this legislation were valid, all would lose heavily; some would be financially ruined. So a large number of the purchasers organized the New England Mississippi Company for the purpose of defending their interests. A written opinion upon the validity of their titles was procured from Alexander Hamilton, who was then practicing law in New York and directing the Federalist Party throughout

---

[1] Ames to Gore, Feb. 24, 1795, Ames, I, 168. Ames's alarm, however, was that the Georgia land sale " threatens Indian, Spanish, and civil, wars." The immorality of the transaction appears to have been unknown to him.

[2] Haskins, 30.

the Nation. He was still regarded by most Federalists, and by nearly all moneyed men, as the soundest lawyer, as well as the ablest statesman, in America.

Hamilton's opinion was brief, simple, convincing, and ideally constructed for perusal by investors. It stated the facts of the enactment of the sale law, the fulfillment of the conditions of it by the purchasers, and the passage of the rescinding act. Hamilton declared this latter act to be invalid because it plainly violated the contract clause of the Constitution. "Every grant . . whether [from] . . a state or an individual, is virtually a contract." The rescinding act was therefore null, and "the courts of the United States . . will be likely to pronounce it so." [1]

Soon after its passage, President Washington had received a copy of the Georgia land sale act. He transmitted it to Congress with a short Message,[2] stating that the interests of the United States were involved. His principal concern, however, and that of Congress also, was about the Indians. It was feared that depredations by whites would cause another outbreak of the natives. A resolution was adopted authorizing the President to obtain from Georgia the cession of her "claim to the whole or any part of the land within the . . Indian boundaries," and recommending that he prevent the making of treaties by individuals or States "for the extinguishment of the Indian title." But not a word was said in Washington's Message, or in the debate in Con-

[1] Harper, 109. Hamilton's opinion is dated March 25, 1796. In Harper's pamphlet it is incorrectly printed 1795.

[2] *Annals*, 3d Cong. 1st and 2d Sess. 1231.

gress, about the invalidity of the Georgia sale law
or the corrupt methods employed to secure the enactment of it.[1]

Two bills to protect the Indians failed of passage.[2]
Just before adjournment the House adopted a Senate
resolution which had been offered by Senator Rufus
King of New York, requesting that the Attorney-
General report to the Senate all data bearing on
Georgia's title to the territory sold to the land
companies; but again the invalidity of the sale law
was not even suggested, and the corruption of the
Georgia Legislature was not so much as referred to.[3]

A year later, Charles Lee, Washington's Attorney-
General, transmitted to Congress an exhaustive report containing all facts.[4] This report was referred
to a special committee, headed by Senator Aaron
Burr of New York, who, on May 20, 1796, reported
a resolution authorizing the President to treat with
Georgia for the cession of the territory.[5] Once more
no attention was paid to the fraud in the sale act,
or to the rescinding act of the Georgia Legislature.

But when the public finally learned of the "Yazoo
Fraud" and of the repudiation by the Georgia Legislature of the corrupt law, the whole country was
deeply stirred. A war of pamphlets broke out and
was waged by both sides with vigor and ability.
Abraham Bishop of New Haven, Connecticut, wrote
a comprehensive answer to the prospectus of the
land companies, and copies of this pamphlet, which

[1] *Annals*, 3d Cong. 1st and 2d Sess. 1251-54. The Georgia act was
transmitted to Washington privately.

[2] *Ib.* 1255, 1262-63.   [3] *Ib.* 1282-83.

[4] *Am. State Papers, Public Lands*, I, 341.   [5] *Ib.* 71.

appeared in four parts, were widely circulated.[1] Georgia had no fee in the lands, said Bishop.[2] Sales to "innocent purchasers" could not give them what Georgia had no right to sell. Neither could such a device validate fraud. Much litigation had already grown out of the swindle, and the Georgia rescinding act had "brought . . matters to a crisis, and one decision of the supreme court of the United States may probably influence the decisions of lower courts." [3] Bishop discussed brilliantly, and at length, every possible question involved. The power of the State to pass and repeal laws was "wholly uncontrolable," [4] he asserted. The history of other dishonest and imprudent speculations was examined — the South Sea Bubble, the Mississippi Bubble,[5] and the interposition of the legislative power of Great Britain in the one case and of France in the other. Should like power be denied in America? Georgia's rescinding act "nipt in the bud a number of aspiring swindlers." [6] Courts could not overthrow such legislation. The "sacredness of contracts" was the favorite cloak of fraud. Bishop urged buyers to resist the recovery of money pledged in their purchase notes and, by so doing, to restore "millions of dollars . . to the channels of industry." [7]

Hard upon the publication of the first number of Bishop's pamphlet followed one for the land companies and investors. This had been written by Robert Goodloe Harper of Maryland a few months after Hamilton had rendered his opinion that the

---

[1] Bishop's pamphlet was called *Georgia Speculation Unveiled.*
[2] Bishop, 6.   [3] *Ib.* 11.   [4] *Ib.*   [5] *Ib.* 29–32.   [6] *Ib.* 92.   [7] *Ib.* 144.

Georgia grant was inviolable.[1] It was an able and learned performance. The title of Georgia to the lands was carefully examined and held to be indefeasible. The sale of 1795 was set forth and the fact disclosed that Georgia had appropriated one hundred thousand dollars of the purchase money immediately upon the receipt of it.[2] It was pointed out that the rescinding act ignored this fact.[3]

Harper argued that only the courts could determine the validity and meaning of a law, and that no Legislature could annul a grant made by a previous one. To the Judiciary alone belonged that power.[4] The sale law was a contract, fully executed; one party to it could not break that compact.[5] If Georgia thought the sale act unconstitutional, she should have brought suit in the United States Court to determine that purely judicial question. The same was true as to the allegations of fraud and corruption in the passage of the measure. If any power could do so, the courts and they alone could decide the effect of fraud in procuring the enactment of a law. But even the courts were barred from investigating that question: if laws could be invalidated because of the motives of members of lawmaking bodies, "what a door would be opened to fraud and uncertainty of every kind!"[6]

[1] Harper's opinion bears, opposite his signature, this statement: "Considered at New-York August 3d, 1796." Beyond all doubt it had been submitted to Hamilton — perhaps prepared in collaboration with him. Harper was himself a member of one of the purchasing companies and in the House he later defended the transaction. (See *Annals*, 5th Cong. 2d Sess. 1277.)

[2] Harper, 16. [3] *Ib*. 14. [4] *Ib*. 49–50.

[5] *Ib*. 50. Here Harper quotes Hamilton's opinion.

[6] *Ib*. 50–53. Harper's pamphlet is valuable as containing, in com-

Finally, after a long altercation that lasted for nearly three years, Congress enacted a law authorizing the appointment of commissioners to settle the disputes between the National Government and Georgia, and also to secure from that truculent sovereignty the cession to the Nation of the lands claimed by the State.[1] In the somewhat extended debate over the bill but little was said about the invalidity of the Yazoo sale, and the corruption of the Legislature that directed it to be made was not mentioned.[2]

Under this act of Congress, Georgia ceded her rights over the disputed territory for one million, two hundred and fifty thousand dollars; provided, however, that the Nation should extinguish the Indian titles, settle British and Spanish claims, ulti-

pact form, all the essential documents relating to Georgia's title as well as the sale and rescinding acts. Other arguments on both sides appeared. One of the ablest of these was a pamphlet by John E. Anderson and William J. Hobby, attorneys of Augusta, Georgia, and published at that place in 1799 "at the instance of the purchasers." It is entitled: *The Contract for the Purchase of the Western Territory Made with the Legislature of Georgia in the Year 1795, Considered with a Reference to the Subsequent Attempts of the State to Impair its Obligations.*

[1] See report of Attorney-General Charles Lee, April 26, 1796, *Am. State Papers, Public Lands,* I, 34; report of Senator Aaron Burr, May 20, 1796, *ib.* 71; report of Senator James Ross, March 2, 1797, *ib.* 79.

[2] Except by John Milledge of Georgia, who declared that "there was no legal claim upon . . any part of that territory." Robert Goodloe Harper said that that question "must be determined in a Court of Justice," and argued for an "amicable settlement" of the claims. He himself once had an interest in the purchase, but had disposed of it three years before when it appeared that the matter must come before Congress (*Annals,* 5th Cong. 2d Sess. 1277–78); the debate occupied parts of two days (see also *ib.* 1298–1313). In view of the heated controversy that afterward occurred, it seems scarcely credible that almost no attention was given in this debate to the fraudulent character of the transaction.

mately admit the vast domain as a State of the
Union, and reserve five million acres for the purpose
of quieting all other demands. A later law [1] directed
the National commissioners, who had negotiated this
arrangement with Georgia, to investigate and report
upon the claims of individuals and companies to
lands within the territory thus ceded to the United
States.

At once the purchasers from the land companies,
especially the New England investors, besieged Congress to devote part of this five million acres to the
salvage of their imperiled money. The report of the
commissioners [2] was wise, just, and statesmanlike.
It was laid before the House on February 16, 1803.
Although the titles of the claimants could "not be
supported," still, because most of the titles had been
acquired in good faith, and because it would be injurious to everybody, including the Nation, to leave
the matter unsettled, the report recommended the
accommodation of the dispute on terms that would
save innocent purchasers at least a part of the
money they had paid or legally engaged to pay. [3]

When a bill to carry out the recommendations of
the commission for the payment of the Yazoo claim-

[1] May 10 1800, Sess. I, chap. 50, *U.S. Statutes at Large*, II, 69.

[2] The entire commission was composed of three of the five members
of Jefferson's Cabinet, to wit: James Madison, Secretary of State;
Albert Gallatin, Secretary of the Treasury; and Levi Lincoln, Attorney-General.

[3] Report of the Commissioners, *Am. State Papers, Public Lands*, I,
132–35. "The interest of the United States, the tranquillity of those
who may hereafter inhabit that territory, and various equitable considerations which may be urged in favor of most of the present claimants, render it expedient to enter into a compromise on reasonable
terms."

ants came before the House, John Randolph offered
a resolution that went directly to the heart of the
controversy and of all subsequent ones of like nature.
It declared that "when the governors of any people
shall have betrayed" their public trust for their own
corrupt advantage, it is the "inalienable right" of
that people "to abrogate the act thus endeavoring
to betray them." Accordingly the Legislature of
Georgia had passed the rescinding act. This was
entirely legal and constitutional because "a subsequent Legislature of an individual State has an undoubted right to repeal any act of a preceding Legislature, provided such repeal be not forbidden by the
constitution of such State, or of the United States."
Neither the fundamental law of Georgia nor of the
Nation forbade the repeal of the corrupt law of 1795.
Claims under this nullified and "usurped" law were
not recognized by the compact of cession between
Georgia and the United States, "nor by any act
of the Federal Government." Therefore, declared
Randolph's resolution, "no part of the five millions
of acres reserved for satisfying and quieting claims
. . shall be appropriated to quiet or compensate any
claims" derived under the corrupt legislation of the
Georgia Legislature of 1795.[1] After a hot fight, consideration of the resolutions was postponed until the
next session; but the bill authorizing the commissioners to compromise with the Yazoo claimants also
went over.[2]

The matter next came up for consideration in the
House, just before the trial in the Senate of the

---

[1] *Annals*, 8th Cong. 1st Sess. 1039–40. [2] *Ib.* 1099–1122, 1131–70.

impeachment of Justice Samuel Chase. A strong and influential lobby was pressing the compromise. The legislative agents of the New England Mississippi Company [1] presented its case with uncommon ability. In a memorial to Congress [2] they set forth their repeated applications to President, Congress, and the commissioners for protection. They were, they said, "constantly assured" that the rights of the claimants would be respected; and that it was expressly for this purpose that the five million acres had been reserved. For years they had attended sittings of the commissioners and sessions of Congress "at great cost and heavy expense."

Would not Congress at last afford them relief? If a "judicial decision" was desired, let Congress enact a law directing the Supreme Court to decide as to the validity of their title and they would gladly submit the matter to that tribunal. It was only because Congress seemed to prefer settlement by compromise that they again presented the facts and reasons for establishing their rights. So once more every aspect of the controversy was discussed with notable ability and extensive learning in Granger and Morton's brochure. [3]

[1] Perez Morton and Gideon Granger. Morton, like Granger, was a Republican and a devoted Jeffersonian. He went annually to Washington to lobby for the Yazoo claimants and assiduously courted the President. In Boston the Federalists said that his political activity was due to his personal interest in the Georgia lands. (See *Writings, J. Q. A.*: Ford, III, 51–53.)

[2] *Memorial of the Agents of the New England Mississippi Company to Congress, with a Vindication of their Title at Law annexed.*

[3] This document, issued in pamphlet form in 1804, is highly important. There can be little doubt that Marshall read it attentively, since it proposed a submission of the acrimonious controversy to the Supreme Court.

The passions of John Randolph, which had never grown cold since as a youth, a decade previously, he had witnessed the dramatic popular campaign in Georgia — and which during 1804 had been gathering intense heat — now burst into a furious flame. Unfortunately for Jefferson, the most influential agent of the New England claimants was the one Administration official who had most favors to bestow — Gideon Granger of Connecticut, the Postmaster-General.[1] He was the leader of the lobby which the New England Mississippi Company had mustered in such force. And Granger now employed all the power of his department, so rich in contracts and offices, to secure the passage of a bill that would make effectual the recommendations of Jefferson's commissioners.

As the vote upon it drew near, Granger actually appeared upon the floor of the House soliciting votes for the measure. Randolph's emotions were thus excited to the point of frenzy — the man was literally beside himself with anger. He needed to husband all his strength for the conduct of the trial of Chase[2] and to solidify his party, rather than to waste his physical resources, or to alienate a single Republican. On the report of the Committee of Claims recommending the payment of the Yazoo claimants, one of the most virulent and picturesque debates in the history of the American Congress began.[3] Randolph took the floor, and a "fire and brimstone speech"[4] he made.

---

[1] The Postmaster-General was not made a member of the Cabinet until 1829.

[2] See *supra*, chap. IV.

[3] *Annals*, 8th Cong. 2d Sess. 1023.   [4] Cutler, II, 182.

"Past experience has shown that this is one of those subjects which pollution has sanctified," he began. "The press is gagged." The New England claimants innocent purchasers! "Sir, when that act of stupendous villainy was passed in 1795 . . it caused a sensation scarcely less violent than that produced by the passage of the stamp act." Those who assert their ignorance of "this infamous act" are gross and willful liars.[1] To a "monstrous anomaly" like the present case, cried Randolph, "narrow maxims of municipal jurisprudence ought not, and cannot be applied. . . Attorneys and judges do not decide the fate of empires." [2]

Randolph mercilessly attacked Granger, and through him the Administration itself. Granger's was a practiced hand at such business, he said. He was one of " the applicants by whom we were beset" in the Connecticut Reserve scheme, " by which the nation were swindled out of some three or four millions of acres of land, which, like other bad titles, had fallen into the hands of innocent purchasers." Granger "seems to have an unfortunate knack of buying bad titles. His gigantic grasp embraces with one hand the shores of Lake Erie,[3] and stretches with the other to the Bay of Mobile.[4] Millions of

---

[1] *Annals*, 8th Cong. 2d Sess. 1024. To such extravagance and inaccuracy does the frenzy of combat sometimes drive the most honest of men. When he made these assertions, John Randolph knew that scores of purchasers from the land companies had invested in absolute good faith and before Georgia had passed the rescinding act. His tirade done, however, this inexplicable man spoke words of sound though misapplied statesmanship.

[2] *Ib.* 1029–30.

[3] Referring to Granger's speculations in the Western Reserve.

[4] The Yazoo deal.

acres are easily digested by such stomachs. . . They buy and sell corruption in the gross." They gamble for "nothing less than the patrimony of the people." Pointing his long, bony finger at Granger, Randolph exclaimed: "Mr. Speaker, . . this same agent is at the head of an Executive department of our Government. . . This officer, possessed of how many snug appointments and fat contracts, let the voluminous records on your table, of the mere names and dates and sums declare, . . this officer presents himself at your bar, at once a party and an advocate."[1]

The debate continued without interruption for four full days. Every phase of the subject was discussed exhaustively. The question of the power of the Legislature to annul a contract; of the power of the Judiciary to declare a legislative act void because of corruption in the enactment of it; the competency of Congress to pass upon such disputed points — these questions, as well as that of the innocence of the purchasers, were elaborately argued.

The strongest speech in support of the good faith of the New England investors was made by that venerable and militant Republican and Jeffersonian, John Findley of Pennsylvania.[2] He pointed out that the purchase by members of the Georgia Legislature of the lands sold was nothing unusual — everybody knew "that had been the case in Pennsylvania and other states." Georgia papers did not circulate in

[1] *Annals*, 8th Cong. 2d Sess. 1031.

[2] Findley was one of those who led the fight against the ratification of the Constitution in the Pennsylvania Convention. (See vol. I, 327-38, of this work.)

New England; how could the people of that section know of the charges of corruption and the denial of the validity of the law under which the lands were sold?

Those innocent purchasers had a right to trust the validity of the title of the land companies — the agents had exhibited the deeds executed by the Governor of Georgia, the law directing the sale to be made, and the Constitution of the State. What more could be asked? "The respectability of the characters of the sellers" was a guarantee "that they could not themselves be deceived and would not deceive others." Among these, said Findley, was an eminent Justice of the Supreme Court,[1] a United States Senator,[2] and many other men of hitherto irreproachable standing. Could people living in an old and thickly settled State, far from the scene of the alleged swindle, with no knowledge whatever that fraud had been charged, and in need of the land offered — could they possibly so much as suspect corruption when such men were members of the selling companies?

Moreover, said Findley — and with entire accuracy — not a Georgia official charged with venality had been impeached or indicted. The truth was that if the Georgia Legislature had not passed the rescinding act the attention of Congress would never have been called to the alleged swindle. Then, too, everybody knew "that one session of a Legislature cannot annul the contracts made by the preceding session"; for did not the National Constitution

[1] James Wilson.   [2] James Gunn.

forbid any State from passing a law impairing the obligation of contracts? [1]

Randolph outdid himself in daring and ferocity when he again took the floor. His speech struck hostile spectators as "more outrageous than the first." [2] He flatly charged that a mail contract had been offered to a member of the House, who had accepted it, but that it had been withdrawn from him when he refused to agree to support the compromise of the Yazoo claims. Randolph declared that the plot to swindle Georgia out of her lands "was hatched in Philadelphia and New York (and I believe Boston . .) and the funds with which it was effected were principally furnished by moneyed capitalists in those towns." [3]

At last the resolution was adopted by a majority of 63 to 58,[4] and Randolph, physically exhausted and in despair at his overthrow as dictator of the House, went to his ineffective management of the Chase impeachment trial.[5] He prevented for the time being, however, the passage of the bill to carry out the compromise with the Yazoo claimants. He had mightily impressed the people, especially those of Virginia. The Richmond *Enquirer*, on October 7, 1806, denounced the Yazoo fraud and the compromise of the investors' claims as a "stupendous scheme of plunder." Senator Giles, in a private conversation with John Quincy Adams, asserted that "not a man from that State, who should give any

[1] *Annals*, 8th Cong. 2d Sess. 1080–89.
[2] Cutler, II, 182.
[3] *Annals*, 8th Cong. 2d Sess. 1100–08.
[4] *Ib.* 1173.   [5] See *supra*, chap. IV.

countenance to the proposed compromise, could obtain an election after it." He avowed that "nothing since the Government existed had so deeply
affected him." [1]

The debate was published fully in the newspapers
of Washington, and it is impossible that Marshall
did not read it and with earnest concern. As has
already been stated, the first case involving the sale
of these Georgia lands had been dropped because of
the Eleventh Amendment to the Constitution, abolishing the right to sue a state in the National courts.
Moreover, Marshall was profoundly interested in
the stability of contractual obligations. The repudiation of these by the Legislature of Virginia had powerfully and permanently influenced his views upon
this subject. [2] Also, Marshall's own title to part of
the Fairfax estate had more than once been in
jeopardy. [3] At that very moment a suit affecting the
title of his brother to certain Fairfax lands was
pending in Virginia courts, and the action of the
Virginia Court of Appeals in one of these was soon
to cause the first great conflict between the highest
court of a State and the supreme tribunal of the
Nation. [4] No man in America, therefore, could have
followed with deeper anxiety the Yazoo controversy
than did John Marshall.

Again and again, session after session, the claimants presented to Congress their prayers for relief.
In 1805, Senator John Quincy Adams of Massachu-

[1] *Memoirs, J. Q. A.*: Adams, I, 343.
[2] See vol. I, 224–41, of this work.
[3] *Ib.* 191, 196; and vol. II, 206.
[4] **Martin** *vs.* Hunter's Lessees; see vol. IV, chap. III, of this work.

setts and Senator Thomas Sumter of South Carolina
urged the passage of a bill to settle the claims. This
led Senator James Jackson of Georgia to deliver "a
violent invective against the claims, without any
specific object." [1] After Jackson's death the measure
passed the Senate by a vote of 19 to 11, but was
rejected in the House by a majority of 8 out of a
total of 116. [2]

Among the lawyers who went to Washington for
the New England Mississippi Company was a young
man not yet thirty years of age, Joseph Story of
Massachusetts, who on his first visit spent much
time with Madison, Gallatin, and the President. [3]
On a second visit, Story asked to address the House
on the subject, but that body refused to hear him. [4]

From the first the New England investors had
wished for a decision by the courts upon the validity
of their titles and upon the effect of the rescinding
act of the Georgia Legislature; but no way had
occurred to them by which they could secure such
a determination from the bench. The Eleventh
Amendment prevented them from suing Georgia;
and the courts of that State were, as we have seen,
forbidden by the rescinding act from entertaining
such actions.

To secure a judicial expression, the Boston claimants arranged a "friendly" suit in the United States

[1] *Memoirs, J. Q. A.*: Adams, I, 381; also see *ib.* 389, 392, 404–05,
408–09, 417–19.
[2] Haskins, 38.
[3] Story to Fay, May 30, 1807, Story, I, 150–53; and see Cabot to
Pickering, Jan. 28, 1808, Lodge: *Cabot*, 377.
[4] *Annals*, 10th Cong. 1st Sess. 1601–13.

Court for the District of Massachusetts. One John Peck of Boston had been a heavy dealer in Georgia lands.[1] On May 14, 1803, he had either sold or pretended to sell to one Robert Fletcher of Amherst, New Hampshire, fifteen thousand acres of his holdings for the sum of three thousand dollars. Immediately Fletcher brought suit against Peck for the recovery of this purchase money; but the case was "continued by consent" for term after term from June, 1803, until October, 1806.[2]

The pleadings[3] set forth every possible phase of the entire subject which could be considered judicially. Issues were joined on all points except that of the title of Georgia to the lands sold.[4] On this question a jury, at the October term, 1806, returned as a special verdict a learned and bulky document. It recited the historical foundations of the title to the territory in dispute; left the determination of the question to the court; and, in case the judge should decide that Georgia's claim to the lands sold was not valid, found for the plaintiff and assessed his damages at the amount alleged to have been paid to Peck.

Thereafter the case was again "continued by consent" until October, 1807, when Associate Justice William Cushing of the Supreme Court, sitting as Circuit Judge, decided in Peck's favor every question raised by the pleadings and by the jury's special verdict. Fletcher sued out a writ of error to the

---

[1] See Abstract, *Am. State Papers, Public Lands*, I, 220–34.

[2] Records, U.S. Circuit Court, Boston.

[3] Judge Chappell asserts that the pleadings showed, on the face of them, that the case was feigned. (See Chappell, 135–36.)

[4] Fletcher *vs.* Peck, 6 Cranch, 87–94.

Supreme Court of the United States, and so this controversy came before John Marshall. The case was argued twice, the first time, March 1–4, 1809, by Luther Martin for Fletcher and by Robert Goodloe Harper and John Quincy Adams for Peck. There was no decision on the merits because of a defect of pleadings which Marshall permitted counsel to remedy.[1]

During this argument the court adjourned for two hours to attend the inauguration of James Madison. For the third time Marshall administered the Presidential oath. At the ball that night, Judge Livingston told Adams that the court had been reluctant "to decide the case at all, as it appeared manifestly made up for the purpose of getting the Court's judgment upon all the points." The Chief Justice himself had mentioned the same thing to Cranch.

Adams here chronicles an incident of some importance. After delivering the court's opinion on the pleadings, Marshall "added verbally, that, circumstanced as the Court are, only five judges attending,[2] there were difficulties which would have prevented them from giving any opinion at this term had the pleadings been correct; and the Court the more readily forbore giving it, as from the complexion of the pleadings they could not but see that at the time when the covenants were made the parties had notice of the acts covenanted against."[3]

The cause was argued again a year later. This

---

[1] Fletcher vs. Peck, 6 Cranch, 127.

[2] Justices Chase and Cushing were absent because of illness.

[3] Memoirs, J. Q. A.: Adams, I, 546–47.

time Joseph Story, so soon thereafter appointed an Associate Justice, took the place of John Quincy Adams. Martin's address was technical and, from the record, appears to have been perfunctory.[1] On behalf of Peck, two thirds of the argument for the soundness of his title was devoted to the demonstration of the validity of that of Georgia. If that were sound, said Story, the Legislature had a right to sell the land, and a subsequent Legislature could not cancel the contract when executed. The Judiciary alone could declare what a law is or had been. Moreover, the National Constitution expressly forbade a State to pass an act impairing the obligation of contracts. To overthrow a law because it was corruptly enacted "would open a source of litigation which could never be closed." However, "the parties now before the court are innocent of the fraud, if any has been practiced. They were bona fide purchasers, for a valuable consideration, without notice of fraud. They cannot be affected by it."[2]

On March 16, 1810, Marshall delivered the opinion of the majority of the Supreme Court. In this he laid the second stone in the structure of American Constitutional law which bears his name. He held that the Georgia rescinding act was a violation of the contract clause of the Constitution, and in doing so asserted that courts cannot examine the motives

---

[1] *Memoirs, J. Q. A.*: Adams, i, 115.

On this occasion Martin was so drunk that the court adjourned to prevent him from completing his argument. (See *Md. Hist. Soc. Fund-Pub. No. 24*, 35.) This was the first time that drink seems to have affected him in the discharge of his professional duties. (See *supra*, footnote to 185–86.)

[2] 6 Cranch, 123.

that induce legislators to pass a law. In arriving at these profoundly important conclusions his reasoning was as follows:

Did the Georgia sale act of 1795 violate the Constitution of that State? An act of a legislature was not to be set aside "lightly" on "vague conjecture" or "slight implication." There was no ground for asserting that the Georgia Legislature transcended its constitutional powers in passing the sale act.[1] Had the corruption of the Legislature destroyed the title of Peck, an innocent purchaser? It was, cautiously said Marshall, doubtful "how far the validity of a law depends upon the motives of its framers," particularly when the act challenged authorized a contract that was executed according to the terms of it. Even if such legislation could be set aside on the ground of fraud in the enactment of it, to what extent must the impurity go?

"Must it be direct corruption, or would interest or undue influence of any kind be sufficient? Must the vitiating cause operate on a majority, or on what number of the members? Would the act be null, whatever might be the wish of the nation, or would its obligation or nullity depend upon the public sentiment?"

The State of Georgia did not bring this action; nor, "by this count" of the complaint, did it appear that the State was dissatisfied. On the face of the pleadings a purchaser of Georgia land declares that the seller had no title because "some of the members of the legislature were induced to vote in favor

[1] 6 Cranch, 128-29.

of the law, which constituted the contract [with the original grantees], by being promised an interest in it, and that therefore the act is a mere nullity." A tribunal "sitting as a court of law" cannot decide, in a suit between private parties, that the law of a State "is a nullity in consequence of the impure motives which influenced certain members of the legislature which passed the law." [1] Conceding, for the sake of argument, that "the original transaction was infected with fraud," the purchasers from the land companies were innocent according to the records before the court. Yet, if the rescinding act were valid, it "annihilated their rights. . . The legislature of Georgia was a party to this transaction; and for a party to pronounce its own deed invalid" was an assertion "not often heard in courts of justice." It was true, as urged, that "the real party . . are the people"; but they can act only through agents whose "acts must be considered as the acts of the people." Should these agents prove unfaithful, the people can choose others to undo the nefarious work, "if their contracts be examinable" by legislation. [2]

Admit that the State "might claim to itself the power of judging in its own case, yet there are certain great principles of justice . . that ought not to be entirely disregarded." Thus, at first, Marshall rested his opinion on elementary "principles of justice," rather than on the Constitution. These "principles" required that an innocent purchaser should not suffer. "If there be any concealed defect, arising from the conduct of those who had held the

[1] 6 Cranch, 130–31. [2] *Ib*. 132–33.

property long before he acquired it, of which he had
no notice, that concealed defect cannot be set up
against him. He has paid his money for a title good
at law; he is innocent, whatever may be the guilt of
others, and equity will not subject him to the penalties attached to that guilt. All titles would be insecure, and the intercourse between man and man
would be very seriously obstructed, if this principle
be overturned." The John Marshall who sat in the
Virginia Legislature [1] is speaking now.

Even if the Legislature could throw aside all "rules
of property," still the rescinding act is "supported
by its power alone, and the same power may divest
any other individual of his lands, if it shall be the
will of the legislature so to exert it." To make this
perfectly clear, Marshall defined the theory relied
upon by the opponents of the Yazoo fraud — "The
principle is this: that a legislature may, by its own
act, divest the vested estate of any man whatever,
for reasons which shall, by itself, be deemed sufficient." [2]

Supposing that the Georgia sale act had been procured by fraud; nevertheless, "the grant, when issued,
conveyed an estate in fee-simple to the grantee,
clothed with all the solemnities which law can bestow. This estate was transferable; and those who
purchased parts of it were not stained by that guilt
which infected the original transaction." They could
not, therefore, be made to suffer for the wrong of
another.

Any legislature can, of course, repeal the acts of a

[1] See vol. i, 202, of this work.   [2] 6 Cranch, 133–34.

preceding one, and no legislature can limit the powers of its successor. "But, if an act be done under a law, a succeeding legislature cannot undo it. The past cannot be recalled by the most absolute power." The purchase of estates from the land companies was, by virtue of law, "a fact, and cannot cease to be a fact," even if the State should deny that it was a fact.

"When, then, a law is in its nature a contract, where absolute rights have vested under that contract, a repeal of the law cannot divest those rights." If it can, such a power is "applicable to the case of every individual in the community." Regardless of written constitutions, the "nature of society and of government" prescribes "limits to the legislative power." But "where are they to be found, if the property of an individual, fairly and honestly acquired, may be seized without compensation?" Again Marshall founds his reasoning, not on the Constitution, but on fundamental principles. At last, however, he arrives at the Constitution.

Georgia was not a single sovereign power, but "a part of a large empire, . . a member of the American Union; and that Union has a constitution . . which imposes limits to the legislatures of the several states, which none claim a right to pass." Had the Legislature of Georgia overstepped those limits? "Is a grant a contract?" The answer to that depended upon the definition of a contract. On this decisive point Marshall cited Blackstone: "A contract executed . . differs in nothing from a grant." This was the exact case presented by the Georgia sale act and the fulfillment, by the purchasers, of the conditions of it. "A party is, therefore, always estopped by his own grant," one obligation of which is that he shall never attempt "to re-assert that right" thus disposed of.

By this reasoning Marshall finally came to the conclusion that the Constitution plainly covered the case. That instrument did not distinguish between grants by individuals and those by States. If a State could not pass a law impairing the obligation of contracts between private persons, neither could it invalidate a contract made by itself.

Indeed, as everybody knew, said Marshall, "the framers of the constitution viewed, with some apprehension, the violent acts which might grow out of the feelings of the moment; and that the people of the United States, in adopting that instrument, have manifested a determination to shield themselves and their property from the effects of those sudden and strong passions to which men are exposed." Therefore, it was provided in America's fundamental law that "no state shall pass any bill of attainder, ex post facto law, or law impairing the obligation of contracts." [1]

Such limitations, declared Marshall, constitute a bill of rights for the people of each State. Would any one pretend to say that a State might enact an *ex post facto* law or pass a bill of attainder? Certainly not! How then could anybody pretend that a State could by legislation annul a contract?

Thus far the opinion of the court was unanimous. [2]

[1] 6 Cranch, 137–38.   [2] *Ib.* 139.

As to the Indian title, Justice Johnson dissented. On the want of power of the Georgia Legislature to annul the sale act of 1795, the Republican Associate. Justice was, however, even more emphatic than the soft-spoken Federalist Chief Justice. But he ended by a rebuke which, if justified, and if the case had not been so important and the situation so critical, probably would have required the peremptory dismissal of the appeal and the disbarment of counsel appearing in the cause. Justice Johnson intimated — all but formally charged — that the case was collusive.

"I have been very unwilling," he said, "to proceed to the decision of this cause at all. It appears to me to be[ar] strong evidence, upon the face of it, of being a mere feigned case. It is our duty to decide upon the rights but not upon the speculations of parties. My confidence, however, in the respectable gentlemen who have been engaged for the parties, had induced me to abandon my scruples, in the belief that they would never consent to impose a mere feigned case upon this court." [1]

One cannot patiently read these words. Far better had Justice William Johnson denounced Fletcher *vs*. Peck for what everybody believed it to be, and what it really was, or else had refrained from raising the question, than in these unctuous sentences to have shifted the responsibility upon the shoulders of the attorneys who appeared before the Supreme Bench. The conclusion seems inescapable that had not Jefferson, who placed Johnson on the

[1] 6 Cranch, 147–48.

Supreme Bench, and Jefferson's Secretary of State and political legatee, James Madison, ardently desired the disposition which Marshall made of the case, Justice Johnson would have placed on record a stronger statement of the nature of this litigation.

The fact that Marshall rendered an opinion, under the circumstances, is one of the firmest proofs of his greatness. As in Marbury *vs.* Madison, the supremacy of the National Judiciary had to be asserted or its inferiority conceded, so in Fletcher *vs.* Peck, it was necessary that the Nation's highest court should plainly lay down the law of public contract, notify every State of its place in the American system, and announce the limitations which the National Constitution places upon each State.

Failure to do this would have been to sanction Georgia's rescinding act, to encourage other States to take similar action, and to render insecure and litigious numberless titles acquired innocently and in good faith, and multitudes of contracts entered into in the belief that they were binding. A weaker man than John Marshall, and one less wise and courageous, would have dismissed the appeal or decided the case on technical points.

Marshall's opinion did more than affect the controversy in Congress over the Yazoo lands. It announced fundamental principles for the guidance of the States and the stabilizing of American business.[1]

[1] At the risk of iteration, let it again be stated that, in Fletcher *vs.* Peck, Marshall declared that a grant by a State, accepted by the grantees, is a contract; that the State cannot annul this contract, because the State is governed by the National Constitution which forbids any State to pass any law "impairing the obligation of contracts";

It increased the confidence in him of the conservative elements and of all Nationalists. But, for the
same reason, it deepened the public distrust of him
and the popular hostility toward him.

Although Marshall's opinion gave steadiness to
commercial intercourse at a time when it was sadly
needed, checked for the moment a flood of contract-
breaking laws, and asserted the supremacy of Nationalism over Localism, it also strengthened many
previous speculations that were at least doubtful
and some that were corrupt.[1] Moreover, it furnished
the basis for questionable public grants in the future.
Yet the good effects of it fairly outweighed the bad.
Also it taught the people to be careful in the choice
of their representatives in all legislative bodies; if
citizens will not select honest and able men as their
public agents, they must suffer the consequences of
their indifference to their own affairs.

Whatever may be thought of other aspects of this
case, it must be conceded that Marshall could not
have disobeyed the plain command of the Constitution which forbids any State to impair the obligation of contracts. That the Georgia Legislature was
guilty of such violation even Jefferson's appointee,
Justice Johnson, declared more emphatically than

that even if the contract clause were not in the Constitution, fundamental principles of society protect vested rights; and that the courts
cannot inquire into the motives of legislators no matter how corrupt
those motives may be.

[1] For the first two decades of the National Government land frauds
were general. See, for example, letter of Governor Harrison of Indiana, Jan. 19, 1802, *Am. State Papers, Public Lands*, I, 123; report of
Michael Leib, Feb. 14, 1804, *ib.* 189; and letter of Amos Stoddard,
Jan. 10, 1804, *ib.* 193–94.

did Marshall himself. If Johnson had asserted that
a legislative grant, accepted by the grantee, was not
a contract, Marshall's opinion would have been
fatally wounded.

It had now been Marshall's fate to deliver opinions
in three cases [1] which helped to assure his future
fame, but which, at the moment, were highly unwelcome to the people. Throughout the country,
at the end of the first decade of the nineteenth century, a more unpopular person could not have been
found than that wise, brave, gentle man, the Chief
Justice of the United States.

Marshall's opinion and the decision of the court
had no practical effect whatever, so far as the legal
result of it was concerned, but it had some influence in the settlement of the controversy by Congress. The Eleventh Congress was in session when
Fletcher *vs.* Peck was decided, and the New England
Yazoo claimants immediately presented another petition for relief. Soon after Marshall's opinion was
published, Randolph moved that the New England
memorial be referred to the Committee of Claims
with instructions to report to the House. The matter, he said, must not go by default. He wanted
nothing "done, directly or indirectly, by any act of
commission or omission, that should give any the
slightest degree of countenance to that claim."

Randolph thus brought Marshall's opinion before
the House: "A judicial decision, of no small importance, had, during the present session of Congress,
taken place in relation to that subject." To let the

[1] Marbury *vs.* Madison, the Burr trial, and Fletcher *vs.* Peck.

business rest, particularly at this time, "would wear the appearance abroad of acquiescence [by the House] in that judicial decision." The Yazoo claimants must not be allowed to profit in this way by the action of the Supreme Court as they would surely do if not prevented, since "never has a claim been pressed upon the public with such pertinacity, with such art, with such audacity." [1]

George M. Troup of Georgia, slender, handsome, fair-haired,[2] then thirty years old and possessing all the fiery aggressiveness of youth, sprang to his feet to add his reproof of Marshall and the Supreme Court. He declared that the opinion of the Chief Justice, in Fletcher *vs.* Peck, was a pronouncement "which the mind of every man attached to Republican principles must revolt at." [3]

Because the session was closing and from pressure of business, Randolph withdrew his motion to refer the memorial to the Committee, and offered another: "That the prayer of the petition of the New England Mississippi Land Company is unreasonable, unjust, and ought not to be granted." This, if passed, would amount to a condemnation by the House of the decision of the Supreme Court of the United States. All Federalists and conservative Republicans combined to defeat it, and the resolution was lost by a vote of 46 yeas to 54 nays.[4]

But Troup would not yield. On December 17 he insisted that the National Government should resist by force of arms the judgment of the Supreme

---

[1] *Annals*, 11th Cong. 2d Sess. 1881.
[2] Harden: *Life of George M. Troup*, 9.
[3] *Annals*, 11th Cong. 2d Sess. 1882.   [4] *Ib.*

Court. The title to the lands was in the United States, he said, yet the court had decided it to be in the Yazoo claimants. "This decision must either be acquiesced in or resisted by the United States. . . If the Government . . would not submit to this decision, . . what course could be taken but to employ the whole military force . . to eject all persons not claiming under the authority of the United States?". Should those "in whose behalf" Marshall's opinion was rendered, take possession, either the National Government must "remove them by . . military power, or tamely acquiesce in the lawless aggression." [1]

But Marshall and the Supreme Court were to be attacked still more openly and violently. Strengthened by the decision in Fletcher *vs.* Peck, the Yazoo claimants pressed Congress harder than ever for payment. On January 20, 1813, a bill from the Senate providing for the payment of the claims came up for consideration in the House.

Troup instantly took the floor, moved its rejection and delivered such an excoriation of the Supreme Court as never before was or has since been heard in Congress. He began by reciting the details of the "hideous corruption." Such legislation was void *ab initio.* The original speculators had made fortunes out of the deal, and now Congress was asked to make the fortunes of the second-hand speculators. For years the House had, most righteously, repelled their audacious assaults; but now they had devised a new weapon of attack.

[1] *Annals,* 11th Cong. 3d Sess. 415.

They had secured the assistance of the Judiciary. "Two of the speculators combined and made up a fictitious case, a feigned issue for the decision of the Supreme Court," asserted Troup. "They presented precisely those points for the decision of the Court which they wished the Court to decide, and the Court did actually decide them as the speculators themselves would have decided them if they had been in the place of the Supreme Court.

"The first point was, whether the Legislature of Georgia had the *power* to sell the territory.

"Yes, said the Judges, they had.

"Whether by the Yazoo act an estate did vest in the original grantees?

"Yes, said the Judges, it did.

"Whether it was competent to any subsequent Legislature to set aside the act on the ground of fraud and corruption?

"No, said the Judges, it was not. . . No matter, say the Judges, what the nature or extent of the corruption, . . be it ever so nefarious, it could not be set aside. . .

"The [legal] maxim that third purchasers without notice shall not be affected by the fraud of the original parties" had, declared Troup, been wielded by the Judges for the benefit of the speculators and to the ruin of the country.

"Thus, sir, by a maxim of English law are the rights and liberties of the people of this country to be corruptly bartered by their Representatives.

"It is this decision of the Judges which has been made the basis of the bill on your table — a decision shocking to every free Government, sapping the foundations of all your constitutions, and annihilating at a breath the best hope of man.

"Yes, sir," exclaimed the deeply stirred and sincerely angered Georgian, "it is proclaimed by the Judges, and is now to be sanctioned by the Legislature, that the Representatives of the people may corruptly betray the people, may corruptly barter their rights and those of their posterity, and the people are wholly without any kind of remedy whatsoever.

"It is this monstrous and abhorrent doctrine which must startle every man in the nation, that you ought promptly to discountenance and condemn."

In such fashion the enraged Troup ran on; and he expressed the sentiments of the vast majority of the inhabitants of the United States. The longer the Georgia champion of popular justice and the rights of the States talked, the more unrestrained became his sentiments and his expression of them: "If, Mr. Speaker, the arch-fiend had in . . his hatred to mankind resolved the destruction of republican government on earth, he would have issued a decree like that of the judges" — the opinion of John Marshall in Fletcher *vs.* Peck. "Why . . do the judges who passed this decision live and live unpunished? . . The foundations of the Republic are shaken and the judges sleep in tranquillity at home. . . The question . . had been so often discussed" that it was "well understood by every man in the nation." Troup prophesied, therefore, that "no party in this country, however deeply seated in power, can long survive the adoption of this measure." [1]

[1] *Annals*, 12th Cong. 2d Sess. 856–59.

But the Federalist-Jeffersonian Yazoo coalition held firm and Troup's motion to reject the Senate Yazoo bill was lost by a vote of 55 to 59.[1] The relief bill was delayed, however, and the claimants were compelled to nurse their eighteen-year-old disappointment until another session of Congress convened.

The following year the bill to settle the Yazoo claims was again introduced in the Senate and passed by that body without opposition. On February 28, 1814, the measure reached the House.[2] On the second reading of it, Troup despairingly moved that the bill be rejected. The intrepid and resourceful John Randolph had been beaten in the preceding Congressional election, the House no longer echoed with his fearless voice, and his dominant personality no longer inspired his followers or terrified his enemies. Troup could not bend the mighty bow that Randolph had left behind and that he alone could draw. But the dauntless Georgian did his best. Once more he went over the items of this "circle of fraud," as he branded it. Success of the "plunderers" now depended on the affirmation by Congress of Marshall's opinion, which, said Troup, "overturns Republican Government. You cannot, you dare not, sanctify this doctrine." If you do so, then "to talk of the rights of the people after this is insult and mockery."[3]

Long did Troup argue and denounce. He could not keep his eager fingers from the throat of John Marshall and the Supreme Court. "The case of

---

[1] *Annals*, 12th Cong. 2d Sess. 860.
[2] *Annals*, 13th Cong. 2d Sess. 1697.   [3] *Ib.* 1840–42.

Fletcher and Peck was a decision of a feigned issue, made up between two speculators, to decide certain points, in the decision of which they were interested. . . Whenever it is conceded that it is competent to the Supreme Court, in a case between A and B, to take from the United States fifty [*sic*] millions of acres of land, it will be time for the Government to make a voluntary surrender of the public property to whosoever will have it. . . Sir, I am tired and disgusted with this subject." [1]

Robert Wright of Maryland urged the passage of the bill. "He . . dwelt . . on the sanctity of the title of the present claimants under the decision of the Supreme Court, against whose awards he hoped never to see the bayonet employed. He feared not to advocate this bill on account of the clamor against it. Let justice be done though the heavens fall." [2]

Weaker and ever weaker grew the assaults of the opponents against Marshall's opinion and the bill to reimburse the Yazoo claimants. In every case the speakers supported or resisted the bill solely according to the influence of their constituents. Considerations of local politics, and not devotion to the Constitution or abhorrence of fraud, moved the Representatives. The House voted, 56 to 92, against Troup's motion to reject the bill. [3] Finally the measure was referred to a select committee, with instructions to report. [4] Almost immediately this committee reported in favor of the Yazoo claimants. [5] No time was lost and the friends of the bill now crowded

---

[1] *Annals*, 13th Cong. 2d Sess. 1848. [2] *Ib.* 1850.
[3] *Ib.* 1855.   [4] *Ib.* 1858–59.   [5] *Ib.* 1873–75.

the measure to a vote with all the aggressive confidence of an assured majority. By a vote of 84 yeas to 76 nays, five millions of dollars were appropriated for reimbursement to the purchasers of the Yazoo lands.[1]

Daniel Webster, who was serving his first term in the House and supported the bill, thus describes the situation at the time of its passage: "The Yazoo bill is through, passed by eight majority. It excited a great deal of feeling. All the Federalists supported the bill, and some of the Democrats. Georgians, and some Virginians and Carolinians, opposed it with great heat. . . Our feeling was to get the Democratic support of it." [2]

Thus John Marshall's great opinion was influential in securing from Congress the settlement of the claims of numerous innocent investors who had, in good faith, purchased from a band of legislative corruptionists. Of infinitely more importance, however, is the fact that Marshall's words asserted the power of the Supreme Court of the United States to annul State laws passed in violation of the National Constitution, and that throughout the Republic a fundamental principle of the law of public contract was established.

[1] *Annals*, 13th Cong. 2d Sess. 1925; see also Sess. I, chap. 39, March 31, 1814, *U.S. Statutes at Large*, III, 117.

[2] Daniel to Ezekiel Webster, March 28, 1814, *Private Correspondence of Daniel Webster:* Webster, 244.

END OF VOLUME III

APPENDIX

APPENDIX A

APPLICATIONS from different persons suffering prosecution under the act usually called the Sedition act, claimed my early attention to that instrument. our country has thought proper to distribute the powers of it's government among three equal & independent authorities, constituting each a check on one or both of the others, in all attempts to impair it's constitution. to make each an effectual check, it must have a right in cases which arise within the line of it's proper functions, where, equally with the others, it acts in the last resort & without appeal, to decide on the validity of an act according to it's own judgment, & uncontrouled by the opinions of any other department. we have accordingly, in more than one instance, seen the opinions of different departments in opposition to each other, & no ill ensue. the constitution moreover, as a further security for itself, against violation even by a concurrence of all the departments, has provided for it's own reintegration by a change of the persons exercising the functions of those department. Succeeding functionaries have the same right to judge of the conformity or non-conformity of an act with the constitution, as their predecessors who past it. for if it be against that instrument it is a perpetual nullity. uniform decisions indeed, sanctioned by successive functionaries, by the public voice, and by repeated elections would so strengthen a construction as to render highly responsible a departure from it. On my accession to the administration, reclamations against the Sedition act were laid before me by individual citizens, claiming the protection of the constitution against the Sedition act. called on by the position in which the nation had placed me, to exercise in their behalf my free & independent judgment, I took the act into consideration, compared it with the constitution, viewed it under every aspect of which I thought it susceptible, and gave to it all the attention which the magnitude of the case demanded. on mature deliberation, in the presence of the nation, and under the tie of the solemn oath which binds

[1] See 51–53 of this volume.

me to them & to my duty, I do declare that I hold that act to be in palpable & unqualified contradiction to the constitution. considering it then as a nullity, I have relieved from oppression under it those of my fellow-citizens who were within the reach of the functions confided to me. in recalling our footsteps within the limits of the Constitution, I have been actuated by a zealous devotion to that instrument. it is the ligament which binds us into one nation. It is, to the national government, the law of it's existence, with which it began, and with which it is to end. infractions of it may sometimes be committed from inadvertence, sometimes from the panic, or passions of a moment. to correct these with good faith, as soon as discovered, will be an assurance to the states that, far from meaning to impair that sacred charter of it's authorities, the General government views it as the principle of it's own life.[1]

[1] Jefferson MSS. Lib. Cong.

APPENDIX B

LETTER OF JOHN TAYLOR "OF CAROLINE" TO JOHN BRECKEN-
RIDGE CONTAINING ARGUMENTS FOR THE REPEAL OF THE
FEDERALIST NATIONAL JUDICIARY ACT OF 1801[1]

VIRGINIA — CAROLINE — Dec[r] 22[d] 1801

DEAR SIR

An absence from home, when your letter arrived, has been
the cause which delayed this answer.

I confess that I have not abstracted myself from the political
world, but I must at the same time acknowledge, that this kind
of world, of which I am a member, is quite distinct from that
in which your country has placed you. Mine is a sort of metaphysical world, over which the plastick power of the imagination is unlimited — yours, being only physical, cannot be
modulated by fancy. The ways of mine are smooth & soft;
of yours, rugged & thorny. And a most prosperous traveller
into the political world which I inhabit, generally becomes
unfortunate if he wanders into the region of which you are
now a resident. Yet, as a solicitation for the continuance of
your correspondence, I will venture upon a short excursion
out of my own atmosphere, in relation to the subject you
state.

By way of bringing the point into plain view, I will suppose
some cases. Suppose a congress and president should conspire
to erect five times as many courts & judges, as were made by
the last law, meerly for the sake of giving salaries to themselves
or their friends, and should annex to each office, a salary of
100,000 dollars. Or suppose a president in order to reward his
counsel on an impeachment, and the members of the senate who
voted for his acquittal, had used his influence with the legisla
ture to erect useless tribunals, paid by him in fees or bribes.
Or, lastly, suppose a long list of courts and judges to be established, without any ill intention, but meerly from want of intellect in the legislature, which from experience are found to be
useless, expensive and unpopular. Are all these evils originating either in fraud or error, remediless under the principles of
your constitution?

[1] See footnote to 58 of this volume.

The first question is, whether the *office* thus established, is to continue.

The second, whether the officer is to continue, after the office is abolished, as being unnecessary.

Congress are empowered "from *time to time* to ordain & establish inferior courts."

The law for establishing the present inferior courts, is a legislative construction, affirming that under this clause, congress may *abolish* as well as create these *judicial offices;* because it does expressly *abolish* the then existing inferior courts, for the purpose of making way for the present.

It is probable that this construction is correct, but it is equally pertinent to our object, whether it is or not. If it is, then the present inferior courts may be abolished, as constitutionally as the last; if it is not, then the law for abolishing the former courts, and establishing the present, was unconstitutional, and being so, is undoubtedly repealable.

Thus the only ground which the present inferior courts can take, is, that congress may from time to time, regulate, create or abolish such courts, as the public interest may dictate, because such is the very tenure under which they exist.

The second question is, whether the officer is to continue after the office is abolished, as being useless or pernicious.

The constitution declares "that the judge shall hold his *office* during good behavior." Could it mean, that he should hold this *office* after it was *abolished?* Could it mean that his tenure should be limited by behaving well in an office, which did not exist?

It must either have intended these absurdities, or admit of a construction which will avoid them. This construction obviously is, that the officer should hold that which he might hold, namely, an existing office, so long as he did that which he might do, namely, his duty in that office; and not that he should hold an office, which did not exist, or perform duties not sanctioned by law. If therefore congress can abolish the courts, as they did by the last law, the officer dies with his office, unless you allow the constitution to intend impossibilities as well as absurdities. A construction bottomed upon either, overthrows the benefits of language and intellect.

The article of the constitution under consideration closes with an idea, which strongly supports my construction.

The salary is to be paid "during their continuance in office."

This limitation of salary is perfectly clear and distinct. It literally excludes the idea of paying a salary, when the officer is not in office; and it is undeniably certain, that he cannot be in office, when there is no office. There must have been some other mode by which the officer should cease to be in office, than that of *bad behaviour*, because, if this had not been the case, the constitution would have directed "that the judges should hold their offices *and salaries* during good behaviour," instead of directing "that they should" hold the salaries during *their continuance* in office. This could only be an abolition of the office itself, by which the salary would cease with the office, tho' the judge might have conducted himself unexceptionably.

This construction certainly coincides with the public opinion, and the principles of the constitution. By neither is the idea for a moment tolerated, of maintaining burthensome sinecure offices, to enrich unfruitful individuals.

Nor is it incompatible with the "good behaviour" tenure, when its origin is considered. It was invented in England, to counteract the influence of the crown over the judges, and we have rushed into the principle with such precipitancy, in imitation of this our general prototype, as to have outstript monarchists, in our efforts to establish a judicial oligarchy; their judges being removable by a joint vote of Lords & commons, and ours by no similar or easy process.

The tenure however is evidently bottomed upon the idea of securing the honesty of Judges, whilst exercising the office, and not upon that of sustaining useless or pernicious offices, for the sake of Judges. The regulation of offices in England, and indeed of inferior offices in most or all countries, depends upon the legislature; it is a part of the detail of the government, which necessarily devolves upon it, and is beyond the foresight of a constitution, because it depends on variable circumstances. And in England, a regulation of the courts of justice, was never supposed to be a violation of the "good behaviour" tenure.

If this principle should disable congress from erecting tribunals which temporary circumstances might require, without entailing them upon the society after these circumstances by ceasing, had converted them in grievances, it would be used in a mode, contemplated neither in its original or duplicate.

Whether courts are erected by regard to the administration of justice, or with the purpose of rewarding a meritorious faction, the legislature may certainly abolish them without infringing the constitution, whenever they are not required by the administration of justice, or the merit of the faction is exploded, and their claim to reward disallowed.

With respect to going into the judiciary system farther at present, the length of this trespass forbids it, and perhaps all ideas tending towards the revision of our constitution would be superfluous, as I fear it is an object not now to be attained. All my hopes upon this question rest I confess with Mr: Jefferson, and yet I know not how far he leans towards the revision. But he will see & the people will feel, that his administration bears a distinct character, from that of his predecessor, and of course discover this shocking truth, that the nature of our government depends upon the complection of the president, and not upon the principles of the constitution. He will not leave historians to say "this was a good president, but like a good Roman Emperor he left the principles of the government unreformed, so that his country remained exposed to eternal repetitions of those oppressions after his death, which he had himself felt and healed during his life."

And yet my hopes are abated by some essays signed "Solon" published at Washington, and recommending amendments to the constitution. They are elegantly written, but meerly skim along the surface of the subject, without touching a radical idea. They seem to be suggested by the pernicious opinion, that the administration only has been chargeable with the defectiveness of our operating government heretofore. Who is the author of these pieces?

Nothing can exceed our exultation on account of the president's message, and the countenance of congress — nothing can exceed the depression of the monarchists. They deprecate political happiness — we hope for the president's aid to place it on a rock before he dies.

It would have given me great pleasure to have seen you'here, and I hope it may be still convenient for you to call. I close with your proposal to correspond, if the political wanderings of a man, almost in a state of vegitation, will be accepted for that interesting detail of real affairs, with which you propose occasionally to treat me. I am, with great regard, Dr Sir

Yr: mo: ob^t Sev^t

JOHN TAYLOR[1]

---

[1] Breckenridge MSS. Lib. Cong.

APPENDIX C

Holmes *vs.* Walton (November, 1779, New Jersey), before Chief Justice David Brearly. (See Austin Scott in *American Historical Review*, IV, 456 *et seq.*) If Marshall ever heard of this case, it was only because Paterson, who was Associate Justice with Marshall when the Supreme Court decided Marbury *vs.* Madison, was attorney-general in New Jersey at the time Holmes *vs.* Walton was decided. Both Brearly and William Paterson were members of the Constitutional Convention of 1787. (See Corwin, footnote to 41-42.)

Commonwealth *vs.* Caton (November, 1782, 4 Call, 5-21), a noted Virginia case. (See Tyler, I, 174-75.) The language of the court in this case is merely *obiter dicta;* but George Wythe and John Blair were on the Bench, and both of them were afterwards members of the Constitutional Convention. Blair was appointed by President Washington as one of the Associate Justices of the Supreme Court.

As to the much-talked-of Rhode Island case of Trevett *vs.* Weeden (September, 1786; see Arnold: *History of Rhode Island*, II, 525-27, Varnum's pamphlet, *Case of Trevett vs. Weeden*, and Chandler's *Criminal Trials*, II, 269-350), it is improbable that Marshall had any knowledge whatever of it. It arose in 1786 when the country was in chaos; no account of it appeared in the few newspapers that reached Virginia, and Varnum's description of the incident — for it can hardly be called a case — could scarcely have had any circulation outside of New England. It was referred to in the Constitutional Convention at Philadelphia in 1787, but the journals of that convention were kept secret until many years after Marbury *vs.* Madison was decided.

It is unlikely that the recently discussed case of Bayard *vs.* Singleton (North Carolina, November, 1787, 1 Martin, 48-51), ever reached Marshall's attention except by hearsay.

[1] See 118-19 of this volume.

The second Hayburn case (August, 1792, 2 Dallas, 409; and see *Annals*, 2d Cong. 2d Sess. 1319–22). For a full discussion of this important case see particularly Professor Max Farrand's analysis in the *American Historical Review* (XIII, 283–84), which is the only satisfactory treatment of it. See also Thayer: *Cases on Constitutional Law* (1, footnote to 105).

Kamper *vs.* Hawkins (November, 1793, 1 Va. Ca. 20 *et seq.*), a case which came directly under Marshall's observation.

Van Horne's Lessee *vs.* Dorrance (April, 1795, 2 Dallas, 304), in which Justice Paterson of the Supreme Court said all that Marshall repeated in Marbury *vs.* Madison upon the power of the Judiciary to declare legislation void.

Calder *vs.* Bull (August, 1798, 3 Dallas, 386–401), in which, however, the Court questioned its power to annul legislation. Cooper *vs.* Telfair (February, 1800, 4 Dallas, 14). These last two cases and the Hayburn Case had been decided by justices of the Supreme Court.

Whittington *vs.* Polk (Maryland, April, 1802, 1 Harris and Johnson, 236–52). Marshall surely was informed of this case by Chase who, as Chief Justice of Maryland, decided it. The report, however, was not published until 1821. (See McLaughlin: *The Courts, the Constitution, and Parties*, 20–23.) In his opinion in this case Justice Chase employed precisely the same reasoning used by Marshall in Marbury *vs.* Madison to show the power of courts to declare invalid legislative acts that violate the Constitution.

The old Court of Appeals, under the Articles of Confederation, denounced as unconstitutional the law that assigned circuit duties to the judges of that appellate tribunal; and this was cited by Thomas Morris of New York and by John Stanley of South Carolina in the judiciary debate of 1802.[1]

As to the statement of Chief Justice, later Governor Thomas Hutchinson of Massachusetts, in 1765, and the ancient British precedents, cited by Robert Ludlow Fowler in the *American Law Review* (XXIX, 711–25), it is positive that Marshall never had an intimation that any such pronouncements ever had been made.

Neither, in all likelihood, had Marshall known of the highly advertised case of Rutgers *vs.* Waddington, decided by a New York justice of the peace in 1784 (see *American Law Review*, XIX, 180), and the case of Bowman *vs.* Middleton (South Caro-

---

[1] See footnote 5 to p. 74 of this volume.

lina, May, 1792, 1 Bay, 252–55) which was not printed until 1809. (See McLaughlin, 25–26.) The same may be said of the North Carolina controversy, State vs. ——, decided in April, 1794 (1 Haywood, 28–40), and of Lindsay *et al vs.* Commissioners (South Carolina, October, 1796, 2 Bay, 38–62), the report of which was not printed until 1811.

For a scholarly treatment of the matter from an historical and legally professional point of view, see *Doctrine of Judicial Review* by Professor Edward S. Corwin of the Department of History and Politics, Princeton University; also *The Courts, the Constitution, and Parties,* by Professor Andrew C. McLaughlin of the Department of History, University of Chicago. The discussion by these scholars is thorough. All cases are critically examined, and they omit only the political exigency that forced Marshall's opinion in Marbury *vs.* Madison.

The student should also consult the paper of William M. Meigs, "The Relation of the Judiciary to the Constitution," in the *American Law Review* (xix, 175–203), and that of Frank E. Melvin, "The Judicial Bulwark of the Constitution," in the *American Political Science Review* (viii, 167–203).

Professor Charles A. Beard's *The Supreme Court and the Constitution* contains trustworthy information not readily accessible elsewhere, as well as sound comment upon the whole subject.

Judicial Power and Unconstitutional Legislation, by Brinton Coxe, although published in 1893, is still highly valuable. And *Power of Federal Judiciary over Legislation,* by J. Hampden Dougherty, will be profitable to the student.

Marbury *vs.* Madison is attacked ably, if petulantly, by Dean Trickett, "Judicial Nullification of Acts of Congress," in the *North American Review* (clxxxv, 848 *et seq.*), and also by James B. McDonough, "The Alleged Usurpation of Power by the Federal Courts," in the *American Law Review* (xlvi, 45–59). An ingenious and comparatively recent dissent from the theory of judicial supervision of legislation is the argument of Chief Justice Walter Clark of the Supreme Court of North Carolina, "Government by Judges." (See Senate Document No. 610, 63d Congress, 2d Session.)

With regard to the possible effect on American law of foreign assertions of the supremacy of the Judiciary, particularly that of France, the Address of James M. Beck of the New York Bar, before the Pennsylvania Bar Association on June 29, 1915, and reported in the Twenty-first Annual Report of that Association (222–51), is a careful and exhaustive study.

APPENDIX D

TEXT, AS GENERALLY ACCEPTED, OF THE CIPHER LETTER OF
AARON BURR TO JAMES WILKINSON, DATED JULY 29, 1806[1]

YOUR letter postmarked thirteenth May, is received. At
length I have obtained funds, and have actually commenced.
The Eastern detachments, from different points and under
different pretences, will rendezvous on the Ohio first of November. Everything internal and external favors our views. Naval
protection of England is secured. Truxtun is going to Jamaica
to arrange with the admiral on that station. It will meet us
at the Mississippi. England, a navy of the United States, are
ready to join, and final orders are given to my friends and followers. It will be a host of choice spirits. Wilkinson shall be
second to Burr only; Wilkinson shall dictate the rank and promotion of his officers. Burr will proceed westward first August,
never to return. With him goes his daughter; her husband will
follow in October, with a corps of worthies. Send forthwith an
intelligent and confidential friend with whom Burr may confer;
he shall return immediately with further interesting details;
this is essential to concert and harmony of movement. Send a
list of all persons known to Wilkinson west of the mountains
who could be useful, with a note delineating their characters.
By your messenger send me four or five commissions of your
officers, which you can borrow under any pretence you please;
they shall be returned faithfully. Already are orders given to
the contractor to forward six months' provisions to points
Wilkinson may name; this shall not be used until the last moment, and then under proper injunctions. Our object, my dear
friend, is brought to a point so long desired. Burr guarantees
the result with his life and honor, with the lives and honor and
the fortunes of hundreds, the best blood of our country. Burr's
plan of operation is to move down rapidly from the Falls, on
the fifteenth of November, with the first five hundred or a
thousand men, in light boats now constructing for that purpose;
to be at Natchez between the fifth and fifteenth of December,
there to meet you; there to determine whether it will be expedient in the first instance to seize on or pass by Baton Rouge.

[1] See 307–09, 352–55, of this volume.

On receipt of this send Burr an answer. Draw on Burr for all expenses, etc. The people of the country to which we are going are prepared to receive us; their agents, now with Burr, say that if we will protect their religion, and will not subject them to a foreign Power, that in three weeks all will be settled. The gods invite us to glory and fortune; it remains to be seen whether we deserve the boon. The bearer of this goes express to you. He is a man of inviolable honor and perfect discretion, formed to execute rather than project, capable of relating facts with fidelity, and incapable of relating them otherwise; he is thoroughly informed of the plans and intentions of Burr, and will disclose to you as far as you require, and no further. He has imbibed a reverence for your character, and may be embarrassed in your presence; put him at ease, and he will satisfy you.

APPENDIX E

WHO is Blennerhassett? A native of Ireland, a man of letters, fled from the storms of his own country to find quiet in ours. His history shows that war is not the natural element of his mind. If it had been, he never would have exchanged Ireland for America. So far is an army from furnishing the society natural and proper to Mr. Blennerhassett's character, that on his arrival in America, he retired even from the population of the Atlantic States, and sought quiet and solitude in the bosom of our Western forests.

But he carried with him taste and science and wealth; and lo, the desert smiled! Possessing himself of a beautiful island in the Ohio, he rears upon it a palace and decorates it with every romantic embellishment of fancy. A shrubbery, that Shenstone might have envied, blooms around him. Music, that might have charmed Calypso and her nymphs, is his. An extensive library spreads its treasures before him. A philosophical apparatus offers to him all the secrets and mysteries of nature. Peace, tranquillity, and innocence shed their mingled delights around him. And to crown the enchantment of the scene, a wife, who is said to be lovely even beyond her sex and graced with every accomplishment that can render it irresistible, had blessed him with her love and made him the father of several children. The evidence would convince you, that this is but a faint picture of the real life.

In the midst of all this peace, this innocent simplicity and this tranquillity, this feast of the mind, this pure banquet of the heart, the destroyer comes; he comes to change this paradise into a hell. Yet the flowers do not wither at his approach. No monitory shuddering through the bosom of their unfortunate possessor warns him of the ruin that is coming upon him. A stranger presents himself. Introduced to their civilities by the high rank which he had lately held in his country, he soon finds his way to their hearts, by the dignity and elegance of his demeanor, the light and beauty of his conversation and the seductive and fascinating power of his address.

[1] See 495–97 of this volume.

The conquest was not difficult. Innocence is ever simple and credulous. Conscious of no design itself, it suspects none in others. It wears no guard before its breast. Every door and portal and avenue of the heart is thrown open, and all who choose it enter. Such was the state of Eden when the serpent entered its bowers.

The prisoner, in a more engaging form, winding himself into the open and unpractised heart of the unfortunate Blenner-hassett, found but little difficulty in changing the native char-acter of that heart and the objects of its affection. By degrees he infuses into it the poison of his own ambition. He breathes into it the fire of his own courage; a daring and desperate thirst for glory; an ardour panting for great enterprises, for all the storm and bustle and hurricane of life.

In a short time the whole man is changed, and every object of his former delight is relinquished. No more he enjoys the tranquil scene; it has become flat and insipid to his taste. His books are abandoned. His retort and crucible are thrown aside. His shrubbery blooms and breathes its fragrance upon the air in vain; he likes it not. His ear no longer drinks the rich melody of music; it longs for the trumpet's clangor and the cannon's roar. Even the prattle of his babes, once so sweet, no longer affects him; and the angel smile of his wife, which hitherto touched his bosom with ecstasy so unspeakable, is now unseen and unfelt.

Greater objects have taken possession of his soul. His imagi-nation has been dazzled by visions of diadems, of stars and garters and titles of nobility. He has been taught to burn with restless emulation at the names of great heroes and conquerors. His enchanted island is destined soon to relapse into a wilder-ness; and in a few months we find the beautiful and tender partner of his bosom, whom he lately permitted not the winds of summer to visit too roughly, we find her shivering at mid-night, on the winter banks of the Ohio and mingling her tears with the torrents, that froze as they fell.

Yet this unfortunate man, thus deluded from his interest and his happiness, thus seduced from the paths of innocence and peace, thus confounded in the toils that were deliberately spread for him and overwhelmed by the mastering spirit and genius of another — this man, thus ruined and undone and made to play a subordinate part in this grand drama of guilt and treason, this man is to be called the principal offender.

while *he*, by whom he was thus plunged in misery, is compara, tively innocent, a mere accessory! Is this reason? Is it law? Is it humanity? Sir, neither the human heart nor the human understanding will bear a perversion so monstrous and absurd! So shocking to the soul! So revolting to reason! Let Aaron Burr then not shrink from the high destination which he has courted, and having already ruined Blennerhassett in fortune, character and happiness forever, let him not attempt to finish the tragedy by thrusting that ill-fated man between himself and punishment.[1]

[1] *Burr Trials*, II, 96–98.

APPENDIX F

ESSENTIAL PART OF MARSHALL'S OPINION ON CONSTRUCTIVE
TREASON DELIVERED AT THE TRIAL OF AARON BURR, ON
MONDAY, AUGUST 31, 1807[1]

THE place in which a crime was committed is essential to an indictment, were it only to shew the jurisdiction of the court. It is also essential for the purpose of enabling the prisoner to make his defence. . . This necessity is rendered the stronger by the constitutional provision that the offender "shall be tried in the state and district wherein the crime shall have been committed," and by the act of congress which requires that twelve petty jurors at least shall be summoned from the county where the offence was committed.

A description of the particular manner in which the war was levied seems also essential to enable the accused to make his defence. The law does not expect a man to be prepared to defend every act of his life which may be suddenly and without notice alleged against him. In common justice the particular fact with which he is charged ought to be stated, and stated in such a manner as to afford a reasonable certainty of the nature of the accusation and the circumstances which will be adduced against him.

.   .   .   .

Treason can only be established by the proof of overt acts; and . . those overt acts only which are changed in the indictment can be given in evidence, unless perhaps as corroborative testimony after the overt acts are proved. That clause in the constitution too which says that in all criminal prosecutions the accused shall enjoy the right "to be informed of the nature and cause of the accusation" is considered as having a direct bearing on this point. It secures to him such information as will enable him to prepare for his defence.

It seems then to be perfectly clear that it would not be sufficient for an indictment to allege generally that the accused had levied war against the United States. The charge must be more particularly specified by laying what is termed an overt act of levying war. . .

[1] See *supra*, chap IX.

If it be necessary to specify the charge in the indictment, it would seem to follow, irresistibly, that the charge must be proved as laid. . . Might it be otherwise, the charge of an overt act would be a mischief instead of an advantage to the accused. It would lead him from the true cause and nature of the accusation instead of informing him respecting it.

But it is contended on the part of the prosecution that, although the accused had never been with the party which assembled at Blennerhassett's island, and was, at the time, at a great distance, and in a different state, he was yet legally present, and therefore may properly be charged in the indictment as being present in fact.

It is therefore necessary to inquire whether in this case the doctrine of constructive presence can apply.

It is conceived by the court to be possible that a person may be concerned in a treasonable conspiracy and yet be legally, as well as actually absent while some one act of the treason is perpetrated. If a rebellion should be so extensive as to spread through every state in the union, it will scarcely be contended that every individual concerned in it is legally present at every overt act committed in the course of that rebellion. It would be a very violent presumption indeed, . . to presume that even the chief of the rebel army was legally present at every such overt act.

If the main rebel army, with the chief at its head, should be prosecuting war at one extremity of our territory, say in New-Hampshire — if this chief should be there captured and sent to the other extremity for the purpose of trial — if his indictment instead of alleging an overt act, which was true in point of fact, should allege that he had assembled some small party, which in truth he had not seen, and had levied war by engaging in a skirmish in Georgia at a time when in reality he was fighting a battle in New-Hampshire — if such evidence would support such an indictment by the fiction that he was legally present though really absent, all would ask to what purpose are those provisions in the constitution, which direct the place of trial and ordain that the accused shall be informed of the nature and cause of the accusation?

But that a man may be legally absent, who has counselled or procured a treasonable act, is proved by all those books which treat upon the subject; and which concur in declaring that such a person is a principal traitor, not because he was legally present, but because in treason all are principals. Yet the indictment, speaking upon general principles, would charge him according to the truth of the case. . .

If the conspirator had done nothing which amounted to levying of war, and if by our constitution the doctrine that an accessory becomes a principal be not adopted, in consequence of which the conspirator could not be condemned under an indictment stating the truth of the case, it would be going very far to say that this defect, if it be termed one, may be cured by an indictment stating the case untruly.

. . . .

In point of law then, the man, who incites, aids, or procures a treasonable act, is not merely in consequence of that incitement, aid or procurement, legally present when that act is committed.

If it do not result, from the nature of the crime, that all who are concerned in it are legally present at every overt act, then each case depends upon its own circumstances; and to judge how far the circumstances of any case can make him legally present, who is in fact absent, the doctrine of constructive presence must be examined.

. . . .

The whole treason laid in this indictment is the levying of war in Blennerhassett's island; and the whole question to which the inquiry of the court is now directed is whether the prisoner was legally present at that fact.

I say this is the whole question; because the prisoner can only be convicted on the overt act laid in the indictment. With respect to this prosecution, it is as if no other overt act existed.

If other overt acts can be inquired into, it is for the sole purpose of proving the particular fact charged. It is as evidence of the crime consisting of this particular fact, not as establishing the general crime by a distinct fact.

The counsel for the prosecution have charged those engaged in the defence with considering the overt act as the treason, whereas it ought to be considered solely as the evidence of the treason; but the counsel for the prosecution seem themselves not to have sufficiently adverted to this clear principle; that though the overt act may not be itself the treason, it is the sole act of that treason which can produce conviction. It is the sole point in issue between the parties. And the only division of that point, if the expression be allowed, which the court is now examining, is the constructive presence of the prisoner at the fact charged. . .

Had the prisoner set out with the party from Beaver for Blennerhassett's island, or perhaps had he set out for that place, though not from Beaver, and had arrived in the island, he would have been present at the fact. Had he not arrived in the island, but had taken a position near enough to coöperate with those on the island, to assist them in any act of hostility, or to aid them if attacked, the question whether he was constructively present would be a question compounded of law and fact, which would be decided by the jury, with the aid of the court, so far as respected the law. In this case the accused would have been of the particular party assembled on the island, and would have been associated with them in the particular act of levying war said to have been committed on the island.

But if he was not with the party at any time before they reached the island — if he did not join them there, or intend to join them there — if his personal coöperation in the general plan was to be afforded elsewhere, at a great distance, in a different state — if the overt acts of treason to be performed by him were to be distinct overt acts — then he was not of the particular party assembled at Blennerhassett's island, and was not constructively present, aiding and assisting in the particular act which was there committed.

The testimony on this point, so far as it has been delivered, is not equivocal. There is not only no evidence that the accused was of the particular party which assembled on Blennerhassett's island; but the whole evidence shows he was not of that party.

In felony then, admitting the crime to have been completed on the island, and to have been advised, procured, or commanded by the accused, he would have been incontestably an accessory and not a principal.

But in treason, it is said, the law is otherwise, because the theatre of action is more extensive.

The reasoning applies in England as strongly as in the United States. While in '15 and '45 the family of Stuart sought to regain the crown they had forfeited, the struggle was for the whole kingdom; yet no man was ever considered as legally present at one place, when actually at another; or as aiding in one transaction, while actually employed in another.

With the perfect knowledge that the whole nation may be

the theatre of action, the English books unite in declaring that he, who counsels, procures or aids treason, is guilty accessorially and solely in virtue of the common law principle, that what will make a man an accessory in felony makes him a principal in treason. So far from considering a man as constructively present at every overt act of the general treason in which he may have been concerned, the whole doctrine of the books limits the proof against him to those particular overt acts of levying war with which he is charged.

What would be the effect of a different doctrine? Clearly that which has been stated. If a person levying war in Kentucky, may be said to be constructively present and assembled with a party carrying on war in Virginia at a great distance from him, then he is present at every overt act performed anywhere. He may be tried in any state on the continent, where any overt act has been committed. He may be proved to be guilty of an overt act laid in the indictment in which he had no personal participation, by proving that he advised it, or that he committed other acts.

This is, perhaps, too extravagant to be in terms maintained. Certainly it cannot be supported by the doctrines of the English law.

. . . .

In conformity with principle and with authority then, the prisoner at the bar was neither legally nor actually present at Blennerhassett's island; and the court is strongly inclined to the opinion that without proving an actual or legal presence by two witnesses, the overt act laid in this indictment cannot be proved.

But this opinion is controverted on two grounds.

The first is, that the indictment does not charge the prisoner to have been present.

The second, that although he was absent, yet if he caused the assemblage, he may be indicted as being present, and convicted on evidence that he caused the treasonable act.

The first position is to be decided by the indictment itself. . . The court understands it to be directly charged that the prisoner did assemble with the multitude and did march with them. . . The charges of this special indictment therefore must be proved as laid, and no evidence which proves the crime in a form substantially different can be received. . .

But suppose the law to be as is contended by the counsel for the United States. Suppose an indictment, charging an individual with personally assembling among others and thus levying war, may be satisfied with the proof that he caused the assemblage. What effect will this law have upon this case?

The guilt of the accused, if there be any guilt, does not consist in the assemblage; for he was not a member of it. The simple fact of assemblage no more affects one absent man than another.

His guilt then consists in procuring the assemblage, and upon this fact depends his criminality. The proof relative to the character of an assemblage must be the same whether a man be present or absent. In general, to charge any individual with the guilt of an assemblage, the fact of his presence must be proved: it constitutes an essential part of the overt act.

If then the procurement be substituted in the place of presence, does it not also constitute an essential part of the overt act? must it not also be proved? must it not be proved in the same manner that presence must be proved?

If in one case the presence of the individual make the guilt of the assemblage his guilt, and in the other case the procurement by the individual make the guilt of the assemblage his guilt, then presence and procurement are equally component parts of the overt act, and equally require two witnesses.

Collateral points may, say the books, be proved according to the course of the common law; but is this a collateral point? Is the fact, without which the accused does not participate in the guilt of the assemblage if it were guilty, a collateral point? This cannot be.

The presence of the party, where presence is necessary, being a part of the overt act must be positively proved by two witnesses. No presumptive evidence, no facts from which presence may be conjectured or inferred will satisfy the constitution and the law.

If procurement take the place of presence and become part of the overt act, then no presumptive evidence, no facts from which the procurement may be conjected or inferred, can satisfy the constitution and the law.

The mind is not to be led to the conclusion that the individual was present by a train of conjectures, of inferences or of reasoning; the fact must be proved by two witnesses.

Neither, where procurement supplies the want of presence, is the mind to be conducted to the conclusion that the accused procured the assembly, by a train of conjectures of inferences or of reasoning; the fact itself must be proved by two witnesses, and must have been committed within the district.

If it be said that the advising or procurement of treason is a secret transaction, which can scarcely ever be proved in the manner required by this opinion, the answer which will readily suggest itself is, that the difficulty of proving a fact will not justify conviction without proof. Certainly it will not justify conviction without a direct and positive witness in a case where the constitution requires two.

The more correct inference from this circumstance would seem to be, that the advising of the fact is not within the constitutional definition of the crime. To advise or procure a treason is in the nature of conspiring or plotting treason, which is not treason in itself. . .

The 8th amendment to the constitution has been pressed with great force. . . The accused cannot be said to be "informed of the nature and cause of the accusation" unless the indictment give him that notice which may reasonably suggest to him the point on which the accusations turns [sic], so that he may know the course to be pursued in his defence.

It is also well worthy of consideration that this doctrine, so far as it respects treason, is entirely supported by the operation of the common law, which is said to convert the accessory before the fact into the principal, and to make the act of the principal his act. The accessory before the fact is not said to have levied war. He is not said to be guilty under the statute, but the common law attaches to him the guilt of that fact which he has advised or procured; and, as contended, makes it his act.

This is the operation of the common law not the operation of the statute. It is an operation then which can only be performed where the common law exists to perform: it is the creature of the common law, and the creature presupposes its creator. To decide then that this doctrine is applicable to the United States would seem to imply the decision that the United States, as a nation, have a common law which creates and defines the punishment of crimes accessorial in their nature. It would imply the further decision that these accessorial crimes are not in the case of treason excluded by the definition of treason given in the constitution. . .

I have said that this doctrine cannot apply to the United States without implying those decisions respecting the common

law which I have stated; because, should it be true as is contended that the constitutional definition of treason comprehends him who advises or procures an assemblage that levies
war, it would not follow that such adviser or procurer might be
charged as having been present at the assemblage.

If the adviser or procurer be within the definition of levying
war, and independent of the agency of the common law do actually levy war, then the advisement of procurement is an overt
act of levying war. If it be the overt action which he is to be
convicted, then it must be charged in the indictment; for he
can only be convicted on proof of the overt acts which are
charged.

To render this distinction more intelligible let it be recollected, that although it should be conceded that since the statutes of William and Mary he who advises or procures a treason
may, in England, be charged as having committed that treason
by virtue of the common law operation, which is said so far as
respects the indictment to unite the accessorial to the principal offence and permit them to be charged as one, yet it can
never be conceded that he who commits one overt act under
the statute of Edward can be charged and convicted on proof
of another overt act.

If then procurement be an overt act of treason under the constitution, no man can be convicted for the procurement under
an indictment charging him with actually assembling, whatever may be the doctrine of the common law in the case of an
accessorial offender.[1]

[1] *Burr Trials*, ii, 424–38.

WORKS CITED IN THIS VOLUME

WORKS CITED IN THIS VOLUME

The material given in parentheses and following certain titles indicates the form in which those titles have been cited in the footnotes.

Acts and Laws. *See* United States Statutes.

ADAMS, HENRY. History of the United States of America. 9 vols. New York. 1889–1911. (Adams: *U.S.*)

—— John Randolph. Boston. 1892. [American Statesmen series.] (Adams: *Randolph.*)

—— Life of Albert Gallatin. Philadelphia. 1879. (Adams: *Gallatin.*)

ADAMS, HENRY, *editor.* Documents relating to New-England Federalism, 1800–1815. Boston. 1877. (*N.E. Federalism:* Adams.)

ADAMS, JOHN. *See* Old Family Letters.

ADAMS, JOHN QUINCY. Memoirs. Edited by Charles Francis Adams. 12 vols. Philadelphia. 1874–77. (*Memoirs, J. Q. A.:* Adams.)

—— Writings. Edited by Worthington Chauncey Ford. 5 vols. New York. 1913–15. (*Writings, J. Q. A.:* Ford.)

ADDISON, ALEXANDER. Trial on an Impeachment by the House of Representatives before the Senate of the Commonwealth of Pennsylvania. Reported by Thomas Lloyd, stenographer. Lancaster. 1803. (*Addison Trial.*)

ALLEN, GARDNER WELD. Our Navy and the Barbary Corsairs. Boston. 1905.

ALLIBONE, SAMUEL AUSTIN. Dictionary of English Literature and British and American Authors. 3 vols. Philadelphia. 1870–71.

AMBLER, CHARLES HENRY. Thomas Ritchie — A Study in Virginia Politics. Richmond. 1913.

American Historical Association. Annual Report. 1896, vol. II; 1913, vol. II. Washington, D.C.

American Historical Review. Vol. IV–XIX, inclusive, 1899–1914. New York. (*Am. Hist. Rev.*)

American Law Review. Vol. I, 1867; Boston. Vols. XIX, XXIX, XLVI, 1885, 1895, 1912; St. Louis. (*Am. Law Rev.*)

American Political Science Review. Vol. VIII, 1914; vol. IX, 1915. Baltimore. (*Am. Pol. Sci. Rev.*)

American State Papers. Documents, Legislative and Executive, of the Congress of the United States. Selected and edited under the Authority of Congress. 38 vols. Washington. 1832–61. [Citations in this work are from "Foreign Relations" (*Am. State Papers, For. Rel.*); "Miscellaneous." (*Am. State Papers, Misc.*); and "Public Lands."]

AMES, FISHER. Works. Edited by Seth Ames. 2 vols. Boston. 1854. (Ames.)

ANDERSON, DICE ROBINS. William Branch Giles: A Study in the Politics of Virginia and the Nation from 1790 to 1830. Menasha [Wisconsin]. 1914. (Anderson.)

ANDERSON, JOHN E., *and* HOBBY, WILLIAM J. Contract for the Western Territory made with the Legislature of Georgia in the year 1795, considered with a Reference to the subsequent Attempts of the State to impair its Obligation. Augusta. 1799.

ARNOLD, SAMUEL GREENE. History of the State of Rhode Island and Providence Plantations. 2 vols. New York. 1860.

Athenæum; Journal of Literature, Science, and the Fine Arts. (Weekly.) 1835. London.

BASSETT, JOHN SPENCER. Life of Andrew Jackson. 2 vols. New York. 1911.

BAY, ELIHU HALL. Reports of Cases argued and determined in the Superior Courts of Law in the State of South Carolina. Vols. I and II, 1809, 1811. New York.

BAYARD, JAMES ASHETON. Papers, from 1796 to 1815. Edited by Elizabeth Donnan. [Annual Report of the American Historical Association for the year 1913, vol. II.] Washington. 1915. (*Bayard Papers:* Donnan.)

BEARD, CHARLES AUSTIN. Economic Origins of Jeffersonian Democracy. New York. 1915. (Beard: *Econ. Origins Jeff. Dem.*)

—— Supreme Court and the Constitution. New York. 1912.

BEVERIDGE, ALBERT JEREMIAH. Life of John Marshall. 4 vols. Boston. 1916–19.

BIDDLE, ALEXANDER. *See* Old Family Letters.

BISHOP, ABRAHAM. Georgia Speculation Unveiled. [Two pamphlets, in two parts each.] Hartford. 1797–98. (Bishop.)

Blackwood's Magazine. Vol. XVII, 1822. Edinburgh and London.

Blennerhassett Papers, embodying the private Journal of Harman Blennerhassett. Edited by William H. Safford. Cincinnati. 1864. (*Blennerhassett Papers:* Safford.)

BOTTA, CARLO GIUSEPPE GUGLIELMO. History of the War of the Independence of the United States of America. Translated from the Italian by George Alexander Otis. 3 vols. Philadelphia. 1820.

BOUVIER, JOHN. Law Dictionary and Concise Encyclopedia. Third Revision by Francis Rawle. 3 vols. Kansas City and St. Paul. 1914.

BRADY, JOSEPH PLUNKETT. Trial of Aaron Burr. New York. 1913.

BROCKENBROUGH, WILLIAM, *and* HOLMES, HUGH. Collection of Cases decided by the General Court of Virginia, chiefly relating to the penal laws of the Commonwealth, commencing in the year 1789 and ending in 1814. [Also known as the first volume of Virginia Cases.] Philadelphia. 1815. (Va. Cases.)

BRYAN, WILHELMUS BOGART. History of the National Capital from its Foundation through the Period of the Adoption of the Organic Act. 2 vols. New York. 1914–16. (Bryan.)

BURR, AARON. Private Journal: Reprinted in full from the original manuscript in the library of William Keeney Bixby of St. Louis, Missouri. 2 vols. Rochester. 1903.

—— Trials, for Treason and for a Misdemeanor. Reported by David Robertson, stenographer. 2 vols. Philadelphia. 1808. (*Burr Trials.*)

 And see Brady, Joseph Plunkett; Davis, Matthew Livingston; Jenkinson, Isaac; McCaleb, Walter Flavius; Parton, James.

CABOT, GEORGE. *See* Lodge, Henry Cabot.

CALL, DANIEL. Reports of Cases argued and decided in the Court of Appeals of Virginia. Vol. IV. Richmond. 1833. (Call.)

CARSON, HAMPTON LAWRENCE. Supreme Court of the United States: Its History. 2 vols. Philadelphia. 1891. (Carson.)

CHANDLER, PELEG WHITMAN. American Criminal Trials. 2 vols. Boston. 1844.

CHANNING, EDWARD. History of the United States. Vols. 1–4. New York. 1905–17. (Channing: *U.S.*)

—— Jeffersonian System, 1801–11. [Vol. 12 of "The American Nation, a History," edited by Albert Bushnell Hart.] New York and London. 1906. (Channing: *Jeff. System.*)

CHAPPELL, ABSALOM HARRIS. Miscellanies of Georgia, Historical, Biographical, Descriptive, etc. Atlanta. 1874. (Chappell.)

CHASE, SAMUEL. Trial, before the High Court of Impeachment, composed of the Senate of the United States, for charges exhibited against him by the House of Representatives . . for high Crimes and Misdemeanors. Reported by Charles Evans, stenographer. Baltimore. 1805. (*Chase Trial.*)

CHASTELLUX, FRANÇOIS JEAN, MARQUIS DE. Travels in North America in the years 1780–81–82. New York. 1828.

CLARK, DANIEL. Proofs of the Corruption of Gen. James Wilkinson and of his Connexion with Aaron Burr. Philadelphia. 1809. (Clark: *Proofs.*)

CLARK, JOSHUA VICTOR HOPKINS. Onondaga; or Reminiscences of Earlier and Later Times; being a Series of Historical Sketches relative to Onondaga; with Notes on the Several Towns in the County, and Oswego. 2 vols. Syracuse. 1849. (Clark: *Onondaga.*)

CLAY, HENRY. Private Correspondence. Edited by Calvin Colton. New York. 1855. (*Priv. Corres.*: Colton.)

—— Works. Edited by Calvin Colton. 7 vols. New York. 1897. (*Works:* Colton.)

CLEVELAND, CATHERINE CAROLINE. Great Revival in the West, 1797–1805. Chicago. 1916.

COLTON, CALVIN, *editor.* See Clay, Henry. Private Correspondence, and Works.

CONGRESS. *See* United States Congress.

CORWIN, EDWARD SAMUEL. Doctrine of Judicial Review — Its Legal and Historical Basis and other Essays. Princeton. 1914. (Corwin.)

COX, ISAAC JOSLIN. West Florida Controversy, 1798–1813. Baltimore. 1918. (Cox.)

COXE, BRINTON. Essay on Judicial Power and Unconstitutional Legislation, being a Commentary on Parts of the Constitution of the United States. Philadelphia. 1893.

CRANCH, WILLIAM. Reports of Cases argued and adjudged in the Supreme Court of the United States, 1801–08. 6 vols. New York. 1812.

—— Same February term, 1810. Vol. VI. New York. 1812. *Also* Cases argued and decided in the Supreme Court of the United States and others. [Lawyers' edition.] 1, 2, 3, 4 Cranch, Book II. 5, 6, 7, 8, 9 Cranch, Book III. Edited and annotated by Stephen K. Williams and Walter Malins Rose. Rochester. 1901. (Cranch.)

CUTLER, WILLIAM PARKER, *and* JULIA PERKINS. Life, Journals, and Correspondence of Menasseh Cutler. 2 vols. Cincinnati. 1888. (Cutler.)

DALLAS, ALEXANDER JAMES. Reports of Cases ruled and adjudged in the several Courts of the United States and of Pennsylvania. Vols. 2, 3, 4. Philadelphia. 1798, 1799, 1835. *Also* Cases argued and decided in the Supreme Court of the United States and others. [Lawyers' edition.] 1, 2, 3, 4 Dallas, Book I. Edited and annotated by Stephen K. Williams and Walter Malins Rose. Rochester. 1901. (Dallas.)

DAVIS, JOHN CHANDLER BANCROFT, *reporter*. *See* United States Supreme Court.

DAVIS, MATTHEW LIVINGSTON. Memoirs of Aaron Burr. 2 vols. New York. 1836. (Davis.)

Debate in the House of Representatives of the Territory of Orleans, on a Memorial to Congress, respecting the illegal conduct of General Wilkinson. New Orleans. 1807.

Debates in the Several State Conventions. See Elliot, Jonathan.

DILLON, JOHN FORREST, *compiler and editor*. John Marshall. Life, Character, and Judicial Services, as portrayed in the Centenary Proceedings throughout the United States in Marshall's Day. 1901. 3 vols. Chicago. 1903. (Dillon.)

DODD, WILLIAM EDWARD. Life of Nathaniel Macon. Raleigh. 1903. (Dodd.)

DONNAN, ELIZABETH, *editor*. *See* Bayard Papers.

DOUGHERTY, JOHN HAMPDEN. Power of Federal Judiciary over Legislation. New York. 1912.

DWIGHT, NATHANIEL. Signers of the Declaration of Independence. New York. 1895. (Dwight.)

EATON, WILLIAM. Life, principally collected from his correspondence and other manuscripts. Edited by Charles Prentiss. Brookfield. 1813. (*Eaton:* Prentiss.)

ELLIOT, JONATHAN. Debates in the several State Conventions, on the Adoption of the Federal Constitution, as recommended by the General Convention at Philadelphia in 1787. 5 vols. Washington. 1836–45.

EVANS, CHARLES, *reporter. See* Chase, Samuel. Trial.

FARRAND, MAX, *editor. See* Records of the Federal Convention.

Federalist, The. Commentary on the Constitution of the United States from original text of Alexander Hamilton, John Jay, and James Madison. Edited by Henry Cabot Lodge. New York. 1895.

First Forty Years of Washington Society. See Hunt, Gaillard.

FORD, PAUL LEICESTER, *editor. See* Jefferson, Thomas. Works.

FORD, WORTHINGTON CHAUNCEY, *editor. See* Adams, John Quincy. Writings.

GALLATIN, ALBERT. *See* Adams, Henry.

GARLAND, HUGH ALFRED. Life of John Randolph of Roanoke. 2 vols. New York. 1851.

GIBBS, GEORGE, *editor.* Memoirs of the Administrations of Washington and John Adams. *See* Wolcott, Oliver.

GILES, WILLIAM BRANCH. *See* Anderson, Dice Robins.

GIRARD, STEPHEN. *See* McMaster, John Bach.

Great American Lawyers. See Lewis, William Draper.

Green Bag: An Entertaining Magazine for Lawyers. Edited by Horace Williams Fuller. Vol. II, 1890. Boston.

GREENE, NATHANAEL. *See* Johnson, William.

GRIGSBY, HUGH BLAIR. History of the Virginia Federal Convention of 1788, with a Biographical Sketch of the Author and Illustrative Notes. Edited by Robert Alonzo Brock. 2 vols. [Collections of the Virginia Historical Society, new series, vols. IX and X.] Richmond. 1890–91.

—— Virginia Convention of 1829–30. Richmond. 1854.

Gulf States Historical Magazine. Vol. II, 1903. Montgomery [Ala.].

HAMILTON, ALEXANDER. *See* Lodge, Henry Cabot.

HAMMOND, JABEZ DELANO. History of Political Parties in the State of New York from the Ratification of the Federal Constitution to December, 1840. Albany. 1842.

HARDEN, EDWARD JENKINS. Life of George Michael Troup. Savannah. 1859.

HARPER, ROBERT GOODLOE. Case of the Georgia Sales on the Mississippi considered with a Reference to Law Authorities and Public Acts, and an Appendix containing certain Extracts, Records, and Official Papers. Philadelphia. 1797. (Harper.)

HARRIS, JOEL CHANDLER. Georgia from the Invasion of De Soto to recent Times. New York. 1896. (Harris.)

HARRIS, THOMAS, and JOHNSON, REVERDY. Reports of Cases argued and determined in the General Court and Court of Appeals of the State of Maryland from 1800 to 1805 inclusive. Vol. I. Annapolis. 1821. (Harris and Johnson.)

HASKINS, CHARLES HOMER. Yazoo Land Companies. [Reprinted from the papers of the American Historical Association for October, 1891.] New York. 1891. (Haskins.)

HAYWOOD, JOHN. Reports of Cases adjudged in the Superior Courts of Law and Equity of the State of North Carolina from the year 1789 to the year 1798. Halifax. 1799.

HENRY, WILLIAM WIRT. Patrick Henry. Life, Correspondence and Speeches. 3 vols. New York. 1891.

HILDRETH, RICHARD. History of the United States of America. 6 vols. New York. 1854–55. (Hildreth.)

Historical and Philosophical Society of Ohio. Quarterly Publication. Vol. IX, Nos. 1 and 2; January and April, 1914. Cincinnati. (Quarterly Pub. Hist. and Phil. Soc. Ohio.)

HOWARD, BENJAMIN CHEW. Reports of Cases argued and adjudged in the Supreme Court of the United States, December term, 1856. Vol. XIX. Washington. 1857. (Howard.)

HOYT, WILLIAM HENRY, editor. See Murphey, Archibald Debow.

HUDSON, FREDERIC. Journalism in the United States from 1690 to 1872. New York. 1873. (Hudson.)

HUGHES, ROBERT WILLIAM. Reports of Cases decided in the Courts of the Fourth Judicial Circuit sitting in Admiralty. Vol. V, edited by Robert Morton Hughes. New York. 1883.

HUNT, GAILLARD, *editor*.   First Forty Years of Washington Society, portrayed by the Family Letters of Mrs. Samuel Harrison Smith.   New York.   1906.   (Hunt.)

INDIANA TERRITORY.   Laws of the Indiana Territory, 1801–06 inclusive.   Paoli [Indiana].   1886.

IREDELL, JAMES.   Life and Correspondence.   Edited by Griffith John McRee.   2 vols.   New York.   1857–58.   (*Iredell:* McRee.)

IRVING, PIERRE MUNROE.   Life and Letters of Washington Irving.   4 vols.   New York.   1869.   (Irving.)

JACKSON, ANDREW.   *See* Bassett, John Spencer; Parton, James.

JAY, JOHN.   Correspondence and Public Papers.   Edited by Henry Phelps Johnston.   4 vols.   New York.   1890–93.   [Letter-press edition.]   (*Jay:* Johnston.)

JEFFERSON, THOMAS.   Memoir, Correspondence, and Miscellanies.   Edited by Thomas Jefferson Randolph.   Charlottesville.   1829.   (*Jefferson:* Randolph.)

—— Works.   Edited by Paul Leicester Ford.   12 vols.   New York.   1904–05.   [Federal edition.]   (*Works:* Ford.)

—— Writings.   Edited by Henry Augustine Washington.   Washington.   1853–54.   (*Jefferson:* Washington.)

See Parton, James; Randall, Henry Stephens.

JENKINSON, ISAAC.   Aaron Burr.   His Personal and Political Relations with Thomas Jefferson and Alexander Hamilton.   Richmond [Indiana].   1902.   (Jenkinson.)

JOHNSON, ALLEN.   Union and Democracy.   Boston.   1915.

JOHNSON, WILLIAM.   Sketches of the Life and Correspondence of Nathanael Greene.   2 vols.   Charleston.   1822.

JOHNSTON, HENRY PHELPS, *editor*.   *See* Jay, John.

JONES, CHARLES COLCOCK, *and* DUTCHER, SALEM.   Memorial History of Augusta, Georgia.   Syracuse.   1890.

KENNEDY, JOHN PENDLETON.   Memoirs of the Life of William Wirt.   2 vols.   Philadelphia.   1849.   (Kennedy.)

KING, RUFUS.   Life and Correspondence, comprising his Letters, Private and Official, his Public Documents and his Speeches.   Edited by Charles Ray King.   6 vols.   New York.   1894–1900.   [Letterpress edition.]   (King.)

KNIGHT, LUCIAN LAMAR.   Georgia's Landmarks, Memorials and Legends.   2 vols.   Atlanta.   1913–14.

LA ROCHEFOUCAULD-LIANCOURT, FRANÇOIS ALEXANDRE FRÉ-
DÉRIC, DUC DE. Travels through the United States of
North America. 4 vols. London. 1800. (La Roche-
foucauld-Liancourt.)

LEWIS, WILLIAM DRAPER, *editor*. Great American Lawyers:
A History of the Legal Profession in America. 8 vols.
Philadelphia. 1907–09. (*Great American Lawyers:* Lewis.)

Literary Magazine and American Register. Vol. II, April to
December, inclusive, 1804. Philadelphia.

LODGE, HENRY CABOT. Alexander Hamilton. Boston. 1882.
[American Statesmen series.]

—— Life and Letters of George Cabot. Boston. 1877.
(Lodge: *Cabot.*)

LODGE, HENRY CABOT, *editor*. *See* Federalist.

MCCALEB, WALTER FLAVIUS. Aaron Burr Conspiracy. New
York. 1903. (McCaleb.)

MCHENRY, JAMES. *See* Steiner, Bernard Christian.

MCLAUGHLIN, ANDREW CUNNINGHAM. Courts, the Constitution and Parties. Studies in Constitutional History and
Politics. Chicago. 1912. (McLaughlin.)

MACLAY, SAMUEL. Journal. Annotated by John Franklin
Meginness. Williamsport. 1887. (*Maclay's Journal.*)

MCMASTER, JOHN BACH. History of the People of the United
States from the Revolution to the Civil War. 8 vols.
New York. 1883–1914. (McMaster: *U.S.*)

—— Life and Times of Stephen Girard, Merchant and Mariner.
2 vols. Philadelphia and London. 1918.

MACON, NATHANIEL. *See* Dodd, William Edward.

MCREE, GRIFFITH JOHN, *editor*. *See* Iredell, James.

MANUSCRIPTS:
Breckenridge, John. Library of Congress.
Dreer, Ferdinand Julius. Pennsylvania Historical Society.
Etting, Frank Marx. Pennsylvania Historical Society.
Hopkinson, Joseph. Possession of Edward P. Hopkinson,
Philadelphia.
Jefferson, Thomas. Library of Congress.
Kent, James. Library of Congress.
Letters in Relation to the Burr Conspiracy. Library of
Congress. (Letters in Relation.)
Letters of the Corresponding Secretary. (Marshall to John
Eliot.) Massachusetts Historical Society.

Miscellaneous. New York Public Library.

Peters, Richard. Pennsylvania Historical Society.

Pickering, Timothy. Massachusetts Historical Society.

Plumer, William. Library of Congress. [The Plumer Papers are listed in several divisions, as "Congress," "Diary," "Journal," "Letters," "Register," and "Repository."]

Records of the United States Circuit Court, Boston, Mass.

Records of the United States Circuit Court, Richmond, Va.

Wilkinson, James. Chicago Historical Society.

MARSHALL FAMILY. *See* Paxton, William McClung.

MARSHALL, JOHN. Life of George Washington. [1st edition.] 5 vols. Philadelphia. 1805–07. (Marshall, 1st ed.)

—— Same. [2d edition.] 2 vols. Philadelphia. 1840. (Marshall, 2d ed.)

—— Same. [School edition.] Philadelphia. 1838. (Marshall, school ed.)

    And see Beveridge, Albert Jeremiah; Dillon, John Forrest; Paxton, William McClung.

MARTIN, FRANÇOIS XAVIER. Notes of a few decisions in the Superior Courts of the State of North-Carolina, and in the Circuit Court of the U[nited] States, for North-Carolina District. Newbern. 1797. (Martin.)

MARTINEAU, HARRIET. Retrospect of Western Travel. 2 vols. London and New York. 1838.

Maryland Historical Society. Fund-Publications. No. 24, 1887. Baltimore. (*Md. Hist. Soc. Fund-Pub.*)

Massachusetts Historical Society. Proceedings. Boston. (*Mass. Hist. Soc. Proc.*)

MASSACHUSETTS. Senate Journal, 1798–99. Vol. XIX. Manuscript volume, Massachusetts State Library.

MEGINNESS, JOHN FRANKLIN, *annotator*. *See* Maclay, Samuel. Journal.

Messages and Papers of the Presidents, 1789–1897. *See* Richardson, James Daniel.

Monthly Anthology and Boston Review. Vol. V. 1808. Boston.

MOORE, THOMAS. Poetical Works, collected by himself, with a Memoir. 6 vols. Boston. 1856.

MORDECAI, SAMUEL. Richmond in By-Gone Days, being the Reminiscences of An Old Citizen. Richmond. 1856. (Mordecai.)

MORISON, JOHN HOPKINS. Life of the Hon. Jeremiah Smith. Boston. 1845. (Morison: *Smith.*)

MORISON, SAMUEL ELIOT. Life and Letters of Harrison Gray
    Otis, Federalist, 1765–1848. 2 vols. Boston. 1913.
    (Morison: *Otis*.)

MORRIS, GOUVERNEUR. Diary and Letters. Edited by Anne
    Cary Morris. 2 vols. New York. 1888. (Morris.)

MURPHEY, ARCHIBALD DEBOW. Papers. Edited by William
    Henry Hoyt. [Publications of the North Carolina His-
    torical Commission.] 2 vols. Raleigh. 1914.

New England Mississippi Land Company. Memorial of the
    Agents to Congress, with a Vindication of their Title at
    Law annexed. Washington. 1804.

NEWSPAPERS:

Baltimore, Md.:   *American*, issues of November 4, 5, 6,
                     1807.

Boston, Mass.:   *Columbian Centinel*, issues of January
                     23, February 16, March 27, 30, 1799, Feb-
                     ruary 6, 17, April 2, 7, 1802. *Independ-
                     ent Chronicle*, issues of February 11, 14,
                     18, 25, 1799, May 12, July 10, 1800,
                     March 15, April 26, 1802, March 10,
                     June 30, 1803.
                     *J. Russell's Gazette — Commercial and Po-
                     litical* (later known as the *Boston Gazette*
                     and the *Boston Commercial Gazette*), is-
                     sue of January 28, 1799.
                     New England Palladium, issues of March
                     12, 23, 1802.

Richmond, Va.:   *Enquirer*, issues of April 10, 28, May 8,
                     November 6, 24, December 1, 4, 8, 12,
                     1807.

Washington, D.C.: *Federalist*, issues of February 13, 20, 22,
                     March 3, 1802, January 8, 1805.

New York Review. Vols. II and III. 1838. New York.

New York State Library Bulletin. Vol. IV, 1900. New York.

North American Review. Vol. 46, 1838; Boston. Vol. 185,
    1907; New York.

North Carolina Booklet. Vol. XVII, 1917. Raleigh.

Old Family Letters. Copied from the Originals for Alexander
    Biddle. Series A. Philadelphia. 1892.

OTIS, HARRISON GRAY. *See* Morison, Samuel Eliot.

PARTON, JAMES. Life and Times of Aaron Burr. New York.
1858. (Parton: *Burr.*)
—— Life of Andrew Jackson. 3 vols. New York. 1861.
(Parton: *Jackson.*)
—— Life of Thomas Jefferson. Boston. 1874.
PAXTON, WILLIAM MCCLUNG. Marshall Family. Cincinnati.
1885. (Paxton.)
Pennsylvania Bar Association. Report of the Twenty-first
Annual Meeting, 1915. Philadelphia.
PETERS, RICHARD, JR. Reports of Cases argued and adjudged
in the Supreme Court of the United States, January term,
1828. Vol. I. Philadelphia. 1828. (Peters.)
PICKERING, TIMOTHY. Review of the Correspondence be-
tween the Hon. John Adams and the late William Cun-
ningham, Esq., beginning in 1803 and ending in 1812.
Salem. 1824
PICKETT, ALBERT JAMES. History of Alabama, and inciden-
tally of Georgia and Mississippi, from the earliest period.
2 vols. Charleston. 1851. (Pickett.)
PLUMER, WILLIAM. Life. Begun by William Plumer, Jr.,
completed and edited, with a sketch of the author's
life, by Andrew Preston Peabody. Boston. 1857.
(Plumer.)
PRENTISS, CHARLES, *editor.* *See* Eaton, William. Life.
PRIEST, WILLIAM. Travels in the United States of America,
1793–97. London. 1802.

QUINCY, EDMUND. Life of Josiah Quincy of Massachusetts.
Boston. 1867. (Quincy.)

RAMSEY, JAMES GATTYS MCGREGOR. Annals of Tennessee
to the End of the Eighteenth Century. Charleston. 1853.
RANDALL, HENRY STEPHENS. Life of Thomas Jefferson. 3
vols. New York. 1858. (Randall.)
RANDOLPH, JOHN. Adams, Henry; Garland, Hugh Alfred.
RANDOLPH, THOMAS JEFFERSON, *editor.* *See* Jefferson, Thomas.
Records of the Federal Convention of 1787. Edited by Max
Farrand. 3 vols. New Haven. 1911. (*Records Fed.
Conv.*: Farrand.)
RICHARDSON, JAMES DANIEL, *compiler.* A Compilation of
Messages and Papers of the Presidents, 1789–1897. 10
vols. Washington. 1896–99. (Richardson.)

RITCHIE, THOMAS. *See* Ambler, Charles Henry.
ROBERTSON, DAVID, *reporter*. *See* Burr, Aaron. Trials.

SAFFORD, WILLIAM HARRISON, *editor*. *See* Blennerhassett Papers.
SCOTT, LIEUT.-GENERAL [WINFIELD]. Memoirs. Written by Himself. 2 vols. New York. 1864.
SEMPLE, ROBERT BAYLOR. History of the Rise and Progress of the Baptists in Virginia. Richmond. 1810.
SHELTON, WILLIAM HENRY. Jumel Mansion, being a Full History of the House on Harlem Heights built by Roger Morris before the Revolution, together with some Account of its more Notable Occupants. Boston. 1916.
SINGLETON, ESTHER. Story of the White House. 2 vols. New York. 1907.
SMITH, GEORGE GILLMAN. Story of Georgia and the Georgia People, 1732 to 1800. Macon. 1900. (Smith.)
SMITH, JEREMIAH. *See* Morison, John Hopkins.
SMITH, MRS. SAMUEL HARRISON. *See* Hunt, Gaillard.
SMITH, WILLIAM STEUBEN, *and* OGDEN, SAMUEL GOUVERNEUR. Trials for Misdemeanors. Reported by Thomas Lloyd, stenographer. New York. 1807. (*Trials of Smith and Ogden*.)
South Carolina Historical and Genealogical Magazine. Vol. VII, 1906. Charleston.
Southwestern Historical Quarterly. Vol. XVII, 1909. Austin. (*Southwestern Hist. Quarterly*.)
SPARKS, JARED, *editor*. *See* Washington, George.
State of Facts, showing the Right of Certain Companies to the Lands lately purchased by them from the State of Georgia. United States. 1795.
State Trials. Complete Collection of State Trials and Proceedings for High-Treason, and other Crimes and Misdemeanors; from the Reign of King Richard II. to the End of the Reign of King George I. [1377–1727.] 6 vols. London. 1730. (*State Trials Richard II. to George I.*)
Statutes at Large. *See* United States Statutes.
STEINER, BERNARD CHRISTIAN. Life and Correspondence of James McHenry. Cleveland. 1907.
STEVENS, THADDEUS. *See* Woodburn, James Albert.
STEVENS, WILLIAM BACON. History of Georgia from its First Discovery by Europeans to the Adoption of the Present

Constitution in 1798. 2 vols. Vol. I, New York, 1847.
Vol. II, Philadelphia, 1859. (Stevens.)

STORY, JOSEPH. Life and Letters. Edited by William Wetmore Story. 2 vols. Boston. 1851. (Story.)

SUPREME COURT. *See* United States Supreme Court.

THAYER, JAMES BRADLEY. Cases on Constitutional Law. 4 vols. Cambridge. 1894–95.

—— John Marshall. Boston. 1904. [Riverside Biographical Series.]

TROUP, GEORGE MICHAEL. *See* Harden, Edward Jenkins.

TUCKER, George. Life of Thomas Jefferson. 2 vols. Philadelphia. 1837. (Tucker.)

TYLER, LYON GARDINER. Letters and Times of the Tylers. 3 vols. Richmond. 1884–96. (Tyler.)

UNITED STATES CONGRESS. Debates and Proceedings, First Congress, First Session, March 3, 1789, to Eighteenth Congress, First Session, May 27, 1824. [Known as the Annals of Congress.] 42 vols. Washington. 1834–56. (*Annals.*)

—— Documents, Legislative and Executive. *See* American State Papers.

—— History of the Last Session of Congress, which commenced on the seventh of December, 1801. [Taken from the *National Intelligencer.*] Washington. 1802. (*Hist. Last Sess. Cong. which commenced 7th Dec. 1801.*)

UNITED STATES SENATE. Document No. 610. 63d Congress, 2d Session. Washington. 1914.

—— Journal of the Executive Proceedings of the Senate of the United States of America, from the Commencement of the First to the Termination of the Nineteenth Congress. 3 vols. Washington. 1828. (*Journal Exec. Proc. Senate.*)

United States Statutes at Large. Vols. I, II, III. Boston. 1850. (*U.S. Statutes at Large.*)

UNITED STATES SUPREME COURT. Cases adjudged in the Supreme Court at October term, 1883. Reported by John Chandler Bancroft Davis. Vol. III. New York and Albany. 1884.

   See also Cranch, William; Dallas, Alexander James; Howard, Benjamin Chew; Peters, Richard, Jr.; Wallace, John William.

VAN SANTVOORD, GEORGE. Sketches of the Lives and Judicial Services of the Chief-Justices of the Supreme Court of the United States. New York. 1854.

VARNUM, JAMES MITCHELL. The Case of Trevett against Weeden, on Information and Complaint, for refusing Paper Bills in Payment for Butcher's Meat, in Market, at par with Specie, tried before the Honourable Superior Court, in the County of Newport. Also the Case of the Judges of Said Court before the Honourable General Assembly. Providence. 1787.

VERMONT. Records of the Governor and Council of the State of Vermont. 8 vols. Montpelier. 1873–80.

VIRGINIA. Journal of the House of Delegates of the Commonwealth of Virginia. Begun and held at the Capitol in the City of Richmond on Monday, the third of December, 1798. Richmond. 1798.

Virginia Cases. See Brockenbrough, William, and Holmes, Hugh.

WALLACE, JOHN WILLIAM. Cases argued and adjudged in the Supreme Court of the United States, December term, 1865. Vol. III. Washington. 1866.

—— Same, December term, 1871. Vol. XIII. Washington. 1872. (Wallace.)

WARREN, CHARLES. History of the American Bar. Boston. 1911. (Warren.)

WASHINGTON, GEORGE. Writings. Selected and published from the Original Manuscripts with a Life of the Author. Edited by Jared Sparks. 12 vols. Boston. 1836.
And see Marshall, John.

WASHINGTON, HENRY AUGUSTINE, *editor. See* Jefferson, Thomas.

WEBSTER, DANIEL. Private Correspondence. Edited by Fletcher Webster. 2 vols. Boston. 1857.

WHARTON, ANNE HOLLINGSWORTH. Social Life in the Early Republic. Philadelphia. 1902. (Wharton: *Social Life.*)

WHARTON, FRANCIS. State Trials of the United States during the Administrations of Washington and Adams, with references. Philadelphia. 1849. (Wharton: *State Trials.*)

WHITE, GEORGE. Statistics of the State of Georgia. Savannah. 1849.

WILKINSON, JAMES. Memoirs of my Own Times. 3 vols. Philadelphia. 1816.

—— Proofs of the Corruption of. *See* Clark, Daniel.

And see Debate in the House of Representatives of the Territory of Orleans.

WILSON, JAMES. Works. Edited by Bird Wilson. 3 vols. Philadelphia. 1804.

WIRT, WILLIAM. Letters of the British Spy. Baltimore. No date.

—— Memoirs. *See* Kennedy, John Pendleton.

WOLCOTT, OLIVER. Memoirs of the Administrations of Washington and John Adams. Edited from the papers of Oliver Wolcott by George Gibbs. 2 vols. New York. 1846. (Gibbs.)

WOODBURN, JAMES ALBERT. Life of Thaddeus Stevens. Indianapolis. 1913.

WROTH, LAWRENCE COUNSELMAN. Parson Weems, Biographical and Critical Study. Baltimore. 1911.

THE LIFE OF JOHN MARSHALL

VOLUME IV

The Building of the Nation

1815–1835

CONTENTS

at Raleigh — Marshall's devotion to his wife — His religious belief —
His children — Life at Oak Hill — Generosity — Member of Quoit
Club — His "lawyer dinners" — Delights in the reading of poetry
and fiction — Familiarity and friendliness — Joseph Story first
meets the Chief Justice — Is captivated by his personality — Marshall's dignity in presiding over Supreme Court — Quickness at repartee — Life in Washington — Marshall and Associate Justices live
together in same boarding-house — His dislike of publicity — Honorary degrees conferred — Esteem of his contemporaries — His personality — Calmness of manner — Strength of intellect — His irresistible charm — Likeness to Abraham Lincoln — The strong and
brilliant bar practicing before the Supreme Court — Legal oratory of
the period — Length of arguments — Joseph Story — His character
and attainments — Birth and family — A Republican — Devotion
to Marshall — Their friendship mutually helpful — Jefferson fears
Marshall's influence on Story — Edward Livingston sues Jefferson
for one hundred thousand dollars — Circumstances leading to
Batture litigation — Jefferson's desire to name District Judge
in Virginia — Jefferson in letter attacks Marshall — He disputes
appointment of John Tyler to succeed Cyrus Griffin — Death of Justice Cushing of the Supreme Court — Jefferson tries to name Cushing's successor — He objects to Story — Madison wishes to comply
with Jefferson's request — His consequent difficulty in filling place
— Appointment of Story — Jefferson prepares brief on Batture case
— Public interest in case — Case is heard — Marshall's opinion
reflects on Jefferson — Chancellor Kent's opinion — Jefferson and
Livingston publish statements — Marshall ascribes Jefferson's animosity in subsequent years to the Batture litigation.

Marshall uniformly upholds acts of Congress even when he thinks
them unwise and of doubtful constitutionality — The Embargo,
Non-Importation, and Non-Intercourse laws — Marshall's slight
knowledge of admiralty law — His dependence on Story — Marshall is supreme only in Constitutional law — High rank of his opinions on international law — Examples: The Schooner Exchange;
U. S. *vs.* Palmer; The Divina Pastora; The Venus; The Nereid —
Scenes in the court-room — Appearance of the Justices — William
Pinkney the leader of the American bar — His learning and eloquence — His extravagant dress and arrogant manner — Story's admiration of him — Marshall's tribute — Character of the bar — Its
members statesmen as well as lawyers — The attendance of women
at arguments — Mrs. Smith's letter — American Insurance Co.
et al. vs. David Canter — Story delivers the opinion in Martin *vs.*
Hunter's Lessee — Reason for Marshall's declining to sit in that
case — The Virginia Republican organization — The great political triumvirate, Roane, Ritchie, and Taylor — The Fairfax litigation
— The Marshall purchase of a part of the Fairfax estate — Separate
purchases of James M. Marshall — The Marshall and Virginia "compromise" — Virginia Court of Appeals decides in favor of Hunter —

National Supreme Court reverses State court — The latter's bold defiance of the National tribunal — Marshall refuses to sit in the case of the Granville heirs — History of the Granville litigation — The second appeal from the Virginia Court in the Fairfax-Martin-Hunter case — Story's great opinion in Fairfax's Devisee vs. Hunter's Lessee — His first Constitutional pronouncement — Its resemblance to Marshall's opinions — The Chief Justice disapproves one ground of Story's opinion — His letter to his brother — Anger of the Virginia judges at reversal of their judgment — The Virginia Republican organization prepares to attack Marshall.

February and March, 1819, mark an epoch in American history — Marshall, at that time, delivers three of his greatest opinions — He surveys the state of the country — Beholds terrible conditions — The moral, economic, and social breakdown — Bad banking the immediate cause of the catastrophe — Sound and brilliant career of the first Bank of the United States — Causes of popular antagonism to it — Jealousy of the State banks — Jefferson's hostility to a central bank — John Adams's description of State banking methods — Opposition to rechartering the National institution — Congress refuses to recharter it — Abnormal increase of State banks — Their great and unjustifiable profits — Congress forced to charter second Bank of the United States — Immoral and uneconomic methods of State banks — Growth of "private banks" — Few restrictions placed on State and private banks and none regarded by them — Popular craze for more "money" — Character and habits of Western settlers — Local banks prey upon them — Marshall's personal experience — State banks control local press, bar, and courts — Ruthless foreclosures of mortgages and incredible sacrifices of property — Counterfeiting and crime — People unjustly blame Bank of the United States for their financial misfortunes — It is, at first, bad, and corruptly managed — Is subsequently well administered — Popular demand for bankruptcy laws — State "insolvency" statutes badly drawn and ruinously executed — Speculators use them to escape the payment of their liabilities while retaining their assets — Foreclosures and sheriff's sales increase — Demand for "stay laws" in Kentucky — Marshall's intimate personal knowledge of conditions in that State — States begin to tax National Bank out of existence — Marshall delivers one of his great trilogy of opinions of 1819 on contract, fraud, and banking — Effect of the decision of the Supreme Court in Sturges vs. Crowninshield.

The Dartmouth College case affected by the state of the country — Marshall prepares his opinion while on his vacation — His views well known — His opinion in New Jersey vs. Wilson — Eleazar Wheelock's frontier Indian school — The voyage and mission of

tion" — Marshall is acutely alarmed by Roane's attacks — He
writes a dull and petulant newspaper defense of his brilliant opinion
— Regrets his controversial effort and refuses to permit its republication — The Virginia Legislature passes resolutions denouncing
his opinion and proposing a new tribunal to decide controversies between States and the Nation — The slave power joins the attack
upon Marshall's doctrines — Ohio aligns herself with Virginia —
Ohio's dramatic resistance to the Bank of the United States —
Passes extravagantly drastic laws — Adopts resolutions denouncing Marshall's opinions and defying the National Government —
Pennsylvania, Tennessee, Indiana, Illinois also demand a new
court — John Taylor "of Caroline" writes his notable book, *Construction Construed* — Jefferson warmly approves it — Declares the
National Judiciary to be a "subtle corps of sappers and miners
constantly working underground to undermine the foundations of
our confederated fabric."

Relation of slavery and Marshall's opinions — The South threatens
war: "I behold a brother's sword crimsoned with a brother's
blood" — Northern men quail — The source and purpose of Marshall's opinion in Cohens *vs.* Virginia — The facts in that case —
A trivial police court controversy — The case probably "arranged" — William Pinkney and David B. Ogden appear for
the Cohens — Senator James Barbour, for Virginia, threatens secession: "With them [State Governments], it is to determine how
long their [National] government shall endure" — Marshall's opinion
is an address to the American people — The grandeur of certain
passages: "A Constitution is framed for ages to come and is
designed to approach immortality" — The Constitution is vitalized by a "conservative power" within it — Independence of the
Judiciary necessary to preservation of the Republic — Marshall
directly replies to the assailants of Nationalism: "The States are
members of one great empire" — Marshall originates the phraseology, "a government of, by, and for the people" — Publication
of the opinion in Cohens *vs.* Virginia arouses intense excitement
— Roane savagely attacks Marshall under the *nom de guerre* of
"Algernon Sidney" — Marshall is deeply angered — He writes
Story denouncing Roane's articles — Jefferson applauds and encourages attacks on Marshall — Marshall attributes to Jefferson
the assaults upon him and the Supreme Court — The incident of
John E. Hall and his *Journal of American Jurisprudence* — John
Taylor again assails Marshall's opinions in his second book,
Tyranny Unmasked — He connects monopoly, the protective
tariff, internal improvements, "exclusive privileges," and emancipation with Marshall's Nationalist philosophy — Jefferson
praises Taylor's essay and declares for armed resistance to National "usurpation": "The States must meet the invader foot to
foot" — Senator Richard M. Johnson of Kentucky, in Congress,
attacks Marshall and the Supreme Court — Offers an amend-

CONTENTS

Widespread expressions of sorrow—Only one of condemnation—
The long-continued mourning in Virginia — Marshall's old club resolves never to fill his place or increase its membership — Story's
"inscription for a cenotaph" and the words Marshall wrote for
his tomb.

LIST OF ABBREVIATED TITLES MOST FREQUENTLY CITED

All references here are to the List of Authorities at the end of this volume

Adams: *U.S.* *See* Adams, Henry. History of the United States.

Ambler: *Ritchie.* *See* Ambler, Charles Henry. Thomas Ritchie: A Study in Virginia Politics.

Ames: Ames. *See* Ames, Fisher. Works.

Anderson. *See* Anderson, Dice Robins. William Branch Giles.

Babcock. *See* Babcock, Kendric Charles. Rise of American Nationality, 1811–1819.

Bayard Papers: Donnan. *See* Bayard, James Asheton. Papers from 1796 to 1815. Edited by Elizabeth Donnan.

Branch Historical Papers. *See* John P. Branch Historical Papers.

Catterall. *See* Catterall, Ralph Charles Henry. Second Bank of the United States.

Channing: *Jeff. System.* *See* Channing, Edward. Jeffersonian System, 1801–1811.

Channing: *U.S.* *See* Channing, Edward. History of the United States.

Curtis. *See* Curtis, George Ticknor. Life of Daniel Webster.

Dewey. *See* Dewey, Davis Rich. Financial History of the United States.

Dillon. *See* Dillon, John Forrest. John Marshall: Life, Character, and Judicial Services.

E. W. T.: Thwaites. *See* Thwaites, Reuben Gold. Early Western Travels.

Farrar. *See* Farrar, Timothy. Report of the Case of the Trustees of Dartmouth College against William H. Woodward.

Hildreth. *See* Hildreth, Richard. History of the United States of America.

Hunt: *Livingston.* *See* Hunt, Charles Havens. Life of Edward Livingston.

Kennedy. *See* Kennedy, John Pendleton. Memoirs of the Life of William Wirt.

King. *See* King, Rufus. Life and Correspondence. Edited by Charles R. King.

Lodge: *Cabot.* *See* Lodge, Henry Cabot. Life and Letters of George Cabot.

Lord. *See* Lord, John King. A History of Dartmouth College, 1815–1909.

McMaster. *See* McMaster, John Bach. A History of the People of the United States.

Memoirs, J.Q.A.: Adams. *See* Adams, John Quincy. Memoirs. Edited by Charles Francis Adams.

Morison: *Otis.* *See* Morison, Samuel Eliot. Life and Letters of Harrison Gray Otis.

Morris. *See* Morris, Gouverneur. Diary and Letters. Edited by Anne Cary Morris.

N.E. Federalism: Adams. *See* Adams, Henry. Documents relating to New-England Federalism, 1800–1815.

Parton: *Jackson.* *See* Parton, James. Life of Andrew Jackson.

Plumer. *See* Plumer, William, Jr. Life of William Plumer.

Priv. Corres.: Webster. *See* Webster, Daniel. Private Correspondence. Edited by Fletcher Webster.

Quincy: *Quincy.* *See* Quincy, Edmund. Life of Josiah Quincy of Massachusetts.

Randall. *See* Randall, Henry Stephens. Life of Thomas Jefferson.

Records Fed. Conv.: Farrand. *See* Records of the Federal Convention of 1787. Edited by Max Farrand.

Richardson. *See* Richardson, James Daniel. A Compilation of the Messages and Papers of the Presidents, 1789–1897.

Shirley. *See* Shirley, John M. The Dartmouth College Causes and the Supreme Court of the United States.

Story. *See* Story, Joseph. Life and Letters. Edited by William Wetmore Story.

Sumner: *Hist. Am. Currency.* *See* Sumner, William Graham. A History of American Currency.

Sumner: *Jackson.* *See* Sumner, William Graham. Andrew Jackson. As a Public Man.

Tyler: *Tyler.* *See* Tyler, Lyon Gardiner. Letters and Times of the Tylers.

Works: Ford. *See* Jefferson, Thomas. Works. Edited by Paul Leicester Ford.

Writings: Adams. *See* Gallatin, Albert. Writings. Edited by Henry Adams.

Writings: Hunt. *See* Madison, James. Writings. Edited by Gaillard Hunt.

THE LIFE OF JOHN MARSHALL

THE LIFE OF JOHN MARSHALL

CHAPTER I

THE PERIOD OF AMERICANIZATION

Great Britain is fighting our battles and the battles of mankind, and France is combating for the power to enslave and plunder us and all the world. (Fisher Ames.)

Though every one of these Bugbears is an empty Phantom, yet the People seem to believe every article of this bombastical Creed. Who shall touch these blind eyes. (John Adams.)

The object of England, long obvious, is to claim the ocean as her domain. (Jefferson.)

I am for resistance by the *sword*. (Henry Clay.)

INTO the life of John Marshall war was strangely woven. His birth, his young manhood, his public services before he became Chief Justice, were coincident with, and affected by, war. It seemed to be the decree of Fate that his career should march side by side with armed conflict, and that the final phase of that career should open with a war — a war, too, which brought forth a National consciousness among the people and demonstrated a National strength hitherto unsuspected in their fundamental law.

Yet, while American Nationalism was Marshall's one and only great conception, and the fostering of it the purpose of his life, he was wholly out of sympathy with the National movement that led to our second conflict with Great Britain, and against the continuance of it. He heartily shared the opinion of the Federalist leaders that the War of 1812 was unnecessary, unwise, and unrighteous.

By the time France and England had renewed

hostilities in 1803, the sympathies of these men had become wholly British. The excesses of the French Revolution had started them on this course of feeling and thinking. Their detestation of Jefferson, their abhorrence of Republican doctrines, their resentment of Virginia domination, all hastened their progress toward partisanship for Great Britain. They had, indeed, reverted to the colonial state of mind, and the old phrases, "the mother country," "the protection of the British fleet," [1] were forever on their lips.

These Federalists passionately hated France; to them France was only the monstrous child of the terrible Revolution which, in the name of human rights, had attacked successfully every idea dear to their hearts — upset all order, endangered all property, overturned all respectability. They were sure that Napoleon intended to subjugate the world; and that Great Britain was our only bulwark against the aggressions of the Conqueror — that "varlet" whose "patron-saint [is] Beelzebub," as Gouverneur Morris referred to Napoleon. [2]

So, too, thought John Marshall. No man, except his kinsman Thomas Jefferson, cherished a prejudice more fondly than he. Perhaps no better example of first impressions strongly made and tenaciously retained can be found than in these two men. Jefferson was as hostile as Marshall was friendly to Great Britain; and they held exactly opposite sentiments toward France. Jefferson's strongest title

[1] "The navy of Britain is our shield." (Pickering: *Open Letter* [Feb. 16, 1808] *to Governor James Sullivan*, 8; *infra*, 5, 9–10, 25–26, 45–46.)

[2] *Diary and Letters of Gouverneur Morris:* Morris, II, 548.

to immortality was the Declaration of Independence; nearly all of his foreign embroilments had
been with British statesmen. In British conservatism he had found the most resolute opposition to
those democratic reforms he so passionately championed, and which he rightly considered the manifestations of a world movement.[1]

And Jefferson adored France, in whose entrancing
capital he had spent his happiest years. There his
radical tendencies had found encouragement. He
looked upon the French Revolution as the breaking
of humanity's chains, politically, intellectually, spiritually.[2] He believed that the war of the allied governments of Europe against the new-born French
Republic was a monarchical combination to extinguish the flame of liberty which France had lighted.

Marshall, on the other hand, never could forget his
experience with the French. And his revelation of
what he had endured while in Paris had brought him
his first National fame.[3] Then, too, his idol, Washington, had shared his own views — indeed, Marshall had been instrumental in the formation of
Washington's settled opinions. Marshall had championed the Jay Treaty, and, in doing so, had necessarily taken the side of Great Britain as opposed to
France.[4] His business interests [5] powerfully inclined
him in the same direction. His personal friends were
the ageing Federalists.

[1] Jefferson to D'Ivernois, Feb. 6, 1795, *Works of Thomas Jefferson:*
Ford, VIII, 165.

[2] Jefferson to Short, Jan. 3, 1793, *ib.* VII, 203; same to Mason,
Feb. 4, 1791, *ib.* VI, 185.

[3] See vol. II, 354, of this work.

[4] *Ib.* 133-39.   [5] The Fairfax transaction.

He had also become obsessed with an almost religious devotion to the rights of property, to steady
government by "the rich, the wise and good,"[1] to
"respectable" society. These convictions Marshall
found most firmly retained and best defended in the
commercial centers of the East and North. The
stoutest champions of Marshall's beloved stability
of institutions and customs were the old Federalist leaders, particularly of New England and New
York. They had been his comrades and associates
in bygone days and continued to be his intimates.

In short, John Marshall had become the personification of the reaction against popular government
that followed the French Revolution. With him and
men of his cast of mind, Great Britain had come to
represent all that was enduring and good, and France
all that was eruptive and evil. Such was his outlook on social and political life when, after these
traditional European foes were again at war, their
spoliations of American commerce, violations of
American rights, and insults to American honor
once more became flagrant; and such continued to
be his opinion and feeling after these aggressions
had become intolerable.

Since the adoption of the Constitution, nearly
all Americans, except the younger generation, had
become re-Europeanized in thought and feeling.
Their partisanship of France and Great Britain
relegated America to a subordinate place in their
minds and hearts. Just as the anti-Federalists and

---

[1] The phrase used by the Federalists to designate the opponents of
democracy.

their successors, the Republicans, had been more
concerned in the triumph of revolutionary France
over "monarchical" England than in the maintenance of American interests, rights, and honor, so
now the Federalists were equally violent in their
championship of Great Britain in her conflict with
the France of Napoleon. Precisely as the French
partisans of a few years earlier had asserted that
the cause of France was that of America also,[1]
the Federalists now insisted that the success of
Great Britain meant the salvation of the United
States.

"Great Britain is fighting our battles and the battles of mankind, and France is combating for the
power to enslave and plunder us and all the world,"[2]
wrote that faithful interpreter of extreme New
England Federalism, Fisher Ames, just after the
European conflict was renewed. Such opinions were
not confined to the North and East. In South Carolina, John Rutledge was under the same spell.
Writing to "the head Quarters of good Principles," Boston, he avowed that "I have long considered England as but the advanced guard of our
Country. . . If they fall we do."[3] Scores of quotations from prominent Federalists expressive of the
same views might be adduced.[4] Even the assault on

[1] See vol. II, 24–27, 92–96, 106–07, 126–28, of this work.

[2] Ames to Dwight, Oct. 31, 1803, *Works of Fisher Ames:* Ames,
I, 330; and see Ames to Gore, Nov. 16, 1803, *ib.* 332; also Ames to
Quincy, Feb. 12, 1806, *ib.* 360.

[3] Rutledge to Otis, July 29, 1806, Morison: *Life and Letters of
Harrison Gray Otis,* I, 282.

[4] The student should examine the letters of Federalists collected
in Henry Adams's *New-England Federalism;* those in the *Life and*

the Chesapeake did not change or even soften them.[1]
On the other hand, the advocates of France as
ardently upheld her cause, as fiercely assailed Great
Britain.[2]

Never did Americans more seriously need emancipation from foreign influence than in the early decades of the Republic — never was it more vital to their well-being that the people should develop an American spirit, than at the height of the Napoleonic Wars.

Upon the renewal of the European conflict, Great Britain announced wholesale blockades of French ports,[3] ordered the seizure of neutral ships wherever found carrying on trade with an enemy of England;[4] and forbade them to enter the harbors of immense stretches of European coasts.[5] In reply, Napoleon declared the British Islands to be under blockade, and ordered the capture, in any waters whatsoever of all ships that had entered British harbors.[6] Great Britain responded with the Orders in Council of 1807 which, in effect, prohib-

Correspondence of Rufus King; in Lodge's *Life and Letters of George Cabot;* in the *Works of Fisher Ames* and in Morison's *Otis.*

[1] See Adams: *History of the United States,* IV, 29.

[2] Once in a long while an impartial view was expressed: "I think myself sometimes in an Hospital of Lunaticks, when I hear some of our Politicians eulogizing Bonaparte because he humbles the English; & others worshipping the latter, under an Idea that they will shelter us, & take us under the Shadow of their Wings. They would join, rather, to deal us away like Cattle." (Peters to Pickering, Feb. 4, 1807, Pickering MSS. Mass. Hist. Soc.)

[3] See Harrowby's Circular, Aug. 9, 1804, *American State Papers, Foreign Relations,* III, 266.

[4] See Hawkesbury's Instructions, Aug. 17, 1805, *ib.*

[5] Fox to Monroe, April 8 and May 16, 1806, *ib.* 267.

[6] The Berlin Decree, Nov. 21, 1806, *ib.* 290–91.

ited the oceans to neutral vessels except such as traded directly with England or her colonies; and even this commerce was made subject to a special tax to be paid into the British treasury.[1] Napoleon's swift answer was the Milan Decree,[2] which, among other things, directed all ships submitting to the British Orders in Council to be seized and confiscated in the ports of France or her allies, or captured on the high seas.

All these "decrees," "orders," and "instructions" were, of course, in flagrant violation of international law, and were more injurious to America than to all other neutrals put together. Both belligerents bore down upon American commerce and seized American ships with equal lawlessness.[3] But, since Great Britain commanded the oceans,[4] the United States suffered far more severely from the depredations of that Power.[5] Under pressure of conflict, Great

[1] Orders in Council, Jan. 7 and Nov. 11, 1807, *Am. State Papers, For. Rel.* III, 267–73; and see Channing: *Jeffersonian System*, 199.

[2] Dec. 17, 1807, *Am. State Papers, For. Rel.* III, 290.

[3] Adams: *U.S.* v, 31.

[4] "England's naval power stood at a height never reached before or since by that of any other nation. On every sea her navies rode, not only triumphant, but with none to dispute their sway." (Roosevelt: *Naval War of 1812,* 22.)

[5] See Report, Secretary of State, July 6, 1812, *Am. State Papers, For. Rel.* III, 583-85.

"These decrees and orders, taken together, want little of amounting to a declaration that every neutral vessel found on the high seas, whatsoever be her cargo, and whatsoever foreign port be that of her departure or destination, shall be deemed lawful prize." (Jefferson to Congress, Special Message, March 17, 1808, *Works:* Ford, XI, 20.)

"The only mode by which either of them [the European belligerents] could further annoy the other . . was by inflicting . . the torments of starvation. This the contending parties sought to accomplish by putting an end to all trade with the other nation." (Channing: *Jeff. System* 169.)

Britain increased her impressment[1] of American
sailors. In effect, our ports were blockaded.[2]

Jefferson's lifelong prejudice against Great Britain [3]
would permit him to see in all this nothing but a
sordid and brutal imperialism. Not for a moment did
he understand or consider the British point of view.
England's "intentions have been to claim the ocean
as her conquest, & prohibit any vessel from navigating it but on . . tribute," he wrote.[4] Nevertheless,
he met Great Britain's orders and instructions with
hesitant recommendations that the country be put
in a state of defense; only feeble preliminary steps
were taken to that end.

[1] Theodore Roosevelt, who gave this matter very careful study,
says that at least 20,000 American seamen were impressed. (Roosevelt, footnote to 42.)

"Hundreds of American citizens had been taken by force from
under the American flag, some of whom were already lying beneath
the waters off Cape Trafalgar." (Adams: *U.S.* III, 202.)

See also Babcock: *Rise of American Nationality*, 76–77; and Jefferson to Crawford, Feb. 11, 1815, *Works:* Ford, XI, 451.

[2] See Channing: *Jeff. System*, 184–94. The principal works on the
War of 1812 are, of course, by Henry Adams and by Alfred Mahan.
But these are very extended. The excellent treatments of that period
are the *Jeffersonian System*, by Edward Channing, and *Rise of American Nationality*, by Kendric Charles Babcock, and *Life and Letters
of Harrison Gray Otis*, by Samuel Eliot Morison. The latter work
contains many valuable letters hitherto unpublished.

[3] But see Jefferson to Madison, Aug. 27, 1805, *Works:* Ford, X,
172–73; same to Monroe, May 4, 1806, *ib.* 262–63; same to same, Oct.
26, 1806, *ib.* 296–97; same to Lincoln, June 25, 1806, *ib.* 272; also
see Adams: *U.S.* III, 75. While these letters speak of a temporary
alliance with Great Britain, Jefferson makes it clear that they are
merely diplomatic maneuvers, and that, if an arrangement was made,
a heavy price must be paid for America's coöperation.

Jefferson's letters, in general, display rancorous hostility to Great
Britain. See, for example, Jefferson to Paine, Sept. 6, 1807, *Works:*
Ford, X, 493; same to Leib, June 23, 1808, *ib.* XI, 34–35; same to Meigs,
Sept. 18, 1813, *ib.* 334–35; same to Monroe, Jan. 1, 1815, *ib.* 443.

[4] Jefferson to Dearborn, July 16, 1810, *ib.* 144.

The President's principal reliance was on the device of taking from Great Britain her American markets. So came the Non-Importation Act of April, 1806, prohibiting the admission of those products that constituted the bulk of Great Britain's immensely profitable trade with the United States.[1] This economic measure was of no avail — it amounted to little more than an encouragement of successful smuggling.

When the Leopard attacked the Chesapeake,[2] Jefferson issued his proclamation reciting the "enormity" as he called it, and ordering all British armed vessels from American waters.[3] The spirit of America was at last aroused.[4] Demands for war rang throughout the land.[5] But they did not come from the lips of Federalists, who, with a few exceptions, protested loudly against any kind of retaliation.

John Lowell, unequaled in talent and learning among the brilliant group of Federalists in Boston, wrote a pamphlet in defense of British conduct.[6]

[1] *Annals*, 9th Cong. 1st Sess. 1259–62; also see "An Act to Prohibit the Importation of Certain Goods, Wares, and Merchandise," chap. 29, 1806, *Laws of the United States*, IV, 36–38.

[2] See vol. III, 475–76, of this work.

[3] Jefferson's Proclamation, July 2, 1807, *Works:* Ford, X, 434–47; and *Messages and Papers of the Presidents:* Richardson, I, 421–24.

[4] "This country has never been in such a state of excitement since the battle of Lexington." (Jefferson to Bowdoin, July 10, 1807, *Works:* Ford, X, 454; same to De Nemours, July 14, 1807, *ib.* 460.)
For Jefferson's interpretation of Great Britain's larger motive for perpetrating the Chesapeake crime, see Jefferson to Paine, Sept. 6, 1807, *ib.* 493.

[5] Adams: *U.S.* IV, 38.

[6] Lowell: *Peace Without Dishonor — War Without Hope:* by "A Yankee Farmer," 8. The author of this pamphlet was the son of one of the new Federal judges appointed by Adams under the Federalist Judiciary Act of 1801.

It was an uncommonly able performance, bright, informed, witty, well reasoned. "Despising the threats of prosecution for treason," he would, said Lowell, use his right of free speech to save the country from an unjustifiable war. What did the Chesapeake incident, what did impressment of Americans, what did anything and everything amount to, compared to the one tremendous fact of Great Britain's struggle with France? All thoughtful men knew that Great Britain alone stood between us and that slavery which would be our portion if France should prevail.[1]

Lowell's sparkling essay well set forth the intense conviction of nearly all leading Federalists. Giles was not without justification when he branded them as "the mere Anglican party."[2] The London press had approved the attack on the Chesapeake, applauded Admiral Berkeley, and even insisted upon war against the United States.[3] American Federalists were not far behind the *Times* and the *Morning Post*.

Jefferson, on the contrary, vividly stated the thought of the ordinary American: "The English being equally tyrannical at sea as he [Bonaparte] is on land, & that tyranny bearing on us in every point of either honor or interest, I say, 'down with Eng-

---

[1] See *Peace Without Dishonor — War Without Hope*, 39–40.

[2] Giles to Monroe, March 4, 1807; Anderson: *William Branch Giles — A Study in the Politics of Virginia, 1790–1830*, 108.

Thomas Ritchie, in the Richmond *Enquirer*, properly denounced the New England Federalist headquarters as a "hot-bed of treason." (*Enquirer*, Jan. 24 and April 4, 1809, as quoted by Ambler: *Thomas Ritchie — A Study in Virginia Politics*, 46.)

[3] Adams: *U.S.* IV, 41–44, 54.

land' and as for what Buonaparte is then to do to us, let us trust to the chapter of accidents, I cannot, with the Anglomen, prefer a certain present evil to a future hypothetical one." [1]

But the President did not propose to execute his policy of "down with England" by any such horrid method as bloodshed. He would stop Americans from trading with the world — that would prevent the capture of our ships and the impressment of our seamen. [2] Thus it was that the Embargo Act of December, 1807, and the supplementary acts of January, March, and April, 1808, were passed. [3] All exportation by sea or land was rigidly forbidden under heavy penalties. Even coasting vessels were not allowed to continue purely American trade unless heavy bond was given that landing would be made exclusively at American ports. Flour could be shipped by sea only in case the President thought it necessary to keep from hunger the population of any given port. [4]

[1] Jefferson to Leiper, Aug. 21, 1807, *Works:* Ford, x, 483–84.

Jefferson tenaciously clung to his prejudice against Great Britain: "The object of England, long obvious, is to claim the ocean as her domain. . . We believe no more in Bonaparte's fighting merely for the liberty of the seas, than in Great Britain's fighting for the liberties of mankind." (Jefferson to Maury, April 25, 1812, *ib.* xi, 240–41.) He never failed to accentuate his love for France and his hatred for Napoleon.

[2] "During the present paroxysm of the insanity of Europe, we have thought it wisest to break off all intercourse with her." (Jefferson to Armstrong, May 2, 1808, *ib.* 30.)

[3] "Three alternatives alone are to be chosen from. 1. Embargo. 2. War. 3. Submission and tribute, &. wonderful to tell, the last will not want advocates." (Jefferson to Lincoln, Nov. 13, 1808, *ib.* 74.)

[4] See Act of December 22, 1807 (*Annals,* 10th Cong. 1st Sess. 2814–15); of January 9, 1808 (*ib.* 2815–17); of March 12, 1808 (*ib.* 2839–42); and of April 25, 1808 (*ib.* 2870–74); Treasury Circulars of

Here was an exercise of National power such as
John Marshall had never dreamed of. The effect
was disastrous. American ocean-carrying trade was
ruined; British ships were given the monopoly of
the seas.[1] And England was not "downed," as Jefferson expected. In fact neither France nor Great
Britain relaxed its practices in the least.[2]

The commercial interests demanded the repeal of
the Embargo laws,[3] so ruinous to American shipping,
so destructive to American trade, so futile in re-
dressing the wrongs we had suffered. Massachusetts was enraged. A great proportion of the tonnage of the whole country was owned in that State
and the Embargo had paralyzed her chief industry.
Here was a fresh source of grievance against the
Administration and a just one. Jefferson had, at
last, given the Federalists a real issue. Had they

May 6 and May 11, 1808 (*Embargo Laws*, 19-20, 21-22); and Jefferson's letter "to the Governours of Orleans, Georgia, South Carolina,
Massachusetts and New Hampshire," May 6, 1808 (*ib.* 20-21).

Joseph Hopkinson sarcastically wrote: "Bless the Embargo —
thrice bless the Presidents distribution Proclamation, by which his
minions are to judge of the appetites of his subjects, how much food
they may reasonably consume, and who shall supply them . . whether
under the Proclamation and Embargo System, a child may be lawfully born without a clearing out at the Custom House." (Hopkinson to Pickering, May 25, 1808, Pickering MSS. Mass. Hist.
Soc.)

[1] Professor Channing says that "the orders in council had been
passed originally to give English ship-owners a chance to regain some
of their lost business." (Channing: *Jeff. System*, 261.)

[2] Indeed, Napoleon, as soon as he learned of the American Embargo laws, ordered the seizure of all American ships entering French
ports because their captains or owners had disobeyed these American statutes and, therefore, surely were aiding the enemy. (Armstrong to Secretary of State, April 23, postscript of April 25, 1808,
Am. State Papers, For. Rel. III, 291.)

[3] Morison: *Otis*, II, 10-12; see also Channing: *Jeff. System*, 183.

availed themselves of it on economic and purely American grounds, they might have begun the rehabilitation of their weakened party throughout the country. But theirs were the vices of pride and of age — they could neither learn nor forget; could not estimate situations as they really were, but only as prejudice made them appear to be.

As soon as Congress convened in November, 1808, New England opened the attack on Jefferson's retaliatory measures. Senator James Hillhouse of Connecticut offered a resolution for the repeal of the obnoxious statutes. "Great Britain was not to be threatened into compliance by a rod of coercion," he said.[1] Pickering made a speech which might well have been delivered in Parliament.[2] British maritime practices were right, the Embargo wrong, and principally injurious to America.[3] The Orders in Council had been issued only after Great Britain "had witnessed . . these atrocities" committed by Napoleon and his plundering armies, "and seen the

[1] *Annals*, 10th Cong. 2d Sess. 22.

The intensity of the interest in the Embargo is illustrated by Giles's statement in his reply to Hillhouse that it "almost . . banish[ed] every other topic of conversation." (*Ib.* 94.)

[2] Four years earlier, Pickering had plotted the secession of New England and enlisted the support of the British Minister to accomplish it. (See vol. III, chap. VII, of this work.) His wife was an Englishwoman, the daughter of an officer of the British Navy. (Pickering and Upham: *Life of Timothy Pickering*, I, 7; and see Pickering to his wife, Jan. 1, 1808, *ib.* IV, 121.) His nephew had been Consul-General at London under the Federalist Administrations and was at this time a merchant in that city. (Pickering to Rose, March 22, 1808, *New-England Federalism:* Adams, 370.) Pickering had been, and still was, carrying on with George Rose, recently British Minister to the United States, a correspondence all but treasonable. (Morison: *Otis*, II, 6.)

[3] *Annals*, 10th Cong. 2d Sess. 175, 177–78.

deadly weapon aimed at her vitals." Yet Jefferson
had acted very much as if the United States were a
vassal of France.[1]

Again Pickering addressed the Senate, flatly charging that all Embargo measures were "in exact conformity with the views and wishes of the French
Emperor, . . the most ruthless tyrant that has
scourged the European world, since the Roman Empire fell!" Suppose the British Navy were destroyed
and France triumphant over Great Britain — to the
other titles of Bonaparte would then "be added
that of Emperor of the Two Americas"; for what
legions of soldiers "could he not send to the United
States in the thousands of British ships, were they
also at his command?"[2]

As soon as they were printed, Pickering sent
copies of these and speeches of other Federalists to
his close associate, the Chief Justice of the United
States. Marshall's prompt answer shows how far he
had gone in company with New England Federalist
opinion.

"I thank you very sincerely," he wrote "for the
excellent speeches lately delivered in the senate. ..
If sound argument & correct reasoning could save
our country it would be saved. Nothing can be
more completely demonstrated than the inefficacy
of the embargo, yet that demonstration seems to
be of no avail. I fear most seriously that the same
spirit which so tenaciously maintains this measure
will impel us to a war with the only power which
protects any part of the civilized world from the

[1] *Annals*, 10th Cong. 2d Sess. **193**.   [2] *Ib*. **279–82**.

despotism of that tyrant with whom we shall then be ravaged."[1]

Such was the change that nine years had wrought in the views of John Marshall. When Secretary of State he had arraigned Great Britain for her conduct toward neutrals, denounced the impressment of American sailors, and branded her admiralty courts as habitually unjust if not corrupt.[2] But his hatred of France had metamorphosed the man.

Before Marshall had written this letter, the Legislature of Massachusetts formally declared that the continuance of the Embargo would "endanger . . the union of these States."[3] Talk of secession was steadily growing in New England.[4] The National Government feared open rebellion.[5] Only one eminent Federalist dissented from these views of the party leaders which Marshall also held as fervently as they. That man was the one to whom he owed his place on the Supreme Bench. From his retirement in Quincy, John Adams watched the growing excitement with amused contempt.

"Our Gazettes and Pamphlets," he wrote, "tell us that Bonaparte . . will conquer England, and command all the British Navy, and send I know not how many hundred thousand soldiers here and con-

[1] Marshall to Pickering, Dec. 19, 1808, Pickering MSS. Mass. Hist. Soc.

[2] See vol. II, 509–14, of this work.   [3] Morison: *Otis*, II, 3–4.

[4] "The tories of Boston openly threaten insurrection." (Jefferson to Dearborn, Aug. 9, 1808, *Works:* Ford, XI, 40.) And see Morison: *Otis*, II, 6; *Life and Correspondence of Rufus King:* King, V, 88; also see Otis to Quincy, Dec. 15, 1808, Morison: *Otis*, II, 115.

[5] Monroe to Taylor, Jan. 9, 1809, *Branch Historical Papers*, June, 1908, 298.

quer from New Orleans to Passamaquoddy. Though every one of these Bugbears is an empty Phantom, yet the People seem to believe every article of this bombastical Creed and tremble and shudder in Consequence. Who shall touch these blind eyes?"[1]

On January 9, 1809, Jefferson signed the "Force Act," which the Republican Congress had defiantly passed, and again Marshall beheld such an assertion of National power as the boldest Federalist of Alien and Sedition times never had suggested. Collectors of customs were authorized to seize any vessel or wagon if they suspected the owner of an intention to evade the Embargo laws; ships could be laden only in the presence of National officials, and sailing delayed or prohibited arbitrarily. Rich rewards were provided for informers who should put the Government on the track of any violation of the multitude of restrictions of these statutes or of the Treasury regulations interpretative of them. The militia, the army, the navy were to be employed to enforce obedience.[2]

Along the New England coasts popular wrath swept like a forest fire. Violent resolutions were passed.[3] The Collector of Boston, Benjamin Lincoln, refused to obey the law and resigned.[4] The Legislature of

---

[1] Adams to Rush, July 25, 1808, *Old Family Letters*, 191–92.

[2] *Annals*, 10th Cong. 2d Sess. III, 1798–1804.

[3] Morison: *Otis*, II, 10. These resolutions denounced "'all those who shall assist in enforcing on others the arbitrary & unconstitutional provisions of this [Force Act]' .. as 'enemies to the Constitution of the United States and of this State, and hostile to the Liberties of the People.'" (Boston Town Records, 1796–1813, as quoted in *ib.*; and see McMaster: *History of the People of the United States*, III, 328.)

[4] McMaster, III, 329.

Massachusetts passed a bill denouncing the "Force
Act" as unconstitutional, and declaring any officer
entering a house in execution of it to be guilty of a
high misdemeanor, punishable by fine and imprisonment.[1] The Governor of Connecticut declined the
request of the Secretary of War to afford military
aid and addressed the Legislature in a speech bristling with sedition.[2] The Embargo must go, said the
Federalists, or New England would appeal to arms.
Riots broke out in many towns. Withdrawal from
the Union was openly advocated.[3] Nor was this
sentiment confined to that section. "If the question were barely *stirred* in New England, some States
would drop off the Union like fruit, *rotten ripe*,"
wrote A. C. Hanson of Baltimore.[4] Humphrey
Marshall of Kentucky declared that he looked to
"BOSTON . . the Cradle, and SALEM, the nourse, of
American Liberty," as "the source of reformation,
or should that be unattainable, of disunion."[5]

Warmly as he sympathized with Federalist opinion
of the absurd Republican retaliatory measures, and
earnestly as he shared Federalist partisanship for
Great Britain, John Marshall deplored all talk of

[1] McMaster, III, 329–30; and see Morison: *Otis*, II, 4.
  The Federalist view was that the "Force Act" and other extreme
portions of the Embargo laws were "so violently and palpably unconstitutional, as to render a reference to the judiciary absurd"; and
that it was "the inherent right of the people to resist measures
fundamentally inconsistent with the principles of just liberty and the
Social compact." (Hare to Otis, Feb. 10, 1814, Morison: *Otis*, II,
175.)

[2] McMaster, III, 331–32.   [3] Morison: *Otis*, II, 3, 8.

[4] Hanson to Pickering, Jan. 17, 1810, *N.E. Federalism*: Adams, 382.

[5] Humphrey Marshall to Pickering, March 17, 1809, Pickering MSS.
Mass. Hist. Soc.

secession and sternly rebuked resistance to National authority, as is shown in his opinion in Fletcher *vs.* Peck,[1] wherein he asserted the sovereignty of the Nation over a State.

Another occasion, however, gave Marshall a better opportunity to state his views more directly, and to charge them with the whole force of the concurrence of all his associates on the Supreme Bench. This occasion was the resistance of the Legislature and Governor of Pennsylvania to a decree of Richard Peters, Judge of the United States Court for that district, rendered in the notable and dramatic case of Gideon Olmstead. During the Revolution, Olmstead and three other American sailors captured the British sloop Active and sailed for Egg Harbor, New Jersey. Upon nearing their destination, they were overhauled by an armed vessel belonging to the State of Pennsylvania and by an American privateer. The Active was taken to Philadelphia and claimed as a prize of war. The court awarded Olmstead and his comrades only one fourth of the proceeds of the sale of the vessel, the other three fourths going to the State of Pennsylvania, to the officers and crew of the State ship, and to those of the privateer. The Continental Prize Court reversed the decision and ordered the whole amount received for sloop and cargo to be paid to Olmstead and his associates.

This the State court refused to do, and a litigation began which lasted for thirty years. The funds were invested in United States loan certificates, and these were delivered by the State Judge to the State Treas-

[1] See vol. III, chap. X, of this work.

urer, David Rittenhouse, upon a bond saving the
Judge harmless in case he, thereafter, should be compelled to pay the amount in controversy to Olmstead.
Rittenhouse kept the securities in his personal possession, and after his death they were found among
his effects with a note in his handwriting that they
would become the property of Pennsylvania when
the State released him from his bond to the Judge.

In 1803, Olmstead secured from Judge Peters an
order to the daughters of Rittenhouse who, as his executrixes, had possession of the securities, to deliver
them to Olmstead and his associates. This proceeding of the National court was promptly met by an
act of the State Legislature which declared that
the National court had "usurped" jurisdiction, and
directed the Governor to "protect the just rights of
the state . . from any process whatever issued out
of any federal court." [1]

Peters, a good lawyer and an upright judge, but a
timorous man, was cowed by this sharp defiance and
did nothing. The executrixes held on to the securities. At last, on March 5, 1808, Olmstead applied to
the Supreme Court of the United States for a rule
directed to Judge Peters to show cause why a mandamus should not issue compelling him to execute
his decree. Peters made return that the act of the
State Legislature had caused him "from prudential
. . motives . . to avoid embroiling the government
of the United States and that of Pennsylvania." [2]

Thus the matter came before Marshall. On February 20, 1809, just when threats of resistance to the

[1] 5 Cranch, 133.   [2] *Ib.* 117.

"Force Act" were sounding loudest, when riots were in progress along the New England seaboard, and a storm of debate over the Embargo and Non-Intercourse laws was raging in Congress, the Chief Justice delivered his opinion in the case of the United States *vs.* Peters.[1] The court had, began Marshall, considered the return of Judge Peters "with great attention, and with serious concern." The act of the Pennsylvania Legislature challenged the very life of the National Government, for, "if the legislatures of the several states may, at will, annul the judgments of the courts of the United States, and destroy the rights acquired under those judgments, the constitution itself becomes a solemn mockery, and the nation is deprived of the means of enforcing its laws by the instrumentality of its own tribunals."

These clear, strong words were addressed to Massachusetts and Connecticut no less than to Pennsylvania. They were meant for Marshall's Federalist comrades and friends — for Pickering, and Gore, and Morris, and Otis — as much as for the State officials in Lancaster. His opinion was not confined to the case before him; it was meant for the whole country and especially for those localities where National laws were being denounced and violated, and National authority defied and flouted. Considering the depth and fervor of Marshall's feelings on the whole policy of the Republican régime, his opinion in United States *vs.* Judge Peters was signally brave and noble.

[1] 5 Cranch, 135.

Forcible resistance by a State to National authority! "So fatal a result must be deprecated by all; and the people of Pennsylvania, *not less than the citizens of every other state*, must feel a deep interest in resisting principles so destructive of the Union, and in averting consequences so fatal to themselves." Marshall then states the facts of the controversy and concludes that "the state of Pennsylvania can possess no constitutional right" to resist the authority of the National courts. His decision, he says, "is not made without extreme regret at the necessity which has induced the application." But, because "it is a solemn duty" to do so, the "mandamus must be awarded."[1]

Marshall's opinion deeply angered the Legislature and officials of Pennsylvania.[2] When Judge Peters, in obedience to the order of the Supreme Court, directed the United States Marshal to enforce the decree in Olmstead's favor, that official found the militia under command of General Bright drawn up around the house of the two executrixes. The dispute was at last composed, largely because President Madison rebuked Pennsylvania and upheld the National courts.[3]

---

[1] 5 Cranch, 136, 141. (Italics the author's.)

[2] The Legislature of Pennsylvania adopted a resolution, April 3, 1809, proposing an amendment to the National Constitution for the establishment of an "impartial tribunal" to decide upon controversies between States and the Nation. (*State Documents on Federal Relations:* Ames, 46–48.) In reply Virginia insisted that the Supreme Court, "selected from those . . who are most celebrated for virtue and legal learning," was the proper tribunal to decide such cases. (*Ib.* 49–50.) This Nationalist position Virginia reversed within a decade in protest against Marshall's Nationalist opinions. Virginia's Nationalist resolution of 1809 was read by Pinkney in his argument of Cohens *vs.* Virginia. (See *infra,* chap. VI.)

[3] See Madison to Snyder, April 13, 1809, *Annals,* 11th Cong. 2d Sess. 2269; also McMaster, v, 403–06.

A week after the delivery of Marshall's opinion, the most oppressive provisions of the Embargo Acts were repealed and a curious non-intercourse law enacted.[1] One section directed the suspension of all commercial restrictions against France or Great Britain in case either belligerent revoked its orders or decrees against the United States; and this the President was to announce by proclamation. The new British Minister, David M. Erskine, now tendered apology and reparation for the attack on the Chesapeake and positively assured the Administration that, if the United States would renew intercourse with Great Britain, the British Orders in Council would be withdrawn on June 10, 1809. Immediately President Madison issued his proclamation stating this fact and announcing that after that happy June day, Americans might renew their long and ruinously suspended trade with all the world not subject to French control.[2]

The Federalists were jubilant.[3] But their joy was quickly turned to wrath — against the Administration. Great Britain repudiated the agreement of her Minister, recalled him, and sent another charged with rigid and impossible instructions.[4] In deep humiliation, Madison issued a second proclamation reciting the facts and restoring to full operation against Great Britain all the restrictive commercial and maritime laws remaining on the statute

[1] *Annals*, 10th Cong. 2d Sess. 1824–30.

[2] Erskine to Smith, April 18 and 19, 1809, *Am. State Papers, For. Rel.* iii, 296.

[3] Adams: *U.S.* v, 73–74; see also McMaster, iii, 337.

[4] Adams: *U.S.* v, 87–89, 112.

books.[1] At a banquet in Richmond, Jefferson proposed a toast: "The freedom of the seas!"[2]

Upon the arrival of Francis James Jackson, Erskine's successor as British Minister, the scenes of the Genêt drama[3] were repeated. Jackson was arrogant and overbearing, and his instructions were as harsh as his disposition.[4] Soon the Administration was forced to refuse further conference with him. Jackson then issued an appeal to the American people in the form of a circular to British Consuls in America, accusing the American Government of trickery, concealment of facts, and all but downright falsehood.[5] A letter of Canning to the American Minister at London[6] found its way into the Federalist newspapers, "doubtless by the connivance of the British Minister," says Joseph Story. This letter was, Story thought, an "infamous" appeal to the American people to repudiate their own Government, "the old game of Genêt played over again."[7]

[1] Proclamation of Aug. 9, 1809, *Am. State Papers, For. Rel.* III, 304.

[2] Tyler: *Letters and Times of the Tylers*, I, 229. For an expression by Napoleon on this subject, see Adams: *U.S.* v, 137.

[3] See vol. II, 28–29, of this work.

[4] "The appointment of Jackson and the instructions given to him might well have justified a declaration of war against Great Britain the moment they were known." (Channing: *Jeff. System*, 237.)

[5] Circular, Nov. 13, 1809, *Am. State Papers, For. Rel.* III, 323; *Annals*, 11th Cong. 2d Sess. 743.

[6] Canning to Pinkney, Sept. 23, 1808, *Am. State Papers, For. Rel.* III, 230–31.

[7] Story to White, Jan. 17, 1809, *Life and Letters of Joseph Story*. Story, I, 193–94. There were two letters from Canning to Pinkney, both dated Sept. 23, 1808. Story probably refers to one printed in the *Columbian Centinel*, Boston, Jan. 11, 1809.

"It seems as if in New England the federalists were forgetful of all the motives for union & were ready to destroy the fabric which has been raised by the wisdom of our fathers. Have they altogether lost the

Furious altercations arose all over the country.
The Federalists defended Jackson. When the elections came on, the Republicans made tremendous
gains in New England as well as in other States,[1]
a circumstance that depressed Marshall profoundly.
In December an acrimonious debate arose in Congress over a resolution denouncing Jackson's circular
letter as a "direct and aggravated insult and affront
to the American people and their Government." [2]
Every Federalist opposed the resolution. Josiah
Quincy of Massachusetts declared that every word
of it was a "falsehood," and that the adoption of
it would call forth "severe retribution, perhaps in
war" from Great Britain.[3]

Disheartened, disgusted, wrathful, Marshall wrote
Quincy: "The Federalists of the South participate
with their brethren of the North in the gloomy an-
ticipations which your late elections must inspire.
The proceedings of the House of Representatives already demonstrate the influence of those elections on
the affairs of the Union. I had supposed that the late
letter to Mr. Armstrong,[4] and the late seizure [by

memory of Washington's farewell address? .. The riotous proceedings in some towns .. no doubt .. are occasioned by the instigation
of men, who keep behind the curtain & yet govern the wires of the
puppet shew." (Story to his brother, Jan. 3, 1809, Story MSS. Mass.
Hist. Soc.)

"In New England, and even in New York, there appears a spirit
hostile to the existence of our own government." (Plumer to Gilman,
Jan. 24, 1809, Plumer: *Life of William Plumer*, 368.)

[1] Adams: *U.S.* v, 158.

[2] *Annals*, 11th Cong. 2d Sess. 481.

[3] *Ib.* 943. The resolution was passed over the strenuous resistance
of the Federalists.

[4] Probably that of Madison, July 21, 1808, *Annals*, 10th Cong.
2d Sess. 1681.

the French] of an American vessel, simply because she was an American, added to previous burnings, ransoms, and confiscations, would have exhausted to the dregs our cup of servility and degradation; but these measures appear to make no impression on those to whom the United States confide their destinies. To what point are we verging?" [1]

Nor did the Chief Justice keep quiet in Richmond. "We have lost our resentment for the severest injuries a nation ever suffered, because of their being so often repeated. Nay, Judge Marshall and Mr. Pickering & Co. found out Great Britain had given us no cause of complaint," [2] writes John Tyler. And ever nearer drew the inevitable conflict.

Jackson was unabashed by the condemnation of Congress, and not without reason. Wherever he went, more invitations to dine than he could accept poured in upon him from the "best families"; banquets were given in his honor; the Senate of Massachusetts adopted resolutions condemning the Administration and upholding Jackson, who declared that the State had "done more towards justifying me to the world than it was possible . . that I or any other person could do." [3] The talk of secession grew.[4] At

[1] Marshall to Quincy, April 23, 1810, Quincy: *Life of Josiah Quincy*, 204.

[2] Tyler to Jefferson, May 12, 1810, Tyler: *Tyler*, I, 247; and see next chapter.

[3] Adams: *U.S.* v, 212–14; and see Morison: *Otis*, II, 18–19.

[4] Turreau, then the French Minister at Washington, thus reported to his Government: "To-day not only is the separation of New England openly talked about, but the people of those five States wish for this separation, pronounce it, openly prepare it, will carry it out under British protection"; and he suggests that "perhaps the moment has come for forming a party in favor of France in the Central and

a public banquet given Jackson, Pickering proposed the toast: "The world's last hope — Britain's fast-anchored isle!" It was greeted with a storm of cheers. Pickering's words sped over the country and became the political war cry of Federalism.[1] Marshall, who in Richmond was following "with anxiety" all political news, undoubtedly read it, and his letters show that Pickering's words stated the opinion of the Chief Justice.[2]

Upon the assurance of the French Foreign Minister that the Berlin and Milan Decrees would be revoked after November 1, 1810, President Madison, on November 2, announced what he believed to be Napoleon's settled determination, and recommended the resumption of commercial relations with France and the suspension of all intercourse with Great Britain unless that Power also withdrew its injurious and offensive Orders in Council.[3]

When at Washington, Marshall was frequently in

Southern States, whenever those of the North, having given themselves a separate government under the support of Great Britain, may threaten the independence of the rest." (Turreau to Champagny, April 20, 1809, as quoted in Adams: *U.S.* v, 36.)

[1] For account of Jackson's reception in Boston and the effects of it, see Adams: *U.S.* 215-17, and Morison: *Otis*, 20-22.

[2] On the other hand, Jefferson, out of his bottomless prejudice against Great Britain, drew venomous abuse of the whole British nation: "What is to restore order and safety on the ocean?" he wrote; "the death of George III? Not at all. He is only stupid; . . his ministers . . ephemeral. But his nation is permanent, and it is that which is the tyrant of the ocean. The principle that force is right, is become the principle of the nation itself. They would not permit an honest minister, were accident to bring such an one into power, to relax their system of lawless piracy." (Jefferson to Rodney, Feb. 10, 1810, *Works:* Ford, xi, 135-36.)

[3] Champagny, Duke de Cadore, to Armstrong, Aug. 5, 1810 (*Am. State Papers, For. Rel.* iii, 386-87), and Proclamation, Nov. 2, 1810 (*ib.* 392); and see Adams: *U.S.* v, 303-04.

Pickering's company. Before the Chief Justice left for Richmond, the Massachusetts Senator had lent him pamphlets containing part of John Adams's "Cunningham Correspondence." In returning them, Marshall wrote that he had read Adams's letters "with regret." But the European war, rather than the "Cunningham Correspondence," was on the mind of the Chief Justice: "We are looking with anxiety towards the metropolis for political intelligence. Report gives much importance to the communications of Serrurier [the new French Minister],[1] & proclaims him to be charged with requisitions on our government, a submission to which would seem to be impossible. . . I will flatter myself that I have not seen you for the last time. Events have so fully demonstrated the correctness of your opinions on subjects the most interesting to our country that I cannot permit myself to believe the succeeding legislature of Massachusetts will deprive the nation of your future services." [2]

As the Federalist faith in Great Britain grew stronger, Federalist distrust of the youthful and growing American people increased. Early in 1811, the bill to admit Louisiana was considered. The Federalists violently resisted it. Josiah Quincy declared that "if this bill passes, the bonds of this Union are virtually dissolved; that the States which compose it are free from their moral obligations, and that, as it will be the right of all, so it will be the duty of some, to prepare definitely for a separation

[1] Adams: *U.S.* v, 346.
[2] Marshall to Pickering, Feb. 22, 1811, Pickering MSS. Mass. Hist. Soc.

— amicably if they can, violently if they must."[1]
Quincy was the embodiment of the soul of Localism: "The first public love of my heart is the Commonwealth of Massachusetts. There is my fireside;
there are the tombs of my ancestors."[2]

The spirit of American Nationalism no longer
dwelt in the breasts of even the youngest of the
Federalist leaders. Its abode now was the hearts of
the people of the West and South; and its strongest
exponent was a young Kentuckian, Henry Clay,
whose feelings and words were those of the heroic
seventies. Although but thirty-three years old, he
had been appointed for the second time to fill an
unexpired term in the National Senate. On February 22, 1810, he addressed that body on the country's wrongs and duty: "Have we not been for years
contending against the tyranny of the ocean?" We
have tried "*peaceful* resistance. . . When this is abandoned without effect, I am for resistance by the
sword."[3] Two years later, in the House, to which he
was elected immediately after his term in the Senate
expired, and of which he was promptly chosen
Speaker, Clay again made an appeal to American
patriotism: "The real cause of British aggression was
not to distress an enemy, but to destroy a rival!"[4]

[1] *Annals*, 11th Cong. 3d Sess. 525.
Daniel Webster was also emphatically opposed to the admission
of new States: "Put in a solemn, decided, and spirited Protest
against making new States out of new Territories. Affirm, in direct
terms, that New Hampshire has never agreed to favor political con-
nexions of such intimate nature, with any people, out of the limits
of the U.S. as they existed at the time of the compact." (Webster to
his brother, June 4, 1813, *Letters of Daniel Webster:* Van Tyne, 37.)

[2] *Annals*, 11th Cong. 3d Sess. 542.   [3] *Ib.* 1st and 2d Sess. 579–82.
[4] *Annals*, 12th Cong. 1st Sess. 601; also see Adams: *U.S.* v, 189–90.

he passionately exclaimed. Another Patrick Henry had arisen to lead America to a new independence.

Four other young Representatives from the West and South, John C. Calhoun, William Lowndes, Langdon Cheves, and Felix Grundy were as hot for war as was Henry Clay.[1]

Clay's speeches, extravagant, imprudent, and grandiose, had at least one merit: they were thoroughly American and expressed the opinion of the first generation of Americans that had grown up since the colonies won their freedom. Henry Clay spoke their language. But it was not the language of the John Marshall of 1812.

Eventually the Administration was forced to act. On June 1, 1812, President Madison sent to Congress his Message which briefly, and with moderation, stated the situation.[2] On June 4, the House passed a bill declaring war on Great Britain. Every Federalist but three voted against it.[3] The Senate

---

[1] Adams: *U.S.* v, 316.

[2] Richardson, I, 499–505; *Am. State Papers, For. Rel.* III,.567–70.

[3] *Annals*, 12th Cong. 1st S ss. 1637. The Federalists who voted for war were: Joseph Kent of Maryland, James Morgan of New Jersey, and William M. Richardson of Massachusetts.

Professor Channing thus states the American grievances: "Inciting the Indians to rebellion, impressing American seamen and making them serve on British war-ships, closing the ports of Europe to American commerce, these were the counts in the indictment against the people and government of Great Britain." (Channing: *Jeff. System*, 260.) See also *ib.* 268, and Jefferson's brilliant statement of the causes of the war, Jefferson to Logan, Oct. 3, 1813, *Works: Ford*, XI, 338–39.

"The United States," says Henry Adams, "had a superfluity of only too good causes for war with Great Britain." (Adams: *Life of Albert Gallatin*, 445.) Adams emphasizes this: "The United States had the right to make war on England with or without notice, either for her past spoliations, her actual blockades, her Orders in Council other than blockades, her Rule of 1756, her impressments, or her

made unimportant amendments which the House accepted;[1] and thus, on June 18, war was formally declared.

At the Fourth of July banquet of the Boston Federalists, among the toasts, by drinking to which the company exhilarated themselves, was this sentiment: "*The Existing War* — The Child of Prostitution, may no American acknowledge it legitimate."[2] Joseph Story was profoundly alarmed: "I am thoroughly convinced," he wrote, "that the leading Federalists meditate a severance of the Union."[3] His apprehension was justified: "Let the Union be severed. Such a severance presents no terrors to me," wrote the leading Federalist of New England.[4]

While opposition to the war thus began to blaze into open and defiant treason in that section,[5] the

attack on the 'Chesapeake,' not yet redressed, — possibly also for other reasons less notorious." (Adams: *U.S.* v, 339.) And see Roosevelt, chaps. I and II.

[1] *Annals*, 12th Cong. 1st Sess. 1675–82.

[2] Salem *Gazette*, July 7, 1812, as quoted in Morison: *Otis*, I, 298.

[3] Story to Williams, Aug. 24, 1812, Story, I, 229.

[4] Pickering to Pennington, July 12, 1812, *N.E. Federalism:* Adams, 389.

[5] Of course the National courts were attacked: "Attempts . . are made . . to break down the Judiciary of the United States through the newspapers, and mean and miserable insinuations are made to weaken the authority of its judgments." (Story to Williams, Aug. 3, 1813, Story, I, 247.) And again: "Conspirators, and traitors are enabled to carry on their purposes almost without check." (Same to same, May 27, 1813, *ib.* 244.) Story was lamenting that the National courts had no common-law jurisdiction. Some months earlier he had implored Nathaniel Williams, Representative in Congress from Story's district, to "induce Congress to give the Judicial Courts of the United States power to punish all crimes . . against the Government. . . Do not suffer conspiracies to destroy the Union." (Same to same, Oct. 8, 1812, *ib.* 243.)

Jefferson thought the people were loyal: "When the questions of separation and rebellion shall be nakedly proposed . . the Gores and

old-time Southern Federalists, who detested it no
less, sought a more practical, though more timid, way
to resist and end it. "Success in this War, would most
probably be the worst kind of ruin," wrote Benjamin Stoddert to the sympathetic James McHenry.
"There is but one way to save our Country . . change
the administration — . . this can be affected by
bringing forward another Virgn. as the competitor of
Madison." For none but a Virginian can get the
Presidential electors of that State, said Stoddert.

"There is, then, but one man to be thought of as
the candidate of the Federalists and of all who were
against the war. That man is John Marshall." Stoddert informs McHenry that he has written an article for a Maryland Federalist paper, the *Spirit of
Seventy-Six*, recommending Marshall for President.
"This I have done, because . . every body else . .
seems to be seized with apathy . . and because I felt
it sacred duty." [1]

Stoddert's newspaper appeal for Marshall's nomination was clear, persuasive, and well reasoned. It
opened with the familiar Federalist arguments
against the war. It was an "*offensive* war," which
meant the ruin of America. "Thus thinking . . I feel
it a solemn duty to my countrymen, to name JOHN
MARSHALL, as a man as highly gifted as any other in
the United States, for the important office of Chief
Magistrate; and more likely than any other to com-

the Pickerings will find their levees crowded with silk stocking gentry,
but no yeomanry." (Jefferson to Gerry, June 11, 1812, *Works : Ford,
XI, 257.)

[1] Stoddert to McHenry, July 15, 1812, Steiner: *Life and Correspondence of James McHenry*, 581–83.

mand the confidence, and unite the votes of that description of men, of all parties, who desire nothing from government, but that it should be wisely and faithfully administered. . .

"The sterling integrity of this gentleman's character and his high elevation of mind, forbid the suspicion, that he could descend to be a mere party President, or less than the President of the whole people: — but one objection can be urged against him by candid and honorable men: He is a Virginian, and Virginia has already furnished more than her full share of Presidents — This objection in less critical times would be entitled to great weight; but situated as the world is, and as we are, the only consideration now should be, who amongst our ablest statesmen, can best unite the suffrages of the citizens of all parties, in a competition with Mr. Madison, whose continuance in power is incompatible with the safety of the nation? . .

"It may happen," continues Stoddert, "that this our beloved country may be ruined for want of the services of the great and good man I have been prompted by sacred duty to introduce, from the mere want of energy among those of his immediate countrymen [Virginians], who think of his virtues and talents as I do; and as I do of the crisis which demands their employment.

" If in his native state men of this description will act in concert, & with a vigor called for by the occasion, and will let the people fairly know, that the contest is between John Marshall, peace, and a new order of things; and James Madison, Albert Gallatin and war, with war taxes, war loans, and all the other dreadful evils of a war in the present state of the world, my life for it they will succeed, and by a considerable majority of the independent votes of Virginia."

Stoddert becomes so enthusiastic that he thinks victory possible without the assistance of Marshall's own State: "Even if they fail in Virginia, the very effort will produce an animation in North Carolina, the middle and Eastern states, that will most probably secure the election of John Marshall. At the worst nothing can be lost but a little labour in a good cause, and everything may be saved, or gained for our country." Stoddert signs his plea "A Maryland Farmer." [1]

In his letter to McHenry he says: "They vote for electors in Virga. by a general ticket, and I am thoroughly persuaded that if the men in that State, who prefer Marshall to Madison, can be animated into Exertion, he will get the votes of that State. What little I can do by private letters to affect this will be done." Stoddert had enlisted one John Davis, an Englishman — writer, traveler, and generally a rolling stone — in the scheme to nominate Marshall. Davis, it seems, went to Virginia on this mission. After investigating conditions in that State, he had informed Stoddert "that if the Virgns. have nerve to believe it will be agreeable to the Northern & E. States, he is sure Marshall will get the Virga. votes." [2]

[1] "To the Citizens of the United States," in the *Spirit of Seventy-Six*, July 17, 1812.

[2] Stoddert refers to this person as "Jo Davies." By some this has been thought to refer to Marshall's brother-in-law, "Jo" Daveiss of

Stoddert dwells with the affection and anxiety of parentage upon his idea of Marshall for President: "It is not because I prefer Marshall to several other men, that I speak of him — but because I am well convinced it is vain to talk of any other man, and Marshall is a Man in whom Fedts. may confide — Perhaps indeed he is the man for the crisis, which demands great good sense, a great firmness under the garb of great moderation." He then urges McHenry to get to work for Marshall — "support a cause [election of a peace President] on which all that is dear to you depends."[1] Stoddert also wrote two letters to William Coleman of New York, editor of the *New York Evening Post*, urging Marshall for the Presidency.[2]

Twelve days after Stoddert thus instructed McHenry, Marshall wrote strangely to Robert Smith of Maryland. President Madison had dismissed Smith from the office of Secretary of State for inefficiency in the conduct of our foreign affairs and for intriguing with his brother, Senator Samuel Smith, and others against the Administration's foreign

Kentucky. But the latter was killed in the Battle of Tippecanoe, November 7, 1811.

While the identity of Stoddert's agent cannot be established with certainty, he probably was one John Davis of Salisbury, England, as described in the text. "Jo" was then used for John as much as for Joseph; and Davis was frequently spelled "Davies." A John or "Jo" Davis or Davies, an Englishman, was a very busy person in America during the first decade of the nineteenth century. (See Loshe: *Early American Novel*, 74–77.) Naturally he would have been against the War of 1812, and he was just the sort of person that an impracticable man like Stoddert would have chosen for such a mission.

[1] Stoddert to McHenry, July 15, 1812, Steiner, 582.
[2] See King, v, 266.

policy.[1] Upon his ejection from the Cabinet, Smith proceeded to "vindicate" himself by publishing a dull and pompous "Address" in which he asserted that we must have a President "of energetic mind, of enlarged and liberal views, of temperate and dignified deportment, of honourable and manly feelings, and as efficient in maintaining, as sagacious in discerning the rights of our much-injured and insulted country."[2] This was a good summary of Marshall's qualifications.

When Stoddert proposed Marshall for the Presidency, Smith wrote the Chief Justice, enclosing a copy of his attack on the Administration. On July 27, 1812, more than five weeks after the United States had declared war, Marshall replied: "Although I have for several years forborn to intermingle with those questions which agitate & excite the feelings of party, it is impossible that I could be inattentive to passing events, or an unconcerned observer of them." But "as they have increased in their importance, the interest, which as an American I must take in them, has also increased; and the declaration of war has appeared to me, as it has to you, to be one of those portentous acts which ought to concentrate on itself the efforts of all those who can take an active part in rescuing their country from the ruin it threatens.

"All minor considerations should be waived; the lines of subdivision between parties, if not absolutely effaced, should at least be convened for a time;

---

[1] Adams: *U.S.* v, 375–78.
[2] Smith: *An Address to the People of the United States*, 42–43.

and the great division between the friends of peace & the advocates of war ought alone to remain. It is an object of such magnitude as to give to almost every other, comparative insignificance; and all who wish peace ought to unite in the means which may facilitate its attainment, whatever may have been their differences of opinion on other points." [1]

Marshall proceeds to analyze the causes of hostilities. These, he contends, were Madison's subserviency to France and the base duplicity of Napoleon. The British Government and American Federalists had, from the first, asserted that the Emperor's revocation of the Berlin and Milan Decrees was a mere trick to entrap that credulous French partisan, Madison; and this they maintained with ever-increasing evidence to support them. For, in spite of Napoleon's friendly words, American ships were still seized by the French as well as by the British.

In response to the demand of Joel Barlow, the new American Minister to France, for a forthright statement as to whether the obnoxious decrees against neutral commerce had or had not been revoked as to the United States, the French Foreign Minister delivered to Barlow a new decree. This document, called " The Decree of St. Cloud," declared that the former edicts of Napoleon, of which the American Government complained, "are definitively, and to date from the 1st day of November last [1810], considered as not having existed [*non avenus*] in regard to American vessels." The "decree" was dated April 28,

---

[1] Marshall to Smith, July 27, 1812, Dreer MSS. "American Lawyers," Pa. Hist. Soc.

1811, yet it was handed to Barlow on May 10, 1812. It expressly stated, moreover, that Napoleon issued it because the American Congress had, by the Act of May 2, 1811, prohibited "the vessels and merchandise of Great Britain . . from entering into the ports of the United States." [1]

General John Armstrong, the American Minister who preceded Barlow, never had heard of this decree; it had not been transmitted to the French Minister at Washington; it had not been made public in any way. It was a ruse, declared the Federalists when news of it reached America — a cheap and tawdry trick to save Madison's face, a palpable falsehood, a clumsy afterthought. So also asserted Robert Smith, and so he wrote to the Chief Justice.

Marshall agreed with the fallen Baltimore politician. Continuing his letter to Smith, the longest and most unreserved he ever wrote, except to Washington and to Lee when on the French Mission,[2] the Chief Justice said: "The view you take of the edict purporting to bear date of the 28th of April 1811 appears to me to be perfectly correct. . . I am astonished, if in these times any thing ought to astonish, that the same impression is not made on all." Marshall puts many questions based on dates, for the purpose of exposing the fraudulent nature of the French decree and continues:

"Had France felt for the United States any portion of that respect to which our real importance entitles us, would she have failed to give this proof of it? But

---

[1] *Am. State Papers, For. Rel.* III, 603; and see Channing: *U.S.* IV, 449.
[2] See vol. II, 243–44, 245–47, of this work.

regardless of the assertion made by the President in his Proclamation of the 2ᵈ of Novʳ 1810, regardless of the communications made by the Executive to the Legislature, regardless of the acts of Congress, and regardless of the propositions which we have invariably maintained in our diplomatic intercourse with Great Britain, the Emperor has given a date to his decree, & has assigned a motive for its enactment, which in express terms contradict every assertion made by the American nation throughout all the departments of its government, & remove the foundation on which its whole system has been erected.

"The motive for this offensive & contemptuous proceeding cannot be to rescue himself from the imputation of continuing to enforce his decrees after their formal repeal because this imputation is precisely as applicable to a repeal dated the 28ᵗʰ of April 1811 as to one dated the 1ˢᵗ of November 1810, since the execution of those decrees has continued after the one date as well as after the other. Why then is this obvious fabrication such as we find it? Why has Mʳ Barlow been unable to obtain a paper which might consult the honor & spare the feelings of his government? The answer is not to be disguised. Bonaparte does not sufficiently respect us to exhibit for our sake, to France, to America, to Britain, or to the world, any evidence of his having receded one step from the position he had taken.

"He could not be prevailed on, even after we had done all he required, to soften any one of his acts so far as to give it the appearance of his having advanced one step to meet us. That this step, or rather

the appearance of having taken it, might save our
reputation was regarded as dust in the balance.
Even now, after our solemn & repeated assertions
that our discrimination between the belligerents is
founded altogether on a first advance of France—on
a decisive & unequivocal repeal of all her obnoxious
decrees; after we have engaged in a war of the most
calamitous character, avowedly, because France had
repealed those decrees, the Emperor scorns to countenance the assertion or to leave it uncontradicted.

"He avers to ourselves, to our selected enemy, &
to the world, that, whatever pretexts we may assign
for our conduct, he has in fact ceded nothing, he has
made no advance, he stands on his original ground &
we have marched up to it. We have submitted, completely submitted; & he will not leave us the poor
consolation of concealing that submission from ourselves. But not even our submission has obtained
relief. His cruizers still continue to capture, sink,
burn & destroy.

"I cannot contemplate this subject without excessive mortification as well at the contempt with
which we are treated as at the infatuation of my
countrymen. It is not however for me to indulge
these feelings though I cannot so entirely suppress
them as not sometimes though rarely to allow them
a place in a private letter." Marshall assures Smith
that he has "read with attention and approbation"
the paper sent him and will see to its "republication." [1]

[1] Marshall to Smith, July 27, 1812, Dreer MSS. "American Lawyers," Pa. Hist. Soc.
A single quotation from the letters of Southern Federalists will
show how accurately Marshall interpreted Federalist feeling during

From reading Marshall's letter without a knowledge of the facts, one could not possibly infer that America ever had been wronged by the Power with which we were then at war. All the strength of his logical and analytical mind is brought to bear upon the date and motives of Napoleon's last decree. He wrote in the tone and style, and with the controversial ability of his state papers, when at the head of the Adams Cabinet. But had the British Foreign Secretary guided his pen, his indictment of France and America could not have been more unsparing. His letter to Smith was a call to peace advocates and British partisans to combine to end the war by overthrowing the Administration.

This unfortunate letter was written during the long period between the adjournment of the Supreme Court in March, 1812, and its next session in February of the following year. Marshall's sentiments are in sharp contrast with those of Joseph Story, whose letters, written from his Massachusetts home, strongly condemn those who were openly opposing the war. "The present," he writes, "was the last occasion which patriotism ought to have sought to create divisions." [1]

Apparently the Administration did not know of Marshall's real feelings. Immediately after the declaration of war, Monroe, who succeeded Smith as Secretary of State, had sent his old personal friend,

the War of 1812: "Heaven grant that . . our own Country may not be found ultimately, a solitary friend of this great Robber of Nations." (Tallmadge to McHenry, May 30, 1813, Steiner, 598.) The war had been in progress more than ten months when these words were written.

[1] Story to Williams, Oct. 8, 1812, Story, I, 243.

the Chief Justice, some documents relating to the war. If Marshall had been uninformed as to the causes that drove the United States to take militant action, these papers supplied that information. In acknowledging receipt of them, he wrote Monroe:

"On my return to day from my farm where I pass a considerable portion of my time in *laborious relaxation*, I found a copy of the message of the President of the 1st inst accompanied by the report of the Committee of foreign relations & the declaration of war against Great Britain, under cover from you.

"Permit me to subjoin to my thanks for this mark of your attention my fervent wish that this momentous measure may, in its operation on the interest & honor of our country, disappoint only its enemies. Whether my prayer be heard or not I shall remain with respectful esteem," etc.[1]

Cold as this letter was, and capable as it was of double interpretation, to the men sorely pressed by the immediate exigencies of combat, it gave no inkling that the Chief Justice of the United States was at that very moment not only in close sympathy with the peace party, but was actually encouraging that party in its efforts to end the war.[2]

Just at this time, Marshall must have longed for seclusion, and, by a lucky chance, it was afforded him. One of the earliest and most beneficial effects of the Non-Importation, Embargo, and Non-Inter-

[1] Marshall to Monroe, June 25, 1812, Monroe MSS. Lib. Cong.
[2] Marshall, however, was a member of the "Vigilance Committee" of Richmond, and took an important part in its activities. (*Virginia Magazine of History and Biography*, VII, 230–31.)

course laws that preceded the war, was the heavily increased migration from the seaboard States to the territories beyond the Alleghanies. The dramatic story of Burr's adventures and designs had reached every ear and had turned toward the Western country the eyes of the poor, the adventurous, the aspiring; already thousands of settlers were taking up the new lands over the mountains. Thus came a practical consideration of improved means of travel and transportation. Fresh interest in the use of waterways was given by Fulton's invention, which seized upon the imagination of men. The possibilities of steam navigation were in the minds of all who observed the expansion of the country and the growth of domestic commerce.

Before the outbreak of war, the Legislature of Virginia passed an act appointing commissioners "for the purpose of viewing certain rivers within this Commonwealth," [1] and Marshall was made the head of this body of investigators. Nothing could have pleased him more. It was practical work on a matter that interested him profoundly, and the renewal of a subject which he had entertained since his young manhood.[2]

This tour of observation promised to be full of va-

[1] *Report of the Commissioners appointed to view Certain Rivers within the Commonwealth of Virginia, 5.*

[2] A practicable route for travel and transportation between Virginia and the regions across the mountains had been a favorite project of Washington. The Potomac and James River Company, of which Marshall when a young lawyer had become a stockholder (vol. I, 218, of this work), was organized partly in furtherance of this project. The idea had remained active in the minds of public men in Virginia and was, perhaps, the one subject upon which they substantially agreed.

riety and adventure, tinged with danger, into forests, over mountains, and along streams and rivers not yet thoroughly explored. For a short time Marshall would again live over the days of his boyhood. Most inviting of all, he would get far away from talk or thought of the detested war. Whether the Presidential scheming in his behalf bore fruit or withered, his absence in the wilderness was an ideal preparation to meet either outcome.

In his fifty-seventh year Marshall set out at the head of the expedition, and a thorough piece of work he did. With chain and spirit level the route was carefully surveyed from Lynchburg to the Ohio. Sometimes progress was made slowly and with the utmost labor. In places the scenes were "awful and discouraging."

The elaborate report which the commission submitted to the Legislature was written by Marshall. It reads, says the surveyor of this division of the Chesapeake and Ohio Railway,[1] "as an account of that survey of 1869, when I pulled a chain down the rugged banks of New River." Practicable sections were accurately pointed out and the methods by which they could best be utilized were recommended with particular care.

Marshall's report is alive with far-seeing and statesmanlike suggestions. He thinks, in 1812, that steamboats can be run successfully on the New River, but fears that the expense will be too great. The

[1] Much of the course selected by Marshall was adopted in the building of the Chesapeake and Ohio Railway. In 1869, Collis P. Huntington made a trip of investigation over part of Marshall's route. (Nelson: *Address — The Chesapeake and Ohio Railway*, 15.)

velocity of the current gives him some anxiety, but "the currents of the Hudson, of the Mohawk, and of the Mississippi, are very strong; and . . a practice so entirely novel as the use of steam in navigation, will probably receive great improvement."

The expense of the undertaking must, he says, depend on the use to be made of the route. Should the intention be only to assist the local traffic of the "upper country down the James river," the expense would not be great. But, "if the views of the legislature shall extend to a free commercial intercourse with the western states," the route must compete with others then existing "or that may be opened." In that case "no improvement ought to be undertaken but with a determination to make it complete and effectual." If this were done, the commerce of Kentucky, Ohio, and even a part of Southwestern Pennsylvania would pour through Virginia to the Atlantic States. This was a rich prize which other States were exerting themselves to capture. Moreover, such "commercial intercourse" would bind Virginia to the growing West by "strong ties" of "friendly sentiments," and these were above price. "In that mysterious future which is in reserve, and is yet hidden from us, events may occur to render" such a community of interest and mutual regard "too valuable to be estimated in dollars and cents."

Marshall pictures the growth of the West, "that extensive and fertile country . . increasing in wealth and population with a rapidity which baffles calculation." Not only would Virginia profit by opening a great trade route to the West, but the Nation

would be vastly benefited. "Every measure which
tends to cement more closely the union of the eastern with the western states" would be invaluable to
the whole country. The military uses of "this central channel of communication" were highly important: "For the want of it, in the course of the last
autumn, government was reduced to the necessity of
transporting arms in waggons from Richmond to
the falls of the Great Kanawha," and "a similar
necessity may often occur."[1]

When Marshall returned to Richmond, he found
the country depressed and in turmoil. The war had
begun dismally for the Americans. Our want of
military equipment and training was incredible and
assured those disasters that quickly fell upon us.
The Federalist opposition to the war grew ever
bolder, ever more bitter. The Massachusetts House
of Representatives issued an "Address" to the people, urging the organization of a "*peace party*," ad-
juring "loud and deep .. disapprobation of this war,"
and demanding that nobody enlist in the army.[2]
Pamphlets were widely circulated, abusing the
American Government and upholding the British
cause. The ablest of these, "Mr. Madison's War,"
was by John Lowell of Boston.

The President, he said, "impelled" Congress to
declare an "offensive" war against Great Britain.
Madison was a member of "the *French* party."
British impressment was the pursuance of a sound
policy; the British doctrine — once a British subject,

[1] *Report of the Commissioners appointed to view Certain Rivers
within the Commonwealth of Virginia*, 38–39.

[2] Niles: *Weekly Register*, ii, 418.

always a British subject — was unassailable. The
Orders in Council were just; the execution of them
"moderation" itself. On every point, in short, the
British Government was right; the French, diabolical; the American, contemptible and wrong. How
trivial America's complaints, even if there was a
real basis for them, in view of Great Britain's unselfish struggle against "the gigantic dominion of
France."

If that Power, "swayed" by that satanic genius,
Napoleon, should win, would she not take Nova
Scotia, Canada, Louisiana, the Antilles, Florida,
South America? After these conquests, would not
the United States, "the only remaining republic,"
be conquered. Most probably. What then ought
America to do? "In war offensive and unjust, the
citizens are not only obliged not to take part, but
by the laws of God, and of civil society, they are
bound to abstain." What were the rights of citizens
in war-time? To oppose the war by tongue and pen,
if they thought the war to be wrong, and to refuse to
serve if called "contrary to the Constitution." [1]

Such was the Federalism of 1812–15, such the arguments that would have been urged for the election
of Marshall had he been chosen as the peace candidate. But the peace Republicans of New York
nominated the able, cunning, and politically corrupt

[1] Lowell: *Mr. Madison's War:* by "A New England Farmer."
A still better illustration of Federalist hostility to the war and the
Government is found in a letter of Ezekiel Webster to his brother
Daniel: "Let gamblers be made to contribute to the support of this
war, which was declared by men of no better principles than them-
selves." (Ezekiel Webster to Daniel Webster, Oct. 29, 1814, Van
Tyne, 53.) Webster here refers to a war tax on playing-cards.

De Witt Clinton; and this man, who had assured the Federalists that he favored an "honourable peace" with England,[1] was endorsed by a Federalist caucus as the anti-war standard-bearer,[2] though not without a swirl of acrimony and dissension.

But for the immense efforts of Clinton to secure the nomination, and the desire of the Federalists and all conservatives that Marshall should continue as Chief Justice,[3] it is possible that he might have been named as the opponent of Madison in the Presidential contest of 1812. "I am far enough from desiring Clinton for President of the United States," wrote Pickering in the preceding July; "I would infinitely prefer another Virginian — if Judge Marshall could be the man.' [4]

Marshall surely would have done better than Clinton, who, however, carried New York, New Jersey, Delaware, Maryland, and all the New England States except Vermont. The mercantile classes would have rallied to Marshall's standard more enthusiastically than to Clinton's. The lawyers generally would have worked hard for him. The Federalists, who accepted Clinton with repugnance, would have exerted themselves to the utmost for Marshall, the ideal representative of Federalism. He was personally very strong in North Carolina; the capture of Pennsylvania might have been possible;[5] Vermont might have given him her votes.

[1] Harper to Lynn, Sept. 25, 1812, Steiner, 584.
[2] See McMaster, IV, 199–200.   [3] Morison: *Otis*, I, 399.
[4] Pickering to Pennington, July 22, 1812, *N.E. Federalism:* Adams, 389.
[5] The vote of Pennsylvania, with those cast for Clinton, would have elected Marshall.

The Federalist resistance to the war grew more determined as the months wore on. Throughout New
England the men of wealth, nearly all of whom were
Federalists, declined to subscribe to the Government loans.[1] The Governors of the New England
States refused to aid the National Government with
the militia.[2] In Congress the Federalists were obstructing war measures and embarrassing the Government in every way their ingenuity could devise.
One method was to force the Administration to tell
the truth about Napoleon's pretended revocation of
his obnoxious decree. A resolution asking the President to inform the House "when, by whom, and in
what manner, the first intelligence was given to this
Government" of the St. Cloud Decree, was offered
by Daniel Webster,[3] who had been elected to Congress from New Hampshire as the fiercest youthful
antagonist of the war in his State.[4] The Republicans agreed, and Webster's resolution was passed by
a vote of 137 yeas to only 26 nays.[5]

In compliance the President transmitted a long report. It was signed by the Secretary of State, James
Monroe, but bears the imprint of Madison's lucid
mind. The report states the facts upon which Congress was compelled to declare war and demonstrates

[1] Babcock, 157; and see Dewey: *Financial History of the United
States*, 133.

[2] For an excellent statement of the conduct of the Federalists at
this time see Morison: *Otis*, II, 53–66. "The militia of Massachusetts, seventy thousand in enrolment, well-drilled, and well-equipped,
was definitely withdrawn from the service of the United States in
September, 1814." (Babcock, 155.) Connecticut did the same thing.
(*Ib.* 156.)

[3] *Annals*, 13th Cong. 1st Sess. 302.

[4] See McMaster, IV, 213–14.   [5] *Annals*, 13th Cong. 1st Sess. 302

that the Decree of St. Cloud had nothing to do with
our militant action, since it was not received until
more than a month after our declaration of war.
Then follow several clear and brilliant paragraphs
setting forth the American view of the causes and
purposes of the war.[1]

Timothy Pickering was not now in the Senate. The
Republican success in Massachusetts at the State
election of 1810 had given the Legislature to that
party,[2] and the pugnacious Federalist leader was
left at home. There he raged and intrigued and wrote
reams of letters. Monroe's report lent new fury to
his always burning wrath, and he sent that document,
with his malediction upon it, to John Marshall at
Richmond. In reply the Chief Justice said that the
report "contains a labored apology for France but
none for ourselves. It furnishes no reason for our
tame unmurmuring acquiescence under the double
insult of withholding this paper [Decree of St. Cloud]
from us & declaring in our face that it has been put
in our possession.

"The report is silent on another subject of still
deeper interest. It leaves unnoticed the fact that the
Berlin & Milan decrees were certainly not repealed
by that insidious decree of April since it had never
been communicated to the French courts and cruizers, & since their cruizers had at a period subsequent
to the pretended date of that decree received orders

---

[1] *Am. State Papers, For. Rel.* III, 609–12.

[2] The Republican victory was caused by the violent British partisanship of the Federalist leaders. In spite of the distress the people
suffered from the Embargo, they could not, for the moment, tolerate
Federalist opposition to their own country. (See Adams: *U.S.* v, 215.)

to continue to execute the offensive decrees on American vessels.

"The report manifests no sensibility at the disgraceful circumstances which tend strongly to prove that this paper was fabricated to satisfy the importunities of Mr. Barlow, was antedated to suit French purposes; nor at the contempt manifested for the feelings of Americans and their government, by not deigning so to antedate it as to save the credit of our Administration by giving some plausibility to their assertion that the repeal had taken place on the 1st of Nov^r — But this is a subject with which I dare not trust myself."

The plight of the American land forces, the splendid and unrivaled victories of the American Navy, apparently concerned Marshall not at all. His eyes were turned toward Europe; his ears strained to catch the sounds from foreign battle-fields.

"I look with anxious solicitude — with mingled hope & fear," he continues, "to the great events which are taking place in the north of Germany. It appears probable that a great battle will be fought on or near the Elbe & never had the world more at stake than will probably depend on that battle.

"Your opinions had led me to hope that there was some prospect for a particular peace for ourselves. My own judgement, could I trust it, would tell me that peace or war will be determined by the events in Europe."[1]

---

[1] Marshall to Pickering, Dec. 11, 1813, Pickering MSS. Mass. Hist. Soc.

The "great battle" which Marshall foresaw had been fought nearly eight weeks before his letter was written. Napoleon had been crushingly defeated at Leipzig in October, 1813, and the British, Prussian, and other armies which Great Britain had combined against him, were already invading France. When, later, the news of this arrived in America, it was hailed by the Federalists with extravagant rejoicings.[1]

Secession, if the war were continued, now became the purpose of the more determined Federalist leaders. It was hopeless to keep up the struggle, they said. The Administration had precipitated hostilities without reason or right, without conscience or sense.[2] The people never had favored this wretched conflict; and now the tyrannical Government, failing to secure volunteers, had resorted to conscription — an "infamous" expedient resorted to in brutal violation of the Constitution.[3] So came the Hartford

---

[1] Morison: *Otis*, ii, 54–56.

[2] "CURSE THIS GOVERNMENT! I would march at 6 days notice for Washington . . and I would swear upon the *altar* never to return till Madison was buried under the ruins of the capitol." (Herbert to Webster, April 20, 1813, Van Tyne, 27.)

[3] The Federalists frantically opposed conscription. Daniel Webster, especially, denounced it. "Is this [conscription] . . consistent with the character of a free Government? . . No, Sir. . . The Constitution is libelled, foully libelled. The people of this country have not established . . such a fabric of despotism. . .

"Where is it written in the Constitution . . that you may take children from their parents . . & compel them to fight the battles of any war, in which the folly or the wickedness of Government may engage it? . . Such an abominable doctrine has no foundation in the Constitution."

Conscription, Webster said, was a gambling device to throw the dice for blood; and it was a "horrible lottery." "May God, in his compassion, shield me from . . the enormity of this guilt." (See

Convention which the cool wisdom of George Cabot saved from proclaiming secession.[1]

Of the two pretenses for war against Great Britain, the Federalists alleged that one had been removed even before we declared war, and that only the false and shallow excuse of British impressment of American seamen remained. Madison and Monroe recognized this as the one great remaining issue, and an Administration pamphlet was published asserting the reason and justice of the American position. This position was that men of every country have a natural right to remove to another land and there become citizens or subjects, entitled to the protection of the government of the nation of their adoption. The British principle, on the contrary, was that British subjects could never thus expatriate themselves, and that, if they did so, the British Government could seize them wherever found, and by force compel them to serve the Empire in any manner the Government chose to direct.

Monroe's brother-in-law, George Hay, still the United States Attorney for the District of Virginia, was selected to write the exposition of the American

Webster's speech on the Conscription Bill delivered in the House of Representatives, December 9, 1814, Van Tyne, 56–68; see also Curtis: *Life of Daniel Webster*, I, 138.)

Webster had foretold what he meant to do: "Of course we shall oppose such usurpation." (Webster to his brother, Oct. 30, 1814, Van Tyne, 54.) Again: "The conscription has not come up — if it does it will cause a storm such as was never witnessed here" [in Washington]. (Same to same, Nov. 29, 1814, *ib.* 55.)

[1] See Morison: *Otis*, II, 78–199. Pickering feared that Cabot's moderation would prevent the Hartford Convention from taking extreme measures against the Government. (See Pickering to Lowell, Nov. 7, 1814, *N.E. Federalism:* Adams, 406.)

view. It seems probable that his manuscript was carefully revised by Madison and Monroe, and perhaps by Jefferson.[1] Certainly Hay stated with singular precision the views of the great Republican triumvirate. The pamphlet was entitled "A Treatise on Expatriation." He began: "I hold in utter reprobation the idea that a man is bound by an obligation, permanent and unalterable, to the government of a country which he has abandoned and his allegiance to which he has solemnly adjured."[2]

Immediately John Lowell answered.[3] Nothing keener and more spirited ever came from the pen of that gifted man. "The presidential pamphleteer," as Lowell called Hay, ignored the law. The maxim, once a subject always a subject, was as true of America as of Britain. Had not Ellsworth, when Chief Justice, so decided in the famous case of Isaac Williams?[4] Yet Hay sneered at the opinion of that distinguished jurist.[5]

Pickering joyfully dispatched Lowell's brochure to Marshall, who lost not a moment in writing of his admiration. "I had yesterday the pleasure of receiv-

[1] Some sentences are paraphrases of expressions by Jefferson on the same subject. For example: "I hold the right of expatriation to be inherent in every man by the laws of nature, and incapable of being rightfully taken from him even by the united will of every other person in the nation." (Jefferson to Gallatin, June 26, 1806, *Works:* Ford, x, 273.) Again: "Our particular and separate grievance is only the impressment of our citizens. We must sacrifice the last dollar and drop of blood to rid us of that badge of slavery." (Jefferson to Crawford, Feb. 11, 1815, *ib.* xi, 450–51.) This letter was written at Monticello the very day that the news of peace reached Washington.

[2] Hay: *A Treatise on Expatriation*, 24.

[3] Lowell: *Review of 'A Treatise on Expatriation'*: by "A Massachusetts Lawyer." [4] See vol. iii, chap. i, of this work.

[5] See *Review of 'A Treatise on Expatriation*,' 6.

ing your letter of the 8th accompanying Mr Lowell's very masterly review of the treatise on expatriation. I have read it with great pleasure, & thank you very sincerely for this mark of your recollection.

"Could I have ever entertained doubts on the subject, this review would certainly have removed them. Mingled with much pungent raillery is a solidity of argument and an array of authority which in my judgement is entirely conclusive. But in truth it is a question upon which I never entertained a *scintilla* of doubt; and have never yet heard an argument which ought to excite a doubt in any sound and reflecting mind. It will be to every thinking American a most afflicting circumstance, should our government on a principle so completely rejected by the world proceed to the execution of unfortunate, of honorable, and of innocent men." [1]

Astonishing and repellent as these words now appear, they expressed the views of every Federalist lawyer in America. The doctrine of perpetual allegiance was indeed then held and practiced by every government except our own,[2] nor was it rejected by the United States until the Administration became Republican. Marshall, announcing the opinion of the Supreme Court in 1804, had held that an alien could take lands in New Jersey because he had lived in that State when, in 1776, the Legislature passed a law making all residents citizens.[3] Thus he had declared that an American citizen did not cease to be

[1] Marshall to Pickering, April 11, 1814, Pickering MSS. Mass. Hist. Soc.

[2] See Channing: *Jeff. System*, 170–71.

[3] M'Ilvaine *vs.* Coxe's Lessee, 4 Cranch, 209.

such because he had become the subject of a foreign power. Four years later, in another opinion involving expatriation, he had stated the law to be that a British subject, born in England before 1775, could not take, by devise, lands in Maryland, the statute of that State forbidding aliens from thus acquiring property there.[1] In both these cases, however, Marshall refrained from expressly declaring in terms against the American doctrine.

Even as late as 1821 the Chief Justice undoubtedly retained his opinion that the right of expatriation did not exist,[2] although he did not say so in express terms. But in Marshall's letter on Lowell's pamphlet he flatly avows his belief in the principle of perpetual allegiance, any direct expression on which he so carefully avoided when deciding cases involving it.

Thus the record shows that John Marshall was as bitterly opposed to the War of 1812 as was Pickering or Otis or Lowell. So entirely had he become one of "the aristocracy of talents of reputation, & of property," as Plumer, in 1804, had so accurately styled the class of which he himself was then a member,[3] that Marshall looked upon all but one subject then before the people with the eyes of confirmed reaction. That subject was Nationalism. To that supreme cause he was devoted with all the passion of his deep and powerful nature; and in the service of that cause he was soon to do much more than he had already performed.

[1] Dawson's Lessee *vs.* Godfrey, 4 Cranch, 321.

[2] Case of the Santissima Trinidad *et al.*, 1 Brockenbrough, 478–87; and see 7 Wheaton, 283.

[3] Plumer to Livermore, March 4, 1804, Plumer MSS. Lib. Cong.

Our second war with Great Britain accomplished
none of the tangible and immediate objects for which
it was fought. The British refused to abandon "the
right" of impressment; or to disclaim the British
sovereignty of the oceans whenever they chose to
assert it; or to pay a farthing for their spoliation of
American commerce. On the other hand, the British
did not secure one of their demands.[1] The peace
treaty did little more than to end hostilities.

But the war achieved an inestimable good — it de-
Europeanized America. It put an end to our thinking and feeling only in European terms and emotions.
It developed the spirit of the new America, born
since our political independence had been achieved,
and now for the first time emancipated from the intellectual and spiritual sovereignty of the Old World.
It had revealed to this purely American generation
a consciousness of its own strength; it could exult in
the fact that at last America had dared to fight.

The American Navy, ship for ship, officer for officer, man for man, had proved itself superior to
the British Navy, the very name of which had hitherto been mentioned only in terror or admiration
of its unconquerable might. In the end, raw and
untrained American troops had beaten British regu-
lars. American riflemen of the West and South had

---

[1] For example, the British "right" of impressment must be formally
and plainly acknowledged in the treaty; an Indian dominion was to
be established, and the Indian tribes were to be made parties to the
settlements; the free navigation of the Mississippi was to be guaranteed to British vessels; the right of Americans to fish in Canadian
waters was to be ended. Demands far more extreme were made by the
British press and public. (See McMaster, IV, 260–74; and see especially Morison: *Otis*, II, 171.)

overwhelmed the flower of all the armies of Europe.
An American frontier officer, Andrew Jackson, had
easily outwitted some of Great Britain's ablest and
most experienced professional generals. In short,
on land and sea America had stood up to, had really
beaten, the tremendous Power that had overthrown
the mighty Napoleon.

Such were the feelings and thoughts of that Young
America which had come into being since John Marshall had put aside his Revolutionary uniform and
arms. And in terms very much like those of the
foregoing paragraph the American people generally
expressed their sentiments.

Moreover, the Embargo, the Non-Intercourse and
Non-Importation Acts, the British blockades, the
war itself, had revolutionized the country econom-
ically and socially. American manufacturing was
firmly established. Land travel and land traffic
grew to proportions never before imagined, never
before desired. The people of distant sections became acquainted.

The eyes of all Americans, except those of the aged
or ageing, were turned from across the Atlantic Ocean
toward the boundless, the alluring West — their
thoughts diverted from the commotions of Europe
and the historic antagonism of foreign nations, to the
economic conquest of a limitless and virgin empire
and to the development of incalculable and untouched resources, all American and all their own.

The migration to the West, which had been increasing for years, now became almost a folk movement. The Eastern States were drained of their

young men and women. Some towns were almost depopulated.[1] And these hosts of settlers carried into wilderness and prairie a spirit and pride that had not been seen or felt in America since the time of the Revolution. But their high hopes were to be quickly turned into despair, their pride into ashes; for a condition was speedily to develop that would engulf them in disaster. It was this situation which was to call forth some of the greatest of Marshall's Constitutional opinions. This forbidding future, however, was foreseen by none of that vast throng of homeseekers crowding every route to the "Western Country," in the year of 1815. Only the rosiest dreams were theirs and the spirited consciousness that they were Americans, able to accomplish all things, even the impossible.

It was then a new world in which John Marshall found himself, when, in his sixtieth year, the war which he so abhorred came to an end. A state of things surrounded him little to his liking and yet soon to force from him the exercise of the noblest judicial statesmanship in American history. From the extreme independence of this new period, the intense and sudden Nationalism of the war, the ideas of local sovereignty rekindled by the New England Federalists at the dying fires that Jefferson and the Republicans had lighted in 1798, and from the play of conflicting interests came a reaction against Nationalism which it was Marshall's high mission to check and to turn into channels of National power, National safety, and National well-being.

[1] McMaster, IV, 383–88.

CHAPTER II

MARSHALL AND STORY

Either the office was made for the man or the man for the office.
(George S. Hillard.)

I am in love with his character, positively in love. (Joseph Story.)

In the midst of these gay circles my mind is carried to my own fireside and to my beloved wife. (Marshall.)

Now the man Moses was very meek, above all the men which were upon the face of the earth. (Numbers XII, 3.)

"IT will be difficult to find a character of firmness enough to preserve his independence on the same bench with Marshall." [1] So wrote Thomas Jefferson one year after he had ceased to be President. He was counseling Madison as to the vacancy on the Supreme Bench and one on the district bench at Richmond, in filling both of which he was, for personal reasons, feverishly concerned.

We are now to ascend with Marshall the mountain peaks of his career. Within the decade that followed after the close of our second war with Great Britain, he performed nearly all of that vast and creative labor, the lasting results of which have given him that distinctive title, the Great Chief Justice. During that period he did more than any other one man ever has done to vitalize the American Constitution; and, in the performance of that task, his influence over his associates was unparalleled. [2]

[1] Jefferson to Madison, May 25, 1810, *Works:* Ford, XI, 140.
"There is no man in the court that strikes me like Marshall. . . I have never seen a man of whose intellect I had a higher opinion." (Webster to his brother, March 28, 1814, *Private Correspondence of Daniel Webster:* Webster, I, 244.)

[2] "In the possession of an ordinary man . . it [the office of Chief

When Justices Chase and Cushing died and their successors Gabriel Duval[1] and Joseph Story were appointed, the majority of the Supreme Court, for the first time, became Republican. Yet Marshall continued to dominate it as fully as when its members were of his own political faith and views of government.[2] In the whole history of courts there is no parallel to such supremacy. Not without reason was that tribunal looked upon and called "Marshall's Court." It is interesting to search for the sources of his strange power.

These sources are not to be found exclusively in the strength of Marshall's intellect, surpassing though it was, nor yet in the mere dominance of his will. Joseph Story was not greatly inferior to Marshall in mind and far above him in accomplishments, while William Johnson, the first Justice of the Supreme Court appointed by Jefferson, was as determined as Marshall and was "strongly imbued with the principles of southern democracy, bold, independent, eccentric, and sometimes harsh."[3] Nor did learning give Marshall his commanding influence. John Jay and Oliver Ellsworth were his superiors in that respect; while Story so infinitely surpassed him in erudition that, between the two men, there is nothing but contrast. Indeed, Marshall had no "learning"

Justice] would be very apt to disgrace him." (Story to McLean, Oct. 12, 1835, Story, II, 208.)

[1] Justice Duval's name is often, incorrectly, spelled with two "l's."

[2] "No man had ever a stronger influence upon the minds of others." (*American Jurist*, XIV, 242.)

[3] Ingersoll: *Historical Sketch of the Second War between the United States and Great Britain*, 2d Series, I, 74.

at all in the academic sense;[1] we must seek elsewhere for an explanation of his peculiar influence.

This explanation is, in great part, furnished by
Marshall's personality. The manner of man he was,
of course, is best revealed by the well-authenticated
accounts of his daily life. He spent most of his time
at Richmond, for the Supreme Court sat in Washington only a few weeks each year. He held circuit
court at Raleigh as well as at the Virginia Capital,
but the sessions seldom occupied more than a fortnight each. In Richmond, then, his characteristics
were best known; and so striking were they that
time has but little dimmed the memory of them.

Marshall, the Chief Justice, continued to neglect his
dress and personal appearance as much as he did
when, as a lawyer, his shabby attire so often "brought
a blush" to the cheeks of his wife,[2] and his manners
were as "lax and lounging" as when Jefferson called
them proofs of a "profound hypocrisy."[3] Although
no man in America was less democratic in his ideas
of government, none was more democratic in his
contact with other people. To this easy bonhomie
was added a sense of humor, always quick to appreciate an amusing situation.

When in Richmond, Marshall often did his own
marketing and carried home the purchases he made.
The tall, ungainly, negligently clad Chief Justice,
ambling along the street, his arms laden with pur-

---

[1] "He was not, in any sense of the word, a learned man." (George
S. Hillard in *North American Review*, XLII, 224.)

[2] See vol. I, 163, of this work; also *Southern Literary Messenger*,
XVII, 154; and Terhune: *Colonial Homesteads*, 92.

[3] See vol. II, 139, of this work.

chases, was a familiar sight.[1] He never would hurry, and habitually lingered at the market-place, chatting with everybody, learning the gossip of the town, listening to the political talk that in Richmond never ceased, and no doubt thus catching at first hand the drift of public sentiment.[2] The humblest and poorest man in Virginia was not more unpretentious than John Marshall.

No wag was more eager for a joke. One day, as he loitered on the outskirts of the market, a newcomer in Richmond, who had never seen Marshall, offered him a small coin to carry home for him a turkey just purchased. Marshall accepted, and, with the bird under his arm, trudged behind his employer. The incident sent the city into gales of laughter, and was so in keeping with Marshall's ways that it has been retold from one generation to another, and is to-day almost as much alive as ever.[3] At another time the Chief Justice was taken for the butcher. He called on a relative's wife who had never met him, and who had not been told of his plain dress and rustic manners. Her husband wished to sell a calf and she expected the butcher to call to make the trade. She saw Marshall approaching, and judging by his appearance that he was the butcher, she directed the servant to tell him to go to the stable where the animal was awaiting inspection.[4]

It was Marshall's custom to go early every morning to a farm which he owned four miles from Richmond. For the exercise he usually walked, but, when he

---

[1] Mordecai: *Richmond in By-Gone Days*, 64.   [2] Terhune, 91.

[3] *Ib.* 92; and see Howe: *Historical Collections of Virginia*, 266.

[4] *Green Bag*, VIII, 486.

wished to take something heavy, he would ride. A stranger coming upon him on the road would have thought him one of the poorer small planters of the vicinity. He was extremely fond of children and, if he met one trudging along the road, he would take the child up on the horse and carry it to its destination. Often he was seen riding into Richmond from his farm, with one child before and another behind him.[1]

Bishop Meade met Marshall on one of these morning trips, carrying on horseback a bag of clover seed.[2] On another, he was seen holding on the pommel a jug of whiskey which he was taking out to his farm-hands. The cork had come out and he was using his thumb as a stopper.[3] He was keenly interested in farming, and in 1811 was elected President of the Richmond Society for Promotion of Agriculture.[4]

The distance from Richmond to Raleigh was, by road, more than one hundred and seventy miles. Except when he went by stage,[5] as he seldom did, it must have taken a week to make this journey. He traveled in a primitive vehicle called a stick gig, drawn by one horse which he drove himself, seldom taking a servant with him.[6] Making his slow way

[1] Personal experience related by Dr. William P. Palmer to Dr. J. Franklin Jameson, and by him to the author.

[2] Meade: *Old Churches, Ministers and Families of Virginia*, II, 222.

[3] *Magazine of American History*, XII, 70; also *Green Bag*, VIII, 486.

[4] Anderson, 214.

[5] The stage schedule was much shorter, but the hours of travel very long. The stage left Petersburg at 3 A.M., arrived at Warrenton at 8 P.M., left Warrenton at 3 A.M., and arrived at Raleigh the same night. (Data furnished by Professor Archibald Henderson.) The stage was seldom on time, however, and the hardships of traveling in it very great. Marshall used it only when in extreme haste, a state of mind into which he seldom would be driven by any emergency.

[6] Mordecai, 64–65. Bishop Meade says of Marshall on his trips to Fauquier County, "Servant he had none." (Meade, II, 222.)

through the immense stretches of tar pines and sandy fields, the Chief Justice doubtless thought out the solution of the problems before him and the plain, clear, large statements of his conclusions which, from the bench later, announced not only the law of particular cases, but fundamental policies of the Nation. His surroundings at every stage of the trip encouraged just such reflection — the vast stillness, the deep forests, the long hours, broken only by some accident to gig or harness, or interrupted for a short time to feed and rest his horse, and to eat his simple meal.

During these trips, Marshall would become so abstracted that, apparently, he would forget where he was driving. Once, when near the plantation of Nathaniel Macon in North Carolina, he drove over a sapling which became wedged between a wheel and the shaft. One of Macon's slaves, working in an adjacent field, saw the predicament, hurried to his assistance, held down the sapling with one hand, and with the other backed the horse until the gig was free. Marshall tossed the negro a piece of money and asked him who was his owner. "Marse Nat. Macon," said the slave. "He is an old friend," said Marshall; "tell him how you have helped me," giving his name. When the negro told his master, Macon said: "That was the great Chief Justice Marshall, the biggest lawyer in the United States." The slave grinned and answered: "Marse Nat., he may be de bigges' lawyer in de United States, but he ain't got sense enough to back a gig off a saplin'." [1]

[1] As related by M. D. Haywood, Librarian of the Supreme Court of North Carolina, to Professor Archibald Henderson and by him to the author; and see *Harper's Magazine*, LXX, 610; *World's Work*, I, 395.

At night he would stop at some log tavern on the route, eat with the family and other guests, if any were present, and sit before the fireplace after the meal, talking with all and listening to all like the simple and humble countryman he appeared to be. Since the minor part of his time was spent in court, and most of it about Richmond, or on the road to and from Raleigh, or journeying to his Fauquier County plantation and the beloved mountains of his youth where he spent the hottest part of each year, it is doubtful whether any other judge ever maintained such intimate contact with people in the ordinary walks of life as did John Marshall.

The Chief Justice always arrived at Raleigh stained and battered from travel.[1] The town had a population of from three hundred to five hundred.[2] He was wont to stop at a tavern kept by a man named Cooke and noted for its want of comfort; but, although the inn got worse year after year, he still frequented it. Early one morning an acquaintance saw the Chief Justice go to the woodpile, gather an armful of wood and return with it to the house. When they met later in the day, the occurrence was recalled. "Yes," said Marshall, "I suppose it is not convenient for Mr. Cooke to keep a servant; so I make up my own fires."[3]

The Chief Justice occupied a small room in which were the following articles: "A bed, . . two split-bot-

---

[1] Judge James C. MacRae in *John Marshall — Life, Character and Judicial Services:* Dillon, II, 68.

[2] As late as April, 1811, the population of Raleigh was between six hundred and seven hundred. Nearly all the houses were of wood. By 1810 there were only four brick houses in the town.

[3] *Magazine of American History*, XII, 69.

tom chairs, a pine table covered with grease and ink, a cracked pitcher and broken bowl." The host ate with his guests and used his fingers instead of fork or knife.[1] When court adjourned for the day, Marshall would play quoits in the street before the tavern "with the public street characters of Raleigh," who were lovers of the game.[2]

He was immensely popular in Raleigh, his familiar manners and the justice of his decisions appealing with equal force to the bar and people alike. Writing at the time of the hearing of the Granville case,[3] John Haywood, then State Treasurer of North Carolina, testifies: "Judge Marshall . . is greatly respected here, as well on account of his talents and uprightness as for that sociability and ease of manner which render all happy and pleased when in his company."[4]

In spite of his sociability, which tempted him, while in Richmond, to visit taverns and the law offices of his friends, Marshall spent most of the day in his house or in the big yard adjoining it, for Mrs. Marshall's affliction increased with time, and the Chief Justice, whose affection for his wife grew as her illness advanced, kept near her as much as possi-

---

[1] Account of eye-witness as related by Dr. Kemp P. Battle of Raleigh to Professor Henderson and by him to the author.

Another tavern was opened about 1806 by one John Marshall. He had been one of the first commissioners of Raleigh, serving until 1797. He was no relation whatever to the Chief Justice. As already stated (vol. I, footnote to 15, of this work) the name was a common one.

[2] Mr. W. J. Peele of Raleigh to Professor Henderson.

[3] See *infra*, 154–56.

[4] Haywood to Steele, June 19, 1805. (MS. supplied by Professor Henderson.)

ble. In Marshall's grounds and near his house were
several great oak and elm trees, beneath which was
a spring; to this spot he would take the papers in
cases he had to decide and, sitting on a rustic bench
under the shade, would write many of those great
opinions that have immortalized his name.[1]

Mrs. Marshall's malady was largely a disease of
the nervous system and, at times, it seemingly
affected her mind. It was a common thing for the
Chief Justice to get up at any hour of the night and,
without putting on his shoes lest his footfalls might
further excite his wife, steal downstairs and drive
away for blocks some wandering animal — a cow,
a pig, a horse — whose sounds had annoyed her.[2]
Even upon entering his house during the daytime,
Marshall would take off his shoes and put on soft
slippers in the hall.[3]

She was, of course, unequal to the management of
the household. When the domestic arrangements
needed overhauling, Marshall would induce her to
take a long drive with her sister, Mrs. Edward Carrington, or her daughter, Mrs. Jacquelin B. Harvie,
over the still and shaded roads of Richmond. The
carriage out of sight, he would throw off his coat and

[1] *World's Work*, i, 395. This statement is supported by the testimony of Mr. Edward V. Valentine of Richmond, who has spent many
years gathering and verifying data concerning Richmond and its early
citizens. It is also confirmed by the Honorable James Keith, until
recently President of the Court of Appeals of Virginia, and by others
of the older residents of Richmond. For some opinions thus written,
see chaps. iv, v, and vi of this volume.

[2] *Green Bag*, viii, 484. Sympathetic Richmond even ordered the
town clock and town bell muffled. (Meade, ii, 222.)

[3] Statements of two eye-witnesses, Dr. Richard Crouch and William
F. Gray, to Mr. Edward V. Valentine and by him related to the author.

vest, roll up his shirt-sleeves, twist a bandanna hand-kerchief about his head, and gathering the servants, lead as well as direct them in dusting the walls and furniture, scrubbing the floors and setting the house in order.[1]

Numerous incidents of this kind are well authenti-cated. To this day Marshall's unselfish devotion to his infirm and distracted wife is recalled in Rich-mond. But nobody ever heard the slightest word of complaint from him; nor did any act or expression of countenance so much as indicate impatience.

In his letters Marshall never fails to admonish his wife, who seldom if ever wrote to him, to care for her health. "Yesterday I received Jacquelin's let-ter of the 12th informing me that your health was at present much the same as when I left Richmond," writes Marshall.[2] "John [Marshall's son] passed through this city a day or two past, & although I did not see him I had the pleasure of hearing from Mr. Washington who saw him . . that you were as well as usual."[3] In another letter Marshall says: "Do my dearest Polly let me hear from you through someone of those who will be willing to write for you."[4] Again he says: "I am most anxious to know how you do but no body is kind enough to gratify my wishes. . . I looked eagerly for a letter to day but no letter came. . . You must not fail when you go to Chiccahominy [Marshall's farm near Richmond]

[1] Accounts given Professor J. Franklin Jameson by old residents of Richmond, and by Professor Jameson to the author.
[2] Marshall to his wife, Washington, Feb. 16, 1818, MS.
[3] Same to same, March 12, 1826, MS.
[4] Same to same, Feb. 19, 1829, MS.

. . to carry out blankets enough to keep you comfortable. I am very desirous of hearing what is doing there but as no body is good enough to let me know how you do & what is passing at home I could not expect to hear what is passing at the farm." [1] Indeed, only one letter of Marshall's has been discovered which indicates that he had received so much as a line from his wife; and this was when, an old man of seventy-five, he was desperately ill in Philadelphia.[2] Nothing, perhaps, better reveals the sweetness of his nature than his cheerful temper and tender devotion under trying domestic conditions.[3]

His "dearest Polly" was intensely religious, and Marshall profoundly respected this element of her character.[4] The evidence as to his own views and feelings on the subject of religion, although scanty, is definite. He was a Unitarian in belief and therefore never became a member of the Episcopal church, to which his parents, wife, children, and all other relatives belonged. But he attended services, Bishop Meade informs us, not only because "he was a sincere friend of religion," but also because he wished

[1] Marshall to his wife, Washington, Jan. 30, 1831, MS.

[2] See *infra*, chap. x.

[3] Mrs. Marshall did not write to her children, it would seem. When he was in Richmond, the Chief Justice himself sent messages from her which were ordinary expressions of affection.

"Your mother is very much gratified with the account you give from yourself and Claudia of all your affairs & especially of your children and hopes for its continuance. She looks with some impatience for similar information from John. She desires me to send her love to all the family including Miss Maria and to tell you that this hot weather distresses her very much & she wishes you also to give her love to John & Elizabeth & their children." (Marshall to his son James K. Marshall, Richmond, July 3, 1827, MS.)

[4] See vol. I, footnote to 189, of this work.

"to set an example." The Bishop bears this testimony: "I can never forget how he would prostrate his tall form before the rude low benches, without backs, at Coolspring Meeting-House,[1] in the midst of his children and grandchildren and his old neighbors." When in Richmond, Marshall attended the Monumental Church where, says Bishop Meade, "he was much incommoded by the narrowness of the pews. . . Not finding room enough for his whole body within the pew, he used to take his seat nearest the door of the pew, and, throwing it open, let his legs stretch a little into the aisle."[2]

It is said, however, that his daughter, during her last illness, declared that her father late in life was converted, by reading Keith on Prophecy, to a belief in the divinity of Christ; and that he determined to "apply for admission to the communion of our Church . . but died without ever communing."[3] There is, too, a legend about an astonishing flash of eloquence from Marshall — "a streak of vivid lightning" — at a tavern, on the subject of religion.[4] The impression said to have been made by Marshall on this occasion was heightened by his appearance when he arrived at the inn. The shafts of his ancient gig were broken and "held together by withes formed from the bark of a hickory sapling"; he was negligently dressed, his knee buckles loosened.[5]

In the tavern a discussion arose among some young men concerning "the merits of the Christian reli-

---

[1] In Leeds Parish, near Oakhill, Fauquier County.
[2] Meade, II, 221-22.
[3] *Green Bag*, VIII, 487.
[4] Howe, 275-76.   [5] *Ib.*

gion." The debate grew warm and lasted "from six o'clock until eleven." No one knew Marshall, who sat quietly listening. Finally one of the youthful combatants turned to him and said: "Well, my old gentleman, what think you of these things?" Marshall responded with a "most eloquent and unanswerable appeal." He talked for an hour, answering "every argument urged against" the teachings of Jesus. "In the whole lecture there was so much simplicity and energy, pathos and sublimity, that not another word was uttered." The listeners wondered who the old man could be. Some thought him a preacher; and great was their surprise when they learned afterwards that he was the Chief Justice of the United States.[1]

His devotion to his wife illustrates his attitude toward women in general, which was one of exalted reverence and admiration. "He was an enthusiast in regard to the domestic virtues," testifies Story. "There was . . a romantic chivalry in his feelings, which, though rarely displayed, except in the circle of his most intimate friends, would there pour out itself with the most touching tenderness." He loved to dwell on the "excellences," "accomplishments," "talents," and "virtues" of women, whom he looked upon as "the friends, the companions, and the equals of man." He tolerated no wit at their expense, no fling, no sarcasm, no reproach. On no phase of Marshall's character does Story place so

[1] This story was originally published in the *Winchester Republican*. The incident is said to have occurred at McGuire's hotel in Winchester. The newspaper account is reproduced in the Charleston (S.C.) edition (1845) of Howe's book, 275-76.

much emphasis as on his esteem for women.[1] Harriet Martineau, too, bears witness that "he maintained through life and carried to his grave, a reverence for woman as rare in its kind as in its degree."[2] "I have always believed that national character as well as happiness depends more on the female part of society than is generally imagined," writes Marshall in his ripe age to Thomas White.[3]

Commenting on Story's account, in his centennial oration on the first settlement of Salem, of the death of Lady Arbella Johnson, Marshall expresses his opinion of women thus: "I almost envy the occasion her sufferings and premature death have furnished for bestowing that well-merited eulogy on a sex which so far surpasses ours in all the amiable and attractive virtues of the heart, — in all those qualities which make up the sum of human happiness and transform the domestic fireside into an elysium. I read the passage to my wife who expressed such animated approbation of it as almost to excite fears for that exclusive admiration which husbands claim as their peculiar privilege Present my compliments to M[rs] Story and say for me that a lady receives the highest compliment her husband can pay her when he expresses an exalted opinion of the sex, because the world will believe that it is formed on the model he sees at home."[4]

Ten children were born to John Marshall and

[1] Joseph Story in Dillon, III, 364–66.
[2] Martineau: *Retrospect of Western Travels*, I, 150.
[3] *North American Review*, xx, 444–45.
[4] Marshall to Story, Oct. 29, 1828, *Proceedings, Massachusetts Historical Society*, 2d Series, xiv, 337–38.

Mary Ambler, of whom six survived, five boys and one girl.[1] By 1815 only three of these remained at home; Jacquelin, twenty-eight years old, James Keith, fifteen, and Edward, ten years of age. John was in Harvard, where Marshall sent all his sons except Thomas, the eldest, who went to Princeton.[2] The daughter, Mary, Marshall's favorite child, had married Jacquelin B. Harvie and lived in Richmond not far from Marshall's house.[3] Four other children had died early.

"You ask," Marshall writes Story, "if Mrs Marshall and myself have ever lost a child. We have lost four, three of them bidding fairer for health and life than any that have survived them. One, a daughter about six or seven . . was one of the most fascinating children I ever saw. She was followed within a fortnight by a brother whose death was attended by a circumstance we can never forget.

"When the child was supposed to be dying I tore the distracted mother from the bedside. We soon afterwards heard a voice in the room which we considered as indicating the death of the infant. We believed him to be dead. [I went] into the room and found him still breathing. I returned [and] as the pang of his death had been felt by his mother and [I] was confident he must die, I concealed his being alive and prevailed on her to take refuge with her

[1] Thomas, born July 21, 1784; Jacquelin Ambler, born December 3, 1787; Mary, born September 17, 1795; John, born January 15, 1798; James Keith, born February 13, 1800; Edward Carrington, born January 13, 1805. (Paxton: *Marshall Family*, Genealogical Chart.)

[2] Edward Carrington was the only son to receive the degree of A.B. from Harvard (1826).

[3] Paxton, 100.

mother who lived the next door across an open square from her.

"The child lived two days, during which I was agonized with its condition and with the occasional hope, though the case was desperate, that I might enrapture his mother with the intelligence of his restoration to us. After the event had taken place his mother could not bear to return to the house she had left and remained with her mother a fortnight.

"I then addressed to her a letter in verse in which our mutual loss was deplored, our lost children spoken of with the parental feeling which belonged to the occasion, her affection for those which survived was appealed to, and her religious confidence in the wisdom and goodness of Providence excited. The letter closed with a pressing invitation to return to me and her children." [1]

All of Marshall's sons married, settled on various parts of the Fairfax estate, and lived as country gentlemen. Thomas was given the old homestead at Oak Hill, and there the Chief Justice built for his eldest son the large house adjacent to the old one where he himself had spent a year before joining the army under Washington. [2] To this spot Marshall went every year, visiting Thomas and his other sons who lived not far apart, seeing old friends, wandering along Goose Creek, over the mountains, and among the haunts where his first years were spent.

Here, of course, he was, in bearing and appearance, even less the head of the Nation's Judiciary than he

---

[1] Marshall to Story, June 26, 1831, *Proceedings, Mass. Hist. Soc.* 2d Series, xiv, 344–46.

[2] See vol. i, 55–56, of this work.

was in Richmond or on the road to Raleigh. He was emphatically one of the people among whom he sojourned, familiar, interested, considerate, kindly and sociable to the last degree. Not one of his sons but showed more consciousness of his own importance than did John Marshall; not a planter of Fauquier, Warren, and Shenandoah Counties, no matter how poorly circumstanced, looked and acted less a Chief Justice of the United States. These characteristics, together with a peculiar generosity, made Marshall the most beloved man in Northern Virginia.

Once, when going from Richmond to Fauquier County, he overtook one of his Revolutionary comrades. As the two rode on together, talking of their war-time experiences and of their present circumstances, it came out that this now ageing friend of his youth was deeply in debt and about to lose all his possessions. There was, it appeared, a mortgage on his farm which would soon be foreclosed. After the Chief Justice had left the inn where they both had stopped for refreshments, an envelope was handed to his friend containing Marshall's check for the amount of the debt. His old comrade-in-arms quickly mounted his horse, overtook Marshall, and insisted upon returning the check. Marshall refused to take it back, and the two friends argued the matter, which was finally compromised by Marshall's agreeing to take a lien upon the land. But this he never foreclosed.[1]

This anecdote is highly characteristic of Marshall. He was infinitely kind, infinitely considerate.

[1] Howe (Charleston, S.C., ed. of 1845), 266.

Bishop Meade, who knew him well, says that he "was a most conscientious man in regard to some things which others might regard as too trivial to be observed." On one of Meade's frequent journeys with Marshall between Fauquier County and the "lower country," they came to an impassable stretch of road. Other travelers had taken down a fence and gone through the adjoining plantation, and the Bishop was about to follow the same route. Marshall refused — "He said we had better go around, although each step was a plunge, adding that it was his duty, as one in office, to be very particular in regard to such things." [1]

When in Richmond the one sport in which he delighted was the pitching of quoits. Not when a lawyer was he a more enthusiastic or regular attendant of the meetings of the Quoit Club, or Barbecue Club, [2] under the trees at Buchanan's Spring on the outskirts of Richmond, than he was when at the height of his fame as Chief Justice of the United States. More personal descriptions of Marshall at these gatherings have come down to us than exist for any other phase of his life. Chester Harding, the artist, when painting Marshall's portrait during the summer of 1826, spent some time in the Virginia Capital, and attended one of the meetings of the Quoit Club. It was a warm day, and presently Marshall, then in his seventy-second year, was seen coming, his coat on his arm, fanning himself with his hat. Walking straight up to a bowl of mint julep, he poured a

[1] Meade, II, 222.
[2] Tyler: *Tyler*, I, 220; and see vol. II, 182–83, of this work.

tumbler full of the liquid, drank it off, said, "How are you, gentlemen?" and fell to pitching quoits with immense enthusiasm. When he won, says Harding, "the woods would ring with his triumphant shout." [1]

James K. Paulding went to Richmond for the purpose of talking to the Chief Justice and observing his daily life. He was more impressed by Marshall's gayety and unrestraint at the Quoit Club than by anything else he noted. "The Chief-Justice threw off his coat," relates Paulding, "and fell to work with as much energy as he would have directed to the decision of . . the conflicting jurisdiction of the General and State Governments." During the game a dispute arose between two players "as to the quoit nearest the meg." Marshall was agreed upon as umpire. "The Judge bent down on one knee and with a straw essayed the decision of this important question, . . frequently biting off the end of the straw" for greater accuracy. [2]

The morning play over, the club dinner followed. A fat pig, roasted over a pit of coals, cold meats, melons, fruits, and vegetables, were served in the old Virginia style. The usual drinks were porter, toddy, [3] and the club punch made of "lemons, brandy, rum, madeira, poured into a bowl one-third filled with ice

[1] White: *A Sketch of Chester Harding, Artist*, 195–96.

[2] *Lippincott's Magazine*, II, 624. Paulding makes this comment on Marshall: "In his hours of relaxation he was as full of fun and as natural as a child. He entered into the spirit of athletic exercises with the ardor of youth; and at sixty-odd years of age was one of the best quoit-players in Virginia." (*Ib.* 626.)

[3] *American Turf Register and Sporting Magazine* (1829), I, 41–42; and see Mordecai, 188–89.

(no water), and sweetened." [1] In addition, champagne and other wines were sometimes provided. [2]
At these meals none of the witty company equaled
Marshall in fun-making; no laugh was so cheery and
loud as his. Not more was John Marshall the chief
of the accomplished and able men who sat with him
on the Supreme Bench at Washington than, even in
his advancing years, he was the leader of the convivial spirits who gathered to pitch quoits, drink julep
and punch, tell stories, sing songs, make speeches,
and play pranks under the trees of Richmond.

Marshall dearly loved, when at home, to indulge in
the giving of big dinners to members of the bench
and bar. In a wholly personal sense he was the best-
liked man in Richmond. The lawyers and judges
living there were particularly fond of him, and the
Chief Justice thoroughly reciprocated their regard.
Spencer Roane, Judge of the Virginia Court of Appeals, seems to have been the one enemy Marshall
had in the whole city. Indeed, Roane and Jefferson
appear to have been the only men anywhere who
ever hated him personally. Even the testy George
Hay reluctantly yielded to his engaging qualities.
When at the head of the Virginia bar, Marshall had
been one of those leading attorneys who gave the attractive dinners that were so notable and delightful
a feature of life in Richmond. After he became Chief
Justice, he continued this custom until his "lawyer
dinners" became, among men, the principal social
events of the place.

[1] Recipe for the Quoit Club punch, *Green Bag*, VIII, 482. This recipe was used for many years by the Richmond Light Infantry Blues.
[2] See vol. II, 183, of this work.

Many guests sat at Marshall's board upon these occasions. Among them were his own sons as well as those of some of his guests. These dinners were repetitions within doors of the Quoit Club entertainments, except that the food was more abundant and varied, and the cheering drinks were of better quality — for Marshall prided himself on this feature of hospitality, especially on his madeira, of which he was said to keep the best to be had in America. Wit and repartee, joke, story and song, speech and raillery, brought forth volleys of laughter and roars of applause until far into the morning hours.[1] Marshall was not only at the head of the table as host, but was the leader of the merriment.[2]

His labors as Chief Justice did not dull his delight in the reading of poetry and fiction, which was so keen in his earlier years.[3] At the summit of his career, when seventy-one years old, he read all of Jane Austen's works, and playfully reproved Story for failing to name her in a list of authors given in his Phi Beta Kappa oration at Harvard. "I was a little mortified," he wrote Story, "to find that you had not admitted the name of Miss Austen into your list of favorites. I had just finished reading her novels when I received your discourse, and was so much pleased with them that I looked in it for her name, and was rather disappointed at not finding it. Her flights are not lofty, she does not soar on eagle's wings, but she is pleasing, interesting, equable, and

[1] On these occasions Mrs. Marshall spent the nights at the house of her daughter or sister.

[2] For an extended description of Marshall's "lawyer dinners" see Terhune, 85-87.   [3] See vol. I, 44-45, 153-54, of this work.

yet amusing. I count on your making some apology for this omission." [1]

Story himself wrote poetry, and Marshall often asked for copies of his verses.[2] "The plan of life I had formed for myself to be adopted after my retirement from office," he tells Story, "is to read nothing but novels and poetry."[3] That this statement genuinely expressed his tastes is supported by the fact that, among the few books which the Chief Justice treasured, were the novels of Sir Walter Scott and an extensive edition of the British poets.[4] While his chief intellectual pleasure was the reading of fiction, Marshall liked poetry even better; and he committed to memory favorite passages which he quoted as comment on passing incidents. Once when he was told that certain men had changed their opinions as a matter of political expediency, he repeated Homer's lines:

> "Ye gods, what havoc does ambition make
> 'Mong all your works." [5]

During the six or eight weeks that the Supreme Court sat each year, Marshall was the same in manner and appearance in Washington as he was among his neighbors in Richmond — the same in dress, in habits, in every way. Once a practitioner sent his little son to Marshall's quarters for some legal papers. The boy was in awe of the great man. But the Chief Justice, detecting the feelings of the lad, remarked:

[1] Marshall to Story, Nov. 26, 1826, Story, i, 506.

[2] Story to his wife, Feb. 26, 1832, *ib.* ii, 84.

[3] Marshall to Story, Sept. 30, 1829, *Proceedings, Mass. Hist. Soc.* 2d Series, xiv, 341.

[4] Statement of Miss Elizabeth Marshall of Leeds Manor to the author.   [5] Meade, i, footnote to 99.

"Billy, I believe I can beat you playing marbles; come into the yard and we will have a game." Soon the Chief Justice of the United States and the urchin were hard at play.[1]

If he reached the court-room before the hour of convening court, he sat among the lawyers and talked and joked as if he were one of them;[2] and, judging from his homely, neglected clothing, an uninformed onlooker would have taken him for the least important of the company. Yet there was about him an unconscious dignity that prevented any from presuming upon his good nature, for Marshall inspired respect as well as affection. After their surprise and disappointment at his ill attire and want of impressiveness,[3] attorneys coming in contact with him were unfailingly captivated by his simplicity and charm.

It was thus that Joseph Story, when a very young lawyer, first fell under Marshall's spell. "I love his laugh," he wrote; "it is too hearty for an intriguer, — and his good temper and unwearied patience are equally agreeable on the bench and in the study."[4] And Marshall wore well. The longer and more intimately men associated with him, the greater their fondness for him. "I am in love with his character, positively in love," wrote Story after twenty-four

[1] World's Work, i, 395.

[2] Gustavus Schmidt in Louisiana Law Journal (1841), i, No. 1, 85–86. Mr. Schmidt's description is of Marshall in the court-room at Richmond when holding the United States Circuit Court at that place. Ticknor, Story, and others show that the same was true in Washington.

[3] Quincy: Figures of the Past, 242–43.

[4] Story to Fay, Feb. 25, 1808, Story, i, 166–67.

years of close and familiar contact.[1] He "rises . . with the nearest survey," again testified Story in a magazine article.[2]

When, however, the time came for him to open court, a transformation came over him. Clad in the robes of his great office, with the Associate Justices on either side of him, no king on a throne ever appeared more majestic than did John Marshall. The kindly look was still in his eye, the mildness still in his tones, the benignity in his features. But a gravity of bearing, a firmness of manner, a concentration and intentness of mind, seemed literally to take possession of the man, although he was, and appeared to be, as unconscious of the change as he was that there was anything unusual in his conduct when off the bench.[3]

Marshall said and did things that interested other people and caused them to talk about him. He was noted for his quick wit, and the bar was fond of repeating anecdotes about him. "Did you hear what the Chief Justice said the other day?" — and then the story would be told of a bright saying, a quick repartee, a picturesque incident. Chief Justice Gibson of Pennsylvania, when a young man, went to Marshall for advice as to whether he should accept a position offered him on the State Bench. The young attorney, thinking to flatter him, remarked that the Chief Justice had "reached the acme of judicial distinction." "Let me tell you what that

[1] Story to Martineau, Oct. 8, 1835, Story, ii, 205.

[2] *Ib.* i, 522.

[3] Gustavus Schmidt in *Louisiana Law Journal* (1841), i, No. 1, 85–86.

means, young man," broke in Marshall. "The acme
of judicial distinction means the ability to look a
lawyer straight in the eyes for two hours and not
hear a damned word he says." [1]

Wherever he happened to be, nothing pleased
Marshall so much as to join a convivial party at dinner or to attend any sort of informal social gathering. On one occasion he went to the meeting of a
club at Philadelphia, held in a room at a tavern
across the hall from the bar. It was a rule of the club
that every one present should make a rhyme upon
a word suddenly given. As he entered, the Chief
Justice observed two or three Kentucky colonels
taking their accustomed drink. When Marshall appeared in the adjoining room, where the company
was gathered, he was asked for an extemporaneous
rhyme on the word "paradox." Looking across the
hall, he quickly answered:

> "In the Blue Grass region,
> A 'Paradox' was born,
> The corn was full of kernels
> And the 'colonels' full of corn." [2]

But Marshall heartily disliked the formal society
of the National Capital. He was, of course, often invited to dinners and receptions, but he was usually
bored by their formality. Occasionally he would
brighten his letters to his wife by short mention of
some entertainment. "Since being in this place,"

---

[1] Related to the author by Mr. Sussex D. Davis of the Philadelphia
bar.

[2] Related to the author by Thomas Marshall Smith of Baltimore,
a descendant of Marshall. Mr. Smith says that this story has been
handed down through three generations of his family.

he writes her, " I have been more in company than I wish. . . I have been invited to dine with the President with our own secretaries & with the minister of France & tomorrow I dine with the British minister. . . In the midst of these gay circles my mind is carried to my own fireside & to my beloved wife." [1]

Again: "Soon after dinner yesterday the French Chargé d'affaires called upon us with a pressing invitation to be present at a party given to the young couple, a gentleman of the French legation & the daughter of the secretary of the navy who are lately married. There was a most brilliant illumination which we saw and admired, & then we returned." [2] Of a dinner at the French Legation he writes his wife, it was "rather a dull party. Neither the minister nor his lady could speak English and I could not speak French. You may conjecture how far we were from being sociable. Yesterday I dined with M[r] Van Buren the secretary of State. It was a grand dinner and the secretary was very polite, but I was rather dull through the evening. I make a poor return for these dinners. I go to them with reluctance and am bad company while there. I hope we have seen the last, but I fear we must encounter one more. [3] With the exception of these parties my time was never passed with more uniformity. I rise early, pour [sic] over law cases, go to court and return at

[1] Marshall to his wife, Feb. 14, 1817, MS.

[2] Same to same, Jan. 4, 1823, MS.

[3] For excellent descriptions of Washington society during Marshall's period see the letters of Moss Kent, then a Representative in Congress. These MSS. are in the Library of Congress. Also see Story to his wife, Feb. 7, 1810, Story, i, 196.

the same hour and pass the evening in consultation with the Judges." [1]

Chester Harding relates that, when he was in Washington making a full-length portrait of the Chief Justice, [2] Marshall arrived late for the sitting, which had been fixed for eight o'clock in the evening. He came without a hat. Congressman Storrs and one or two other men, having seen Marshall, bareheaded, hurrying by their inn with long strides, had "followed, curious to know the cause of such a strange appearance." But Marshall simply explained to the artist that the consultation lasted longer than usual, and that he had hurried off without his hat. When the Chief Justice was about to go home, Harding offered him a hat, but he said, "Oh, no! it is a warm night, I shall not need one." [3]

No attorney practicing in the Supreme Court was more unreserved in social conversation than was the Chief Justice. Sometimes, indeed, on a subject that appealed to him, Marshall would do all the talking, which, for some reason, would occasionally be quite beyond the understanding of his hearer. Of one such exhibition Fisher Ames remarked to Samuel Dexter: "I have not understood a word of his argument for

[1] Marshall to his wife, Jan. 30, 1831, MS.

[2] This was painted for the Boston Athenæum. See frontispiece in vol. III. The other portrait by Harding, painted in Richmond (see *supra*, 76), was given to Story who presented it to the Harvard Law School.

[3] White: *Sketch of Chester Harding*, 194–96.

For the Chief Justice to lose or forget articles of clothing was nothing unusual. "He lost a coat, when he dined at the Secretary of the Navy's," writes Story who had been making a search for Marshall's missing garment. (Story to Webster, March 18, 1828, Story MSS. Mass. Hist. Soc.)

half an hour." "And I," replied the leader of the Massachusetts bar, "have been out of my depth for an hour and a half."[1]

The members of the Supreme Court made life as pleasant for themselves as they could during the weeks they were compelled to remain in "this dismal" place, as Daniel Webster described the National Capital. Marshall and the Associate Justices all lived together at one boarding-house, and thus became a sort of family. "We live very harmoniously and familiarly,"[2] writes Story, one year after his appointment. "My brethren are very interesting men," he tells another friend. We "live in the most frank and unaffected intimacy. Indeed, we are all united as one, with a mutual esteem which makes even the labors of Jurisprudence light."[3]

Sitting about a single table at their meals, or gathered in the room of one of them, these men talked over the cases before them. Not only did they "moot every question as" the arguments proceeded in court, but by "familiar conferences at our lodgings often come to a very quick, and . . accurate opinion, in a few hours," relates that faithful chronicler of their daily life, Joseph Story.[4] Story appears to have been even more impressed by the comradery of the members of the Supreme Court than by the difficulty of the cases they had to decide.

None of them ever took his wife with him to Washington, and this fact naturally made the personal relations of the Justices peculiarly close. "The

---

[1] Story, II, 504–05.   [2] Story to Williams, Feb. 16, 1812, *ib.* I, 214.
[3] Story to Fay, Feb. 24, 1812, *ib.* 215.   [4] *Ib.*

Judges here live with perfect harmony," Story reiterates, "and as agreeably as absence from friends and from families could make our residence. Our intercourse is perfectly familiar and unconstrained, and our social hours when undisturbed with the labors of law, are passed in gay and frank conversation, which at once enlivens and instructs." [1]

This "gay and frank conversation" of Marshall and his associates covered every subject — the methods, manners, and even dress of counsel who argued before them, the fortunes of public men, the trend of politics, the incident of the day, the gossip of society. "Two of the Judges are widowers," records Story, "and of course objects of considerable attraction among the ladies of the city. We have fine sport at their expense, and amuse our leisure with some touches at match-making. We have already ensnared one of the Judges, and he is now (at the age of forty-seven) violently affected with the tender passion." [2]

Thus Marshall, in his relation with his fellow occupants of the bench, was at the head of a family as much as he was Chief of a court. Although the discussion of legal questions occurred continuously at the boarding-house, each case was much more fully examined in the consultation room at the Capitol. There the court had a regular "consultation day" devoted exclusively to the cases in hand. Yet, even on these occasions, all was informality, and wit and humor brightened the tediousness. These "consul-

[1] Story to his wife, March 5, 1812, Story, I, 217.
[2] Same to same, March 12, 1812, *ib*. 219.

tations" lasted throughout the day and sometimes into the night; and the Justices took their meals while the discussions proceeded. Amusing incidents, some true, some false, and others a mixture, were related of these judicial meetings. One such story went the rounds of the bar and outlived the period of Marshall's life.

"We are great ascetics, and even deny ourselves wine except in wet weather," Story dutifully informed his wife. "What I say about the wine gives you our rule; but it does sometimes happen that the Chief Justice will say to me, when the cloth is removed, 'Brother Story, step to the window and see if it does not look like rain.' And if I tell him that the sun is shining brightly, Judge Marshall will sometimes reply, 'All the better, for our jurisdiction extends over so large a territory that the doctrine of chances makes it certain that it must be raining somewhere.'" [1]

When, as sometimes happened, one of the Associate Justices displeased a member of the bar, Marshall would soothe the wounded feelings of the lawyer. Story once offended Littleton W. Tazewell of Virginia by something said from the bench. "On my return from court yesterday," the Chief Justice hastened to write the irritated Virginian, "I informed Mr Story that you had been much hurt at an expression used in the opinion he had delivered in the case of the Palmyra. He expressed equal surprize and regret on the occasion, and declared that the

---

[1] *Magazine of American History*, XII, 69; and see Quincy: *Figures of the Past*, 189–90. This tale, gathering picturesqueness as it was passed by word of mouth during many years, had its variations.

words which had given offense were not used or understood by him in an offensive sense. He assented without hesitation to such modification of them as would render them in your view entirely unexceptionable." [1]

As Chief Justice, Marshall shrank from publicity, while printed adulation aggravated him. "I hope to God they will let me alone 'till I am dead," he exclaimed, when he had reached that eminence where writers sought to portray his life and character. [2]

He did, however, appreciate the recognition given from time to time by colleges and learned societies. In 1802 Princeton conferred upon him the honorary degree of LL.D.; in 1806 he received the same degree from Harvard and from the University of Pennsylvania in 1815. In 1809, as we have seen, he was elected a corresponding member of the Massachusetts Historical Society; on January 24, 1804, he was made a member of the American Academy of Arts and Sciences; and, in 1830, was elected to the American Philosophical Society. All these honors Marshall valued highly.

This, then, was the man who presided over the Supreme Court of the United States when the decisions of that tribunal developed the National powers of the Constitution and gave stability to our National life. His control of the court was made so easy for the Justices that they never resented it; often, perhaps, they did not realize it. The influence of his strong, deep, clear mind was powerfully aided

[1] Marshall to Tazewell, Jan. 20, 1827, MS.
[2] Wirt to Delaplaine, Nov. 5, 1818, Kennedy: *Memoirs of the Life of William Wirt*, II. 85.

by his engaging personality. To agree with him was a pleasure.

Marshall's charm was as great as his intellect; he was never irritable; his placidity was seldom ruffled; not often was his good nature disturbed. His "great suavity, or rather calmness of manner, cannot readily be conceived," testifies George Bancroft.[1] The sheer magnitude of his views was, in itself, captivating, and his supremely lucid reasoning removed the confusion which more complex and subtle minds would have created in reaching the same conclusion. The elements of his mind and character were such, and were so combined, that it was both hard and unpleasant to differ with him, and both easy and agreeable to follow his lead.

Above all other influences upon his associates on the bench, and, indeed, upon everybody who knew him, was the sense of trustworthiness, honor, and uprightness he inspired.[2] Perhaps no public man ever stood higher in the esteem of his contemporaries for noble personal qualities than did John Marshall.

When reviewing his constructive work and marveling at his influence over his judicial associates, we must recall, even at the risk of iteration, the figure revealed by his daily life and habits — "a man who is tall to awkwardness, with a large head of

[1] Bancroft to his wife, Jan. 23, 1832, Howe: *Life and Letters of George Bancroft*, I, 202.

[2] Even Jefferson, in his bitterest attacks, never intimated anything against Marshall's integrity; and Spencer Roane, when assailing with great violence the opinion of the Chief Justice in M'Culloch *vs.* Maryland (see *infra*, chap. VI), paid a high tribute to the purity of his personal character.

hair, which looked as if it had not been lately tied or combed, and with dirty boots," [1] a body that seemed "without proportion," and arms and legs that "dangled from each other and looked half dislocated," dressed in clothes apparently "gotten from some antiquated slop-shop of second-hand raiment . . the coat and breeches cut for nobody in particular." [2] But we must also think of such a man as possessed of "style and tones in conversation uncommonly mild, gentle, and conciliating." [3] We must think of his hearty laughter, his "imperturbable temper," [4] his shyness with strangers, his quaint humor, his hilarious unreserve with friends and convivial jocularity when with intimates, his cordial warm-heartedness, unassuming simplicity and sincere gentleness to all who came in contact with him — a man without "an atom of gall in his whole composition." [5] We must picture this distinctive American character among his associates of the bench in the Washington boarding-house no less than in court, his luminous mind guiding them, his irresistible personality drawing from them a real and lasting affection. We must bear in mind the trust and confidence which so powerfully impressed those who knew the man. We must imagine a person very much like Abraham Lincoln.

[1] Ticknor to his father, Feb. 1, 1815, Ticknor: *Life, Letters, and Journals of George Ticknor*, I, 33.

[2] Description from personal observation, as quoted in Van Santvoord: *Lives and Judicial Services of the Chief Justices*, footnote to 363.

[3] Ticknor to his father, as cited in note 1, *supra*.

[4] *Memoirs of John Quincy Adams:* Adams, IX, 243.

[5] Wirt to Carr, Dec. 30, 1827, Kennedy, 240. For Story's estimate of Marshall's personality see Dillon, III, 363–66.

Indeed, the resemblance of Marshall to Lincoln is striking. Between no two men in American history is there such a likeness. Physically, intellectually, and in characteristics, Marshall and Lincoln were of the same type. Both were very tall men, slender, loose-jointed, and awkward, but powerful and athletic; and both fond of sport. So alike were they, and so identical in their negligence of dress and their total unconsciousness of, or indifference to, convention, that the two men, walking side by side, might well have been taken for brothers.

Both Marshall and Lincoln loved companionship with the same heartiness, and both had the same social qualities. They enjoyed fun, jokes, laughter, in equal measure, and had the same keen appreciation of wit and humor. Their mental qualities were the same. Each man had the gift of going directly to the heart of any subject; while the same lucidity of statement marked each of them. Their style, the simplicity of their language, the peculiar clearness of their logic, were almost identical. Notwithstanding their straightforwardness and amplitude of mind, both had a curious subtlety. Some of Marshall's opinions and Lincoln's state papers might have been written by the same man. The "Freeholder" questions and answers in Marshall's congressional campaign, and those of Lincoln's debate with Douglas, are strikingly similar in method and expression.

Each had a genius for managing men; and Marshall showed the precise traits in dealing with the members of the Supreme Court that Lincoln displayed in the Cabinet.

Both were born in the South, each on the eve of a great epoch in American history when a new spirit was awakening in the hearts of the people. Although Southern-born, both Marshall and Lincoln sympathized with and believed in the North; and yet their manners and instinct were always those of the South. Marshall was given advantages that Lincoln never had; but both were men of the people, were brought up among them, and knew them thoroughly. Lincoln's outlook upon life, however, was that of the humblest citizen; Marshall's that of the well-placed and prosperous. Neither was well educated, but each acquired, in different ways, a command of excellent English and broad, plain conceptions of government and of life. Neither was a learned man, but both created the materials for learning.

Marshall and Lincoln were equally good politicians; but, although both were conservative in their mental processes, Marshall lost faith in the people's steadiness, moderation, and self-restraint; and came to think that impulse rather than wisdom was too often the temporary moving power in the popular mind, while the confidence of Lincoln in the good sense, righteousness, and self-control of the people became greater as his life advanced. If, with these distinctions, Abraham Lincoln were, in imagination, placed upon the Supreme Bench during the period we are now considering, we should have a good idea of John Marshall, the Chief Justice of the United States.

It is, then, largely the personality of John Marshall that explains the hold, as firm and persistent as it was gentle and soothing, maintained by him upon the Associate Justices of the Supreme Court; and it is this, too, that enables us to understand his immense popularity with the bar — a fact only second in importance to the work he had to do, and to his influence upon the men who sat with him on the bench.

For the lawyers who practiced before the Supreme Court at this period were most helpful to Marshall.[1] Many of them were men of wide and accurate learning, and nearly all of them were of the first order of ability. No stronger or more brilliant bar ever was arrayed before any bench than that which displayed its wealth of intellect and resources to Marshall and his associates.[2] This assertion is strong, but wholly justified. Oratory of the finest quality, though of the old rhetorical kind, filled the courtroom with admiring spectators, and entertained Marshall and the other Justices, as much as the solid reasoning illuminated their minds, and the exhaustive learning informed them.

[1] "He was solicitous to hear arguments, and not to decide causes without hearing them. And no judge ever profited more by them. No matter whether the subject was new or old; familiar to his thoughts or remote from them; buried under a mass of obsolete learning, or developed for the first time yesterday — whatever was its nature, he courted argument, nay, he demanded it." (Story in Dillon, III, 377; and see vol. II, 177–80, of this work.)

[2] See Story's description of Harper, Duponceau, Rawle, Dallas, Ingersoll, Lee, and Martin (Story to Fay, Feb. 16, 1808, Story, I, 162–64); and of Pinkney (notes *supra*); also see Warren: *History of the American Bar*, 257–63. We must remember, too, that Webster, Hopkinson, Emmet, Wirt, Ogden, Clay, and others of equal ability and accomplishments, practiced before the Supreme Court when Marshall was Chief Justice.

Marshall encouraged extended arguments; often demanded them. Frequently a single lawyer would speak for two or three days. No limit of time was put upon counsel.[1] Their reputation as speakers as well as their fame as lawyers, together with the throngs of auditors always present, put them on their mettle. Rhetoric adorned logic; often encumbered it. A conflict between such men as William Pinkney, Luther Martin of Maryland, Samuel Dexter of Massachusetts, Thomas Addis Emmet of New York, William Wirt of Virginia, Joseph Hopkinson of Pennsylvania, Jeremiah Mason of New Hampshire, Daniel Webster, Henry Clay, and others of scarcely less distinction, was, in itself, an event. These men, and indeed all the members of the bar, were Marshall's friends as well as admirers.

The appointment of Story to the Supreme Bench was, like the other determining circumstances in Marshall's career, providential.

Few characters in American history are more attractive than the New England lawyer and publicist who, at the age of thirty-two, took his place at Marshall's side on the Supreme Bench. Hand

[1] Story relates that a single case was argued for nine days. (Story to Fay, Feb. 16, 1808, Story, I, 162.)

In the Charlestown Bridge case, argued in 1831, the opening counsel on each side occupied three days. (Story to Ashmun, March 10, 1831, *ib.* II, 51.)

Four years later Story writes: "We have now a case .. which has been under argument eight days, and will probably occupy five more." (Story to Fay, March 2, 1835, *ib.* 193.)

In the lower courts the arguments were even longer. "This is the fourteenth day since this argument was opened. Pinkney .. promised to speak only two hours and a half. He has now spoken two days, and is, at this moment, at it again for the third day." (Wirt to his wife, April 7, 1821, Kennedy, II, 119.)

some, vivacious, impressionable, his mind was a storehouse of knowledge, accurately measured and systematically arranged. He read everything, forgot nothing. His mental appetite was voracious, and he had a very passion for research. His industry was untiring, his memory unfailing. He supplied exactly the accomplishment and toilsomeness that Marshall lacked. So perfectly did the qualities and attainments of these two men supplement one another that, in the work of building the American Nation, Marshall and Story may be considered one and the same person.

Where Marshall was leisurely, Story was eager. If the attainments of the Chief Justice were not profuse, those of his young associate were opulent. Marshall detested the labor of investigating legal authorities; Story delighted in it. The intellect of the older man was more massive and sure; but that of the youthful Justice was not far inferior in strength, or much less clear and direct in its operation. Marshall steadied Story while Story enriched Marshall. Each admired the other, and between them grew an affection like that of father and son.

Story's father, Elisha Story, was a member of the Republican Party, a rare person among wealthy and educated men in Massachusetts at the time Jefferson founded that political organization. The son tells us that he "naturally imbibed the same opinions," which were so reprobated that not "more than four or five lawyers in the whole state . . *dared* avow themselves republicans. The very name was odious."[1]

[1] Story, I, 96.

Joseph Story was born in Marblehead, Massachusetts, September 18, 1779, one of a family of eighteen children, seven by a first wife and eleven by a second. He was the eldest son of the second wife, who had been a Miss Pedrick, the daughter of a rich merchant and shipowner.[1]

No young member of the Massachusetts bar equaled Joseph Story in intellectual gifts and acquirements. He was a graduate of Harvard, and few men anywhere had a broader or more accurate education. His personality was winning and full of charm. Yet, when he began practice at Salem, he was "persecuted" with "extreme . . virulence" because of his political opinions.[2] He became so depressed by what he calls "the petty prejudices and sullen coolness of New England, . . bigoted in opinion and satisfied in forms," where Federalism had "persecuted . . [him] unrelentingly for . . [his] political principles," that he thought seriously of going to Baltimore to live and practice his profession. He made headway, however, in spite of opposition; and, when the growing Republican Party, "the whole" of which he says were his "warm advocates,"[3] secured the majority of his district, Story was sent to Congress. "I was . . of course a supporter of the administration of Mr. Jefferson and Mr. Madison," although not "a

---

[1] Story, i, 2. Elisha Story is said to have been one of the "Indians" who threw overboard the tea at Boston; and he fought at Lexington. When the Revolution got under way, he entered the American Army as a surgeon and served for about two years, when he resigned because of his disgust with the management of the medical department. (*Ib.*)

[2] Story to Duval, March 30, 1803, *ib.* 102.

[3] Story to Williams, June 6, 1805, *ib.* 105–06.

mere slave to the opinions of either." In exercising
what he terms his "independent judgment," [1] Story
favored the repeal of the Embargo, and so earned,
henceforth, the lasting enmity of Jefferson.[2]

Because of his recognized talents, and perhaps
also because of the political party to which he belonged, he was employed to go to Washington as
attorney for the New England and Mississippi Company in the Yazoo controversy.[3] It was at this
period that the New England Federalist leaders began to cultivate him. They appreciated his ability,
and the assertion of his "independent principles"
was to their liking. Harrison Gray Otis was quick
to advise that seasoned politician, Robert Goodloe
Harper, of the change he thought observable in
Story, and the benefit of winning his regard. "He is
a young man of talents, who commenced Democrat
a few years since and was much fondled by his
party," writes Otis. "He discovered however too
much sentiment and honor to go *all lengths* . . and
a little attention from the right sort of people will
be very useful to him & to us." [4]

The wise George Cabot gave Pickering the same
hint when Story made one of his trips to Washington
on the Yazoo business. "Though he is a man whom
the Democrats support," says Cabot, "I have seldom
if ever met with one of sounder mind on the principal
points of national policy. He is well worthy the civil
attention of the most respectable Federalists." [5]

---

[1] Story, i, 128.　　　[2] At first, Story supported the Embargo.
[3] See vol. iii, chap. x, of this work.
[4] Otis to Harper, April 19, 1807, Morison: *Otis*, i, 283.
[5] Cabot to Pickering, Jan. 28, 1808, Lodge: *Cabot*, 377.

It was while in the Capital, as attorney before Congress and the Supreme Court in the Georgia land controversy, that Story, then twenty-nine years old, met Marshall; and impulsively wrote of his delight in the "hearty laugh," "patience," consideration, and ability of the Chief Justice. On this visit to Washington the young Massachusetts lawyer took most of his meals with the members of the Supreme Court.[1] At that time began the devotion of Joseph Story to John Marshall which was to prove so helpful to both for more than a generation, and so influential upon the Republic for all time.

That Story, while in Washington, had copiously expressed his changing opinions, as well as his disapproval of Jefferson's Embargo, is certain; for he was "a very great talker," [2] and stated his ideas with the volubility of his extremely exuberant nature. "At this time, as in after life," declares Story's son, "he was remarkable for fulness and fluency of conversation. It poured out from his mind . . sparkling, and exhaustless. Language was as a wide open sluice, through which every feeling and thought rushed forth. . . It would be impossible to give an idea of his conversational powers." [3]

It was not strange, then, that Jefferson, who was eager for all gossip and managed to learn everything that happened, or was said to have happened, in Washington, heard of Story's association with the Federalists, his unguarded talk, and especially his admiration for the Chief Justice. It was plain to

[1] Story to Fay, Feb. 16, 1808, Story, i, 162.
[2] Moss Kent to James Kent, Feb. 1, 1817, Kent MSS. Lib. Cong.
[3] Story, i, 140.

Jefferson that such a person would never resist Marshall's influence.

In Jefferson's mind existed another objection to Story which may justly be inferred from the situation in which he found himself when the problem arose of filling the place on the Supreme Bench vacated by the death of Justice Cushing. Story had made a profound study of the law of real estate; and, young though he was, no lawyer in America equaled him, and few in England surpassed him, in the intricate learning of that branch of legal science. This fact was well known to the bar at Washington as well as to that of Massachusetts. Therefore, the thought of Story on the Supreme Bench, and under Marshall's influence, made Jefferson acutely uncomfortable; for the former President was then engaged in a lawsuit involving questions of real estate which, if decided against him, would, as he avowed, ruin him. This lawsuit was the famous Batture litigation. It was this predicament that led Jefferson to try to control the appointment of the successor to Cushing, whose death he declared to be "a Godsend" [1] to him personally; and also to dictate the naming of the district judge at Richmond to the vacancy caused by the demise of Judge Cyrus Griffin.

In the spring of 1810, Edward Livingston, formerly of New York and then of New Orleans, brought suit in the United States Court for the District of Virginia against Thomas Jefferson for damages to the amount of one hundred thousand dollars.

[1] Jefferson to Gallatin, Sept. 27, 1810, *Works:* Ford, xi, footnote to 152–54.

This was the same Livingston who in Congress had been the Republican leader in the House when Marshall was a member of that body.[1] Afterwards he was appointed United States Attorney for the District of New York and then became Mayor of that city. During the yellow fever epidemic that scourged New York in 1803, Livingston devoted himself to the care of the victims of the plague, leaving the administration of the Mayor's office to a trusted clerk. In time Livingston, too, was stricken. During his illness his clerk embezzled large sums of the public money. The Mayor was liable and, upon his recovery, did not attempt to evade responsibility, but resigned his office and gave all his property to make good the defalcation. A heavy amount, however, still remained unpaid; and the discharge of this obligation became the ruling purpose of Livingston's life until, twenty years afterward, he accomplished his object.

His health regained, Livingston went to New Orleans to seek fortune anew. There he soon became the leader of the bar. When Wilkinson set up his reign of terror in that city, it was Edward Livingston who swore out writs of habeas corpus for those illegally imprisoned and, in general, was the most vigorous as well as the ablest of those who opposed Wilkinson's lawless and violent measures.[2] Jefferson had been displeased that Livingston had not shown more enthusiasm for him, when, in 1801, the Federalists had tried to elect Burr to the Presidency,

[1] See vol. II, 461–74, of this work.
[2] See vol. III, chap. VI, of this work.

and bitterly resented Livingston's interference with Wilkinson's plans to "suppress treason" in New Orleans.

One John Gravier, a lifelong resident of that city, had inherited from his brother Bertrand certain real estate abutting the river. Between this and the water the current had deposited an immense quantity of alluvium. The question of the title to this river-made land had never been raised, and everybody used it as a sort of common wharf front. Alert for opportunities to make money with which fully to discharge the defalcation in the New York Mayor's office, Livingston investigated the rightful ownership of the batture, as the alluvial deposit was termed; satisfied himself that the title was in Gravier; gave an opinion to that effect, and brought suit for the property as Gravier's attorney.[1] While the trial of Aaron Burr was in progress in Richmond, the Circuit Court in New Orleans rendered judgment in favor of Gravier,[2] who then conveyed half of his rights to his attorney, apparently as a fee for the recovery of the batture.

Livingston immediately began to improve his property, whereupon the people became excited and drove away his workmen. Governor Claiborne refused to protect him and referred the whole matter to Jefferson. The President did not direct the Attorney-General to bring suit for the possession of the batture — the obvious and the legal form of procedure. Indeed, the title to the property was not so much as examined. Jefferson did not even take into

---

[1] Hunt: *Life of Edward Livingston*, 138.   [2] *Ib.* 140.

consideration the fact that, if Livingston was not the rightful owner of the batture, it might belong to the City of New Orleans. He merely assumed that it was National property; and, hastily acting under a law against squatters on lands belonging to the United States, he directed Secretary of State Madison to have all persons removed from the disputed premises. Accordingly, the United States Marshal was ordered to eject the "intruder" and his laborers. This was done; but Livingston told his men to return to their work and secured an injunction against the Marshal from further molesting them. That official ignored the order of the court and again drove the laborers off the batture.

Livingston begged the President to submit the controversy to arbitration or to judicial decision, but Jefferson was deaf to his pleas. The distracted lawyer appealed to Congress for relief.[1] That body ignored his petition.[2] He then brought suit against the Marshal in New Orleans for the recovery of his property. Soon afterward he brought another in Virginia against Jefferson for one hundred thousand dollars damages. Such, in brief outline, was the beginning of the famous "Batture Controversy," in which Jefferson and Livingston waged a war of pamphlets for years.

When he learned that Livingston had begun action against him in the Federal court at Richmond, Jefferson was much alarmed. In anticipation of the death of Judge Cyrus Griffin, Governor John Tyler

---

[1] *Annals*, 10th Cong. 2d Sess. 702.
[2] *Annals*, 11th Cong. 1st and 2d Sess. 323, 327--49, 418–19, 1373, 1617–18, 1694–1702.

had written Jefferson that, while he "never did apply for an office," yet "Judge Griffin is in a low state of health, and holds my old office." Tyler continues: "I really hope the President will chance to think of me . . in case of accidents, and if an opportunity offers, lay me down softly on a bed of *roses in my latter days*." He condemns Marshall for his opposition to the War of 1812, and especially for his reputed statement that Great Britain had done nothing to justify armed retaliation on our part.[1] "Is it possible," asks Tyler, "that a man who can assert this, can have any true sense of sound veracity? And yet these sort of folks retain their stations and consequence in life."[2]

Immediately Jefferson wrote to President Madison: "From what I can learn Griffin cannot stand it long, and really the state has suffered long enough by having such a cypher in so important an office, and infinitely the more from the want of any counterpoint to the rancorous hatred which Marshall bears to the government of his country, & from the cunning & sophistry within which he is able to enshroud himself. It will be difficult to find a character of firmness enough to preserve his independence on the same bench with Marshall. Tyler, I am certain, would do it. . . A milk & water character . . would be seen as a calamity. Tyler having been the former state judge of that court too, and removed to make way for so wretched a fool as Griffin,[3] has a kind of right of reclamation."

[1] See *supra*, 25, 35–41.
[2] Tyler to Jefferson, May 12, 1810, Tyler: *Tyler*, i, 246–47.
[3] Cyrus Griffin was educated in England; was a member of the

Jefferson gives other reasons for the appointment of Tyler, and then addresses Madison thus: "You have seen in the papers that Livingston has served a writ on me, stating damages at 100,000. D. . . I shall soon look into my papers to make a state of the case to enable them to plead." Jefferson hints broadly that he may have to summon as witnesses his "associates in the proceedings," one of whom was Madison himself.

He concludes this astounding letter in these words: "It is a little doubted that his [Livingston's] knolege [*sic*] of Marshall's character has induced him to bring this action. His twistifications of the law in the case of Marbury, in that of Burr, & the late Yazoo case shew how dexterously he can reconcile law to his personal biasses: and nobody seems to doubt that he is ready prepared to decide that Livingston's right to the batture is unquestionable, and that I am bound to pay for it with my private fortune." [1]

The next day Jefferson wrote Tyler that he had "laid it down as a law" to himself "never to embarrass the President with any solicitations." Yet, in Tyler's case, says Jefferson, "I . . have done it with all my heart, and in the full belief that I serve him

first Legislature of Virginia after the Declaration of Independence; was a delegate to the Continental Congress in 1778–81, and again in 1787–88, and was President of that body during the last year of his service. He was made President of the Supreme Court of Admiralty, and held that office until the court was abolished. When the Constitution was adopted, and Washington elected President, one of his first acts, after the passage of the Ellsworth Judiciary Law, was to appoint Judge Griffin to the newly created office of Judge of the United States Court for the District of Virginia. It is thus evident that Jefferson's statement was not accurate.

[1] Jefferson to Madison, May 25, 1810, *Works*: Ford, xi, 139–41.

and the public in urging the appointment." For,
Jefferson confides to the man who, in case Madison
named him, would, with Marshall, hear the suit,
"we have long enough suffered under the base prostitution of the law to party passions in one judge,
and the imbecility of another.

"In the hands of one [Marshall] the law is nothing
more than an ambiguous text, to be explained by his
sophistry into any meaning which may subserve
his personal malice. Nor can any milk-and-water associate maintain his own independence, and by a firm
pursuance of what the law really is, extend its protection to the citizens or the public. . . And where you
cannot induce your colleague to do what is right,
you will be firm enough to hinder him from doing
what is wrong, and by opposing sense to sophistry,
leave the juries free to follow their own judgment." [1]

Upon the death of Judge Griffin in the following
December, John Tyler was appointed to succeed
him.

On September 13, 1810, William Cushing, Associate
Justice of the Supreme Court, died. Only three Federalists now remained on the Supreme Bench, Samuel
Chase, Bushrod Washington, and John Marshall.
The other Justices, William Johnson of South Carolina, Brockholst Livingston of New York, and Thomas
Todd of Kentucky, were Republicans, appointed
by Jefferson. The selection of Cushing's successor
would give the majority of the court to the Republican Party for the first time since its organization.

---

[1] Jefferson to Tyler, May 26, 1810, Tyler: *Tyler*, I, 247–48; also
Works: Ford, XI, footnote to 141–43.

That Madison would fill the vacancy by one of his
own following was certain; but this was not enough
to satisfy Jefferson, who wanted to make sure that
the man selected was one who would not fall under
Marshall's baleful influence. If Griffin did not die in
time, Jefferson's fate in the batture litigation would
be in Marshall's hands.

Should Griffin be polite enough to breathe his
last promptly and Tyler be appointed in season, still
Jefferson would not feel safe — the case might go
to the jury, and who could tell what their verdict
would be under Marshall's instructions? Even Tyler
might not be able to "hinder" Marshall "from wrong
doing"; for nothing was more probable than that,
no matter what the issue of the case might be, it
would be carried to the Supreme Court if any ground
for appeal could be found. Certainly Jefferson would
take it there if the case should go against him. It was
vital, therefore, that the latest vacancy on the Supreme Bench should also be filled by a man on whom
Jefferson could depend.

The new Justice must come from New England,
Cushing having presided over that circuit. Republican lawyers there, fit for the place, were at that
time extremely hard to find. Jefferson had been
corresponding about the batture case with Gallatin,
who had been his Secretary of the Treasury and continued in that office under Madison. The moment
he learned of Cushing's death, Jefferson wrote to
Gallatin in answer to a letter from that able man,
admitting that "the Batture . . could not be within
the scope of the law . . against squatters," under

color of which Livingston had been forcibly ousted
from that property. Jefferson adds: "I should so
adjudge myself; yet I observe many opinions otherwise, and in defence against a spadassin it is lawful to use all weapons." The case is complex;
still no unbiased man "can doubt what the issue
of the case ought to be. What it will be, no one
can tell.

"The judge's [Marshall's] inveteracy is profound,
and his mind of that gloomy malignity which will
never let him forego the opportunity of satiating it
on a victim. His decisions, his instructions to a jury,
his allowances and disallowances and garblings of
evidence, must all be subjects of appeal. . . And to
whom is my appeal? From the judge in Burr's case
to himself and his associate judges in the case of
Marbury v. Madison.

"Not exactly, however. I observe old Cushing is
dead. . . The event is a fortunate one, and so timed
as to be a Godsend to me. I am sure its importance
to the nation will be felt, and the occasion employed
to complete the great operation they have so long
been executing, by the appointment of a decided
Republican, with nothing equivocal about him. But
who will it be?"

Jefferson warmly recommends Levi Lincoln, his
former Attorney-General. Since the new Justice
must come from New England, "can any other bring
equal qualifications? . . I know he was not deemed
a profound common lawyer; but was there ever a
profound common lawyer known in one of the
Eastern States? There never was, nor never can be,

one from those States. . . Mr. Lincoln is . . as learned
in their laws as any one they have." [1]

After allowing time for Gallatin to carry this message to the President, Jefferson wrote directly to
Madison. He congratulates him on "the revocation
of the French decrees"; abuses Great Britain for her
"principle" of "the exclusive right to the sea by conquest"; and then comes to the matter of the vacancy
on the Supreme Bench.

"Another circumstance of congratulation is the
death of Cushing," which "gives an opportunity of
closing the reformation [the Republican triumph of
1800] by a successor of unquestionable republican
principles." Jefferson suggests Lincoln. "Were he
out of the way," then Gideon Granger ought to be
chosen, "tho' I am sensible that J.[ohn] R.[andolph]
has been able to lessen the confidence of many in
him.[2] . . As the choice must be of a New Englander,
. . I confess I know of none but these two characters."
Of course there was Joseph Story, but he is "unquestionably a tory," and "too young."[3]

Madison strove to follow Jefferson's desires. Cushing's place was promptly offered to Lincoln, who de-

---

[1] Jefferson to Gallatin, Sept. 27, 1810, *Works:* Ford, xi, footnote
to 152–54.

[2] Gideon Granger, as Jefferson's Postmaster-General, had lobbied
on the floor of the House for the Yazoo Bill, offering government contracts for votes. He was denounced by Randolph in one of the most
scathing arraignments ever heard in Congress. (See vol. iii, 578–79,
of this work.)

[3] Jefferson to Madison, Oct. 15, 1810, *Works:* Ford, xi, 150–52.
Granger was an eager candidate for the place, and had asked Jefferson's
support. In assuring him that it was given, Jefferson tells Granger
of his "esteem & approbation," and adds that the appointment of "a
firm unequivocating republican" is vital. (Jefferson to Granger, Oct.
22, 1810, *ib.* footnote to 155.)

clined it because of approaching blindness. Granger, of course, was impossible — the Senate would not have confirmed him. So Alexander Wolcott, "an active Democratic politician of Connecticut," of mediocre ability and "rather dubious . . character," [1] was nominated; but the Senate rejected him. It seemed impossible to find a competent lawyer in New England who would satisfy Jefferson's requirements. John Quincy Adams, who had deserted the Federalist Party and acted with the Republicans, and who was then Minister to Russia, was appointed and promptly confirmed. Jefferson himself had not denounced Marshall so scathingly as had Adams in his report to the Senate on the proposed expulsion of Senator John Smith of Ohio. [2] It was certain that he would not, as Associate Justice, be controlled by the Chief Justice. But Adams preferred to continue in his diplomatic post, and refused the appointment.

Thus Story became the only possible choice. After all, he was still believed to be a Republican by everybody except Jefferson and the few Federalist leaders who had been discreetly cultivating him. At least his appointment would not be so bad as the selection of an out-and-out Federalist. On November 18, 1811, therefore, Joseph Story was made an Associate Justice of the Supreme Court of the United States. In Massachusetts his appointment "was ridiculed and condemned." [3]

Although Jefferson afterward declared that he

---

[1] Hildreth: *History of the United States*, vi, 241; and see Adams *U.S.* v, 359–60.

[2] See vol. iii, 541–43, of this work.   [3] Story, i, 212.

"had a strong desire that the public should have
been satisfied by a trial on the merits," [1] he was willing that his counsel should prevent the case from
coming to trial if they could. Fearing, however, that
they would not succeed, Jefferson had prepared, for
the use of his attorneys, an exhaustive brief covering
his version of the facts and his views of the law.
Spencer Roane, Judge of the Virginia Court of Appeals, and as hot a partisan of Jefferson as he was
an implacable enemy of Marshall, read this manuscript and gave Tyler "some of the outlines of it."
Tyler explains this to Jefferson after the decision in
his favor, and adds that, much as Tyler wanted to
get hold of Jefferson's brief, still, "as soon as I had
received the appointment . . (which I owe to your
favor in great measure), it became my duty to shut
the door against every observation which might in
any way be derived from either side, lest the impudent British faction, who had enlisted on Livingston's side, might suppose an undue influence had
seized upon me." [2]

The case aroused keen interest in Virginia and, indeed, throughout the country. Jefferson was still the
leader of the Republican Party and was as much beloved and revered as ever by the great majority of the
people. When, therefore, he was sued for so large a
sum of money, the fact excited wide and lively attention. That the plaintiff was such a man as Edward
Livingston gave sharper edge to the general interest.
Especially among lawyers, curiosity as to the out-

[1] Jefferson to Wirt, April 12, 1812, *Works*: Ford, xi, 227.
[2] Tyler to Jefferson, May 17, 1812, Tyler: *Tyler*, i, 263.

come was keen. In Richmond, of course, "great
expectation was excited."

When the case came on for hearing, Tyler was so
ill from a very painful affliction that he could scarcely
sit through the hearing; but he persisted because he
had "determined to give an opinion." The question
of jurisdiction alone was argued and only this was
decided. Both judges agreed that the court had no
jurisdiction, though Marshall did so with great reluctance. He wished "to carry the cause to the Supreme Court, by adjournment or somehow or other;
but," says Tyler in his report to Jefferson, "I pressed
the propriety of [its] being decided." [1]

Marshall, however, delivered a written opinion in
which he gravely reflected on Jefferson's good faith
in avoiding a trial on the merits. If the court, upon
mere technicality, were prevented from trying and
deciding the case, "the injured party may have a
clear right without a remedy"; and that, too, "in a
case where a person who has done the wrong, and
who ought to make the compensation, is within the
power of the court." The situation created by Jefferson's objection to the court's jurisdiction was unfortunate: "Where the remedy is against the person,
and is within the power of the court, I have not yet
discerned a reason, other than a technical one, which
can satisfy my judgment" why the case should not
be tried and justice done.

"If, however," continues Marshall, "this technical reason is firmly established, if all other judges respect it, I cannot venture to disregard it," no matter

[1] Tyler to Jefferson, May 17, 1812, Tyler: *Tyler*, I, 263–64.

how wrong in principle and injurious to Livingston the Chief Justice might think it. If Lord Mansfield, "one of the greatest judges who ever sat upon any bench, and who has done more than any other, to remove those technical impediments which .. too long continued to obstruct the course of substantial justice," had vainly attempted to remove the very "technical impediments" which Jefferson had thrown in Livingston's way, Marshall would not make the same fruitless effort.

To be sure, the technical point raised by Jefferson's counsel was a legal fiction derived from "the common law of England"; but "this common law has been adopted by the legislature of Virginia"; and "had it not been adopted, I should have thought it in force." Thus Marshall, by innuendo, blames Jefferson for invoking, for his own protection, a technicality of that very common law which the latter had so often and so violently denounced. For the third time Marshall deplores the use of a technicality "which produces the inconvenience of a clear right without a remedy." "Other judges have felt the weight of this argument, and have struggled ineffectually against" it; so, he concluded, "I must submit to it." [1]

Thus it was that Jefferson at last escaped; for it was nothing less than an escape. What a decision on the merits of the case would have been is shown by the opinion of Chancellor Kent, stated with his characteristic emphasis. Jefferson was anxious that the public should think that he was in the right. "Mr. Livingston's suit having gone off on the plea to the

[1] 1 Brockenbrough, 206-12.

jurisdiction, it's foundation remains of course unex-
plained to the public. I have therefore concluded to
make it public thro' the . . press. . . I am well satisfied
to be relieved from it, altho' I had a strong desire
that the public should have been satisfied by a trial
on the merits."[1] Accordingly, Jefferson prepared his
statement of the controversy and, curiously enough,
published it just before Livingston's suit against the
United States Marshal in New Orleans was approaching decision. To no other of his documents did he
give more patient and laborious care. Livingston
replied in an article [2] which justified the great reputation for ability and learning he was soon to acquire
in both Europe and America.[3] Kent followed this
written debate carefully. When Livingston's answer
appeared, Kent wrote him: "I read it eagerly and
studied it thoroughly, with a re-examination of
Jefferson as I went along; and I should now be
as willing to subscribe my name to the validity of
your title and to the atrocious injustice you have
received as to any opinion contained in Johnson's
Reports."[4]

---

[1] Jefferson to Wirt, April 12, 1812, *Works:* Ford, xi, 226–27. On
the Batture controversy see Hildreth, vi, 143–48.

[2] The articles of both Jefferson and Livingston are to be found in
Hall's *American Law Journal* (Philadelphia, 1816), vol. v, 1–91, 113–
289. A brief but valuable summary of Livingston's reply to Jefferson
is found in Hunt: *Livingston,* 143–80. For an abstract of Jefferson's
attack, see Randall: *Life of Thomas Jefferson,* iii, 266–68.

[3] See Hunt: *Livingston,* 276–80.

[4] Kent to Livingston, May 13, 1814, Hunt: *Livingston,* 181–82.
Kent was appointed Chancellor of the State of New York, Feb. 25,
1814. His opinions are contained in *Johnson's Chancery Reports,* to
which he refers in this letter.

For twenty years Livingston fought for what he believed to be his
.ights to the batture, and, in the end, was successful; but in such

Marshall's attitude in the Batture litigation intensified Jefferson's hatred for the Chief Justice, while Jefferson's conduct in the whole matter still further deepened Marshall's already profound belief that the great exponent of popular government was dishonest and cowardly. Story shared Marshall's views; indeed, the Batture controversy may be said to have furnished that personal element which completed Story's forming antagonism to Jefferson. "Who . . can remember, without regret, his conduct in relation to the batture of New Orleans?" wrote Story many years afterward.[1]

The Chief Justice attributed the attacks which Jefferson made upon him in later years to his opinion in Livingston *vs.* Jefferson, and to the views he was known to have held as to the merits of that case and Jefferson's course in relation to it. "The Batture will never be forgotten," wrote the Chief Justice some years later when commenting on the attacks upon the National Judiciary which he attributed to

fashion that the full value of the property was only realized by his family long after his death.

Notwithstanding Jefferson's hostility, Livingston grew in public favor, was elected to the Louisiana State Legislature and then to Congress, where his work was notable. Later, in 1829, he was chosen United States Senator from that State; and, after serving one term, was appointed Secretary of State by President Jackson. In this office he prepared most of the President's state papers and wrote Jackson's great Nullification Proclamation in 1832.

Livingston was then sent as Minister to France and, by his brilliant conduct of the negotiations over the French Spoliation Claims, secured the payment of them. He won fame throughout Europe and Spanish America by his various works on the penal code and code of procedure. In the learning of the law he was not far inferior to Story and Kent.

Aside from one or two sketches, there is no account of his life except an inadequate biography by Charles H. Hunt.

[1] Story, I, 186.

Jefferson.[1] Again: "The case of the mandamus [2] may be the cloak, but the batture is recollected with still more resentment." [3]

Events thus sharpened the hostility of Jefferson and his following to Marshall, but drew closer the bonds between the Chief Justice and Joseph Story. Once under Marshall's pleasing, steady, powerful influence, Story sped along the path of Nationalism until sometimes he was ahead of the great constructor who, as he advanced, was building an enduring and practicable highway.

[1] Marshall to Story, Sept. 18, 1821, *Proceedings, Mass. Hist. Soc.* 2d series, xiv, 330; and see *infra*, 363–64.

[2] Marbury *vs.* Madison.

[3] Marshall to Story, July 13, 1821, *Proceedings, Mass. Hist. Soc.* 2d series, xiv, 328–29.

CHAPTER III

INTERNATIONAL LAW

It was Marshall's lot in more than one case to blaze the way in the establishment of rules of international conduct. (John Bassett Moore.)

The defects of our system of government must be remedied, not by the judiciary, but by the sovereign power of the people.
(Judge William H. Cabell of the Virginia Court of Appeals.)

I look upon this question as one which may affect, in its consequences, the permanence of the American Union.
(Justice William Johnson of the Supreme Court.)

WHILE Marshall unhesitatingly struck down State laws and shackled State authority, he just as firmly and promptly upheld National laws and National authority. In Marbury *vs.* Madison he proclaimed the power of National courts over Congressional legislation so that the denial of that power might not be admitted at a time when, to do so, would have yielded forever the vital principle of Judiciary supervision.[1] But that opinion is the significant exception to his otherwise unbroken practice of recognizing the validity of acts of Congress.

He carried out this practice even when he believed the law before him to be unwise in itself, injurious to the Nation, and, indeed, of extremely doubtful constitutionality. This course was but a part of Marshall's Nationalist policy. The purpose of his life was to strengthen and enlarge the powers of the National Government; to coördinate into harmonious operation its various departments; and to make it in fact, as well as in principle, the agent of

[1] See vol. III, chap. III, of this work.

a people constituting a single, a strong, and efficient Nation.

A good example of his maintenance of National laws is his treatment of the Embargo, Non-Importation, and Non-Intercourse Acts. The hostility of the Chief Justice to those statutes was, as we have seen, extreme; the political party of which he was an ardent member had denounced them as unconstitutional; his closest friends thought them invalid. He himself considered them to be, if within the Constitution at all, on the periphery of it; [1] he believed them to be ruinous to the country and meant as an undeserved blow at Great Britain upon whose victory over France depended, in his opinion, the safety of America and the rescue of imperiled civilization.

Nevertheless, not once did Marshall, in his many opinions, so much as suggest a doubt of the validity of those measures, when cases came before him arising from them and requiring their interpretation and application. Most of these decisions are not now of the slightest historical importance. [2] His opinions relating to the Embargo are, indeed, tiresome

[1] This is a fair inference from the statement of Joseph Story in his autobiography: "I have ever considered the embargo a measure, which went to the utmost limit of constructive power under the Constitution. It stands upon the extreme verge of the Constitution, being in its very form and terms an unlimited prohibition, or suspension of foreign commerce." (Story, I, 185–86.) When it is remembered that after Story was made Associate Justice his views became identical with those of Marshall on almost every subject, it would seem likely that Story expressed the opinions of the Chief Justice as well as his own on the constitutionality of the Embargo.

[2] See, for instance, the case of William Dixon *et al. vs.* The United States, 1 Brockenbrough, 177; United States *vs.* ——, *ib.* 195; the case of the Fortuna, *ib.* 299; the case of the Brig Caroline, *ib.* 384; Thomson and Dixon *vs.* United States (case of the Schooner Patriot), *ib.* 407.

and dull, with scarcely a flash of genius to brighten
them. Now and then, but so rarely that search for
it is not worth making, a paragraph blazes with the
statement of a great principle. In the case of the
Ship Adventure and Her Cargo, one such statesmanlike expression illuminates the page. The Non-
Intercourse Law forbade importation of British
goods "from any foreign port or place whatever."
The British ship Adventure had been captured by a
French frigate and given to the master and crew of an
American brig which the Frenchmen had previously
taken. The Americans brought the Adventure into
Norfolk, Virginia, and there claimed the proceeds of
ship and cargo. The United States insisted that ship
and cargo should be forfeited to the Government because brought in from "a foreign place." But, said
Marshall on this point: "The broad navigable ocean,
which is emphatically and truly termed the great
highway of nations, cannot . . be denominated 'a
foreign place.' . . The sea is the common property of
all nations. It belongs equally to all. None can appropriate it exclusively to themselves; nor is it 'foreign' to any." [1]

Where special learning, or the examination of the
technicalities and nice distinctions of the law were required, Marshall did not shine. Of admiralty law in
particular he knew little. The preparation of opinions in such cases he usually assigned to Story who,
not unjustly, has been considered the father of American admiralty law.[2] Also, in knowledge of the intricate law of real estate, Story was the superior of

---

[1] 1 Brockenbrough, 241.   [2] See Warren, 279.

Marshall and, indeed, of all the other members of
the court. Story's preëminence in most branches of
legal learning was admitted by his associates, all
of whom gladly handed over to the youthful Justice
more than his share of work. Story was flattered
by the recognition. "My brethren were so kind as
to place confidence in my researches," [1] he tells his
friend Judge Samuel Fay.

During the entire twenty-four years that Marshall
and Story were together on the Supreme Bench the
Chief Justice sought and accepted the younger man's
judgment and frankly acknowledged his authority
in every variety of legal questions, excepting only
those of international law or the interpretation of the
Constitution. "I wish to consult you on a case which
to me who am not versed in admiralty proceedings
has some difficulty," Marshall writes to Story in
1819. [2] In another letter Marshall asks Story's help
on a "question of great consequence." [3] Again and
again he requests the assistance of his learned junior
associate. [4] Sometimes he addresses Story as though
that erudite Justice were his superior. [5] Small wonder that John Marshall should declare that Story's
"loss would be irreparable" to the Supreme Bench,
if he should be appointed to the place made vacant by
the death of Chief Justice Parker of Massachusetts. [6]

[1] Story to Fay, April 24, 1814, Story, i, 261.
[2] Marshall to Story, May 27, 1819, *Proceedings, Mass. Hist. Soc.*
2d Series, xiv, 325. This was the case of the Little Charles.
[3] Same to same, July 13, 1819, *ib.* 326.
[4] Same to same, June 15, 1821, *ib.* 327; Sept. 18, 1821, *ib.* 331; Dec.
9, 1823, *ib.* 334; June 26, 1831, *ib.* 344.
[5] Same to same, July 2, 1823, *ib.* 331-33.
[6] Same to same, Oct. 15, 1830, *ib.* 342.

Only in his expositions of the Constitution did Marshall take supreme command. If he did anything preëminent, other than the infusing of life into that instrument and thus creating a steadying force in the rampant activities of the young American people, it was his contributions to international law, which were of the highest order.[1]

The first two decades of his labors as Chief Justice were prolific in problems involving international relations. The capture of neutral ships by the European belligerents; the complications incident to the struggle of Spanish provinces in South America for independence; the tangle of conflicting claims growing out of the African slave trade — the unsettled questions arising from all these sources made that period of Marshall's services unique in the number, importance, and novelty of cases requiring new and authoritative announcements of the law of nations. An outline of three or four of his opinions in such cases will show the quality of his work in that field of legal science and also illustrate his broad conception of some of the fundamentals of American statesmanship in foreign affairs.

His opinion in the case of the Schooner Exchange lays down principles which embrace much more than was involved in the question immediately before the court [2] — a practice habitual with Marshall and dis-

[1] John Bassett Moore, in his *Digest of International Law*, cites Marshall frequently and often uses passages from his opinions. Henry Wheaton, in his *Elements of International Law*, sometimes quotes Marshall's language as part of the text.

[2] Professor John Bassett Moore, in a letter to the author, says that he considers Marshall's opinion in this case his greatest in the realm of international law.

tinguishing him sharply from most jurists. The vessel in controversy, owned by citizens of Maryland, was, in 1810, captured by a French warship, armed, and taken into the French service. The capture was made under one of the decrees of Napoleon when the war between Great Britain and France was raging fiercely. This was the Rambouillet Decree of March 23, 1810, which because of the Non-Intercourse Act of March 1, 1809, ordered that American ships, entering French ports, be seized and sold.[1] The following year the Exchange, converted into a French national war-craft under the name of the Balaou, manned by a French crew, commanded by a French captain, Dennis M. Begon, put into the port of Philadelphia for repairs of injuries sustained in stress of weather. The former owners of the vessel libeled the ship, alleging that the capture was illegal and demanding their property.

In due course this case came before Marshall who, on March 3, 1812, delivered a long and exhaustive opinion, the effect of which is that the question of title to a ship having the character of a man-of-war is not justiciable in the courts of another country. The Chief Justice begins by avowing that he is "exploring an unbeaten path" and must rely, mainly, on "general principles." A nation's jurisdiction within its own territory is "necessarily exclusive and absolute. It is susceptible of no limitation not imposed by itself." The nation itself must consent to any restrictions upon its "full and complete power . . within its own territories."

[1] *Am. State Papers, For. Rel.* III, 384.

Nations are "distinct sovereignties, possessing equal rights and equal independence"; and, since mutual intercourse is for mutual benefit, "all sovereigns have consented" in certain cases to relax their "absolute and complete jurisdiction within their respective territories. . . Common usage, and . . common opinion growing out of that usage" may determine whether such consent has been given. [1] Even when a nation has not expressly stipulated to modify its jurisdiction, it would be guilty of bad faith if "suddenly and without previous notice" it violated "the usages and received obligations of the civilized world."

One sovereign is not "amenable" to another in any respect, and "can be supposed to enter a foreign territory only under an express license, or in the confidence that the immunities belonging to his independent sovereign station, though not expressly stipulated, are reserved by implication, and will be extended to him." From the facts that sovereigns have "perfect equality and absolute independence," and that mutual intercourse and "an interchange of good offices with each other" are to their common advantage, flows a class of cases in which all sovereigns are "understood to waive the exercise of a part of that complete exclusive territorial jurisdiction" which is "the attribute of every nation."

One of these cases "is admitted to be the exemption of the person of the sovereign from arrest or detention within a foreign territory. If he enters that territory with the knowledge and license of its sover-

[1] 7 Cranch, 136.

eign, that license, although containing no stipulation
exempting his person from arrest, is universally understood to imply such stipulation." [1] The protection of foreign ministers stands "on the same principles." The governments to which they are accredited
need not expressly consent that these ministers shall
receive immunity, but are "supposed to assent to
it." This assent is implied from the fact that, "without such exemption, every sovereign would hazard
his own dignity by employing a public minister
abroad. . . Therefore, a consent to receive him, implies a consent" that he shall be exempt from the
territorial jurisdiction of the nation to which he is
sent. [2]

The armies of one sovereign cannot pass through
the territory of another without express permission;
to do so would be a violation of faith. Marshall here
enters into the reasons for this obvious rule. But the
case is far otherwise, he says, as to "ships of war
entering the ports of a friendly power." The same
dangers and injuries do not attend the entrance of
such vessels into a port as are inseparable from the
march of an army through a country. But as to foreign vessels, "if there be no prohibition," of which
notice has been given, "the ports of a friendly nation are considered as open to the public ships of
all powers with whom it is at peace, and they are
supposed to enter such ports and to remain in them
while allowed to remain, under the protection of the
government of the place." [3] Marshall goes into a long
examination of whether the rule applies to ships of

[1] 7 Cranch, 137.   [2] *Ib.* 138–39.   [3] *Ib.* 141.

war, and concludes that it does. So the Exchange, now an armed vessel of France, rightfully came into the port of Philadelphia and, while there, is under the protection of the American Government.

In this situation can the title to the vessel be adjudicated by American courts? It cannot, because the schooner "must be considered as having come into the American territory under an implied promise, that while necessarily within it, and demeaning herself in a friendly manner, she should be exempt from the jurisdiction of the country." [1]

Over this general question there was much confusion and wrangling in the courts of various countries, but Marshall's opinion came to be universally accepted, and is the foundation of international law on that subject as it stands to-day. [2]

Scarcely any other judicial act of Marshall's life reveals so clearly his moral stature and strength. He was, as he declared, "exploring an unbeaten path," and could have rendered a contrary decision, sustaining it with plausible arguments. Had he allowed his feelings to influence his judgment; had he permitted his prejudices to affect his reason; had he heeded the desires of political friends — his opinion in the case of the Exchange would have been the reverse of what it was.

In the war then desolating Europe, he was an intense partisan of Great Britain and bitterly hostile to France. [3] He hated Napoleon with all the vigor of his being. He utterly disapproved of what he

---

[1] 7 Cranch, 147.　　[2] See John Bassett Moore in Dillon, I, 521–23.
[3] See *supra*, chap. I.

believed to be the Administration's truckling, or, at least, partiality, to the Emperor. Yet here was a ship, captured from Americans under the orders of that "satanic" ruler, a vessel armed by him and in his service. The emotions of John Marshall must have raged furiously; but he so utterly suppressed them that clear reason and considerations of statesmanship alone controlled him.

In the South American revolutions against Spain, American sailors generally and, indeed, the American people as a whole, ardently sympathized with those who sought to establish for themselves free and independent governments. Often American seamen took active part in the conflicts. On one such occasion three Yankee mariners, commissioned by the insurrectionary government of one of the revolting provinces, attacked a Spanish ship on the high seas, overawed the crew, and removed a large and valuable cargo. The offending sailors were indicted and tried in the United States Court for the District of Massachusetts.

Upon the many questions arising in this case, United States *vs.* Palmer,[1] the judges, Story of the Supreme Court, and John Davis, District Judge, disagreed and these questions were certified to the Supreme Court for decision. One of these questions was: What, in international law, is the status of a revolting province during civil war?[2] In an extended and closely reasoned opinion, largely devoted to the construction of the act of Congress on piracy, the Chief Justice lays down the rule that the relation

[1] 3 Wheaton, 610–44.   [2] *Ib.* 614.

of the United States to parts of countries engaged in internecine war is a question which must be determined by the political departments of the Government and not by the Judicial Department. Questions of this kind "belong . . to those who can declare what the law shall be; who can place the nation in such a position with respect to foreign powers as to their own judgment shall appear wise; to whom are entrusted all its foreign relations. . . In such contests a nation may engage itself with the one party or the other; may observe absolute neutrality; may recognize the new state absolutely; or may make a limited recognition of it.

"The proceeding in courts must depend so entirely on the course of the government, that it is difficult to give a precise answer to questions which do not refer to a particular nation. It may be said, generally, that if the government remains neutral, and recognizes the existence of a civil war, its courts cannot consider as criminal those acts of hostility which war authorizes, and which the new government may direct against its enemy To decide otherwise, would be to determine that the war prosecuted by one of the parties was unlawful, and would be to arraign the nation to which the court belongs against that party. This would transcend the limits prescribed to the judicial department." [1] So the Yankee "liberators" were set free.

Another instance of the haling of American citizens before the courts of the United States for having taken part in the wars of South American coun-

[1] 3 Wheaton, 634–35.

tries for liberation was the case of the Divina Pastora. This vessel was captured by a privateer manned and officered by Americans in the service of the United Provinces of Rio de la Plata. An American prize crew was placed on board the Spanish vessel which put into the port of New Bedford in stress of weather and was there libeled by the Spanish Consul. The United States District Court awarded restitution, the Circuit Court affirmed this decree, and the case was appealed to the Supreme Court.

Marshall held that the principle announced in the Palmer case governed the question arising from the capture of the Divina Pastora. "The United States, having recognized the existence of a civil war between Spain and her colonies, but remaining neutral, the courts of the Union are bound to consider as lawful those acts which war authorizes." Captures by privateers in the service of the revolting colonies are "regarded by us as other captures, jure belli, are regarded," unless our neutral rights or our laws or treaties are violated.[1]

The liberal statesman and humanitarian in Marshall on matters of foreign policy is often displayed in his international utterances. In the case of the Venus,[2] he dissented from the harsh judgment of the majority of the court, which clearly stated the cold law as it existed at the time, "that the property of an American citizen domiciled in a foreign country became, on the breaking out of war with that country, immediately confiscable as enemy's property, even though it was shipped before he had knowledge of

[1] 4 Wheaton, 63-64.   [2] 8 Cranch, 253-317.

the war." [1] Surely, said Marshall, that rule ought
not to apply to a merchant who, when war breaks
out, intends to leave the foreign country where he
has been doing business. Whether or not his property is enemy property depends not alone on his residence in the enemy country, but also on his intention
to remain after war begins. But it is plain that evidence of his intention can seldom, if ever, be given
during peace and that it can be furnished only "after
the war shall be known to him." Of consequence,
"justice requires that subsequent testimony shall be
received to prove a pre-existing fact." [2]

It is not true that extended residence in a foreign
country in time of peace is evidence of intention to
remain there permanently. "The stranger merely
residing in a country during peace, however long
his stay, . . cannot . . be considered as incorporated
into that society, so as, immediately on a declaration
of war, to become the enemy of his own." [3] Even
the ancient writers on international law concede this
principle. But modern commerce has sensibly influenced international law and greatly strengthened
the common sense and generally accepted considerations just mentioned. All know, as a matter of everyday experience, that "merchants, while belonging
politically to one society, are considered commer-
cially as the members of another." [4] The real motives of the merchant should be taken into account.

Of the many cases in which Marshall rendered
opinions touching upon international law, however,

---

[1] John Bassett Moore in Dillon, I, 524.
[2] 8 Cranch, 289.   [3] *Ib*. 291–92.   [4] *Ib*. 293.

that of the Nereid [1] is perhaps the best known. The descriptions of the arguments in that controversy, and of the court when they were being made, are the most vivid and accurate that have been preserved of the Supreme Bench and the attorneys who practiced before it at that time. Because of this fact an account of the hearing in this celebrated case will be helpful to a realization of similar scenes.

The burning of the Capitol by the British in 1814 left the Supreme Court without its basement room in that edifice; at the time the case of the Nereid was heard, and for two years afterward,[2] that tribunal held its sessions in the house of Elias Boudinot Caldwell, the clerk of the court, on Capitol Hill.[3] Marshall and the Associate Justices sat "inconveniently at the upper end" of an uncomfortable room "unfit for the purpose for which it is used." [4] In the space before the court were the counsel and other lawyers who had gathered to hear the argument. Back of them were the spectators. On the occasion of this hearing, the room was well filled by members of the legal profession and by laymen, for everybody looked forward to a brilliant legal debate.

Nor were these expectations vain. The question

---

[1] 9 Cranch, 388 *et seq.*

[2] Until the February session of 1817. This room was not destroyed or injured by the fire, but was closed while the remainder of the Capitol was being repaired. In 1817, the court occupied another basement room in the Capitol, where it continued to meet until February, 1819, when it returned to its old quarters in the room where the library of the Supreme Court is now situated. (Bryan: *History of the National Capital*, II, 39.)

[3] *Ib.*, I, 632. Mr. Bryan says that this house still stands and is now known as 204–06 Pennsylvania Avenue, S.E.

[4] Ticknor to his father, Feb. 1815, Ticknor, I, 38.

was as to whether a certain cargo owned by neutrals,
but found in an enemy ship, should be restored. The
claimants were represented by J. Ogden Hoffman
of New York and the universally known and talked
of Thomas Addis Emmet, the Irish patriot whose pathetic experiences, not less than his brilliant talents,
appealed strongly to Americans of that day. For the
captors appeared Alexander J. Dallas of Pennsylvania and that strangest and most talented advocate of his time, William Pinkney of Maryland,
exquisite dandy and profound lawyer,[1] affected fop
and accomplished diplomat, insolent as he was able,
haughty[2] as he was learned.

George Ticknor gives a vivid description of the
judges and lawyers. Marshall's neglected clothing
was concealed by his flowing black robes, and his un-
kempt hair was combed, tied, and "fully powdered."
The Associate Justices were similarly robed and
powdered, and all "looked dignified." Justice Bushrod Washington, "a little sharp-faced gentleman
with only one eye, and a profusion of snuff distributed over his face," did not, perhaps, add to the
impressive appearance of the tribunal; but the noble

---

[1] "His opinions had almost acquired the authority of judicial decisions." (Pinkney: *Life of William Pinkney*, quotation from Robert
Goodloe Harper on title-page.)

[2] "He has . . a dogmatizing absoluteness of manner which passes
with the million, . . for an evidence of power; and he has acquired
with those around him a sort of papal infallibility." (Wirt to Gilmer,
April 1, 1816, Kennedy, i, 403.)

Wirt's estimate of Pinkney must have been influenced by professional jealousy, for men like Story and Marshall were as profoundly
affected by the Maryland legal genius as were the most emotional
spectators. See the criticisms of Wirt's comments on Pinkney by his
nephew, Rev. William Pinkney, in his *Life of William Pinkney*, 116-22.

features and stately bearing of William Johnson,
the handsome face and erect attitude of young
Joseph Story, and the bald-headed, scholarly looking Brockholst Livingston, sitting beside Marshall,
adequately filled in the picture of which he was the
center.

Opinions were read by Marshall and Story, but
evidently they bored the nervous Pinkney, who
"was very restless, frequently moved his seat, and,
when sitting, showed by the convulsive twitches of
his face how anxious he was to come to the conflict.
At last the judges ceased to read, and he sprang into
the arena like a lion who has been loosed by his keep-
ers on the gladiator that awaited him." This large,
stout man wore "corsets to diminish his bulk," used
"cosmetics . . to smooth and soften a skin growing
somewhat wrinkled and rigid with age," and dressed
"in a style which would be thought foppish in a
much younger man." [1] His harsh, unmusical voice,
grating and high in tone, no less than his exaggerated
fashionable attire, at first repelled; but these defects
were soon forgotten because of "his clear and forcible manner" of speaking, "his powerful and commanding eloquence, occasionally illuminated with
sparkling lights, but always logical and appropriate,
and above all, his accurate and discriminating law
knowledge, which he pours out with wonderful precision." [2]

Aloof, affected, overbearing [3] as he was, Pinkney

---

[1] Ticknor to his father, Feb. [day omitted] 1815, Ticknor, I, 38–40.

[2] Story to Williams, Feb. 16, 1812, Story, I, 214; and March 6, 1814, *ib.* 252.

[3] "At the bar he is despotic and cares as little for his colleagues or

overcame prejudice and compelled admiration "by force of eloquence, logic and legal learning and by the display of naked talent," testifies Ticknor, who adds that Pinkney "left behind him . . all the public speaking I had ever heard." [1] Emmet, the Irish exile, "older in sorrows than in years," with "an appearance of premature age," and wearing a "settled melancholy in his countenance," spoke directly to the point and with eloquence as persuasive as that of Pinkney was compelling.[2] Pinkney had insulted Emmet in a previous argument, and Marshall was so apprehensive that the Irish lawyer would now attack his opponent that Justice Livingston had to reassure the Chief Justice.[3]

The court was as much interested in the oratory as in the arguments of the counsel. Story's letters are rich in comment on the style and manner of the leading advocates. At the hearing of a cause at about the same time as that of the Nereid, he tells his wife that Pinkney and Samuel Dexter of Massachusetts "have called crowded houses; all the belles of the city have attended, and have been entranced for hours." Dexter was "calm, collected, and forcible, appealing to the judgment." Pinkney, "vivacious, sparkling, and glowing," although not "as close in his logic as Mr. Dexter," but "step[ping]

adversaries as if they were men of wood." (Wirt to Gilmer, April 1, 1816, Kennedy, i, 403.)

The late Roscoe Conkling was almost the reincarnation of William Pinkney. In extravagance of dress, haughtiness of manner, retentiveness of memory, power and brilliancy of mind, and genuine eloquence, Pinkney and Conkling were well-nigh counterparts.

[1] Ticknor to his father, Feb. 21, 1815, Ticknor, i, 40.
[2] *Ib.* Feb. 1815, 39–40.   [3] Pinkney, 100–01.

aside at will from the path, and strew[ing] flowers of rhetoric around him." [1]

The attendance of women at arguments before the Supreme Court had as much effect on the performance of counsel at this period as on the oratory delivered in House and Senate. One of the belles of Washington jotted down what took place on one such occasion. "Curiosity led me, . . to join the female crowd who throng the court room. A place in which I think women have no business. . . One day Mr. Pinckney [*sic*] had finished his argument and was just about seating himself when Mrs. Madison and a train of ladies enter'd, — he recommenced, went over the same ground, using fewer arguments, but scattering more flowers. And the day I was there I am certain he thought more of the female part of his audience than of the court, and on concluding, he recognized their presence, when he said, 'He would not weary the court, by going thro a long list of cases to prove his argument, as it would not only be fatiguing to them, but inimical to the laws of good taste, which *on the present occasion*, (bowing low) he wished to obey." [2]

---

[1] Story to his wife, March 10, 1814, Story, i, 253.

[2] Mrs. Samuel Harrison Smith to Mrs. Kirkpatrick, March 13, 1814, *First Forty Years of Washington Society:* Hunt, 96.

Pinkney especially would become eloquent, even in an argument of dry, commercial law, if women entered the court-room. "There were ladies present — and Pinkney was expected to be eloquent at all events. So, the mode he adopted was to get into his tragical tone in discussing the construction of an act of Congress. Closing his speech in this solemn tone he took his seat, saying to me, with a smile — 'that will do for the ladies.' " (Wirt to Gilmer, April 1, 1816, Kennedy, i, 404.)

The presence of women affected others no less than Pinkney. "Web-

This, then, is a fairly accurate picture of the
Supreme Court of the United States when the great
arguments were made before it and its judgments
delivered through the historic opinions of Marshall
— such the conduct of counsel, the appearance of
the Justices, the auditors in attendance. Always,
then, when thinking of the hearings in the Supreme
Court while he was Chief Justice, we must bear in
mind some such scene as that just described.

William Pinkney, the incomparable and enigmatic, passed away in time; but his place was taken
by Daniel Webster, as able if not so accomplished,
quite as interesting from the human point of view,
and almost as picturesque. The lively, virile Clay
succeeded the solid and methodical Dexter; and a
procession of other eminent statesmen files past our
eyes in the wake of those whose distinction for the
moment had persuaded their admirers that their
equals never would be seen again. It is essential to
an understanding of the time that we firmly fix in
our minds that the lawyers, no less than the judges,
of that day, were publicists as well as lawyers. They
were, indeed, statesmen, having deep in their minds
the well-being of their Nation even more than the
success of their clients.

Briefly stated, the facts in the case of the Nereid
were as follows: More than a year after our second
war with Great Britain had begun, one Manuel Pinto
of Buenos Aires chartered the heavily armed British

ster, Wirt, Taney . . and Emmet, are the combatants, and a bevy of
ladies are the promised and brilliant distributors of the prizes," writes
Story of an argument in the Supreme Court many years later. (Story
to Fay, March 8, 1826, Story, i, 493.)

merchant ship, the Nereid, to take a cargo from London to the South American city and another back to the British metropolis. The Nereid sailed under the protection of a British naval convoy. The outgoing cargo belonged partly to Pinto, partly to other Spaniards, and partly to British subjects. When approaching Madeira an American privateer attacked the Nereid and, after a brief fight, captured the British vessel and took her to New York as a prize. The British part of the cargo was condemned without contest. That part belonging to Pinto and the other Spaniards was also awarded to the captors, but over the earnest opposition of the owners, who appealed to the Supreme Court. The arguments before the Supreme Court were long and uncommonly able. Those of Pinkney and Emmet, however, contained much florid "eloquence." [1]

Space permits no summary of these addresses; the most that can be given here is the substance of Marshall's very long and tedious opinion which is of no historical interest, except that part of it dealing with international law. The Chief Justice stated this capital question: "Does the treaty between Spain and the United States subject the goods of either party, being neutral, to condemnation as enemy property, if found by the other in a vessel of an enemy? That treaty stipulates that neutral bottoms shall make neutral goods, but contains no stipulation that enemy bottoms shall communicate the hostile character to the cargo. It is contended by the captors that the

---

[1] This is illustrated by the passage in Pinkney's argument to which Marshall in his opinion paid such a remarkable tribute (see *infra*, 141).

two principles are so completely identified that the stipulation of the one necessarily includes the other."

It was, said Marshall, "a part of the original law of nations" that enemy goods in friendly vessels "are prize of war," and that friendly goods in enemy vessels must be restored if captured. The reason of this rule was that "war gives a full right to capture the goods of an enemy, but gives no right to capture the goods of a friend." Just as "the neutral flag constitutes no protection to enemy property," so "the belligerent flag communicates no hostile character to neutral property." The nature of the cargo, therefore, "depends in no degree" upon the ship that carries it.[1]

Unless treaties expressly modified this immemorial law of nations there would, declared Marshall, "seem to be no necessity" to suppose that an exception was intended. "Treaties are formed upon deliberate reflection"; if they do not specifically designate that a particular item is to be taken out of the "ancient rule," it remains within it. "The agreement [in the Spanish treaty] that neutral bottoms shall make neutral goods is . . a concession made by the belligerent to the neutral"; as such it is to be encouraged since "it enlarges the sphere of neutral commerce, and gives to the neutral flag a capacity not given to it by the law of nations."

On the contrary, a treaty "stipulation which subjects neutral property, found in the bottom of an enemy, to condemnation as prize of war, is a concession made by the neutral to the belligerent. It narrows

[1] 9 Cranch, 418–19.

the sphere of neutral commerce, and takes from the neutral a privilege he possessed under the law of nations." However, a government can make whatever contracts with another that it may wish to make. "What shall restrain independent nations from making such a compact" as they please? [1]

Suppose that, regardless of "our treaty with Spain, considered as an independent measure, the ordinances of that government would subject American property, under similar circumstances, to confiscation." Ought Spanish property, for that reason, to be "condemned as prize of war"? That was not a question for courts to decide: "Reciprocating to the subjects of a nation, or retaliating on them its unjust proceedings towards our citizens, is a political, not a legal measure. It is for the consideration of the government, not of its courts. The degree and the kind of retaliation depend entirely on considerations foreign to this tribunal."

The Government is absolutely free to do what it thinks best: "It is not for its courts to interfere with the proceedings of the nation and to thwart its views. It is not for us to depart from the beaten track prescribed for us, and to tread the devious and intricate path of politics." He and his associates had no difficulty, said Marshall, in arriving at these conclusions. "The line of partition" between "belligerent rights and neutral privileges" is "not so distinctly marked as to be clearly discernible." [2] Nevertheless, the neutral part of the Nereid's cargo must "be governed by the principles which would apply to it had

[1] 9 Cranch, 419–20.   [2] Ib. 422–23.

the Nereid been a general ship." That she was armed, that she fought to resist capture, did not charge the cargo with the belligerency of the ship, since the owners of the cargo had nothing to do with her armed equipment or belligerent conduct.

It is "universally recognized as the original rule of the law of nations" that a neutral may ship his goods on a belligerent vessel. This right is "founded on the plain and simple principle that the property of a friend remains his property wherever it may be found." [1] That it is lodged in an armed belligerent ship does not take it out of this universal rule. The plain truth is, declares Marshall, that "a belligerent has a perfect right to arm in his own defense; and a neutral has a perfect right to transport his goods in a belligerent vessel." Such merchandise "does not cease to be neutral" because placed on an armed belligerent ship, nor when that vessel exercises the undoubted belligerent right forcibly to resist capture by the enemy.

Shipping goods on an armed belligerent ship does not defeat or even impair the right of search. "What is this right of search? Is it a substantive and independent right wantonly, and in the pride of power, to vex and harass neutral commerce, because there is a capacity to do so?" No! It is a right "essential . . to the exercise of . . a full and perfect right to capture enemy goods and articles going to their enemy which are contraband of war. . . It is a mean justified by the end," and "a right . . ancillary to the greater right of capture."

[1] 9 Cranch, 425.

For a neutral to place "his goods in the vessel of an armed enemy" does not connect him with that enemy or give him a "hostile character." Armed or unarmed, "it is the right and the duty of the carrier to avoid capture and to prevent a search." Neither arming nor resistance is "chargeable to the goods or their owner, where he has taken no part" in either.[1] Pinkney had cited two historical episodes, but Marshall waved these aside as of no bearing on the case. "If the neutral character of the goods is forfeited by the resistance of the belligerent vessel, why is not the neutral character of the passengers," who did not engage in the conflict, "forfeited by the same cause?"[2]

In the case of the Nereid, the goods of the neutral shipper were inviolable. Pinkney had drawn a horrid picture of the ship, partly warlike, partly peaceful, displaying either character as safety or profit dictated.[3] But, answers Marshall, falling into something

---

[1] 9 Cranch, 426-29.   [2] Ib. 428-29.

[3] "We .. have Neutrality, soft and gentle and defenceless in herself, yet clad in the panoply of her warlike neighbours—with the frown of defiance upon her brow, and the smile of conciliation upon her lip — with the spear of Achilles in one hand and a lying protestation of innocence and helplessness unfolded in the other. Nay, .. we shall have the branch of olive entwined around the bolt of Jove, and Neutrality in the act of hurling the latter under the deceitful cover of the former...

"Call you that Neutrality which thus conceals beneath its appropriate vestment the giant limbs of War, and converts the charter-party of the compting-house into a commission of marque and reprisals; which makes of neutral trade a laboratory of belligerent annoyance; which .. warms a torpid serpent into life, and places it beneath the footsteps of a friend with a more appalling lustre on its crest and added venom in its sting." (Wheaton: *Some Account of the Life, Writings, and Speeches of William Pinkney*, 463, 466.)

Pinkney frankly said that his metaphors, "hastily conceived and hazarded," were inspired by the presence of women "of this mixed and (for a court of judicature) *uncommon* audience." (*Ib.* 464-65.)

Except for this exhibition of rodomontade his address was a wonder-like the rhetoric of his youth,[1] "the Nereid has not that centaur-like appearance which has been ascribed to her. She does not rove over the ocean hurling the thunders of war while sheltered by the olive branch of peace." Her character is not part neutral, part hostile. "She is an open and declared belligerent; claiming all the rights, and subject to all the dangers of the belligerent character." One of these rights is to carry neutral goods which were subject to "the hazard of being taken into port" in case of the vessel's capture — in the event of which they would merely be "obliged to seek another conveyance." The ship might lawfully be captured and condemned; but the neutral cargo within it remained neutral, could not be forfeited, and must be returned to its owners.[2]

But Marshall anoints the wounds of the defeated Pinkney with a tribute to the skill and beauty of his oratory and argument: "With a pencil dipped in the most vivid colors, and guided by the hand of a master, a splendid portrait has been drawn exhibiting this vessel and her freighter as forming a single figure, composed of the most discordant materials of peace and war. So exquisite was the skill of the artist, so dazzling the garb in which the figure was presented, that it required the exercise of that cold investigating faculty which ought always to belong to those who sit on this bench, to discover its only imperfection; its want of resemblance." [3]

ful display of reasoning and erudition. His brief peroration was eloquence of the noblest order. (See entire speech, Wheaton: *Pinkney*, 455–516.)

[1] See vol. I, 72, 195, of this work. [2] 9 Cranch, 430–31. [3] *Ib.* 430.

Such are examples of Marshall's expositions of international law and typical illustrations of his method in statement and reasoning. His opinion in the case of the Nereid is notable, too, because Story dissented [1] — and for Joseph Story to disagree with John Marshall was a rare event. Justice Livingston also disagreed, and the British High Court of Admiralty maintained the contrary doctrine. But the principle announced by Marshall, that enemy bottoms do not make enemy goods and that neutral property is sacred, remained and still remains the American doctrine. Indeed, by the Declaration of Paris in 1856, the principle thus announced by Marshall in 1815 is now the accepted doctrine of the whole world.

Closely akin to the statesmanship displayed in his pronouncements upon international law, was his assertion, in Insurance Co. *vs.* Canter,[2] that the Nation has power to acquire and to govern territory. The facts of this case were that a ship with a cargo of cotton, which was insured, was wrecked on the coast of Florida after that territory had been ceded to the United States and before it became a State of the Union. The cotton was saved, and taken to Key West, where, by order of a local court acting under

[1] "Never in my whole life was I more entirely satisfied that the Court were wrong in their judgment. I hope Mr. Pinkney will . . publish his admirable argument . . it will do him immortal honor." (Story to Williams, May 8, 1815, Story, I, 256.)

Exactly the same question as that decided in the case of the Nereid was again brought before the Supreme Court two years later in the case of the Atalanta. (3 Wheaton, 409.) Marshall merely stated that the former decision governed the case. (*Ib.* 415.)

[2] The American Insurance Company *et al. vs.* David Canter, 1 Peters, 511–46.

a Territorial law, it was sold at auction to satisfy claims for salvage. Part of the cotton was purchased by one David Canter, who shipped it to Charleston, South Carolina, where the insurance companies libeled it. The libelants contended, among other things, that the Florida court was not competent to order the auction sale because the Territorial act was "inconsistent" with the National Constitution. After a sharp and determined contest in the District and Circuit Courts of the United States at Charleston, in which Canter finally prevailed, the case was taken to the Supreme Court.[1]

Was the Territorial act, under which the local court at Key West ordered the auction sale, valid? The answer to that question, said Marshall, in delivering the opinion of the court, depends upon "the relation in which Florida stands to the United States." Since the National Government can make war and conclude treaties, it follows that it "possesses the power of acquiring territory either by conquest or treaty . . Ceded territory becomes a part of the nation to which it is annexed"; but "the relations of the inhabitants to each other [do not] undergo any change." Their allegiance is transferred; but the law "which regulates the intercourse and general conduct of individuals remains in force until altered by the newly created power of the state." [2]

The treaty by which Spain ceded Florida to the United States assures to the people living in that Territory "the enjoyment of the privileges, rights, and immunities" of American citizens; "they do not

---

[1] 1 Peters, 511–46.   [2] *Ib.* 542.

however, participate in political power; they do not
share in the government till Florida shall become
a state. In the meantime Florida continues to be a
Territory of the United States, governed by virtue
of that clause in the Constitution which empowers
Congress 'to make all needful rules & regulations
respecting the territory or other property belonging
to the United States.'" [1]

The Florida salvage act is not violative of the Constitution. The courts upon which that law confers
jurisdiction are not "Constitutional Courts; . . they
are legislative Courts, created in virtue of the general right of sovereignty which exists in the government, or in virtue of that clause which enables
Congress to make all needful rules and regulations respecting the territory belonging to the United States.
. . Although admiralty jurisdiction can be exercised,
in the States, in those courts only" which are authorized by the Constitution, the same limitation
does not extend to the Territories. In legislating for
them, Congress exercises the combined powers of the
general and of a state government. [2]

Admirable and formative as were Marshall's opinions of the law of nations, they received no attention
from the people, no opposition from the politicians,
and were generally approved by the bar. At the very
next term of the Supreme Court, after the decision
in the case of the Nereid, an opinion was delivered
by Story that aroused more contention and had
greater effect on the American Nation than had all
the decisions of the Supreme Court on international

---

[1] 1 Peters, 542.   [2] *Ib.* 546.

law up to that time. This was the opinion in the famous case of Martin *vs.* Hunter's Lessee.

It was Story's first exposition of Constitutional law and it closely resembles Marshall's best interpretations of the Constitution. So conspicuous is this fact that the bench and bar generally have adopted the view that the Chief Justice was, in effect, the spiritual author of this commanding judicial utterance.[1] But Story had now been by Marshall's side on the Supreme Bench for four years and, in his ardent way, had become more strenuously Nationalist, at least in expression, than Marshall.[2]

That the Chief Justice himself did not deliver this opinion was due to the circumstance that his brother, James M. Marshall, was involved in the controversy; was, indeed, a real party in interest. This fact, together with the personal hatred of Marshall by the head of the Virginia Republican organization, had much to do with the stirring events that attended and followed this litigation.

[1] Story wrote George Ticknor that Marshall "concurred in every word of it." (Story to Ticknor, Jan. 22, 1831, Story, II, 49.)

[2] "Let us extend the national authority over the whole extent of power given by the Constitution. Let us have great military and naval schools; an adequate regular army; the broad foundations laid of a permanent navy; a national bank; a national system of bankruptcy; a great navigation act; a general survey of our ports, and appointments of port-wardens and pilots; Judicial Courts which shall embrace the . . justices of the peace, for the commercial and national concerns of the United States. By such enlarged and liberal institutions, the Government of the United States will be endeared to the people . . Let us prevent the possibility of a division, by creating great national interests which shall bind us in an indissoluble chain." (Story to Williams, Feb. 22, 1815, *ib.* I, 254.)

Later in the same year Story repeated these views and added: "I most sincerely hope that a national newspaper may be established at Washington." (Story to Wheaton, Dec. 13, 1815, *ib.* 270–71.)

At the time of the Fairfax-Hunter controversy,
Virginia was governed by one of the most efficient
party organizations ever developed under free institutions. Its head was Spencer Roane, President of
the Court of Appeals, the highest tribunal in the
State, an able and learned man of strong prejudices
and domineering character. Jefferson had intended
to appoint Roane Chief Justice of the United States
upon the expected retirement of Ellsworth.[1] But
Ellsworth's timely resignation gave Adams the opportunity to appoint Marshall. Thus Roane's highest ambition was destroyed and his lifelong dislike of
Marshall became a personal and a virulent animosity.

Roane was supported by his cousin, Thomas
Ritchie, editor of the Richmond *Enquirer*, the most
influential of Southern newspapers, and, indeed, one
of the most powerful journals in the Nation. Another of the Virginia junto was John Taylor of Caroline County, a brilliant, unselfish, and sincere man.
Back of this triumvirate was Thomas Jefferson with
his immense popularity and his unrivaled political
sagacity. These men were the commanding officers
of a self-perpetuating governmental system based
on the smallest political unit, the County Courts.
These courts were made up of justices of the peace
appointed by the Governor. Vacancies in the County
Courts were filled only on the recommendation of the
remaining members.[2] These justices of the peace
also named the men to be sent to the State Legislature which appointed the Governor and also chose

[1] Professor William E. Dodd, in *Am. Hist. Rev.* xii, 776.
[2] For fuller description of the Virginia County Court system, see
chap. ix of this volume.

the members of the Court of Appeals who held office for life.[1] A perfect circle of political action was thus formed, the permanent and controlling center of which was the Court of Appeals.

These, then, were the judge, the court, and the party organization which now defied the Supreme Court of the United States. By one of those curious jumbles by which Fate confuses mortals, the excuse for this defiance of Nationalism by Localism arose from a land investment by Marshall and his brother. Thus the fact of the purchase of the larger part of the Fairfax estate [2] is woven into the Constitutional development of the Nation.

Five years before the Marshall syndicate made this investment,[3] one David Hunter obtained from Virginia a grant of seven hundred and eighty-eight acres of that part of the Fairfax holdings known as "waste and ungranted land." [4] The grant was made under the various confiscatory acts of the Virginia Legislature passed during the Revolution. These acts had not been carried into effect, however, and in 1783 the Treaty of Peace put an end to subsequent proceedings under them.

Denny Martin Fairfax, the devisee of Lord Fairfax, denied the validity of Hunter's grant from the

[1] On the Virginia Republican machine, Roane, Ritchie, etc., see Dodd in *Am. Hist. Rev.* xii, 776–77; and in *Branch Hist. Papers,* June, 1903, 222; Smith in *ib.* June, 1905, 15; Thrift in *ib.* June, 1908, 183; also Dodd: *Statesmen of the Old South,* 70 *et seq.*; Anderson, 205; Turner: *Rise of the New West,* 60; Ambler: *Ritchie,* 27, 82.

[2] Several thousand acres of the Fairfax estate were not included in this joint purchase. (See *infra,* 150.)

[3] 1793–94. See vol. ii, 202–11, of this work.

[4] April 30, 1789. See Hunter *vs.* Fairfax's Devisee, 1 Munford, 223.

State on the ground that Virginia did not execute her confiscatory statutes during the war, and that all lands and property to which those laws applied were protected by the Treaty of Peace. In 1791, two years after he obtained his grant and eight years after the ratification of the treaty, Hunter brought suit in the Superior Court at Winchester [1] against Fairfax's devisee for the recovery of the land. The action was under the ancient form of legal procedure still practiced, and bore the title of "Timothy Trititle, Lessee of David Hunter, *vs.* Denny Fairfax," Devisee of Thomas, Lord Fairfax.[2] The facts were agreed to by the parties and, on April 24, 1794, the court decided against Hunter,[3] who appealed to the Court of Appeals at Richmond.[4] Two years later, in May, 1796, the case was argued before Judges Roane, Fleming, Lyons, and Carrington.[5] Meanwhile the Jay Treaty had been ratified, thus confirming the guarantees of the Treaty of Peace to the holders of titles of lands which Virginia, in her confiscatory acts, had declared forfeited.

At the winter session, 1796–97, of the Virginia Legislature, Marshall, acting for his brother and

[1] For the district composed of Frederick, Berkeley, Hampshire, Hardy, and Shenandoah Counties.

[2] Order Book, Superior Court, No. 2, 43, Office of Clerk of Circuit Court, Frederick Co., Winchester, Va.

[3] The judges rendering this decision were St. George Tucker and William Nelson, Jr. (*Ib.*)

[4] In making out the record for appeal the fictitious name of Timothy Trititle was, of course, omitted, so that in the Court of Appeals and in the appeals to the Supreme Court of the United States the title of the case is Hunter *vs.* Fairfax's Devisee, instead of "Timothy Trititle, Lessee of David Hunter," *vs.* Fairfax's Devisee, and Martin *vs.* Hunter's Lessee.

[5] 1 Munford, 223.

brother-in-law, as well as for himself, agreed to execute deeds to relinquish their joint claims "to the
waste and unappropriated lands in the Northern
Neck" upon condition that the State would confirm
the Fairfax title to lands specifically appropriated [1]
by Lord Fairfax or by his devisee. But for the statement made many years later by Judges Roane and
Fleming, of the Court of Appeals, that this adjustment covered the land claimed by Hunter, it would
appear that Marshall did not intend to include it in
the compromise,[2] even if, as seems improbable, it was
a part of the Marshall syndicate's purchase; for the
decision of the court at Winchester had been against
Hunter, and after that decision and before the compromise, the Jay Treaty had settled the question of
title.

On October 18, 1806, the Marshall syndicate, having finally made the remaining payments for that
part of the Fairfax estate purchased by it — fourteen
thousand pounds in all — Philip Martin, the devisee
of Denny M. Fairfax, executed his warranty to John
and James M. Marshall and their brother-in-law,
Rawleigh Colston; and this deed was duly recorded
in Fauquier, Warren, Frederick, and Shenandoah

[1] See vol. II, footnote to 209, of this work.

[2] The adjustment was made because of the memorial of about two
hundred settlers or squatters (mostly Germans) on the wild lands who
petitioned the Legislature to establish title in them. David Hunter was
not one of these petitioners. Marshall agreed to execute deeds "extinguishing" the Fairfax title "so soon as the conveyance shall be
transmitted to me from Mr. Fairfax." (Marshall to the Speaker of the
House of Delegates, Va., Nov. 24, 1796. See vol. II, footnote to 209,
of this work.) The Fairfax deed to the Marshalls was not executed
until ten years after this compromise. (Land Causes, 1833, 40, Records in Office of Clerk of Circuit Court, Fauquier Co., Va.)

Counties, where the Fairfax lands were situated.[1] Nearly ten years before this conveyance, James M. Marshall separately had purchased from Denny Martin Fairfax large quantities of land in Shenandoah and Hardy Counties where the Hunter grant probably was situated.[2]

[1] Two years later, on October 5, 1808, the Marshall brothers effected a partition of the estate between themselves on the one part and their brother-in-law on the other part, the latter receiving about forty thousand acres. (Deed Book 36, 302, Records in Office of Clerk of Circuit Court, Frederick Co., Va.)

[2] On August 30, 1797, Denny Martin Fairfax conveyed to James M. Marshall all the Fairfax lands in Virginia "save and except . . the manor of Leeds." (See Marshall *vs.* Conrad, 5 Call, 364.) Thereafter James M. Marshall lived in Winchester for several years and made many conveyances of land in Shenandoah and Berkeley Counties. For instance, Nov. 12, 1798, to Charles Lee, Deed Book 3, 634, Records in Office of Clerk of Circuit Court, Frederick County, Va.; Jan. 9, 1799, to Henry Richards, *ib.* 549; Feb. 4, 1799, to Joseph Baker, Deed Book 25, *ib.* 561; March 30, 1799, to Richard Miller, Deed Book 3, *ib.* 602, etc.

All of these deeds by James M. Marshall and Hester, his wife, recite that these tracts and lots are parts of the lands conveyed to James M. Marshall by Denny Martin Fairfax on August 30, 1797. John Marshall does not join in any of these deeds. Apparently, therefore, he had no personal interest in the tract claimed by Hunter.

In a letter to his brother Marshall speaks of the Shenandoah lands as belonging to James M. Marshall: "With respect to the rents due Denny Fairfax before the conveyance to you I should suppose a recovery could only be defeated by the circumstance that they passed to you by the deed conveying the land." (Marshall to his brother, Feb. 13, 1806, MS.)

At the time when the Fairfax heir, Philip Martin, executed a deed to the Marshall brothers and Rawleigh Colston, conveying to them the Manor of Leeds, the lands involved in the Hunter case had been owned by James M. Marshall exclusively for nearly ten years.

After the partition with Colston, October 5, 1808, John and James M. Marshall, on September 5, 1809, made a partial division between themselves of Leeds Manor, and Goony Run Manor in Shenandoah County, the latter going to James M. Marshall.

These records apparently establish the facts that the "compromise" of 1796 was not intended to include the land claimed by Hunter; that James M. Marshall personally owned most of the lands about Win-

It would seem that James M. Marshall continued in peaceful possession of the land, the title to which the Winchester court had decreed to be in the Fairfax devisee and not in Hunter. When Denny M. Fairfax died, he devised his estate to his younger brother [1] Major-General Philip Martin. About the same time he made James M. Marshall his administrator, with the will annexed, apparently for the purpose of enabling him to collect old rents.[2] For thirteen years and six months the case of Hunter vs. Fairfax's Devisee slumbered in the drowsy archives of the Virginia Court of Appeals. In the autumn of 1809, however, Hunter demanded a hearing of it and, on October 25, of that year, it was reargued.[3] Hunter was represented by John Wickham, then the acknowledged leader of the Virginia bar, and by another lawyer named Williams.[4] Daniel Call appeared for the Fairfax devisee.

chester; and that John Marshall had no personal interest whatever in the land in controversy in the litigation under review.

This explains the refusal of the Supreme Court, including even Justice Johnson, to take notice of the compromise of 1796. (See *infra*, 157.)

[1] When Lord Fairfax devised his Virginia estate to his nephew, Denny Martin, he required him to take the name of Fairfax.

[2] Order Book, Superior Court of Frederick Co. Va., III, 721.

[3] 1 Munford, 223. The record states that Judge Tucker did not sit on account of his near relationship to a person interested.

[4] It should be repeated that David Hunter was not one of the destitute settlers who appealed to the Legislature in 1796. From the records it would appear that he was a very prosperous farmer and landowner who could well afford to employ the best legal counsel, as he did throughout the entire litigation. As early as 1771 we find him selling to Edward Beeson 536 acres of land in Frederick County. (Deed Book 15, 213, Office of Clerk of Circuit Court, Frederick County, Va.) The same Hunter also sold cattle, farming implements, etc., to a large amount. (Deeds dated Nov. 2, 1771, Deed Book cited above, 279, 280.) These transactions took place eighteen years before Hunter secured

The following spring[1] the Court of Appeals decided in favor of Hunter, reversing the judgment of the lower court rendered more than sixteen years before. In his opinion Roane, revealing his animosity to Marshall, declared that the compromise of 1796 covered the case. "I can never consent that the appellees,[2] after having got the benefit thereof, should refuse to submit thereto, or pay the equivalent; the consequence of which would be, that the Commonwealth would have to remunerate the appellant for the land recovered from him! Such a course cannot be justified on the principles of justice and good faith; and, I confess, I was not a little surprised that the objection should have been raised in the case before us."[3]

from Virginia the grant of Fairfax lands, twenty-five years before the Marshall compromise of 1796, thirty-eight years before Hunter employed Wickham to revive his appeal against the Fairfax devisee, forty-two years prior to the first arguments before the Supreme Court, and forty-five years before the final argument and decision of the famous case of Martin vs. Hunter's Lessee. So, far from being a poor, struggling, submissive, and oppressed settler, David Hunter was one of the most well-to-do, acquisitive, determined, and aggressive men in Virginia.

[1] April 23, 1810.

[2] By using the plural "appellees," Roane apparently intimates that Marshall was personally interested in the case; as we have seen, he was not. There was of record but one appellee, the Fairfax devisee.

[3] 1 Munford, 232.

The last two lines of Roane's language are not clear, but it would seem that the "objection" must have been that the Marshall compromise did not include the land claimed by Hunter and others, the title to which had been adjudged to be in Fairfax's devisee before the compromise. This is, indeed, probably the meaning of the sentence of Roane's opinion; otherwise it is obscure. It would appear certain that the Fairfax purchasers did make just this objection. Certainly they would have been foolish not to have done so if the Hunter land was not embraced in the compromise.

To this judgment the Fairfax devisee [1] obtained
from the Supreme Court of the United States [2] a writ
of error to the Virginia court under Section 25 of
the Ellsworth Judiciary Act, upon the ground that
the case involved the construction of the Treaty of
Peace with Great Britain and the Jay Treaty, the
Virginia court having held against the right claimed
by Fairfax's devisee under those treaties. [3]

The Supreme Court now consisted of two Federalists, Washington and Marshall, and five Republicans, Johnson, Livingston, Story, and Duval; and
Todd, who was absent from illness at the decision
of this cause. Marshall declined to sit during the arguments, or to participate in the deliberations and

[1] Since James M. Marshall was the American administrator of the
will of Denny M. Fairfax, and also had long possessed all the rights and
title of the Fairfax heir to this particular land, it doubtless was he
who secured the writ of error from the Supreme Court.

[2] 1 Munford, 238.

[3] 7 Cranch, 608–09, 612. The reader should bear in mind the provisions of Section 25 of the Judiciary Act, since the validity and meaning of it are involved in some of the greatest controversies hereafter
discussed. The part of that section which was in controversy is as
follows:

"A final judgment or decree in any suit, in the highest court of law
or equity of a state in which a decision in the suit could be had, where
is drawn in question the validity of a treaty or statute of, or an authority exercised under the United States, and the decision is against their
validity; or where is drawn in question the validity of a statute of, or an
authority exercised under any state, on the ground of their being repugnant to the constitution, treaties or laws of the United States, and
the decision is in favor of such their validity; or where is drawn in
question the construction of any clause of the constitution, or of a
treaty, or statute of, or commission held under the United States, and
the decision is against the title, right, privilege or exemption specially
set up or claimed by either party, under such clause of the said constitution, treaty, statute or commission, may be re-examined and reversed or affirmed in the supreme court of the United States upon a
writ of error."

conclusions of his associates. Indeed, throughout this litigation the Chief Justice may almost be said to have leaned backward. It was with good reason that Henry S. Randall, the biographer and apologist of Jefferson, went out of his way to laud Marshall's "stainless private character" and pay tribute to his "austere public and private virtue." [1]

Eight years before the Hunter-Fairfax controversy was first brought to the Supreme Court, the case of the Granville heirs against William R. Davie, Nathaniel Allen, and Josiah Collins, was tried at the June term, 1805, of the United States Court at Raleigh, North Carolina. Marshall, as Circuit Judge, sat with Potter, District Judge. The question was precisely that involved in the Fairfax title. The grant to Lord Granville [2] was the same as that to Lord Fairfax. [3] North Carolina had passed the same confiscatory acts against alien holdings as Virginia. [4] Under these statutes, Davie, Allen, and Collins obtained grants to parts of the Granville estate [5] identical with that of Hunter to a part of the Fairfax estate in Virginia.

Here was an excellent opportunity for Marshall to decide the Fairfax controversy once and for all. Nowhere was his reputation at that time higher than in North Carolina, nowhere was he more admired and trusted. [6] That his opinion would have been ac-

---

[1] Randall, II, 35–36.

[2] For a full and painstaking account of the Granville grant, and the legislation and litigation growing out of it, see Henry G. Connor in *University of Pennsylvania Law Review*, vol. 62, 671 *et seq.*

[3] See vol. I, 192, of this work.

[4] Connor in *Univ. of Pa. Law Rev.* vol. 62, 674–75.

[5] *Ib.* 676.   [6] See *supra*, 69.

cepted by the State authorities and acquiesced in by
the people, there can be no doubt.[1] But the Chief
Justice flatly stated that he would take no part in
the trial because of an "opinion . . formed when he
was very deeply interested (alluding to the cause of
Lord Fairfax in Virginia). He could not consistently
with his duty and the delicacy he felt, give an opinion in the cause." [2]

[1] This highly important fact is proved by the message of Governor
David Stone to the Legislature of North Carolina in which he devotes
much space to the Granville litigation and recommends "early provision to meet the justice of the claim of her [North Carolina's] citizens
for remuneration in case of a decision against the sufficiency of the
title derived from herself." The "possibility" of such a decision is apparent "when it is generally understood that a greatly and deservedly
distinguished member of that [the Supreme] Court, has already formed
an unfavorable opinion, will probably enforce the consideration that
it is proper to make some eventual provision, by which the purchasers from the State, and those holding under that purchase, may
have justice done them." (Connor in *Univ. of Pa. Law Rev.* vol. 62,
690–91.)

From this message of Governor Stone it is clear that the State expected a decision in favor of the Granville heirs, and that the Legislature and State authorities were preparing to submit to that decision.

[2] *Raleigh Register*, June 24, 1805, as quoted by Connor in *Univ. of
Pa. Law Rev.* vol. 62, 689.

The jury found against the Granville heirs. A Mr. London, the
Granville agent at Wilmington, still hoped for success: "The favorable
sentiments of Judge Marshall encourage me to hope that we shall
finally succeed," he writes William Gaston, the Granville counsel.
Nevertheless, "I think the Judge's reasons for withdrawing from the
cause partakes more of political acquiescence than the dignified, official independence we had a right to expect from his character. He
said enough to convince our opponents he was unfavorable to their
construction of the law and, therefore, should not have permitted incorrect principles to harass our clients and create expensive delays.
Mr. Marshall had certainly no interest in our cause, he ought to have
governed the proceedings of a Court over which he presided, according
to such opinion — it has very much the appearance of shirking to popular impressions."

London ordered an appeal to be taken to the Supreme Court of the
United States, remarking that "it is no doubt much in our favor what

The case of Fairfax's Devisee *vs.* Hunter's Lessee
was argued for the former by Charles Lee of Richmond and Walter Jones of Washington, D.C.
Robert Goodloe Harper of Baltimore appeared for
Hunter. On both sides the argument was mainly
upon the effect on the Fairfax title of the Virginia
confiscatory laws; of the proceedings or failure to
proceed under them; and the bearing upon the
controversy of the two treaties with Great Britain.
Harper, however, insisted that the court consider
the statute of Virginia which set forth and confirmed
the Marshall compromise.

On March 15, 1813, Story delivered the opinion
of the majority of the court, consisting of himself and
Justices Washington, Livingston, Todd, and Duval.
Johnson, alone, dissented. Story held that, since
Virginia had not taken the prescribed steps to acquire
legal possession of the land before the Treaty of
Peace, the State could not do so afterward. "The
patent of the original plaintiff [Hunter] . . issued im-

has already dropt from the Chief Justice." (London to Gaston, July 8,
1805, as quoted by Connor in *Univ. of Pa. Law Rev.* vol. 62, 690.)

He was, however, disgusted with Marshall. "I feel much chagrin
that we are put to so much trouble and expense in this business, and
which I fear is in great degree to be attributed to the Chief Justice's
delivery." (Same to same, April 19, 1806, as quoted by Connor in *ib.*
691.)

For more than ten years the appeal of the Granville heirs from the
judgment of the National Court for the District of North Carolina reposed on the scanty docket of the Supreme Court awaiting call for argument by counsel. Finally on February 4, 1817, on motion of counsel
for the Granville heirs, the case was stricken from the docket. The
reason for this action undoubtedly was that William Gaston, counsel
for the Granville heirs, had been elected to Congress, was ambitious
politically, was thereafter elected judge of the Supreme Court of North
Carolina; none of these honors could possibly have been achieved had
he pressed the Granville case.

providently and passed no title whatever." To up-
hold Virginia's grant to Hunter "would be selling
suits and controversies through the whole country."[1]
It was not necessary, said Story, to consider the
Treaty of Peace, since "we are well satisfied that
the treaty of 1794 [2] completely protects and confirms
the title of Denny Fairfax."[3]

In his dissenting opinion Justice Johnson ignored
the "compromise" of 1796, holding that the grant by
the State to Hunter extinguished the right of Fairfax's devisee.[4] He concurred with Story and Washington, however, in the opinion that, on the face of
the record, the case came within Section 25 of the
Judiciary Act; that, therefore, the writ of error had
properly issued, and that the title must be inquired
into before considering "how far the . . treaty . . is
applicable to it."[5] Accordingly the mandate of the
Supreme Court was directed to the judges of the Virginia Court of Appeals, instructing them "to enter
judgment for the appellant, Philip Martin [the Fairfax devisee]." Like all writs of the Supreme Court,
it was, of course, issued in the name of the Chief
Justice.[6]

Hot was the wrath of Roane and the other judges
of Virginia's highest court when they received this
order from the National tribunal at Washington.
At their next sitting they considered whether to
obey or to defy the mandate. They called in "the
members of the bar generally," and the question

[1] 7 Cranch, 625.
[2] The Jay Treaty. See vol. II, 113–15, of this work.
[3] 7 Cranch, 627.   [4] *Ib.* 631.
[5] *Ib.* 632.   [6] For mandate see 4 Munford, 2–3.

"was solemnly argued" at Richmond for six consecutive days.[1] On December 16, 1815, the decision was published. The Virginia judges unanimously declined to obey the mandate of the Supreme Court of the United States. Each judge rendered a separate opinion, and all held that so much of Section 25 of the National Judiciary Act as "extends the appellate jurisdiction of the Supreme Court to this court, is not in pursuance of the constitution of the United States." [2]

But it was not only the Virginia Court of Appeals that now spoke; it was the entire Republican partisan machine, intensively organized and intelligently run, that brought its power to bear against the highest tribunal of the Nation. Beyond all possible doubt, this Republican organization, speaking through the supreme judiciary of the State, represented public sentiment, generally, throughout the Old Dominion. Unless this political significance of the opinions of the Virginia judges be held of higher value than their legal quality, the account of this historic controversy deserves no more than a brief paragraph stating the legal point decided.

The central question was well set forth by Judge Cabell thus: Even where the construction of a treaty is involved in the final decision of a cause by the highest court of a State, that decision being against the title of the party claiming under the treaty, can Congress "confer on the Supreme Court of the United States, a power to *re-examine, by way of appeal or writ of error, the decision of the state Court; to*

[1] March 31, April 1 to April 6, 1814. (4 Munford, 3.)   [2] *Ib.* 58.

affirm or reverse that decision; and in case of reversal, to command the state Court to enter and execute a judgment different from that which it had previously rendered?" [1]

Every one of the judges answered in the negative. The opinion of Judge Cabell was the ablest, and stated most clearly the real issue raised by the Virginia court. Neither State nor National Government is dependent one upon the other, he said; neither can act *"compulsively"* upon the other. Controversies might arise between State and National Governments, "yet the constitution has provided no umpire, has erected no tribunal by which they shall be settled." Therefore, the National court could not oblige the State court to "enter a judgment not its own." [2] The meaning of the National "Constitution, laws and treaties, . . must, in cases coming before State courts, be decided by the State Judges, *according to their own judgments, and upon their own responsibility."* [3] National tribunals belong to one sovereignty; State tribunals to a different sovereignty — neither is *"superior"* to the other; neither can command or instruct the other. [4]

Grant that this interpretation of the Constitution results in conflicts between State and Nation and even deprives the "general government . . of the power of executing its laws and treaties"; even so, "the defects of our system of government must be remedied, not by the judiciary, but by the sovereign power of the people." The Constitution must be amended by the people, not by judicial interpre-

[1] 4 Munford, 7. [2] *Ib.* 8–9. [3] *Ib.* 11. [4] *Ib.* 12.

tation;[1] yet Congress, in Section 25 of the Judiciary Act, "attempts, in fact, to make the State Courts *Inferior Federal Courts.*" The appellate jurisdiction conferred on the Supreme Court, and the word *"supreme"* itself, had reference to inferior National courts and not to State courts.[2]

Judge Roane's opinion was very long and discussed extensively every phase of the controversy. He held that, in giving National courts power over State courts, Section 25 of the Ellsworth Judiciary Act violated the National Constitution. If National courts could control State tribunals, it would be a "plain case of the judiciary of one government correcting and reversing the decisions of that of another." [3] The Virginia Court of Appeals "is bound, to follow its own convictions . . any thing in the decisions, or supposed decisions, of any other court, to the contrary notwithstanding." Let the court at Winchester, therefore, be instructed to execute the judgment of the State Court of Appeals.[4]

Such was the open, aggressive, and dramatic defiance of the Supreme Court of the United States by the Court of Appeals of Virginia. Roane showed his opinion to Monroe, who approved it and sent it to Jefferson at Monticello. Jefferson heartily commended Roane,[5] whereat the Virginia judge was "very much flattered and gratified." [6]

Promptly Philip Martin, through James M. Marshall, took the case to the Supreme Court by means

---

[1] 4 Munford, 15.   [2] *Ib.* 133.   [3] *Ib.* 38.   [4] *Ib.* 54.

[5] Jefferson to Roane, Oct. 12, 1815, *Works:* Ford, xi, 488–90.

[6] Roane to Jefferson, Oct. 28, 1815, *Branch Hist. Papers*, June, 1905, 131–32.

of another writ of error. It now stood upon the docket of that court as Martin *vs.* Hunter's Lessee. Again Marshall refused to sit in the case. St. George Tucker of Virginia, one of the ablest lawyers of the South, and Samuel Dexter, the leader of the Massachusetts bar, appeared for Hunter.[1] As Harper had done on the first appeal, both Tucker and Dexter called attention to the fact that the decision of the Virginia Court of Appeals did not rest exclusively upon the Treaty of Peace, which alone in this case would have authorized an appeal to the Supreme Court.[2]

Story delivered the court's opinion, which was one of the longest and ablest he ever wrote. The Constitution was not ordained by the States, but "emphatically . . by 'the people of the United States.'[3] . . Its powers are expressed in general terms, leaving to the legislature, from time to time, to adopt its own means to effectuate legitimate objects, and to mold and model the exercise of its powers, as its own wisdom and the public interests should require."[4] Story then quotes Sections 1 and 2 of Article III of the Constitution,[5] and continues: Thus is "the voice

[1] The employment of these expensive lawyers is final proof of Hunter's financial resources.

[2] 1 Wheaton, 317, 318.   [3] *Ib.* 324.   [4] *Ib.* 326–27.

[5] The sections of the Constitution pertaining to this dispute are as follows:

"Article III, Section 1. The judicial Power of the United States, shall be vested in one supreme Court, and in such inferior Courts as the Congress may from time to time ordain and establish. The Judges, both of the supreme and inferior Courts, shall hold their Offices during good Behaviour, and shall, at stated Times, receive for their Services a Compensation, which shall not be diminished during their Continuance in Office.

"Section 2. The judicial Power shall extend to all Cases, in Law

of the whole American people solemnly declared, in establishing one great department of that government which was, in many respects, national, and in all, supreme." Congress cannot disregard this Constitutional mandate. At a length which, but for the newness of the question, would be intolerable, Story demonstrates that the Constitutional grant of judiciary powers is "imperative." [1]

What, then, is the "nature and extent of the appellate jurisdiction of the United States"? It embraces "every case . . not exclusively to be decided by way of original jurisdiction." There is nothing in the Constitution to "restrain its exercise over state tribunals in the enumerated cases. . . It is the case, . . and not the court, that gives the jurisdiction." [2] If the appellate power does not extend to State courts having concurrent jurisdiction of specified cases, then that power does "not extend to all, but to some, cases" — whereas the Constitution declares that it extends to all other cases than those over which the Supreme Court is given original jurisdiction. [3]

With great care Story shows the "propriety" of this construction. [4] Then, with repetitiousness after the true Marshall pattern, he reasserts that the

and Equity, arising under this Constitution, the Laws of the United States, and Treaties made, or which shall be made, under their Authority; — to all Cases affecting Ambassadors, other public Ministers and Consuls; — to all Cases of admiralty and maritime Jurisdiction; — to Controversies to which the United States shall be a Party; — to Controversies between two or more States; — between a State and Citizens of another State; — between Citizens of different States; — between Citizens of the same State claiming Lands under Grants of different States, and between a State, or the Citizens thereof, and foreign States, Citizens or Subjects."

[1] 1 Wheaton, 328.   [2] *Ib.* 337–38.   [3] *Ib.* 339.   [4] *Ib.* 341.

Constitution acts on States as well as upon individuals, and gives many instances where the "sovereignty" of the States are "restrained." State judges are not independent "in respect to the powers granted to the United States";[1] and the appellate power of the Nation extends to the State courts in cases prescribed in Section 25 of the Judiciary Act; for the Constitution does not limit this power and "we dare not interpose a limitation where the people have not been disposed to create one."[2]

The case decided on the former record, says Story, is not now before the court. "The question now litigated is not upon the construction of a treaty, but upon the constitutionality of a statute of the United States, which is clearly within our jurisdiction." However, "from motives of a public nature," the Supreme Court would "re-examine" the grounds of its former decision.[3] After such reëxamination, extensive in length and detail, he finds the first decision of the Supreme Court to have been correct.

Story thus notices the Marshall adjustment of 1796: "If it be true (as we are informed)" that the compromise had been effected, the court could not take "judicial cognizance" of it "unless spread upon the record." Aside from the Treaty of Peace, the Fairfax title "was, at all events, perfect under the treaty of 1794."[4] In conclusion, Story announces: "It is the opinion of the whole court that the judgment of the Court of Appeals of Virginia, rendered on the mandate in this cause, be reversed, and the

[1] 1 Wheaton, 343-44.   [2] *Ib.* 351.   [3] *Ib.* 355.   [4] *Ib.* 360.

judgment of the District Court, held at Winchester, be, and the same is hereby affirmed." [1]

It has been commonly supposed that Marshall practically dictated Story's two opinions in the Fairfax-Hunter controversy, and certain writers have stated this to be the fact. As we have seen, Story himself, fifteen years afterwards, declared that the Chief Justice had "concurred in every word of the second opinion"; yet in a letter to his brother concerning the effect of Story's opinion upon another suit in the State court at Winchester, involving the same question, Marshall says: "The case of Hunter & Fairfax is very absurdly put on the treaty of 94." [2]

[1] 1 Wheaton, 362.

[2] Marshall to his brother, July 9, 1822, MS. Parts of this long letter are of interest: "Although Judge White [of the Winchester court] will, of course, conform to the decision of the court of appeals against the appellate jurisdiction of the Supreme court, & therefore deny that the opinion in the case of Fairfax & Hunter is binding, yet he must admit that the supreme court is the proper tribunal for expounding the treaties of the United States, & that its decisions on a treaty are binding on the state courts, whether they possess the appellate jurisdiction or not... The exposition of any state law by the courts of that state, are considered in the courts of all the other states, and in those of the United States, as a correct exposition, not to be reexamined.

"The only exception to this rule is when the statute of a state is supposed to violate the constitution of the United States, in which case the courts of the Union claim a controuling & supervising power. Thus any construction made by the courts of Virginia on the statute of descents or of distribution, or on any other subject, is admitted as conclusive in the federal courts, although those courts might have decided differently on the statute itself. The principle is that the courts of every government are the proper tribunals for construing the legislative acts of that government.

"Upon this principle the Supreme court of the United States, independent of its appellate jurisdiction, is the proper tribunal for construing the laws & treaties of the United States; and the construction of that court ought to be received every where as the right construction. The Supreme court of the United States has settled the con-

Justice Johnson dissented in an opinion as inept
and unhappy as his dissent in Fletcher *vs.* Peck.[1]
He concurs in the judgment of his brethren, but, in
doing so, indulges in a stump speech in which
Nationalism and State Rights are mingled in astounding fashion. The Supreme Court of the United
States, he says, "disavows all intention to decide on
the right to issue compulsory process to the state
courts." To be sure, the Supreme Court is "supreme
over persons and cases as far as our judicial powers
extend," but it cannot assert "any compulsory control over the state tribunals." He views "this question as one . . which may affect, in its consequences,
the permanence of the American Union," since the
Nation and "one of the greatest states" are in collision. The "general government must cease to
exist" if the Virginia doctrine shall prevail, but "so
firmly" was he "persuaded that the American people
can no longer enjoy the blessings of a free government, whenever the state sovereignties shall be prostrated at the feet of the general government," that
he " could borrow the language of a celebrated orator,
and exclaim: 'I rejoice that Virginia has resisted.' " [2]

struction of the treaty of peace to be that lands at that time held by
British subjects were not escheatable or grantable by a state . . I refer
particularly to Smith v The State of Maryland 6th Cranch Jackson v
Clarke 3 Wheaton & Orr v Hodgson 4 Wheaton. The last case is explicit & was decided unanimously, Judge Johnson assenting.

"This being the construction of the highest court of the government
which is a party to the treaty is to be considered by all the world as its
true construction unless Great Britain, the other party, should con-
trovert it. The court of appeals has not denied this principle. The
dicta of Judge Roane respecting the treaty were anterior to this constitutional construction of it."

[1] See vol. III, chap. X, of this work.   [2] 1 Wheaton, 362–63

Nevertheless, Johnson agrees with the judgment of his associates and, in doing so, delivers a Nationalist opinion, stronger if possible than that of Story.[1]

The public benefits and the historic importance of the decision was the assertion of the supremacy of the Supreme Court of the Nation over the highest court of any State in all cases where the National Constitution, laws and treaties — "the supreme law of the land" — are involved. The decision of the Supreme Court in Martin *vs.* Hunter's Lessee went further than any previous judicial pronouncement to establish the relation between National courts and State tribunals which now exists and will continue as long as the Republic endures.

When the news of this, the first Constitutional opinion ever delivered by Story, got abroad, he was mercilessly assailed by his fellow Republicans as a "renegade." [2] Congress refused to increase the salaries of the members of the Supreme Court,[3] who found it hard to live on the compensation allowed them,[4] and Story seriously considered resigning from the bench and taking over the Baltimore practice of Mr. Pinkney, who soon was to be appointed Minister

[1] Johnson's opinion was published in the *National Intelligencer*, April 16, 1816, as an answer to Roane's argument. (Smith in *Branch Hist. Papers*, June, 1905, 23.)

[2] Story, I, 277.

[3] *Annals*, 14th Cong. 1st Sess. 194, 231–33.

A bill was reported March 22, 1816, increasing the salaries of all government officials. The report of the committee is valuable as showing the increased cost of living. (*Ib.*)

[4] Nearly three years after the decision of Martin *vs.* Hunter's Lessee, Story writes that the Justices of the Supreme Court are "*starving in splendid poverty.*" (Story to Wheaton, Dec. 9, 1818, Story, I, 313.)

to Russia.[1] The decision aroused excitement and indignation throughout Virginia. Roane's popularity increased from the Tide Water to the Valley.[2] The Republican organization made a political issue of the judgment of the National tribunal at Washington. Judge Roane issued his orders to his political lieutenants. The party newspapers, led by the *Enquirer*, inveighed against the "usurpation" by this distant Supreme Court of the United States, a foreign power, an alien judiciary, unsympathetic with Virginia, ignorant of the needs of Virginians.

This conflict between the Supreme Court of the United States and the Court of Appeals of Virginia opened another phase of that fundamental struggle which war was to decide — a fact without knowledge of which this phase of American Constitutional history is colorless.

Not yet, however, was the astute Virginia Republican triumvirate ready to unloose the lightnings of Virginia's wrath. That must be done only when the whole South should reach a proper degree of emotion. This time was not long to be delayed. Within three years Marshall's opinion in M'Culloch *vs.* Maryland was to give Roane, Ritchie, and Taylor their cue to come upon the stage as the spokesmen of Virginia and the entire South, as the champions, indeed, of Localism everywhere throughout America. Important were the parts they played in the drama of Marshall's judicial career.

[1] Story to White, Feb. 26, 1816, Story, I, 278; and see Story to Williams, May 22, 1816, *ib.* 279.
[2] Ambler: *Sectionalism in Virginia*, 103.

CHAPTER IV

FINANCIAL AND MORAL CHAOS

Like a dropsical man calling out for water, water, our deluded citizens are calling for more banks. (Jefferson.)

Merchants are crumbling to ruin, manufactures perishing, agriculture stagnating and distress universal. (John Quincy Adams.)

If we can believe our Democratic editors and public declaimers it [Bank of the United States] is a Hydra, a Cerberus, a Gorgon, a Vulture, a Viper.
(William Harris Crawford.)

Where one prudent and honest man applies for [bankruptcy] one hundred rogues are facilitated in their depredations. (Hezekiah Niles.)

Merchants and traders are harassed by twenty different systems of laws, prolific in endless frauds, perjuries and evasions. (Harrison Gray Otis.)

THE months of February and March, 1819, are memorable in American history, for during those months John Marshall delivered three of his greatest opinions. All of these opinions have had a determinative effect upon the political and industrial evolution of the people; and one of them [1] has so decisively influenced the growth of the Nation that, by many, it is considered as only second in importance to the Constitution itself. At no period and in no land, in so brief a space of time, has any other jurist or statesman ever bestowed upon his country three documents of equal importance. Like the other fundamental state papers which, in the form of judicial opinions, Marshall gave out from the Supreme Bench, those of 1819 were compelled by grave and dangerous conditions, National in extent.

It was a melancholy prospect over which Marshall's broad vision ranged, when from his rustic

[1] M'Culloch vs. Maryland, see infra, chap. VI.

bench under his trees at Richmond, during the spring and autumn of 1818, he surveyed the situation in which the American people found themselves. It was there, or in the quiet of the Blue Ridge Mountains where he spent the summer months, that he formed the outlines of those charts which he was soon to present to the country for its guidance; and it was there that at least one of them was put on paper.

The interpretation of John Marshall as the constructing architect of American Nationalism is not satisfactorily accomplished by a mere statement of his Nationalist opinions and of the immediate legal questions which they answered. Indeed, such a narrative, by itself, does not greatly aid to an understanding of Marshall's immense and enduring achievements. Not in the narrow technical points involved, some of them diminutive and all uninviting in their formality; not in the dreary records of the law cases decided, is to be found the measure of his monumental service to the Republic or the meaning of what he did. The state of things which imperatively demanded the exercise of his creative genius and the firm pressure of his steadying hand must be understood in order to grasp the significance of his labors.

When the Supreme Court met in February, 1819, almost the whole country was in grievous turmoil; for nearly three years conditions had been growing rapidly worse and were now desperate. Poverty, bankruptcy, chicanery, crime were widespread and increasing. Thrift, prudence, honesty, and order had seemingly been driven from the hearts and minds of most of the people; while speculation, craft, and

unscrupulous devices were prevalent throughout all
but one portion of the land. Only New England had
largely escaped the universal curse that appeared to
have fallen upon the United States; and even that
section was not untouched by the economic and
social plague that had raged and was becoming more
deadly in every other quarter.

While it is true that a genuine democratizing evolution was in progress, this fact does not explain the
situation that had grown up throughout the country.
Neither does the circumstance that the development
of land and resources was going forward in haphaz-
ard fashion, at the hands of a new population hard
pressed for money and facilities for work and communication, reveal the cause of the appalling state
of affairs. It must frankly be said of the conditions,
to us now unbelievable, that they were due partly to
the ignorance, credulity, and greed of the people;
partly to the spirit of extravagance; partly to the
criminal avarice of the financially ambitious; partly
to popular dread of any great centralized moneyed
institution, however sound; partly to that pest of all
democracies, the uninformed and incessant demagogue whipping up and then pandering to the passions of the multitude; partly to that scarcely less
dangerous creature in a Republic, the fanatical doc-
trinaire, proclaiming the perfection of government
by word-logic and insisting that human nature shall
be confined in the strait-jacket of verbal theory.
From this general welter of moral and economic de-
bauchery, Localism had once more arisen and was
eagerly reasserting its domination.

The immediate cause of the country's plight was an utter chaos in banking. Seldom has such a financial motley ever covered with variegated rags the backs of a people. The confusion was incredible; but not for a moment did the millions who suffered, blame themselves for their tragic predicament. Now praising banks as unfailing fountains of money, now denouncing banks as the sources of poisoned waters, clamoring for whatever promised even momentary relief, striking at whatever seemingly denied it, the people laid upon anything and anybody but themselves and their improvidence, the responsibility for their distress.

Hamilton's financial plans [1] had proved to be as successful as they were brilliant. The Bank of the United States, managed, on the whole, with prudence, skill, and honesty, [2] had fulfilled the expectations of its founders. It had helped to maintain the National credit by loans in anticipation of revenue; it had served admirably, and without compensation, as an agent for collecting, safeguarding, and transporting the funds of the Government; and, more important than all else, it had kept the currency, whether its own notes or those of private banks, on a sound specie basis. It had, indeed, "acted as the general guardian of commercial credit" and, as such, had faithfully and wisely performed its duties. [3]

But the success of the Bank had not overcome the

---

[1] See vol. II, 60, of this work.

[2] Sumner: *History of American Currency*, 63.

[3] See Memorial of the Bank for a recharter, April 20, 1808 (*Am. State Papers, Finance*, II, 301), and second Memorial, Dec. 18, 1810 (*ib.* 451–52). Every statement in these petitions was true. See also Dewey: *Financial History of the United States*, 100, 101.

original antagonism to a great central moneyed institution. Following the lead of Jefferson, who had
insisted that the project was unconstitutional,[1] Madison, in the first Congress, had opposed the bill to
incorporate the first Bank of the United States. Congress had no power, he said, to create corporations.[2]
After twelve years of able management, and in spite
of the good it had accomplished, Jefferson still considered it, potentially, a monster that might overthrow the Republic. "This institution," he wrote in
the third year of his Presidency, "is one of the most
deadly hostility existing, against the principles &
form of our Constitution. . . An institution like this,
penetrating by it's branches every part of the Union,
acting by command & in phalanx, may, in a critical
moment, upset the government. . . What an obstruction could not this bank of the U. S., with all it's
branch banks, be in time of war?"[3]

The fact that most of the stock of the Bank had
been bought up by Englishmen added to the un-
popularity of the institution.[4] Another source of hostility was the jealousy of State banks, much of the
complaint about "unconstitutionality" and "foreign ownership" coming from the agents and friends
of these local concerns. The State banks wished for
themselves the profits made by the National Bank
and its branches, and they chafed under the wise

[1] See vol. II, 70–71, of this work.

[2] *Annals*, 1st Cong. 2d. Sess. 1945. By far the strongest objection
to a National bank, however, was that it was a monopoly inconsistent
with free institutions.

[3] Jefferson to Gallatin, Dec. 13, 1803, *Works:* Ford: x, 57.

[4] "Fully two thirds of the Bank stock . . were owned in England." (Adams: *U.S.* v, 328.)

regulation of their note issues, which the existence of the National system compelled.

For several years these State banks had been growing in number and activity.[1] When, in 1808, the directors of the Bank of the United States asked for a renewal of its charter, which would expire in 1811, and when the same request was made of Congress in 1809, opposition poured into the Capital from every section of the country. The great Bank was a British institution, it was said; its profits were too great; it was a creature of Federalism, brought forth in violation of the Constitution. Its directors, officers, and American stockholders were Federalists; and this fact was the next most powerful motive for the overthrow of the first Bank of the United States.[2]

Petitions to Congress denounced it and demanded its extinction. One from Pittsburgh declared "that your memorialists are 'the People of the United States,'" and asserted that the Bank "held in bondage thousands of our citizens," kept the Government "in duress," and subsidized the press, thus "thronging" the Capital with lobbyists who in general were the "head-waters of corruption."[3] The Legislatures of many States "instructed" their Senators and "earnestly requested" their Representatives in Congress to oppose a new charter for the expiring National institution. Such resolutions came from Pennsylvania, from Virginia, from Massachusetts.[4]

[1] Dewey, 127; and Pitkin: *Statistical View of the Commerce of the United States*, 130–32.
[2] Adams: *U.S.* v, 328–29.
[3] *Annals*, 11th Cong. 3d Sess. 118–21.
[4] *Ib.* 153, 201, 308; and see Pitkin, 421.

The State banks were the principal contrivers of all
this agitation.[1] For instance, the Bank of Virginia,
organized in 1804, had acquired great power and,
but for the branch of the National concern at Richmond, would have had almost the banking monopoly of that State. Especially did the Virginia Bank
desire to become the depository of National funds[2]
— a thing that could not be accomplished so long as
the Bank of the United States was in existence.[3] Dr.
John Brockenbrough, the relative, friend, and political associate of Spencer Roane and Thomas Ritchie,
was the president of this State institution, which
was a most important part of the Republican machine in Virginia. Considering the absolute control
held by this political organization over the Legislature, it seems probable that the State bank secured
the resolution condemnatory of the Bank of the
United States.

Certainly the General Assembly would not have
taken any action not approved by Brockenbrough,
Roane, and Ritchie. Ritchie's *Enquirer* boasted that
it "was the first to denounce the renewal of the bank
charter."[4] In the Senate, William H. Crawford
boldly charged that the instructions of the State Legislatures were "induced by motives of avarice";[5]
and Senator Giles was plainly embarrassed in his
attempt to deny the indictment.[6]

[1] Adams: *U.S.* v, 327–28. "They induced one State legislature after
another to instruct their senators on the subject." Pitkin, 422.

[2] Ambler: *Ritchie*, 26–27, 52.   [3] *Ib.* 67.

[4] *Branch Hist. Papers*, June, 1903, 179.

[5] *Annals*, 11th Cong. 3d Sess. 145.

[6] "It is true, that a branch of the Bank of the United States . is
established at Norfolk; and that a branch of the Bank of Virginia is

Nearly all the newspapers were controlled by the State banks;[1] they, of course, denounced the National Bank in the familiar terms of democratic controversy and assailed the character of every public man who spoke in behalf of so vile and dangerous an institution.[2] It was also an ideal object of assault for local politicians who bombarded the Bank with their usual vituperation. All this moved Senator Crawford, in his great speech for the rechartering of the Bank, to a scathing arraignment of such methods.[3]

In spite of conclusive arguments in favor of the Bank of the United States on the merits of the question, the bill to recharter that institution was de-

also established there. But these circumstances furnish no possible motive of avarice to the Virginia Legislature. . . They have acted . . from the purest and most honorable motives." (*Annals*, 11th Cong. 3d Sess. 200.)

[1] Pitkin, 421.

[2] The "newspapers teem with the most virulent abuse." (James Flint's Letters from America, in *Early Western Travels*: Thwaites, IX, 87.) Even twenty years later Captain Marryat records: "The press in the United States is licentious to the highest possible degree, and defies control. . . Every man in America reads his newspaper, and hardly any thing else." (Marryat: *Diary in America*, 2d Series, 56–59.)

[3] "The Democratic presses . . have . . teemed with the most scurrilous abuse against every member of Congress who has dared to utter a syllable in favor of the renewal of the bank charter." Any member supporting the bank "is instantly charged with being bribed, . . with being corrupt, with having trampled upon the rights and liberties of the people, . . with being guilty of perjury."

According to "the rantings of our Democratic editors . . and the denunciations of our public declaimers," the bank "exists under the form of every foul and hateful beast and bird, and creeping thing. It is an *Hydra*; it is a *Cerberus*; it is a *Gorgon*; it is a *Vulture*; it is a *Viper*. . .

"Shall we tamely act under the lash of this tyranny of the press? . . I most solemnly protest . . To tyranny, under whatever form it may be exercised, I declare open and interminable war . . whether the tyrant is an irresponsible editor or a despotic Monarch." (*Annals*, 11th Cong. 3d Sess. 145.)

feated in the House by a single vote,[1] and in the Senate by the casting vote of the Vice-President, the aged George Clinton.[2] Thus, on the very threshold of the War of 1812, the Government was deprived of this all but indispensable fiscal agent; immense quantities of specie, representing foreign bank holdings, were withdrawn from the country; and the State banks were given a free hand which they soon used with unrestrained license.

These local institutions, which, from the moment the failure of the rechartering of the National Bank seemed probable, had rapidly increased in number, now began to spring up everywhere.[3] From the first these concerns had issued bills for the loan of which they charged interest. Thus banking was made doubly profitable. Even those banks, whose note issues were properly safeguarded, achieved immense profits. Banking became a mania.

"The Banking Infatuation pervades all America," wrote John Adams in 1810. "Our whole system of Banks is a violation of every honest Principle of Banks. . . A Bank that issues Paper at Interest is a Pickpocket or a Robber. But the Delusion will have its Course. You may as well reason with a Hurricane. An Aristocracy is growing out of them, that will be as fatal as The Feudal Barons, if unchecked in Time. . . Think of the Number, the Offices, Stations, Wealth, Piety and Reputations of the Persons in all the States, who have made Fortunes by these Banks, and then you will see how deeply rooted the evil is. The Number of Debtors who hope to pay

---

[1] *Annals*, 11th Cong. 3d Sess. 826.   [2] *Ib.* 347.   [3] Pitkin, 430.

their debts by this Paper united with the Creditors
who build Pallaces in our Cities, and Castles for
Country Seats, by issuing this Paper form too im-
pregnable a Phalanx to be attacked by any Thing
less disciplined than Roman Legions." [1]

Such was the condition even before the expiration
of the charter of the first Bank. But, when the restraining and regulating influence of that conservative and ably managed institution was removed altogether, local banking began a course that ended in
a mad carnival of roguery, to the ruin of legitimate
business and the impoverishment and bankruptcy
of hundreds of thousands of the general public.

The avarice of the State banks was immediately
inflamed by the war necessities of the National Government. Desperate for money, the Treasury exchanged six per cent United States bonds for the
notes of State banks.[2] The Government thus lost
five million dollars from worthless bank bills.[3] These
local institutions now became the sole depositories
of the Government funds which the National Bank
had formerly held.[4] Sources of gain of this kind were
only extra inducements to those who, by wit alone,
would gather quick wealth to set up more local banks.
But other advantages were quite enough to appeal
to the greedy, the dishonest, and the adventurous.

Liberty to pour out bills without effective restriction as to the amount or security; to loan such

---

[1] Adams to Rush, Dec. 27, 1810, *Old Family Letters*, 272.
[2] Sumner: *Andrew Jackson*, 229.   [3] Dewey, 145.
[4] Twenty-one State banks were employed as Government depositories after the destruction of the first Bank of the United States
(*Ib.* 128.)

"rags" to any who could be induced to borrow; to collect these debts by foreclosure of mortgages or threats of imprisonment of the debtors — these were some of the seeds from which grew the noxious financial weeds that began to suck the prosperity of the country. When the first Bank of the United States was organized there were only three State banks in the country. By 1800, there were twenty-eight; by 1811, they had more than trebled,[1] and most of the eighty-eight State institutions in exist-ence when the first National Bank was destroyed had been organized after it seemed probable that it would not be granted a recharter.

So rapidly did they increase and so great were their gains that, within little more than a year from the demise of the first Bank of the United States, John Adams records: "The Profits of our Banks to the advantage of the few, at the loss of the many, are such an enormous fraud and oppression as no other Nation ever invented or endured. Who can compute the amount of the sums taken out of the Pocketts of the Simple and hoarded in the Purses of the cunning in the course of every year? .. If Rumour speaks the Truth Boston has and will emulate Philadelphia in her Proportion of Bankruptcies."[2]

Yet Boston and Philadelphia banks were the soundest and most carefully conducted of any in the whole land. If Adams spoke extravagantly of the methods and results of the best managed financial institutions of the country, he did not exaggerate

---

[1] Dewey, 127.

[2] Adams to Rush, July 3, 1812, *Old Family Letters*, 299.

conditions elsewhere. From Connecticut to the Mississippi River, from Lake Erie to New Orleans, the craze for irresponsible banking spread like a contagious fever. The people were as much affected by the disease as were the speculators. The more "money" they saw, the more "money" they wanted. Bank notes fell in value; specie payments were suspended; rates of exchange were in utter confusion and constantly changing. From day to day no man knew, with certainty, what the "currency" in his pocket was worth. At Vincennes, Indiana, in 1818, William Faux records: "I passed away my 20 dollar note of the rotten bank of Harmony, Pennsylvania, for five dollars only!"[1]

The continuance of the war, of course, made this financial situation even worse for the Government than for the people. It could not negotiate its loans; the public dues were collected with difficulty, loss, and delay; the Treasury was well-nigh bankrupt. "The Department of State was so bare of money as to be unable to pay even its stationery bill."[2] In 1814, when on the verge of financial collapse, the Administration determined that another Bank of the United States was absolutely necessary to the conduct of the war.[3] Scheme after scheme was proposed, wrangled over, and defeated.

One plan for a bank[4] was beaten "after a day of the most tumultuous proceedings I ever saw," testi-

---

[1] William Faux's Journal, *E. W. T.*: Thwaites, XI, 207.
[2] Speech of Hanson in the House, Nov. 28, 1814, *Annals*, 13th Cong 3d Sess. 656.
[3] Catterall: *Second Bank of the United States*, 13–17.
[4] Calhoun's bill.

fies Webster.[1] Another bill passed,[2] but was vetoed
by President Madison because it could not aid in
the rehabilitation of the public credit, nor "provide
a circulating medium during the war, nor . . furnish
loans, or anticipate public revenue."[3] When the war
was over, Madison timidly suggested to Congress the
advisability of establishing a National bank "that
the benefits of a uniform national currency should be
restored."[4] Thus, on April 10, 1816, two years after
Congress took up the subject, a law finally was enacted and approved providing for the chartering
and government of the second Bank of the United
States.[5]

Within four years, then, of the refusal of Congress
to recharter the sound and ably managed first Bank
of the United States, it was forced to authorize
another National institution, endowed with practically the same powers possessed by the Bank which
Congress itself had so recently destroyed.[6] But the
second establishment would have at least one advantage over the first in the eyes of the predominant political party — a majority of the officers
and directors of the Bank would be Republicans.[7]

[1] Webster to his brother, Nov. 29, 1814, Van Tyne, 55.

[2] Webster's bill.

[3] *Annals*, 13th Cong. 3d Sess. 189–91; Richardson, I, 555–57.

[4] Richardson, I, 565–66. Four years afterwards President Monroe
told his Secretary of State, John Quincy Adams, that Jefferson, Madison, and himself considered all Constitutional objections to the Bank
as having been "settled by twenty years of practice and acquiescence
under the first bank." (*Memoirs, J. Q. A.*: Adams, IV, 499, Jan. 8,
1820.)

[5] *Annals*, 14th Cong. 1st Sess. 280–81.

[6] *Annals*, 1st Cong. 2d and 3d Sess. 2375–82; and 14th Cong. 1st
Sess. 1812–25; also Dewey, 150–51.

[7] Catterall, 22.

During their four years of "financial liberty" the number of State banks had multiplied. Those that could be enumerated in 1816 were 246.[1] In addition to these, scores of others, most of them "pure swindles,"[2] were pouring out their paper.[3] Even if they had been sound, not half of them were needed.[4] Nearly all of them extended their wild methods. "The Banks have been going on, as tho' the day of reckoning would never come," wrote Rufus King of conditions in the spring of 1816.[5]

The people themselves encouraged these practices. The end of the war released an immense quantity of English goods which flooded the American market. The people, believing that devastated Europe would absorb all American products, and beholding a vision of radiant prosperity, were eager to buy. A passion for extravagance swept over America;[6] the country was drained of specie by payments for exports.[7] Then came a frenzy of speculation. "The people were wild; . . reason seemed turned topsy turvey."[8]

The multitude of local banks intensified both these manias by every device that guile and avarice could suggest. Every one wanted to get rich at the expense of some one else by a mysterious process, the nature of

---

[1] Dewey, 144.   [2] Sumner: *Hist. Am. Currency*, 70.

[3] In November, 1818, Niles estimated that there were about four hundred banks in the country with eight thousand "managers and clerks," costing $2,000,000, annually. (Niles, xv, 162.)

[4] "The present multitude of them . . is no more fitted to the condition of society, than a long-tailed coat becomes a sailor on shipboard." (*Ib.* xi, 130.)

[5] King to his son, May 1, 1816, King, vi, 22.

[6] King to Gore, May 14, 1816, *Ib.* 23–25.

[7] Niles, xiv, 109.   [8] *Ib.* xvi, 257.

which was not generally understood beyond the fact that it involved some sort of trickery. Did any man's wife and family want expensive clothing — the local bank would loan him bills issued by itself, but only on good security. Did any man wish to start some unfamiliar and alluring enterprise by which to make a fortune speedily — if he had a farm to mortgage, the funds were his. Was a big new house desired? The money was at hand — nothing was required to get it but the pledge of property worth many times the amount with which the bank "accommodated" him.[1]

Indeed, the local banks urged such "investments," invited people with property to borrow, laid traps to ensnare them. "What," asked Hezekiah Niles, "is to be the end of such a business? — Mammoth fortunes for the *wise*, wretched poverty for the *foolish*. . . Lands, lots, houses — stock, farming utensils and household furniture, under custody of the sheriff — SPECULATION IN A COACH, HONESTY IN THE JAIL."[2]

Many banks sent agents among the people to hawk their bills. These were perfectly good, the harpies would assure their victims, but they could now be had at a heavy discount; to buy them was to make a large profit. So the farmer, the merchant, even the laborer who had acquired a dwelling of his own, were induced to mortgage their property or sell it outright in exchange for bank paper that often proved to be worthless.[3]

Frequently these local banks ensnared prosperous farmers by the use of "cappers." Niles prints con-

[1] Niles, XVI, 257.   [2] *Ib.* XIV, 110.   [3] *Ib.* 195–96.

spicuously as "A True Story"[1] the account of a
certain farmer who owned two thousand acres, well
improved and with a commodious residence and
substantial farm buildings upon it. Through his land
ran a stream affording good water power. He was
out of debt, prosperous, and contented. One day he
went to a town not many miles from his plantation.
There four pleasant-mannered, well-dressed men
made his acquaintance and asked him to dinner,
where a few directors of the local bank were present.
The conversation was brought around to the profits
to be made in the milling business. The farmer was
induced to borrow a large sum from the local bank
and build a mill, mortgaging his farm to secure
the loan. The mill was built, but seldom used because there was no work for it to do; and, in the
end, the two thousand acres, dwelling, buildings,
mill, and all, became the property of the bank directors.[2]

This incident is illustrative of numerous similar
cases throughout the country, especially in the
West and South. Niles thus describes banking
methods in general: "At first they throw out money
profusely, to all that they believe are *ultimately*
able to return it; nay, they wind round some like ser-
pents to tempt them to borrow — . . they then affect
to draw in their notes, . . money becomes scarce,
and notes of hand are *shaved* by them to meet bank
engagements; it gets worse — the *consummation*

[1] "Niles' *Weekly Register* is . . an excellent repository of facts and
documents." (Jefferson to Crawford, Feb. 11, 1815, *Works:* Ford, xi,
453.)
[2] Niles, xiv, 426–28.

originally designed draws nigh, and farm after farm, lot after lot, house after house, are sacrificed." [1]

So terrifying became the evil that the Legislature of New York, although one of the worst offenders in the granting of bank charters, was driven to appoint a committee of investigation. It reported nothing more than every honest observer had noted. Money could not be transmitted from place to place, the committee said, because local banks had "engrossed the whole circulation in their neighborhood," while their notes abroad had depreciated. The operations of the bankers "immediately within their vicinity" were ruinous: "Designing, unprincipled speculator[s] .. impose on the credulity of the honest, industrious, unsuspecting .. by their specious flattery and misrepresentation, obtaining from them borrowed notes and endorsements, until the ruin is consummated, and their farms are sold by the sheriff." [2]

Some banks committed astonishing frauds, "such as placing a partial fund in a distant bank to redeem their paper" and then "issuing an emission of notes signed with ink of a different shade, at the same time giving secret orders to said bank not to pay the notes thus signed." Bank paper, called *"facility notes,"* was issued, but "payable in neither money, country produce, or any thing else that has body or shape." Bank directors even terrorized merchants who did not submit to their practices. In one typical case all persons were denied discounts who traded at a cer-

[1] Niles, xiv, 2-3.

[2] "Report of the Committee on the Currency of this [New York] State," Feb. 24, 1818, *ib.* 39-42; also partially reproduced in *American History told by Contemporaries:* Hart, iii, 441-45.

tain store, the owner of which had asked for bank bills that would be accepted in New York City, where they had to be remitted — this, too, when the offending merchant kept his account at the bank.

The committee describes, as illustrative of banking chicanery, the instance of "an aged farmer," owner of a valuable farm, who, "wishing to raise the sum of one thousand dollars, to assist his children, was told by a director, he could get it out of the bank . . and that he would endorse his note for him." Thus the loan was made; but, when the note expired, the director refused to obtain a renewal except upon the payment of one hundred dollars in addition to the discount. At the next renewal the same condition was exacted and also "a judgment . . in favor of said director, and the result was, his farm was soon after sold without his knowledge by the sheriff, and purchased by the said director for less than the judgment." [1]

Before the second Bank of the United States opened its doors for business, the local banks began to gather the first fruits of their labors. By the end of 1816 suits upon promissory notes, bonds, and mortgages, given by borrowers, were begun. Three fourths of all judgments rendered in the spring of 1818 by the Supreme Court of the State of New York alone were "in favor of banks, against real property." [2] Suits and judgments of this kind grew ever more frequent.

In such fashion was the country hastened toward the period of bankruptcy. Yet the people in general

[1] "Report of Committee on the Currency," New York, *supra*, 184.
[2] Niles, xiv, 108.

still continued to demand more "money." The worse the curse, the greater the floods of it called for by the body of the public. "Like a dropsical man calling out for water, water, our deluded citizens are clamoring for more banks. . . We are now taught to believe that legerdemain tricks upon paper can produce as solid wealth as hard labor in the earth," wrote Jefferson when the financial madness was becoming too apparent to all thoughtful men.[1]

Practically no restrictions were placed upon these financial freebooters,[2] while such flimsy regulations as their charters provided were disregarded at will.[3] There was practically no publicity as to the management and condition of even the best of these banks;[4] most of them denied the right of any authority to inquire into their affairs and scorned to furnish information as to their assets or methods.[5] For years the Legislatures of many States were controlled by these institutions; bank charters were secured by the worst methods of legislative manipulation; lobbyists thronged the State Capitols when the General Assemblies were in session; few, if any, lawmaking bodies of the States were without officers, directors, or agents of local banks among their membership.[6]

---

[1] Jefferson to Yancey, Jan. 6, 1816, *Works:* Ford, XI, 494.

[2] Dewey, 144; and Sumner: *Hist. Am. Currency,* 75.

[3] Niles proposed a new bank to be called "THE RAGBANK OF THE UNIVERSE," main office at *"Lottery-ville,"* and branches at *"Hookstown," "Owl Creek," "Botany Bay,"* and *"Twisters-burg."* Directors were to be empowered also "to put offices on wheels, on ship-board, or in balloons"; stock to be "one thousand million of old shirts." (Niles, XIV, 227.)

[4] Dewey, 144.   [5] *Ib.* 153–54.

[6] Flint's Letters, *E. W. T.*: Thwaites, IX, 136; and see "Report of the Committee on the Currency," New York, *supra,* 184.

Thus bank charters were granted by wholesale and they were often little better than permits to plunder the public. During the session of the Virginia Legislature of 1816–17, twenty-two applications for bank charters were made.[1] At nearly the same time twenty-one banks were chartered in the newly admitted and thinly peopled State of Ohio.[2] The following year forty-three new banks were authorized in Kentucky.[3] In December, 1818, James Flint found in Kentucky, Ohio, and Tennessee a "vast host of fabricators, and venders of base money."[4] All sorts of "companies" went into the banking business. Bridge companies, turnpike companies, manufacturing companies, mercantile companies, were authorized to issue their bills, and this flood of paper became the "money" of the people; even towns and villages emitted "currency" in the form of municipal notes. The City of Richmond, Virginia, in 1815, issued "small paper bills for change, to the amount of $29,948."[5] Often bills were put in circulation of denominations as low as six and one fourth cents.[6]

---

[1] Tyler: *Tyler*, i, 302; Niles, xi, 130.

[2] Niles, xi, 128.

[3] *Ib.* iv, 109; Collins: *Historical Sketches of Kentucky*, 88.

These were in addition to the branches of the Bank of Kentucky and of the Bank of the United States. Including them, the number of chartered banks in that State was fifty-eight by the close of 1818. Of the towns where new banks were established during that year, Burksville had 106 inhabitants; Barboursville, 55; Hopkinsville, 131; Greenville, 75; thirteen others had fewer than 500 inhabitants. The "capital" of the banks in such places was never less than $100,000, but that at Glasgow, with 244 inhabitants, had a capital of $200,000, and several other villages were similarly favored. For full list see Niles, xiv, 109.

[4] Flint's Letters, *E. W. T.*: Thwaites, ix, 133.   [5] Niles, xvii, 85.

[6] John Woods's Two Years' Residence, *E. W. T.*: Thwaites, x, 236.

Rapidly the property of the people became encumbered to secure their indebtedness to the banks.

A careful and accurate Scotch traveler thus describes their methods: "By lending, and otherwise emitting their engravings, they have contrived to mortgage and buy much of the property of their neighbours, and to appropriate to themselves the labour of less moneyed citizens. . . Bankers gave in exchange for their paper, that of *other banks, equally good with their own.* . . The holder of the paper may comply in the barter, or keep the notes . , ; but he finds it too late to be delivered from the snare. The people committed the lapsus, when they accepted of the gew-gaws clean from the press. . . The deluded multitude have been basely duped." [1] Yet, says Flint, "every one is afraid of bursting the bubble." [2]

As settlers penetrated the Ohio and Indiana forests and spread over the Illinois prairies, the banks went with them and "levied their contributions on the first stroke of the axe." [3] Kentucky was comparatively well settled and furnished many emigrants to the newer regions north of the Ohio River. Rough log cabins were the abodes of nearly all of the people [4]

---

[1] Flint's Letters, *E. W. T.*: Thwaites, ix, 133–34.

[2] *Ib.* 136.   [3] Niles, xiv, 162.

[4] Woods's Two Years' Residence, *E. W. T.*: Thwaites, x, 274–78: and Flint's Letters, *ib.* ix, 69.

In southwestern Indiana, in 1818, Faux "saw nothing . . but miserable log holes, and a mean ville of eight or ten huts or cabins, sadly neglected farms, and indolent, dirty, sickly, wild-looking inhabitants." (Faux's Journal, Nov. 1, 1818, *ib.* xi, 213–14.) He describes Kentucky houses as "miserable holes, having one room only," where "all cook, eat, sleep, breed, and die, males and females, all together." (*Ib.* 185, and see 202.)

who, for the most part, lived roughly,[1] drank heavily,[2] were poorly educated.[3] They were, however, hospitable, generous, and brave; but most of them preferred to speculate rather than to work.[4] Illness was general, sound health rare.[5] "I hate the prairies. . . I would not have any of them of a gift, if I must be compelled to live on them," avowed an English emigrant.[6]

In short, the settlers reproduced most of the features of the same movement in the preceding generation.[7] There was the same squalor, suspicion,

[1] For shocking and almost unbelievable conditions of living among the settlers see Faux's Journal, *E. W. T.*: Thwaites, XI, 226, 231, 252–53, 268–69.

[2] "We landed for some whiskey; for our men would do nothing without." (Woods's Two Years' Residence, *ib.* X, 245, 317.) "Excessive drinking seems the all-pervading, easily-besetting sin." (Faux's Journal, Nov. 3, 1818, *ib.* XI, 213.) This continued for many years and was as marked in the East as in the West. (See Marryat, 2d Series, 37–41.)

There was, however, a large and ever-increasing number who hearkened to those wonderful men, the circuit-riding preachers, who did so much to build up moral and religious America. Most people belonged to some church, and at the camp meetings and revivals, multitudes received conviction.

The student should carefully read the *Autobiography of Peter Cartwright*, edited by W. P. Strickland. This book is an invaluable historical source and is highly interesting. See also Schermerhorn and Mills: *A Correct View of that part of the United States which lies west of the Allegany Mountains, with regard to Religion and Morals. Great Revival in the West*, by Catharine C. Cleveland, is a careful and trustworthy account of religious conditions before the War of 1812. It has a complete bibliography.

[3] Flint's Letters, *E. W. T.*: Thwaites, 153; also Schermerhorn and Mills, 17–18.

[4] "Nature is the agriculturist here [near Princeton, Ind.]; speculation instead of cultivation, is the order of the day amongst men." (Thomas Hulme's Journal, *E. W. T.*: Thwaites, X, 62; see Faux's Journal, *ib.* XI, 227.)

[5] Faux's Journal, *ib.* 216, 236, 242–43.   [6] *Ib.* 214.

[7] See vol. I, chap. VII, of this work.

credulity, and the same combativeness,[1] the same
assertion of superiority over every other people on
earth,[2] the same impatience of control, particularly
from a source so remote as the National Government.[3] "The people speak and seem as if they were
without a government, and name it only as a bugbear," wrote William Faux.[4]

Moreover, the inhabitants of one section knew lit-

[1] Flint's Letters, *E. W. T.*: Thwaites, ix, 87; Woods's Two Years
Residence, *ib.* x, 255. "I saw a man this day . . his nose bitten off close
down to its root, in a fight with a nose-loving neighbour." (Faux's
Journal, *ib.* xi, 222; and see Strickland, 24-25.)

[2] The reports of American conditions by British travelers, although
from unsympathetic pens and much exaggerated, were substantially
true. Thus Europe, and especially the United Kingdom, conceived for
Americans that profound contempt which was to endure for generations.

"Such is the land of Jonathan," declared the *Edinburgh Review* in an
analysis in 1820 (xxxiii, 78-80) of a book entitled *Statistical Annals of
the United States*, by Adam Seybert. "He must not . . allow himself to
be dazzled by that galaxy of epithets by which his orators and newspaper scribblers endeavour to persuade their supporters that they are
the greatest, the most refined, the most enlightened, and the most
moral people upon earth. . . They have hitherto given no indications
of genius, and made no approaches to the heroic, either in their morality or character. . .

"During the thirty or forty years of their independence, they have
done absolutely nothing for the Sciences, for the Arts, for Literature,
or even for statesman-like studies of Politics or Political Economy. . .
In the four quarters of the globe, who reads an American book? or
goes to an American play? or looks at an American picture or statue?
What does the world yet owe to American physicians or surgeons?
What new substances have their chemists discovered? or what old
ones have they analyzed? What new constellations have been discovered by the telescopes of Americans? — what have they done in the
mathematics? . . under which of the old tyrannical governments of
Europe is every sixth man a Slave, whom his fellow-creatures may buy
and sell and torture?"

[3] Nevertheless, these very settlers had qualities of sound, clean
citizenship; and beneath their roughness and crudity were noble as-
pirations. For a sympathetic and scholarly treatment of this phase of
the subject see Pease: *Frontier State*, i, 69.

[4] Faux's Journal, *E. W. T.*: Thwaites, xi, 246.

tle or nothing of what those in another were doing. "We are as ignorant of the temper prevailing in the Eastern States as the people of New Holland can be," testifies John Randolph in 1812.[1] Even a generation after Randolph made this statement, Frederick Marryat records that "the United States . . comprehend an immense extent of territory, with a population running from a state of refinement down to one of positive barbarism. . . The inhabitants of the cities . . know as little of what is passing in Arkansas and Alabama as a cockney does of the manners and customs of . . the Isle of Man." [2] Communities were still almost as segregated as were those of a half-century earlier.[3] Marryat observes, a few years later, that "to write upon America *as a nation* would be absurd, for nation . . it is not." [4] Again, he notes in his journal that "the mass of the citizens of the United States have . . a very great dislike to all law except . . the decision of the majority." [5]

These qualities furnished rich soil for cultivation by demagogues, and small was the husbandry required to produce a sturdy and bellicose sentiment of Localism. Although the bills of the Bank of the United States were sought for,[6] the hostility to that National institution was increased rather than diminished by the superiority of its notes over those of the local money mills. No town was too small for a bank. The fact that specie payments were not exacted "indicated every village in the United

---

[1] Randolph to Quincy, Aug. 16, 1812, Quincy: *Quincy*, 270.
[2] Marryat, 2d Series, 1.   [3] See vol. I, chap. VII, of this work.
[4] Marryat, 1st Series, 15.   [5] Marryat, 2d Series, 176.
[6] Woods's Two Years' Residence, *E. W. T.*: Thwaites, x, 325.

States, where there was a 'church, a tavern and a blacksmith's shop,' as a suitable site for a *bank*, and justified any persons in establishing one who could raise enough to pay the *paper maker* and *engraver*." [1]

Not only did these chartered manufactories of currency multiply, but private banks sprang up and did business without any restraint whatever. Niles was entirely within the truth when he declared that nothing more was necessary to start a banking business than plates, presses, and paper.[2] Often the notes of the banks, private or incorporated, circulated only in the region where they were issued.[3] In 1818 the "currency" of the local banks of Cincinnati was "mere waste paper . . out of the city." [4] The people had to take this local "money" or go without any medium of exchange. When the notes of distant banks were to be had, the people did not know the value of them. "Notes current in one part, are either refused, or taken at a large discount, in another," wrote Flint in 1818.[5]

In the cities firms dealing with bank bills printed

---

[1] Niles, xiv, 2.

[2] See McMaster, iv, 287. This continued even after the people had at last become suspicious of unlicensed banks. In 1820, at Bloomington, Ohio, a hamlet of "ten houses . . in the edge of the prairie . . a [bank] company was formed, plates engraved, and the bank notes brought to the spot." Failing to secure a charter, the adventurers sold their outfit at auction, fictitious names were signed to the notes, which were then put into fraudulent circulation. (Flint's Letters, *E. W. T.*: Thwaites, ix, 310.)

[3] *Ib.* 130–31.

[4] Faux's Journal, Oct. 11, 1818, *E. W. T.*: Thwaites, xi, 171. Faux says that even in Cincinnati itself the bank bills of that town could be exchanged at stores "only 30 or 40 per centum below par, or United States' paper."

[5] Flint's Letters, *E. W. T.*: Thwaites, ix, 132–36.

lists of them with the market values, which changed from day to day.[1] Sometimes the county courts fixed rates of exchange; for instance, the County Court of Norfolk County, Virginia, in March, 1816, decreed that the notes of the Bank of Virginia and the Bank of South Carolina were worth their face value, while the bills of Baltimore and Philadelphia and the District of Columbia were below par.[2] Merchants had to keep lists on which was estimated the value of bank bills and to take chances on the constant fluctuations of them.[3] "Of upwards of a hundred banks that lately figured in Indiana, Ohio, Kentucky, and Tennessee, the money of two is now only received in the land-office, in payment for public lands," testifies Flint, writing from Jeffersonville, Indiana, in March, 1820. "Discount," he adds, "varies from thirty to one hundred per cent."[4] By September, 1818, two thirds of the bank bills sent to Niles in payment for the *Register* could not "be passed for money."[5]

"Chains" of banks were formed by which one member of the conspiracy would redeem its notes only by paying out the bills of another. Thus, if a man presented at the counter of a certain bank the bills issued by it, he was given in exchange those of another bank; when these were taken to this second

---

[1] In Baltimore Cohens's "lottery and exchange office" issued a list of nearly seventy banks, with rates of prices on their notes. The circular gave notice that the quotations were good for one day only. (Niles, xiv, 396.) At the same time G. & R. Waite, with offices in New York, Philadelphia, and Baltimore, issued a list covering the country from Connecticut to Ohio and Kentucky. (*Ib.* 415.) The rates as given by this firm differed greatly from those published by Cohens.

[2] *Ib.* x, 80.   [3] Sumner: *Jackson*, 229.

[4] Flint's Letters, *E. W. T.*: Thwaites, ix, 219.   [5] Niles, xv, 60.

institution, they were exchanged for the bills of a third bank, which redeemed them with notes of the first.[1] For instance, Bigelow's bank at Jefferson-ville, Indiana, redeemed its notes with those of Pi-att's bank at Cincinnati, Ohio; this, in turn, paid its bills with those of a Vincennes sawmill and the saw-mill exchanged its paper for that of Bigelow's bank.[2]

The redemption of their bills by the payment of specie was refused even by the best State banks, and this when the law positively required it. Niles esti-mated in April, 1818, that, although many banks were sound and honestly conducted, there were not "half a dozen banks in the United States that are able to pay their debts *as théy are payable.*" [3]

All this John Marshall saw and experienced. In 1815, George Fisher [4] presented to the Bank of Virginia ten of its one-hundred-dollar notes for re-demption, which was refused. After several months' delay, during which the bank officials ignored a summons to appear in court, a distringas [5] was secured. The President of the bank, Dr. Brocken-brough, resisted service of the writ, and the "Sheriff then called upon the by-standers, as a *posse comi-tatus,*" to assist him. Among these was the Chief Justice of the United States. Fisher had hard work in finding a lawyer to take his case; for months no member of the bar would act as his attorney.[6] For

---

[1] Niles, xiv, 193–96; also xv, 434.   [2] *Ib.* xvii, 164.   [3] *Ib.* xiv, 108.

[4] A wealthy Richmond merchant who had married a sister of Marshall's wife. (See vol. ii, 172, of this work.)

[5] A writ directing the sheriff to seize the goods and chattels of a person to compel him to satisfy an obligation. Bouvier (Rawle's ed.) i, 590.

[6] Richmond *Enquirer*, Jan. 16, 1816.

What was the outcome of this incident does not appear. Professor

in Virginia as elsewhere — even less than in many States — the local banks were the most lucrative clients and the strongest political influence; and they controlled the lawyers as well as the press.

In June, 1818, for instance, a business man in Pennsylvania had accumulated several hundred dollars in bills of a local bank which refused to redeem them in specie or better bills. Three justices of the peace declined to entertain suit against the bank and no notary public would protest the bills. In Maryland, at the same time, a man succeeded in bringing an action against a bank for the redemption of some of its bills; but the cashier, while admitting his own signature on the notes, swore that he could not identify that of the bank's president, who had absented himself.[1]

Counterfeiting was widely practiced and, for a time, almost unpunished; a favorite device was the raising of notes, usually from five to fifty dollars. Bills were put in circulation purporting to have been issued by distant banks that did not exist, and never had existed. In a single week of June, 1818, the country newspapers contained accounts of twenty-eight cases of these and similar criminal operations.[2] Sometimes a forger or counterfeiter was caught; at Plattsburg, New York, one of these had twenty different kinds of fraudulent notes, "well executed."[3]

Sumner says that the bank was closed for a few days, but soon opened and went on with its business. (Sumner: *Hist. Am. Currency*, 74–75.) Sumner fixes the date in 1817, two years after the event.

[1] Niles, xiv, 281.   [2] *Ib.* 314–15.

[3] *Ib.* 333; and for similar cases, see *ib.* 356, 396–97, 428–30. All these accounts were taken from newspapers at the places where criminals were captured.

In August, 1818, Niles estimates that "the notes of
at least ONE HUNDRED banks in the United States are
counterfeited." [1] By the end of the year an organized
gang of counterfeiters, forgers, and distributors of
their products covered the whole country. [2] Counter-
feits of the Marine Bank of Baltimore alone were
estimated at $1,000,000; [3] one-hundred-dollar notes
of the Bank of Louisiana were scattered far and wide. [4]
Scarcely an issue of any newspaper appeared without
notices of these depredations; [5] one half of the remittances sent Niles from the West were counter-
feit. [6]

Into this chaos of speculation, fraud, and financial fiction came the second Bank of the United
States. The management of it, at the beginning, was
adventurous, erratic, corrupt; its officers and directors countenanced the most shameful manipulation of the Bank's stock; some of them participated
in the incredible jobbery. [7] Nothing of this, however, was known to the country at large for many
months, [8] nor did the knowledge of it, when revealed,
afford the occasion for the popular wrath that soon
came to be directed against the National Bank. This
public hostility, indeed, was largely produced by
measures which the Bank took to retrieve the early
business blunders of its managers.

These blunders were appalling. As soon as it

[1] Niles, xiv, 428.   [2] Ib. xvi, 147–48; also, ib. 360, 373, 390.
[3] Ib. 179.   [4] Ib. 210.   [5] Ib. 208.   [6] Ib. 210.
[7] See Catterall, 39–50.
[8] The frauds of the directors and officers of the Bank of the United
States were used, however, as the pretext for an effort to repeal its
charter. On Feb. 9, 1819, James Johnson of Virginia introduced a resolution for that purpose. (Annals, 15th Cong. 2d Sess. iii, 1140–42.)

opened in 1817, the Bank began to do business on the
inflated scale which the State banks had established;
by over-issue of its notes it increased the inflation,
already blown to the bursting point. Except in New
England, where its loans were moderate and well
secured, it accommodated borrowers lavishly. The
branches were not required to limit their business to
a fixed capital; in many cases, the branch officers and
directors, incompetent and swayed by local interest
and feeling,[1] issued notes as recklessly as did some
of the State banks. In the West particularly, and
also in the South, the loans made were enormous.
The borrowers had no expectation of paying them
when due, but of renewing them from time to time,
as had been the practice under State banking.

The National branches in these regions showed a
faint gleam of prudence by refusing to accept bills
of notoriously unsound local banks. This undemocratic partiality, although timidly exercised, aroused
to activity the never-slumbering hostility of these
local concerns. In the course of business, however,
bills of most State banks accumulated to an immense
amount in the vaults of the branches of the Bank
of the United States. When, in spite of the disposition of the branch officers to extend unending and
unlimited indulgence to the State banks and to borrowers generally, the branches finally were compelled
by the parent Bank to demand payment of loans and
redemption of bills of local banks held by it; and
when, in consequence, the State banks were forced
to collect debts due them, the catastrophe, so long

[1] See Catterall, 32.

preparing, fell upon sections where the vices of State banking had been practiced most flagrantly.

Suits upon promissory notes, bonds and mortgages, already frequent, now became incessant; sheriffs were never idle. In the autumn of 1818, in a single small county [1] of Delaware, one hundred and fifty such actions were brought by the banks. In addition to this, records the financial chronicler of the period, "their vaults are loaded with bonds, mortgages and other securities, held *in terrorem* over the heads of several hundreds more." [2] At Harrisburg, Pennsylvania, one bank brought more than one hundred suits during May, 1818;[3] a few months later a single issue of one country newspaper in Pennsylvania contained advertisements of eighteen farms and mills at sheriff's sale; a village newspaper in New York advertised sixty-three farms and lots to be sold under the sheriff's hammer.[4] "Currency" decreased in quantity; unemployment was amazing; scores of thousands of men begged for work; throngs of the idle camped near cities and subsisted on charity.[5]

All this the people laid at the doors of the National Bank, while the State banks,[6] of course, encouraged the popular animosity. Another order of the National concern increased the anger of the people and of the State banks against it. For more than a year the parent institution and its branches had redeemed all notes issued by them wherever presented. Since the notes from the West and South

---

[1] New Castle County.   [2] Niles, xv, 162.   [3] *Ib.* 59.   [4] *Ib.* 418.
[5] Flint's Letters, *E. W. T.*: Thwaites, ix, 226.
[6] They, too, asserted that institution to be the author of their woes. (Niles, xvii, 2.)

flowed to the North and East [1] in payment for the manufactures and merchandise of these sections, this universal redemption became impossible. So, on August 28, 1818, the branches were directed to refuse all notes except their own. [2]

Thus the Bank, "like an *abandoned* mother, . . BASTARDIZED its offspring," [3] said the enemies of the National Bank, among them all State banks and most of the people. The enforcement of redemption of State bank bills, the reduction of the volume of "currency," were the real causes of the fury with which the Bank of the United States and its branches was now assailed. That institution was the monster, said local orators and editors; its branches were the tentacles of the Octopus, heads of the Hydra. [4] "The 'branches' are execrated on all hands," wrote an Ohio man. "We *feel* that to the policy pursued by them, we are indebted for all the evils we experience for want of a circulating medium." [5]

The popular cry was for relief. More money, not less, was needed, it was said; and more banks that could and would loan funds with which to pay debts. If the creditor would not accept the currency thus procured, let laws be passed that would compel him to do so, or prevent him from collecting what his contract called for. Thus, with such demands upon their lips, and in the midst of a storm of lawsuits, the people entered at last that inevitable period of bank-

[1] Catterall, 33–37.
[2] *Ib.* 51–53; and see Niles. xv, 25.   [3] Catterall, 33.
[4] Monster, Hydra, Cerberus, Octopus, and names of similar import were popularly applied to the Bank of the United States. (See Crawford's speech, *supra*, 175.)
[5] Niles, xv, 5.

ruptcy to which for years they had been drawing nearer and for which they were themselves largely responsible.

Bankruptcy laws had already been enacted by some States; and if these acts had not been drawn for the benefit of speculators in anticipation of the possible evil day, the "insolvency" statutes certainly had been administered for the protection of rich and dishonest men who wished to escape their liabilities, and yet to preserve their assets. In New York[1] the debtor was enabled to discharge all accounts by turning over such property as he had; if he owed ten thousand dollars, and possessed but fifty dollars, his debt was cancelled by the surrender of that sum. For the honest and prudent man the law was just, since no great discrepancy usually existed between his reported assets and his liabilities. But lax administration of it afforded to the dishonest adventurer a shield from the righteous consequences of his wrongdoing.

The "bankruptcies" of knavish men were common operations. One merchant in an Eastern city "failed," but contrived to go on living in a house for which he "was offered $200,000 in real money."[2] Another in Philadelphia became "insolvent," yet had $7000 worth of wine in his cellar at the very time he was going through "bankruptcy."[3] A merchant tailor in the little town of York, Pennsylvania, resorted to bankruptcy to clear himself of eighty four thousand dollars of debt.[4]

---

[1] Act of April 3, 1811, *Laws of New York, 1811*, 205–21.
[2] Niles, xvi, 257.   [3] *Ib.*   [4] *Ib.* xvii, 147.

In their speculations adventurous men counted on the aid of these legislative acts for the relief of debtors. "Never . . have any . . laws been more productive of crime than the insolvent laws of Maryland," testifies Niles.[1] One issue of the *Federal Gazette* contained six columns of bankruptcy notices, and these were only about "one-third of the persons" then "'going through our mill.'" Several "bankrupts" had been millionaires, and continued to "*live in splendid affluence*, . . their wives and children, or some kind relative, having been made rich through their swindlings of the people."[2] Many "insolvents" were bankers; and this led Niles to propose that the following law be adopted:

"'Whereas certain persons . . *unknown*, have petitioned for the establishment of a bank at ——:

"'Be it enacted, that . . these persons, . . shall have liberty to become BANKRUPTS, and may legally swindle as much as they can.'"[3]

In a Senate debate in March, 1820, for a proposed new National Bankruptcy Act,[4] Senator Harrison Gray Otis of Massachusetts moderately stated the results of the State insolvency laws. "Merchants and traders . . are harassed and perplexed by twenty

---

[1] "I have known several to *calculate* upon the 'relief' from them, just as they would do on an accommodation at bank, or on the payment of debts due to them! If we succeed in such and such a thing, say they — very well; if not, we can get the benefit of the insolvent laws . . Where one prudent and honest man applies for such benefit, one hundred rogues are facilitated in their depredations." (Niles, XVII, 115.)

[2] *Ib.*   [3] *Ib.* xv, 283.

[4] The bankruptcy law which Marshall had helped to draw when in Congress (see vol. II, 481–82, of this work) had been repealed in 1803. (*Annals*, 8th Cong. 1st Sess. 215, 625, 631. For reasons for the repeal see *ib.* 616–22.)

different systems of municipal laws, often repugnant to each other and themselves; always defective; seldom executed in good faith; prolific in endless frauds, perjuries, and evasions; and never productive of . . any sort of justice, to the creditor. Nothing could be . . comparable to their pernicious effects upon the public morals." [1] Senator Prentiss Mellen, of the same State, described the operation of the bankruptcy mill thus: "We frequently witness transactions, poisoned throughout with fraud . . in which *all* creditors are deceived and defrauded. . . The man *pretends* to be a bankrupt; and having converted a large portion of his property into money . . he . . closes his doors; . . goes through the form of offering to give up all his property, (though secretly retaining thousands,) on condition of receiving a discharge from his creditors. . . In a few months, or perhaps weeks, he recommences business, and finds himself . . with a handsome property at command." [2]

Senator James Burrill, Jr., of Rhode Island was equally specific and convincing. He pictured the career of a dishonest merchant, who transfers property to relatives, secures a discharge from the State bankruptcy courts, and "in a few days . . resumes his career of folly, extravagance, and rashness. . . Thus the creditors are defrauded, and the debtor, in many cases, lives in affluence and splendor." [3] Flint records that "mutual credit and confidence are almost torn up by the roots." [4]

[1] *Annals*, 16th Cong. 1st Sess. 505.   [2] *Ib.* 513.   [3] *Ib.* 517–18.
[4] Flint's Letters, *E. W. T.*: Thwaites, ix, 225.
In reviewing *Sketches of America* by Henry Bradshaw Fearon, an Englishman who traveled through the United States, the *Quarterly*

It was soon to be the good fortune of John Marshall to declare such State legislation null and void because in violation of the National Constitution. Never did common honesty, good faith, and fair dealing need such a stabilizing power as at the moment Marshall furnished to the American people. In most parts of the country even insolvency laws did not satisfy debtors; they were trying to avoid the results of their own acts by securing the enactment of local statutes that repealed the natural laws of human intercourse — of statutes that expressed the momentary wish of the uncomfortable, if honest, multitude, but that represented no less the devices of the clever and unscrupulous. Fortunate, indeed, was it for the United States, at this critical time in its development, that one department of the Government could not be swayed by the passion of the hour, and thrice happy that the head of that department was John Marshall.

The impression made directly on Marshall by what took place under his very eyes in Virginia was strengthened by events that occurred in Kentucky. All his brothers and sisters, except two, besides numerous cousins and relatives by marriage, lived there. Thus he was advised in an intimate and personal way of what went forward in that State.[1]

Review of London scathingly denounced the frauds perpetrated by means of insolvent laws. (*Quarterly Review*, xxi, 165.)

[1] None of these letters to Marshall have been preserved. Indeed, only a scant half-dozen of the original great number of letters written him even by prominent men during his long life are in existence. For those of men like Story and Pickering we are indebted to copies preserved in their papers.

Marshall, at best, was incredibly negligent of his correspondence

The indebtedness of Kentucky State banks, and of individual borrowers to the branches of the National Bank located in that Commonwealth, amounted to more than two and one half millions of dollars.[1] "This is the *trifling* sum which the people of Kentucky are called upon to pay in *specie!*"[2] exclaimed a Kentucky paper. The people of that State owed the local banks about $7,000,000 more, while the total indebtedness to all financial institutions within Kentucky was not far from $10,000,000.[3] The sacrifice of property for the satisfaction of mortgages grew ever more distressing. At Lexington, a house and lot, for which the owner had refused $15,000, brought but $1300 at sheriff's sale; another costing $10,000 sold under the hammer for $1500.[4] Even slaves could be sold only at a small fraction of their ordinary market price.

It was the same in other States. Within Marshall's personal observation in Virginia the people were forced to eat the fruits of their folly. "Lands in this State cannot now be sold for a year's rent," wrote Jefferson.[5] A farm near Easton, Pennsylvania, worth $12,500, mortgaged to secure a debt of $2500, was taken by the lender on foreclosure for the amount of the loan. A druggist's stock of the retail value of $10,000 was seized for rent by the landlord and sold for $400.[6] In Virginia a little later a farm

as he was of all other ordinary details of life. Most other important men of the time kept copies of their letters; Marshall kept none; and if he preserved those written to him, nearly all of them have disappeared.

[1] Niles, xv, 385.   [2] *Ib.*   [3] *Ib.* xvi, 261.   [4] *Ib.* xvii, 85.
[5] Jefferson to Adams, Nov. 7, 1819, *Works:* Ford, xii, 145.
[6] Niles, xvii, 85.

of three hundred acres with improvements worth, at the lowest estimate, $1500, sold for $300; two wagon horses costing $200 were sacrificed for $40.

Mines were shut down, shops closed, taxes unpaid. "The debtor . . gives up his land, and, ruined and undone, seeks a home for himself and his family in the western wilderness." [1] John Quincy Adams records in his diary: "Staple productions . . are falling to . . less than half the prices which they have lately borne, the merchants are crumbling to ruin, the manufactures perishing, agriculture stagnating, and distress universal in every part of the country." [2]

During the summer and autumn of 1818, the popular demand for legislation that would suspend contracts, postpone the payment of debts, and stay the judgment of courts, became strident and peremptory. "Our greatest real evil is the question between debtor and creditor, into which the banks have plunged us deeper than would have been possible without them," testifies Adams. "The bank debtors are everywhere so numerous and powerful that they control the newspapers throughout the Union, and give the discussion a turn extremely erroneous, and prostrate every principle of political economy." [3]

This was especially true of Kentucky. Throughout the State great assemblages were harangued by oratorical "friends of the people." "The reign of political quackery was in its glory." [4] Why the

---

[1] Niles, XVII, 185.
[2] *Memoirs, J. Q. A.*: Adams, May 27, 1819, IV, 375.
[3] *Ib.* 391.   [4] Collins, 88.

scarcity of money when that commodity was most needed? Why the lawsuits for the collection of debts, the enforcement of bonds, the foreclosure of mortgages, instead of the renewal of loans, to which debtors had been accustomed? Financial manipulation had done it all. The money power was responsible for the misery of the people. Let that author and contriver of human suffering be suppressed.

What could be easier or more just than to enact legislation that would lift the burden of debt that was crushing the people? The State banks would not resist — were they not under the control of the people's Legislature? But they were also at the mercy of that remorseless creature of the National Government, the Bank of the United States. That malign Thing was the real cause of all the trouble.[1] Let the law by which Congress had given illegitimate life to that destroyer of the people's well-being be repealed. If that could not be done because so many of the National Legislature were corruptly interested in the Bank, the States had a sure weapon with which to destroy it — or at least to drive it out of business in every member of the Union.

That weapon was taxation. Let each Legislature, by special taxes, strangle the branches of the National Bank operating in the States. So came a popular determination to exterminate, by State action, the second Bank of the United States. Na-

---

[1] "The disappointment is altogether ascribed to the Bank of the U. S." (King to Mason, Feb. 7, 1819, King, VI, 205.) King's testimony is uncommonly trustworthy. His son was an officer of the branch of Chillicothe, Ohio.

tional power should be brought to its knees by local authority! National agencies should be made helpless and be dispatched by State prohibition and State taxation! The arm of the National Government should be paralyzed by the blows showered on it when thrusting itself into the affairs of "sovereign" States! Already this process was well under way.

The first Constitution of Indiana, adopted soon after Congress had authorized the second Bank of the United States, prohibited any bank chartered outside the State from doing business within its borders.[1] During the very month that the National Bank opened its doors in 1817, the Legislature of Maryland passed an act taxing the Baltimore branch $15,000 annually. Seven months afterward the Legislature of Tennessee enacted a law that any bank not chartered under its authority should pay $50,000 each year for the privilege of banking in that State. A month later Georgia placed a special tax on branches of the Bank of the United States.

The Constitution of Illinois, adopted in August, 1818, forbade the establishment of any but State banks. In December of that year North Carolina taxed the branch of the National Bank in that State $5000 per annum. A few weeks later Kentucky laid an annual tax of $60,000 on each of the two branches of the Bank of the United States located at Lexington and Frankfort. Three weeks before John Marshall delivered his opinion in M'Culloch *vs.* Maryland, Ohio enacted a statute placing a yearly

[1] See Article x, Section 1, Constitution of Indiana, as adopted June 29, 1816.

tax of $50,000 on each of the two National Bank branches then doing business in that State.[1]

Thus the extinction of the second Bank of the United States by State legislation appeared to be inevitable. The past management of it had well deserved this fate; but earnest efforts were now in operation to recover it from former blunders and to retrieve its fortunes. The period of corruption was over, and a new, able, and honest management was about to take charge. If, however, the States could destroy this National fiscal agency, it mattered not how well it might thereafter be conducted, for nothing could be more certain than that the local influence of State banks always would be great enough to induce State Legislatures to lay impossible burdens on the National Bank.

Such, then, was the situation that produced those opinions of Marshall on insolvency, on contract, and on a National bank, delivered during February and March of 1819; such the National conditions which confronted him during the preceding summer and autumn. He could do nothing to ameliorate these conditions, nothing to relieve the universal unhappiness, nothing to appease the popular discontent. But he could establish great National principles, which would give steadiness to American business, vitality to the National Government; and which would encourage the people to practice honesty, prudence, and thrift. And just this John Marshall did. When considering the enduring work he performed at this time, we must have in our thought

[1] See Catterall, 64–65, and sources there cited.

the circumstances that made that work vitally necessary.

One of the earliest cases decided by the Supreme
Court in 1819 involved the Bankrupt Law of New
York. On November 25, 1817, Josiah Sturges [1] of
Massachusetts sued Richard Crowninshield of New
York in the United States Circuit Court for the
District of Massachusetts to recover upon two promissory notes for the sum of $771.86 each, exe-
cuted March 22, 1811, just twelve days before the
passage, April 3, 1811, of the New York statute
for the relief of insolvent debtors. The defendant
pleaded his discharge under that act. The judges
were divided in opinion on the questions whether
a State can pass a bankrupt act, whether the New
York law was a bankrupt act, and whether it impaired the obligations of a contract. These questions were, accordingly, certified to the Supreme
Court.

The case was there argued long and exhaustively
by David Daggett and Joseph Hopkinson for Sturges
and by David B. Ogden and William Hunter for
Crowninshield. In weight of reasoning and full citation of authority, the discussion was inferior only
to those contests before the Supreme Bench which
have found a place in history.

On February 17, 1819, Marshall delivered the
unanimous opinion of the court. [2] Do the words of
the Constitution, "Congress shall have power . .
to establish . . uniform laws on the subject of

---

[1] Spelled *Sturgis* on the manuscript records of the Supreme Court.
[2] 4 Wheaton, 192.

bankruptcies throughout the United States" take from the States the right to pass such laws?

Before the adoption of the Constitution, begins Marshall, the States "united for some purposes, but, in most respects, sovereign," could "exercise almost every legislative power." The powers of the States under the Constitution were not defined in that instrument. "These powers proceed, not from the people of America, but from the people of the several states; and remain, after the adoption of the constitution, what they were before, except so far as they may be abridged" by the Nation's fundamental law.

While the "mere grant of a power to Congress" does not necessarily mean that the States are forbidden to exercise the same power, such concurrent power does not extend to "every possible case" not expressly prohibited by the Constitution. "The confusion resulting from such a practice would be endless." As a general principle, declares the Chief Justice, "whenever the terms in which a power is granted to Congress, or the nature of the power, required that it should be exercised exclusively by Congress, the subject is as completely taken from the state legislatures as if they had been expressly forbidden to act on it." [1]

Does this general principle apply to bankrupt laws? Assuredly it does. Congress is empowered to "establish uniform laws on the subject throughout the United States." Uniform National legislation is "incompatible with state legislation" on the same

[1] 4 Wheaton, 192–93.

subject. Marshall draws a distinction between bankrupt and insolvency laws, although "the line of partition between them is not so distinctly marked" that it can be said, "with positive precision, what belongs exclusively to the one, and not to the other class of laws." [1]

He enters upon an examination of the nature of insolvent laws which States may enact, and bankrupt laws which Congress may enact; and finds that "there is such a connection between them as to render it difficult to say how far they may be blended together. . . A bankrupt law may contain those regulations which are generally found in insolvent laws"; while "an insolvent law may contain those which are common to a bankrupt law." It is "obvious," then, that it would be a hardship to "deny to the state legislatures the power of acting on this subject, in consequence of the grant to Congress." The true rule — "certainly a convenient one" — is to "consider the power of the states as existing over such cases as the laws of the Union may not reach." [2]

But, whether this common-sense construction is adopted or not, it is undeniable that Congress may exercise a power granted to it or decline to exercise it. So, if Congress thinks that uniform bankrupt laws "ought not to be established" throughout the country, surely the State Legislatures ought not, on that account, to be prevented from passing bankrupt acts. The idea of Marshall, the statesman, was that it was better to have bankrupt laws of some kind than none at all. "It is not the mere existence

[1] 4 Wheaton, 194.   [2] *Ib.* 195.

of the power [in Congress], but its exercise, which is incompatible with the exercise of the same power by the states. It is not the right to establish these uniform laws, but their actual establishment, which is inconsistent with the partial acts of the states." [1]

Even should Congress pass a bankrupt law, that action does not extinguish, but only suspends, the power of the State to legislate on the same subject. When Congress repeals a National bankrupt law it merely "removes a disability" of the State created by the enactment of the National statute, and lasting only so long as that statute is in force. In short, "until the power to pass uniform laws on the subject of bankruptcies be exercised by Congress, the states are not forbidden to pass a bankrupt law, provided it contain no principle which violates the 10th section of the first article of the constitution of the United States." [2]

Having toilsomely reached this conclusion, Marshall comes to what he calls "the great question on which the cause must depend": Does the New York Bankrupt Law "impair the obligation of contracts"?[3]

What is the effect of that law? It "liberates the person of the debtor, and discharges him from all liability for any debt previously contracted, on his surrendering his property in the manner it prescribes." Here Marshall enters upon that series of expositions of the contract clause of the Constitu-

---

[1] 4 Wheaton, 196.

[2] "No State shall . . emit Bills of Credit; make any Thing but gold and silver Coin a Tender in Payment of Debts; pass any . . ex post facto Law, or Law impairing the Obligation of Contracts."

[3] 4 Wheaton, 196–97.

tion which, next to the Nationalism of his opinions, is, perhaps, the most conspicuous feature of his philosophy of government and human intercourse.[1] "What is the obligation of a contract? and what will impair it?" [2]

It would be hard to find words "more intelligible, or less liable to misconstruction, than those which are to be explained." With a tinge of patient impatience, the Chief Justice proceeds to define the words "contract," "impair," and "obligation," much as a weary school teacher might teach the simplest lesson to a particularly dull pupil.

"A contract is an agreement in which a party undertakes to do, or not to do, a particular thing. The law binds him to perform his undertaking, and this is, of course, the obligation of his contract. In the case at bar, the defendant has given his promissory note to pay the plaintiff a sum of money on or before a certain day. The contract binds him to pay that sum on that day; and this is its obligation. Any law which releases a part of this obligation, must, in the literal sense of the word, impair it. Much more must a law impair it which makes it totally invalid, and entirely discharges it.

"The words of the constitution, then, are express, and incapable of being misunderstood. They admit of no variety of construction, and are acknowledged to apply to that species of contract, an engagement between man and man, for the payment of money, which has been entered into by these parties." [3]

[1] For the proceedings in the Constitutional Convention on this clause, see vol. III, chap. x, of this work.

[2] 4 Wheaton, 197.   [3] *Ib.* 197–98.

What are the arguments that such law does not violate the Constitution? One is that, since a contract "can only bind a man to pay to the full extent of his property, it is an implied condition that he may be discharged on surrendering the whole of it." This is simply not true, says Marshall. When a contract is made, the parties to it have in mind, not only existing property, but "future acquisitions. Industry, talents and integrity, constitute a fund which is as confidently trusted as property itself. Future acquisitions are, therefore, liable for contracts; and to release them from this liability impairs their obligation." [1]

Marshall brushes aside, almost brusquely, the argument that the only reason for the adoption of the contract clause by the Constitutional Convention was the paper money evil; that the States always had passed bankrupt and insolvent laws; and that if the framers of the Constitution had intended to deprive the States of this power, "insolvent laws would have been mentioned in the prohibition."

No power whatever, he repeats, is conferred on the States by the Constitution. That instrument found them "in possession" of practically all legislative power and either prohibited "its future exercise entirely," or restrained it "so far as national policy may require."

While the Constitution permits States to pass bankrupt laws "until that power shall be exercised by Congress," the fundamental law positively for-

---

[1] 4 Wheaton, 198.

bids the States to "introduce into such laws a
clause which discharges the obligations the bankrupt has entered into. It is not admitted that,
without this principle, an act cannot be a bankrupt
law; and if it were, that admission would not change
the constitution, nor exempt such acts from its
prohibitions." [1]

There was, said Marshall, nothing in the argument
that, if the framers of the Constitution had intended
to "prohibit the States from passing insolvent
laws," they would have plainly said so. "It was not
necessary, nor would it have been safe" for them to
have enumerated "particular subjects to which the
principle they intended to establish should apply."

On this subject, as on every other dealt with in
the Constitution, fundamental principles are set
out. What is the one involved in this case? It is
"the inviolability of contracts. This principle was
to be protected in whatsoever form it might be
assailed. To what purpose enumerate the particular
modes of violation which should be forbidden, when
it was intended to forbid all? . . The plain and simple
declaration, that no state shall pass any law impairing the obligation of contracts, includes insolvent laws and all other laws, so far as they
infringe the principle the convention intended to
hold sacred, and no farther." [2]

At this point Marshall displays the humanitarian
which, in his character, was inferior only to the
statesman. He was against imprisonment for debt,
one of the many brutal customs still practiced.

[1] 4 Wheaton, 199.   [2] *Ib.* 200.

"The convention did not intend to prohibit the passage of all insolvent laws," he avows. "To punish honest insolvency by imprisonment for life, and to make this a constitutional principle, would be an excess of inhumanity which will not readily be imputed to the illustrious patriots who framed our constitution, nor to the people who adopted it. . . Confinement of the debtor may be a punishment for not performing his contract, or may be allowed as a means of inducing him to perform it. But the state may refuse to inflict this punishment, or may withhold this means and leave the contract in full force. Imprisonment is no part of the contract, and simply to release the prisoner does not impair its obligation." [1]

Following his provoking custom of taking up a point with which he had already dealt, Marshall harks back to the subject of the reason for inserting the contract clause into the Constitution. He restates the argument against applying that provision to State insolvent laws — that, from the beginning, the Colonies and States had enacted such legislation; that the history of the times shows that "the mind of the convention was directed to other laws which were fraudulent in their character, which enabled the debtor to escape from his obligation, and yet hold his property, not to this, which is beneficial in its operation."

But, he continues, "the spirit of . . a constitution" is not to be determined solely by a partial view of the history of the times when it was adopted

[1] 4 Wheaton, 200–01.

— "the spirit is to be collected chiefly from its words." And "it would be dangerous in the extreme to infer from extrinsic circumstances, that a case for which the words of an instrument expressly provide, shall be exempted from its operation." Where language is obscure, where words conflict, "construction becomes necessary." But, when language is clear, words harmonious, the plain meaning of that language and of those words is not "to be disregarded, because we believe the framers of that instrument could not intend what they say." [1]

The practice of the Colonies, and of the States before the Constitution was adopted, was a weak argument at best. For example, the Colonies and States had issued paper money, emitted bills of credit, and done other things, all of which the Constitution prohibits. "If the long exercise of the power to emit bills of credit did not restrain the convention from prohibiting its future exercise, neither can it be said that the long exercise of the power to impair the obligation of contracts, should prevent a similar prohibition." The fact that insolvent laws are not forbidden "by name" does not exclude them from the operation of the contract clause of the Constitution. It is "a principle which is to be forbidden; and this principle is described in as appropriate terms as our language affords." [2]

Perhaps paper money was the chief and impelling reason for making the contract clause a part of the National Constitution. But can the operation of that clause be confined to paper money? "No court

[1] 4 Wheaton, 202.   [2] *Ib.* 203-04.

can be justified in restricting such comprehensive words to a particular mischief to which no allusion is made." The words must be given "their full and obvious meaning." [1] Doubtless the evils of paper money directed the Convention to the subject of contracts; but it did far more than to make paper money impossible thereafter. "In the opinion of the convention, much more remained to be done. The same mischief might be effected by other means. To restore public confidence completely, it was necessary not only to prohibit the use of particular means by which it might be effected, but to prohibit the use of any means by which the same mischief might be produced. The convention appears to have intended to establish a great principle, that contracts should be inviolable. The constitution therefore declares, that no state shall pass 'any law impairing the obligation of contracts.'" [2] From all this it follows that the New York Bankruptcy Act of 1812 is unconstitutional because it impaired the obligations of a contract.

The opinion of the Chief Justice aroused great excitement.[3] It, of course, alarmed those who had been using State insolvent laws to avoid payment of their debts, while retaining much of their wealth. It also was unwelcome to the great body of honest, though imprudent, debtors who were struggling to lighten their burdens by legislation. But the more thoughtful, even among radicals, welcomed Marshall's pronouncement. Niles approved it heartily.[4]

---

[1] 4 Wheaton, 205.   [2] *Ib*. 206.   [3] Niles, xvi, 76.

[4] "It will probably, make some great revolutions in property, and

Gradually, surely, Marshall's simple doctrine grew in favor throughout the whole country, and is to-day a vital and enduring element of American thought and character as well as of Constitutional law.

As in Fletcher *vs.* Peck, the principle of the inviolability of contracts was applied where a State and individuals are parties, so the same principle was now asserted in Sturges *vs.* Crowninshield as to State laws impairing the obligation of contracts between man and man. At the same session, in the celebrated Dartmouth College case,[1] Marshall announced that this principle also covers charters granted by States. Thus did he develop the idea of good faith and stability of engagement as a life-giving principle of the American Constitution.

raise up many from penury . . and cause others to descend to the condition that becomes *honest men*, by compelling a payment of their debts — as every honest man ought to be compelled to do, if ever able. . . It ought not to be at any one's discretion to say when, or under what *convenient* circumstances, he will *wipe off* his debts, by the benefit of an insolvent law — as some do every two or three years; or, just as often as they can get credit enough to make any thing by it." (Niles. XVI, 2.)

[1] See *infra*, next chapter.

CHAPTER V

THE DARTMOUTH COLLEGE CASE

Such a contract, in relation to a publick institution would be absurd and contrary to the principles of all governments.
(Chief Justice William M. Richardson.)

It would seem as if the state legislatures have an invincible hostility to the sacredness of charters. (Marshall.)

Perhaps no judicial proceedings in this country ever involved more important consequences. (*North American Review*, 1820.)

It is the legitimate business of government to see that contracts are fulfilled, that charters are kept inviolate, and the foundations of human confidence not rudely or wantonly disturbed. (John Fiske.)

JUST before Marshall delivered his opinion in Sturges *vs.* Crowninshield, he gave to the Nation another state paper which profoundly influenced the development of the United States. It was one of the trilogy of Constitutional expositions which make historic the February term, 1819, of the Supreme Court of the United States. This pronouncement, like that in the bankruptcy case, had to do with the stability of contract. Both were avowals that State Legislatures cannot, on any pretext, overthrow agreements, whether in the form of engagements between individuals or franchises to corporations. Both were meant to check the epidemic of repudiatory legislation which for three years had been sweeping over the land and was increasing in virulence at the time when Marshall prepared them. The Dartmouth opinion was wholly written in Virginia during the summer, autumn, or winter of 1818; and it is probable that the greater part of the opinion in

Sturges *vs.* Crowninshield was also prepared when the Chief Justice was at home or on his vacation.

Marshall's economic and political views, formed as a young man,[1] had been strengthened by every event that had since occurred until, in his sixty-fifth year, those early ideas had become convictions so deep as to pervade his very being. The sacredness of contract, the stability of institutions, and, above all, Nationalism in government, were, to John Marshall, articles of a creed as holy as any that ever inspired a religious enthusiast.

His opinion of contract had already been expressed by him not only in the sensational case of Fletcher *vs.* Peck,[2] but far more rigidly two years later, 1812, in the important case of the State of New Jersey *vs.* Wilson.[3] In 1758, the Proprietary Government of New Jersey agreed to purchase a tract of land for a band of Delaware Indians, provided that the Indians would surrender their title to all other lands claimed by them in New Jersey. The Indians agreed and the contract was embodied in an act of the Legislature, which further provided that the lands purchased for the Indians should "not hereafter be subject to any tax, any law, usage or custom to the contrary thereof, in any wise notwithstanding."[4] The contract was then executed, the State purchasing lands for the Indians and the latter relinquishing the lands claimed by them.

After forty years the Indians, wishing to join other Delawares in New York, asked the State of

---

[1] See vol. I, 147, 231, of this work.
[2] See vol. III, chap. x, of this work.
[3] 7 Cranch, 164.   [4] *Ib.* 165.

New Jersey to authorize the sale of their lands. This was done by an act of the Legislature, and the lands were sold. Soon after this, another act was passed which repealed that part of the Act of 1758 exempting the lands from taxation. Accordingly the lands were assessed and payment of the tax demanded. The purchasers resisted and, the Supreme Court of New Jersey having held valid the repealing act, took the case to the Supreme Court of the United States.

In a brief opinion, in which it is worthy of particular note that the Supreme Court was unanimous, Marshall says that the Constitution protects "contracts to which a state is a party, as well as . . contracts between individuals. . . The proceedings [of 1758] between the then colony . . and the Indians . . is certainly a contract clothed in forms of unusual solemnity." The exemption of the lands from taxation, "though for the benefit of the Indians, is annexed, by the terms which create it, to the land itself, not to their persons." This element of the contract was valuable to the Indians, since, "in the event of a sale, on which alone the question could become material, the value [of the lands] would be enhanced" by the exemption.

New Jersey "might have insisted on a surrender of this privilege as the sole condition on which a sale of the property should be allowed"; but this had not been done and the land was sold "with the assent of the state, with all its privileges and immunities. The purchaser succeeds, with the assent of the state, to all the rights of the Indians. He stands, with respect to this land, in their place, and claims the benefit of their contract. This contract is certainly impaired by a law which would annul this essential part of it." [1]

After his opinions in Fletcher *vs.* Peck and in New Jersey *vs.* Wilson, nobody could have expected from John Marshall any other action than the one he took in the Dartmouth College case. [2]

The origins of the Dartmouth controversy are tangled and obscure. When on December 23, 1765, a little ocean-going craft, of which a New England John Marshall [3] was skipper, set sail from Boston Harbor for England with Nathaniel Whitaker and Samson Occom on board, [4] a succession of curious events began which, two generations afterward, terminated in one of the most influential decisions ever rendered by a court. Whitaker was a preacher and a disciple of George Whitefield; Occom was a young Indian, converted to Christianity by one Eleazar Wheelock, and endowed with uncommon powers of oratory.

Wheelock had built up a wilderness school to which were admitted Indian youth, in whom he became increasingly interested. Occom was one product of his labors, and Wheelock sent him to England as a living, speaking illustration of what his school

---

[1] 7 Cranch, 166–67.

[2] This was true also of the entire court, since all the Justices concurred in Marshall's opinions in both cases as far as the legislative violations of the contract clause were concerned.

[3] He was not at all related to the Chief Justice. See vol. I, footnote to 15–16, of this work.

[4] Chase: *History of Dartmouth College and the Town of Hanover, New Hampshire*, I, 49.

could do if given financial support. Whitaker went
with the devout and talented Indian as the business
agent.[1]

Their mission was to raise funds for the prosecution of this educational and missionary work on the
American frontier. They succeeded in a manner
almost miraculous. Over eleven thousand pounds
were soon raised,[2] and this fund was placed under
the control of the Trustees, at the head of whom
was the Earl of Dartmouth, one of the principal
donors.[3] From this circumstance the name of this
nobleman was given to Wheelock's institution.

On December 13, 1769, John Wentworth, Royal
Governor of the Province of New Hampshire,
granted to Wheelock a charter for his school. It
was, of course, in the name of the sovereign, but it is
improbable that George III ever heard of it.[4] This
charter sets forth the successful efforts of Wheelock,
"at his own expense, on his own estate," to establish
a charity school for Indian as well as white youth,
in order to spread "the knowledge of the great Re-
deemer among their savage tribes"; the contributions to the cause; the trust, headed by Dartmouth
— and all the other facts concerning Wheelock's
adventure. Because of these facts the charter
establishes "DARTMOUTH COLLEGE" for the education of Indians, to be governed by "one body
corporate and politick, . . by the name of the
TRUSTEES OF DARTMOUTH COLLEGE."

---

[1] Chase, 45–48.   [2] Ib. 59.   [3] Ib. 54–55.

[4] Dartmouth and the English Trustees opposed incorporation and
the Bishops of the Church of England violently resisted Wheelock's
whole project. (Ib. 90.)

These Trustees are constituted "forever hereafter . . in deed, act, and name a body corporate and politick," and are empowered to buy, receive, and hold lands, "jurisdictions, and franchises, for themselves and their successors, in fee simple, or otherwise howsoever." In short, the Trustees are authorized to do anything and everything that they may think proper. Wheelock is made President of the College, and given power to "appoint, . . by his last will" whomever he chooses to succeed himself as President of the College.

The charter grants to the Trustees and to "their successors forever," or "the major part of any seven or more of them convened," the power to remove and choose a President of the College, and to fill any vacancy in the Board of Trustees occasioned by death, or "removal," or any other cause. All this is to be done if seven Trustees, or a majority of seven, are present at any meeting. Also this majority of seven of the twelve Trustees, if no more attend a meeting, are authorized to make all laws, rules, and regulations for the College. Other powers are granted, all of which the Trustees and their successors are "to have and to hold . . forever." [1] Under this charter, Dartmouth College was established and, for nearly half a century, governed and managed.

Eleazar Wheelock died in 1779, when sixty-eight

[1] Farrar: *Report of the Case of the Trustees of Dartmouth College against William H. Woodward*, 11, 16; also see Charter of Dartmouth College, Chase, 639–49. (Although the official copy of the charter appears in Chase's history, the author cites Farrar in the report of the case; the charter also is cited from his book.)

years of age.[1] By his will he made his son John his
successor as President of the College.[2] This young
man, then but twenty-five years of age, was a Colonel
of the Revolutionary Army.[3] He hesitated to accept
the management of the institution, but the Trustees
finally prevailed upon him to do so.[4] The son was as
strong-willed and energetic as the father, and gave
himself vigorously to the work to which he had thus
been called.

Within four years troubles began to gather about
the College. They came from sources as strange as
human nature itself, and mingled at last into a compound of animosities, prejudices, ambitions, jealousies, as curious as any aggregation of passions ever
arranged by the most extravagant novelist. It is
possible here to mention but briefly only a few of the
circumstances by which the famous Dartmouth
quarrel may be traced. A woman, one Rachel Murch,
complained to the church at Hanover, where Dartmouth College was situated, that a brother of the
congregation, one Samuel Haze, had said of her,
among other things, that her "character was . . as
black as Hell."[5] This incident grew into a sectarian warfare that, by the most illogical and human

---

[1] Chase, 556.   [2] See Wheelock's will, *ib.* 562.

[3] Young Wheelock was very active in the Revolution. He was a
member of the New Hampshire Assembly in 1775, a Captain in the
army in 1776, a Major the following year, and then Lieutenant-Colonel,
serving on the staff of General Horatio Gates until called from military service by the death of his father in 1779. (See Smith: *History
of Dartmouth College*, 76.)

[4] Chase, 564.

[5] Rachel Murch "To yᵉ Session of yᵉ Church of Christ in Hanover,"
April 26, 1783, Shirley: *Dartmouth College Causes and the Supreme
Court of the United States,* 67.

processes, eventuated in arraigning the Congregationalists, or "established" Church, on one side and
all other denominations on the other.[1]

Into this religious quarrel the economic issue entered, as it always does. The property of ministers
of the "standing order," or "State religion," was
exempt from taxation while that of other preachers
was not.[2] Another source of discord arose out of
the question as to whether the College Professor of
Theology should preach in the village church. Coincident with this grave problem were subsidiary ones
concerning the attendance of students at village
worship and the benches they were to occupy. The
fates threw still another ingredient of trouble into
the cauldron. This was the election in 1793, as one
of the Trustees, of Nathaniel Niles, whom Jefferson,
with characteristic exuberance of expression, once
declared to be "the ablest man I ever knew."[3]

Although a lawyer by profession, Niles had taken
a course in theology when a student, his instructor
being a Dr. Joseph Bellamy. Both the elder Wheelock and Bellamy had graduated from Yale and had
indulged in some bitter sectarian quarrels, Bellamy
as a Congregationalist and Wheelock as a Presbyterian. From tutor and parent, Niles and the younger
Wheelock inherited this religious antagonism. Moreover, they were as antipathetic by nature as they
were bold, uncompromising, and dominant. Niles
eventually acquired superior influence over his fel-

[1] Shirley, 66–70.
[2] *Ib.* 70–75. Only three of the scores of Congregationalist ministers
in New Hampshire were Republicans. (*Ib.* 70.)
[3] *Ib.* 82.

low Trustees, and thereafter no friend of President
Wheelock was elected to the Board.[1]

An implacable feud arose. Wheelock asked the
Legislature to appoint a committee to investigate
the conduct of the College. This further angered the
Trustees. By this time the warfare in the one college in the State had aroused the interest of the
people of New Hampshire and, indeed, of all New
England, and they were beginning to take sides.
This process was hastened by a furious battle of
pamphlets which broke out in 1815. This logomachy
of vituperation was opened by President Wheelock
who wrote an unsigned attack upon the Trustees.[2]
Another pamphlet followed immediately in support
of that of Wheelock.[3]

The Trustees quickly answered by means of two
pamphlets.[4] The Wheelock faction instantly replied.[5] With the animosity and diligence of political,
religious, and personal enemies, the adherents of the
hostile factions circulated these pamphlets among
the people, who became greatly excited. On August
26, 1815, the Trustees removed Wheelock from the
office of President,[6] and thereby increased the public
agitation. Two days after Wheelock's removal, the

---

[1] Shirley, 81, 84–85.

[2] *Sketches of the History of Dartmouth College and Moors' Charity
School.*

[3] *A Candid, Analytical Review of the Sketches of the History of Dartmouth College.*

[4] *Vindication of the Official Conduct of the Trustees,* etc., and *A
True and Concise Narrative of the Origin and Progress of the Church
Difficulties,* by Benoni Dewey, James Wheelock, and Benjamin J
Gilbert.

[5] *Answer to the "Vindication,"* etc., by Josiah Dunham.

[6] Lord: *History of Dartmouth College,* 73–77.

upon the managem
tution. The Gove
empowered to app
existing Board of T
one; and authoriz
and report to the
once in every five
the charter and br
trol of the Legislat

The bitterness o
legislation was inte
House entered up
emphatic protest.²
orate resolutions,
of the law and a
action. Among th
that it violated th
Constitution was
summing up their
that "if the act .
effect, every liter
hereafter hold its
not according to
of law, but accord
sure of every succ

¹ Act of June 27, Law
687–90.

The temper of the R
adopted June 29, 1816,
and Representatives in
inducements to avarice
ing power," and "conta
of New Hampshire, 181
² Journal, House of I
³ Resolutions of the

Trustees elected as his successor the Reverend Francis Brown of Yarmouth, Maine.¹

During these years of increasing dissension, political parties were gradually drawn into the controversy; at the climax of it, the Federalists found themselves supporting the cause of the Trustees and the Republicans that of Wheelock. In a general, and yet quite definite, way the issue shaped itself into the maintenance of chartered rights and the established religious order, as against reform in college management and equality of religious sects. Into this issue was woven a contest over the State Judiciary. The Judiciary laws of New Hampshire were confused and inadequate and the courts had fallen in dignity. During the Republican control of the State, Republicans had been appointed to all judicial positions.² When, in 1813, the Federalists recovered supremacy, they, in turn, enacted a statute, the effect of which was the ousting of the Republican judges and the appointment of Federalists in their stead.³ The Republicans made loud and savage outcry against this Federalist "outrage."

Upon questions so absurdly incongruous a political campaign raged throughout New Hampshire

¹ Lord, 78.
² In 1811 the salary of Chief Justices of the Court of Common Pleas for four of the counties was fixed at $200 a year; and that of the other Justices of those courts at $180. "The Chief Justice of said court in Grafton County, $180, and the other Justices in that court $160." (Act of June 21, Laws of New Hampshire, 1811, 33.)
³ Acts of June 24 and Nov. 5, Laws of New Hampshire, 1813, 6–19; Barstow: History of New Hampshire, 363–64; Morison: Life of Jeremiah Smith, 265–67. This law was, however, most excellent. It established a Supreme Court and systematized the entire judicial system.

during the
1816, the R
ernor,[1] and
Legislature.
and the ma
introduced.
the name of
increased t
twenty-one,
Overseers w
tees, and di
to report a

[1] This was tl
He was first ch
the failing and
and had since b
[2] The numbe
polled in the hi
[3] See Act of
repealed the Fed
by those acts.
The burning
up by this Legis
the Reverend I
only three vote
was, for that se
The "Toleratio
tock: *History of*
is omitted from
[4] In his Mess
Dartmouth Coll
charter relating
a free governm
Jefferson, who r
the use of the n
them answer the
generally inculc
tions .. had a r
in fine, that th
(Jefferson to Pl

In later resolutions the old Trustees declined to accept the provisions of the law, "but do hereby expressly refuse to act under the same."[1] The Governor and Council promptly appointed Trustees and Overseers of the new University; among the latter was Joseph Story. The old Trustees were defiant and continued to run the College. When the winter session of the Legislature met, Governor Plumer sharply denounced their action;[2] and two laws were passed for the enforcement of the College Acts, the second of which provided that any person assuming to act as trustee or officer of the College, except as provided by law, should be fined $500 for each offense.[3]

The Trustees of the University "removed" the old Trustees of the College and the President, and the professors who adhered to them.[4] Each side took its case to the people.[5] The new régime ousted the old faculty from the College buildings and the faculty of the University were installed in them. Wheelock was elected President of the State institution.[6] The College faculty procured quarters in

[1] Lord, 96.

[2] "It is an important question and merits your serious consideration whether a law passed and approved by all the constituted authorities of the State shall be carried into effect, or whether *a few individuals* not vested with *any judicial authority* shall be permitted to declare your statutes *dangerous and arbitrary, unconstitutional and void:* whether a *minority* of the trustees of a literary institution formed for the education of your children shall be encouraged to inculcate the doctrine of resistance to the law and their example tolerated in disseminating principles of insubordination and rebellion against government." (Plumer's Message, Nov. 20, 1816, Lord, 103.)

[3] Acts of Dec. 18 and 26, 1816, *Laws of New Hampshire, 1816,* 74–75; see also Lord, 104.)

[4] Lord, 111–12.   [5] *Ib.* 112–15.   [6] *Ib.* 115.

Rowley Hall near by, and there continued their work, the students mostly adhering to them.[1]

The College Trustees took great pains to get the opinion of the best lawyers throughout New Hampshire,[2] as well as the advice of their immediate counsel, Jeremiah Mason, Jeremiah Smith, and Daniel Webster, the three ablest members of the New England bar, all three of them accomplished politicians.[3]

William H. Woodward, who for years had been Secretary and Treasurer of the College, had in his possession the records, account books, and seal. As one of the Wheelock faction he declined to recognize the College Trustees and acted with the Board of the University. The College Trustees removed him from his official position on the College Board;[4] and on February 8, 1817, brought suit against him in the Court of Common Pleas of Grafton County for the recovery of the original charter, the books of record and account, and the common seal — all of the value

[1] Lord, 121. So few students went with the University that it dared not publish a catalogue. (*Ib.* 129.)

[2] *Ib.* 92.

[3] One of the many stories that sprang up in after years about Webster's management of the case is that, since the College was founded for the education of Indians and none of them had attended for a long time, Webster advised President Brown to procure two or three. Brown got a number from Canada and brought them to the river beyond which were the College buildings. While the party were rowing across, the young Indians, seeing the walls and fearing that they were to be put in prison, gave war whoops, sprang into the stream, swam to shore and fled. So Webster had to go on without them. (Harvey: *Reminiscences and Anecdotes of Daniel Webster*, 111–12.) There is not the slightest evidence to support this absurd tale. (Letters to the author from Eugene F. Clark, Secretary of Dartmouth College, and from Professor John K. Lord, author of *History of Dartmouth College*.)

[4] Lord, 99.

of $50,000. By the consent of the parties the case was taken directly before the Superior Court of Appeals, and was argued upon an agreed state of facts returned by the jury in the form of a special verdict.[1]

There were two arguments in the Court of Appeals, the first during May and the second during September, 1817. The court consisted of William M. Richardson, Chief Justice, and Samuel Bell and Levi Woodbury, Associate Justices, all Republicans appointed by Governor Plumer.

Mason, Smith, and Webster made uncommonly able and learned arguments. The University was represented by George Sullivan and Ichabod Bartlett, who, while good lawyers, were no match for the legal triumvirate that appeared for the College.[2] The principle upon which Marshall finally overthrew the New Hampshire law was given a minor place[3] in the plans as well as in the arguments of Webster, Mason, and Smith.

The Superior Court of Appeals decided against the College. The opinion, delivered by Chief Justice Richardson, is able and persuasive. "A corporation, all of whose franchises are exercised for publick purposes, is a publick corporation" — a gift to such a corporation "is in reality a gift to the publick."[4] The

[1] Farrar, 1.

[2] These arguments are well worth perusal. (See Farrar, 28–206; also 65 N.H. Reports, 473–624.)

[3] For instance, Mason's argument, which is very compact, consists of forty-two pages of which only four are devoted to "the contract clause" of the National Constitution and the violation of it by the New Hampshire College Act. (Farrar, 28–70; 65 N.H. 473–502.)

[4] Farrar, 212–13· 65 N.H. 628–29.

corporation of Dartmouth College is therefore public. "Who has any private interest either in the objects or the property of this institution?" If all its "property . . were destroyed, the loss would be exclusively publick." The Trustees, as individuals, would lose nothing. "The office of trustee of Dartmouth College is, in fact, a publick trust, as much so as the office of governor, or of judge of this court." [1]

No provision in the State or National Constitution prevents the control of the College by the Legislature. The Constitutional provisions cited by counsel for the College [2] "were, most manifestly, intended to protect private rights only." [3] No court has ever yet decided that such a charter as that of Dartmouth College is in violation of the contract clause of the National Constitution, which "was obviously intended to protect private rights of property, and embraces all contracts relating to private property." This clause "was not intended to limit the power of the states" over their officers or "their own civil institutions"; [4] otherwise divorce laws would be void. So would acts repealing or modifying laws under which the judges, sheriffs, and other officers were appointed.

Even if the royal charter is a contract, it does not, cannot forever, prevent the Legislature from modifying it for the general good (as, for instance, by increasing the number of trustees) "however strongly the publick interest might require" this to be done. "Such a contract, in relation to a publick institution,

---

[1] Farrar, 214–15; 65 N.H. 630   [2] The contract clause.
[3] Farrar, 216; 65 N.H. 631.   [4] Farrar, 228–29; 65 N.H. 639.

would . . be absurd and repugnant to the principles
of all government. The king had no power to make
such a contract," and neither has the Legislature.
If the act of June 27 had provided that "the twenty-
one trustees should forever have the exclusive controul of this institution, and that no future legislature should add to their number," it would be as
invalid as an act that the "number of judges of this
court should never be augmented." [1]

It is against "sound policy," Richardson affirmed,
to place the great institutions of learning "within
the absolute controul of a few individuals, and out
of the controul of the sovereign power. . . It is a
matter of too great moment, too intimately connected with the publick welfare and prosperity, to
be thus entrusted in the hands of a few." [2] So the
New Hampshire court adjudged that the College
Acts were valid and binding upon the old Trustees
"without acceptance thereof, or assent thereto by
them." And the court specifically declared that
such legislation was "not repugnant to the constitution of the United States." [3]

Immediately the case was taken to the Supreme
Court by writ of error, which assigned the violation
of the National Constitution by the College Acts as
the ground of appeal. [4] On March 10, 1818, Webster
opened the argument before a full bench. [5] Only a
few auditors were present, and these were lawyers [6]

---

[1] Farrar, 231; 65 N.H. 641.   [2] Farrar, 232; 65 N.H. 642.
[3] Farrar, 235.   [4] Ib.
[5] Webster was then thirty-six years of age.
[6] Goodrich's statement in Brown: *Works of Rufus Choate: With
a Memoir of his Life*, I, 515.

who were in Washington to argue other cases.[1]
Stirred as New Hampshire and the New England
States were by the College controversy, the remainder of the country appears to have taken no interest
in it. Indeed, west and south of the Hudson, the
people seem to have known nothing of the quarrel.
The Capital was either ignorant or indifferent.
Moreover, Webster had not, as yet, made that great
reputation, in Washington, as a lawyer as well as an
orator which, later, became his peculiar crown of
glory. At any rate, the public was not drawn to the
court-room on that occasion.[2]

The argument was one of the shortest ever made
in a notable case before the Supreme Court during
the twenty-eight years of its existence up to this
time. Not three full days were consumed by counsel
on both sides — a space of time frequently occupied
by a single speaker in hearings of important causes.[3]

In talents, bearing, and preparation the attorneys

[1] They were Rufus Greene Amory and George Black of Boston,
David B. Ogden and "a Mr. Baldwin from New York," Thomas
Sergeant and Charles J. Ingersoll of Philadelphia, John Wickham,
Philip Norborne, Nicholas and Benjamin Watkins Leigh of Virginia,
and John McPherson Berrien of Georgia. (Webster to Sullivan,
Feb. 27, 1818, *Priv. Corres.*: Webster, I, 273.)

[2] Brown, I, 515. Story makes no comment on the argument of the
Dartmouth case — a pretty sure sign that it attracted little attention
in Washington. Contrast Story's silence as to this argument with his
vivid description of that of M'Culloch *vs.* Maryland (*infra*, chap. VI).
Goodrich attributes the scant attendance to the fact that the court
sat "in a mean apartment of moderate size"; but that circumstance
did not keep women as well as men from thronging the room when a
notable case was to be heard or a celebrated lawyer was to speak. (See
description of the argument of the case of the Nereid, *supra*, 133–34.)

[3] For example, in M'Culloch *vs.* Maryland, Luther Martin spoke
for three days. (Webster to Smith, Feb. 28, 1819, Van Tyne, 80; and
see *infra*, chap. VI.)

for the College were as much superior to those for the University as, in the Chase impeachment trial, the counsel for the defense were stronger than the House managers.[1] Indeed, the similarity of the arguments in the Chase trial and in the Dartmouth case, in respect to the strength and preparation of opposing counsel, is notable; and in both cases the victory came to the side having the abler and better-prepared advocates. With Webster for the College was Joseph Hopkinson of Philadelphia, who had so distinguished himself in the Chase trial exactly thirteen years earlier. Hopkinson was now in his forty-ninth year, the unrivaled leader of the Philadelphia bar and one of the most accomplished of American lawyers.[2]

It would seem incredible that sensible men could have selected such counsel to argue serious questions before any court as those who represented the University in this vitally important controversy. The obvious explanation is that the State officials and the University Trustees were so certain of winning that they did not consider the employment of powerful and expensive attorneys to be necessary.[3] In fact, the belief was general that the contest was practi-

[1] See vol. III, chap. IV, of this work.

[2] The College Trustees at first thought of employing Luther Martin to assist Webster in the Supreme Court (Brown to Kirkland, Nov. 15, 1817, as quoted by Warren in *American Law Review*, XLVI, 665). It is possible that Hopkinson was chosen instead, upon the advice of Webster, who kept himself well informed of the estimate placed by Marshall and the Associate Justices on lawyers who appeared before them. Marshall liked and admired Hopkinson, had been his personal friend for years, and often wrote him. When Peters died in 1828, Marshall secured the appointment of Hopkinson in his place. (Marshall to Hopkinson, March 16, 1827, and same to same [no date, but during 1828], Hopkinson MSS.)

[3] It was considered to be a "needless expense" to send the original counsel, Sullivan and Bartlett, to Washington. (Lord, 140.)

cally over and that the appeal of the College to the Supreme Court was the pursuit of a feeble and forlorn hope.

Even after his powerful and impressive argument in the Supreme Court, Webster declared that he had never allowed himself "to indulge any great hopes of success." [1] It was not unnatural, then, that the State and the University should neglect to employ adequate counsel.

John Holmes, a Representative in Congress from that part of Massachusetts which afterward became the State of Maine, appeared for the University. He was notoriously unfitted to argue a legal question of any weight in any court. He was a busy, agile, talkative politician of the roustabout, hail-fellow-well-met variety, "a power-on-the-stump" orator, gifted with cheap wit and tawdry eloquence. [2]

Associated with Holmes was William Wirt, recently appointed Attorney-General. At that particular time Wirt was all but crushed by overwork, and without either leisure or strength to master the case and prepare an argument. [3] Never in Wirt's life did

---

[1] Webster to McGaw, July 27, 1818, Van Tyne, 77.

[2] Shirley, 229–32. The fact that Holmes was employed plainly shows the influence of "practical politics" on the State officials and the Trustees of the University. The Board voted December 31, 1817, "to take charge of the case." Benjamin Hale, one of the new Trustees, was commissioned to secure other counsel if Holmes did not accept. Apparently Woodward was Holmes's champion: "I have thought him extremely ready . . [a] good lawyer, inferior to D. W. only in point of oratory." (Woodward to Hall, Jan. 18, 1818, Lord, 139–40.) Hardly had Hale reached Washington than he wrote Woodward: "Were you sensible of the low ebb of Mr. Holmes' reputation here, you would . . be unwilling to trust the cause with him." (Hale to Woodward, Feb. 15, 1818, ib. 139.)

[3] "It is late at night — the fag-end of a hard day's work. My eyes,

he appear in any case so poorly equipped as he was in the Dartmouth controversy.[1]

Webster's address was a combination of the arguments made by Mason and Smith in the New Hampshire court. Although the only question before the Supreme Court was whether the College Acts violated the contract clause of the Constitution, Webster gave comparatively scant attention to it; or, perhaps it might be said that most of his argument was devoted to laying the foundation for his brief reasoning on the main question. In laying this foundation, Webster cleverly brought before the court his version of the history of the College, the situation in New Hampshire, the plight of institutions like Dartmouth, if the College Acts were permitted to stand.

The facts were, said Webster, that Wheelock had founded a private charity; that, to perpetuate this, the charter created a corporation by the name of "The Trustees of Dartmouth College," with the powers, privileges, immunities, and limitations set forth in the charter. That instrument provided for no public funds, but only for the perpetuation an

hand and mind all tired. . . I have been up till midnight, at work every night, and still have my hands full. . . I am now worn out . extremely fatigued. . . The Supreme Court is approaching. It will half kill you to hear that it will find me unprepared." (Wirt to Carr, Jan. 21, 1818, Kennedy, II, 73–74.) Wirt had just become Attorney-General. Apparently he found the office in very bad condition. The task of putting it in order burdened him. He was compelled to do much that was not "properly [his] duty." (*Ib.* 73.) His fee in the Dartmouth College case did not exceed $500. (Hale to Plumer, Jan. 1818, Lord, 140.)

[1] "He seemed to treat this case as if his side could furnish nothing but declamation." (Webster to Mason, March 13, 1818, *Priv. Cor-res.*: Webster, I, 275.)

convenient management of the private charity. For nearly half a century the College "thus created had existed, uninterruptedly, and usefully." Then its happy and prosperous career was broken by the rude and despoiling hands of the Legislature of the State which the College had so blessed by the education of New Hampshire youth.

What has the Legislature done to the College? It has created a new corporation and transferred to it "all the *property, rights, powers, liberties and privileges* of the old corporation." The spirit and the letter of the charter were wholly changed by the College Acts.[1] Moreover, the old Trustees "are to be *punished*" for not accepting these revolutionary laws. A single fact reveals the confiscatory nature of these statutes: Under the charter the president, professors, and tutors of the College had a right to their places and salaries, "subject to the twelve trustees alone"; the College Acts change all this and make the faculty "accountable to new masters."

If the Legislature can make such alterations, it can abolish the charter "rights and privileges altogether." In short, if this legislation is sustained, the old Trustees "have no *rights, liberties, franchises, property or privileges*, which the legislature may not revoke, annul, alienate or transfer to others whenever it sees fit." Such acts are against "common right" as well as violations of the State and National Constitutions.[2]

Although, says Webster, nothing is before the court

[1] Farrar, 241; 65 N.H. 596; 4 Wheaton, 534; and see Curtis, I, 163–66.

[2] Farrar, 242–44; 65 N.H. 597–98; 4 Wheaton, 556–57.

but the single question of the violation of the National Constitution, he will compare the New Hampshire laws with "fundamental principles" in order
that the court may see "their true nature and character." Regardless of written constitutions, "these
acts are not the exercise of a power properly legislative." They take away "vested rights"; but this
involves a "forfeiture . . to . . declare which is the
proper province of the judiciary." [1] Dartmouth College is not a civil but "an *eleemosynary* corporation,"
a "private charity"; and, as such, not subject to the
control of public authorities.[2] Does Dartmouth College stand alone in this respect? No! Practically all
American institutions of learning have been "established . . by incorporating governours, or trustees.
. . All such corporations are . . in the strictest legal
sense a private charity." Even Harvard has not
"any surer title than Dartmouth College. It may,
to-day, have more friends; but to-morrow it may
have more enemies. Its legal rights are the same. So
also of Yale College; and indeed of all others." [3]

From the time of Magna Charta the privilege of
being a member of such eleemosynary corporations
"has been the object of legal protection." To contend that this privilege may be "taken away," because the Trustees derive no "pecuniary benefit"
from it, is "an extremely narrow view." As well say
that if the charter had provided that each Trustee
should be given a "commission on the disbursement
of the funds," his status and the nature of the cor-

---

[1] Farrar, 244; 65 N.H. 598–99; 4 Wheaton, 558–59.
[2] Farrar, 248; 65 N.H. 600–01; 4 Wheaton, 563–64.
[3] Farrar, 255–56; 65 N.H. 605–06; 4 Wheaton, 567–68.

poration would have been changed from public to private. Are the rights of the Trustees any the less sacred "because they have undertaken to administer it [the trust] gratuitously? . . As if the law regarded no rights but the rights of money, and of visible tangible property!" [1]

The doctrine that all property "of which the use may be beneficial to the publick, belongs therefore to the publick," is without principle or precedent. In this very matter of Dartmouth College, Wheelock might well have "conveyed his property to trustees, for precisely such uses as are described in this charter" — yet nobody would contend that any Legislature could overthrow such a private act. "Who ever appointed a legislature to administer his charity? Or who ever heard, before, that a gift to a *college*, or *hospital*, or an *asylum*, was, in reality, nothing but a gift to the state?" [2]

Vermont has given lands to the College; was this a gift to New Hampshire? "What hinders Vermont . . from resuming her grants," upon the ground that she, equally with New Hampshire, is "the representative of the publick?" In 1794, Vermont had "granted to the respective towns in that state, certain glebe lands lying within those towns *for the sole use and support of religious worship.*" Five years later, the Legislature of that State repealed this grant; "but this court declared [3] that the act of

[1] Farrar, 258–59; 65 N.H. 607–08; 4 Wheaton, 571–72.

[2] Farrar, 260–61; 65 N.H. 609; 4 Wheaton, 571.

[3] In Terrett *vs.* Taylor, 9 Cranch, 45 *et seq.* Story delivered the unanimous opinion of the Supreme Court in this case. This fact was well known at the time of the passage of the College Acts; and, in

1794, 'so far as it granted the glebes to the towns, *could not afterwards be repealed by the legislature, so as to divest the rights of the towns under the grant.*'" [1]

So with the Trustees of Dartmouth College. The property entrusted to them was "private property"; and the right to "administer the funds, and . . govern the college was a *franchise* and *privilege*, solemnly granted to them," which no Legislature can annul. "The use being publick in no way diminishes their legal estate in the property, or their title to the franchise." Since "the acts in question violate property, . . take away privileges, immunities, and franchises, . . deny to the trustees the protection of the law," and "are retrospective in their operation," they are, in all respects, "against the constitution of New Hampshire." [2]

It will be perceived by now that Webster relied chiefly on abstract justice. His main point was that, if chartered rights could be interfered with at all, such action was inherently beyond the power of the Legislature, and belonged exclusively to the Judiciary. In this Webster was rigidly following Smith and Mason, neither of whom depended on the violation of the contract clause of the National Constitution any more than did Webster.

Well did Webster know that the Supreme Court of the United States could not consider the violation of a State constitution by a State law. He merely

view of it, there is difficulty in understanding how Story could have been expected to support the New Hampshire legislation. (See *infra*, 257.)

[1] Farrar, 262; 65 N.H. 609–10; 4 Wheaton, 574–75.
[2] Farrar, 273; 65 N.H. 617; 4 Wheaton, 588.

indulged in a device of argument to bring before Marshall and the Associate Justices those "fundamental principles," old as Magna Charta, and embalmed in the State Constitution, which protect private property from confiscation.[1] Toward the close of his argument, Webster discusses the infraction of the National Constitution by the New Hampshire College Acts, a violation the charge of which alone gave the Supreme Court jurisdiction over the case.

What, asks Webster, is the meaning of the words, "no state shall pass any . . law impairing the obligation of contracts"? Madison, in the *Federalist*, clearly states that such laws "'are contrary to the first principles of the social compact, and to every principle of sound legislation.'" But this is not enough. "Our own experience," continues Madison, "has taught us . . that additional fences" should be erected against spoliations of "personal security and private rights." This was the reason for inserting the contract clause in the National Constitution — a provision much desired by the "sober people of America," who had grown "weary of the fluctuating policy" of the State Governments and beheld with anger "that sudden changes, and legislative interferences in cases affecting personal rights, become jobs in the hands of enterprising and influential speculators." These, said Webster, were the words of James Madison in Number 44 of the *Federalist*.

High as such authority is, one still more exalted and final has spoken, and upon the precise point

[1] Farrar, 246–47; 65 N.H. 598–600; 4 Wheaton, 557–59.

now in controversy. That authority is the Supreme Court itself. In Fletcher *vs.* Peck [1] this very tribunal declared specifically that "a *grant* is a contract, within the meaning of this provision; and that a grant by a state is also a contract, as much as the grant of an individual." [2] This court went even further when, in New Jersey *vs.* Wilson, [3] it decided that "a grant by a state before the revolution is as much to be protected as a grant since." [4] The principle announced in these decisions was not new, even in America. Even before Fletcher *vs.* Peck and New Jersey *vs.* Wilson, this court denied [5] that a Legislature "can repeal statutes creating private corporations, or confirming to them property already acquired under the faith of previous laws, and by such repeal can vest the property of such corporations exclusively in the state, or dispose of the same to such purposes as they please, without the consent or default of the corporators . . ; and we think ourselves standing upon the principles of *natural justice*, upon the *fundamental laws of every free government*, upon the spirit and letter of the constitution of the United States, and upon the decisions of the most respectable judicial tribunals, in resisting such a doctrine." [6]

From the beginning of our Government until this

---

[1] See vol. III, chap. x, of this work.

[2] Farrar, 273–74; 65 N.H. 618–19; 4 Wheaton, 591–92.

[3] *Supra*, 223.   [4] Farrar, 275; 65 N.H. 619; 4 Wheaton, 591.

[5] In Terrett *vs.* Taylor, see *supra*, footnote to 243.

[6] Farrar, 275; 65 N.H. 619; 4 Wheaton, 591. (Italics the author's.) It will be observed that Webster puts the emphasis upon "natural justice" and "fundamental laws" rather than upon the Constitutional point.

very hour, continues Webster, such has been the uniform language of this honorable court. The principle that a Legislature cannot "repeal statutes
creating private corporations" must be considered
as settled. It follows, then, that if a Legislature cannot repeal such laws entirely, it cannot repeal them
in part — cannot "impair them, or essentially alter
them without the consent of the corporators." [1] In
the case last cited [2] the property granted was land;
but the Dartmouth charter "is embraced within the
very terms of that decision," since "a grant of corporate powers and privileges is as much a *contract* as
a grant of land." [3]

Even the State court concedes that if Dartmouth
College is a private corporation, "its rights stand on
the same ground as those of an individual"; and
that tribunal rests its judgment against the College
on the sole ground that it is a public corporation.[4]

Dartmouth College is not the only institution
affected by this invasion of chartered rights. "Every
college, and all the literary institutions of the
country" are imperiled. All of them exist because
of "the inviolability of their charters." Shall their
fate depend upon "the rise and fall of popular
parties, and the fluctuations of political opinions"?
If so, "colleges and halls will . . become a theatre
for the contention of politicks. Party and faction
will be cherished in the places consecrated to piety
and learning."

---

[1] Farrar, 276; 65 N.H. 619–20; 4 Wheaton, 592.
[2] Terrett *vs.* Taylor.   [3] Farrar, 277; 65 N.H. 620; 4 Wheaton, 592.
[4] Farrar, 280; 65 N.H. 622. The two paragraphs containing these
statements of Webster are omitted in *Wheaton's Reports.*

"We had hoped, earnestly hoped," exclaimed Webster, "that the State court would protect Dartmouth College. That hope has failed. It is here, that those rights are now to be maintained, or they are prostrated forever." He closed with a long Latin quotation, not a word of which Marshall understood, but which, delivered in Webster's sonorous tones and with Webster's histrionic power, must have been prodigiously impressive.[1]

Undoubtedly it was at this point that the incomparable actor, lawyer, and orator added to his prepared peroration that dramatic passage which has found a permanent place in the literature of emotional eloquence. Although given to the world a quarter of a century after Webster's speech was delivered, and transmitted through two men of vivid and creative imaginations, there certainly is some foundation for the story. Rufus Choate in his "Eulogy of Webster," delivered at Dartmouth College in 1853, told, for the first time, of the incident as narrated to him by Professor Chauncey A. Goodrich, who heard Webster's argument. When Webster had apparently finished, says Goodrich, he "stood for some moments silent before the Court, while every eye was fixed intently upon him." At length, addressing the Chief Justice, Webster delivered that famous peroration ending: "'Sir, you may destroy this little Institution; it is weak; it is in your hands! I know it is one of the lesser lights in the literary horizon of our country. You may put it out. But if you do so, you must carry through your work!

[1] Farrar, 282–83; 65 N.H. 624; 4 Wheaton, 599.

You must extinguish, one after another, all those great lights of science which, for more than a century, have thrown their radiance over our land!

"'It is, Sir, as I have said, a small College. And yet, *there are those who love it* —— '" [1]

Then, testifies Goodrich, Webster broke down with emotion, his lips quivered, his cheeks trembled, his eyes filled with tears, his voice choked. In a "few broken words of tenderness" he spoke of his love for Dartmouth in such fashion that the listeners were impressed with "the recollections of father, mother, brother, and all the trials and privations through which he had made his way into life." [2]

Goodrich describes the scene in the court-room, "during these two or three minutes," thus: "Chief Justice Marshall, with his tall and gaunt figure bent over as if to catch the slightest whisper, the deep furrows of his cheek expanded with emotion, and eyes suffused with tears; Mr. Justice Washington at his side, — with his small and emaciated frame, and countenance more like marble than I ever saw on any other human being, — leaning forward with an eager, troubled look; and the remainder of the Court, at the two extremities, pressing, as it were, toward a single point, while the audience below were wrapping themselves round in closer folds beneath the bench to catch each look, and every movement of the speaker's face." Recovering "his

[1] Brown, I, 516.
[2] *Ib.* 516–17. This scene, the movement and color of which grew in dignity and vividness through the innumerable repetitions of it, caught the popular fancy. Speeches, poems, articles, were written about the incident. It became one of the chief sources from which the idolaters of Webster drew endless adulation of that great man.

composure, and fixing his keen eye on the Chief
Justice," Webster, "in that deep tone with which
he sometimes thrilled the heart of an audience,"
exclaimed:

"'Sir, I know not how others may feel,' (glancing
at the opponents of the College before him,) 'but,
for myself, when I see my Alma Mater surrounded,
like Cæsar in the senate-house, by those who are
reiterating stab upon stab, I would not, for this
right hand, have her turn to me, and say, *Et tu
quoque, mi fili!*'" [1]

Exclusive of his emotional finish, Webster's whole
address was made up from the arguments of Jeremiah
Mason and Jeremiah Smith in the State court. [2] This
fact Webster privately admitted, although he never
publicly gave his associates the credit. [3]

[1] See Brown, I, 517; Curtis, I, 169–71.
Chauncey Allen Goodrich was in his twenty-eighth year when he
heard Webster's argument. He was sixty-three when he gave Choate the
description which the latter made famous in his "Eulogy of Webster."
[2] Compare their arguments with Webster's. See Farrar 28–70; 104–
61; 238–84.
[3] "Your notes I found to contain the whole matter. They saved
me great labor; but that was not the best part of their service; they
put me in the right path. . . The only new aspect of the argument was
produced by going into cases to prove these ideas, which indeed lie at the
very bottom of your argument." (Webster to Smith, March 14, 1818,
Priv. Corres.: Webster, I, 276–77; and see Webster to Mason, March
22, 1818, *ib.* 278.)
A year later, after the case had been decided, when the question of
publishing Farrar's *Report* of all the arguments and opinions in the
Dartmouth College case was under consideration, Webster wrote
Mason: "My own interest would be promoted by *preventing* the Book.
I shall strut well enough in the Washington Report, & if the 'Book'
should not be published, the world would not know where I borrowed
my plumes — But I am still inclined to have the Book — One reason
is, that you & Judge Smith may have the credit which belongs to you."
(Webster to Mason, April 10, 1819, Van Tyne, 80.)
Farrar's *Report* was published in August, 1819. It contains the

When Farrar's "Report," containing Mason's argument, was published, Story wrote Mason that he was "exceedingly pleased" with it. "I always had a desire that the question should be put upon the broad basis you have stated; and it was a matter of regret that we were so stinted in jurisdiction in the Supreme Court, that half the argument could not be met and enforced. You need not fear a comparison of your argument with any in our annals."[1] Thus Story makes plain, what is apparent on the face of his own and Marshall's opinion, that he considered the master question involved to be that the College Acts were violative of fundamental principles of government. Could the Supreme Court have passed upon the case without regard to the Constitution, there can be no doubt that the decision would have been against the validity of the New Hampshire laws upon the ground on which Mason, Smith, and Webster chiefly relied.

Webster, as we have seen, had little faith in winning on the contract clause and was nervously anxious that the controversy should be presented to the Supreme Court by means of a case which would give that tribunal greater latitude than was afforded by the "stinted jurisdiction" of which Story complained. Indeed, Story openly expressed impatience that the court was restricted to a consideration of the contract clause. Upon his return to Massa-

pleadings and special verdict, the arguments of counsel, opinions, and the judgments in the State and National courts, together with valuable appendices. The Farrar *Report* is indispensable to those who wish to understand this celebrated case from the purely legal point of view.

[1] Story to Mason, Oct. 6, 1819, Story, I, 323.

chusetts after the argument, Story as much as told Webster that another suit should be brought which could be taken to the Supreme Court, and which would permit the court to deal with all the questions raised by the New Hampshire College Acts. Webster's report of this conversation is vital to an understanding of the views of the Chief Justice, as well as of those of Story, since the latter undoubtedly stated Marshall's views as well as his own. "I saw Judge Story as I came along," Webster reported to Mason. "He is evidently expecting a case which shall present all the questions. It is not of great consequence whether the actions or action, go up at this term, except that it would give it an earlier standing on the docket next winter.

"The question which we must raise in one of these actions, is, 'whether, by the *general principles of our governments*, the State Legislatures be not restrained from divesting vested rights?' This, of course, independent of the constitutional provision respecting contracts. On this question [the maintenance of vested rights by "general principles"] I have great confidence in a decision on the right side. This is the proposition with which you began your argument at Exeter, and which I endeavored to state from your minutes at Washington. . . On *general* principles, I am very confident the court at Washington would be with us." [1]

---

[1] Webster to Mason, April 28, 1818, *Priv. Corres.*: Webster, I, 282-83. (Italics the author's.) In fact three such suits were brought early in 1818 on the ground of diverse citizenship. (Shirley, 2-3.) Any one of them would have enabled the Supreme Court to have passed on the "general principles" of contract and government. These cases

Holmes followed Webster. "The God-like Daniel" could not have wished for a more striking contrast to himself. In figure, bearing, voice, eye, intellect, and personality, the Maine Congressman, politician, and stump-speaker, was the antithesis of Webster. For three hours Holmes declaimed "the merest stuff that was ever uttered in a county court." [1] His "argument" was a diffuse and florid repetition of the opinion of Chief Justice Richardson, and was one of those empty and long-winded speeches which Marshall particularly disliked.

Wirt did his best to repair the damage done by Holmes; but he was so indifferently prepared,[2] and

had they arrived on time, would have afforded Story his almost frantically desired opportunity to declare that legislation violative of contracts was against "natural right" — an opinion he fervently desired to give. But the wiser Marshall saw in the case, as presented to the Supreme Court on the contract guarantee of the Constitution, the occasion to declare, in effect, that these same fundamental principles are embraced in the contract clause of the written Constitution of the American Nation.

[1] Webster to Mason, March 13, 1818, *Priv. Corres.*: Webster, I, 275.

"Every body was grinning at the folly he uttered. Bell could not stand it. He seized his hat and went off." (Webster to Smith, March 14, 1818, *ib.* 277; and see Webster to Brown, March 11, 1818, Van Tyne, 75–76.)

Holmes "has attempted as a politician . . such a desire to be admired by *everybody*, that he has ceased for weeks to be regarded by *anybody*. . . In the Dartmouth College Cause, he sunk lower at the bar than he had in the Hall of Legislature." (Daggett to Mason, March 18, 1818, Hillard: *Memoir and Correspondence of Jeremiah Mason*, 199.)

The contempt of the legal profession for Holmes is shown by the fact that in Farrar's *Report* but four and one half pages are given to his argument, while those of all other counsel for Woodward (Sullivan and Bartlett in the State court and Wirt in the Supreme Court) are published in full.

[2] "He made an apology for himself, that he had not had time to study the case, and had hardly thought of it, till it was called on." (Webster to Mason, March 13, 1818, *Priv. Corres.*: Webster, I, 275–76.)

so physically exhausted, that, breaking down in the midst of his address, he asked the court to adjourn that he might finish next day;[1] and this the bored and weary Justices were only too willing to do. Wirt added nothing to the reasoning and facts of Richardson's opinion which was in the hands of Marshall and his associates.

The argument was closed by Joseph Hopkinson; and here again Fate acted as stage manager for Dartmouth, since the author of "Hail Columbia"[2] was as handsome and impressive a man as Webster, though of an exactly opposite type. His face was that of the lifelong student, thoughtful and refined. His voice, though light, had a golden tone. His manner was quiet, yet distinguished.

Joseph Hopkinson showed breeding in every look, movement, word, and intonation.[3] He had a beautiful and highly trained mind, equipped with immense and accurate knowledge systematically arranged.[4] It is unfortunate that space does not permit even a brief *précis* of Hopkinson's admirable argument.[5] He quite justified Webster's assur-

---

[1] "Before he concluded he became so exhausted . . that he was obliged to request the Court to indulge him until the next day." (*Boston Daily Advertiser*, March 23, 1818.)

"Wirt . . argues a good cause well. In this case he said more nonsensical things than became him." (Webster to Smith, March 14, 1818, *Priv. Corres.*: Webster, I, 277.)

[2] Hopkinson wrote this anthem when Marshall returned from France. (See vol. II, 343, of this work.)

[3] This description of Hopkinson is from Philadelphia according to traditions gathered by the author.

[4] Choate says that Webster called to his aid "the ripe and beautiful culture of Hopkinson." (Brown, I, 514.)

[5] The same was true of Hopkinson's argument for Chase. (See vol. III, chap. IV, of this work.)

ance to Brown that "Mr. Hopkinson . . will do all that man can do." [1]

At eleven o'clock of March 13, 1818, the morning after the argument was concluded, Marshall announced that some judges were of "different opinions, and that some judges had not formed opinions; consequently, the cause must be continued." [2] On the following day the court adjourned.

Marshall, Washington, and Story [3] were for the College, Duval and Todd were against it, and Livingston and Johnson had not made up their minds. [4] During the year that intervened before the court again met in February, 1819, hope sprang up in the hearts of Dartmouth's friends, and they became incessantly active in every legitimate way. Webster's

[1] Webster to Brown, March 11, 1818, Van Tyne, 75–76.

After Hopkinson's argument Webster wrote Brown: "Mr. Hopkinson understood every part of the cause, and in his argument did it great justice." (Webster to Brown, March 13, 1818, *Priv. Corres.*: Webster, I, 274; and see Webster to Mason, March 13, 1818, *ib.* 275–76.)

"Mr. Hopkinson closed the cause for the College with great ability, and in a manner which gave perfect satisfaction and delight to all who heard him." (*Boston Daily Advertiser*, March 23, 1818.)

It was expected that the combined fees of Webster and Hopkinson would be $1000, "not an unreasonable compensation." (Marsh to Brown, Nov. 22, 1817, Lord, 139.) Hopkinson was paid $500. (Brown to Hopkinson, May 4, 1819, Hopkinson MSS.)

At their first meeting after the decision, the Trustees, "feeling the inadequacy" of the fees of all the lawyers for the College, asked Mason, Smith, Webster, and Hopkinson to sit for their portraits by Gilbert Stuart, the artist to be paid by the Trustees. (Shattuck to Hopkinson, Jan. 4, 1835, enclosing resolution of the Trustees, April 4, 1819, attested by Miles Olcott, secretary, Hopkinson MSS.; also, Webster to Hopkinson, May 9, 1819, *ib.*)

[2] Webster to Smith, March 14, 1818, *Priv. Corres.*: Webster, I, 577.

[3] Many supposed that Story was undecided, perhaps opposed to the College. In fact, he was as decided as Marshall. (See *infra*, 257–58, 275 and footnote.)

[4] Webster to Smith, March 14, 1818, *Priv. Corres.*: Webster, I, 577.

argument was printed and placed in the hands of all influential lawyers in New England.

Chancellor James Kent of New York was looked upon by the bench and bar of the whole country as the most learned of American jurists and, next to Marshall, the ablest.[1] The views of no other judge were so sought after by his fellow occupants of the bench. Charles Marsh of New Hampshire, one of the Trustees of the College and a warm friend of Kent, sent him Webster's argument. While on a vacation in Vermont Kent had read the opinion of Chief Justice Richardson and, "on a hasty perusal of it," was at first inclined to think the College Acts valid, because he was "led by the opinion to assume the fact that Dartmouth College was a public establishment for purposes of a general nature."[2] Webster's argument changed Kent's views.

During the summer of 1818, Justice Johnson, of the National Supreme Court, was in Albany, where Kent lived, and conferred with the Chancellor about the Dartmouth case. Kent told Johnson that he thought the New Hampshire College Acts to be

---

[1] For example, William Wirt, Monroe's Attorney-General, in urging the appointment of Kent, partisan Federalist though he was, to the Supreme Bench to succeed Justice Livingston, who died March 19, 1823, wrote that "Kent holds so lofty a stand everywhere for almost matchless intellect and learning, as well as for spotless purity and high-minded honor and patriotism, that I firmly believe the nation at large would approve and applaud the appointment." (Wirt to Monroe, May 5, 1823, Kennedy, II, 153.)

[2] Kent to Marsh, Aug. 26, 1818, Shirley, 263. Moreover, in 1804, Kent, as a member of the New York Council of Revision, had held that "charters of incorporation containing grants of personal and municipal privileges were not to be essentially affected without the consent of the parties concerned." (Record of Board, as quoted in ib. 254.)

against natural right and in violation of the contract clause of the National Constitution.[1] It seems fairly certain also that Livingston asked for the Chancellor's opinion, and was influenced by it.

Webster sent Story, with whom he was on terms of cordial intimacy, "five copies of our argument." Evidently Webster now knew that Story was unalterably for the College, for he adds these otherwise startling sentences: "If you send one of them to each of such of the judges as you think proper, you will of course do it in the manner least likely to lead to a feeling that any indecorum has been committed by the plaintiffs." [2]

In some way, probably from the fact that Story was an intimate friend of Plumer, a rumor had spread, before the case was argued, that he was against the College Trustees. Doubtless this impression was strengthened by the fact that Governor Plumer had appointed Story one of the Board of Overseers of the new University. No shrewder politician than Plumer ever was produced by New England. But Story declined the appointment.[3] He had been compromised, however, in the eyes of both sides. The friends of the College were discouraged, angered, frightened.[4] In great apprehension,

[1] Shirley, 253. Shirley says that Kent "agreed to draw up an opinion for Johnson in this case."

[2] Webster to Story, Sept. 9, 1818, *Priv. Corres.*: Webster. I, 287.

[3] Lord, 143.

[4] "The folks in this region are frightened... It is ascertained that Judge Story .. is the original framer of the law... They suppose that on this account the cause is hopeless before the Sup. Ct. of U. S. This is, however, report." (Murdock to Brown, Dec. 27, 1817, *ib.* 142.)

Murdock mentions Pickering as one of those who believed the

Charles Marsh, one of the College Trustees, wrote
Hopkinson of Story's appointment as Overseer of
the University and of the rumor in circulation. Hopkinson answered heatedly that he would object to
Story's sitting in the case if the reports could be
confirmed.[1]

Although the efforts of the College to get its case
before Kent were praiseworthy rather than reprehensible, and although no smallest item of testimony
had been adduced by eager searchers for something
unethical, nevertheless out of the circumstances just
related has been woven, from the materials of eager
imaginations, a network of suspicion involving the
integrity of the Supreme Court in the Dartmouth
decision.[2]

rumors about Story. This explains much. The soured old Federalist
was an incessant gossip and an indefatigable purveyor of rumors concerning any one he did not like, provided the reports were bad enough
for him to repeat. He himself would, with great facility, apply the
black, if the canvas were capable of receiving it; and he could not forget that Story, when a young man, had been a Republican.

[1] Hopkinson to Marsh, Dec. 31, 1817, Shirley, 274–75.

[2] This is principally the work of John M. Shirley in his book *Dartmouth College Causes and the Supreme Court of the United States*. The
volume is crammed with the results of extensive research, strange
conglomeration of facts, suppositions, inferences, and insinuations,
so inextricably mingled that it is with the utmost difficulty that the
painstaking student can find his way.

Shirley leaves the impression that Justices Johnson and Livingston
were improperly worked upon because they consulted Chancellor
Kent. Yet the only ground for this is that Judge Marsh sent Webster's argument to Kent, who was Marsh's intimate friend; and
that the Reverend Francis Brown, President of Dartmouth, went
to see Kent, reported that his opinion was favorable to the College,
and that the effect of this would be good upon Johnson and Livingston.

From the mere rumor, wholly without justification, that Story was
at first against the College — indeed, had drawn the College Acts (for
so the rumor grew, as rumors always grow) — Shirley would have us

Meanwhile the news had spread of the humiliating failure before the Supreme Court of the flamboyant Holmes and the tired and exhausted Wirt as contrasted with the splendid efforts of Webster and Hopkinson. The New Hampshire officials and the University at last realized the mistake they had made in not employing able counsel, and resolved to remedy their blunder by securing the acknowledged leader of the American bar whose primacy no judge or lawyer in the country denied. They did what they should have done at the beginning — they retained William Pinkney of Maryland.

Traveling with him in the stage during the autumn of 1818, Hopkinson learned that the great lawyer had been engaged by the University. Moreover, with characteristic indiscretion, Pinkney told Hopkinson that he intended to request a reargument at the approaching session of the Supreme

believe, without any evidence whatever, that some improper influence was exerted over Story.

Because Webster said that there was something "left out" of the report of his argument, Shirley declares that for a whole hour Webster spoke as a Federalist partisan in order to influence Marshall. (Shirley, 237.) But such an attempt would have been resented by every Republican member of the court and, most of all, by Marshall himself. Moreover, Marshall needed no such persuasion, nor, indeed, persuasion of any kind. His former opinions showed where he stood; so did the views which he had openly and constantly avowed since he was a member of the Virginia House of Burgesses in 1783. The something "left out" of Webster's reported argument was, of course, his extemporaneous and emotional peroration described by Goodrich.

These are only a very few instances of Shirley's assumptions. Yet, because of the mass of data his book contains, and because of the impossibility of getting out of them a connected narrative without the most laborious and time-consuming examination, together with the atmosphere of wrongdoing with which Shirley manages to surround the harried reader, his volume has had a strong and erroneous effect upon general opinion.

Court. In alarm, Hopkinson instantly wrote Webster,[1] who was dismayed by the news. Of all men
the one Webster did not want to meet in forensic
combat was the legal Colossus from Baltimore.[2]

Pinkney applied himself to the preparation of the
case with a diligence and energy uncommon even for
that most laborious and painstaking of lawyers. Apparently he had no doubt that the Supreme Court
would grant his motion for a reargument. It was
generally believed that some of the Justices had
not made up their minds; rearguments, under such
circumstances, were usually granted and sometimes
required by the court; and William Pinkney was
the most highly regarded by that tribunal of all
practitioners before it. So, on February 1, 1819, he
took the Washington stage at Baltimore, prepared at
every point for the supreme effort of his brilliant
career.[3]

Pinkney's purpose was, of course, well advertised
by this time. By nobody was it better understood
than by Marshall and, indeed, by every Justice of

[1] Hopkinson to Webster, Nov. 17, 1818, *Priv. Corres.*: Webster,
I, 288–89. "I suppose he expects to do something very extraordinary
in it, as he says Mr. Wirt 'was not strong enough for it, has not back
enough.'" (*Ib.* 289.)

[2] Both Hopkinson and Webster resolved to prevent Pinkney from
making his anticipated argument. (*Ib.*)

[3] Not only did Pinkney master the law of the case, but, in order to
have at his command every practical detail of the controversy, he kept
Cyrus Perkins, who succeeded Woodward, deceased, as Secretary of
the University Trustees, under continuous examination for an entire
week. Perkins knew every possible fact about the College controversy
and submitted to Pinkney the whole history of the dispute and also
all documents that could illuminate the subject. "Dr. Perkins had
been a week at Baltimore, conferring with Mr. Pinkney." (Webster to
Mason, Feb. 4, 1819, Hillard, 213; and see Shirley, 203.)

the Supreme Court. All of them, except Duval and Todd, had come to an agreement and consented to the opinion which Marshall had prepared since the adjournment the previous year.[1] None of them were minded to permit the case to be reopened. Most emphatically John Marshall was not.

When, at eleven o'clock, February 2, 1819, the marshal of the court announced "The Honorable, the Chief Justice and the Associate Justices of the Supreme Court of the United States," Marshall, at the head of his robed associates, walked to his place, he beheld Pinkney rise, as did all others in the room, to greet the court. Well did Marshall know that, at the first opportunity, Pinkney would ask for a re-argument.

From all accounts it would appear that Pinkney was in the act of addressing the court when the Chief Justice, seemingly unaware of his presence, placidly announced that the court had come to a decision and began reading his momentous opinion.[2] After a few introductory sentences the Chief Justice came abruptly to the main point of the dispute:

"This court can be insensible neither to the magnitude nor delicacy of this question. The validity of a legislative act is to be examined; and the opinion

[1] This fact was unknown to anybody but the Justices themselves. "No public or general opinion seems to be formed of the opinion of any particular judge." (Webster to Brown, Jan. 10, 1819, *Priv. Corres.*: Webster, I, 299.)

[2] "On Tuesday morning, he [Pinkney] being in court, as soon as the judges had taken their seats, the Chief Justice said that in vacation the judges had formed opinions in the College case. He then immediately began reading his opinion, and, of course, nothing was said of a second argument." (Webster to Mason, Feb. 4, 1819, Hillard 213.)

of the highest law tribunal of a state is to be revised:
an opinion which carries with it intrinsic evidence
of the diligence, of the ability, and the integrity,
with which it was formed. On more than one occasion this court has expressed the cautious circumspection with which it approaches the consideration
of such questions; and has declared that, in no doubtful case would it pronounce a legislative act to be
contrary to the constitution.

"But the American people have said, in the constitution of the United States, that 'no state shall pass
any bill of attainder, *ex post facto* law, or law impairing the obligation of contracts.' In the same
instrument they have also said, 'that the judicial
power shall extend to all cases in law and equity arising under the constitution.' On the judges of this
court, then, is imposed the high and solemn duty of
protecting, from even legislative violation, those
contracts which the constitution of our country
has placed beyond legislative control; and, however
irksome the task may be, this is a duty from which
we dare not shrink." [1]

Then Marshall, with, for him, amazing brevity,
states the essential provisions of the charter and of
the State law that modified it; [2] and continues, almost curtly: "It can require no argument to prove
that the circumstances of this case constitute a
contract." On the faith of the charter "large contributions" to "a religious and literary institution"
are conveyed to a corporation created by that charter. Indeed, in the very application it is stated

[1] 4 Wheaton, 625.   [2] *Ib.* 626–27.

that these funds will be so applied. "Surely in this transaction every ingredient of a complete and legitimate contract is to be found." [1]

This being so, is such a contract "protected" by the Constitution, and do the New Hampshire College Acts impair that contract? Marshall states clearly and fairly Chief Justice Richardson's argument that to construe the contract clause so broadly as to cover the Dartmouth charter would prevent legislative control of public offices, and even make divorce laws invalid; and that the intention of the framers of the Constitution was to confine the operation of the contract clause to the protection of property rights, as the history of the times plainly shows. [2]

All this, says Marshall, "may be admitted." The contract clause "never has been understood to embrace other contracts than those which respect property, or some object of value, and confer rights which may be asserted in a court of justice." Divorce laws are not included, of course — they merely enable a court, "not to impair a marriage contract, but to liberate one of the parties because it has been broken by the other."

The "point on which the cause essentially depends" is "the true construction" of the Dartmouth charter. If that instrument grants "political power," creates a "civil institution" as an instrument of government; "if the funds of the college be public property," or if the State Government "be alone interested in its transactions," the Legislature may do

[1] 4 Wheaton, 627.   [2] *Ib.* 627–28.

what it likes "unrestrained" by the National Constitution.[1]

If, on the other hand, Dartmouth "be a private eleemosynary institution," empowered to receive property "for objects unconnected with government," and "whose funds are bestowed by individuals on the faith of the charter; if the donors have stipulated for the future disposition and management of those funds in the manner prescribed by themselves," the case becomes more difficult.[2] Marshall then sets out compactly and clearly the facts relating to the establishment of Wheelock's school; the granting and acceptance of the charter; the nature of the College funds which "consisted entirely of private donations." These facts unquestionably show, he avows, that Dartmouth College is "an eleemosynary, and, as far as respects its funds, a private corporation."[3]

Does the fact that the purpose of the College is the education of youth make it a public corporation? It is true that the Government may found and control an institution of learning. "But is Dartmouth College such an institution? Is education altogether in the hands of government?" Are all teachers public officers? Do gifts for the advancement of learning "necessarily become public property, so far that the will of the legislature, not the will of the donor, becomes the law of donation?"[4]

[1] 4 Wheaton, 629–30.　　　　[2] Ib. 630.
[3] Ib. 631–34. The statement of facts and of the questions growing out of them was by far the best work Marshall did. In these statements he is as brief, clear, and pointed as, in his arguments, he is prolix, diffuse, and repetitious.　　　　[4] Ib. 634.

Certainly Eleazar Wheelock, teaching and supporting Indians "at his own expense, and on the voluntary contributions of the charitable," was not a public officer. The Legislature could not control his money and that given by others, merely because Wheelock was using it in an educational charity. Whence, then, comes "the idea that Dartmouth College has become a public institution? . . Not from the source" or application of its funds. "Is it from the act of incorporation?" [1]

Such is the process by which Marshall reaches his famous definition of the word "corporation": "A corporation is an artificial being, invisible, intangible, and existing only in contemplation of law. . . It possesses only those properties which the charter of its creation confers upon it. . . Among the most important are immortality, and . . individuality. . . By these means, a perpetual succession of individuals are capable of acting for the promotion of the particular object, like one immortal being. . . But . . it is no more a state instrument than a natural person exercising the same powers would be." [2]

This, says Marshall, is obviously true of all private corporations. "The objects for which a corporation is created are universally such as the government wishes to promote." Why should a private charity, incorporated for the purpose of education, be excluded from the rules that apply to other corporations? An individual who volunteers to teach is not a public officer because of his personal devotion to

[1] 4 Wheaton, 635–36.   [2] *Ib.* 636.

education; how, then, is it that a corporation formed for precisely the same service "should become a part of the civil government of the country?" Because the Government has authorized the corporation "to take and to hold property in a particular form, and for particular purposes, has the Government a consequent right substantially to change that form, or to vary the purposes to which the property is to be applied?" Such an idea is without precedent. Can it be supported by reason? [1]

Any corporation for any purpose is created only because it is "deemed beneficial to the country; and this benefit constitutes the consideration, and, in most cases, the sole consideration for the grant." This is as true of incorporated charities as of any other form of incorporation. Of consequence, the Government cannot, subsequently, assume a power over such a corporation which is "in direct contradiction to its [the corporate charter's] express stipulations." So the mere fact "that a charter of incorporation has been granted" does not justify a Legislature in changing "the character of the institution," or in transferring "to the Government any new power over it."

"The character of civil institutions does not grow out of their incorporation, but out of the manner in which they are formed, and the objects for which they are created. The right to change them is not founded on their being incorporated, but on their being the instruments of government, created for its purposes. The same institutions, created for the same objects,

[1] 4 Wheaton, 637.

though not incorporated, would be public institutions, and, of course, be controllable by the legislature. The incorporating act neither gives nor prevents this control. Neither, in reason, can the incorporating act change the character of a private eleemosynary institution." [1]

For whose benefit was the property of Dartmouth College given to that institution? For the people at large, as counsel insist? Read the charter. Does it give the State "any exclusive right to the property of the college, any exclusive interest in the labors of the professors?" Does it not rather "merely indicate a willingness that New Hampshire should enjoy those advantages which result to all from the establishment of a seminary of learning in the neighborhood? On this point we think it impossible to entertain a serious doubt." For the charter shows that, while the spread of education and religion was the object of the founders of the College, the "particular interests" of the State "never entered into the minds of the donors, never constituted a motive for their donation." [2]

It is plain, therefore, that every element of the problem shows "that Dartmouth College is an eleemosynary institution, incorporated for the purpose of perpetuating . . the bounty of the donors, to the specified objects of that bounty"; that the Trustees are legally authorized to perpetuate themselves and that they are "not public officers"; that, in fine, Dartmouth College is a "seminary of education, incorporated for the preservation of its

[1] 4 Wheaton, 638–39.   [2] *Ib.* 639–40

property, and the perpetual application of that property to the objects of its creation." [1]

There remains a question most doubtful of "all that have been discussed." Neither those who have given money or land to the College, nor students who have profited by those benefactions, "complain of the alteration made in its charter, or think themselves injured by it. The trustees alone complain, and the trustees have no beneficial interest to be protected." Can the charter "be such a contract as the constitution intended to withdraw from the power of state legislation?" [2]

Wheelock and the other philanthropists who had endowed the College, both before and after the charter was granted, made their gifts "for something . . of inestimable value — . . the perpetual application of the fund to its object, in the mode prescribed by themselves. . . The corporation . . stands in their place, and distributes their bounty, as they would themselves have distributed it, had they been immortal." Also the rights of the students "collectively" are "to be exercised . . by the corporation." [3]

The British Parliament is omnipotent. Yet had it annulled the charter, even immediately after it had been granted and conveyances made to the corporation upon the faith of that charter, "so that the living donors would have witnessed the disappointment of their hopes, the perfidy of the transaction would have been universally acknowledged." Nevertheless, Parliament would have had the power to

---

[1] 4 Wheaton, 640–41.   [2] *Ib.* 641.   [3] *Ib.* 642–43.

perpetrate such an outrage. "Then, as now, the donors would have had no interest in the property; .. the students .. no rights to be violated;.. the trustees .. no private, individual, beneficial interest in the property confided to their protection." But, despite the legal power of Parliament to destroy it, "the contract would at that time have been deemed sacred by all."

"What has since occurred to strip it of its inviolability? Circumstances have not changed it. In reason, in justice, and in law, it is now what it was in 1769." The donors and Trustees, on the one hand, and the Crown on the other, were the original parties to the arrangement stated in the charter, which was "plainly a contract" between those parties. To the "rights and obligations" of the Crown under that contract, "New Hampshire succeeds."[1] Can such a contract be impaired by a State Legislature?

"It is a contract made on a valuable consideration.

"It is a contract for the security and disposition of property.

"It is a contract, on the faith of which real and personal estate has been conveyed to the corporation.

"It is then a contract within the letter of the constitution, and within its spirit also, unless" the nature of the trust creates "a particular exception, taking this case out of the prohibition contained in the constitution."

It is doubtless true that the "preservation of rights of this description was not particularly in the view of the framers of the constitution when the

[1] 4 Wheaton, 643.

clause under consideration was introduced into that instrument," and that legislative interferences with contractual obligations "of more frequent recurrence, to which the temptation was stronger, and of which the mischief was more extensive, constituted the great motive for imposing this restriction on the state legislatures.

"But although a particular and a rare case may not . . induce a rule, yet it must be governed by the rule, when established, unless some plain and strong reason for excluding it can be given. It is not enough to say that this particular case was not in the mind of the convention when the article was framed, nor of the American people when it was adopted. It is necessary to go farther, and to say that, had this particular case been suggested, the language [of the contract clause] would have been so varied as to exclude it, or it would have been made a special exception." [1]

Can the courts now make such an exception? "On what safe and intelligible ground can this exception stand?" Nothing in the language of the Constitution; no "sentiment delivered by its contemporaneous expounders . . justify us in making it."

Does "the nature and reason of the case itself . . sustain a construction of the constitution, not warranted by its words?" The contract clause was made a part of the Nation's fundamental law "to give stability to contracts." That clause in its "plain import" comprehends Dartmouth's charter. Does public policy demand a construction which

[1] 4 Wheaton, 644.

will exclude it? The fate of all similar corporations is involved. "The law of this case is the law of all." [1] Is it so necessary that Legislatures shall "new-model" such charters "that the ordinary rules of construction must be disregarded in order to leave them exposed to legislative alteration?"

The importance attached by the American people to corporate charters like that of Dartmouth College is proved by "the interest which this case has excited." If the framers of the Constitution respected science and literature so highly as to give the National Government exclusive power to protect inventors and writers by patents and copyrights, were those statesman "so regardless of contracts made for the advancement of literature as to intend to exclude them from provisions made for the security of ordinary contracts between man and man?" [2]

No man ever did or will found a college, "believing at the time that an act of incorporation constitutes no security for the institution; believing that it is immediately to be deemed a public institution, whose funds are to be governed and applied, not by the will of the donor, but by the will of the legislature. All such gifts are made in the pleasing, perhaps delusive hope, that the charity will flow forever in the channel which the givers have marked out for it."

Since every man finds evidence of this truth "in his own bosom," can it be imagined that "the framers of our constitution were strangers" to the same universal sentiment? Although "feeling

[1] 4 Wheaton, 645.   [2] *Ib.* 646–47.

the necessity . . of giving permanence and security to contracts," because of the "fluctuating" course and "repeated interferences" of Legislatures which resulted in the "most perplexing and injurious embarrassments," did the framers of the Constitution nevertheless deem it "necessary to leave these contracts subject to those interferences?" Strong, indeed, must be the motives for making such exceptions.[1]

Finally, Marshall declares that the "opinion of the court, after mature deliberation, is, that this is a contract, the obligation of which cannot be impaired without violating the Constitution of the United States."[2]

Do the New Hampshire College Acts impair the obligations of Dartmouth's charter? That instrument gave the Trustees "the whole power of governing the college"; stipulated that the corporation "should continue forever"; and "that the number of trustees should forever consist of twelve, and no more." This contract was made by the Crown, a power which could have made "no violent alteration in its essential terms, without impairing its obligation."

The powers and duties of the Crown were, by the Revolution, "devolved on the people of New Hampshire." It follows that, since the Crown could not change the charter of Dartmouth without impairing the contract, neither can New Hampshire. "All contracts, and rights, respecting property, remained unchanged by the revolution."[3]

[1] 4 Wheaton, 647–48.   [2] *Ib.* 650.   [3] *Ib.* 651.

As to whether the New Hampshire College Acts radically alter the charter of Dartmouth College, "two opinions cannot be entertained." The State takes over the government of the institution. "The will of the state is substituted for the will of the donors, in every essential operation of the college. . . The charter of 1769 exists no longer" — the College has been converted into "a machine entirely subservient to the will of government," instead of the "will of its founders." [1] Therefore, the New Hampshire College laws "are repugnant to the constitution of the United States." [2]

On account of the death of Woodward, who had been Secretary and Treasurer of the University, and formerly held the same offices in the College against whom the College Trustees had brought suit, Webster moved for judgment *nunc pro tunc;* and judgment was immediately entered accordingly.

Not for an instant could Webster restrain the expression of his joy. Before leaving the courtroom he wrote his brother: "All is safe. . . The opinion was delivered by the Chief Justice. It was very able and very elaborate; it goes the whole length, and leaves not an inch of ground for the University to stand on." [3] He informed President Brown that "all is safe and certain. . . I feel a load removed from my shoulders much heavier than they have been accustomed to bear." [4] To Mason, Webster describes Marshall's manner: "The Chief

---

[1] 4 Wheaton, 652–53.   [2] *Ib.* 654.

[3] Webster "in court" to his brother, Feb. 2, 1819, *Priv. Corres.:* Webster, I, 300.

[4] Webster to Brown, Feb. 2, 1819, *ib.*

Justice's opinion was in his own peculiar way. He reasoned along from step to step; and, not referring to the cases [cited], adopted the principles of them, and worked the whole into a close, connected, and very able argument." [1]

At the same time Hopkinson wrote Brown in a vein equally exuberant: "Our triumph . . has been complete. Five judges, only six attending, concur not only in a decision in our favor, but in placing it upon principles broad and deep, and which secure corporations of this description from legislative despotism and party violence for the future. . . I would have an inscription over the door of your building, 'Founded by Eleazar Wheelock, Refounded by Daniel Webster.'" [2] The high-tempered Pinkney was vocally indignant. "He talked . . and blustered" ungenerously, wrote Webster, "because . . the party was in a fever and he must do something for his fees. As he could not talk *in* court, he therefore talked *out* of court." [3]

As we have seen, Marshall had prepared his opinion under his trees at Richmond and in the mountains during the vacation of 1818; and he had barely time to read it to his associates before the opening of court at the session when it was delivered. But he afterward submitted the manuscript to Story, who made certain changes, although enthusiastically praising it. "I am much obliged," writes Marshall,

[1] Webster to Mason, Feb. 4, 1819, Hillard, 213–14. Webster adds: "Some of the other judges, I am told, have drawn opinions with more reference to authorities." (*Ib.* 214.)

[2] Hopkinson to Brown, Feb. 2, 1819, *Priv. Corres.*: Webster, I, 301.

[3] Webster to Mason, April 13, 1819, Hillard, 223.

"by the alterations you have made in the Dartmouth College case & am highly gratified by what you say respecting it." [1]

Story also delivered an opinion upholding the charter [2] — one of his ablest papers. It fairly bristles with citations of precedents and historical examples. The whole philosophy of corporations is expounded with clearness, power, and learning. Apparently Justice Livingston liked Story's opinion even more than that of Marshall. Story had sent it to Livingston, who, when returning the manuscript, wrote: It "has afforded me more pleasure than can easily be expressed. It was exactly what I had expected from you, and hope it will be adopted without alteration." [3]

At the time of the Dartmouth decision little attention was paid to it outside of New Hampshire and

[1] Marshall to Story, May 27, 1819, *Proceedings, Mass. Hist. Soc.* 2d Series, xiv, 324–25.

[2] 4 Wheaton, 666–713.

[3] Livingston to Story, Jan. 24, 1819, Story, i, 323. This important letter discredits the rumor that Story at first thought the College Acts valid.

Story sent copies of his opinion to eminent men other than his associates on the Supreme Bench, among them William Prescott, father of the historian, a Boston lawyer highly esteemed by the leaders of the American bar. "I have read your opinion with care and great pleasure," writes Prescott. "In my judgment it is supported by the principles of our constitutions, and of all free governments, as well as by the authority of adjudged cases. As one of the public, I thank you for establishing a doctrine affecting so many valuable rights and interests, with such clearness and cogency of argument, and weight of authority as must in all probability prevent its ever being again disturbed. I see nothing I should wish altered in it. I hope it will be adopted without diminution or subtraction. You have placed the subject in some strong, and to me, new lights, although I had settled my opinion on the general question years ago." (Prescott to Story, Jan. 9, 1819, *ib* 324.)

Massachusetts.[1] The people, and even the bar, were too much occupied with bank troubles, insolvency, and the swiftly approaching slavery question, to bother about a small New Hampshire college. The profound effect of Marshall's opinion was first noted in the *North American Review* a year after the Chief Justice delivered it. "Perhaps no judicial proceedings in this country ever involved more important consequences, . . than the case of Dartmouth College."[2]

Important, indeed, were the "consequences" of the Dartmouth decision. Everywhere corporations were springing up in response to the necessity for larger and more constant business units and because of the convenience and profit of such organizations. Marshall's opinion was a tremendous stimulant to this natural economic tendency. It reassured investors in corporate securities and gave confidence and steadiness to the business world. It is undeniable and undenied that America could not have been developed so rapidly and solidly without the power which the law as announced by Marshall gave to industrial organization.

One result of his opinion was, for the period, of even higher value than the encouragement it gave to private enterprise and the steadiness it brought to business generally; it aligned on the side of Nationalism all powerful economic forces operating through corporate organization. A generation passed before railway development began in Amer-

---

[1] For instance, the watchful Niles does not even mention it in his all-seeing and all-recording *Register*. Also see Warren, 377.

[2] *North American Review* (1820), x, 83.

ica; but Marshall lived to see the first stage of
the evolution of that mighty element in American
commercial, industrial, and social life; and all of
that force, except the part of it which was directly
connected with and under the immediate influence of the slave power, was aggressively and most
effectively Nationalist.

That this came to be the fact was due to Marshall's Dartmouth opinion more than to any other
single cause. The same was true of other industrial
corporate organizations. John Fiske does not greatly
exaggerate in his assertion that the law as to corporate franchises declared by Marshall, in subjecting
to the National Constitution every charter granted
by a State "went farther, perhaps, than any other
in our history toward limiting State sovereignty and
extending the Federal jurisdiction." [1]

Sir Henry Sumner Maine has some ground for
his rather dogmatic statement that the principle of
Marshall's opinion "is the basis of credit of many
of the great American Railway Incorporations," and
"has . . secured full play to the economical forces
by which the achievement of cultivating the soil of
the North American Continent has been performed."
Marshall's statesmanship is, asserts Maine, "the
bulwark of American individualism against democratic impatience and Socialistic fantasy." [2] Such
views of the Dartmouth decision are remarkably
similar to those which Story himself expressed soon
after it was rendered. Writing to Chancellor Kent

---

[1] Fiske: *Essays, Historical and Literary*, I, 379.
[2] Maine: *Popular Government*, 248.

Story says: "Unless I am very much mistaken the principles on which that decision rests will be found to apply with an extensive reach to all the great concerns of the people, and will check any undue encroachments upon civil rights, which the passions or the popular doctrines of the day may stimulate our State Legislatures to adopt." [1]

The court's decision, however, made corporate franchises infinitely more valuable and strengthened the motives for procuring them, even by corruption. In this wise tremendous frauds have been perpetrated upon negligent, careless, and indifferent publics; and "enormous and threatening powers," selfish and non-public in their purposes and methods, have been created.[2] But Marshall's opinion put the public on its guard. Almost immediately the States enacted laws reserving to the Legislature the right to alter or repeal corporate charters; and the constitutions of several States now include this limitation on corporate franchises. Yet these reservations did not, as a practical matter, nullify or overthrow Marshall's philosophy of the sacredness of contracts.

Within the last half-century the tendency has been strongly away from the doctrine of the Dartmouth decision, and this tendency has steadily become more powerful. The necessity of modifying and even abrogating legislative grants, more freely than is secured by the reservation to do so contained in State constitutions and corporate charters, has further restricted the Dartmouth decision. It is this necessity that has

---

[1] Story to Kent, Aug. 21, 1819, Story, i, 331.
[2] See Cooley: *Constitutional Limitations* (6th ed.), footnote to 335.

produced the rapid development of "that well-known but undefined power called the police power," [1] under which laws may be passed and executed, in disregard of what Marshall would have called contracts, provided such laws are necessary for the protection or preservation of life, health, property, morals, or order. The modern doctrine is that "the Legislature cannot, by any contract, divest itself of the power to provide for these objects. . . They are to be attained and provided for by such appropriate means as the legislative discretion may devise. That discretion can no more be bargained away than the power itself." [2]

Aside from the stability which this pronouncement of the Chief Justice gave to commercial transactions in general, and the confidence it inspired throughout the business world, the largest permanent benefit of it to the American people was to teach them that faith once plighted, whether in private contracts or public grants, must not and cannot be broken by State legislation; that, by the fundamental law which they themselves established for their own government, they as political entities are forbidden to break their contracts by enacting statutes, just as, by the very spirit of the law, private persons are forbidden to break their contracts. If it be said that their representatives may betray the people, the plain answer is that the people must learn to elect honest agents.

For exactly a century Marshall's Dartmouth opin-

[1] Butchers' Union, etc. *vs.* Crescent City, etc. 111 U.S. 750.
[2] Beer Company *vs.* Massachusetts, 97 U.S. 25; and see Fertilizing Co. *vs.* Hyde Park, *ib.* 659.

ion has been assailed and the Supreme Court itself
has often found ways to avoid its conclusions. But
the theory of the Chief Justice has shown amazing
vitality. Sixty years after Marshall delivered it, Chief
Justice Waite declared that the principles it announced are so "imbedded in the jurisprudence of
the United States as to make them to all intents
and purposes a part of the Constitution itself." [1]
Thirty-one years after Marshall died, Justice Davis
avowed that "a departure from it [Marshall's doc-
trine] *now* would involve dangers to society that
cannot be foreseen, would shock the sense of justice
of the country, unhinge its business interests, and
weaken, if not destroy, that respect which has always been felt for the judicial department of the
Government." [2] As late as 1895, Justice Brown asserted that it has "become firmly established as a
canon of American jurisprudence." [3]

It was a principle which Marshall introduced into
American Constitutional law, and, fortunately for
the country, that principle still stands; but to-day
the courts, when construing a law said to impair the
obligation of contracts, most properly require that
it be established that the unmistakable purpose of
the Legislature is to make an actual contract for a
sufficient consideration. [4]

[1] Stone *vs*. Mississippi, October, 1879, 11 Otto (101 U.S.) 816.
[2] The Binghamton Bridge, December, 1865, 3 Wallace, 73.
[3] Pearsall *vs*. Great Northern Railway, 161 U.S. 660.
[4] More has been written of Marshall's opinion in this case than of
any other delivered by him except that in Marbury *vs*. Madison.
For recent discussions of the subject see Russell: "Status and Tendencies of the Dartmouth College Case," *Am. Law Rev.* xxx, 322–56,
an able, scholarly, and moderate paper; Doe: "A New View of the

It is highly probable that in the present state of the country's development, the Supreme Court would not decide that the contract clause so broadly protects corporate franchises as Marshall held a century ago. In considering the Dartmouth decision, however, the state of things existing when it was rendered must be taken into account. It is certain that Marshall was right in his interpretation of corporation law as it existed in 1819; right in the practical result of his opinion in that particular case; and, above all, right in the purpose and effect of that opinion on the condition and tendency of the country at the perilous time it was delivered.

Dartmouth College Case," *Harvard Law Review*, VI, 161–81, a novel and well-reasoned article; Trickett: "The Dartmouth College Paralogism," *North American Review*, XL, 175–87, a vigorous radical essay; Hall: "The Dartmouth College Case," *Green Bag*, XX, 244–47, a short but brilliant attack upon the assailants of Marshall's opinion; Jenkins: "Should the Dartmouth College Decision be Recalled," *Am. Law Rev.* LI, 711–51, a bright, informed, and thorough treatment from the extremely liberal point of view. A calm, balanced, and convincing review of the effect of the Dartmouth decision on American economic and social life is that of Professor Edward S. Corwin in his *Marshall and the Constitution*, 167–72. When reading these comments, however, the student should, at the same time, carefully reëxamine Marshall's opinion.

CHAPTER VI

VITALIZING THE CONSTITUTION

The crisis is one which portends destruction to the liberties of the American people. (Spencer Roane.)

The constitutional government of this republican empire cannot be practically enforced but by a fair and liberal interpretation of its powers.
(William Pinkney.)

The Judiciary of the United States is the subtle corps of sappers and miners constantly working under ground to undermine the foundations of our confederated fabric. (Jefferson.)

The government of the Union is emphatically and truly a government of the people. In form and substance it emanates from them. Its powers are granted by them, and are to be exercised directly on them and for their benefit.
(Marshall.)

ALTHOUGH it was the third of the great causes to be decided by the Supreme Court in the memorable year, 1819, M'Culloch *vs.* Maryland was the first in importance and in the place it holds in the development of the American Constitution. Furthermore, in his opinion in this case John Marshall rose to the loftiest heights of judicial statesmanship. If his fame rested solely on this one effort, it would be secure.

To comprehend the full import of Marshall's opinion in this case, the reader must consider the state of the country as described in the fourth chapter of this volume. While none of his expositions of our fundamental law, delivered in the critical epoch from 1819 to 1824, can be entirely understood without knowledge of the National conditions that produced them, this fact must be especially borne in mind when reviewing the case of M'Culloch *vs.* Maryland.

Like most of the controversies in which Marshall's Constitutional opinions were pronounced, M'Culloch *vs.* Maryland came before the Supreme Court on an agreed case. The facts were that Congress had authorized the incorporation of the second Bank of the United States; that this institution had instituted a branch at Baltimore; that the Legislature of Maryland had passed an act requiring all banks, established "without authority from the state," to issue notes only on stamped paper and only of certain denominations, or, in lieu of these requirements, only upon the payment of an annual tax of fifteen thousand dollars; that, in violation of this law, the Baltimore branch of the National Bank continued to issue its notes on unstamped paper without paying the tax; and that on May 8, 1818, John James, "Treasurer of the Western Shore," had sued James William M'Culloch, the cashier of the Baltimore branch, for the recovery of the penalties prescribed by the Maryland statute.[1]

The immediate question was whether the Maryland law was Constitutional; but the basic issue was the supremacy of the National Government as against the dominance of State Governments. Indeed, the decision of this case involved the very existence of the Constitution as an "ordinance of Nationality," as Marshall so accurately termed it.

At no time in this notable session of the Supreme Court was the basement room, where its sittings

---

[1] These penalties were forfeits of $500 for every offense — a sum that would have aggregated hundreds of thousands, perhaps millions of dollars, in the case of the Baltimore branch, which did an enormous business. The Maryland law also provided that "every person having any agency in circulating" any such unauthorized note of the Bank should be fined one hundred dollars. (Act of Feb. 11, 1818, *Laws of Maryland*, 174.)

were now again held, so thronged with auditors as it was when the argument in M'Culloch *vs.* Maryland took place. "We have had a crowded audience of ladies and gentlemen," writes Story toward the close of the nine days of discussion. "The hall was full almost to suffocation, and many went away for want of room."[1]

Webster opened the case for the Bank. His masterful argument in the Dartmouth College case the year before had established his reputation as a great Constitutional lawyer as well as an orator of the first class. He was attired in the height of fashion, tight breeches, blue cloth coat, cut away squarely at the waist, and adorned with large brass buttons, waistcoat exposing a broad expanse of ruffled shirt with high soft collar surrounded by an elaborate black stock.[2]

The senior counsel for the Bank was William Pinkney. He was dressed with his accustomed foppish elegance, and, as usual, was nervous and impatient. Notwithstanding his eccentricities, he was Webster's equal, if not his superior, except in physical presence and the gift of political management. With Webster and Pinkney was William Wirt, then Attorney-General of the United States, who had arrived at the fullness of his powers.

Maryland was represented by Luther Martin, still Attorney-General for that State, then seventy-five years old, but a strong lawyer despite his half-

[1] Story to White, March 3, 1819, Story, I, 325.

[2] Webster always dressed with extreme care when he expected to make a notable speech or argument. For a description of his appearance on such an occasion see Sargent: *Public Men and Events*, I, 172.

century, at least, of excessive drinking. By his side was Joseph Hopkinson of Philadelphia, now fifty years of age, one of the most learned men at the American bar. With Martin and Hopkinson was Walter Jones of Washington, who appears to have been a legal genius, his fame obliterated by devotion to his profession and unaided by any public service, which so greatly helps to give permanency to the lawyer's reputation. All told, the counsel for both sides in M'Culloch *vs.* Maryland were the most eminent and distinguished in the Republic.

Webster said in opening that Hamilton had "exhausted" the arguments for the power of Congress to charter a bank and that Hamilton's principles had long been acted upon. After thirty years of acquiescence it was too late to deny that the National Legislature could establish a bank.[1] With meticulous care Webster went over Hamilton's reasoning to prove that Congress can "pass all laws 'necessary and proper' to carry into execution powers conferred on it." [2]

Assuming the law which established the Bank to be Constitutional, could Maryland tax a branch of that Bank? If the State could tax the Bank at all, she could put it out of existence, since a "power to tax involves . . a power to destroy" [3] — words that Marshall, in delivering his opinion, repeated as his own. The truth was, said Webster, that, in taxing the Baltimore branch of the National Bank, Maryland taxed the National Government itself.[4]

Joseph Hopkinson, as usual, made a superb argu-

[1] 4 Wheaton, 323.   [2] *Ib*. 324.   [3] *Ib*. 327.   [4] *Ib*. 328.

ment — a performance all the more admirable as an
intellectual feat in that, as an advocate for Maryland, his convictions were opposed to his reasoning.[1]
Walter Jones was as thorough as he was lively, but
he did little more than to reinforce the well-nigh perfect argument of Hopkinson.[2] On the same side the
address of Luther Martin deserves notice as the last
worthy of remark which that great lawyer ever made.
Old as he was, and wasted as were his astonishing
powers, his argument was not much inferior to those
of Webster, Hopkinson, and Pinkney. Martin showed
by historical evidence that the power now claimed
for Congress was suspected by the opponents of
the Constitution, but denied by its supporters and
called "a dream of distempered jealousy." So came
the Tenth Amendment; yet, said Martin, now,
"we are asked to engraft upon it [the Constitution]
powers . . which were disclaimed by them [the advocates of the Constitution], and which, if they had
been fairly avowed at the time, would have prevented
its adoption."[3]

Could powers of Congress be inferred as a necessary means to the desired end? Why, then, did the
Constitution *expressly* confer powers which, of necessity, must be implied? For instance, the power
to declare war surely implied the power to raise
armies; and yet that very power was granted in specific terms. But the power to create corporations
"is not expressly delegated, either as an end or a
means of national government."[4]

[1] 4 Wheaton, 330 *et seq.*   [2] *Ib.* 362 *et seq.*
[3] *Ib.* 272–73.   [4] *Ib.* 374

When Martin finished, William Pinkney, whom Marshall declared to be "the greatest man he had ever seen in a Court of justice," [1] rose to make what proved to be the last but one of the great arguments of that unrivaled leader of the American bar of his period. To reproduce his address is to set out in advance the opinion of John Marshall stripped of Pinkney's rhetoric which, in that day, was deemed to be the perfection of eloquence. [2]

For three days Pinkney spoke. Few arguments ever made in the Supreme Court affected so profoundly the members of that tribunal. Story describes the argument thus: "Mr. Pinkney rose on Monday to conclude the argument; he spoke all that day and yesterday, and will probably conclude to-day. I never, in my whole life, heard a greater speech; it was worth a journey from Salem to hear it; his elocution was excessively vehement, but his eloquence was overwhelming. His language, his style, his figures, his arguments, were most brilliant and sparkling. He spoke like a great statesman and patriot, and a sound constitutional lawyer. All the cobwebs of sophistry and metaphysics about State rights and State sovereignty he brushed away with a mighty besom." [3]

Indeed, all the lawyers in this memorable contest appear to have surpassed their previous efforts at

---

[1] Tyler: *Memoir of Roger Brooke Taney*, 141.

[2] The student should carefully examine Pinkney's argument. Although the abstract of it given in Wheaton's report is very long, a painstaking study of it will be helpful to a better understanding of the development of American Constitutional law. (4 Wheaton, 377–400.)

[3] Story to White, March 3, 1819, Story, I, 324–25.

the bar. Marshall, in his opinion, pays this tribute to all their addresses: "Both in maintaining the affirmative and the negative, a splendor of eloquence, and strength of argument seldom, if ever, surpassed, have been displayed." [1]

After he had spoken, Webster, who at that moment was intent on the decision of the Dartmouth College case,[2] became impatient. "Our Bank argument goes on — & threatens to be long," he writes Jeremiah Mason.[3] Four days later, while Martin was still talking, Webster informs Jeremiah Smith: "We are not yet thro. the Bank question. Martin has been *talking 3 ds*. Pinkney replies tomorrow & that finishes — I set out for home next day." [4] The arguments in M'Culloch *vs*. Maryland occupied nine days.[5]

Four days before the Bank argument opened in the Supreme Court, the House took up the resolution offered by James Johnson of Virginia to repeal the Bank's charter.[6] The debate over this proposal continued until February 25, the third day of the argument in M'Culloch *vs*. Maryland. How, asked Johnson, had the Bank fulfilled expectations and promises? "What . . is our condition? Surrounded by one universal gloom. We are met by the tears of the widow and the orphan." [7] Madison has "cast a shade" on his reputation by signing the Bank Bill

[1] 4 Wheaton, 426.   [2] See *supra*, chap. v.
[3] Webster to Mason, Feb. 24, 1819, Van Tyne, 78–79.
[4] Webster to Smith, Feb. 28, 1819, *ib.* 79–80.
[5] From February 22 to February 27 and from March 1 to March 3, 1819.
[6] February 18, 1819. See *Annals*, 15th Cong. 2d Sess. 1240.
[7] *Ib.* 1242.

— that "act of usurpation." Under the common law the charter " is forfeited." [1]

The Bank is a "mighty corporation," created "to overawe . . the local institutions, that had dealt themselves almost out of breath in supporting the Government in times of peril and adversity." The financial part of the Virginia Republican Party organization thus spoke through James Pindall of that State. [2]

William Lowndes of South Carolina brilliantly defended the Bank, but admitted that its "early operation" had been "injudicious." [3] John Tyler of Virginia assailed the Bank with notable force. "This charter has been violated," he said; "if subjected to investigation before a court of justice, it will be declared null and void." [4] David Walker of Kentucky declared that the Bank "is an engine of favoritism — of stock jobbing" — a machine for "binding in adamantine chains the blessed, innocent lambs of America to accursed, corrupt European tigers." [5] In spite of all this eloquence, Johnson's resolution was defeated, and the fate of the Bank left in the hands of the Supreme Court.

On March 6, 1819, before a few spectators, mostly lawyers with business before the court, Marshall read his opinion. It is the misfortune of the biographer that only an abstract can be given of this epochal state paper — among the very first of the greatest judicial utterances of all time. [6] It was de-

---

[1] *Annals,* 15th Cong. 2d Sess. 1249–50.   [2] *Ib.* 1254.
[3] *Ib.* 1286.   [4] *Ib.* 1311.   [5] *Ib.* 1404–06.
[6] "Marshall's opinion in M'Culloch *vs.* Maryland, is perhaps the most celebrated Judicial utterance in the annals of the English speaking world." (*Great American Lawyers:* Lewis, ii, 363.)

livered only three days after Pinkney concluded his
superb address.

Since it is one of the longest of Marshall's opinions
and, by general agreement, is considered to be his
ablest and most carefully prepared exposition of the
Constitution, it seems not unlikely that much of it
had been written before the argument. The court
was very busy every day of the session and there
was little, if any, time for Marshall to write this
elaborate document. The suit against M'Culloch
had been brought nearly a year before the Supreme
Court convened; Marshall undoubtedly learned of
it through the newspapers; he was intimately familiar with the basic issue presented by the litigation;
and he had ample time to formulate and even to
write out his views before the ensuing session of the
court. He had, in the opinions of Hamilton and Jefferson,[1] the reasoning on both sides of this fundamental controversy. It appears to be reasonably
probable that at least the framework of the opinion
in M'Culloch *vs.* Maryland was prepared by Marshall when in Richmond during the summer, autumn,
and winter of 1818–19.

The opening words of Marshall are majestic: "A
sovereign state denies the obligation of a law . . of
the Union. . . The constitution of our country, in its
most . . vital parts, is to be considered; the conflicting powers of the government of the Union and of its

---

[1] As the biographer of Washington, Marshall had carefully read
both Hamilton's and Jefferson's Cabinet opinions on the constitutionality of a National bank. Compare Hamilton's argument (vol.
II, 72–74, of this work) with Marshall's opinion in M'Culloch *vs.*
Maryland.

members, . . are to be discussed; and an opinion given, which may essentially influence the great operations of the government." [1] He cannot "approach such a question without a deep sense of . . the awful responsibility involved in its decision. But it must be decided peacefully, or remain a source of hostile legislation, perhaps of *hostility of a still more serious nature.*" [2] In these solemn words the Chief Justice reveals the fateful issue which M'Culloch *vs.* Maryland foreboded.

That Congress has power to charter a bank is not "an open question. . . The principle . . was introduced at a very early period of our history, has been recognized by many successive legislatures, and has been acted upon by the judicial department . . as a law of undoubted obligation. . . An exposition of the constitution, deliberately established by legislative acts, on the faith of which an immense property has been advanced, ought not to be lightly disregarded."

The first Congress passed the act to incorporate a National bank. The whole subject was at the time debated exhaustively. "The bill for incorporating the bank of the United States did not steal upon an unsuspecting legislature, & pass unobserved," says Marshall. Moreover, it had been carefully examined with "persevering talent" in Washington's Cabinet. When that act expired, "a short experience of the embarrassments" suffered by the country "induced the passage of the present law." He must be intrepid, indeed, who asserts that "a measure adopted under

[1] 4 Wheaton, 400.   [2] *Ib.* (Italics the author's.)

these circumstances was a bold and plain usurpation, to which the constitution gave no countenance." [1]

But Marshall examines the question as though it were "entirely new"; and gives an historical account of the Constitution which, for clearness and brevity, never has been surpassed. [2] Thus he proves that "the government proceeds directly from the people; . . their act was final. It required not the affirmance, and could not be negatived, by the state governments. The constitution when thus adopted . . bound the state sovereignties." The States could and did establish "a league, such as was the confed-

[1] 4 Wheaton, 400–02.

[2] "In discussing this question, the counsel for the state of Maryland have deemed it of some importance, in the construction of the constitution, to consider that instrument not as emanating from the people, but as the act of sovereign and independent states. The powers of the general government, it has been said, are delegated by the states, who alone are truly sovereign; and must be exercised in subordination to the states, who alone possess supreme dominion.

"It would be difficult to sustain this proposition. The convention which framed the constitution was indeed elected by the state legislatures. But the instrument, when it came from their hands, was a mere proposal, without obligation, or pretensions to it. It was reported to the then existing Congress of the United States, with a request that it might ' be submitted to a convention of delegates, chosen in each state, by the people thereof, under the recommendation of its legislature, for their assent and ratification.' This mode of proceeding was adopted; and by the convention, by Congress, and by the state legislatures, the instrument was submitted to the people.

" They acted upon it in the only manner in which they can act safely, effectively, and wisely, on such a subject, by assembling in convention. It is true, they assembled in their several states — and where else should they have assembled? No political dreamer was ever wild enough to think of breaking down the lines which separate the states, and of compounding the American people into one common mass. Of consequence, when they act, they act in their states. But the measures they adopt do not, on that account, cease to be the measures of the people themselves, or become the measures of the state governments. From these conventions the constitution derives its whole authority." (4 Wheaton, 402–03.)

eration. . . But when, 'in order to form a more perfect union,' it was deemed necessary to change this alliance into an effective government, . . acting directly on the people," it was the people themselves who acted and established a fundamental law for their government.[1]

The Government of the American Nation is, then, "emphatically, and truly, a government of the people. In form and in substance it emanates from them. Its powers are granted by them, and are to be exercised directly on them, and for their benefit"[2] — a statement, the grandeur of which was to be enhanced forty-four years later, when, standing on the battle-field of Gettysburg, Abraham Lincoln said that "a government of the people, by the people, for the people, shall not perish from the earth."[3]

To be sure, the States, as well as the Nation, have certain powers, and therefore "the supremacy of their respective laws, when they are in opposition, must be settled." Marshall proceeds to settle that basic question. The National Government, he begins, "is supreme within its sphere of action. This would

[1] 4 Wheaton, 403–04.   [2] *Ib.* 405.

[3] The Nationalist ideas of Marshall and Lincoln are identical; and their language is so similar that it seems not unlikely that Lincoln paraphrased this noble passage of Marshall and thus made it immortal. This probability is increased by the fact that Lincoln was a profound student of Marshall's Constitutional opinions and committed a great many of them to memory.

The famous sentence of Lincoln's Gettysburg Address was, however, almost exactly given by Webster in his Reply to Hayne: "It is . . the people's Government; made for the people: made by the people; and answerable to the people." (*Debates*, 21st Cong. 1st Sess. 74; also Curtis, I, 355–61.) But both Lincoln and Webster merely stated in condensed and simpler form Marshall's immortal utterance in M'Culloch *vs.* Maryland. (See also *infra*, chap. x.)

seem to result necessarily from its nature." For "it is the government of all; its powers are delegated by all; it represents all, and acts for all. Though any one state may be willing to control its operations, no state is willing to allow others to control them. The nation, on those subjects on which it can act, must necessarily bind its component parts." Plain as this truth is, the people have not left the demonstration of it to "mere reason" — for they have, "in express terms, decided it by saying" that the Constitution, and the laws of the United States which shall be made in pursuance thereof, "shall be the supreme law of the land," and by requiring all State officers and legislators to "take the oath of fidelity to it." [1]

The fact that the powers of the National Government enumerated in the Constitution do not include that of creating corporations does not prevent Congress from doing so. "There is no phrase in the instrument which, like the articles of confederation, *excludes* incidental or implied powers; and which requires that everything granted shall be expressly and minutely described. . . A constitution, to contain an accurate detail of all the subdivisions of which its great powers will admit, and of all the means by which they may be carried into execution, would partake of a prolixity of a legal code, and could scarcely be embraced by the human mind. It would probably never be understood by the public."

The very "nature" of a constitution, "therefore.

[1] 4 Wheaton, 405–06.

requires, that only its great outlines should be marked, its important objects designated, and the minor ingredients which compose those *objects be deduced from the nature of the objects themselves*." In deciding such questions "we must never forget," reiterates Marshall, "that it is a *constitution* we are expounding." [1]

This being true, the power of Congress to establish a bank is undeniable — it flows from "the great powers to lay and collect taxes; to borrow money; to regulate commerce; to declare and conduct a war; and to raise and support armies and navies." Consider, he continues, the scope of the duties of the National Government: "The sword and the purse, all the external relations, and no inconsiderable portion of the industry of the nation, are entrusted to its government... A government, entrusted with such ample powers, on the due execution of which the happiness and prosperity of the nation so vitally depends, must also be entrusted with ample means for their execution. The power being given, it is the interest of the nation to facilitate its execution. It can never be their interest, and cannot be presumed to have been their intention, to clog and embarrass its execution by withholding the most appropriate means." [2]

At this point Marshall's language becomes as exalted as that of the prophets: "Throughout this vast republic, from the St. Croix to the Gulf of Mexico, from the Atlantic to the Pacific, revenue is to be collected and expended, armies are to be

[1] 4 Wheaton, 406–07. (Italics the author's.)   [2] *Ib.*, 407–08.

marched and supported. The exigencies of the
nation may require that the treasure raised in the
north should be transported to the south, that
raised in the east conveyed to the west, or that this
order should be reversed." Here Marshall the
soldier is speaking. There is in his words the blast
of the bugle of Valley Forge. Indeed, the pen with
which Marshall wrote M'Culloch *vs.* Maryland was
fashioned in the army of the Revolution.[1]

The Chief Justice continues: "Is that construction of the constitution to be preferred which would
render these operations difficult, hazardous, and expensive?" Did the framers of the Constitution "when
granting these powers for the public good" intend
to impede "their exercise by withholding a choice
of means?" No! The Constitution "does not profess to enumerate the means by which the powers
it confers may be executed; nor does it prohibit
the creation of a corporation, if the existence of
such a being be essential to the beneficial exercise
of those powers." [2]

Resorting to his favorite method in argument,
that of repetition, Marshall again asserts that the
fact that "the power of creating a corporation is one
appertaining to sovereignty and is not expressly conferred on Congress," does not take that power from
Congress. If it does, Congress, by the same reasoning, would be denied the power to pass most laws;
since "all legislative powers appertain to sovereignty." They who say that Congress may not
select "any appropriate means" to carry out its

[1] See vol. I, 72, of this work.   [2] 4 Wheaton, 408–09.

admitted powers, "take upon themselves the burden of establishing that exception." [1]

The establishment of the National Bank was a means to an end; the power to incorporate it is "as incidental" to the great, substantive, and independent powers expressly conferred on Congress as that of making war, levying taxes, or regulating commerce. [2] This is not only the plain conclusion of reason, but the clear language of the Constitution itself as expressed in the "necessary and proper" clause [3] of that instrument. Marshall treats with something like contempt the argument that this clause does not mean what it says, but is "really restrictive of the general right, which might otherwise be implied, of selecting means for executing the enumerated powers" — a denial, in short, that, without this clause, Congress is authorized to make laws. [4] After conferring on Congress all legislative power, "after allowing each house to prescribe its own course of proceeding, after describing the manner in which a bill should become a law, would it have entered into the mind . . of the convention that an express power to make laws was necessary to enable the legislature to make them?" [5]

In answering the old Jeffersonian argument that, [6] under the "necessary and proper" clause, Congress can adopt only those means absolutely "necessary"

---

[1] 4 Wheaton, 409–10.   [2] *Ib.* 411.

[3] "The Congress shall have Power . . to make all Laws which shall be necessary and proper for carrying into Execution the foregoing Powers, and all other Powers vested by this Constitution in the Government of the United States, or in any Department or Officer thereof." (Constitution of the United States, Article i, Section 8.)

[4] 4 Wheaton, 412.   [5] *Ib.* 413.   [6] See vol. ii, 71, of this work.

to the execution of express powers, Marshall devotes an amount of space which now seems extravagant. But in 1819 the question was unsettled and acute; indeed, the Republicans had again made it a political issue. The Chief Justice repeats the arguments made by Hamilton in his opinion to Washington on the first Bank Bill.[1]

Some words have various shades of meaning, of which courts must select that justified by "common usage." "The word 'necessary' is of this description. . . It admits of all degrees of comparison. . . A thing may be necessary, very necessary, absolutely or indispensably necessary." For instance, the Constitution itself prohibits a State from "laying 'imposts or duties on imports or exports, except what may be *absolutely* necessary for executing its inspection laws '"; whereas it authorizes Congress to "'make all laws which shall be necessary and 'proper'" for the execution of powers expressly conferred.[2]

Did the framers of the Constitution intend to forbid Congress to employ "*any*" means "which might be appropriate, and which were conducive to the end"? Most assuredly not! "The subject is the execution of those great powers on which the welfare of a nation essentially depends." The "necessary and proper" clause is found "in a constitution intended to endure for ages to come, and, consequently, to be adapted to the various crises of human affairs. . . To have declared that the best means shall not be used, but those alone without which

---

[1] Vol. II, 72–74, of this work.   [2] 4 Wheaton, 414.

the power given would be nugatory, would have been to deprive the legislature of the capacity to avail itself of experience, to exercise its reason, and to accommodate its legislation to circumstances." [1]

The contrary conclusion is tinged with "insanity." Whence comes the power of Congress to prescribe punishment for violations of National laws? No such general power is expressly given by the Constitution. Yet nobody denies that Congress has this general power, although "it is expressly given in some cases," such as counterfeiting, piracy, and "offenses against the law of nations." Nevertheless, the specific authorization to provide for the punishment of these crimes does not prevent Congress from doing the same as to crimes not specified. [2]

Now comes an example of Marshall's reasoning when at his best — and briefest.

"Take, for example, the power 'to establish post-offices and post-roads.' This power is executed by the single act of making the establishment. But, from this has been inferred the power and duty of carrying the mail along the post-road, from one post-office to another. And, from this implied power, has again been inferred the right to punish those who steal letters from the post-office, or rob the mail. It may be said, with some plausibility, that the right to carry the mail, and to punish those who rob it, is not indispensably necessary to the establishment of a post-office and post-road. This right is indeed essential to the beneficial exercise of the power, but not indispensably necessary to its

[1] 4 Wheaton, 415.   [2] *Ib.* 416–17.

existence. So, of the punishment of the crimes of
stealing or falsifying a record or process of a court
of the United States, or of perjury in such court.
To punish these offenses is certainly conducive to
the due administration of justice. But courts may
exist, and may decide the causes brought before
them, though such crimes escape punishment.

"The baneful influence of this narrow construction on all the operations of the government, and
the absolute impracticability of maintaining it
without rendering the government incompetent to
its great objects, might be illustrated by numerous
examples drawn from the constitution, and from
our laws. The good sense of the public has pronounced, without hesitation, that the power of
punishment appertains to sovereignty, and may be
exercised whenever the sovereign has a right to act,
as incidental to his constitutional powers. It is a
means for carrying into execution all sovereign
powers, and may be used, although not indispensably necessary. It is a right incidental to the power,
and conducive to its beneficial exercise." [1]

To attempt to prove that Congress *might* execute
its powers without the use of other means than
those absolutely necessary would be "to waste time
and argument," and "not much less idle than to
hold a lighted taper to the sun." It is futile to speculate upon imaginary reasons for the "necessary and
proper" clause, since its purpose is obvious. It "is
placed among the powers of Congress, not among
the limitations on those powers. Its terms purport

[1] 4 Wheaton, 417–18.

to enlarge, not to diminish the powers vested in the government. . . If no other motive for its insertion can be suggested, a sufficient one is found in the desire to remove all doubts respecting the right to legislate on the vast mass of incidental powers which must be involved in the constitution, if that instrument be not a splendid bauble." [1]

Marshall thus reaches the conclusion that Congress may "perform the high duties assigned to it, in the manner most beneficial to the people." Then comes that celebrated passage — one of the most famous ever delivered by a jurist: "Let the end be legitimate, let it be within the scope of the constitution, and all means which are appropriate, which are plainly adapted to that end, which are not prohibited, but consist with the letter and spirit of the constitution, are constitutional." [2]

Further on the Chief Justice restates this fundamental principle, without which the Constitution would be a lifeless thing: "Where the law is not prohibited, and is really calculated to effect any of the objects entrusted to the government, to undertake here to inquire into the degree of its necessity, would be to pass the line which circumscribes the judicial department, and to tread on legislative ground. The court disclaims all pretensions to such a power." [3]

The fact that there were State banks with whose business the National Bank might interfere, had nothing to do with the question of the power of Congress to establish the latter. The National

[1] 4 Wheaton, 419–21.   [2] *Ib.* 421.   [3] *Ib.* 423.

Government does not depend on State Governments "for the execution of the great powers assigned to it. Its means are adequate to its ends." It can choose a National bank rather than State banks as an agency for the transaction of its business; "and Congress alone can make the election."

It is, then, "the unanimous and decided opinion" of the court that the Bank Act is Constitutional. So is the establishment of the branches of the parent bank. Can States tax these branches, as Maryland has tried to do? Of course the power of taxation "is retained by the states," and "is not abridged by the grant of a similar power to the government of the Union." These are "truths which have never been denied."

With sublime audacity Marshall then declares that "such is the paramount character of the constitution that its capacity to withdraw any subject from the action of even this power, is admitted." [1] This assertion fairly overwhelms the student, since the States then attempting to tax out of existence the branches of the National Bank did not admit, but emphatically denied, that the National Government could withdraw from State taxation any taxable subject whatever, except that which the Constitution itself specifically withdraws.

"The States," argues Marshall, "are expressly forbidden" to tax imports and exports. This being so, "the same paramount character would seem to restrain, as it certainly may restrain, a state from such other exercise of this [taxing] power, as is in

[1] 4 Wheaton, 424–25.

its nature incompatible with, and repugnant to, the constitutional laws of the Union. A law, absolutely repugnant to another, as entirely repeals that other as if express terms of repeal were used."

In this fashion Marshall holds, in effect, that Congress can restrain the States from taxing certain subjects not mentioned in the Constitution as fully as though those subjects were expressly named.

It is on this ground that the National Bank claims exemption "from the power of a state to tax its operations." Marshall concedes that "there is no express provision [in the Constitution] for the case, but the claim has been sustained on a principle which so entirely pervades the constitution, is so intermixed with the materials which compose it, so interwoven with its web, so blended with its texture, as to be incapable of being separated from it without rendering it into shreds." [1]

This was, indeed, going far — the powers of Congress placed on "a principle" rather than on the language of the Constitution. When we consider the period in which this opinion was given to the country, we can understand — though only vaguely at this distance of time — the daring of John Marshall. Yet he realizes the extreme radicalism of the theory of Constitutional interpretation he is thus advancing, and explains it with scrupulous care.

"This great principle is that the constitution and the laws made in pursuance thereof are supreme; that they control the constitution and laws of the respective states, and cannot be controlled by them. From this, which may be almost termed an axiom,

[1] 4 Wheaton, 425–26.

other propositions are deduced as corollaries, on the truth or error of which . . the cause is supposed to depend." [1]

That "cause" was not so much the one on the docket of the Supreme Court, entitled M'Culloch *vs.* Maryland, as it was that standing on the docket of fate entitled Nationalism *vs.* Localism. And, although Marshall did not actually address them, everybody knew that he was speaking to the disunionists who were increasing in numbers and boldness. Everybody knew, also, that the Chief Justice was, in particular, replying to the challenge of the Virginia Republican organization as given through the Court of Appeals of that State. [2]

The corollaries which Marshall deduced from the principle of National supremacy were: "1st. That a power to create implies a power to preserve. 2d. That a power to destroy, if wielded by a different hand, is hostile to, and incompatible with these powers to create and to preserve. 3d. That where this repugnancy exists, that authority which is supreme must control, not yield to that over which it is supreme." [3]

It is "too obvious to be denied," continues Marshall that, if permitted to exercise the power, the States can tax the Bank "so as to destroy it." The power of taxation is admittedly "sovereign"; but the taxing power of the States "is subordinate to, and may be controlled by the constitution of the United States. How far it has been controlled by that instrument must be a question of construction. In

[1] 4 Wheaton, 426.   [2] See *supra*, 158 *et seq.*   [3] 4 Wheaton, 426.

making this construction, no principle not declared can be admissible, which would defeat the legitimate operations of a supreme government. It is of the very essence of supremacy to remove all obstacles to its action within its own sphere, and so to modify every power vested in subordinate governments as to exempt its own operations from their own influence. This effect need not be stated in terms. It is so involved in the declaration of supremacy, so necessarily implied in it, that the expression of it could not make it more certain. We must, therefore, keep it [the principle of National supremacy] in view while construing the constitution." [1]

Unlimited as is the power of a State to tax objects within its jurisdiction, that State power does not "extend to those means which are employed by Congress to carry into execution powers conferred on that body by the people of the United States . . powers . . given . . to a government whose laws . . are declared to be supreme. . . The right never existed [in the States] . . to tax the means employed by the government of the Union, for the execution of its powers." [2]

Regardless of this fact, however, can States tax instrumentalities of the National Government? It cannot be denied, says Marshall, that "the power to tax involves the power to destroy; that the power to destroy may defeat . . the power to create; that there is a plain repugnance, in conferring on one government a power to control the constitutional measures of another, which other, with respect to

[1] 4 Wheaton, 427.   [2] *Ib.* 429-30.

those very measures, is declared to be supreme over that which exerts the control." [1]

Here Marshall permits himself the use of sarcasm, which he dearly loved but seldom employed. The State Rights advocates insisted that the States can be trusted not to abuse their powers — confidence must be reposed in State Legislatures and officials; they would not destroy needlessly, recklessly. "All inconsistencies are to be reconciled by the magic of the word CONFIDENCE," says Marshall. "But," he continues, "is this a case of 'confidence'? Would the people of any one state trust those of another with a power to control the most insignificant operations of their state government? We know they would not."

By the same token the people of one State would never consent that the Government of another State should control the National Government "to which they have confided the most important and most valuable interests. In the legislature of the Union alone, are all represented. The legislature of the Union alone, therefore, can be trusted by the people with the power of controlling measures which concern all, in the confidence that it will not be abused. This, then, is not a case of confidence." [2]

The State Rights theory is "capable of arresting all the measures of the government, and of prostrating it at the foot of the states." Instead of the National Government being "supreme," as the Constitution declares it to be, "supremacy" would be transferred "in fact, to the states"; for, "if the

[1] 4 Wheaton, 431.   [2] *Ib.*

states may tax one instrument, employed by the
government in the execution of its powers, they may
tax any and every other instrument. They may tax
the mail; they may tax the mint; they may tax
patent-rights; they may tax the papers of the cus-
tom-house; they may tax judicial process; they may
tax all the means employed by the government, to
an excess which would defeat all the ends of government. This was not intended by the American people. They did not design to make their government
dependent on the states."

The whole question is, avows Marshall, "in truth,
a question of supremacy." If the anti-National
principle that the States can tax the instrumentalities of the National Government is to be sustained,
then the declaration in the Constitution that it and
laws made under it "shall be the supreme law of the
land, is empty and unmeaning declamation." [1]

Maryland had argued that, since the taxing power
is, at least, "concurrent" in the State and National
Governments, the States can tax a National bank as
fully as the Nation can tax State banks. But, remarks Marshall, "the two cases are not on the same
reason." The whole American people and all the
States are represented in Congress; when they
tax State banks, "they tax their constituents; and
these taxes must be uniform. But, when a state taxes
the operations of the government of the United
States, it acts upon institutions created, not by their
own constituents, but by people over whom they
claim no control. It acts upon the measures of a

[1] 4 Wheaton, 432–33.

government created by others as well as themselves, for the benefit of others in common with themselves.

"The difference is that which always exists, and always must exist, between the action of the whole on a part, and the action of a part on the whole — between the laws of a government declared to be supreme, and those of a government which, when in opposition to those laws, is not supreme. . . The states have no power, by taxation or otherwise, to retard, impede, burden, or in any manner control the operations of the constitutional laws enacted by Congress to carry into execution the powers vested in the general government." [1]

For these reasons, therefore, the judgment of the Supreme Court was that the Maryland law taxing the Baltimore branch of the National Bank was "contrary to the constitution . . and void"; that the judgment of the Baltimore County Court against the branch bank "be reversed and annulled," and that the judgment of the Maryland Court of Appeals affirming the judgment of the County Court also "be reversed and annulled." [2]

In effect John Marshall thus rewrote the fundamental law of the Nation; or, perhaps it may be more accurate to say that he made a written instrument a living thing, capable of growth, capable of keeping pace with the advancement of the American people and ministering to their changing necessities. This greatest of Marshall's treatises on government may well be entitled the "Vitality of the Constitution." Story records that Marshall's opinion aroused great

[1] 4 Wheaton, 435–36. [2] *Ib.* 437.

political excitement;[1] and no wonder, since the Chief
Justice announced, in principle, that Congress had
sufficient power to "emancipate every slave in the
United States" as John Randolph declared five
years later.[2]

Roane, Ritchie, Taylor, and the Republican organization of Virginia had anticipated that the Chief
Justice would render a Nationalist opinion; but they
were not prepared for the bold and crushing blows
which he rained upon their fanatically cherished theory of Localism. As soon as they recovered from their
surprise and dismay, they opened fire from their
heaviest batteries upon Marshall and the National
Judiciary. The way was prepared for them by a
preliminary bombardment in the *Weekly Register* of
Hezekiah Niles.

This periodical had now become the most widely
read and influential publication in the country; it
had subscribers from Portland to New Orleans, from
Savannah to Fort Dearborn. Niles had won the confidence of his far-flung constituency by his honesty,
courage, and ability. He was the prototype of Horace Greeley, and the *Register* had much the same
hold on its readers that the *Tribune* came to have
thirty years later.

In the first issue of the *Register*, after Marshall's
opinion was delivered, Niles began an attack upon
it that was to spread all over the land. "A deadly
blow has been struck at the *sovereignty of the states*,
and from a quarter so far removed from the people
as to be hardly accessible to public opinion," he

[1] Story to his mother, March 7, 1819, Story, I, 325–26.
[2] See *infra*, 420; also 325–27; 338–39, 534–37.

wrote. "The welfare of the union has received a more dangerous wound than fifty *Hartford* conventions . . could inflict." Parts of Marshall's opinion are "*incomprehensible*. But perhaps, as some people ell us of what *they* call the *mysteries* of religion, the *common people* are not to understand them, such things being reserved only for the *priests ! !*" [1]

The opinion of the Chief Justice was published in full in Niles's *Register* two weeks after he delivered it,[2] and was thus given wider publicity than any judicial utterance previously rendered in America. Indeed, no pronouncement of any court, except, perhaps, that in Gibbons *vs.* Ogden,[3] was read so generally as Marshall's opinion in M'Culloch *vs.* Maryland, until the publication of the Dred Scott decision thirty-eight years later. Niles continues his attack in the number of the *Register* containing the Bank opinion:

It is "more important than any ever before pronounced by that exalted tribunal — a tribunal so far removed from the people, that some seem to regard it with a species of that awful reverence in which the inhabitants of Asia look up to their princes." [4] This exasperated sentence shows the change that Marshall, during his eighteen years on the bench, had wrought in the standing and repute of the Supreme Court.[5] The doctrines of the Chief Justice amount to this, said Niles — "congress may grant *monopolies*" at will, "if the *price* is paid for them, or without any pecuniary consideration at all." As for

---

[1] Niles, xvi, 41–44.   [2] *Ib.* 68–76.   [3] See *infra*, chap. viii.
[4] Niles, xvi, 65.   [5] See vol. iii, 130–31, of this work.

the Chief Justice personally, he "has not added . .
to his stock of reputation by writing it — *it is excessively labored.*" [1]

Papers throughout the country copied Niles's bitter criticisms,[2] and public opinion rapidly crystallized against Marshall's Nationalist doctrine. Every
where the principle asserted by the Chief Justice
became a political issue; or, rather, his declaration,
that that principle was law, made sharper the controversy that had divided the people since the framing
of the Constitution.

In number after number of his *Register* Niles, pours
his wrath on Marshall's matchless interpretation.
It is "far more dangerous to the union and happiness
of the people of the United States than . . *foreign
invasion.*[3] . . Certain nabobs in Boston, New York,
Philadelphia and Baltimore, . . to secure the passage
of an act of *incorporation*, . . fairly purchase the souls
of some members of the national legislature with
money, as happened in Georgia, or secure the votes of
others by making them *stockholders*, as occurred in
New York, and the act is passed.[4] . . We call upon
the people, the honest people, who hate *monopolies*
and *privileged orders*, to arise in their strength and
purge our political temple of the *money-changers*
and those who sell *doves* — causing a reversion to
the original purity of our system of government,

[1] Niles, xvi, 65.

[2] *Ib.* 97. For instance, the *Natchez Press*, in announcing its intention to print Marshall's whole opinion, says that, if his doctrine prevails, "the independence of the individual states . . is obliterated at
one fell sweep." No country can remain free "that tolerates incorporated banks, in any guise." (*Ib.* 210.)

[3] *Ib.* 103.

[4] *Ib.* 104.

that the faithful centinel may again say, 'ALL'S WELL!'" [1]

Extravagant and demagogical as this language of Niles's now seems, he was sincere and earnest in the use of it. Copious quotations from the *Register* have been here made because it had the strongest influence on American public opinion of any publication of its time. Niles's *Register* was, emphatically, the mentor of the country editor. [2]

At last the hour had come when the Virginia Republican triumvirate could strike with an effect impossible of achievement in 1816 when the Supreme Court rebuked and overpowered the State appellate tribunal in Martin *vs.* Hunter's Lessee. [3] Nobody outside of Virginia then paid any attention to that decision, so obsessed was the country by speculation and seeming prosperity. But in 1819 the collapse had come; poverty and discontent were universal; rebellion against Nationalism was under way; and the vast majority blamed the Bank of the United States for all their woes. Yet Marshall had upheld "the monster." The Virginia Junto's opportunity had arrived.

No sooner had Marshall returned to Richmond than he got wind of the coming assault upon him. On March 23, 1819, the *Enquirer* published his opinion in full. The next day the Chief Justice wrote Story: "Our opinion in the Bank case has aroused the sleeping spirit of Virginia, if indeed it ever sleeps.

---

[1] Niles, XVI, 105.

[2] Niles's attack on Marshall's opinion in M'Culloch *vs.* Maryland ran through three numbers. (See *ib.* 41–44; 103–05; 145–47.)

[3] See *supra*, 161–67.

It will, I understand, be attacked in the papers with some asperity, and as those who favor it never write for the publick it will remain undefended & of course be considered as *damnably heretical*." [1] He had been correctly informed. The attack came quickly.

On March 30, Spencer Roane opened fire in the paper of his cousin Thomas Ritchie, the *Enquirer*,[2] under the *nom de guerre* of "Amphictyon." His first article is able, calm, and, considering his intense feelings, fair and moderate. Roane even extols his enemy:

"That this opinion is very able every one must admit. This was to have been expected, proceeding as it does from a man of the most profound legal attainments, and upon a subject which has employed his thoughts, his tongue, and his pen, as a politician, and an historian for more than thirty years. The subject, too, is one which has, perhaps more than any other, heretofore drawn a broad line of distinction between the two great parties in this country, on which line no one has taken a more distinguished and decided rank than the judge who has thus expounded the supreme law of the land. It is not in my power to carry on a contest upon such a subject with a man of his gigantic powers." [3]

Niles had spoken to " the plain people "; Roane is now addressing the lawyers and judges of the country. His essay is almost wholly a legal argument.

[1] Marshall to Story, March 24, 1819, *Proceedings, Mass. Hist. Soc.* 2d Series, xiv, 324.

[2] See *supra*, 146.

[3] *Enquirer*, March 30, 1819, as quoted in *Branch Hist. Papers*, June, 1905, 52–53.

It is based on the Virginia Resolutions of 1799 and gives the familiar State Rights arguments, applying them to Marshall's opinion.[1] In his second article Roane grows vehement, even fiery, and finally exclaims that Virginia " never will *employ force to support her doctrines till other measures have entirely failed.*" [2]

His attacks had great and immediate response. No sooner had copies of the *Enquirer* containing the first letters of Amphictyon reached Kentucky than the Republicans of that State declared war on Marshall. On April 20, the *Enquirer* printed the first Western response to Roane's call to arms. Marshall's principles, said the Kentucky correspondent, "must raise an alarm throughout our widely extended empire. . . The people must rouse from the lap of Delilah and prepare to meet the Philistines. . . No mind can compass the extent of the encroachments upon State and individual rights which may take place under the principles of this decision." [3]

Even Marshall, a political and judicial veteran in his sixty-fifth year, was perturbed. "The opinion in the Bank case continues to be denounced by the democracy in Virginia," he writes Story, after the second of Roane's articles appeared. "An effort is certainly making to induce the legislature which will meet in December to take up the subject & to pass resolutions not very unlike those which were called forth by the alien & sedition laws in 1799.

[1] *Branch Hist. Papers*, June, 1905, 51–63.
[2] *Enquirer*, April 2, 1819, as quoted in *Branch Hist. Papers*, June, 1905, 76. (Italics the author's.)
[3] *Enquirer*, April 20, 1819, as quoted in *ib.* 76.

Whether the effort will be successful or not may perhaps depend in some measure on the sentiments of our sister states. To excite this ferment the opinion has been grossly misrepresented; and where its argument has been truly stated it has been met by principles one would think too palpably absurd for intelligent men.

"But," he gloomily continues, "prejudice will swallow anything. If the principles which have been advanced on this occasion were to prevail the constitution would be converted into the old confederation." [1]

As yet Roane had struck but lightly. He now renewed the Republican offensive with greater spirit. During June, 1819, the *Enquirer* published four articles signed "Hampden," from Roane's pen. Ritchie introduced the "Hampden" essays in an editorial in which he urged the careful reading of the exposure "of the alarming errors of the Supreme Court. . . Whenever State rights are threatened or invaded, Virginia will not be the last to sound the tocsin." [2]

Are the people prepared "to give *carte blanche* to our federal rulers"? asked Hampden. Amendment of the Constitution by judicial interpretation is taking the place of amendment by the people. Infamous as the methods of National judges had been during the administration of Adams, "the most abandoned of our rulers," Marshall and his associates have done worse. They have given "a

[1] Marshall to Story, May 27, 1819, *Proceedings, Mass. Hist. Soc.* 2d Series, XIV, 325.

[2] *Enquirer*, June 11, 1819, as quoted in *Branch Hist. Papers*, June, 1905, footnote to 77.

general letter of attorney to the future legislators of
the Union. . . That man must be a deplorable idiot ·
who does not see that there is no . . difference" between an "*unlimited* grant of power and a grant
limited in its terms, but accompanied with *unlimited*
means of carrying it into execution. . . The crisis is
one which portends destruction to the liberties of
the American people." Hampden scoldingly adds:
"If Mason or Henry could lift their patriot heads
from the grave, . . they would almost exclaim, with
Jugurtha, 'Venal people! you will soon perish if you
can find a purchaser.'" [1]

For three more numbers Hampden pressed the
Republican assault on Marshall's opinion. The
Constitution is a "*compact*, to which the *States* are
the parties." Marshall's argument in the Virginia
Convention of 1788 is quoted,[2] and his use of certain
terms in his "Life of Washington" is cited.[3] If the
powers of the National Government ought to be
enlarged, "let this be the act of the *people*, and not
that of subordinate agents." [4] The opinion of the
Chief Justice repeatedly declares "that the general
government, though limited in its powers, is supreme." Hampden avows that he does "not understand this jargon. . . The *people* only are supreme.[5]
. . Our general government . . is as much a . . 'league'
as was the former confederation." Therefore, the

---

[1] *Enquirer*, June 11, 1819, as quoted in *Branch Hist. Papers*, June,
1905, 77–82.
[2] *Enquirer*, June 15, 1819, as quoted in *ib.* 85; also *Enquirer*, June
18, 1819, as quoted in *ib.* 95.
[3] *Enquirer*, June 15, 1819, as quoted in *ib.* 91.
[4] *Ib.* 87; also *Enquirer*, June 18, 1819, as quoted in *ib.* 96–97.
[5] *Ib.* 98.

Virginia Court of Appeals, in Hunter *vs.* Fairfax, declared an act of Congress "unconstitutional, although it had been sanctioned by the opinion of the Supreme Court of the United States." Pennsylvania, too, had maintained its "sovereignty." [1]

Hampden has only scorn for "*some* of the judges" who concurred in the opinion of the Chief Justice. They "had before been accounted republicans. . . Few men come out from high places, as pure as they went in." [2] If Marshall's doctrine stands, "the triumph over our liberties will be . . easy and complete." What, then, could "arrest this calamity"? Nothing but an "appeal" to the people. Let this majestic and irresistible power be invoked. [3]

That he had no faith in his own theory is proved by the rather dismal fact that, more than two months before Marshall "violated the Constitution" and "endangered the liberties" of the people by his Bank decision, Roane actually arranged for the purchase, as an investment for his son, of $4900 worth of the shares of the Bank of the United States, and actually made the investment. [4] This transaction, consummated even before the argument

[1] *Enquirer*, June 22, 1819, as quoted in *Branch Hist. Papers*, June, 1905, 116.

[2] *Ib.* 118.

[3] *Ib.* 121. Madison endorsed Roane's attacks on Marshall. (See Madison to Roane, Sept. 2, 1819, *Writings of James Madison:* Hunt, VIII, 447–53.)

[4] See Roane to his son, Jan. 4, 1819, *Branch Hist. Papers*, June, 1905, 134; and same to same, Feb. 4, 1819, *ib.* 135.

Eighteen days before Marshall delivered his opinion Roane again writes his son: "I have to-day deposited in the vaults of the Virga. bank a certificate in your name for 50 shares U. S. bank stock, as per memo., by Mr. Dandridge Enclosed. The shares cost, as you will see, $98 each." (Roane to his son, Feb. 16, 1819, *ib.* 136.)

in M'Culloch *vs.* Maryland, shows that Roane, the
able lawyer, was sure that Marshall would and ought
to sustain the Bank in its controversy with the States
that were trying to destroy it. Moreover, Dr. John
Brockenbrough, President of the Bank of Virginia,
actually advised the investment.[1]

It is of moment, too, to note at this point the
course taken by Marshall, who had long owned
stock in the Bank of the United States. As soon as
he learned that the suit had been brought which, of
a certainty, must come before him, the Chief Justice
disposed of his holdings.[2]

So disturbed was Marshall by Roane's attacks
that he did a thoroughly uncharacteristic thing.
By way of reply to Roane he wrote, under the *nom
de guerre* of "A Friend of the Union," an elaborate defense of his opinion and, through Bushrod
Washington, procured the publication of it in the
Union of Philadelphia, the successor of the *Gazette
of the United States*, and the strongest Federalist
newspaper then surviving.

On June 28, 1819, the Chief Justice writes Washington: "I expected three numbers would have concluded my answer to Hampden but I must write
two others which will follow in a few days. If the
publication has not commenced I could rather wish

[1] Roane to his son, note 4, p. 317.

[2] The entire transaction is set out in letters of Benjamin Watkins
Leigh to Nicholas Biddle, Aug. 21, Aug. 28, Sept. 4, and Sept. 13,
1837; and Biddle to Leigh, Aug. 24 and 25, Sept. 7 and Sept. 15, 1837.
(Biddle MSS. in possession of Professor R. C. McGrane of the University of Ohio, to whose courtesy the author is indebted for the
use of this material. These letters appear in full in the *Correspondence of Nicholas Biddle:* McGrane, 283–89, 291–92, published in September, 1919, by Houghton Mifflin Company, Boston.)

the signature to be changed to 'A Constitutionalist.'
A Friend of the Constitution is so much like a Friend
of the Union that it may lead to some suspicion of
identity. . . I hope the publication has commenced
unless the Editor should be unwilling to devote so
much of his paper to this discussion. The letters of
Amphyction & of Hampden have made no great
impression in Richmond but they were designed for
the country [Virginia] & have had considerable influence there. I wish the refutation to be in the
hands of some respectable members of the legislature
as it may prevent some act of the assembly [torn —
probably "both"] silly & wicked. If the publication
be made I should [like] to have two or three sets of
the papers to hand if necessary. I will settle with
you for the printer." [1]

The reading of Marshall's newspaper effort is
exhausting; a summary of the least uninteresting
passages will give an idea of the whole paper. The
articles published in the *Enquirer* were intended,
so he wrote, to inflict "deep wounds on the constitution," are full of "mischievous errours," and are
merely new expressions of the old Virginia spirit of
hostility to the Nation. The case of M'Culloch *vs.*
Maryland serves only as an excuse "for once more
agitating the publick mind, and reviving those unfounded jealousies by whose blind aid ambition
climbs the ladder of power." [2]

---

[1] Marshall to Bushrod Washington, June 28, 1819. This letter is
unsigned, but is in Marshall's unmistakable handwriting and is endorsed by Bushrod Washington, "C. Just. Marshall." (Marshall
MSS. Lib. Cong.)

[2] *Union*, April 24, 1819.

After a long introduction, Marshall enters upon his defense which is as wordy as his answer to the Virginia Resolutions. He is sensitive over the charge, by now popularly made, that he controls the Supreme Court, and cites the case of the Nereid to prove that the Justices give dissenting opinions whenever they choose. "The course of every tribunal must necessarily be, that the opinion which is to be delivered as the opinion of the court, is previously submitted to the consideration of all the judges; and, if any part of the reasoning be disapproved, it must be so modified as to receive the approbation of all, before it can be delivered as the opinion of all."

Roane's personal charges amount to this: "The chief justice . . is a federalist; who was a politician of some note before he was judge; and who with his tongue and his pen supported the opinions he avowed." With the politician's skill Marshall uses the fact that the majority of the court, which gave the Nationalist judgment in M'Culloch *vs.* Maryland, were Republicans — "four of whom [Story, Johnson, Duval, and Livingston] have no political sin upon their heads; — who in addition to being eminent lawyers, have the still greater advantage of being sound republicans; of having been selected certainly not for their federalism, by Mr Jefferson, and Mr Madison, for the high stations they so properly fill." For eight tedious columns of diffuse repetition Marshall goes on in defense of his opinion.[1]

When the biographer searches the daily life of a

[1] *Union*, April 24, 1819.

man so surpassingly great and good as Marshall, he hopes in no ungenerous spirit to find some human frailty that identifies his hero with mankind. The Greeks did not fail to connect their deities with humanity. The leading men of American history have been ill-treated in this respect — for a century they have been held up to our vision as superhuman creatures to admire whom was a duty, to criticize whom was a blasphemy, and to love or understand whom was an impossibility.

All but Marshall have been rescued from this frigid isolation. Any discovery of human frailty in the great Chief Justice is, therefore, most welcome. Some small and gracious defects in Marshall's character have appeared in the course of these volumes; and this additional evidence of his susceptibility to ordinary emotion is very pleasing. With all his stern repression of that element of his character, we find that he was sensitive in the extreme; in reality, thirsting for approval, hurt by criticism. In spite of this desire for applause and horror of rebuke, however, he did his duty, knowing beforehand that his finest services would surely bring upon him the denunciation and abuse he so disliked. By such peevishness as his anonymous reply in the *Union* to Roane's irritating attacks, we are able to get some measure of the true proportions of this august yet very human character.

When Marshall saw, in print, this controversial product of his pen, he was disappointed and depressed. The editor had, he avowed, so confused the manuscript that it was scarcely intelligible. At any rate, Marshall did not want his defense reproduced in New England. Story had heard of the article in the *Union*, and wrote Marshall that he wished to secure the publication of it. The Chief Justice replied:

"The piece to which you allude was not published in Virginia. Our patriotic papers admit no such political heresies. It contained, I think, a complete demonstration of the fallacies & errors contained in those attacks on the opinion of the Court which have most credit here & are supposed to proceed from a high source,[1] but was so mangled in the publication that those only who had bestowed close attention to the subject could understand it.

"There were two numbers[2] & the editor of the Union in Philadelphia, the paper in which it was published, had mixed the different numbers together so as in several instances to place the reasoning intended to demonstrate one proposition under another. The points & the arguments were so separated from each other, & so strangely mixed as to constitute a labyrinth to which those only who understood the whole subject perfectly could find a clue."[3]

It appears that Story insisted on having at least Marshall's rejoinder to Roane's first article reproduced in the Boston press. Again the Chief Justice evades the request of his associate and confidant:

---

[1] Marshall means that Jefferson inspired Roane's attacks.

[2] Marshall had written five essays, but the editor condensed them into two numbers.

[3] Marshall to Story, May 27, 1819, *Proceedings, Mass. Hist. Soc.* 2d Series, xiv, 325.

"I do not think a republication of the piece you mention in the Boston papers to be desired, as the antifederalism of Virginia will not, I trust, find its way to New England. I should also be sorry to see it in Mr. Wheaton's [1] appendix because that circumstance might lead to suspicions regarding the author & because I should regret to see it republished in its present deranged form with the two centres transposed." [2]

For a brief space, then, the combatants rested on their arms, but each was only gathering strength for the inevitable renewal of the engagement which was to be sterner than any previous phases of the contest.

Soon after the convening of the first session of the Virginia Legislature held subsequent to the decision of M'Culloch *vs.* Maryland, Roane addressed the lawmakers through the *Enquirer*, now signing himself "Publicola." He pointed out the "absolute disqualification of the supreme court of the U. S. to decide with impartiality upon controversies between the General and State Governments"; [3] and, to " ensure *unbiassed* " decisions, insisted upon a Constitutional amendment to establish a tribunal "(as occasion may require) " appointed partly by the States and partly by the National Government, " with *appellate* jurisdiction from the present supreme court." [4]

Promptly a resolution against Marshall's opinion

[1] Henry Wheaton, Reporter of the Supreme Court.
[2] Marshall to Story, July 13, 1819, *Proceedings, Mass. Hist. Soc.* 2d Series, xiv, 326.
[3] *Enquirer*, Jan. 30, 1821.   [4] *Ib.* Feb. 1, 1821.

was offered in the House of Delegates.[1] This note-worthy paper was presented by Andrew Stevenson, a member of the "committee for Courts of Justice." [2] The resolutions declared that the doctrines of M'Culloch *vs.* Maryland would "undermine the pillars of the Constitution itself." The provision giving to the judicial power "*all cases* arising *under the Constitution*" did not "extend to questions which would amount to a subversion of the constitution itself, by the usurpation of one contracting party on another." But Marshall's opinion was calculated to "change the whole character of the government." [3]

Sentences from the opinion of the Chief Justice are quoted, including the famous one: "Let the end be legitimate, . . and all the means which are appropriate, . . which are not prohibited, . . are constitutional." Did not such expressions import that Congress could "conform the constitution to their own designs" by the exercise of "unlimited and uncontrouled" power? The ratifying resolution of the Constitution by the Virginia Convention of 1788 is quoted.[4] Virginia's voice had been heard to the same effect in the immortal Resolutions of 1799. Her views had been endorsed by the country

---

[1] *Journal*, House of Delegates, Virginia, 1819–20, 56–59.

[2] *Ib.* 9.   [3] *Ib.* 57.

[4] This resolution declared that Virginia assented to the Constitution only on condition that "Every power *not granted*, remains with the people, and at their will; *that therefore no right of any denomination can be cancelled, abridged, restrained, or modified*, by the congress, by the senate, or house of representatives acting in any capacity; by the President or any department, or officer of the United States, except in those instances in which power is given by the constitution for those purposes." (*Journal*, House of Delegates, Virginia, 1819–20, 58.)

in the Presidential election of 1800 — that "great
revolution of principle." Her Legislature, therefore,
"enter their most solemn protest, against the decision of the supreme court, and of the principles
contained in it."

In this fashion the General Assembly insisted on
an amendment to the National Constitution "creating a *tribunal*" authorized to decide questions relative to the "powers of the general and state governments, under the compact." The Virginia Senators
are, therefore, instructed to do their best to secure
such an amendment and "to resist on every occasion" attempted legislation by Congress in conflict
with the views set forth in this resolution or those
of 1799 "which have been re-considered, and are
fully and entirely approved of by this Assembly."
The Governor is directed to transmit the resolutions
to the other States.[1]

At this point Slavery and Secession enter upon
the scene. Almost simultaneously with the introduction of the resolutions denouncing Marshall and
the Supreme Court for the judgment and opinion
in M'Culloch *vs.* Maryland, other resolutions were
offered by a member of the House named Baldwin
denouncing the imposition of restrictions on Missouri (the prohibition of slavery) as a condition of admitting that Territory to the Union. Such action by
Congress would "excite feelings eminently hostile
to the fraternal affection and prudent forbearance
which ought ever to pervade the confederated
union." [2] Two days later, December 30, the same

---

[1] *Journal*, House of Delegates, Virginia, 1819–20, 59.   [2] *Ib.* 76.

delegate introduced resolutions to the effect that
only the maintenance of the State Rights principle
could "preserve the confederated union," since
"no government can long exist which lies at the
mercy of another"; and, inferentially, that Marshall's opinion in M'Culloch *vs.* Maryland had violated that principle.[1]

A yet sterner declaration on the Missouri question
quickly followed, declaring that Congress had no
power to prohibit slavery in that State, and that
"Virginia will support the good people of Missouri
in their just rights . . and will co-operate with them
in resisting with manly fortitude any attempt
which Congress may make to impose restraints or
restrictions as the price of their admission" to the
Union.[2] The next day these resolutions, strengthened by amendment, were adopted.[3] On February
12, 1820, the resolutions condemning the Nationalist doctrine expounded by the Chief Justice in the
Bank case also came to a vote and passed, 117
ayes to 38 nays.[4] They had been amended and re-
amended,[5] but, as adopted, they were in substance
the same as those originally offered by Stevenson.
Through both these sets of resolutions — that on
the Missouri question and that on the Bank decision — ran the intimation of forcible resistance to
National authority. Introduced at practically the
same time, drawn and advocated by the same men,
passed by votes of the same members, these important declarations of the Virginia Legislature were

[1] *Journal*, House of Delegates, Virginia, 1819–20, 85.
[2] *Ib.* 105.   [3] *Ib.* 108–09.   [4] *Ib.* 179.   [5] *Ib.* 175–78.

meant to be and must be considered as a single expression of the views of Virginia upon National policy.

In this wise did the Legislature of his own State repudiate and defy that opinion of John Marshall which has done more for the American Nation than any single utterance of any other one man, excepting only the Farewell Address of Washington. In such manner, too, was the slavery question brought face to face with Marshall's lasting exposition of the National Constitution. For, it should be repeated, in announcing the principles by virtue of which Congress could establish the Bank of the United States, the Chief Justice had also asserted, by necessary inference, the power of the National Legislature to exact the exclusion of slavery as a condition upon which a State could be admitted to the Union. At least this was the interpretation of Virginia and the South.

The slavery question did not, to be sure, closely touch Northern States, but their local interests did. Thus it was that Ohio aligned herself with Virginia in opposition to Marshall's Nationalist statesmanship, and in support of the Jeffersonian doctrine of Localism. In such fashion did the Ohio Bank question become so intermingled with the conflict over Slavery and Secession that, in the consideration of Marshall's opinions at this time, these controversies cannot be separated. The facts of the Ohio Bank case must, therefore, be given at this point.[1]

Since the establishment at Cincinnati, early in 1817, of a branch of the Bank of the United States,

---

[1] For Marshall's opinion in this controversy see *infra*, 347 *et seq.*

Ohio had threatened to drive it from the State by
a prohibitive tax. Not long before the argument of
M'Culloch *vs.* Maryland in the Supreme Court, the
Ohio Legislature laid an annual tax of $50,000 on
each of the two branches which, by that time, had
been established in that State.[1] On February 8, 1819,
only four days previous to the hearing of the Maryland case at Washington, and less than a month before Marshall delivered his opinion, the Ohio law-
makers passed an act directing the State Auditor,
Ralph Osborn, to charge this tax of $50,000 against
each of the branches, and to issue a warrant for the
immediate collection of $100,000, the total amount
of the first year's tax.

This law is almost without parallel in severity,
peremptoriness, and defiant contempt for National
authority. If the branches refused to pay the tax,
the Ohio law enjoined the person serving the State
Auditor's warrant to seize all money or property belonging to the Bank, found on its premises or elsewhere. The agent of the Auditor was directed to
open the vaults, search the offices, and take everything of value.[2]

Immediately the branch at Chillicothe obtained
from the United States District Court, then in

---

[1] The second branch was established at Chillicothe.

[2] Chap. 83, *Laws of Ohio, 1818–19*, 1st Sess. 190–99.

Section 5 of this act will give the student the spirit of this autocratic law. This section made it the "duty" of the State agent collecting the tax, after demand on and refusal of the bank officers to pay
the tax, if he cannot readily find in the bank offices the necessary
amount of money, "to go into each and any other room or vault . .
and to every closet, chest, box or drawer in such banking house, to
open and search," and to levy on everything found. (*Ib.* 193.)

session at that place, an injunction forbidding
Osborn from collecting the tax;[1] but the bank's
counsel forgot to have a writ issued to stay the
proceedings. Therefore, no order of the court was
served; instead a copy of the bill praying that the
Auditor be restrained, together with a subpœna to
answer, was sent to Osborn. These papers were not,
of course, an injunction, but merely notice that one
had been applied for. Thinking to collect the tax
before the injunction could be issued, Osborn forthwith issued his Auditor's warrant to one John L.
Harper to collect the tax immediately. Assisted by
a man named Thomas Orr, Harper entered the
Chillicothe branch of the Bank of the United States,
opened the vaults, seized all the money to be found,
and deposited it for the night in the local State bank.
Next morning Harper and Orr loaded the specie,
bank notes, and other securities in a wagon and
started for Columbus.[2]

The branch bank tardily obtained an order from
the United States Court restraining Osborn, the
State Auditor, and Harper, the State agent, from delivering the money to the State Treasurer and from
making any report to the Legislature of the collection of the tax. This writ was served on Harper as he
and Orr were on the road to the State Capital with
the money. Harper simply ignored the writ, drove

---

[1] A private letter to Niles says that when it was found that an injunction had been granted, the friends of the bank rejoiced, "wine
was drank freely and mirth abounded." (Niles, xvii, 85.) This explains the otherwise incredible negligence of the bank's attorneys in
the proceedings next day.

[2] Niles, xvii, 85–87, reprinting account as published in the *Chillicothe Supporter*, Sept. 22, 1819, and the *Ohio Monitor*, Sept. 25, 1819.

on to Columbus, and handed over to the State Treasurer the funds which he had seized at Chillicothe.

Harper and Orr were promptly arrested and imprisoned in the jail at Chillicothe.[1] Because of technical defects in serving the warrant for their arrest and in the return of the marshal, the prisoners were set free.[2] An order was secured from the United States Court directing Osborn and Harper to show cause why an attachment should not be issued against them for having disobeyed the court's injunction not to deliver the bank's money to the State Treasurer. After extended argument, the court issued the attachment, which, however, was not made returnable until the January term, 1821.

Meanwhile the Virginia Legislature passed its resolutions denouncing Marshall's opinion in M'Culloch vs. Maryland, and throughout the country the warfare upon the Supreme Court began. The Legislature of Ohio acted with a celerity and boldness that made the procedure of the Virginia Legislature seem hesitant and timid. A joint committee was speedily appointed and as promptly made its report. This report and the resolutions recommended by it were adopted without delay and transmitted to the Senate of the United States.[3]

The Ohio declaration is drawn with notable ability. A State cannot be sued — the true meaning of the Constitution forbids, and the Eleventh Amendment specifically prohibits, such procedure.

[1] Niles, xvii, 147.   [2] Ib. 338.
[3] Report of Committee made to the Ohio Legislature and transmitted to Congress. (Annals, 16th Cong. 2d Sess. 1685 et seq.)

a powerful group of States were acting in concert and that others ardently sympathized with them.

At this point, in different fashion, Virginia spoke again, this time by the voice of that great protagonist of Localism, John Taylor of Caroline, the originator of the Kentucky Resolutions,[1] and the most brilliant mind in the Republican organization of the Old Dominion. Immediately after Marshall's opinion in M'Culloch vs. Maryland, and while the Ohio conflict was in progress, he wrote a book in denunciation and refutation of Marshall's Nationalist principles. The editorial by Thomas Ritchie, commending Taylor's book, declares that "the crisis has come"; the Missouri question, the Tariff question, the Bank question, have brought the country to the point where a decision must be made as to whether the National Government shall be permitted to go on with its usurpations. "If there is any book capable of arousing the people, it is the one before us."

Taylor gave to his volume the title "Construction Construed, and Constitutions Vindicated." The phrases "exclusive interests" and "exclusive privileges" abound throughout the volume. Sixteen chapters compose this classic of State Rights philosophy. Five of them are devoted to Marshall's opinion in M'Culloch vs. Maryland; the others to theories of government, the state of the country, the protective tariff, and the Missouri question. The principles of the Revolution, avows Taylor, "are the keys of construction" and "the locks of liberty.[2]

[1] See vol. II, 397, of this work.
[2] Taylor: *Construction Construed, and Constitutions Vindicated*, 9.

.. No form of government can foster a fanaticism for wealth, without being corrupted." Yet Marshall's ideas establish "the despotick principle of a gratuitous distribution of wealth and poverty by law." [1]

If the theory that Congress can create corporations should prevail, "legislatures will become colleges for teaching the science of getting money by monopolies or favours." [2] To pretend faith in Christianity, and yet foster monopoly, is "like placing Christ on the car of Juggernaut." [3] The framers of the National Constitution tried to prevent the evils of monopoly and avarice by "restricting the powers given to Congress" and safeguarding those of the States; "in fact, by securing the freedom of property." [4]

Marshall is enamored of the word "sovereignty," an "equivocal and illimitable word," not found in "the declaration of independence, nor the federal constitution, nor the constitution of any single state"; all of them repudiated it "as a traitor of civil rights." [5] Well that they had so rejected this term of despotism! No wonder Jugurtha exclaimed, "Rome was for sale," when "the government exercised an absolute power over the national property." Of course it would "find purchasers." [6] To this condition Marshall's theories will bring America.

Whence this effort to endow the National Government with powers comparable to those of a monarchy? Plainly it is a reaction — "many wise and good men, .. alarmed by the illusions of Rousseau

---

[1] Taylor: *Construction Construed*, 11–12. Taylor does not, of course, call Marshall by name, either in this book or in his other attacks on the Chief Justice.

[2] *Ib.* 15.   [3] *Ib.* 16   [4] *Ib.* 18.   [5] *Ib.* 25–26   [6] *Ib.* 28.

and Godwin, and the atrocities of the French revolution, honestly believe that these [democratic] principles have teeth and claws, which it is expedient to draw and pare, however constitutional they may be; without considering that such an operation will subject the generous lion to the wily fox; . . subject liberty and property to tyranny and fraud." [1]

In chapter after chapter of clever arguments, illumined by the sparkle of such false gems as these quotations, Taylor prepares the public mind for his direct attack on John Marshall. He is at a sad disadvantage; he, "an unknown writer," can offer only "an artless course of reasoning" against the "acute argument" of Marshall's opinion, concurred in by the members of the Supreme Court whose "talents," "integrity," "uprightness," and "erudition" are universally admitted.[2] The essence of Marshall's doctrine is that, although the powers of the National Government are limited, the means by which they may be executed are unlimited. But, "as ends may be made to beget means, so means may be made to beget ends, until the co-habitation shall rear a progeny of unconstitutional bastards, which were not begotten by the people." [3]

Marshall had said that "'the creation of a corporation appertains to sovereignty.'" This is the language of tyranny. The corporate idea crept into British law "wherein it hides the heart of a prostitute under the habiliments of a virgin." [4] But since, in America, only the people are "sovereign," and, to use Marshall's own words, the power to create

---

[1] Taylor: *Construction Construed*, 77.   [2] *Ib*. 79.   [3] *Ib*. 84.   [4] *Ib*. 87.

corporations "appertains to sovereignty," it follows that neither State nor National Governments can create corporations.[1]

The Chief Justice is a master of the "science of verbality" by which the Constitution may be rendered "as unintelligible, as a single word would be made by a syllabick dislocation, or a jumble of its letters; and turn it into a reservoir of every meaning for which its expounder may have occasion."

Where does Marshall's "artifice of verbalizing" lead?[2] To an "artificially reared, a monied interest . . which is gradually obtaining an influence over the federal government," and "craftily works upon the passions of the states it has been able to delude" [on the slavery question], "to coerce the defrauded and discontented states into submission." For this reason talk of civil war abounds. "For what are the states talking about disunion, and for what are they going to war among themselves? To create or establish a monied sect, composed of privileged combinations, as an aristocratical oppressor of them all."[3] Marshall's doctrine that Congress may bestow "exclusive privileges" is at the bottom of the Missouri controversy. "Had the motive . . never existed, the discussion itself would never have existed; but if the same cause continues, more fatal controversies may be expected."[4]

[1] Taylor: *Construction Construed*, 89.   [2] *Ib*. 161.   [3] *Ib*. 233.
[4] *Ib*. 237.

It is interesting to observe that Taylor brands the protective tariff as one of the evils of Marshall's Nationalist philosophy. "It destroys the division of powers between federal and state governments, . . it violates the principles of representation, . . it recognizes a sovereign power over property, . . it destroys the freedom of labour, . . it taxes

Finally Taylor hurls at the Nation the challenge of the South, which the representatives of that section, from the floor of Congress, quickly repeated in threatenings of civil war.[1] "There remains a right, anterior to every political power whatsoever, . . the natural right of self-defence. . . It is allowed, on all hands, that danger to the slave-holding states lurks in their existing situation, . . and it must be admitted that the right of self-defence applies to that situation. . . I leave to the reader the application of these observations."[2]

Immediately upon its publication, Ritchie sent a copy of Taylor's book to Jefferson, who answered that he knew "before reading it" that it would prove "orthodox." The attack upon the National courts could not be pressed too energetically: "The judiciary of the United States is the subtle corps of sappers and miners constantly working under ground to undermine the foundations of our confederated fabric. . . An opinion is huddled up in conclave, perhaps by a majority of one, delivered as if unanimous, and with the silent acquiescence of lazy and timid associates, by a crafty chief judge, who sophisticates the law to his mind, by the turn of his own reasoning."[3]

the great mass of capital and labour, to enrich the few; . . it increases the burden upon the people . . increases the mass of poverty; . . it impoverishes workmen and enriches employers; . . it increases the expenses of government, . . it deprives commerce of the freedom of exchanges, . . it corrupts congress . . generates the extremes of luxury and poverty." (Taylor: *Construction Construed*, 252–53.)

[1] See *infra*, 340–42; and see *infra*, chap. x.

[2] Taylor: *Construction Construed*, 314.

[3] Jefferson to Ritchie, Dec. 25, 1820, *Works :* Ford, xii, 176–78. He declined, however, to permit publication of his endorsement of Taylor's book. (*Ib.*)

CHAPTER VII

THREATS OF WAR

Cannot the Union exist unless Congress and the Supreme Court shall make banks and lotteries? (John Taylor "of Caroline.")

If a judge can repeal a law of Congress, by declaring it unconstitutional, is not this the exercise of political power? (Senator Richard M. Johnson.)

The States must shield themselves and meet the invader foot to foot.
(Jefferson.)

The United States . . . form a single nation. In war we are one people. In making peace we are one people. In all commercial regulations we are one and the same people. (Marshall.)

The crisis has arrived contemplated by the framers of the Constitution.
(Senator James Barbour.)

THE appeals of Niles, Roane, and Taylor, and the defiant attitude toward Nationalism of Virginia, Ohio, Pennsylvania, and other States, expressed a widespread and militant Localism which now manifested itself in another and still more threatening form. The momentous and dramatic struggle in Congress over the admission of Missouri quickly followed these attacks on Marshall and the Supreme Court.

Should that Territory come into the Union only on condition that slavery be prohibited within the new State, or should the slave system be retained? The clamorous and prophetic debate upon that question stirred the land from Maine to Louisiana. A division of the Union was everywhere discussed, and the right of a State to secede was boldly proclaimed.

In the House and Senate, civil war was threatened. "I fear this subject will be an ignited spark, which, communicated to an immense mass of combustion, will produce an explosion that will shake this Union to its centre. . . The crisis has arrived, contemplated

by the framers of the Constitution. . . This portentous subject, twelve months ago, was a little speck
scarcely visible above the horizon; it has already
overcast the heavens, obscuring every other object;
materials are everywhere accumulating with which
to render it darker." [1] In these bombastic, yet serious words Senator James Barbour of Virginia, when
speaking on the Missouri question on January 14,
1820, accurately described the situation.

"I behold the father armed against the son, . . a
brother's sword crimsoned with a brother's blood, . .
our houses wrapt in flames," exclaimed Senator
Freeman Walker of Georgia. "If Congress . . impose the restriction contemplated [exclusion of
slavery from Missouri], . . consequences fatal to the
peace and harmony of this Union will . . result." [2]
Senator William Smith of South Carolina asked "if,
under the misguided influence of fanaticism and
humanity, the impetuous torrent is once put in motion, what hand short of Omnipotence can stay it?" [3]
In picturing the coming horrors Senator Richard
Mentor Johnson of Kentucky declared that "the
heart sickens, the tongue falters." [4]

In the House was heard language even more sanguinary. "Let gentlemen beware!" exclaimed Robert Raymond Reid of Georgia; for to put limits on
slavery was to implant "envy, hatred, and bitter
reproaches, which

> ' Shall grow to clubs and naked swords,
>   To murder and to death.' . .

---

[1] *Annals*, 16th Cong. 1st Sess. 107–08.
[2] *Ib.* 175.   [3] *Ib.* 275.   [4] *Ib.* 359.

Sir, the firebrand, which is even now cast into your
society, will require blood . . for its quenching." [1]

Only a few Northern members answered with
spirit. Senator Walter Lowrie of Pennsylvania preferred "a dissolution of this Union" rather than "the
extension of slavery." [2] Daniel Pope Cook of Illinois
avowed that "the sound of disunion . . has been
uttered so often in this debate, . . that it is high time
. . to adopt measures to prevent it. . . Such declarations . . will have no . . effect upon me. . . Is it . .
the intention of gentlemen to arouse . . the South to
rebellion?" [3] For the most part, however, Northern
Representatives were mild and even hopeful. [4]

Such was the situation concerning which John
Marshall addressed the American people in his
epochal opinion in the case of Cohens *vs.* Virginia.
The noble passages of that remarkable state paper
were inspired by, and can be understood only in the
light of, the crisis that produced them. Not in
the mere facts of that insignificant case, not in the
precise legal points involved, is to be found the

---

[1] *Annals*, 16th Cong. 1st Sess. 1033.

[2] *Ib.* 209. The Justices of the Supreme Court followed the proceedings in Congress with the interest and accuracy of politicians. (See,
for example, Story's comments on the Missouri controversy, Story to
White, Feb. 27, 1820, Story, I, 362.)

[3] *Annals*, 16th Cong. 1st Sess. 1106–07.

[4] For instance, Joshua Cushman of Massachusetts was sure that,
instead of disunion, "the Canadas, with New Brunswick and Nova
Scotia, allured by the wisdom and beneficence of our institutions, will
stretch out their hands for an admission into this Union. The Floridas
will become a willing victim. Mexico will mingle her lustre with the
federal constellation. South America . . will burn incense on our . .
altar. The Republic of the United States shall have dominion from
sea to sea, . . from the river Columbia to the ends of the earth. The
American Eagle . . will soar aloft to the stars of Heaven." (*Ib.* 1309.)

inspiration of Marshall's transcendent effort on this
occasion. Indeed, it is possible, as the Ohio Legislature and the Virginia Republican organization soon
thereafter charged, that Cohens *vs*. Virginia was
"feigned" for the purpose of enabling Marshall to
assert once more the supremacy of the Nation.

If the case came before Marshall normally, without
design and in the regular course of business, it was
an event nothing short of providential. If, on the
contrary, it was "arranged" so that Marshall could
deliver his immortal Nationalist address, never was
such contrivance so thoroughly justified. While the
legal profession has always considered this case to
be identical, judicially, with that of Martin *vs*. Hunter's Lessee, it is, historically, a part of M'Culloch *vs*.
Maryland and of Osborn *vs*. The Bank. The opinion
of John Marshall in the Cohens case is one of the
strongest and most enduring strands of that mighty
cable woven by him to hold the American people
together as a united and imperishable nation.

Fortunate, indeed, for the Republic that Marshall's fateful pronouncement came forth at such a
critical hour, even if technicalities were waived in
bringing before him a case in which he could deliver
that opinion. For, in conjunction with his exposition
in M'Culloch *vs*. Maryland, it was the most powerful answer that could be given, and from the source
of greatest authority, to that defiance of the National
Government and to the threats of disunion then
growing ever bolder and more vociferous. Marshall's
utterances did not still those hostile voices, it is true,
but they gave strength and courage to Nationalists

and furnished to the champions of the Union arguments of peculiar force as coming from the supreme tribunal of the Nation.

Could John Marshall have seen into the future he would have beheld Abraham Lincoln expounding from the stump to the farmers of Illinois, in 1858, the doctrines laid down by himself in 1819 and 1821.

Briefly stated, the facts in the case of Cohens *vs*. Virginia were as follows: The City of Washington was incorporated under an act of Congress [1] which, among other things, empowered the corporation to "authorize the drawing of lotteries for effecting any important improvements in the city which the ordinary funds or revenue thereof will not accomplish," to an amount not to exceed ten thousand dollars, the object first to be approved by the President. [2] Accordingly a city ordinance was passed, creating "The National Lottery" and authorizing it to sell tickets and conduct drawings.

By an act of the Virginia Legislature [3] the purchase or sale within the State of lottery tickets, except those of lotteries authorized by the laws of Virginia, was forbidden under penalty of a fine of one hundred dollars for each offense.

[1] May 3, 1802, *U.S. Statutes at Large*. This act, together with a supplementary act (May 4, 1812, *ib.*), is a vivid portrayal of a phase of the life of the National Capital at that period. See especially Section VI.

[2] Lotteries had long been a favorite method of raising funds for public purposes. As a member of the Virginia House of Delegates, Marshall had voted for many lottery bills. (See vol. II, footnote 1, to 56, of this work.) For decades after the Constitution was adopted, lotteries were considered to be both moral and useful.

[3] Effective January 21, 1820.

On June 1, 1820, "P. J. & M. J. Cohen, . . being evil-disposed persons," violated the Virginia statute by selling to one William H. Jennings in the Borough of Norfolk two half and four quarter lottery tickets "of the National Lottery, to be drawn in the city of Washington, that being a lottery not authorized by the laws of this commonwealth," as the information of James Nimmo, the prosecuting attorney, declared.[1]

At the quarterly session of the Court of Norfolk, held September 2, 1820, the case came on for hearing before the Mayor, Recorder, and Aldermen of said borough and was decided upon an agreed case "in lieu of a special verdict," which set forth the sale of the lottery tickets, the Virginia statute, the act of Congress incorporating the City of Washington, and the fact that the National Lottery had been established under that act.[2] The Norfolk Court found the defendants guilty and fined them in the sum of one hundred dollars. This paltry amount could not have paid one twentieth part of the fees which the eminent counsel who appeared for the Cohens would, ordinarily, have charged.[3] The case was carried to the Supreme Court on a writ of error.

[1] 6 Wheaton, 266–67. [2] *Ib.* 268–90.

[3] William Pinkney was at this time probably the highest paid lawyer in America. Five years before he argued the case of Cohens *vs.* Virginia, his professional income was $21,000 annually (Story to White, Feb. 26, 1816, Story, I, 278), more than four times as much as Marshall ever received when leader of the Richmond bar (see vol. II, 201, of this work). David B. Ogden, the other counsel for the Cohens, was one of the most prominent and successful lawyers of New York. See Warren, 303–04.

Another interesting fact in this celebrated case is that the Norfolk Court fined the Cohens the minimum allowed by the Virginia statute.

On behalf of Virginia, Senator James Barbour of that State [1] moved that the writ of error be dismissed, and upon this motion the main arguments were made and Marshall's principal opinion delivered. In concluding his argument, Senator Barbour came near threatening secession, as he had done in the Senate: "Nothing can so much endanger it [the National Government] as exciting the hostility of the state governments. With them it is to determine how long this government shall endure." [2]

In opening for the Cohens, David B. Ogden of New York denied that "there is any such thing as a sovereign state, independent of the Union." The authority of the Supreme Court "extends . . to all cases arising under the constitution, laws, and treaties of the United States." [3] Cohens *vs.* Virginia was such a case.

Upon the supremacy of the Supreme Court over State tribunals depended the very life of the Nation, declared William Pinkney, who appeared as the principal counsel for the Cohens. Give up the appellate jurisdiction of National courts "from the decisions of the state tribunals" and "every other branch of federal authority might as well be surrendered. To part with this, leaves the Union a mere league or confederacy." [4] Long, brilliantly, convincingly, did

They could have been fined at least $800, $100 for each offense — perhaps should have been fined that amount had the law been strictly observed. Indeed, the Virginia Act permitted a fine to the extent of "the whole sum of money proposed to be raised by such lottery." (6 Wheaton, 268.)

[1] Barbour declined a large fee offered him by the State. (Grigsby: *Virginia Convention of 1829–30.*)

[2] 6 Wheaton, 344.   [3] *Ib.* 347.   [4] *Ib.* 354.

Pinkney speak. The extreme State Rights arguments were, he asserted, "too wild and extravagant"[1] to deserve consideration.

Promptly Marshall delivered the opinion of the court on Barbour's motion to dismiss the writ of error. The points made against the jurisdiction of the Supreme Court were, he said: "1st. That a state is a defendant. 2d. That no writ of error lies from this court to a state court. 3d. . . that this court . . has no right to review the judgment of the state court, because neither the constitution nor any law of the United States has been violated by that judgment."[2]

The first two points "vitally . . affect the Union," declared the Chief Justice, who proceeds to answer the reasoning of the State judges when, in Hunter vs. Fairfax's Devisee, they hurled at the Supreme Court Virginia's defiance of National authority.[3] Marshall thus states the Virginia contentions: That the Constitution has "provided no tribunal for the final construction of itself, or of the laws or treaties of the nation; but that this power may be exercised . . by the courts of every state of the Union. That the constitution, laws, and treaties, may receive as many constructions as there are states; and that this is not a mischief, or, if a mischief, is irremediable."[4]

Why was the Constitution established? Because the "American States, as well as the American people, have believed a close and firm Union to be essential to their liberty and to their happiness. They

---

[1] 6 Wheaton, 375. For a better report of Pinkney's speech see Wheaton: *Pinkney*, 612–16.

[2] *Ib.* 376.   [3] See *supra*, 157–58.   [4] 6 Wheaton, 377.

have been taught by experience, that this Union cannot exist without a government for the whole; and they have been taught by the same experience that this government would be a mere shadow, that must disappoint all their hopes, unless invested with large portions of that sovereignty which belongs to independent states." [1]

The very nature of the National Government leaves no doubt of its supremacy "in all cases where it is empowered to act"; that supremacy was also expressly declared in the Constitution itself, which plainly states that it, and laws and treaties made under it, "' shall be the supreme law of the land; and the judges in every state shall be bound thereby; anything in the constitution or laws of any state to the contrary notwithstanding.'"

This supremacy of the National Government is a Constitutional "principle." And why were "ample powers" given to that Government? The Constitution answers: "In order to form a more perfect union, establish justice, ensure domestic tranquillity, provide for the common defense, promote the general welfare." [2]

The "limitations on the sovereignty of the states" were made for the same reason that the "supreme government" of the Nation was endowed with its broad powers. In addition to express limitations on State "sovereignty" were many instances " where, perhaps, *no other power is conferred on Congress than a conservative power to maintain the principles* established in the constitution. The maintenance of these

[1] 6 Wheaton, 380. [2] *Ib.* 381.

principles in their purity, is certainly among the great duties of the government." [1]

Marshall had been Chief Justice of the United States for twenty years, and these were the boldest and most extreme words that he had spoken during that period. Like all men of the first rank, Marshall met in a great way, and without attempt at compromise, a great issue that could not be compromised — an issue which, everywhere, at that moment, was challenging the existence of the Nation. There must be no dodging, no hedging, no equivocation. Instead, there must be the broadest, frankest, bravest declaration of National powers that words could express. For this reason Marshall said that these powers might be exercised even as a result of "a conservative power" in Congress "to maintain the principles established in the constitution."

The Judicial Department is an agency essential to the performance of the "great duty" to preserve those "principles." "It is authorized to decide all cases of every description, arising under the constitution or laws of the United States." Those cases in which a State is a party are not excepted. There are cases where the National courts are given jurisdiction solely because a State is a party, and regardless of the subject of the controversy; but in all cases involving the Constitution, laws, or treaties of the Nation, the National tribunals have jurisdiction, regardless of parties. [2]

"Principles" drawn from the very "*nature of government*" require that "the judicial power . .

[1] 6 Wheaton, 382. (Italics the author's.)   [2] *Ib.* 382.

must be co-extensive with the legislative, and must
be capable of deciding every judicial question which
grows out of the constitution and laws" — not that
"it is fit that it should be so; but . . that this fit-
ness" is an aid to the right interpretation of the
Constitution.[1]

What will be the result if Virginia's attitude is
confirmed? Nothing less than the prostration of the
National Government "at the feet of every state in
the Union. . . . Each member will possess a veto on
the will of the whole." Consider the country's experience. Assumption [2] had been deemed unconstitutional by some States; opposition to excise
taxes had produced the Whiskey Rebellion; [3] other
National statutes "have been questioned partially,
while they were supported by the great majority of
the American people." [4] There can be no assurance
that such divergent and antagonistic actions may
not again be taken. State laws in conflict with National laws probably will be enforced by State
judges, since they are subject to the same prejudices
as are the State Legislatures — indeed, "in many
states the judges are dependent for office and for
salary on the will of the legislature." [5]

The Constitution attaches first importance to the
"independence" of the Judiciary; can it have been
intended to leave to State "tribunals, where this independence may not exist," cases in which " a state
shall prosecute an individual who claims the protection of an act of Congress?" Marshall gives

---

[1] 6 Wheaton, 384–85. (Italics the author's.)
[2] See vol. II, 66, of this work.
[3] 6 Wheaton, 87.   [4] Ib. 385–86.   [5] Ib. 387.

examples of possible collisions between National and State authority, in ordinary times, as well as in exceptional periods.[1] Even to-day it is obvious that the Chief Justice was denouncing the threatened resistance by State officials to the tariff laws, a fact of commanding importance at the time when Marshall's opinion in Cohens *vs.* Virginia was delivered.

At this point he rises to the heights of august eloquence: "A constitution is framed for ages to come, and is designed to approach immortality as nearly as human institutions can approach it. Its course cannot always be tranquil. It is exposed to storms and tempests, and its framers must be unwise statesmen indeed, if they have not provided it . . with the means of self-preservation from the perils it may be destined to encounter. No government ought to be so defective in its organization as not to contain within itself the means of securing the execution of its own laws against other dangers than those which occur every day."

Marshall is here replying to the Southern threats of secession, just as he rebuked the same spirit when displayed by his New England friends ten years earlier.[2] Then turning to the conflict of courts, he remarks, as though the judicial collision is all that he has in mind: "A government should repose on its own courts, rather than on others." [3]

He recalls the state of the country under the Confederation when requisitions on the States were

---

[1] 6 Wheaton, 386–87.
[2] See U.S. *vs.* Peters, *supra*, 18 *et seq.*   [3] 6 Wheaton, 387–88.

"habitually disregarded," although they were "as constitutionally obligatory as the laws enacted by the present Congress." In view of this fact is it improbable that the framers of the Constitution meant to give the Nation's courts the power of preserving that Constitution, and laws made in pursuance of it, "from all violation from every quarter, so far as judicial decisions can preserve them"? [1]

Virginia contends that if States wish to destroy the National Government they can do so much more simply and easily than by judicial decision — "they have only not to elect senators, and it expires without a struggle"; and that therefore the destructive effect on the Nation of decisions of State courts cannot be taken into account when construing the Constitution.

To this Marshall makes answer: "Whenever hostility to the existing system shall become universal, it will be also irresistible. The people made the constitution, and the people can unmake it. It is the creature of their own will, and lives only by their will. But this supreme and irresistible power to make or to unmake, resides only in the whole body of the people; not in any sub-division of them. The attempt of any of the parts to exercise it is usurpation, and ought to be repelled by those to whom the people have delegated their power of repelling it. The acknowledged inability of the government, then, to sustain itself against the public will, and, by force or otherwise, to control the whole nation, is no sound argument in support of its constitutional

[1] 6 Wheaton, 388.

inability to preserve itself against a section of the nation acting in opposition to the general will." [1]

This is a direct reply to the Southern arguments in the Missouri debate which secessionists were now using wherever those who opposed National laws and authority raised their voices. John Marshall is blazing the way for Abraham Lincoln. He speaks of a "section" instead of a State. The Nation, he says, may constitutionally preserve itself "against a section." And this right of the Nation rests on "principles" inherent in the Constitution. But in Cohens *vs.* Virginia no "section" was arrayed against the Nation — on the record there was nothing but a conflict of jurisdiction of courts, and this only by a strained construction of a municipal lottery ordinance into a National law.

The Chief Justice is exerting to the utmost his tremendous powers, not to protect two furtive peddlers of lottery tickets, but to check a powerful movement that, if not arrested, must destroy the Republic. Should that movement go forward thereafter, it must do so over every Constitutional obstacle which the Supreme Court of the Nation could throw in its way. In Cohens *vs.* Virginia, John Marshall stamped upon the brow of Localism the brand of illegality. If this is not the true interpretation of his opinion in that case, all of the exalted language he used is mere verbiage.

Marshall dwells on "the subordination of the parts to the whole." The one great motive for establishing the National Judiciary "was the pres-

[1] 6 Wheaton, 389–90.

ervation of the constitution and laws of the United
States, so far as they can be preserved by judicial
authority." [1]

Returning to the technical aspects of the controversy, Marshall points out that the Supreme Court
plainly has appellate jurisdiction of the Cohens
case: "If a state be a party, the jurisdiction of this
court is original; if the case arise under a [National]
constitution or a [National] law, the jurisdiction is
appellate. But a case to which a state is a party
may arise under the constitution or a law of the
United States." [2] That would mean a double jurisdiction. Marshall, therefore, shows, at provoking
length,[3] that the appellate jurisdiction of the Supreme
Court "in all cases arising under the constitution,
laws, or treaties of the United States, was not
arrested by the circumstance that a state was a
party"; [4] and in this way he explains that part of
his opinion in Marbury *vs.* Madison, in which he
reasoned that Section 13 of the Ellsworth Judiciary
Act was unconstitutional.[5]

Marshall examines the Eleventh Amendment
and becomes, for a moment, the historian, a rôle in
which he delighted. "The states were greatly indebted" at the close of the Revolution; the Constitution was opposed because it was feared that
their obligations would be collected in the National
courts. This very thing happened. "The alarm
was general; and, to quiet the apprehensions that
were so extensively entertained, this amendment

---

[1] 6 Wheaton, 390–91.   [2] *Ib.* 393.   [3] *Ib.* 394–404.
[4] *Ib.* 405.   [5] See vol. III. 127–28, of this work.

was . . adopted." But "its motive was not to maintain the sovereignty of a state from the degradation supposed to attend a compulsory appearance
before the tribunal of the nation." It was to prevent
creditors from suing a State — "no interest could be
felt in so changing the relations between the whole and
its parts, as to strip the government of the means
of protecting, by the instrumentality of its courts,
the constitution and laws from active violation." [1]

With savage relish the Chief Justice attacks and
demolishes the State Rights theory that the Supreme Court cannot review the judgment of a
State court "in any case." That theory, he says,
"considers the federal judiciary as completely foreign to that of a state; and as being no more connected with it, in any respect whatever, than the
court of a foreign state." [2] But "the United States
form, for many, and for most important purposes, a
single nation. . . In war, we are one people. In making peace, we are one people. In all commercial
regulations, we are one and the same people. In
many other respects, the American people are one;
and the government which is alone capable of controlling and managing their interests in all these
respects, is the government of the Union.

"It is their government, and in that character
they have no other. America has chosen to be, in
many respects, and to many purposes, a nation; and
for all these purposes, her government is complete;
to all these objects, it is competent. The people
have declared, that in the exercise of all powers

[1] 6 Wheaton, 406–07.   [2] *Ib.* 413.

given for these objects it is supreme. It can, then, in effecting these objects, legitimately control all individuals or governments within the American territory. The Constitution and laws of a state, so far as they are repugnant to the Constitution and laws of the United States, are absolutely void.

"These states are constituent parts of the United States. They are members of one great empire." [1] The National Court alone can decide all questions arising under the Constitution and laws of the Nation. "The uniform decisions of this court on the point now under consideration," he continues, "have been assented to, with a single exception,[2] by the courts of every state in the Union whose judgments have been revised." [3]

As to the lottery ordinance of the City of Washington, Congress has exclusive power to legislate for the District of Columbia and, in exercising that power, acts "as the legislature of the Union." The Constitution declares that it, and all laws made under it, constitute "the supreme law of the land." [4] Laws for the government of Washington are, therefore, parts of this "supreme law" and "bind the nation. . . Congress legislates, in the same forms, and in the same character, in virtue of powers of equal obligation, conferred in the same instrument, when exercising its exclusive powers of legislation, as well as when exercising those which are limited." [5]

The Chief Justice gives examples of the exclusive powers of Congress, all of which are binding through-

---

[1] 6 Wheaton, 413–14.   [2] Fairfax's Devisee *vs.* Hunter, *supra,* 157–60.
[3] 6 Wheaton, 420.   [4] *Ib.* 424.   [5] *Ib.* 425–26.

out the Republic. "Congress is not a local legislature, but exercises this particular power [to legislate for the District of Columbia], like all its other
powers, in its high character, as the legislature of
the Union." [1] The punishment of the Cohens for
selling tickets of the National Lottery, created by
the City of Washington under authority of an act
of Congress, involves the construction of the Constitution and of a National law. The Supreme Court,
therefore, has jurisdiction of the case, and the motion to dismiss the writ of error is denied.

Marshall having thus established the jurisdiction
of the Supreme Court to hear and decide the case,
it was argued "on the merits." Again David B.
Ogden appeared for the Cohens and was joined by
William Wirt as Attorney-General. For Virginia
Webster took the place of Senator Barbour. The
argument was upon the true construction of the act
of Congress authorizing the City of Washington to
establish a lottery; and upon this Marshall delivered
a second opinion, to the effect that the lottery
ordinance was "only co-extensive with the city"
and a purely local affair; that the court at Norfolk
had a right to fine the Cohens for violating a law
of Virginia; and that its judgment must be affirmed. [2]

So ended, as far as the formal record goes, the
famous case of Cohens *vs.* Virginia. On its merits it
amounted to nothing; the practical result of the
appeal was nothing; but it afforded John Marshall
the opportunity to tell the Nation its duty in a
crowning National emergency.

[1] 6 Wheaton, 429.   [2] *Ib.* 445–47.

Intense was the excitement and violent the rage
in the anti-Nationalist camp when Marshall's opinion was published. Ritchie, in his paper, demanded
that the Supreme Court should be abolished.[1] The
Virginia Republican organization struck instantly,
Spencer Roane wielding its sword. The *Enquirer*
published a series of five articles between May 25
and June 8, 1821, inclusive, signed "Algernon Sidney," Roane's latest *nom de plume.*

"The liberties and constitution of our country
are . . deeply and vitally endangered by the fatal
effects" of Marshall's opinion. "Appointed in one
generation it [the Supreme Court] claims to make
laws and constitutions for another."[2] The unanimity of the court can be explained only on the
ground of "a culpable apathy in the other judges,
or a confidence not to be excused, in the principles
and talents of their chief." Sidney literally wastes
reams of paper in restating the State Rights arguments. He finds a malign satisfaction in calling the
Constitution a "compact," a "league," a "treaty"
between "sovereign governments."[3]

National judges have "*no* interest in the government or laws of any state but that of which they are
citizens," asserts Sidney. "As to every other state
but that, they are, completely, aliens and foreigners."[4] Virginia is as much a foreign nation as Russia[5] so far as jurisdiction of the Supreme Court over

[1] Ambler: *Ritchie*, 81.

[2] *Enquirer*, May 25, 1821, as quoted in *Branch Hist. Papers*, June,
1906, 78, 85.

[3] *Enquirer*, May 25 and May 29, 1821, as quoted in *ib.* 89, 100.

[4] *Enquirer*, May 29, 1821, as quoted in *ib.* 101.

[5] *Enquirer*, June 21, 1821, as quoted in *ib.* 110.

the judgments of State courts is concerned. Marshall's doctrine "is the blind and absolute despotism which exists in an army, or is exercised by a tyrant over his slaves." [1]

The apostate Republican Justices who concurred with Marshall are denounced, and with greater force, by reason of a tribute paid to the hated Chief Justice: "How else is it that they also go to all lengths with the ultra-federal leader who is at the head of their court? That leader is honorably distinguished from you messieurs judges. He is true to his former politics. He has even pushed them to an extreme never until now anticipated. He must be equally delighted and *surprised* to find his *Republican* brothers going with him" — a remark as true as it was obvious. "How is it . . that they go with him, not only as to the results of his opinions, but as to all the points and positions contained in the most lengthy, artful and alarming opinions?" Because, answers Sidney, they are on the side of power and of "the government that feeds them." [2]

What Marshall had said in the Virginia Constitutional Convention of 1788 refutes his opinions now. "Great principles then operated on his luminous mind, not hair-splitting quibbles and verbal criticisms." [3] The "artifices" of the Chief Justice render his opinions the more dangerous. [4]

If the anger of John Marshall ever was more aroused than it was by Roane's assaults upon him, no evidence of the fact exists. Before the last number

[1] *Branch Hist. Papers*, June, 1906, 119.   [2] *Ib.* 123–24.
[3] *Enquirer*, June 5, 1821, as quoted in *Branch Hist. Papers*, June, 1906, 146–47.   [4] *Ib.* 182–83.

of the Algernon Sidney essays appeared, the Chief Justice confides his wrathful feelings to the devoted and sympathetic Story: "The opinion of the Supreme Court in the Lottery case has been assaulted with a degree of virulence transcending what has appeared on any former occasion. Algernon Sidney is written by the gentleman who is so much distinguished for his feelings towards the Supreme Court, & if you have not an opportunity of seeing the Enquirer I will send it to you.

"There are other minor gentry who seek to curry favor & get into office by adding their mite of abuse, but I think for coarseness & malignity of invention Algernon Sidney surpasses all party writers who have ever made pretensions to any decency of character. There is on this subject no such thing as a free press in Virginia, and of consequence the calumnies and misrepresentations of this gentleman will remain uncontradicted & will by many be believed to be true. He will be supposed to be the champion of state rights, instead of being what he really is, the champion of dismemberment." [1]

When Roane's articles were finished, Marshall wrote Story: "I send you the papers containing the essays of Algernon Sidney. Their coarseness & malignity would designate the author if he was not avowed. The argument, if it may be called one, is, I think, as weak as its language is violent & prolix. Two other gentlemen [2] have appeared in the papers on this sub-

---

[1] Marshall to Story, June 15, 1821, *Proceedings, Mass. Hist. Soc.* 2d Series, XIV, 327–28.

[2] Marshall refers to three papers published in the *Enquirer* of May 15 and 22, and June 22, the first two signed "Somers" and the third

ject, one of them is deeply concerned in pillaging the purchasers of the Fairfax estate in which goodly work he fears no other obstruction than what arises

signed "Fletcher of Saltoun." It is impossible to discover who these writers were. Their essays, although vicious, are so dull as not to be worth the reading, though Jefferson thought them "luminous and striking." (Jefferson to Johnson, June 12, 1823, *Works:* Ford, XII, 252, footnote.)

"Somers," however, is compelled to admit the irresistible appeal of Marshall's personality. "Superior talents and address will forever attract the homage of inferior minds." (*Enquirer*, May 15, 1821.)

"The Supreme court . . have rendered the constitution the sport of legal ingenuity. . . . Its meaning is locked up from the profane vulgar, and distributed only by the high priests of the temple." (*Ib.* May 22, 1821.)

"Fletcher of Saltoun" is intolerably verbose: "The victories . . of courts . . though bloodless, are generally decisive. . . The progress of the judiciary, though slow, is steady and untiring as the foot of time."

The people act as though hypnotized, he laments — "the powerful mind of the chief justice has put forth its strength, and we are quiet as if touched by the wand of enchantment; — we fall prostrate before his genius as though we had looked upon the dazzling brightness of the shield of Astolfo. — Triumphant indeed has been this most powerful effort of his extraordinary mind. His followers exult — those who doubted, have yielded; even the faithful are found wavering, and the unconvinced can find no opening in his armor of defense."

This writer points out Marshall's "abominable inconsistencies," but seems to be himself under the spell of the Chief Justice: "I mention not this to the disadvantage of the distinguished individual who has pronounced these conflicting opinions. No man can have a higher respect for the virtues of his character, or greater admiration of the powers of his mind."

Alas for the change that time works upon the human intellect! Consider Marshall, the young man, and Marshall, the Chief Justice! "How little did he, at that early day, contemplate the possibility of his carrying the construction of the constitution to an extent so far beyond even what he then renounced!" [*sic.*]

Thereupon "Fletcher of Saltoun" plunges into an ocean of words concerning Hamilton's theories of government and Marshall's application of them. He announces this essay to be the first of a series; but, luckily for everybody, this first effort exhausted him. Apparently he, too, fell asleep under Marshall's "wand," for nothing more came from his drowsy pen. (*Ib.* June 22, 1821.)

from the appellate power of the Supreme Court, & the other is a hunter after office who hopes by his violent hostility to the Union, which in Virginia assumes the name of regard for state rights, & by his devotion to Algernon Sidney, to obtain one. In support of the sound principles of the constitution & of the Union of the States, not a pen is drawn. In Virginia the tendency of things verges rapidly to the destruction of the government & the re-establishment of a league of sovereign states. I look elsewhere for safety." [1]

Another of the "minor gentry" of whom Marshall complained was William C. Jarvis, who in 1820 had written a book entitled "The Republicans," in which he joined in the hue and cry against Marshall because of his opinion in M'Culloch *vs.* Maryland. Jarvis sent a copy of his book to Jefferson who, in acknowledging the receipt of it, once more spoke his mind upon the National Judiciary. To Jarvis's statement that the courts are "the ultimate arbiters of all constitutional questions," Jefferson objected.

It was "a very dangerous doctrine indeed, and one which would place us under the despotism of an oligarchy," wrote the "Sage of Monticello." "The constitution has erected no such single tribunal, knowing that to whatever hands confided, with the corruptions of time and party, its members would become despots. . . If the legislature fails to pass" necessary laws — such as those for taking of the census, or the payment of judges; or even if "they

---

[1] Marshall to Story, July 13, 1821, *Proceedings, Mass. Hist. Soc.* 2d Series, XIV, 329.

fail to meet in congress, the judges cannot issue their mandamus to them."

So, concludes Jefferson, if the President does not appoint officers to fill vacancies, "the judges cannot force him." In fact, the judges "can issue their mandamus . . to no executive or legislative officer to enforce the fulfilment of their official duties, any more than the president or legislature may issue orders to the judges. . . When the legislature or executive functionaries act unconstitutionally, they are responsible to the people in their elective capacity. The exemption of the judges from that is quite dangerous enough." [1]

This letter by Jefferson had just been made public, and Story, who appears to have read everything from the Greek classics to the current newspaper gossip, at once wrote Marshall. The Chief Justice replied that Jefferson's view "rather grieves than surprizes" him. But he could not "describe the surprize & mortification" he felt when he learned that Madison agreed with Jefferson "with respect to the judicial department. For Mr Jefferson's opinion as respects this department it is not difficult to assign the cause. He is among the most ambitious, & I suspect among the most unforgiving of men. His great power is over the mass of the people, & this power is chiefly acquired by professions of democracy. Every check on the wild impulse of the moment is a check on his own power, & he is unfriendly to the source from which it flows. He looks of course with ill will at an independent judiciary.

[1] Jefferson to Jarvis, Sept. 28, 1820, *Works:* Ford, xii, 162–63.

"That in a free country with a written constitution any intelligent man should wish a dependent judiciary, or should think that the constitution is not a law for the court as well as for the legislature would astonish me, if I had not learnt from observation that with many men the judgement is completely controuled by the passions." [1]

To Jefferson, Marshall ascribes Roane's attacks upon the Supreme Court: "There is some reason to believe that the essays written against the Supreme Court were, in a degree at least, stimulated by this gentleman, and that although the coarseness of the language belongs exclusively to the author, its acerbity has been increased by his communications with the great Lama of the mountains. He may therefore feel himself . . required to obtain its republication in some place of distinction." [2]

John E. Hall was at that time the publisher at Philadelphia of *The Journal of American Jurisprudence*. Jefferson had asked Hall to reprint Roane's articles, and Hall had told Story, who faithfully reported to Marshall. "I am a little surprized at the request which you say has been made to Mr Hall, although there is no reason for my being so. The settled hostility of the gentleman who has made that request to the judicial department will show itself in that & in every other form which he believes will conduce to its object. For this he has several motives, & it is not among the weakest that the department would never lend itself as a tool to work for his political power. . .

---

[1] Marshall to Story, July 13, 1821, *Proceedings, Mass. Hist. Soc.* 2d Series, xiv, 328–29.

[2] Same to same, Sept. 18, 1821, *ib.* 330.

"What does Mr Hall purpose to do?" asks Marshall. "I do not suppose you would willingly interfere so as to prevent his making the publication, although I really think it is in form & substance totally unfit to be placed in his law journal. I really think a proper reply to the request would be to say that no objection existed to the publication of any law argument against the opinion of the Supreme Court, but that the coarseness of its language, its personal & official abuse & its tedious prolixity constituted objections to the insertion of Algernon Sidney which were insuperable. If, however, Mr Hall determines to comply with this request, I think he ought, unless he means to make himself a party militant, to say that he published that piece by particular request, & ought to subjoin the masterly answer of Mr Wheaton. I shall wish to know what course Mr Hall will pursue." [1]

Roane's attacks on Marshall did not appear in Hall's law magazine!

Quitting such small, unworthy, and prideful considerations, Marshall rises for a moment to the great issue which he met so nobly in his opinions in M'Culloch *vs.* Maryland and in Cohens *vs.* Virginia. "A deep design," he writes Story, "to convert our government into a mere league of states has taken strong hold of a powerful & violent party in Virginia. The attack upon the judiciary is in fact an attack upon the union. The judicial department is well understood to be that through which the govern-

---

[1] Marshall to Story, July 13, 1821, *Proceedings, Mass. Hist. Soc* 2d Series, XIV, 329–30.

ment may be attacked most successfully, because it is without patronage, & of course without power. And it is equally well understood that every subtraction from its jurisdiction is a vital wound to the government itself. The attack upon it therefore is a masked battery aimed at the government itself.

"The whole attack, if not originating with Mr Jefferson, is obviously approved & guided by him. It is therefore formidable in other states as well as in this, & it behoves the friends of the union to be more on the alert than they have been. An effort will certainly be made to repeal the 25th sec. of the judicial act." [1] Marshall's indignation at Roane exhausted his limited vocabulary of resentment. Had he possessed Jefferson's resources of vituperation, the literature of animosity would have been enriched by the language Marshall would have indulged in when the next Republican battery poured its volleys upon him.

No sooner had Roane's artillery ceased to play upon Marshall and the Supreme Court than the roar of Taylor's heavy guns was again heard. In a powerful and brilliant book, called "Tyranny Unmasked," he directed his fire upon the newly proposed protective tariff, "this sport for capitalists and death for the rest of the nation." [2] The theory of the Chief Justice that there is a "supreme federal power" over the States is proved false by the proceedings of the Constitutional Convention at Phila-

---

[1] Marshall to Story, July 13, 1821, *Proceedings, Mass. Hist. Soc* 2d Series, XIV, 330–31.

[2] Taylor: *Tyranny Unmasked*, 89.

delphia in 1787. Certain members then proposed to give the National Government a veto over the acts of State Governments.[1] This proposal was immediately rejected. Yet to-day Marshall proclaims a National power, "infinitely more objectionable," which asserts that the Supreme Court has "a negative or restraining power over the State governments."[2]

A protective tariff is only another monstrous child of Marshall's accursed Nationalism, that prolific mother of special favors for the few. By what reasoning is a protective tariff made Constitutional? By the casuistry of John Marshall, that "present fashionable mode of construction, which considers the constitution as a lump of fine gold, a small portion of which is so malleable as to cover the whole mass. By this golden rule for manufacturing the constitution, a particular power given to the Federal Government may be made to cover all the rights reserved to the people and the States;[3] a limited jurisdiction given to the Federal Courts is made to cover all the State Courts;[4] and a legislative power over ten miles square is malleated over the whole of the United States,[5] as a single guinea may be beaten out so as to cover a whole house."[6] Such is the method by which a protective tariff is made Constitutional.

For one hundred and twenty-one scintillant and learned pages Taylor attacks this latest creation of National "tyranny." The whole Nationalist system

[1] This was Madison's idea. See vol. i, 312, of this work.
[2] Taylor: *Tyranny Unmasked*, 33.   [3] M'Culloch *vs.* Maryland.
[4] Martin *vs.* Hunter's Lessee and Cohens *vs.* Virginia.
[5] Cohens *vs.* Virginia.   [6] Taylor: *Tyranny Unmasked*, 132–33.

is "tyranny," which it is his privilege to "unmask,"
and the duty of all true Americans to destroy.[1] Marshall's Constitutional doctrine "amounts to the insertion of the following article in the constitution:
'Congress shall have power, with the assent of the
Supreme Court, to exercise or usurp, and to prohibit the States from exercising, any or all of the
powers reserved to the States, whenever they [Con-
gress] shall deem it convenient, or for the general
welfare.'"[2] Such doctrines invite "civil war."[3]

By Marshall's philosophy "the people are made
the prey of exclusive privileges." In short, under
him the Supreme Court has become the agent of
special interests.[4] "Cannot the Union subsist unless
Congress and the Supreme Court shall make banks
and lotteries?"[5]

Jefferson eagerly read Roane's essays and Taylor's book and wrote concerning them: "The judiciary
branch is the instrument which, working like gravity, without intermission, is to press us at last into
one consolidated mass. Against this I know no one
who, equally with Judge Roane himself, possesses
the power and the courage to make resistance; and
to him I look, and have long looked, as our strongest
bulwark."

At this point Jefferson declares for armed resistance to the Nation in even stronger terms than those
used by Roane or Taylor: "If Congress fails to
shield the States from dangers so palpable and so im-

---

[1] Taylor: *Tyranny Unmasked*, 133–254. Taylor was the first to state
fully most of the arguments since used by the opponents of protective tariffs.

[2] *Ib.* 260.   [3] *Ib.* 285.   [4] *Ib.* 305.   [5] *Ib.* 341.

minent, the States must shield themselves, and meet
the invader foot to foot. . . This is already half done
by Colonel Taylor's book" which "is the most effectual retraction of our government to its original principles which has ever yet been sent by heaven to our
aid. Every State in the Union should give a copy to
every member they elect, as a standing instruction,
and ours should set the example." [1]

Until his death the aged politician raged continuously, except in one instance,[2] at Marshall and the
Supreme Court because of such opinions and decisions as those in the Bank and Lottery cases. He
writes Justice Johnson that he "considered . . ma-
turely" Roane's attacks on the doctrines of Cohens
vs. Virginia and they appeared to him "to pulverize
every word which had been delivered by Judge Marshall, of the extra-judicial part of his opinion." If
Roane "can be answered, I surrender human reason
as a vain and useless faculty, given to bewilder, and
not to guide us. . . This practice of Judge Marshall,
of travelling out of his case to prescribe what the law

[1] Jefferson to Thweat, Jan. 19, 1821, *Works:* Ford, xii, 196–97.

Wirt, though a Republican, asserted that "the functions to be performed by the Supreme Court . . are among the most difficult and
perilous which are to be performed under the Constitution. They
demand the loftiest range of talents and learning and a soul of Roman
purity and firmness. The questions which come before them frequently involve the fate of the Constitution, the happiness of the
whole nation." (Wirt to Monroe, May 5, 1823, Kennedy, ii, 153.)

Wirt, in this letter, was urging the appointment of Kent to the
Supreme Bench, notwithstanding the Federalism of the New York
Chancellor. "Federal politics are no way dangerous on the bench of
the Supreme Court," adds Wirt. (*Ib.* 155.)

[2] His strange failure to come to Roane's support in the fight, over
the Judiciary amendments to the Constitution, in the Virginia Legislature during the session of 1821–22. (See *infra,* 371.)

would be in a moot case not before the court, is very irregular and censurable." [1]

Again Jefferson writes that, above all other officials, those who most need restraint from usurping legislative powers are "the judges of what is commonly called our General Government, but what I call our Foreign department. . . A few such doctrinal decisions, as barefaced as that of the Cohens," may so arouse certain powerful States as to check the march of Nationalism. The Supreme Court "has proved that the power of declaring what the law is, *ad libitum*, by sapping and mining, slily and without alarm, the foundations of the Constitution, can do what open force would not dare to attempt." [2]

So it came to pass that John Marshall and the Supreme Court became a center about which swirled the forces of a fast-gathering storm that raged with increasing fury until its thunders were the roar of cannon, its lightning the flashes of battle. Broadly speaking, slavery and free trade, State banking and debtors' relief laws were arraigned on the side of Localism; while slavery restriction, national banking, a protective tariff, and security of contract were marshaled beneath the banner of Nationalism. It was an assemblage of forces as incongruous as human nature itself.

The Republican protagonists of Localism did not content themselves with the writing of enraged letters or the publication of flaming articles and books.

[1] Jefferson to Johnson, June 12, 1823, *Works:* Ford, xii, footnote to 255–56.

[2] Jefferson to Livingston, March 25, 1825, Hunt: *Livingston,* 295-97.

They were too angry thus to limit their attacks, and they were politicians of too much experience not to crystallize an aroused public sentiment. On December 12, 1821, Senator Richard M. Johnson of Kentucky, who later was honored by his party with the Vice-Presidency, offered an amendment to the Constitution that the Senate be given appellate jurisdiction in all cases where the Constitution or laws of a State were questioned and the State desired to defend them; and in all cases "where the judicial power of the United States shall be so construed as to extend to any case . . arising under" the National Constitution, laws, or treaties.[1]

Coöperating with Johnson in the National Senate, Roane in Virginia, when the Legislature of that State met, prepared amendments to the National Constitution which, had they been adopted by the States, would have destroyed the Supreme Court. He declares that he takes this step "with a view to aid" the Congressional antagonists of Nationalism and the Supreme Court, "or rather to lead, on this important subject." The amendments "will be copied by another hand & circulated among the members. I would not wish to injure the great Cause, by being known as the author. My name would damn them, as I believe, nay hope, with the *Tories*." Roane asks his correspondent to "jog your Chesterfield Delegates . . and other good republicans," and complains that "Jefferson & Madison hang back too much, in this great Crisis." [2]

[1] *Annals*, 17th Cong. 1st Sess. 68.
[2] Roane to Thweat, Dec. 24, 1821, Jefferson MSS. Lib. Cong.

On Monday, January 14, 1822, Senator Johnson took the floor in support of his proposition to reduce the power of the Supreme Court. "The conflicts between the Federal judiciary and the sovereignty of the States," he said, "are become so frequent and alarming, that the public safety" demands a remedy. "The Federal judiciary has assumed a guardianship over the States, even to the controlling of their peculiar municipal regulations." [1] The "basis of encroachment" is Marshall's "doctrine of Federal supremacy . . established by a judicial tribunal which knows no change. Its decisions are predicated upon the principle of perfection, and assume the character of immutability. Like the laws of the Medes and Persians, they live forever, and operate through all time." What shall be done? An appeal to the Senate "will be not only harmless, but beneficial." It will quiet "needless alarms . . restore . . confidence . . preserve . . harmony." There is pressing need to tranquillize the public mind concerning the National Judiciary,[2] a department of the government which is a denial of our whole democratic theory. "Some tribunal should be established, responsible to the people, to correct their [the Judges'] aberrations."

Why should not the National Judiciary be made answerable to the people? No fair-minded man can deny that the judges exercise legislative power. "If a judge can repeal a law of Congress, by declaring it unconstitutional, is not this the exercise of political power? If he can declare the laws of a State

---

[1] *Annals*, 17th Cong. 1st Sess. 69–70.　　[2] *Ib.* 71–72.

unconstitutional and void, and, in one moment, subvert the deliberate policy of that State for twenty-four years, as in Kentucky, affecting its whole landed property, . . is not this the exercise of political power? All this they have done, and no earthly power can investigate or revoke their decisions."[1] The Constitution gives the National Judiciary no such power — that instrument "is as silent as death upon the subject." [2]

How absurd is the entire theory of judicial independence! Why should not Congress as properly declare the decisions of the National courts unconstitutional as that the courts should do the same thing to acts of Congress or laws of States? Think of it as a matter of plain common sense — "forty-eight Senators, one hundred and eighty-eight Representatives, and the President of the United States, all sworn to maintain the Constitution, have concurred in the sentiment that the measure is strictly conformable to it. Seven judges, irresponsible to any earthly tribunal for their decisions, revise the measure, declare it unconstitutional, and effectually destroy its operation. Whose opinion shall prevail? that of the legislators and President, or that of the Court?" [3]

The Supreme Court, too, has gently exercised the principle of judicial supervision over acts of Congress; has adjudged that Congress has a free hand in choosing means to carry out powers expressly granted to that body. But consider the conduct of the Supreme Court toward the States: "An irresponsible judiciary" has ruthlessly struck down State

[1] *Annals,* 17th Cong. 1st Sess. 74–75.   [2] *Ib.* 79.   [3] *Ib.* 79–80.

law after State law; has repeatedly destroyed the decisions of State courts. Look at Marshall's opinions
in M'Culloch *vs.* Maryland, in the Dartmouth College case, in United States *vs.* Peters, in Sturges *vs.*
Crowninshield, in Cohens *vs.* Virginia — smallest,
but perhaps worst of all, in Wilson *vs.* New Jersey.
The same principle runs through all these pronouncements; — the States are nothing, the Nation everything.[1]

Webster, in the House, heard of Johnson's speech
and promptly wrote Story: "Mr. Johnson of Ken-
tucky . . has dealt, they say, pretty freely with the
supreme court. Dartmouth College, Sturges and
Crowninshield, *et cetera*, have all been demolished.
To-morrow he is to pull to pieces the case of the
Kentucky betterment law. Then Governor [Senator]
Barber [Barbour] is to annihilate Cohens *v.* Virginia.
So things go; but I see less reality in all this smoke
than I thought I should, before I came here." [2]

It would have been wiser for Webster to have listened carefully to Johnson's powerful address than to
have sneered at it on hearsay, for it was as able as it
was brave; and, erroneous though it was, it stated
most of the arguments advanced before or since
against the supervisory power of the National Judiciary over the enactments of State Legislatures and
the decisions of State courts.

When the Kentucky Senator resumed his speech
the following day, he drove home his strongest
weapon — an instance of judicial interference with

[1] *Annals*, 17th Cong. 1st Sess. 84–90.
[2] Webster to Story, Jan. 14, 1822, *Priv. Corres.*: Webster, I, 320.

State laws which, indeed, at first glance appeared to have been arbitrary, autocratic, and unjust. The agreement between Virginia and Kentucky by which the latter was separated from the parent Commonwealth provided that "all private rights and interests of lands" in Kentucky "derived from the laws of Virginia, shall remain valid . . and shall be determined by the laws now existing" in Virginia.[1]

In 1797 the Kentucky Legislature enacted that persons occupying lands in that State who could show a clear and connected title could not, without notice of any adverse title, upon eviction by the possessor of a superior title, be held liable for rents and profits during such occupancy.[2] Moreover, all permanent improvements made on the land must, in case of eviction, be deducted from the value of the land and judgment therefor rendered in favor of the innocent occupant and against the successful claimant. On January 31, 1812, this "occupying claimant" law, as it was called, was further strengthened by a statute providing that any person "seating and improving" lands in Kentucky, believing them "to be his own" because of a claim founded on public record, should be paid for such seating and improvements by any person who thereafter was adjudged to be the lawful owner of the lands.

Against one such occupant, Richard Biddle, the heirs of a certain John Green brought suit in the

[1] Ordinance of Separation, 1789.

[2] Act of Feb. 27, *Laws of Kentucky, 1797:* Littell, 641–45. See also Act of Feb. 28 (*ib.* 652–71), apparently on a different subject; and, especially, Act of March 1 (*ib.* 682–87). Compare Act of 1796 (*ib.* 392–420); and Act of Dec. 19, 1796 (*ib.* 554–57). See also in *ib.* general land laws.

United States Court for the District of Kentucky, and the case was certified to the Supreme Court on a division of opinion of the judges. The case was argued and decided at the same term at which Marshall delivered his opinion in Cohens *vs.* Virginia. Story delivered the unanimous opinion of the court: that the Kentucky "occupying claimant" laws violated the separation "compact" between Virginia and Kentucky, because, "by the *general principles of law*, and from the necessity of the case, titles to real estate can be determined only by the laws of the state under which they were acquired." [1] Unfortunately Story did not specifically base the court's decision on the contract clause of the Constitution, but left this vital point to inference.

Henry Clay, "as *amicus curiæ*," moved for a rehearing because the rights of numerous occupants of Kentucky lands "would be irrevocably determined by this decision," and because Biddle had permitted the case "to be brought to a hearing without appearing by his counsel, and without any argument on that side of the question." [2] In effect, Clay thus intimated that the case was feigned. The motion was granted and Green *vs.* Biddle was awaiting reargument when Senator Johnson made his attack on the National Judiciary.

Johnson minutely examined the historical reasons for including the contract clause in the National Constitution, "in order to understand perfectly well the mystical influence" of that provision. [3] It never

---

[1] 8 Wheaton, 11–12. (Italics the author's.)　　[2] *Ib.* 18.
[3] *Annals*, 17th Cong. 1st Sess. 96–98.

was intended to affect such legislation as the Kentucky land system. The intent and meaning of the contract clause is, that "you shall not declare to-day that contract void, .. which was made yesterday under the sanction of law." [1] Does this simple rule of morality justify the National courts in annulling measures of public policy "which the people have solemnly declared to be expedient"? [2] The decision of the Supreme Court in Green vs. Biddle, said Johnson, "prostrates the deliberate" course which Kentucky has pursued for almost a quarter of a century, "and affects its whole landed interest. The effect is to legislate for the people; to regulate the interior policy of that community, and to establish their municipal code as to real estate." [3]

If such judicial supremacy prevails, the courts can "establish systems of policy by judicial decision." What is this but despotism? "I see no difference, whether you take this power from the people and give it to your judges, who are in office for life, or grant it to a King for life." [4]

The time is overripe, asserts Johnson, to check judicial usurpation — already the National Judiciary has struck down laws of eight States.[5] The career of this judicial oligarchy must be ended. "The

---

[1] *Annals*, 17th Cong. 1st Sess. 102.
[2] *Ib.* 103.   [3] *Ib.* 104.   [4] *Ib.* 108.
[5] Georgia, Fletcher vs. Peck (see vol. III, chap. x, of this work); Pennsylvania, U.S. vs. Peters (*supra*, chap. I); New Jersey, New Jersey vs. Wilson (*supra*, chap. v); New Hampshire, Dartmouth College vs. Woodward (*supra*, chap. v); New York, Sturges vs. Crowninshield (*supra*, chap. IV); Maryland, M'Culloch vs. Maryland (*supra*, chap. VI); Virginia, Cohens vs. Virginia (*supra*, chap. VII); Kentucky, Green vs. Biddle (*supra*, this chapter).

security of our liberties demands it." Let the jurisdiction of National courts be specifically limited; or
let National judges be subject to removal upon address of both Houses of Congress; or let their commissions be vacated "after a limited term of service";
or, finally, "vest a controlling power in the Senate . .
or some other body who shall be responsible to the
elective franchise." [1]

The Kentucky Legislature backed its fearless
Senator;[2] but the Virginia Assembly weakened at
the end. Most of the Kentucky land titles, which the
Supreme Court's decision had protected as against
the "occupying claimants," were, of course, held
by Virginians or their assignees. Virginia conservatives, too, were beginning to realize the wisdom of
Marshall's Nationalist policy as it affected all their
interests, except slavery and tariff taxation; and
these men were becoming hesitant about further
attacks on the Supreme Court. Doubtless, also,
Marshall's friends were active among the members
of the Legislature. Roane understood the situation
when he begged friends to "jog up" the apathetic,
and bemoaned the quiescence of Jefferson and Madison. His proposed amendments were lost, though
by a very close vote.[3]

[1] *Annals*, 17th Cong. 1st Sess. 113.
[2] Niles, XXI, 404.
[3] *Ib.* The resolutions, offered by John Wayles Eppes, Jefferson's
son-in-law, "*instructed*" Virginia's Senators and requested her Representatives in Congress to "procure" these amendments to the Constitution:

1. The judicial power shall not extend to any power "not expressly
granted . . or *absolutely* necessary for carrying the same into execution."

2. Neither the National Government nor any department thereof

Nevertheless, the Virginia Localists carried the fight to the floors of Congress. On April 26, 1822, Andrew Stevenson, one of Roane's lieutenants and now a member of the National House, demanded the repeal of Section 25 of the Ellsworth Judiciary Act which gave the Supreme Court appellate jurisdiction over the State courts. But Stevenson was unwontedly mild. He offered his resolution "in a spirit of peace and forbearance. . . It was . . due to those States, in which the subject has been lately so much agitated, as well as to the nation, to have it . . decided." [1]

As soon as Congress convened in the winter of 1823, Senator Johnson renewed the combat; but he had become feeble, even apologetic. He did not mean to reflect "upon the conduct of the judges, for he believed them to be highly enlightened and intelligent." Nevertheless, their life tenure and irresponsibility required that some limit should be fixed to their powers. So he proposed that the membership of the Supreme Court be increased to ten, and that at least seven Justices should concur in any opinion involving the validity of National or State laws. [2]

shall have power to bind "*conclusively*" the States in conflicts between Nation and State.

3. The judicial power of the Nation shall never include "*any* case in which a State shall be a party," except controversies between States; nor cases involving the rights of a State "to which such a state shall ask to become a party."

4. No appeal to any National court shall be had from the decisions of any State court.

5. Laws applying to the District of Columbia or the Territories, which conflict with State laws, shall not be enforceable within State jurisdiction. (Niles, XXI, 404.)

[1] *Annals*, 17th Cong. 1st Sess. 1682.

[2] *Ib.*, 18th Cong. 1st Sess. 28.

Four months later, Senator Martin Van Buren reported from the Judiciary Committee, a bill "that no law of any of the States shall be rendered invalid, without the concurrence of at least five Judges of the Supreme Court; their opinions to be separately expressed." [1] But the friends of the Judiciary easily overcame the innovators; the bill was laid on the table; [2] and for that session the assault on the Supreme Court was checked. At the next session, however, Kentucky again brought the matter before Congress. Charles A. Wickliffe, a Representative from that State, proposed that writs of error from the Supreme Court be "awarded to either party," regardless of the decision of the Supreme Court of any State. [3] Webster, on the Judiciary Committee, killed Wickliffe's resolution with hardly a wave of his hand. [4]

After a reargument of Green *vs.* Biddle, lasting an entire week, [5] the Supreme Court stood to its guns and again held the Kentucky land laws unconstitutional. Yet so grave was the crisis that the decision was not handed down for a whole year. This time the opinion of the court was delivered on February 27, 1823, by Bushrod Washington, who held that the contract clause of the National Constitution was violated, but plainly considered that "the principles of law and reason" [6] were of more importance in this case than the Constitutional pro-

---

[1] *Annals*, 18th Cong. 1st Sess. 336.   [2] *Ib.* 419.   [3] *Ib.* 915.

[4] Webster, from the Judiciary Committee, which he seems to have dominated, merely reported that Wickliffe's proposed reform was "not expedient."   (*Annals*, 18th Cong. 1st Sess. 1291.)

[5] March 7 to 13, 1822, inclusive.   [6] 8 Wheaton, 75.

vision. Washington's opinion displays the alarm of
the Supreme Court at the assaults upon it: "We
hold ourselves answerable to God, our consciences
and our country, to decide this question according
to the dictates of our best judgment, be the consequences of the decision what they may." [1]

Kentucky promptly replied. In his Message to
the Legislature, Governor John Adair declared that
the Kentucky decisions of the Supreme Court struck
at "the right of the people to govern themselves."
The National authority can undoubtedly employ
force to "put down insurrection," but "that . . day,
when the government shall be compelled to resort
to the bayonet to compel a state to submit to its
laws, will not long precede an event of all others to
be deprecated." [2]

One of Marshall's numerous Kentucky kinsmen,
who was an active member of the Legislature,
stoutly protested against any attack on the Supreme
Court; nevertheless he offered a resolution reciting the grievances of the State and proposing an address "to the supreme court of the United States,
in full session," against the decision and praying for
"its total and definitive reversal." [3] What! exclaimed
John Rowan, another member of the Legislature,
shall Kentucky again petition "like a degraded prov-

---

[1] 8 Wheaton, 93. Johnson dissented. (*Ib.* 94–107.) Todd of Kentucky was absent because of illness, a circumstance that greatly
worried Story, who wrote the sick Justice: "We have missed you
exceedingly during the term and particularly in the Kentucky causes.
. . We have had . . tough business" and "wanted your firm vote
on many occasions." (Story to Todd, March 24, 1823, Story, I,
422–23.)

[2] Niles, xxv, 203–05.   [3] *Ib.* 206.

ince of Rome"?[1] He proposed counter-resolutions
that the Legislature "do . . most solemnly PRO-
TEST . . against the erroneous, injurious, and degrading doctrines of the opinion . . in . . Green and
Biddle."[2] When modified, Rowan's resolutions,
one of which hinted at forcible resistance to the
mandate of the Supreme Court, passed by heavy
majorities.[3] Later resolutions openly threatened to
"call forth the physical power of the state, to resist
the execution of the decisions of the court," which
were "considered erroneous and unconstitutional."[4]

In the same year that the Supreme Court decided
the Kentucky land case, Justice Johnson aroused
South Carolina by a decision rendered in the United
States District Court of that State. One Henry
Elkison, a negro sailor and a British subject, was
taken by the sheriff of the Charleston district, from
the British ship Homer; and imprisoned under a
South Carolina law which directed the arrest and
confinement of any free negro on board any ship
entering the ports of that State, the negro to be
released only when the vessel departed.[5] Johnson
wrathfully declared that the "unconstitutionality
of the law . . will not bear argument" — nobody
denied that it could not be executed "without
clashing with the general powers of the United
States, to regulate commerce." Thereupon, one of
the counsel for the State said that the statute must
and would be enforced; and "that if a dissolution [sic]
of the union must be the alternative he was ready

---

[1] Niles, xxv, 205. [2] *Ib.* 261. [3] *Ib.* 275–76. [4] *Ib.* xxix, 228–29.
[5] *Ib.* xxv, 12; and see Elkison *vs.* Deliesseline, 8 *Federal Cases,* 493

to meet it" — an assertion which angered Johnson who delivered an opinion almost as strong in its Nationalism as those of Marshall.[1]

Throughout South Carolina and other slaveholding States, the action of Justice Johnson inflamed the passions of the white population. "A high state of excitement exists," chronicles Niles.[2] Marshall, of course, heard of the outcry against his associate and promptly wrote Story: "Our brother Johnson, I perceive, has hung himself on a democratic snag in a hedge composed entirely of thorny state rights in South Carolina. . . You . . could scarcely have supposed that it [Johnson's opinion] would have excited so much irritation as it seems to have produced. The subject is one of much feeling in the South. . . The decision has been considered as another act of judicial usurpation; but the sentiment has been avowed that if this be the constitution, it is better to break that instrument than submit to the principle. . . Fuel is continually adding to the fire at which *exaltées* are about to roast the judicial department."[3]

The Governor and Legislature of South Carolina fiercely maintained the law of the State — it was to them a matter of "self-preservation." Niles was distressingly alarmed. He thought that the collision of South Carolina with the National Judiciary threatened to disturb the harmony of the Republic as much as the Missouri question had done.[4]

[1] Niles, xxv, 13–16. [2] *Ib.* 12; and see especially *ib.* xxvii, 242–43.
[3] Marshall to Story, Sept. 26, 1823, Story MSS. Mass. Hist. Soc.
[4] Niles, xxvii, 242. The Senate of South Carolina resolved by a vote of six to one that the duty of the State to "guard against insubordination or insurrection among our colored population . . is para-

This, then, was the situation when the Ohio Bank case reached the Supreme Court.[1] Seven States were formally in revolt against the National Judiciary, and others were hostile. Moreover, the protective Tariff of 1824 was under debate in Congress; its passage was certain, while in the South ever-growing bitterness was manifesting itself toward this plundering device of Nationalism as John Taylor branded it. In the House Southern members gave warning that the law might be forcibly resisted.[2] The first hints of Nullification were heard. Time and again Marshall's Nationalist construction of the Constitution was condemned. To the application of his theory of government was laid most of the abuses of which the South complained ; most of the dangers the South apprehended.

Thus again stands out the alliance of the various forces of Localism — slavery, State banking, debtors' relief laws, opposition to protective tariffs — which confronted the Supreme Court with threats of physical resistance to its decrees and with the ability to carry out those threats.

mount to all *laws*, all *treaties*, all *constitutions* . . and will never, by this state, be renounced, compromised, controlled or participated with any power whatever."

Johnson's decision is viewed as "an unconstitutional interference" with South Carolina's slave system, and the State "will, on this subject, . . make common cause with . . other southern states similarly circumstanced in this respect." (Niles, xxvii, 264.) The House rejected the savage language of the Senate and adopted resolutions moderately worded, but expressing the same determination. (*Ib.* 292.)

[1] For the facts in Osborn *vs.* The Bank of the United States, see *supra*, 328-329.

[2] See, for instance, speech of John Carter of South Carolina. (*Annals*, 18th Cong. 1st Sess. 2097 ; and upon this subject, generally, see *infra*, chap. x.)

Two arguments were had in Osborn *vs.* The Bank of the United States, the first by Charles Hammond and by Henry Clay for the Bank; [1] the second by John C. Wright, Governor Ethan Allen Brown, and Robert Goodloe Harper, for Ohio, and by Clay, Webster, and John Sergeant for the Bank. Arguments on both sides were notable, but little was presented that was new. Counsel for Ohio insisted that the court had no jurisdiction, since the State was the real party against which the proceedings in the United States Court in Ohio were had. Clay made the point that the Ohio tax, unlike that of Maryland, "was a confiscation, and not a tax. . . Is it possible," he asked, "that . . the law of the whole may be defeated . . by a single part?" [2]

On March 19, 1824, Marshall delivered the opinion of the court. All well-organized governments, he begins, "must possess, within themselves, the means of expounding, as well as enforcing, their own laws." The makers of the Constitution kept constantly in view this great political principle. The Judiciary Article "enables the judicial department to receive jurisdiction to the full extent of the constitution, laws, and treaties of the United States. . . That power is capable of acting only when the subject is submitted to it by a party who asserts his rights in the form prescribed by law. It then becomes a case " over which the Constitution gives jurisdiction to the National courts. "The suit of The Bank of the United States *v.* Osborn *et al.*, is a

[1] Who appeared for Ohio on the first argument is not disclosed by the records.

[2] 9 Wheaton, 795–96.

case, and the question is, whether it arises under a law of the United States." [1]

The fact that other questions are involved does not "withdraw a case" from the jurisdiction of the National courts; otherwise, "almost every case, although involving the construction of a [National] law, would be withdrawn; and a clause in the constitution, relating to a subject of vital importance to the government and expressed in the most comprehensive terms, would be construed to mean almost nothing."

It is true that the Constitution specifies the cases in which the Supreme Court shall have original jurisdiction, but nowhere in the Constitution is there any "prohibition" against Congress giving the inferior National courts original jurisdiction; such a restriction is not "insinuated." Congress, then, can give the National Circuit Courts "original jurisdiction, in any case to which the appellate jurisdiction [of the Supreme Court] extends." [2]

At this particular period of our history this was, indeed, a tremendous expansion of the power of Congress and the National Judiciary. Marshall flatly declares that Congress can invest the inferior National courts with any jurisdiction whatsoever which the Constitution does not prohibit. It marks another stage in the development of his Constitutional principle that the National Government not only has all powers expressly granted, but also all powers not expressly prohibited. For that is just what Marshall's reasoning amounts to during these crucial years.

[1] 9 Wheaton, 818–19.   [2] *Ib.* 819–21.

No matter, continues the Chief Justice, how many questions, other than that affecting the Constitution or laws, are involved in a case; if any National question "forms an ingredient of the original cause," Congress can "give the circuit courts jurisdiction of that cause." The Ohio Bank case "is of this description." All the Bank's powers, functions, and duties are conferred or imposed by its charter, and "that charter is a law of the United States... Can a being, thus constituted, have a case which does not arise literally, as well as substantially, under the law?" [1]

If the Bank brings suits on a contract, the very first, the "foundation" question is, "has this legal entity a right to sue?.. This depends on a law of the United States" — a fact that can never be waived. "Whether it be in fact relied on or not, in the defense, it is still a part of the cause, and may be relied on." [2] Assume, as counsel for Ohio assert, that "the case arises on the contract"; still, "the validity of the contract depends on a law of the United States... The case arises emphatically under the law. The act of Congress is its foundation... The act itself is the first ingredient in the case; is its origin; is that from which every other part arises." [3]

Marshall concedes that the State is directly interested in the suit and that, if the Bank could have done so, it ought to have made the State a party. "But this was not in the power of the bank," because the Eleventh Amendment exempts a State from being sued in such a case. So the "very diffi-

[1] 9 Wheaton, 823.   [2] Ib. 823-24.   [3] Ib. 824-25.

cult question" arises, "whether, in such a case, the court may act upon the agents employed by the state, and on the property in their hands." [1]

Just what will be the result if the National courts have not this power? "A denial of jurisdiction forbids all inquiry into the nature of the case," even of "cases perfectly clear in themselves; . . where the government is in the exercise of its best-established and most essential powers." If the National courts have no jurisdiction over the agents of a State, then those agents, under the "authority of a [State] law void in itself, because repugnant to the constitution, may arrest the execution of any law in the United States" — this they may do without any to say them nay. [2]

In this fashion Marshall leads up to the serious National problem of the hour — the disposition of some States, revealed by threats and sometimes carried into execution, to interfere with the officers of the National Government in the execution of the Nation's laws. According to the Ohio-Virginia-Kentucky idea, those officers "can obtain no protection from the judicial department of the government. The carrier of the mail, the collector of the revenue, [3] the marshal of a district, the recruiting officer, may all be inhibited, under ruinous penalties, from the performance of their respective duties"; and not one of them can "avail himself of the preventive justice of the nation to protect him in the performance of his duties." [4]

[1] 9 Wheaton, 846–47.   [2] *Ib.* 847.
[3] Marshall here refers to threats to resist forcibly the execution of the Tariff of 1824. See *infra*, 535–36.   [4] 9 Wheaton, 847–48.

Addressing himself still more directly to those who were flouting the authority of the Nation and preaching resistance to it, Marshall uses stern language. What is the real meaning of the anti-National crusade; what the certain outcome of it? "Each member of the Union is capable, at its will, of attacking the nation, of arresting its progress at every step, of acting vigorously and effectually in the execution of its designs, while the nation stands naked, stripped of its defensive armor, and incapable of shielding its agent or executing its laws, otherwise than by proceedings which are to take place after the mischief is perpetrated, and which must often be ineffectual, from the inability of the agents to make compensation."

Once more Marshall cites the case of a State "penalty on a revenue officer, for performing his duty," and in this way warns those who are demanding forcible obstruction of National law or authority, that they are striking at the Nation and that the tribunals of the Nation will shield the agents and officers of the Nation: " If the courts of the United States cannot rightfully protect the agents who execute every law authorized by the constitution, from the direct action of state agents in the collecting of penalties, they cannot rightfully protect those who execute any law." [1]

Here, in judicial language, was that rebuke of the spirit of Nullification which Andrew Jackson was soon to repeat in words that rang throughout the land and which still quicken the pulses of Americans. What is the great question before the court in the case of Osborn

[1] 9 Wheaton, 848–49.

vs. The Bank of the United States; what, indeed, the great question before the country in the controversy between recalcitrant States and the imperiled Nation? It is, says Marshall, "whether the constitution of the United States has provided a tribunal which can peacefully and rightfully protect those who are employed in carrying into execution the laws of the Union, from the attempts of a particular state to resist the execution of those laws."

Ohio asserts that "no preventive proceedings whatever," no action even to stay the hand of a State agent from seizing property, no suit to recover it from that agent, can be maintained because it is brought "substantially against the State itself, in violation of the 11th amendment of the constitution." Is this true? "Is a suit, brought against an individual, for any cause whatever, a suit against a state, in the sense of the constitution?" [1] There are many cases in which a State may be vitally interested, as, for example, those involving grants of land by different States.

If the mere fact that the State is "interested" in, or affected by, a suit makes the State a party, "what rule has the constitution given, by which this interest is to be measured?" No rule, of course! Is then the court to decide the *degree* of "interest" necessary to make a State a party? Absurd! since the court would have to examine the "whole testimony of a cause, inquiring into, and deciding on, the extent of a State's interest, without having a right to exercise any jurisdiction in the case." [2]

[1] 9 Wheaton, 849. [2] *Ib.* 852–53.

At last he affirms that it may be "laid down as a
rule which admits of no exception, that, in all cases
where jurisdiction depends on the party, it is the
party *named in the record.*" Therefore, the Eleventh
Amendment is, "of necessity, limited to those suits
in which a state is a party *on the record.*" [1] In the
Ohio Bank case, it follows that, "the state not being
a party on the record, and the court having jurisdiction over those who are parties on the record, the
true question is, not one of jurisdiction, but whether"
the officers and agents of Ohio are "only nominal
parties" or whether "the court ought to make a decree" against them. [2] The answer to this question
depends on the constitutionality of the Ohio tax law.
Although that exact point was decided in M'Culloch
vs. Maryland, [3] "a revision of that opinion has been
requested; and many considerations combine to induce a review of it." [4]

Maryland and Ohio claim the right to tax the
National Bank as an "individual concern . . having
private trade and private profit for its great end and
principal object." But this is not true; the Bank is
a "public corporation, created for public and national purposes"; the fact that it transacts "private
as well as public business" does not destroy its character as the "great instrument by which the fiscal
operations of the government are effected." [5] Obviously the Bank cannot live unless it can do a general business as authorized by its charter. This being
so, the right to transact such business "is necessary

---

[1] 9 Wheaton, 857. (Italics the author's.)   [2] *Ib.* 858.
[3] See *supra,* chap. VI.   [4] 9 Wheaton, 859.   [5] *Ib.* 859–60.

to the legitimate operations of the government, and was constitutionally and rightfully engrafted on the institution." Indeed, the power of the Bank to engage in general banking is "the vital part of the corporation; it is its soul." As well say that, while the human body must not be touched, the "vivifying principle" which "animates" it may be destroyed, as to say that the Bank shall not be annihilated, but that the faculty by which it exists may be extinguished.

For a State, then, to tax the Bank's "faculties, its trade and occupation, is to tax the Bank itself. To destroy or preserve the one, is to destroy or preserve the other." [1] The mere fact that the National Government created this corporation does not relieve it from "state authority"; but the "operations" of the Bank "give its value to the currency in which all the transactions of the government are conducted." In short, the Bank's business is "inseparably connected" with the "transactions" of the Government. "Its corporate character is merely an incident, which enables it to transact that business more beneficially." [2]

The Judiciary "has no will, in any case" — no option but to execute the law as it stands. "Judicial power, as contradistinguished from the power of the laws, has no existence. Courts are the mere instruments of the law, and can will nothing." They can exercise no "discretion," except that of "discerning the course prescribed by law; and, when that is discerned, it is the duty of the court to follow it.

---

[1] 9 Wheaton, 861–62.   [2] *Ib.* 862–63.

Judicial power is never exercised for the purpose of giving effect to the will of the judge; always for the purpose of giving effect to the will of the legislature." [1] This passage, so wholly unnecessary to the decision of the case or reasoning of the opinion, was inserted as an answer to the charges of judicial "arrogance" and "usurpation."

In conclusion, Marshall holds that the Ohio law taxing the National Bank's branches is unconstitutional and void; that the State is not a "party on the record"; that Osborn, Harper, Currie, and Sullivan are "incontestably liable for the full amount of the money taken out of the Bank"; that this money may be pursued, since it "remained a distinct deposit" — in fact, was "kept untouched, in a trunk, by itself, .. to await the event of the pending suit respecting it." [2] The judgment of the lower court that the money must be restored to the Bank was right; but the judgment was wrong in charging interest against the State officers, since they "were restrained by the authority of the Circuit Court from using" the money, taken and held by them.[3]

So everybody having an immediate personal and practical interest in that particular case was made happy, and only the State Rights theorists were discomfited. It was an exceedingly human situation, such as Marshall, the politician, managed to create in his disposition of those cases that called for his highest judicial statesmanship. No matter how acutely he irritated party leaders and forced upon them unwelcome issues, Marshall contrived to sat-

[1] 9 Wheaton, 866. [2] *Ib.* 868–69. [3] *Ib.* 871.

isfy the persons immediately interested in most of the cases he decided.

The Chief Justice himself was a theorist — one of the greatest theorists America has produced; but he also had an intimate acquaintance with human nature, and this knowledge he rightly used, in the desperate conflicts waged by him, to leave his antagonists disarmed of those weapons with which they were wont to fight.

Seemingly Justice Johnson dissented; but, burning with anger at South Carolina's defiance of his action in the negro sailor case, he strengthened Marshall's opinion in his very "dissent." This is so conspicuously true that it may well be thought that Marshall inspired Johnson's "disagreement" with his six brethren of the Supreme Court. Whether the decision was "necessary or unnecessary originally," begins Johnson, " a *state of things has now grown up, in some of the states*, which renders all the protection necessary, that the general government can give to this bank." [1] He makes a powerful and really stirring appeal for the Bank, but finally concludes, on technical grounds, that the Supreme Court has no jurisdiction.[2]

Immediately the fight upon the Supreme Court was renewed in Congress. On May 3, 1824, Representative Robert P. Letcher of Kentucky rose in the House and proposed that the Supreme Court should be forbidden by law to hold invalid any provision

----

[1] 9 Wheaton, 871–72. (Italics the author's.) In reality Johnson is here referring to the threats of physical resistance to the proposed tariff law of 1824. (See *infra*, chap. x.)

[2] *Ib.* 875–903.

of a State constitution or statute unless five out of
the seven Justices concurred, each to give his opinion
"separately and distinctly," if the court held against
the State.[1] Kentucky, said Letcher, had been deprived of "equal rights and privileges." How? By
"*construction.* . . Yes, construction! Its mighty powers are irresistible; . . it creates new principles; . . it
destroys laws long since established; and it is daily
acquiring new strength."[2] John Forsyth of Georgia
proposed as a substitute to Letcher's resolutions
that, for the transaction of business, "a majority
of the quorum" of the Supreme Court "shall be a
majority of the whole court, including the Chief
Justice." A long and animated debate[3] ensued
in which Clay, Webster, Randolph, and Philip P.
Barbour, among others, took part.

David Trimble of Kentucky declared that "no
nation ought to submit, to an umpire of minorities.[4]
. . If less than three-fourths of the States cannot
amend the Constitution, less than three-fourths of
the judges ought not to construe it" — for judicial
constructions are "explanatory amendments" by
which "the person and property of every citizen
must stand or fall."[5]

So strong had been the sentiment for placing some
restraint on the National Judiciary that Webster,

[1] *Annals*, 18th Cong. 1st Sess. 2514.   [2] *Ib.* 2519–20.
[3] *Ib.* 2527. This debate was most scantily reported. Webster wrote
of it: "We had the Supreme Court before us yesterday. . . A debate
arose which lasted all day. Cohens *v.* Virginia, Green and Biddle, &c.
were all discussed. . . The proposition for the concurrence of five
judges will not prevail." (Webster to Story, May 4, 1824, *Priv.
Corres.*: Webster, i, 350.)
[4] *Annals*, 18th Cong. 1st Sess. 2538.   [5] *Ib.* 2539.

astute politician and most resourceful friend of the
Supreme Court, immediately offered a resolution
that, in any cause before the Supreme Court where
the validity of a State law or Constitution is drawn
in question "on the ground of repugnancy to the
Constitution, treaties, or laws, of the United States,
no judgment shall be pronounced or rendered until
a majority of all the justices . . legally competent
to sit, . . shall concur in the opinion." [1]

But Marshall's opinion in Gibbons *vs.* Ogden [2]
had now reached the whole country and, for the time
being, changed popular hostility to the Supreme
Court into public favor toward it. The assault in
Congress died away and Webster allowed his soothing resolution to be forgotten. When the attack on
the National Judiciary was again renewed, the language of its adversaries was almost apologetic.

---

[1] *Annals*, 18th Cong. 1st Sess. 2541.

Throughout this session Webster appears to have been much disturbed. For example, as early as April 10, 1824, he writes Story:
"I am exhausted. When I look in the glass, I think of our old New
England saying, 'As thin as a shad.' I have not vigor enough left,
either mental or physical, to try an action for assault and battery.
. . I shall call up some bills reported by our [Judiciary] committee. . .
The gentlemen of the West will propose a clause, requiring the assent
of a majority of all the judges to a judgment, which pronounces a
state law void, as being in violation of the constitution or laws of the
United States. Do you see any great evil in such a provision? Judge
Todd told me he thought it would give great satisfaction in the West.
In what phraseology would you make such a provision?" (Webster to
Story, April 10, 1824, *Priv. Corres.*: Webster, I, 348–49.)

[2] See next chapter.

CHAPTER VIII

COMMERCE MADE FREE

Marshall's decision involved in its consequences the existence of the Union.
(John F. Dillon.)

Opposing rights to the same thing cannot exist under the Constitution of our country. (Chancellor Nathan Sanford.)

Sir, we shall keep on the windward side of treason, but we must combine to resist these encroachments, — and that effectually. (John Randolph.)

That uncommon man who presides over the Supreme Court is, in all human probability, the ablest Judge now sitting on any judicial bench in the world.
(Martin Van Buren.)

At six o'clock in the evening of August 9, 1803, a curious assembly of curious people was gathered at a certain spot on the banks of the Seine in Paris. They were gazing at a strange object on the river— the model of an invention which was to affect the destinies of the world more powerfully and permanently than the victories and defeats of all the armies that, for a dozen years thereafter, fought over the ancient battle-fields of Europe from Moscow to Madrid. The occasion was the first public exhibition of Robert Fulton's steamboat.

France was once more gathering her strength for the war which, in May, Great Britain had declared upon her; and Bonaparte, as First Consul, was in camp at Boulogne. Fulton had been experimenting for a long time, and the public exhibition now in progress would have been made months earlier had not an accident delayed it. His activities had been reported to Bonaparte, who promptly ordered members of the Institute [1] to attend the exhibition and report to him on the practicability of the invention, which,

[1] Institut national des sciences et des arts.

he wrote, and in italics, "*may change the face of the world.*" [1] Prominent, therefore, among the throng were these learned men, doubting and skeptical as mere learning usually is.

More conspicuous than Bonaparte's scientific agents, and as interested and confident as they were indifferent or scornful, was a tall man of distinguished bearing, whose powerful features, bold eyes, aggressive chin, and acquisitive nose indicated a character of unyielding determination, persistence, and hopefulness. This was the American Minister to France, Robert R. Livingston of New York, who, three months before, had conducted the Louisiana Purchase. By his side was Fulton himself, a man of medium height, slender and erect, whose intellectual brow and large, speculative eyes indicated the dreamer and contriver.

The French scientists were not impressed, and the French Government dropped consideration of the subject. But Fulton and Livingston were greatly encouraged. An engine designed by Fulton was ordered from a Birmingham manufacturer and, when constructed, was shipped to America.

For many years inventive minds had been at work on the problem of steam navigation. Because of the cost and difficulties of transportation, and the ever-growing demand for means of cheap and easy water carriage, the most active and fruitful efforts to solve the problem had been made in America. [2] Livingston,

---

[1] Dickinson: *Robert Fulton, Engineer and Artist,* 156–57; also see Thurston: *Robert Fulton,* 113.

[2] See Dickinson, 126–32; also Knox: *Life of Robert Fulton,* 72–86; and Fletcher: *Steam-Ships,* 19–24.

then Chancellor of New York, had taken a deep and practical interest in the subject.[1] He had constructed a boat on the Hudson, and was so confident of success that, five years before the Paris experiments of Fulton, he had procured from the New York Legislature an act giving him the exclusive right for twenty years to navigate by steamboats the streams and other waters of the State, provided that, within a year, he should build a boat making four miles an hour against the current of the Hudson.[2] The only difficulty Livingston encountered in securing the passage of this act was the amused incredulity of the legislators. The bill "was a standing subject of ridicule" and had to run the gamut of jokes, jeers, and raillery.[3] The legislators did not object to granting a monopoly on New York waters for a century or for a thousand years,[4] provided the navigation was by steam; but they required, in payment to themselves, the price of derision and laughter.

[1] Dickinson, 134–35; Knox, 90–93.

[2] Act of March 27, 1798, *Laws of New York, 1798*, 382–83. This act, however, was merely the transfer of similar privileges granted to John Fitch on March 19, 1787, to whom, rather than to Robert Fulton, belongs the honor of having invented the steamboat. It was printed in the *Laws of New York* edited by Thomas Greenleaf, published in 1792, i, 411; and also appears as Appendix A to "A Letter, addressed to Cadwallader D. Colden, Esquire," by William Alexander Duer, the first biographer of Fulton. (Albany, 1817.) Duer's pamphlet is uncommonly valuable because it contains all the petitions to, and the acts of, the New York Legislature concerning the steamboat monopoly.

[3] Reigart: *Life of Robert Fulton*, 163. Nobody but Livingston was willing to invest in what all bankers and business men considered a crazy enterprise. (*Ib.* 100–01.)

[4] Knox, 93. It should be remembered, however, that the granting of monopolies was a very common practice everywhere during this period. (See Prentice: *Federal Power over Carriers and Corporations*, 60–65.)

Livingston failed to meet in time the conditions of the steamboat act, but, with Livingston tenacity,[1] persevered in his efforts to build a practicable vessel. When, in 1801, he arrived in Paris as American Minister, his mind was almost as full of the project as of his delicate and serious official tasks.

Robert Fulton was then living in the French Capital, working on his models of steamboats, submarines, and torpedoes, and striving to interest Napoleon in his inventions.[2] Livingston and Fulton soon met; a mutual admiration, trust, and friendship followed and a partnership was formed.[3] Livingston had left his interests in the hands of an alert and capable agent, Nicholas J. Roosevelt, who, in 1803, had no difficulty in securing from the now hilarious New York Legislature an extension of Livingston's monopoly for twenty years upon the same terms as the first.[4] Livingston resigned his office and returned home. Within a year Fulton joined his partner.

The grant of 1803 was forfeited like the preceding one, because its conditions had not been complied with in time, and another act was passed by the Legislature reviving the grant and extending it for two years.[5] Thus encouraged and secured, Fulton and Livingston put forth every effort, and on Monday, August 17, 1807, four years and eight days after the dramatic exhibition on the river Seine in Paris,

---

[1] Compare with his brother's persistence in the Batture controversy, *supra*, 100–15.

[2] Dickinson, 64–123; Knox, 35–44.

[3] Knox, 93; see also Dickinson, 136.

[4] Act of April 5, 1803, *Laws of New York, 1802–04*, 323–24.

[5] Act of April 6, 1807, *Laws of New York, 1807–09*, 213–14.

the North River,[1] the first successful steamboat,
made her voyage up the Hudson from New York
to Albany[2] and the success of the great enterprise
was assured.

On April 11, 1808, a final law was enacted by the
New York Legislature. The period of ridicule had
passed; the members of that body now voted with
serious knowledge of the possibilities of steam navigation. The new act provided that, for each new
boat "established" on New York waters by Livingston and Fulton and their associates, they should
be "entitled to five years prolongation of their
grant *or contract* with this state," the "whole term"
of their monopoly not to exceed thirty years. All
other persons were forbidden to navigate New York
waters by steam craft without a license from Livingston and Fulton; and any unlicensed vessel, "together with the engine, tackle and apparel thereof,"
should be forfeited to them.[3]

Obedient to "the great god, Success," the public
became as enthusiastic and friendly as it had been
frigid and hostile and eagerly patronized this pleasant, cheap, and expeditious method of travel. The
profits quickly justified the faith and perseverance of
Livingston and Fulton. Soon three boats were running between New York and Albany. The fare each
way was seven dollars and proportionate charges
were made for intermediate landings, of which there

[1] The North River was afterward named the Clermont, which
was the name of Livingston's county seat. (Dickinson, 230.)

[2] The country people along the Hudson thought the steamboat
a sea monster or else a sign of the end of the world. (Knox, 110–11.)

[3] Act of April 11, 1808, *Laws of New York, 1807–09*, 407–08.
(Italics the author's.)

were eleven.[1] Immediately the monopoly began operating steam ferryboats between New York City and New Jersey.[2] Having such solid reason for optimism, Livingston and Fulton, with prudent foresight, leaped half a continent and placed steamboats on the Mississippi, the traffic of which they planned to control by securing from the Legislature of Orleans Territory the same exclusive privileges for steam navigation upon Louisiana waters, which included the mouth of the Mississippi,[3] that New York had granted upon the waters of that State. Nicholas J. Roosevelt was put in charge of this enterprise, and in an incredibly short time the steamboat New Orleans was ploughing the turgid and treacherous currents of the great river.[4]

[1] Dickinson, 233–34.

[2] *Ib.* 234–36. The thoroughfare in New York, at the foot of which these boats landed, was thereafter named Fulton Street. (*Ib.* 236.)

[3] See *infra*, 414.

[4] Dickinson, 230. From the first Roosevelt had been associated with Livingston in steamboat experiments. He had constructed the engine for the craft with which Livingston tried to fulfill the conditions of the first New York grant to him in 1798. Roosevelt was himself an inventor, and to him belongs the idea of the vertical wheel for propelling steamboats which Fulton afterward adopted with success. (See J. H. B. Latrobe, in *Maryland Historical Society Fund-Publication*, No. 5, 13–14.)

Roosevelt was also a manufacturer and made contracts with the Government for rolled and drawn copper to be used in war-vessels. The Government failed to carry out its agreement, and Roosevelt became badly embarrassed financially. In this situation he entered into an arrangement with Livingston and Fulton that if the report he was to make to them should be favorable, he was to have one third interest in the steamboat enterprise on the Western waters, while Livingston and Fulton were to supply the funds.

The story of his investigations and experiments on the Ohio and Mississippi glows with romance. Although forty-six years old, he had but recently married and took his bride with him on this memorable

It was not long, however, before troubles came —
the first from New Jersey. Enterprising citizens of

journey. At Pittsburgh he built a flatboat and on this the newly
wedded couple floated to New Orleans; the trip, with the long and
numerous stops to gather information concerning trade, transportation, the volume and velocity of various streams, requiring six months'
time.

Before proceeding far Roosevelt became certain of success. Discovering coal on the banks of the Ohio, he bought mines, set men at
work in them, and stored coal for the steamer he felt sure would be
built. His expectation was justified and, returning to New York from
New Orleans, he readily convinced Livingston and Fulton of the
practicability of the enterprise and was authorized to go back to Pittsburgh to construct a steamboat, the design of which was made by
Fulton. By the summer of 1811 the vessel was finished. It cost
$38,000 and was named the New Orleans.

Late in September, 1811, the long voyage to New Orleans was begun, the only passengers being Roosevelt and his wife. A great crowd
cheered them as the boat set out from Pittsburgh. At Cincinnati the
whole population greeted the arrival of this extraordinary craft. Mr.
and Mrs. Roosevelt were given a dinner at Louisville, where, however, all declared that while the boat could go down the river, it never
could ascend. Roosevelt invited the banqueters to dine with him on
the New Orleans the next night and while toasts were being drunk
and hilarity prevailed, the vessel was got under way and swiftly proceeded upstream, thus convincing the doubters of the power of the
steamboat.

From Louisville onward the voyage was thrilling. The earthquake
of 1811 came just after the New Orleans passed Louisville and this
changed the river channels. At another time the boat took fire and
was saved with difficulty. Along the shore the inhabitants were torn
between terror of the earthquake and fright at this monster of the
waters. The crew had to contend with snags, shoals, sandbars, and
other obstructions. Finally Natchez was reached and here thousands of people gathered on the bluffs to witness this triumph of
science.

At last the vessel arrived at New Orleans and the first steamboat
voyage on the Ohio and Mississippi was an accomplished fact. The
experiment, which began two years before with the flatboat voyage of
a bride and groom, ended at the metropolis of the Southwest in the
marriage of the steamboat captain to Mrs. Roosevelt's maid, with
whom he had fallen in love during this thrilling and historic voyage.
(See Latrobe, in *Md. Hist. Soc. Fund-Pub.* No. 6. A good summary
of Latrobe's narrative is given in Preble: *Chronological History of the
Origin and Development of Steam Navigation,* 77–81.)

that State also built steamboats; but the owners of
any vessel entering New York waters, even though
acting merely as a ferry between Hoboken and New
York City, must procure a license from Livingston
and Fulton or forfeit their boats. From discontent at
this condition the feelings of the people rose to resentment and then to anger. At last they determined
to retaliate, and early in 1811 the New Jersey Legislature passed an act authorizing the owner of any
boat seized under the New York law, in turn to capture and hold any steam-propelled craft belonging
"in part or in whole" to any citizen of New York;
"which boat . . shall be forfeited . . to the . . owner
. . of such . . boats which may have been seized"
under the New York law.[1]

New York was not slow to reply. Her Legislature
was in session when that of New Jersey thus declared
commercial war. An act was speedily passed providing that Livingston and Fulton might enforce at
law or in equity the forfeiture of boats unlicensed by
them, "as if the same had been tortiously and wrong-
fully taken out of their possession"; and that when
such a suit was brought the defendants should be
enjoined from running the boat or "removing the
same or any part thereof out of the jurisdiction of
the court." [2]

Connecticut forbade any vessel licensed by Livingston and Fulton from entering Connecticut waters.[3] The opposition to the New York steamboat
monopoly was not, however, confined to other

[1] Act of Jan. 25, 1811, *Acts of New Jersey, 1811*, 298–99.
[2] Act of April 9, 1811, *Laws of New York, 1811*, 368–70.
[3] *Laws of Connecticut*, May Sess. 1822, chap. XXVIII.

States. Citizens of New York defied it and began to
run steam vessels on the Hudson.[1] James Van Ingen
and associates were the first thus to challenge the
exclusive "contract," as the New York law termed
the franchise which the State had granted to Livingston and Fulton. Suit was brought against Van
Ingen in the United States Circuit Court in New
York, praying that Livingston and Fulton be
"quieted in the possession," or in the exclusive right,
to navigate the Hudson secured to them by two
patents.[2] The bill was dismissed for want of jurisdiction. Thus far the litigation was exclusively
a State controversy. Upon the face of the record
the National element did not appear; yet it was the
governing issue raised by the dispute.

Immediately Livingston and Fulton sued Van
Ingen and associates in the New York Court of
Chancery, praying that they be enjoined from operating their boats. In an opinion of great ability and
almost meticulous learning, Chancellor John Lansing
denied the injunction; he was careful, however, not
to base his decision on a violation of the commerce
clause of the National Constitution by the New
York steamboat monopoly act. He merely held
that act to be invalid because it was a denial of a
natural right of all citizens alike to the free navigation of the waters of the State. In such fashion the
National question was still evaded.

[1] Dickinson, 244.
[2] Livingston *et al. vs.* Van Ingen *et al.*, 1 Paine, 45–46. Brockholst
Livingston, Associate Justice of the Supreme Court, sat in this case
with William P. Van Ness (the friend and partisan of Burr), and delivered the opinion.

The Court of Errors[1] reversed the decree of Chancellor Lansing. Justice Yates and Justice Thompson delivered State Rights opinions that would have done credit to Roane.[2] At this point the National consideration develops. The opinion of James Kent, then Chief Justice, was more moderate in its denial of National power over the subject. Indeed, Kent appears to have anticipated that the Supreme Court would reverse him. Nevertheless, his opinion was the source of all the arguments thereafter used in defense of the steamboat monopoly. Because of this fact; because of Kent's eminence as a jurist; and because Marshall so crushingly answered his arguments, a *précis* of them must be given. It should be borne in mind that Kent was defending a law which, in a sense, was his own child; as a member of the New York Council of Revision, he had passed upon and approved it before its passage.

There could have been "no very obvious constitutional objection" to the steamboat monopoly act, began Kent, "or it would not so repeatedly have escaped the notice of the several branches of the government [3] when these acts were under consideration." [4] There had been five acts all told; [5] that of 1798 would surely have attracted attention since it

---

[1] The full title of this tribunal was the "Court for the Trial of Impeachments and the Correction of Errors." It was the court of last resort, appeals lying to it from the Supreme Court of Judicature and from the Court of Chancery. It consisted of the Justices of the Supreme Court of Judicature and a number of State Senators. A more absurdly constituted court cannot well be imagined.

[2] 9 Johnson, 558, 563.

[3] The State Senate, House, Council of Revision, and Governor.

[4] 9 Johnson, 572.

[5] Those enacted in 1798, 1803, 1807, 1808, and 1811.

was the first to be passed on the subject after the National Constitution was adopted. It amounted to "a legislative exposition" of State powers under the new National Government.

Members of the New York Legislature of 1798 had also been members of the State Convention that ratified the Constitution, and "were masters of all the critical discussions" attending the adoption of that instrument. This was peculiarly true of that "exalted character," John Jay, who was Governor at that time; and "who was distinguished, as well in the *council of revision*, as elsewhere, for the scrupulous care and profound attention with which he examined every question of a constitutional nature." [1] The Act of 1811 was passed after the validity of the previous ones had been challenged and "was, therefore, equivalent to a declaratory opinion of high authority, that the former laws were valid and constitutional." [2]

The people of New York had not "alienated" to the National Government the power to grant exclusive privileges. This was proved by the charters granted by the State to banks, ferries, markets, canal and bridge companies. "The legislative power in a *single, independent government*, extends to every proper object of power, and is limited only by its own constitutional provisions, or by the fundamental principles of all government, and the unalienable rights of mankind." [3] In what respect did the steamboat monopoly violate any of these restrictions? In

---

[1] 9 Johnson, 573. Jay as Governor was Chairman of the Council of Revision, of which Kent was a member.
[2] *Ib.* 572.   [3] *Ib.* 573. (Italics the author's.)

no respect. "It interfered with no man's property."
Everybody could freely use the waters of New York
in the same manner that he had done before. So
there was "no violation of first principles." [1]

Neither did the New York steamboat acts violate
the National Constitution. State and Nation are
"supreme within their respective constitutional
spheres." It is true that when National and State
laws "come directly in contact, as when they are
aimed at each other," those of the State "must
yield"; but State Legislatures cannot all the time
be on the watch for some possible future collision.
The only "safe rule of construction" is this: "If any
given power was originally vested in this State, if it
has not been exclusively ceded to Congress, or if the
exercise of it has not been prohibited to the States,
we may then go on in the exercise of the power until
it comes practically in collision with the actual exercise of some congressional power." [2]

The power given Congress to regulate commerce is
not, "in express terms, exclusive, and the only prohibition upon the States" in this regard concerns the
making of treaties and the laying of tonnage import or export duties. All commerce within a State
is "exclusively" within the power of that State. [3]
Therefore, New York's steamboat grant to Livingston and Fulton is valid. It conflicts with no act of
Congress, according to Kent, who cannot "perceive
any power which . . can lawfully carry to that extent." If Congress has any control whatever over

---

[1] 9 Johnson, 574.   [2] *Ib.* 575–76.
[3] *Ib.* 577–78.

New York waters, it is concurrent with that of the
State, and even then, "no further than may be
incidental and requisite to the due regulation of
commerce between the States, and with foreign
nations." [1]

Kent then plunges into an appalling mass of authorities, in dealing with which he delighted as much
as Marshall recoiled from the thought of them. [2] So
Livingston and Fulton's steamboat monopoly was
upheld. [3]

But what were New York waters and what were
New Jersey waters? Confusion upon this question
threatened to prevent the monopoly from gathering
fat profits from New Jersey traffic. Aaron Ogden, [4]
who had purchased the privilege of running ferryboats from New York to certain points on the New
Jersey shore, combined with one Thomas Gibbons,
who operated a boat between New Jersey landings,
to exchange passengers at Elizabethtown Point in
the latter State. Gibbons had not secured the per-

[1] 9 Johnson, 578, 580.   [2] *Ib.* 582–88.

[3] All the Senators concurred except two, Lewis and Townsend,
who declined giving opinions because of relationship with the parties
to the action. (*Ib.* 589.)

[4] Ogden protested against the Livingston-Fulton steamboat monopoly in a Memorial to the New York Legislature. (See Duer, 94–97.)
A committee was appointed and reported the facts as Ogden stated
them; but concluded that, since New York had granted exclusive
steamboat privileges to Livingston, "the honor of the State requires
that its faith should be preserved." However, said the committee, the
Livingston-Fulton boats "are in substance the invention of John
Fitch," to whom the original monopoly was granted, after the expiration of which "the right to use" steamboats "became common to all
the citizens of the United States." Moreover, the statements upon
which rested the Livingston monopoly of 1798 "were not true in
fact," Fitch having forestalled the claims of the Livingston pretensions
(*Ib.* 103–04.)

mission of the New York steamboat monopoly to
navigate New York waters. By his partnership with
Ogden he, in reality, carried passengers from New
York to various points in New Jersey. In fact,
Ogden and Gibbons had a common traffic agent in
New York who booked passengers for routes, to
travel which required the service of the boats of both
Ogden and Gibbons.

So ran the allegations of the bill for an injunction
against the offending carriers filed in the New York
Court of Chancery by the steamboat monopoly in
the spring of 1819. Ogden answered that his license
applied only to waters "*exclusively* within the state
of *New-York*," and that the waters lying between the
New Jersey ports "are within the jurisdiction of *New
Jersey*." Gibbons admitted that he ran a boat between New Jersey ports under "a coasting *license*"
from the National Government. He denied, however, that the monopoly had "any exclusive right"
to run steamboats from New York to New Jersey.
Both Ogden and Gibbons disclaimed that they ran
boats in combination, or by agreement with each
other.[1]

Kent, now Chancellor, declared that a New York
statute [2] asserted jurisdiction of the State over "the
whole of the river Hudson, southward of the northern
boundary of the city of New-York, and the whole of
the bay between Staten Island and Long or Nassau
Island." He refused to enjoin Ogden because he

---

[1] 4 Johnson's *Chancery Reports*, 50–51. The reader must not confuse the two series of Reports by Johnson; one contains the decisions of
the Court of Errors; the other, those of the Court of Chancery.

[2] Act of April 6, 1808, *Laws of New York, 1807–09*, 313–15.

operated his boat under license of the steamboat
monopoly; but did enjoin Gibbons "from navigating the waters in the bay of New-York, or Hudson
river, between Staten Island and Powles Hook." [1]

Ogden was content, but Gibbons, thoroughly angered by the harshness of the steamboat monopoly
and by the decree of Chancellor Kent, began to run
boats regularly between New York and New Jersey in
direct competition with Ogden.[2] To stop his former
associate, now his rival, Ogden applied to Chancellor
Kent for an injunction. As in the preceding case,
Gibbons again set up his license from the National
Government, asserting that by virtue of this license
he was entitled to run his boats "in the coasting
trade between ports of the same state, or of different
states," and could not be excluded from such traffic
"by any law or grant of any particular state, on any
pretence to an exclusive right to navigate the waters
of any particular state by steam-boats." Moreover,
pleaded Gibbons, the representatives of Livingston
and Fulton had issued to Messrs. D. D. Tompkins,
Adam Brown, and Noah Brown a license to navigate
New York Bay; and this license had been assigned
to Gibbons.[3]

Kent held that the act of Congress,[4] concerning
the enrollment and licensing of vessels for the coasting trade, conferred no right "incompatible with an
exclusive right in Livingston and Fulton" to navigate New York waters.[5] The validity of the steam-

---

[1] 4 Johnson's *Chancery Reports*, 51, 53.
[2] *Ib.* 152.   [3] *Ib.* 154.
[4] Act of Feb. 18, 1793, *U.S. Statutes at Large*, I, 305–18.
[5] 4 Johnson's *Chancery Reports*, 156.

boat monopoly laws had been settled by the decision of the Court of Errors in Livingston *vs.* Van Ingen.[1] If a National law gave to all vessels, "duly licensed" by the National Government, the right to navigate all waters "within the several states," despite State laws to the contrary, the National statute would "overrule and set aside" the incompatible legislation of the States. "The only question that could arise in such a case, would be, whether the [National] law was constitutional." But that was not the situation; "there is no collision between the act of Congress and the acts of this State, creating the steam-boat monopoly." At least "some judicial decision of the supreme power of the Union, acting upon those laws, in direct collision and conflict" with them, is necessary before the courts of New York "can retire from the support and defence of them."[2]

Undismayed, Gibbons lost no time in appealing to the New York Court of Errors, and in January, 1820, Justice Jonas Platt delivered the opinion of that tribunal. Immediately after the decision in Livingston *vs.* Van Ingen, he said, many, who formerly had resisted the steamboat monopoly law, acquiesced in the judgment of the State's highest court and secured licenses from Livingston and Fulton. Ogden was one of these. The Court of Errors rejected Gibbons's defense, followed Chancellor Kent's opinion, and affirmed his decree.[3]

Thus did the famous case of Gibbons *vs.* Ogden reach the Supreme Court of the United States; thus

---

[1] 9 Johnson, 507 *et seq.*
[2] 4 Johnson's *Chancery Reports*, 158–59.   [3] 17 Johnson, 488 *et seq.*

was John Marshall given the opportunity to deliver the last but one of his greatest nation-making opinions — an opinion which, in the judgment of most lawyers and jurists, is second only to that in M'Culloch *vs.* Maryland in ability and statesmanship. By some, indeed, it is thought to be superior even to that state paper.

The Supreme Court, the bar, and the public anticipated an Homeric combat of legal warriors when the case was argued, since, for the first time, the hitherto unrivaled Pinkney was to meet the new legal champion, Daniel Webster, who had won his right to that title by his efforts in the Dartmouth College case and in M'Culloch *vs.* Maryland.[1] It was expected that the steamboat monopoly argument would be made at the February session of 1821, and Story wrote to a friend that "the arguments will be very splendid." [2]

But, on March 16, 1821, the case was dismissed because the record did not show that there was a final decree in the court "from which said appeal was made." [3] On January 10, 1822, the case was again docketed, but was continued at each term of the Supreme Court thereafter until February, 1824. Thus, nearly four years elapsed from the time the appeal was first taken until argument was heard.[4]

By the time the question was at last submitted to

---

[1] See *supra*, 240–50, 284–86.
[2] Story to Fettyplace, Feb. 28, 1821, Story, I, 397.
[3] Records Supreme Court, MS.
[4] The case was first docketed, June 7, 1820, as Aaron Ogden *vs.* Thomas *Gibbins*, and the defective transcript was filed October 17, of the same year. When next docketed, the title was correctly given, Thomas Gibbons *vs.* Aaron Ogden. (*Ib.*)

Marshall, transportation had become the most pressing and important of all economic and social problems confronting the Nation, excepting only that of slavery; nor was any so unsettled, so confused.

Localism had joined hands with monopoly — at the most widely separated points in the Republic, States had granted "exclusive privileges" to the navigation of "State waters." At the time that the last steamboat grant was made by New York to Livingston and Fulton, in 1811, the Legislature of the Territory of Orleans passed, and Governor Claiborne approved, an act bestowing upon the New York monopoly the same exclusive privileges conferred by the New York statute. This had been done soon after Nicholas J. Roosevelt had appeared in New Orleans on the bridge of the first steamboat to navigate the Mississippi. Whoever operated any steam vessel upon Louisiana waters without license from Livingston and Fulton must pay them $5000 for each offense, and also forfeit the boat and equipment.[1]

The expectations of Livingston and Fulton of a monopoly of the traffic of that master waterway were thus fulfilled. When, a few months later, Louisiana was admitted to the Union, the new State found herself bound by this monopoly from which, however, it does not appear that she wished to be released. Thus Livingston and Fulton held the keys to the two American ports into which poured the greatest volume of domestic products for export, and from which the largest quantity of foreign trade found its way into the interior.

[1] Act of April 19, 1811, *Acts of Territory of Orleans, 1811,* 112-18.

Three years later Georgia granted to Samuel Howard of Savannah a rigid monopoly to transport merchandise upon Georgia waters in all vessels "or rafts" towed by steam craft.[1] Anybody who infringed Howard's monopoly was to forfeit $500 for each offense, as well as the boat and its machinery. The following year Massachusetts granted to John Langdon Sullivan the "exclusive rights to the Connecticut river within this Commonwealth for the use of his patent steam towboats for . . twenty-eight years." [2] A few months afterwards New Hampshire made a like grant to Sullivan.[3] About the same time Vermont granted a monopoly of navigation in the part of Lake Champlain under her jurisdiction.[4] These are some examples of the general tendency of States and the promoters of steam navigation to make commerce pay tribute to monopoly by the exercise of the sovereignty of States over waters within their jurisdiction. Retaliation of State upon State again appeared — and in the same fashion that wrecked the States under the Confederation.[5]

But this ancient monopolistic process could not keep pace with the prodigious development of water

---

[1] Act of Nov. 18, 1814, *Laws of Georgia, 1814,* October Sess. 28–30.

[2] Act of Feb. 7, 1815, *Laws of Massachusetts, 1812–15,* 595.

[3] Act of June 15, 1815, *Laws of New Hampshire, 1815,* II, 5.

[4] Act of Nov. 10, 1815, *Laws of Vermont, 1815,* 20.

[5] Ohio, for example, passed two laws for the "protection" of its citizens owning steamboats. This act provided that no craft propelled by steam, operated under a license from the New York monopoly, should land or receive passengers at any point on the Ohio shores of Lake Erie unless Ohio boats were permitted to navigate the waters of that lake within the jurisdiction of New York. For every passenger landed in violation of these acts the offender was made subject to a fine of $100. (Chap. xxv, Act of Feb. 18, 1822, and chap. II, Act of May 23, 1822, *Laws of Ohio, 1822.*)

travel and transportation by steamboat. On every river, on every lake, glided these steam-driven vessels. Their hoarse whistles startled the thinly settled wilderness; or, at the landings on big rivers flowing through more thickly peopled regions, brought groups of onlookers to witness what then were considered to be marvels of progress.[1]

By 1820 seventy-nine steamboats were running on the Ohio between Pittsburgh and St. Louis, most of them from 150 to 650 tons burden. Pittsburgh, Cincinnati, and Louisville were the chief places where these boats were built, though many were constructed at smaller towns along the shore.[2] They carried throngs of passengers and an ever-swelling volume of freight. Tobacco, pork, beef, flour, cornmeal, whiskey — all the products of the West[3] were borne to market on the decks of steamboats which, on the return voyage, were piled high with manufactured goods.

River navigation was impeded, however, by snags, sandbars, and shallows, while the traffic overland was made difficult, dangerous, and expensive by atrocious roads. Next to the frantic desire to unburden themselves of debt by "relief laws" and other

---

[1] Niles's *Register* for these years is full of accounts of the building, launching, and departures and arrivals of steam craft throughout the whole interior of the country.

[2] See Blane: *An Excursion Through the United States and Canada,* by "An English Gentleman," 119–21. For an accurate account of the commercial development of the West see also Johnson: *History of Domestic and Foreign Commerce,* I, 213–15.

On March 1, 1819, Flint saw a boat on the stocks at Jeffersonville, Indiana, 180 feet long, 40 feet broad, and of 700 tons burden. (Flint's Letters, in *E. W. T.*: Thwaites, IX, 164.)

[3] Blane, 118.

forms of legislative contract-breaking, the thought uppermost in the minds of the people was the improvement of means of communication and transportation. This popular demand was voiced in the second session of the Fourteenth Congress. On December 16, 1816, John C. Calhoun brought the subject before the House.[1] Four days later he reported a bill to devote to internal improvements "the bonus of the National bank and the United States's share of its dividends."[2] It met strenuous opposition, chiefly on the ground that Congress had no Constitutional power to expend money for such purposes.[3] An able report was made to the House based on the report of Secretary Gallatin in 1808. The vital importance of "internal navigation" was pointed out,[4] and the bill finally passed.[5]

The last official act of President James Madison was the veto of this first bill for internal improvements passed by Congress. The day before his second term as President expired, he returned the bill with the reasons for his disapproval of it. He did this, he explained, because of the "insuperable difficulty . . in reconciling the bill with the Constitution." The power "proposed to be exercised by the bill" was not "enumerated," nor could it be deduced "by any just interpretation" from the power of Congress "to make laws necessary and proper" for the execution of powers expressly conferred on Congress. "The power to regulate com-

[1] *Annals*, 14th Cong. 2d Sess. 296.   [2] *Ib.* 361.
[3] See debate in the House, *ib.* 851–923; and in the Senate, *ib.* 166–70.
[4] *Ib.* 924–33.   [5] March 1, 1817, *ib.* 1052.

merce among the several States can not include a power to construct roads and canals, and to improve the navigation of water courses." Nor did the "'common defense and general welfare'" clause justify Congress in passing such a measure.[1]

But not thus was the popular demand to be silenced. Hardly had the next session convened when the subject was again taken up.[2] On December 15, 1817, Henry St. George Tucker of Virginia, chairman of the Select Committee appointed to investigate the subject, submitted an uncommonly able report ending with a resolution that the Bank bonus and dividends be expended on internal improvements "with the assent of the States."[3] For two weeks this resolution was debated.[4] Every phase of the power of Congress to regulate commerce was examined. And so the controversy went on year after year.

Three weeks before the argument of Gibbons *vs.* Ogden came on in the Supreme Court, a debate began in Congress over a bill to appropriate funds for surveying roads and canals, and continued during all the time that the court was considering the case. It was going on, indeed, when Marshall delivered his opinion and lasted for several weeks. Once more the

[1] Veto Message of March 3, 1817, Richardson, i, 584–85.

[2] Monroe gingerly referred to it in his First Inaugural Address. (Richardson, ii, 8.) But in his First Annual Message he dutifully followed Madison and declared that "Congress do not possess the right" to appropriate National funds for internal improvements. So this third Republican President recommended an amendment to the Constitution "which shall give to Congress the right in question." (*Ib.* 18.)

[3] *Annals*, 15th Cong. 1st Sess. 451–60.

[4] *Ib.* 1114–1250, 1268–1400.

respective powers of State and Nation over internal improvements, over commerce, over almost everything, were threshed out. As was usual with him, John Randolph supplied the climax of the debate.

Three days previous to the argument of Gibbons *vs.* Ogden before Marshall and his associates, Randolph arose in the House and delivered a speech which, even for him, was unusually brilliant. In it he revealed the intimate connection between the slave power and opposition to the National control of commerce. Randolph conceded the progress made by Nationalism through the extension of the doctrine of implied powers. The prophecy of Patrick Henry as to the extinction of the sovereignty, rights, and powers of the State had been largely realized, he said. The promises of the Nationalists, made in order to secure the ratification of the Constitution, and without which pledges it never would have been adopted, had been contemptuously broken, he intimated. He might well have made the charge outright, for it was entirely true.

Randolph laid upon Madison much of the blame for the advancement of implied powers; and he arraigned that always weak and now ageing man in an effective passage of contemptuous eloquence.[1]

[1] "All the difficulties under which we have labored and now labor on this subject have grown out of a fatal admission" by Madison "which runs counter to the tenor of his whole political life, and is expressly contradicted by one of the most luminous and able State papers that ever was written [the Virginia Resolutions] — an admission which gave a sanction to the principle that this Government had the power to charter the present colossal Bank of the United States. Sir, . . that act, and one other which I will not name. Madison's War

When, in the election of 1800, continued Randolph, the Federalists were overthrown, and "the construction of the Constitution according to the Hamiltonian version" was repudiated, "did we at that day dream, . . that a new sect would arise after them, which would so far transcend Alexander Hamilton and his disciples, as they outwent Thomas Jefferson, James Madison, and John Taylor of Caroline? This is the deplorable fact: such is now the actual state of things in this land; . . it speaks to the senses, so that every one may understand it." [1] And to what will all this lead? To this, at last: "If Congress possesses the power to do what is proposed by this bill [appropriate money to survey roads and canals], . . they may *emancipate every slave in the United States* [2] — and with stronger color of reason than they can exercise the power now contended for."

Let Southern men beware! If "a coalition of knavery and fanaticism . . be got up on this floor, I ask gentlemen, who stand in the same predicament as I do, to look well to what they are now doing — to the colossal power with which they are now arm-

Message in 1812], bring forcibly home to my mind a train of melancholy reflections on the miserable state of our mortal being:

> ' In life's last scenes, what prodigies surprise!
> Fears of the brave, and follies of the wise.
> From Marlborough's eyes the streams of dotage flow,
> And Swift expires a driv'ler and a show.'

"Such is the state of the case, Sir. It is miserable to think of it — and we have nothing left to us but to weep over it." (*Annals*, 18th Cong. 1st Sess. 1301.)

Randolph was as violently against the War of 1812 as was Marshall, but he openly proclaimed his opposition.

[1] *Ib.*   [2] Italics the author's.

ing this Government." [1] And why, at the present moment, insist on this "new construction of the Constitution? . . Are there not already causes enough of jealousy and discord existing among us? . . Is this a time to increase those jealousies between different quarters of the country already sufficiently apparent?"

In closing, Randolph all but threatened armed rebellion: "Should this bill pass, one more measure only requires to be consummated; and then we, who belong to that unfortunate portion of this Confederacy which is south of Mason and Dixon's line, . . have to make up our mind to perish . . or we must resort to the measures which we first opposed to British aggressions and usurpations — to maintain that independence which the valor of our fathers acquired, but which is every day sliding from under our feet. . . Sir, this is a state of things that cannot last. . . We shall keep on the windward side of treason — but we must combine to resist, and that effectually, these encroachments." [2]

Moreover, Congress and the country, particularly the South, were deeply stirred by the tariff question; in the debate then impending over the Tariff of 1824, Nationalism and Marshall's theory of Constitutional construction were to be denounced in language almost as strong as that of Randolph on internal improvements. [3] The Chief Justice and his associates were keenly alive to this agitation; they well knew that the principles to be upheld in

---

[1] *Annals*, 18th Cong. 1st Sess. 1308.
[2] *Ib*. 1310–11. The bill passed, 115 yeas to 86 nays. (*Ib*. 1468–69.)
[3] See *infra*, 535–36.

Gibbons *vs.* Ogden would affect other interests and concern other issues than those directly involved in that case.

So it was, then, when the steamboat monopoly case came on for hearing, that two groups of interests were in conflict. State Sovereignty standing for exclusive privileges as chief combatant, with Free Trade and Slavery as brothers in arms, confronted Nationalism, standing at that moment for the power of the Nation over all commerce as the principal combatant, with a Protective Tariff and Emancipation as its most effective allies. Fate had interwoven subjects that neither logically nor naturally had any kinship.[1]

The specific question to be decided was whether the New York steamboat monopoly laws violated that provision of the National Constitution which bestows on Congress the "power to regulate commerce among the several States."

The absolute necessity of a general supervision of commerce was the sole cause of the Convention at Annapolis, Maryland, in 1786, which resulted in the Constitutional Convention in Philadelphia the following year.[2] Since the adoption of uniform

---

[1] See *infra*, chap. x.

[2] See vol. i, 310–12, of this work; also Marshall: *Life of George Washington*, 2d ed. ii, 105–06, 109–10, 125. And see Madison's "Preface to Debates in the Convention of 1787." (*Records of the Federal Convention:* Farrand, iii, 547.) "The want of authy. in Congs. to regulate Commerce had produced in Foreign nations particularly G. B. a monopolizing policy injurious to the trade of the U. S. and destructive to their navigation. . . The same want of a general power over Commerce led to an exercise of this power separately, by the States, wch not only proved abortive, but engendered rival, conflicting and angry regulations."

commercial regulations was the prime object of the Convention, there was no disagreement as to, or discussion of, the propriety of giving Congress full power over that subject. Every draft except one [1] of the Committee of Detail, the Committee of Style, and the notes taken by members contained some reference to a clause to that effect.[2]

The earliest exposition of the commerce clause of the Constitution by any eminent National authority, therefore, came from John Marshall. In his opinion in Gibbons *vs.* Ogden he spoke the first and last authoritative word on that crucial subject.

Pinkney was fatally ill when the Supreme Court convened in 1822 and died during that session. His death was a heavy blow to the steamboat monopoly, and his loss was not easily made good. It was finally decided to employ Thomas J. Oakley, Attorney-General of New York, a cold, clear reasoner, and carefully trained lawyer, but lacking imagination,

---

[1] *Records, Fed. Conv.*: Farrand, ii, 143. The provision in this draft is very curious. It declares that "a navigation act shall not be passed, but with the consent of (eleven states in) $<\frac{2}{3}$d. of the Members present of$>$ the senate and (10 in) $<$the like No. of$>$ the house of representatives."

[2] *Ib.* 135, 157, 569, 595, 655. Roger Sherman mentioned interstate trade only incidentally. Speaking of exports and imports, he said that "the oppression of the uncommercial States was guarded agst. by the power to regulate trade between the States." (*Ib.* 308.)

Writing in 1829, Madison said that the commerce clause "being in the same terms with the power over foreign commerce, the same extent, if taken literally, would belong to it. Yet it . . grew out of the abuse of the power by the importing States in taxing the non-importing, and was intended as a negative and preventive provision against injustice among the States themselves, rather than as a power to be used for the positive purposes of the General Government, in which alone, however, the remedial power could be lodged." (Madison to Cabell, Feb. 13, 1829, *ib.* iii, 478.)

warmth, or breadth of vision.[1] He was not an adequate
substitute for the masterful and glowing Pinkney.

When on February 4, 1824, the argument at last
was begun, the interest in the case was so great that,
although the incomparable Pinkney was gone, the
court-room could hold but a small part of those who
wished to hear that brilliant legal debate. Thomas
Addis Emmet, whose "whole soul" was in the case,
appeared for the steamboat monopoly and made in
its behalf his last great argument. With him came
Oakley, who was expected to perform some marvelous intellectual feat, his want of attractive qualities of speech having enhanced his reputation as a
thinker. Wirt reported that he was "said to be one
of the first logicians of the age."[2]

Gibbons was represented by Webster who, says
Wirt, "is as ambitious as Cæsar," and "will not be
outdone by any man, if it is within the compass of
his power to avoid it."[3] Wirt appeared with Webster against the New York monopoly. The argument
was opened by Webster; and never in Congress or
court had that surprising man prepared so carefully
— and never so successfully.[4] Of all his legal argu-

---

[1] See *Monthly Law Reporter*, New Series, x, 177.
[2] Wirt to Carr, Feb. 1, 1824, Kennedy, II, 164.   [3] *Ib.*
[4] "Reminiscence," that betrayer of history, is responsible for the
fanciful story, hitherto accepted, that Webster was speaking on the tariff in the House when he was suddenly notified that Gibbons *vs.* Ogden
would be called for argument the next morning; and that, swiftly concluding his great tariff argument, he went home, took medicine, slept
until ten o'clock that night, then rose, and in a strenuous effort worked
until 9 A.M. on his argument in the steamboat case; and that this was
all the preparation he had for that glorious address. (Ticknor's reminiscences of Webster, as quoted by Curtis, I, 216–17.)

On its face, Webster's argument shows that this could not have
been true. The fact was that Webster had had charge of the case in

ments, that in the steamboat case is incontestably
supreme. And, as far as the assistance of associate
counsel was concerned, Webster's address, unlike
that in the Dartmouth College case, was all his
own. It is true that every point he made had been
repeated many times in the Congressional debates
over internal improvements, or before the New
York courts in the steamboat litigation. But these
facts do not detract from the credit that is rightfully
Webster's for his tremendous argument in Gibbons
vs. Ogden.

He began by admissions—a dangerous method and
one which only a man of highest power can safely employ. The steamboat monopoly law had been "deliberately re-enacted," he said, and afterwards had the
"sanction" of various New York courts, "than which
there were few, if any, in the country, more justly entitled to respect and deference." Therefore he must,
acknowledged Webster, "make out a clear case" if
he hoped to win.[1]

the Supreme Court for three years; and that, since the argument was
twice before expected, he had twice before prepared for it.

The legend about his being stopped in his tariff speech is utterly
without foundation. The debate on that subject did not even begin
in the House until February 11, 1824 (*Annals*, 18th Cong. 1st Sess.
1470), three days after the argument of Gibbons *vs.* Ogden was concluded; and Webster did not make his famous speech on the Tariff Bill
of 1824 until April 1–2, one month after the steamboat case had been
decided. (*Ib.* 2026–68.)

Moreover, as has been stated in the text, the debate on the survey
of roads and canals was on in the House when the argument in Gibbons *vs.* Ogden was heard; had been in progress for three weeks previously and continued for some time afterward; and in this debate
Webster did not participate. Indeed, the record shows that for more
than a week before the steamboat argument Webster took almost no
part in the House proceedings. (*Ib.* 1214–1318.)

[1] 9 Wheaton, 3.

What was the state of the country with respect to transportation? Everybody knew that the use of steamboats had become general; everywhere they plied over rivers and bays which often formed the divisions between States. It was inevitable that the regulations of such States should be "hostile" to one another. Witness the antagonistic laws of New York, New Jersey, and Connecticut. Surely all these warring statutes were not "consistent with the laws and constitution of the United States." If any one of them were valid, would anybody "point out where the state right stopped?" [1]

Webster carefully described the New York steamboat monopoly laws, the rights they conferred, and the prohibitions they inflicted.[2] He contended, among other things, that these statutes violated the National Constitution. "The power of Congress to regulate commerce was complete and entire," said Webster, "and to a certain extent necessarily exclusive." [3] It was well known that the "immediate" reason and "prevailing motive" for adopting the Constitution was to "rescue" commerce "from the embarrassing and destructive consequences resulting from the legislation of so many different states, and to place it under the protection of a uniform law." [4] The paramount object of establishing the present Government was "to benefit and improve" trade. This, said Webster, was proved by the undisputed history of the period preceding the Constitution.[5]

What commerce is to be regulated by Congress?

[1] 9 Wheaton, 4–5.　[2] *Ib.* 6–9.　[3] *Ib.* 9.　[4] *Ib.* 11.　[5] *Ib.* 11–12.

Not that of the several States, but that of the Nation
as a "unit." Therefore, the regulation of it "must
necessarily be complete, entire and uniform. Its
character was to be described in the flag which
waved over it, *E Pluribus Unum*." Of consequence,
Congressional regulation of commerce must be
"exclusive." Individual States cannot "assert a
right of concurrent legislation, . . without manifest
encroachment and confusion." [1]

If New York can grant a monopoly over New
York Bay, so can Virginia over the entrance of
the Chesapeake, so can Massachusetts over the bay
bearing the name and under the jurisdiction of that
State. Worse still, every State may grant "an exclusive right of entry of vessels into her ports." [2]

Oakley, Emmet, and Wirt exhausted the learning
then extant on every point involved in the controversy. Not even Pinkney at his best ever was more
thorough than was Emmet in his superb argument
in Gibbons *vs.* Ogden. [3]

The small information possessed by the most careful and thorough lawyers at that time concerning
important decisions in the Circuit Courts of the
United States, even when rendered by the Chief Justice himself, is startlingly revealed in all these arguments. Only four years previously, Marshall, at
Richmond, had rendered an opinion in which he asserted the power of Congress over commerce as em-

[1] 9 Wheaton, 14.   [2] *Ib.* 24.
[3] The student should carefully read these three admirable arguments, particularly that of Emmet. All of them deal with patent law
as well as with the commerce clause of the Constitution. (See
9 Wheaton, 33–135.) The argument lasted from February 4 to February 9 inclusive.

phatically as Webster or Wirt now insisted upon it. This opinion would have greatly strengthened their arguments, and undoubtedly they would have cited it had they known of it. But neither Wirt nor Webster made the slightest reference to the case of the Brig Wilson *vs.* The United States, decided during the May term, 1820.

One offense charged in the libel of that vessel by the National Government was, that she had brought into Virginia certain negroes in violation of the laws of that State and in contravention of the act of Congress forbidding the importation of negroes into States whose laws prohibited their admission. Was this act of Congress Constitutional? The power to pass such a law is, says Marshall, "derived entirely" from that clause of the Constitution which "enables Congress, 'to regulate commerce with foreign nations, and among the several States.'" [1] This power includes navigation. The authority to forbid foreign ships to enter our ports comes exclusively from the commerce clause. "If this power over vessels is not in Congress, where does it reside? Does it reside in the States?

"No American politician has ever been so extravagant as to contend for this. No man has been wild enough to maintain, that, although the power to regulate commerce, gives Congress an unlimited power over the cargoes, it does not enable that body to control the vehicle in which they are imported: that, while the whole power of commerce is vested in Congress, the state legislatures may confiscate

[1] 1 Brockenbrough, 430–31.

every vessel which enters their ports, and Congress is unable to prevent their entry."

The truth, continues Marshall, is that "even an empty vessel, or a packet, employed solely in the conveyance of passengers and letters, may be regulated and forfeited" under a National law. "There is not, in the Constitution, one syllable on the subject of navigation. And yet, every power that pertains to navigation has been . . rightfully exercised by Congress. From the adoption of the Constitution, till this time, the universal sense of America has been, that the word commerce, as used in that instrument, is to be considered a generic term, comprehending navigation, or, that a control over navigation is necessarily incidental to the power to regulate commerce." [1]

Here was a weapon which Webster could have wielded with effect, but he was unaware that it existed — a fact the more remarkable in that both Webster and Emmet commented, in their arguments, upon State laws that prohibited the admission of negroes.

But Webster never doubted that the court's decision would be against the New York steamboat monopoly laws. "Our Steam Boat case is not yet decided, but it *can go but one way*," he wrote his brother a week after the argument.[2]

On March 2, 1824, Marshall delivered that opinion which has done more to knit the American people into an indivisible Nation than any other one

---

[1] 1 Brockenbrough, 431–32.
[2] Webster to his brother, Feb. 15, 1824, Van Tyne, 102.

force in our history, excepting only war. In Marbury *vs.* Madison he established that fundamental principle of liberty that a permanent written constitution controls a temporary Congress; in Fletcher *vs.* Peck, in Sturges *vs.* Crowninshield, and in the Dartmouth College case he asserted the sanctity of good faith; in M'Culloch *vs.* Maryland and Cohens *vs.* Virginia he made the Government of the American people a living thing; but in Gibbons *vs.* Ogden he welded that people into a unit by the force of their mutual interests.

The validity of the steamboat monopoly laws of New York, declares Marshall, has been repeatedly upheld by the Legislature, the Council of Revision, and the various courts of that State, and is "supported by great names — by names which have all the titles to consideration that virtue, intelligence, and office, can bestow." [1] Having paid this tribute to Chancellor Kent — for every word of it was meant for that great jurist — Marshall takes up the capital question of construction.

It is urged, he says, that, before the adoption of the Constitution, the States "were sovereign, were completely independent, and were connected with each other only by a league. This is true. But when these allied sovereigns converted their league into a government, when they converted their Congress of Ambassadors, deputed to deliberate on their common concerns, and to recommend measures of general utility, into a legislature, empowered to enact laws . . the whole character" of the States "under-

[1] 9 Wheaton, 186.

went a change, the extent of which must be determined by a fair consideration" of the Constitution.

Why ought the powers "expressly granted" to the National Government to be "construed strictly," as many insist that they should be? "Is there one sentence in the constitution which gives countenance to this rule?" None has been pointed out; none exists. What is meant by "a strict construction"? Is it "that narrow construction, which would cripple the government and render it unequal to the objects for which it is declared to be instituted,[1] and to which the powers given, as fairly understood, render it competent"? The court cannot adopt such a rule for expounding the Constitution.[2]

Just as men, "whose intentions require no concealment," use plain words to express their meaning, so did "the enlightened patriots who framed our constitution," and so did "the people who adopted it." Surely they "intended what they have said." If any serious doubt of their meaning arises, concerning the extent of any power, "the objects for which it was given . . should have great influence in the construction."[3]

Apply this common-sense rule to the commerce clause of the Constitution.[4] What does the word

[1] "WE THE PEOPLE of the United States, in Order to form a more perfect Union, establish Justice, insure domestic Tranquility, provide for the common defence, promote the general Welfare, and secure the Blessings of Liberty to ourselves and our Posterity, do ordain and establish this CONSTITUTION for the United States of America." (Preamble to the Constitution of the United States.)

[2] 9 Wheaton, 187–88.   [3] Ib. 188–89.

[4] "The Congress shall have Power . . to regulate Commerce with foreign Nations, and among the Several States, and with the Indian Tribes." (Constitution of the United States, Article I, Section 8.)

'commerce" mean? Strict constructionists, like
the advocates of the New York steamboat monopoly, "limit it to . . buying and selling . . and do
not admit that it comprehends navigation." But
why not navigation? "Commerce . . is traffic, but
it is something more; it is intercourse." If this is not
true, then the National Government can make no
law concerning American vessels — "yet this power
has been exercised from the commencement of the
government, has been exercised with the consent of
all, and has been understood by all to be a commercial regulation. All America understands . . the
word 'commerce' to comprehend navigation. . .
The power over commerce, including navigation,
was one of the primary objects for which the people
of America adopted their government. . . The attempt to restrict it [the meaning of the word "commerce"] comes too late."

Was not the object of the Embargo, which "engaged the attention of every man in the United
States," avowedly "the protection of commerce? . .
By its friends and its enemies that law was treated
as a commercial, not as a war measure." Indeed, its
very object was "the avoiding of war." Resistance
to it was based, not on the denial that Congress can
regulate commerce, but on the ground that "a perpetual embargo was the annihilation, and not the
regulation of commerce." This illustration proves
that "the universal understanding of the American
people" was, and is, that "a power to regulate navigation is as expressly granted as if that term had been
added to the word 'commerce.'" [1]

[1] 9 Wheaton, 192–93.

Nobody denies that the National Government
has unlimited power over foreign commerce — "no
sort of trade can be carried on between this country
and any other, to which this power does not extend."
The same is true of commerce among the States.
The power of the National Government over trade
with foreign nations, and "among" the several
States, is conferred in the same sentence of the
Constitution, and "must carry the same meaning
throughout the sentence. . . The word 'among'
means intermingled with." So "commerce among
the states cannot stop at the external boundary line
of each state, but may be introduced into the interior." This does not, of course, include the "completely interior traffic of a state." [1]

Everybody knows that foreign commerce is that
of the whole Nation and not of its parts. "Every
district has a right to participate in it. The deep
streams which penetrate our country in every direction, pass through the interior of almost every state
in the Union." The power to regulate this commerce
"must be exercised whenever the subject exists.
If it exists within a state, if a foreign voyage may
commence or terminate within a state, then the
power of Congress may be exercised within a state."[2]

If possible, "this principle . . is still more clear,
when applied to commerce 'among the several
states.' They either join each other, in which case
they are separated by a mathematical line, or they
are remote from each other, in which case other
states lie between them. . . Can a trading expedition

---

[1] 9 Wheaton, 193–94.   [2] *Ib.* 195.

between two adjoining states commence and terminate outside of each?" The very idea is absurd. And must not commerce between States "remote" from one another, pass through States lying between them? The power to regulate this commerce is in the National Government.[1]

What is this power to "regulate commerce"? It is the power "to prescribe the rule by which commerce is to be governed. This power . . is complete in itself, may be exercised to its utmost extent, and acknowledges no limitations, other than are prescribed in the constitution;" and these do not affect the present case. Power over interstate commerce "is vested in Congress as absolutely as it would be in a single government" under a Constitution like ours. There is no danger that Congress will abuse this power, because "the wisdom and the discretion of Congress, their identity with the people, and the influence which their constituents possess at election, are, in this, as in many other instances, as that, for example, of declaring war, the sole restraints on which they [the people] have relied, to secure them from its abuse. They are restraints on which the people must often rely solely, in all representative governments." The upshot of the whole dispute is, declares Marshall, that Congress has power over navigation "within the limits of every state . . so far as that navigation may be, in any manner, connected" with foreign or interstate trade.[2]

Marshall tries to answer the assertion that the power to regulate commerce is concurrent in Con-

[1] 9 Wheaton, 195–96.   [2] *Ib.* 196–97.

Obviously, however, the National Government "in the exercise of its express powers, that, for example, of regulating [foreign and interstate] commerce . . may use means that may also be employed by a state, . . that, for example, of regulating commerce within the state." The National coasting laws, though operating upon ports within the same State, imply "no claim of a direct power to regulate the purely internal commerce of a state, or to act directly on its system of police." State laws on these subjects, although of the "same character" as those of Congress, do not flow from the same source whence the National laws flow, "but from some other, which remains with the state, and may be executed by the same means." Although identical measures may proceed from different powers, "this does not prove that the powers themselves are identical." [1]

It is inevitable in a "complex system" of government like ours that "contests respecting power must arise" between State and Nation. But this "does not prove that one is exercising, or has a right to exercise, the powers of the other." [2] It cannot be inferred from National statutes requiring National officials to "conform to, and assist in the execution of the quarantine and health laws of a state . . that a state may rightfully regulate commerce"; such laws flow from "the acknowledged power of a state, to provide for the health of its citizens." Nevertheless, "Congress may control the state [quarantine and health] laws, so far as it may be necessary to control them, for the regulation of commerce." [3]

[1] 9 Wheaton, 203–04.   [2] *Ib.* 204–05.   [3] *Ib.* 205–06.

Marshall analyzes, at excessive length, National and State laws on the importation of slaves, on pilots, on lighthouses,[1] to show that such legislation does not justify the inference that "the states possess, concurrently" with Congress, "the power to regulate commerce with foreign nations and among the states."

In the regulation of "their own purely internal affairs," States may pass laws which, although in themselves proper, become invalid when they interfere with a National law. Is this the case with the New York steamboat monopoly acts? Have they "come into collision with an act of Congress, and deprived a citizen of a right to which that act entitles him"? If so, it matters not whether the State laws are the exercise of a concurrent power to regulate commerce, or of a power to "regulate their domestic trade and police." In either case, "the acts of New York must yield to the law of Congress." [2]

This truth is "founded as well on the nature of the government as on the words of the constitution." The theory that if State and Nation each rightfully pass conflicting laws on the same subject, "they affect the subject, and each other, like equal opposing powers," is demolished by the "supremacy" of the Constitution and "of the laws made in pursuance of it. The nullity of *any act*, inconsistent with the constitution, is produced by the declaration that the constitution is the supreme law." So when a State statute, enacted under uncontrovertible State powers, conflicts with a law, treaty, or the Constitution

[1] 9 Wheaton, 206–09.   [2] *Ib.* 209–10.

of the Nation, the State enactment "must yield
to it." [1]

It is not the Constitution, but "those laws whose
authority is acknowledged by civilized man throughout the world" that "confer the right of intercourse
between state and state. . . The constitution found
it an existing right, and gave to Congress the power
to regulate it. In the exercise of this power, Congress has passed an act" regulating the coasting
trade. Any law "must imply a power to exercise the
right" it confers. How absurd, then, the contention
that, while the State of New York cannot prevent a
vessel licensed under the National coasting law, when
proceeding from a port in New Jersey to one in New
York, "from enjoying . . all the privileges conferred
by the act of Congress," nevertheless, the State of
New York "can shut her up in her own port, and
prohibit altogether her entering the waters and ports
of another state"! [2]

A National license to engage in the coasting trade
gives the right to navigate between ports of different
States. [3] The fact that Gibbons's boats carried passengers only did not make those vessels any the less
engaged in the coasting trade than if they carried
nothing but merchandise — "no clear distinction
is perceived between the power to regulate vessels
employed in transporting men for hire, and property for hire. . . A coasting vessel employed in the
transportation of passengers, is as much a portion
of the American marine as one employed in the

[1] 9 Wheaton, 210–11. (Italics the author's.)
[2] *Ib.* 211–12.   [3] *Ib.* 214.

transportation of a cargo." [1] Falling into his characteristic over-explanation, Marshall proves the
obvious by many illustrations. [2]

However the question as to the nature of the
business is beside the point, since the steamboat
monopoly laws are based solely on the method of
propelling boats — "whether they are moved by
steam or wind. If by the former, the waters of New
York are closed against them, though their cargoes
be dutiable goods, which the laws of the United
States permit them to enter and deliver in New
York. If by the latter, those waters are free to them,
though they should carry passengers only." What
is the injury which Ogden complains that Gibbons
has done him? Not that Gibbons's boats carry passengers, but only that those vessels "are moved by
steam."

"The writ of injunction and decree" of the State
court "restrain these [Gibbons's] licensed vessels,
not from carrying passengers, but from being moved
through the waters of New York by steam, for any
purpose whatever." Therefore, "the real and sole
question seems to be, whether a steam machine, in
actual use, deprives a vessel of the privileges conferred by a [National] license." The answer is easy
— indeed, there is hardly any question to answer:
"The laws of Congress, for the regulation of commerce, do not look to the principle by which vessels
are moved." [3]

Steamboats may be admitted to the coasting trade
"in common with vessels using sails. They are . .

---

[1] 9 Wheaton, 215–16.   [2] *Ib.* 216–18.   [3] *Ib.* 218–20.

entitled to the same privileges, and can no more
be restrained from navigating waters, and entering
ports which are free to such vessels, than if they
were wafted on their voyage by the winds, instead
of being propelled by the agency of fire. The one
element may be as legitimately used as the other,
for every commercial purpose authorized by the
laws of the Union; and the act of a state inhibiting
the use of either to any vessel having a license under
the act of Congress comes . . in direct collision with
that act." [1]

Marshall refuses to discuss the question of Fulton's patents since, regardless of that question,
the cause must be decided by the supremacy of
National over State laws that regulate commerce
between the States.

The Chief Justice apologizes, and very properly,
for taking so "much time . . to demonstrate propositions which may have been thought axioms. It is
felt that the tediousness inseparable from the endeavor to prove that which is already clear, is im-
putable to a considerable part of this opinion. But
it was unavoidable." The question is so great, the
judges, from whose conclusions "we dissent," are so
eminent,[2] the arguments at the bar so earnest, an
"unbroken" statement of principles upon which the
court's judgment rests so indispensable, that Marshall feels that nothing should be omitted, nothing
taken for granted, nothing assumed.[3]

Having thus placated Kent, Marshall turns upon

[1] 9 Wheaton, 221.
[2] Marshall is here referring particularly to Chancellor Kent.
[3] 9 Wheaton, 221–22.

his Virginia antagonists: "Powerful and ingenious minds, taking, as postulates, that the powers expressly granted to the government of the Union, are to be contracted, by construction, into the narrowest possible compass, and that the original powers of the States are retained, if any possible construction will retain them, may, by a course of well digested, but refined and metaphysical reasoning, founded on these premises, *explain away the constitution of our country, and leave it a magnificent structure indeed, ,o look at, but totally unfit for use.*

"They may so entangle and perplex the understanding, as to obscure principles which were before thought quite plain, and induce doubts where, if the mind were to pursue its own course, none would be perceived.

"In such a case, it is peculiarly necessary to recur to safe and fundamental principles to sustain those principles, and, when sustained, to make them the tests of the arguments to be examined." [1]

So spoke John Marshall, in his seventieth year, when closing the last but one of those decisive opinions which vitalized the American Constitution, and assured for himself the grateful and reverent homage of the great body of the American people as long as the American Nation shall endure. It is pleasant to reflect that the occasion for this ultimate effort of Marshall's genius was the extinction of a monopoly.

Marshall, the statesman, rather than the judge, appears in his opinion. While avowing the most determined Nationalism in the body of his opinion,

[1] 9 Wheaton, 222. (Italics the author's.)

he is cautious, nevertheless, when coming to close grips with the specific question of the respective rights of Gibbons and Ogden. He is vague on the question of concurrent powers of the States over commerce, and rests the concrete result of his opinion on the National coasting laws and the National coasting license to Gibbons.

William Johnson, a Republican, appointed by Jefferson, had, however, no such scruples. In view of the strong influence Marshall had, by now, acquired over Johnson, it appears to be not improbable that the Chief Justice availed himself of the political status of the South Carolinian, as well as of his remarkable talents, to have Johnson state the real views of the master of the Supreme Court.

At any rate, Johnson delivered a separate opinion so uncompromisingly Nationalist that Marshall's Nationalism seems hesitant in comparison. In it Johnson gives one of the best statements ever made, before or since, of the regulation of commerce as the moving purpose that brought about the American Constitution. That instrument did not originate liberty of trade: "The law of nations . . pronounces all commerce legitimate in a state of peace, until prohibited by positive law." So the power of Congress over that vital matter "must be exclusive; it can reside but in one potentate; and hence, the grant of this power carries with it the whole subject, leaving nothing for the state to act upon." [1]

Commercial laws! Were the whole of them "repealed to-morrow, all commerce would be lawful."

[1] 9 Wheaton, 227.

The authority of Congress to control foreign commerce is precisely the same as that over interstate
commerce. The National power over navigation is
not "incidental to that of regulating commerce; . .
it is as the thing itself; inseparable from it as vital
motion is from vital existence. . . Shipbuilding, the
carrying trade, and the propagation of seamen, are
such vital agents of commercial prosperity, that the
nation which could not legislate over these subjects
would not possess power to regulate commerce." [1]

Johnson therefore finds it "impossible" to agree
with Marshall that freedom of interstate commerce
rests on any such narrow basis as National coasting
law or license: "I do not regard it as the foundation
of the right set up in behalf of the appellant [Gibbons].
If there was any one object riding over every other
in the adoption of the constitution, it was to keep
the commercial intercourse among the states free
from all invidious and partial restraints. . . If the
[National] licensing act was repealed to-morrow,"
Gibbons's right to the free navigation of New York
waters "would be as strong as it is under this
license." [2]

So it turned out that the first man appointed for
the purpose of thwarting Marshall's Nationalism,
expressed, twenty years after his appointment,
stronger Nationalist sentiments than Marshall himself was, as yet, willing to avow openly. Johnson's
astonishing opinion in Gibbons *vs.* Ogden is conclusive proof of the mastery the Chief Justice had
acquired over his Republican associate, or else of

---

[1] 9 Wheaton, 228–30.   [2] *Ib.* 231–32.

the conquest by Nationalism of the mind of the South Carolina Republican.

For the one and only time in his career on the Supreme Bench, Marshall had pronounced a "popular" opinion. The press acclaimed him as the deliverer of the Nation from thralldom to monopoly. His opinion, records the *New York Evening Post*, delivered amidst "the most unbroken silence" of a "courtroom . . crowded with people," was a wonderful exhibition of intellect — "one of the most powerful efforts of the human mind that has ever been displayed from the bench of any court. Many passages indicated a profoundness and a forecast in relation to the destinies of our confederacy peculiar to the great man who acted as the organ of the court. The steamboat grant is at an end." [1]

Niles published Marshall's opinion in full,[2] and in this way it reached, directly or indirectly, every paper, big and little, in the whole country, and was reproduced by most of them. Many journals contained long articles or editorials upon it, most of them highly laudatory. The *New York Evening Post* of March 8 declared that it would "command the assent of every impartial mind competent to embrace the subject." Thus, for the moment, Marshall was considered the benefactor of the people and the defender of the Nation against the dragon of monopoly. His opinion in Gibbons *vs.* Ogden changed into applause that disfavor which his opinion in M'Culloch *vs.* Maryland had evoked.

[1] *New York Evening Post*, March 5, 1824, as quoted in Warren, 395.
[2] Niles, XXVI, 54–62.

Only the Southern political leaders saw the "danger"; but so general was the satisfaction of the public that they were, for the most part, quiescent as to Marshall's assertion of Nationalism in this particular case.

But few events in our history have had a larger and more substantial effect on the well-being of the American people than this decision, and Marshall's opinion in the announcement of it. New York instantly became a free port for all America. Steamboat navigation of American rivers, relieved from the terror of possible and actual State-created monopolies, increased at an incredible rate; and, because of two decades of restraint and fear, at abnormal speed.[1]

New England manufacturers were given a new life, since the transportation of anthracite coal — the fuel recently discovered and aggravatingly needed — was made cheap and easy. The owners of factories, the promoters of steamboat traffic, the innumerable builders of river craft on every navigable stream in the country, the farmer who wished to send his products to market, the manufacturer who sought quick and inexpensive transportation of his wares — all acclaimed Marshall's decision because all found in it a means to their own interests.

The possibilities of transportation by steam railways soon became a subject of discussion by enterprising men, and Marshall's opinion gave them tre-

[1] For example, steamboat construction on the Ohio alone almost doubled in a single year, and quadrupled within two years. (See table in Meyer-MacGill: *History of Transportation in the United States*, etc., 108.)

mendous encouragement. It was a guarantee that
they might build railroads across State lines and be
safe from local interference with interstate traffic.
Could the Chief Justice have foreseen the development of the railway as an agency of Nationalism, he
would have realized, in part, the permanent and
ever-growing importance of his opinion — in part,
but not wholly; for the telegraph, the telephone, the
oil and gas pipe line were also to be affected for the
general good by Marshall's statesmanship as set
forth in his outgiving in Gibbons vs. Ogden.

It is not immoderate to say that no other judicial
pronouncement in history was so wedded to the inventive genius of man and so interwoven with the
economic and social evolution of a nation and a
people. After almost a century, Marshall's Nationalist theory of commerce is more potent than ever;
and nothing human is more certain than that it will
gather new strength as far into the future as forecast can penetrate.

At the time of its delivery, nobody complained of
Marshall's opinion except the agents of the steamboat monopoly, the theorists of Localism, and the
slave autocracy. All these influences beheld, in Marshall's statesmanship, their inevitable extinction.
All correctly understood that the Nationalism expounded by Marshall, if truly carried out, sounded
their doom.

Immediately after the decision was published, a
suit was brought in the New York Court of Equity,
apparently for the purpose of having that tribunal
define the extent of the Supreme Court's holding.

John R. Livingston secured a coasting license for the Olive Branch, and sent the boat from New York to Albany, touching at Jersey and unloading there two boxes of freight. The North River Steamboat Company, assignee of the Livingston-Fulton monopoly, at once applied for an injunction.[1] The matter excited intense interest, and Nathan Sanford, who had succeeded Kent as Chancellor, took several weeks to "consider the question." [2]

He delivered two opinions, the second almost as Nationalist as that of Marshall. "The law of the United States is supreme. . . The state law is annihilated, so far as the ground is occupied by the law of the union; and the supreme law prevails, as if the state law had never been made. The supremacy of constitutional laws of the union, and the nullity of state laws inconsistent with such laws of the union, are principles of the constitution of the United States. . . So far as the law of the union acts upon the case, the state law is extinguished. . . Opposing rights to the same thing, can not co-exist under the constitution of our country." [3] But Chancellor Sanford held that, over commerce exclusively within the State, the Nation had no control.

Livingston appealed to the Court of Errors, and in February, 1825, the case was heard. The year intervening since Marshall delivered his opinion had witnessed the rise of an irresistible tide of public sentiment in its favor; and this, more influential than all arguments of counsel even upon an "in-

[1] 1 Hopkins's *Chancery Reports*, 151.
[2] *Ib*. 198.   [3] 3 Cowen, 716–17.

dependent judiciary," was reflected in the opinion
delivered by John Woodworth, one of the judges
of the Supreme Court of that State. He quotes
Marshall liberally, and painstakingly analyzes his
opinion, which, says Woodworth, is confined to
commerce among the States to the exclusion of that
wholly within a single State. Over this latter trade
Congress has no power, except for "national purposes," and then only where such power is "'expressly given . . or is clearly incidental to some
power expressly given.'" [1]

Chief Justice John Savage adopted the same
reasoning as did Justice Woodworth, and examined
Marshall's opinion with even greater particularity,
but arrived at the same conclusion. Savage adds,
however, "a few general remarks," and in these he
almost outruns the Nationalism of Marshall. "The
constitution . . should be so construed as best to
promote the great objects for which it was made";
among them a principal one was "'to form a more
perfect union,'" etc. [2] The regulation of commerce
among the States "was one great and leading inducement to the adoption" of the Nation's fundamental law. [3] "We are the citizens of two distinct,
yet connected governments. . . The powers given to
the general government are to be first satisfied."

To the warning that the State Governments
"will be swallowed up" by the National Government, Savage declares, "my answer is, if such
danger exists, the states should not provoke a
termination of their existence, by encroachments

[1] 3 Cowen, 731–34.   [2] *Ib.* 750.   [3] *Ib.*

on their part." [1]   In such ringing terms did Savage endorse Marshall's opinion in Gibbons *vs.* Ogden.

The State Senators "concurred" automatically in the opinion of Chief Justice Savage, and the decree of Chancellor Sanford, refusing an injunction on straight trips of the Olive Branch between New York landings, but granting one against commerce of any kind with other States, was affirmed.

So the infinitely important controversy reached a settlement that, to this day, has not been disturbed. Commerce among the States is within the exclusive control of the National Government, including that which, though apparently confined to State traffic, affects the business transactions of the Nation at large. The only supervision that may be exercised by a State over trade must be wholly confined to that State, absolutely without any connection whatever with intercourse with other States.

One year after the decision of Gibbons *vs.* Ogden, the subject of the powers and duties of the Supreme Court was again considered by Congress. During February, 1825, an extended debate was held in the Senate over a bill which, among other things, provided for three additional members of that tribunal. [2] But the tone of its assailants had mellowed. The voice of denunciation now uttered words of deference, even praise. Senator Johnson, while still com-

---

[1] 3 Cowen, 753–54.

[2] This bill had been proposed by Senator Richard M. Johnson of Kentucky at the previous session (*Annals*, 18th Cong. 1st Sess, 575) as an amendment to a bill reported from the Judiciary Committee by Senator Martin Van Buren (*ib.* 336).

plaining of the evils of an "irresponsible" Judiciary, softened his attack with encomium: "Our nation has ever been blessed with a most distinguished Supreme Court, . . eminent for moral worth, intellectual vigor, extensive acquirements, and profound judicial experience and knowledge. . . Against the Federal Judiciary, I have not the least malignant emotion." [1] Senator John H. Eaton of Tennessee said that Virginia's two members of the Supreme Court (Marshall and Bushrod Washington) were "men of distinction, . . whose decisions carried satisfaction and confidence." [2]

Senator Isham Talbot of Kentucky paid tribute to the "wise, mild, and guiding influence of this solemn tribunal." [3] In examining the Nationalist decisions of the Supreme Court he went out of his way to declare that he did not mean "to cast the slightest shade of imputation on the purity of intention or the correctness of judgment with which justice is impartially dispensed from this exalted bench." [4]

This remarkable change in the language of Congressional attack upon the National Judiciary became still more conspicuous at the next session in the debate upon practically the same bill and various amendments proposed to it. Promptly after Congress convened in December, 1825, Webster himself reported from the Judiciary Committee of the House

[1] *Debates*, 18th Cong. 2d Sess. 527–33.   [2] *Ib.* 588.   [3] *Ib.* 609.
[4] *Ib.* 614.

After considerable wrangling, the bill was reported favorably from the Judiciary Committee (*ib.* 630), but too late for further action at that session.

a bill increasing to ten the membership of the Supreme Court and rearranging the circuits.[1] This measure passed substantially as reported.[2]

When the subject was taken up in the Senate, Senator Martin Van Buren in an elaborate speech pointed out the vast powers of that tribunal, unequaled and without precedent in the history of the world — powers which, if now "presented for the first time," would undoubtedly be denied by the people.[3] Yet, strange as it may seem, opposition has subsided in an astonishing manner, he said; even those States whose laws have been nullified, "after struggling with the giant strength of the Court, have submitted to their fate." [4]

Indeed, says Van Buren, there has grown up "a sentiment . . of idolatry for the Supreme Court . . which claims for its members an almost entire exemption from the fallibilities of our nature." The press, especially, is influenced by this feeling of worship. Van Buren himself concedes that the Justices have "talents of the highest order and spotless integrity." Marshall, in particular, deserves unbounded praise and admiration: "That . . uncommon man who now presides over the Court . . is, in all human probability, the ablest Judge now sitting upon any judicial bench in the world." [5]

---

[1] *Debates*, 19th Cong. 1st Sess. 845.

[2] Four days after the House adopted Webster's bill (*ib.* 1149), he wrote his brother: "The judiciary bill will probably pass the Senate, as it left our House. There will be no difficulty in finding perfectly safe men for the new appointments. The contests on those constitutional questions in the West have made men fit to be judges." (Webster to his brother, Jan. 29, 1826, *Priv. Corres.*: Webster, I, 401.)

[3] *Debates*, 19th Cong. 1st Sess. 417-18.   [4] *Ib.* 419.   [5] *Ib.* 420-21.

The fiery John Rowan of Kentucky, now Senator from that State, and one of the boldest opponents of the National Judiciary, offered an amendment requiring that "seven of the ten Justices of the Supreme Court shall concur in any judgement or decree, which denies the validity, or restrains the operation, of the Constitution, or law of any of the States, or any provision or enaction in either." [1] In advocating his amendment, however, Rowan, while still earnestly attacking the "encroachments" of the Supreme Court, admitted the "unsuspected integrity" of the Justices upon which "suspicion has never scowled. . . The present incumbents are above all suspicion; obliquity of motive has never been ascribed to any of them." [2] Nevertheless, he complains of "a judicial superstition — which encircles the Judges with infallibility." [3]

This seemingly miraculous alteration of public opinion, manifesting itself within one year from the violent outbursts of popular wrath against Marshall and the National Judiciary, was the result of the steady influence of the conservatives, unwearyingly active for a quarter of a century; of the natural reaction against extravagance of language and conduct shown by the radicals during that time; of the realization that the Supreme Court could be resisted only by force continuously exercised; and, above all, of the fundamental soundness and essential justness

---

[1] *Debates*, 19th Cong. 1st Sess. 423–24.   [2] *Ib*. 436.

[3] *Ib*. 442. Rowan's amendment was defeated (*ib*. 463). Upon disagreements between the Senate and House as to the number and arrangement of districts and circuits, the entire measure was lost. In the House it was "indefinitely postponed" by a vote of 99 to 89 (*ib*. 2648); and in the Senate the bill was finally laid on the table (*ib*. 784).

of Marshall's opinions, which, in spite of the local and transient hardship they inflicted, in the end appealed to the good sense and conscience of the average man. Undoubtedly, too, the character of the Chief Justice, which the Nation had come to appreciate, was a powerful element in bringing about the alteration in the popular concept of the Supreme Court.

But, notwithstanding the apparent diminution of animosity toward the Chief Justice and the National Judiciary, hatred of both continued, and within a few years showed itself with greater violence than ever. How Marshall met this recrudescence of Localism is the story of his closing years.

When, in Gibbons vs. Ogden, Marshall established the supremacy of Congress over commerce among the States, he also announced the absolute power of the National Legislature to control trade with foreign nations. It was not long before an opportunity was afforded him to apply this principle, and to supplement his first great opinion on the meaning of the commerce clause, by another pronouncement of equal power and dignity. By acts of the Maryland Legislature importers or wholesalers of imported goods were required to take out licenses, costing fifty dollars each, before they could sell "by wholesale, bale or package, hogshead, barrel, or tierce." Non-observance of this requirement subjected the offender to a fine of one hundred dollars and forfeiture of the amount of the tax.[1]

Under this law Alexander Brown and his partners,

---

[1] 12 Wheaton, 420.

George, John, and James Brown, were indicted in the City Court of Baltimore for having sold a package of foreign dry goods without a license. Judgment against the merchants was rendered; and this was affirmed by the Court of Appeals. The case was then taken to the Supreme Court on a writ of error and argued for Brown & Co. by William Wirt and Jonathan Meredith, and for Maryland by Roger Brooke Taney [1] and Reverdy Johnson. [2]

On March 12, 1827, the Chief Justice delivered the opinion of the majority of the court, Justice Thompson dissenting. The only question, says Marshall, is whether a State can constitutionally require an importer to take out a license "before he shall be permitted to sell a bale or package" of imported goods. [3] The Constitution prohibits any State from laying imposts or duties on imports or exports, except what may be "absolutely necessary for executing its inspection laws." The Maryland act clearly falls within this prohibition: "A duty on imports . . is not merely a duty on the act of importation, but is a duty on the thing imported. . .

"There is no difference," continues Marshall, "between a power to prohibit the sale of an article and a power to prohibit its introduction into the country. . . No goods would be imported if none

[1] Taney, leading counsel for Maryland, had just been appointed Attorney-General of that State, and soon afterwards was made Attorney-General of the United States. He succeeded Marshall as Chief Justice. (See *infra*, 460.)

[2] Johnson was only thirty-one years old at this time, but already a leader of the Baltimore bar and giving sure promise of the distinguished career he afterward achieved.

[3] 12 Wheaton, 436.

could be sold." The power which can levy a small
tax can impose a great one — can, in fact, prohibit
the thing taxed: "Questions of power do not depend
on the degree to which it may be exercised." [1] He
admits that "there must be a point of time when the
prohibition [of States to tax imports] ceases and the
power of the State to tax commences"; but "this
point of time is [not] the instant that the articles
enter the country." [2]

Here Marshall becomes wisely cautious. The
power of the States to tax and the "restriction"
on that power, "though quite distinguishable when
they do not approach each other, may yet, like the
intervening colors between white and black, approach so nearly as to perplex the understanding,
as colors perplex the vision in marking the distinction between them. Yet the distinction exists, and
must be marked as cases arise. Till they do arise, it
might be premature to state any rule as being universal in its application. It is sufficient for the present, to say, generally, that, when the importer has
so acted upon the thing imported that it has become
incorporated and mixed up with the mass of property in the country, it has, perhaps, lost its distinctive character as an import, and has become subject
to the taxing power of the State; but while remaining the property of the importer, in his warehouse, in
the original form or package in which it was imported, a tax upon it is too plainly a duty on imports
to escape the prohibition in the constitution." [3]

[1] 12 Wheaton, 437–39.   [2] *Ib.* 441.   [3] *Ib.* 441–42.

It is not true that under the rule just stated, the
State is precluded from regulating its internal trade
and from protecting the health or morals of its citizens. The Constitutional inhibition against State
taxation of imports applies only to "the form in
which it was imported." When the importer sells
his goods "the [State] law may treat them as it
finds them." Measures may also be taken by the
State concerning dangerous substances like gunpowder or "infectious or unsound articles" — such
measures are within the "police power, which unquestionably remains, and ought to remain, with
the States." But State taxation of imported articles
in their original form is a violation of the clause of
the Constitution forbidding States to lay any imposts or duties on imports and exports.[1]

Such taxation also violates the commerce clause.
Marshall once more outlines the reasons for inserting that provision into the Constitution, cites his
opinion in Gibbons *vs*. Ogden, and again declares
that the power of Congress to regulate commerce
"is co-extensive with the subject on which it acts
and cannot be stopped at the external boundary of a
State, but must enter its interior." This power,
therefore, "must be capable of authorizing the sale
of those articles which it introduces." In almost the
same words already used, the Chief Justice reiterates that goods would not be imported if they could
not be sold. "Congress has a right, not only to authorize importation, but to authorize the importer
to sell." A tariff law "offers the privilege [of im-

[1] 12 Wheaton, 443–44.

portation] for sale at a fixed price to every person who chooses to become a purchaser." By paying the duty the importer makes a contract with the National Government — "he . . purchase[s] the privilege to sell."

"The conclusion, that the right to sell is connected with the law permitting importation, as an inseparable incident, is inevitable." To deny that right "would break up commerce." The power of a State "to tax its own citizens, or their property within its territory," is "acknowledged" and is "sacred"; but it cannot be exercised "so as to obstruct or defeat the power [of Congress] to regulate commerce." When State laws conflict with National statutes, "that which is not supreme must yield to that which is supreme" — a "great and universal truth . . inseparable from the nature of things," which "the constitution has applied . . to the often interfering powers of the general and State governments, as a vital principle of perpetual operation."

The States, through the taxing power, "cannot reach and restrain the action of the national government . . — cannot reach the administration of justice in the Courts of the Union, or the collection of the taxes of the United States, or restrain the operation of any law which Congress may constitutionally pass — . . cannot interfere with any regulation of commerce." Otherwise a State might tax "goods in their transit through the State from one port to another for the purpose of re-exportation"; or tax articles "passing through it from one State to another, for the purpose of traffic"; or tax "the transportation of articles passing from the State itself to another State for commercial purposes." Of what avail the power given Congress by the Constitution if the States may thus "derange the measures of Congress to regulate commerce"?

Marshall is here addressing South Carolina and other States which, at that time, were threatening retaliation against the manufacturers of articles protected by the tariff.[1] He pointedly observes that the decision in M'Culloch *vs.* Maryland is "entirely applicable" to the present controversy, and adds that "we suppose the principle laid down in this case to apply equally to importations from a sister State."[2]

The principles announced by Marshall in Brown *vs.* Maryland have been upheld by nearly all courts that have since dealt with the subject of commerce. But there has been much "distinguishing" of various cases from that decision; and, in this process, the application of his great opinion has often been modified, sometimes evaded. In some cases in which Marshall's statesmanship has thus been weakened and narrowed, local public sentiment as to questions that have come to be considered moral, has been influential. It is fortunate for the Republic that considerations of this kind did not, in such fashion, impair the liberty of commerce among the States before the American Nation was firmly established. When estimating our indebtedness to John Marshall, we must have in mind the state of

[1] See *infra*, 536–38.   [2] 12 Wheaton, 448–49.

the country at the time his Constitutional expositions were pronounced and the inevitable and ruinous effect that feebler and more restricted assertions
of Nationalism would then have had.

Seldom has a triumph of sound principles and of
sound reasoning in the assertion of those principles
been more frankly acknowledged than in the tribute which Roger Brooke Taney inferentially paid to
John Marshall, whom he succeeded as Chief Justice.
Twenty years after the decision of Brown *vs.* Maryland, Taney declared: "I at that time persuaded
myself that I was right. . . But further and more
mature reflection has convinced me that the rule
laid down by the Supreme Court is a just and safe
one, and perhaps the best that could have been
adopted for preserving the right of the United
States on the one hand, and of the States on the
other, and preventing collision between them." [1]

Chief Justice Taney's experience has been that of
many thoughtful men who, for a season and when
agitated by intense concern for a particular cause or
policy, have felt Marshall to have been wrong in
this, that, or the other of his opinions.   Frequently,
such men have, in the end, come to the steadfast
conclusion that they were wrong and that Marshall
was right.

[1] 5 Howard, 575.

CHAPTER IX

THE SUPREME CONSERVATIVE

If a judge becomes odious to the people, let him be removed.
(William Branch Giles.)

Our wisest friends look with gloom to the future. (Joseph Story.)

I have always thought, from my earliest youth till now, that the greatest scourge an angry Heaven ever inflicted upon an ungrateful and a sinning people, was an ignorant, a corrupt, or a dependent judiciary. (Marshall.)

"I was in a very great crowd the other evening at Mrs Adams' drawing room, but I see very few persons there whom I know & fewer still in whom I take any interest. A person as old as I am feels that his home is his place of most comfort, and his old wife the companion in the world in whose society he is most happy.

"I dined yesterday with Mr. Randolph. He is absorbed in the party politics of the day & seems as much engaged in them as he was twenty five years past. It is very different with me. I long to leave this busy bustling scene & to return to the tranquility of my family & farm. Farewell my dearest Polly. That Heaven may bless you is the unceasing prayer of your ever affectionate

"J. MARSHALL." [1]

This letter to his ageing and afflicted wife, written in his seventy-second year, reveals Marshall's state of mind as he entered the final decade of his life. While the last of his history-making and nation-building opinions had been delivered, the years still before

[1] Marshall to his wife, March 12, 1826, MS.

him were to be crowded with labor as arduous and scenes as picturesque as any during his career on the Bench. It was to be a period of disappointment and grief, but also of that supreme reward for sound and enduring work which comes from recognition of the general and lasting benefit of that work and of the greatness of mind and nobility of character of him who performed it.

For twenty years the Chief Justice had not voted. The last ballot he had cast was against the reëlection of Jefferson in 1804. From that time forward until 1828, he had kept away from the polls. In the latter year he probably voted for John Quincy Adams, or rather against Andrew Jackson, who, as Marshall thought, typified the recrudescence of that unbridled democratic spirit which he so increasingly feared and distrusted.[1]

[1] Nevertheless he watched the course of politics closely. For instance: immediately after the House had elected John Quincy Adams to the Presidency, Marshall writes his brother a letter full of political gossip. He is surprised that Adams was chosen on the first ballot; many think Kremer's letter attacking Clay caused this unexpectedly quick decision, since it "was & is thought a sheer calumny; & the resentment of Clay's friends probably determined some of the western members who were hesitating. It is supposed to have had some influence elsewhere. The vote of New York was not decided five minutes before the ballots were taken."

Marshall tells his brother about Cabinet rumors — Crawford has refused the Treasury and Clay has been offered the office of Secretary of State. "It is meer [sic] common rumor" that Clay will accept. "Mr. Adams will undoubtedly wish to strengthen himself in the west," and Clay is strong in that section unless Kremer's letter has weakened him. The Chief Justice at first thought it had, but "on reflection" doubts whether it will "make any difference." (Marshall to his brother, Feb. 14, 1825, MS.) Marshall here refers to the letter of George Kremer, a Representative in Congress from Pennsylvania. Kremer wrote an anonymous letter to the Columbian Observer in which he asserted that Clay had agreed to deliver votes to Adams as the price

Yet, even in so grave a crisis as Marshall believed
the Presidential election of 1828 to be, he shrank
from the appearance of partisanship. The *Marylander*, a Baltimore Democratic paper, published an
item quoting Marshall as having said: "I have not
voted for twenty years; but I shall consider it a
solemn duty I owe my country to go to the polls and
vote at the next presidential election — for should
Jackson be elected, I shall look upon the government
as virtually dissolved." [1]

This item was widely published in the Administration newspapers, including the Richmond *Whig
and Advertiser.* To this paper Marshall wrote, denying the statement of the Baltimore publication:
"Holding the situation I do . . I have thought it
right to abstain from any public declarations on
the election; . . I admit having said in private that
though I had not voted since the establishment of
the general ticket system, and had believed that I
never should vote during its continuance, I might
probably depart from my resolution in this instance,
from the strong sense I felt of the injustice of the

of Clay's appointment to the office of Secretary of State. After much
bluster, Kremer admitted that he had no evidence whatever to support his charge; yet his accusation permanently besmirched Clay's
reputation. (For an account of the Kremer incident see Sargent, I,
67–74, 123–24.)

Out of the Kremer letter grew a distrust of Clay which he never
really lived down. Some time later, John Randolph seized an opportunity to call the relation between President Adams and his Secretary
of State "the coalition of Blifil and Black George — the combination,
unheard of till then, of the Puritan with the blackleg." The bloodless,
but not the less real duel, that followed, ended this quarrel, though
the unjust charges never quite died out. (Schurz: *Henry Clay*, I, 273–
74.)

[1] Baltimore *Marylander*, March 22, 1828.

charge of corruption against the President & Secretary of State: I never did use the other expressions ascribed to me." [1] This "card" the *Enquirer* reproduced, together with the item from the *Marylander*, commenting scathingly upon the methods of Adams's supporters.

Clay, deeply touched, wrote the Chief Justice of his appreciation and gratitude; but he is sorry that Marshall paid any attention to the matter "because it will subject you to a part of that abuse which is so indiscriminately applied to .. everything standing in the way of the election of a certain individual." [2]

Marshall was sorely worried. He writes Story that the incident "provoked" him, "not because I have any objection to its being known that my private judgement is in favor of the re-election of Mr Adams, but because I have great objections to being represented in the character of a furious partisan. Intemperate language does not become my age or office, and is foreign from my disposition and habits. I was therefore not a little vexed at a publication which represented me as using language which could be uttered only by an angry party man."

He explains that the item got into the *Marylander* through a remark of one of his nephews "who was on the Adams convention" at Baltimore, to the effect that he had heard Marshall say that, although he had "not voted for upwards of twenty years" he "should probably vote at the ensuing election." His nephew wrote a denial, but it was not published. So, con-

---

[1] *Enquirer*, April 4, 1828.
[2] Meaning Jackson. Clay to Marshall, April 8, 1828, MS.

cludes Marshall, "I must bear the newspaper scurrility which I had hoped to escape, and which is generally reserved for more important personages than myself. It is some consolation that it does not wound me very deeply." [1]

It would seem that Marshall had early resolved to go to any length to deprive the enemies of the National Judiciary of any pretext for attacking him or the Supreme Court because of any trace of partisan activity on his part. One of the largest tasks he had set for himself was to create public confidence in that tribunal, and to raise it above the suspicion that party considerations swayed its decisions. He had seen how nearly the arrogance and political activity of the first Federalist judges had wrecked the Supreme Court and the whole Judicial establishment, and had resolved, therefore, to lessen popular hostility to courts, as far as his neutral attitude to party controversies could accomplish that purpose.

It thus came about that Marshall refrained even from exercising his right of suffrage from 1804 to 1828 — perhaps, indeed, to the end of his life, since it is not certain that he voted even at the election of 1828. Considering the intensity of his partisan feelings, his refusal to vote, during nearly all the long period when he was Chief Justice, was a real sacrifice, the extent of which may be measured by the fact that, according to his letter to Story, he did not even vote against Madison in 1812, notwithstanding the violence of his emotions aroused by the war. [2]

[1] Marshall to Story, May 1, 1828, *Proceedings, Mass. Hist. Soc.* 2d Series, xiv, 336–37.

[2] See chap. i of this volume.

On March 4, 1829, Marshall administered the oath of office to the newly elected President, Andrew Jackson. No two men ever faced one another more unlike in personality and character. The mild, gentle, benignant features of the Chief Justice contrasted strongly with the stern, rigid, and aggressive countenance of "Old Hickory." The one stood for the reign of law; the other for autocratic administration. In Jackson, whim, prejudice, hatred, and fierce affections were dominant; in Marshall, steady, level views of life and government, devotion to order and regularity, abhorrence of quarrel and feud, constancy and evenness in friendship or conviction, were the chief elements of character. Moreover, the Chief Justice personified the static forces of society; the new President was the product of a fresh upheaval of democracy, not unlike that which had placed Jefferson in power.

Marshall had administered the Presidential oath seven times before — twice each to Jefferson, Madison, and Monroe, and once to John Quincy Adams. And now he was reading the solemn words to the passionate frontier soldier from whose wild, undisciplined character he feared so much. Marshall briefly writes his wife about the inauguration: "We had yesterday a most busy and crowded day. People have flocked to Washington from every quarter of the United States. When the oath was administered to the President the computation is that 12 or 15000 people were present — a great number of them ladies. A great ball was given at night to celebrate the election. I of course did not attend it. The affliction of our son [1] would have been sufficient to restrain me had I even felt a desire to go." [2] In a previous letter to his wife he forecast the crowds and commotion: "The whole world it is said will be here. . . I wish I could leave it all and come to you. How much more delightful would it be to me to sit by your side than to witness all the pomp and parade of the inauguration." [3]

Much as he had come to dislike taking part in politics or in public affairs, except in the discharge of his judicial duties, Marshall was prevailed upon to be a delegate to the Virginia Constitutional Convention of 1829–30. He refused, at first, to stand for the place and hastened to reassure his "dearest Polly." "I am told," he continues in his letter describing Jackson's induction into office, "by several that I am held up as a candidate for the convention. I have no desire to be in the convention and do not mean to be a candidate. I should not trouble you with this did I not apprehend that the idea of my wishing to be in the convention might prevent some of my friends who are themselves desirous of being in it from becoming candidates. I therefore wish you to give this information to Mr. Harvie.[4] . . Farewell my dearest Polly. Your happiness is always nearest the heart of your J. Marshall." [5]

He yielded, however, and wrote Story of his disgust at having done so: "I am almost ashamed of

[1] Thomas, whose wife died Feb. 2, 1829. (Paxton, 92.)
[2] Marshall to his wife, March 5 [1829], MS.
[3] Same to same, Feb. 1, 1829, MS.
[4] Jacquelin B. Harvie, who married Marshall's daughter, Mary.
[5] Marshall to his wife, March 5 [1829], MS.

my weakness and irresolution when I tell you that
I am a member of our convention. I was in earnest
when I told you that I would not come into that
body, and really believed that I should adhere to
that determination; but I have acted like a girl addressed by a gentleman she does not positively dislike, but is unwilling to marry. She is sure to yield
to the advice and persuasion of her friends. . . The
body will contain a great deal of eloquence as well
as talent, and yet will do, I fear, much harm with
some good. Our freehold suffrage is, I believe,
gone past redemption. It is impossible to resist the
influence, I had almost said contagion of universal
example." [1]

For fifty-three years Virginia had been governed
under the constitution adopted at the beginning of
the Revolution. As early as the close of this war the
injustice and inadequacy of the Constitution of 1776
had become evident, and, as a member of the House
of Delegates, Marshall apparently had favored the
adoption of a new fundamental law for the State. [2]
Almost continuously thereafter the subject had
been brought forward, but the conservatives always had been strong enough to defeat constitutional reform.

On July 12, 1816, in a letter to Samuel Kercheval,
one of the ablest documents he ever produced,
Jefferson had exposed the defects of Virginia's constitution which, he truly said, was without "leading
principles." It denied equality of representation;

---

[1] Marshall to Story, June 11, 1829, *Proceedings, Mass. Hist. Soc.*
2d Series, XIV, 338–39.
[2] See vol. I, 216–17, of this work.

the Governor was neither elected nor controlled by the people; the higher judges were "dependent on none but themselves." With unsparing severity Jefferson denounces the County Court system.

Clearly and simply he enumerates the constructive reforms imperatively demanded, beginning with "General Suffrage" and "Equal representation," on which, however, he says that he wishes "to take no public share" because that question "has become a party one." Indeed, at the very beginning of this brilliant and well-reasoned letter, Jefferson tells Kercheval that it is "for your satisfaction only, and not to be quoted before the public." [1]

But Kercheval handed the letter around freely and proposed to print it for general circulation. On hearing of this, Jefferson was "alarmed" and wrote Kercheval harshly, repeating that the letter was not to be given out and demanding that the original and copies be recalled.[2] This uncharacteristic perturbation of the former President reveals in startling fashion the bitterness of the strife over the calling of the convention, and over the issues confronting that body in making a new constitution for Virginia.

Of the serious problems to be solved by the Convention of 1829–30, that of suffrage was the most important. Up to that time nobody could vote in Virginia except white owners of freehold estates. Counties, regardless of size, had equal representation

---

[1] Jefferson to Kercheval, July 12, 1816, *Works:* Ford, XII, 3–15.
[2] Same to same, Oct. 8, 1816, *ib.* footnote to 17.

in the House of Delegates. This gave to the eastern
and southern slaveholding sections of the State, with
small counties having few voters, an immense preponderance over the western and northwestern
sections, with large counties having many voters.
On the other hand, the rich slavery districts paid
much heavier taxes than the poorer free counties.[1]

Marshall was distressed by every issue, to settle
which the convention had been called. The question of the qualification for suffrage especially agitated him. Immediately after his election to the
convention, he wrote Story of his troubles and misgivings: "We shall have a good deal of division and
a good deal of heat, I fear, in our convention. The
freehold principle will, I believe, be lost. It will,
however, be supported with zeal. If that zeal should
be successful I should not regret it. If we find that a
decided majority is against retaining it I should prefer making a compromise by which a substantial
property qualification may be preserved in exchange
for it.

"I fear the excessive [torn — probably, democratic
spirit, coin]cident to victory after a hard fought
battle continued to the last extremity may lead to
universal suffrage or something very near it. What
is the prop[erty] qualification for your Senate?
How are your Senators apportioned on the State?
And how does your system work? The question

---

[1] At the time of the convention the eastern part of the State paid,
on the average, more than three times as much in taxes per acre as
the west. The extremes were startling — the trans-Alleghany section
(West Virginia) paid only 92 cents for every $8.43 paid by the Tide-
water. (*Proceedings and Debates of the Virginia State Convention of
1829-30*, 214, 258, 660-61.)

whether white population alone, or white population compounded with taxation, shall form the basis of representation will excite perhaps more interest than even the freehold suffrage. I wish we were well through the difficulty." [1]

The Massachusetts Constitutional Convention had been held nearly a decade before that of Virginia. The problem of suffrage had troubled the delegates almost as much as it now perplexed Marshall. The reminiscent Pickering writes the Chief Justice of the fight made in 1820 by the Massachusetts conservatives against "the conceited innovators." Story had been a delegate, and so had John Adams, fainting with extreme age, but rich with the wisdom of his eighty-five years: "He made a short, but very good speech," begging the convention to retain the State Senate as "the representative of *property;* . . the number of Senators in each district was proportioned to its direct taxes to the State revenue — and not to its population. Some democrats desired that the number of Senators should be apportioned not according to the taxation, but exclusively to the population. This, Mr. Adams and all the most intelligent and considerate members opposed." [2]

Ultra-conservative as Marshall was, strongly as he felt the great body of the people incapable of self-government, he was deeply concerned for the well-being of what he called "the mass of the people." The best that can be done for them, he says in a

---

[1] Marshall to Story, July 3, 1829, *Proceedings, Mass. Hist. Soc.* 2d Series, xiv, 340–41.

[2] Pickering to Marshall, Dec. 26, 1828, Pickering MSS. Mass. Hist. Soc.; see also Story, i, 386–96.

letter to Charles F. Mercer, is to educate them. "In governments entirely popular" general education "is more indispensable .. than in an other." The labor problem troubles him sorely. When population becomes so great that "the surplus hands" must turn to other employment, a grave situation will arise.

"As the supply exceeds the demand the price of labour will cheapen until it affords a bare subsistence to the labourer. The superadded demands of a family can scarcely be satisfied and a slight indisposition, one which suspends labour and compensation for a few days produces famine and pauperism. How is this to be prevented?" Education may be relied on "in the present state of our population, and for a long time to come. . . But as our country fills up how shall we escape the evils which have followed a dense population?" [1]

The Chief Justice went to the Virginia Convention a firm supporter of the strongest possible property qualification for suffrage. On the question of slavery, which arose in various forms, he had not made his position clear. The slavery question, as a National matter, perplexed and disturbed Marshall. There was nothing in him of the humanitarian reformer, but there was everything of the statesman. He never had but one, and that a splendid, vision.

The American Nation was his dream; and to the realization of it he consecrated his life. A full generation after Marshall wrote his last despairing

---

[1] Marshall to Mercer, April 7, 1827, Chamberlain MSS. Boston Pub. Lib.

word on slavery, Abraham Lincoln expressed the conviction which the great Chief Justice had entertained: "I would save the Union. I would save it the shortest way under the Constitution... If I could save the Union without freeing any slave, I would do it; and if I could save it by freeing some and leaving others alone, I would also do that. What I do about slavery and the colored race, I do because I believe it helps to save the Union." [1]

Pickering, the incessant, in one of his many and voluminous letters to Marshall which the ancient New Englander continued to write as long as he lived, had bemoaned the existence of slavery — one of the rare exhibitions of Liberalism displayed by that adamantine Federalist conservative. Marshall answered: "I concur with you in thinking that nothing portends more calamity & mischief to the Southern States than their slave population. Yet they seem to cherish the evil and to view with immovable prejudice & dislike every thing which may tend to diminish it. I do not wonder that they should resist any attempt, should one be made, to interfere with the rights of property, but they have a feverish jealousy of measures which may do good without the hazard of harm that is, I think, very unwise." [2]

Marshall heartily approved the plan of the American Colonization Society to send free negroes back to Africa. The Virginia branch of that organization

[1] Lincoln to Greeley, Aug. 22, 1862, *Complete Works of Abraham Lincoln:* Nicolay and Hay, II, 227–28.

[2] Marshall to Pickering, March 20, 1826, *Proceedings, Mass. Hist. Soc.* 2d Series, XIV, 321.

was formed in 1829, the year of the State Constitutional Convention, and Marshall became a member.
Two years later he became President of the Virginia
branch, with James Madison, John Tyler, Abel P.
Upshur, and other prominent Virginians as Vice-
Presidents.[1] In 1831, Marshall was elected one of
twenty-four Vice-Presidents of the National society,
among whom were Webster, Clay, Crawford, and
Lafayette.[2]

The Reverend R. R. Gurley, Secretary of this
organization, wrote to the more eminent members
asking for their views. Among those who replied
were Lafayette, Madison, and Marshall. The Chief
Justice says that he feels a "deep interest in the . .
society," but refuses to "prepare any thing for
publication." The cause of this refusal is "the
present state of [his] family"[3] and a determination
"long since formed . . against appearing in print
on any occasion." Nevertheless, he writes Gurley
a letter nearly seven hundred words in length.

Marshall thinks it "extremely desirable" that the
States shall pass "permanent laws" affording financial aid to the colonization project. It will be "also
desirable" if this legislation can be secured "to
incline the people of color to migrate." He had
thought for a long time that it was just possible
that more negroes might like to go to Liberia than

---

[1] *Fifteenth Annual Report, Proceedings, American Colonization Society.* The abolitionists, later, mercilessly attacked the Colonization
Society. (See Wilson: *Rise of the Slave Power,* i, 208 *et seq.*)

[2] *Fourteenth Annual Report, Proceedings, American Colonization
Society.*

[3] His wife's illness. She died soon afterwards. See *infra,* 524–25.

"can be provided for with the funds [of] the Society"; therefore he had "suggested, some years past," to the managers, "to allow a small additional bounty in lands to those who would pay their passage in whole or in part."

To Marshall it appears to be of "great importance to retain the countenance and protection of the General Government. Some of our cruizers stationed on the coast of Africa would, at the same time, interrupt the slave trade — a horrid traffic detested by all good men — and would protect the vessels and commerce of the Colony from pirates who infest those seas. The power of the government to afford this aid is not, I believe, contested." He thinks the plan of Rufus King to devote part of the proceeds from the sale of public lands to a fund for the colonization scheme, "the most effective that can be devised." Marshall makes a brief but dreary argument for this method of raising funds for the exportation of the freed blacks.

He thus closes this eminently practical letter: "The removal of our colored population is, I think, a common object, by no means confined to the slave States, although they are more immediately interested in it. The whole Union would be strengthened by it, and relieved from a danger, whose extent can scarcely be estimated." Furthermore, says the Chief Justice, "it lessens very much . . the objection in a political view to the application of this ample fund [from the sale of the public domain], that our lands are becoming an object for which the States are to scramble, and which threatens to sow the seeds of discord among us instead of being what they might be — a source of national wealth." [1]

Marshall delivered two opinions in which the question of slavery was involved, but they throw little light on his sentiments. In the case of the Antelope he held that the slave trade was not prohibited by international law as it then existed; but since the court, including Story and Thompson, both bitter antagonists of slavery, was unanimous, the views of Marshall cannot be differentiated from those of his associates. Spain and Portugal claimed certain negroes forcibly taken from Spanish and Portuguese slavers by an American slaver off the coast of Africa. After picturesque vicissitudes the vessel containing the blacks was captured by an American revenue cutter and taken to Savannah for adjudication.

In due course the case reached the Supreme Court and was elaborately argued. The Government insisted that the captured negroes should be given their liberty, since they had been brought into the country in violation of the statutes against the importation of slaves. Spain and Portugal demanded

---

[1] Marshall to Gurley, Dec. 14, 1831, *Fifteenth Annual Report, Proceedings, American Colonization Society*, pp. vi–viii.

In a letter even less emotional than Marshall's, Madison favored the same plan. (*Ib.* pp. v, vi.) Lafayette, with his unfailing floridity, says that he is "proud . . of the honor of being one of the Vice Presidents of the Society," and that "the progressing state of our Liberia establishment is . . a source of enjoyment, and the most lively interest" to him. (*Ib.* p. v.)

At the time of his death, Marshall was President of the Virginia branch of the Society, and his ancient enemy, John Tyler, who succeeded him in that office, paid a remarkable tribute to the goodness and greatness of the man he had so long opposed. (Tyler: *Tyler*, I, 567–68.)

them as slaves "acquired as property .. in the regular course of legitimate commerce." [1] It was not surprising that opinion on the slave trade was "unsettled," said Marshall in delivering the opinion of the court.

All "Christian and civilized nations .. have been engaged in it. . . Long usage, and general acquiescence" have sanctioned it.[2] America had been the first to "check" the monstrous traffic. But, whatever its feelings or the state of public opinion, the court "must obey the mandate of the law." [3] He cites four English decisions, especially a recent one by Sir William Scott, the effect of all being that the slave trade "could not be pronounced contrary to the law of nations." [4]

Every nation, therefore, has a right to engage in it. Some nations may renounce that right sanctioned by "universal assent." But other nations cannot be bound by such "renunciation." For all nations, large and small, are equal — "Russia and Geneva have equal rights." No one nation "can rightfully impose a rule on another .. none can make a law of nations; and this traffic remains lawful to those whose governments have not forbidden it. . . It follows, that a foreign vessel engaged in the African slave trade, captured on the high seas in time of peace, by an American cruiser, and brought in for adjudication, would be restored." [5]

Four months before Marshall was elected a member of the Virginia Constitutional Convention, he

[1] 10 Wheaton, 114.
[2] *Ib*. 115. Marshall delivered this opinion March 15, 1825.
[3] *Ib*. 114.   [4] *Ib*. 118–19.   [5] *Ib*. 122–23.

delivered another opinion involving the legal status of slaves. Several negroes, the property of one Robert Boyce, were on a steamboat, the Teche, which was descending the Mississippi. The vessel took fire and those on board, including the negroes, escaped to the shore. Another steamboat, the Washington, was coming up the river at the time, and her captain, in response to appeals from the stranded passengers of the burning vessel, sent a yawl to bring them to the Washington. The yawl was upset and the slaves drowned. The owner of them sued the owner of the Washington for their value. The District Court held that the doctrine of common carriers did not apply to human beings; and this was the only question before the Supreme Court, to which Boyce appealed.

"A slave . . cannot be stowed away as a common package," said Marshall in his brief opinion. "The responsibility of the carrier should be measured by the law which is applicable to passengers, rather than by that which is applicable to the carriage of common goods. . . The law applicable to common carriers is one of great rigor. . . It has not been applied to living men, and . . ought not to be applied to them." Nevertheless, "the ancient rule 'that the carrier is liable only for ordinary neglect,' still applies" to slaves. Therefore the District Court was right in its instructions to the jury.[1]

The two letters quoted and the opinions expressing the unanimous judgment of the Supreme Court are all the data we have as to Marshall's views on slav-

[1] 2 Peters, 150–56.

ery. It appears that he regretted the existence of
slavery, feared the results of it, saw no way of getting
rid of it, but hoped to lessen the evil by colonizing in
Africa such free black people as were willing to go
there. In short, Marshall held the opinion on slavery
generally prevailing at that time. He was far more
concerned that the Union should be strengthened,
and dissension in Virginia quieted, than he was
over the problem of human bondage, of which he
saw no solution.

When he took his seat as a delegate to the Virginia
Constitutional Convention of 1829–30, a more determined conservative than Marshall did not live.
Apparently he did not want anything changed —
especially if the change involved conflict — except,
of course, the relation of the States to the Nation.
He was against a new constitution for Virginia;
against any extension of suffrage; against any modification of the County Court system except to
strengthen it; against a free white basis of representation; against legislative interference with
business. His attitude was not new, nor had he
ever concealed his views.

His opinions of legislation and corporate property,
for instance, are revealed in a letter written twenty
years before the Convention of 1829–30. In withdrawing from some Virginia corporation because the
General Assembly of the State had passed a law for
the control of it, Marshall wrote: "I consider the interference of the legislature in the management of
our private affairs, whether those affairs are committed to a company or remain under individual

direction, as equally dangerous and unwise. I have always thought so and I still think so. I may be compelled to subject my property to these interferences, and when compelled I shall submit; but I will not voluntarily expose myself to the exercise of a power which I think so improperly usurped." [1]

Two years before the convention was called, Marshall's unyielding conservatism was displayed in a most conspicuous manner. In Sturges *vs.* Crowninshield,[2] a State law had been held invalid which relieved creditors from contracts made before the passage of that law. But, in his opinion in that case, Marshall used language that also applied to contracts made after the enactment of insolvency statutes; and the bench and bar generally had accepted his statement as the settled opinion of the Supreme Court. But so acute had public discontent become over this rigid doctrine, so strident the demand for bankrupt laws relieving insolvents, at least from contracts made after such statutes were enacted, that the majority of the Supreme Court yielded to popular insistence and, in Ogden *vs.* Saunders,[3] held that "an insolvent law of a State does not

[1] Marshall to Greenhow, Oct. 17, 1809, MSS. "Judges and Eminent Lawyers," Mass. Hist. Soc.

[2] See *supra*, 202–18, of this volume.

[3] 12 Wheaton, 214 *et seq.* John Saunders, a citizen of Kentucky, sued George M. Ogden, a citizen of Louisiana, on bills of exchange which Ogden, then a citizen of New York, had accepted in 1806, but which were protested for non-payment. The defendant pleaded a discharge granted by a New York court under the insolvent law of that State enacted in 1801. (*Ib.*) On the manuscript records of the Supreme Court, Saunders is spelled *Sanders.* After the case was filed, the death of Ogden was suggested, and his executors, Charles Harrod and Francis B. Ogden, were substituted.

impair the obligation of future contracts between its citizens." [1]

For the first time in twenty-seven years the majority of the court opposed Marshall on a question of Constitutional law. The Chief Justice dissented and delivered one of the most powerful opinions he ever wrote. The very "nature of our Union," he says, makes us "one people, as to commercial objects." [2] The prohibition in the contract clause "is complete and total. There is no exception from it.[3] . . Insolvent laws are to operate on a future, contingent unforseen event." [4] Yet the majority of the court hold that such legislation enters into subsequent contracts "so completely as to become a . . part" of them. If this is true of one law, it is true of "every other law which relates to the subject."

But this would mean, contends Marshall, that a vital provision of the Constitution, "one on which the good and the wise reposed confidently for securing the prosperity and harmony of our citizens, would lie prostrate, and be construed into an inanimate, inoperative, unmeaning clause." The construction of the majority of the court would "convert an inhibition to pass laws impairing the obligation of contracts into an inhibition to pass retrospective laws." [5] If the Constitution means this, why is it not so expressed? The mischievous laws which caused the insertion of the contract clause "embraced future contracts, as well as those previously formed." [6]

[1] Washington, Johnson, Thompson, and Trimble each delivered long opinions supporting this view. (12 Wheaton, 254–331, 358–369.)
[2] *Ib*. 334.   [3] *Ib*. 335.   [4] *Ib*. 337.   [5] *Ib*. 356.   [6] *Ib*. 357.

The gist of Marshall's voluminous opinion in Ogden *vs.* Saunders is that the Constitution protects all contracts, past or future, from State legislation which in any manner impairs their obligation.[1] Considering that even the rigidly conservative Bushrod Washington, Marshall's stanch supporter, refused to follow his stern philosophy, in this case, the measure and character of Marshall's conservatism are seen when, in his seventy-fifth year, he helped to frame a new constitution for Virginia.

Still another example of Marshall's rock-like conservatism and of the persistence with which he held fast to his views is afforded by a second dissent from the majority of the court at the same session. This time every one of the Associate Justices was against him, and Story delivered their unanimous opinion. The Bank of the United States had sued Julius B. Dandridge, cashier of the Richmond branch, and his sureties, on his official bond. Marshall, sitting as Circuit Judge, had held that only the written record of the bank's board of directors, that they approved and accepted the bond, could be received to prove that Dandridge had been legally authorized to act as cashier.

The Supreme Court reversed Marshall's judgment, holding that the authorization of an agent by a corporation can be established by presumptive evidence,[2] an opinion that was plainly sound and which stated the law as it has continued to be ever since. But despite the unanimity of his brethren, the clear

---

[1] Story and Duval concurred with Marshall.

[2] 12 Wheaton, 65–90.

and convincing opinion of Story, the disapproval of his own views by the bench, bar, and business men of the whole country, Marshall would not yield. "The Ch: Jus: I fear will *die hard*," wrote Webster, who was of counsel for the bank.[1]

In a very long opinion Marshall insists that his decision in the Circuit Court was right, fortifying his argument by more than thirty citations. He begins by frank acknowledgment of the discontent his decision in the Circuit Court has aroused: "I should now, as is my custom, when I have the misfortune to differ with this court, acquiesce silently in its opinion, did I not believe that the judgment of the circuit court of Virginia gave general surprise to the profession, and was generally condemned." Corporations, "being destitute of human organs," can express themselves only by writing. They must act through agents; but the agency can be created and proved only by writing.

Marshall points out the serious possibilities to those with whom corporations deal, as well as to the corporations themselves, of the acts of persons serving as agents without authority of record.[2] Powerful as his reasoning is, it is based on mistaken premises inapplicable to modern corporate transactions; but his position, his method, his very style, reveal the stubborn conservative at bay, bravely defending himself and his views.

This, then, was the John Marshall, who, in his old age, accepted the call of men as conservative as

---

[1] Webster to Biddle, Feb. 20, 1827, *Writings and Speeches of Webster:* (Nat. ed.) XVI, 140.

[2] 12 Wheaton, 90–116.

himself to help frame a new constitution for Virginia.
On Monday, October 5, 1829, the convention met
in the House of Delegates at Richmond. James Madison, then in his seventy-ninth year, feeble and
wizened, called the members to order and nominated James Monroe for President of the convention. This nomination was seconded by Marshall.
These three men, whose careers since before the
Revolution and throughout our formative period,
had been more distinguished, up to that time, than
had that of any American then living, were the most
conspicuous persons in that notable Assembly.
Giles, now Governor of the State, was also a member; so were Randolph, Tyler, Philip P. Barbour,
Upshur, and Tazewell. Indeed, the very ablest men
in Virginia had been chosen to make a new constitution for the State. In the people's anxiety to
select the best men to do that important work,
delegates were chosen regardless of the districts in
which they lived.[1]

To Marshall, who naturally was appointed to the
Judiciary Committee,[2] fell the task of presenting to
the convention the first petition of non-freeholders
for suffrage.[3] No more impressive document was
read before that body. It stated the whole democratic argument clearly and boldly.[4] The first
report received from any committee was made by
Marshall and also was written by him.[5] It provided

[1] Grigsby: *Virginia Convention of 1829–30;* and see Ambler: *Sectionalism in Virginia*, 145. Chapter v of Professor Ambler's book is devoted exclusively to the convention. Also see preface to *Debates Va. Conv.* iii; and see Dodd, in *American Journal of Sociology*, xxvi, no. 6, 735 *et seq.*; and Anderson, 229–36.   [2] *Debates, Va. Conv.* 23.
[3] *Ib.* 25.   [4] *Ib.* 25–31.   [5] Statement of Marshall. (*Ib.* 872.)

for the organization of the State Judiciary, but did not seek materially to change the system of appointments of judges.

Two sentences of this report are important: "No modification or abolition of any Court, shall be construed to deprive any Judge thereof of his office"; and, "Judges may be removed from office by a vote of the General Assembly: but two-thirds of the whole number of each House must concur in such vote." [1] Marshall promptly moved that this report be made the order of the day and this was done.

Ranking next to the question of the basis of suffrage and of representation was that of judiciary reform. To accomplish this reform was one of the objects for which the convention had been called. At that time the Judiciary of Virginia was not merely a matter of courts and judges; it involved the entire social and political organization of that State. No more essentially aristocratic scheme of government ever existed in America. Coming down from Colonial times, it had been perpetuated by the Revolutionary Constitution of 1776. It had, in practical results, some good qualities and others that were evil, among the latter a well-nigh faultless political mechanism. [2]

The heart of this system was the County Courts. Too much emphasis cannot be placed on this fact. These local tribunals consisted of justices of the peace who sat together as County Courts for the hearing and decision of the more important cases. They were almost always the first men of their coun-

[1] *Debates, Va. Conv.* 33.   [2] See *supra*, 146, 147.

ties, appointed by the Governor for life; vacancies
were, in practice, filled only on the recommendation
of the remaining justices. While the Constitution
of 1776 did not require the Governor to accept the
nominations of the County Courts for vacancies in
these offices, to do so had been a custom long established.[1]

For this acquiescence of the Governor in the recommendation of the County Courts, there was a very
human reason of even weightier influence than that
of immemorial practice. The Legislature chose the
Governor; and the justices of the peace selected, in
most cases, the candidates for the Legislature —
seldom was any man elected by the people to the
State Senate or House of Delegates who was not
approved by the County Courts. Moreover, the
other county offices, such as county clerks and sheriffs, were appointed by the Governor only on the
suggestion of the justices of the peace; and these
officials worked in absolute agreement with the local
judicial oligarchy. In this wise members of Congress
were, in effect, named by the County Courts, and
the Legislature dared not and did not elect United
States Senators of whom the justices of the peace
disapproved.

The members of the Court of Appeals, appointed
by the Governor, were never offensive to these minor
county magistrates, although the judges of this highest tribunal in Virginia, always able and learned men
holding their places for life, had great influence over
the County Courts, and, therefore, over the Gover-

[1] See Giles's speech, *Debates, Va. Conv.* 604–05.

ner and General Assembly also. Nor was this the
limit of the powers of the County Courts. They fixed
the county rate of taxation and exercised all local
legislative and executive as well as judicial power.[1]

In theory, a more oligarchic system never was devised for the government of a free state; but in practice, it responded to the variations of public opinion
with almost the precision of a thermometer. For
example, nearly all the justices of the peace were
Federalists during the first two years of Washington's Administration; yet the State supported Henry
against Assumption, and, later, went over to Jefferson as against Washington and Henry combined.[2]

Rigid and self-perpetuating as was the official
aristocracy which the Virginia judicial system had
created, its members generally attended to their
duties and did well their public work.[3] They lived
among the people, looked after the common good,
composed disputes between individuals; soothed
local animosities, prevented litigation; and administered justice satisfactorily when, despite their preventive efforts, men would bring suits. But the
whole scheme was the very negation of democracy.[4]

While, therefore, this judicial-social-political plan
worked well for the most part, the idea of it was
offensive to liberal-minded men who believed in
democracy as a principle. Moreover, the official

[1] See Ambler: *Sectionalism in Virginia,* 139.

[2] See vol. II, 62–69, of this work.

[3] Serious abuses sprang up, however. In the convention, William
Naylor of Hampshire County charged that the office of sheriff was sold
to the highest bidder, sometimes at public auction. (*Debates, Va.
Conv.* 486; and see Anderson, 229.)

[4] See Marshall's defense of the County Court system, *infra,* 491.

oligarchy was more powerful in the heavy slaveholding, than in the comparatively "free labor," sections; it had been longer established, and it better
fitted conditions, east of the mountains.

So it came about that there was, at last, a demand
for judicial reform. Seemingly this demand was
not radical — it was only that the self-perpetuating
County Court system should be changed to appointments by the Governor without regard to recommendations of the local justices; but, in reality, this
change would have destroyed the traditional aristocratic organization of the political, social, and to
a great extent the economic, life of Virginia.

On every issue over which the factions of this
convention fought, Marshall was reactionary and
employed all his skill to defeat, whenever possible,
the plans and purposes of the radicals. In pursuing
this course he brought to bear the power of his now
immense reputation for wisdom and justice. Perhaps no other phase of his life displays more strikingly his intense conservatism.

The conclusion of his early manhood — reluctantly avowed after Washington, following the Revolution, had bitterly expressed the same opinion,[1]
that the people, left to themselves, are not capable
of self-government — had now become a profound
moral belief. It should again be stated that most of
Marshall's views, formed as a young lawyer during
the riotous years between the achievement of Independence and the adoption of the Constitution,
had hardened, as life advanced, into something

[1] See vol. i, 302, of this work.

like religious convictions. It is noteworthy, too, that, in general, Madison, Giles, and even Monroe, now stood with Marshall.

The most conspicuous feature of those fourteen weeks of tumultuous contest, as far as it reveals Marshall's personal standing in Virginia, was the trust, reverence, and affection in which he was held by all members, young and old, radical and conservative, from every part of the State. Speaker after speaker, even in the fiercest debates, went out of his way to pay tribute to Marshall's uprightness and wisdom.[1]

Marshall spoke frequently on the Judiciary; and, at one point in a debate on the removal of judges, disclosed opinions of historical importance. Although twenty-seven years had passed since the repeal of the Federalist Judiciary Act of 1801,[2] Marshall would not, even now, admit that repeal to be Constitutional. Littleton W. Tazewell, also a mem-

[1] For example, Thomas R. Joynes of Accomack County, who earnestly opposed Marshall in the Judiciary debate, said that no man felt "more respect" than he for Marshall's opinions which are justly esteemed "not only in this Convention, but throughout the United States." (*Debates, Va. Conv.* 505.) Randolph spoke of "the very great weight" which Marshall had in the convention, in Virginia, and throughout the Nation. (*Ib.* 500.) Thomas M. Bayly of Accomack County, while utterly disagreeing with the Chief Justice on the County Court system, declared that Marshall, "as a lawyer and Judge, is without a rival." (*Ib.* 510.) Richard H. Henderson of Loudoun County called the Chief Justice his "political father" whose lessons he delighted to follow, and upon whose "wisdom, . . virtue, . . prudence" he implicitly relied. (Henderson's statement as repeated by Benjamin W. Leigh, *ib.* 544.) Charles F. Mercer of the same county "expressed toward Judge Marshall a filial respect and veneration not surpassed by the ties which had bound him to a natural parent." (*Ib.* 563.) Such are examples of the expressions toward Marshall throughout the prolonged sessions of the convention.

[2] See vol. III, chap. II, of this work.

ber of the Judiciary Committee, asserted that, under the proposed new State Constitution, the Legislature could remove judges from office by abolishing the courts. John Scott of Fauquier County asked Marshall what he thought of the ousting of Federalist judges by the Republicans in 1802.

The Chief Justice answered, "with great, very great repugnance," that throughout the debate he had "most carefully avoided" expressing any opinion on that subject. He would say, however, that "he did not conceive the Constitution to have been at all definitely expounded by a single act of Congress." Especially when "there was no union of Departments, but the Legislative Department alone had acted, and acted but once," ignoring the Judicial Department, such an act, "even admitting that act not to have passed in times of high political and party excitement, could never be admitted as final and conclusive." [1]

Tazewell was of "an exactly opposite opinion" — the Repeal Act of 1802 "was perfectly constitutional and proper." Giles also disagreed with Marshall. Should "a public officer . . receive the public money any longer than he renders service to the public"? [2] Marshall replied with spirit. No serious question can be settled, he declared, by mere "confidence of conviction, but on the reason of the case." All that he asked was that the Judiciary Article of the proposed State Constitution should go forth, "uninfluenced by the opinion of any individual: let those, whose duty it was to settle the

[1] *Debates, Va. Conv.* 871–72.   [2] *Ib.* 872–74.

interpretation of the Constitution, decide on the Constitution itself." [1] After extended debate [2] and some wrangling, Marshall's idea on this particular phase of the subject prevailed. [3]

The debate over the preservation of the County Court system, for which Marshall's report provided, was long and acrimonious, and a résumé of it is impossible here. Marshall stoutly supported these local tribunals; their "abolition will affect our whole internal police. . . No State in the Union, has hitherto enjoyed more complete internal quiet than Virginia. There is no part of America, where . . less of ill-feeling between man and man is to be found than in this Commonwealth, and I believe most firmly that this state of things is mainly to be ascribed to the practical operation of our County Courts." The county judges "consist in general of the best men in their respective counties. They act in the spirit of peace-makers, and allay, rather than excite the small disputes . . which will sometimes arise among neighbours." [4]

Giles now aligned himself with Marshall as a champion of the County Court system. In an earnest defense of it he went so far as to reflect on the good sense of Jefferson. Everybody, said Giles,

---

[1] *Debates, Va. Conv.* 873.   [2] See *infra*, 493–501.

[3] Accordingly the following provision was inserted into the Constitution: "No law abolishing any court shall be construed to deprive a Judge thereof of his office, unless two-thirds of the members of each House present concur in the passing thereof; but the Legislature may assign other Judicial duties to the Judges of courts abolished by any law enacted by less than two-thirds of the members of each House present." (Article v, Section 2, Constitution of Virginia, 1830.)

[4] *Debates, Va. Conv.* 505.

knew that that "highly respectable man .. dealt very much in theories." [1]

During the remainder of the discussion on this subject, Marshall rose frequently, chiefly, however, to guide the debate.[2] He insisted that the custom of appointing justices of the peace only on nomination of the County Courts should be written into the constitution. The Executive ought to appoint *all* persons recommended by "a County Court, taken as a whole." Marshall then moved an amendment to that effect.[3]

This was a far more conservative idea than was contained in the old constitution itself. "Let the County Court who now recommended, have power also to appoint: for there it ended at last," said William Campbell of Bedford County. Giles was for Marshall's plan: "The existing County Court system" threw "power into the hands of the middle class of the community," he said; and it ought to be fortified rather than weakened.

Marshall then withdrew his astonishing amendment and proposed, instead, that the advice and "consent of the Senate" should not be required for appointments of county justices, thus utterly eliminating all legislative control over these important appointments; and this extreme conservative proposition was actually adopted without dissent.[4] Thus

---

[1] *Debates, Va. Conv.* 509.

[2] *Ib.* 524, 530, 531, 533, 534.   [3] *Ib.* 604–05.

[4] *Ib.* 605. The provision as it finally appeared in the constitution was that these "appointments shall be made by the Governor, on the recommendation of the respective County Courts." (Article v, Section 7, Constitution of Virginia, 1830.)

the very foundation of Virginia's aristocratic political organization was greatly strengthened.

Concerning the retention of his office by a judge after the court had been abolished, Marshall made an earnest and impressive speech. What were the duties of a judge? "He has to pass between the Government and the man whom that Government is prosecuting: between the most powerful individual in the community, and the poorest and most unpopular. It is of the last importance, that in the exercise of these duties, he should observe the utmost fairness. Need I press the necessity of this? Does not every man feel that his own personal security and the security of his property depends on that fairness?

"The Judicial Department comes home in its effects to every man's fireside: it passes on his property, his reputation, his life, his all. Is it not, to the last degree important, that he should be rendered perfectly and completely independent, with nothing to influence or controul him but God and his conscience?

"You do not allow a man to perform the duties of a juryman or a Judge, if he has one dollar of interest in the matter to be decided: and will you allow a Judge to give a decision when his office may depend upon it? when his decision may offend a powerful and influential man?

"Your salaries do not allow any of your Judges to lay up for his old age: the longer he remains in office, the more dependant he becomes upon his office. He wishes to retain it; if he did not wish to retain it, he would not have accepted it. And will you make me believe that if the manner of his decision may affect the tenure of that office, the man himself will not be affected by that consideration? . . The whole good which may grow out of this Convention, be it what it may, will never compensate for the evil of changing the tenure of the Judicial office."

Barbour had said that to presume that the Legislature would oust judges because of unpopular decisions, was to make an unthinkable imputation. But "for what do you make a Constitution?" countered Marshall. Why provide that "no bill of attainder, or an *ex post facto* law, shall be passed? What a calumny is here upon the Legislature," he sarcastically exclaimed. "Do you believe, that the Legislature will pass a bill of attainder, or an *ex post facto* law? Do you believe, that they will pass a law impairing the obligation of contracts? If not, why provide against it? . .

"You declare, that the Legislature shall not take private property for the public use, without just compensation. Do you believe, that the Legislature will put forth their grasp upon private property, without compensation? Certainly I do not. There is as little reason to believe they will do such an act as this, as there is to believe, that a Legislature will offend against a Judge who has given a decision against some favourite opinion and favourite measure of theirs, or against a popular individual who has almost led the Legislature by his talents and influence.

"I am persuaded, there is at least as much danger that they will lay hold on such an individual, as that they will condemn a man to death for doing that which, when he committed it, was no crime. The gentleman says, it is impossible the Legislature should ever think of doing such a thing. Why then expunge the prohibition? . . This Convention can do nothing that would entail a more serious evil upon Virginia, than to destroy the tenure by which her Judges hold their offices." [1]

An hour later, the Chief Justice again addressed the convention on the independence of the Judiciary. Tazewell had spoken much in the vein of the Republicans of 1802.[2] "The independence of all those who try causes between man and man, and between a man and his Government," answered Marshall, "can be maintained only by the tenure of their office. Is not their independence preserved under the present system? None can doubt it. Such an idea was never heard of in Virginia, as to remove a Judge from office." Suppose the courts at the mercy of the Legislature? "What would then be the condition of the court, should the Legislature prosecute a man, with an earnest wish to convict him? . . If they may be removed at pleasure, will any lawyer of distinction come upon your bench?

"No, Sir. I have always thought, from my earliest youth till now, that the greatest scourge an angry Heaven ever inflicted upon an ungrateful and a sinning people, was an ignorant, a corrupt, or a dependent Judiciary. Will you draw down this

[1] *Debates, Va. Conv.* 615–17.   [2] See vol. III, chap. II, of this work.

curse upon Virginia? Our ancestors thought so: we thought so till very lately; and I trust the vote of this day will shew that we think so still." [1]

Seldom in any parliamentary body has an appeal been so fruitful of votes. Marshall's idea of the inviolability of judicial tenure was sustained by a vote of 56 to 29, Madison voting with him. [2]

Lucas P. Thompson of Amherst County moved to strike out the provision in Marshall's Judiciary Article that the abolition of a court should not "deprive any Judge thereof of his office." [3] Thus the direct question, so fiercely debated in Congress twenty-seven years earlier, [4] was brought before the convention. It was promptly decided, and against the views and action of Jefferson and the Republicans of 1802. By a majority of 8 out of a total of 96, [5] the convention sustained the old Federalist idea that judges should continue to hold their positions and receive their salaries, even though their offices were abolished.

Before the vote was taken, however, a sharp debate occurred between Marshall and Giles. To keep judges in office, although that office be destroyed, "was nothing less than to establish a privileged corps in a free community," said Giles. Marshall had said "that a Judge ought to be responsible only to God and to his own conscience." Although "one of the first objects in view, in calling this Convention, was to make the Judges responsible — not nominally, but really responsible," Marshall

---

[1] *Debates, Va. Conv.* 619. [2] *Ib.* 618–19. [3] *Ib.* 726.
[4] See vol. III, chap. II, of this work. [5] *Debates, Va. Conv.* 731.

actually proposed to establish "a *privileged order* of men." Another part of Marshall's plan, said Giles, required the concurrent vote of both Houses of the Legislature to remove a judge from the bench. "This was inserted, for what?" To prevent the Legislature from removing a judge "whenever his conduct had been such, that he became unpopular and odious to the people" — the very power the Legislature ought to have.[1]

In reply, Marshall said that he would not, at that time, discuss the removal of judges by the Legislature, but would confine himself "directly to the object before him," as to whether the abolition of a court should not deprive the judge of his office. Giles had fallen into a strange confusion — he had treated "the office of a Judge, and the Court in which he sat, as being . . indissolubly united." But, asked Marshall, were the words "office and Court synonymes"? By no means. The proposed Judiciary Article makes the distinction when it declares that though the *court* be abolished, the judge still holds his *office*. "In what does the office of a Judge consist? . . in his constitutional capacity to receive Judicial power, and to perform Judicial Duties. . .

"If the Constitution shall declare that when the court is abolished, he shall still hold" his office, "there is no inconsistency in the declaration. . . What creates the office?" An election to it by the Legislature and a commission by the Governor. "When these acts have been performed, the Judges are in office. Now, if the Constitution shall say

[1] *Debates, Va. Conv.* 726–27.

that his office shall continue, and he shall perform
Judicial duties, though his court may be abolished,
does he, because of any modification that may be
made in that court, cease to be a Judge? . .

"The question constantly recurs — do you mean
that the Judges shall be removable at the will of the
Legislature? The gentleman talks of responsibility.
Responsibility to what? to the will of the Legislature? can there be no responsibility, unless your
Judges shall be removable at pleasure? will nothing
short of this satisfy gentlemen? Then, indeed, there
is an end to independence. The tenure during good
behaviour, is a mere imposition on the public belief
— a sound that is kept to the ear — and nothing
else. The consequences must present themselves to
every mind. There can be no member of this body
who does not feel them.

"If your Judges are to be removable at the will of
the Legislature, all that you look for from fidelity,
from knowledge, from capacity, is gone and gone
forever." Seldom did Marshall show more feeling
than when pressing this point; he could not "sit
down," he said, without "noticing the morality" of
giving the Legislature power to remove judges from
office. "Gentlemen talk of sinecures, and privileged
orders — with a view, as it would seem, to cast
odium on those who are in office.

"You seduce a lawyer from his practice, by which
he is earning a comfortable independence, by promising him a certain support for life, unless he shall be
guilty of misconduct in his office. And after thus
seducing him, when his independence is gone, and

the means of supporting his family relinquished, you will suffer him to be displaced and turned loose on the world with the odious brand of sinecure-pensioner — privileged order — put upon him, as a lazy drone who seeks to live upon the labour of others. This is the course you are asked to pursue."

The provisions of the Judiciary Article before the convention secure ample responsibility. "If not, they can be made [to do] so. But is it not new doctrine to declare, that the Legislature by merely changing the name of a court or the place of its meeting, may remove any Judge from his office? The question to be decided is, and it is one to which we must come, whether the Judges shall be permanent in their office, or shall be dependent altogether upon the breath of the Legislature." [1]

Giles answered on the instant. In doing so, he began by a tribute to Marshall's "standing and personal excellence" which were so great "that he was willing to throw himself into the background, as to any weight to be attached to his [Giles's] own opinion." Therefore, he would "rely exclusively on the merits" of the controversy. Marshall had not shown "that it was not an anomaly to have the court out of being, and an office pertain[ing] to the court in being. . . It was an anomaly in terms."

Giles "had, however, such high respect" for Marshall's standing, "that he always doubted his own opinion when put in opposition" to that of the Chief Justice. He had not intended, he avowed, "to throw reproach upon the Judges in office." Far be it from

[1] *Debates, Va. Conv.* 727–29.

him to reflect "in the least degree on their honour and integrity." His point was that, by Marshall's plan, "responsibility was rather avoided than sought to be secured." Giles was willing to risk his liberty thus far — "if a Judge became odious to the people, let him be removed from office." [1]

The debate continued upon another amendment by Thompson. Viewing the contest as a sheer struggle of minds, the conservatives were superior to the reformers,[2] and steadily they gained votes.[3]

Again Marshall spoke, this time crossing swords with Benjamin W. S. Cabell and James Madison, over a motion of the former that judges whose courts were abolished, and to whom the Legislature assigned no new duties, should not receive salaries: "There were upwards of one hundred Inferior Courts in Virginia. . . No gentleman could look at the dockets of these courts, and possibly think" that the judges would ever have no business to transact.

Cabell's amendment "stated an impossible case," said Marshall, — a " case where there should be no controversies between man and man, and no crimes committed against society. It stated a case that could not happen — and would the convention encounter the real hazard of putting almost every Judge in the Commonwealth in the power of the Legislature, for the sake of providing for an impossible case?" [4] But in spite of Marshall's opposition, Cabell's amendment was adopted by a vote of 59

[1] *Debates, Va. Conv.* 729–30.
[2] See especially the speech of Benjamin Watkins Leigh, *ib.* 733–37.
[3] See *ib.* for ayes and noes, 740, 741, 742, 744, 748.
[4] *Ib.* 764.

to 36.[1] Two weeks later, however, the convention reversed itself by two curious and contradictory votes.[2] So in the end Marshall won.

The subject of the Judiciary did not seriously arise again until the vote on the adoption of the entire constitution was imminent. As it turned out, the constitution, when adopted, contained, in substance, the Judiciary provisions which Marshall had written and reported at the beginning of that body's deliberations.[3]

The other and the commanding problem, for the solution of which the convention had been called, was made up of the associated questions of suffrage, taxation, and representation. Broadly speaking, the issue was that of white manhood suffrage and representation based upon the enumeration of whites, as against suffrage determined by property and taxation, representation to be based on an enumeration which included three fifths of the slave population.[4]

On these complex and tangled questions the State and the convention were divided; so fierce were the contending factions, and so diverse were opinions on various elements of the confused problem, especially among those demanding reform, that at times no solution seemed possible. The friends of reform were fairly well organized and coöperated in a spirit of

---

[1] *Debates, Va. Conv.* 767.   [2] *Ib.* 880.

[3] Compare Marshall's report (*ib.* 33) with Article v of the constitution (*ib.* 901-02; and see *supra*, 491, note 2.)

[4] Contrast Marshall's resolutions (*Debates, Va. Conv.* 39-40), which expressed the conservative stand, with those of William H. Fitzhugh of Fairfax County (*ib.* 41-42), of Samuel Claytor of Campbell County (*ib.* 42), of Charles S. Morgan of Monongalia (*ib.* 43-44), and of Alexander Campbell of Brooke County (*ib.* 45-46), which state the views of the radicals.

unity uncommon to liberals. But, as generally happens, the conservatives had much better discipline, far more harmony of opinion and conduct. The debate on both sides was able and brilliant.[1]

Finally the convention seemingly became deadlocked. Each side declared it would not yield.[2] Then came the inevitable reaction — a spirit of conciliation mellowed everybody. Sheer human nature, wearied of strife, sought the escape that mutual accommodation alone afforded. The moment came for which Marshall had been patiently waiting. Rising slowly, as was his wont, until his great height seemed to the convention to be increased, his soothing voice, in the very gentleness of its timbre, gave a sense of restfulness and agreement so grateful to, and so desired by, even the sternest of the combatants.

"No person in the House," began the Chief Justice, "can be more truly gratified than I am, at seeing the spirit that has been manifested here today; and it is my earnest wish that this spirit of conciliation may be acted upon in a fair, equal and honest manner, adapted to the situation of the different parts of the Commonwealth, which are to be affected."

The warring factions, said Marshall, were at last

[1] See, for instance, the speech of John R. Cooke of Frederick County for the radicals (*Debates, Va. Conv.* 54–65), of Abel P. Upshur of Northampton for the conservatives (*ib.* 65–79), of Philip Doddridge of Brooke County for the radicals (*ib.* 79–89), of Philip P. Barbour of Orange County for the conservatives (*ib.* 90–98), and especially the speeches of Benjamin Watkins Leigh for the conservatives (*ib.* 151–74, 544–48). Indeed, the student cannot well afford to omit any one of the addresses in this remarkable contest.

[2] It is at this point that we see the reason for Jefferson's alarm thirteen years before the convention was called. (*See supra,* 469.)

in substantial accord. "That the Federal numbers
[the enumeration of slaves as fixed in the National
Constitution] and the plan of the white basis shall be
blended together so as to allow each an equal portion of power, seems to be very generally agreed to."
The only difference now was that one faction insisted on applying this plan to both Houses of the
Legislature, while the other faction would restrict
the white basis to the popular branch, leaving the
Senate to be chosen on the combined free white and
black slave enumeration.

This involves the whole theory of property. One
gentleman, in particular, "seems to imagine that we
claim nothing of republican principles, when we claim
a representation for property." But "republican
principles" do not depend on "the naked principle
of numbers." On the contrary, "the soundest principles of republicanism do sanction some relation
between representation and taxation. . . The two
ought to be connected. . . This was the principle of
the revolution. . . This basis of Representation is . .
so important to Virginia" that everybody had
thought about it before this convention was called.

"Several different plans were contemplated. The
basis of white population alone; the basis of free
population alone; a basis of population alone; a basis
compounded of taxation and white population, (or
which is the same thing, a basis of Federal numbers:)
. . Now, of these various propositions, the basis of
white population, and the basis of taxation alone are
the two extremes." But, "between the free population, and the white population, there is almost no

difference: Between the basis of total population and the basis of taxation, there is but little difference."

Frankly and without the least disguise of his opinions, Marshall admitted that he was a conservative of conservatives: ",The people of the East," of whom he avowed himself to be one, "thought that they offered a fair compromise, when they proposed the compound basis of population and taxation, or the basis of the Federal numbers. We thought that we had republican precedent for this — a precedent given us by the wisest and truest patriots that ever were assembled: but that is now past.

"We are now willing to meet on a new middle ground." Between the two extremes "the majority is too small to calculate upon. . . We are all uncertain as to the issue. But all know this, that if either extreme is carried, it must leave a wound in the breast of the opposite party which will fester and rankle, and produce I know not what mischief." The conservatives were now the majority of the convention, yet they were again willing to make concessions. Avoiding both extremes, Marshall proposed, "as a compromise," that the basis of representation "shall be made according to an exact compound of the two principles, of the white basis and of the Federal numbers, according to the Census of 1820." [1]

Further debate ensued, during which animosity seemed about to come to life again, when the Chief Justice once more exerted his mollifying influence. "Two propositions respecting the basis of Representation have divided this Convention almost equally,"

[1] *Debates, Va. Conv.* 497-500.

he said. "The question has been discussed, until discussion has become useless. It has been argued, until argument is exhausted. We have now met on the ground of compromise." It is no longer a matter of the triumph of either side. The only consideration now is whether the convention can agree on some plan to lay before the people "with a reasonable hope that it may be adopted. Some concession must be made on both sides. . . What is the real situation of the parties?" Unquestionably both are sincere. "To attempt now to throw considerations of principle into either scale, is to add fuel to a flame which it is our purpose to extinguish. We must lose sight of the situation of parties and state of opinion, if we make this attempt."

The convention is nearly evenly balanced. At this moment those favoring a white basis only have a trembling majority of two. This may change — the reversal of a single vote would leave the House "equally divided."

The question must be decided "one way or the other"; but, if either faction prevails by a bare majority, the proposed constitution will go to the people from an almost equally divided convention. That means a tremendous struggle, a riven State. Interests in certain parts of the Commonwealth will surely resist "with great force" a purely white basis of representation, especially if no effective property qualification for suffrage is provided. This opposition is absolutely certain "unless human nature shall cease to be what it has been in all time."

No human power can forecast the result of further

contest. But one thing is certain: "To obtain a just compromise, concession must not only be mutual — it must be equal also. . . Each ought to concede to the other as much as he demands from that other. . . There can be no hope that either will yield more than it gets in return."

The proposal that white population and taxation "mixed" with Federal numbers in "equal proportions" shall "form the basis of Representation in both Houses," is equal and just. "All feel it to be equal." Yet the conservatives now go still further — they are willing to place the House on the white basis and apply the mixed basis to the Senate only. Why refuse this adjustment? Plainly it will work well for everybody: "If the Senate would protect the East, will it not protect the West also?"

Marshall's satisfaction was "inexpressible" when he heard from both sides the language of conciliation. "I hailed these auspicious appearances with as much joy, as the inhabitant of the polar regions hails the re-appearance of the sun after his long absence of six tedious months. Can these appearances prove fallacious? Is it a meteor we have seen and mistaken for that splendid luminary which dispenses light and gladness throughout creation? ·It must be so, if we cannot meet on equal ground. If we cannot meet on the line that divides us equally, then take the hand of friendship, and make an equal compromise; it is vain to hope that any compromise can be made." [1]

The basis of representation does not appear in the

[1] *Debates, Va. Conv.* 561–62.

constitution, the number of Senators and Representatives being arbitrarily fixed by districts and counties; but this plan, in reality, gave the slaveholding sections almost the same preponderance over the comparatively non-slaveholding sections as would have resulted from the enumeration of three fifths of all slaves in addition to all whites.[1]

While the freehold principle was abandoned, as Marshall foresaw that it would be, the principle of property qualification as against manhood suffrage was triumphant.[2] With a majority against them, the conservatives won by better management, assisted by the personal influence of the Chief Justice, to which, on most phases of the struggle, was added that of Madison and Giles.

Nearly a century has passed since these happenings, and Marshall's attitude now appears to have been that of cold reaction; but he was as honest as he was outspoken in his resistance to democratic reforms. He wanted good government, safe government. He was not in the least concerned in the rule of the people as such. Indeed, he believed that the more they directly controlled public affairs the worse the business of government would be conducted.

He feared that sheer majorities would be unjust, intolerant, tyrannical; and he was certain that they would be untrustworthy and freakishly changeable. These convictions would surely have dictated his course in the Virginia Constitutional Convention of 1829–30, had no other considerations influenced him.

[1] Constitution of Virginia, 1830, Article III, Sections 1 and 2.
[2] *Ib.* Article III, Section 14.

But, in addition to his long settled and ever-petrifying conservative views, we must also take into account the conditions and public temper existing in Virginia ninety years ago. Had the convention reached any other conclusion than that to which Marshall gently guided it, it is certain that the State would have been torn by dissension, and it is not improbable that there would have been bloodshed. All things considered, it seems unsafe to affirm that Marshall's course was not the wisest for that immediate period and for that particular State.

Displaying no vision, no aspiration, no devotion to human rights, he merely acted the uninspiring but necessary part of the practical statesman dealing with an existing and a very grave situation. If Jefferson could be so frightened in 1816 that he forbade the public circulation of his perfectly sound views on the wretched Virginia Constitution of 1776,[1] can it be wondered at that the conservative Marshall in 1830 wished to compose the antagonisms of the warring factions?

The fact that the Nation was then facing the possibility of dissolution [2] must also be taken into account. That circumstance, indeed, influenced Marshall even more than did his profound conservatism. There can be little doubt that, had either the radicals or the conservatives achieved an outright victory, one part of Virginia would have separated from the other and the growing sentiment for disunion would have received a powerful impulse.

[1] See *supra*, 469.   [2] See next chapter.

Hurrying from Richmond to Washington when the convention adjourned, Marshall listened to the argument of Craig *vs.* Missouri; and then delivered one of the strongest opinions he ever wrote — the only one of his Constitutional expositions to be entirely repudiated by the Supreme Court after his death. The case grew out of the financial conditions described in the fourth chapter of this volume.

When Missouri became a State in 1821, her people found themselves in desperate case. There was no money. Banks had suspended, and specie had been drained to the Eastern commercial centers. The simplest business transactions were difficult, almost impossible. Even taxes could not be paid. The Legislature, therefore, established loan offices where citizens, by giving promissory notes, secured by mortgage or pledge of personal property, could purchase loan certificates issued by the State. These certificates were receivable for taxes and other public debts and for salt from the State salt mines. The faith and resources of Missouri were pledged for the redemption of the certificates which were negotiable and issued in denominations not exceeding ten dollars or less than fifty cents. In effect and in intention, the State thus created a local circulating medium of exchange.

On August 1, 1822, Hiram Craig and two others gave their promissory notes for $199.99 in payment for loan certificates. On maturity of these notes the borrowers refused to pay, and the State sued them; judgment against them was rendered in the trial court and this judgment was affirmed by the Supreme Court of Missouri. The case was taken, by writ of error, to the Supreme Court of the United States, where the sole question to be decided was the constitutionality of the Missouri loan office statutes.

Marshall's associates were now Johnson, Duval, Story, Thompson, McLean, and Baldwin; the last two recently appointed by Jackson. It was becoming apparent that the court was growing restive under the rigid practice of the austere theory of government and business which the Chief Justice had maintained for nearly a generation. This tendency was shown in this case by the stand taken by three of the Associate Justices. Marshall was in his seventy-sixth year, but never did his genius shine more resplendently than in his announcement of the opinion of the Supreme Court in Craig *vs*. Missouri.[1]

He held that the Missouri loan certificates were bills of credit, which the National Constitution prohibited any State to issue. "What is a bill of credit?" It is "any instrument by which a state engages to pay money at a future day; thus including a certificate given for money borrowed. . . To 'emit bills of credit' conveys to the mind the idea of issuing paper intended to circulate through the community, for its ordinary purposes, as money, which paper is redeemable at a future day."[2] The Chief Justice goes into the history of the paper money evil that caused the framers of the Constitution to forbid the States to "emit bills of credit."

[1] March 12, 1830.   [2] 4 Peters, 432.

Such currency always fluctuates. "Its value is continually changing; and these changes, often great and sudden, expose individuals to immense loss, are the sources of ruinous speculations, and destroy all confidence between man and man." To "cut up this mischief by the roots . . the people declared, in their Constitution, that no state should emit bills of credit. If the prohibition means anything, if the words are not empty sounds, it must comprehend the emission of any paper medium by a state government, for the purpose of common circulation." [1]

Incontestably the Missouri loan certificates are just such bills of credit. Indeed, the State law itself "speaks of them in this character." That the statute calls them certificates instead of bills of credit does not change the fact. How absurd to claim that the Constitution "meant to prohibit names and not things! That a very important act, big with great and ruinous mischief, which is expressly forbidden . . may be performed by the substitution of a name." The Constitution is not to be evaded "by giving a new name to an old thing." [2]

It is nonsense to say that these particular bills of credit are lawful because they are not made legal tender, since a separate provision applies to legal tender. The issue of legal tender currency, and also bills of credit, is equally and separately forbidden: "To sustain the one because it is not also the other; to say that bills of credit may be emitted if they be not made a tender in payment of debts; is . . to expunge that distinct, independent prohibition." [3]

[1] 4 Peters, 432.   [2] *Ib.* 433.   [3] *Ib.* 434.

In a well-nigh perfect historical summary, Marshall reviews experiments before and during the Revolution in bills of credit that were made legal tender, and in others that were not — all "productive of the same effects," all equally ruinous in results.[1] The Missouri law authorizing the loan certificates, for which Craig gave his promissory note, is "against the highest law of the land, and . . the note itself is utterly void." [2]

The Chief Justice closes with a brief paragraph splendid in its simple dignity and power. In his argument for Missouri, Senator Thomas H. Benton had used violent language of the kind frequently employed by the champions of State Rights: "If . . the character of a sovereign State shall be impugned," he cried, "contests about civil rights would be settled amid the din of arms, rather than in these halls of national justice." [3]

To this outburst Marshall replies: The court has been told of "the dangers which may result from" offending a sovereign State. If obedience to the Constitution and laws of the Nation "shall be calculated to bring on those dangers . . or if it shall be indispensable to the preservation of the union, and consequently of the independence and liberty of these states; these are considerations which address themselves to those departments which may with perfect propriety be influenced by them. This department can listen only to the mandates of law; and can tread only that path which is marked out by duty." [4]

---

[1] 4 Peters, 434–36.   [2] *Ib.* 437.   [3] *Ib.* 420.   [4] *Ib.* 438.

In this noble passage Marshall is not only re-
buking Benton; he is also speaking to the advocates
of Nullification, then becoming clamorous and threatening; he is pointing out to Andrew Jackson the path
of duty.[1]

Justices Johnson, Thompson, and McLean afterwards filed dissenting opinions, thus beginning the
departure, within the Supreme Court, from the
stern Constitutional Nationalism of Marshall. This
breach in the court deeply troubled the Chief Justice during the remaining four years of his life.

Johnson thought "that these certificates are of
a truly amphibious character." The Missouri law
"does indeed approach as near to a violation of the
Constitution as it can well go without violating its
prohibition, but it is in the exercise of an unquestionable right, although in rather a questionable
form." So, on the whole, Johnson concluded that
the Supreme Court had better hold the statute
valid.[2]

"The right of a State to borrow money cannot be
questioned," said Thompson; that is all the Missouri scheme amounts to. If these loan certificates
are bills of credit, so are "all bank notes, issued either
by the States, or under their authority."[3] Justice
McLean pointed out that Craig's case was only one
of many of the same kind. "The solemn act of a
State . . cannot be set aside . . under a doubtful
construction of the Constitution.[4] . . It would be as
gross usurpation on the part of the federal govern-

---

[1] See 552–58.   [2] 4 Peters, 438–44.
[3] *Ib.* 445–50.   [4] *Ib.* 458.

ment to interfere with State rights by an exercise
of powers not delegated, as it would be for a State
to interpose its authority against a law of the
Union." [1]

In Congress attacks upon Marshall and the Supreme Court now were renewed — but they grew
continuously feebler. At the first session after the
decision of the Missouri loan certificate case, a bill
was introduced to repeal the provision of the Judiciary Act upon which the National powers of
the Supreme Court so largely depended. "If the
twenty-fifth section is repealed, the Constitution
is practically gone," declared Story. "Our wisest
friends look with great gloom to the future." [2]

Marshall was equally despondent, but his political vision was clearer. When he read the dissenting
opinions of Johnson, Thompson, and McLean, he
wrote Story: "It requires no prophet to predict
that the 25th section [of the Judiciary Act] is to
be repealed, or to use a more fashionable phrase
to be nullified by the Supreme Court of the United
States." [3] He realized clearly that the great tribunal, the power and dignity of which he had done
so much to create, would soon be brought under
the control of those who, for some years at least,
would reject that broad and vigorous Nationalism which he had steadily and effectively asserted

[1] 4 Peters, 464.

[2] Story to Ticknor, Jan. 22, 1831, Story, II, 49. Nevertheless Story
did not despair. "It is now whispered, that the demonstrations of public opinion are so strong, that the majority [of the Judiciary Commit-
tee] will conclude not to present their report." (Ib.)

[3] Marshall to Story, Oct. 15, 1830, Proceedings, Mass. Hist. Soc.
2d Series, XIV, 342.

during almost a third of a century. One more vacancy on the Supreme Bench and a single new appointment by Jackson would give the court to the opponents of Marshall's views. Before he died, the Chief Justice was to behold two such vacancies.[1]

On January 24, 1831, William R. Davis of South Carolina presented the majority report of the Judiciary Committee favoring the repeal of that section of the Judiciary Act under which the Supreme Court had demolished State laws and annihilated the decisions of State courts.[2] James Buchanan presented the minority report.[3] A few minutes' preliminary discussion revealed the deep feeling on both sides. Philip Doddridge of Virginia declared that the bill was of "as much importance as if it were a proposition to repeal the Union of these States." William W. Ellsworth of Connecticut avowed that it was of "overwhelming magnitude."[4]

Thereupon the subject was furiously debated. Thomas H. Crawford of Pennsylvania considered Section 25 of the Judiciary Act, to be as "sacred" as the Constitution itself.[5] Henry Daniel of Kentucky asserted that the Supreme Court "stops at nothing to obtain power." Let the "States . . prepare for the worst, and protect themselves against the assaults of this gigantic tribunal."[6]

William Fitzhugh Gordon of Virginia, recently elected, but already a member of the Judiciary Com-

---

[1] See *infra*, 584.   [2] *Debates*, 21st Cong. 2d Sess. 532.
[3] *Ib*. 535.   [4] *Ib*. 534.   [5] *Ib*. 659.   [6] *Ib*. 665.

mittee, stoutly defended the report of the majority: "When a committee of the House had given to a subject the calmest and maturest investigation, and a motion is made to print their report, a gentleman gets up, and, in a tone of alarm, denounces the proposition as tantamount to a motion to repeal the Union." Gordon repudiated the very thought of dismemberment of the Republic — that "palladium of our hopes, and of the liberties of mankind."

As to the constitutionality of Section 25 of the Judiciary Act — "could it be new, especially to a Virginia lawyer"? when the Virginia Judiciary, with Roane at its head, had solemnly proclaimed the illegality of that section. And had not Georgia ordered her Governor to resist the enforcement of that provision of that ancient act of Congress? "I declare to God . . that I believe nothing would tend so much to compose the present agitation of the country . . as the repeal of that portion of the judiciary act." Gordon was about to discuss the nefarious case of Cohens *vs.* Virginia when his emotions overcame him — "he did not wish . . to go into the merits of the question." [1]

Thomas F. Foster of Georgia said that the Judiciary Committee had reported under a "galling fire from the press"; quoted Marshall's unfortunate language in the Convention of 1788; [2] and insisted that the "vast and alarming" powers of the Supreme Court must be bridled. [3]

---

[1] *Debates*, 21st Cong. 2d Sess. 620–21.
[2] *Ib.* 731, 748; and see vol. I, 454–55, of this work.
[3] *Debates*, 21st Cong. 2d Sess. 739.

But the friends of the court overwhelmed the supporters of the bill, which was rejected by a vote of 138 to 51.[1] It was ominous, however, that the South stood almost solid against the court and Nationalism.

[1] *Debates*, 21st Cong. 2d Sess. 542.

This was the last formal attempt, but one, made in Congress during Marshall's lifetime, to impair the efficiency of National courts. The final attack was made by Joseph Lecompte, a Representative from Kentucky, who on January 27, 1832, offered a resolution instructing the Judiciary Committee to "inquire into the expediency of amending the constitution . . so that the judges of the Supreme Court, and of the inferior courts, shall hold their offices for a limited term of years." On February 24, the House, by a vote of 141 to 27, refused to consider Lecompte's resolution, ignoring his plea to be allowed to explain it. (*Debates*, 22d Cong. 1st Sess. 1856–57.) So summary and brusque — almost contemptuous — was the rejection of Lecompte's proposal, as almost to suggest that personal feeling was an element in the action taken by the House.

CHAPTER X

THE FINAL CONFLICT

Liberty and Union, now and forever, one and inseparable. (Daniel Webster.)

Fellow citizens, the die is now cast. Prepare for the crisis and meet it as becomes men and freemen. (South Carolina Ordinance of Nullification.)

The Union has been prolonged thus far by miracles. I fear they cannot continue. (Marshall.)

It is time to be old,
To take in sail. (Emerson.)

THE last years of Marshall's life were clouded with sadness, almost despair. His health failed; his wife died; the Supreme Court was successfully defied; his greatest opinion was repudiated and denounced by a strong and popular President; his associates on the Bench were departing from some of his most cherished views; and the trend of public events convinced him that his labor to construct an enduring nation, to create institutions of orderly freedom, to introduce stability and system into democracy, had been in vain.

Yet, even in this unhappy period, there were hours of triumph for John Marshall. He heard his doctrine of Nationalism championed by Daniel Webster, who, in one of the greatest debates of history, used Marshall's arguments and almost his very words; he beheld the militant assertion of the same principle by Andrew Jackson, who, in this instance, also employed Marshall's reasoning and method of statement; and he witnessed the sudden flowering of public appreciation of his character and services.

During the spring of 1831, Marshall found himself, for the first time in his life, suffering from acute pain. His Richmond physician could give him no relief; and he became so despondent that he determined to resign immediately after the ensuing Presidential election, in case Jackson should be defeated, an event which many then thought probable. In a letter about the house at which the members of the Supreme Court were to board during the next term, Marshall tells Story of his purpose: "Being . . a bird of passage, whose continuance with you cannot be long, I did not chuse to permit my convenience or my wishes to weigh a feather in the permanent arrangements. . . But in addition, I felt serious doubts, although I did not mention them, whether I should be with you at the next term.

"What I am about to say is, of course, in perfect confidence which I would not breathe to any other person whatever. I had unaccountably calculated on the election of P[residen]t taking place next fall, and had determined to make my continuance in office another year dependent on that event.

"You know how much importance I attach to the character of the person who is to succeed me, and calculate the influence which probabilities on that subject would have on my continuance in office. This, however, is a matter of great delicacy on which I cannot and do not speak.

"My erroneous calculation of the time of the election was corrected as soon as the pressure of official duty was removed from my mind, and I had nearly decided on my course, but recent events produce such real uncertainty respecting the future as to create doubts whether I ought not to await the same chances in the fall of 32 which I had intended to await in the fall of 31." [1]

Marshall steadily became worse, and in September he went to Philadelphia to consult the celebrated physician and surgeon, Dr. Philip Syng Physick, who at once perceived that the Chief Justice was suffering from stone in the bladder. His affliction could be relieved only by the painful and delicate operation of lithotomy, which Dr. Physick had introduced in America. From his sick-room Marshall writes Story of his condition during the previous five months, and adds that he looks "with impatience for the operation." [2] He is still 'concerned about the court's boarding-place and again refers to his intention of leaving the Bench: "In the course of the summer . . I found myself unequal to the effective consideration of any subject, and had determined to resign at the close of the year. This determination, however, I kept to myself, being determined to remain master of my own conduct." Story had answered Marshall's letter of June 26, evidently protesting against the thought of the Chief Justice giving up his office.

Marshall replies: "On the most interesting part of your letter I have felt, and still feel, great difficulty. You understand my general sentiments on that subject as well as I do myself. I am most earnestly attached to the character of the department, and to the wishes and convenience of those with whom it has been my pride and my happiness to be associated for so many years. I cannot be insensible to

[1] Marshall to Story, June 26, 1831, *Proceedings, Mass. Hist. Soc.* 2d Series, xiv, 344–45.

[2] Same to same, Oct. 12, 1831, *ib.* 346–48.

'the gloom which lours over us. I have a repugnance to abandoning you under such circumstances which is almost invincible. But the solemn convictions of my judgement sustained by some pride of character admonish me not to hazard the disgrace of continuing in office a mere inefficient pageant." [1]

Had Adams been reëlected in 1828, there can be no doubt that Marshall would have resigned during that Administration; and it is equally certain that, if Jackson had been defeated in 1832, the Chief Justice would have retired immediately. The Democratic success in the election of that year determined him to hold on in an effort to keep the Supreme Court, as long as possible, unsubmerged by the rising tide of radical Localism. Perhaps he also clung to a desperate hope that, during his lifetime, a political reaction would occur and a conservative President be chosen who could appoint his successor.

When Marshall arrived at Philadelphia, the bar of that city wished to give him a dinner, and, by way of invitation, adopted remarkable resolutions expressing their grateful praise and affectionate admiration. The afflicted Chief Justice, deeply touched, declined in a letter of singular grace and dignity: "It is impossible for me . . to do justice to the feelings with which I receive your very flattering address; . . to have performed the official duties assigned to me by my country in such a manner as to acquire the approbation of" the Philadelphia bar, "affords me the highest gratification of which I am capable, and is

[1] Marshall to Story, Oct. 12, 1831, *Proceedings, Mass. Hist. Soc.* 2d Series, xiv, 347. A rumor finally got about that Marshall contemplated resigning. (See Niles, xl, 90.)

more than an ample reward for the labor which those
duties impose." Marshall's greatest satisfaction, he
says, is that he and his associates on the Supreme
Bench "have never sought to enlarge the judicial
power beyond its proper bounds, nor feared to carry
it to the fullest extent that duty required." [1] The
members of the bar then begged the Chief Justice
to receive them "in a body" at "the United States
Courtroom"; and also to "permit his portrait to be
taken" by "an eminent artist of this city." [2]

With anxiety, but calmness and even good humor,
Marshall awaited the operation. Just before he went
to the surgeon's table, Dr. Jacob Randolph, who
assisted Dr. Physick, found Marshall eating a hearty
breakfast. Notwithstanding the pain he suffered,
the Chief Justice laughingly explained that, since it
might be the last meal he ever would enjoy, he had
determined to make the most of it. He understood
that the chances of surviving the operation were
against him, but he was eager to take them, since he
would rather die than continue to suffer the agony
he had been enduring.

While the long and excruciating operation went
on, by which more than a thousand calculi were
removed, Marshall was placid, "scarcely uttering
a murmur throughout the whole procedure." The

[1] The resolutions of the bar had included the same idea, and Marshall emphasized it by reiterating it in his response.

[2] Hazard's *Pennsylvania Register*, as quoted in Dillon, III, 430–33.
The artist referred to was either Thomas Sully, or Henry Inman, who
had studied under Sully. During the following year, Inman painted
the portrait and it was so excellent that it brought the artist his first
general recognition. The original now hangs in the rooms of the Philadelphia Law Association. A reproduction of it appears as the frontispiece of this volume.

physicians ascribed his recovery "in a great degree
. . to his extraordinary self possession, and to the calm
and philosophical views which he took of his case." [1]

Marshall writes Story about his experience and
the results of the treatment, saying that he must
take medicine "continually to prevent new forma-
tions," and adding, with humorous melancholy, that
he "must submit too to a severe and most unsoci-
able regimen." He cautions Story to care for his
own health, which Judge Peters had told him was
bad. "Without your vigorous and powerful co-operation I should be in despair, and think the 'ship must
be given up.'" [2]

On learning of his improved condition, Story writes
Peters from Cambridge: "This seems to me a special
interposition of Providence in favor of the Constitution. . . He is beloved and reverenced here beyond
all measure, though not beyond his merits. Next to
Washington he stands the idol of all good men." [3]

While on this distressing visit to Philadelphia,
Marshall writes his wife two letters — the last letters
to her of which any originals or copies can be found.
"I anticipate with a pleasure which I know you will
share the time when I may sit by your side by our
tranquil fire side & enjoy the happiness of your
society without inflicting on you the pain of witnessing my suffering. . . I am treated with the most flattering attentions in Philadelphia. They give me pain,

[1] Randolph: *A Memoir on the Life and Character of Philip Syng Physick, M.D.* 97–99.

[2] Marshall to Story, Nov. 10, 1831, *Proceedings, Mass. Hist. Soc.* 2d Series, XIV, 348–49.

[3] Story to Peters, Oct. 29, 1831, Story, II, 70.

the more pain as the necessity of declining many of them may be ascribed to a want of sensibility." [1]

His recovery assured, Marshall again writes his wife: "I have at length risen from my bed and am able to hold a pen. The most delightful use I can make of it is to tell you that I am getting well . . from the painful disease with which I have been so long affected. . . Nothing delights me so much as to hear from my friends and especially from you. How much was I gratified at the line from your own hand in Mary's letter.[2] . . I am much obliged by your offer to lend me money.[3] I hope I shall not need it but can not as yet speak positively as my stay has been longer and my expenses greater than I had anticipated on leaving home. Should I use any part of it, you may be assured it will be replaced on my return. But this is a subject on which I know you feel no solicitude. . . God bless you my dearest Polly love to all our friends. Ever your most affectionate J. Marshall." [4]

On December 25, 1831, his "dearest Polly" died. The previous day, she hung about his neck a locket containing a wisp of her hair. For the remainder of his life he wore this memento, never parting with it night or day.[5] Her weakness, physical and mental, which prevailed throughout practically the whole of

[1] Marshall to his wife, Oct. 6, 1831, MS.

[2] This is the only indication in any of Marshall's letters that his wife had written him.

[3] Mrs. Marshall had a modest fortune of her own, bequeathed to her by her uncle. She invested this quite independently of her husband. (Leigh to Biddle, Sept. 7, 1837, McGrane, 289.)

[4] Marshall to his wife, Nov. 8, 1831, MS.

[5] Terhune, 98. This locket is now in the possession of Marshall's granddaughter, Miss Emily Harvie of Richmond.

their married life, inspired in Marshall a chivalric
adoration. On the morning of the first anniversary
of her death, Story chanced to go into Marshall's
room and "found him in tears. He had just finished
writing out for me some lines of General Burgoyne,
of which he spoke to me last evening as eminently
beautiful and affecting. . . I saw at once that he
had been shedding tears over the memory of his own
wife, and he has said to me several times during the
term, that the moment he relaxes from business he
feels exceedingly depressed, and rarely goes through
a night without weeping over his departed wife. . . I
think he is the most extraordinary man I ever saw,
for the depth and tenderness of his feelings." [1]

[1] Story to his wife, March 4, 1832, Story, II, 86–87.

Soon after the death of his wife, Marshall made his will "entirely
in [his] . . own handwriting." A more informal document of the kind
seldom has been written. It is more like a familiar letter than a legal
paper; yet it is meticulously specific. "I owe nothing on my own
account," he begins. (He specifies one or two small obligations as
trustee for women relatives and as surety for "considerable sums" for
his son-in-law, Jacquelin B. Harvie.) The will shows that he owns
bank and railroad stock and immense quantities of land. He equally
divides his property among his children, making special provision
that the portion of his daughter Mary shall be particularly safeguarded.

One item of the will is curious: "I give to each of my grandsons
named John one thousand acres, part of my tract of land called Canaan
lying in Randolph county. If at the time of my death either of my
sons should have no son living named John, then I give the thousand
acres to any son he may have named Thomas, in token for my love
for my father and veneration for his memory. If there should be no
son named John or Thomas, then I give the land to the eldest son and
if no sons to the daughters."

He makes five additions to his will, three of which he specifically
calls "codicils." One of these is principally "to emancipate my faithful servant Robin and I direct his emancipation if he *chuses* to conform
to the laws on that subject, requiring that he should leave the state
or if permission can be obtained for his continuing to reside in it."
If Robin elects to go to Liberia, Marshall gives him one hundred dol-

But Marshall had also written something which he did not show even to Story — a tribute to his wife:

"This day of joy and festivity to the whole Christian world is, to my sad heart, the anniversary of the keenest affliction which humanity can sustain. While all around is gladness, my mind dwells on the silent tomb, and cherishes the remembrance of the beloved object which it contains.

"On the 25th of December, 1831, it was the will of Heaven to take to itself the companion who had sweetened the choicest part of my life, had rendered toil a pleasure, had partaken of all my feelings, and was enthroned in the inmost recess of my heart. Never can I cease to feel the loss and to deplore it. Grief for her is too sacred ever to be profaned on this day, which shall be, during my existence, marked by a recollection of her virtues.

"On the 3d of January, 1783, I was united by the holiest bonds to the woman I adored. From the moment of our union to that of our separation, I never ceased to thank Heaven for this its best gift. Not a moment passed in which I did not consider her as a blessing from which the chief happiness of my life was derived. This never-dying sentiment, originating in love, was cherished by a long and close observation of as amiable and estimable qualities as ever adorned

lars. "If he does not go there I give him fifty dollars." In case it should be found "impracticable to liberate" Robin, "I desire that he may choose his master among my sons, or if he prefer my daughter that he may be held in trust for her and her family as is the other property bequeathed in trust for her, and that he may always be treated as a faithful and meritorious servant." (Will and Codicils of John Marshall, Records of Henrico County, Richmond, and Fauquier County, Warrenton, Virginia.)

the female bosom. To a person which in youth was very attractive, to manners uncommonly pleasing, she added a fine understanding, and the sweetest temper which can accompany a just and modest sense of what was due to herself.

"She was educated with a profound reverence for religion, which she preserved to her last moments. This sentiment, among her earliest and deepest impressions, gave a colouring to her whole life. Hers was the religion taught by the Saviour of man. She was a firm believer in the faith inculcated by the Church (Episcopal) in which she was bred.

"I have lost her, and with her have lost the solace of my life! Yet she remains still the companion of my retired hours, still occupies my inmost bosom. When alone and unemployed, my mind still recurs to her. More than a thousand times since the 25th of December, 1831, have I repeated to myself the beautiful lines written by General Burgoyne, under a similar affliction, substituting 'Mary' for 'Anna':

" ' Encompass'd in an angel's frame,
     An angel's virtues lay:
 Too soon did Heaven assert its claim
     And take its own away!
 My Mary's worth, my Mary's charms,
     Can never more return!
 What now shall fill these widow'd arms?
     Ah, me! my Mary's urn!
     Ah, me! ah, me! my Mary's urn!' " [1]

After his wife's death, Marshall arranged to live at "Leeds Manor," Fauquier County, a large house

[1] Meade, II, footnote to 222. It would seem that Marshall showed this tribute to no one during his lifetime except, perhaps, to his children. At any rate, it was first made public in Bishop Meade's book in 1857.

on part of the Fairfax estate which he had given to his son, James Keith Marshall. A room, with very thick walls to keep out the noise of his son's many children, was built for him, adjoining the main dwelling. Here he brought his library, papers, and many personal belongings. His other sons and their families lived not far away; "Leeds Manor" was in the heart of the country where he had grown to early manhood; and there he expected to spend his few remaining years.[1] He could not, however, tear himself from his Richmond home, where he continued to live most of the time until his death.[2]

When fully recovered from his operation, Marshall seemed to acquire fresh strength. He "is in excellent health, never better, and as firm and robust in mind as in body," Story informs Charles Sumner.[3]

The Chief Justice was, however, profoundly depressed. The course that President Jackson was then pursuing — his attitude toward the Supreme Court in the Georgia controversy,[4] his arbitrary and violent rule, his hostility to the second Bank of the United States — alarmed and distressed Marshall.

The Bank had finally justified the brightest predictions of its friends. Everywhere in the country its notes were as good as gold, while abroad they were often above par.[5] Its stock was owned in every

---

[1] Statements to the author by Miss Elizabeth Marshall of "Leeds Manor," and by Judge J. K. N. Norton of Alexandria, Va.

[2] Statement to the author by Miss Emily Harvie. Most of Marshall's letters to Story during these years were written from Richmond.

[3] Story to Sumner, Feb. 6, 1833, Story, II, 120.   [4] See *infra*, 540–51.

[5] See Catterall, 407, 421–22, 467; and see especially Parton: *Jackson*, III, 257–58.

nation and widely distributed in America.[1] Up to the time when Jackson began his warfare upon the Bank, the financial management of Nicholas Biddle had been as brilliant as it was sound.[2]

But popular hostility to the Bank had never ceased. In addition to the old animosity toward any central institution of finance, charges were made that directors of certain branches of the Bank had used their power to interfere in politics. As implacable as they were unjust were the assaults made by Democratic politicians upon Jeremiah Mason, director of the branch at Portsmouth, New Hampshire. Had the Bank consented to Mason's removal, it is possible that Jackson's warfare on it would not have been prosecuted.[3]

The Bank's charter was to expire in 1836. In his first annual Message to Congress the President briefly called attention to the question of rechartering the institution. The constitutionality of the Bank Act was doubtful at best, he intimated, and the Bank certainly had not established a sound and uniform currency.[4] In his next Message, a year later, Jackson repeated more strongly his attack upon the Bank.[5]

Two years afterwards, on the eve of the Presidential campaign of 1832, the friends of the Bank in Congress passed, by heavy majorities, a bill extend-

---

[1] Catterall, Appendix IX, 508.

[2] *Ib.* chaps. V and VII. Biddle was appointed director of the Bank by President Monroe in 1819, and displayed such ability that, in 1823, he was elected president of the institution. Not until he received information that Jackson was hostile to the Bank did Biddle begin the morally wrong and practically unwise policy of loaning money without proper security to editors and members of Congress.

[3] Parton: *Jackson*, III, 260. [4] Richardson, II, 462. [5] *Ib.* 528–29.

ing the charter for fifteen years after March 3, 1836, the date of its expiration.[1] The principal supporters of this measure were Clay and Webster and, indeed, most of the weighty men in the National Legislature. But they were enemies of Jackson, and he looked upon the rechartering of the Bank as a personal affront.

On July 4, 1832, the bill was sent to the President. Six days later he returned it with his veto. Jackson's veto message was as able as it was cunning. Parts of it were demagogic appeals to popular passion; but the heart of it was an attack upon Marshall's opinions in M'Culloch *vs.* Maryland and Osborn *vs.* The Bank.

The Bank is a monopoly, its stockholders and directors a "privileged order"; worse still, the institution is rapidly passing into the hands of aliens —"already is almost a third of the stock in foreign hands." If we must have a bank, let it be "*purely American.*" This aristocratic, monopolistic, un-American concern exists by the authority of an unconstitutional act of Congress. Even worse is the rechartering act which he now vetoed.

The decision of the Supreme Court in the Bank cases, settled nothing, said Jackson. Marshall's opinions were, for the most part, erroneous and "ought not to control the co-ordinate authorities of this Government. The Congress, the Executive, and the Court must each for itself be guided by its own opinion of the Constitution. . . It is as much the

---

[1] See Catterall, 235. For account of the fight for the Bank Bill see *ib.* chap. x.

duty of the House of Representatives, of the Senate, and of the President to decide upon the constitutionality of any bill or resolution which may be presented to them for passage or approval as it is of the supreme judges when it may be brought before them for judicial decision.

"The opinion of the judges has no more authority over Congress than the opinion of Congress has over the judges, and on that point the President is independent of both. The authority of the Supreme Court must not, therefore, be permitted to control the Congress or the Executive when acting in their legislative capacities, but to have only such influence as the force of their reasoning may deserve." [1]

But, says Jackson, the court did not decide that "all features of this corporation are compatible with the Constitution." He quotes — and puts in italics — Marshall's statement that "*where the law is not prohibited and is really calculated to effect any of the objects intrusted to the Government, to undertake here to inquire into the degree of its necessity would be to pass the line which circumscribes the judicial department and to tread on legislative ground.*" This language, insists Jackson, means that "it is the exclusive province of Congress and the President to decide whether the particular features of this act are *necessary* and *proper* . . and therefore constitutional, or *unnecessary* and *improper*, and therefore unconstitutional." [2] Thereupon Jackson points out what he considers to be the defects of the bill.

Congress has no power to "grant exclusive privi-

[1] Richardson, II, 580–82.   [2] *Ib.* 582–83.

leges or monopolies," except in the District of Columbia and in the matter of patents and copyrights. "Every act of Congress, therefore, which attempts, by grants of monopolies or sale of exclusive privileges for a limited time, or a time without limit, to restrict or extinguish its own discretion in the choice of means to execute its delegated powers, is equivalent to a legislative amendment of the Constitution, and palpably unconstitutional." [1] Jackson fiercely attacks Marshall's opinion that the States cannot tax the National Bank and its branches.

The whole message is able, adroit, and, on its face, plainly intended as a campaign document.[2] A shrewd appeal is made to the State banks. Popular jealousy and suspicion of wealth and power are skillfully played upon: "The rich and powerful" always use governments for "their selfish purposes." When laws are passed "to grant titles, gratuities, and exclusive privileges, to make the rich richer and the potent more powerful, the humble members of society — the farmers, mechanics, and laborers — who have neither the time nor the means of securing like favors to themselves, have a right to complain of the injustice of their Government.

"There are no necessary evils in government," says Jackson. "Its evils exist only in its abuses. If it would confine itself to equal protection, and, as

---

[1] Richardson, ii, 584.

[2] Jackson's veto message was used with tremendous effect in the Presidential campaign of 1832. There cannot be the least doubt that the able politicians who managed Jackson's campaign and, indeed, shaped his Administration, designed that the message should be put to this use. These politicians were William B. Lewis, Amos Kendall, Martin Van Buren, and Samuel Swartwout.

Heaven does its rains, shower its favors alike on the high and the low, the rich and the poor, it would be an unqualified blessing" — thus he runs on to his conclusion.[1]

The masses of the people, particularly those of the South, responded with wild fervor to the President's assault upon the citadel of the "money power." John Marshall, the defender of special privilege, had said that the Bank law was protected by the Constitution; but Andrew Jackson, the champion of the common people, declared that it was prohibited by the Constitution. Hats in the air, then, and loud cheers for the hero who had dared to attack and to overcome this financial monster as he had fought and beaten the invading British!

Marshall was infinitely disgusted. He informs Story of Virginia's applause of Jackson's veto: "We are up to the chin in politics. Virginia was always insane enough to be opposed to the Bank of The United States, and therefore hurras for the veto. But we are a little doubtful how it may work in . Pennsylvania. It is not difficult to account for the part New York may take. She has sagacity enough to see her interest in putting down the present bank. Her mercantile position gives her a controul, a commanding controul, over the currency and the exchanges of the country, if there be no Bank of The United States. Going for herself she may approve this policy; but Virginia ought not to drudge for her benefit." [2]

[1] Richardson, ii, 590–91.

[2] Marshall to Story, Aug. 2, 1832, *Proceedings, Mass. Hist. Soc.* 2d Series, xiv, 349–51.

Jackson did not sign the bill for the improvement of rivers and harbors, passed at the previous session of Congress, because, as he said, he had not "sufficient time .. to examine it before the adjournment." [1] Everybody took the withholding of his signature as a veto. [2] This bill included a feasible project for making the Virginia Capital accessible to seagoing vessels. Even this action of the President was applauded by Virginians:

"We show our wisdom most strikingly in approving the veto on the harbor bill also," Marshall writes Story. "That bill contained an appropriation intended to make Richmond a seaport, which she is not at present, for large vessels fit to cross the Atlantic. The appropriation was whittled down in the House of Representatives to almost nothing. . . Yet we wished the appropriation because we were confident that Congress when correctly informed, would add the necessary sum. This too is vetoed; and for this too our sagacious politicians are thankful. We seem to think it the summit of human wisdom, or rather of American patriotism, to preserve our poverty." [3]

During the Presidential campaign of 1832, Marshall all but despaired of the future of the Republic.

[1] Richardson, II, 638. There was a spirited contest in the House over this bill. (See *Debates*, 22d Cong. 1st Sess. 2438–44, 3248–57, 3286.) It reached the President at the end of the session, so that he had only to refuse to sign it, in order to kill the measure.

[2] In fact Jackson did send a message to Congress on December 6, 1832, explaining his reasons for having let the bill die. (Richardson, II, 638–39.)

[3] Marshall to Story, Aug. 2, 1832, *Proceedings, Mass. Hist. Soc.* 2d Series, XIV, 350.

The autocracy of Jackson's reign; the popular enthusiasm which greeted his wildest departures from
established usage and orderly government; the state
of the public mind, indicated everywhere by the encouragement of those whom Marshall believed to be
theatrical and adventurous demagogues — all these
circumstances perturbed and saddened him.

And for the time being, his fears were wholly justified. Triumphantly reëlected, Jackson pursued
the Bank relentlessly. Finally he ordered that the
Government funds should no longer be deposited in
that hated institution. Although that desperate act
brought disaster on business throughout the land,
it was acclaimed by the multitude. In alarm and
despair, Marshall writes Story: "We [Virginians] are
insane on the subject of the Bank. Its friends, who
are not numerous, dare not, a few excepted, to avow
themselves."[1]

But the sudden increase and aggressiveness of
disunion sentiment oppressed Marshall more heavily
than any other public circumstance of his last years.
The immediate occasion for the recrudescence of

[1] Marshall to Story, Dec. 3, 1834, *Proceedings, Mass. Hist. Soc.* 2d
Series, xiv, 359.

The outspoken and irritable Kent expressed the conservatives'
opinion of Jackson almost as forcibly as Ames stated their views of
Jefferson: "I look upon Jackson as a detestable, ignorant, reckless,
vain and malignant Tyrant. . . This American Elective Monarchy
frightens me. The Experiment, with its foundations laid on universal
Suffrage and an unfettered and licentious Press is of too violent a nature for our excitable People. We have not in our large cities, if we have
in our country, moral firmness enough to bear it. *It racks the machine
too much.*" (Kent to Story, April 11, 1834, Story MSS. Mass. Hist.
Soc.) In this letter Kent perfectly states Marshall's convictions, which
were shared by nearly every judge and lawyer in America who was
not "in politics."

Localism was the Tariff. Since the Tariff of 1816 the South had been discontented with the protection afforded the manufacturers of the North and East; and had made loud outcry against the protective Tariff of 1824. The Southern people felt that their interests were sacrificed for the benefit of the manufacturing sections; they believed that all that they produced had to be sold in a cheap, unprotected market, and all that they purchased had to be bought in a dear, protected market; they were convinced that the protective tariff system, and, indeed, the whole Nationalist policy, meant the ruin of the South.

Moreover, they began to see that the power that could enact a protective tariff, control commerce, make internal improvements, could also control slavery — perhaps abolish it.[1] Certainly that was "the spirit" of Marshall's construction of the Constitution, they said. "Sir," exclaimed Robert S. Garnett of Virginia during the debate in the House on the Tariff of 1824, "we must look very little to consequences if we do not perceive in the spirit of this construction, combined with the political fanaticism of the period, reason to anticipate, at no distant day, the usurpation, on the part of Congress, of the right to legislate upon a subject which, if you once touch, will inevitably throw this country into revolution — I mean that of slavery. . . Can whole nations be mistaken? When I speak of nations, I mean Virginia, the Carolinas, and other great Southern commonwealths."[2]

John Carter of South Carolina warned the House

---

[1] See *supra*, 420.   [2] *Annals*, 18th Cong. 1st Sess. 2097.

not to pass a law "which would, as to this portion of the Union, be registered on our statute books as a dead letter." [1] James Hamilton, Jr., of the same State, afterwards a Nullification Governor, asked: "Is it nothing to weaken the attachment of one section of this confederacy to the bond of Union? . . Is it nothing to sow the seeds of incurable alienation?" [2]

The Tariff of 1828 alarmed and angered the Southern people to the point of frenzy. "The interests of the South have been . . shamefully sacrificed!" cried Hayne in the Senate. "Her feelings have been disregarded; her wishes slighted; her honest pride insulted!" [3] So enraged were Southern Representatives that, for the most part, they declined to speak. Hamilton expressed their sentiments. He disdained to enter into the "chaffering" about the details of the bill.[4] "You are coercing us to inquire, whether we can afford to belong to a confederacy in which severe restrictions, tending to an ultimate prohibition of foreign commerce, is its established policy.[5] . . Is it . . treason, sir, to tell you that there is a condition of public feeling throughout the southern part of this confederacy, which no prudent man will treat with contempt, and no man who loves his country will not desire to see allayed? [6] . . I trust, sir, that this cup may pass from us. . . But, if an adverse destiny should be ours — if we are doomed to drink 'the waters of bitterness,' in their utmost woe, . . South Carolina will be found on the side of those principles, standing firmly, on the very ground which

[1] *Annals*, 18th Cong. 1st Sess. 2163.   [2] *Ib.* 2208.
[3] *Debates*, 20th Cong. 1st Sess. 746.   [4] *Ib.* 2431.
[5] *Ib.* 2434.   [6] *Ib.* 2435.

is canonized by that revolution which has made us what we are, and imbued us with the spirit of a free and sovereign people." [1]

Retaliation, even forcible resistance, was talked throughout the South when this "Tariff of Abominations," as the Act of 1828 was called, became a law. The feeling in South Carolina especially ran high. Some of her ablest men proposed that the State should tax all articles [2] protected by the tariff. Pledges were made at public meetings not to buy protected goods manufactured in the North. At the largest gathering in the history of the State, resolutions were passed demanding that all trade with tariff States be stopped. [3] Nullification was proposed. [4] The people wildly acclaimed such a method of righting their wrongs, and Calhoun gave to the world his famous "Exposition," a treatise based on the Jeffersonian doctrine of thirty years previous. [5]

A little more than a year after the passage of the Tariff of 1824, and the publication of Marshall's opinions in Osborn vs. The Bank and Gibbons vs. Ogden, Jefferson had written Giles of the "encroachments" by the National Government, particularly by the Supreme Court and by Congress. How should these invasions of the rights of the States be checked? "Reason and argument? You might as well reason

---

[1] Debates, 20th Cong. 1st Sess. 2437.

[2] This was the plan of George McDuffie. Calhoun approved it. (Houston: A Critical Study of Nullification in South Carolina, 70–71.)

[3] Ib.　　　　　　　　　[4] Ib. 75.

[5] Calhoun's "Exposition" was reported by a special committee of the South Carolina House of Representatives on December 19, 1828. It was not adopted, however, but was printed, and is included in Statutes at Large of South Carolina, edited by Thomas Cooper, I, 247–73.

and argue with the marble columns encircling them [Congress and the Supreme Court]. . . Are we then *to stand to our arms?* . . No. That must be the last resource." But the States should denounce the acts of usurpation "until their accumulation shall overweigh that of separation." [1] Jefferson's letter, written only six months before his death, was made public just as the tide of belligerent Nullification was beginning to rise throughout the South.[2]

At the same time defiance of National authority came also from Georgia, the cause being as distinct from the tariff as the principle of resistance was identical. This cause was the forcible seizure, by Georgia, of the lands of the Cherokee Indians and the action of the Supreme Court in cases growing out of Georgia's policy and the execution of it.

By numerous treaties between the National Government and the Cherokee Nation, the Indians were guaranteed protection in the enjoyment of their lands. When Georgia, in 1802, ceded her claim to that vast territory stretching westward to the Mississippi, it had been carefully provided that the lands of the Indians should be preserved from seizure or entry without their consent, and that their rights should be defended from invasion or disturbance. The Indian titles were to be extinguished, however, as soon as this could be done peaceably, and without inordinate expense.

In 1827, these Georgia Cherokees, who were highly civilized, adopted a constitution, set up a

---

[1] Jefferson to Giles, Dec. 26, 1825, *Works:* Ford, XII, 425–26.
[2] Niles, XXV, 48.

government of their own modeled upon that of the
United States, and declared themselves a sovereign
independent nation.[1] Immediately thereafter the
Legislature of Georgia passed resolutions declaring
that the Cherokee lands belonged to the State "absolutely" — that the Indians were only "tenants
at her will"; that Georgia had the right to, and
would, extend her laws throughout her "conventional limits," and "coerce obedience to them from all
descriptions of people, be they white, red, or black."[2]

Deliberately, but without delay, the State enacted
laws taking over the Cherokee lands, dividing them
into counties, and annulling "all laws, usages and customs" of the Indians.[3] The Cherokees appealed to
President Jackson, who rebuffed them and upheld
Georgia.[4] Gold was discovered in the Indian country, and white adventurers swarmed to the mines.[5]
Georgia passed acts forbidding the Indians to hold
courts, or to make laws or regulations for the tribe.
White persons found in the Cherokee country without a license from the Governor were, upon conviction, to be imprisoned at hard labor for four years.
A State guard was established to "protect" the
mines and arrest any one "detected in a violation
of the laws of this State." [6] Still other acts equally
oppressive were passed.[7]

[1] See Phillips: *Georgia and State Rights*, in *Annual Report, Am. Hist.
Ass'n* (1901), ii, 71.

[2] Resolution of Dec. 27, 1827, *Laws of Georgia, 1827*, 249; and
see Phillips, 72.

[3] Act of Dec. 20, *Laws of Georgia, 1828*, 88–89.

[4] Parton: *Jackson*, iii, 272.   [5] Phillips, 72.

[6] Act of Dec. 22, *Laws of Georgia, 1830*, 114–17.

[7] Act of Dec. 23, *ib.* 118; Dec. 21, *ib.* 127–43; Dec. 22, *ib.* 145–46.

On the advice of William Wirt, then Attorney-General of the United States, and of John Sergeant of Philadelphia, the Indians applied to the Supreme Court for an injunction to stop Georgia from executing these tyrannical statutes. The whole country was swept by a tempest of popular excitement. South and North took opposite sides. The doctrine of State Rights, in whose name internal improvements, the Tariff, the Bank, and other Nationalist measures had been opposed, was invoked in behalf of Georgia.

The Administration tried to induce the Cherokees to exchange their farms, mills, and stores in Georgia for untamed lands in the Indian Territory. The Indians sent a commission to investigate that far-off region, which reported that it was unfit for agriculture and that, once there, the Cherokees would have to fight savage tribes.[1] Again they appealed to the President; again Jackson told them that Georgia had absolute authority over them. Angry debates arose in Congress over a bill to send the reluctant natives to the wilds of the then remote West.[2]

Such was the origin of the case of The Cherokee Nation *vs.* The State of Georgia.[3] At Wirt's request,

---

[1] Wirt to Carr, June 21, 1830, Kennedy, II, 292–93.

[2] See *Debates*, 21st Cong. 1st Sess. 309–57, 359–67, 374–77, 994–1133. For the text of this bill as it passed the House see *ib.* 1135–36. It became a law May 28, 1830. (*U.S. Statutes at Large*, IV, 411.) For an excellent account of the execution of this measure see Abel: *The History of the Events Resulting in Indian Consolidation West of the Mississippi River, Annual Report, Am. Hist. Ass'n*, 1906, I, 381–407. This essay, by Dr. Anne Héloise Abel, is an exhaustive and accurate treatment of the origin, development, and execution of the policy pursued by the National and State Governments toward the Indians. Dr. Abel attaches a complete bibliography and index to her brochure.

[3] 5 Peters, 1.

Judge Dabney Carr laid the whole matter before Marshall, Wirt having determined to proceed with it or to drop it as the Chief Justice should advise. Marshall, of course, declined to express any opinion on the legal questions involved: "I have followed the debate in both houses of Congress, with profound attention and with deep interest, and have wished, most sincerely, that both the executive and legislative departments had thought differently on the subject. Humanity must bewail the course which is pursued, whatever may be the decision of policy." [1]

Before the case could be heard by the Supreme Court, Georgia availed herself of an opportunity to show her contempt for the National Judiciary and to assert her "sovereign rights." A Cherokee named George Tassels was convicted of murder in the Superior Court of Hall County, Georgia, and lay in jail

[1] Marshall to Carr, 1830, Kennedy, II, 296–97.

As a young man Marshall had thought so highly of Indians that he supported Patrick Henry's plan for white amalgamation with them. (See vol. I, 241, of this work.) Yet he did not think our general policy toward the Indians had been unwise. They were, he wrote Story, "a fierce and dangerous enemy whose love of war made them sometimes the aggressors, whose numbers and habits made them formidable, and whose cruel system of warfare seemed to justify every endeavour to remove them to a distance from civilized settlements. It was not until after the adoption of our present government that respect for our own safety permitted us to give full indulgence to those principles of humanity and justice which ought always to govern our conduct towards the aborigines when this course can be pursued without exposing ourselves to the most afflicting calamities. That time, however, is unquestionably arrived, and every oppression now exercised on a helpless people depending on our magnanimity and justice for the preservation of their existence impresses a deep stain on the American character. I often think with indignation on our disreputable conduct (as I think) in the affair of the Creeks of Georgia." (Marshall to Story, Oct. 29, 1829, *Proceedings, Mass. Hist. Soc.* 2d Series, XIV, 337–38.)

until the sentence of death should be executed. A writ of error from the Supreme Court was obtained, and Georgia was ordered to appear before that tribunal and defend the judgment of the State Court.

The order was signed by Marshall. Georgia's reply was as insulting and belligerent as it was prompt and spirited. The Legislature resolved that "the interference by the chief justice of the supreme court of the U. States, in the administration of the criminal laws of this state, . . is a flagrant violation of her rights"; that the Governor "and every other officer of this state" be directed to "disregard any and every mandate and process . . purporting to proceed from the chief justice or any associate justice of the supreme court of the United States"; that the Governor be "authorised and required, with all the force and means . . at his command . . to resist and repel any and every invasion from whatever quarter, upon the administration of the criminal laws of this state"; that Georgia refuses to become a party to "the case sought to be made before the supreme court"; and that the Governor, "by express," direct the sheriff of Hall County to execute the law in the case of George Tassels.[1]

Five days later, Tassels was hanged,[2] and the Supreme Court of the United States, powerless to vindicate its authority, defied and insulted by a "sovereign" State, abandoned by the Administration, was humiliated and helpless.

When he went home on the evening of January 4, 1831, John Quincy Adams, now a member of

---

[1] Niles, xxxix, 338. [2] *Ib.* 353.

Congress, wrote in his diary that "the resolutions of the legislature of Georgia setting at defiance the Supreme Court of the United States are published and approved in the Telegraph, the Administration newspaper at this place. . . The Constitution, the laws and treaties of the United States are prostrate in the State of Georgia. Is there any remedy for this state of things? None. Because the Executive of the United States is in League with the State of Georgia. . . This example . . will be imitated by other States, and with regard to other national interests — perhaps the tariff. . . The Union is in the most imminent danger of dissolution. . . The ship is about to founder." [1]

Meanwhile the Cherokee Nation brought its suit in the Supreme Court to enjoin the State from executing its laws, and at the February term of 1831 it was argued for the Indians by Wirt and Sergeant. Georgia disdained to appear — not for a moment would that proud State admit that the Supreme Court of the Nation could exercise any authority whatever over her.[2]

On March 18, 1831, Marshall delivered the opinion of the majority of the court, and in it he laid down the broad policy which the Government has unwaveringly pursued ever since. At the outset the Chief Justice plainly stated that his sympathies were with the Indians,[3] but that the court could not examine the merits or go into the moralities of the contro-

[1] *Memoirs, J. Q. A.*: Adams, VIII, 262–63.

[2] The argument for the Cherokee Nation was made March 12 and 14, 1831.

[3] 5 Peters, 15.

versy, because it had no jurisdiction. The Cherokees sued as a foreign nation, but, while they did indeed constitute a separate state, they were not a foreign nation. The relation of the Indians to the United States is "unlike that of any other two people in existence." The territory comprises a "part of the United States." [1]

In our foreign affairs and commercial regulations, the Indians are subject to the control of the National Government. "They acknowledge themselves in their treaties to be under the protection of the United States." They are not, then, foreign nations, but rather "domestic dependent nations. . . They are in a state of pupilage." Foreign governments consider them so completely under our "sovereignty and dominion" that it is universally conceded that the acquisition of their lands or the making of treaties with them would be "an invasion of our territory, and an act of hostility." By the Constitution power is given Congress to regulate commerce among the States, with foreign nations, and with Indian tribes, these terms being "entirely distinct." [2]

The Cherokees not being a foreign nation, the Supreme Court has no jurisdiction in a suit brought by them in that capacity, said Marshall. Furthermore, the court was asked "to control the Legislature of Georgia, and to restrain the exertion of its physical force" — a very questionable "interposition," which "savors too much of the exercise of political power to be within the proper province

[1] 5 Peters, 16–17.   [2] *Ib.* 17–18.

of the judicial department." In "a proper case with proper parties," the court might, perhaps, decide "the mere question of right" to the Indian lands. But the suit of the Cherokee Nation against Georgia is not such a case.

Marshall closes with a reflection upon Jackson in terms much like those with which, many years earlier, he had so often rebuked Jefferson: "If it be true that the Cherokee Nation have rights, this is not the tribunal in which those rights are to be asserted. If it be true that wrongs have been inflicted, and that still greater are to be apprehended, this is not the tribunal which can redress the past or prevent the future." [1]

In this opinion the moral force of Marshall was displayed almost as much as in the case of the Schooner Exchange. [2] He was friendly to the whole Indian race; he particularly detested Georgia's treatment of the Cherokees; he utterly rejected the State Rights theory on which the State had acted; and he could easily have decided in favor of the wronged and harried Indians, as the dissent of Thompson and Story proves. But the statesman and jurist again rose above the man of sentiment, law above emotion, the enduring above the transient.

[1] 5 Peters, 20. Justice Smith Thompson dissented in an opinion of immense power in which Story concurred. These two Justices maintained that in legal controversies, such as that between the Cherokees and Georgia, the Indian tribe must be treated as a foreign nation. (*Ib.* 50–80.)

Thompson's opinion was as Nationalist as any ever delivered by Marshall. It well expressed the general opinion of the North, which was vigorously condemnatory of Georgia as the ruthless despoiler of the rights of the Indians and the robber of their lands.

[2] See *supra,* 121–25.

As a "foreign state" the Indians had lost, but the constitutionality of Georgia's Cherokee statutes had not been affirmed. Wirt and Sergeant had erred as to the method of attacking that legislation. Another proceeding by Georgia, however, soon brought the validity of her expansion laws before the Supreme Court. Among the missionaries who for years had labored in the Cherokee Nation was one Samuel A. Worcester, a citizen of Vermont. This brave minister, licensed by the National Government, employed by the American Board of Commissioners for Foreign Missions, appointed by President John Quincy Adams to be postmaster at New Echota, a Cherokee town, refused, in company with several other missionaries, to leave the Indian country.

Worcester and a Reverend Mr. Thompson were arrested by the Georgia guard. The Superior Court of Gwinnett County released them, however, on a writ of habeas corpus, because, both being licensed missionaries expending National funds appropriated for civilizing Indians, they must be considered as agents of the National Government. Moreover, Worcester was postmaster at New Echota. Georgia demanded his removal and inquired of Jackson whether the missionaries were Government agents. The President assured the State that they were not, and removed Worcester from office.[1]

Thereupon both Worcester and Thompson were promptly ordered to leave the State. But they and some other missionaries remained, and were arrested; dragged to prison — some of them with

[1] Phillips, 79.

chains around their necks; [1] tried and convicted.
Nine were pardoned upon their promise to depart
forthwith from Georgia. But Worcester and one
Elizur Butler sternly rejected the offer of clemency
on such a condition and were put to hard labor in
the penitentiary.

From the judgment of the Georgia court, Worcester and Butler appealed to the Supreme Court of
the United States. Once more Marshall and Georgia
confronted each other; again the Chief Justice faced
a hostile President far more direct and forcible than
Jefferson, but totally lacking in the subtlety and skill
of that incomparable politician. Thrilling and highly
colored accounts of the treatment of the missionaries
had been published in every Northern newspaper;
religious journals made conspicuous display of soul-
stirring narratives of the whole subject; feeling in
the North ran high; resentment in the South rose
to an equal degree.

This time Georgia did more than ignore the Supreme Court as in the case of George Tassels and in
the suit of the Cherokee Nation; she formally refused to appear; formally denied the right of that
tribunal to pass upon the decisions of her courts. [2]
Never would Georgia so "compromit her dignity as
a sovereign State," never so "yield her rights as a
member of the Confederacy." The new Governor,
Wilson Lumpkin, avowed that he would defend
those rights by every means in his power. [3] When
the case of Worcester vs. Georgia came on for hearing before the Supreme Court, no one answered for

[1] See McMaster, vi, 47–50.   [2] Phillips, 81.   [3] Ib. 80–81.

the State. Wirt, Sergeant, and Elisha W. Chester appeared for the missionaries as they had for the Indians.[1] Wirt and Sergeant made extended and powerful arguments.[2]

Marshall's opinion, delivered March 3, 1832, is one of the noblest he ever wrote. "The legislative power of a State, the controlling power of the Constitution and laws of the United States, the rights, if they have any, the political existence of a once numerous and powerful people, the personal liberty of a citizen, are all involved," begins the aged Chief Justice.[3] Does the act of the Legislature of Georgia, under which Worcester was convicted, violate the Constitution, laws, and treaties of the United States?[4] That act is "an assertion of jurisdiction over the Cherokee Nation."[5]

He then goes into a long historical review of the relative titles of the natives and of the white discoverers of America; of the effect upon these titles of the numerous treaties with the Indians; of the acts of Congress relating to the red men and their lands; and of previous laws of Georgia on these subjects.[6] This part of his opinion is the most extended and exhaustive historical analysis Marshall ever made in any judicial utterance, except that on the law of treason during the trial of Aaron Burr.[7]

Then comes his condensed, unanswerable, brilliant conclusion: "A weaker power does not surrender its independence, its rights to self-govern-

[1] 6 Peters, 534–35.
[2] Story to his wife, Feb. 26, 1832, Story, II, 84.
[3] 6 Peters, 536.   [4] Ib. 537–42.   [5] Ib. 542.   [6] Ib. 542–61.
[7] See vol. III, 504–13, of this work.

ment, by associating with a stronger, and taking its protection. A weak state, in order to provide for its safety, may place itself under the protection of one more powerful, without stripping itself of the right of self-government, and ceasing to be a state. . . The Cherokee Nation . . is a distinct community, occupying its own territory . . in which the laws of Georgia can have no force, and which the citizens of Georgia have no right to enter but with the assent of the Cherokees themselves, or in conformity with treaties, and with the acts of Congress. The whole intercourse between the United States and this nation is by our Constitution and laws vested in the government of the United States."

The Cherokee Acts of the Georgia Legislature "are repugnant to the constitution, laws and treaties of the United States. They interfere forcibly with the relations established between the United States and the Cherokee Nation." This controlling fact the laws of Georgia ignore. They violently disrupt the relations between the Indians and the United States; they are equally antagonistic to acts of Congress based upon these treaties. Moreover, "the forcible seizure and abduction" of Worcester, "who was residing in the nation with its permission and by authority of the President of the United States, is also a violation of the acts which authorize the chief magistrate to exercise this authority."

Marshall closes with a passage of eloquence almost equal to, and of higher moral grandeur than, the finest passages in M'Culloch *vs.* Maryland and in Cohens *vs.* Virginia. So the decision of the court was that the judgment of the Georgia court be "reversed and annulled." [1]

Congress was intensely excited by Marshall's opinion; Georgia was enraged; the President agitated and belligerent. In a letter to Ticknor, written five days after the judgment of the court was announced, Story accurately portrays the situation: "The decision produced a very strong sensation in both houses; Georgia is full of anger and violence. . . Probably she will resist the execution of our judgement, & if she does I do not believe the President will interfere. . . The Court has done its duty. Let the nation do theirs. If we have a government let its commands be obeyed; if we have not it is as well to know it at once, & to look to consequences." [2]

Story's forecast was justified. Georgia scoffed at Marshall's opinion, flouted the mandate of the Supreme Court. "Usurpation!" cried Governor Lumpkin. He would meet it "with the spirit of determined resistance." [3] Jackson defied the Chief Justice. "John Marshall has made his decision: — *now let him enforce it!*" the President is reported to have said.[4] Again the Supreme Court found itself powerless; the judgment in Worcester *vs.* Georgia came to nothing; the mandate was never obeyed, never heeded.[5]

---

[1] 6 Peters, 561–63.

[2] Story to Ticknor, March 8, 1832, Story, II, 83.

[3] Lumpkin's Message to the Legislature, Nov. 6, 1832, as quoted in Phillips, 82.

[4] Greeley: *The American Conflict*, I, 106; and see Phillips, 80.

[5] When the Georgia Legislature first met after the decision of the Worcester case, acts were passed to strengthen the lottery and distribution of Cherokee lands (Acts of Nov. 14, 22, and Dec. 24, 1832,

For the time being, Marshall was defeated; Nationalism was prostrate; Localism erect, strong, aggressive. Soon, however, Marshall and Nationalism were to be sustained, for the moment, by the man most dreaded by the Chief Justice, most trusted by Marshall's foes. Andrew Jackson was to astound the country by the greatest and most illogical act of his strange career — the issuance of his immortal Proclamation against Nullification.

Georgia's very first assertion of her "sovereignty" in the Indian controversy had strengthened South Carolina's fast growing determination to resist the execution of the Tariff Law. On January 25, 1830, Senator Robert Young Hayne of South Carolina, in his brilliant challenge to Webster, set forth the philosophy of Nullification: "Sir, if, the measures of the Federal Government were less oppressive, we should still strive against this usurpation. The

Laws of Georgia, 1832, 122–25, 126, 127) and to organize further the Cherokee territory under the guise of protecting the Indians. (Act of Dec. 24, 1832, *ib.* 102–05.) Having demonstrated the power of the State and the impotence of the highest court of the Nation, the Governor of Georgia, one year after Marshall delivered his opinion, pardoned Worcester and Butler, but not without protests from the people.

Two years later, Georgia's victory was sealed by a final successful defiance of the Supreme Court. One James Graves was convicted of murder; a writ of error was procured from the Supreme Court; and a citation issued to Georgia as in the case of George Tassels. The high spirit of the State, lifted still higher by three successive triumphs over the Supreme Court, received the order with mingled anger and derision. Governor Lumpkin threatened secession: "Such attempts, if persevered in, will eventuate in the dismemberment and overthrow of our great confederacy," he told the Legislature. (Governor Lumpkin's Special Message to the Georgia Legislature, Nov. 7, 1834, as quoted in Phillips, 84.)

The Indians finally were forced to remove to the Indian Territory. (See Phillips, 83.) Worcester went to his Vermont home.

South is acting on a principle she has always held sacred — resistance to unauthorized taxation." [1]

Webster's immortal reply, so far as his Constitutional argument is concerned, is little more than a condensation of the Nationalist opinions of John Marshall stated in popular and dramatic language. Indeed, some of Webster's sentences are practically mere repetitions of Marshall's, and his reasoning is wholly that of the Chief Justice.

"We look upon the States, not as separated, but as united under the same General Government, having interests, common, associated, intermingled. In war and peace, we are one; in commerce, one; because the authority of the General Government reaches to war and peace, and to the regulation of commerce." [2]

What is the capital question in dispute? It is this: "Whose prerogative is it to decide on the constitutionality or unconstitutionality of the laws?" [3] Can States decide? Can States "annul the law of Congress"? Hayne, expressing the view of South Carolina, had declared that they could. He had based his argument upon the Kentucky and Virginia Resolu-

---

[1] *Debates*, 21st Cong. 1st Sess. 58. The debate between Webster and Hayne occurred on a resolution offered by Senator Samuel Augustus Foot of Connecticut, "that the Committee on Public Lands be instructed to inquire into the expediency of limiting for a certain period the sales of public lands," etc. (*Ib.* 11.) The discussion of this resolution, which lasted more than three months (see *ib.* 11–302), quickly turned to the one great subject of the times, the power of the National Government and the rights of the States. It was on this question that the debate between Webster and Hayne took place.

[2] *Ib.* 64. Compare with Marshall's language in Cohens *vs.* Virginia, *supra*, 355.

[3] *Debates*, 21st Cong. 1st Sess. 73.

tions — upon the theory that the States, and not the people, had created the Constitution; that the States, and not the people, had established the General Government.

But is this true? asked Webster. He answered by paraphrasing Marshall's words in M'Culloch *vs.* Maryland: "It is, sir, the people's constitution, the people's Government; made for the people; made by the people; and answerable to the people.[1] The people . . have declared that this Constitution shall be the supreme law.[2] . . Who is to judge between the people and the Government?"[3]

The Constitution settles that question by declaring that "the judicial power shall extend to all cases arising under the Constitution and laws."[4] Because of this the Union is secure and strong. "Instead of one tribunal, established by all, responsible to all, with power to decide for all, shall constitutional questions be left to four and twenty popular bodies, each at liberty to decide for itself, and none bound to respect the decisions of others?"[5]

Then Webster swept grandly forward to that famous peroration ending with the words which in

[1] See Marshall's statement of this principle, *supra*, 293, 355.

[2] *Debates*, 21st Cong. 1st Sess. 74.
This was the Constitutional theory of the Nationalists. As a matter of fact, it was not, perhaps, strictly true. There can be little doubt that a majority of the people did not favor the Constitution when adopted by the Convention and ratified by the States. Had manhood suffrage existed at that time, and had the Constitution been submitted directly to the people, it is highly probable that it would have been rejected. (See vol. i, chaps. ix–xii, of this work.)

[3] *Debates*, 21st Cong. 1st Sess. 76. See chap. iii, vol. iii, of this work.

[4] *Debates*, 21st Cong. 1st Sess. 78.

[5] *Ib.* See Marshall's opinion in Cohens *vs.* Virginia, *supra*, 347–57.

time became the inspiring motto of the whole American people: "Liberty *and* Union, now and forever, one and inseparable!" [1]

Immediately after the debate between Hayne and Webster, Nullification gathered force in South Carolina. Early in the autumn of 1830, Governor Stephen Decatur Miller spoke at a meeting of the Sumter district of that State. He urged that a State convention be called for the purpose of declaring null and void the Tariff of 1828. Probably the National courts would try to enforce that law, he said, but South Carolina would "refuse to sustain" it. Nullification involved no danger, and if it did, what matter! — "those who fear to defend their rights, have none. Their property belongs to the banditti: they are only tenants at will of their own firesides." [2]

Public excitement steadily increased; at largely attended meetings ominous resolutions were adopted. "The attitude which the federal government continues to assume towards the southern states, calls for decisive and unequivocal resistance." So ran a typical declaration of a gathering of citizens of Georgetown, South Carolina, in December, 1830. [3]

In the Senate, Josiah Stoddard Johnston of Louisiana, but Connecticut-born, made a speech denouncing the doctrine of Nullification, asserting the supremacy of the National Government, and declaring that the Supreme Court was the final judge of the constitutionality of legislation. "It has fulfilled the design of its institution; . . it has given form and consistency to the constitution, and uniformity to

[1] *Debates*, 21st Cong. 1st Sess. 80.　[2] Niles, xxxix, 118.　[3] *Ib.* 330.

the laws." [1] Nullification, said Johnston, means "either disunion, or civil war; or, in the language of the times, disunion and blood." [2]

The Louisiana Senator sent his speech to Marshall, who answered that "it certainly is not among the least extraordinary of the doctrines of the present day that such a question [Nullification] should be seriously debated." [3]

All Nullification arguments were based on the Kentucky and Virginia Resolutions. Madison was still living, and Edward Everett asked him for his views. In a letter almost as Nationalist as Marshall's opinions, the venerable statesman replied at great length and with all the ability and clearness of his best years.

The decision by States of the constitutionality of acts of Congress would destroy the Nation, he wrote. Such decision was the province of the National Judiciary. While the Supreme Court had been criticized, perhaps justly in some cases, "still it would seem that, with but few exceptions, the course of the judiciary has been hitherto sustained by the predominant sense of the nation." It was absurd to deny the "supremacy of the judicial power of the U. S. & denounce at the same time nullifying power in a State. . . A law of the land" cannot be supreme "without a supremacy in the exposition & execution of the law." Nullification was utterly destructive of the Constitution and the Union.[4]

This letter, printed in the *North American Re-*

[1] *Debates*, 21st Cong. 1st Sess. 287.   [2] *Ib.* 285.

[3] Marshall to Johnston, May 22, 1830. MSS. "Society Collection," Pa. Hist. Soc.

[4] Madison to Everett, Aug. 28, 1830, *Writings:* Hunt, IX, 383–403.

view,[1] made a strong impression on the North, but it only irritated the South. Marshall read it "with peculiar pleasure," he wrote Story: "Mr Madison . . is himself again. He avows the opinions of his best days, and must be pardoned for his oblique insinuations that some of the opinions of our Court are not approved. Contrast this delicate hint with the language Mr Jefferson has applied to us. He [Madison] is attacked . . by our Enquirer, who has arrayed his report of 1799 against his letter. I never thought that report could be completely defended; but Mr Madison has placed it upon its best ground, that the language is incautious, but is intended to be confined to a mere declaration of opinion, or is intended to refer to that ultimate right which all admit, to resist despotism, a right not exercised under a constitution, but in opposition to it." [2]

At a banquet on April 15, 1830, in celebration of Jefferson's birthday, Jackson had given a warning not to be misunderstood except by Nullifiers who had been blinded and deafened by their new political religion. "The Federal Union; — it must be preserved," was the solemn and inspiring toast proposed by the President. Southern leaders gave no heed. They apparently thought that Jackson meant to endorse Nullification, which, most illogically, they always declared to be the only method of preserving the Union peaceably.

Their denunciation of the Tariff grew ever louder; their insistence on Nullification ever fiercer, ever

---

[1] *North American Review* (1830), XXXI, 537–46.

[2] Marshall to Story, Oct. 15, 1830, *Proceedings, Mass. Hist. Soc.* 2d Series, XIV, 342–43.

more determined. To a committee of South Carolina Union men who invited him to their Fourth of
July celebration at Charleston in 1831, Jackson sent
a letter which plainly informed the Nullifiers that if
they attempted to carry out their threats, the National Government would forcibly suppress them.[1]

At last the eyes of the South were opened. At last
the South understood the immediate purpose of that
enigmatic and self-contradictory man who ruled
America, at times, in the spirit of the Czars of
Russia; at times, in the spirit of the most compromising of opportunists.

Jackson's outgiving served only to enrage the
South and especially South Carolina. The Legislature of that State replied to the President's letter
thus: "Is this Legislature to be schooled and rated by
the President of the United States? Is it to legislate
under the sword of the Commander-in-Chief? .. This
is a confederacy of sovereign States, and each may
withdraw from the confederacy when it chooses."[2]

Marshall saw clearly what the outcome was likely
to be, but yielded slowly to the despair so soon to
master him. "Things to the South wear a very
serious aspect," he tells Story. "If we can trust appearances the leaders are determined to risk all the
consequences of dismemberment. I cannot entirely
dismiss the hope that they may be deserted by
their followers — at least to such an extent as to
produce a pause at the Rubicon. They undoubtedly
believe that Virginia will support them. I think they

---

[1] Jackson to the Committee, June 14, 1831, Niles, XL, 351.
[2] *State Doc. Fed. Rel.*: Ames, 167–68.

are mistaken both with respect to Virginia and North Carolina. I do not think either State will embrace this mad and wicked measure. New Hampshire and Maine seem to belong to the tropics. It is time for New Hampshire to part with Webster and Mason. She has no longer any use for such men." [1]

As the troubled weeks passed, Marshall's apprehension increased. Story, profoundly concerned, wrote the Chief Justice that he could see no light in the increasing darkness. "If the prospects of our country inspire you with gloom," answered Marshall, "how do you think a man must be affected who partakes of all your opinions and whose geographical position enables him to see a great deal that is concealed from you? I yield slowly and reluctantly to the conviction that our constitution cannot last. I had supposed that north of the Potowmack a firm and solid government competent to the security of rational liberty might be preserved. Even that now seems doubtful. The case of the south seems to me to be desperate. Our opinions are incompatible with a united government even among ourselves. The union has been prolonged thus far by miracles. I fear they cannot continue." [2]

Congress heeded the violent protest of South Carolina — perhaps it would be more accurate to say that Congress obeyed Andrew Jackson. In 1832 it reduced tariff duties; but the protective policy was retained. The South was infuriated — if the principle were recognized, said Southern men, what could

[1] Marshall to Story, Aug. 2, 1832, *Proceedings, Mass. Hist. Soc.* 2d Series, xiv, 350.
[2] Same to same, Sept. 22, 1832, *ib.* 351–52.

they expect at a later day when this capitalistic, manufacturing North would be still stronger and the unmoneyed and agricultural South still weaker?

South Carolina especially was frantic. The spirit of the State was accurately expressed by R. Barnwell Smith at a Fourth of July celebration: "If the fire and the sword of war are to be brought to our dwellings, . . let them come! Whilst a bush grows which may be dabbled with blood, or a pine tree stands to support a rifle, let them come!" [1] At meetings all over the State treasonable words were spoken. Governor James Hamilton, Jr., convened the Legislature in special session and the election of a State convention was ordered.

"Let us act, next October, at the ballot box — next November, in the state house — and afterwards, should any further action be necessary, let it be where our ancestors acted, *in the field of battle*"; [2] such were the toasts proposed at banquets, such the sentiments adopted at meetings.

On November 24, 1832, the State Convention, elected [3] to consider the new Tariff Law, adopted the famous Nullification Ordinance which declared that the Tariff Acts of 1828 and 1832 were "null, void, and no law"; directed the Legislature to take measures to prevent the enforcement of those acts within South Carolina; forbade appeal to the Supreme Court of the United States from South Carolina courts in any case where the Tariff Law was involved; and required all State officers, civil and military, to

[1] Niles, XLII, 387.   [2] *Ib.* 388.
[3] Under Act of Oct. 26, 1832, *Statutes at Large of South Carolina*: Cooper, I, 309–10.

take oath to "obey, execute and enforce this Ordinance, and such act or acts of the Legislature as may be passed in pursuance thereof."

The Ordinance set forth that "we, the People of South Carolina, . . *Do further Declare,* that we will not submit to the application of force, on the part of the Federal Government, to reduce this State to obedience; but that we will consider" any act of the National Government to enforce the Tariff Laws "as inconsistent with the longer continuance of South Carolina in the Union: and that the People of this State . . will forthwith proceed to organize a separate Government, and to do all other acts and things which sovereign and independent States may of right do."[1]

Thereupon the Convention issued an address to the people.[2] It was long and, from the Nullification point of view, very able; it ended in an exalted, passionate appeal: "Fellow citizens, the die is now cast. NO MORE TAXES SHALL BE PAID HERE. . . Prepare for the crisis, and . . meet it as becomes men and freemen. . . Fellow citizens, DO YOUR DUTY TO YOUR COUNTRY, AND LEAVE THE CONSEQUENCES TO GOD."[3]

Excepting only at the outbreak of war could a people be more deeply stirred than were all Americans by the desperate action of South Carolina. In the North great Union meetings were held, fervid speeches made, warlike resolutions adopted. The South, at first, seemed dazed. Was war at hand? This was the question every man asked of his neighbor. A pamphlet on the situation, written by

---

[1] *Statutes at Large of South Carolina:* Cooper, I, 329–31.
[2] *Ib.* 434–45. [3] *Ib.* 444–45; also Niles, XLIII, 219–20.

some one in a state of great emotion, had been sent to Marshall, and Judge Peters had inquired about it, giving at the same time the name of the author.

"I am not surprised," answered Marshall, "that he [the author] is excited by the doctrine of nullification. It is well calculated to produce excitement in all. . . Leaving it to the courts and the custom house will be leaving it to triumphant victory, and to victory which must be attended with more pernicious consequences to our country and with more fatal consequences to its reputation than victory achieved in any other mode which rational men can devise." [1] If Nullification must prevail, John Marshall preferred that it should win by the sword rather than through the intimidation of courts.

Jackson rightly felt that his reëlection meant that the country in general approved of his attitude toward Nullification as well as that toward the Bank. He promptly answered the defiance of South Carolina. On December 10, 1832, he issued his historic Proclamation. Written by Edward Livingston,[2] Secretary of State, it is one of the ablest of American state papers. Moderate in expression, simple in style, solid in logic, it might have been composed by Marshall himself. It is, indeed, a restatement of Marshall's Nationalist reasoning and conclusions. Like the argument in Webster's Reply to Hayne, Jackson's Nullification Proclamation was a repetition of those views of the Constitution and of the nature of the American Government for which Mar-

---

[1] Marshall to Peters, Dec. 3, 1832, Peters MSS. Pa. Hist. Soc.
[2] See *supra*, footnote to 115.

shall had been fighting since Washington was made President.

As in Webster's great speech, sentences and paragraphs are in almost the very words used by Marshall in his Constitutional opinions, so in Jackson's Proclamation the same parallelism exists. Gently, but firmly, and with tremendous force, in the style and spirit of Abraham Lincoln rather than of Andrew Jackson, the Proclamation makes clear that the National laws will be executed and resistance to them will be put down by force of arms.[1]

The Proclamation was a triumph for Marshall. That the man whom he distrusted and of whom he so disapproved, whose election he had thought to be equivalent to a dissolution of the Union, should turn out to be the stern defender of National solidarity, was, to Marshall, another of those miracles which so often had saved the Republic. His disapproval of Jackson's rampant democracy, and whimsical yet arbitrary executive conduct, turned at once to hearty commendation.

"Since his last proclamation and message," testifies Story, "the Chief Justice and myself have become his warmest supporters, and shall continue so just as long as he maintains the principles contained in them. Who would have dreamed of such an occurrence?"[2] Marshall realized, nevertheless, that even the bold course pursued by the President could not permanently overcome the secession convictions of the Southern people.

---

[1] Richardson, II, 640–56; Niles, XLIII, 260–64.
[2] Story to his wife, Jan. 27, 1833, Story, II, 119.

The Union men of South Carolina who, from the beginning of the Nullification movement, had striven earnestly to stay its progress, rallied manfully.[1] Their efforts were futile — disunion sentiment swept the State. "With . . indignation and contempt," with "defiance and scorn," most South Carolinians greeted the Proclamation [2] of the man who, only three years before, had been their idol. To South Carolinians Jackson was now "a tyrant," a would-be "Cæsar," a "Cromwell," a "Bonaparte." [3]

The Legislature formally requested Hayne, now Governor, to issue a counter-proclamation,[4] and adopted spirited resolutions declaring the right of any State "to secede peaceably from the Union." One count in South Carolina's indictment of the President was thoroughly justified — his approval of Georgia's defiance of Marshall and the Supreme Court. Jackson's action, declared the resolutions, was the more "extraordinary, that he has silently, and . . with entire approbation, witnessed our sister state of Georgia avow, act upon, and carry into effect, even to the taking of life, principles identical with those now denounced by him in South Carolina." The Legislature finally resolved that the State would "repel force by force, and, relying upon the blessing of God, will maintain its liberty at all hazards." [5]

Swiftly Hayne published his reply to the President's Proclamation. It summed up all the arguments for the right of a State to decide the constitu-

---

[1] Niles, XLIII, 266–67.   [2] *Ib.* 287.   [3] *Ib.*
[4] *Statutes at Large of South Carolina:* Cooper, I, 355.   [5] *Ib.* 356–57.

tionality of acts of Congress, that had been made since the Kentucky Resolutions were written by Jefferson — that "great Apostle of American liberty . . who has consecrated these principles, and left them as a legacy to the American people, recorded by his own hand." It was Jefferson, said Hayne, who had first penned the immortal truth that "NULLIFICATION" of unconstitutional acts of Congress was the "RIGHTFUL REMEDY" of the States.[1]

In his Proclamation Jackson had referred to the National Judiciary as the ultimate arbiter of the constitutionality of National laws. How absurd such a claim by such a man, since that doctrine "has been denied by none more strongly than the President himself" in the Bank controversy and in the case of the Cherokees! "And yet when it serves the purpose of bringing odium on South Carolina, 'his native State,' the President has no hesitation in regarding the attempt of a State to release herself from the controul of the Federal Judiciary, in a matter affecting her sovereign rights, as a violation of the Constitution." [2]

In closing, Governor Hayne declares that "the time has come when it must be seen, whether the people of the several States have indeed lost the spirit of the revolution, and whether they are to become the willing instruments of an unhallowed despotism. In such a sacred cause, South Carolina will feel that she is not striking for her own, but the liberties of the Union and the RIGHTS OF MAN." [3]

[1] *Statutes at Large of South Carolina:* Cooper, I, 362.
[2] *Ib.* 360.   [3] *Ib.* 370.

Instantly [1] the Legislature enacted one law to prevent the collection of tariff duties in South Carolina; [2] another authorizing the Governor to "order into service the whole military force of this State" to resist any attempt of the National Government to enforce the Tariff Acts. [3] Even before Hayne's Proclamation was published, extensive laws had been passed for the reorganization of the militia, and the Legislature now continued to enact similar legislation. In four days fourteen such acts were passed. [4]

The spirit and consistency of South Carolina were as admirable as her theory was erroneous and narrow. If she meant what she had said, the State could have taken no other course. If, moreover, she really intended to resist the National Government, Jackson had given cause for South Carolina's militant action. As soon as the Legislature ordered the calling of the State Convention to consider the tariff, the President directed the Collector at Charleston to use every resource at the command of the Government to collect tariff duties. The commanders of the forts at Charleston were ordered to be in readiness to repel any attack. General Scott was sent to the scene of the disturbance. Military and naval dispositions were made so as to enable the National Government to strike quickly and effectively. [5]

Throughout South Carolina the rolling of drums and blare of bugles were heard. Everywhere was

---

[1] December 20, the same day that Hayne's Proclamation appeared.
[2] *Statutes at Large of South Carolina:* Cooper, I, 271–74.
[3] *Ib.* VIII, 562–64.   [4] *Ib.* 562–98.
[5] Parton: *Jackson,* III, 460–61, 472; Bassett: *Life of Andrew Jackson,* 564; MacDonald: *Jacksonian Democracy,* 156.

seen the blue cockade with palmetto button.[1] Volunteers were called for,[2] and offered themselves by thousands; in certain districts "almost the entire population" enlisted.[3] Some regiments adopted a new flag, a banner of red with a single black star in the center.[4]

Jackson attempted to placate the enraged and determined State. In his fourth annual Message to Congress he barely mentioned South Carolina's defiance, but, for the second time, urgently recommended a reduction of tariff duties. Protection, he said, "must be ultimately limited to those articles of domestic manufacture which are indispensable to our safety in time of war. . . Beyond this object we have already seen the operation of the system productive of discontent."[5]

Other Southern States, although firmly believing in South Carolina's principles and sympathetic with her cause, were alarmed by her bold course. Virginia essayed the rôle of mediator between her warlike sister and the "usurping" National Government. In his Message to the Legislature, Governor John Floyd stoutly defended South Carolina — "the land of Sumpter [sic] and of Marion." "Should force be resorted to by the federal government, the horror of the scenes hereafter to be witnessed cannot now be pictured. . . What surety has any state for her existence as a sovereign, if a difference of opinion should be punished by the sword as treason?" The situation calls for a reference of the whole ques-

---

[1] Parton: *Jackson*, III, 459. [2] Niles, XLIII, 312. [3] *Ib.* 332.
[4] Parton: *Jackson*, III, 472. [5] Richardson, II, 598–99.

tion to "the PEOPLE of the states. On you depends
in a high degree the future destiny of this republic.
It is for you now to say whether the brand of civil
war shall be thrown into the midst of these states." [1]

Mediative resolutions were instantly offered for the
appointment of a committee "to take into consideration the relations existing between the state of South
Carolina and the government of the United States,"
and the results to each and to Virginia flowing from
the Ordinance of Nullification and Jackson's Proclamation. The committee was to report "such measures as . . it may be expedient for Virginia to adopt
— the propriety of recommending a general convention to the states — and such a declaration of our
views and opinions as it may be proper for her to
express in the present fearful impending crisis, for
the protection of the right of the states, the restoration of harmony, and the preservation of the union." [2]

Only five members voted against the resolution. [3]

The committee was appointed and, on December
20, 1832, reported a set of resolutions — "worlds of
words," as Niles aptly called them — disapproving
Jackson's Proclamation; applauding his recommendation to Congress that the tariff be reduced; re-
gretting South Carolina's hasty action; deprecating
"the intervention of arms on either side"; entreat-
ing "our brethren in S. Carolina to pause in their
career"; appealing to Jackson "to withstay the
arm of force"; instructing Virginia Senators and requesting Virginia Representatives in Congress to do
their best to "procure an immediate reduction of the

[1] Niles, XLIII, 275.   [2] Ib.   [3] Ib. 276.

tariff"; and appointing two commissioners to visit
South Carolina with a view to securing an adjustment
of the dispute.[1]

With painful anxiety and grave alarm, Marshall,
then in Richmond, watched the tragic yet absurd
procession of events. Much as the doings and sayings
of the mediators and sympathizers with Nullification irritated him, serious as were his forebodings, the
situation appealed to his sense of humor. He wrote
Story an account of what was going on in Virginia.
No abler or more accurate statement of the conditions and tendencies of the period exists. Marshall's
letter is a document of historical importance. It reveals, too, the character of the man.

It was written in acknowledgment of the receipt
of "a proof sheet" of a page of Story's "Commentaries on the Constitution of the United States,"
dedicating that work to Marshall. "I am . . deeply
penetrated," says Marshall, "by the evidence it affords of the continuance of that partial esteem and
friendship which I have cherished for so many years,
and still cherish as one of the choicest treasures of
my life. The only return I can make is locked up in
my own bosom, or communicated in occasional conversation with my friends." He congratulates Story
on having finished his "Herculean task." He is sure
that Story has accomplished it with ability and "correctness," and is "certain in advance" that he will
read "every sentence with entire approbation. It
is a subject on which we concur exactly. Our opin-

---

[1] Niles, XLIII, 394–96. The resolutions, as adopted, provided for
only one commissioner. (See *infra*, 573.)

ions on it are, I believe, identical. Not so with Virginia or the South generally."

Marshall then relates what has happened in Richmond: "Our legislature is now in session, and the dominant party receives the message of the President to Congress with enthusiastic applause. Quite different was the effect of his proclamation. That paper astonished, confounded, and for a moment silenced them. In a short time, however, the power of speech was recovered, and was employed in bestowing on its author the only epithet which could possibly weigh in the scales against the name of 'Andrew Jackson,' and countervail its popularity.

"Imitating the Quaker who said the dog he wished to destroy was mad, they said Andrew Jackson had become a Federalist, even an ultra Federalist. To have said he was ready to break down and trample on every other department of the government would not have injured him, but to say that he was a Federalist — a convert to the opinions of Washington, was a mortal blow under which he is yet staggering.

"The party seems to be divided. Those who are still true to their President pass by his denunciation of all their former theories; and though they will not approve the sound opinions avowed in his proclamation are ready to denounce nullification and to support him in maintaining the union. This is going a great way for them — much farther than their former declarations would justify the expectation of, and much farther than mere love of union would carry them.

"You have undoubtedly seen the message of our

Governor and the resolutions reported by the committee to whom it was referred — a message and resolutions which you will think skillfully framed had the object been a civil war. They undoubtedly hold out to South Carolina the expectation of support from Virginia; and that hope must be the foundation on which they have constructed their plan for a southern confederacy or league.

"A want of confidence in the present support of the people will prevent any direct avowal in favor of this scheme by those whose theories and whose secret wishes may lead to it; but the people may be so entangled by the insane dogmas which have become axioms in the political creed of Virginia, and involved so inextricably in the labyrinth into which those dogmas conduct them, as to do what their sober judgement disapproves.

"On Thursday these resolutions are to be taken up, and the debate will, I doubt not, be ardent and tempestuous enough. I pretend not to anticipate the result. Should it countenance the obvious design of South Carolina to form a southern confederacy, it may conduce to a southern league — never to a southern government. Our theories are incompatible with a government for more than a single State. We can form no union which shall be closer than an alliance between sovereigns.

"In this event there is some reason to apprehend internal convulsion. The northern and western section of our State, should a union be maintained north of the Potowmack, will not readily connect itself with the South. At least such is the present belief of their most intelligent men. Any effort on their part to separate from Southern Virginia and unite with a northern confederacy may probably be punished as treason. 'We have fallen on evil times.'".

Story had sent Marshall, Webster's speech at Faneuil Hall, December 17, 1832, in which he declared that he approved the "general principles" of Jackson's Proclamation, and that "nullification . . is but another name for civil war." "I am," said Webster, "for the Union as it is; . . for the Constitution as it is." He pledged his support to the President in "maintaining this Union." [1]

Marshall was delighted: "I thank you for Mr Webster's speech. Entertaining the opinion he has expressed respecting the general course of the administration, his patriotism is entitled to the more credit for the determination he expressed at Faneuil Hall to support it in the great effort it promises to make for the preservation of the union. No member of the then opposition avowed a similar determination during the Western Insurrection, which would have been equally fatal had it not been quelled by the well timed vigor of General Washington.

"We are now gathering the bitter fruits of the tree even before that time planted by Mr Jefferson, and so industriously and perseveringly cultivated by Virginia." [2]

Marshall's predictions of a tempestuous debate over the Virginia resolutions were fulfilled. They were, in fact, "debated to death," records Niles.

---

[1] *Writings and Speeches of Daniel Webster* (Nat. ed.) XIII, 40–42.

[2] Marshall to Story, Dec. 25, 1832, *Proceedings, Mass. Hist. Soc.* 2d Series, XIV, 352–54.

"It would seem that the genuine spirit of 'ancient *dominionism*' would lead to a making of speeches, even in 'the cave of the Cyclops when forging thunderbolts,' instead of striking the hammers from the hands of the workers of iniquity. Well — the matter was debated, and debated and debated. . . The proceedings . . were measured by the *square yard*." At last, however, resolutions were adopted.

These resolutions "respectfully requested and entreated" South Carolina to rescind her Ordinance of Nullification; "respectfully requested and entreated" Congress to "modify" the tariff; reaffirmed Virginia's faith in the principles of 1798-99, but held that these principles did not justify South Carolina's Ordinance or Jackson's Proclamation; and finally, authorized the appointment of one commissioner to South Carolina to communicate Virginia's resolutions, expressing at the same time, however, "our sincere good will to our sister state, and our anxious solicitude that the kind and respectful recommendations we have addressed to her, may lead to an accommodation of all the difficulties between that state and the general government." [1] Benjamin Watkins Leigh was unanimously elected to be the ambassador of accommodation. [2]

So it came about that South Carolina, anxious to extricate herself from a perilous situation, yet ready to fight if she could not disentangle herself with honor, took informal steps toward a peaceful adjust-

[1] Niles, XLIII, 396-97; also *Statutes at Large of South Carolina:* Cooper, I, 381-83.

[2] Niles, XLIII, 397. For the details of Leigh's mission see *ib.* 377-93; also *Statutes at Large of South Carolina:* Cooper, I, 384-94.

ment of the dispute; and that Jackson and Congress, equally wishing to avoid armed conflict, were eager to have a tariff enacted that would work a "reconciliation." On January 26, 1833, at a meeting in Charleston, attended by the first men of the State of all parties, resolutions, offered by Hamilton himself, were adopted which, as a practical matter, suspended the Ordinance of Nullification that was to have gone into effect on February 1. Vehement, spirited, defiant speeches were made, all ending, however, in expressions of hope that war might be avoided. The resolutions were as ferocious as the most bloodthirsty Secessionist could desire; but they accepted the proposed "beneficial modification of the tariff," and declared that, "pending the process" of reducing the tariff, "all . . collision between the federal and state authorities should be sedulously avoided on both sides." [1]

The Tariff Bill of 1833 — Clay's compromise — resulted. Jackson signed it; South Carolina was mollified. For the time the storm subsided; but the net result was that Nullification triumphed [2] — a National law had been modified at the threat of a State which was preparing to back up that threat by force.

Marshall was not deceived. "Have you ever seen anything to equal the exhibition in Charleston and in the far South generally?" he writes Story. "Those people pursue a southern league steadily or they are insane. They have caught at Clay's bill, if their conduct is at all intelligible, not as a real accommoda-

---

[1] Niles, XLIII, 380–82.   [2] See Parton: *Jackson*, III, 475–82.

tion, a real adjustment, a real relief from actual or supposed oppression, but as an apology for avoiding the crisis and deferring the decisive moment till the other States of the South will unite with them." [1] Marshall himself was for the compromise Tariff of 1833, but not because it afforded a means of preventing armed collision: "Since I have breathed the air of James River I think favorably of Clay's bill. I hope, if it can be maintained, that our manufactures will still be protected by it." [2]

The "settlement" of the controversy, of course, satisfied nobody, changed no conviction, allayed no hostility, stabilized no condition. The South, though victorious, was nevertheless morose, indignant — after all, the principle of protection had been retained. "The political world, at least our part of it, is surely moved *topsy turvy*," Marshall writes Story in the autumn of 1833. "What is to become of us and of our constitution? Can the wise men of the East answer that question? Those of the South perceive no difficulty. Allow a full range to state rights and state sovereignty, and, in their opinion, all will go well." [3]

Placid as was his nature, perfect as was the coordination of his powers, truly balanced as were his intellect and emotions, Marshall could not free his mind of the despondency that had now settled upon him. Whatever the subject upon which he wrote to friends, he was sure to refer to the woeful state of the country, and the black future it portended.

[1] Marshall to Story, April 24, 1833, *Proceedings, Mass. Hist. Soc.* 2d Series, xiv, 356–57.

[2] *Ib.*   [3] Same to same, Nov. 16, 1833, *ib.* 358.

Story informed him that an abridged edition of his own two volumes on the Constitution would soon be published. "I rejoice to hear that the abridgement of your Commentaries is coming before the public," wrote Marshall in reply, "and should be still more rejoiced to learn that it was used in all our colleges and universities. The first impressions made on the youthful mind are of vast importance; and, most unfortunately, they are in the South all erroneous. Our young men, generally speaking, grow up in the firm belief that liberty depends on construing our Constitution into a league instead of a government; that it has nothing to fear from breaking these United States into numerous petty republics. Nothing in their view is to be feared but that bugbear, consolidation; and every exercise of legitimate power is construed into a breach of the Constitution. Your book, if read, will tend to remove these prejudices." [1]

A month later he again writes Story: "I have finished reading your great work, and wish it could be read by every statesman, and every would-be statesman in the United States. It is a comprehensive and an accurate commentary on our Constitution, formed in the spirit of the original text. In the South, we are so far gone in political metaphysics, that I fear no demonstration can restore us to common sense. The word 'State Rights,' as expounded by the resolutions of '98 and the report of '99, construed by our legislature, has a charm against which all reasoning is vain.

---

[1] Marshall to Story, June 3, 1833, *Proceedings, Mass. Hist. Soc.* 2d Series, XIV, 358.

"Those resolutions and that report constitute the creed of every politician, who hopes to rise in Virginia; and to question them, or even to adopt the construction given by their author [Jefferson] is deemed political sacrilege. The solemn . . admonitions of your concluding remarks [1] will not, I fear, avail as they ought to avail against this popular frenzy." [2]

He once more confides to his beloved Story his innermost thoughts and feelings. Story had sent the Chief Justice a copy of the *New England Magazine* containing an article by Story entitled "Statesmen: their Rareness and Importance," in which Marshall was held up as the true statesman and the poor quality of the generality of American public men was set forth in scathing terms.

Marshall briefly thanks Story for the compliment paid him, and continues: "It is in vain to lament, that the portrait which the author has drawn of our political and party men, is, in general, true. Lament it as we may, much as it may wound our vanity or our pride, it is still, in the main, true; and will, I fear, so remain. . . In the South, political prejudice is too strong to yield to any degree of merit; and the great body of the nation contains, at least appears to me to contain, too much of the same ingredient.

"To men who think as you and I do, the present is gloomy enough; and the future presents no cheering prospect. The struggle now maintained in every

---

[1] Story ends his *Commentaries on the Constitution of the United States* by a fervent, passionate, and eloquent appeal for the preservation, at all hazards, of the Constitution and the Union.

[2] Marshall to Story, July 31, 1833, Story, II, 135-36.

State in the Union seems to me to be of doubtful issue; but should it terminate contrary to the wishes of those who support the enormous pretensions of the Executive, should victory crown the exertions of the champions of constitutional law, what serious and lasting advantage is to be expected from this result?

"In the South (things may be less gloomy with you) those who support the Executive do not support the Government. They sustain the personal power of the President, but labor incessantly to impair the legitimate powers of the Government. Those who oppose the violent and rash measures of the Executive (many of them nullifiers, many of them seceders) are generally the bitter enemies of a constitutional government. Many of them are the avowed advocates of a league; and those who do not go the whole length, go great part of the way. What can we hope for in such circumstances? As far as I can judge, the Government is weakened, whatever party may prevail. Such is the impression I receive from the language of those around me." [1]

During the last years of Marshall's life, the country's esteem for him, slowly forming through more than a generation, manifested itself by expressions of reverence and affection. When he and Story attended the theater, the audience cheered him.[2] His sentiment still youthful and tender, he wept over Fanny Kemble's affecting portrayal of Mrs. Haller in "The Stranger."[3] To the very last Marshall per-

---

[1] Marshall to Story, Oct. 6, 1834, Story, II, 172–73.
[2] Story to his wife, Jan. 20, 1833, *ib.* 116.   [3] *Ib.* 117.

formed his judicial duties thoroughly, albeit with a heavy heart. He "looked more vigorous than usual," and "seemed to revive and enjoy anew his green old age," testifies Story.[1]

It is at this period of his career that we get Marshall's account of the course he pursued toward his malignant personal and political enemy, Thomas Jefferson. Six years after Jefferson's death,[2] Major Henry Lee, who hated that great reformer even more than Jefferson hated Marshall, wrote the Chief Justice for certain facts, and also for his opinion of the former President. In his reply Marshall said:

"I have never allowed myself to be irritated by Mʳ Jeffersons unprovoked and unjustifiable aspersions on my conduct and principles, nor have I ever noticed them except on one occasion[3] when I thought myself called on to do so, and when I thought that declining to enter upon my justification might have the appearance of crouching under the lash, and admitting the justice of its infliction."[4]

Intensely as he hated Jefferson, attributing to him, as Marshall did, most of the country's woes, the Chief Justice never spoke a personally offensive word concerning his radical cousin.[5] On the other hand, he never uttered a syllable of praise or appreciation of Jefferson. Even when his great antagonist

---

[1] Story to his wife, Jan. 20, 1833, Story, ii, 116.

[2] July 4, 1826.

[3] Jefferson's attacks on Marshall in the X. Y. Z. affair. (See vol. ii, 359–63, 368–69, of this work.)

[4] Marshall to Major Henry Lee, Jan. 20, 1832, MSS. Lib. Cong. In no collection, but, with a few unimportant letters, in a portfolio marked "M," sometimes referred to as "Marshall Papers."

[5] *Green Bag*, viii, 463.

died, no expression of sorrow or esteem or regret or admiration came from the Chief Justice. Marshall could not be either hypocritical or vindictive; but he could be silent.

Holding to the old-time Federalist opinion that Jefferson's principles were antagonistic to orderly government; convinced that, if they prevailed, they would be destructive of the Nation; believing the man himself to be a demagogue and an unscrupulous if astute and able politician — Marshall, nevertheless, said nothing about Jefferson to anybody except to Story, Lee, and Pickering; and, even to these close friends, he gave only an occasional condemnation of Jefferson's policies.

The general feeling toward Marshall, especially that of the bench and bar, during his last two years is not too strongly expressed in Story's dedication to the Chief Justice of his "Commentaries on the Constitution of the United States." Marshall had taken keen interest in the preparation of Story's masterpiece and warned him against haste. "Precipitation ought carefully to be avoided. This is a subject on which I am not without experience." [1]

Story begins by a tribute "to one whose youth was engaged in the arduous enterprises of the Revolution; whose manhood assisted in framing and supporting the national Constitution; and whose maturer years have been devoted to the task of unfolding its powers, and illustrating its principles." As the expounder of the Constitution, "the common consent of your

---

[1] Marshall to Story, July 3, 1829, *Proceedings, Mass. Hist. Soc.* 2d Series, XIV, 340.

countrymen has admitted you to stand without a rival. Posterity will assuredly confirm, by its deliberate award, what the present age has approved, as an act of undisputed justice.

"But," continues Story, "I confess that I dwell with even more pleasure upon the entirety of a life adorned by consistent principles, and filled up in the discharge of virtuous duty; where there is nothing to regret, and nothing to conceal; no friendships broken; no confidence betrayed; no timid surrenders to popular clamor; no eager reaches for popular favor. Who does not listen with conscious pride to the truth, that the disciple, the friend, the biographer of Washington, still lives, the uncompromising advocate of his principles?" [1]

Excepting only the time of his wife's death, the saddest hours of his life were, perhaps, those when he opened the last two sessions of the Supreme Court over which he presided. When, on January 13, 1834, the venerable Chief Justice, leading his associate justices to their places, gravely returned the accustomed bow of the bar and spectators, he also, perforce, bowed to temporary events and to the iron, if erratic, rule of Andrew Jackson. He bowed, too, to time and death. Justice Washington was dead,

---

[1] Story to Marshall, January, 1833, Story, ii, 132–33. This letter appears in Story's *Commentaries on the Constitution*, immediately after the title-page of volume i.

Story's perfervid eulogium did not overstate the feeling — the instinct — of the public. Nathan Sargent, that trustworthy writer of reminiscences, testifies that, toward the end of Marshall's life, his name had "become a household word with the American people implying greatness, purity, honesty, and all the Christian virtues." (Sargent, i, 299.)

Johnson was fatally ill, and Duval, sinking under age and infirmity, was about to resign.

Republicans as Johnson and Duval were, they had, generally, upheld Marshall's Nationalism. Their places must soon be filled, he knew, by men of Jackson's choosing — men who would yield to the transient public pressure then so fiercely brought to bear on the Supreme Court. Only Joseph Story could be relied upon to maintain Marshall's principles. The increasing tendency of Justices Thompson, McLean, and Baldwin was known to be against his unyielding Constitutional philosophy. It was more than probable that, before another year, Jackson would have the opportunity to appoint two new Justices — and two cases were pending that involved some of Marshall's dearest Constitutional principles.

The first of these was a Kentucky case [1] in which almost precisely the same question, in principle, arose that Marshall had decided in Craig *vs.* Missouri. [2] The Kentucky Bank, owned by the State, was authorized to issue, and did issue, bills which were made receivable for taxes and other public dues. The Kentucky law furthermore directed that an endorsement and tender of these State bank notes should, with certain immaterial modifications, satisfy any judgment against a debtor. [3] In short, the Legislature had authorized a State currency — had emitted those bills of credit, expressly forbidden by the National Constitution.

Another case, almost equally important, came

[1] Briscoe *vs.* The Commonwealth's Bank of the State of Kentucky, **8** Peters, 118 *et seq.*   [2] See *supra*, 509–13.

[3] Act of Dec. 25, *Laws of Kentucky, 1820*, 183–88.

from New York.[1] To prevent the influx of impoverished foreigners, who would be a charge upon the
City of New York, the Legislature had enacted that
the masters of ships arriving at that port should report to the Mayor all facts concerning passengers.
The ship captain must remove those whom the
Mayor decided to be undesirable.[2] It was earnestly
contended that this statute violated the commerce
clause of the Constitution.

Both cases were elaborately argued; both, it was
said, had been settled by former decisions — the
Kentucky case by Craig *vs.* Missouri, the New York
case by Gibbons *vs.* Ogden and Brown *vs.* Maryland.
The court was almost equally divided. Thompson,
McLean, and Baldwin thought the Kentucky and
New York laws Constitutional; Marshall, Story,
Duval, and Johnson believed them invalid. But
Johnson was absent because of his serious illness.
No decision, therefore, was possible.

Marshall then announced a rule of the court,
hitherto unknown by the public: "The practice of
this court is not (except in cases of absolute necessity)
to deliver any judgment in cases where constitutional questions are involved, unless four judges concur in opinion, thus making the decision that of a
majority of the whole court. In the present cases
four judges do not concur in opinion as to the constitutional questions which have been argued. The
court therefore direct these cases to be re-argued at

[1] The Mayor, Aldermen and Commonalty of the City of New York
vs. Miln, 8 Peters, 121 *et seq.*

[2] 11 Peters, 104. This was the first law against unrestricted immigration.

the next term, under the expectation that a larger number of the judges may then be present." [1]

The next term! When, on January 12, 1835, John Marshall for the last time presided over the Supreme Court of the United States, the situation, from his point of view, was still worse. Johnson had died and Jackson had appointed James M. Wayne of Georgia in his place. Duval had resigned not long before the court convened, and his successor had not been named. Again the New York and Kentucky cases were continued, but Marshall fully realized that the decision of them must be in opposition to his firm and pronounced views. [2]

[1] 8 Peters, 122.

[2] These cases were not decided until 1837, when Roger Brooke Taney of Maryland took his seat on the bench as Marshall's successor. Philip Pendleton Barbour of Virginia succeeded Duval. Of the seven Justices, only one disciple of Marshall remained, Joseph Story.

In the New York case the court held that the State law was a local police regulation. (11 Peters, 130–43; 144–53.) Story dissented in a signally able opinion of almost passionate fervor.

"I have the consolation to know," he concludes, "that I had the entire concurrence . . of that great constitutional jurist, the late Mr. Chief Justice Marshall. Having heard the former arguments, his deliberate opinion was that the act of New York was unconstitutional, and that the present case fell directly within the principles established in the case of Gibbons v. Ogden." (Ib. 153–61.)

In the Kentucky Bank case, decided immediately after the New York immigrant case, Marshall's opinion in Craig vs. Missouri was completely repudiated, although Justice McLean, who delivered the opinion of the court (ib. 311–28), strove to show that the judgment was within Marshall's reasoning.

Story, of course, dissented, and never did that extraordinary man write with greater power and brilliancy. When the case was first argued in 1834, he said, a majority of the court "were decidedly of the opinion" that the Kentucky Bank Law was unconstitutional. "In principle it was thought to be decided by the case of Craig v. The State of Missouri." Among that majority was Marshall — "a name never to be pronounced without reverence." (Ib. 328.)

In closing his great argument, Story says that the frankness and

It is doubtful whether history shows more than a few examples of an aged man, ill, disheartened, and knowing that he soon must die, who nevertheless continued his work to the very last with such scrupulous care as did Marshall. He took active part in all cases argued and decided and actually delivered the opinion of the court in eleven of the most important.[1] None of these are of any historical interest; but in all of them Marshall was as clear and vigorous in reasoning and style as he had been in the immortal Constitutional opinions delivered at the height of his power. The last words Marshall ever uttered as Chief Justice sparkle with vitality and high ideals. In Mitchel *et al. vs.* The United States,[2] a case involving land titles in Florida, he said, in ruling on a motion to continue the case: "Though the hope of deciding causes to the mutual satisfaction of parties would be chimerical, that of convincing them that the case has been fully and fairly considered . . may be sometimes indulged. Even this is not always attainable. In the excite-

fervor of his language are due to his "reverence and affection" for Marshall. "I have felt an earnest desire to vindicate his memory. . . I am sensible that I have not done that justice to his opinion which his own great mind and exalted talents would have done. But . . I hope that I have shown that there were solid grounds on which to rest his exposition of the Constitution. *His saltem accumulem donis, et fungar inani munere.*" (11 Peters, 350.)

[1] Lessee of Samuel Smith *vs.* Robert Trabue's Heirs, 9 Peters, 4–6; U.S. *vs.* Nourse, *ib.* 11–32; Caldwell *et al. vs.* Carrington's Heirs, *ib.* 87–105; Bradley *vs.* The Washington, etc. Steam Packet Co. *ib.* 107–16; Delassus *vs.* U.S. *ib.* 118–36; Chouteau's Heirs *vs.* U.S. *ib.* 137–46; U.S. *vs.* Clarke, *ib.* 168–70; U.S. *vs.* Huertas, *ib.* 171–74; Field *et al. vs.* U.S. *ib.* 182–203; Mayor, etc. of New Orleans *vs.* De Armas and Cucullo, *ib.* 224–37; Life and Fire Ins. Co. of New York *vs.* Adams, *ib.* 571–605.

[2] *Ib.* 711–63.

ment produced by ardent controversy, gentlemen view the same object through such different media that minds, not infrequently receive therefrom precisely opposite impressions. The Court, however, must see with its own eyes, and exercise its own judgment, guided by its own reason." [1]

At last Marshall had grave intimations that his life could not be prolonged. Quite suddenly his health declined, although his mind was as strong and clear as ever. "Chief Justice Marshall still possesses his intellectual powers in very high vigor," writes Story during the last session of the Supreme Court over which his friend and leader presided. "But his physical strength is manifestly on the decline; and it is now obvious, that after a year or two, he will resign, from the pressing infirmities of age. . . What a gloom will spread over the nation when he is gone! His place will not, nay, it cannot be supplied." [2]

As the spring of 1835 ripened into summer, Marshall grew weaker. "I pray God," wrote Story in agonies of apprehension, "that he may long live to bless his country; but I confess that I have many fears whether he can be long with us. His complaints are, I am sure, incurable, but I suppose that they may be alleviated, unless he should meet with some accidental cold or injury to aggravate them. Of these, he is in perpetual danger, from his imprudence as well as from the natural effects of age." [3]

In May, 1835, Kent went to Richmond in order to see Marshall, whom "he found very emaciated,

---

[1] 9 Peters, 723.   [2] Story to Fay, March 2, 1835, Story, II, 193.
[3] Story to Peters, May 20, 1835, ib. 194.

feeble & dangerously low. He injured his Spine by a Post Coach fall & oversetting. . . He . . made me *Promise to see him at Washington next Winter.*" [1]

Kent wrote Jeremiah Smith of New Hampshire that Marshall must soon die. Smith was overwhelmed with grief "because his life, at this time especially, is of incalculable value." Marshall's "views . . of our national affairs" were those of Smith also. "Perfectly just in themselves they now come to us confirmed by the dying attestation of one of the greatest and best of men." [2]

Marshall's "incurable complaint," which so distressed Story, was a disease of the liver.[3] Finding his health failing, he again repaired to Philadelphia for treatment by Dr. Physick. When informed that the prospects for his friend's recovery were desperate, Story was inconsolable. "Great, good and excellent man!" he wrote. "I shall never see his like again! His gentleness, his affectionateness, his glorious virtues, his unblemished life, his exalted talents, leave him without a rival or a peer." [4]

At six o'clock in the evening of Monday, July 6, 1835, John Marshall died, in his eightieth year, in the city where American Independence was proclaimed and the American Constitution was born — the city which, a patriotic soldier, he had striven to protect and where he had received his earliest national recognition. Without pain, his mind as clear and strong as ever, he "met his fate with the forti-

[1] Kent's Journal, May 16, 1835, Kent MSS. Lib. Cong.
[2] Smith to Kent, June 13, 1835, Kent MSS. Lib. Cong.
[3] Randolph: *Physick*, 100–01.
[4] Story to Peters, June 19, 1835, Story, II, 199–200.

tude of a Philosopher, and the resignation of a Christian," testifies Dr. Nathaniel Chapman, who was present.[1] By Marshall's direction, the last thing taken from his body after he expired was the locket which his wife had hung about his neck just before she died.[2] The morning after his death, the bar of Philadelphia met to pay tribute to Marshall, and at half-past five of the same day a town meeting was held for the same purpose.[3]

Immediately afterward, his body was sent by boat to Richmond. The bench, bar, and hundreds of citizens of Philadelphia accompanied the funeral party to the vessel. During the voyage a transfer was made to another craft.[4] A committee, consisting of Major-General Winfield Scott, of the United States Army, Henry Baldwin, Associate Justice of the Supreme Court, Richard Peters, formerly Judge for the District of Pennsylvania, John Sergeant, Edward D. Ingraham, and William Rawle, of the Philadelphia bar, went to Richmond.

In the late afternoon of July 9, 1835, the steamboat Kentucky, bearing Marshall's body, drew up at the Richmond wharf. Throughout the day the bells had been tolling, the stores were closed, and, as the vessel came within sight, a salute of three guns was fired.

---

[1] Chapman to Brockenbrough, July 6, 1835, quoted in the Richmond *Enquirer*, July 10, 1835. Marshall died "at the Boarding House of Mrs. Crim, Walnut street below Fourth." (Philadelphia *Inquirer*, July 7, 1835.) Three of Marshall's sons were with him when he died. His eldest son, Thomas, when hastening to his father's bedside, had been killed in Baltimore by the fall upon his head of bricks from a chimney blown down by a sudden and violent storm. Marshall was not informed of his son's death.

[2] Terhune, 98.

[3] Philadelphia *Inquirer*, July 7, 1835.   [4] Niles, XLVIII, 322.

All Richmond assembled at the landing. An immense procession marched to Marshall's house,[1] where he had requested that his body be first taken, and then to the "New Burying Ground," on Shockoe Hill. There Bishop Richard Channing Moore of the Episcopal Church read the funeral service, and Jchn Marshall was buried by the side of his wife.

When his ancient enemy and antagonist, the Richmond *Enquirer*, published the news of Marshall's death, it expressed briefly its true estimate of the man. It would be impossible, said the *Enquirer*, to over-praise Marshall's "brilliant talents." It would be "a more grateful incense" to his memory to say "that he was as much beloved as he was respected. . . There was about him so little of 'the insolence of office,' and so much of the benignity of the man, that his presence always produced . . the most delightful impressions. There was something irresistibly winning about him." Strangers could hardly be persuaded that "in the plain, unpretending . . man who told his anecdote and enjoyed the jest — they had been introduced to the Chief Justice of the United States, whose splendid powers had filled such a large space in the eye of mankind." [2]

The Richmond *Whig and Public Advertiser* said that "no man has lived or died in this country, save its father George Washington alone, who united such a warmth of affection for his person, with so deep and unaffected a respect for his character, and admiration for his great abilities. No man ever bore

---

[1] Richmond *Enquirer*, July 10, 1835.   [2] *Ib.*

public honors with so meek a dignity. . . It is hard
. . to conceive of a more perfect character than his,
for who can point to a vice, scarcely to a defect —
or who can name a virtue that did not shine conspicuously in his life and conduct?" [1]

The day after the funeral the citizens of Richmond
gathered at and about the Capitol, again to honor the
memory of their beloved neighbor and friend. The
resolutions, offered by Benjamin Watkins Leigh, declared that the people of Richmond knew "better
than any other community can know" Marshall's
private and public "virtues," his "wisdom," "simplicity," "self-denial," "unbounded charity," and
"warm benevolence towards all men." Since nothing
they can say can do justice to "such a man," the
people of Richmond "most confidently trust, to
History alone, to render due honors to his memory,
by a faithful and immortal record of his wisdom, his
virtues and his services." [2]

All over the country similar meetings were held,
similar resolutions adopted. Since the death of
Washington no such universal public expressions
of appreciation and sorrow had been witnessed. [3]
The press of the country bore laudatory editorials
and articles. Even Hezekiah Niles, than whom no
man had attacked Marshall's Nationalist opinions
more savagely, lamented his death, and avowed
himself unequal to the task of writing a tribute to

[1] Richmond *Whig and Public Advertiser*, July 10, 1835.
[2] Richmond *Enquirer*, July 14, 1835.
[3] See Sargent, I, 299. If the statements in the newspapers and magazines of the time are to be trusted, even the death of Jefferson called
forth no such public demonstrations as were accorded Marshall.

Marshall that would be worthy of the subject. "'A great man has fallen in Israel,'" said Niles's *Register*. "Next to WASHINGTON, only, did he possess the reverence and homage of the heart of the American people." [1]

One of the few hostile criticisms of Marshall's services appeared in the *New York Evening Post* over the name of "Atlantic." [2] This paper had, by now, departed from the policy of its Hamiltonian founder. "Atlantic" said that Marshall's "political doctrines . . were of the ultra federal or aristocratic kind. . . With Hamilton" he "distrusted the virtue and intelligence of the people, and was in favor of a strong and vigorous General Government, at the expense of the rights of the States and of the people." While he was "sincere" in his beliefs and "a good and exemplary man" who "truly loved his country . . he has been, all his life long, a stumbling block . . in the way of democratic principles. . . His situation . . at the head of an important tribunal, constituted in utter defiance of the very first principles of democracy, has always been . . an occasion of lively regret. That he is at length removed from that station is a source of satisfaction." [3]

The most intimate and impressive tributes came, of course, from Virginia. Scarcely a town in the State that did not hold meetings, hear orations, adopt resolutions. For thirty days the people of Lynchburg

---

[1] Niles, XLVIII, 321.

[2] Undoubtedly William Leggett, one of the editors. See Leggett: *A Collection of Political Writings*, II, 3–7.

[3] As reprinted in Richmond *Whig and Public Advertiser*, July 14, 1835.

wore crape on the arm.[1] Petersburg honored "the Soldier, the Orator, the Patriot, the Statesman, the Jurist, and above all, the good and virtuous man."[2] Norfolk testified to his "transcendent ability, perfect integrity and pure patriotism."[3] For weeks the Virginia demonstrations continued. That at Alexandria was held five weeks after his death. "The flags at the public square and on the shipping were displayed at half mast; the bells were tolled . . during the day, and minute guns fired by the Artillery"; there was a parade of military companies, societies and citizens, and an oration by Edgar Snowden.[4]

The keenest grief of all, however, was felt by Marshall's intimates of the Quoit Club of Richmond. Benjamin Watkins Leigh proposed, and the club resolved, that, as to the vacancy caused by Marshall's death, "there should be no attempt to fill it ever; but that the number of the club should remain one less than it was before his death."[5]

Story composed this "inscription for a cenotaph":

"To Marshall reared — the great, the good, the wise;
Born for all ages, honored in all skies;
His was the fame to mortals rarely given,
Begun on earth, but fixed in aim on heaven.
Genius, and learning, and consummate skill,
Moulding each thought, obedient to the will;
Affections pure, as e'er warmed human breast,
And love, in blessing others, doubly blest;

---

[1] Richmond *Enquirer*, July 21, 1835.　　[2] *Ib.*　　[3] *Ib.* July 17, 1835.
[4] Alexandria *Gazette*, Aug. 13, 1835, reprinted in the Richmond *Enquirer*, Aug. 21, 1835.
[5] Magruder: *John Marshall*, 282.

Virtue unspotted, uncorrupted truth,
Gentle in age, and beautiful in youth; —
These were his bright possessions. These had power
To charm through life and cheer his dying hour.
Are these all perished? No! but snatched from time,
To bloom afresh in yonder sphere sublime.
Kind was the doom (the fruit was ripe) to die,
Mortal is clothed with immortality." [1]

Upon his tomb, however, were carved only the words he himself wrote for that purpose two days before he died, leaving nothing but the final date to be supplied:

JOHN MARSHALL

The son of Thomas and Mary Marshall
Was born on the 24th of
September, 1755; intermarried
with Mary Willis Ambler
the 3d of January, 1783;
departed this life the 6th day
of July, 1835.

---

[1] Story, II, 206.

THE END

WORKS CITED IN THIS VOLUME

WORKS CITED IN THIS VOLUME

The material given in parentheses and following certain titles indicates the form in which those titles have been cited in the footnotes.

ABEL, ANNIE HÉLOISE. The History of Events resulting in Indian Consolidation west of the Mississippi. [Volume 1 of *Annual Report of the American Historical Association* for 1906.]

ADAMS, HENRY. History of the United States of America from 1801 to 1817. 9 vols. New York. 1889–93. (Adams: *U.S.*)

—— Life of Albert Gallatin. Philadelphia. 1879. (Adams: *Gallatin.*)

ADAMS, HENRY, *editor*. Documents relating to New England Federalism, 1800–15. Boston. 1877. (*N.E. Federalism:* Adams.)

—— *See also* Gallatin, Albert. Writings.

ADAMS, JOHN. *See* Old Family Letters.

ADAMS, JOHN QUINCY. Memoirs. Edited by Charles Francis Adams. 12 vols. Philadelphia. 1874–77. (*Memoirs, J. Q. A.:* Adams.)

AMBLER, CHARLES HENRY. Sectionalism in Virginia, from 1776 to 1861. Chicago. 1910.

—— Thomas Ritchie: A Study in Virginia Politics. Richmond. 1913. (Ambler: *Ritchie.*)

AMBLER, CHARLES HENRY, *editor*. *See* John P. Branch Historical Papers.

American Colonization Society. Annual Reports, 1–72. 1818–89.

American Historical Review. Managing Editor, J. Franklin Jameson. Vols. 1–24. New York. 1896–1919. (*Am. Hist. Rev.*)

American Jurist and Law Magazine. 28 vols. Boston. 1829–43.

American Law Journal. Edited by John E. Hall. 6 vols. Baltimore. 1808–17.

American State Papers. Documents, Legislative and Executive, of the Congress of the United States. Selected and edited under the Authority of Congress. 38 vols. Washington. 1832–61. [Citations in this work are from "Foreign Relations" (*Am. State Papers, For. Rel.*); and "Finance" (*Am. State Papers, Finance*).]

American Turf Register and Sporting Magazine. Edited by J. S. Skinner. 7 vols. Baltimore. 1830–40.

AMES, FISHER. Works. Edited by Seth Ames. 2 vols. Boston. 1854. (*Ames:* Ames.)

AMES, HERMAN VANDENBURG, editor. State Documents on Federal Relations: The States and the United States. Philadelphia. 1906. (*State Doc. Fed. Rel.*: Ames.)

ANDERSON, DICE ROBINS. William Branch Giles: A Study in the Politics of Virginia and the Nation, from 1790–1830. Menasha, Wis. 1914. (Anderson.)

BABCOCK, KENDRIC CHARLES. Rise of American Nationality, 1811–1819. New York. 1906. [Volume 13 of *The American Nation: A History.*] (Babcock.)

BANCROFT, GEORGE. *See* Howe, M. A. DeWolfe.

BARSTOW, GEORGE. History of New Hampshire. Concord, 1842. (Barstow.)

BASSETT, JOHN SPENCER. Life of Andrew Jackson. 2 vols. New York. 1911.

BAYARD, JAMES ASHETON. Papers from 1796 to 1815. Edited by Elizabeth Donnan. [Volume 2 of *Annual Report of the American Historical Association* for 1913.] (*Bayard Papers:* Donnan.)

BIDDLE, ALEXANDER. *See* Old Family Letters.

BIDDLE, NICHOLAS. Correspondence. Edited by Reginald C. McGrane. Boston. 1919.

BLANE, WILLIAM NEWNHAM. An Excursion through the United States and Canada during the Years 1822–23. By an English Gentleman. London. 1824.

Branch Historical Papers. *See* Dodd, W. E.

BROCKENBROUGH, JOHN W., reporter. Reports of Cases decided by the Honourable John Marshall, in the Circuit Court of the United States, for the District of Virginia and North Carolina, from 1802 to 1833 inclusive. 2 vols. Philadelphia. 1837. (Brockenbrough.)

BROWN, SAMUEL GILMAN. Life of Rufus Choate. Boston. 1870. (Brown.)

BRYAN, WILHELMUS BOGART. A History of the National Capital. 2 vols. New York. 1914–16. (Bryan.)

CABOT, GEORGE.   *See* Lodge, Henry Cabot.

CALL, DANIEL.   Reports of the Court of Appeals, Virginia [1779–1818].   6 vols.   Richmond.   1801–33.

CARTWRIGHT, PETER.   Autobiography of Peter Cartwright, the Backwoods Preacher.   Edited by W. P. Strickland.   New York.   1856.

CATTERALL, RALPH CHARLES HENRY.   Second Bank of the United States.   Chicago.   1903.   [Decennial Publications of the University of Chicago.]   (Catterall.)

CHANNING, EDWARD.   A History of the United States.   Vols. 1–4.   New York.   1905–17.   (Channing: *U.S.*)

—— Jeffersonian System, 1801–1811.   New York.   1906.   [Volume 12 of *The American Nation: A History.*]   (Channing: *Jeff. System.*)

CHASE, FREDERICK.   A History of Dartmouth College, and the Town of Hanover, New Hampshire.   Edited by John King Lord.   2 vols.   [Vol. 2: A History of Dartmouth College, 1815–1909.   By John King Lord.]   Cambridge. 1891.   1913.

CHOATE, RUFUS.   *See* Brown, Samuel Gilman.

CLAY, HENRY.   *See* Schurz, Carl.

CLEVELAND, CATHERINE CAROLINE.   Great Revival in the West, 1797–1805.   Chicago.   1916.

COLLINS, LEWIS.   Historical Sketches of Kentucky.   Cincinnati. 1847.   (Collins.)

CONNECTICUT.   Public Statute Laws of the State of Connecticut.   May Sessions 1822, 1823, 1825, 1826.   Hartford.   n. d.

COOLEY, THOMAS MCINTYRE.   A Treatise on the Constitutional Limitations which rest upon the Legislative Power of the States of the American Union.   Boston.   1868.

COOPER, THOMAS, *editor.*   Statutes at Large of South Carolina. Vols. 1–5.   Columbia, S.C.   1836.

CORWIN, EDWARD SAMUEL.   John Marshall and the Constitution.   New Haven.   1919.

COTTON, JOSEPH P., JR., *editor.*   Constitutional Decisions of John Marshall.   2 vols.   New York.   1905.

COWEN, EZEKIEL, *reporter.*   Reports of Cases argued and determined in the Supreme Court .. of the State of New York. 9 vols.   Albany.   1824–30.   (Cowen.)

CRANCH, WILLIAM, *reporter.*   Reports of Cases argued and adjudged in the Supreme Court of the United States. 9 vols.   New York.   1812–17.   (Cranch.)

CURTIS, GEORGE TICKNOR. Life of Daniel Webster. 2 vols.
New York. 1870. (Curtis.)

DEWEY, DAVIS RICH. Financial History of the United States.
New York. 1903. [American Citizen Series.] (Dewey.)

DICKINSON, H. W. Robert Fulton, Engineer and Artist: His
Life and Works. London. 1913. (Dickinson.)

DILLON, JOHN FORREST, *compiler and editor.* John Marshall:
Life, Character and Judicial Services, as portrayed in the
Centenary Proceedings throughout the United States on
Marshall Day. 1901. 3 vols. Chicago. 1903. (Dillon.)

DODD, WILLIAM EDWARD, *editor. See* John P. Branch Historical Papers.

——— Statesmen of the Old South. New York. 1911.

DONNAN, ELIZABETH, *editor. See* Bayard, James A. Papers.

DUER, WILLIAM ALEXANDER. A Letter addressed to Cadwallader D. Colden, Esquire. In Answer to the Strictures
contained in his "Life of Robert Fulton," etc. Albany
1817.

Edinburgh Review.

EMBARGO LAWS, with the Message from the President, upon
which they were founded. Boston. 1809.

FARMER, JOHN. Sketches of the Graduates of Dartmouth
College. Concord. 1832. 1834. [In *New Hampshire
Historical Society.* Collections. Volumes 3 and 4.]

FARRAND, MAX, *editor. See* Records of the Federal Convention
of 1787.

FARRAR, TIMOTHY, *reporter.* Report of the Case of the Trustees
of Dartmouth College against William H. Woodward.
Portsmouth, N.H. 1819. (Farrar.)

Federal Cases: Cases, Circuit and District Courts, United
States [1789–1880]. St. Paul. 1894–97.

First Forty Years of Washington Society. See Hunt, Gaillard.

Fiske, John. Essays Historical and Literary. 2 vols. New
York. 1902.

FLANDERS, HENRY. Lives and Times of the Chief Justices of
the Supreme Court of the United States. 2 vols. Philadelphia. 1881.

FLETCHER, R. A. Steam-Ships. The Story of Their Development to the Present Day. Philadelphia. 1910.

FORD, PAUL LEICESTER, *editor*.   *See* Jefferson, Thomas. Works.

FULTON, ROBERT.   *See* Dickinson, H. W.; Knox, Thomas W.; Reigart, J. Franklin; Thurston, Robert H.

GALLATIN, ALBERT. Writings. Edited by Henry Adams. 3 vols. Philadelphia. 1879. (*Writings:* Adams.)
    See also Adams, Henry.

GEORGIA. Acts of the General Assembly of the State of Georgia, at an Annual Session, in October and November, 1814. Milledgeville, Ga. 1814.

GILES, WILLIAM BRANCH.   *See* Anderson, Dice Robins.

Great American Lawyers.   *See* Lewis, William Draper.

GREELEY, HORACE. The American Conflict. 2 vols. Hartford. 1864. 1867.

Green Bag, The: An Entertaining Magazine for Lawyers. Edited by Horace W. Fuller. Boston. 1889–1914. (*Green Bag.*)

GRIGSBY, HUGH BLAIR. The Virginia Convention of 1829–1830. Richmond. 1854.

HARDING, CHESTER. A Sketch of Chester Harding, Artist. Drawn by his own Hand. Edited by Margaret Eliot White. Boston. 1890.

Harper's Magazine.

HART, ALBERT BUSHNELL, *editor*. American History told by Contemporaries. 4 vols. New York. 1897–1901.

—— The American Nation: A History. 27 volumes. New York. 1904–1908.

Harvard Law Review.

HARVEY, PETER. Reminiscences and Anecdotes of Webster. Boston. 1877.

HAY, GEORGE. A Treatise on Expatriation. Washington. 1814.

HILDRETH, RICHARD. History of the United States of America. 6 vols. New York. 1854–55. (Hildreth.)

HILLARD, GEORGE STILLMAN. Memoir and Correspondence of Jeremiah Mason. Cambridge. 1873. (Hillard.)

HOPKINS, SAMUEL M., *reporter*. Reports of Cases argued and determined in the Court of Chancery of the State of New York. Albany. 1839.

HOUSTON, DAVID FRANKLIN. A Critical Study of Nullification in South Carolina. New York. 1896 [Harvard Historical Studies.] (Houston.)

HOWARD, BENJAMIN CHEW. Reports of Cases argued and adjudged in the Supreme Court of the United States, 1843–60. 24 vols. Philadelphia. 1852–[61].

HOWE, HENRY. Historical Collections of Virginia. Charleston, S.C. 1845. (Howe.)

HOWE, MARK ANTONY DeWOLFE, JR. Life and Letters of George Bancroft. 2 vols. New York. 1908.

HUNT, CHARLES HAVENS. Life of Edward Livingston. New York. 1864. (Hunt: *Livingston.*)

HUNT, GAILLARD, *editor.* First Forty Years of Washington Society, portrayed by the Family Letters of Mrs. Samuel Harrison Smith. New York. 1906.

—— *See* Madison, James. Writings.

INDIANA. Revised Laws of Indiana, adopted and enacted by the General Assembly at their Eighth Session. Corydon. 1824.

INGERSOLL, CHARLES JARED. History of the Second War between the United States of America and Great Britain. (Second Series.) 2 vols. Philadelphia. 1853.

JACKSON, ANDREW. *See* Bassett, John Spencer; Parton, James; Sumner, William Graham.

JEFFERSON, THOMAS. Works. Edited by Paul Leicester Ford. 12 vols. New York. 1904–05. [Federal Edition.] (*Works:* Ford.)
  See Randall, Henry Stephens.

John P. Branch Historical Papers, issued by the Randolph-Macon College. Vols. 1–5. [Edited by W. E. Dodd and C. H. Ambler.] Ashland, Va. 1901–18. (Branch Historical Papers.)

JOHNSON, EMORY RICHARD, *and others.* History of Domestic and Foreign Commerce of the United States. 2 vols. Washington. 1915. [Carnegie Institution of Washington. Publications.]

JOHNSON, WILLIAM, *reporter.* Reports of Cases adjudged in the Court of Chancery of New-York, 1814–23. 7 vols. Albany. 1816–24. (Johnson's *Chancery Reports.*)

—— Reports of Cases argued and determined in the Supreme Court . . in the State of New-York (1806–22), 20 vols. New York and Albany. 1808–23. (Johnson.)

KENNEDY, JOHN PENDLETON. Memoirs of the Life of William Wirt. 2 vols. Philadelphia. 1849. (Kennedy.)

KING, RUFUS. Life and Correspondence. Edited by Charles R. King. 6 vols. New York. 1894–1900. (King.)

KNOX, THOMAS W. Life of Robert Fulton and a History of Steam Navigation. New York. 1896.

LANMAN, CHARLES. Private Life of Daniel Webster. New York. 1852.

LEGGETT, WILLIAM. A Collection of Political Writings. 2 vols. New York. 1840.

LEWIS, WILLIAM DRAPER, editor. Great American Lawyers: A History of the Legal Profession in America. 8 vols. Philadelphia. 1907–09.

LINCOLN, ABRAHAM. Complete Works. Edited by John G. Nicolay and John Hay. 12 vols. New York. 1894–1905.

Lippincott's Magazine of Literature, Science and Education.

LITTELL, WILLIAM. The Statute Law of Kentucky: with Notes, Prælections, and Observations on the Public Acts. 3 vols. Frankfort (Ky.), 1809.

LIVINGSTON, EDWARD. *See* Hunt, Charles Havens.

LODGE, HENRY CABOT. Daniel Webster. Boston. 1883. [American Statesmen.]

—— Life and Letters of George Cabot. Boston. 1877. (Lodge: *Cabot.*)

LORD, JOHN KING. A History of Dartmouth College, 1815–1909. Being the second volume of History of Dartmouth College and the Town of Hanover, New Hampshire, begun by Frederick Chase. Concord, N.H. 1913. (Lord.)

LOSHE, LILLIE DEMING. The Early American Novel. New York. 1907. [Columbia University. Studies in English.]

Louisiana Law Journal. Edited by Gustavus Schmidt. Volume 1, nos. 1–4. New Orleans. 1841.

LOWELL, JOHN. Mr. Madison's War. By a New England Farmer (*pseud.*). Boston. 1812.

—— Peace Without Dishonour — War Without Hope. By a Yankee Farmer (*pseud.*). Boston. 1807.

—— Review of a Treatise on Expatriation by George Hay, Esquire. By a Massachusetts Lawyer (*pseud.*). Boston 1814.

McCLINTOCK, JOHN NORRIS. History of New Hampshire. Boston. 1888.

McCORD, DAVID JAMES, *editor*. Statutes at Large of South Carolina. Vols 6 to 10. Columbia, S.C. 1839–41.

MacDONALD, WILLIAM. Jacksonian Democracy, 1829–1837. New York. 1906. [Volume 15 of *The American Nation: A History.*]

McGRANE, REGINALD C., *editor*. *See* Biddle, Nicholas. Correspondence.

McHENRY, JAMES. *See* Steiner, Bernard Christian.

McMASTER, JOHN BACH. A History of the People of the United States from the Revolution to the Civil War. 8 vols. New York. 1883–1913. (McMaster.)

MADISON, JAMES. Writings. Edited by Gaillard Hunt. 9 vols. New York. 1900–1910. (*Writings*: Hunt.)

Magazine of American History.

MAGRUDER, ALLAN BOWIE. John Marshall. Boston. 1885. [American Statesmen.]

MAINE, *Sir* HENRY. Popular Government. London. 1885.

MANUSCRIPTS:

  Chamberlain MSS. Boston Public Library.

  Dreer MSS. Pennsylvania Historical Society.

  Frederick Co., Va., Deed Book; Order Book.

  Jefferson MSS. Library of Congress.

  "Judges and Eminent Lawyers" Collection. Massachusetts Historical Society.

  Kent MSS. Library of Congress.

  Marshall MSS. Library of Congress.

  Monroe MSS. Library of Congress.

  Peters MSS. Pennsylvania Historical Society.

  Pickering MSS. Massachusetts Historical Society.

  Plumer MSS. Library of Congress.

  "Society Collection." Pennsylvania Historical Society.

  Story MSS. Massachusetts Historical Society.

  Supreme Court Records.

MARRYAT, FREDERICK. A Diary in America, with Remarks on its Institutions. 2 vols. Philadelphia. 1839.

—— Second Series of A Diary in America, with Remarks on its Institutions. Philadelphia. 1840.

MARSHALL, JOHN. Letters of Chief Justice Marshall to Timothy Pickering and Joseph Story. [From Pickering Papers and Story Papers. *Massachusetts Historical Society.*

Proceedings. Second Series. Vol. xiv, pp. 321–360.]
(*Proceedings, Mass. Hist. Soc*).
> *See* Corwin, Edward Samuel; Cotton, Joseph P., Jr.;
Dillon, John Forrest; Magruder, Allan Bowie.

MARTINEAU, HARRIET. Retrospect of Western Travel. 2 vols.
London. 1838.

MARYLAND. Laws made and passed by the General Assembly
of the State of Maryland. Annapolis, Md. 1818.

Maryland Historical Society Fund-Publications. Baltimore.
(*Md. Hist. Soc. Fund-Pub.*)

MASON, JEREMIAH. *See* Hillard, George S.

MASSACHUSETTS. Laws of the Commonwealth of Massa-
chusetts, passed at the several Sessions of the General
Court, beginning 26th May, 1812, and ending on the 2d
• March, 1815. Boston. 1812–15.

Massachusetts Historical Society. Proceedings. *See* Marshall,
John. Letters.

MEADE, *Bishop* WILLIAM. Old Churches, Ministers, and
Families of Virginia. 2 vols. Richmond. 1910. (Meade.)

Monthly Law Reporter. Edited by John Lowell. Vol. xx. New
Series, vol. x. Boston. 1858.

MOORE, JOHN BASSETT. Digest of International Law. 8 vols.
Washington. 1906.

MORDECAI, SAMUEL. Richmond in By-Gone Days, being the
Reminiscences of an old Citizen. Richmond. 1856.
(Mordecai.)

MORISON, JOHN HOPKINS. Life of the Hon. Jeremiah Smith.
Boston. 1845.

MORISON, SAMUEL ELIOT. Life and Letters of Harrison Gray
Otis, Federalist, 1765–1848. 2 vols. Boston. 1913.
(Morison: *Otis*.)

MORRIS, GOUVERNEUR. Diary and Letters. Edited by Anne
Cary Morris. 2 vols. London. 1888. (Morris.)

MORSE, JOHN TORREY, JR., *editor*. American Statesmen. 40
vols. Boston. 1882–1917.

MUNFORD, WILLIAM, *reporter*. Report of Cases argued and
determined in the Supreme Court of Appeals of Virginia
[1810–1820]. 6 vols. New York. 1812–21. (Munford.)

NELSON, JAMES POYNTZ. Address: The Chesapeake and Ohio
Railway. [Before the Railway Men's Improvement Society, New York City, January 27, 1916.] n. p., n. d.

NEW HAMPSHIRE. Journal of the House of Representatives of the State of New-Hampshire, at their session begun and holden at Concord, on the first Wednesday of June, A.D. 1816. Concord. 1816.

—— Laws of the State of New Hampshire. Exeter. 1815–16.

—— Public Laws of the State of New-Hampshire passed at a session of the General Court begun and holden at Concord on the fifth day of June, 1811. Concord. 1811.

—— Public Laws of the State of New-Hampshire passed at a session of the General Court begun and holden at Concord on the first Wednesday of June, 1813. Concord. 1813.

—— Public Laws of the State of New-Hampshire passed at a session of the General Court begun and holden at Concord on Wednesday the 27th day of October, 1813. Concord. 1813.

NEW JERSEY. Acts of the Thirty-fifth General Assembly of the State of New-Jersey. Trenton. 1811.

NEWSPAPERS:

Baltimore, Md.	*Marylander*, March 22, 1828.
Boston, Mass.	*Columbian Centinel*, January 11, 1809.
	Daily Advertiser, March 23, 1818.
	Spirit of Seventy-Six, July 17, 1812.
Philadelphia, Pa.	*Inquirer*, July 7, 1835.
	The Union: The United States Gazette and True American, April 24, 1819.
Richmond, Va.	*Enquirer*, January 16, 1816; January 30, February 1, May 15, 22, June 22, 1821; April 4, 1828; July 10, 14, 17, 21, August 21, 1835.
	Whig and Public Advertiser, July 10, 14, 1835.

NEW YORK. Laws of the State of New-York, passed at the Twenty-first and Twenty-second Sessions of the Legislature. Albany. 1798.

—— Laws of the State of New-York, passed at the Twenty-fifth, Twenty-sixth, and Twenty-seventh Sessions of the Legislature. Albany. 1804.

—— Laws of the State of New-York passed at the Thirtieth, Thirty-first, and Thirty-second Sessions of the Legislature. Albany. 1809.

—— Laws of the State of New-York, passed at the Thirty-fourth Session of the Legislature. Albany. 1811.

NICOLAY, JOHN GEORGE *and* HAY, JOHN, *editors*. *See* Lincoln, Abraham. Works.

Niles's Weekly Register. Baltimore. 1811–1849.

North American Review.

OHIO. Acts of the State of Ohio, passed at the First Session of the Seventeenth General Assembly. Chillicothe. 1819.

—— Acts passed at the First Session of the Twentieth General Assembly of the State of Ohio. Columbus. 1822.

—— Acts passed at the Second Session of the Twentieth General Assembly of the State of Ohio; and . . at the First Session of the Twenty-first General Assembly. Columbus. 1822–23.

Old Family Letters. Copied from the Originals for Alexander Biddle. Philadelphia. 1892.

ORLEANS TERRITORY. Acts passed at the Second Session of the Third Legislature of the Territory of Orleans. New Orleans, La. 1811.

OTIS, HARRISON GRAY. . *See* Morison, Samuel Eliot.

PARTON, JAMES. Life of Andrew Jackson. 3 vols. Boston 1861. (Parton: *Jackson*.)

PAXTON, WILLIAM McCLUNG. Marshall Family. Cincinnati. 1885.

PEASE, THEODORE CALVIN. The Frontier State, 1818–1848. Springfield. 1918. [Volume 2 of *Centennial History of Illinois*.]

PECQUET DU BELLET, KATE LOUISE NOÉMIE. Some Prominent Virginia Families. 4 vols. Lynchburg, Va. 1907. (Pecquet du Bellet.)

PETERS, RICHARD, JR., *reporter*. Reports of Cases argued and adjudged in the Supreme Court of the United States, 1828–43. 17 vols. Philadelphia. 1828–43. (Peters.)

PHILLIPS, ULRICH BONNELL. Georgia and State Rights. Washington. 1902. [Volume 2 of *Annual Report of the American Historical Association* for 1901.]

PHYSICK, PHILIP SYNG. *See* Randolph, Jacob.

PICKERING, OCTAVIUS, *and* UPHAM, CHARLES WENTWORTH. Life of Timothy Pickering. 4 vols. Boston. 1867–73.

PICKERING, TIMOTHY. A Letter . . to James Sullivan, Governor of Massachusetts. Boston. 1808.

—— Life. *See* Pickering, Octavius, and Upham, Charles W.

PINKNEY, WILLIAM. *See* Pinkney, William; Wheaton, Henry.

PINKNEY, WILLIAM. Life of William Pinkney. New York. 1853.

PITKIN, TIMOTHY. A Statistical View of the Commerce of the United States of America. New Haven. 1835. (Pitkin.)

PLUMER, WILLIAM, *Governor*. *See* Plumer, William, Jr.

PLUMER, WILLIAM, JR. Life of William Plumer, edited, with a Sketch of the Author's Life, by A. P. Peabody. Boston. 1857. (Plumer.)

PREBLE, GEORGE HENRY. A Chronological History of the Origin and Development of Steam Navigation. Philadelphia. 1895.

PRENTICE, EZRA PARMALEE. Federal Power over Carriers and Corporations. New York. 1907.

Quarterly Review. London.

QUINCY, EDMUND. Life of Josiah Quincy of Massachusetts. Boston. 1867. (Quincy: *Quincy*.)

QUINCY, JOSIAH, *d.* 1864. *See* Quincy, Edmund.

QUINCY, JOSIAH, *d.* 1882. Figures of the Past, from the Leaves of Old Journals. Boston. 1883.

RANDALL, HENRY STEPHENS. Life of Thomas Jefferson. 3 vols. New York. 1858. (Randall.)

RANDOLPH, JACOB. A Memoir on the Life and Character of Philip Syng Physick, M.D. Philadelphia. 1839. (Randolph: *Physick*.)

Records of the Federal Convention of 1787. Edited by Max Farrand. 3 vols. New Haven. 1911. (*Records Fed. Conv.*: Farrand.)

REIGART, J. FRANKLIN. Life of Robert Fulton. Philadelphia. 1856.

RICHARDSON, JAMES DANIEL, *compiler*. A Compilation of the Messages and Papers of the Presidents, 1789–1897. 10 vols. Washington. 1900. (Richardson.)

RITCHIE, THOMAS. *See* Ambler, Charles Henry.

ROOSEVELT, THEODORE. Naval War of 1812. New York. 1882. (Roosevelt.)

SARGENT, NATHAN. Public Men and Events, from 1817 to 1853. 2 vols. Philadelphia. 1875. (Sargent.)

SCHERMERHORN, JOHN F., *and* MILLS, SAMUEL J. A Correct View of that Part of the United States which lies west of the Allegany Mountains, with regard to Religion and Morals. Hartford. 1814.

SCHURZ, CARL. Henry Clay. 2 vols. Boston. 1887. [American Statesmen.]

SHIRLEY, JOHN M. The Dartmouth College Causes and the Supreme Court of the United States. St. Louis. 1879. (Shirley.)

SMITH, BAXTER PERRY. The History of Dartmouth College. Boston. 1878.

SMITH, ROBERT. An Address to the People of the United States. London. 1811.

SMITH, *Mrs.* SAMUEL HARRISON. *See* Hunt, Gaillard.

SOUTH CAROLINA. Statutes at Large. *See* McCord, David James.

Southern Literary Messenger. Richmond, Va. 1834–64.

STEINER, BERNARD CHRISTIAN. Life and Correspondence of James McHenry. Cleveland. 1907. (Steiner.)

STORY, JOSEPH. Life and Letters. Edited by William Wetmore Story. 2 vols. Boston. 1851. (Story.)

STRICKLAND, WILLIAM PETER, *editor.* *See* Cartwright, Peter. Autobiography. (Strickland.)

SUMNER, WILLIAM GRAHAM. Andrew Jackson. As a Public Man. Boston. 1882. [American Statesmen.] (Sumner: *Jackson.*)

—— A History of American Currency. New York. 1875. (Sumner: *Hist. Am. Currency.*)

TANEY, ROGER BROOKE. *See* Tyler, Samuel.

TAYLOR, JOHN. Construction Construed and Constitutions Vindicated. Richmond. 1820. (Taylor: *Construction Construed.*)

—— New Views of the Constitution of the United States. Washington. 1823.

—— Tyranny Unmasked. Washington. 1822. (Taylor: *Tyranny Unmasked.*)

TERHUNE, MARY VIRGINIA HAWES. Some Colonial Homesteads and their Stories. By Marion Harland (*pseud.*). 2 vols. New York. 1912. (Terhune.)

THOMAS, DAVID. Travels through the Western Country in 1816. Auburn, N.Y. 1819.

THURSTON, ROBERT HENRY. Robert Fulton: His Life and its Results. New York. 1891.

THWAITES, REUBEN GOLD, editor. Early Western Travels. 32 vols. Cleveland, 1904–07. (*E. W. T.*: Thwaites.)

TICKNOR, GEORGE. Life, Letters, and Journals. Edited by Anna Ticknor and George S. Hillard. 2 vols. Boston. 1876. (Ticknor.)

TURNER, FREDERICK JACKSON. Rise of the New West, 1819–1829. New York. 1906. [Volume 14 of *The American Nation: A History*.]

TYLER, LYON GARDINER. Letters and Times of the Tylers. 2 vols. Richmond. 1884. (*Tyler*: Tyler.)

TYLER, SAMUEL. Memoir of Roger Brooke Taney, Chief Justice of the Supreme Court of the United States. Baltimore. 1872.

UNITED STATES CONGRESS. Debates and Proceedings in the Congress of the United States. First Congress, First Session, to eighteenth Congress, First Session; Mar. 3, 1789 to May 27, 1824. [Known as the Annals of Congress.] 42 vols. Washington. 1834–56. (*Annals*.)

—— Register of Debates. Eighteenth Congress, Second Session — Twenty-fifth Congress, First Session. 29 vols. Washington. 1825–37. (*Debates*.)

—— Laws of the United States of America. 5 vols. Washington. 1816.

—— Statutes at Large.

UNITED STATES SUPREME COURT. Reports of Cases adjudged. *University of Pennsylvania Law Review and American Law Register.*

VAN SANTVOORD, GEORGE. Sketches of the Lives and Judicial Services of the Chief-Justices of the Supreme Court of the United States. New York. 1854.

VAN TYNE, CLAUDE HALSTEAD, editor. See Webster, Daniel. Letters.

VERMONT. Laws passed by the Legislature of the State of Vermont at their Session at Montpelier on the second Thursday of October, 1815. Windsor. n. d.

VIRGINIA. Journals of the House of Delegates. Richmond. 1819.

—— Proceedings and Debates of the Virginia State Convention of 1829–30. Richmond. 1830. (*Debates, Va. Conv.*)

—— Report of the Commissioners appointed to view certain

Rivers within the Commonwealth of Virginia, John Marshall, Chairman. Printed, 1816.

VIRGINIA. Reports of Cases argued and decided in the Court of Appeals. Richmond. 1833.

Virginia Branch Colonization Society. Report. 1832.

Virginia Magazine of History and Biography. 25 vols. Richmond. 1893–1917.

WALLACE, JOHN WILLIAM. Cases argued and adjudged in the Supreme Court of the United States, 1863–74. 23 vols. Washington, 1870–76.

WARREN, CHARLES. History of the American Bar. Boston. 1911. (Warren.)

WEBSTER, DANIEL. Letters of Daniel Webster, from Documents owned principally by the New Hampshire Historical Society. Edited by Claude H. Van Tyne. New York. 1902. (Van Tyne.)

—— Private Correspondence. Edited by Fletcher Webster. 2 vols. Boston. 1857. (*Priv. Corres.*: Webster.)

—— *See* Curtis, George Ticknor; Harvey, Peter; Lanman, Charles; Lodge, Henry Cabot; Wilkinson, William Cleaver.

WENDELL, JOHN LANSING, *reporter*. Reports of Cases argued and determined in the Supreme Court of Judicature . . of the State of New York. 26 vols. Albany. 1829–42.

WHEATON, HENRY. A Digest of the Decisions of the Supreme Court of the United States from 1789 to February Term, 1820. New York. 1821.

—— Elements of International Law, with a Sketch of the History of the Science. Philadelphia. 1836.

—— Some Account of the Life, Writings, and Speeches of William Pinkney. Philadelphia. 1826. (Wheaton: *Pinkney.*)

WHEATON, HENRY, *reporter*. Reports of Cases argued and adjudged in the Supreme Court of the United States, 1816–27. 12 vols. Philadelphia. 1816–27. (Wheaton.)

WILKINSON, WILLIAM CLEAVER. Daniel Webster: A Vindication. New York. 1911.

WILSON, HENRY. Rise and Fall of the Slave Power in America. 3 vols. Boston. 1872.

WIRT, WILLIAM. *See* Kennedy, John Pendleton.

World's Work.

GENERAL INDEX

GENERAL INDEX

ABRAHAM LINCOLN

1809 – 1858

BY ALBERT J. BEVERIDGE

Below are given a few typical extracts from reviews of this superb work — perhaps the greatest of all American biographies.

'As a picture of the times I know no other book equal to it. . . . Mr. Beveridge has overlooked nothing of importance, and instead of being overcome by the weight of his facts has handled and arranged them in masterly fashion. . . . The book should be in every library and read by every American.' *James Truslow Adams in the New York Sun.*

'Beveridge has introduced us to the Lincoln of reality . . . done with passionate intensity and meticulous attention to the most minute details. . . . This book is much mellower than the Marshall, but the brilliant analysis, the keen characterizations, the rare powers of recreating a dead day, the dramatic recitals are here in abundance.' — *Claude G. Bowers in the New York World.*

'A monumental achievement.' — *Rev. William E. Barton, biographer of Lincoln, in the Christian Science Monitor.*

'It is the simple truth to say that Beveridge's Lincoln stands alone in its treatment of the Illinois lawyer's preparation for the Presidency. The author's own experience in politics, the opportunity that came to him to devote years to this work, added to rare personal and literary gifts, made success natural and inevitable. He will have no rivals. Comparisons are uncalled-for; it would be like comparing the man-made monuments that we know of with the Pyramids.' — *Dr. Albert J. Shaw in the Review of Reviews.*

ILLUSTRATED, 2 VOLS., $12.50